Masterpieces of World Philosophy

Masterpieces
of
World Philosophy

Edited by
Frank N. Magill

Selection by John K. Roth
With an Introduction by John K. Roth

HarperCollins*Publishers*

FIRST EDITION

Library of Congress Cataloging-in-Publication Data

Masterpieces of world philosophy / Frank N. Magill, editor. — 1st ed.
    p.   cm.
  Includes bibliographical references and index.
  ISBN 0-06-270051-0
  1. Philosophy.   2. Philosophy—Bibliography.   I. Magill, Frank
Northen, 1907– .
B75.M37   1990
100—dc20.   89-46545

92 93 94 RRD 10 9 8 7 6 5 4

CONTENTS

ON READING MASTERPIECES OF PHILOSOPHY IN A CHANGING WORLD

> *In its turn every philosophy will suffer a deposition.*
> *Alfred North Whitehead,* Process and Reality, *1929*

This book contains essays about works that deserve to be called masterpieces of world philosophy. One of those masterpieces, Alfred North Whitehead's *Process and Reality*, claims that "every philosophy will suffer a deposition." If Whitehead is correct, philosophies come and go. None has the last word, but each contributes to a conversation destined to continue as long as people ask questions that seek understanding and wisdom.

Our world might be one where only a single masterpiece of philosophy exists—the one that states everything that should be said and does so truthfully, once and for all, without any need for correction, revision, or elaboration. The history of philosophy and human experience in general, however, indicate that ours is not such a world. Neither do we possess nor are we likely to obtain the truth once and for all, without any need for correction, revision, or elaboration. In our changing world no philosophy can be *the* masterpiece, because no single philosophy can reign supremely. Yet searches for truth continue, and we need *masterpieces* of philosophy to guide us. Fortunately, they exist; more may be on the way as well. To shed further light on those claims, and on the contents of this book, consider the following issues: (1) What is philosophy? (2) What makes a masterpiece of world philosophy? (3) How might it help to read such works, and indeed the treatments of them found here, in a changing world?

Philosophers do not always agree when they are asked what philosophy is, but few would deny that philosophy revolves around questions. Nor would they be likely to dispute the claim made by Immanuel Kant, the author of more than one of the masterpieces discussed in this book, who held that philosophy is centrally concerned with three of them: What can I know? What should I do? What may I hope?

"Do you really know Fred or Carol?" "What do you know about the stock market or baseball?" "How do you know that your boss or teacher wants a report next week?" "What makes you say that this sculpture is beautiful and that painting is ugly?" We sometimes answer such questions without thinking twice, but we may not respond quite so easily when we look more deeply into what is involved when we claim to know or to possess knowledge. We realize that mistakes happen. There is also a difference between opinion and warranted belief; our perceptions of truth and falsity differentiate our judgments. "I'm not sure," or "I can't say." The questions people ask us often produce those responses and make us wonder what it is to know.

In response to the question "What can I know?" philosophers urge us to analyze how we think and how we decide what to believe. They also recommend how we *should* think and propose beliefs we *ought* to hold. Everyday experience contains a similar mixture. We deal constantly with factual matters, but we also make value judgments that focus on good and evil, right and wrong, virtue and vice. In short, we try to figure out what we ought to do. Many factors enter into such evaluations: our cultural background, religious training, the influences of parents, teachers, and friends, to mention only a few. Philosophers take all those features into account, but in exploring the variations on the question "What should I do?" they want to learn whether our attitudes about right and wrong simply are the reflections of culture or rest on critically appraised foundations. They wonder, for example, whether all men and women have rights and duties in common. Philosophers seek to discover what a good life involves and to see if the qualities that make life good are valid regardless of time and place. They also ask whether human history makes progress in achieving what is good.

Sometimes we wonder whether justice will prevail or whether society can make progress in achieving what is good. A natural response to such questioning is "I hope so." To hope for something is to want it, even to yearn for it. At times hope involves the anticipation or expectation that we will get what we want, but we also realize that hope differs from certainty. A person may hope to be successful in business, but such hope indicates an understanding that one may not be successful. What does occur may be so contrary to a person's desire that he or she reaches the point of "hoping against hope," which means sustaining a desire even though the likelihood of its fulfillment is remote. But when circumstances turn far enough against desire, one may reach a point of hopelessness.

When Immanuel Kant identified "What may I hope?" as one of philosophy's fundamental questions, he recognized a decisive feature of human existence. Humanity possesses purposeful awareness. We exist in the present and with a past, but we also move into the future. Although a sense of possibility is an essential part of our lives, possibility is also a fickle companion. Even if we are free to act, we neither know nor control completely what comes to be. The future attracts us; it also makes us anxious. This makes us beings who hope, who long for things that we may never obtain.

What we hope for can vary tremendously. Sometimes we hope for very concrete things: a better job, for example, or a new car or a good grade. Even when these hopes are fulfilled, however, they are rarely ends in themselves. Typically we hope for particular things because they are the means to fulfill a larger, if less articulated, aim. Where hope is concerned, Kant and many other philosophers are especially interested in the larger dimensions of hope, which involve questions about life's meaning, death, and perhaps God.

The questions that concern human beings cover a vast area. They range from a curiosity about life's details to reflection about the nature of the universe. We come to realize that some things appear and disappear while others tend to last. We note how many ways of life there are, some more powerful, important, and valuable than others. What is ultimately real and lasting? How did this world of ours come to be? How do our lives fit into the scheme of things? What is at stake in such questions is the degree to which we are entitled to trust that human existence is significant.

In sum, philosophy reflects and shows how questions and questionings are vital to our lives. Everything in life hinges on whether any person can rightly claim to possess knowledge. Hardly an hour passes without questions being raised as to whether we ought to do some things and not others. These issues keep us thinking about the future. Questions about the meaning and destiny of our lives—individually and collectively—are never far from our attention.

The global and historical variety of philosophers and philosophies represented in this book tells us that philosophy does not yield final answers on which everyone agrees. On the contrary, philosophers approach and answer the questions of philosophy in diverse ways, which suggests that no one philosophy is completely correct. If that circumstance means that *the* masterpiece of philosophy will never be, it leaves the door open for the masterpieces of world philosophy. What, however, qualifies a work of philosophy for such consideration?

One fascinating approach to that question comes from William James, another philosopher discussed here. "The history of philosophy," observed James, "is to a great extent that of a certain clash of human temperament." Philosophy, he thought, is intimately related to how we "see" the world. Much that we see is shared and apparently the same, and yet our seeing is not identical. Philosophers belong to human communities, and they depend on others. Yet, in the final analysis, they are not inclined to let anyone else do their seeing for them. They state their own views, believing that what needs to be said is different in some significant way from anything else that has been said before. No two philosophers agree on everything. They are different persons, who see differently, and therefore they want their thoughts to be different, too. Otherwise their writings would make far less sense than they do.

INTRODUCTION

From such differences the masterpieces of world philosophy are made. Not every piece of philosophy, of course, fits that description, but a few rise to prominence—though not necessarily to permanent prominence. At least two factors loom large when that happens. First, a masterpiece of world philosophy is obviously one that stands the test of time. It continues to be referred to, read, and studied. The writings of Confucius or Plato come to mind as primary examples in this regard. Their durability considerably exceeds that of writings from the nineteenth or twentieth centuries that are included in this book. Sifting and sorting continues. Although a volume of essays about the masterpieces of world philosophy published a century from now is still likely to include essays on Confucius and Plato, its entries from much more recent times might be considerably revised.

In the long or short run, how does a philosophical work pass the test of time? The answer depends on the philosopher's "seeing" and, in particular, on seeing differently. What drives philosophers to write is the conviction that someone else has seen something important but also inadequately or mistakenly. A correction is needed and in view. Plato influenced Aristotle, and the latter saw things *differently*. Hume awakened Kant from "dogmatic slumbers," and philosophy took a lasting Kantian turn. No philosopher works in a vacuum. Each is provoked by someone else. But a masterpiece emerges only when the result of that provocation makes a turning point in thought that, in turn, provokes not one mind but a community of them. To put the point in terms of the epigraph by Whitehead with which this introduction began, a masterpiece of world philosophy deposes what preceded it and, in turn, becomes itself a subject for depositioning. This depositioning, however, is not disappearing. The masterpiece's influence lingers on. Far from being completely eclipsed, the philosophical masterpiece continues to find a place—sometimes more prominent, sometimes less so—in the ongoing and expanding conversation that comprises what Whitehead liked to call the "adventures of ideas." An important part of those adventures, incidentally, lives in the fact that the masterpiece does not always contain exactly what the philosopher thought he or she saw. "Before Columbus set sail for America," Whitehead wrote, "he had dreamt of the Far East, and of the round world, and of the trackless ocean. Adventure rarely reaches its predetermined end. Columbus never reached China. But he discovered America." Often the masterpieces of world philosophy turn out to be voyages of discovery like that. If so, there is drama in philosophy. Its masterpieces tell a story that goes beyond their individuality. Taken together they establish a narrative in which we readers, too, are invited to take part. That invitation suggests some ways of reading the masterpieces of philosophy, or essays about them, in a changing world.

Philosophy is a kind of literature. Like a novel or a poem, philosophical writing—sometimes it does employ fictional or poetic forms—will have controlling ideas. Often these themes are questions, and one way to track down a philosopher's themes is to identify the questions that form the heart of the matter under consideration. Philosophy lives and dies with questions. A philosopher feels or poses a problem and tries to deal with it, that's all. Of course, there are many questions and many ways of putting the same question, but questions are never far behind the scenes, and if you can isolate them and puzzle out why these questions are significant for the philosopher, then you are on the way to having the counterpart to theme in a novel or poem. While you are on this trail, it will not hurt to ask: Are these questions mine, too? Should they be? Why?

Philosophy is sometimes portrayed as an objective, dispassionate, unemotional pursuit of truth. The misleading qualities of that description are unmasked when it becomes apparent that philosophical writings are rhetorical, too. They are out to persuade—even if the persuasion is only that of issuing an invitation to inquire with them—and thus their voices are not emotionless. Some philosophers are more forthright about this than others, but you will feel and understand better the tone of a philosopher's work if you wonder: How is this writer trying to show me that his or her questions are important and that his or her reflections on them are pertinent? You will learn something about your own temperament if you turn the question on yourself: Is the philosopher succeeding with me? Am I skeptical, convinced, angry, exasperated, excited by these ideas and the distinctive "voice" in which they are expressed?

Argument is philosophy's counterpart to plot. We can ask of a novel: What is the plot? How does it unfold? Where does it lead? How is it developed? Substituting argument, the same can be done with philosophy. In exploring a philosopher's argument, seek an overview of what the writer is trying to say. Then trace the movement from question to answer, from answer to question, from point to point. As with the other hints outlined here, the structure of the essays in this book encourages reading of that kind.

With exceptions such as Plato's dialogues, philosophical writing rarely seems to have a cast of characters aside from the philosophers themselves. That quality forms perhaps the most striking difference between philosophical essays and novels or short stories. Yet, if you think about the situation further, there are "characters" in philosophy, too. They exist, for example, as *ideas*. Their variety can be at least as great as the persons who make a novel move. Assumptions, hypotheses, conclusions, resolutions—these are some of the major character-ideas to identify and analyze in philosophical works. What convictions does a philosopher take for granted—and why? What is the "character" of the hypotheses that he or she wants to explore, and how are they developed? What conclusions does a thinker draw; how is a dilemma resolved—if it is? Those questions can produce an inquiry that identifies the cast of philosophical thought. If you go on to ask yourself whether the writer's "characters" are believable, you will begin to have some clues about the validity of his or her thought and of your own as well.

If plot stands to argument as character does to idea, then consider the ways in which philosophers use ideas to form an argument and also develop their arguments so as to lend force to the ideas that they want to advance. Questions such as the following suggest themselves as tools for analysis in this area: If the philosopher's assumptions (like a novelist's *dramatis personae*) were different, could the argument come out the same? Are the philosopher's ideas "lined up" so as to yield a result that he or she already has in mind? Or do the philosopher's "characters"—as they are introduced and interrogated——actually make the argument happen as you read? To what degree does the philosopher have a "plot outline" before he or she writes, and to what degree does it seem that he or she is developing ideas to explore where they lead—as a novelist's characters may be said to lead the novelist?

Philosophers are usually much concerned about *how* you get from one idea to another. That concern involves concepts such as reasoning, inference, and evidence. So if the *structure* of a philosophical work is the target, the objective is to discern the forms of reasoning and inference and the patterns in which the writer presents and organizes evidence for his or her position. In a word, we are looking for clues about the thinker's *logic*. Just as in a poem or novel, there can be great variety in the structure of a philosophical work. Some thinkers, for instance, make appeals to self-evident truths and then seek to deduce other truths from them. Other philosophers not only refuse to make these moves; they argue against the possibility of doing so. Some thinkers believe that the worst thing one can do is to contradict oneself. Others, less sure of the powers of reason or of the rationality of reality itself, delight in paradox, provided that it is controlled for pushing thought along and does not result from gross mistakes. Some philosophers are more "dialectical" than others, creating conflicts comparable to those in a novel or play. They reach a conclusion only to throw things up in the air again by further questioning. But other philosophers will drive for their goal and then attempt to secure it against every adversary. If you can sense a philosophy's structure, you will learn much about how the philosopher is thinking and indeed about *what* he or she thinks. When you ask "Would I do it the same way?" you will begin to understand yourself better, too.

In the pages that follow, you will meet philosophers from ancient China and twentieth century Europe, from the United States and the Roman Empire, and from a vast array of times and places in between. Their thoughts will be as different as the languages in which they spoke or wrote them. Yet they share many goals, and none is more pronounced than that of understanding ourselves better. The pursuit of that adventure is the most important reason to read—and to read about—masterpieces of philosophy in a changing world.

John K. Roth

Masterpieces of World Philosophy

THE ANALECTS OF CONFUCIUS (Lun Yü)

Author: Confucius (c. 551-c. 479 B.C.)
Type of work: Ethics, political philosophy, epistemology
First transcribed: Late sixth or early fifth century B.C.

Principal Ideas Advanced

Jen, *the ideal relationship among human beings, is the perfect virtue of men.*
Man is basically close to jen *by his very nature, but his action should be controlled by* li, *the rules of propriety.*
The chun-tzu, *or ideal man, is one who practices* jen *in accordance with* li; *consequently, he treasures and seeks the* tao, *the right Way.*

Confucius, to whom most of the sayings in the *Analects* are ascribed, was a descendant of an influential family of the state of Lu in the present-day Eastern Chinese province of Shantung. His family name was K'ung. His own names were Ch'iu and Chung-ni. Later he was known as K'ung Fu-tzu, meaning Master K'ung, out of respect. At the time of his birth, his family was already in reduced circumstances, but he could boast of a long line of illustrious ancestors, dating all the way back to pre-Chou dynasty times. Because of Confucius' fame, his family history is perhaps the most complete and extensive genealogy in the world. Today a man named K'ung Te-ch'eng, officially recognized as the seventy-seventh generation descendant of Confucius, still lives in Taiwan.

Orphaned at an early age, Confucius went to work while still in his teens. He held a number of minor posts in the government and in the employ of the nobility. His service record and his self-cultivation soon won for him wide recognition. Students gathered around him for instruction in ethics, literature, and the art of government service. He was particularly respected for his knowledge of ancient rituals. Among his followers were men of diverse interests and temperaments. As myth and legend grew around the historical Confucius through the years, the biographical details of his life make the story of the ancient sage anything but monotonous. Confucius is said to have had to put up with one student who was too stingy to let his master borrow his umbrella; consequently, Confucius was drenched in the rain at least once. Confucius, so the legend says, had constantly to restrain a second student whose hot temper involved himself and his master in frequent difficulties. Confucius is believed to have had a narrow escape from a third disciple whose reaction against his master's ceaseless moralistic admonitions amounted to a murderous intent.

Confucius divided his time among lecturing to his students, editing reading materials for his students, and trying to persuade the men in government to adopt his ideas. If he failed in the last, he certainly succeeded remarkably well in the first two tasks, as his *Analects* (the *Lun Yü*) and its lasting influence testify. Being a collection of remembered dialogues recorded by his disciples and their pupils, there is clearly a question about the accuracy of the statements in the *Analects*. In addition, the extremely terse style of these dialogues lends itself to a variety of interpretations. However, upon a careful perusal of these sayings, many key ideas of the Confucian system emerge with clarity.

Of the central cluster of ideas that are discernible in Confucian thought, the idea of *jen* is perhaps the greatest in importance. *Jen* is the foundation of Confucian ethics because *jen* stands for the ideal relationship among human beings. The etymological significance of the Chinese character *jen* yields a key to this idea: the symbols that form this character mean "two human beings," hence the suggestion of "the ideal relationship between any two human beings." *Jen* suggests gentility, magnanimity, humanity, goodness of character, and benevolence. The last sense is the one most frequently used to translate this term. In short, *jen* is the perfect virtue of human beings; it is the only road to the peace and harmony of a society. He who embraces the principle of *jen* will treat people gently and humanely; and for him everything will go well.

In answering his disciples' questions on the existence and functions of *jen*, Confucius stressed the importance not only of internalizing the principles of *jen* to make them a part of man's natural disposition, but also of putting them into daily practice. He wanted his students to practice courtesy, magnanimity, good faith, diligence, and kindness everywhere and all the time. He came close to advocating an infinite compassion when he summed up his own exposition with a succinct command: to practice *jen* is to "love mankind" universally. Most frequently Confucius emphasized that *jen* was not a lofty metaphysical abstraction beyond the comprehension of the ordinary person. On the contrary, he insisted that *jen* lay close at hand for everyone to grasp. The difficulty, as he saw it, was that few people could remain firm for long. Even among his distinguished disciples he mentioned only one who succeeded in practicing *jen* with constancy.

One detects a note of earnestness that verges on religious fervor when Confucius speaks of the importance of *jen*. With unmistakable clarity he asserts that good men sacrifice their lives in order to maintain *jen* and that never would they alter *jen* in order to survive any crisis. In this light the Confucian principles of *jen* become more than relative standards of desirable social behavior; they are notions of absolute right and justice. But, Confucius explains, the seeds of these notions are not to be found outside man's basic nature. Without anywhere giving a clear statement on his view on man's nature, Confucius nevertheless reveals his assumption that men are born basically the same and that direct expressions of the original nature of man approach much closer to *jen* than any affectation could. There is only one condition that Confucius insists on: any direct expression of one's own nature would have to be restrained by *li* (the rules of propriety) in order to adhere to the principles of *jen.*

Strictly speaking, the rules of propriety, the *li,* taken literally could mean rites, etiquette, good form, or decorum, but clearly Confucius uses this term to mean more than mere outward expressions of formality. As an expert and an authority on ancient rites, Confucius preferred to have his students look beyond the music and pomp, the "jade and silk," and other features usually accompanying the rituals. In the *Analects* he stresses the essence of *li* as the distinguishing quality of man without which man and wild animals would be the same and human society would cease to exist. He also tells his own son to study *li* because if man does not know *li* he does not know how to behave like a man.

Li, consequently is upheld as the evidence of man's civilization. *Li* is essential to sophisticated, cultured, and orderly living, which is the central aim of the Confucian social teachings. With *li* man can tame the wild animal in him and make himself a better member of society. In more than one statement Confucius suggests the psychological use of *li* to bring calm and poise to man at critical moments. *Li* is the Confucian prescription to save society from chaos and disorder.

True to his status as a self-appointed bearer of traditional culture, Confucius does not spare any effort to impress his students with the importance of rituals. He himself would not eat unless the meal was presented and the seat arranged in the proper manner; he would not walk on foot when he kept company with the dignitaries; he would not look, listen, speak, or move until he was sure his every action was in accordance with the rules of propriety (*li*). Indeed, his own sayings and other statements about him in this book show us a man of meticulous care for proper manners. One feels that Confucius purposely did so to dramatize the cultural heritage of his state of Lu, which was closely linked to the Chou dynasty. In his philosophy Confucius champions a revival of the Chou institutions which in his political vision represent a golden past. Of course, it must be remembered that Confucius holds the spirit, the appropriateness, and the sincerity behind the rites above the formalities. He instructs his students to observe simplicity, not lavish display, as the general principle of all rites, and to ascertain the genuine sentiment behind any ritual observance, rather than the mere physical presence of etiquette. The spirit of *li*, according to Confucius, obtains only when the man practicing *li* has *jen*. Here the two key Confucian ideas come together to form the basis for the cult of *chün-tzu*.

Originally *chün-tzu* meant no more than "the son of the lord." Its more extensive use acquired for it the broader meaning of "any man of good breeding." In the repeated appearance of this term in the Confucian statements, the element of "good breeding" or family origin is no longer stressed and *chün-tzu* becomes simply "good man" or "the best of men" in contradistinction with *hsiao-jen*, "small man" or "petty man." The sense of the term in the *Analects* can also be quite adequately expressed as "the superior man" in contrast to the "inferior man."

Confucius paints in *chün-tzu* a picture of the ideal man. This perfect man has a thorough understanding of *jen* and constantly practices it. He acts according to *li*, and the rules of propriety are so much a part of his nature that he never can violate them. His uprightness, or the expressions of his genuine nature, is perfectly blended with that proper amount of refinement, so that he is neither pedantic nor rustic. In dealing with others he is warm-mannered. He has a will of steel and his appearance is always calm because his *jen* keeps him from anxieties, his wisdom guards him against perplexities, and his courage dispels any possible fear. While the petty-minded people think of profit, he, the *chün-tzu*, is always mindful of what is right. He may not possess much technical knowledge about details but his mind is capable of grasping what is essential and significant. Above all, the *chün-tzu* treasures and seeks the *tao*.

The Confucian *tao* is vastly different from the *tao* of mystic Taoism. Confucius speaks of the *tao* of the ancient sage-kings, meaning the Way to an ideal government and society, and of the *tao* of a virtuous man, meaning the right Way of being a man. At times Confucius treats the word *tao* as another name for righteousness and sagacity. As he does with *jen*, Confucius also speaks of *tao* with occasional outbursts of pious feeling. Thus, we hear him declare, "He who hears of *tao* in the morning may die content at night." In these instances Confucius does come close to expressing a religious dedication.

On the whole Confucius' silence on the supernatural is eloquent. In the *Analects*, he does not defend, nor does he attempt to destroy, the prevailing ideas about the world of the spirits. Instead, he unequivocally instructs his disciples to keep their minds on the affairs of men and not to be bothered by questions about the spirits. He informs them that they must first learn enough about life before they inquire into life hereafter, and he himself throughout his life remained too busy studying this world to deal with the other world. When his student asks him about the relationship between the rites and the spirits, Confucius' answer is that since sincerity is the essence of the rituals, one must conduct the sacrificial rites to one's ancestors "as if they were present," and to the spirits also "as if they were present." Beyond this, so says Confucius, one should not go. It is enough "to respect the spirits and stay away from them."

Small wonder that one of his disciples declares his disappointment in trying to learn Confucius' expositions on "Heaven's ways." Confucius may be suspected of dodging the question, he may also be suspected of having no formulated ideas about the spirits, but he cannot be accused of total silence on the question of Heaven. For in many passages in this book Confucius refers to Heaven, sometimes as an invincible moral force, at other times as a Supreme Being, willful and purposeful.

Heaven to Confucius is the Supreme Being that decides in favor of the moral and the right, and Confucius envisages himself as having been commissioned by the Heavenly authority to perpetuate the sage-king's Way on earth. So he declares, when his life is threatened by the people of K'uang, "If Heaven is not going to let this culture decline, what can the people of K'uang do to me?" On another occasion of distress, Confucius comforts his friends by saying, "Heaven has created this virtue in me; what can Huan T'ui do to me?" That Confucius views Heaven's will as always in favor of the good and always beneficial is further evinced in his statement about the regularity of the seasons and the thriving of myriad creatures. This statement has been taken by many students of Confucianism as a proof of Confucius' belief in the spontaneity of a universal amoral force that is omnipotent. This view could be correct, but if one judges by the majority of Confucius' remarks concerning Heaven, the force of the foregoing statement still tends to describe Heaven as a beneficent force that works benevolently without "elaborate explanations."

Heaven's *tao* in Confucian terms is Heaven's Way or Heaven's Will. This Will is supreme and above man's interference. If Confucius' use of the term Heaven is perfectly consistent, then Heaven's Will should also be moral and in favor of the good. Here another Confucian term is introduced, the *ming*. *Ming* could mean either a command or a destiny. When it appears in connection with Heaven as "Heaven's *ming*," it usually means Heaven's command, or Heaven's Will. When it appears alone, *ming* could mean fate or destiny. What makes Confucius' position on Heaven's Will unclear is his statement that if the Way (*tao*) is to prevail, it is fate (*ming*); and if the Way is to fail, it is also fate (*ming*). If this is the same *ming* as Heaven's command, then Heaven may not always be intent on making the Great Way prevail. This idea is what is generally understood as Confucian fatalism. In other words, fate as a shadowy necessity beyond the comprehension and control of human beings also appears in Confucian thought.

Enough is said in the *Analects* to illuminate some other Confucian ideals with regard to social and political institutions. The importance of the family as the microcosm of society is clearly implied when Confucius reminds his students to practice filial piety within the family before trying to learn how to read and write well. The significance of filial piety in the Confucian system as seen in the *Analects*, however, is not as great as has been generally believed. In his book Confucius describes this virtue as important because a man respectful toward his parents is not likely to violate the law and order of society, also because to be thankful to one's parents is a good sentiment that should be encouraged. But to uphold filial piety as the supreme human virtue is not Confucius' intent in this book; rather, it is a later development in the Confucian school of thought, elaborated

and reinterpreted by the Confucian commentators on these texts. Confucius himself does not preach total, blind obedience to one's parents. He sees the virtue of a son shielding his sheep-stealing father, but he also teaches the son to remonstrate, mildly but persistently, with his erring father.

As an educator, Confucius was equally earnest in teaching his students, regardless of their social status and family origins. He believed in the equal teachability of men, but he recognized the difference in intellect and talent among men. In the *Analects* he accepts those "who are born with knowledge" as the best, and those who learn after industrious study as the second type of mind. Nowhere in this book does Confucius suggest that everybody is born socially equal and is entitled to the right to rule himself. He urges the ruler to learn the right Way to govern; he urges his students to learn to be the best ministers possible in order to assist the ruler. Confucius' view on the function of the government is that government must rule by moral excellence—a view that anticipates the whole political philosophy of Mencius.

Confucius' remark about men "born with knowledge" is extremely provocative, but unfortunately the *Analects* does not yield any adequate exposition on Confucius' view of knowledge. In discussing how to study, Confucius acknowledges his own intention "to observe and commit to memory what is observed," because he confesses that he "cannot do anything without knowing about it first." When these statements are examined together, Confucius does hint at the possibility that some people are born with knowledge; hence, these people can act spontaneously without the effort of learning how to act and without being aware of their knowledge. But Confucius carefully declines the company of people of such super intellect, and he admits that the source of his knowledge is observation and intensive study. He also rules out the attainment of knowledge through meditation without the aid of books because once he "tried to think the whole day without eating and the whole night without sleeping, but nothing came of it." Furthermore, he does not separate the attainment of knowledge from action and practice.

More important than the relation between action and knowledge is the exact identification of name with actuality, according to the Confucian teachings. The times were chaotic and the social order was confused. Hence, Confucius urged the king to behave like a king and the minister to act as one of his rank should. If the name is not correctly applied, says Confucius, then language is no longer a medium of communication. Consequently, nothing can be accomplished and men will not even know where to "put their hands or feet." From a moralistic start with a practical aim, the Confucian doctrine of rectification of names developed into a serious effort to define terms. Confucius' concern with this matter reveals his underlying assumption that the name is not just a representation of a thing, but is the very essence of the thing itself. The germ of this idea can be found in pre-Confucian thought in China's high antiquity, but Confucius' effort has added significance to this idea and made it an important development in Chinese philosophy.

In spite of its brevity and limited bulk, the *Analects* remains throughout the centuries the most authentic and rewarding source for the study of Confucius the man and his thought. In addition to the key ideas of original Confucianism, the book also illumines certain aspects of life in ancient China. The fragments of dialogues between Confucius and a few political leaders show the role the intellectuals played in a society where values were undergoing dramatic change. The dialogues also reveal how totally without restraint the states vied for supremacy in a power struggle that followed the collapse of an ancient feudal order.

The fact that certain key statements in the *Analects* have been interpreted in different ways has certainly contributed to the survival of the Confucian system. There is something in this book for everyone, from the most radical to the most conservative, if he searches hard for it. Indeed, much has been read back into the Confucian teachings, and what Confucius did actually teach has been, as a result, distorted. In spite of differences of interpretation, it seems important to note that Confucius valued most highly an orderly, peaceful, and harmonious society. To this goal he channeled all his thought and teaching. His *tao* was the Way to achieve this ideal; his *te* (virtue) was his claim that he had been invested with the knowledge of the Way; his *wen* (refinement, cultural heritage) was the heritage of institutions prevailing in an imaginary golden past derived from the ancient texts. To be sure, Confucius insisted that society would not be peaceful if each individual man did not behave properly, according to his social station. This meant that for Confucius the individual was important, but only insofar as he could help to bring about peace and harmony in society. If Confucius speculated on the position of man in the universe or dealt with other metaphysical matters, there is no sufficient evidence in this book.

Pertinent Literature

Creel, H. G. *Confucius and the Chinese Way*. New York: Harper & Row Publishers, 1960.

Although H. G. Creel's work is not exclusively a commentary on the *Analects*, it is a helpful book for anyone interested in acquiring a general understanding of the historical background of the classic; and it is illuminating for those who have little or no knowledge of Chinese culture.

As a scholar in ancient Chinese history, Creel has made extensive use of authentic sources, both pre-Confucian texts and those written within two centuries after Confucius' death. While two-thirds of the book is devoted to historical backgrounds and the influence of Confucius, the remainder provides a vivid account of this Chinese sage and his ideas. Creel covers the subject in seven sections: "Biography," "The Man," "The Disciples," "The Teacher," "The Scholar," "The Philosopher," and "The Reformer."

In the section entitled "The Teacher," Creel gives a very lucid explanation of the function of *li* (rituals, rites, or proprieties) in education. *Li*, as Creel interprets it, marks the distinction between the civilized man and the rude barbarian who gives immediate vent to his impulses. When *li* is properly performed, it confines a person's behavior to socially acceptable and functional channels. It is therefore a method of guiding and facilitating human relations.

Creel explains that the function of music was given considerable weight by Confucius, since a great many ceremonies are accompanied by music. Creel then compares Confucius to Plato, indicating that both philosophers considered music a matter of concern not only to the individual but also to the state. Both philosophers held that certain kinds of music (the harmonic) should be encouraged, while certain other kinds should be eliminated.

The most important section for our purpose is the one entitled "The Philosopher." It is unfortunate that the author is more a historian or sinologist than a scholar in philosophy. Creel's attempt to avoid mixing Neo-Confucianism with the original philosophy of Confucius is both legitimate and desirable. In doing so, however, Creel may have committed a mistake he would have liked to avoid, that of reading ancient Taoism into Confucianism. He considers that the central concept in the philosophy of Confucius is that of the Way—*tao*. Creel employs his philological knowledge to give an account of the varieties of the meanings of *tao*. He quotes heavily from Lorraine Creel's interpretation of the Way from a sociological viewpoint; and he finally comes to the conclusion that the Way sums up the philosophy of Confucius.

After considering the Way, Creel turns to other concepts of the *Analects*. He argues that Confucius emphasized "peace of mind." (This is further evidence that he has read Taoistic ideas into Confucius.) While discussing the principle of "reciprocity," Creel compares Confucius to Immanuel Kant. This comparison is legitimate, provided that we do not allow the similarities to obscure the significant differences. Unfortunately, the striking differences between these two philosophers have escaped Creel's attention. Kant holds to the supremacy of reason, while Confucius maintains the primacy of the human heart. The leading concept in the *Analects* is *jen*, which is mentioned in the classic more than a hundred times. It is unfortunate that this important concept is dealt

with by Creel only in the documentary notes in the back of the book.

The word *Jen* has been translated into English as "Good," "Love," "Humanity," "Benevolence," "Virtue," "Manhood-at-its-Best," "Man-to-Man-ness," "Human-heartedness," and the like; yet the essence of *jen* is love or human feeling. It is not the feeling that we call "impulse" or "instinct." It is instinctive feeling tranquilized, directed, and transformed through education. Mencius interpreted *jen* as "human heart." When *jen* is so conceived, it can be defined as the cultivated feeling which distinguishes a human being from other forms of biological beings. With *jen* as the central concept, other concepts in the *Analects* can be defined in terms of *jen*. For example, *hsiao* (filial piety) means the cultivated feeling toward one's parents; *chung* (loyalty) means the cultivated feeling toward one's superiors, lords, country, even one's own goal; *li* (rites, rituals) means the behavioral norms through which one's cultivated feeling is expressed; *yi* (propriety or righteousness) means the proper point (or due degree) at which one's cultivated feeling is expressed; and *chün-tzu* (noble man) means the kind of personality in which cultivated feeling has attained maximum development. If *li* is defined as the behavioral norms in terms of which *jen* is expressed, we can see clearly a logical unity holding these two major concepts together. In the *Analects*, Confucius categorically maintained that the practice of *li* is a path leading to the attainment of *jen*. (*Analects*, XII, 1.) So, *li* and *jen* form an inseparable means-ends continuum which constitutes the very foundation of the philosophy of Confucius.

It has commonly been held that Confucius was seeking merely to revive the ways of antiquity. Creel, on the contrary, holds that since Confucius recognized the human institutions change and develop, he was quite ready to make or accept changes if desirable and necessary. In this regard, Creel is correct, for he gains support from textual evidence. In defending Confucius as a "reformer," however, he appears to have read American democracy into the views of this ancient Chinese sage.

Fingarette, Herbert. *Confucius—The Secular as Sacred.* New York: Harper & Row Publishers, 1972.

Although he makes no acknowledgment of his debt to H. G. Creel, Herbert Fingarette's book provides a development of Creel's basic ideas. Creel argued that religious and secular activities were not widely separated in ancient China and, accordingly, Fingarette intelligently uses "The Secular as Sacred" as the subtitle of his book. Creel's book provides a lucid interpretation of the function of *li* in education, while Fingarette has taken up *li* as the key concept of the philosophy of Confucius and (with the help of John Chan) has tactfully designed the cover of his book with the character of *li*. Creel maintained that the Way sums up the philosophy of Confucius, while Fingarette argues that the idea of a Way is congenial to the central Confucian notion of *li*, and that the *li* may be thought of as "the map or the specific road-system which is Tao." Finally, Creel regarded Confucius as a reformer, while Fingarette holds that Confucius was the creator of a new ideal, not simply an apologist or modifier of earlier views.

The striking difference between Creel and Fingarette is that the former is a sinologist and historian while the latter is a scholar in philosophy, working within the analytic tradition. A historian delves into the richness of culture and then synoptically sums up his piecemeal studies. An analytic philosopher, on the other hand, is able to elaborate on a small topic and expand it into a long treatise with conceptual sophistication. Creel's work is, no doubt, a result of many years of painstaking studies of Chinese culture, while Fingarette's is an intelligent product accomplished through the use of philosophic analysis in the Western tradition.

Fingarette's fundamental handicap is that he lacks a substantial background in Chinese culture. He has endowed *li* with holy nature and magic power throughout his book without realizing that his theme has been established on a more solid humanistic ground in the ancient Confucian classic *Li Chi (The Book of Rites)*. According to *Li Chi*, *li* consists of more than rote rituals or rites; it is a method of education established by the sages with vision and purpose. This teleological view of *li* was explained in the *Li Chi*: "The sages invented *li* to educate people. . . . It is for fixation of relations, settlement of doubts, determination of sameness and differences, and distinction between right and wrong." It is just because *li* was developed by the sages with a teleological view that it has holy and magic power. (The Chinese word for "holy" is *shêng*, which connotes more of wisdom than holiness.)

A significant contribution of Fingarette's treatise is that he rightly points out that in Confucian philosophy the concepts of choice and responsibility are not confined to a moral context. However, Fingarette's emphasis on conforming to the Way does not go far enough. The problem of choice between conflicting duties arises only when one employs reason or reflective thinking. This has been an acute problem in Western culture where reason rules supreme, but the problem does not arise in a culture where the cultivation of feeling occupies the central place in education. If a person's feeling has been properly cultivated in accordance with *li*, he resolves dilemmas of choice easily through feeling; the problem is not made more difficult through reason. In any case, the concept of the individual as an independent metaphysical entity does not exist in Chinese thought. Instead, the Chinese always conceive an individual within as a network of human relations. Thus, when an individual person follows a proper relational channel, he does not need to bother to reason or calculate about individual choices.

Fingarette emphasizes the concept of *jen.*. He argues that *li* and *jen* are two aspects of the same thing. The former directs attention to traditional social patterns of conduct while the latter focuses on the person as the one who in pursuing patterns of conduct maintains social relationships. The concept of *li* is very clearly explained, but the concept of *jen* remains somewhat obscure. Fingarette's failure to explicate *jen* may well be due to his maintaining a rigid distinction between the psychological and the philosophical, an uncriticized but popular tendency among contemporary philosophers.

Fingarette's treatise is a landmark of American scholarship in the field of Chinese studies, where

Chinese philosophy has not attracted sufficient attention. Fingarette's sophisticated essay can be seen as a breakthrough of Confucian philosophy in Western scholarship. With this perceptive treatise, the philosophy of the *Analects* is given a proper opportunity to be studied by philosophers of the modern West. In addition, this essay can be considered as an original philosophical treatise of the author, inspired by the great sage of ancient China.

Additional Recommended Reading

Confucius. *Analects*. Edited and translated by D. C. Lau. Middlesex, England: Penguin Books, 1979. Very scholarly translation with informative introductory essay, bibliography, and appendixes.

_____. *The Analects of Confucius*. Edited and translated by Arthur Waley. London: George Allen & Unwin, 1938. Beautiful translation with literary qualities; yet Waley's interpretation of *jen* is clouded in mysticism.

_____. *The Wisdom of Confucius*. Edited and translated by Lin Yutang. New York: The Modern Library, 1938. An excellent anthology of Confucian classical writings, including Lin's own beautiful translation of the *Analects*. Very well-written introductory essays and notes.

Creel, H. G. *Chinese Thought: From Confucius to Mao Tsê-tung*. Chicago: University of Chicago Press, 1953. Lucidly written, the ideas of the *Analects* are thoughtfully presented in summary form in a chapter.

Fung Yu-lan. *A History of Chinese Philosophy*. Translated by Derk Bodde. Princeton, New Jersey: Princeton University Press, 1952-1953. The ideas of the *Analects* in general and the concept of *jen* in particular are adequately presented in the relevant chapter of this scholarly work.

Hall, David L. and Roger T. Ames. *Thinking Through Confucius*. Albany: State University of New York Press, 1987. Helps to make the thought of Confucius more accessible.

Tu Wei-ming. "*Li* as Process of Humanization," in *Philosophy East and West*. XXII, no. 2 (April, 1972), pp. 187-201. A well-reasoned essay establishing the relation between *li* and *jen*, a pair of leading concepts in the *Analects* and the Confucian tradition.

Wing-tsit Chan. "The Evolution of the Confucian Concept of *Jen*," in *Philosophy East and West*. IV, no. 4 (January, 1955), pp. 295-319. The most extensive and scholarly study of the concept of *jen*, the leading idea in the *Analects* and the Confucian tradition.

Wu, Joseph. "The Son Being Witness Against the Father—A Paradox in the *Confucian Analects*," in *Clarification and Enlightenment: Essays in Comparative Philosophy*. Washington, D.C.: University Press of America, 1978. In solving the paradox, this essay includes a philosophical interpretation of *jen* as "cultivated feeling." The relation between *jen* and some other major concepts in the *Analects* are given a clear definition in terms of *jen*.

BHAGAVAD GITA

Author: Unknown
Type of work: Theology, metaphysics, ethics
First transcribed: Probably between fifth and second century B.C.

Principal Ideas Advanced

One's true self is one's undying soul which is divine in nature.

Even though one's phenomenal nature is a projection of the ever-active matter (prakrti), *one can avoid the inherent bondage of a material mode of existence by cultivating even-mindedness and detachment.*

Practice of detachment is possible through self-knowledge and devotion to God and is to be initiated in the performance of righteous acts which uphold social order.

Such practice of detachment leads to freedom from the fetters of action through the conquest of human passion and ego-consciousness, and contributes to an awakening of one's latent divinity by taking one closer to God.

Whenever righteousness declines and lawlessness abounds, God descends into this world in human form to restore order; he is the Supreme Person, the personified Absolute Being, who is the abode of all beings; yet he remains distinct from his creation in power and personality.

The *Bhagavad Gita*, the most revered text in Hinduism, literally means "Song of the Lord." The spiritual poem consists of the God-incarnate Krishna's discourse with a despondent warrior, Arjuna. Throughout the discourse, the *Gita* attempts to synthesize the various ideas in the Hindu philosophy of its time into its own brand of theism. Yet, in spite of its philosophical profundity, it remains a delightfully easy-to-read poem with an almost lyrical beauty. This is one important reason for its appeal to people of all levels of understanding.

Composed of eighteen chapters, the *Gita* is itself a small part of the vast epic, *The Mahabharata*. Although its authorship is unknown, there is speculation that it was written by more than one person because of its comprehensive, if not eclectic, scope. In addition, it seems to have been inserted into the larger epic over a period of time. Like its authorship, the *Gita*'s exact date of composition is subject to question. The extensive use of Upanishadic and early Samkhya ideas in the poem and lack of reference for any of the six orthodox systems of Hindu philosophy suggest that it was composed between these two periods, somewhere between the fifth and the second century B.C.

To understand the *Gita*'s importance in the Hindu tradition requires some familiarity with dominant trends and ideas in Hinduism itself. Broadly speaking, the Hindu tradition makes a distinction between the pursuit of God as the personified Supreme Being, to be reached primarily through devotion, and the mystical quest for the undifferentiated One. In the latter tradition, it is believed that any characterization of the supreme reality, including identifying it as God with his various attributes in their perfection, is an attempt to impose limitations on the Absolute which is beyond name and form. The supremely real is to be known through an exalted type of direct intuitive awareness that transcends all relativity and conceptual limitations. In ancient India, this view was taught in the Upanishads, which asserted an identity between a person's true self (*atman*) and the Absolute (*Brahman*). According to this philosophy, a mystical, nondiscursive knowledge of such an identity is the ultimate experience of one's life. Such a realization liberates one from material bondage.

A seeker of God in theistic Hinduism, on the other hand, strives for God-realization through self-surrender, devoted service, and rituals. He sees God as the Supreme Person with many-splendored attributes who never lets a devotee down. This is the view which finds its most definitive expression in the philosophy of the *Gita*, composed at a time when the Hindu religion was trying to make a comeback with its own answer to the Buddha's practical philosophy. The Buddha's emergence had been made possible mainly because of the post-Upanishadic slump in the Hindu tradition. At that time, the common people were bewildered by the excesses of the Vedic sacrificial ritualism and by the all-too-nebulous metaphysical teachings of self-realization (*atma-jñana*) as found in the Upanishads. What they needed and were looking for was a practical guide to everyday living and a philosophy of salvation understandable in human terms. Hence came the Buddha, and a few centuries later a resurgence of Hinduism, made possible through the popular appeal of the *Gita* and through the emergence of the *dharma* texts, which contained systematic explanations of household and social duties.

The *Gita* emphasized the element of loving devotion (*bhakti*) to a personal God in a tradition which was by that time all too ready for it. As opposed to the Vedic hierarchy, the promise of salvation was offered to all people who would put their faith in Krishna. The importance of self-knowledge was de-emphasized but not denied; rather, such knowledge was to be blended with selfless action and devotion. The *Gita* found meaning in diverse spiritual orientations and put them together into its own broad conception of religious quest, thereby making its philosophy appeal to a wide range of people.

The *Gita*'s story is set in the dramatic context of a war in which the good and the evil sides are clearly marked. Krishna, the human-incarnate of the Hindu god Vishnu, is the charioteer of Arjuna, who is the most gifted warrior on the good side which is destined to overcome the evil forces. When the two sides are about to engage in the war, Arjuna, realizing that the war means killing some of his own relatives and benefactors with the other side, becomes dejected and refuses to fight. In order to advise Arjuna that he

should do what must be done, Krishna gives his sermon which constitutes the body of the *Gita*. The dramatic setting of the story in the battlefield is highly symbolic. It is suggestive of the spiritual struggle of a human soul in which Arjuna, the confused self, looks for an excuse to withdraw from the battle, but Krishna, the Divine in man, charioteers the soul.

To get Arjuna back to his task, Krishna starts his teaching with the Samkhya idea that a man's true self, which is his soul, is eternal and indestructible. The initial thrust of his message is to persuade Arjuna to get out of his despondency; hence, some of Krishna's points, at this stage, are meant more as persuasive appeals than as spiritual insights. Accordingly, the idea that a man's true self is eternal is used, to start with, to convince Arjuna that he should not be perturbed by the prospect of the mere physical death he might cause to people; after all, their souls are indestructible. (However shocking this ploy might seem because it is an apparent rationalization for killing, it should be understood in its proper perspective. Arjuna is faced with a crisis of resolve: he is rightfully assigned to do something which he now finds unnerving, improper, and distasteful. To show him the importance of doing his duty (*svadharma*) and of not being swayed by external considerations in the face of what must be done, Krishna teaches him how to accept the inevitable in the right spirit.)

The rightness of Arjuna's fighting the battle, since he is a warrior by caste, is not really in question. It was already decided that to fight was the only right and honorable option available to Arjuna and his clan. Arjuna's last-minute self-doubt and his consequent decision not to fight are, then, indications of failure of nerve and weakness of resolve on his part. As a result, it is Krishna's task to see that Arjuna comes out of his confusion and secures the necessary strength to do what must be done. Being Arjuna's guru and a shrewd judge of human character, Krishna knows that a confused person like Arjuna who is in need of help will not be impressed by a reasoned discourse on the rightness of a proposed course of actions, nor by a gospel of spiritual wisdom. Rather, what he needs is some reassurance and practical persuasions. Accordingly, Krishna tries to provide them both by using, almost to the point of sophistry, the deeply cherished Hindu ideas of the imperishability of soul and the inevitability of death and reincarnation. He also tries to appeal to Arjuna's honor by reminding him of his caste duty to fight a just war and by citing the possible consequence of his being branded as a coward if he backs out of the battle at the last moment.

Gradually, however, Krishna takes Arjuna to progressively higher planes of awakening by leaving out sophistry and the appeal to his base emotions and by providing more substantive discourses on human nature, life's goal, and God. This practical teaching procedure, in which the teacher comes down to the disciple's level and then gradually takes him to a deeper understanding of the issues commensurate with his ability, is a standard feature in a guru-disciple relationship in Hinduism. In such teaching, many of the earlier points of persuasion, meant to take one out of one's spiritual lethargy, are to be ignored or grown out of in a later phase of realization. Krishna's initial effort to make Arjuna come back to his senses, together with his later offering of more profound discourses, serves as an excellent demonstration of this progressive teaching technique.

It is seemingly ironic that the *Gita*, which is one of the most definitive texts on love and nonviolence, starts with an apparent rationalization for killing. However, the irony disappears when it is understood that Arjuna is not really given a lesson on killing but is told to differentiate between real love and false compassion, to understand death and not be afraid of it, and to realize that there is much more to a person than his fleeting nature and perishable body—namely, his undying soul which is divine in nature. Because these points are presented in the context of a battle and in the initial guise of the advice to kill, they illustrate the real-life import of the teachings and dramatize the importance of spiritual serenity in the midst of unnerving situations. Like the progressive teaching method, the advocacy of spirituality in juxtaposition to material concerns is another technique in the Hindu tradition, a technique also exemplified by the explicitly erotic sculptures on the walls of even the most pious Hindu temples.

In order to emphasize the need for even-mindedness as a prelude to having control over oneself in the midst of action and hence to being able to better perform action, Krishna moves on to a discourse of detachment in action. In the course of his teaching it becomes clear that such detachment is not only necessary if one is to be unperturbed by extraneous considerations while performing action, but also if one is to attain purity of soul and conquest of passion and ego-consciousness. These in turn are said to be conducive to spiritual liberation (*moksa*), man's ultimate salvation.

Krishna initially develops the idea of detachment by elaborating on the nature of work and its "fruit" (*phala*). He advocates right attitude toward work to avoid its inherent bondage, and illustrates the fundamental difference between eternal, nonactive human souls and transient, ever-active matter, which is the real locus of action. Perhaps the most celebrated account of detachment in any Hindu scripture is contained in the second chapter of the *Gita*, where Krishna asks Arjuna to set his heart only upon his work and never on its fruit or result. A man who is moved by success or failure, Arjuna is told, is not an even-minded person settled in wisdom. To be mentally detached from one's work one need not renounce work or be indifferent to what must be done; rather, one is asked to be indifferent to the *fruits* of one's action. That is, after taking utmost care in doing what is right, one must not worry or be apprehensive about the results, for, according to Krishna, one has access only to one's work, not to its results.

In the later chapters Krishna points out that the results of work must be surrendered to God as sacrifice; any outcome must be acceptable as God's gift. The emergence of the totality of God in the *Gita* is a gradual but sure one: it starts in Chapter IV and goes on until Chapter XV, climaxing in the eleventh chapter where Krishna reveals his divine form to Arjuna in all its terrifying majesty. These chapters contain discourses on God's nature, the nature of soul and matter and their relation to God, and, above all, the importance of loving self-devotion to God. They also dwell on the idea of work in the spirit of sacrifice as a means to detachment.

The Vedas prescribed undertaking sacrificial rituals to obtain the desirables from the gods. The Upanishads de-emphasized the rituals, substituting inward subjective quest in their place. The *Gita* reintroduced the notion of sacrifice, but not in the Vedic sense. If work cannot be avoided because the world is sustained by work, and yet if attachment to its fruit creates fetters (*karma*), then the way out, according to the *Gita*, is through a detached performance of one's work where God is the object to whom the result is offered as sacrifice. The cardinal teaching in the *Gita* seems to be that doing one's work in the right spirit, as sacrifice, involves an integrated discipline (*yoga*) of action, knowledge, and, above all, devotion, and that such a *yoga* not only enables one to undertake activities without anxiety for gain and safety but is also a spiritual exercise which takes one closer to God.

Accompanying the idea of personal devotion in the *Gita* is the notion of divine incarnation (*avataravada*). In Chapter IV, Krishna declares that whenever righteousness declines and lawlessness arises, he appears in this world in human form to set things right. This idea is especially important to a devotee because it provides a personal touch to one of the persistent themes of the *Gita*, which is that God's laws are moral laws and whoever strives to establish righteousness (*dharma*) is actually doing God's service and is dear to him. It reveals that God is concerned about what goes on in his creation, and, therefore, it conveys hope to the faithful. In the context of this declaration it makes all the more sense why Arjuna is asked to engage in action to uphold righteousness, and why, in the *Gita*, so much emphasis is placed on the importance of devoted performance of righteous work, in the spirit of sacrifice, as the preferred means to God-realization.

The idea of divine incarnation, popular among the Hindus, has helped them view all prophets of all religions as fulfilling the divine promise, and thus it has made them generally tolerant toward other religions. In fact, the *Gita* itself champions this attitude: throughout its gradual unfolding of the supremacy and priority of God, Krishna repeatedly mentions that whenever one shows devotion to God in whatever form, God responds to him likewise. Although the *Gita* favors an integrated *yoga* of devotion which

is to be carried through wisdom and proper action, it leaves room for other forms of devotion; and, what is more, it also acknowledges paths to spiritual freedom even without devotion. In Chapter XII Krishna admits that the seekers of wisdom who strive after the Upanishadic "Unmanifest" also reach God; but he thinks that the path of devotion to a personal God is an easier one. However, he declares that if the *Gita*'s preferred path is not suitable for someone, then that person should resort to another method.

The *Gita* repeatedly asserts the fundamental difference between a person's true self, which is his soul and which is nonactive by nature, and the ever-active material nature (*prakrti*) which forms his body and mind (the subtle body). However, the *Gita* avoids a Samkhya-type dualism, which is the basis of the later philosophy of the Yoga, by postulating a personified Absolute Being, God, who manifests himself both in selves and matter (which are parts of him) and yet remains distinct from them in power and personality. *Isvara*, the personal god who is symbolized as Lord Vishnu and whose incarnate is Krishna, is the creative aspect of this Supreme Being; it is through *Isvara* that he creates and sustains the world and dwells in everything. *Brahman*, the Upanishadic Absolute, is said to be the unmanifest form of the *Gita*'s God, the Supreme Person (*purusottama*); yet the *Gita* insists that God is more than all his forms.

Consistent with this position which asserts the supremacy of God over everything else, the *Gita* makes God the abode of *Brahman*. Philosophical difficulties aside, what is clearly evident in these characterizations is an attempt to meet the Upanishadic challenge by making a personified Absolute Being the foundation of all possible beings, including the one immutable *Brahman*, and by making devotion not only a viable but also the most important path to the realization of this highest reality. The *Gita*'s whole idea is to demonstrate that love of God, so far from being just a convenient device disposable at the dawn of knowledge, is also the very anchor of such knowledge, which, without it, is inadequate.

One of the major themes conveyed by Krishna's message to Arjuna is that human beings and everything else have a divine essence because everything is created out of God's being. Hence, an important aspect of the religious quest in the *Gita* is to realize one's own divine essence and to share in God's mode of being through an experience of one's essential unity with the divine source. In that sense the liberating experience in the *Gita* has a definite mystical flavor; but, unlike a Upanishadic mystic who strives for the experience of oneness with *Brahman* primarily through a meditative quest, the seeker of God in the *Gita* cultivates detachment in his performance of righteous acts which uphold social order. The *Gita*'s insistence on the importance of self-knowledge is not meant to shift the emphasis from society to hermitage, nor is its call for devotion to God to be taken as signifying a priority for the life hereafter. In fact, perhaps the greatest contribution of the *Gita* is that it provides a religious justification for continuing a socially committed life of action.

Pertinent Literature

The Bhagavad Gita. Translated by Franklin Edgerton. Cambridge, Massachusetts: Harvard University Press, 1972.

Franklin Edgerton's translation of the *Gita* is perhaps the most celebrated of all English translations, and rightly so. It demonstrates the rare combination of being literal yet poetic, a quality which is difficult to achieve in translating a religious poem which has deep cultural roots. Overall, the translation comes close to the text's original style and spirit.

Edgerton believes that the task of an interpreter should be to indicate the relations between various ideas found in the text, with as few comments on his part as possible. The *Gita*, being primarily a mystical poem, does not provide a logical or thoroughly systematic treatment of the issues. Although it needs some interpretation, Edgerton lets the poem stand on its own as much as possible. Despite the seeming simplicity of the *Gita*'s language, the general understanding of its philosophy has widely varied. Therefore, even though the *Gita* has been translated and interpreted many times, Edgerton felt that another attempt was needed. However, he acknowledges that the final interpretation of the poem will never be written.

In tracing the historical origin of the *Gita*'s ideas, Edgerton points out that the earliest of all Hindu literature, the *Hymns of the Rig Veda*, although mostly polytheistic in nature, contains speculation about the notion of an impersonal, nontheistic One. However, according to Edgerton, Upanishadic monism is the real beginning of the speculative trend of the later, classical Hinduism. Along with such speculation arose a need for a more personal, theistic emphasis; this yearning found its culmination in the *Gita*. Nevertheless, Edgerton notes that even the *Gita*'s monotheistic deity shows a blend of these two trends, for, according to him, the Upanishadic Absolute is also a part of the *Gita*'s deity.

Edgerton calls the *Gita*'s God the First Principle of the universe, distinct from all things, yet encompassing everything. Because of every man's intrinsic god-nature, due to God's immanence in his creation, the *Gita* views it as a man's duty to treat others as himself. However, Edgerton notes that most often in the *Gita* such duty is not specified; one is simply asked to undertake a task in the spirit of doing one's duty, whatever that duty may be. He also observes that the injunction to do no harm to any living creature, even though implicit in the *Gita*'s doctrine of God's immanence in his creation and generally accepted in most other Hindu systems, is not adequately emphasized in the *Gita*.

The *Gita* distinguishes three paths leading to salvation, each emphasizing knowledge, or disciplined activity, or devotion to God. Even though the *Gita* generally admits the importance of knowledge in spiritual awakening, it seems to prefer the path of detached action over that of knowledge because it is believed to be an easier way to attain salvation. However, Edgerton points out, the *Gita* considers the path of devotion to God as an even easier way; hence, it is the most favored of all in the *Gita*. At times the

Gita seems to indicate that each of the paths invariably leads to the others, thus implying that, no matter what path one takes, the way to salvation really consists of an integrated *yoga* of knowledge, disciplined action, and devotion. In fact, the characteristics of a true devotee described in the *Gita* are very much like those ascribed to a man of disciplined action or of knowledge.

The Bhagavad Gita. Edited and translated by Eliot Deutsch. New York: Holt, Rinehart and Winston, 1968.

The *Gita* has been translated into English many times, both by Indian and Western scholars. However, until recently it had not been translated and commented upon by a professional Western philosopher with specifically Western students of philosophy in mind. Eliot Deutsch's stated reason for undertaking another study of the *Gita* was to fill this gap. Overall, the book is primarily a philosophical study, perhaps one of only two or three of its kind. It is divided into three parts: the first part critically introduces some of the main concepts found in the *Gita*; the second contains the author's own English translation of the text, along with notes; and the third portion consists of four philosophical essays on the *Gita*.

In the translation Deutsch retains a few important Sanskrit terms in Roman script because he believes that it is almost impossible to find their adequate English equivalents. These key words are explained in the first part of the book so that the reader is aware of the various traditional lines of thought which the words represent and which the *Gita* incorporates into its own philosophy. The faithful and readable translation is remarkably precise, partly because Deutsch retains these important terms in the original Sanskrit.

Deutsch characterizes the *Gita*'s philosophy as personalized monism or nondualistic theism and notes that these descriptions, incomprehensible as they may seem because of the incompatible ideas expressed in the conjoined terms, are permissible in view of the *Gita*'s special metatheology. With regard to the *Gita*'s doctrine of divine descent into human form, Deutsch looks for some deeper symbolic meaning and finds it in the idea that Krishna is Arjuna's divine self calling for spiritual awakening. Arjuna as the symbolic embodiment of a confused soul looking for guidance in a crisis of faith is gradually taken to higher levels of understanding, consistent with his ability at each stage of learning, through the progressive teaching technique which is extensively used in the *Gita*.

Many interpreters have presumed that the *Gita* is a systematic philosophical treatise with a logically coherent metaphysical structure; others have thought that it is a mere poem meant to appeal to the emotions. Deutsch's philosophical essays in the third part of the book are written in a spirit which tries to avoid both these extremes. According to Deutsch, the core teaching of the *Gita* is about a very special discipline of action (*karma-yoga*) which also necessarily involves devotion (*bhakti*) and knowledge (*jnana*). Such teaching does not find value in the practice of the Vedic ceremonial religion meant for attaining egocentric desires. The *Gita* approves such practice only when it is undertaken in the spirit of *karma-yoga* to fulfill one's social duties (*dharma*).

Deutsch also deals with the problem of freedom and determinism, which is a basic issue in Indian philosophy in general and in the *Gita* in particular. The *Gita* states that man, as an empirical, phenomenal being, lacks freedom in several ways. He, like everything else in nature, is bound by its forces and is predestined by God's will. Further, in accordance with the law of *karma*, he is determined by his own past actions. Yet, Deutsch observes, the *Gita* categorically affirms man's divinity and holds that man, as a spiritual being, is capable of attaining the highest freedom (*moksa*). The *Gita*'s favored path leading to such freedom is the integrated pursuit of disciplined action, devoted self-surrender to God, and knowledge.

Deutsch thinks that the *Gita*'s teachings have an existential urgency about them; consequently, even though they are synthetic and not strikingly original, they are appealing. They also have an enduring value because, according to Deutsch, they find meaning in every possible spiritual orientation and urge people of all temperaments to pursue their self-fulfillment in a manner appropriate to their needs.

The Bhagavadgita. Translated by Sarvepalli Radhakrishnan. London: George Allen & Unwin, 1948.

According to Sarvepalli Radhakrishnan, the pressing need of today's world is the reconciliation of mankind. The *Gita*, in his judgment, is specially suited for this purpose, because the *Gita* espouses a spiritual philosophy which incorporates many types of religious consciousness into a unified quest and thus embodies man's perennial search for the Divine. Radhakrishnan views his interpretation of the *Gita* as a restatement of the timeless truth contained in the text; he thinks that such interpretation is needed if a great ancient scripture is to be of living value in today's world.

The *Gita*, according to Radhakrishnan, draws on various living elements of Hinduism. Even though the *Gita*'s answer to the problem of human action, posed at the opening section of the text, is not altogether a new one, it is stated with a new emphasis. Radhakrishnan views the *Gita* more as a religious scripture containing profound philosophical ideas than as a philosophical treatise *per se*. He points out, for example, that the *Gita* does not provide any logical arguments regarding the nature and existence of the ultimate reality, because, as primarily concerned with practical spirituality, the *Gita* values personal experience and faith more than philosophic dialectic. Nevertheless, the *Gita* sounds convincing without being unduly dogmatic because it provides an eloquent account of a philosophy of life based on an insightful observation of human nature and human predicaments.

Radhakrishnan's interpretation of the *Gita*'s message is greatly influenced by the Upanishadic ideas found in Saykara's monistic Vedanta philosophy. Samkara himself wrote a commentary on the *Gita*— the oldest extant commentary on the poem—and Radhakrishnan cites it often both in his interpretation of the *Gita*'s ideas and in his notes to the translation of the text. He justifies the blend of the Upanishadic and the *Gita*'s ideas in his interpretation on the ground that the *Gita* itself supports the Upanishadic view in many passages. Such an Upanishadic emphasis, however, often distorts the *Gita*'s metaphysical position.

For example, the *Gita*'s God, the Supreme Person (*Purusottama*), is not only the Lord of the universe but, ontologically, is also the abode of the Upanishadic *Brahman*. Consequently, Radhakrishnan's characterization of the *Gita*'s God as the Upanishadic *Isvara*, the creative manifestation of the unmanifest *Brahman*, does not agree with the *Gita*'s insistence that God is the supreme reality. In the Upanishads, as interpreted by Samkara, *Isvara* is the finite manifestation of *Brahman*; hence it lacks ontological supremacy.

Radhakrishnan rightly points out that even though there is textual evidence that Krishna as a historical person actually lived, the historicity of Krishna is irrelevant in appreciating the eternal message of the *Gita*. Regarding the question of how the *Gita* can identify a historical person with the Supreme, Radhakrishnan has two answers. The first answer is based on the Upanishadic theme that a liberated person sees himself as essentially one with the Absolute, and the other is the doctrine of divine incarnation (*avatara-vada*) in the *Gita*. In the former context, the identity between a person and the Supreme is not so much a limitation of the Absolute Spirit within the bonds of the finite as it is the elevation of human nature to the realm of the infinite. With regard to the latter, even though the doctrine is viewed as expressing the idea of God's descent into man, Radhakrishnan notes the Upanishadic theme that both creation and incarnation belong to the world of manifestation and do not affect the unmanifest Absolute Spirit. Reading this idea into the *Gita*, he concludes that Krishna is the Absolute *as though* born and embodied.

Radhakrishnan observes that the symbolic meaning of the *Gita*'s doctrine of divine incarnation is the eternal presence of the Divine consciousness in human beings, for the *Gita* teaches us that the human nature, properly cultivated, can become an instrument of the Divine will and find spiritual freedom. Such liberation does not consist in isolating the Divine from the mere human, but in transfiguring the whole man.

Additional Recommended Reading

The Bhagavad Gita. Edited and translated by A. L. Herman. Springfield, Illinois: Charles C. Thomas, 1973. A provocative philosophical examination of the problems raised in the *Gita*, which is treated here primarily as a philosophical text.

The Bhagavad-Gita: An English Translation and Commentary. Edited and translated by W. Douglas P. Hill. London: Oxford University Press, 1928. Perhaps the most readable translation, along with a commentary and a long scholarly introduction.

The Bhagavad-Gita: With a Commentary Based on the Original Sources. Edited and translated by R. C. Zaehner. Oxford: Clarendon Press, 1969. An excellent and detailed exposition of the *Gita*'s central ideas, with a faithful translation and a useful appendix.

Bhagavad-Gita as It Is. Edited and translated by A. C. Bhaktivedanta. Los Angeles: The Bhaktivedanta Book Trust, 1968. The *Gita* introduced, translated, and commented upon by the founder of the Krishna consciousness movement in the West.

Feuerstein, G. A. *Introduction to the Bhagavad-Gita: Its Philosophy and Cultural Setting.* London: Rider & Company, 1975. Contains a detailed introduction and perceptive essays on the *Gita*'s essential doctrines.

Sharma, Arvind. *The Hindu Gita: Ancient and Classical Interpretation of the Bhagavadgita.* Peru, Illinois: Open Court, 1986. A helpful account of the varied ways in which these classical Hindu texts have been interpreted.

DEMOCRITUS: FRAGMENTS

Author: Democritus of Abdera (c. 460-c. 370 B.C.)
Type of work: Philosophy of nature
First transcribed: Probably fourth century B.C.

Principal Ideas Advanced

Since nothing can come from nothing, and change really occurs, and motion requires a void, reality must consist of atoms moving in a void.

The only inherent properties of atoms are size, shape, and solidity; color, sweetness, bitterness, and other such qualities are attributed to objects because of the sensations occurring within experiencing organisms, but such qualities have no existence in objects.

The sensations that come from experiencing various kinds of atoms vary according to the shapes of the atoms.

The best form of government is the democratic.

The wise man is one who limits his ambition according to his ability.

In all probability credit for the fundamental ideas of the atomic theory—Greek speculation's greatest achievement—should go to Leucippus of Miletus rather than to his pupil Democritus. But we know almost nothing of Leucippus.

Rational speculation about the nature of the world began not earlier than the sixth century B.C. Four or five generations later it had progressed, in Democritus, to an essentially correct account of the nature of matter. This amazing fact has led to both exaggeration and underestimation of the Greek achievement. On the one hand, some people conclude that science stood still until the revival of the atomic theory in the seventeenth century. On the other, scientists especially are prone to point out that modern atomic physics rests on evidence derived from careful quantitative experimentation of which the Greeks knew nothing; therefore, it is said, the ancient theory was merely a lucky guess—and the Greeks made all possible guesses. A brief review of the development of early Greek physics will show that while Democritus did not have Dalton's reasons for asserting that the world consists of atoms moving in the void, he nevertheless had some very good ones. Knowing these, we shall be able to compare ancient and modern atomism less superficially and misleadingly.

The men of Miletus, especially Anaximander, who made the break with mythological world accounts in the early sixth century B.C. took over from previous creation myths two important assumptions. First, these Milesians accepted the belief that there *was* a creation, or rather a development: the world was not always as it is now, but had in the beginning been something simple and homogeneous, like the "chaos" of the myths. Differentiation, complexity, and organization have a history. Second, the Milesians accepted the theory that there exists an impersonal force making for order and "justice" in the universe at large. The Milesians were the first philosophers because they dispensed altogether with the "will of the gods" as an explanatory principle, because they assumed that the natural forces that made the universe what it is were of a kind still operative. The problem, as they conceived it, was to identify the original simple world-stuff, out of which all things had come, and to describe the process which had differentiated and organized it into the present world. Not "divine" inspiration but ordinary human reason, they thought, was capable of solving the problem. And since conclusions based on reasons invite criticism and modification, unlike revelations which can be only accepted or rejected, the history of rational speculation was progressive.

In addition to the ideas of ultimate oneness, development, and "justice" inherited from religion, the earliest philosophers assumed with "common sense" that nothing can come out of nothing, or be absolutely destroyed, and that our senses reveal to us directly the constituents of the world, at least as it is now. We feel heat and cold; we taste sweetness and bitterness; we see red and green. Heat, cold, sweetness, bitterness, red, and green are therefore *parts* of the objective world; together they make it up. *We* should say that these are *qualities* of matter, but early Greek thought does not make this distinction; "the hot," "the cold," "the wet," "the dry," and so on, in various combinations, *are* the stuff of things. One must simply find out the unity underlying this diversity.

Thus, for example, Anaximenes, the third of the Milesian "physicists," held that the fundamental stuff is Mist. Everything is really Mist; the things that do not appear to be Mist are Mist that has been thickened or thinned. Very thin Mist is fire; Mist somewhat thickened is water; thickened still more it is stone.

There is an inconsistency here which Parmenides (in effect) pointed out. No doubt the theory of Anaximenes squares with observation, for fire, when cooled and "thickened," becomes smoke and smoke is easy to regard, at this stage of thought, as a kind of fog or Mist. Condensed Mist is water, and water thickened still more becomes ice, a solid, a kind of stone. But is the theory compatible with logic? Fire is (identical with) "the hot and dry"; water is (identical with) "the cold and wet." How, then, can the one be transformed into the other without violating the fundamental principle that nothing can come from nothing? Where did the *cold* come from? Where has the *hot* gone? If cold and hot are thought of (so to speak) as substances, it seems that there can be no satisfactory answer to this question. Something has come out of "nothing"; something has disappeared into "nothing." Worse still, as Parmenides saw, if there is ultimately just one stuff, that stuff must be just the kind of stuff it is, so that it cannot logically be both hot and cold, both wet and dry. Therefore *change is impossible*. If things seem to change (as they do), this must be mere illusion, for logic pronounces it contradictory.

It is important to see that Parmenides was right, *given his assumptions* of monism, nothing-from-nothing, and identity of things and qualities. Parmenides had another argument (a fallacious one) to show that the kind of change called motion cannot really occur. It is this: If a thing moves, there must be room for it to move into—that is, there must be empty space. But there cannot be any empty space, for empty space would be just "nothing," "that which is not," and the assertion that there is empty space amounts to saying "That which is not, is," a statement of contradiction.

The philosophers Empedocles and Anaxagoras tried to develop systems which would meet the logical objections of Parmenides without flying in the face of common sense. They argued that motion could occur without empty space if the moving thing *displaced* what was in front of it, as a fish swims in water. For the rest, they abandoned monism. Empedocles said that there are six basic stuffs, while Anaxagoras held that there are an infinity—as many stuffs as there are sensible discriminations—and all things are made by the mixture and separation of these stuffs.

The philosophy of Anaxagoras successfully met Parmenides' criticism, but at too high a price. While it is hard to say precisely just what it is that we are asking for when we demand an explanation of something, at any rate it is clear that an explanation is not satisfactory unless in *some* sense the ideas used in the explanation are simpler, or more unified, than the thing to be explained. But if one's explanatory principles are as diverse as the things to be explained, the requirement cannot be met. "Flour is a mixture in which flour-stuff predominates, and water is a mixture in which water-stuff predominates, and the two make bread because when they are mixed and baked the bread-stuff in both of them comes to the fore." This may be true, but it is too easy, and it does not *explain* anything.

Leucippus and Democritus discovered a better way of answering Parmenides. As to motion, Leucippus flatly declared that "nothing" *does* exist; while Democritus more appropriately dismissed Parmenides' quibble with another: " 'Hing' exists no more than 'not-hing,' " the point of the joke being that if " 'Nothing does not exist" is a truth of *logic*, elimination of the double negative must also produce a logical truth: "'Hing' does exist." But "hing," so far from existing, is not even a word. (Greek for "nothing" is "meden," of which "mé" means "not," while "den" has no meaning in isolation.)

There is, then, a void, and things that move in it. These things are *atoms*— "uncuttables." Each separate atom is like the "reality" of Parmenides, uncreated, indestructible, unchanging. The matter in an atom is homogeneous, and nothing can happen to one internally; that is, each atom is infinitely hard. Atoms differ from one another in size and shape—that is all. They do not differ in color, for instance, but not because they are all the *same* color. They do so because they have no color at all (not even black or gray). Similarly for heat, moisture, taste, and odor. Atoms have always been (and always will be) in motion—"like the motes in a sunbeam." They jostle one another, and in their jostlings, two kinds of processes occur that result in the "coming-into-being" of the large-scale aggregates with which we are familiar. One is vortex motion, the effect of which is to separate random aggregates according to likenesses, the heavier—that is, the bigger—atoms going to the center, the lighter ones to the periphery. The other process is the hooking on to each other by atoms of like configurations.

One atom can affect another only by colliding with it; and the outcome of a collision (hooking, or change of direction or speed) is *determined* by the sizes, shapes, and velocities of the atoms involved in the collision. But the sizes and shapes are eternal, and the velocities in their turn are outcomes of previous collisions. Therefore, there is no such thing as "chance" in nature; "Nothing happens at random," Leucippus pronounced in the one sentence of his that has survived, "but everything from a rationale and by necessity." Ideally, explanation should consist in finding out the laws of motion and impact and using these to show how one atomic configuration came about from a previous one. Such a complex act is of course impossible; however, Democritus sought to apply the fundamental idea of *mechanical causation* to observable phenomena.

There is an ancient story that illustrates his method and points up its difference from traditional concepts. Considerable interest had been aroused by the extraordinary death of a prominent man. When he was strolling along a beach, an eagle had dropped a turtle on his head. *Why*? It was recalled that an oracle had said that he would die of "a bolt from Zeus." This had been thought to be a prediction of death by a stroke of lightning. But someone pointed out that the eagle was sacred to Zeus; thus, the oracle was fulfilled. This satisfied most Greeks, but not Democritus. *He* went to the beach and observed the habits of eagles. He found that they were fond of turtle meat. In order to get at it, an eagle would seize a turtle in his talons, fly into the air with it, and drop it on a rock to crack the shell. This observation, together with the fact that the deceased had been bald, provided an explanation that satisfied Democritus. The curious event was shown to be one item in a natural regularity or pattern. It was unnecessary to postulate the purposes of unseen beings to account for the fact. Aristotle complained, quite unjustifiably, that Democritus "reduced the explanation of nature to the statement, 'Thus it happened formerly also.' " The fact is that Democritus understood the character of scientific explanation far better than did Aristotle.

In sum, Democritus' reason for asserting that reality consists of atoms moving in the void is that this statement can be *deduced* from the premises: (1) nothing can come from nothing, (2) change really occurs, and (3) motion requires a void. That explanation must be mechanistic also follows from these assumptions if it is further allowed that all interaction is impact. Democritus' mechanism was also the culmination of the rejection of animistic and supernatural will-forces by all his philosophical predecessors.

Democritus' atomism, and still more his mechanism, agree in principle with the fundamental tenets of modern physical science. (By "in principle" it is meant to rule out as inessential, though important, such differences as that the particles of the present-day physicists are wave-packets or whatever, and fuzzy, and hookless; what is essential is the concept of matter as somehow granular, and that physical processes are analyzable into redistributions of energy among these grains.) What modern physicists have that Democritus lacked is a conception of controlled, quantitative experimentation, together with a technique of mathematical manipulation of the data. For this reason, Democritus, though he declared that he would "rather discover one causal explanation than gain the kingdom of the Persians," failed utterly to add to detailed knowledge of nature. In fact, he was much behind his own times, still believing, for instance, that the earth is a flat disc, though the Pythagoreans had long understood its sphericity. In detailed explanations, Democritus could do no better than this: "Thunder is produced by an unstable mixture forcing the cloud enclosing it to move downward. Lightning is a clashing together of clouds by which the fire-producing atoms rubbing against each other are assembled through the porous mass into one place and pass out. And the thunderbolt occurs when the motion is forced by the very pure, very fine, uniform and 'closely-packed' fire-producing atoms, as he himself calls them." (The foregoing is an ancient paraphrase, not a quotation from Democritus.) It must be admitted that this account is no worse than any other prior to Franklin, and a considerable improvement over "Zeus is angry."

"By convention color, by convention sweet, by convention bitter; but in reality atoms and void." Thus Democritus states his theory. The atoms alone are real, and their only inherent qualities (we can use this word now, for Democritus distinguished for the first time clearly between thing and quality) are size, shape, and solidity. Then what about color, sweet, bitter, and the rest? They are "by convention." What does this mean? Democritus held that a man's soul consists of particularly fine and spherical, hence mobile, atoms. When certain "images" from the external world—the images being, of course, themselves assemblages of atoms—impinge on the soul atoms, a sensation is produced. The sensation occurs only within the ensouled body; hence, is not "out there" because the external world is colorless and odorless. This is a part of the meaning of "by convention," a phrase that might be rendered as "subjective." The sensations are also subjective in the sense that they lead us to suppose, falsely, that the world is colored and odorous.

"There are two forms of knowledge, one genuine, one obscure. Of the obscure sort are all these: sight, hearing, smell, taste, touch. The genuine is distinguished from this. . . . Whenever the obscure cannot sense any farther into the minute by seeing or hearing or smelling or tasting or touching, but [it is necessary to pursue the investigation] more finely, [then the genuine, which has a finer organ of knowing,] comes up." The organ of "genuine knowledge" would seem to be the "Pure Reason" that led Democritus to deduce the atomic nature of matter. But Democritus was worried, as well he might have been, about the "obscure." He portrayed the senses speaking thus to the mind: " 'Wretched mind, getting from us your confidences you cast us down? That is your own downfall.' " For the information on which even the atomic theory is based is, after all, derived ultimately from observation through the senses.

If reality consists of matter with only its "primary qualities," what kind of reality do sensation, and thought, and consciousness in general have? This problem besets all forms of materialism and is often alleged (wrongly) to be fatal to it as a world view. Democritus spent much effort in trying to account for sensations on atomic principles. Thus, he claimed that sour fluids consist of angular and twisted atoms, while honey is made of rounded, rather large ones. This was, of course, inconsistent with his claim that tastes are subjective effects. He could have patched up the account to some extent by considering not only the atomic constitution of the food but also that of the tongue which interacts with it; but there is no evidence that he did so. Perhaps it was despair at this problem that led him to exclaim, "In reality we know nothing. For truth is in a depth."

Materialists *should* say that sensations are not *things* at all; but Democritus held that they are illusory things. This, at any rate, is the impression we get from ancient discussions of his theory of knowledge. It may be mistaken, for the accounts all come from hostile critics who may well have misunderstood or misrepresented the great Abderite.

Unlike most Greek philosophers, Democritus was a partisan of democracy. He said: "Poverty in a democracy is as much preferable to so-called prosperity in an autocracy as freedom is to slavery." By "democracy" he meant a constitutional government, directed by public-spirited, intelligent men in the interest of all citizens.

Democritus was one of the most prolific authors of antiquity, having written, we are told, more than sixty works. All have perished. The fragments that remain fill about ten pages of ordinary print, of which eight are concerned with ethics, politics, education, and child-rearing. (Democritus thought it a risky and thankless business to have children.) Many of the ethical reflections are unbearably platitudinous: "In good fortune it is easy to find a friend, in misfortune hardest of all." Others are shrewd and worldly wise: "If you cannot understand the compliments, conclude that you are being flattered." The general tenor of the maxims is advocacy of "cheerfulness," that is, of prudence, contentment with what one has, not worrying too much: "He who would be cheerful must not busy himself with many things, either by himself or in company; and whatever he busies himself with, he should not choose what is beyond his own power and nature. But he should be so on his guard that when a stroke of fortune tempts him to excess, he puts it aside, and does not grasp at what is beyond his powers. For being well-filled is better than being stuffed." There are some fragments, however, that rise quite above this pedestrian level, embodying, in fact, teachings often credited to others, and used unfairly to belabor crude "Materialism":

"Refrain from wrongdoing not from fear but from duty."

"The doer of injustice is unhappier than the sufferer. "

"Goodness is not merely in refraining from being unjust, but in not even wishing to be."

"The cause of error is ignorance of the better."

Pertinent Literature

Cleve, Felix M. *The Giants of Pre-Sophistic Greek Philosophy: An Attempt to Reconstruct Their Thoughts.* The Hague, The Netherlands: Martinus Nijhoff, 1969.

In a fascinating chapter on Leucippus of Miletus and Democritus of Abdera, Felix Cleve has attempted to reconstruct Democritus' theories through a new analysis of the fragments and by posing a series of searching questions about interpretations of his positions that had been proposed by his successors. Cleve concentrates especially upon Democritus' physical theories and on his theory of sensation, ignoring completely his moral theories and his famous aphorisms. He is particularly careful to avoid confusing the theories of Democritus with those of his famous successor, Epicurus, whom he accuses of having "bowdlerized" and "jumbled up" the true Democritean theory and thereby confused almost everyone for thousands of years. The following is a summary of Cleve's account of the most important points in Democritus' theory.

Atoms are unchangeable in several important respects. First, they are indivisible, and thus can never become smaller than they are at any given moment. Second, they never alter their shape or their size. Finally, they cannot grow by "adhesion"; that is, particles of similar shape cannot adhere to the smooth sides of one another. They form compounds not by adhesion or what we would call magnetic or gravitational attraction, but by irregularities on their surfaces—hooks and eyes of various sizes and shapes—which fit into similar projections and crevices on the surfaces of other atoms. Thus, by a purely mechanical process, atoms grasp one another as they move through space, catching more and more until rather large aggregates are formed. Although most atoms are very tiny, some of them are of gigantic size. The word "atom" simply means *indivisible*, not *minute*, as we are sometimes inclined to suppose. The gigantic atoms form the nuclei of the stars, according to Democritus.

Epicurus accounted for the conglomeration of atoms in a way that is strangely reminiscent of the modern theory of Werner Heisenberg, sometimes known as the indeterminacy or uncertainty principle. The Heisenberg principle was inspired by the fact that microscopic particles are observed to dart suddenly and unpredictably from their paths. Epicurus suggested that originally atoms were falling in parallel lines through the void of space, but that every now and then, for no apparent reason, they would suddenly veer out of their downward paths and move into the paths of other atoms. These sudden deviations would frequently result in collisions which would in turn bring about the connection of one atom with another. According to Cleve, this was not the theory adopted by Democritus. Democritus believed that the atoms were moving in every possible direction. Indeed, each atom has a motion peculiar to itself. Since Democritus believed that space is infinite, there was no reason for him to suppose that there is an absolute "up" or "down," so it would have made no sense for him to assume that atoms were falling through the void—*falling* requiring a presupposition of some "downward" direction in which the motion is proceeding. Since the atoms proceed in parallel paths, in perpendicular paths, and in paths that crisscross in every imaginable way, it is inevitable that they will collide with one another and eventually form larger conglomerations.

Why does an atom move? Because it is its nature to do so. It moves not because of gravity or because it is attracted to or repelled by anything else; rather, its motion is as much an inherent quality of itself as its shape is. Democritus made no attempt to explain the atom's motion (an omission for which he was taken to task by Aristotle and others), simply because he felt that there was no reason to explain it. It was merely a brute fact. Since the atoms are moving in random directions, each one with its own velocity, and each one in a straight line, it followed, according to Democritus, that space must be infinite. For were it not, the atoms would constantly be crashing into the outer boundaries of space only to bounce off and head in the opposite direction, a conclusion which Democritus evidently felt was absurd.

Moreover, from the infinity of space it followed that there must be an infinite number of atoms; for with an infinite amount of space in which to dash about, the atoms would eventually be spread so thin that very little of any consequence would be left after a certain amount of time had passed. And since there is an infinite number of atoms and an infinite amount of space in which they may do whatever they do, there is no reason to suppose that there is only one world. Therefore, Democritus drew the logical conclusion that there are infinitely many worlds. And since he could see no reason why the atoms should necessarily form similar conglomerations in various parts of the infinite void, he concluded that the infinite worlds could have an infinite number of varieties.

Inasmuch as each of the atoms possesses a natural motion, the question inevitably arises: How can we account for the fact that some objects, at least, are quite stable and seem not to be in motion at all? The answer, it appears, is that even though the aggregate is at rest, each of the particles of which it is composed is nevertheless in constant motion—a theory not very far from that with which we are familiar from modern atomic theory.

The atomists advanced a number of arguments to bolster their theory, the principal ones being:

(a) If there were no empty spaces (that is, if the world were a plenum, or if objects were perfectly solid with no empty spaces between their parts), it would be impossible to account for motion.

(b) The expansion and contraction of solids is inexplicable except under the theory that they are composed of solid particles separated by empty spaces which are widened during expansion and narrowed during contraction.

(c) Organic objects (animals and plants) can grow without merely developing thicker and thicker tissues and without losing their shapes only because some particles separate from one another, making room for others.

Whether these arguments are fully persuasive is another matter. The most persuasive, perhaps, is this:

(d) Ashes thrown into a vessel that is full of water will not cause the water to overflow. Nor will soluble salts added to a vessel full of water cause the water to overflow. Therefore (they reasoned), the particles of ashes or salts must be moving into the empty spaces between the particles of water.

The atoms possess size, shape, velocity, and resistance to penetration, according to the atomists, but not color, flavor, smell, or other properties. The atomists also said that the atoms are "apathetic," that is, unfeeling, by which they meant that they are not alive. In this respect, Democritus and his colleagues initiated an important departure from the other early Greek philosophers, who seem to have believed that all matter was in some sense alive.

In order to account for life and consciousness, Democritus assumed that fire atoms carry sensation and will, and that they are the force behind such biological functions as growth, automotion, nutrition, and the like ("automotion" meaning motion which is initiated by an act of will, of course, as distinguished from the purely automatic motions of atoms and inorganic matter). The loss of fire atoms accounts, in turn, for death. Consciousness and sensation are purely bodily functions. For Democritus, there is no immaterial soul or spirit, since only atoms —that is, material particles—and the void exist.

In attempting to explain vision, Democritus' predecessors—and also some of the great philosophers who came after him, including Plato—imagined that somewhere between the eye and the object being perceived, there is a meeting of two rays, one proceeding from the eye and being projected outward, and the other proceeding from the object and radiating outward. Democritus, however, concluded that vision takes place in or on the eye alone. Atoms bombarding an object (say, a cube) bounce off it again and form a pattern like that of the object itself. Some of these atoms then strike the eye of the perceiver, converging to a very narrow focus, entering the eye and finally appearing in the pupil. In other words, a picture of the object is reflected from the object itself to the eye, and what is seen is that reflection as it touches the eye.

Cleve goes on to discuss more modern theories of vision and other forms of perception—but that is no longer the philosophy of Democritus, who anticipated in rather remarkable ways many of the general theories which modern science has adopted— although of course, he had no way of anticipating their detailed development.

Bailey, Cyril. *The Greek Atomists and Epicurus.* Oxford: Clarendon Press, 1928.

Cyril Bailey's study of the Greek atomists concentrates on the philosophies of Leucippus, Democritus, and Epicurus. Bailey was led to an examination of the ideas of the former two philosophers as a preparation for an account of what he calls the "comprehensive system" of Epicurus.

In a brief biographical account of Democritus, Bailey agrees with most of the authorities in presuming Democritus to have been a student of Leucippus and in thinking it unlikely that he studied with Anaxagoras or the Pythagoreans. The nickname "Wisdom" (*sophia*) was given to Democritus, Bailey remarks, because of the philosopher's "universal knowledge." (The more familiar title, "The Laughing Philosopher," called attention to Democritus' "good-natured amusement at 'the vain efforts' of men. . . .")

Bailey provides an account of the works attributed to Democritus and emphasizes the wide range of the philosopher's interests: ethics, physics (including works on the physical universe, man, the mind, and sensation), logic, mathematics, astronomy, geography, music, literary criticism, the philosophy of language, medicine, agriculture, and a study of "history" or investigation. The most important part of this encyclopedic effort, according to Bailey, is Democritus' atomic theory, learned from Leucippus but related to the other areas of human knowledge so as to allow him to "see it in truer proportion" and attach to the atomic theory a moral theory that, as Bailey writes, "contained the germs of a cheerful and good-hearted philosophy of imperturbability. . . ." Bailey puts major emphasis on Democritus' atomic theory, his discussion of the soul, sensation, and thought, and the ethics. He also discusses Democritus' views concerning the cosmic whirl, the world, the gods, and theory of knowledge.

The central presupposition of Democritus' atomic theory, as derived from Leucippus, is that "ultimate existence" consists of "infinite indivisible particles in an infinite void." To this basic idea Democritus added the principle that "nothing is created out of the non-existent or is destroyed into the non-existent." Bailey points out that this principle provides the foundation for the atomistic account of the physical universe. Two more important principles were contributed by Democritus to the elaboration of the basic atomistic view: the principle that the universe is infinite because it was not created and the principle that "by necessity are foreordained all things that were and are and are to come." This latter principle, the principle of causal necessity, involves a strict causal determinism. Hence, Democritus was prepared to argue against the popular philosophical view that presented chance as a feature of physical reality and also against various metaphysical and religious views that posited "mysterious, semi-religious" forces. Bailey repeatedly describes Democritus as a thinker who held faithfully to the basic atomistic ideas he inherited but who, as a "man of the world," continually added to and modified the ideas so as to make them coherent and illuminating.

In agreement with Leucippus, Democritus argued for the permanence of individual atoms, but he departed from the line of proof advanced by Leucippus which based the proof of the indestructability of the atoms on their extreme smallness. Democritus relied in his proof of indestructability on the hardness of the atoms and, indeed, rebelled against the emphasis on smallness even to the point of insisting that some atoms are "very large" and that (as reported by one authority) "there might be an atom as big as the world."

As for the problem of accounting for the motion of the atoms, Democritus did not, like Epicurus, posit a universal downward fall, nor maintain, as some atomists did, that motion results from the heaviness of the atoms or from some blow (although heaviness affects the character and direction of movement); instead, Democritus argued that motion is eternal, that there was no beginning of motion, and hence that there is no need to look for a primary efficient cause.

Bailey emphasizes Democritus' contributions to the discussion of the differences of atomic shapes and their effect on the compounding or union of the atoms.

Bailey points out that Democritus agreed with Leucippus in regarding the soul as corporeal and as

being of the nature of fire (hence, composed of spherical atoms, the most mobile kind). Democritus accounted for the motion of the body by presupposing the causal effectiveness of soul atoms in motion: the moving soul actually made the body move. Death results when in the course of breathing the soul atoms are expired; the body, no longer able to sense or move, is then without life. The soul atoms disperse upon being breathed out; hence, the soul dies as does the body. Democritus conceived of mind as made up of the same kind of spherical atoms that make up the soul; but although the soul is distributed in the body and makes sensation and movement possible, the mind atoms are concentrated in the breast and produce the kind of sensation that is called thought.

According to Bailey, the word that is crucial to Democritus' moral ideas is the term "cheerfulness." By "cheerfulness" is not meant pleasure, Bailey argues, for Democritus maintained that the "good and true" is the same for all persons but that the "pleasant" varies from one to another; "cheerfulness" refers to the state of mind that is best for human beings as human, a state of imperturbability, of "undisturbed serenity." The emphasis is on the state of *mind*, not on physical pleasure, a state of the body. Hence, although in some ways Democritus' ethics anticipates that of Epicurus, in other ways Democritus' views are significantly different. Throughout his ethics Democritus emphasized the superiority of the soul over the body, and he urged that human beings seek not "every pleasure but that which is concerned with the beautiful." (The "beautiful" is understood by reference to the soul's preferences.) The body of Democritus' ethics was accordingly directed toward the consideration of practical ways of achieving cheerfulness, and it emphasized the virtues of moderation, friendship, and generosity, as well as other "positive" virtues that were extolled as providing aids to the cheerfulness of the mind.

Bailey concludes that in many ways Democritus' mind was superior to that of Epicurus and that, "in not a few respects," with Democritus "Atomism as such reached its highest development in Greece."

Additional Recommended Reading

Burnet, John. *Early Greek Philosophy*. London: A. and C. Black, 1948. Includes the fragments as well as a very good commentary and an account of Democritus' life.

Burnet, John. *Greek Philosophy; Thales to Plato*. London: Macmillan and Company, 1953. Includes a brief account of Democritus' philosophy.

Furley, David J. "The Atomists' Reply to the Eleatics," in *The Pre-Socratics: A Collection of Critical Essays.* Edited by Alexander P. D. Mourelatos. Garden City, New York: Anchor Press/Doubleday, 1974, pp. 504-526. Focuses on the question of whether Democritus and Leucippus were merely physical atomists, holding that the atoms are physically unsplittable, or whether they held that the atoms were also theoretically (mathematically) indivisible as well.

Vlastos, Gregory. "Ethics and Physics in Democritus," in *The Philosophical Review,* LIV, no. 6 (November, 1945), pp. 578-592; and LV, no. 1 (January, 1946), pp. 53-64. A study of Democritus' ethical as well as his physical theories and of the connections between them.

EUTHYPHRO

Author: Plato (427-347 B.C.)
Type of work: Ethics, philosophy of religion
First transcribed: Probably one of the early dialogues

Principal Ideas Advanced

Socrates has been charged by Meletus with corrupting the youth of Athens and with inventing new gods; and he seeks to learn from Euthyphro, who is prosecuting his own father for murder, the distinction between piety and impiety.

Euthyphro suggests that piety is prosecuting the unjust, those who have committed such crimes as murder or sacrilege; impiety is failure to prosecute such persons.

But Socrates points out that this is an example, not a definition; and thus Euthyphro suggests that piety is whatever is pleasing to the gods, and impiety is whatever is displeasing to them.

But Socrates rejects Euthyphro's definition on the ground that the gods do not agree in attitude concerning the acts of men, nor is it satisfactory to say that the pious is what all the gods love, for the pertinent question concerns the nature of piety in virtue of which the gods love it.

If, as Euthyphro then claims, piety is paying careful attention to the gods, by means of prayer and worship, for the benefit of man, then piety seems to be loved by the gods even though it is of no benefit to the gods; but this runs counter to the previous claim that piety is good not simply because the gods love it.

The *Euthyphro* deals with some of the events culminating in Socrates' trial and death, portraying Socrates just before his trial. The *Euthyphro* forms a sequence with the dialogues, the *Apology* (dealing with the trial), the *Crito* (dealing with Socrates' incarceration after his conviction), and the *Phaedo* (dealing with the execution of Socrates by the drinking of the poison hemlock).

The *Euthyphro* is one of the best examples of the Socratic method. Socrates is portrayed as seeking wisdom about the meaning of the terms "piety" and "impiety" so that he can defend himself against the charge of being impious. Euthyphro, presumably, knows what these terms mean, Socrates tries to learn from him by asking questions and by asking him to define the terms. Each answer given by Euthyphro is scrutinized by Socrates and found to be faulty. Euthyphro complains that Socrates will not let his statements "stand still." Instead, by his persistent questioning, he makes the statements "move away," until Euthyphro no longer knows what to say. He

finally quits the discussion, refusing to recognize his own ignorance concerning the matter in question, and refusing to see how dangerous it is for him, or for anyone else, to act on the basis of such complete ignorance.

The discussion begins when Socrates and Euthyphro meet at the Porch of the King Archon, where cases dealing with crimes affecting the state religion are judged. Euthyphro expresses surprise at encountering Socrates in such a place. The latter explains that he is there because he has been charged with corrupting the youth of Athens, and with inventing new gods while not believing in the old, official ones. In contrast, Euthyphro has come to court to charge his own father with murder. Socrates suggests that Euthyphro must be very wise if he knows that he is right in prosecuting his own father. Such wisdom about what is right and wrong can be of great assistance to Socrates in his own case, so he requests details from Euthyphro.

The charge that Euthyphro is bringing against his

own father is based on a very strange story. A drunken laborer, who worked on the family farm, killed one of the slaves. Euthyphro's father caught the murderer, tied him up, and threw him into a ditch. The father then sent a messenger to Athens to find out what to do. While waiting for an answer, he completely neglected the bound murderer, who died from cold and hunger before the messenger returned. Euthyphro's family insisted that the father did not actually kill the laborer, and even if he had, the laborer was a murderer anyway, so he probably deserved death. Also, they maintained, Euthyphro should not get involved, because it is impious for a son to charge his own father with murder. Euthyphro, on the other hand, insisted that he was doing the right thing.

Socrates is so impressed by Euthyphro's assurance that what he is doing is right and pious, that he asks Euthyphro to instruct him so that he will be able to go to his own trial and explain to his accusers and his judges what is right and wrong. Since piety and impiety must have the same characteristics in all actions that are pious or impious, Socrates asks Euthyphro to explain the distinction between piety and impiety.

The first definition that Euthyphro offers is that piety consists of doing what he is doing; namely, prosecuting an unjust person who has committed a serious crime, even if such a person is a parent. Impiety, on the other hand, consists of not prosecuting such an individual. To justify what he is doing, Euthyphro also points out that the Greek god, Zeus, bound up his own father, Cronos, for committing the crime of devouring some of his children, and that Cronos also punished his father for wrongdoing.

Socrates points out that Euthyphro's statement does not actually constitute a definition of "piety," but only an illustration of one pious action. Such a statement does not really help in ascertaining if other actions are pious or impious. What is needed, instead of an example, is a statement of the essential characteristic of piety that makes all pious actions pious. Such a statement would allow one to classify all actions, since it would provide a general standard by which to judge which actions are pious and which are not. (As Plato points out over and over again in his dialogues, one does not actually know a general concept like "piety," "justice," "courage," and so on, if one can only cite examples of pious, just, or courageous activity. One cannot even be sure that these are examples of what one thinks, unless one also knows the meaning of the concepts; hence, the general knowledge is crucial for identifying and comprehending the particular examples with which we are acquainted.)

Euthyphro sees that he has not given a satisfactory definition of the term "piety" by citing the example of his case against his father. So, he offers a more general statement about "piety," saying that "what is pleasing to the gods is pious, and what is not pleasing to them is impious." Socrates congratulates him for giving him the kind of answer he wanted. All that remains, he states, is to find out if this definition is the true one. The truth will be ascertained by asking questions about the definition given.

Since Euthyphro accepts all the Greek mythological tales about quarrels and disagreements among the gods, Socrates asks him whether the gods disagree about matters of fact or matters of value. The latter, says Euthyphro. Then, Socrates argues, they are disagreeing about what pleases or displeases them. The same action is pleasing to some gods and displeasing to others, and hence, according to Euthyphro's second definition of "piety," that which is pleasing to the gods, the same action can be both pious and impious.

Euthyphro insists that this contradictory conclusion does not follow because the gods all agree on certain matters, such as that if one man unjustly kills another, he is to be punished. The gods may all agree, Socrates admits, about certain universal laws regarding punishment, but a disagreement still exists among both men and gods as to which cases fall under these laws. They disagree in their evaluations of various acts, some saying the acts are just, some that they are unjust. Even if Euthyphro is sure in his own case that the gods agree that his father's action was unjust, and that Euthyphro's action is just, it is still evident that Euthyphro's second definition of "piety" is inadequate. In view of the fact that the gods disagree about some of the actions that are pleasing or displeasing to them, an action cannot be pious simply because it pleases some gods, since the same action would have to be classed as "impious" if it displeased other gods.

A third definition is presented to overcome the problem of divine disagreements. Something is pious if *all* the gods love it, and it is impious if they *all* hate it. In cases where there is disagreement among the gods, the item in question is to be classed as neither pious nor impious.

Socrates immediately begins examining this new definition by raising the most serious point that is brought up in the dialogue. He asks Euthyphro whether the gods love piety because it is pious, or whether it is pious because the gods love it. The question at issue is whether the basic characteristic that determines piety is the fact that the gods love it, or whether piety has in itself some characteristic which accounts for the fact that the gods love it. (In a more general form this question was debated in the Middle Ages, when philosophers asked whether, if something is good, it is so because God wills it or whether God wills it because it is good. Is goodness an independent value, or is it dependent upon the divine will? It was pointed out that if the latter be true, the Ten Commandments are good and right only because God decreed them; if he had decreed the exact opposite, then the opposite would be good and right, if goodness is simply whatever God wills.)

Euthyphro holds that the gods love piety because it is pious. Socrates then shows him that he has not offered a definition, but only an effect of piety in pointing out that the gods love it. Since, according to Euthyphro, piety has certain characteristics that make it what it is, and since it is because of those characteristics that the gods love it, then he still has not given an adequate definition of "piety." He still has not revealed what the essential characteristics are that make it what it is.

Then Socrates asks Euthyphro once more to tell him what Euthyphro claims to know—namely, what piety and impiety are. By this point in the discussion, Euthyphro is bewildered; he complains that whatever he says in answer to Socrates' persistent questioning just gets up and moves away. His words and his ideas do not seem able to stay fixed and permanent. Socrates then offers to help by suggesting another way of approaching the problem.

He asks Euthyphro whether whatever is pious

must also be just. When Euthyphro gives an affirmative answer, Socrates inquires whether piety is the same as justice, or whether piety is only part of what constitutes justice. The latter, he is told. In turn, Socrates demands to know what part of justice piety is. If he could find out, he tells Euthyphro, then he could go to his own trial and show his accusers that they should not prosecute him for impiety, since he would then know what piety is and would act accordingly.

In answering the question, Euthyphro offers another definition of "piety" and states that righteousness and piety are that part of justice dealing with the careful attention which should be paid to the gods. The remaining portion of justice deals with the careful attention that ought to be paid to men. Socrates requests a clarification of the meaning of the phrase, "careful attention." A clarification is needed, he points out, because in most cases where careful attention is paid to some object, like a horse or a person, the object is benefited or improved by the attention. Is this also true of the gods? Are they benefited or improved by piety? No. Therefore, it must be a different kind of attention that is involved.

To make his point clear, Euthyphro says that the kind of attention he has in mind is that which slaves pay their masters. Then, Socrates points out, piety is a type of service to the gods. Every service aims at accomplishing something. A doctor's service produces health; a shipwright's service produces a ship. But what does piety, which now seems to be a service, produce? Generally speaking, Euthyphro answers, the principal result achieved through piety, by means of words and actions in prayer and sacrifice that are acceptable to the gods, is the preservation of the state and of private families. The results of impiety are the undermining and destruction of everything.

In terms of this latest answer, Socrates again asks what piety and impiety are. Euthyphro now seems to be offering the view that piety is a science of prayer and sacrifice, a science that deals with asking of the gods and giving to them. Euthyphro insists this is exactly what he means, so Socrates proceeds to explore this latest definition of piety. To ask rightly of the gods is to ask of them what we need from them, and to give rightly to the gods is to give to them what they need from us. When Euthyphro agrees to this view Socrates points out that piety is the art of carrying on business between the gods and men. But it is a strange kind of business, since one side, man's, appears to receive all of the benefits. We are obviously benefited by what the gods give us. But what do we give in return? Also, are the gods benefited by it?

Euthyphro answers that what we give in return are honor and praise, which are gifts acceptable to the gods. Then, Socrates argues, piety is acceptable to the gods, but it does not benefit them, nor is it loved by them. Euthyphro disagrees and insists that nothing is more loved by the gods than piety. So, Socrates asserts, piety means that which is loved by gods. Euthyphro agrees wholeheartedly.

Socrates then goes on to show Euthyphro that he has simply been talking around in a circle, and it is his own fault that his words will not stay put. They had agreed earlier in the discussion that the gods love piety because it is pious, and it is not pious because the gods love it. The fact that the gods love it is an effect of its nature and not its essential characteristic. Hence, there must be something which constitutes the fundamental characteristic of piety, that makes it what it is and causes the gods to love it. Either this conclusion is wrong, or Euthyphro has yet to answer the question, "What is piety?" Then Socrates begins all over again by asking that question.

Socrates points out once more that Euthyphro must know the answer in order to pursue his case against his father. Surely, he would not risk doing the wrong thing and offending the gods. Euthyphro wearily protests that he has no more time for the discussion, and he must rush off about his business. Socrates protests that he is left without the help he needs for his trial so that he can report that he knows what piety is, and hence will not commit any impieties in the future. At this point the dialogue ends.

The *Euthyphro* is one of the several superb short early dialogues that portray Socrates exposing the ignorance of supposedly wise men. When pressed, they are shown not to know what they are talking about. They cannot define basic concepts they deal with, such as "piety," "justice," and "courage," yet they are sure that what they are doing is pious, or just, or courageous. They are unwilling to undertake the difficult task of seeking to discover the meanings and natures of these terms. Their actions, based on their ignorance, can be disastrous, as is illustrated by both Euthyphro's charges against his father and the impending trial of Socrates.

Pertinent Literature

Beckman, James. *The Religious Dimension of Socrates' Thought.* (The Canadian Corporation for Studies in Religion.) Waterloo, Canada: Wilfrid Laurier University Press, 1979.

The *Euthyphro* has to do with religion in two ways. In the first place, the dialogue is about religion. It takes place between Euthyphro and Socrates when they chance upon each other before King Archon's office. They are both involved in legal cases, which have brought them there. Euthyphro is going to prosecute his father for murder; Socrates is to be indicted for apostasy and the corruption of youth. These are all religious offenses. Socrates steers their talk about their impending trials to the basic question involved in their respective cases, the question of what constitutes piety, and he does his best to keep their conversation on this topic.

In the second place, apart from the religious nature of their topic, Socrates' engagement in the conversation is itself a religious act for him. It is a holy act of laying bare Euthyphro's confusion and inconsistency on a topic of mutual importance. It is an act of subjecting to critical examination not just a professional statement or a theoretical position, but an entire personality, an entire way of life. The dialogue as a whole illustrates what Socrates in the *Apology* calls the sacred conduct of philosophy which he could not abandon without being impious. In short, the *Euthyphro* exhibits Socrates' religious conception of philosophy at work.

James Beckman's *The Religious Dimension of Socrates' Thought*, a comprehensive and systematic treatise on the historical Socrates' religiousness, explains the background of religious thought for the *Euthyphro* and examines the form and content of this dialogue. Because of his attention to historical details and scholarly treatment of secondary literature, Beckman's book is not easy reading, but his insights and synoptic scope make it rewarding. In the first and preliminary chapter he examines several putative sources of our knowledge of the historical Socrates and concludes that in Plato's early Socratic dialogues, including the *Euthyphro*, we have the only reliable literary representation of the character of Socratic philosophy in action. Accordingly, we may regard the Socrates of Plato's drama as a faithful re-creation of Socrates, Plato's teacher—not in historical details and exact wording, to be sure, but faithful to the spirit of Socrates' philosophical conduct and his principal articles of belief.

In the next chapter Beckman examines Socrates' religious or theological utterances and arguments in Plato's early dialogues in order to reconstruct a positive picture of the Socratic conception of religion. Since among the early dialogues the *Euthyphro*, together with the *Apology*, receives the focus of Beckman's attention here, this section of his work pertains directly to what we have observed above— namely, that the *Euthyphro* is a religious document in two ways: one by virtue of its topic, the other by virtue of Socrates' engagement in the dialogue as a religious mission.

In the third and last chapter Beckman goes beyond the positive evidence to consider that negative dimension of Socrates' philosophy which takes the highly idiosyncratic forms of pervasive irony, profession of ignorance, and silence. The key to the hidden motives underlying Socrates' negativity, argues Beckman, lies in the transcendence and ultimate indescribability of the Forms. In conclusion, Beckman assesses Socrates' religious philosophy in the context of the evolving tradition of Hellenic culture. The thesis central to his assessment is that with Socrates and Plato the Forms have replaced the Homeric gods as the transcendent embodiment of supreme values. This chapter helps the reader to discern how Euthy-

phro's beliefs and attitudes reflect the Homeric tradition, and how Socrates is in effect criticizing and transforming the Homeric values in reacting to Euthyphro as he does.

For Socrates, how is piety or holiness related to the gods? To this fundamental question Beckman takes three approaches in his discussion of the *Euthyphro* in Chapter 2.

First, accepting Socrates' suggestion that piety might be defined by differentiating that part of justice which is piety from the rest of it, Euthyphro defines piety as right service to the gods as distinguished from right service to men. Socrates' critique ensues: if "service" here means taking care, Euthyphro's understanding would have to be that the gods are improved by our care. If, alternatively, "service to the gods" means our assistance in their work, what work might that be? And if it means transactions with them through prayer and sacrifice, what kind of commodity could possibly be appropriate? The lesson to be derived from Socrates' critique here, Beckman suggests, is that since there is nothing to give to the gods, there is no reason to suppose piety to be a distinct part of the justice. Moreover, since the gods' work is to mete out justice in the world, piety and justice cannot be differentiated. Hence, the traditional view that religion is a matter of how we transact business with gods rather than with mankind must be rejected.

The dialogue makes the point that the belief that there is one and the same Form, piety, by virtue of which all pious acts are pious conflicts with a theological voluntarism which claims that a pious act is pious because the gods love it. Socrates holds the former view and rejects the latter. The upshot is that, for Socrates, piety is logically prior to the gods; we can know what piety is and be pious ourselves without learning what the gods love. Moreover, if the gods are to be perfect, it is by satisfying the criteria of Forms. Socrates professes his ignorance of the authenticity of stories about the gods, expresses his disinclination to accept the stories, and regards this agnostic attitude as the reason for the charge of impiety against him.

A question may arise about Socrates' agnosticism, Beckman suggests. What motivates it, a pious acknowledgment of the limitation of human knowledge or a philosophical rationalism? But the distinction between faith and reason presupposed by this question is alien to Socrates. For him, philosophy is religion. Thus, his objection to Euthyphro's mythological conception of piety is both philosophical and religious. The tragedy is that Socrates was condemned to death for irreligion precisely because of religiousness.

Allen, R. E. *Plato's 'Euthyphro' and the Earlier Theory of Forms.* London: Routledge & Kegan Paul, 1970.

In R. E. Allen's view, what we find in the *Euthyphro* is not a doctrine but an inquiry, not the outcome of a successful investigation but the process of investigation itself; and this process is not brought to successful conclusion. What is sought is the definition of holiness. Euthyphro proposes several definitions, but one after another they turn out to be unacceptable. They are found to conflict with Euthyphro's other beliefs, or they fail to satisfy Socrates' requirements for successful definition. The dialogue exemplifies a special brand of philosophical investigation called dialectic, and it is as an exercise in dialectic that Allen treats the dialogue.

There is an opposing view that the failure to reach a satisfactory definition of holiness is merely ostensible, and that the dialogue does point to a conception of holiness by means of a riddle, clues to which are embedded in the dialogue. We have seen this view in operation in James Beckman's attempt to puzzle out Socrates' conception of religion in the *Euthyphro.* Such attempts, according to Allen, are "heady"; they inevitably lead to invention.

As the title of his work indicates, Allen is concerned with the status of Plato's theory of Forms in the *Euthyphro* as well as with the dialectic in it. The status of the theory has been debated among scholars largely with regard to differentiating Socrates' thought from Plato's and tracing the course of development of Plato's philosophy throughout his long writing career. The *Euthyphro* belongs to the early period of his career, while most works in which the doctrine of Forms is prominent belong to his middle period. On the issue of the status of the theory in the *Euthyphro,* some argue that the dialogue involves no ontological commitment to Forms, and that what is there called "form" is a concept or the meaning of a word rather than an objective entity. Others disagree, maintaining that the conception of Form in the *Euthyphro* is the same as that in such middle-period dialogues as the *Phaedo, Phaedrus, Republic,* and *Symposium.* Allen's view on this issue is intermediate between these two extremes. He holds that the *Euthyphro* does involve commitment to Forms but that, unlike the theory in the middle dialogues, the theory here does not presuppose the metaphysical view of two separate worlds: one, of tangible objects related as a copy to the original; the other, a world of intangible but intelligible Forms.

But how can Allen, believing as he does that Plato presents no doctrine but an exercise in dialectic in the *Euthyphro,* claim that this doctrine can be found in it? His answer to this crucial question is this: Socratic dialectic is not used to present a body of truths; it is an activity of criticism and exploration. But such activity follows a determinate course; certain moves are disallowed, others are required. In the very conduct of dialectic, appeals are made to rules and principles; and these rules and principles reflect aspects of the theory.

Allen's book consists of a translation of the *Euthyphro* interspersed with comments, together with an essay on the earlier theory of Forms. His running commentary brings into relief details of Socratic dialectic at work in the *Euthyphro* and thus serves to ground the essay textually on the earlier theory of Forms. In the essay Allen formulates the theory, draws its implications with particular attention to dialectic, and compares and contrasts the earlier and the middle-period theories.

The aim of dialectic in the *Euthyphro* is to define holiness. In pursuing the definition Socrates makes the following assumptions:

1. The Form, holiness, exists as an objective entity.
2. This Form is a universal, the same in everything holy.
3. It is the essence or essential cause of holy things.

4. It serves as a universal and objective standard for judging what things are holy and what things are not.

These assumptions, pertaining to holiness here, can be generalized to other Forms. The assumptions so generalized constitute the earlier theory of Forms. Thus Allen lists the elements of the theory as follows:

1. Forms as objective entities
2. Forms as universals
3. Forms as essences
4. Forms as standards

From these elements Allen draws noteworthy consequences. First, since Forms are objective entities and the objects of Socratic definition, Socratic definition is real definition; it is not of words, thoughts, or concepts, but of the natures of things. Second, since a Form is a universal, one cannot, as Euthyphro tries to do, define it by producing its instances. Third, since a Form is the essential cause of its instances, it cannot be defined by a distinguishing mark of the instances. Thus holiness cannot be defined by stating, as Euthyphro does, that all the gods love holy things. Finally, since Forms are standards of our judgment, our correct moral judgment and our well-being itself ultimately depend on our knowledge of Forms. In this sense dialectic is moral inquiry into the nature of things.

Allen draws a further implication from the conception of Form as essential cause. The Form, by virtue of which its instances are what they are, is ontologically prior to the instances. In this sense it is transcendent. For this reason Allen rejects Aristotle's testimony which, according to Allen's construction, says that in the early dialogues Forms are immanent, whereas in the middle dialogues they are transcendent. In their transcendent status Forms do not differ between the early and middle dialogues, Allen argues. It is in the approach to transcendence that they differ. In the early dialogues transcendent Forms emerge as assumptions underlying dialectic; in the middle dialogues they are the product of reflection on the possibility and nature of dialectic.

Additional Recommended Reading

Guthrie, W. K. C. *A History of Greek Philosophy*. Vol. 4. Cambridge: Cambridge University Press, 1975. A comprehensive discussion of Plato the man and of each of his early and middle-period dialogues.

Irwin, Terence. *Plato's Moral Theory*. Oxford: Clarendon Press, 1977. A systematic exposition and critical evaluation of Plato's moral theory in his early and middle dialogues.

Plato. *Euthyphro, Apology of Socrates and Crito*. Edited by John Burnet. Oxford: Clarendon Press, 1924. A standard edition of the Greek text accompanied by notes with philological and historical details.

Santas, Gerasimos Xenophon. *Socrates: Philosophy in Plato's Early Dialogues*. London: Routledge & Kegan Paul, 1979. An analytic study of the Platonic Socrates' method and arguments concerning ethics and politics.

Versényi, Laszlo. *Socratic Humanism*. New Haven, Connecticut: Yale University Press, 1963. An existentialist approach to Socrates' quest for the nature of man.

Vlastos, Gregory, ed. *The Philosophy of Socrates: A Collection of Critical Essays*. Garden City, New York: Doubleday & Company, 1971. A collection of recent contributions to our understanding of the philosophy of Socrates in Plato's early dialogues.

APOLOGY

Author: Plato (427-347 B.C.)
Type of work: Ethics
First transcribed: Probably one of the early dialogues

Principal Ideas Advanced

The oracle at Delphi declared Socrates to be the wisest of all men, and Socrates suggested that if he were superior to other men in wisdom, it was only because he was aware of his own ignorance.

Defending himself against the charge of impiety and corrupting the young, Socrates argued that the pretenders to wisdom, whom he exposed by his critical questioning, must have spread rumors about him in order to discredit him.

Socrates maintained that it would have been foolish for him to corrupt the very persons with whom he associated, for everyone knows that corrupt and evil persons harm even those who have once befriended them.

If to point out the weaknesses in a state is to do the state a service, Socrates argued, then he had better be rewarded for performing the function of gadfly to the state.

After having been condemned to death, Socrates declared that death is not to be feared, for either it is annihilation, or it is a change to a better world where one might converse with noble souls.

The word "apology," as it appears in the title of this famous dialogue, means "a defense," not a request for forgiveness. In meeting the accusation that he had corrupted the youth of Athens, Socrates did not for a moment assume an apologetic air, but with courageous faith in the worth of philosophy set forth the principles by which he governed his life.

The dialogue—which is Plato's creation, and Plato knew Socrates and had grown to love him both as a teacher and a man—assumes the worth of Socrates' life and the rightness of his acts, especially of those acts of criticism which aroused the enmity of Socrates' accusers. The *Apology* is one of three dialogues describing the final days of perhaps the greatest hero in the history of philosophy, one who took philosophy seriously enough to die for it. The *Apology* reports the trial and condemnation of Socrates, the *Crito* his reasons for refusing to escape from prison, and the *Phaedo* his last conversations and death. To read the dialogues in that order is to gain some understanding of the significance of Socrates' identification of wisdom with virtue, and some conception of the nobility of his character.

As the *Apology* opens, the prosecution, for which Meletus is the spokesman, has already stated its case. Meletus was probably merely the spokesman for the chief instigator of the trial, Anytus, respected leader of the restored democracy; the third accuser, Lycon, is barely mentioned in the dialogue. Meletus speaks only a few words, the other accusers none, but Socrates repeats the charges made against him. He begins by pointing out that almost everything they have said is false, especially their warning to the court implying that Socrates is a persuasive speaker, unless they mean by that one who speaks truth. His words will be unpremeditated but spoken with confidence in the justice of his cause; it is to truth that the jury should attend, just as it is the speaker's duty to state only the truth. There are actually two sets of charges against him, Socrates says: the present ones of impiety and corruption of the young, and some ancient ones his audience heard as children and which should now be refuted.

The latter were made by accusers largely unknown, except for Aristophanes in his burlesque of Socrates in the comedy, *The Clouds* (which was written in fun rather than ill will). These accusations were that Socrates had theories about and conducted investigations into the heavens and things below the earth (that is, pursued physical sciences), and that he could make weaker arguments appear to overcome the stronger and taught others to do the same (that is, he was a sophist). Such accusations are dangerous, Socrates argues, because uncritical listeners assume that such inquirers must be atheists. But the accusations are false, for Socrates has no knowledge of physics, not from disdain but from lack of interest. Socrates asks whether anyone present ever heard him discussing these matters. As to the charge that he has taught others professionally for fees, this, too, is false. Socrates professes (ironically) to admire Sophists such as Gorgias, Prodicus, and Hippias, who are able to persuade youths to forsake their usual company, which is free, and come to them for training in social skills, for large fees. Still, people will wonder how Socrates got this reputation if the accusations are false, so he will explain.

Perhaps he does have some degree of human wisdom, though that of the sophists is undoubtedly superhuman! The tale he will tell now concerning the kind of wisdom he does have may seem exaggerated, but judgment should be reserved until the end: Chaerephon, an old friend known to all, asked the oracle at Delphi if anyone were wiser than Socrates, and the answer was "No!" Such an answer puzzled Socrates —surely the god was speaking in riddles, for he could not be lying. So Socrates set out to see whether he could disprove the oracle by finding a wiser man. He examined a politician with a great reputation for, and the conceit of, wisdom. Not only was the man not wise, but he resented Socrates' attempt to show him that he was not. Socrates came away realizing that at least he was himself wiser in awareness of his own ignorance. Others who heard the politician's examination resented the inquiry, too, but Socrates felt it a religious duty to determine the oracle's meaning. Having queried other politicians with the same effect, he went next to the poets and found that they could not even expound their own works. Not wisdom, then, but instinct or inspiration must be the source of poetry. Proceeding to the skilled craftsmen Socrates discovered here a kind of technical knowl-

edge he did not possess, but these men prided themselves so on their special competence that they mistakenly thought themselves expert on everything else. Naturally, Socrates' exposé of the ignorance of others made him unpopular with them, even though it was really to their good.

When bystanders heard him examine pretenders to wisdom, it was assumed that he had the knowledge, lack of which he uncovered in those questioned, even though this was not true. But the real meaning of the oracle and the upshot of Socrates' search was that God alone is really wise, and human wisdom is of relatively little value. The oracle used Socrates' name merely to make a point: "The wisest of you men is he who has realized, like Socrates, that in respect of wisdom he is really worthless." (Perhaps what Socrates actually meant here is that admission of one's errors and present lack of understanding is a necessary prerequisite of learning, for neither in theory nor in practice does Socrates deny that true wisdom is one of man's highest goods.) Thus in exposing ignorance, Socrates continues, he obeys a divine command.

Socrates tells the court that young men of leisure, having heard him questioning their elders to the latter's discomfort, have tried to imitate his techniques and have aroused further hostility which has redounded to Socrates' discredit. When victims irritated at exposure are asked what Socrates has done or taught to mislead the young, however, they have no specific evidence and so "they fall back on the stock charges against any philosopher: that he teaches his pupils about things in the heavens and below the earth, and to disbelieve in gods, and to make the weaker argument defeat the stronger." It is thus because he has revealed the truth about them in plain language that the earlier calumniators have spread these rumors about Socrates, which are the underlying causes of the present attack by Meletus, Anytus, and Lycon.

Before we turn to Socrates' reply to the latter, it would be well to realize, as Professor A. E. Taylor points out, that the prosecution could not afford to present its real complaint against him. The pretext of "corruption of the young" concerned his supposed influence, discouraging unquestioning loyalty to the democracy, on former associates (Alcibiades, Critias, Charmides, and others) who had opposed the state. The charge of "irreligion" was probably related to the mutilation, in 415 B.C., of all the Athenian statues of Hermes on the night before Alcibiades led the military expedition to Sicily, for which Alcibiades was blamed, probably falsely. But these matters were excluded from the jurisdiction of the present court by the Act of Oblivion which Anytus had sponsored. According to this act, offenses occurring under the old democracy had received general amnesty. During the year of Socrates' trial, 399 B.C., Anytus defended another person against charges of "irreligion," so it is unlikely that he actually held such a grievance against Socrates. It is likely, Professor Taylor suggests, that Anytus regarded Socrates' influence as dangerous to the restored democracy and, consequently, as one which had better be removed. Hence the trumped-up charges, the use of Meletus as mouthpiece, and the prosecution's unwillingness and inability to explain or substantiate the accusations made in public.

Consequently, on trial, Socrates exercises his argumentative abilities with humor and irony to show how ridiculous the prosecution's case is. He turns specifically to the charges of Meletus, stating them as follows: "Socrates is guilty of corrupting the minds of the young, and of believing in deities of his own invention instead of the gods recognized by the State." (Professor Taylor writes that this passage means that Socrates did not worship the official gods rather than that he did not believe in them, and that he practiced unfamiliar rites.)

Socrates now takes the line that Meletus must be joking about a serious matter in which he really has no interest. Who, he queries, exercises the best influence on the young? By a series of questions he leads Meletus to say that it is the whole Athenian citizenry—except Socrates. But this is very odd; in fact, it is exactly opposite to the case of training horses, in which the many are incompetent and only a few expert trainers improve the animals.

Furthermore, since Meletus must admit that evil people harm their associates, he must also admit that Socrates would be unbelievably stupid not to know that by corrupting his young acquaintances he would only be brewing trouble for himself; now either

Socrates has not been a bad influence, or if so, it must have been unintentional. If the latter, however, what Socrates deserves according to the usual procedure is that he be given private admonition rather than punishment. But far from instructing Socrates, Meletus has avoided his company until now.

How, specifically, has Socrates corrupted the young, especially in regard to teaching belief in new deities? Does he believe in gods different from those of the state or in none at all? Meletus takes the latter alternative. Socrates suggests that Meletus has deliberately and flippantly contradicted himself in order to test Socrates' logical prowess. It is charged both that Socrates believes in no gods and that he believes in new deities, that he is an atheist and yet believes in "supernatural activities" (this refers to Socrates' famous divine "sign," or inner voice). Now one cannot believe in activities without an actor, and if Socrates believes in supernatural activities, he must believe in supernatural beings. Thus, either Meletus was trying Socrates' wit or he was desperate for a genuine charge against him.

At this point Socrates acknowledges that his destruction will be caused by the general hostility aroused by his conduct, not by these flimsy accusations, but that he has no regret for his behavior. A good man must not busily calculate the chances of life and death, but must concern himself with acting rightly. It would be most inconsistent if, after loyal military service through several engagements, Socrates were to fail through fear of death an assignment given by God himself to the philosophic life. To fear death implies knowledge of what occurs afterward, another form of the pretense to know what one does not; but to disobey a superior, human or divine, is a known evil.

Were it suggested that Socrates be acquitted on condition that he desist from his philosophical questionings, he would reply that, much as he appreciates the offer, he must still pursue his duty to God, asking Athenians, "Are you not ashamed that you give your attention to acquiring as much money as possible, and similarly with reputation and honour, and give no attention or thought to truth and understanding and the perfection of your soul?" Actually, Socrates conceives his divine service as the greatest benefit ever to fall on Athens, since he urges men to put the welfare of their souls above all else. If the Athenians kill him, they will inflict more harm on themselves; Socrates believes that divine law prevents injury by an evil to a good man. Of course they can banish or kill his body, but such acts do no harm to the soul, except of course to the soul of the evildoer.

Here Socrates introduces the famous "gadfly" metaphor. Comical as it sounds, he says, "God has appointed me to this city, as though it were a large thoroughbred horse which because of its great size is inclined to be lazy and needs the stimulation of some stinging fly" ("gadfly," in the Jowett translation). "It seems to me that God has attached me to this city to perform the office of such a fly; and all day long I never cease to settle here, there, and everywhere, rousing, persuading, reproving every one of you. You will not easily find another like me, gentlemen, and if you take my advice you will spare my life. I suspect, however, that before long you will awake from your drowsing, and in your annoyance you will take Anytus' advice and finish me off with a single slap; and then you will go on sleeping till the end of your days, unless God in his care for you sends someone to take my place." (While such a description of his mission might be misinterpreted as conceited, careful study of its context and of other Socratic dialogues will convince the reader that it is only the frank self-appraisal of a prophet.) As Socrates adds, proof of the sincerity of what he has said and done lies in the obvious fact of his poverty; he has neglected his private affairs in order to fulfill his duty.

Should someone ask why Socrates has not addressed himself to the state at large with his advice, the answer is that he has been forbidden to do so by the divine voice to which Meletus' charge made implicit reference and which comes to him occasionally to warn against a course of action. In regard to a political career its warning was evidently provident, for otherwise Socrates would have been dead long ago—no man, he says, can conscientiously oppose a government by the masses and champion justice and live long. He would not act wrongly in obedience to any authority, as is evidenced by the few occasions of his public office. When a member of the Council under the old democracy, he alone opposed the un-

constitutional trial of ten military commanders *en bloc,* thus risking denunciation and arrest. Later, under the oligarchy, he disobeyed an unjust order to participate in the arrest of Leon of Salamis and probably would have been executed had not the government fallen.

Toward the end of his defense, Socrates repeats that he has never taught professionally nor privately, but has allowed rich and poor to exchange questions and answers with him, and, consequently, cannot be held responsible for the good or bad career of any individual. If some of those who have listened to his discourse have been corrupted by him, Socrates challenges them to bear witness now. That no one comes is ample evidence that Meletus lies. This constitutes Socrates' defense; he will not appeal, as is usual with defendants, to the sympathy of the jury by exhibiting his children and friends. To do so would be unfitting for one of Socrates' reputation. Besides, the defendant's business is to convince the jury by facts and argument rather than by sentiment, and the jury is to decide justly, not hand out verdicts as favors. Were he to ask them to perjure themselves as jurors, this in itself would convict him of guilt. Thus Socrates ends his speech and places himself in his judges' and God's hands.

When the verdict is brought in, it is "Guilty," though obtained by a small margin, about 280 to 220. Meletus proposes the death penalty (although scholars believe Socrates' accusers did not wish to kill him but only to silence or banish him, since according to current practices several alternatives of escape were open). It was customary for the convicted defendant to propose an alternate penalty and for the jury to choose which one would be enacted. But Socrates will not admit guilt; what then is his desert? Since he has not cared for money, a comfortable home, high rank, or secret societies—all the things having popular appeal—and has instead devoted himself to his mission to Athens, he says it would therefore be appropriate that he be maintained at state expense as a public benefactor. Certainly he deserves this treatment more than do Olympic horse racers!

Of course Socrates does not expect this suggestion to be taken seriously in spite of its justice. What of other possibilities? He rejects that of imprisonment, which is a known evil compared to death, which is of uncertain value. As to banishment, it is clear that he would find no more welcome in other societies than he has in Athens, for his conduct and its results would be the same. Again, he cannot give up philosophy and "mind his own business," for "to let no day pass without discussing goodness and all the other subjects about which you hear me talking and examining both myself and others is really the very best thing that a man can do, and . . . life without this sort of examination is not worth living. . . ." As to a fine, it is not likely that what he could afford would be acceptable. At this point Plato, Crito, Critobulus, and Apollodorus offer to pay a fine thirty times that which Socrates suggests, which offer he transmits to the court.

But the jury decides on the death penalty instead, and Socrates makes his final remarks. He reminds that part of the jury voting for death that nature would soon have brought about what they wished, but as it is, they will incur blame for having killed a wise man, whether he is one or not. His condemnation has resulted not from paucity of argument but from his bearing: he has not been brazen or servile, nor has he catered to their pleasure. The real difficulty is not to elude death but to outrun vice; Socrates, the old man, has been caught by the former, but they have been captured by the latter; his condemnation is by the court, but they are convicted of their wickedness by Truth. Hoping to stop his mouth by death, they will find that criticism of their actions will increase—the only escape for them is to become good men.

To those voting for acquittal, he notes that in nothing he has done this day has the inner voice opposed him, whereas in the past it sometimes stopped him in the middle of a sentence. This is clear evidence that the outcome is good and that even death is no evil. Death must be either total annihilation, in which case it is an unbroken rest, or else a change to another world; and if it is true as reported that one can there converse with the great men of time past, how rewarding! To meet Homer, Hesiod, or the great heroes of the old days, especially those similarly condemned to death unjustly, would be worth dying for again and again. To talk and argue with them would be happiness beyond description, and presumably one is not killed there for asking questions.

Socrates concludes by encouraging the friendly jurors with the belief that "nothing can harm a good man either in life or after death, and his fortunes are not a matter of indifference to the gods." He has no ill will for those who condemned him, although they are guilty of intent to harm him. As a final favor Socrates asks that his hearers treat his sons as he has treated the Athenians: if they put anything before goodness, or are self-deceived about their virtues, he asks that the jurors take their "revenge by plaguing them as I plagued you. . . ."

So ends Plato's story of the legal but unjust trial of one regarded as philosophy's first martyr. The authenticity of his report has been questioned, but scholars have pointed out that many people present at the trial, including hostile critics, would have read Plato's account and detected any substantial deviation from the facts. We may therefore regard it as an essentially accurate record of the serenity, wit, courage, and steadfastness of a philosopher whose justness gave him composure in the face of those who cheated him of life.

Pertinent Literature

Plato. *Plato's Euthyphro, Apology of Socrates, and Crito.* Edited by John Burnet. Oxford: Clarendon Press, 1924.

No one can get far in the study of Socrates before he meets references to the John Burnet-A. E. Taylor hypothesis. Historians reconstructing the life and work of Socrates must make up their minds concerning the value to be placed on various sources—Plato, Aristotle, Xenophon, Diogenes Laertius, and others. Plato is always impressive; but there is frequently a question of how far Plato is putting his own thoughts into the mouth of his mentor. Burnet chose to take Plato's account of Socrates at face value, not only in the *Apology* but also in all the dialogues. The latter, says Burnet, may or may not have taken place, but we must assume "that they should not misrepresent the personality and beliefs of Socrates." Accordingly, for Burnet (and for Taylor, who adopted the same principle) Socrates was not merely the quiz master of the early dialogues but the author of most of the logical, psychological, and metaphysical doctrines that are usually credited to Plato.

As we might expect, Burnet regards the *Apology* as historically accurate; but his thesis also has interesting implications for interpreting the document. One of the difficulties in the way of accepting Plato's account of Socrates' speech arises from the assumption that Socrates lacked the rhetorical training necessary to put together and deliver the defense with which he is here credited. Burnet, without suggesting that what we have is anything like a verbatim report, nevertheless maintains that Socrates conducted the argument substantially as Plato represents him as doing. After all, if Socrates was as familiar with the principles and practice of public speaking as he is represented as being in the *Phaedrus*, it is not difficult to imagine his inventing this defense, including the ironic introduction in which he plays with the notion that he is not much of a public speaker.

In Burnet's opinion, it was true that Socrates, in his youth, engaged in the physical speculations attributed to him by Aristophanes in the *Clouds*. Closely connected with the society which Anaxagoras had left behind him when he himself was forced to leave Athens, Socrates "must have known all there was to know about such things, only—it did not seem to him to be knowledge"; hence, all that he meant to deny in the *Apology* is that he ever "talked about these matters in public." Anaxagoras, although protected by Pericles and surrounded by such men as Phidias, Herodotus, and Euripides, had been charged with impiety for saying that the sun is a fiery stone and that the moon was made of earth and had hills and valleys; and in the popular mind Socrates was saddled with similar views.

There was, however, another side to Socrates. If the opinions expressed in the *Phaedo* and in the

Republic are to be taken as historical, Socrates steeped himself in the teachings of the Pythagoreans and other Orphics. According to Burnet, it was this "ascetic and psychical side" of Socrates that had attracted young men like Chaerephon. Moreover, this explains what Socrates meant when he talked, at the trial, about God having assigned him "the post of living a life of philosophy." It is clear, says Burnet, that he did not use the term "philosophy" in the popular sense but in the deeper sense which it had among the Pythagoreans.

Here, in Burnet's opinion, is the essential background for understanding the overriding ethical concern which made Socrates cross-examine everyone he met concerning the kind of life he was leading. Socrates, says Burnet, was the first Greek to speak of the soul (psyche) as "the seat of knowledge and ignorance, goodness and badness," and to draw the inference that the chief duty of everyone is the care or tendency of his own soul.

People pursue wealth or honor instead of following truth and understanding, said Socrates; that is, they are ruled by the appetitive and spirited parts of the soul rather than by reason. But it ought to be otherwise: for goodness does not come from wealth but "it is goodness that makes money and everything else good for man." Similarly, in respect to the state, Socrates sought to persuade men to put wisdom and justice before wealth and national glory. "Here we have in a nutshell the political theory of Socrates developed in the *Republic*, according to which the 'care of the city' is in principle the same as the 'care of oneself.' "

For Burnet, Orphicism provides the basis for understanding Socrates' conviction that no evil is permitted to happen to the good man and of his "hope that death is a good." The view common among the citizens of Athens was that death is annihilation; but, for the benefit of sympathetic hearers whom he addresses in his final speech, Socrates develops the Orphic doctrine that the purified soul, itself divine, departs to be with the gods. The language which he uses, says Burnet, is technical. "Hope" is the Orphic equivalent to the Christian "faith," and what Socrates says here about death being "a change and migration of the soul from this world to another" is substantially the same doctrine which, in his death-cell, he would explain as his personal faith. "In view of this," says Burnet, "I cannot regard the doctrine of the *Phaedo* as Platonic rather than Socratic."

Hackforth, Reginald. *The Composition of Plato's Apology.* Cambridge: Cambridge University Press, 1933.

Reginald Hackforth believes that Plato set out with the intention of giving his readers a "substantial reproduction" of Socrates' defense and that, on the whole, he has done so. The main exception comes in the latter half of the long defense speech, where Plato must have thought the actual speech was inadequate to his purpose, "namely the presentation of Socrates as he saw him," and decided to give full play to his own feelings, "retaining however just enough of the form of *apologia* to meet the minimum demands of verisimilitude."

Hackforth suggests that Socrates, in his speech before the court, must have dealt specifically with each charge in the indictment. In Plato's account he answers the first charge (impiety) but not the second charge (corrupting the young). Hackforth thinks that Socrates did deal with the corruption charge in the course of interrogating Meletus. In Xenophon's *Apology* we are told that when Meletus mentions that one of the charges is persuading young men to listen to him rather than to their parents, Socrates acknowledges the truth of the charge and proceeds to justify his conduct. Perhaps Plato saw this as a weakness and, for this reason, transformed the actual interrogation into a typically Socratic dialogue, representing Meletus as not understanding the meaning of corruption. In doing so, however, Plato made it impossible for himself to return to Socrates' original line of defense.

The first charge, as Hackforth points out, had two parts: the negative charge that Socrates did not believe in the gods of the City, and the positive charge that he introduced strange deities. Socrates' defense against the charge of unbelief was to repudiate utterly the popular notion which lay behind Aristophanes' lampoon, that he was a nature-philosopher, a sophist, and a disbeliever in the gods. Hackforth explicitly rejects the contention of John Burnet and A. E. Taylor that Socrates was a speculative philosopher and denies that he made light of the allegations against him in the *Clouds*. Burnet has superimposed the Socrates of the *Phaedo* on the *Apology*, whereas in Hack-

forth's opinion the Socrates of the *Apology* is perfectly convincing, so that any evidence which conflicts with his statement that he never had anything to do with physical speculations must not be set aside. Comparing the Socrates of the *Apology* with the Socrates of *Phaedo*, Hackforth says that if they had not been assigned the same name no one would have suspected they were meant to be the same man.

Hackforth takes the charge of introducing new deities to refer to Socrates' divine sign. In contrast to Burnet, he argues that the charge was indeed concerned with new gods and not merely with new (Orphic) rites. Hackforth denies that Socrates ever believed in any gods other than those of Olympus and holds that he was punctilious in his religious duties. Like his contemporary Euripides, he was a rationalist and was not shackled by popular beliefs; but his humility was incompatible with dogmatic opposition to traditional wisdom. "The unexamined life is not worth living," said Socrates; but he also said that "human wisdom is worth little or nothing for only God is wise."

What was Socrates' defense against the charge of introducing new gods? Plato has not told us. According to Hackforth the explanation may be simply that Socrates convinced his judges on this point and that, by the time the *Apology* was written, the absurdity of supposing that Socrates' divine voice was incompatible with traditional religion had become apparent.

Socrates' reference to the oracle of Apollo has given some trouble to readers of the *Apology*. It is introduced in order to explain Socrates' practice of interrogating everyone who had any pretension to wisdom. We are told that Socrates undertook this practice with a view to refuting the oracle; elsewhere, however, Socrates says that in interrogating his fellow citizens, he is obeying the god's bidding, that he is helping the god, that he is performing a divine service. Hackforth suggests that Plato himself is responsible for the confusion. Granted that Socrates took the oracle seriously, it was Plato who invented the connection between the oracle and Socrates' sense of mission. Presumably Socrates had never explained his conviction that he would be disobeying God if he ceased his practice of questioning himself and others; and Plato, convinced that it originated with the oracle, believed that introducing this information into the *Apology* could not fail to put Socrates' practice in a favorable light.

Hackforth does not doubt that the story of Chaerephon and the oracle is true and that it was connected with the practice of cross-examining public figures which had brought so much enmity on his head. According to Hackforth's reconstruction, there was a period when, having abandoned his brief interest in natural philosophy, Socrates gathered a small group with whom he discussed moral and religious questions. It was Socrates' insights that led Chaerephon to ask the oracle whether anyone was wiser than Socrates. Puzzled by the answer, Socrates began examining reputedly wise men. Then came a break in his practice, caused partly by the war and partly by doubts as to whether his practice might not be doing more harm than good. But after the war (and after the presentation of Aristophanes' *Clouds*) he resumed his public mission, this time talking with everyone who was interested and approaching moral questions in a more positive fashion than before. This outline, says Hackforth, explains the connection between the oracle and the "destructive side" of Socrates' practice without making the oracle the real fount and origin of his mission.

In the two brief speeches which follow the defense, Plato's report is substantially true. The note of arrogance in the way Socrates spoke of himself as too honest to be a politician and said that instead of being fined he should be given a pension must be historical because it puzzled Xenophon. How, he asks, could Socrates have ruined his defense by taunting his judges in this way? And he can think of no other reply than that Socrates must have decided that by being put to death he would avoid the ills of old age. Plato saw deeper into Socrates' motives, recognizing that although an acquittal would have been welcome Socrates did not wish it at the expense of compromising his life work.

According to Hackforth, Socrates was agnostic concerning man's prospects after death. In an appendix devoted to Taylor's recent book *Socrates*, he challenges Taylor's claim that Socrates clearly attested his belief in immortality, citing earlier passages in which Socrates says "no one knows whether death may not be the greatest good," and contrasting the reticent tone of the *Apology* with that of the *Phaedo* in which the "Platonic Socrates" speaks of "the good hope that there is a future . . . a far better future for the good than for the evil."

Additional Recommended Reading

Blum, Alan F. *Socrates: The Original and Its Images*. London: Routledge & Kegan Paul, 1978. Chapter VII, "The Oracle," is a popular study of the *Apology*.

Friedländer, Paul. "The Apology," in *Plato*. Vol. II. New York: Pantheon Books, 1964, pp. 157-172. Emphasis is placed on the philosopher's existence—piety, linked with justice, courage, and wisdom.

Nussbaum, Martha. *The Fragility of Goodness: Luck and Ethics in Greek Tragedy and Philosophy*. Cambridge, England: Cambridge University Press, 1986. Shows the links between Greek drama and moral philosophy.

Oldfather, W. A. "Socrates in Court," in *Classical Weekly*. XXXI, no. 21 (1938), pp. 203-211. Develops the view that Socrates probably said little at his trial.

Taylor, A. E. *Socrates*. New York: D. Appelton, 1933. A reconstruction of the life and teaching of Socrates, with special attention to the early period.

Vlastos, Gregory, ed. *The Philosophy of Socrates*. Garden City, New York: Doubleday-Anchor, 1971. Except for Vlastos' introductory paper, the articles are addressed to readers with special knowledge. A. P. Lacey's "Our Knowledge of Socrates," pp. 22-49, and K. J. Dover's "Socrates in the *Clouds*," pp. 50-77, bear upon the *Apology*.

West, Thomas G. *Plato's Apology of Socrates*. Ithaca, New York: Cornell University Press, 1979. Argues that Plato used Socrates' defense, which was a failure, to show the inevitable tensions between philosophy and the demands of the state.

CRITO

Author: Plato (427-347 B.C.)
Type of work: Ethics
First transcribed: Probably one of the early dialogues

Principal Ideas Advanced

Although Socrates has been unjustly accused of corrupting the young and has been sentenced to death, he refuses to escape because to escape would be to break an implicit agreement with the State to abide by its laws and judgments.

He argues that the important thing is not to live, but to live honorably.

It is never right to defend oneself against injury by an act of retaliation.

To remain in a state, after having been reared and educated under its laws, is, in effect, to agree to abide by its laws.

If Socrates were to escape a punishment legally decided upon by the State, he could no longer conduct himself as a philosopher devoted to justice and the love of wisdom.

The *Crito* is a relatively short dialogue which should be read in conjunction with and between the *Apology* and the *Phaedo*. The *Apology* gives an account of Socrates' trial and condemnation; the *Phaedo* describes his last conversations and death; the *Crito* recounts a friend's urgent plea for Socrates to avail himself of the ample opportunity to escape and the latter's justification on moral grounds for remaining in prison voluntarily, although the execution will occur two days after the present one. The dialogue is probably meant to explain Socrates' personal reasons for taking this course of inaction, rather than to prescribe a universally applicable norm for the individual unjustly condemned by the State, and some writers have suggested that Plato himself would probably have chosen to escape rather than to accept the sentence. Yet profound political, social, and moral issues are raised to which there are no easy solutions; their complications are such that readers may find their own judgments falling on either side of an exceedingly fine line.

When the dialogue opens, Socrates has been in prison a month, for no death sentences could be carried out in Athens during the annual voyage of the State vessel to Delos, in commemoration of the legendary deliverance of the city from the Minotaur by Theseus. But the ship is reportedly about to return, and Crito, having arrived at the prison before dawn, is waiting for Socrates to awake, in order to break the news and try to persuade him to escape while there is yet time. It is typical of Socrates that he slumbers peacefully while Crito is wakeful and desperate, and that in the ensuing discussion it is Socrates who is the more rational and objective, though it is his own life which is at stake.

Crito's reasons for urging Socrates to escape, though perhaps on a less lofty plane than the latter's rebuttal, are not specious but are rather quite practical and persuasive. It is the weight of these, plus that of the circumstances under which Socrates was condemned, which gives the dialogue its moral significance. Crito begins by pointing out that if Socrates dies, an irreplaceable friend will have been lost, and besides, Crito will gain a reputation for loving money more than his friends, since many people will think he could have saved Socrates had he only been willing to put up the necessary cash; they will not believe that Socrates stayed in prison voluntarily.

Socrates answers that men of reason will believe only the truth; why should one regard majority opinion? Crito then points out that popular opinion is not to be taken lightly, which fact is confirmed by Socrates' present circumstances. But the philosopher replies that common people, unfortunately, are of limited capacity to do evil—since otherwise they could likewise do great good; actually they can make one neither wise nor stupid. (Here again we note the Socratic identification of wisdom and virtue, and his belief that no real evil can happen to a good man even if his body is destroyed.)

Crito acquiesces in this point but continues by assuring Socrates that he need not be concerned about any consequences to his friends if he chooses to escape (which apparently would have been quite easy under the circumstances, if not actually desired or intended by those who brought Socrates to trial). They are prepared to risk a large fine, loss of property, or other punishment. There is plenty of money available to buy off informers, and Crito knows men who will take Socrates out of the country for a moderate fee. Not only Crito's money, but also that of Simmias and Cebes—foreigners who would not be so liable to punishment—is at Socrates' disposal. At his trial Socrates had rejected banishment to a foreign society, but Crito assures him of comfort and protection among friends in Thessaly.

Furthermore, he continues, Socrates will do a wrong in voluntarily neglecting to save his life; he will be inflicting on himself the penalty his enemies wished. And what of his young sons? Will he not be failing them by leaving their education unfinished and deserting them to the lot of orphans? Crito finishes his argument by expressing once more his concern for the reputation both Socrates and his friends will incur if he refuses escape, a reputation for cowardice and lack of initiative resulting from (1) Socrates' unnecessary appearance in court (it was customary for Athenians whose conviction was probable to leave the country before trial), (2) the manner in which the defense was made (Socrates had refused all compromise and had deliberately taken a position which might, and did, result in conviction), and (3) the present situation, which will suggest sheer bungling and lack of spirit. In short, the suffering of Socrates' death will be augmented by disgrace.

To all this Socrates makes a reply remarkable for its calm, detached, and rational tenor. Much as he appreciates Crito's concern, he points out that his choice to face death is not a sudden impulse; his practice has always been to follow the course reason shows to be best. The question, then, is whether the opinions he has previously adopted are still true or whether their truth has been altered by the turn of events. We must not be frightened into a change of outlook, he reassures Crito, by imprisonment, loss of goods, or execution. With characteristic but kindly irony Socrates asks Crito to consider the matter with him, for since Crito is in no danger of death he is more likely to be impartial and objective!

Is it not true, he asks, that only some opinions are tenable and not all, that those to be respected are the good ones, and that these belong to the wise? And is it not the case that the opinions of the few qualified experts, rather than those of the masses, are to be regarded, as is illustrated in the case of athletic training? If this is true in general, then it follows that in the present case Socrates and Crito should be concerned only with what the expert in right and wrong will think, not with what the majority will say. The fact that the latter have the powers of life and death in their hands is irrelevant to the argument.

In the considerations which follow, it is clear that Socrates is not at all interested in discussing the possibility or the means of escape, but rather its rightness or wrongness. His premises are that ". . . the really important thing is not to live, but to live well. . . . And . . . to live well means the same thing as to live honourably or rightly." Critos's concern about expense, reputation, and the upbringing of Socrates' children are those of the common people, whose attitudes and acts are unrelated to reason. Socrates says: "Our real duty . . . is to consider one question only. . . . Shall we be acting rightly in paying money and showing gratitude to these people who are going to rescue me, and in escaping . . . or shall we really be acting wrongly in doing all this? If it becomes clear that such conduct is wrong, I cannot help thinking that the question whether we are sure to die, or to suffer any other ill effect . . . if we stand our ground and take no action, ought not to weigh with us at all in comparison with the risk of doing what is wrong."

Wrongdoing, Socrates holds, is reprehensible not merely on most but on all occasions; there are no exceptions. While most people think it natural and right to return wrongs done them, Socrates disagrees: ". . . it is never right to do a wrong or return a wrong or defend one's self against injury by retaliation. . . ." If this is so, and it is agreed that one should always fulfill morally right agreements, then it follows, Socrates concludes, that it would be wrong for him to leave without an official discharge by the State, for he would be doing the State an injury by breaking an implicit agreement with it. He explains what he means by personifying the Athenian Laws and Constitution and imagining the dialogue which might occur between them and himself were he to favor escape.

They would first point out to him that such an act would subvert the Laws and the State; the latter cannot subsist if its legal decisions are to be set aside for the benefit of individuals. But suppose that Socrates should retort that the proposed escape was in reprisal for the wrong done him by the State? The answer of the Laws to this would be that not only was there no provision made for such evasion and insubordination, but Socrates is under agreement to abide by the State's judgments. He has no legitimate complaint against them, the Laws continue, but rather positive obligations to abide by them. The Laws, by sanctioning the marriage of his parents, in a sense gave him life itself; they also provided a proper education for him. He is thus their child and servant, and as such does not have rights equal to theirs, any more than a son has the right to rebel against his father. Indeed, ". . . compared with your mother and father and all the rest of your ancestors your country is something far more precious, more venerable, more sacred, and held in greater honour both among gods and among all reasonable men. . . ." Whatever it orders one must do, unless he can justly persuade it otherwise (and of course, during the trial Socrates failed to persuade the jury, though he was confident he might have done so if given more time).

Now, in spite of all the blessings vouchsafed to Athenian citizens, the Laws continue, any young man upon reaching maturity may evaluate the political order and the administration of justice, and if he disapproves, he is free to leave the State with all his possessions. If, on the other hand, he surveys the political and judicial arrangement and voluntarily stays, his act is equivalent to an agreement to abide by the State's commands—or rather its proposals, since they are not blunt dictates and the citizen has the choice of either obeying or persuading the State to change its decision. If Socrates should run away now, he would be more blameworthy than any other Athenian: his implicit agreement to abide by the law has been more explicit than that of any other citizen because he above all has remained at home, never crossing the border except while on military duty. Although he admired Sparta and Crete because of their good governments and respect for law, he has never emigrated to those city-states. And again, during the trial when the defendant was given the customary opportunity to propose an alternative penalty, Socrates did not choose banishment. His covenant with the State was thus made freely, consciously, and under no stress in relation to time—after all, he has spent seventy years in Athens.

Furthermore, the Laws ask, what will Socrates gain by escaping? The risk of banishment or loss of property would be inflicted upon his friends. If he entered well-ordered states, he would be regarded as a lawbreaker by their citizens and would confirm the jury's opinion of him. But if he chose to go to states with little or no respect for law and order, would that kind of life be worthwhile? He could not continue to converse as usual about goodness in persons and governments, for it would be hypocrisy to do so. He would not want to rear his children in such an environment, and if they remained in Athens, they would be more likely to receive good care with Socrates dead than with him alive illegally and in exile. Surely his friends, if true to their profession, would care for them.

In conclusion the Laws advise Socrates, ". . . do not think more of your chiidren or of your life or of anything else than you think of what is right; so that when you enter the next world you may have all this to plead in your defence before the authorities there." To disobey by escaping will not really better either his friends or Socrates in this world or the next. "As it is, you will leave this place, when you do, as the victim of a wrong done not by us, the Laws, but by your fellowmen." But if he retaliates and returns evil for evil, breaking his agreement and wronging himself, his friends, his country, and the Laws themselves, he will incur the wrath of the Laws both here and in the next life.

Socrates thus concludes the speeches he has put in the mouth of the Laws and asks Crito whether he has anything to say in opposition to these arguments, which seem so persuasive that Socrates professes to be scarcely able to hear any others. Since Crito offers no refutation, the matter is decided: Socrates will obey the law even though it means his death.

Few readers will leave the *Crito* without making a personal judgment on Socrates' decision and his justification for it. The difficulty of making an adequate one is complicated by several factors: Socrates' trial, as far as we know, was legal. As Professor A. E. Taylor notes in discussing the *Apology*, the real reasons for which Socrates was prosecuted concerned matters for which general amnesty had been extended by the Act of Oblivion, and so the court could not have jurisdiction over these; hence the failure of Anytus and Meletus, Socrates' accusers, to explain their charges. However, though the ostensible charges were thus specious, and though Socrates showed them to be ridiculous, the jury had voted in proper order to convict him, and so the letter of the law had been fulfilled. The very fact that this case clearly showed that an innocent and supremely good man could be condemned unjustly under the law and hence that the law needed revision was cited as an excellent reason for escape, but Socrates argued that such reform should be demanded at a time other than that at which his own fate was affected in order that

reform would not be motivated by mere favoritism.

But—as Socrates makes the Laws say in the present dialogue—it is not the laws but the men administering them who wronged him. Socrates argued that respect for law in general is more valuable than one man's life lost by maladministration.

This again is a delicate point. Had the miscarriage of justice occurred merely through ignorance—though of course Socrates regarded vice as a kind of ignorance—it would have been easier to accept the sacrifice. But the reader finds it difficult to avoid feeling that the court is more intent on ridding Athens of Socrates than it is on reaching a just verdict. It is true that Socrates argued that were he to evade the death penalty, people would think him insincere in his former teaching about integrity and obedience to the law—but Crito might well have turned one of his own statements against him by replying that it is only what reasonable and wise men think that really matters. Nevertheless, the example set by escape might have been harmful to men of less comprehension.

Socrates perceived the value of consistency and stability in the State and its dispensation of justice. A state does not consist merely of the persons administering and living in it at any given time; to function best a state must have a continuity transcending the irregularities of individual fortunes. Presumably this was Socrates' intent in valuing the State above parents and ancestors, though modern Western readers may feel that Socrates revered the State too much. But whether the reader agrees with Socrates' decision here, he can hardly fail to admire the philosopher's devotion to principal, nor deny that the nobility of such a death enhances life for the living.

Pertinent Literature

Woozley, A. D. "Socrates on Disobeying the Law," in *The Philosophy of Socrates*. Edited by Gregory Vlastos. Garden City, New York: Anchor Books, 1971.

It is clear that the *Crito* and the *Apology* are closely connected. The most obvious connection is that they form two adjacent items in a sequence of dialogues which Plato wrote to show Socrates' char-

acter and behavior during his trial and death. This group of writings includes the *Euthyphro* at one end and the *Phaedo* at the other. Of course, it need not be the case that the dialogues were written in that sequence, and it is certain that the *Phaedo* is later than the others. Nevertheless, the best evidence and reasoning show that the *Apology* and the *Crito* were written fairly early in Plato's dialogue-writing career. Moreover, it seems eminently reasonable to presume that it was Plato's aim in those early works to portray Socrates more or less as he was.

Given those assumptions about the two dialogues, a pressing problem arises. A. D. Woozley was not the first to notice this matter, but he has certainly been the chief instrument in making it an important issue in modern Socratic/Platonic studies.

The problem is this. In the *Apology*, when explaining to the court what his life has involved, Socrates imagines the court proposing to acquit him on the condition that he give up his questioning ideas; that is, that he give up doing philosophy. His response to that offer is that if he were to be acquitted with that condition, he would not change his behavior no matter what the consequences. For Socrates to have said that would have amounted to his declaring that he would disobey the court if they handed down a conditional decision. The court did not make that decision, and consequently in the dialogue Socrates is portrayed as in prison waiting for the death sentence to be carried out. His friend Crito proposes to help him escape. Socrates proceeds to argue that it would be wrong for him to escape, and one of the arguments he uses is that escaping would mean that he would be violating a legitimate order of the court. That is, he argues that disobedience of a court order is wrong and so he refuses to escape.

It certainly seems as if, although Socrates at his trial declared that as a matter of principle he would disobey a certain court order, only a month later he argues that it is in principle wrong to disobey procedurally correct legal commands, even one threatening one's own life. The problem, in consequence, is how one resolves, if at all, that (seeming) contradiction in Socrates' views.

In addressing this problem, Woozley argues that there is no possibility that one of these apparently inconsistent positions is not being genuinely Socratic or that Socrates changed his mind in the interval between trial and prison. Hence, there remain only two choices. Either the inconsistency was not noticed or there really is no inconsistency. Woozley regards the first choice as wholly implausible—a man of principle such as Socrates could hardly fail to see such an inconsistency. The solution depends on finding a way of treating the two situations so that they are seen not to be in conflict, and Woozley believes he has found such a way.

The difference between the two situations Woozley finds to reside in matters of openness of action and persuasion. In the *Apology* Socrates says he would disobey a restraining court order by openly going about his business and trying to persuade Athens of her wrong behavior. However, to escape, as Crito proposes, would be to evade the law by *stealth* and would do nothing to try to reason the state out of wrongful conduct. Hence, Woozley holds that under certain circumstances Socrates condones genuine civil disobedience, openly breaking the law, in an attempt to persuade the state to alter its behavior.

Santas, Gerasimos Xenophon. *Socrates: Philosophy in Plato's Early Dialogues.* London: Routledge & Kegan Paul, 1979.

In his study of Socrates, Gerasimos Xenophon Santas picks up the problem developed by A. D. Woozley, the question of whether there is a contradiction between the *Apology* and the *Crito* concerning Socrates' conclusions as to whether he should disobey court orders.

Several things should be noted before looking at Santas' way of solving the problem. First, in his discussion of this issue, as in all the other ones

discussed throughout the book, Santas is especially concerned to set out Socrates' arguments in full detail and in approved official form. That is the nature of the book he has attempted to write. Second, he emphatically says he disagrees with the solution proposed by Woozley in his essay. Third, despite Santas' claim that his solution is different from Woozley's, there is a great deal of similarity between the two positions. This is not to say that there are no differences, even significant ones. Rather, the reader should be warned that the differences lie in matters of comparative detail. The two authors agree that there is no contradiction between the two dialogues and also agree in the general line of solution to the seeming inconsistency.

The advantage of looking carefully at Santas' work in connection with this issue is that he patiently goes over all the relevant arguments so that one can see how Socrates comes to his conclusions and how Santas arrives at his conclusions.

To discover whether Socrates contradicted his assertions in the *Apology* by what he argued while in prison, it is necessary, Santas holds, to consider both the arguments in the *Crito* which lead to the conclusion that it would be wrong for him to escape and the arguments in the *Apology* which are used to support his claim that he would continue to philosophize even if ordered to stop. There are two central lines of argument in the *Crito* leading to the conclusion that escape would be wrong. Although both are difficult to reconstruct in detail (a task which Santas does very well), the main lines are clear. He argues that to escape, given all the circumstances, would be (1) to do harm to the state and so violate a moral principle which says one ought not do harm and (2) to break

an agreement with the city and so violate a principle concerning the rightness of keeping agreements. The arguments in the *Apology* which bear upon this issue are more diffuse that those in the *Crito* and so are even more difficult to set out fully, but again the main points are clear. Socrates concludes that if he were given an acquittal with the proviso that he cease doing philosophy, he would refuse to cease for the reason that to cease philosophizing would be to disobey God and to stop doing what is the greatest good for the city,

The question now is "How do the arguments of the *Crito* apply to the case in the *Apology*, and vice versa?" Santas holds that the *Crito*'s arguments do not *fully* apply to the situation envisioned in the trial, and, just as important, that they do not mention *all* the relevant facts in that situation, especially the question of obedience to God. Hence, those arguments do not show Socrates to have come to the wrong decision when defending himself before the court. On the other hand, the arguments in the *Apology* do support his later decision not to escape; hence, there is no contradiction in that direction either. Socrates' behavior was consistent—civil disobedience was not ruled out by the arguments of the *Crito*.

Woozley, A. D. *Law and Obedience: The Arguments of Plato's* Crito. London: Duckworth, 1979.

In the same year that Gerasimos Xenophon Santas' book critical of A. D. Woozley's earlier argument was published, Woozley himself had published a full-length study of the *Crito*. This is the only work given over to nothing else but an examination of the *Crito*, a fact which is not surprising since the dialogue is so short. Woozley, of course, reexamines the ground covered by his earlier paper (and also that covered by Santas). However, as the issue of Socrates' inconsistency concerning civil disobedience is not the only issue worthy of notice in connection with the dialogue, let us look at Woozley's discussion of another matter arising from the *Crito*.

Crito gives his long-time friend Socrates several reasons for escaping. Socrates first rejects those reasons and then turns around and constructs his own argument to show that it would be wrong to escape.

It is interesting, both for the light it throws on his views and on his character, to consider how Socrates rejects the reasons why he should escape. Here one should consult the second chapter of Woozley's book.

Woozley mentions four reasons advanced by Crito for escaping. The surprising fact is that three of those reasons are never directly responded to by Socrates. The three are these: (1) if Socrates does not escape but remains to die, Crito will be losing a friend he can never hope to replace; (2) by staying and dying, Socrates would allow to happen what his enemies want to happen; and (3) if Socrates does not escape he will be failing his children by failing to see them properly educated and reared. The only place where Socrates even alludes to these considerations is at 48c where he dismisses all that kind of talk as irrelevant to the situation, a dismissal which Woozley notes as "hardhearted."

The fourth reason, which Crito is very much concerned with and which Socrates does spend time criticizing, is about reputations. If Socrates does not escape, then Crito and Socrates' other friends will acquire reputations as men too miserly or too cowardly to help their friend escape. Woozley is first of all interested in considering whether this is proposed as a *moral* reason for escaping. His conclusion is that it *was* most likely intended to be a moral consideration: that a man's reputation, especially that of a friend, should undeservedly be allowed to suffer by one's actions is something that morally matters.

What was Socrates' response to that argument? As Woozley says, Socrates treats Crito's worry about the reputation of Crito and others with contempt. And Woozley sees that since Crito made his point as part of a moral argument, it is difficult to hold that Socrates acted properly in simply casting the argument aside, in saying (in effect) "Don't worry about your reputation, unless it is your reputation in the eyes of people who know what they are talking about." Woozley, in fact, wants to defend Crito's position that the weight of public opinion must sometimes be considered significant even if what the public believes is wrong. Sometimes to refuse to take public opinion into account may have a serious effect if the public is mistaken or ill-informed.

On the other hand, Woozley does think that there is a flaw in Crito's argument, although it is one which Socrates seems not to have noticed. The flaw, according to Woozley, is that in fact Crito's reputation would not be likely to suffer much since Socrates was not popular; friends of Socrates were not likely to be much blamed for not having assisted in an escape.

While Socrates emerges impressively from most of the dialogues (even though making mistakes of reasoning at times), it is evident from Woozley's account of the response to Crito that there were flaws in Socrates' character. Woozley's assessment is that Socrates was not at his best in the exchange with Crito about the reasons given for escaping.

Additional Recommended Reading

Allen, R. E. "Law and Justice in Plato's *Crito*," in *The Journal of Philosophy*. LXIX, no. 18 (October 5, 1972), pp. 557-567.

Cohen, Carl. *Civil Disobedience*. New York: Columbia University Press, 1971.

Murphy, Jeffrie G. "The Socratic Theory of Legal Fidelity," in *Violence and Aggression in the History of Ideas*. Edited by P. R. Wiener and John Fisher. New Brunswick, New Jersey: Rutgers University Press, 1974. Three interesting further comments on the conflict between civil law and moral justice.

PHAEDO

Author: Plato (427-347 B.C.)
Type of work: Metaphysics
First transcribed: Probably one of the middle dialogues

Principal Ideas Advanced

The philosopher is always pursuing death, for the body hinders the soul's search for knowledge, and death would bring about a separation of body and soul.

The philosopher attempts to acquire knowledge of the Ideas—those eternal forms which are copied by individual things—but to gain such knowledge he must practice a kind of death, freeing the soul so that it can discover Ideas.

Surely the soul survives the death of the body, for opposites are generated out of opposites, and life is the opposite of death.

Furthermore, we have certain ideas (such as the idea of equality) which could not have been acquired in this life; hence, we must have existed, as souls, prior to being born; we recollect the Ideas we encountered before our birth.

The *Phaedo* (named after the narrator in the dialogue) is Plato's literary and philosophical monument to the death, and to the life, of his master, Socrates. An excellent way to begin the study of philosophy is with this account of the end of the first member in the great trio in Greek thought, as written by the second. It describes the philosophic way of life as Socrates and consequently Plato saw it, explaining how the philosopher, so unlike other men in many ways, differs also in being unafraid of death. Its account of the soul's immortality ranges from the fanciful myth about the various destinies of good and evil souls to what is perhaps Socrates'—and certainly Plato's—most fundamental theory, the doctrine of forms. While the *Phaedo* must be complimented by the other Platonic dialogues in order to round out the picture of Socrates as a man and as a philosopher, it suggests powerfully the influence he and Plato have jointly exercised in the history of Western thought.

The work consists of one dialogue within another; at the request of a friend, Phaedo recounts the conversation between Socrates and his companions and the final events of the day Socrates' unjust death sentence is executed. The inner dialogue occurs chiefly between the master and two of the several followers present, Simmias and Cebes. Quite naturally the talk turns to the true philosopher's attitude toward death.

Since Socrates appears willing to die and to justify this willingness, the question is raised: is suicide legitimate? Socrates' answer is that since men belong to the gods, the occasion of our death is in their hands, not ours. But Cebes objects that if life is divinely directed, its continuance is desirable and the voluntary escape from it would be folly. Socrates explains, however, that he expects to enjoy the company of other good and wise gods and men after death.

But a stronger defense of his position is requested. Socrates surprises his listeners by asserting that the philosopher is always pursuing death, and that it would hence be most inconsistent, now that death is at hand, to shun it. Simmias laughingly agrees that most people think the philosophic life is and deserves to be a kind of death, but he desires clarification. Socrates explains that the philosopher seeks and enjoys the pleasures of the body—those of food, drink, sex, and adornment—only to the extent that they are necessary to life, and beyond this despises them. The bodily senses, desires, and feelings hinder the soul's search for knowledge of true existence. Thought is clearest, then, when the influence of the body is least felt, or when there is the greatest possible separation between body and soul ("soul" in this context includes "mind"). But what is such separation, when completed, but death itself? Hence the philosopher—whose object is truth beheld with the clear eye of the soul, not with the befuddled vision of the physical organ—is constantly practicing a kind of death.

In elaborating this position Socrates introduces the famous doctrine of forms (variously described as "essences," "absolutes," and "Ideas." The last term does not have the connotation of the common English word, and hence the others are preferable). For each class of objects and qualities (or at least for many classes) there is an absolute form or essence which is the true nature and reality shared by particular members of the class. For example, there are absolute justice, beauty, goodness, greatness, health, strength. A beautiful object, say, is beautiful not in itself but by participation to some degree in the very essence of beauty. Each absolute is pure or self-identical, unique, eternal, and perfect in its kind since ultimately it *is* the kind in reality and not simply by definition for the sake of classification (although it may serve the latter purpose for the reader who rejects the Platonic metaphysics). A healthy man, for instance, becomes now more, now less healthy and eventually loses health altogether in death, but health is what it is without relation to time. Particular things, Plato explains elsewhere, are real only on a secondary level because they are changeable and perishable; they exist only by virtue of the ideal patterns they so variously but never perfectly copy.

Socrates asks now, how are such forms known? Certainly not, strictly speaking, by the senses; with the eye we see only this or that imperfectly beautiful thing, or observe persons merely more or less just, whereas beauty, justice, and the other absolutes are adequately apprehended only by an arduous and purely intellectual process : ". . . he attains to the purest knowledge of them who goes to each with the mind alone, not introducing or intruding in the act of thought, sight or any other sense together with rea-

son, but with the very light of the mind in her own clearness searches into the very truth of each." But if forms are known by mind alone, wisdom concerning true being can mature only after death, when the mind is wholly freed.

But it has not yet been established that the soul survives; Cebes expresses the common fear that upon bodily death the soul simply disperses into nothing. Socrates therefore offers a number of considerations supporting his confidence in immortality. (One translator of the dialogue suggests that Plato does not attempt a logical proof of this belief, but even in the translation phrases such as "sufficient proof" and "logical necessity" occur. It is true, however, that the arguments used vary greatly in plausibility for a modern reader.)

It is observable, Socrates holds, that all things which are "generated" or which come into and pass out of being are generated from their opposites. Particular (rather than absolute) opposites give way to each other: that which becomes weaker must have been stronger, the worse comes from the better, and so on. Thus we find all through nature both opposite states and the processes of coming into them; otherwise, if all things passed into conditions from which there was no return, the universe would become utterly static. Imagine, for example, a world in which waking was followed only by sleeping, or in which the processes of composition were never varied by those of division. Granted this point, Socrates argues that since life and death and living and dying are opposites, and it is certain that the living die, according to this universal law of nature the living must return from the dead, and therefore the dead must exist somewhere prior to return.

Cebes now suggests that the same implication follows from Socrates' familiar account of knowledge as recollection: knowledge of true being (that is, of the forms) turns out to be a recognition of what was known in a previous existence. Let us consider our comprehension of equality, for example. If we see two similar objects we may judge that they are equal or nearly so, but how do we recognize this relative equality? Such a judgment presupposes a concept of equality *per se* to serve as a standard for comparison. The concept of perfect equality cannot be derived from sensory observation because physical objects are never precisely equal. At the same time, however—and here Socrates tempers the extreme rationalism of the earlier account of knowledge of absolutes—we are reminded of absolute equality by the sight of imperfectly equal things; sensation is thus a necessary but not a sufficient condition of this recognition. But since we have sensation at birth, knowledge of essences must be prior to the present life; it is recollection of what we had once known and had forgotten when the soul took on a body. It is clear then that preexistence of the soul and that of the absolutes are equally certain.

Nevertheless, say Simmias and Cebes, we still have insufficient proof that the soul continues to exist *after* physical death. But Socrates reminds them that the latter argument, plus the one concerning opposites, does prove the point, for if the soul exists before birth (that is, in a state of "death" relative to bodily existence) and the living come from the dead, even as the dead come from the living, the soul thus exists both before and after the various bodies into which it is born. But noticing that Simmias and Cebes still evince the natural human uneasiness about the soul's future, Socrates adds another and perhaps sounder argument.

It hinges on comparison of the nature of the soul as compared to that of the body, and it concludes that if they are materially different, there is no reason to assign them a common fate. In general the composite or compound is unstable, subject to change and hence to dissolution, whereas the uncompounded or simple must be indissoluble, as are the invisible, simple, self-existent, and unchanging forms. Comparison of body and soul shows that body is like all other compound and perishable physical objects, but soul resembles the absolutes in some ways and presumably will share their permanence. This dichotomy of soul and body appears in the knowing process: if the soul relies on sensation she is dragged down to earth, as it were—to the unstable and the confused; but if she relies on her own reason she approaches the pure and eternal. Communion with the immutable breeds similarity: ". . . the soul is in the very likeness of the divine, and immortal, and intellectual, and uniform, and indissoluble, and unchangeable. . . ."

This conclusion leads Socrates to descriptions of the soul's fate after death which approach and finally cross the border between philosophy and fiction, but which, like many of Plato's myths, allegorically state significant hypotheses and profound insights. The soul's future, he says, will depend on its degree of purity in the present. Those impure souls enthralled by love of sensual pleasures and by evil passions are so weighed down by the corporeal that they may be reincarnated in animals similarly miserable in nature, such as in asses or wolves. The moderately virtuous soul might be given the body of an admirable social animal such as the ant or the bee, or perhaps even another human body. But only those souls purified of all bodily taint through philosophy may enter immediately into the blissful company of the gods and escape further reincarnation.

Philosophy is thus not merely an academic discipline or a profession; in the Platonic view it is a way of life and even the soul's salvation. Socrates describes the soul as previously shackled to the body, hoodwinked by the senses, enslaved by its own desires; worst of all, it is deceived about true reality by opinions influenced by pleasure and pain—it mistakes violence of emotion for evidence of truth. Philosophy offers release from this deception and teaches the soul to rely on her own intellectual resources. Thus, "she will calm passion, and follow reason, and dwell in the contemplation of her, beholding the true and divine. . . ."

After the almost poetic heights Socrates reaches in this account, he displays the equanimity of the truly philosophical inquirer when Simmias and Cebes still have serious doubts which he encourages them to broach. Simmias' objection presupposes the Pythagorean concept of the soul as a sort of harmony or attunement of the elements of the body, obtaining when these are in proper tension or proportion. By analogy to his previous arguments, Socrates would have to argue that the harmony of a lyre—which harmony is also invisible, perfect, and divine—could survive the destruction of the instrument. But the absurdity of this suggests the absurdity of the belief that the soul exists when the body is destroyed. Cebes adds that while the soul may survive several deaths and reincarnations, yet it is possible that it finally wears out as does a body that has survived several coats.

These objections seem so cogent to the audience, just now persuaded by Socrates' train of thought, that a despair of the success of any argument whatever sets in. But Socrates warns his friends of the dangers of misology; just as one may become a misanthropist by overconfidence in men, followed by disillusionment, so may one learn to distrust all argument by accepting conclusions hastily and without sufficient attention to logic, only to discover their falsity later. But instead of adopting a cynically skeptical position that no arguments are valid, no truths about reality discoverable, we should think that the difficulty is our lack of ability, which can be improved by further effort. It is fallacious to attribute the invalidity of our own thinking to reason itself, and folly thus to forfeit the very possibility of learning the truth.

Socrates then proceeds to answer Simmias' objection by showing that it is inconsistent with previous and present admissions. Harmony or attunement is not prior to the elements organized or tuned, but the soul has been shown to exist prior to the body. Simmias cannot hold, therefore, both that knowledge is recollection and that the soul is harmony. Furthermore, harmony occurs in degrees; an instrument may be more or less in tune. But we do not think that souls are more or less souls either in themselves or relative to others. Again, if the soul were a harmony, it could contain no vice, which is inharmonious, and consequently all souls would be equally good, which of course is absurd. And finally, if soul were a harmony of bodily elements, it would be dependent upon them, but as a matter of fact the soul, especially the wise one, acts as a governor of the body, and hence is sometimes out of harmony with it.

To meet Cebes' objection that the soul may eventually deteriorate and vanish, Socrates appeals once more to the doctrine of forms to elaborate a theory of causation relevant to the problem. In his youth, he remembers, he studied physicalistic and mechanistic theories of causal explanation of human life and behavior. But the detail (and presumably the mutual inconsistencies) of these frustrated and confused him. A gleam of hope appeared in the Anaxagorean view that Mind (as universal rather than human) orders and causes all things, which philosophy Socrates thought would show that everything was ordered for the best. If one wished to discover the ultimate causes for the shape of the earth, the positions and movements of the heavenly bodies, he need only refer to the highest good which these arrangements serve. But to his disappointment Socrates found Anaxagoras falling back on the familiar physical causes.

These offer partial but inadequate explanation of his own present behavior, Socrates continues. Of course he is engaging in his present activities in prison by means of bones, muscles, and their functions, but these are not the true causes of his behavior, which are that the Athenians have condemned him to die and he has thought it right to refuse escape and accept the penalty. Mechanistic philosophers ignore the distinction between conditions and causes (or between what Aristotle was later to call efficient and final causes); "of the obligatory and containing power of the good they think nothing. . . ." But since Socrates claims that he has been unable to discover what the nature of the best is, he offers a substitute causal theory.

While his procedure of adopting it may appear too rationalistic, further qualifications reveal much affinity to later scientific thought. His method is to select the theory judged most sound and then to accept or reject particular propositions by reference to it. But the original hypothesis is not wholly arbitrary; it can be justified either by derivation from an established theory, or (to judge from Socrates' practice) by examining its consequences for any inconsistencies. With this explanation Socrates accounts for his present assumption of the theory of forms.

We recall that an implication of the theory is that participation in the forms accounts for the characteristics of objects; Socrates insists that for him this is the only intelligible *cause* assignable. Indeed, it applies to the very processes of becoming: there is "no other way in which anything comes into existence except by participation in its own proper essence. . . ." Now two chief characteristics of forms are uniqueness and simplicity: they cannot admit their opposites. Furthermore, some particulars are so constituted that it is impossible they should admit forms opposite to those especially characteristic of their own natures; for example, the number two, having the form "even," cannot remain two and admit the form "odd." Now when we realize that what renders body alive is soul and nothing else, it appears that soul has an essential relation to life and hence cannot admit its opposite, death, any more than fire can admit cold. Hence, again the soul has been proved to be immortal, this time to the satisfaction of all those present.

It follows, then, that the soul deserves the greatest care in the present life, preparatory to the next. Socrates proceeds to give an imaginative description of the details of life after death and the various regions good and evil souls will occupy. The orthodox Christian reader will find here a number of counterparts anticipating his own traditions of heaven, hell, and even purgatory. Socrates adds, however, that "A man of sense ought not to say, nor will I be very confident, that the description which I have given of the soul and her mansions is exactly true. But I do say that, inasmuch as the soul is shown to be immortal, he may venture to think, not improperly or unworthily, that something of the kind is true." The chief point is again that "there is no release or salvation from evil except the attainment of the highest virtue and wisdom."

That Socrates has by his own virtue and wisdom escaped the evil of fear of death is now abundantly evident. When the discussion is finished and he has bidden his family goodbye, only Socrates among the entire assembly keeps his composure as the final preparations are made. Admonishing his friends to restrain their sorrow (which Plato has made contagious even today), Socrates quaffs the cup of poison as cheerfully as if it were wine.

Whether or not the reasoning associated with his attitude seems entirely valid, and some of it judged formally certainly is not, there is much in the Socratic teaching which is enduringly sound and recurrently fruitful. Some doctrines, such as that of the forms, may be rejected as metaphysics while renewed as logic or epistemology. But theory aside, none can gainsay the value of Socrates' visionary courage, or fail to wish it perpetual in the human race. For an adequate intimation of the master's immortality, however, one must return to its original description by his most eminent disciple.

Pertinent Literature

Vlastos, Gregory. "Reasons and Causes in the *Phaedo*," in *The Philosophical Review*. LXXVIII, no. 3 (July, 1969), pp. 291-325.

The part of the *Phaedo* (95E-105C) in which Socrates explains his new method of hypothesis, although recognized as fundamental for understanding Plato's metaphysics and epistemology, has been interpreted in many ways and today is often dismissed as dealing with pseudoproblems. Gregory Vlastos thinks that, if one fundamental misunderstanding is cleared up, the passage does its author credit. That misunderstanding arises from the careless habit of using "cause" to translate the Greek *aitia*. One meets the difficulty again in connection with Aristotle's so-called "four causes," only one of which, the "efficient cause," is a cause in the English sense of the word. Vlastos suggests that we can best preserve the extension of the Greek word if we reformulate expressions containing *aitia* as answers to why-questions. In this way we make it clear that *aitiai* are not properly "causes" but rather are "becauses" or reasons. "Because" may point to an event, to a lawlike connection, to a purpose, or to an entailment. Any of these could be called in Greek an *aitia*.

When Cebes, viewing the soul as a physical object, expressed the fear that like everything else in nature the soul must eventually waste away, Socrates told of his own youthful disappointment with the theories of naturalists, such as Democritus and Anaxagoras, which made use only of material and mechanical *aitiai*. Socrates then explained the new theory which he had devised according to which Forms or Ideas functioned as *aitiai*. Vlastos regards this as an important new insight: speaking through Socrates, Plato called attention to the ambiguity of the concept of *aitia*, and sorted out its import in different categorial contexts. Unfortunately, interpreters of Plato have failed to recognize what he was doing and have charged him with the very fault which he was the first to expose. Aristotle, for example, says that in the *Phaedo* Forms are treated like generative causes and he criticizes Plato for making the Form Health, rather than the physician, the cause of the patient's recovery. Modern scholars, Vlastos says, too often make the same mistake.

As a basis for discussion, Vlastos takes the following statement: ". . . each of the Forms exists and it is in virtue of participating in them that other things are named after them" (102A10-B2). Here, besides the relation, participation, three sets of variables are used: Forms, individual persons or things, and immanent characters which have the same names as their respective Forms. The hypothesis is that for any character (F) of any individual (x) there exists a Form (Φ), and that x has the character F if and only if x participates in Φ.

In the *Phaedo*, Socrates uses this hypothesis to give two answers to the question, "Why is x F?" The first answer, which he calls the safe and simpleminded answer, offers the Form as the *aitia*. This interpretation holds the solution for the series of perplexities with which philosophical naturalism had left Socrates confronted: for example, the puzzle of why things which were one and one, became two when placed together. The difficulty disappeared when he came to see that questions of arithmetic require different *aitiai* than do physical questions. If we call things two, it is because we view them as participating in the Dyad; if we call them one, it is because we view them as participating in Unity—not because of the distance between them, or their proximity. In general, we can speak of a figure as a square or of an object as beautiful or of a law as just only because of the ontological dependence of temporal things on eternal Forms. This dependence, however, is not a causal relation. The Form Squareness does not bring squares into existence any more than the Form Ideal City brings into existence ideal cities. Although Forms are metaphysical *aitiai*, it is not their ontological status but their logical content that makes them useful in answering questions.

The safe but simpleminded answer to the question, "Why is x F?," is, "Because x participates in Φ." A more clever and bolder answer is, "Because x participates in Γ," when Γ "brings on," or, as we might say, "entails" Φ. Thus, "Why is x odd?" could be answered, "Because x is three," the reasoning being that because x is three it participates in Threeness, and because Threeness entails Oddness, then x must be odd. Other pairs of Forms mentioned are Fire-Heat and Fever-Sickness; and the answer is bold and clever because it does, in some fashion, connect physical causality with logical entailment. We infer, for example, that a man is sick because he has a fever. Does this mean that, for Plato, the Form Fever is the cause of a man's being sick? Not directly, says Vlastos. Plato is saying that causal connections in the physical world are what they are and are intelligible to us only because there exist incorporeal, immutable objects, the relations between which we can know.

That Plato's analysis could hold no interest for the natural scientist Vlastos is quick to recognize; he also remarks that any attempt to find in the laws of nature the same necessity which obtains in formal reasoning is unpopular with philosophers in our times. But the atomist Leucippus had said that "nothing happens at random, but everything by reason and by necessity"; and Plato was right in pointing out that if one looks for necessity in nature he will not find it by observing regularities. Even in modern times, says Vlastos, not all have agreed with David Hume that the laws of nature are radical contingencies; and he cites Brand Blanshard, who says, in *The Nature of Thought*, that "being causally connected involve(s) being connected by a relation of logical necessity."

Plato. *Plato, Phaedo*. Translated by R. Hackforth. Cambridge: Cambridge University Press, 1955.

This excellent book contains a brief but incisive introduction, a lucid and accurate translation, and a running commentary which sheds light on obscure and difficult passages and places the dialogue in its proper historical and philosophical context.

R. Hackforth denies that the fundamental purpose

of the dialogue is to prove that the human soul is immortal, although it is of course obvious that much of it is devoted to arguments designed to prove that thesis. Nor is it to expound the doctrine of the Forms, although that too occupies a considerable amount of space in the dialogue. It is, rather, to extend and deepen Socrates' principal teaching: that man's supreme concern is the watchful care or "tendance" of his soul—that is, the development of deeper insights into moral and spiritual values and application of those insights to individual conduct. Such insights are attained through philosophy, according to both Socrates and Plato, and are the conditions essential for genuine happiness.

According to Hackforth, the emphasis upon purification of the soul, with the concomitant doctrine of flight from the body and all material things, as well as contempt for the world that is perceived by the senses, is not purely negative and does not lead to an extreme form of asceticism. By being fused with the doctrine of the Forms or Ideas, the principal doctrines of the *Phaedo* lead to a rather different conception of human happiness than one would find in pure asceticism. The soul's proper activity is the apprehension of the Forms, the universals, and through that activity it achieves the only kind of joy or satisfaction of which it is truly capable. In order to reach the utmost pinnacle of such achievement, it is necessary for the philosopher to be rid of the fetters of the body, which merely impede the soul in its quest; hence, the renunciation of physical pleasures and desires and the "training for death" which Socrates recommends.

The ethical principles advocated in the *Phaedo* are very individualistic, according to Hackforth, and for that reason very much different from the concerns Plato demonstrated in the *Republic*. Hackforth concludes from this and from other evidence that the *Phaedo* was written some time before the *Republic*, and probably before the *Symposium* as well; for in these (later) dialogues the concern shifts from exclusive preoccupation with the welfare of the individual and his soul to social and political questions, such as the nature of justice in the state.

Furthermore, the theories on the nature of the soul in the *Phaedo* and the *Republic* are quite different from one another. In the *Phaedo*, the soul is very much like the eternal Forms—simple, noncomposite, and eternal. In the *Republic*, however, Plato goes to great lengths to "prove" that the soul is composed of three distinct "parts," each of them possessing different attributes and exercising different kinds of power or influence upon the whole. Moral conflict is characterized in the *Republic* as a kind of disharmony or discord between the various parts of the soul, each of them attempting to usurp a function more properly belonging to another. But in the *Phaedo* moral conflict is conceived as a struggle between the pure, rational soul and the body, which is by its very nature irrational and shot through with passions and desires. In the *Phaedo*, the soul opposes the body's irrational fears and desires; in the *Republic*, those fears and desires arise within the soul itself and must be controlled by its rational element.

Moreover, Hackforth finds in the *Phaedo* a hint of Plato's mysticism—that is, of his theory that the soul's activity goes beyond the mere cognition of its objects. The soul also seeks to possess its objects and to satisfy a powerful desire for them. This desire for possession and unification is reminiscent of the kind of love, the union of the lover with the beloved, described so vividly in the *Symposium* and again in the *Republic*, where Plato has Socrates tell how the philosopher approaches and is finally united with "that which truly is." This mystical idea is only hinted at in the *Phaedo*, but according to Hackforth its brooding presence is unmistakable.

Unlike many of the dialogues, the *Phaedo* contains no conceited interlocutor who suffers deflation at the hands of Socrates—no Gorgias, no Thrasymachus, no Protagoras, no Polus. This is of course appropriate for the setting of the dialogue, which was a gathering of Socrates' most intimate associates, grieving already over the imminent execution of their great teacher. Hackforth notes that in contrast to the rapierlike thrusts of Socrates' logic in other dialogues, he is depicted here as serene and confident, and the discussion proceeds in a quiet and somber manner, except for occasional bits of quiet humor— as when Socrates responds to Cebes's question as to the manner of his burial, "Bury me as you like, if you can catch me."

In his commentary, Hackforth notes that the myth

toward the end of the *Phaedo* is designed to reinforce the fundamental point of the dialogue—the tendance of the soul as the principal obligation of the philosopher. The intellectual and moral process of purging our souls from the taint of the body can help to bring about that unity of goodness and happiness which is the goal of the philosopher's life. The myth itself is similar in important respects to the myths about the judgment of souls in the *Gorgias*, the myth of Er in the *Republic*, and the myth of the supracelestial region in the *Phaedrus*. The myth in the *Phaedo*, according to Hackforth, is to extend our mental horizons beyond this life and beyond the small corner of the earth which we know from experience. The hollow in which people live (Tartarus) is comparable, in many important respects, to the cave that Plato describes in the *Republic*. Those who live in the hollow imagine that they are dwelling on the surface of the earth, and they suppose that the impure air they breathe is the heaven, while in fact the true surface of the earth, a much more beautiful place, is beyond their reach, and the true heaven is almost beyond their imagining. The true earth is the habitation of righteous souls that have not quite reached the state of perfection required for ascent to the ultimate reality, the highest and purest state of being.

Unlike the myths of the *Phaedrus* and the *Republic*, where three classes of souls are distinguished (curable sinners, incurable sinners, and the righteous), this myth introduces five classes, the additional ones being those who are "indifferently good" and those who have been purified by philosophy and are therefore to be removed from the perpetual cycle of birth and death and rebirth. And here, according to Hackforth, comes the climax of the *Phaedo*'s message: "But now, Simmias, having regard to all these matters of our tale, we must endeavour ourselves to have part in goodness and intelligence while this life is ours; for the prize is glorious, and great is our hope thereof."

Additional Recommended Reading

Castañeda, Héctor-Neri. "Plato's *Phaedo* Theory of Relations," in *Journal of Philosophic Logic*. 1, nos. 3/4 (Aug., 1972), pp. 467-480. A discussion of 102B7-C4, with special reference to the distinction between relations and qualities.

Cobb, William S., Jr. "Anamnesis: Platonic Doctrine or Sophistic Absurdity?," in *Dialogue: Canadian Philosophical Revue*. XII, no. 4 (December, 1973), pp. 604-628. An analysis of the passages in the *Phaedo* and other dialogues in which the doctrine of recollection is discussed, concluding that it is not a solution to an epistemological problem, but a step in rebutting certain sophistic claims.

Cornford, Francis Macdonald. "The Mystical Tradition," in *From Religion to Philosophy: A Study in the Origins of Western Speculations*. New York: Harper & Row Publishers, 1957, especially pp. 245-263. An excellent, informative discussion of Plato's theory of immortality and his theory of the Forms, with comparisons between the *Phaedo* and Plato's other works; helpful historical notes.

Epp, Ronald H. "Some Observations on the Platonic Concept of Katharsis in the Phaedo," in *Kinesis*. 1, no. 2 (Spring, 1969), pp. 82-91. An attempt to mediate between those who believe that immortality is the main issue in the *Phaedo* and those who believe that it is something else.

Flew, Antony. "Survival and Immortality," in *An Introduction to Western Philosophy: Ideas and Argument from Plato to Sartre*. Indianapolis: Bobbs-Merrill, 1971, pp. 125-167. Excerpts from the *Phaedo* and other dialogues, with a sympathetic but skeptical analysis by a master of philosophical analysis, complete with appropriate references to *Alice in Wonderland*.

REPUBLIC

Author: Plato (427-347 B.C.)
Type of work: Political philosophy, metaphysics, epistemology
First transcribed: Probably one of the middle dialogues

Principal Ideas Advanced

The question arises, "What is justice?" and after some unacceptable answers, Thrasymachus suggests that justice is whatever is to the interest of the stronger party (since the stronger party makes the laws and enforces them); but Socrates argues that rulers sometimes err and that, in any case, the art of government, like other arts, is directed to the interests of those to be affected, the people themselves.

Socrates claims that the just man, provided he has knowledge, can rule both himself and others, and that the concern of the just man is not for himself alone.

To clarify the idea of justice and to prove its worth, Socrates leads a discussion concerning justice in the state; he constructs the idea of an ideal state, one which exhibits justice.

Any state needs guardians (rulers), auxiliaries (soldiers), and workers; each class does its proper business without interfering with the others; analogously, the just man is one in whom the three elements of his nature—the rational, the spirited, and the appetitive—are harmonized.

The ideal republic is one in which the classes are carefully built up by controlled breeding, education, and selection; society is communized in order to eliminate quarrels about personal property.

The guardians of the state should be educated as philosophers, having been prepared by training in music and gymnastic.

The *Republic* of Plato, perhaps the greatest single treatise written on political philosophy, has influenced strongly the thought of Western man concerning questions of justice, rule, obedience, and the good life. This is true whether one agrees with Plato's answer or, if dissatisfied, seeks a different solution. The work is also undoubtedly the best introduction to Plato's philosophy in general. Not only does it contain his ideas on the state and man, but also his famous theory of forms, his theory of knowledge, and his views of the role of music and poetry in society. Nor does he condescend in this introduction, for he presents on each of the philosophical questions mentioned a penetrating analysis which demands careful study on the part of the reader. Socrates and his illustrious student Plato force one by their dialectical technique of question and answer, of definition and exception, to take an active part in the philosophical enterprise.

The work is divided into ten books, or chapters, written as a dialogue with Socrates as the main character. One cannot fail to catch the magnificence that must be present in Plato's literary and philosophical style, for all of the available translations indicate passages of great force and beauty.

The opening book of the *Republic* is concerned with the question, "What is justice?" Invited by Polemarchus to the home of his father Cephalus, Socrates and others (among them Glaucon, Adeimantus, and Thrasymachus) begin, in an easy fashion, the search for an answer. A general but vague definition is defended, first by Cephalus and then by his son, Polemarchus, to the effect that justice consists in restoring what one has received from another. Socrates asks if this definition would apply in a situation in which weapons borrowed from a friend were demanded by him when quite obviously he was no longer of sound mind. It is a homely example of the type that Socrates loved to give; and, as usual, when examined, it raises important considerations. Justice, among other things, involves not only property but also conditions, such as a sound mind, which cannot be merely assumed.

The next attempt is: justice is doing good to friends and harm to enemies. But knowledge is needed in order to be able to judge who our friends and enemies are. The definition is then modified: do good to the just and harm to the unjust. Socrates brings up a point in objection which is a central feature of many of his discussions of the good life. He argues that doing harm to the unjust makes them worse than they are. He holds that it can never be just to make a man worse than he is by doing harm to him.

The most serious discussion of this book and one which sets the tone for the remainder of the *Republic* occurs next. Thrasymachus, who had been sitting by listening to the argument with ill-concealed distaste, impetuously breaks in and takes it up. He presents a position which has since been stated many times: justice is that which is to the advantage or interest of the stronger party, the reason being that the stronger party makes the laws. Socrates begins to attack this definition: for instance, he points out that a man does not always know what his interest is or wherein it lies. When the stronger errs in his judgment, then what? Thrasymachus replies that the ruler is not a ruler when he errs. (Note that in admitting this, Thrasymachus has already moved away from his original position and toward that of Socrates that might alone does not make right, for it is might together with some kind of knowledge capable of preventing errors that makes right.) Socrates presses his advantage further. Whenever we consider an art and its practice, be it medicine, piloting a ship, or ruling, it is done so not for the sake of the art or for its practitioner but for those who are to receive its benefits, be they patients, passengers, or the ruled.

Thrasymachus angrily declares that anyone but a philosopher could see that society "honors" the man of power over the powerless. Corrupt men with impunity dissolve contracts, and pay no taxes. People may privately proclaim the virtues of justice but publicly the opposite prevails, and men are admired and respected for daring to practice that which is ordinarily frowned upon. In fact, Thrasymachus claims, the tyrant is the happiest of men. Here Socrates points out that Thrasymachus has challenged the whole conduct of living.

Socrates repeats the point that an art is practiced for the benefit of those for whom its services are intended and not for the benefit of the practitioner. Any payment received for practicing an art is independent of the aim of the art. In ruling, the benefit is for the ruled, not the ruler. No man rules willingly; he accepts the responsibility only because he fears to be ruled by a worse man. Thrasymachus replies that ideal justice is a virtue that a man of intelligence cannot afford, whereas what is called "injustice" is in reality only good prudence. Under questioning, Thrasymachus admits that the just man does not try to get the better of other just men, but rather of unjust men who are his opposites in character. "Get the better of" appears to mean "take advantage of" in the widest possible sense. Even to instruct someone is somehow to take advantage of him. In a vein much like the one taken above, Socrates argues that in every form of knowledge and ignorance (every art or its lack), the man who knows tries to benefit those who do not know, not those who know. When the ignorant are in control, not knowing the art, they do not know in what way to practice it or on whom. Hence, they try to get the better of all—be they wise or ignorant. For Socrates, knowing one's art and for whom it is intended is a sign of virtue. "Virtue" appears to mean "the proper function of anything"; what the proper function of a thing is, however, demands appropriate study and knowledge. We saw that those who are just try to get the better of only those who are unjust and of no others, whereas the unjust try to get the better of all. The latter, then, are the ignorant and the ineffectual; the former, the intelligent, and hence the wise and the good. The soul's virtue is found in proper rule of the individual. The just man with knowledge can rule both himself and others, whereas the unjust man, factitious, disrupted, and not knowing what to do and what not to do, can rule neither himself nor others.

The first book ends as Socrates reminds his disputants that they have been getting ahead of themselves; it is a bit foolish to talk about justice (a virtue) when they have not yet defined it.

In Book II, Glaucon and Adeimantus press Socrates to prove that the just life is worth living, and Glaucon illustrates his wish by means of the legend of Gyges's ring. Gyges, so the story goes, gained possession of a ring which, when turned, made its wearer invisible. With this advantage he was able to practice evil with impunity. Socrates is to consider an individual with the advantage of a Gyges and contrast him with one who in life is his opposite. It is his task to show that the life of the just man, no matter what indignities he suffers, is worth living; nay, more, that it is preferable to that of Gyges. He is to show that virtue is its own reward no matter what the consequences.

Socrates, with misgivings, takes on the task. He suggests, inasmuch as they are searching for something not easily found, justice, that they turn to a subject which will most readily exhibit it. The state is analogous to the individual, and justice, once found in the state, will apply also to its counterpart, the individual.

He begins his quest by a kind of pseudo-historical analysis of the state. Men are not self-sufficient and thus cannot supply themselves with all the necessities of life. But by pooling their resources, and by having each man do what he is best suited to do, they will provide food, shelter, and clothing for themselves. The city thus started engages in exporting and importing, sets up markets, and steadily advances from its simple beginnings. (It should be pointed out that the *states* in ancient Greece bore a strong resemblance to the *cities* of today, both in size and population, but were independent units.) From simple needs, the people pass increasingly to luxurious wants. Since the necessities of life are no longer sufficient, the people turn to warfare to accumulate booty. Armies are needed and a new professional is born: the soldier, with appropriate characteristics. The soldiers must be as watchdogs; gentle to their friends and fierce to their enemies. (Note that in discussing the characteristics of the soldiers, a spirited group that forms only a part of the state, and analogously, a spirited part of the individual, Socrates suggests a feature formerly given as a possible definition of "justice.") The soldier must know his friends—the citizenry—and his ene-

mies, the barbarians, and be good to the one and harm the other. This may be an aspect of justice, but it is not the complete definition. The state also needs rulers, or guardians, who are to be carefully selected and trained.

Plato holds music and gymnastics to be a significant part of the guardian training. He concludes Book II and takes up much of Book III with arguments for censorship of the tales of Hesiod and Homer, especially any wherein the gods, who ought to be examples of noble, virtuous beings, are presented as deceitful, lustful, brutal, and petty. He believed that Greek society was in the decline, that moral behavior was no longer understood or practiced by the Athenians, and that, to a large measure, the degrading tales of the gods were responsible. He no doubt mistook a symptom for a cause. The moral decline of a people involves many things of which trashy literature is only a sign; the desire for such things cannot be cured by censorship; the principle involved in censorship has other consequences which are as bad as the social evils that Plato hoped to cure. He thought, as many today do, that the young imitate in their behavior the activities they see in the imitative arts. If they read stories in which the "heroes" are immoral, if they see plays in which the protagonists are effeminate and slavish, then they will tend to act similarly. Plato argues that the guardians may know of such people, but to act as they do will bring about bad habits. Furthermore, to imitate means to do or be more than one thing—that is, to be both that which one imitates and also one's own self—and in this society it is enough to do or be one thing and that well.

In order to convince the inhabitants of this state that men are fit for one and only one job—to be either guardians (rulers), auxiliaries (soldiers), or workers—the rulers will institute a "noble lie." This lie or myth will be to the effect that men are molded by the gods to be one of the three types noted. Plato likens these classes to gold, silver, and bronze and holds that the people are to look upon themselves as having these "metals" in their makeup from birth. There will be some "mobility" between classes if ability is discovered, but generally they will remain static.

In Book IV, Socrates holds that the city should be neither too wealthy nor too poor, neither too large nor too small, neither too populous nor too few: one in which men and women have equal opportunity and in which each does that task for which he is best suited. Such a city will be wise and brave, temperate and just. These are the cardinal virtues, and so we are well on our way toward finding in the city those virtues we had hoped to see in the individual.

In the city, wisdom is found in the rule of the guardian; in the individual, in the rule of intelligence. To function properly, we saw, is to be virtuous. This, to Plato, is the essence of wisdom, especially since acting virtuously takes knowledge. Courage is a way of preserving the values of the city through education. Knowing what to fear and what not to fear, a knowledge gained through law, characterizes courage. Temperance is a kind of order; the naturally better part of the soul controls the worst part, as in the city the naturally superior part governs the inferior. Thus, the intelligence of the few controls the passions of the many, as a man's intelligence governs his appetites through his will. Justice, lastly, is found in the truth that each one must practice the one thing for which his nature is best suited. To do one's "business" and not to meddle with others, to have and to do that which is one's own—that is justice. Although within the class of artisans there may be some mixing of tasks—the carpenter may perform some other craft—there cannot be mixing of the classes of gold, silver, or bronze.

In Book V, Plato discusses his famous "three waves" which are needed if the ideal state is to be possible. From those who show the proper aptitude the rulers are to be selected, women as well as men. This is the first wave. The second wave is that communal life must be shared by the ruling class. Marriage and children will be held in common. All within a certain age group are to be designated "parents," a younger group, "children" and "brothers and sisters," and so on. Plato argues that family loyalty is an asset which, when practiced on a public scale, will retain its value, whereas the deficits of private family life, such as the factiousness between families, will have been eliminated. "Mine" and "not mine" now will apply to the same things. The ruler will arrange communal marriages by lot; unknown to the betrothed, however, the lottery will be fraudu-

lently arranged for reasons of eugenics. Another myth or lie is told for the state's benefit.

The third wave, and most difficult to bring about, is that philosophers must be kings, or kings, philosophers. If this can occur, then political power and intellectual wisdom will be combined so that justice may prevail. (Recall Socrates' discussion with Thrasymachus; only when knowledge and power are joined in the ruler can true advantage or benefit befall the ruled. It is now Plato's task to characterize the philosopher and define the kind of knowledge needed.)

In Books VI and VII, he presents three magnificent analogies to explain his meaning. But first his complicated theory of forms should be mentioned. Plato believed that those features which objects of a certain kind have in common, for example, the features common to varied art objects, all beautiful, are all related to a single perfect ideal, or form, which he called "the feature itself," in this case "beauty itself." This is an intellectual reality properly "seen" by the rational element of the soul, just as the many instances are perceived by sight or by means of the other senses. The good itself, the highest of all forms, is the proper object of the philosopher's quest.

In his first analogy, Plato likens the good to the sun. Just as the sun provides light so that we may see physical objects, the good provides "light" so that the soul may perceive intellectual forms.

Plato's second analogy also emphasizes the distinction between the senses and the rational element of the soul as sources of knowing. We are to imagine a line whose length has been divided into two unequal parts; furthermore, these parts are then to be divided in the same proportion as the first division. If we label the line AE, the first point of division C and the other two points of the subdivisions B and D, then the following proportions hold:

$$\frac{CE}{AC} = \frac{DE}{CD} = \frac{BC}{AB}$$

and hence BC = CD. Now what do these segments represent?

The first segment of the original line with its two segments Plato styles "the world of opinion," and he calls the first of its segments "conjecture" (AB) and the second "belief" (BC). As noted, we gain information of this world through our senses. We pass from creatures who let the world come to us with little or no thought (only conjecture)—a world of shadows and reflections—to persons who have beliefs as to what the shadows represent—a world of physical objects such as trees, hammers, houses.

The second segment of the original line is titled "the world of knowledge," and its sections "understanding" and "thinking" respectively; this is the world of forms mentioned in the analogy of the sun. Plato considers mathematics the mental activity most characteristic of *understanding* by the use of images. In geometry we find, among other things, an attempt to define precisely the various mathematical figures (circle, triangle, square, and so forth). Unlike the world of physical objects, which is mutable, these definitions, which state the formal properties of these objects, are unchanging. In *thinking* we find the highest form of mental activity: dialectical thought, or thinking by the use of Ideas. From contemplating the unchanging forms or Ideas of physical things, the mind progresses to the reality of perfect beauty, justice, and goodness. The process of education in the perceptual world moves from bare opinion through belief, a practical rather than a theoretical understanding of the truths of the world of things seen, to understanding and thinking, wherein the eternal truths of the world of things thought are known.

Plato's third analogy is that of the cave. We are to imagine prisoners chained in a cave in a way that all they can see is a wall in front of them. On the wall, shadows appear cast from a parapet behind them where a fire burns and where bearers carry all sorts of objects. This is, of course, analogous to the world of shadows (sense experience) represented by the segment AB of the divided line. Miraculously, a prisoner frees himself and sees the cause of the images and the light that casts them; he is in the world of belief. Noticing an opening which leads out of the cave, he crawls into the sunlight, the world of forms, and is so dazzled that he is blinded. But gradually he adjusts to the light, sees the true reality, the realm of Ideas, and is tempted to remain forever. But he is compelled by a sense of obligation to return to the cave and to instruct the chained. They disbelieve, for all they know is the world of gloom and shadows, and they would jeer him, or worse, tear him to pieces; but he persists and rededicates his life to their instruction. Thus the philosopher, having the world of forms for his contemplation, must return to be king, to rule by a sense of duty, if there is to be justice.

Plato outlines an educational program for the philosopher-king which continues from the music and gymnastics taught the guardians. For ten years he studies arithmetic, geometry, solid geometry, and astronomy. He is in the realm of understanding, and the point of his mathematical training is to prepare him for study of and grasp of ideal forms. For five years he studies dialectical thought so that the ultimate principle of reason, the form of good, shall be known to him. Then, at the age of thirty-five, he begins his period of practical application of these principles, and, after fifteen years he ascends the throne at fifty.

In Book VIII, Plato, after having brought us to a glimpse of the form of the state, discusses its decline. The decline of the state is paralleled by the decline of the individuals who make it up; the state is analogous to the individual. From the rational state we move to the spirited one (the guardians), the chief virtue of which is honor; when the spirited element is again dominated by appetites, then wealth is sought and the oligarchy born. From wealth we go to the government of the many who, overthrowing the few, proclaim the virtues of the group. Appealing to the mob, the demogogue takes over and the full decline of the ideal state and man has occurred. There is a weird similarity; from love of reason to insatiable lust, the state and the individual have degenerated. There is the rule of one in both cases, but we have gone from one who knows what to do and what not to do to one who knows nothing and whose every impulse is his master. The man of intelligence uses his reason to direct his will and thus to control his appetites, but the tyrant controls nothing. He is controlled by his appetites. A man who is slave to his appetites is master of nothing; the man who is master of nothing is the most miserable of men. He is always in pain. Thus Book IX closes, with the passage from true pleasure to pain, from the just man to the unjust.

Socrates has shown Glaucon and Adeimantus what the happy life, the just life, is.

Book X contains the famous Myth of Er, which will not be discussed here, but it also touches somewhat on what Plato means by "Idea" or "form" and on the danger of art in the state. His analysis will be mentioned briefly. To each class of particulars that have something in common, Plato holds there is a form or Idea in which these particulars participate and which gives them their common quality. The quality is a reflection of the Idea; so a bed painted by an artist has as its model a physical bed which has in common with other beds the Idea of "bedness" itself.

There can be but one Idea-form of beds, for if there were another, the two forms would have a third in which they would participate, and so on, *ad infinitum*. Plato's criticism of art as imitation was based on the claim that art is three steps removed from reality (since works of art are copies of the aspects of things, and things are themselves copies of the Ideas).

The *Republic* closes with an argument for the immortality of the soul. The soul's only illness is injustice; yet injustice is not fatal. By loving justice —by harmonizing reason, spirit, and appetite—man can keep his soul healthy, and the soul will prosper forever.

Pertinent Literature

Sachs, David. "A Fallacy in Plato's *Republic*," in *The Philosophical Review*. LXXII, no. 2 (April, 1963), pp. 141-158.

In this provocative essay, David Sachs distinguishes two conceptions of justice that are evident in the *Republic*. The first of these he calls the "vulgar" conception and the other the "Platonic" conception.

The vulgar conception of justice is shared by all of Socrates' interlocutors: Cephalus, Polemarchus, Thrasymachus, Glaucon, and Adeimantus. Justice, according to this conception, consists of not performing certain acts, while injustice consists of performing them—such acts as theft, betrayal, failing to keep promises or agreements, adultery, and neglecting one's parents or the service one owes to the gods. Glaucon's story of Gyges' ring perfectly exemplifies this conception of justice: the unjust man is represented as one who commits seduction and adultery, murder, and treason.

The Platonic view, on the other hand, begins with Socrates' observation that justice is both intrinsically and instrumentally good—that is, that it is desired both for its own sake and for the good effects that it brings about (or so it would seem from the traditional translations, including F.M. Cornford's). Sachs observes that Plato had been accused by some of his critics of not really responding to the question he set for himself, since it would appear that most, if not all, of his answer is designed to respond to the demand

for proof that justice has good effects. It does not seem to respond at all to the demand that he prove that justice is intrinsically good. Sachs explains that Glaucon's classification of goods is more accurately rendered as follows: those which by themselves (or on their own) produce good and nothing else; those which by themselves are productive of good and, in conjunction with other things, have other good effects; and those which by themselves have bad effects and good ones, the latter outweighing the former. In this rendering, then, there is no demand that Socrates prove that justice is intrinsically good, but merely that he show that it produces good and nothing else and that it has no bad effects.

Sachs says that merely proving that justice by itself cannot but be good for the soul of its possessor, and that injustice is evil, is not a sufficient response to the challenge of Glaucon and Adeimantus. Socrates must also show that justice is the soul's *greatest* good, and injustice its greatest evil. In addition, he must show that the just man's life is happier than that of the unjust man—even such men as those described in Glaucon's striking image of the just man who seems to be unjust and is treated accordingly, and the unjust man who seems to be just and is treated accordingly.

It must be remembered also that it is part of Plato's doctrine that to the extent that any man's soul is infected by injustice, he is less happy than the man who is perfectly just, despite the fact that there may be other goods which (one would ordinarily think) would contribute to his happiness. Thus, it would seem that Socrates is required to prove that a man who is ever so slightly unjust is more miserable than the perfectly just man so vividly described by Glaucon—that is, the one who is rotting in prison with his eyes gouged out.

In order for Plato's project to succeed, it is of course essential that he establish that the just man in Plato's sense—that is, the one whose soul is ordered as Socrates describes it—will not behave unjustly in the vulgar sense: that is, he will not commit immoral or criminal acts as those are ordinarily conceived. Moreover, he must prove that those who are just in the vulgar conception are also just in his, since short of this he will not have proved that it is impossible for men to be just in the vulgar sense and still be less happy than those who are not. Sachs argues that Plato did not meet either of these requirements.

Sachs says that Plato frequently *says* that the Platonically just man is least likely of all men to commit immoral acts and most likely to possess the vulgar moral virtues, but he never proves that this is so. It is true, of course, that Plato prescribes the minimal conditions for one's being just—namely, that he possess wisdom or intelligence, courage, and self-control or temperance—but he insists that these virtues are not sufficient for justice in the vulgar sense. The most that can be said, he argues, is that a Platonically just man would not commit crimes in a foolish, unintelligent, cowardly, or uncontrolled way. Plato merely has Socrates assert what he was supposed to have proved without ever bothering to prove it.

As for the second requirement, that Plato show that the ordinarily just man be shown also to be Platonically just, Sachs alleges that Plato not only failed to prove it, but that he also never even considered it. Furthermore, Sachs suggests that such a claim is rather implausible in any case, since it makes perfectly good sense to say that vulgarly just men, such as Cephalus, are *not* just in the Platonic sense.

He concludes, therefore, that the principal goal toward which the *Republic* was directed was not fulfilled and that the entire dialogue is infected with a very serious fallacy.

Wild, John. *Plato's Modern Enemies and the Theory of Natural Law*. Chicago: University of Chicago Press, 1953.

This excellent book is one of a number which were written in response to Karl Popper's charge that Plato was an irrational dogmatist, a "pseudo-rationalist," an authoritarian, indeed, a totalitarian, and also a racist who evinced "nothing but hostility toward the humanitarian ideas of a unity of mankind which transcends race and class." Popper charged that the ideal society described in the *Republic* was strictly regimented with a purely negativistic view of human freedom. Among his many accusations against the *Republic*, Popper alleged that it rested upon an educational monopoly of the ruling class with strict censorship. In this respect, it was fundamentally opposed to the egalitarian, individualistic philosophy of the historical Socrates.

In responding to this last charge, John Wild argues that nothing in the *Republic* provides a legitimate basis for the thesis that free expression of certain opinions is to be suppressed. He concedes that Plato went too far in advocating the censorship of artistic expressions that might have a corrupting influence upon the youth. But nowhere, he says, is it suggested that the nonguardians are to be kept artificially ignorant or deprived of the freedom to express their dissenting opinions. Without the freedom to express one's opinions, he says, the whole concept of Platonic argument and education would be absurd.

As for Plato's alleged dogmatism, Wild responds that Plato was no more dogmatic than anyone who defends his basic philosophical convictions. If it is dogmatic to assert that uncriticized opinion and prejudice are inimical to freedom, then Socrates too was a dogmatist. Nor, according to Wild, was Plato a racist. The rulers of his ideal state, whom Popper called the ruling class, the master race, and "herders of human cattle," were not a hereditary caste selected on racial grounds; nor were they arbitrary rulers. Rather, they were guardians of the "law of nature," which they did not decree by arbitrary fiat, but which they discovered through their philosophical explorations.

Shifting to the attack, Wild denounces Popper's "open society," which Popper had offered as a suitable alternative to Plato's "totalitarian" state, as being either a form of diluted anarchism or as a form of unjustifiable arbitrary rule by the majority—a form of mass tyranny, which Wild considers to be the most dangerous form of repression.

Moreover, Wild argues, Plato should not be attacked for not having been a moral relativist. He was not because he believed that men share a common rational nature and that cooperation is necessary if human life is to be lived satisfactorily. Plato's guardians, he said, are guardians of the law, who must first understand it and then apply it for the benefit of the whole community, including themselves. They are not selected because they belong to an aristocratic class or family, but because of their innate abilities. Furthermore, there is a sense in which they are not properly characterized as a *class* at all, since they are more like public servants or civil servants. They certainly had no special privileges, since they lived arduous lives, were deprived of all material goods other than those that were needed for their bare subsistence, and were utterly devoted to the common good.

Nor were the nonrulers slaves in Plato's society, for a slave properly so called is one whose natural rights are disregarded and violated. The artisans in the Republic, however, were performing productive functions for which they were naturally fitted and were given the same education as all other citizens of Plato's commonwealth. They had all the material goods they needed and indeed enjoyed a higher material standard of living than their supposed masters, the guardians.

Popper's allegations that Plato's "noble lie" was comparable to the activities of the Nazi Propaganda Bureau are grossly exaggerated, since Plato's "noble lie" was not as bad as Popper made it out to be, according to Wild. Some lies (such as the one discussed at the beginning of the *Republic* with Cephalus—that is, lying to a person who has gone mad and is seeking a weapon) are reasonable. A society needs a sense of unity and devotion to the common welfare of all if it is to survive in a healthy state. Some people are not fully capable of understanding the necessity for all the laws and institutions that are necessary for the orderly functioning of a state. Therefore, it is not unreasonable for the guardians to simplify the complex doctrines which lie at the philosophical base of the society's foundations and to clothe them in a patriotic myth. Such myths, Wild says, have been developed in all human communities. Plato's noble lie does convey a kernel of truth: that all men are brothers and that some people are endowed with superior intelligence. It is intended to induce a sense of brotherhood and loyalty to the community, and to that extent, at least, it is morally sound.

The book as a whole is a very thorough and well-documented exposition of many of Plato's most important ideas, including some that are frequently omitted from other expositions of Plato's philosophy; and Wild, who is obviously very sympathetic to Plato, does a masterful job of synthesizing Plato's doctrines and relating them to ideas that were more elaborately developed by later philosophers.

Additional Recommended Reading

Benardete, Seth. *Socrates' Second Sailing: On Plato's Republic.* Chicago: University of Chicago Press, 1989. A novel and insightful treatment of Plato's thought.

Levinson, Ronald B. *In Defense of Plato.* Cambridge, Massachusetts: Harvard University Press, 1953. A detailed response to Plato's modern critics, in cluding particularly Warner Fite, Karl Popper, and R. H. S. Crossman.

Popper, Karl R. *The Open Society and Its Enemies*. London: George Routledge & Sons, 1945. The source of a great intellectual conflict, accusing Plato of a multitude of sins, including the advocacy of totalitarianism and of having been the inspiration for many of the world's worst political thinkers and many of its political troubles.

Robinson, T. M. *Plato's Psychology*. Toronto: University of Toronto Press, 1970. Contains an excellent but somewhat technical analysis of Plato's theory of the soul as expounded in the *Republic*.

Sesonske, Alexander, ed. *Plato's* Republic: *Interpretation and Criticism*. Belmont, California: Wadsworth Publishing Company, 1966. A collection of excellent articles dealing with a number of issues treated in the *Republic*, ranging from Plato's theory of language to his concept of justice.

METAPHYSICS

Author: Aristotle (384-322 B.C.)
Type of work: Metaphysics
First transcribed: Fourth century B.C.

Principal Ideas Advanced

True knowledge is the knowledge of ultimate causes.

There are four types of causes: the formal cause (a plan or type); the final cause (a purpose); the material cause (matter, that which is used); and the efficient cause (that which initiates change).

The study of being as being involves the attempt to discover first principles of explanation.

The individual thing to which properties belong is the only true substance; substances are subjects, but never predicates.

Since properties attach themselves to individuals of a certain kind, the kind may also be called "substance"; thus, the essence of a thing is, in this sense, its substance.

Matter is potentiality, the capacity to be something; matter is unlimited which is able to be limited by form; when matter is limited by form, there is actuality.

Forms, or universals, exist only in things.

The process of change cannot go on to infinity; there must be an unmoved first mover which is eternal substance and actuality; such a first mover is good; it is divine thought thinking only of thought.

Avicenna reported that he had read Aristotle's *Metaphysics* forty times and still had not understood it. Such a comment is illuminating both for metaphysics as a subject matter and for Aristotle's treatise, from which the title for this inquiry has been derived. Both are difficult to understand, but the thinker who would understand this philosophic discipline would do well to start with Aristotle. Baffling as his piece of writing is, it is still the best source of metaphysics. Its structure is puzzling, since it was put together not by Aristotle but by his students from their notes. Nor did Aristotle give the treatise its immortal name. It was placed in the collection of his writings *after* the treatise on *Physics* and so earned the name of *meta* —(after the) physics.

Accidental as this title seems, it still describes the content of the treatise fairly accurately. In modern times much of the *Physics* might be classed as metaphysics (the discussion of the infinite), and some of the topics of the *Physics* are repeated in the *Metaphysics* (change and movement); but still the *Meta-physics* does go beyond the *Physics*. First principles, not the principles of natural movement alone, are the subject now. The *Metaphysics* takes up questions beyond those of physical nature as such and moves on not only to first principles but also to an Unmoved Mover. It is true that the book (the *Metaphysics*) stands somewhat alone in Aristotle's writings. According to the way in which the *Metaphysics* is either bypassed or interpreted, much of the general interpretation of Aristotle's other works will vary. That is, this treatise rightly occupies a metaphysical (basic) position within Aristotle's vast writings.

Book *Alpha*, which begins with the famous sentence, "All men by nature desire to know," is sometimes called the first history of philosophy. In it Aristotle reviews the theories of the pre-Socratics and of Plato, and much information we have about the pre-Socratics actually comes from Aristotle's accounts. Aristotle works out his own theories by a critical appraisal of other doctrines, indicating the strong and the weak points of each theory and incorporating the strong points into his own view.

Aristotle first gives a brief epistemology, describing the modes for gaining knowledge and, finally, for the achievement of wisdom. Such true knowledge can only be a knowledge of causes, particularly of ultimate causes. It is this which leads Aristotle to consider previous theories and types of cause, ending in the famous doctrine of the four kinds of cause: the *formal* cause (the plan); the *final* cause (the purpose); the *material* cause (that which is used); and the *efficient* cause (that which initiates change).

Such a theory of causation is crucial to metaphysics, since what we want is knowledge of truth, and we cannot know truth without its cause. To assure us that this can be obtained, Aristotle must affirm the existence of a first principle and the impossibility of either an infinite series or infinitely various kinds of causes. If it were otherwise, knowledge could not be obtained. Thus, a great deal of the treatise is devoted to proving that the kinds of causes are definite in number and that the existence of a first principle is certain. Knowledge comes through a grasp of causes; but if the kinds of causes were infinite in number, knowledge would be impossible (the mind can handle only finite entities). The disproof of an actual infinite, the limitation of causes to four, and the establishment of the existence of a first cause of motion—all are central if metaphysics is to achieve wisdom.

Book *Beta* turns to the traditional problem of substance. How many basic kinds of entities are there and what is it that is most stable and underlies change? Are the principles which govern both perishable and imperishable things one and the same? "Being" and "unity" are two difficult concepts, and Aristotle considers whether they are themselves substances or merely properties of things. Inevitably he becomes involved in the Platonic theory of forms. Although rejecting forms as substances, Aristotle still agrees with Plato that individuals as such are never knowable and that the knowledge of any individual thing is of its universal properties.

In Book *Gamma* Aristotle begins with the famous definition of metaphysics as the science which investigates "being as being." Other branches of philosophy treat various particular kinds of things, but metaphysics considers the one starting point of all things, the first principles and highest causes. Since being falls immediately into genera, the various sciences correspond to these genera. Yet there are certain properties peculiar to being as such, and the philosopher seeks to discover the truth about these.

To complete such basic inquiry, principles which are certain must first be found, and Aristotle gives us a statement of the principle of noncontradiction here as an example. Few principles can have the certainty which such a principle has, and one cannot demand demonstration of all things. Basic axioms cannot be proved, although they can be established indirectly by intuition or by the impossibility of their opposite being true. The starting point of demonstration cannot be demonstration but something accepted as true in itself. What the metaphysician must develop is a grasp of the basic principles which lie behind all demonstration, and then he ought to demand demonstration only of matters in which such proof is possible. He must grasp the principles of being itself.

At first glance Book *Delta* seems puzzling. Sometimes called the philosopher's lexicon, it appears to be (and is) simply an extended series of definitions of crucial terms. On closer inspection, these terms prove to be the basic metaphysical vocabulary (made up of such terms as "beginning" and "cause"). Metaphysics has always proceeded by spending time on the definition of a few key words. However, instead of attempting to give a single definition for each of these thirty or so terms, what Aristotle does is to list several common or possible meanings which may be given to each term. He does point up the more important meanings and focuses on any of metaphysical significance, but, on the whole, the book is a straightforward analysis of various common meanings given to these philosophically important terms.

The four causes are listed again here (they are not always defined in the same terms). The term "necessity" is of some special interest, since Aristotle uses it in the positive sense ("cannot be otherwise"), very much as Plato uses "eternal," whereas "necessity" for Plato in the *Timaeus* is a symbol of nonrationality and chaos. Here Aristotle denies unity as an overreaching concept and makes it merely an attribute of things. Here, also, is the famous definition of "substance" as the individual thing which is the bearer of properties and is not itself a property.

Aristotle's other doctrines can be seen through these definitions, that priority means complete actuality and absence of potency, that what is complete and excellent is what has attained its end or purpose. We find that Aristotle in defining "accident" is far from being a rigid determinist. Some aspects of the world are necessary, but events without a definite cause (except that of chance) are equally present; they are accidental. Through definitions of crucial terms, Aristotle built an outline of his view of the world's basic structure.

Scholars argue that the *Metaphysics* was not composed as a continuous work; rather, it represents a collection of pieces on similar topics. This becomes evident when, after the "lexicon," the next section begins again on the concept of knowledge through comprehending the principles and causes of things. However, this time we are led into the well-known definition of physics, mathematics, and metaphysics. Physics theorizes about such beings as admit of being moved, but are not separable from matter. Mathematics deals with things which are immovable but presumably do not exist separately, only as embodied in matter. Metaphysics (first science) deals with things which both exist separately and are immovable and eternal. Of the accidental, there can be no scientific treatment whatsoever, in these branches of science or elsewhere.

Next Aristotle returns to the crucial question of substance, which he calls "first in every sense." The essence or the universal, the genus, and the substratum (that which underlies a thing) are all called substance. In deciding which of these meanings of substance is primary, Aristotle is never completely clear. As far as knowledge is concerned, it is clear that essence is prior. However, Aristotle is clear that he does not consider Plato's forms to be self-subsistent substances; forms, or universals, exist only in things. At the other extreme, matter as pure potentiality is unknowable in itself, and it is clear that there is no definition for the individual as such.

The causes of substances are the objects of Aristotle's search, but sensible substances all have matter and are thus subject to potentiality. Essence certainly attaches to the form and to actuality, and in that sense the form of the thing has a prior claim to be called substance. Substance is the primary category and all other categories depend on it. In virtue of the concept of substance all other beings also are said to be. And it is clear that actuality is prior to potency. "Potency" is every principle of movement or rest, whereas substance or form is actuality.

Arguing that eternal things are prior in substance to perishable things, Aristotle next begins his argument for the existence of an eternal prime mover. No eternal things exist potentially (and on these grounds he excludes the existence of an actual infinite). Nothing which is necessary can exist potentially. Yet such eternal and necessary substances must exist, for if these did not exist, nothing would exist. In things which are from the beginning, in eternal things, there is nothing bad, nothing defective, nothing perverted. And how is there to be order unless there is something eternal and independent and permanent? In pursuing the truth one must start from the things that are always in the same state and permit no change.

The process of change cannot go on to infinity. It is necessary that there should be an eternal unmovable substance. It is impossible that movement should either have come into being or cease to be. Movement also is continuous in the sense in which time is. There must, then, be a principle whose very essence is actuality. There is something which moves without being moved, being eternal substance and actuality. The object of a desire moves in this way; it moves without being moved. The final cause, then, produces motion as being loved or desired, but all other things move by being moved.

Such a first mover exists of necessity and its mode of being is good. On such a principle the heavens and the world of nature depend. This substance cannot have any magnitude, being without parts and indivisible. The nature of divine thought is that it thinks of that which is most divine and precious, and it does not change. Change would be for the worse (involving potentiality, as it must). Since it must be of its own nature that divine thought thinks, its thinking is a thinking on thinking. The divine thought and its object of thought are one.

The *Metaphysics* contains at this point Aristotle's

famous consideration of the Platonic forms and his rejection of their separate and eternal existence. Aristotle does not deny that there are universal forms; knowledge requires them. What Aristotle refuses to do is to give them an independent and prior existence outside of particulars. Aristotle then closes the *Metaphysics* with a consideration of the status of mathematical objects. This section has often been a puzzle to scholars, for Aristotle seems to attribute certain views to Plato which are not to be found as such within the extant Platonic dialogues. Here Aristotle treats Platonic forms as if they were all thought by Plato to be numbers. These and other unexpected references to unknown Platonic theories have led scholars to guess that Aristotle knew (as Plato's pupil) of later theories developed by Plato in the Academy but not reflected in the written dialogues. Such a puzzle is only one among many generated by the *Metaphysics*. It is a book both repetitious and vague in some of its theories, as well as unsystematic in its structure. The parts do not all fit together, and yet it has never failed to attract students to its study. It remains the classical source of metaphysics, and its problems and theories continue to be debated. It is impossible to understand the book in its entirety, and it is equally impossible to dismiss it. It remains the classical training ground for learning abstract theorizing on fundamental problems.

Pertinent Literature

Jaeger, Werner. *Aristotle: Fundamentals of the History of His Development.* Translated by Richard Robinson. Oxford: Clarendon Press, 1934.

Werner Jaeger's work is epoch-making in the history of Aristotelian scholarship. Before it first appeared in German in 1923, Aristotle's philosophy was generally viewed historically, as a system of static dogmas. Questions about its origin and maturation were for the most part not raised. Jaeger sought to replace this outlook with a view of Aristotle's thought as a historical process. He accomplished this objective to a remarkable extent with his *Aristotle*, a vivid philosophical biography based on an array of circumstantial evidence. This biography in its basic outline has stood behind most Aristotelian scholarship for the last sixty years. Moreover, Jaeger's approach and method have inspired others to make similar attempts to reconstruct Aristotle's development.

Jaeger believed that Aristotle's life is the key to understanding his philosophy, that his texts could best be understood in the light of his evolving intellectual and emotional preoccupations. Yet Jaeger's biography is dependent on the supposition that the Aristotelian corpus is chronologically stratified, its strata originating from different stages of his development, and that some of his treatises, notably the *Metaphysics*, are similarly stratified. While acknowledging that Jaeger's strategy provides historical explanations of a host of textual difficulties, we may note here that his biography and textual analysis stand or fall together.

Jaeger sees Aristotle as playing a pivotal role in the transition from cosmological or metaphysical picture-thinking to empirical science. Before him, philosophizing had been carried out largely through painting mental pictures of reality, fashioning cosmological myths, and thinking in metaphors. Aristotle was a reformer of philosophy; to make metaphysics viable he subjected it to the tests of conceptual rigor and consistency with empirical facts and thus united in himself philosophy and science. After him, they fell apart. Hellenistic philosophy was devoid of scientific spirit, while Alexandrian science, which is the intellectual heir of Aristotle's empirical orientation, cast aside metaphysics as irrelevant. Later, in their attempt to resolve the conflict between faith and reason, medieval theologians found a sympathetic chord in Aristotle and drew on him. What they perceived in him was the tension with which he held philosophy and science in union.

According to Jaeger, it took Aristotle his entire philosophical career to come to fulfill this pivotal role in classical intellectual history. In fact, Aristotle made possible the transition from Platonic metaphysics to Alexandrian science by mirroring the transition in his own career, for (and this is Jaeger's main thesis) Aristotle began by embracing Plato's idealistic picture-thinking, and went on to criticize it and revise it so as to accommodate the conceptual possibility of empirical science. At the last stage of his development he turned to the practice of scientific research, collecting and describing masses of facts in order to render their natural articulation manifest. What follows sums up Jaeger's account of these three stages of Aristotle's life: as an apprentice, a journeyman, and finally a master.

At the age of seventeen Aristotle joined Plato's Academy and thus began his twenty-year apprenticeship with Plato. What remains of Aristotle's writings assigned to this period by Jaeger shows him to be a Platonist through and through; in value, doctrine, and style of composition Aristotle follows his master's example. Like his master, Aristotle is convinced that there is a world of intelligible ideas over and above this world of tangible objects, and that one must forsake the seeming goods of this world to embrace the higher, imperishable values of the other. These metaphysical and religious aspects of Platonism molded the young Aristotle's mind. He was to spend his intellectual energy for the rest of his life trying to determine his relation to this mold, trying to resolve the conflict between his emotional acceptance of it and his own scientific and analytic tendencies.

With Plato's death in 347 B.C., Aristotle's apprenticeship ended and his traveling years began. Now thirty-seven years old, he left Athens, not to return for thirteen years. This period of Aristotle's career is a transitional stage in which he rejected Platonic ideas and worked to create a new form of Platonism at once conforming to the facts of experience and satisfying his religious needs. This critical development of Platonism took the form of theological ethics, physics, and metaphysics in which a transcendent divinity, the unmoved mover, replaces Platonic ideas.

Theoretically central to this phase of Aristotle's development, Jaeger holds, is the taming of Platonic ideas. Aristotle came to regard the transcendence of ideas as an impossible notion, for nothing universal

possesses independent existence, and ideas are supposed to be universal. Besides, their transcendence fails to explain the knowability and changeability of individual things of our experience. Thus, Plato's doctrine fails to satisfy what Aristotle holds to be a crucial test for adequacy of a metaphysical theory. Nor is materialism, the rival of Platonism, better off in this respect. It seeks to reduce individual things to the matter common to them all. Such a material would be totally amorphous and capable of accepting any kind of determination. But anything totally amorphous would be unintelligible, and nothing exists which is potentially any kind of thing whatsoever. To avoid the Scylla of Plato's transcendent idea and the Charybdis of Democritus' matter, Aristotle's new metaphysics takes idea and matter to be complementary principles: the individual is embodied form or matter informed. As something formed, it is knowable. As something material, it is capable of change. The change it undergoes, however, is not haphazard, for its form functions as the end of change, as the teleological determinant of its course of development. Thus the conception of immanent form, which in a sense is the idea purged of its transcendence, accounts for the knowability and change of the individual thing.

In 335/4 B.C., at the age of fifty, Aristotle returned to Athens and founded his own school, the Lyceum. He presided over it for eleven years, until one year before his death. This period saw the culmination of his development. In the previous period Aristotle revised Plato's doctrine of ideas and thus began to purge his inherited philosophical consciousness of its metaphorical element. In extending this philosophical reform further during his final period, what is most characteristically Aristotelian emerged: empirical science—that is, the collecting, ordering, and describing of particular facts so as to discern universals in the concrete. Having worked out the theory of immanent form, Aristotle put it to use in carrying out positive research. Everywhere, description and analysis began to replace speculation. In ethics, he looked for a foundation in human psychology rather than theology; talk about character traits and conditions for ascribing responsibility replaced talk about the contemplation of the transcendent god. In politics, he supported his theorizing about an ideal state with an extensive documentation of actual constitutions. Leaving behind him an abstract treatment of the general principles of nature and of the universe, he turned to the close observation of animals, admiring the intricate functional unity even of the lowest forms of life. At the culmination of his development Aristotle emerged as a scientist who pursued empirical investigation for its own sake.

Owens, Joseph. *The Doctrine of Being in the Aristotelian "Metaphysics."* Toronto: Pontifical Institute of Mediaeval Studies, 1951.

In this work, Joseph Owens seeks to determine the nature of Aristotelian metaphysics, and he faces squarely the issues this task entails. First, is Aristotelian metaphysics ontology, which investigates the entire range of types of being as its proper subject? Or, is it theology, which contemplates just one definite type of being—the divine? Second, what is the focus of Aristotle's *Metaphysics*? Is it on the nature of ephemeral material objects as treated in the central Books of *Zeta, Eta,* and *Theta*, or on the nature of eternal immaterial entities as discussed in Book *Lambda*? Third, Aristotle himself calls metaphysics "the first philosophy" and "theology" and characterizes it as "the science of first causes" and "the science of being *qua* being." How are we to understand these expressions?

These issues have been controversial. For example, Werner Jaeger (see the preceding review of his *Aristotle*) claimed that the *Metaphysics*, with its theological and ontological components, lacks a unity of doctrine; and he tried to explain this incoherence by attributing the theological to an earlier, and the ontological to a later, stage of Aristotle's development. Some have found the same or a similar doctrinal incoherence but have rejected Jaeger's historical solution. Owens finds no such incoherence, asserting that the ontological notion is nowhere to be found and that the Aristotelian first philosophy is theology. Although the central Books investigate the ontological structure of ephemeral physical objects, they do so, Owens alleges, only as a means of reaching eternal transcendent entities treated in Book *Lambda*. As for the expressions "first causes" and "being *qua* being" which Aristotle uses to characterize the first philosophy, Owens finds the Aristotelian four causes reduced to the formal, and among forms, divinity is the highest; being *qua* being is not being

of any type whatsoever but the ultimate source of being, which is the divine. Thus, concludes Owens, theology can be described, without inconsistency, as the science of first causes and of being *qua* being.

What distinguishes Owens' study, however, is not so much his basic conclusions, which have historical precedents, as his unique method and the care with which he carries out the method in working out details of his conclusions. Because of this strength even those in disagreement with his orientation and basic conclusions regard his work as a classic whose study promotes a better understanding of Aristotle's *Metaphysics*.

Owens' method is premised on a view of the proper order in which the different treatises of the *Metaphysics* should be studied. According to Owens, this order is not the chronological sequence of composition but the "methodical" one, the order of study Aristotle intends for his "hearers" to follow. Only the methodical sequence assures fidelity to Aristotle's intention and gives us a means of tracing a problem in his expository unfolding throughout the various treatises. Owens believes the treatises exhibit a pattern of cross references which sufficiently indicates their methodical sequence.

The key to understanding Aristotle's doctrine of being, according to Owens, is the phenomenon of *"PROS HEN* equivocals" or "equivocals in relation to one thing." Consider Aristotle's own example: things we call healthy—such as a boy, his complexion, and his exercise. Although they can all be said to be healthy, only the boy can possess health. For the essence of health is the integrity of biological function, which only a living organism can possess. And, of course, neither his complexion nor his exercise is itself a living thing. Although they cannot therefore be said to possess health, they can nevertheless be said to be healthy because his complexion is symptomatic of his health and his exercise is conducive to it. In this sense the boy is a primary instance of health while his complexion and exercise are its secondary instances. In general, the secondary instances of *PROS HEN* equivocals are what they are because of different kinds of reference they have to the essence in the primary instance.

Owens sees Aristotle's exposition of the doctrine of being unfolding in three stages. Stage (1): Things said to *be* are *PROS HEN* equivocals, as are things said to be healthy. The boy's complexion and exercise can be said to *be* because they are of the boy who *is*. Here the boy is a primary instance of being; his complexion and exercise, secondary instances. In general, accidents derive their being from the entity ("substance" in the Oxford translation) whose accidents they are. Stage (2): Entities too are *PROS HEN* equivocals. In the physical domain, form, matter, and

their composite can all be called entities, but only form is the primary instance of entity, for to be an entity is to be something determinate, and form is the principle of determination. Stage (3): When physical objects are called entities, it is not their own nature but the nature of transcendent entities that is primarily designated, just as the boy's health is being referred to when his complexion is called healthy. Transcendent entities are pure forms. Hence, they are immaterial, eternal, divine, and completely self-determined. Each kind of physical entity is what it is because in its limited way it imitates and expresses these characteristics of the transcendent.

Owens acknowledges that Aristotle does not carry out Stage 3 but merely projects it. The project, however, is unmistakably clear: it is to bring to light the divine as the proper subject of the first philosophy. Any other kind of entity falls within the scope of the first philosophy only insofar as it expresses divinity.

Additional Recommended Reading

Annas, Julia. *Aristotle's Metaphysics, Books M and N*. Oxford: Clarendon Press, 1976. A literal translation with an introductory essay on Plato's and Aristotle's philosophy of mathematics, plus detailed philosophical notes.

Anscombe, G. E. M. "Aristotle: The Search for Substance," in *Three Philosophers*. Edited by G. E. M. Anscombe and P. T. Geach. Oxford: Blackwell, 1961, pp. 3-63. A sophisticated exegesis of the central books of the *Metaphysics*.

Grene, Marjorie. *A Portrait of Aristotle*. London: Faber & Faber, 1963. A survey of Aristotle's philosophy, including an account of the *Metaphysics* (mainly *Zeta* and *Theta*) which relies on Owens' thesis.

Kirwan, Christopher. *Aristotle's "Metaphysics," Books Gamma, Delta, and Epsilon*. Oxford: Clarendon Press, 1971. A literal translation with detailed philosophical notes.

Owen, G. E. L. "Aristotle on the Snares of Ontology," in *New Essays on Plato and Aristotle*. Edited by Renford Bambrough. London: Routledge & Kegan Paul, 1965, pp. 69-95. A sophisticated discussion of Aristotle's account of the existential use of the verb "to be."

Randall, J. H., Jr. *Aristotle*. New York: Columbia University Press, 1960. A survey of Aristotle's philosophy, including an account of the *Metaphysics*, relying on Jaeger's thesis.

Ross, W. D., ed. *Aristotle's Metaphysics*. Oxford: Clarendon Press, 1924. A standard edition of the Greek text with an introduction and detailed commentary. A knowledge of Greek is needed for the commentary.

ETHICA NICOMACHEA

Author: Aristotle (384-322 B.C.)
Type of work: Ethics
First transcribed: Date unknown; Aristotle's lectures as recorded by his son, Nicomachus

Principal Ideas Advanced

The good is that at which all things aim; the good for man is happiness, and happiness is the realization of man's essential nature.

The virtue, or excellence, of a thing is the full development of the potentialities of its essential nature; since man is essentially a rational animal, the good for man is activity of the soul in accordance with reason.

To act in accordance with reason, to be virtuous, usually involves choosing the mean between extremes of conduct; for example, the virtue courage *is the mean between rashness and cowardice.*

Some kinds of acts are inherently bad and no temperate action is possible in such cases: for example, adultery and murder.

The good life involves friendship with virtuous men and development of the intellectual virtues.

The highest good for man is the contemplative life.

Dante's description of Aristotle as "the master of those who know" has an appropriate ambiguity: it suggests Aristotle's mastery of his predecessors' knowledge and also his influence, paralleled only by Plato's, on his philosophical descendants. Both aspects of this mastery are prominent in the *Ethica Nicomachea*. It is to Aristotle's credit that he gives full recognition to the contributions of other philosophers, and it is to his glory that so many basic ethical ideas of later philosophers are found in this great seminal work. While scholarly explanations of the work differ, it is generally agreed that the work was not intended for publication in its present form; it is a version of Aristotle's ethics as stated by his son, Nicomachus. The *Eudemian Ethics*, a record composed by one of Aristotle's pupils, Eudemus, supplements this work.

The *Nichomachean Ethics* is part of a vast scientific and philosophical system to which a teleological view of the universe is basic: all things are to be understood in terms of their purposes, the ends toward which they tend, ends inherent in their forms and integral to their natures. Defining the end or good of man by reference to his nature, Aristotle's ethics is a

kind of naturalism, but not a reductionism failing to distinguish a higher sense of "nature" from one meaning simply "whatever is or occurs." It thus suggests (though it does not fully develop) the crucial difference between the factual and the ideal. The normative element, the "oughtness," of virtue is determined by the end or good by which virtue is understood. There is thus no nonnatural, self-subsistent, or supernatural source of obligation, but this is no loss to an ethics grounded firmly in the Aristotelian psychology and metaphysics.

Aristotle's psychological approach appears when he begins his investigation of the final good by reference to what he regards as a general fact of human and animal behavior. He cites the dictum of a predecessor that the good is "that at which all things aim." But there are many aims; some goods are desired for themselves, some for the sake of others. To avoid an infinite regression of goods merely instrumental to others, we must presuppose intrinsic goods; and if one appears to be more ultimate than any other, this will be the chief good. Its criteria will be finality and self-sufficiency—it will be valued for its own sake and its achievement will leave nothing to be desired. Everyone agrees, Aristotle notes, that happiness is thus final and self-sufficient; we desire other goods for the sake of this happiness, but never this for the sake of others. But this general agreement is merely verbal; specific descriptions of happiness are so varied that a detailed inquiry is obviously needed.

Among previous theories of the good is that of Aristotle's teacher, Plato, who held that good is a self-subsistent essence, a universal Form or Idea in which all particular good things participate, and by which alone they are good. Aristotle objects, however, that if nothing but this Form is good intrinsically, the good would be both empty of content and unattainable. In the practice of arts and sciences aiming at their own particular ends, it does not seem that a knowledge of this universal good is prerequisite. Hence Aristotle turns to a search for the specifically human good.

This must be found in man's own form and function *qua* man. To understand the latter, we must consider briefly the Aristotelian concept of matter and form, derived but considerably altered from that of Plato. Except for pure matter and pure form, terminal limits posited by the system rather than experienced differences in reality, the matter and form of any given thing are its two aspects of potentiality and actuality, separable only in analysis. Matter is the stuff, form the structure; matter is the *thatness*, form the *whatness*, of things. Matter without form is hardly conceivable, and form without matter is empty abstraction. Form is not mere structure, however, for what a thing is or becomes when its potentialities are actualized depends not only on shape or organization but also on function. The traditional illustration here is that of the acorn, which is a potential oak tree. Relative to the tree, the acorn is matter—an unrealized possibility which will eventuate in the actuality or form, oak tree. But the tree in turn may be matter for a higher form in case, say, it is made into a piece of furniture, and obviously the acorn itself must mature into the form, "oak tree seed," before it can function as material for the future tree. Thus the end or *telos* of the acorn is integral to its nature, and its "good" is to fulfill its formal function well—to become a strong, well shaped tree.

The end of man must likewise be found in form,

which for him is soul. "Soul" here does not have the connotations given it in Christian tradition; it is not an entity but rather a level of function of living bodies. Even plants have the nutritive function or vegetative "soul"; lower animals have this plus a sensory and appetitive or desiderative soul; the human soul has a higher level, the rational. Now the *excellence* or *virtue* of each thing, according to the meaning of the Greek *areté* lies in the efficiency of its peculiar function; therefore "human good turns out to be activity of soul in accordance with virtue, and if there are more than one virtue, in accordance with the best and most complete."

Two broad divisions in the human soul are the irrational and the rational; the former includes the vegetative, over which reason has no direct control, and the appetitive, partially amenable to rational guidance. The rational part includes the calculative and scientific functions. Corresponding to each of these are various kinds of excellence ranged under the two main types, moral and intellectual virtues.

To reach a definition of the first type, Aristotle observes that well-being is achieved through a mean between two extremes, either of which destroys it, as the athlete's fitness is maintained by the proper amount of food, neither too much nor too little. But this is not an arithmetical mean; the proper amount of food for a wrestler would be too much for a businessman. Applying this concept to attitudes, emotions, and conduct, Aristotle develops a relational ethics which is yet not relativistic in the pejorative sense: "Virtue . . . is a state of character concerned with choice, lying in a mean, i.e., the mean relative to us, this being determined by a rational principle . . . by which the man of practical wisdom would determine it. Now it is a mean between two vices, that which depends on excess and that which depends on defect . . . ."

Examples of virtues appropriate to certain activities are as follows:

ACTIVITY OR ATTITUDE
1. Facing death
2. Experiencing pleasure/pain
3. Giving and taking money
4. Attitude toward honor/dishonor

5. Assertion

6. Giving amusement

VICE OF EXCESS

1. Rashness

2. Self-indulgence

3. Prodigality

4. Empty vanity

5. Boastfulness

6. Buffoonery

VIRTUE (MEAN)

1. Courage

2. Temperance

3. Liberality

4. Proper pride

5. Truth telling

6. Ready wit

VICE OF DEFECT

1. Cowardice

2. Insensibility

3. Meanness

4. Undue humility

5. Mock modesty

6. Boorishness

Virtue lies in feeling or acting rightly in relation to time, objects, people, motives, and manner. Though the mean is variable, since some means lie nearer one or the other extreme, there is a mean for most situations—that middle course recognized by the practically wise or good man. Aristotle himself notes, however, that this account of virtue and vice is not exhaustive; there are some acts and passions inherently bad, such as spite or envy, adultery or murder—there are no mean (right) ways of feeling or doing these.

Neither does the theory apply in the same way to a major virtue, justice. As a particular virtue (rather than as the Platonic justice comprehending all other virtues) justice involves the sharing of external goods such as honor or money; and the mean is an intermediate amount, while both extremes are injustice. Distributive justice is a geometrical proportion between persons judged by merit and goods awarded. If A and B are persons and C and D are things, this justice can be formulated thus: A:B: :C:D. Equality here is thus not between persons or quantities; it lies in proportional relation. Rectificatory justice involves only the righting of wrongs in which the gain of one party equals the loss of the other, and the persons themselves are treated as equal. Since Aristotle disclaims universality for the concept of virtue as a mean, the objection of some critics to the inconsistency of his account of justice seems pointless.

The virtues and vices tend to be self-perpetuating; states of character are both causes and effects of corresponding actions. But while both acts and character are voluntary, we are clearly aware of specific choices preceding acts, while development of character is gradual and not so obvious. Nevertheless, we are responsible for both; even ignorance of the right is inexcusable if due to carelessness. The very attractiveness of false goods is due to one's character, just as that which is not really wholesome may appear so to a diseased person. Herein lies the distinguishing feature of the good man: while each character has its own concept of the noble and pleasant, the good man sees "the truth in each class of things, being as it were the norm and measure of them."

Though Aristotle's ethics is not a deontological system, it clearly was intended to develop "the sort of person that the right rule prescribes." The temperate man, for example, "craves for the things he ought, as he ought, and when he ought; and this is what rational principle directs." But the virtuous man is not burdened with a restrictive, puritanical sense of obligation; instead, he enjoys the best life by realizing his highest potentialities as a human being. This is illustrated by Aristotle's description of the properly proud man: pride, a mean between vanity and humility, "seems to be a sort of crown of the virtues; for it makes them greater, and it is not found without them." The proud man thinks himself to be *and is* worthy of great things. He is courageous, honorable and honored, noble, disdainful of the petty, liberal, dignified yet unassuming, frank in expressing his loves and hatreds, a man of few but great deeds. He is independent and incapable of centering his life in another, except for friends.

Aristotle writes at length of friendship's necessity

to the good life. There are three types: friendships based on utility, those maintained for pleasure alone, and those between similarly virtuous men loved because of their goodness. The last kind is highest, rarest, and most durable.

The topic of friendship raises questions of the relations between benevolence and self-love, and here Aristotle anticipates such later writers as Hume and Bishop Joseph Butler. Our estimate of "self-love," he points out, requires distinction between higher and lower senses of the term. Selfish concern for wealth or physical pleasure is of course blameworthy, but the true lover of self is he who seeks that most fitting to his highest nature—the just, temperate, and noble. If all sought for themselves the highest good, virtue, self-love would make for the greatest common welfare. True self-love thus involves beneficence and occasionally sacrifice of wealth or even life itself for the sake of friends and country. Thus the good man needs friends in order to exercise virtue fully.

The good man also needs the second major type of virtue, the intellectual, for the moral involves choice, and choice is defined as "either desiderative reason or ratiocinative desire." Good choice, then, presupposes right desire and true reasoning. The rightness and truth are measured against the right rule by which Aristotle avoids subjectivism: "there is a mark to which the man who has the rule looks . . . there is a standard which determines the mean states which we say are intermediate between excess and defect. . . ." But pure, contemplative intellect does not directly motivate, its end being truth *per se*; therefore it is the practical or productive intellect which aims at the truth in harmony with right desire. *Practical wisdom* is the intellectual virtue most intimately connected with moral virtue: "it is a true and reasoned state of capacity to act with regard to the things that are good or bad for man." It is deliberation about the contingent, not the eternal, for its concern is with selecting the best means to the good life; therefore, it is a function of the productive intellect which can command and sometimes control the irrational soul, the feelings and desires. Practical wisdom is thus a virtue of the calculative level, the lower of the two rational parts of the soul. Since it must not

only calculate the means but recognize the ends, "it is not possible to be good in the strict sense without practical wisdom, nor practically wise without moral virtue." Thus, intellectual virtue is not mere cleverness.

Practical wisdom presupposes *intuitive reason*, which grasps first principles, universals, and ultimate particulars or specific facts, the raw materials with which practical wisdom does its work. Intuitive reason also furnishes the first principles with which the fourth intellectual virtue, *scientific knowledge* (logical or mathematical demonstration) operates. This virtue concerns only the eternal, the logically necessary. But the highest form of wisdom involves not only knowledge of the logical implications of first principles, but also comprehension of the principles themselves. Hence Aristotle, calling *philosophic wisdom* the combination of scientific knowledge and intuitive reason, specifies that it must be directed to the highest objects and be properly completed. From this it follows that it is not directed toward the highest human good, because "man is not the best thing in the world," not as divine, for example, as the heavenly bodies. But though not directed toward the highest human good, it *is* that good. Should a critic object that philosophic wisdom, being merely contemplative, is thus useless, Aristotle reminds us that it makes man happy not as an instrument but as the actualized end, the highest human activity. Practical wisdom's command of the body is not a mark of superiority to contemplation but rather, prepares the way for its coming, as medicine is instrumental to health.

Before one can fully appreciate Aristotle's concept of happiness it is necessary to review his treatment of pleasure, regarded by many philosophers as the *summum bonum*. As usual, Aristotle considers arguments on both sides in some detail. He concludes not only that pleasure is a good, but also that there are cogent reasons for thinking it the chief good: everyone agrees that its opposite, pain, is bad. Both beasts and men aim at pleasure (and at the start Aristotle had accepted the view that "the good is that at which all things aim"); and since pleasure is a necessary accompaniment of each activity carried to its unimpeded fulfillment, happiness would seem to be the fruition in pleasure of at least some or perhaps all of our activities. This latter consideration enters into Aristotle's final formulation of happiness, but there are compelling reasons for denying that pleasure *per se* and without qualifications is the chief good. Pleasures differ in kind, just as do activities, and since there is a pleasure proper to each activity, their values are concomitant. Some pleasures complete acts that are vicious, and some hinder the fulfillment of more worthwhile activities. As Plato argued, it appears that the desirability of pleasure can be augmented by addition of other goods, such as that of wisdom, but one criterion of the final good is self-sufficiency. Pleasure, then, is but an ingredient of that good, happiness.

The modern reader must be careful not to identify this happiness with euphoria. It is a state of being, not just one of feeling. It is an activity, and since virtuous activity is also desirable for its own sake, happiness is virtuous activity. As the chief good, it involves the highest virtue, which, as we have seen, is contemplative. Contemplation is capable of more continuity than other actions, it requires fewer material necessities, its pleasures are pure and lasting. No immediately practical results follow from it, so again it appears to be loved for itself alone. As the highest human activity, it seems most like that of the gods, and indeed it belongs to the most authoritative element in us: "that which is proper to each thing is by nature best and most pleasant for each thing; for man, therefore, the life according to reason is best and pleasantest, since reason more than anything else *is*

man. This life therefore is also the happiest."

While this may strike the modern reader as an overly rationalistic or perhaps academic conclusion, Aristotle tempers it by adding that such happiness requires a complete life, including the satisfaction of bodily needs. He recognizes that few men have the ability or the opportunity to lead the life of contemplation. He claims that happiness on a secondary level is the morally virtuous life, for the moral virtues, after all, directly concern our nature in its "all too human" aspects, since it is a mixture of reason and the irrational appetites. Indeed, most men are incapable of being good through reason and self-discipline alone; they need the aid of legislation. This idea provides the subject of Aristotle's next work, the *Politica*.

If Aristotle's method should appear too speculative for the leading scientists of his day, he reminds his readers that what he has said must be reviewed and tested by reference to the facts, and should it clash with them, it must be considered mere theory. But should the reader adopt this alternative, it must be with reluctance when the theory is seen as an integral part of Aristotle's whole system. To find the most distinctive human excellence in reason and yet to allow for the most tonic exercise of the senses and appetites by conceiving both as the full fruition of man's natural potentialities, and to see this actualization as part of a universally purposeful process, is to share one of philosophy's most stirring ethical convictions.

Pertinent Literature

Sullivan, Roger J. *Morality and the Good Life: A Commentary on Aristotle's* Nicomachean Ethics. Memphis: Memphis State University Press, 1977.

Although Roger J. Sullivan's book is a commentary, it is not arranged to follow the structure of the *Nicomachean Ethics*, the author believing that the various topics hang together better if the whole is treated as a doctrine of human power: what our powers are and how we should develop and use them. We act and we are acted upon in a world the social

dimension of which is of primary importance in our assignment of priorities. The fundamental question is: What kind of life is most worth living? It is possible to give a rational answer, and as we are not behavior machines, it is also possible to act upon that answer.

Half of Sullivan's book, accordingly, is given over

to exposition and discussion of what he takes to be Aristotle's theory of action. The primary distinction is that of action from passion. We are active, Aristotle holds, when we are the sources and begetters of our behavior, as the father is of the child. This is also the sphere of the voluntary, which is that for which we are responsible, and the object of praise and blame. But a doing is not fully an action unless it is intentional and directed to an end. Herein lies the scope for intelligence.

Sullivan presents Aristotle's analysis of action first from the outside, then from the inside. On the outside, there are seven components of action. 1. The agent: Who did it? 2. The type of action performed: What did he do? 3. Persons or things affected: To whom or what did he do it? 4. The manner of acting. 5. (Sometimes) the means used. 6. Circumstances of action: When? Where? For how long? 7. Result: What did he accomplish? In treating the kinds of practical activities, Aristotle begins with the distinction between actions which have ends distinct from themselves, and those done for their own sake (not an exclusive division). Furthermore, some actions are processes having beginning, middle, and end (doctoring, building); others are activities which have no definite stopping place and are complete at every moment (thinking, seeing). Activities, in this special sense, are superior to processes; pleasure is mostly an accompaniment of activities. A further related distinction is that between making and doing. The latter includes all dealings with our fellow men and is therefore the subject of morality. Aristotle's celebrated doctrine of the Mean—which Sullivan deems overrated—is here applicable.

The inner side of action involves three elements: 1. The agent's knowledge or belief about particularities: Did he know what he was doing? What did he think he was doing? 2. The agent's purpose: What was his goal? 3. The agent's motive: Why did he want to do it? These constitute the domain of practical reasoning—deliberation and choice. Reason enters into choice, but cannot be the whole of it, since desire must also operate. Moral excellence, however, requires that we desire what we should desire. According to Sullivan, Aristotle holds that the logical form of practical reasoning is given in the practical syllo-

gism, in which the first premise is a generalization about what should be done in given circumstances, the second is the statement that I am now in those circumstances, and the conclusion is the action. Sullivan defends this analysis against Aristotle's critics, pointing out that the practical syllogism is not intended as descriptive psychology but as logical reconstruction after the fact.

Practical reasoning is an art and the efficient cause of the product. But practical wisdom is not a skill. Skills are capacities for opposites (the doctor can both kill and cure), while moral character, a necessary part of practical wisdom, is not. Practical wisdom is knowing the right thing to do plus having moral character, the desire to live as one ought.

Virtuous activity involves four conditions: knowing what you are doing, doing it willingly, doing it because it is right, and doing it because of the kind of man you are. This is why motives are important in assessing moral worth. The life of the morally excellent man, Aristotle holds, is one of intense pleasure. Sullivan discusses the problem of whether this does not make Aristotle's virtuous man an egoist, inasmuch as he always seeks what is best for himself. The answer is that it is wrong to think of virtue in terms of the selfish/unselfish contrast. The virtuous man indeed loves himself, but it is a consequence of his self-love that he is a social being.

In a chapter entitled "The Integrity of Moral Personality" Sullivan discusses a problem of the relation of reason and desire. Aristotle held that practical wisdom is the excellence of practical reason, which is concerned with choice of means to an end given by desire: we do not choose the end, only the means. Moral excellence is the excellence of desire. Putting these together, we are led, it seems, to the Humean conclusion that reason is the slave of desire—the excellence of reason would be efficiency only. This cannot be right, Sullivan maintains; we evaluate ends as well as means. His explanation of how Aristotle got into this bind depends on Werner Jaeger's thesis of a development in Aristotle's thought away from Socratic intellectualism. Aristotle eventually came to a nondualistic picture of man, which however was not worked out completely when he wrote the *Ethics*; in this book he does not know what to do with the emotions. The way out is to see that practical reason and character both are amalgams of reason and emotion. Aristotle was on his way to this conclusion: his inquiry is moral from the beginning.

After exposition and discussion of Aristotle's views on the nature and method of moral philosophy, moral training, morals and politics, and the problem of weakness of will (topics which do not fit neatly into the theory-of-action organization), Sullivan concludes his book with a chapter, "Morality and the Good Life," treating of the happiness which Aristotle claims is the highest good at which all action ultimately aims. Aristotle maintained that it is possible to set out at least a general description of the good life that will hold for all of us, since we share a common nature. The good life must consist of activities we can and do perform—it must be attainable. Further, it must consist in the best activity open to us, and must therefore be a life of reason. It must be unconditionally and absolutely good; that is, not a

means to something else. The activity must be pleasurable and practiced throughout a man's life. There are certain nonmoral prerequisites: for example, money, strength, and free birth. Scientific activity—the kind of knowing that the first words of the *Metaphysics* declare "all men desire"—is best of all.

Now it seems clear that however excellent scientific activity is, it cannot and ought not to be the whole of the good life. Aristotle says as much in one place (1144a5): it is "only one part of excellence in its entirety." However, as Sullivan notes with dismay, the explicit doctrine laid down in Chapters 7 and 8 of Book X, to the effect that perfect happiness consists in contemplation *only*, any other activity diluting it, "completely contradicts a number of the most fundamental claims about moral practice which he had so carefully constructed and defended throughout the rest of the *Ethics*." Sullivan conjectures here also that this uncompromising intellectualism belongs to the earlier, more Platonic phase of Aristotle's thought.

Cooper, John M. *Reason and Human Good in Aristotle*. Cambridge, Massachusetts: Harvard University Press, 1975.

John M. Cooper's book is a study of the "theoretical backbone" of Aristotle's moral philosophy: his theories of practical reasoning and of human "flourishing" (as the author renders the word usually translated "happiness").

Cooper notes three interconnected difficulties in Aristotle's theory of practical reason: (1) Aristotle's dictum that we deliberate always about means, never about ends, works well enough in technical contexts (the doctor deliberates how, not whether, to cure the patient), but not in specifically moral ones, where Aristotle furnishes no examples. But is not the doctor in the plague city, making up his mind whether to stay or flee, deliberating whether to choose the professional or the personal end? (2) Is Aristotle describing the way practical decisions are arrived at, or is he showing us how to justify or explain them? (3) At what point does deliberation end—when the agent has decided what to do whenever the occasion for doing it may arise, or only when he actually begins to do what he has decided on?

Cooper argues for these conclusions: (1) The true

Aristotelian doctrine is that we never deliberate about ends *as such*. Ends are relative to context; rival ends, between which we must choose, thereby become alternative means to a higher end. The plague doctor is evaluating both his professional status and his skin as alternative means to "flourishing." This is one reason why there has to be an ultimate fixed end in the Aristotelian ethical scheme. (2) A moral action may be performed without deliberation, if it is routine or uncomplicated or if there is insufficient time; but it is "as if" one had deliberated. The practical reasoning may provide backing for the decision if challenged. (3) What is the pattern of practical reasoning? Aristotle seems to offer two paradigms: the first is "I want E; to get E I must have M1; to get M1 I must do M2; I can do M2; so I will do M2 (whenever appropriate)." The other schema is the "practical syllogism": the major premise is a rule, "In E-circumstances do M2"; the minor is the apprehension "I am now in E-circumstances"; and the conclusion is not a proposition at all but the action M2. Here deliberation can be terminated only by action. The former pattern commends itself to common sense and, Cooper maintains, to Aristotle; so the answer to the question is that deliberation is terminated by decision. This may seem a minor point, but Cooper draws from it a corollary of more interest: that the so-called practical syllogism plays no part in practical reasoning, and was not intended by Aristotle to do so. It is "only a way of expressing the content of the intuitive perceptual act by which the agent recognizes the presence and availability for action of the ultimate means previously decided upon." Its further use is in showing how weakness of will is possible: the sufferer from this defect is said to fail to apprehend fully one or the other of its premises.

Concerning ultimate ends, Cooper argues that while commitment to them cannot be based on reasons (for this would lead to endless regress), dialectical considerations can be advanced which tend to show their validity. The knowledge of them that the man of practical wisdom has must be intuitive, just as the knowledge of the basic premises of scientific demonstration are intuited.

Many commentators have objected to Aristotle's notion of a single ultimate end at which all a man's actions (should) aim. Cooper defends Aristotle on the ground that "flourishing" is really a "second-order aim" or principle of assigning priorities. Nevertheless, Aristotle recognizes that some people organize their lives according to some first-order end, such as money. Does he not do so himself, in favor of intellectual contemplation? While the bulk of the *Nicomachean Ethics* is given over to delineation of the "man of practical wisdom" who, it would surely seem, flourishes—displaying justice, friendship, liberality, courage, and all the other moral virtues—still the official definition of flourishing, as activity of the soul in accordance with excellence, adds the qualification "and if there is more than one excellence, then in accordance with the highest." And at the conclusion Aristotle contrasts the practical and contemplative lives and eloquently exhorts his readers to prefer

the latter as "divine," leading Sullivan (see previous entry) and other commentators to charge him with inconsistency. Much of Cooper's book is devoted to an attempt to integrate this intellectualist strain with the moral theory of the rest of the treatise.

In a crucial passage Aristotle contrasts two lives (Cooper makes the important point that they are not aspects of life, like social life and sex life, but whole lives), declaring that of intellectual contemplation to be the "most flourishing," that of "the other sort of virtue" only "flourishing in the second degree." Cooper points out that while the intellectual does not necessarily disregard the moral virtues, he cannot in terms of this contrast assign to them any ultimate value. Is the "other sort" of life supposed to be one into which intellectual contemplation does not enter? Cooper argues for the negative; it is, he thinks, a "mixed life," consisting of both kinds of virtue.

Now Aristotle says of the intellectual life that this "most of all is the human being." In Cooper's interpretation, Aristotle is recommending identification of one's self with one's intellect. The intellectual will not think of himself as a moral person at all—although he may perform moral acts, out of the necessities of the occasion, his real self will not come into play in them. "The 'intellectual life' discussed in the tenth book does not, then, involve the possession of any of the moral virtues."

How could Aristotle have come to hold so surprising a doctrine? Elsewhere, he identifies the person with his mind, but the mind in question is or includes the practical reason. Cooper's theory is that the intellect of Book X is the separable soul of Aristotle's treatise *On the Soul*—an entity which presents correlative puzzles for the interpreter; for while the general doctrine of that treatise is that the soul is the functioning of the body and inseparable from it, the intellectually creative part, of which little is said, comes from "outside" and is separable and immortal.

Additional Recommended Reading

Bambrough, Renford, ed. *New Essays on Plato and Aristotle.* London: Routledge & Kegan Paul, 1965. Contains essays on the *Ethics* by J. L. Ackrill, G. E. M. Anscombe, and Bambrough.

Dover, K. J. *Greek Popular Morality in the Time of Plato and Aristotle.* Berkeley: University of California Press, 1974. Interesting and valuable background material.

Hardie, W. F. R. *Aristotle's Ethical Theory.* Oxford: Clarendon Press, 1968. A full and penetrating commentary by a leading scholar. Sympathetic to Aristotle on a number of issues where he is often attacked.

Joachim, H. H. *Aristotle, the* Nicomachean Ethics: *A Commentary.* Edited by D. A. Rees. Oxford: Clarendon Press, 1951. A standard work.

MacIntyre, Alasdair. *After Virtue: A Study in Moral Theory.* Notre Dame, Indiana: University of Notre Dame Press, 1984. Contrasts Aristotle's approach to ethics with Nietzsche's.

Moravcsik, Julius M. E., ed. *Aristotle: A Collection of Critical Essays.* Notre Dame, Indiana: University of Notre Dame Press, 1968. Contains essays on the *Ethics* by H. A. Pritchard, W. F. R. Hardie, J. L. Austin, and J. O. Urmson.

Oates, Whitney J. *Aristotle and the Problem of Value.* Princeton, New Jersey: Princeton University Press, 1963. The theory of value as Aristotle developed it in various writings. Pages 262-321 are devoted to the *Nicomachean Ethics.*

Ross, W. D. *Aristotle.* New York: Barnes & Noble, 1964. The chapter on the *Ethics* remains the best brief commentary.

Walsh, James J. *Aristotle's Conception of Moral Weakness.* New York: Columbia University Press, 1963. Aristotle's doctrine of *akrasia* (moral weakness). The first two chapters explain Socrates' and Plato's teaching concerning *akrasia.*

POLITICS

Author: Aristotle (384-322 B.C.)
Type of work: Political philosophy
First transcribed: Between 336 and 322 B.C.

Principal Ideas Advanced

The morally virtuous man performs acts according to a rational mean between extremes of excess and deficiency; so also does the state.

The good states are monarchies, aristocracies, and polities (constitutional governments); the corresponding bad states are tyrannies, oligarchies, and radical democracies.

Polities which lean toward the democratic form of government possess the greatest political stability and are least liable to revolutions.

The art of government involves the use of practical wisdom.

Since the best life is one which combines action with contemplation, the ideal state aims at providing sufficient external goods to permit the pursuit of virtue and happiness.

Descriptions of actually existing states are combined, in Aristotle's *Politics*, with judgments about the ideal political community. Its eight separate books make up a work which, most scholars insist, their author never intended as one finished product. There is debate about the ordering of the existing books. But in spite of the work's variety of special topics, several dominant themes and interests prevail throughout. One theme is the characteristic Aristotelian stress on the purposive quality of political life—the view that a state, like any other entity in nature, has a nature understandable in terms of a purpose. Consequently, one cannot properly determine the nature of citizenship unless he first knows what, in general and particular, the state is established to accomplish. Another, yet related, theme concerns the way in which political life is viewed as an important, organized means to the ethical development of its members. Though the state is logically prior to the individual, according to Aristotle, its purpose centers in the production of the maximum human good. The *Politics* presupposes the ethical teachings found in Aristotle's famous work on ethical life. The primary question for Aristotle is not whether men will act politically—since it is their natures so to act—but

rather whether they will act well.

Aristotle's insistence on the natural basis of human political activity accounts for his central concern with the proper education of the state's citizens. Learning is induced by nature, habit, and reason. Education can influence habit and reason by modifying man's natural capacities, directing them to selected ends or kinds of action. Aristotle's conception of the way in which human ethical capacities develop affects what he says about human political roles. Two broad classes of ethical facts exist—one of them moral, the other intellectual. These classes are interdependent. The moral virtues are learned. They result from habitual kinds of conduct. The morally virtuous man performs acts according to a rational mean between extremes of excess and deficiency which require prudential judgments in specific contexts demanding action. The chief aim of the moral virtues is action rather than contemplation, doing rather than theorizing. Political activity expresses the range of virtuous actions insofar as man, as a political animal, must live in associations and devote attention to the family and to the public affairs of a commonwealth.

The matter of what makes good citizenship possible is a complicated one. The reason is that good citizenship must occur in relation to some actually existing state, of which there may be different kinds. Thus, there can be "good" citizens of "bad" states. Good citizenship need not coincide with human goodness. A man who is a good citizen of a bad state will acquire a character which produces acts foreign to the character of the morally good man. Although Aristotle preferred a state which encouraged moral activity on the part of its members, he showed sufficient realism to recognize the possibility of a wide range of states and to admit that citizenship exists as a function of the end sought after by any actually existing state. Aware of the conditions needed to produce an ideal state, Aristotle nevertheless wanted also to describe and to classify existing and possible types of political units.

Aristotle's sense of the variety of political possibilities becomes clear in his criticisms of Plato's utopian scheme sketched so brilliantly in the latter's *Republic*. He disagrees with Plato's abolition of private property and his advocacy of social communism of wives and children. Aristotle insists that Plato's recommendations are wrong in terms of both their end and their means. There can be too great a unity in any existing state. Plato's political thought wrongfully sought after an impossible kind of unity in suggesting abolition of property and the private family. Such recommendations could never lead, as means, to the minimal unity any state requires. They would increase the chances of dissension in the state. Aristotle argues that differentiation of functions is a law of nature—that things actually differ. Political philosophers must accept this fact and not seek to alter the unalterable.

In the *Laws*, written later than the *Republic*, Plato softened some earlier political suggestions by abandoning his theory of social communism. Aristotle also criticizes the *Laws* on several grounds: it fails to discuss foreign relations; it makes new states too large in territory; and it fails to limit property, population, or the respective roles of ruler and subject. Just as Aristotle insists that philosophers must never seek greater certainty in ethics than the subject matter permits, so he argues that the political philosopher must recognize that judgments must conform to an inevitable relativity in types of political systems.

"Since there are many forms of government," Aristotle asserts in Book III of the *Politics*, "there must be many varieties of citizens, and especially of citizens who are subjects. . . ." Nevertheless, he agrees with Plato that the best states—however specialized the functions of their citizens—seek the common interests of all.

When he describes existing states of his own day and age, Aristotle mentions the three which he considers best: Sparta, Crete, and Carthage. During his lifetime Aristotle also directed a study of the various constitutions, showing his interest in the empirical details of political life. Yet his empirically minded studies never paralyzed his independent judgments about the values of what he studied. Thus, Aristotle pointed out that Sparta was fit only for conducting war; the Cretan state was too narrowly a rule of the rich (oligarchy) whose cities remained safe only because of their accidental geographical inaccessibility; and the Carthaginian state relied on a policy of emigration to keep down domestic insurrection. The best existing states fail to measure up to what is possible. Aristotle realized that a description of what exists politically need not suffice either as a basis for classifying possible type of states or as a means of making clear the nature of an ideal state. In various portions of his *Politics* he devotes attention to such matters.

Like Plato, Aristotle claims that there are three broad types of states, each possessing a corresponding possible perversion. The so-called "good" types are monarchy, aristocracy, and polity. The corresponding perversions (or so-called "bad" types) of these are tyranny, oligarchy, and radical democracy. By "radical democracy" Aristotle means a state which permits an absolutely unrestricted manhood suffrage and the right of all, without qualification, to hold office. This classificatory scheme hides a great complexity, especially of degree, since Aristotle thinks both monarchy and aristocracy allow for at least five possible forms. The classification also contains puzzles. One is that though oligarchy is listed as a possible perversion of aristocracy, Aristotle indicates that the best state (practically, though not ideally) is a polity. A polity is defined as a state which mixes rule by the rich with rule by the poor. Ideally, then, a polity requires existence of a significantly entrenched middle class, whose interests moderate the extremes and receive furtherance through the state's machinery. A polity therefore requires a constitution which expresses elements of oligarchical interests.

To achieve a balance between oligarchy and democracy is difficult. The reason is that each type of state emphasizes a different end. Oligarchy rests on the assumption that men's political rights ought not to be equal but rather based proportionately on their possession of wealth. Democracy stresses human equality—that each shall count as one in political affairs. Neither is absolutely correct. Virtue stands as the sole general aim of statecraft, meaning that any form of political organization which produces virtuous conduct is politically justifiable. Aristotle understood that polity results from a compromise. It involves a mixed constitution. Polities may come into being in several different ways, but their constitutions must find a mean which mingles some property qualifications with offices open to lot or election. Aristotle's comments about the value of a polity result, in part, from his unwillingness to consider absolute kingship the best political unit. Admitting that an absolute king who rules according to the spirit of law produces an excellent model for governing, Aristotle suggests that the rule of law receives less abuse if reserved for many citizens. He objects to monarchy because, in his estimation, it evolved as a response to the problems of a primitive social order. Monarchy often becomes simply hereditary. Its additional weaknesses are that it is subject to the passions of a single man and that no king can adequately handle all the affairs of ruling.

The need of continuity and stability in a state receives ample recognition in Aristotle's *Politics*. Yet all political systems are subject to revolutions. Existing forms of government share two general aims—"an acknowledgement of justice and proportionate equality. . . ." Men fail to translate these aims of government into adequate practice, producing conditions from which revolutions spring. In one example, Aristotle shows how the democrat's emphasis on equality leads him to think that men are equal in all things, while the oligarch's insistence on human

inequality spurs him to claim too much for himself. In any state in which both the equalities among men and their inequalities fail to receive proper balancing, hardened parties tend to arise which encourage revolution on behalf of a more thorough realization of their own partial interests. The citizens possessing the highest right to rebel—men who stand out for their virtuous conduct—are those who, by their nature, seem least willing to take part in rebellions.

A student of revolutions needs to understand, first, the general feeling or attitude of those who rebel; second, the specific motivation of any rebellion (its objects); and third, the immediate factors which cause the rebellion. In all revolutions, a general cause exists in the desire for equality. This leads inferiors to revolt in hopes of attaining equality. It also causes men who are genuinely capable to rebel to achieve superiority over those who are in fact not their equals. The motivation for rebellion centers around "the desire of gain and honour, or the fear of dishonour and loss; the authors of them want to divert punishment or dishonour from themselves or their friends." Other causes play important roles. These causes of revolution include contempt, fear, insolence, increase in some aspect of the state which is disproportionate, and excessive superiority. Other kinds of causes of rebellion include intrigues at elections, unjust differences in the elements in the state, lack of care, and neglect of trivial issues over a period of time.

What causes an actual revolution depends often on the type of constitution involved. For example, Aristotle claims that democracies usually enter revolutionary times because of the demagogic intemperance of the leaders. Oligarchic states must guard against revolution-producing causes of two kinds— severe oppression of the people and personal political rivalries between important oligarchs in the state. Revolutions occur in aristocratic states when too few qualify for honors, in constitutional states when the constitution itself permits lack of justice. Aristotle insists that mixed constitutions which lean toward the democratic possess, in general, the greatest stability.

The analysis of the causes of revolutions leads Aristotle to consider how constitutions may be preserved. Obedience to the spirit of existing law requires planned defense in any moderately stable state. Such obedience extends even to small matters. Like Plato, Aristotle shows suspicion of alteration when he writes that "men should guard against the beginning of change. . . ." This remark shows that despite his awareness of variety Aristotle adopted a conservative political stance. In democracies, offices should rotate frequently; and a number of institutions are required in cases where the governing class is numerous. Aristotle advocates a fairly wide personal participation in government. He wrote for a small Greek city-state, limited in territory and numbers. For this reason many of his observations about participation in governing seem irrelevant or foreign to the modern states whose extensive territories require an underpinning of bureaucratic machinery. Aristotle makes clear, however, that magistrates and others who perform public offices should never make money. Public service should exist as a self-justifying activity of the virtuous citizen.

The moral tone of much of Aristotle's treatment of politics is apparent in his recommendations about the qualifications of men who wish to hold office in the state. In each existing state an office holder must show loyalty to the contents of the constitution. He must also possess administrative abilities of a high order and express the kind of virtue that his particular state requires. In the case of democratic governments, Aristotle never makes clear how office holding by lot or election can guarantee that able administrators will rule. He does insist that only those who are citizens can qualify for office, and from the citizen body he excludes slaves and mechanics. Aristotle shares the cultural prejudices of his own age when he confines the virtues of the governing class (the citizen body) to the well-born and the aristocratic. A reliance on common sense runs throughout the *Politics*. Aristotle realizes that, once the purposes of governing are understood in principle, any state requires the practical wisdom of a sound statesman. Individual men must apply their knowledge of principles to specific situations. At this point the art of governing passes beyond the sphere of scientific prediction and control. Indeed, Aristotle makes clear that each and every form of state is subject to change and possible revolution, including the most tyrannically controlled states. He also indicates an unusual sensitivity to the ways in which any political form—say, democracy—must adapt itself to the special geographical and cultural circumstances with which it must in practice operate.

In the final portion of the *Politics* (Books VII and VIII) Aristotle discusses the way in which to form an ideal state as well as the educational practices necessary for its maintenance, once established. The treatment of these issues depends upon Aristotle's conception of man's nature. The human "soul" (psyche) contains an element which is subservient to a rational principle of control. This is the desiring aspect of human nature which is amenable to command and persuasion. Each man also possesses a unique capacity for rational comprehension. The best life, in Aristotle's view, is that which combines action with contemplation. The happy man will enjoy external goods, goods of the body and spiritual (intellectual) goods in some appropriate proportion. Goods of the soul exist as that to which the other goods are a necessary and enjoyable means. Individuals and states need sufficient external goods to permit the pursuit of virtue and happiness. Aristotle treats such a view as axiomatic, beyond argument.

To the question of which is the more preferable, the life of a philosopher or that of a statesman, Aristotle's answer is that political activity is not degrading, though political power can never stand as the highest good. Aristotle claims that natural capacities, developed in a proper order, can lead to the realization of the philosopher's ideal of wisdom. An important aspect of Aristotle's attitude toward the functions of political philosophizing is the manner in which he relates its aims to common sense. The political philosopher acts not so much like the scientific theorist, discovering new theories, as like the practical man who rediscovers the applicability of rules evolved in the history of political communities.

When he discusses the formation of an ideal state, Aristotle considers a small state. Its population and territory must be controlled. There must be a sufficient economic base to make the state self-sufficient. Agricultural workers, mechanics (artisans) and men of commerce are excluded from the body of the citizens. Slaves possess no rights at all. Only soldiers, priests, and rulers qualify for the rights of citizenship.

These groups alone own land. Each citizen, in addition, should perform the functions of soldiering, act as priest, and rule at different periods of his life's cycle. A hard distinction should hold between rulers (citizens) and subjects (non-citizens). In addition, in any ideally formed state, attention is given to the city's planning from the standpoints of utility and beauty.

Education functions to perpetuate the state. Potential citizens learn to obey in order later to know how to rule. The legislative body of the state holds responsibility for the education of the citizens. The aim again is the production of the good man. The humanistic aim of well-rounded human development of all man's capacities is emphasized. Physical fitness is encouraged to stimulate practical and contemplative efforts. The legislative body exercises a moral watchfulness over the content of the music and tales heard by the potential citizens. Legislators control the age of marriage, determine the physical requirements of parentage, decide when exposure takes place (the Greek practice of putting infants out to die), and oversee the duration of existing marriages. These educational arrangements serve, for Aristotle, as necessary ingredients in the political perpetuation of the state.

The lasting features of Aristotle's *Politics* are its emphasis on the moral justification of a state and the way in which its author accepts the inevitability of a wide range of existing states. Through the work also runs a firm defense of common sense as the touchstone of all political philosophizing. Aristotle attempted to make sense out of politics rather than to impress individuals by proffering complicated theories. There can be no blueprint guiding the statesman's prudential judgments. Aristotle's classical work has inspired men in different times and places when political events have forced them to seek sanity rather than drama in their political thought.

Pertinent Literature

Fortenbaugh, W. W. "Aristotle on Slaves and Women," in *Articles on Aristotle.* Vo. 2. Edited by Jonathan Barnes, Malcolm Schofield, and Richard Sorabji. New York: St. Martin's Press, 1977.

Properly understood, W. W. Fortenbaugh says, Aristotle's view on slaves and women is neither the sophistry of a privileged Greek male chauvinist nor the uncritical and misguided conclusion of a biologist who incorrectly assumed that political realities necessarily reflected the way things are by nature. He contends that it was instead an important application to politics of a significant advance in philosophical psychology.

In various passages of the *Politics*, Aristotle compares the utility of slaves to that of tame animals and suggests that the physical differences between slaves and their masters are related to psychological differences between them—that is, to differences in their souls—and that these differences are comparable to the differences between men and animals. Nevertheless, Aristotle insists that slaves *are* human. They possess the capacity to suffer emotions, for example, just as other human beings do; but they are not capable of reasoning as free men can do. Since slaves cannot deliberate, they are incapable of acting with forethought. For this reason, it is best that they assume the role of obedient service, subordinating their physical powers to the higher intelligence of their masters.

This incapacity on the part of those who are fit by nature only to be slaves does not mean that they cannot at least recognize reason when they see it. Like children, who cannot yet reason themselves but are amenable to its persuasive power, slaves can be reasoned with. On practical grounds, then, Aristotle recommends the use of reason with slaves instead of brute punishment, not so much out of respect for the slaves' humanity as from the realization that such a course is more likely to work without provoking undue antagonism. Fortenbaugh concludes that Aristotle's theories on slavery are "neither psychologically foolish nor morally repulsive." He adds that as a matter of fact there are no natural slaves in the world—but in his view, if there were, Aristotle would be on firm ground.

Women are also suited by nature to a subordinate role, according to Aristotle. Their function is not the physical labor that slaves are supposed to perform, but the preservation of the goods that men procure or produce. In order to fill their proper roles, women need the courage of subordination rather than the courage of command, and a kind of temperance that differs significantly from that which is suitable to men.

Slaves are totally incapable of deliberation. Children are temporarily incapable of it, but have the capacity to deliberate in potential form. Women are somewhere between men and children. The emotional part of the soul or personality develops first, and only afterward does the capacity to reason develop. Children and slaves possess the capacity to feel and be moved by emotions, men are capable of overcoming their emotions through the use of reason, and women possess the capacity to reason, although that capacity is so weak relative to their emotive faculties that their emotions generally tend to overcome their reasonable deliberations. For this reason, Aristotle concludes, their reason lacks authority—not because it is inferior to that of men, but because the natural makeup of women is such that they are generally unable to subordinate reason to their passions. Therefore, Aristotle concludes, they are suited by nature to be subordinate to men, and this fact, together with the fact that they are also generally physically weaker than men, leads him to conclude that it is strictly in accordance with the natural order of things that women should lack authority in the political state and that they should be kept occupied with household tasks.

Fortenbaugh concludes that although Aristotle's view of women may be false, it is not merely the creation of a male chauvinist. It is, according to Fortenbaugh, a "thoughtful view" which is logically coherent with Aristotle's psychological theories.

Wheeler, Marcus. "Aristotle's Analysis of the Nature of Political Struggle," in *Articles on Aristotle*. Vol. 2. Edited by Jonathan Barnes, Malcolm Schofield, and Richard Sorabji. New York: St. Martin's Press, 1977.

Aristotle employs the word *stasis* in a number of contexts which suggest that he may be talking about political revolution, insurrection, or sedition, but the commentators and translators have not found a satisfactory explanation of the term. Marcus Wheeler feels that the word "revolution," with the connotations it has acquired by association with the French and Russian Revolutions, is misleading, since the term stasis as used by Aristotle (in *Politics* V, for example) does not suggest social and economic disintegration such as followed those revolutions. By analysis of the term both in Aristotle and in other classical Greek sources, Wheeler attempts to arrive at a more accurate conception of Aristotle's theory of political struggle than has hitherto been evident in the literature.

In Herodotus, for example, there is a suggestion that *stasis* is associated with force or fraud and with unconstitutional behavior. Aristotle, reflecting the views of other Greeks, believed that one of the dominant purposes of an opposition group's attempting to achieve political power by supplanting the dominant group was to effect a change in the constitution of the state. Constitutions were seen not so much as governing societies or as immutable laws, but as instruments employed by the parties in power to effect their programs.

According to Wheeler, Aristotle believed that *stasis* was a manifestation of three factors: (1) inequality, which included not only the demand that some people might make for literal equality, but also the demand that some might make for superiority for the few (namely, their own class); (2) political privilege and profit—particularly the kind of *political* (as opposed to economic) profit that accrues to those who hold political office; and (3) such other factors as resentment of the power of others, fear or contempt of rulers, a disproportionate increase in the size or power of one class over another, and neglect of duty on the part of those who control the government. Aristotle recognized that there were economic as well as political, ideological, and emotional reasons for *stasis*, but he insisted that economic issues were secondary in importance to what he called "the wickedness of mankind," which he considered to be insatiable. In other words, the fundamental cause of *stasis* was to be found in ethical and not in economic conditions.

In Book IV of the *Politics*, for example, Aristotle develops at length the idea that it is important for cities to have a strong middle class because in such cities there is the smallest likelihood of a *stasis* occurring. *Stasis* occurs most often when the rich and the masses are equally balanced with no middle class between them. This, according to Wheeler, is an application to politics of Aristotle's theory of the Mean. As Aristotle himself put it in Book IV of the *Politics*, if the doctrine of the Mean which he enunciated in the *Ethica Nicomachea* is true, "that the happy life is the life according to virtue without impediment, and that virtue is a mean, then the life which is in a mean must be the best." Therefore, he concludes, the best state would be the one in which the possession of goods is in accordance with the principle of the mean.

Wheeler concludes that such traditional translations of *stasis* as "revolution," "class warfare," "sedition," and the like do not adequately convey the full meaning of the Greek word since nothing comparable to *stasis* exists in our political life. In ancient Greece, *stasis* could be anything from a minor clash between fluid groups of citizens to a wholesale massacre of political opponents. The purpose of such conflicts and the unlawful behavior that accompanied them was sometimes the rectification of economic inequalities; but it was more often purely political—an attempt by those who did not have the benefits of political office (including those that were noneconomic) to acquire such benefits. For this reason, a Marxist interpretation of *stasis* as a form of class struggle is completely anachronistic. In addition, according to Wheeler, no one in ancient Greece seriously considered the possibility of a classless society.

Wheeler concludes, finally, that Aristotle's analysis is partly unsound, since it is meaningless to postulate an underlying moral conflict in the way in which it makes sense to postulate an underlying economic conflict. It is sound, he says, since some instances of *stasis* can legitimately be described in terms that are unrelated to economic conflicts.

Additional Recommended Reading

Aristotle. *The Politics of Aristotle*. Edited by William L. Newman. Oxford: Clarendon Press, 1887-1902. The scholarly introduction of Volume One is followed by three volumes of text, notes, and commentary.

Barker, Ernest. *The Political Thought of Plato and Aristotle*. London: Methuen, 1906. Still a useful introduction for the general reader.

Cooper, John M. *Reason and Human Good in Aristotle*. Indianapolis: Hackett Publishing Company, 1986. An important study of Aristotle's metaphysics, ethics, and politics.

Morrall, John B. *Aristotle*. London: George Allen & Unwin, 1977. Aims at presenting "an overall conspectus of Aristotle's political thought" for the student and the general reader.

Mulgan, R. G. *Aristotle's Political Theory: An Introduction for Students of Political Theory*. Oxford: Clarendon Press, 1977. Seeks to bring the major themes and arguments of Aristotle's political theory into sharper focus than they appear in the *Politics* itself.

Ross, W. D. "The *Politics*," in *Aristotle*. New York: Barnes and Noble, 1959. Widely used introduction to Aristotle's thought by a leading scholar.

Voegelin, Eric. *Order and History*. Vol. III. Baton Rouge: Louisiana State University Press, 1957. An original interpretation intended to show that Aristotle correctly understood the task of political science when he constructed his concepts of the *polis* on the socially preexistent symbolism by means of which society understands itself.

MENG TZU

Author: Mencius (Meng Tzu, c. 372-c. 289 B.C.)
Type of work: Ethics
First transcribed: Early third century B.C.

Principal Ideas Advanced

Every human being is born good; hence, if man maintains his original nature he will remain good.

In man's original nature there is a sense of shame, a sense of courtesy, and a sense of right and wrong.

If man relies only on his sense perceptions without subjecting them to the control of the mind, he falls into evil ways and perverts his original nature.

If a man allows the desire for personal gain to overcome his righteousness—his sense of social obligations—he also perverts his nature.

The ideal ruler is considerate of his subjects' interests, and he provides both moral leadership and adequate social welfare.

Any person who practices the principles of humanity and righteousness with sincerity radiates the spiritual influence of the universe.

The exact date and authorship of this collection of philosophical dialogues and anecdotes have remained a subject of dispute for centuries, but there is no doubt about the existence of the man, Mencius (Meng Tzu), in the fourth to third centuries B.C. Behind the legends that have gathered around this magical name, we find a man who taught students, lectured to the rulers of his time, and expounded his political and moral philosophy in much the same way as most of the Confucians did.

When very young, Mencius lost his father, and his mother worked alone at a weaving loom to bring up the young boy. Mencius' childhood education is said to have been of the ideal kind, and his mother has been held in reverence by the Chinese as an ideal mother. It is said that she was so determined to cultivate her son's moral integrity at a very early age that she took extreme caution in her own speech and behavior in front of him. Once their landlord slaughtered a hog. When the young Mencius saw it, he asked his mother why. In jest his mother answered that the landlord was preparing a feast for him. Immediately afterwards she regretted; and in order to correct her untruthful statement she sold her badly needed clothing to buy some meat with which she

actually served him a good dinner. Another time she was distressed by Mencius' fondness for play when she wanted him to concentrate on studies. After some ineffective admonition, she took out a knife and cut the warp on her loom. Since she could no longer weave, the family was without food. This drastic gesture impressed the young boy so much that he never again neglected his studies.

After studying with a disciple of Confucius' grandson, Mencius emerged in his adult life as a recognized standard-bearer of Confucianism. In his expositions on Confucius' teachings, however, Mencius ventured much further in metaphysical speculations than his master ever did. From Mencius, Confucianism gained a fully developed theory on human nature and a clear orientation toward idealism.

Mencius subscribed to the basic Confucian doctrine of *jen* (benevolence), but in elaborating on this doctrine he gave it a metaphysical basis. Confucius urged man to be humane toward others so that society might be harmonious and peaceful; Mencius urged man to be kind to others because, as he says, to be kind is man's natural propensity. Man is born good, and his evil ways are perversions. Every human being has his innate goodness; hence, if he can maintain his original nature, he will remain good. In Mencius' own language, this original good human nature is the "heart of the child," or the untainted heart. If unperverted, the original childlike heart of man will lead him toward the good, just as "water naturally flows downward." If already perverted, man can attain salvation only by returning to his original state of goodness.

How is this innate goodness of man observed? Mencius suggested that we look at the sympathetic feeling that is a part of man's nature. He uses the following illustration: anybody seeing a child about to fall into a well would immediately spring to his aid. He would do this without reflecting on the advantage and disadvantage of his action; he would not think about what merit he would gain if he rescued the child, or what blame he would have to face if he refused to reach out his hand. He would leap to save the child because the peril of the child would spontaneously fill him with a sense of alarm. This example proves the existence of a sense of mercy in every man.

With similar illustrations Mencius argued that he had proved the existence of a sense of shame, a sense of courtesy, and a sense of right and wrong in man's original nature. Together with the sense of mercy, these senses constitute the four good beginnings of man's development. According to Mencius, the sense of mercy is the beginning of *jen* (humanity); the sense of shame should lead man to righteousness; the sense of courtesy, if allowed to develop, would give man decorum; and the sense of right and wrong is the foundation for wisdom. As with man's four limbs, these four senses are already inseparable parts of any man when he is born. Also as with the four limbs, these four senses would develop to their proper healthy proportions if man would cultivate them; otherwise they wither away through misuse or desuetude.

Basing his argument on his observation of the uninstructed child, Mencius asserts in his book that man has intuitive ability and knowledge. He points out that every child "knows" how to love his parents, and as he grows he "knows" how to respect his elder brothers. The former is true *jen* (humanity) and the latter is true *i* (righteousness). Therefore, says Mencius, man is born with the innate knowledge to distinguish the right from the wrong, and the innate ability to act according to the right.

The innate knowledge and ability of man, like his basic senses or feelings, are analogous to the seeds of a plant. To allow these seeds to germinate Mencius brings forth another notion: the "*ts'ai*" of man, or man's "natural powers." Thus if man exhausts his natural powers, he will realize his potential of being good, and he who does evil is failing to exercise his natural powers. Although human nature is basically good, man can be led astray by his contact with the outside world. If man relies only on his sense perceptions (on seeing, hearing, taste, and so forth) without subjecting them to the control of his mind (heart) which is the office of thinking, then he falls into evil ways. Here Mencius' theory of the "mind" is something very comparable to "reason," but we shall also see how the mind of the Mencian doctrine is closely linked to his theory of a mystic *ch'i*. Be it noted here that Mencius in explaining his theory of innate knowledge gives his view on the origin of evil, which is a subject not treated by Confucius himself.

Mencius never speaks of *jen* (humanity or benevolence) without mentioning *i* (righteousness). He is not the first Confucian philosopher to use this term *i*, but the emphasis certainly is his. Although "right," "fair," and "just" are all within the commonly accepted senses of the word "*i*," in Mencius' usage this word most frequently stands for a concrete sense of justice and fairness. Mencius seems to stress the importance of fulfilling one's obligations toward his fellow men. These obligations are social in nature. Thus an unfilial son is not "*i*" because he fails to repay his parents' kindness toward him; and a servant deserting his master is not "*i*" because he fails to repay his master's favors. In this light Mencius' *i* does not suggest anything like the Western abstract concept of righteousness. However, there is at least one place where Mencius does seem to bring in an absolute righteousness. When he warns the ruler not to abuse his subjects, Mencius states that the ruler has an obligation to protect the interest of the people. Since the ruler does not directly owe any favor to the people, Mencius in this case accepts an absolute standard of righteousness even though he fails to define it.

The social basis of the Mencian concept of righteousness creates perplexing problems when social obligations come into conflict with one another. A man is a righteous son to his father and a righteous minister to his king only so long as there is no conflict of interest between his father and his king, but this condition does not always exist. There is an anecdote in this book that illustrates such difficulties. The story concerns a warrior in ancient China who encountered his own former teacher on the battlefield, on the opposite side of no-man's-land. Remembering his obligation toward his former teacher, the warrior should show his respect to his present enemy. But as a loyal soldier to his lord, the warrior should shoot his former teacher to death. Caught in such a dilemma, the warrior won immortality and historical acclaim by a curious compromise. He broke off the points of four of his arrows and shot the arrows at his former teacher. Then he promptly withdrew with a clear conscience.

In contrast to the idea of righteousness Mencius put "*li*," or "profit" (not to be confused with "*li*," or "rules of propriety"). He blamed man's departure from righteousness to seek personal gain for the disorder and unhappiness in society. Greed leads to strife as men, both in and outside the government, go after profit and fight for personal benefit. Only if everyone strives for that which is right and does what he ought to do, can the community of man prosper in peace. This is what Mencius preached to the rulers and to his disciples alike. It should be noted, however, that Mencius did not dismiss the importance of material well-being, and the book is not always clear on how Mencius would draw the distinction between the desirable and the undesirable kind of profit.

That Mencius recognized the need for material well-being is evident in his political and economic ideas. His ideal government is one with both moral leadership and adequate social welfare. Like Confucius himself, Mencius advocated rule by moral excellence and humane feeling. The ruler must be considerate of his subjects' interests. If the ruler is benevolent, the state will prosper because people will not only flock toward it but will also imitate its virtuous way of living. Since benevolent government could bring peace and prosperity to men without the need for any other action, Mencius' theory amounts to rule by moral magnetism.

Mencius was aware of the larger political and economic forces which were at work in society in addition to the moral forces in which he had great confidence. He realized that a state does not exist without people, so he advised the rulers that people must come first, the state second, and the king last. These are his words which the Chinese have been quoting throughout the centuries: "People are the roots of the nation. If the roots are not firm, the nation collapses." Indeed the king must win the "hearts" of his subjects; otherwise, his administration will be doomed. And Mencius urged the ruler to give to and to share with the people what they desire, and not to do to them what they would not like. Since all human beings like the pleasures of life, the king must work to increase the pleasures of life and to share them with his people. Here Mencius clearly accepts public profit and material well-being for everybody as something good and moral which does not violate the principle of righteousness.

With these declarations, Mencius appears as a champion of the people against tyrannical governments. He is particularly remembered for his expressions in support of the people's right to revolt. There is enough in the sayings attributed to Confucius himself that implies this right to rebel. Confucius makes the observance of Heaven's Will a necessary condition for the ruler to keep his throne, and he blames the king's loss of the Heavenly Mandate for the downfall of the former dynasty. Mencius elaborates on this view and makes it explicit. He calls a man without *jen* (benevolence) a scoundrel, and a man without *i* (righteousness) a scourge, both deserving defeat, even death, regardless of their social station.

Much as Mencius championed the people's right to revolt against a tyrannical ruler, this Confucian sage did not believe in self-rule. In his book he upholds a natural division of labor in society on the basis of the different aptitudes of men. There are, he says, two types of men: those of brain and those of brawn. The former work with their minds and are destined to rule, while the latter work with their hands to feed the former and are to be ruled by the former. Thus he affixes an unmistakable stamp of approval on the Confucian attitude that only the literati, who tend to monopolize education and literature, are fit to conduct the affairs of the government.

Mencius argued that between the two types of men there is a basic difference which helps to justify their separate destinies. To state it briefly, this difference lies in the spiritual fortitude of those with education. For Mencius attributes a moral strength to the true scholar who, unlike the uneducated, alone is capable of maintaining a steadfast heart even when he is threatened with financial insecurity. For the ordinary person, an insured material provision is necessary to keep him behaving properly. What the hungry stomachs of the common people would consume first, Mencius is saying here, are moral scruples. Consequently in the *Meng Tzu* Mencius urges the intelligent ruler to look after his people's livelihood first. He demands that the ruler make certain that each farmer has around his house about an acre of land planted in mulberry trees, to enable anyone over fifty to be clothed in silk. Poultry and meat animals should be bred in season so that those over seventy will never lack a meat diet. In addition, Mencius would assign at least fifteen acres of land to any family of eight mouths in order to keep them all well-fed. The establishment of schools to teach the people Confucian principles comes last because principles can take roots only in minds when stomachs are full.

The difference between Mencius and Confucius comes into sharp relief when Mencius leaves the concrete and practical issues of the day to deal with the abstract. As we have said, in the *Meng Tzu* Mencius injects metaphysics into the Confucian system. He does so by going beyond Confucius in accepting Heaven at different times as a Supreme Being with a discerning moral will, or as a fatalistic pattern, or as the authority that creates virtue and sets the standard of righteousness. Mencius starts with his theory of human nature, and asserts that it is Heaven that gives man his innate knowledge contained in his mind (or heart—the Chinese word, *hsin*, means both heart and mind). The mind, or innate knowledge, is what makes man great because by exercising his mind man can come to "know" his original nature. Here we must note the difference between Mencius' theory of untainted heart and the mystic Taoist theory of untampered heart. The latter does not talk about man's mind and its importance.

The mysticism in the system of Mencius begins when he proceeds to tell us that when man exercises his mind to the utmost he will also come to "know" Heaven. The unerring and unwavering attitude to examine oneself in search of one's good nature is called, in Mencian terms, *ch'eng*, or sincerity. A person practicing the principles of humanity and altruism with "sincerity" can succeed in returning to his original nature which is a part of Heaven. Consequently Mencius declares that "All beings are complete within man." He who has attained this state is a perfect man, or a *chün-tzu*. The *chün-tzu* radiates a spiritual influence wherever he appears. Under his influence the ordinary people become good and the state becomes orderly. This spiritual influence, in most cases, is described by Mencius as *ch'i*, or the irresistible, all-pervading force.

The basic senses of the term, *ch'i*, include "air," "all gaseous matters," and "the air that surrounds a person." Mencius uses this term largely in the last sense. He assumes that a man with such an influential air around him must first possess that degree of spiritual perfection described above. In Mencius' ecstatic description of this all-pervading force, claiming that it flows "above and below together with Heaven and Earth," and that it "fills the entire universe between Heaven and Earth," the *ch'i* acquires puzzlingly mystic proportions.

But this Mencian concept of *ch'i* need not be a puzzle if we consider the basis of his theory. According to him, man acquires this all-pervading force by practicing the principles of humanity and morality according to the dictates of Heaven, conceived as a supreme moral voice. The process of acquiring this force, then, is a constant doing of righteous deeds without stop or affectation. Man can do so only when he uses his mind to examine himself and to rediscover the righteous senses (the four basic good senses already discussed) that come with his birth. In this analysis the mystic *ch'i* of Mencius is no more than a moral force stated metaphorically.

These are the basic tenets of an idealistic philosopher who, next to the Sung Dynasty philosopher Chu Hsi (1130-1200), perhaps did the most in establishing Confucianism as the controlling orthodoxy in Chinese thought for at least two millennia. Much, of course, has been read back into his book. Many apologists of Chinese tradition attempt to offer Mencius as the great champion of democracy in Eastern political thought. They cite Mencius' words on the importance of people but they overlook the Mencian pattern of social hierarchy. Almost every rebel in Chinese history quoted Mencius to support his revolt against the government. At the same time every ruler found comfort in this book when he contemplated punitive campaigns to suppress rebellions. Above all, Mencius has been adopted by the Chinese state-socialists as their ancient spokesman.

In the same manner the mystic element in this book has been made use of by different schools of thought. The Taoists have always wanted to include Mencius in their ranks, and they are not entirely without justification. Certain basic elements of Taoist mysticism antedated, or at least coexisted with, Confucian thought. The theory of the all-pervading force of Mencius certainly has a familiar ring to the ears of a Taoist. These problems cannot be tackled before philological studies of the text can establish the indisputable authenticity of any statements attributed to Mencius in this book and can secure other corroborating evidence to make the full implications of these statements clear.

Pertinent Literature

Creel, H. G. *Chinese Thought from Confucius to Mao Tsê-tung*. Chicago: University of Chicago Press, 1953.

H. G. Creel entitles his chapter on Mencius "Mencius and the Emphasis on Human Nature," thereby providing initial emphasis to the point that the ethics of Mencius, based to a considerable degree on the ideas of Confucius, nevertheless rested on the basic assumption that human beings are born good; he claimed that all are born with feelings that impel them toward the good, feelings of "sympathy, shame and dislike, reverence and respect, and recognition of right and wrong." There is nothing wrong with human nature, then; on the contrary, human beings are naturally good and are naturally inclined to do what is morally right. The philosophy of the *Meng Tzu* (Mencius) combines features of Confucianism with this doctrine of innate moral worth; Mencius developed much of what was undeveloped or implicit in the teachings of Confucius, and he devoted a great deal of effort to determining the kind of moral education that kings as well as commoners should receive.

Creel begins his account of Mencius with a review of the practice, in the fourth century B.C., of inviting philosophers to be "guest-officials" at the courts of rulers. The philosophers were paid—as were military advisers, who were also guest-officials. Among those invited to the capital of the state of Liang was the Confucian philosopher Mencius. According to a work of the Han Dynasty, Mencius was also one of more than a thousand scholars who received high salaries at the court of King Hsüan of the state of Ch'i. Mencius was critical of much of the advice given to rulers by visiting philosophers. The followers of Yang Chu were advocates of ethical egoism, urging that each be for himself, thereby denying the authority of the ruler; the followers of Mo Tzu advocated universal love and hence denied the obligation to give priority to the concern for one's father. The truth is that in the fourth century B.C. there were so many philosophical views being represented that the *Chuang Tzu* speaks of "the hundred schools," and Mencius was busy not only advising rulers but also attempting to confound his philosophical opponents and critics.

Knowledge of the views of Mencius is based on the study of the *Mencius (Meng Tzu)*, the work named, as was the practice, for the philosopher whose ideas it presumably represents. Although it is likely that the *Mencius*, like the other Chinese classics in philosophy, is only in part the direct product of the philosopher himself, the work is generally regarded as an authentic rendering of the views of the master, compiled by his disciples. Creel reminds us that Mencius was too late, of course, to have studied with Confucius himself; Mencius regretted this circumstance. (Confucius died about 479 B.C.; Mencius was born about 372 B.C., more than a hundred years later.) But Mencius was able, it is reported, to study with the grandson of Confucius, Tzu-ssu. According to Creel, Mencius' profession of advising rulers was not accidental: he made it his principal business to secure office as philosophical adviser and thus be in a position to put his philosophical and moral principles into practice.

Creel refers repeatedly to I. A. Richards' study of Mencius, *Mencius on the Mind* (1932), and he cites Richards' comment that some of the arguments of Mencius rank with those of Plato. Creel also summarizes Richards' critique of Mencius' manner of argumentation; apparently Mencius was convinced that he had the truth, and there is no evidence that he ever conceded that he had erred; in argument his objective was to persuade, not rationally to convince. Despite his dogmatism and occasional inclination to quibble in order to avoid admitting error, however, Mencius had many admirable features, Creel contends. Mencius put character before worldly success; what is important, he insisted, is that men be noble by emulating the nobility of Heaven.

Rulers should be advised by scholars, Mencius argued, because the true scholar occupies his correct place in the world, walks in the "great way of the world," and practices his principles when in office; such a person cannot be corrupted either by riches, authority, or power. By enunciating this point of view, Creel points out, Mencius advanced the position maintained by Confucius: namely, that rulers should turn over the administration of their governments to persons of virtue, education, and ability. Creel gives numerous examples of Mencius' courage in advising rulers and correcting them when in error or chastising them when at fault. (For example, he told the king of Liang that since his manner of ruling resulted in the starvation of the king's subjects, the king was a murderer.)

Although Mencius was opposed to war, Creel points out, his political program was based on the conviction that virtue brings success and that some-times a righteous war must be waged. Mencius also emphasized the importance of economics in the governing of a state; he advocated an allocation of lands, diversified farming, and the conservation of fisheries and forests. Mencius' political philosophy was based on the ethical principle that the well-being of the people is the end of government. Consequently, rulers should not only strive to be virtuous (and to be assisted in the effort by consultation with scholars) but should also follow the ways of the sage-kings of old, such ideal rulers as Yao, Shun, and Yü.

As has previously been mentioned, Creel emphasizes Mencius' conviction that all human beings are one in nature, and that human nature is inherently good. But Mencius' use of the term "good" is such that unless a person acts in a way that is in harmony with human nature, he is not good. Since it is possible for a person to act in a way that is not in harmony with his nature as human, it is possible for human beings to act wrongly and so to develop morally bad characters. The failure to live in accordance with the requirements of one's nature as human is occasioned by a person's allowing his emotional side to overcome his rational faculties. However, the emotions should not be repressed; properly channeled they motivate right action.

Creel also emphasizes Mencius' claim that education is necessary if virtue is to be possible. Education consists in maintaining one's nature as human, that is, in strengthening one's natural tendency, as rational, to be good in action. The effort to be righteous should continue throughout one's lifetime; only the continuous development of character will insure strength and virtue of character.

The discussion of Mencius closes with comments by Creel on Mencius' declaration that "All things are complete within us." The idea is that if one knows oneself, one knows the essence of all; one knows Heaven. Creel remarks that this line of thought represents a wide divergence from the original Confucian doctrine, which discouraged meditation. There is also some question as to whether Mencius himself had this radical view. In any case, Creel suggests, the passages in question appear to have a Taoist emphasis.

Waley, Arthur. *Three Ways of Thought in Ancient China.* New York: Macmillan Publishing Company, 1939.

The three ways of thought in ancient China considered by Arthur Waley are those of Chuang Tzu, Mencius, and Han Fei Tzu—or, one might perhaps more accurately say, the ways of thought expressed in the three Chinese classics, the *Chuang Tzu,* the *Mencius (Meng Tzu),* and the *Han Fei Tzu.* Waley follows the practice of most writers on the classics of using the name of the thinker honored in the title of a book (which, in many cases, is a collection of writings by various persons) being discussed.

Waley argues that the philosophy and teaching of Mencius centers about his conviction that *jen* (in the sense of moral goodness, which for Mencius, according to Waley, meant compassion) is the natural heritage of human beings; everyone is born with the kind of feeling that leads to right action; everyone, unless corrupted, cares about others and about the right development of himself as a moral being. Hence, for Mencius, the problem of education was the problem of keeping and strengthening such natural feelings. Mencius was practical enough, despite his emphasis on innate goodness, to emphasize the importance of economics, cooperative agriculture, the abolition of the tribute system (that required giving fixed amounts of grain to the king), the need for social collaboration, the abolition of market and frontier taxes, public support for the aged, and schools for moral education.

In a section entitled "Mencius and the Kings," Waley reviews the most characteristic and interesting of the exchanges between Mencius, the philosophical and moral adviser, and the kings who consulted him. One realizes from the survey of interviews that the task of achieving good government through the giving of philosophical advice, a task involving the making of true kings, was an extremely difficult, often fruitless, and for the most part frustrating enterprise. In his consultations with the kings, Mencius emphasized goodness and rightness over profit and success in war; the importance of the king's doing what is right—working for the welfare of his subjects (in that way, the king would be supported by the people and would prosper); the discipline of oneself in order to allow one's inner feelings of sympathy and compassion to affect one's actions; pushing one's good feelings to wider applications; insuring the economic well-being of the people in order that they be able and willing to maintain their principles of right and wrong; and the necessity of seeking a way of peace through allowing Goodness rather than ambition to rule.

Waley judged Mencius as a controversialist to be "nugatory"; he would have failed in almost every effort to persuade had not his opponents in argument been even feebler in argument than he was. Mencius introduced irrelevancies; he avoided the point at issue; he quibbled and deliberately misunderstood. He was at his best, Waley suggests, when he quite simply and directly urged the development and strengthening of natural goodness.

Additional Recommended Reading

Chai, Ch'u and Winberg Chai, eds. and trs. *The Humanist Way in Ancient China: Essential Works of Confucianism.* New York: Bantam Books, 1965. A readable translation, with helpful notes, in paperback. The book includes *The Confucian Analects, The Works of Mencius, The Great Learning,* and *The Doctrine of the Mean,* as well as selections from the *Hsün-tzu,* the *Hsiao ching,* the *Li chi* (Book of Rites), and the *Tung Chung-shu.*

Fung Yu-lan. *The Spirit of Chinese Philosophy.* London: Kegan Paul, Trench, Trubner & Company, 1947. The distinguished philosopher and historian writes of Confucius and Mencius in Chapter I of this excellent survey from Confucius through the author's own philosophy, "The New Li Hsüeh."

_____. "The Period of the Philosophers from the Beginnings to Circa 100 B.C.," in *A History of Chinese Philosophy.* Translated by Derk Bodde. Vol. I. Princeton, New Jersey: Princeton University Press, 1952. An authoritative and thorough account of Mencius, with illustrative passages, is presented in Chapter VI.

Mencius. *The Life and Works of Mencius.* Edited and translated by James Legge. Oxford: Clarendon Press, 1895. A literal but authoritative translation.

_____. *The Sayings of Mencius.* Translated by James Ware. New York: American Library, 1960. A readable, useful edition, in paperback.

Richards, I. A. *Mencius on the Mind.* London: Kegan Paul, Trench, Trubner & Company, 1932. An able and fresh examination of Mencius by one of the authors of *The Meaning of Meaning*; attention is paid to the various uses of language exhibited in the *Mencius.*

CHUANG TZU

Author: Chuang Chou (Chuang Tzu, c. 370-c.285 B.C.)
Type of work: Metaphysics, ethics
First transcribed: c. 300 B.C.

Principal Ideas Advanced

Tao *is the universal way of things, the all-pervading principle of all that exists; the virtue or power of every individual is a manifestation of* tao.

Distinctions between men or things, between right and wrong, are seen to be false once the universal presence of tao *is recognized.*

The only way to salvation is to identify oneself with the orderly process of all being, the tao.

Death is nothing to fear, for man lives as long as his essence, the tao *lives; and the* tao *is eternal.*

The True Man retains the unspoiled simplicity of a child; he does not concern himself with political action, but allows the tao *to take its course; he abstains from intellectual analysis and the study of abstract ideas.*

The man whose name, together with that of Lao Tzu, has become synonymous with classical Taoism was probably one of the many eccentric recluses who challenged the intellectual authority of Confucius during the Warring States period in Chinese history. Disgusted with the prevailing chaos and weary of the self-styled sages' moral preachings, these men saw the only salvation in "letting things be what they are." Legend about Chuang Chou the man tells us of his refusal to serve in the capacity of prime minister, also of his mystic wanderings and cryptic speeches. The anecdotes involving him and the statements attributed to him are extremely imaginative in character; and his words often soar to dazzling metaphysical heights. Like the *Tao Te Ching*, the thirty-three chapters of the *Chuang Tzu* contain much poetry in which we find many images identifiable with the poetic tradition founded in ancient China along the Yangtze River valley, or in relatively southern parts of China.

Like the *Tao Te Ching*, this work also expounds a theory based on the mystic universal principle called *tao*. *Tao* is the beginning of all being; hence, it could be understood as Non-Being. Having no begetter, *tao* is best expressed by what is spontaneous. From these ideas we perceive the workings of *tao* as actually nonactivity, or doing nothing that is not done by itself. In short, *tao* is the all-pervading principle that exists prior to the existence of the universe, and it is to be found in everything, no matter how trivial or base. The manifestation of this first principle in each individual thing is called *te* (virtue, power). *Tao* and *te*, thus, are actually of one essence, the former being the universal essence, and the latter the share of the former deposited in every individual being.

On this mystic concept of *tao*, Chuang Tzu (as Chuang Chou is traditionally known) has constructed his view of the universe. He does so very rarely by direct logical exposition, using instead a multitude of anecdotes, imaginary dialogues, and metaphorical parables. The universe comes into existence in accordance with *tao*, and the myriad beings in the universe each partake of *tao*. In their essence, the loftiest sage and the humblest of men are the same, their distinctions being man-made, impermanent, and never absolute. The Himalayas and the threshold of a peasant's hut are actually of the same height; the greatest of birds, the roc, really has no reason for laughing at the tiniest wren when they compare their ranges of flight. Since each follows its own way as *tao* makes it, each is as important as the other. This is Chuang Tzu's theory of relativity with which he defies the existing social institutions because they draw lines. These lines, in Chuang Tzu's view, are all false, and the concern of the Confucian and the dialectician of his time with the distinction between names and reality he thought totally irrelevant and useless.

Even the notions of right and wrong do not exist for Chuang Tzu. Right is right only because of the existence of wrong; nothing is absolutely right. Furthermore, everything is simultaneously itself (when it looks at itself) and something else (when looked upon by something else); consequently, there cannot be an absolute "this" or "that." Everything is "this" and "that" at the same time.

When someone challenged Chuang Tzu to explain how he could make such an assertion and claim it to be right when his assertion was a denial of the notion of right, Chuang Tzu dismissed the question by saying that he was not concerned with settling such an argument. He did not believe that there was any argument to be settled. He was merely proposing a third course of action or a third view transcending the ordinary right-wrong dualism.

Why is there no need to settle any argument? To begin with, everything follows *tao*. Since *tao* is always right, by virtue of the fact that it always "is so," everything is always right also. If there is conflict, then the conflict itself is also right. Chuang Tzu believed that conflict arises when man departs from *tao* and tries to act contrary to Nature's way. He asserts, without trying to prove his assertion, that everything in the universe is inclined toward order; therefore, he denies the validity of the accepted legends about how the ancient sage-kings "worked" to bring about peace and order. Chuang Tzu preferred to see the abolition of all the man-made social and political institutions because he believed that only then could Nature's way or *tao* prevail. And *tao* will always ultimately prevail; whatever man can do will not make any lasting difference.

Nature's way is constant, and its constancy is revealed in the ceaseless change that cannot be obstructed in the universe. Every being is involved in this process of change, from one species to another, one appearance to another, or one form of its existence to another form of existence. Hence, nothing is improving or degenerating, but everything is in-

volved in this universal cyclical motion. Man is no exception. And the only way to salvation, if it is relevant to speak of salvation in this philosophical system, is for man to understand this process and to identify himself with *tao*. In doing so man would be able to attain the axis of the wheel from which he could view the perpetual disturbance in the universe with transcendental calm. He would, then, achieve tranquillity in chaos. In this very respect Chuang Tzu's system comes close to Buddhism.

Recalling that Chuang Tzu compares man to a clod, one may say that Chuang Tzu's is not a very edifying view of man, but it is consistent with his fundamental concept of *tao*. According to him, man is part of *tao*'s making. Man has a share of *tao* just as a clod of dirt does. If he preserves this share of *tao*, he will not be lost. And the way to cling to *tao* is by retaining one's original unspoiled simplicity—the state of mind of a child.

Chuang Tzu arrives at this conclusion along several lines of argument: First, the commonly accepted cultivation of the mind drives man to acquire a knowledge of artificial distinctions without real meaning. Such knowledge is not true knowledge; the only true knowledge lies in the comprehension of *tao*. Second, the artificial knowledge man acquires serves no other purpose than to create confusion and strife. Man is led by his false sense of righteousness to combat what he erroneously considers wrong. Man is encouraged by his illusion about greatness to strive for what may be actually small. Third, there is nothing that is absolutely complete except *tao* itself. Man's artificial effort to construct anything or create anything is necessarily incomplete. Man cannot attain perfect construction of anything through his own effort. Hence, whatever he undertakes to complete, he leaves something undone. What is more, the moment man makes a move, he injures something, and also himself. Hence, Chuang Tzu insists on the importance of an uncarved block, and he praises the perfection of music from a lute that has no strings.

Consistent with his theory of relativity and cyclical change, Chuang Tzu shows indifference toward death and suggests that there may be great joy after death. He decries the common practice of mourning because, as he puts it, the mourner assumes knowledge of the unknown and pretends his dislike of it. The famous story in Chapter XVIII about the death of Chuang Tzu's wife is a graphic illustration of this attitude. Chuang Tzu refuses to weep; instead, he sits with his legs crossed and beats on an inverted pot to accompany his singing. In this unconventional behavior, Chuang Tzu already expresses his idea about immortality.

Strictly speaking, the question of immortality does not exist in Chuang Tzu's system. If life and death are but phases in an irresistible cycle of change, then there is no difference between the living and the dead, or between the mortal and the immortal. Mortality becomes a problem and a source of sorrow only because man cannot free himself from the artificially constructed straitjacket of his view on life and existence. In the physical sense, man must die and there is no escape. But if man can understand Nature's way and embrace *tao*, then he lives as long as *tao* lives; hence, he is immortal. Chuang Tzu defies death by saying that if (after death) his left arm became a rooster, he would simply use it to mark the time of night. Man may die indeed, but his essence as part of the universal essence lives on forever. This is the metaphysical view of immortality in the *Chuang Tzu*.

There is also a mystic explanation of immortality offered by Chuang Tzu. A man who has succeeded in preserving his original simplicity and in maintaining his share of *tao* is called in Chuang Tzu's terms, a True Man. In order to achieve this stage, man has to rid himself of his intellectual knowledge by "fasting his mind," and "contemplating on emptiness." If he succeeds in forgetting that there are "things" in the world, he will have discarded manmade distinctions in the universe and he will have come close to a union with *tao*. What he senses will be merely an emptiness and a vastness; his appearance will resemble that of the stupid. Then he will have attained the Mysterious Power in Nature.

So far this seems to be only an exaggerated metaphorical statement of Chuang Tzu's vision of perfect self-discipline and cultivation, but the mysticism surrounding him thickens when he goes on to describe the True Man's capacities. The best of these True Men, so says Chuang Tzu, are ethereal. They sense no heat in fire and no chill in ice. They can "mount on clouds, ride on the sun and moon, and wander at ease beyond the seas." Consequently, neither life nor death can affect them. There are many parallel stories told of this kind of spirit-travel in other ancient Chinese writings. They seem to be part of the common primitive Taoist-shamanistic traditions shared by the Chinese, particularly those in the central Yangtze River valley where Chuang Tzu is said to have lived. In this book, we find Chuang Tzu attempting to give a metaphysical explanation to these legends. It seems that he stresses the importance of "preserving oneself" by following the natural bends of things; consequently, one achieves immortality because one does not wear oneself out. This theory is illustrated in his story about the perfect butcher whose carving knife remains perpetually sharp because it always goes between the bones and tissues and never meets any resistance.

While the physical liberation of a True Man, if taken literally, amounts to a mystic vision which can hardly be rationally explained, the liberation of man's mind in the *taoist* fashion is not difficult to comprehend. We have seen that Chuang Tzu has no use for intellectual knowledge. To him "things are what they are," and they do what Nature dictates them to do. Man should live as part of Nature together with all other things in Nature, and desist from his futile pursuit of seeing, reading, and analyzing the universe in abstraction. The moment man ceases to confuse himself with the useless puzzles which his fellow men have created, his mind will be liberated. Then and only then will he be ready to comprehend *tao*.

By emptying his mind of intellectual prejudices, man will be able to see the similarity of all things. Hence, he and the myriad things will be one and he will feel that the universe is within him. Whatever he does or does not do will cause no concern or anxiety. He will thus be free to move in the universe. At this stage his happiness is true and supreme, because there is nothing about him that is not in accord with Nature.

The kind of extreme happiness that Chuang Tzu speaks of is also a result of emotional liberation. Having been intellectually liberated, man no longer sees any cause for alarm, or worry, or sorrow. Following a course completely in accord with Nature, he depends on nothing and seeks nothing. He is totally free. It is this total freedom projected into time and space that Chuang Tzu describes in his stories about the True Man. Chuang Tzu's ideal freedom is threefold: an intellectual liberation from man's prejudices and man-made restrictions, an emotional liberation through a thorough understanding of the way of all lives, and finally a total liberation when man feels no restriction because he accepts every natural course of events.

Although this work does not deal with the various aspects of what has become known as magical Taoism, Chuang Tzu's theory of the True Man and his notion of *ch'i* (gaseous matter, spirit) provide it with ample inspiration. Chuang Tzu's vague formula to achieve True-Manhood mentions the physical discipline of sitting in meditation, and the mental discipline of discarding abstract ideas. He also urges man to "listen" with his *ch'i* or to react to the outside world with his spirit, while sparing his ordinary senses. These suggestions can be related to some primitive practice of breathing exercise to aid mental concentration and ward off distracting influence. It has been said that this aspect of Taoism is a bridge between Chuang Tzu's mysticism and that of Mencius. We must not overlook, however, the fundamental difference between these two philosophers. Both believed in a mystical perfection of man through the cultivation of his *ch'i*, but while Mencius saw the road to salvation through doing socially good deeds, Chuang Tzu absolutely denied the validity of altruism.

A comparison of Chuang Tzu with Lao Tzu will show their parallelism at almost every point. As we have noted, Lao Tzu and Chuang Tzu are recognized as cofounders of the Taoist school of thought, and there is rarely any mention of one without the other. There is nevertheless one important difference between them. In advocating nonactivity, Lao Tzu stresses the difference between two extremes and warns of the disaster that inevitably follows extremity. While in urging the same thing, Chuang Tzu denies any real difference between extremes. Again, Lao Tzu advises the ruler to govern by noninterference because he believes in the inevitable reversal from one extreme to the other; hence, complete lack of rule will automatically bring rule. Chuang Tzu, on

the other hand, believes in noninterference as an ideal for governing because of an alleged propensity toward order in everything.

Insofar as Chuang Tzu repeatedly criticized his contemporary moralists as useless do-gooders, his anti-intellectual attitude was clearly a reaction against the overbearing Confucians and the many other voices which at the time vied with one another in offering political cure-alls and social panaceas. Most of these moralists sought to bring order to society by urging altruism and redefinition of terms; Chuang Tzu was diametrically opposed to such activities. But in opposing his contemporary thinkers, Chuang Tzu was not unconcerned with the signs of his time; he also offered a political recipe of his own which he believed could solve all the prevalent problems. It should be noted that the *Chuang Tzu* remains an extremely important source for the study of many other less well-known schools of thought in ancient China. In several cases, Chuang Tzu's comments on some of his contemporaries provide the only information available on their philosophies.

In many ways this work has exerted even greater influence on the Chinese mind than has the *Tao Te Ching*. It has been able to do so because of the numerous imaginary and metaphorical anecdotes it contains. The metaphysical poetry of the *Tao Te Ching* is fascinating, but often it is too cryptic to be grasped. The metaphors in the *Chuang Tzu*, however, have found their way into the common pool of metaphors in Chinese literature and even in the daily language where, although their original Taoist color has been diluted through use, they have had a subtle influence on the configuration of the Chinese mind. On a higher level, such notions as the purity of man's heart (mind) and the calmness of man's emotions have become the core of quietism that has found eloquent expression in the undying poems of T'ao Ch'ien (365-427) and Wang Wei (699-750). The principles of quietude, simplicity, detachment, and leisureliness which have made these poets immortal also laid the foundation for the development of Ch'an Buddhism in China and for the theory and practice of the Chinese landscape painting—the most important Chinese contribution to art.

On the level of daily life we note the ever-present

balancing influence of this school of thought on the Chinese mind, providing a measure of practical wisdom. Chuang Tzu's allegorical tales on the themes of relativity and cyclical change appear in many later works in infinite variations. For instance, the story about the death of Chuang Tzu's wife appears in a famous seventeenth century collection of traditional short stories; it again appears in an opera still being staged in modern times. One of these stories is always quoted by him who tries to comfort his friend over the loss of a dear one. Another story is used, in the form of a proverb, to advise man never to take worldly affairs too seriously. A third anecdote enables a man to live through the most trying of crises when he recalls and believes in Chuang Tzu's saying that "This, too, is Nature's way."

Pertinent Literature

Hu Shih. *The Development of the Logical Method in Ancient China*. New York: Paragon Book Reprint Corporation, 1963.

In Part IV, "Evolution and Logic," of his penetrating study of Chinese thought, *The Development of the Logical Method in Ancient China*, Hu Shih discusses (in Chapter II) "The Logic of Chuang Tze." By the term "logic" Hu refers to the characteristic method exemplified in the philosophical work of a philosopher; one might say that a philosopher's "logic" is his distinctive way of thinking, of going after the kind of knowledge sought. That this approach is especially helpful for Western scholars is made evident by the consideration that the citation of content, especially when one approaches the content in translation and when the translation is of a language of a radically different sort from one's own, is practically meaningless. What gives language meaning (as Hu and other perceptive commentators realize) is its use within the context of specifiable problems. Hence, to attend to a philosopher's way of thought, his "logic," is to consider what he does with language and what it accomplishes toward the resolution of the problems he confronts.

Hu begins by quoting a passage from the epilogue to the *Chuang Tzu* in which a writer reporting the views of the master summarizes Chuang Tzu's basic position. Among the central ideas of the passage quoted are the following (here paraphrased): There is constant change and becoming—no permanent form and no final goal. One must live in the world as it is and not be bound by anything. There is no difference (except relative to each other) between right and wrong, life and death. There is no beginning and no ending. (How these ideas relate to *tao*, the universal "way," is discussed later on in the chapter.)

The refusal to make distinctions of the kind traditionally taken for granted can be understood as in part an expression of Chuang Tzu's acceptance of the *tao* as the pervasive principle of the universe and in part as an expression of his skepticism concerning the power of the intellect and of discursive logic to reveal anything worth knowing.

Hu points out that Chuang Tzu was a friend and admirer of Hui Shih, the Neo-Mohist dialectician. Hui Shih had insisted that the universe is one, that all things are both similar to one another and different; the principle was termed that of "Great-Similarity-and-Difference." Chuang Tzu regarded Hui Shih as inconsistent in holding to this principle and then attempting to get at the truth through argumentation. Accordingly, Chuang Tzu refused to distinguish between truth and falsity, right and wrong: all such distinctions ignored what might be called the "relativity" involved in the consideration of such matters. True knowledge would come only with a total conception, or, perhaps one should say, with the "seeing" of things without the making of distinctions.

Hu quotes Chuang Tzu's remark that "Great knowledge is comprehensive; little knowledge is always particular. Great speech is noncommittal; small speech makes clever distinctions." To count on the use of speech and the making of distinctions would be to contribute to the obscuring of the *tao*, according to Chuang Tzu. One understands apparent opposites only "in the light of the other." Thus, the passage from *Chuang Tzu* continues, reporting the words of Chuang Tzu, "The Not-Itself comes from the Itself, and the Itself is also caused by the Not-Itself." The principle of the *tao* (termed by Hu as the "cosmic reason") underlies the philosophy of Chuang Tzu, according to Hu. There is an underlying creative unity, a principle of natural evolution, such that apparent oddities and differences are resolved by considering the whole as pervaded by the *tao*.

Chuang Tzu appealed to the unity of the universe as pervaded by *tao* to justify his denial of the legitimacy of logical distinctions. Discussion is futile, disputes are futile, distinctions are futile—if all is one, why attempt to find out how one thing differs from another, or whether a statement is true or false, or whether a judgment is right or wrong? The only answer (a quotation from the *Chuang Tzu* suggests) is to "Reconcile all in the rhythm of nature . . . Aspire to the realm of the Infinite, and take refuge therein."

In the course of his discussion of Chuang Tzu's distinctive method—the "logic" of no-logic, one might say—Hu presumes to recognize a resemblance between Chuang Tzu's position and method and that of G. W. F. Hegel. Chuang Tzu's comments concerning the pervasive influence of cosmic reason in the natural evolution of the universe are compared to Hegel's "The rational is the real, the real, the rational."

Fung Yu-lan. *The Spirit of Chinese Philosophy.* Translated by E. R. Hughes. London: Kegan Paul, Trench, Trubner & Company, 1947.

Fung Yu-lan begins his discussion of Lao Tzu and Chuang Tzu (in Chapter IV) with the interesting comment that "all thoughts dealing with names are on a higher level than the plain man's thoughts." Even the nominalistic claim that only the actual is real and that names are empty (a denial of universals) is on a level of thinking higher than that of the "plain man" who does not even think about names and to whom it would never occur that there are any problems at all involved in the use of names (words).

The Taoists, having been forced by the Logicians (such as Hui Shih and Kung-sun Lung) to think beyond the concrete world of shapes and features, then thought beyond the level of the logicians: they passed from thought about the nameable to thought about the unnameable. Hence, in the first chapter of the *Lao Tzu (Tao Te Ching)*, one reads (Fung reports) that the *tao* that can be named (described) is not the "abiding Tao." A comparable passage in the *Chuang Tzu*, Fung writes, is the proposition, "In the very beginning there was non-being, and non-being has no name."

Fung points out that in Taoism, the *tao* is regarded as *wu* (non-being), while all creation—heaven, earth, and all things—is *yu* (being). Whatever has being can be named, but whatever is nonbeing is nameless. Of course, one uses a name, *tao*, to desig-nate the abiding unnameable, the "Uncarved Block"; but such a name is distinguishable from all other names in that it is the name for the abiding *tao* and hence is an abiding name. And all abiding names, the argument runs, are names that are not really names. The idea of the *tao* is a *formal* idea, Fung argues, in that it is used to designate that which accounts for all things, for the way of things; it is *not* a *positive* term in that it says nothing about the *tao*.

Fung emphasizes Chuang Tzu's view that the usual distinctions people make are entirely relative. Each claim by which another claim is denied is from a particular point of view, relative to which the claim appears to be about an absolute; but the opposing view, equally "narrow" or limited, presents to the one who holds it the same kind of apparent absolute validity. If one "sees things in the light of Heaven"— that is, if one realizes that only an all-encompassing view is dependable and that such a view reconciles apparent opposites and resists distinctions—then one sees the futility of discussion and judgment about the true and false, the right and wrong, and even about such matters as the living and the dead. To view things from the viewpoint of the *tao*, Fung writes, is to use the *tao* to view things. If one uses the *tao* to view things, then differences are seen to "interpenetrate and become one."

Fung repeatedly makes the point that just as the Logicians used dialectic to criticize the ordinary person's attempt to grasp the world of things, so the Taoists used the *tao* (the technique of viewing from the synoptic "viewpoint" of the *tao*) to criticize the Logicians. Arguing with words in order to argue about words is to go beyond the concern with the shapes and features of things; such a move of thought is from the concrete to the abstract and is in that respect "higher." But to avoid the use of words in order to realize the nameless, the *tao*, is even higher. Hence, "Since all things are one, what room is there for speech?" At the same time, according to Fung, the Taoist position and that of Chuang Tzu is not that the view of the common person, however limited, is wrong: from the viewpoint of the *tao*, it has its place. Nor is the view of the Logicians wrong; it is simply limited on a higher level of thought.

The Taoist view involves the paradoxical consequence that the highest knowledge, knowledge of the *tao*, is not knowledge, Fung claims; but from the Taoist viewpoint this is not a paradox; nor is it something to be regretted. All knowledge involves the making of distinctions; to recognize the *tao* is to know the nameless without being able to name it in any positive way—but this is precisely what one must expect if the *tao* is nameless. One concludes, if one follows Chuang Tzu, that knowledge of the *tao* is not knowledge; hence, it is the highest knowledge.

The *Chuang Tzu* provides many references to the procedure by which one "cultivates the Tao," and to cultivate the *tao* means to discard knowledge, to arrive by stages at an undifferentiated state in which time, the self, the others, and things are forgotten— that is, no longer noticed or considered and are thereby to be identified with the "undifferentiable One." One knows the *tao* by achieving a condition identifiable with "the Great Whole."

Fung is careful to distinguish between the "no-knowledge" of ignorance and the "post-gained no-knowledge" which is attained by "forgetting"—that is, in some way setting aside what one knows by the making of distinctions. From the Taoist point of view, Fung writes, *jen* ("human-heartedness") and *yi* ("righteousness") are not enough. These virtues are not rejected, but they must be transcended. One must take two courses at the same time—the course of discarding knowledge and being out of the world, and the course of using knowledge and being in the world. However, Fung concludes, using the Taoist standard, these two courses are not two but one and the same.

Additional Recommended Reading

Beck, Lily Adams. *The Story of Oriental Philosophy.* New York: Farrar and Rinehart, 1928. In Chapters XXV and XXVI Beck discusses Chuang Tzu both as "A Master of the Mystic Way" and as a thinker of "irony and humor."

Creel, H. G. *Chinese Thought from Confucius to Mao Tsê-tung.* Chicago: University of Chicago Press, 1953. Creel discusses the *Chuang Tzu* and the *Lao Tzu* in Chapter VI, "The Mystical Skepticism of the Taoists." Creel provides a Western perspective, clear and probable, on a point of view that tends to resist explication.

Hackett, Stuart C. *Oriental Philosophy: A Westerner's Guide to Eastern Thought.* Madison: University of Wisconsin Press, 1979. In Chapter 2 of Part One, Hackett discusses "Taoism: A Philosophy of Mystical Oneness and Self-Transcendence." Hackett includes the classical expressions of the *Lao Tzu* and the *Chuang Tzu*, and then goes on to a discussion of the Neo-Taoist reconstruction and of certain critical problems of the Taoist philosophy to which he makes a "personal response."

Hughes, E. R. *Chinese Philosophy in Classical Times.* New York: E. P. Dutton, 1942. Hughes's book, always dependable, offers insightful notes and illuminating selections from the *Tao Te Ching* and the *Chuang Tzu*.

PRINCIPAL DOCTRINES and LETTER TO MENOECEUS

Author: Epicurus (c. 342-c. 270 B.C.)
Type of work: Ethics
First transcribed: Third century B.C.

Principal Ideas Advanced

Pleasure is the standard by which every good and every right action is to be judged.

No pleasure is in itself bad, and all pleasures are alike in quality.

Certain natural desires are necessary, and the gratification of such desires is preferable to the gratification of unnecessary natural desires or desires attaching to artificially cultivated tastes.

The three needs of man are equanimity, bodily health and comfort, and the exigencies of life.

To achieve the good life, a life of moderate and enduring pleasure, a man must cultivate the virtues, particularly prudence, and study philosophy.

Death is nothing to fear for while we live death is not with us; and when death comes, we no longer exist.

The *Principal Doctrines* is a collection of forty of the most important articles of Epicurus' teaching, presumably extracted by a disciple from the master's voluminous works. It was widely known in ancient times, and has been preserved to us by Diogenes Laertius (probably third century) in his *Lives and Opinions of Eminent Philosophers*. Together with the *Letter to Menoeceus*, also found in Diogenes' works, it constitutes our only firsthand source for the ethical teachings of Epicurus. The most important supplementary source is Lucretius' poem, *On the Nature of Things* (first century B.C.).

Epicurus' central teaching was that pleasure is the standard by which every good is to be judged. He distinguished between feelings of pleasure and judgments concerning good and right, and he maintained that the latter, insofar as they have meaning, must refer to the former. "For we recognize pleasure as the first good innate in us, and from pleasure we begin every act of choice and avoidance, and to pleasure we return again, using the feeling as the standard by which we judge every good." (*Letter to Menoeceus*.)

No pleasure, said Epicurus, is in itself bad. He maintained that pleasures are all of the same kind. Some pleasures are more intense than others, some last longer, and some satisfy a greater portion of the body; but if these differences could be set aside, one pleasure could not be distinguished from another. Unfortunately, however, the limitations of human existence compel us to distinguish between pleasures. In actuality, the pleasure cannot be chosen in isolation, and the conditions which are necessary to our enjoying some pleasures are also annexed to pains. "For this reason, we do not choose every pleasure, but sometimes pass over many pleasures, when greater discomfort accrues to us as the result of them." (*Letter to Menoeceus*.)

Thus, Epicurus turned his attention to the consideration of desires. Some desires, he said, are natural while others are illusory. By the latter he meant physical desires of the sort which neither arise from any deprivation nor admit of definite satisfaction—desires which attach to artificially cultivated tastes. Already in his day the public supposed that he and his followers pursued the pleasures of profligacy and vice. Such was far from being the case. The reason was that such artificial desires inevitably come into conflict with natural desires which are far more important. Indeed, Epicurus held that not all natural desires are to be satisfied. He distinguished between natural desires which are necessary and those which are merely natural. The necessary ones are so exacting that we are counseled to concentrate on them alone.

The strength of Epicurus' philosophy, as over against the Cyrenaic and other philosophies of pleasure, derives from its deeper understanding of the psychology of human needs. Man has three kinds of needs that will not be denied: equanimity or peace of mind, bodily health and comfort, and the exigencies of life itself. Fortunately, according to Epicurus, few things are necessary in order to sustain life and keep the body in health, and they are comparatively easy to obtain. Illness is unavoidable, but, as he pointed out, acute pain rarely lasts long, and chronic illnesses permit a predominance of pleasure over pain in the flesh. On the whole, Epicurus seems to have expended but little thought on the necessities of life and bodily health. His main concern was with peace of mind, how to avoid unpleasantness from our fellow men, how to escape the pangs of conscience, how to avoid worry about the future, including the life beyond the grave. Such considerations gave Epicurus' philosophy a predominantly somber tone, so much so that he rarely spoke of pleasure except in a negative way, as "freedom from pain in the body and from trouble in the mind." Speaking of the three necessary desires, he said, " The right understanding of these facts enables us to refer all choice and avoidance to the health of the body and the soul's freedom from disturbance, since this is the aim of the life of blessedness." (*Letter to Menoeceus*.)

Thus, while the good in life is always simple and immediate, namely, feelings of pleasure, the art of achieving a life abundant in goodness is one that requires great skill and constant application. To this end, Epicurus recommended two sorts of means: first, the cultivation of virtue; second, the study of philosophy.

Of these two, virtue is the more important. "The man who does not possess the virtuous life cannot possibly live pleasantly," he declared. Among virtues, the chief he held to be prudence, because all other virtues were, in his view, merely special kinds of prudence.

By prudence he meant what Dostoevski once called "solving the problem of existence." It consists in knowing the worth of various satisfactions, on the one hand, and their cost, on the other. Sometimes we have to choose pains in order to secure greater pleasures; for example, having a tooth extracted. Sometimes we have to forego pleasure because of resultant pains; for example, drinking wine when it makes one ill afterward. Epicurus spoke of a scale of comparison which the prudent man must carry about in his mind, by which he judges prospective courses of action in terms of their advantages and disadvantages.

One of the best counsels of prudence, he thought, was to make oneself independent of desire and, to this end, to accustom oneself to simple food and plain surroundings. His motive was not an ascetic one—he saw no good in deprivation for its own sake. But he contended that anyone who has learned to be satisfied with the necessities of life is freed from most of the cares of the future, since changes of fortune are unlikely to reduce a man to starvation, whereas the slightest turn may deprive a man of his luxuries. Moreover, he maintained that there is an actual overplus of pleasure in the abstemious life. Bread and water produce as great pleasures to the man who needs them as the luxuries of a wealthy table do to the reveler. Moreover, plain fare is better for health of body and alertness of mind. Furthermore, the man whose taste is not spoiled by habitual indulgence is better able to appreciate fine food and drink when, at long intervals, these are set before him.

Another counsel of prudence was to retire from the world of human affairs. Epicurus, somewhat like Hobbes, regarded man as the greatest enemy of man. To secure protection from our fellows is a natural want. But how shall one go about it? Epicurus doubted the wisdom of those who undertake to find security by competing for public honor and position. In his opinion, this is not "safe." Instead, he recommended "the immunity which results from a quiet life and the retirement from the world."

It is in connection with the harm which we may expect from our fellow men that Epicurus introduced the virtue of justice. In opposition to the teaching of Plato and Aristotle, but in agreement with that of Democritus, he denied that justice has its foundation in nature. All justice, he said, originates in "a pledge of mutual advantage to restrain men from harming one another and save them from being harmed." It does not exist among primitive tribes, and what is considered just in one country may be quite different from what is considered just in another. In fact, within the same land, as circumstances change, what was once considered just may be so no longer. For the justice of a law ultimately depends on its being to the mutual advantage of both parties to the compact.

Epicurus raised the question which Glaucon raised in Plato's *Republic*, Book II, whether it is not to the advantage of a person secretly to act unjustly if he can do so without detection. The answer is that one can never be confident that he will escape detection, and that anxiety would spoil the fruits of the crime. "The just man is most free from trouble, the unjust most full of trouble."

After virtue, Epicurus considered philosophy the second most important means for securing the life of bliss. "Let no one when young," he wrote to Menoeceus, "delay to study philosophy, nor when he is old grow weary of his study." In these words Epicurus was not recommending philosophy as a solace against the sorrows of existence nor as a diversion which yields a satisfaction of its own. By philosophy Epicurus meant a kind of mental hygiene, based on a naturalistic world view which, if its implications were understood, would free men's minds from superstitious fear and moral anxiety.

The view of nature which recommended itself to him was that of Democritus of Abdera, who denied that the world was created by the gods or that there is any ultimate purpose in life, all things having been formed by the accidental collision of atoms falling through empty space. The man who is convinced that this is the case has, according to Epicurus, two great advantages over those who hold to traditional beliefs: first, he is freed from religious scruples; second, he is freed from the fear of death.

Epicurus did not deny the existence of the gods, which he identified with the heavenly bodies. He held that they are composed of the same fine, smooth atoms which make up the souls of men and are the basis of our reason and feelings; but because the gods are eternal and blessed in their regular motions, Epicurus found no reason to suppose that they are exacting and vengeful toward men, or indeed that they pay any attention to us. The traditional view, that

the gods are the source of human misfortune and of blessedness, he explained as arising from the tendency man has to view other beings as acting like himself. He denied that such a belief is founded on sensation or has any foundation in reason. Eclipses, solstices, and other celestial phenomena which the ancients were accustomed to regard with superstitious awe, he said, are capable of explanation according to natural principles. "For if we pay attention to these we shall rightly trace the causes whence arose our mental disturbance and fear, and by learning the true causes of celestial phenomena and all other occurrences that come to pass from time to time, we shall free ourselves from all which produces the utmost fear in other men." *(Letter to Herodotus,* also cited by Diogenes.)

The fear of death seemed to him as groundless as fear of the gods. Because, at death, the soul-atoms leave man's body and are dispersed through space, a man's consciousness is dissipated, the separate atoms no longer possessing the same power and sentience which they had when together in the bodily sheath. But good and evil consist in sensations and nothing else. Therefore, according to Epicurus, there is nothing terrible in death. And if a man persuades himself of this, the anticipation of death ceases to be painful. "So death, the most terrifying of ills, is nothing to us, since so long as we exist death is not with us; but when death comes, then we do not exist. It does not then concern either the living or the dead, since for the former it is not, and the latter are no more." *(Letter to Menoeceus.)* Nor does the wise man seek length of days. "Just as with food he does not seek simply the larger share and nothing else, but rather the most pleasant, so he seeks to enjoy not the longest period of time but the most pleasant." Such is the sweetness introduced into man's life by the knowledge that death is nothing, that he no longer has any thirst for immortality.

Epicurus was moved to modify the philosophy of Democritus in one respect. The latter held to a strictly deterministic theory of causation; but Epicurus said that, though some events happen by necessity and chance, others are within our control. It was, he said, more foolish to become "a slave to the destiny of the natural philosophers" than to follow the myths about the gods. The myths leave us some hope—the determinists only despair. The part of wisdom in these matters seemed to him, very much as it did to the Stoic Epictetus, to consist in understanding the limits of man's condition and in not expecting more than is reasonable. A man who knows these things laughs at destiny. All that he asks is a companion like himself, and then he "shall live like a god among men."

Pertinent Literature

Bailey, Cyril. *The Greek Atomists and Epicurus*. Oxford: Clarendon Press, 1928.

Cyril Bailey's account is restricted to Epicurus' two surviving works on ethics. Books on Epicurus usually develop other aspects of his philosophy, notably his theory of knowledge and his philosophy of nature. They also supplement the writings preserved by Diogenes Laertius with other materials—fragmentary sayings, and secondhand reports. Moreover, they try to answer questions concerning the historical situation out of which Epicurus' philosophy arose. As these are problems which require special knowledge of Greek and Latin writings, scholarship dealing with Epicurus is largely the preserve of classical philologists.

Bailey, after editing and translating Epicurus' writings, set out to write a general exposition of his system, but was soon convinced that this could be done properly only within the larger context of Greek atomist philosophy. Although he is at pains to show the refinements which Epicurus introduced into the materialism of Leucippus and Democritus (as, for example, when Epicurus endowed atoms with the ability to change direction and gave mind atoms an active role in sensation and conception), Bailey keeps his author firmly in the mechanistic school. In his opinion, Epicurus' major innovation was to adopt a sensationalistic theory of knowledge and to make sensationalism the foundation for his theory of morals.

Much contemporary discussion of Epicurus centers on his criteria of knowledge (sensations, concepts, feelings), mainly on the second criterion. Bailey, who interprets Epicurus as a consistent empiricist, says that by a concept Epicurus meant the impression which the mind retains of a series of sensations of the same kind, and that Epicurus regarded the validity of a concept as deriving from the fact that it is built up of sensations. The third criterion, feeling, is simply a name for pleasures and pains, and serves as a test for rightness in morals in the same way that sight and touch do for truth in knowledge.

According to Bailey, when Epicurus said that, although all pleasures are good, some pleasures are not to be chosen, adding that absence of pain in the body and of fear in the mind count as pleasures, he was thinking not merely of our feelings but also of the bodily processes which give rise to these feelings. Our nature seeks a restful equilibrium, the feeling corresponding to which Epicurus called static pleasure, in contrast to the kinetic pleasures (and pains) which accompany the body's gain (and loss) of needed atoms. In this manner, says Bailey, Epicurus reduced the pursuit of pleasure to rules of hygiene, and envisaged the wise man as one who is not content to be guided in his actions by conventional virtues but who seeks in all things to live according to nature.

Epicurus advised against civic involvement; he also discouraged his followers from assuming family responsibilities, although he gathered his disciples into something resembling a cult and preached to them the joys of fellowship. Bailey has assembled various fragments and testimonies dealing with this topic, many of which suggest that in his relations with close friends Epicurus was generous to the point of sacrifice. The question arises whether, in taking on himself the cares of other persons, Epicurus was not departing from his rule of avoiding unnecessary cares and responsibilities. Bailey thinks that Epicurus was clear in his own mind. The wise man needs the security that he gets from surrounding himself with like-minded men and women: friends serve as a kind of bodyguard, providing a feeling of security even if their assistance is never needed. Although cultivated initially as a means to peace of mind, friendship proves desirable in itself because it gives rise to special pleasures that more than compensate for the trouble it costs. Thus, says Bailey, Epicurus is "consistently egoistic, and though in the matter of friendship there seems to be a momentary wavering toward altruism, it is not enough to disturb the general idea which has been formed."

De Witt, Norman W. *Epicurus and His Philosophy.* Minneapolis: University of Minnesota Press, 1954.

Shortly after Cyril Bailey's book was published, studies began to appear which undertook to reinterpret Epicurus in the light of his times, arguing that his aim was to free men's minds from the Platonic-Aristotelian view that morality is a branch of politics by putting forward a new view of man based on Aristotle's studies of organic life and on the literature of the Hippocratic school. Hailing these studies, Norman W. De Witt introduces his own book as an effort to rescue Epicurus from the injustice of centuries. An account of three of these "injustices" and of De Witt's attempt to correct them will indicate the line his argument takes.

First, historians have been wrong in thinking of Epicurus as an empiricist. Epicurus' second criterion of knowledge, says De Witt, should not be translated as "concept" but as "intuition," because it is the intuition that provides man with innate ideas such as those of justice and divinity. Moreover, according to De Witt, the method used by Epicurus in developing his view of nature was essentially deductive, modeled after that of Euclid. Twelve elementary principles (such as the principles that matter is uncreatable, that matter is indestructible, and that the universe consists of solid bodies and void), culled from the Presocratics, were for Epicurus theorems to be demonstrated, and they served as major premises for his polemic against the Platonists. For example, if the universe consists of solid bodies and the void, there is no place in it for Plato's eternal forms or Ideas.

Second, according to De Witt, it is wrong to think of Epicurus as a mechanist. Where earlier philosophers looked exclusively to celestial motions for their understanding of nature, Epicurus, profiting from Aristotle's study of organic nature, perceived man in the perspective of creative evolution, with a telos or end to which the cumulative experience of the race has taught him to conform.

Finally, De Witt argues, it is wrong to think of Epicurus as an egoist. De Witt finds in the writings of Epicurus different grades of altruism, ranging from general benevolence toward all men to the selfless commitment which binds close friends. Moreover, in this interpretation, Epicurus regarded justice, which he defined as the covenant that men shall not injure one another or be injured, as an innate idea adapting persons to life in society. De Witt suggests that data brought back from India by Alexander's scientific staff showing that elephants do not harm one another would have confirmed Epicurus in the belief that an embryonic idea of justice is present even in gregarious animals.

In sum, De Witt regards Epicurus as a humanistic reformer, equaled only by Auguste Comte. A passion for the increase of human happiness, De Witt writes, dominated all that Epicurus said and did and eventuated in a missionary cult which prefigured all that was best in Christianity.

Rist, J. M. *Epicurus: An Introduction.* Cambridge: Cambridge University Press, 1972.

In this short book, a leading scholar in the field of Hellenistic philosophy tries to bring English readers up to date on Epicurean studies. Much of Cyril Bailey's work, says J. M. Rist, has been superseded, and Norman W. De Witt's book, "essentially a work of special pleading," has failed to win scholarly acceptance. Rist calls his book an introduction because it aims only to set forth the basic tenets of

Epicurus and either avoids specialized problems of interpretation or relegates them to the appendix, where, for example, he discusses De Witt's claim that Epicurus believed in innate ideas. Much of the book has to do with Epicurus' physics, but chapters on pleasure and on friendship relate to his ethics.

Historians still argue over what Epicurus meant by pleasure and pain. Epicurus is on record as saying that we cannot conceive of the good apart from the pleasures of taste, sex, sound, and sight; but this view does not appear to be consistent with his frequent claim that the truest pleasure is not sensuous enjoyment but freedom from pain and anxiety. According to Rist, the apparent conflict is resolved if what Epicurus had in mind when he spoke of bodily pleasure was not the superficial enjoyment that accompanies physical gratification but the vital satisfaction that comes with relieving bodily wants. When Epicurus said that the root of every good is the pleasure of the stomach, possibly he meant no more than that the basic condition of a good life is that one not be hungry or thirsty, and that the person who has learned to avoid such pains and the fears that accompany them is in the best position to secure the pleasures of the mind. In any case, Epicurus' hedonism was of an unusual kind, enabling its author to say on his deathbed that, although experiencing intense pain in a part of his body, he was nevertheless enjoying supreme happiness, because, as Rist explains, "the atomic compounds in his mind and in the rest of his body . . . were free from pain."

Was Epicurus' hedonism egoistic? The answer, says Rist, depends on how we resolve the problem of friendship. The complication here referred to is partly historical—the problem of distinguishing between the views of Epicurus and those of his followers. The latter, in defending devotion to friends against the objections raised by rival schools, explained that although friendships are formed for the sake of personal advantage, they develop into purely altruistic forms so that a person comes to love the friend for the friend's own sake. That Epicurus argued in this way seems to Rist doubtful, for what Epicurus says is not that a man loves the friend for the other's sake but that friendship is desirable for its own sake. Even the latter claim poses problems in a philosopher who maintains that only pleasure is desirable in itself. Rist finds a possible way out of this difficulty by showing that, in the philosophical usage of the time, "desirable in itself" might be applied not merely to things that are ultimately valuable but also to things which lead "directly and without intermediaries" to the good pursued. This would permit us to say that Epicurus valued friendship not merely for the security it provides but also as giving rise to unique satisfactions. Although Epicurus clearly believed that, whatever anxieties and risks are attendant on it, friendship leads to some of the purest pleasures known to man, there is no reason to call these pleasures unselfish or to say that Epicurus was an altruist.

The subject of friendship calls to mind the society which Epicurus organized around himself at Athens, known as "the Garden," from the house-and-garden where close disciples lived and where others met for lectures. Women were members, and Rist suggests that there is no need to assume that relations between men and women were Platonic. More importantly, at a time when the polis had ceased to provide a meaningful social framework, Epicurus was establishing a new kind of society, drawn from every stratum of society—including slaves, "a sect with its own rules and its own standards of authority." This assertion of individual preferences over the traditional claims of the *polis* was, says Rist, truly revolutionary, a rejection of the basic assumptions of Hellenism.

Additional Recommended Reading

Epicurus. *Letters, Principle Doctrines, and Vatican Sayings.* Translated by R. M. Geer. Indianapolis: Bobbs-Merrill, 1964. The basic writings of Epicurus, with helpful notes.

Farrington, Benjamin. *The Faith of Epicurus.* New York: Basic Books, 1967. Leaning on De Witt's interpretation, the author finds affinities between Epicurus and Karl Marx.

Hicks, R. D. *Stoic and Epicurean*. New York: Charles Scribner's Sons, 1910. Chapter V gives the traditional interpretation of Epicurus' ethics.

Panichas, George A. *Epicurus*. New York: Twayne, 1967. An interdisciplinary approach. Includes an annotated bibliography.

TAO TE CHING

Author: Unknown (but erroneously attributed to Lao Tzu, born c. 600 B.C.)
Type of work: Metaphysics, ethics, political philosophy
First transcribed: Late third century B.C.

Principal Ideas Advanced

Tao, *the way, is the nameless beginning of things, the universal principle underlying everything, the supreme, ultimate pattern, and the principle of growth.*

If a man takes possession of the tao, *the universal principle, he becomes a Sage fit for ruling the world.*

By observing Nature man learns to follow Nature's way, the tao.

The man who possesses tao *must hide his power and appear soft and weak, for he who shows his power is without power; and the soft overcomes the hard.*

To attain tao *a man must return to the state of infancy, avoid action, and preserve the breath, the life-force, by breath control.*

Perhaps more than any other ancient Chinese text this work has been a center of philological dispute through the centuries. The first question is its authorship. Legend has identified a Li Erh of the seventh century B.C. as the writer, but more reliable historical records yield only a Li Erh of the fourth century B.C. who could not have done the things attributed to him by numerous biographical accounts, including having been born with a beard and having taught Confucius for a period. It seems that while the historical Li Erh (or another person named Tsung, of the third century B.C.) may have actually expounded some of the ideas in this work, the story is pure fiction that the legendary Li Erh (known as Lao Tan, or Lao Tzu) composed this book all by himself shortly before he vanished beyond the mountains on the back of a blue water buffalo. In fact the *Tao Te Ching* as it has come down to us contains many telltale features which point to its collective authorship; most probably it was not written by any single author, but has grown into its present shape.

An understanding about the authorship of this work is important for a proper grasp of the central ideas behind the eighty-one short but epigrammatic and sometimes cryptic chapters in this work. For however poetically integrated these ideas may be around the central theme of a mystic quietism that dates as far back as the dawning of Chinese history, there are passages in this book alluding to the many different schools of thought that contended for intellectual dominance in the early Warring States period (fifth to third century B.C.). The voice (or voices, hereafter called the "Taoist") speaking behind these epigrams is arguing against the Legalists (some call them Realists), the Confucians, and the Mohists, but the voice also seems to borrow some of the arguments of its rivals. The borrowings are possibly due both to the coexistence of these arguments, as part of the common knowledge of the intellectuals at the time this book was first put together, and to the subsequent interpolations of commentaries that became hopelessly enmeshed with the original text.

A vague notion of the "*tao*" existed among the proto-philosophical ideas in ancient China long before any Taoist, or Mohist, or Confucian expounded their respective views on this concept. It stemmed, apparently, from an early effort of the Chinese mind to search into the mystery of the universe and to discover the reason, if any, behind things. To name the unnameable, the Chinese borrowed this term, *tao*, or the "Way." The ambiguous nature of this term allows it to serve several doctrines. Hence to Confucius *tao* means the sage-king's way to social harmony; to Mo Ti, *tao* means the way to ample supply of staple foods and a populous state, and to Mencius, *tao* means the way to moral (and spiritual) perfection. But to a Taoist, *tao* could mean all these and more.

Throughout this work (and particularly in Chapter XXV), *tao* is described as the nameless beginning of all things, even prior to Heaven and Earth. *Tao* is unchanging and permeates everything; hence, *tao* must be a kind of constant, universal principle that underlies all phenomena. *Tao* has always existed and has no beginning of itself; hence, it must be comparable to the First Cause. Everything in the universe patterns itself after the dictates of a higher being, such as man patterning his ways after those of Heaven. But *tao*, being supreme, follows itself. Hence, it suggests the Ultimate Pattern. *Tao* "is so of itself," without any outside force or influence. Above all, *tao* is "always so" because it is the dynamic principle of change. It dictates the rhythm of growth and decay, but since it is itself the principle of growth it remains constant.

This is a frontal attack against the Legalist. The Legalist divides phenomena into rigid categories, and he demands that the rigidity of his system be maintained at all costs because he sees no other essence of anything except its name. The Taoist points out, in Chapter I, that the named are but the manifestations of essence. They are only the crust. What lies behind them is the real essence which is the source of all mysteries of the universe. In its application, the Taoist argument thus refutes the Legalist's emphasis on rules and regulations as the essential order of things.

As the First Cause and the Ultimate Pattern, *tao* possesses infinite power without being powerful. It does not force anything to follow its way; yet everything by virtue of being itself will of itself follow *tao,* just as water will ultimately flow downward. Any interruption of this Ultimate Pattern can be only temporary. Why, then, should a ruler employ force, as the Legalist insists he must, in order to conquer and reign over the world? Violence contrived by man is against *tao*; if only the king possesses *tao*, all the world will obey him; even Heaven and Earth will bless him and come to his aid.

The Taoist speaks metaphorically of *tao*, identify-ing it as the secret of all secrets, but he also goes on to suggest a way of comprehending *tao*. Since *tao* is the unchanging universal principle that dwells in everything, then everything in its original state reflects *tao*. In man the original state of existence, his infancy, comes closest to this idea. If man does not tamper with his heart (mind), so that his heart remains untainted, he has the best chance of comprehending this mysterious universal principle. Unspoiled, the *tao* in a tree trunk is as great and as efficacious as the *tao* filling the universe, so long as the tree trunk remains an "uncarved block." If carved, the block of wood becomes a few ordinary articles of daily use. But if man takes possession of the universal principle within an "uncarved block," he becomes a Sage fit for ruling the world.

Like the Confucians, the Taoist also talks about the Sages. But the Taoist Sage is not one who studies the classics, disciplines himself according to the rules of propriety, and preaches constantly to the rulers to be benevolent (as is recommended in Confucius' *Lun Yü*). On the contrary, the Taoist Sage has little use for words, because the words of *tao* are "simple and flavorless." He does not occupy himself with such useless motions as seeking audience with the rulers or teaching students, activities which kept the Confucians and the Mohists busy, because "*tao* never does, and yet through it all things are done." The life of the people becomes proportionately impoverished as Confucian rituals and decorum multiply; thieves and bandits redouble at the same rate as the laws are promulgated. The Taoist Sage "does nothing," and the people of themselves behave properly. The anti-intellectual attitude of the Taoist leads him to stress non-activity because only by refraining from useless motions can the state of the "uncarved block" be preserved.

Clearly Nature in its primeval stage is the best example of the "uncarved block." Consequently, unspoiled Nature is regarded by the Taoist as the best place to observe the revelation of the universal principle or *tao*. By observing Nature man learns to follow Nature's way, the way of *tao*. This acceptance of the way of Nature as inevitable and regular and normal leads to an attitude of resignation. It is not a negative attitude undertaken with a deep sigh of regret, but a joyful acceptance of what is the perfect pattern of things and events. The Taoist does not hesitate to discourage man's efforts to undo what Nature has done. He regards such efforts as useless even should man, out of his ignorance and perversion, attempt to disobey the universal principle revealed in Nature. *Tao* is like an immense boat that drifts freely and irresistibly according to its own will, the Taoist says, and thus man does well in avoiding butting his head uselessly against this huge boat, and by riding along in it. In this idea is found the seed of the Chinese concept that the strongest is he that makes use of his enemy's strength—a concept that finds its prosaic expression in the theory of Chinese boxing. Behind this concept lies the reason why the Taoist respects whatever appears to be soft, weak, and yielding.

The multiple metaphors in this work comparing the nature of *tao* to the secret, the "dark," and the "mysterious," are not merely poetic embellishment, but revelations of the strand of primitive quietism in Taoism. Among the proto-philosophical ideas of ancient China there is the notion of *yin-yang* (negative-positive, or female-male), a pair of mutually complementary forces that are at work in and behind all phenomena. The *yin* force or element is characterized as passive, receiving, and meek (at least in appearance). Yet like the idea of the female or mother, *yin* also possesses the potential of infinite creation. Hence the *yin* principle is closer to *tao*. *Tao* is compared to "a ravine that receives all things" and, therefore, has "unlimited power." In consonance with the *yin* characteristics, the man who possesses *tao* (a Sage) must hide his power, for he who shows his power is really without power. A Taoist Sage appears to be soft and weak because it is the "soft that overcomes the hard, and the weak, the strong," and because *tao* itself is unostentatious; *tao* "produces, clothes, and feeds" all beings without claiming mastery over them, yet everything submits itself to *tao*. For the same reason the Taoist praises the infant who is soft and weak and yet is most strong because in him the universal essence is not dissipated and the harmony of *yin* and *yang* is still perfect.

In this concept lies the Taoist relativity of attributes. To a Taoist nothing is absolute except *tao* itself.

Without "short," there cannot be "long." Thus, a Taoist dismisses the validity of the Dialecticians' effort to distinguish the white of a white horse from the white of a white jade. In doing so he also dismisses the Confucian effort to distinguish good from bad as useless trifling. Just as "long and short" have nothing to do with the essence of things, death and life are also two manifestations of what is so of itself (natural). To treasure the good, to prefer the rich, and to cherish life are equally meaningless, equally foolish to one having arrived at *tao*.

Since there is no real difference between acting and not acting, he who does nothing accomplishes most. This concept of non-activity, coupled with the idea that he who "moves not" endures the longest, strengthens the Taoist belief in quietism.

Throughout this book there are repeated hints at a process of attaining *tao*. The Taoist urges man to retain his untainted and untampered heart, and to return to a state of infancy, desirable because of its undissipated essence. The expression for "essence" here is *ch'i*. Generally understood as "gaseous matters," *ch'i* in ancient Chinese cosmology is closely tied in with "spirit" as distinguished from "physical substance." In man, *ch'i* is identified with breath as separate from flesh and bones. The Taoist regards man's *ch'i* as part of the universal *ch'i*, or man's life-force. Hence, to avoid dissipation man must attempt to preserve his life-force, and this effort turns out to be a process of breath control. Indeed the subsequent development of magical Taoism shows many features parallel to the esoteric Indian yoga. And practitioners of Taoist magic can always cite certain passages from this work for authority. For instance, there is at least one line (in Chapter LV) which tends to support the practice of sexual hygiene as a means of achieving *tao*.

Mysticism thickens around the Taoist when he claims that neither poisonous insects nor wild animals can harm the infant, or that by fixing one's gaze in meditation one can achieve longevity. Three aspects are involved in these claims. First, the Taoist actually believes in a certain kind of yoga practice to prolong this life on earth. Second, in the Taoist vocabulary, the word longevity may mean endurance. That which endures in man is his essence, being part of the universal essence. Man may die, but so long as he does not lose his essence, he actually endures. The manifestation of his essence may take different forms, such as a tree or a rock, but his essence remains unchanged, hence his longevity. Third, by promoting life-nurture, the Taoist stood opposed to another school of thought prevailing at that time. Led by a philosopher named Yang Chu, this school advocated total gratification of man's physical senses as the real goal of life and the road to salvation, a doctrine clearly contrary to the Taoist emphasis on quietism.

To be with *tao* is to be free, so the *Tao Te Ching* tells us. Such a man is free because he has the infinite power which enables him to do whatever he pleases while he stays within *tao*. Metaphysically this freedom should mean spiritual emancipation and salvation—a liberation of man from the bondage of his limited orbit in this earthly world. But it can readily be seen how a man with political ambitions or a magical bent of mind could make use of this theory. Thus, we read in this book the mystic references to "travels in spirit" which take a man with *tao* through space and time to ethereal realms. It has been suggested that this book must have had a southern Chinese origin as some passages in it allude to a southern setting; that is, to the south of the Yangtze River. That region was rich in shamanistic tradition, and a book of southern songs, collected at about the same time as the *Tao Te Ching*, contains descriptions of similar "spirit travels." It seems quite certain that these supernatural feats were part of the shamanistic belief common in the Warring States period along the middle reaches of the Yangtze River. The shamans induced trances with prayers and dances as well as through concentration and yoga-like hypnotism. Later in magical Taoism there appears a True Man, a Taoist adept at having acquired the powers to perform these superhuman feats.

As we have suggested, the *Tao Te Ching*, like most Chinese classics originating during the Warring States period, was intended to serve more as a political manual than as a purely metaphysical treatise. However, the metaphysical speculations in this book

are provocative enough to have inspired many developments—some occult, some seriously philosophical—in the history of Chinese thought. The cult of nature is one of them.

Nature in the *Tao Te Ching* is amoral because it is one manifestation of the universal essence. Nature does not house more *tao* than an infant or a tree trunk, yet Nature by its grandeur has a special appeal to the Taoist. The unchanging mountains, as contrasted with the changing affairs of man, symbolize for the Taoist the principle of nonactivity, and a calm lake expresses the idea of quietude. A profound appreciation of Nature, at once aesthetic and mystic, stems from this Taoist attitude and forms the basis of a cult of nature that has played an important role in Chinese poetry and art. In philosophy, the cult of nature became the native stock upon which Indian Mahayana Buddhism was grafted to bear the fruits of Chinese Ch'an (Zen) Buddhism.

Nature also has its violent moods. Its wild destructive forces must have been the inspiration behind the passage in the *Tao Te Ching* that refers to Heaven and Earth as unkind because "they treat all beings like straw dogs," or expendable sacrificial objects. But kindness has no place in *tao* which is "always so" and unchanging. The Taoist making the above remark is not criticizing Nature but rather is stating an actuality. This attitude has encouraged many people to embrace a political absolutism which they justify and defend with the claim that they have attained *tao*.

The esoteric elements in Taoism encouraged the accumulation of magical formulas and alchemy, and through the years they influenced a large area in Chinese folk religion. A city of Taoist gods has been constructed. A Taoist clerical and lay tradition and a library of Taoist scriptures have grown to impressive proportions.

The *Tao Te Ching* deserves credit as an enduring expression of basic Chinese Philosophy. The belief in the existence of a universal principle, having received such eloquent and poetic expressions in this book, leads contemplative minds to search for the profound and the true in Nature and in man himself.

Pertinent Literature

Lao Tzu. *The Way of Life: Lao Tzu.* Edited and translated by R. B. Blakney. New York: New American Library, 1955.

R. B. Blakney was for a long time a Christian missionary in China and had studied the *Tao Te Ching* for thirty years before rendering it into English. Because of its low-cost Mentor paperback edition and the author's fascinating writing style, it has become a most popular translation of the *Tao Te Ching*. In addition to translating the text, Blakney has written a long introduction and extensive paraphrases or comments under each poem (called "chapter" by other scholars).

Blakney consciously rejects *tao* as impersonal and calls it "proto-personal." With straightforwardness, he equates *tao* with the medieval conception of Godhead or Godness. He then calls his readers' attention to the saying of Jesus Christ, "I am the way. . . ." The identification of the Way of God, according to Blakney, has gained biblical support. Blakney may not be mistaken in this view; yet his theme is very misleading. If we interpret *tao* as God or as a Divine being, this is to force Chinese culture to be as religious as the Hebrew and the Hindu traditions. Such an interpretation will undermine the humanistic spirit of Chinese culture and the naturalistic flavor of Taoism. After all, there are striking differences between *tao* and God. First, *tao* is the embodiment of the principle of *wu-wei* or non-action, while God (as recorded in the *Old Testament*) is a deity of tremendous action. Second, a Christian prays to God, but a Taoist never prays to *tao*, which is never an object for worship. Third, Christians often talk about "the will of God," but Chinese people never speak of "the will of Tao." In short, *tao* is far from being a personal deity or a "proto-personal" being, as Blakney wants it to be. As to some philosophers' concept of God as a metaphysical principle, such a

principle is not much different from *tao*; yet the use of "God" in this sense is a violation of the ordinary use of language and thus may lead to confusion in our understanding of a different culture. Accordingly, the God-*tao* analogy is highly misleading and blocks the way to the understanding of Taoism.

The second topic concerns the label "mysticism." Blakney in his introduction regards Yang Chu as the first Chinese mystic and Chuang Chou as the second one. No doubt, from his viewpoint, the *Tao Te Ching* is a great classic of mysticism rather than a masterpiece in philosophy. The problem with Blakney's viewpoint is although religion has been an important cultural force in the West, it does not follow that it should possess the same weight in a non-Western culture. Nevertheless, the label "mysticism" is not entirely mistaken provided that we make a distinction between "religious mysticism" and "aesthetic mysticism" and apply the latter only to Taoism. Chinese culture is predominantly aesthetic and naturalistic. If we link mysticism to Chinese culture, we should be careful enough to make a distinction between the experience of a Christian mystic who had a union with God and the experience of a naturalistic poet who was self-forgettingly intoxicated with the radiance of the sunset. Only through this distinction can we grasp the unique nature of the *Tao Te Ching* as different from a religious scripture.

Blakney's contribution to the study of the *Tao Te Ching* is substantial and significant. His refreshing style certainly should encourage many students to continue serious studies of this masterpiece. His interpretation remains a cardinal example of how Chinese culture can be sympathetically understood by a religionist in Western culture.

Welch, Holmes. *The Parting of the Way: Lao Tzu and the Taoist Movement.* London: Methuen, 1958.

Holmes Welch's book is written with a dual purpose: to promote the understanding of Taoism as an important component of Chinese culture and to pre-

sent the philosophy of Lao Tzu with a consideration of its relevance to the contemporary world. About one fourth of this book (Part Two) is devoted to an exposition of the central themes of the *Tao Te Ching*.

Welch starts with the concept of *wu-wei* (inaction, non-action, and so on) which is the answer offered by Lao Tzu to the social and political problems of his time. *Wu-wei*, in Welch's interpretation, "does not mean to avoid all action, but rather all hostile, aggressive action." What is important is not the action itself, but the attitude behind the action. The attitude behind *wu-wei* is the ideal of *tz'u*—love in the sense of compassion and pity: "For the Christian love is the mainspring of action: for the Taoist it is ostensibly what makes inaction effective." Another implication of the principle of *wu-wei* is timeliness in action. With such a wisdom, one is able to solve a problem before it comes into being. A government of *wu-wei* is to rule by noninterference, together with the abolishment of capital punishment.

The next topic is the concept of "Uncarved Block" (*p'u*), which is one of the most common symbols in the *Tao Te Ching*. *P'u* means wood in its natural form before any craftsman works on it. This signifies the original state of human consciousness which is free from hostility and aggressiveness. What is further implied in this symbol is the near absence of desires, since primitive consciousness knows very little about social vanity or ambition of any kind. In addition, this symbol implies the rejection of public opinion. The Uncarved Block, as Welch sums up, is described by Lao Tzu as "blank, childlike, untutored, dark, nameless," and "to reach it is to 'know oneself,' to 'return to the root from which we grew.' "

The third and last theme in Welch's treatment is the concept of *tao*. Like R. B. Blakney, Welch relies heavily on his Christian background and knowledge

of mysticism in his interpretation. The criticism of Blakney can also apply, at least in part, to Welch. Nevertheless, Welch is quite aware of interpretations on a naturalistic and humanistic basis. Consequently he is free from the mistake of turning *tao* into a personal deity. For him, tao can be conceived as "the laws of nature, the God that exists by the argument from design; not identical with the universe and yet at work everywhere with it." In addition, "Tao is impersonal, 'unkind,' and beyond the reach of prayer." Then, because of his affinity with Christian mysticism, Welch cites the cases of such well-known mystics as St. Angela, St. Teresa, St. John of the Cross, and the authors of the *Upanishads*, emphasizing the similarities between mystical experience and sexual ecstacy. When he comes back to the *Tao Te Ching*, he could not find anything of the same kind because this Chinese classic does not offer any sexual imagery. Still, Welch attempts to establish Taoism as a form of mysticism. To regard Taoism as mysticism, however, is an error, for Chinese culture is fundamentally naturalistic and humanistic. The *Tao Te Ching* is a product of this culture and should be studied as a form of humanistic naturalism or naturalistic humanism.

In the main, in spite of some methodological inadequacies, Welch's book will continue to appeal to both scholars and laymen alike. His comprehensive knowledge of American culture and substantial background in Christianity has made his book attractive to the American general reader. It is a rare intellectual accomplishment by a Western scholar in promoting intercultural understanding and spiritual development for the contemporary world.

Wing-tsit Chan. *The Way of Lao Tzu (Tao Te Ching)*. New York: Bobbs-Merrill, 1963.

In Wing-tsit Chan's book we find substantial scholarship comprising painstaking research in history, philology, and philosophy. In addition to a translation which has synthesized recent scholarly discoveries in textual subtleties, Chan has provided three well-organized and clearly written informative essays: (1) The Philosophy of Tao, (2) Lao Tzu, the Man, and (3) *Lao Tzu*, the Book.

Chan's interpretation of *tao* is a naturalistic one

which is truthful to the character of Chinese culture. After a philological introduction, Chan exposes the metaphysical meanings of *tao* by quoting key passages from the text. Then he presents Han Fei's interpretation of *tao* as the unification of all principles operating in the universe. The concept "Tao as non-being," as Chan explains, is positive in character, although its linguistic form is negative. He then proceeds to analyze the concept of *wu-wei*, which is also positive in nature. In doing so, he is able to link metaphysics and theory of life together. In fact, from *wu* (non-being) to *wu-wei* (non-action), Chan sees a clear logical unity which has escaped many earlier scholars. Again, Chan cites many key passages from the text in the course of his explication. In the main, *wu-wei* is interpreted as "taking no artificial action, noninterference, or letting things take their own course." Chan's naturalistic interpretation is not alone, for he finds a similar viewpoint in the writings of Joseph Needham, who has equated *tao* with the Order of Nature.

After an exposition of the concept of *tao*, Chan explains other concepts of the text. First, *te* is interpreted as "Tao endowed in the individual things." Then he considers symbols such as "water," "the infant," "the female," "the valley," and "the uncarved block." As Chan rightly puts it, they are used as models or symbols for a life according to *tao*; they symbolize the life of simplicity. In addition, "weakness" is cherished as a virtue, of which "water" and "the female" are exemplars.

Scholars have in the past usually emphasized the striking differences between Lao Tzu and Confucius.

Chan does the opposite in order to correct the impression that the two are irreconcilable. After an exposition of their common points, Chan rightly concludes that "It is because of these and other similarities that Taoism and Confucianism run harmoniously parallel throughout Chinese history so that every Chinese is at once a Taoist and a Confucianist."

In addition, Chan has compared Lao Tzu with Chuang Tzu in terms of both differences and similarities. He has also commented on how the *Tao Te Ching* influenced Neo-Taoism, Buddhism, and Neo-Confucianism. He clarifies the distinction between philosophical Taoism and the Taoist religion by an exposition of the origin and development of the latter. In his conclusion, Chan points out that Taoist thinking is still alive among Chinese people today, in spite of the absence of a Taoist school, a book, a theory, or a single Taoist philosopher in the last thousand years.

In the main, Chan's book represents the most accomplished scholarship in the study of the *Tao Te Ching* available in English. It is a rewarding resource, essential for understanding Chinese culture and its philosophy.

Additional Recommended Reading

Chang Ch'i-chün. *Lao Tzu Che hsueh (The Philosophy of Lao Tzu)*. Taipei, Taiwan: Chêng Chung Book Company, 1969. A logically clear exposition by a leading Chinese scholar of the philosophical system implicit in the *Tao Te Ching*.

Chang, Chung-yüan. *Creativity and Taoism: A Study of Chinese Philsophy, Art, and Poetry*. New York: Julian Press, 1963. An interpretation of some practical and cultural aspects of Taoism. There is no sharp demarcation between Philosophical Taoism and the Taoist religion.

Chen, Ellen Marie. *Tao, Nature, Man: A Study of the Key Ideas in the Tao Te Ching*. Fordham University Thesis, 1966. Interesting thesis interpreting *tao* as Mother Nature.

Creel, H. G. *Chinese Thought: From Confucius to Mao Tsê-tung*. Chicago: University of Chicago Press, 1953. The doctrine of Taoism clearly summed up with thought-provoking discussion; lucidly written.

Fung Yu-lan. *A History of Chinese Philosophy*. Translated by Derk Bodde. Princeton, New Jersey: Princeton University Press, 1952-1953. Best history of Chinese philosophy available in English, containing a good summary of the philosophy of the *Tao Te Ching* in Chapter VIII.

Lau, D. C., tr. *Tao Te Ching*. Middlesex, England: Penguin Books, 1963. The translation is done with care, objectivity, and scholarship. The long introduction and lengthy appendix are very informative.

Lin Yutang, ed. and tr. *The Wisdom of Laotse*. New York: Modern Library, 1948. A very readable translation of the *Tao Te Ching*, interspersed with selections from the *Chuang Tzu* which serve as a kind of commentary on the text.

Waley, Arthur. *The Way and Its Power: A Study of the Tao tê Ching and Its Place in Chinese Thought*. London: George Allen & Unwin, 1934. An authoritative translation with a scholarly introduction on historical and linguistic questions. The view that *Tao Te Ching* is primarily a dialogue between quietists and realists (legalists) is too narrow.

Wu, Joseph. "Understanding Taoism: A Chinese Philosopher's Critique," in *Clarification and Enlightenment: Essays in Comparative Philosophy*. Washington, D.C.: University Press of America, 1978. This essay contains a criticism of some serious misconceptions about the *Tao Te Ching*, together with an original interpretation of the theory of *wu-wei* as "disinterested action."

DE RERUM NATURA

Author: Lucretius (Titus Lucretius Carus, c. 98-55 B.C.)
Type of work: Ethics, metaphysics, philosophy of nature
First transcribed: First century B.C.

Principal Ideas Advanced

Nothing is ever generated from nothing; nature consists of atoms moving in void.

Atoms naturally move downward, but when some swerve from their course, collisions occur; free will in human beings is a similar phenomenon.

Everything in nature is different from every other thing; the number of atoms of each shape is infinite, although the shapes of atoms are not infinite in number.

Sensed qualities are produced by combinations of atoms of various shapes, sizes, and weights.

The soul is composed of atoms; hence, at death the soul dies with the body.

Lucretius' *De rerum natura* (*On the Nature of Things*), by general agreement the greatest didactic poem in any language, is an exposition of the philosophy of Epicurus (about 340-270 B.C.). No divergence of doctrine, however minute, is to be found between Lucretius and his master.

After an invocation to Venus, symbolic of the loveliness, fruitfulness, and peace of nature, Lucretius eulogizes Epicurus as the deliverer of mankind from the superstitious terrors of religion: "When human life lay foul before the eyes, crushed on the earth beneath heavy religion, who showed her face from the regions of heaven, glowering over mortals with horrible visage, first a Greek man dared to lift mortal eyes against her and to stand up to her; neither stories of gods nor thunderbolts nor heaven with menacing growl checked him, but all the more they goaded the spirited manliness of his mind, so that he longed to be first to break through the tight locks of nature's portals. Thus the lively force of his mind prevailed, and he journeyed far beyond the flaming walls of the world and traversed the whole immensity with mind and soul, whence victorious he reports to us what limit there is to the power of each thing, and by what law each has its boundary-stone set deep. And so religion in turn is cast down under foot and trampled; the victory exalts us to heaven." (This is,

of course, a great exaggeration of Epicurus' place in the history of free thought.)

Men make themselves miserable through fear of divine caprice in this life, and of hellfire after it. Lucretius argued that the one comes from ignorance of the workings of nature, the other from the false belief in an immortal soul. The cure for both is understanding of materialist philosophy. "Thus of necessity this terror of the mind, these darknesses, not the rays of the sun nor the bright arrows of daylight will disperse, but nature's aspect and her law."

You may think, says Lucretius to Memmius (the Roman official to whom the poem is dedicated), that the materialist philosophy is unholy. Not so: "On the contrary, that very religion has very often given birth to criminal and impious deeds." For instance, the sacrifice of Iphigenia by her father. "*Tantum religio potuit suadere malorum!*—so much of evil has religion been able to put over!"

The first law of nature is: "Nothing is ever generated from nothing, by any divine force." This Lucretius takes to be amply proved by experience. If something could come from nothing, then anything could beget anything, or things would pop up out of season, or grown men and trees would appear all at once. The observed regularity of birth and growth implies fixed seeds of all things, or in other words sufficient causes of all that happens. Nor can anything disappear into nothing; if it could, then already in the infinity of time nothing would be left. "By no means then do any of the things that are seen perish utterly; since Nature refashions one thing out of another, nor permits anything to be born unless aided by the death of something else."

Nature consists of atoms ("seeds," "beginnings"—Lucretius does not use the Greek word) too small to be seen, but nevertheless real; the winds, odors, heat, and cold show that real things can be invisible, while the drying of wet clothes and the gradual wearing away of rings and stones proves that the things we can see are made of tiny particles. Since things move, there must be void space for them to move in. Visible objects contain much void, as is proved by differences in density and by the free passage through apparently solid objects of heat and sound, of water through rocks, and of food through the tissues of the body. Besides atoms and void, there is no third kind of thing; everything else that has a name is either an essential or accidental property of these two.

Atoms are absolutely solid, containing no void within them, hence internally changeless. If they were not, there would be no large-scale objects left by now, for all would have been pulverized in infinite time. Moreover, if things were infinitely divisible, then the sum of things and the least thing would be equal, both containing an equal, since infinite, number of parts—an absurd situation (says Lucretius).

After refuting (what he takes to be) the rival theories of Heraclitus, Empedocles, and Anaxagoras, Lucretius proceeds to prove that the universe is infinite in space. Suppose it were not: then if you went to the edge of it and shot an arrow, what would happen? Either the arrow would stop, because there was something beyond to stop it, or it would not, and again there would be space beyond the presumed boundary. The number of atoms in infinite space is also infinite, for since their general tendency is to fly apart, a finite number in infinite space would have so spread out by now that the average density would be near zero, which is against observation. There is no center to the world, and no antipodes. (All the ancient atomists

continued to hold that the earth is a flat disc, even though schools such as the Pythagoreans and Aristotelians, less scientific in their general principles, had long known better.)

Book I concludes with a famous passage, more applicable to the progressive nature of science than to the fossilized dogmas of Epicureanism: "These things you will learn thus, led on with little trouble; for one thing will grow clear from another, nor will blind night snatch away the road and not let you perceive Nature's ultimates. Thus things will kindle lights for things."

The proem to Book II is the longest ethical passage in the poem, depicting the peaceful serenity of the Epicurean's life, contrasted with the troubled existence of the unenlightened, who in getting and spending lay waste their powers.

Atoms move either by their own weight or by blows from other atoms. Left to themselves, atoms move "downward" (what down means in an infinite, centerless universe we are not told), all at the same speed, faster than light, because the void offers no resistance. No atom, then, would ever have hit another, if it were not for the fact that "at quite an uncertain time and at uncertain places they push out a little from their course." Thus one hits another, the second a third, and so on. Lucretius also employs this "swerve," which is supposed to occur not just "in the beginning" but even now, to account for free will in human beings—in the same way, and as irrelevantly, as some philosophers now try to buttress free will with Heisenberg's uncertainty principle. (Both are irrelevant because whatever we mean by free will, we certainly do not mean capriciousness.)

Everything in nature is different from every other thing: each lamb knows its own mother, one blade of wheat is not exactly like the next. The atoms too differ in their shapes. Lightning, though it is fire, "consists of more subtle and smaller figures." Honey is sweet because, being made of smooth and round bodies, it caresses the tongue and palate, while the hooked atoms of wormwood tear them. (According to atomism, all the senses are varieties of touch.) The *shapes* of atoms are not infinite in number. If they were, Lucretius infers, there would have to be some that were of enormous size. However, the number of atoms of each shape is infinite. Not every kind of particle can link with every other—that would produce monstrosities.

All combustibles contain particles capable of tossing fire abroad. Anything, such as a fruit, that has color, taste, and smell, must contain at least three kinds of constituent atoms. But no atom *by itself* has color, savor, or odor; the properties of atoms are simply solidity, size, shape, and weight. Colors and the other sensed qualities are products of atomic *arrangements*. If colors were embedded in the ultimate constituents of matter, we should be unable to account for their rapid changes without violating the principle nothing-from-nothing. (This is the main point of superiority of ancient atomism to the other schools of "physics.") Lucretius has another argument: since color, as we know, is not essentially bound up with the shape of a thing, if atoms were themselves colored, we should expect all visible things to exist in all possible colors, "even black swans!"

Nor are individual atoms endowed with consciousness. For (1) sense depends on vital motions, and hence depends on birth; (2) heavy blows can produce unconsciousness, which ought not to happen if consciousness were independent of atomic arrangements; (3) pain is the result of a disturbance, but an atom cannot be (internally) disturbed; for (4) otherwise we should be led to all sorts of absurdities, such as that not only a man but his semen would be conscious.

Lucretius makes brilliant use of the atomistic principle that just as an indefinitely large number of meanings can be conveyed by rearranging the few letters of the alphabet, "so also in things themselves, when motion, order, position, and figure are changed, the things also are bound to be changed."

There are other worlds, like this one, in the infinite universe. Indeed, the vastness and complexity of the universe is itself proof that the whole is not governed by gods: it would be too much for them. Or, if you assume intellects adequate for the task, it then becomes inexplicable why there is evil and confusion in the world.

Growth and decay pertain to worlds as much as to individuals. The vital powers of this earth are wearing out. "Indeed, already the broken and effete earth has difficulty in creating little animals, though it once created all the kinds at once, and gave birth to the huge bodies of wild beasts."

Lucretius distinguishes between the mind (*animus, mens*) which is what thinks in us, and the soul (*anima*), which is the vivifying principle: "seeds of wind and hot vapor, which take care that life shall stay in the limbs." Both, of course, are made of atoms, "extremely subtle and minute." They form a unity: "mind and soul are joined to each other and form one nature, but the chief, so to speak, that which rules the whole body, is the Reason. . . . It is situated in the middle region of the chest." Besides atoms of wind, air, and hot vapor, the mind also contains a fourth, unnamed kind of atom, "than which nothing finer or more mobile exists." This "very soul of the whole soul" has to be postulated to account for consciousness, which is the motion of this superfine substance. (Lucretius is a consistent materialist; consciousness is not for him an unexplained product of atomic motions, distinct from them, but, like color, an "accident" of atoms of a certain kind in a certain arrangement. In other words, consciousness is an atomic process.)

Souls differ in their compositions: lions have more heat, deer more wind, oxen more air. Men differ from one another likewise, their temperaments depending on the makeup of their souls. But Lucretius is quick to add: "So tiny are the traces of the natures, which Reason could not dispel from us, that nothing prevents us living a life worthy of the gods."

The soul particles are few in number compared to those of the flesh, as we know from our inability to sense very slight stimuli.

It follows from the atomic nature of the soul that it is dispersed at death; hence consciousness ceases. Lucretius deems this point so important that he reinforces it with a multitude of observations. Lucretius points out that understanding grows with the body and decays with it; that the soul is affected by bodily diseases, besides having some of its own; that mental ills can be cured by material medications; that "dying by pieces" in paralysis, and the twitches of recently severed limbs, show that the soul is divisible and therefore destructible; that there must be *some* soul-fragments left in the body after death, to account for the generation of worms in the corpse; that if the soul is immortal, we should remember our past existences (to the ancients, the immortality of the soul implied preexistence as much as life *post mortem*) and to reply that it loses its memory at the shock of birth "is not, I think, to stray very far from death." Animals have souls appropriate to their bodily constitutions; this is odd on the transmigration hypothesis, even if restricted to intraspecies reincarnations. And it is not only incomprehensible, but ridiculous, that souls should queue up to get into a body. In general, each thing has its appointed place: that of the soul is the body. If the soul were immortal, there would be a tremendous grotesqueness in its being so intimately linked with a mortal thing (as Lucretius contends elsewhere, there could never have been any centaurs, because the disparity in growth rates between the limbs of equine and human beings render them incompatible). Immortal things are so because they cannot be assaulted (atoms), or because they offer no resistance to blows (void), or because there is no room for them to scatter; none of these applies to the soul.

Thus fears of hell are foolish. "Death, therefore, is nothing to us, nor does it concern us in the least, inasmuch as the nature of the mind is held to be mortal. And just as we felt no ill in time gone by when the Carthaginians came from all quarters to the attack, when all things under the high shore of heaven shook and trembled in horror at the fearful tumult of war, and it was in doubt to which of them would fall the rule of all things human by land and sea—so, when we shall not exist, when there shall have been a parting of body and soul by whose union we are made one, you may know that by no means can anything happen to us, who will then not be, nor move our feeling; not if earth is confounded with sea and sea with sky."

The theory of vision in atomism is that objects constantly throw off "idols" or "semblances," very thin films, of which the snake's discarded skin furnishes an example. Such "idols" enter the eye and jostle the atoms of the mind, resulting in vision. The less said about this doctrine—which, as ancient critics pointed out, cannot even explain why we cannot see in the dark, or how we can get the "idol" of an elephant into our eye—the better. Though we may remark that while the Epicurean theory is patently false and ridiculous, its ancient rivals are unintelligible.

All perceptions are true, according to the Epicureans, even those in imagination and dreams—which are perceptions of finer idols that enter the body otherwise than through the eyes. It is in inferences from perception that errors arise. Epicurus consequently held that the gods really do exist, since they are perceived in dreams. They live in the peaceful spaces between the worlds, in "quiet mansions that winds do not shake, neither do clouds drench them with rainstorms nor the white fall of snow disturb them, hardened with bitter frost; ever a cloudless sky covers them, and smiles with light widely diffused." The gods are, in short, ideal Epicureans. The mistake of men is in their false inferences that these beings trouble themselves with *us*, or even know of our existence. *True* (Epicurean) religion consists in taking these blessed beings as models and making one's own life, as far as possible, like theirs.

In discoursing of perception and imagination, Lucretius takes the opportunity to state another important principle of materialist philosophy, the denial of purposive causation. One must not suppose that our organs were created *in order* to perform their appropriate functions: this is "back-to-front perverse reasoning, for nothing at all was born in the body so that we might be able to use it, but what is once born creates its own use."

This book concludes with a discussion of sex, genetics, and embryology, containing the magnificent (but misguided) denunciation of the passion of love as "madness." It is best (we are told) not to fall in love at all; but if you do, you can still be saved if only you will open your eyes to "all the blemishes of mind and body of her whom you desire."

The world was not created by the gods. Suppose they set out to create a world, where could they get the plan for it otherwise than through observation of nature? We are to understand the origin of the world this way: "So many beginnings of things, of many kinds, already from infinite time driven on by blows and by their own weights, have kept on being carried along and hitting together, all trying to unite in all ways, creating whatever conglomerations were possible among them, so that it is no wonder that they have fallen into those dispositions also and come through those passages by which the present sum of things is carried on by renewal." But even if we knew nothing of this concourse of atoms, we ought still to reject the hypothesis of divine creation, on account of the many evils in the world. Most of the earth is uninhabitable sea, mountain, and desert; what can be lived in requires laborious clearing and cultivation, the fruits whereof are uncertain. Why are there wild beasts, diseases, untimely deaths, the helplessness of human infancy?

The world is young, for discoveries—such as the Epicurean philosophy—are still being made. The heavy earth-seeds came together and squeezed out the smoother and rounder which went to make sea, stars, sun, and moon. Lucretius gives five alternative explanations of the revolutions of the heavens; one is free to take his choice, as long as gods are not introduced. The sun and moon are about the size they appear to be (whatever that may mean).

First bushes appeared on the earth's surface, then trees, then, by spontaneous generation, birds and beasts. " Wherever there was an opportune spot, wombs grew, grasping the earth with their roots." Many monsters (though no centaurs) came out of them; in the end, all perished except those few that were capable of feeding and protecting themselves and begetting offspring. (While this account contains the notion of survival of the fittest, it is hardly an improvement over the fantasies of Empedocles, and distinctly inferior to the evolutionary speculations of Anaximander, who in the sixth century B.C. had already freed himself from the prejudice of fixity of species.)

Lucretius next proceeds to a reconstruction of the history of civilization. This passage, which has nothing to do with atomist principles, is a marvel of shrewd deduction, confirmed in almost all its details by modern anthropology and archaeology. His principle of reasoning is that certain discoveries could not

have been made unless others had preceded them; for example, woven textiles must have come after iron, which is necessary for making various parts of the loom. (Of course he was mistaken—but the method is promising.)

Fire came first, and made possible stable family relationships and the development of human sympathy. "Then too neighbors began to join in friendship, anxious neither to harm nor be harmed among themselves." Language arose in these primitive societies, first as mere animal cries, but developing by the assignment of conventional names. Then kings and cities, and property and gold. Then revolts against absolute rulers, leading to the rule of law. Religion, unfortunately, also arose.

Metallurgy was discovered accidentally: first that of copper, silver, and gold, later bronze and iron.

Though this account, quite unlike most ancient philosophies, shows a knowledge of technology and of the idea of progressive development, Lucretius did not consider material progress an unalloyed blessing. Life was on balance no more secure in his day than in times of savagery; then one might be eaten by a wild beast, but one did not have looting armies to contend with. Then one might have poisoned oneself through ignorance; but for Lucretius the danger was that someone else might poison you very skillfully. Lucretius the materialist wrote: " Thus the race of men labors always in vain, and uses up its time of life in idle cares, truly because it has not learned what the limit of getting is, nor at all how far true pleasure can increase. And this, little by little, has raised life up to the height and stirred up from below the great tides of war."

Book VI consists of miscellaneous Epicurean "explanations" of phenomena such as thunder, lightning, and earthquakes, the natural causes of which need to be understood lest they provide material for religion to frighten us with. The poem, left unfinished at its author's death, ends abruptly after a translation of Thucydides' description of the plague at Athens in the second year of the Peloponnesian War.

Pertinent Literature

Latham, R. E. "Introduction," in Lucretius' *Lucretius: The Nature of the Universe*. Baltimore: Penguin Books, 1951.

In his Introduction to his translation of Lucretius, R. E. Latham emphasizes that the perspective expressed by *On the Nature of the Universe* (or: *On the Nature of Things*) developed in a particular type of social milieu. The city-state ideals of liberty, democracy, and national self-sufficiency had lost their attractiveness in a context characterized by despotism and economic and social disorder. The gods retained their institutions without inspiring genuine confidence. Plato and Aristotle seemed no longer relevant. In this setting, Epicurus "preached his gospel of salvation by common sense."

Latham finds the Epicureanism Lucretius expounds "the simplest of all philosophies." It holds, Latham notes, that all the knowledge we have is gained through sensory experience. (How we could know this is so, if it were true—how its being true is compatible with its being known—is not explained.) Nevertheless, things are not quite as we perceive them but as we would perceive them were our sensory capacities greater. Since physical objects are perceived, Latham continues, Lucretius concludes that they exist. That wind also exists, but is not perceived visually, does not, for Lucretius, give grounds for supposing that something exists which is immaterial, or radically different from physical objects. Rather, Latham explains, Lucretius suggests that one can form a picture of the wind as comprised of physical particles, albeit particles too small to be perceived, like smaller versions of flecks of dust in a shaft of sunlight. Enough of such tiny particles beating upon a branch would account for the branch's movements. (A picture so used becomes, in effect, a model which is conceived as a large-scale representation isomorphic with the microstates it represents and renders intelligible.) Thus, Latham notes, Lucretius endeavors to explain whatever exists by reference to (sometimes very small) physical objects, plus space conceived as the absence of objects.

As Latham explains, this requires Lucretius, in all consistency, to adopt particular sorts of positions on a wide variety of issues. He views the mind, for example, as a set of very mobile particles; these particles form patterns in accord with images which, caused by physical objects, impinge upon them. And, Latham continues, Lucretius supposes that the only thing that is good is pleasurable sensation. Thus Lucretius embraces mind-body materialism in metaphysics and hedonism in ethics. Further, Latham notes, Lucretius denies the existence of God and of any intelligent cause of order in the universe, thinking any such view to be a delusion, and he rejects both polytheism and monotheism.

These Epicurean dogmas, Latham suggests, of course have a history, and Lucretius' positions have their historical predecessors. His materialism resembles, and is influenced by, the atomism of the fifth century B.C. writers Leucippus and Democritus. But, Latham contends, one can understand Lucretius without tracing his historical debts. The positions of Epicurus, and so the positions of Lucretius, can be understood as an effort to hold only positions compatible with all knowledge being gained through sensory perception, expressed without any qualifications concerning such extensions of the senses as telescopes and microscopes and the other instruments of science provide—without qualification, that is, save the qualification concerning the acuteness of our senses, noted above.

Epicurus and Lucretius believed that the pagan deities existed, Latham admits, but they had little interest in them; essentially, these philosophers were enemies of the religion of their day with its omens and taboos. Rather, nature itself, without purpose or mind, but orderly and beautiful, received their religious emotions.

In one respect, Latham notes, the Epicurean system seems to involve a metaphysical claim. Lucretius asserts that human beings have freedom of choice. He reasons, Latham in effect suggests, that since human beings, according to this view, are entirely comprised of atoms, if their movements are simple functions of the movements of these atoms, and if these movements are entirely determined, then there is no movement (and so no action) that is other than determined. Hence, it must be the case that (influenced by human choice) some atoms, some times, must swerve somewhat from the path to which they were otherwise ordained.

Nevertheless, Latham tells us, the system is purely materialistic. When ideas or worries are given spatial location in the breast, this is to be construed literally. (Whether claims ascribing spatial location to mental states are coherent can be, and has been, doubted, but this is not our question here.) Further, Latham continues, the same applies to his claim that the source of all thought is composed of heat, air, and wind, plus an unnamed further element, and is located in the breast. The same mixture, although less concentrated, Lucretius conceives to be diffused throughout the limbs; here, too, Latham suggests, we are to take Lucretius literally.

Latham suggests that Lucretius holds that the truth about the nature of things is not hard to discern, and not very different from what it appears to the unaided senses to be. This, Latham contends, aids the expression of his views in pictorial language. And, as distinctions not based on sensory experience are not, for Lucretius, such that it is part of the human essence to make them, Lucretius will at least be free from the temptation to regard such distinctions, being abstract, as therefore being universal or self-evidently true.

Cochrane, Charles N. *Christianity and Classical Culture*. New York: Oxford University Press, 1944.

Charles N. Cochrane sets the thought of Epicurus, as expressed by Lucretius, in its historical context. He reports that in the society to which Lucretius presented Epicurus' thought (Epicurus' dates are 341-270 B.C., Lucretius' dates are 99-55 B.C.) traditional restraints had been thrown aside. The members of the aristocracy, Cochrane tells us, sought new forms of experience and allowed themselves the fullest range of luxury and vice; they sought pleasure in decadence. For others, Cochrane notes, who were not aristocrats, bread and circuses provided a substitute for rich banquets. All in all, Cochrane says, there was "a riot of sensationalism and emotionalism" which promoted political competition and social disintegration.

Cochrane informs us that Lucretius presents "the gospel of Epicurus" to this "distracted world." Lucretius, in Cochrane's opinion, expounds Epicurus charmingly and persuasively with an intent to show the way out of the reigning anarchy. Cochrane sees Lucretius as trying to elicit an order and understanding that rested on a system of thought which could serve as a basis for human life.

He notes that Lucretius traces the cause of the evils and sufferings of his day to belief in the traditional pagan gods. He regards these evils as prompted by a desire to obtain the favor or escape the anger of these beings, who were thought not only to exist but also to control the fate of human beings. Thus, he reports, Lucretius holds that human ills result from hopes and fears which are unreasonable, being based on mistaken views about the world. Lucretius desires to replace such views by an Epicurean science for which ultimate reality—that which depends for its existence on nothing external to or distinct from itself—contains only simple material atoms moving in the void. As Cochrane suggests, such a world is not one in which there is need to placate or propitiate autocratic but invisible rulers of our destinies. As replacement for prior religious aspirations, emancipation from terror of the invisible is offered.

Lucretius insists, Cochrane continues, that such emancipation will not be produced by following desires, but by following reason. More carefully, it will be produced by a rational patterning of one's life in which one seeks the concrete satisfactions of life in the usual human relationships rather than in concourse with the gods. The criterion for satisfactions, Cochrane notes, is, for Lucretius, presence of individual pleasure and absence of individual pain.

As Cochrane presents it, Lucretius' recommendation involves submitting unprotestingly to the mechanical laws in accordance with which nature operates and which are discoverable by observation. This doctrine depends, Cochrane says, on not having concern for the morrow—it involves cutting "the nerve of effort." While he describes Lucretius' purpose in terms of "salvation through enlightenment," he also suggests that the Lucretian perspective provides not a stimulant but a sedative whose purpose was to provide a cure for the ills of imperial society.

This, Cochrane continues, involved Lucretius in seeking for solutions to "the Roman problem" (of decadent disorder), not in Roman, but in Greek thought. This problem was ultimately moral and psychological. To solve it, Cochrane suggests, Lucretius relies on a Greek science which provides his basis for developing an ethic. (The science in question, of course, was Greek atomism in which the world is conceived as comprised of indivisible material atoms in a void.) Lucretius thus not only views nature as mechanistic and as not run by deities, but also views both society and individual as nondivine, removing the aura of mystery from both. In so doing (no doubt with the scientific atomism in mind), Cochrane contends that Lucretius sponsors a sort of moral atomism in which there is no adequate restraint on private choice and no satisfactory ground for social and political cohesion. While hardly anarchistic in intent, Lucretius' (and Epicurus') perspective, Cochrane feels, puts society under suspicion of being the cause of dissatisfactions not present in persons who are uninfluenced by an organized empire. It made nonpolitical ends the aim of human action and found the state to be no more than an economic expedient. This, Cochrane suggests, involved a repudiation of the Roman past and the rejection of a distinctively Roman future.

Lucretius, Cochrane concludes, was the first to appeal only to (a conception of) reason and nature in an attempt to solve the Roman problem, and he thus focused the dispute on principles rather than prejudices; in effect, he issued a challenge to alternative systems of thought to answer his arguments, if possible, on similar terms—a challenge, Cochrane asserts, that Cicero accepted.

Additional Recommended Reading

Bevan, E. R. *Stoics and Sceptics.* New York: Oxford University Press, 1913. An older work by a Gifford Lecturer and first-rate scholar.

Bréhier, Émile. *The Hellenistic and Roman Age.* Translated by Wade Baskin. Chicago: University of Chicago Press, 1965. A discussion of Epicureanism and Roman and Greek philosophy generally.

Cornford, F. M. *Principium Sapiente.* Edited by W. K. C. Guthrie. New York: Harper & Row Publishers, 1965. Subtitled "A Study of the Origins of Greek Philosophical Thought," with many references to Lucretius.

De Witt, Norman W. *Epicurus and His Philosophy.* Cleveland: Meridian Books, 1967. De Witt argues that Epicureanism is an important bridge between Greek philosophy and Christianity.

Latham, R. E. "Lucretius," in *The Encyclopedia of Philosophy.* Edited by Paul Edwards. Vol. V. New York: Macmillan Publishing Company, 1967. A brief discussion of Lucretius' views with a short bibliography.

Rose, H. J. *Religion in Greece and Rome.* New York: Harper and Brothers, 1959. A general discussion of the varieties of Greek and Roman religion.

DISCOURSES and MANUAL

Author: Epictetus (c. 65-c. 135)
Type of work: Ethics
First transcribed: c. 120

Principal Ideas Advanced

The good life is a life of inner tranquillity which comes from conforming to nature—to reason and to truth.
To achieve the good life a man must master his desires, perform his duties, and think correctly concerning himself and the world.
To master desire one has only to bring desires to the level of facts; only what is within a man's power should be of concern to him.
Every man has a duty to others because each man is a citizen of the world, one of its principal parts.
To discover one's duty one should be skilled in elementary logic, in the art of disputation, and in the right use of names.

So far as is known, Epictetus left no philosophical writings. The *Discourses* (or *Diatribes*) is a transcription of some of his lectures made by a pupil, Arrian. Originally there were eight books, of which only four are known to us. The *Manual* (or *Encheiridion*), a condensed selection from the *Discourses*, was also composed by Arrian. The *Manual* is a good résumé of Epictetus' main doctrines, but the Discourses is rewarding for the vivid picture it calls up of Epictetus as a teacher. It catches the vigor and warmth of a wise and witty man in the act of expounding his philosophy informally. He wore his technical equipment lightly as he answered questions concerning practical difficulties, pointed out dangers in contemporary customs, and delivered short homilies suggested by current events.

For Epictetus, the goal of philosophy is not so much to understand the world as to achieve the good life, which, for him, consisted in inner tranquillity. The Stoics, of whom he was a representative, had a well-developed philosophy of nature, based on the Heraclitean doctrine that Logos or Reason governs all change. They were also competent logicians. But their chief interest lay in personal ethics, in which they applied a knowledge of physics and logic. Inner serenity, they held, consists in conforming to nature,

or, which is the same thing, following reason, or, again, discovering and living by the truth. Epictetus alluded to logic from time to time, but only rarely mentioned philosophy of nature. When he spoke of philosophy, he meant "philosophy of life." In his view, the philosopher is the wise man.

Three stages in the achievement of the good life were noted by Epictetus. The first has to do with mastering one's desires, the second with performing one's duties, and the third with thinking correctly concerning one's self and the world. He complained that students are prone to neglect the first two, which are the most important, and to overvalue the third, because students are less concerned with achieving moral excellence than with gaining a reputation as disputants. As a result, the world is flooded with vain, passionate, fault-finding fellows who have so little self-mastery that a mouse can frighten them to death; yet they boast the name of philosopher.

Epictetus put the mastery of desires first because he regarded the main business of philosophy to be the achievement of a tranquil mind. In his view, all perturbations are the result of a disproportion between our wills and the external world. The natural man supposes that happiness is possible only when the external world comes up to his expectations. The philosopher knows that this condition rarely exists, that if we build on any such hope, we are doomed to endless sorrow, which in turn leads to envy and strife. Instead of trying to bring the world up to our desires we should bring our desires to the level of actuality. Happily, this is quite within the realm of possibility because our wants are in our power, as external things are not.

In effect, the philosopher tells himself that things which are not in his power are matters of indifference, and all that matters is the use he can make of them. He may be exiled—that he cannot prevent— but does any man hinder him from going with smiles? He must die—but must he die lamenting? His leg may be fettered—but not even Zeus can overpower his will.

Epictetus recognized the difference between saying these things and doing them, and he sought various means of inculcating the habits of self-mastery. A man should daily write and meditate on extreme situations, such as how to comport himself if a tyrant puts him to torture. When enjoying anything, he should form the habit of calling up contrary appearances; for example, when embracing his child, let him whisper, "Tomorrow you will die." To overcome passions, such as anger, let each one keep a day-book in which he writes down every offense. Such are the concerns in which the philosopher ought to employ most of the time he has for thinking. "Study not to die only, but also to endure torture, and exile, and scourging, and, in a word, to give up all which is not your own." Without such practice, a man will not be prepared when unexpected trials descend upon him.

Epictetus liked to speak of the "handles" which things present to us. "Everything has two handles, the one by which it may be borne, the other by which it may not." He cited the example of a man whose brother uses him unjustly: if the man thinks of the injustice, he will not bear it; if he thinks of him as a brother, he will.

This illustration affords a good transition to the second of Epictetus' main concerns—namely, duty. It was an important part of his teaching that man is not a detached entity, but part of a whole. In a passage which is quite similar to one in the writings of St. Paul

(I Corinthians XII), he compares man to one of the organs of the human body: "Do you know that as a foot is no longer a foot if it is detached from the body, so you are no longer a man if you are separated from other men? For what is a man? A part of a state, of that which first consists of gods and men; then of that which is called next to it, which is a small image of the universal state." The whole duty of man is inscribed here. Man is, as Epictetus liked to say, "a citizen of the world," and not one of the subservient parts—like the lower animals—but "one of the principal parts, for you are capable of comprehending the divine administration and of considering the connection of things." The lower creatures fulfill their functions without knowing what they do. It is the prerogative of man to understand the "connection of things." And in these connections lie his duties.

"Duties," Epictetus said, "are universally measured by relations." Among the most important for the ordinary person he listed: "engaging in public business, marrying, begetting children, venerating God, taking care of parents, and generally, having desires, aversions, pursuits of things and avoidances, in the way in which we ought to do these things, and according to our nature." The Cynics, who were in some respects the predecessors of the Stoics, used to oppose nature to society and to make a great issue of obeying the former and flouting the latter. That the Stoics of Epictetus' day should see their way to including society as part of nature is noteworthy.

But Epictetus was not ready simply to follow conventional conceptions as to what our duties are. The view that man was a citizen of the cosmos before he was a citizen of Rome has important implications. One of these is that all men, in virtue of possessing reason, are "sons of Zeus." Another is that all men are brothers. To the slave-owner, he said, "Will you not bear with your own brother, who has Zeus for his progenitor, and is like a son from the same seeds and of the same descent from above? . . . Will you not remember who you are, and whom you rule, that they are kinsmen, that they are brethren by nature, that they are the offspring of Zeus?" Conversely, the fact that a man happened to wear the emperor's crown was, in itself, no reason for obeying him. One must examine the stamp on the coin, whether it be that of a Trajan—gentle, sociable, tolerant, affectionate—or that of a Nero—passionate, resentful, violent.

As we have duties toward our fellows, so, said Epictetus, we have duties toward the gods: "to have right opinions about them, to think that they exist, and that they administer the All well and justly; and you must fix yourself in this principle, to obey them, and yield to them in everything which happens, and voluntarily to follow it as being accomplished by the wisest intelligence." Epictetus spoke of the place appointed to an individual as being like the role assigned an actor. The actor should not complain about the role—whether it is the part of a lame man or of a magistrate. "For this is your duty, to act well the part that is given to you; but to select the part belongs to another." In another figure, he spoke of God as resembling a trainer of wrestlers who matches his athletes with suitable partners in order to bring out the best in them. Difficulties, in other words, are designed to test our souls. "For what purpose? you may say. Why, that you may become an Olympic conqueror; but it is not accomplished without sweat." Again he varied the figure: "Every man's life is a kind of warfare, and it is long and diversified. You must observe the duty of a soldier and do everything at the nod of the general."

Some of these thoughts seem far removed from the ideal of inner tranquillity which Epictetus had for his ultimate goal. "Give me a man who cares how he shall do anything, not for the obtaining of a thing." Such a passage seems close to the view which urges duty for duty's sake. But Epictetus also said that faithfulness is accompanied by the consciousness of obeying God and performing the acts of a wise and good man. What higher peace is there, he asked, than to be able to say, "Bring now, O Zeus, any difficulty that thou pleasest, for I have means given to me by thee and powers for honoring myself through the things which happen" ?

The third stage in the education of a philosopher, in Epictetus' program, concerns the discipline of logic and disputation. Because right thinking is a prerequisite both to the rational control of appetite and to discovering one's duty to God and man, it is imperative that every man should study to avoid "deception and rashness of judgment." But how far

formal logic is necessary for this purpose was, for Epictetus, an open question. Mostly, logic was useful in debating with sophists and rhetoricians—and with Epicureans. A knowledge of elementary fallacies seemed to him sufficient for most purposes.

Of the problems which arise in connection with moral judgments, three were particularly noticed by Epictetus. The first had to do with right names. If man's duty is prescribed by relations, it is important to see things as they are, "Does a man bathe quickly? Do not say that he bathes badly, but that he bathes quickly." The right name puts the thing in the right light. Like Confucius in his *Analects*, Epictetus urged his disciples to consider what is meant by "father," "son," "man," and "citizen." Right names disclose true relations.

Similarly, inferences should be studied, so that we may not conclude from a proposition more than it really says. Epictetus used as an example the inference, "I am richer than you are, therefore I am better than you." This is invalid. Nothing follows necessarily from the premise except judgments of the order, "I have more possessions than you." Epictetus explained the function of inference as establishing assent, and that of critical thinking as teaching us to withhold assent from what is uncertain.

Finally, it was necessary to learn the art of testing whether particular things are good. According to Epictetus, all men are by nature endowed with common moral conceptions, such as the conceptions of the good and the just; but nature does not teach us to apply these in detail. A man begins to be a philosopher when he observes that people disagree about what is good or when he casts about for some rule by which he may judge between them. There is no simple rule; but there is what Epictetus called "the art of discussion," which draws out the consequences of a man's conception so that he may see whether it agrees or conflicts with what he really wants. If it is maintained that pleasure is the good, ask such questions as these: "Is the good something that we can have confidence in?" Yes. "Can we have confidence in what is insecure?" No. "Is pleasure insecure?" Yes. Here is our answer: pleasure is not the good. Epictetus supposed that his art of discussion was the same as Socrates' dialectic, and he advised his pupils to read

Xenophon's *Symposium* in order to see Socrates in action and "how many quarrels he put an end to."

Socrates was one of those held to be "saints" by the later Stoics. Another was Diogenes the Cynic.

These men were, in Epictetus' view, "messengers from Zeus to men about good and bad things, to show them that they have wandered and are seeking the substance of good and evil where it is not."

Pertinent Literature

Bonhöffer, Adolf. *Epictet und die Stoa*. Stuttgart, Germany: Verlag von Ferdinand Enke, 1890.
_____. *Die Ethik das Stoikers Epictet*. Stuttgart, Germany: Verlag von Ferdinand Enke, 1894.

Having originated during the decline of the Greek city-states about 300 B.C., Stoicism concluded its career as the almost unchallenged philosophy of Imperial Rome. Only fragments remain from the writings of the old Stoics (Zeno, Cleanthes, Chrysippus), and historians have asked how far the late Stoics (Seneca, Epictetus, Marcus Aurelius) adhered to the original teachings of the school. It is well known that the middle Stoics (Panaetius and Posidonius, who influenced Cicero) were eclectic: that is, they combined Stoicism with Platonism and Aristotelianism. Adolf Bonhöffer, in what remains to this day the only comprehensive study of Epictetus, argues that, although Seneca and Marcus Aurelius were eclectic, this was not the case with Epictetus, who was well-grounded in the writings of the founders, especially Chrysippus, and who remained faithful to Stoic principles on such fundamental matters as the nature of the soul and the definition of the human good.

Bonhöffer's two volumes are parts of an essentially single work, one part dealing with psychology, the other with ethics. The first volume consists largely in an examination of the vocabulary used by different Stoic writers in their account of the soul. As opposed to the Platonists and the Aristotelians, Zeno and his followers distinguished eight parts of the soul (the ruling-part, the five external senses, speech, and procreation). In keeping with their primitive materialism, they held that the ruling part (*hegemonikon*) of each soul is pure fire, but that in the other parts of the soul this active element is mixed with the grosser elements that make up the several bodily organs. In this way, orthodox Stoics, including Epictetus, were able to maintain the soul's essential unity throughout

its various functions of knowing, willing, and feeling. The *hegemonikon* perceives by means of the sense and wills according to bodily impulses and desires.

The second volume is a detailed exposition of Epictetus' moral teachings, with notes and appendices comparing his teachings with those of other Stoics. According to Bonhöffer, Epictetus' entire moral doctrine follows from three theses: (1) every creature strives for its own natural good; (2) because man's essence lies in his soul, his natural good is moral or spiritual; (3) undeveloped when he comes into the world, man must use discipline to achieve his natural good. Thus, although Epictetus shared the teleological orientation that characterized Greek philosophy as a whole, he conceived man's good in such a way that the distinction between happiness and virtue tended to disappear. Virtue was looked on as being its own reward.

Actually, virtues in the traditional sense (wisdom, justice, courage, temperance) found no place in Epictetus' teaching. There is, in Stoicism, no conflict between rational and irrational parts of the soul. Every individual, whether wise or foolish, strives necessarily for the satisfaction of his desires. The general notions, good and evil, are innate to rational beings; but only the wise, that is, persons trained in Stoic philosophy, know how to apply them correctly. Once a person understands what is his natural good, he will do what is right by the same necessity with which he formerly did what was wrong. Thus, according to Epictetus, virtue is no more difficult than vice.

Many accounts of Epictetus' teaching never get past the first stage in the philosopher's training; that is, the mastery of desire, neglecting what he has to say about duties. R. D. Hicks, for example, interprets Epictetus as urging his hearers to hold aloof from domestic cares, and says that Epictetus "is marked out amongst Stoics by his renunciation of the world." Not so Bonhöffer, who places his main emphasis on the second stage, which, he says, follows naturally from the first in that, when man's soul is freed from desires of the wrong sort, those desires most proper to its divine nature demand to be realized. Such desires lead a person out of himself and initiate duties—toward self, toward the gods, and toward one's fellows. Although in the providence of God each person has his special calling, most will marry, become parents, perform temple rites, manage property, and hold public office.

According to Bonhöffer, Zeno and his early disciples, although they believed that the wise man ought to play an active part in society, were prevented from putting their principles into practice because existing institutions fell too far short of their ideas as to what constituted natural society. Epictetus' disciples were not burdened with unrealistic expectations. For this philosopher, the eternal *logos* is manifest not merely in nature but in custom as well. The philosopher does everything that his worldly counterpart is called upon to do, but he does it not for the sake of wealth or honor or power, but out of love for his fellow man and in obedience to the gods.

In connection with religious duties, Bonhöffer discusses Epictetus' theology, which, in spite of occasional pantheistic and polytheistic expressions, was essentially theistic. The divine principle which orders nature as a whole and in its several parts was, for Epictetus, a personal God, who thinks, feels, and wills the same as men do, who takes a fatherly interest in each of his creatures, and with whom men may commune. Bonhöffer's only problem is how, with these exalted thoughts, Epictetus could take the temple cult as seriously as he did. Presumably he did not do so merely out of deference to the ignorant masses, because, as Epictetus himself pointed out, the common man, who prays and sacrifices with worldly ends in view, can never arrive at peace with the gods.

The distinction between the common man and the philosopher was fundamental to the Stoics, some of whom went to the extreme of saying that the common man can do nothing right and that the sage can do nothing wrong.

That, says Bonhöffer, was meant to be taken with a grain of salt. Whatever claim they may have made for Socrates or Diogenes, whom they held up as models, neither Zeno nor any major Stoic ever claimed to have reached perfection, but only that as Stoics they were on the right path and were progressing toward the goal.

More, Paul Elmer. "Epictetus," in *Hellenistic Philosophies*. Princeton, New Jersey: Princeton University Press, 1923.

The works of Epictetus have not been neglected by English and American scholars, as the number of translations into English attests. Apart from introductory notices that sometimes accompany these translations, however, Epictetus' thought is usually dealt with in conjuction with that of other Roman Stoics. Paul Elmer More's chapter is a noteworthy exception. As one of a series of volumes called *The Greek Tradition*, in which More traces the relation between Platonism and other post-Socratic philosophies up to their eventual merging in patristic Christianity, *Hellenistic Philosophies* is concerned with what More calls the Socratic heresies—Epicureanism, Stoicism, Neoplatonism, and Pyrrhonism.

The self-sufficiency of Socrates, so greatly admired by his contemporaries, rested, according to More, on three distinct principles: intellectual skepticism, spiritual affirmation, and belief in the identity of virtue and knowledge. Plato preserved the combination, but rival schools left out one or another of the theses. The Stoics, who were impressed with Socrates' optimistic endurance of suffering, failed to see that it was his skepticism that made this optimism possible, and burdened themselves with a dogmatic philosophy of nature which was both materialistic and deterministic.

More finds Epictetus worthy of special study because, although primarily a moralist, he sought to preserve the teachings of Zeno and the old Stoics about nature and the human soul. Plato, with his dualism of spirit and matter, had maintained that the just man is happy while enduring real evils. Zeno, rejecting the dualism, held that for the wise man there are no real evils. Epictetus tried to combine Zeno's metaphysical monism with the ethical dualism demanded by the cry of suffering and the voice of conscience. In doing so, however, he landed in two contradictions: that the world is totally good, yet human experience is full of evil; and that all things are fatally determined, yet man's will is free.

More maintains that Epictetus wavered between two ethical theories, one humanistic, the other naturalistic. Working in the former vein, he treated human good and evil as quite real. As rational beings, men are endowed by nature with the ideas of good and of right, and through experience they learn that some things are harmful and some actions inappropriate. It is right for man, as a living creature, to act in ways that preserve and enhance his life; similarly, it is right for man, as a social being, to uphold human institutions and to assist his neighbor in times of need. In this way, Epictetus combined a sense of social responsibility with the egoistic pursuit of happiness. He did so, however, without allowing any place for sympathy or fellow-feeling; for, true to his tradition, he could not long forget that men are parts of nature and that what seems bad of a finite creature is ultimately indifferent; or, to take the lofty view, "partial ill is universal good." In the end, Epictetus' naturalism prevailed over his humanism, leading him to the same mood of resignation which characterizes the *Bhagavad Gita:* "Without attachment, lay thy hand to thy peculiar work."

The second contradiction arises, like the first, out of Epictetus' attempt to affirm moral categories in a nonmoral universe—this time the categories of freedom and responsibility. More recognizes that Plato himself had a problem bequeathed to him by Socrates' insistence that virtue is identical with knowledge:

how to escape the conclusion that what we call man's will is identical with his most recent impression. According to More, Plato avoided determinism by affirming a transcendent element in the soul that enables man to bring a higher order of truth to bear upon his transient impressions. Superficially, Epictetus did the same thing when he located freedom in the power of reason to give or to withhold assent; but, says More, the reason appealed to by the Stoics contains no transcendent element, being no more than a congeries of impressions acting one on the other, so that "when erroneous opinions affect it concerning things good and evil, there is necessity upon us to act unreasonably."

Certainly Epictetus did not want his students to lapse into moral indifference of the ordinary sort: the pangs of self-reproach were among the sanctions which he used to steer them away from trivial pursuits. Yet at a deeper level all this becomes indifferent; for the good consists in tranquility, and this consists in willing that things be as the divine will has ordered. Thus, at last, Epictetus' moral teachings were swallowed up in adoration. "What else can a lame old man like me do but chant the praise of God? If indeed I were a nightingale, I should sing as a nightingale; if a swan, as a swan; but as I am a rational creature I must praise God. This is my task." This, More points out, is the language not of a philosopher but of a divine; and he quotes the poem by Herbert of Cherbury, "Of all the creatures both in sea and land, only to Man has Thou made known thy ways." Nevertheless, says More, we have to remember that the Being whom Epictetus worshiped was "only a subtle form of matter," that the Providence which he praised was "only another name for mechanical law," and that the rational element in man was "nothing more than a glimmering flame of the universal fire"; and, doing so, we can only lament the estrangement between philosophy and religion which could have been avoided had this noble sect been able to throw off the tyranny of metaphysics.

Additional Recommended Reading

Arnold, E. V. *Roman Stoicism*. Cambridge: Cambridge University Press, 1911. A systematic approach, with no special treatment of individual philosophers.

Epictetus. *Epictetus*. Loeb Classical Library. Translated by W. A. Oldfather. Cambridge, Massachusetts: Harvard University Press, 1925. Greek and English text, with an introduction to Epictetus' life and teaching, and a bibliography.

Hicks, R. D. *Stoic and Epicurean*. New York: Charles Scribner's Sons, 1910. See Index, under "Epictetus."

Rist, J. M., ed. *The Stoics*. Berkeley: University of California Press, 1978. Articles by different scholars dealing with problems in Stoicism.

OUTLINES OF PYRRHONISM

Author: Sextus Empiricus (fl. late second and early third centuries)
Type of work: Skeptical criticism
First transcribed: Early third century

Principal Ideas Advanced

Skeptical arguments are designed to cure dogmatists of the disease of supposing that knowledge is possible.
The skeptic relies upon appearances, and he avoids the error of passing judgment.
To suppose that it is possible to judge truth and falsity is to ignore the relativity of perception and judgment.

The writings of Sextus Empiricus are the only texts that have survived from the Pyrrhonian skeptical movement of ancient times. The movement takes its name from Pyrrho of Elis (c. 367-275 B.C.), who doubted that there is any way by which one can attain knowledge. He urged that judgment be suspended as to whether any particular assertion is true or false. He argued that to suspend judgment leads to a state of indifference toward the world, and to a kind of inner tranquillity which enables one to live at peace in a troubled world.

The actual school of Pyrrhonian thought began much later, in the first century B.C. It developed out of the extreme skepticism that had been prevalent in the Platonic Academy under Arcesilas (c. 315-c. 241 B.C.) and Carneades (c. 213-c. 129 B.C.). The Academic skeptics developed a series of brilliant arguments to show that nothing can be known; they recommended that one live by probabilities. The Pyrrhonists regarded the Academics as being too dogmatic, and the former maintained their doubts, even about the skeptical contention that nothing can be known. Starting with Aenesidemus (c. 100-c. 40 B.C.), who had been a student at the Academy, the Pyrrhonian movement developed in Alexandria, primarily among medical doctors. Aenesidemus and his successors set forth a series of arguments against various dogmatic philosophies, including the Academic skeptics. The arguments purport to show that every dogmatic attempt to gain knowledge leads to difficulties that cannot be resolved. Instead of seek-

ing knowledge, one should suspend judgment, thus gaining peace of mind.

Sextus Empiricus was one of the last leaders of the Pyrrhonian school. Besides the fact that he was a doctor and a teacher, practically nothing is known about him. His writings—probably copies of lectures—consist of compilations of the arguments that his predecessors had worked out on any and all subjects. The *Outlines of Pyrrhonism* is a summary of the Pyrrhonian position, whereas his other works, *Against the Mathematicians* and *Against the Dogmatists,* are much more detailed expositions of the arguments that the school had developed regarding each particular area in which other philosophers had claimed to have discovered true knowledge. Sextus' writings are veritable storehouses of skeptical arguments designed to confound all other philosophers. Although very repetitious, they contain both good and bad arguments.

In the last chapter of the *Outlines of Pyrrhonism*, Sextus explains the uneven character of his book in answering the question why skeptics sometimes propound arguments which lack persuasion. The skeptic, we are told, is a lover of mankind. He is seeking to cure an ailment called "self-conceit and rashness," from which the dogmatic philosophers suffer. Just as doctors employ remedies of different strengths, depending on the condition of the patient, so, too, the skeptic employs arguments of different strengths depending upon how "sick" the dogmatic philosopher is. If the therapy can succeed with a weak argument, good. If the case is severe, a strong argument is needed. Hence, the Pyrrhonist offered a variety of arguments, good and bad, weak and strong, since his avowed aim was to cure the dogmatist of the disease of supposing that he knew something.

The *Outlines of Pyrrhonism* begins by dividing philosophers into three groups: the dogmatists, such as Aristotle and Epicurus, who say that they have discovered the truth; those such as Carneades, who say it cannot be found; and the Pyrrhonian skeptics who keep seeking for it. The aim of the Pyrrhonian arguments is to cure people from holding either of the first two views. Sextus guards himself from being accused of "secret dogmatism" by saying that the statements in his book are not to be taken as positive assertions of what is true, but only as expressions of what *appear* to him to be matters of fact.

Sextus describes skepticism as the ability or mental attitude which opposes appearances, the objects of sense experience, to judgments that can be made about them, so that suspense of judgment is achieved in which we neither affirm nor deny anything. This state is followed by the state of "quietude," in which we are untroubled and tranquil. The various dogmatic schools of Hellenistic philosophy—the Stoic, the Epicurean, and the Academic—were all looking for "peace of mind," and their theories of knowledge and of the real nature of the universe were intended to lead one to mental peace. The skeptics contend that the dogmatists never achieve peace because they worry about never knowing whether their theories are true. But the skeptic who suspends judgment achieves peace of mind, since he escapes such worry.

If the skeptic suspends judgment about everything, how does he live? Sextus answers by declaring that the skeptic accepts the world of sense experience undogmatically. It seems to the skeptic that he sees certain things, has certain feelings, and so on, but he does not know whether such is really the case. He suspends judgment about all that is not immediately evident to him. Then, without judging, he follows nature and custom, so that—for example—when he seems to be hungry, he eats. He has peace of mind, since he does not judge, and he is guided in his life by his experience, his feelings, and the laws and customs of his society.

To achieve this tranquillity, one must first achieve suspension of judgment. Skeptical arguments are offered by Sextus to encourage such suspension. The first of these is the famous ten tropes, or arguments, of Aenesidemus, which show why we should suspend judgment about whether sense objects really are as they appear to be. (Sextus prefaces these and all the other arguments he sets forth with the disclaimer that he is not asserting dogmatically the exact number, nature, or truth of the arguments, but only that it seems to him that they are a set of arguments.) The ten tropes all deal with difficulties in ascertaining when features of our sense experience belong to real objects existing independently of our perceptions.

First, Sextus points out, different animals experience things differently according to the nature of their sense organs. We cannot tell which animal has the correct experience. Second, even among men, the same object is experienced differently, and we have no basis for deciding which man has the correct experience. Third, the same object affects different senses in different ways. Honey is sweet to the tongue, but sticky to the finger. We cannot tell which quality really belongs to the object. Fourth, our impressions of things vary according to our state of mind or our condition. Fifth, things appear different from different positions. Sixth, we never perceive objects individually, but only together with other objects, so that we never know what they are like by themselves. Seventh, objects look different when decomposed or analyzed than they do whole. We cannot judge which is their true nature. Eighth, everything that we perceive is seen relative to its position in space and time, so we do not know what it is like out of position. Ninth, we regard things differently according to whether they occur frequently or rarely. And tenth, since different nations and cultures have different laws and customs, we cannot judge what things are really right or wrong. These ten tropes should lead us to suspend judgment since they show that our sense impressions vary and are different, and we have no means for deciding which are correct ones.

Sextus follows with five additional tropes, or reasons for suspending judgment, attributed to Agrippa, a skeptic of a century earlier. These are more general reasons for doubting dogmatic contentions. First of all, there is interminable controversy about everything, so we cannot tell who is right. Second, every judgment must be proved, if it is to be accepted as true. But the proof will require a further proof, and so on *ad infinitum*. Third, any judgment is relative to the judge, and may not be true of the thing itself. Fourth, the dogmatists must assume something in order to make judgments, but we cannot tell if these assumptions or hypotheses are true. Fifth, the only way to escape from the infinite regress of proofs of proofs, or from starting with some unwarranted hypothesis, is to employ a circular argument in which something that is to be proved is used as part of the proof itself.

Further sets of tropes are offered, including Aenesidemus' arguments against any dogmatic theory of causation. Then the first book of the *Outlines* concludes with an explanation of skeptical terminology (showing how the skeptics can say what they do without making dogmatic assertions) and with a comparison of other Greek philosophies with Pyrrhonian skepticism.

The second and third books of the *Outlines* show why the skeptic suspends judgment with regard to knowledge claims in various specific disciplines. The second book treats problems of logic and the theory of knowledge, while the third is a collection of arguments about theology, metaphysics, mathematics, physics, and ethics. The second book, and its longer exposition in *Against the Logicians,* has attracted much attention in recent years because of the similarity of some of the views expressed to those of David Hume and of the contemporary logical positivists, analysts, and ordinary language philosophers.

The second book first presents the disturbing problem of whether the skeptic can deal with the arguments of the dogmatists without admitting that he, the skeptic, knows something, namely what the opponents are talking about. After contending that he deals only with what seems to be the dogmatists' views, Sextus turns to what he regards as crucial to any theory of true knowledge, the question whether there is any criterion for judging what is true. Philosophers disagree as to whether there is such a criterion. To settle the dispute, a criterion is needed, but it is not known whether one exists. Further, any proposed

criterion of knowledge would have to be judged by another criterion to tell if it were a true one, and that criterion by still another, and so on.

If the dogmatic philosophers insist that man is the judge or criterion of true knowledge, then a problem exists: whether all men or only some are judges of truth. If all, then another criterion is needed to settle disputes among men. If only some, then a criterion is needed to tell which men are proper judges, and under what conditions. The Stoics, for example, claim that the wise man, the Sage, is the judge. But by what standards can one tell *who* is the Sage, and whether what he says is true? Other philosophers say that the criteria are the faculties of sense and reason. But under what conditions are they the criteria? By what standards shall we judge? And whose sense and reason are standards?

It is not even obvious that anything true exists. There is controversy about this matter; so, if somebody asserts that truth exists, he will not be believed unless he offers proof. But is the proof true? Further proof has to be offered. But is *that* true? Unless some criterion of truth can be established, we cannot tell. But how can we ever determine if the criterion is the true one?

Further, one can ask, what sort of truths are they—apparent ones or nonapparent ones? Since there is disagreement about everything (and Sextus appeals to the fact that there have been philosophers who disputed everything), it is not obvious that something is true. If truths are not apparent, some standard is needed for ascertaining what is true, but all of the above difficulties arise when one attempts to apply a standard of truth.

Philosophers, especially the Stoics, maintain that they can gain true knowledge by means of signs or inferences which connect what is obvious or evident with that which is not. What is nonevident, Sextus says, falls into one of three categories: the *temporarily nonevident*, as, for example, that which is on the other side of the wall I am facing; the *naturally nonevident,* those things which can never under any circumstances be perceived, such as the pores in the skin, but which can be inferred from what is evident; and finally, the *absolutely nonevident,* whatever can never be known at all, such as whether the number of stars is odd or even. There is a type of sign, called the "suggestive sign," which connects what is obvious, our immediate experience, with what is temporarily nonevident. Smoke suggests that there is a fire. The skeptic, like anyone else, accepts suggestive signs and acts by them, because this is the natural way of relating present experience to possible future experience. But suggestive signs do not provide true knowledge, only predictions or expectations about the future course of events.

Philosophers hope to gain true knowledge by means of another kind of sign, the "indicative" one. This is defined as "an antecedent judgment in a valid hypothetical syllogism which serves to reveal the consequent." In a syllogism of the form "If A, then B; A, therefore B," A is an indicative sign if it, itself, is evident, if it reveals that B, which is naturally nonevident, is true, and if the syllogism is valid. Sextus offers many arguments against the existence of indicative signs, including the contention that one can determine if a hypothetical syllogism is valid only if one knows whether the consequent is true or false. The consequent in this case is a statement about what is naturally nonevident, which can be revealed only by an indicative sign. Hence, one is always involved in circular reasoning, since it requires knowing what is naturally nonevident to tell if an indicative sign actually exists, and one can tell what is naturally nonevident only by means of indicative signs.

Demonstrative reasoning consists of using signs to reveal conclusions. Hence, similar doubts can be cast as to whether anything at all can be demonstrated or proved. Sextus offers many arguments to show that nothing can be proved, and then, to avoid establishing the negative conclusion, he offers evidence to show that something can be proved. Therefore, one has to suspend judgment on the question.

A very brief criticism is leveled against induction, pointing out that if a general conclusion is drawn from some particular instances, it may be disproved by other cases. If generalizations can properly be made only after a review of *all* particular cases, it is obviously impossible to survey all of the data, and hence, to generalize.

The second book of the *Outlines* examines the claims of various logicians and epistemologists of ancient times, especially the Stoics and Epicureans, and shows reasons for suspending judgment as to whether there is anything that is true, and as to whether there is any method for discovering truths. The third book rapidly surveys the various sciences from theology and metaphysics to mathematics, physics, and ethics, and indicates that in each of these areas the fundamental concepts are meaningless, that the basic principles are open to question, and that, as a result, one must suspend judgment about whether anything can be known in any of these areas.

Though the skeptic accepts the customs of his society, and hence its religious views, undogmatically, Sextus points out that the arguments for the existence of God and for atheism are inconclusive, and that the conceptions of God offered by various philosophers are conflicting and often inconsistent in themselves. Further, various problems, like the problem of evil, cast doubt on the claim that a good, all-knowing deity exists.

With regard to metaphysics and physics, the basic notions, like "cause," "matter," and "body," contain difficulties. We cannot even be sure that anything causes anything else, or that bodies exist. We seem to have no way of gaining indisputable knowledge in this area. And arguments like those of Zeno of Elea, of the fifth century B.C., indicate that paradoxical conclusions can be drawn about the nature of bodies, motion, and so on.

There are also paradoxes with regard to mathematics, such as the odd argument Sextus offers to show that 6 equals 15. The whole equals the sum of its parts. The parts of 6 are 5, 4, 3, 2, and 1. Therefore, 6 equals 15.

The disagreements among philosophers and mathematicians, and the various paradoxical arguments, whether valid or not, that had been developed in ancient times suffice to raise doubts as to whether anything can be known about the world, or about mathematics. Hence, we must again suspend judgment.

When Sextus turns to ethical matters, he points out that philosophers disagree about what is good and bad. There is not even adequate evidence that anything really good or bad exists. The variety of beliefs and opinions about what is good and bad in the various known cultures leads one to suspend judgment about whether there are any objective moral values in the world. (Sextus even points out that some people and some societies condone incest and cannibalism. And who can say that they are wrong?) The skeptic lives undogmatically, not judging whether things are good or bad, but living according to the dictates of nature and society. The skeptic, like others, may suffer from physical pains, but he will avoid the additional mental suffering that results from judging that pains are bad or evil.

The writings of Sextus Empiricus seem to have had little or no influence in their own time and to have been practically unknown during the Middle Ages. Their rediscovery in the Renaissance greatly influenced many modern thinkers from Michel de Montaigne, onward, for Sextus' writings proved to be a treasurehouse of argumentation on all sorts of subjects. Philosophers such as Pierre Gassendi, George Berkeley, and David Hume, among others, used arguments from Sextus in setting forth their own theories. Pierre Bayle contended that modern philosophy began when arguments of Sextus were introduced on the philosophical scene. The arguments of the skeptic continue to stimulate twentieth century minds caught between the power of faith and the faith in power.

Pertinent Literature

Brochard, Victor. *Les Sceptiques grecs.* Paris: J. Vrin, 1932.

Victor Brochard's work, first presented to the French Academy of Moral and Political Studies in 1884, was awarded the Victor Cousin Prize. It has remained the most complete study of ancient skepticism, and it contains just about all the information that is known on the subject. Unfortunately, even though the book has been reprinted in French, it has never been translated into English.

Brochard first covers the early indications of skepticism before Socrates, and in Socrates' attitudes. Next he sets forth what we know about the skepticism of Pyrrho of Elis and his disciple Timon of Phlius. A very large section of the book is devoted to the skepticism of the New Academy, Arcesilaus, and Carneades, and then of the more eclectic successors, Philo of Larissa and Antiochus of Ascalon. The last half of the work, more than two hundred pages, deals with the emergence of Pyrrhonism in the philosophy of Aenesidemus, and as presented by Sextus Empiricus. Brochard's portrayal is as definitive as one could wish; and he cites the relevant historical sources for what is known. The book is indispensable for the facts concerning the history of Greek skepticism. However, the work is more than merely a compendium of historical data, for throughout the book, and especially in the conclusion, Brochard offers his interpretation and evaluation of the various kinds of skepticism.

Pyrrhonism, we are told by Brochard, is a radical doctrine. It is pure phenomenalism in logic, and abstention and renunciation in morality. On the other hand, the skepticism of the New Academy is a doctrine of a just man; it presents precepts of conduct and assigns a goal to human life. This evaluation (which is nearly the opposite of that given by Philip P. Hallie) is then carried over by Brochard to modern philosophical theories. Aenesidemus and Sextus are seen as being like David Hume, while Carneades is compared to Immanuel Kant (except that, as Brochard points out, Carneades lacked Kant's serious moral concern). Ancient Pyrrhonism is portrayed as foreshadowing modern empiricism, while the theory of the New Academy—"looking for a middle term between dogmatism, idealism or sensualism, and pure Pyrrhonism"—is described as a view analogous to that of Kant. So, Brochard claims, the real difference between Pyrrhonism and Academic skepticism is very similar to that between modern positivism and the critical philosophy of Kant.

In his lengthy conclusion, Brochard comes to grips with the many attempts to answer skepticism. Pyrrhonism is treated by Brochard as a greater philosophical danger than Academic skepticism until one realizes that the Pyrrhic arguments are either self-refuting or based on fundamental misunderstandings. If the Pyrrhonist really rejects all theories, he reduces himself to a fool, and even a dogmatic fool. The Pyrrhonist cannot escape this conclusion. On the other hand, the Academic skeptic is a proper kind of dogmatist, evaluating matters according to probabilities. Sextus is described as a dogmatic philosopher with no justification for his dogmatism. The Academic skeptics, instead, are portrayed as proposing their views provisionally, judging according to probabilities. This latter feature, for Brochard, puts the Academics, not the Pyrrhonians, into the camp of modern science.

Brochard then goes on to claim that of all the schools in the history of philosophy, the school of the probabilists has been most unjustly treated. From the days of Carneades to the nineteenth century, they have provided some of the most productive views. From these a positive view of science has developed; and this scientific outlook eliminates the fear of the Pyrrhonian critiques of knowledge. Nevertheless, Brochard writes in conclusion, the skepticism of Pyrrho, Carneades, Aenesidemus, and others has played an important role in the development of modern thought.

Sextus Empiricus. *Scepticism, Man and God: Selections from the Major Writings of Sextus Empiricus.* Edited by Philip P. Hallie. Translated by Sanford G. Etheridge. Middletown, Connecticut: Wesleyan University Press, 1964.

Philip P. Hallie asserts that since most of the histories of philosophy and most of the encyclopedia articles are incorrect in their portrayal of Greek skepticism, this work is needed. In fact, he goes on, most discussions are usually antagonistic to skepticism. Hallie proposes that Classical skepticism be recognized as a significant force in Western thought. He puts forth his case in what he called "A Polemical Introduction." Although the Greek skeptics were hardly the first or only doubters, he writes, they were the ones who realized what doubt consists in and to what it leads. The dangerous implications of doubt may account for skepticism's having been ignored by so many thinkers. Further, Hallie contends, there is also a practical problem: that, unfortunately, only one text of Greek skeptical thought exists—the dry and often dull writings of Sextus Empiricus. Hallie hopes that his new and lively translation will make it easier to come into intellectual contact with Greek skepticism.

The basic misconception that appears in almost all accounts of Greek skepticism is that skeptical doubts lead to inaction or lack of feeling. Hallie insists that skepticism, like Stoicism and Epicurianism, was a practical philosophy aiming at happiness; it was not some kind of paralytic anesthesia, but a way of living. The doubting process, for the skeptics, removed the features that made man's intellectual life difficult, and when this was done, a happy everyday life was possible. Classical skepticism, as presented in Sextus, neither maintained that nothing is true nor employed doubting in order to destroy normal life. Once doubt has accomplished its function, doubt itself is eliminated, and a practical criterion provides a guide for living.

Hallie next reviews the history of ancient skepticism to show how this misconception developed. He sketches the stages of skepticism, beginning with the pre-Academics, principally Pyrrho of Elis and his disciple Timon. The legends about Pyrrho that appear in Diogenes Laertius picture the early skeptic as indifferent or even apathetic to external events, not even getting out of the way of carts or wild animals, lest he admit he *knew* they were dangerous. A different set of stories about Pyrrho portray him as being moderate all the time, even in the face of very dangerous happenings. His student Timon said that Pyrrho was looking for peace of mind. The various tales, however, do not allow for a clear judgment as to what kind of a skeptic Pyrrho was. His student Timon, about whom we have more information, was definitely not indifferent to ordinary events: he was continually attacking other people's beliefs and actions.

After a detailed account of the Academic skeptics, Hallie turns to the movement to which Sextus belonged, the Pyrrhonians. Both the Academics and the Pyrrhonian Aenesidemus organized the skeptical challenge against the dogmatists into systematic sets of arguments. On the more positive side, Aenesidemus described the recollective or suggestive sign as a way we relate immediate experience to other possible events, without having to have genuine knowledge. Sextus, the codifier of Pyrrhonism, showed the skeptic as the "inquirer" (the original meaning of skeptic), dealing with the actual problems of people. He showed how one can live without certainty by living according to nature and in harmony with sense experience and with the laws and customs of one's society. Hallie emphasized that the Pyrrhonian skeptics dealt with experience in a positive way, consistent with loving life.

Selections from various portions of *Sextus' Outlines of Pyrrhonian,* as well as his *Adversus Mathematicos,* grouped around the topics skepticism, man, and God, are presented. Much helpful data and interpretation is offered by Hallie in the footnotes. He has tried to show that skepticism should be recognized as an important tradition from ancient times to Michel de Montaigne, Pierre Bayle, David Hume, and Ludwig Wittgenstein.

Stough, Charlotte L. *Greek Skepticism: A Study in Epistemology.* Berkeley: University of California Press, 1969.

Charlotte L. Stough's *Greek Skepticism* is the most recent analysis of Greek skeptical thought. Although there has been a growing interest and concern with various skeptical problems and arguments, there have been few book-length studies, especially in English. Stough has concentrated on four basic kinds of ancient skepticism: early Pyrrhonism, Academic skepticism, the skepticism of Aenesidemus, and the views of Sextus Empiricus. (Of course, the writings of Sextus are a major source of our knowledge of all four of these points of view.) Stough focuses chiefly on those aspects of skeptical views that can be classified as "epistemological"—those that deal with questions of knowledge, belief, experience, perception, and sensation. The metaphysical, ethical, social, political, and theological views of the different kinds of skeptics are largely set aside.

Although Sextus Empiricus figures throughout the book, principally as a source of information, the specific discussion of his views appears in the fifth chapter. What is emphasized as a significant difference in his views from earlier skeptical ones going back to Pyrrho of Elis is Sextus' empiricism—his emphasis on experience. Using material both from his *Outlines of Pyrrhonism* and from his larger work, *Against the Mathematicians,* Stough shows first that Sextus accepted the empiricist axiom that knowledge originates in sensory experience. He held both that experience causes ideas and that it produces their content. Through sensation we receive the content, and through perception we recognize the experience. Our thinking is about images received through experience. Things that we cannot conceive, such as a line without breadth, cannot be reasoned about. Stough contends that Sextus used the claim that ideas are images as a powerful weapon against dogmatists.

Developing the empiricism in Sextus' views further, Stough points to his use of an empirical verification principle to determine whether a given claim is true. To ascertain whether something is true, we have to be able to verify it in experience. At the same time we have to recognize that experiences are affected by various factors. Thus, we can learn about experienced objects, but not about independent "real" objects.

The identification of impressions with phenomena, Stough writes, is a central feature of Sextus' empiricism, a feature not present in the Pyrrhonian theory of Aenesidemus. Using classifications that have been developed by modern empirical thinkers, Stough shows that many difficulties or even inconsistencies result from Sextus' view. When one asks what an impression is of, no referent is left. All that remains is a subject with its private experience. This view is described by Stough as an extreme form of empiricism.

Next Stough deals with Sextus' theory of signs, by which one experience makes another known. Sextus held that only perceptually associative signs are usable. The so-called indicative signs of Stoic theory go beyond experience. So, Stough shows, Sextus' refusal to admit that there could be any signs other than observable conjections, is part and parcel of his empiricism.

Having neatly portrayed Sextus' empiricism, Stough then shows that Sextus' ultimate epistemological position casts doubt on the validity of inductive, empirical inferences. Induction, which has been such a major feature in empiricism since David Hume, is briefly and quickly disposed of by Sextus. (Many of Sextus' points were later raised by Hume.) Sextus then goes on to argue that nothing is true. Sextus' thoroughgoing skepticism, Stough points out, challenged the criterion of truth of Carneades (that of credibility) and of Aenesidemus (general consent). But in order to reject them as well as those of assorted dogmatists, Sextus apparently had to assume that any empirical statement that can be true or false (the only ones worth discussing) makes a claim about the real external world. Sextus' arguments are geared to show that we have no way to verify such claims. This result seems to follow from the assumption that truth must be connected with real existence.

Stough, in her evaluation of Sextus, asserts that if Sextus could only have gotten beyond the earlier skeptical tradition and seen that truth can be about experiences and not "real" existences, he could have been a phenomenalist (maybe the first one before the eighteenth century) and not just a skeptic. Stough argues that as a complete skeptic Sextus would have had to doubt his own views. She then quotes a famous passage showing that Sextus was the culmination of the line of skeptical thinking that began in the fourth century with Pyrrho of Elis:

> And, again, just as it is not impossible for a man who has climbed up to a high place by a ladder to overturn the ladder with his foot after his ascent, so too it is not unreasonable that the Skeptic, after he had proceeded, as it were by a kind of ladder, to construct the above argument proving that there is no such thing as demonstration, should then also do away with this very argument.

Additional Recommended Reading

Bevan, Edwyn R. *Stoics and Sceptics.* Oxford: Clarendon Press, 1913. A literate and scholarly account of the period.

Chisholm, Roderick. "Sextus Empiricus and Modern Empiricism," in *Philosophy of Science.* VIII, no. 3 (July, 1941), pp. 371-384. An examination of Sextus' empirical method.

Mates, Benson. *Stoic Logic.* Berkeley: University of California Press, 1953. Sextus Empiricus is considered, among others, as contributing to the development of Stoic logic.

Patrick, Mary Mills. *The Greek Sceptics.* New York: Columbia University Press, 1929. A substantial account of skepticism.

_____ . *Sextus Empiricus and Greek Scepticism.* Cambridge: D. Bell, 1899. Here the focus is on Sextus within the context of skepticism.

THE CITY OF GOD

Author: Saint Augustine (Aurelius Augustinus, 354-430)
Type of work: Theology
First transcribed: c. 413-426

Principal Ideas Advanced

The essential nature of man is will, and no man wills the true God to be God unless he is touched by Divine Grace.

Theology is faith seeking understanding; man has faith in order that he may understand.

History has at its beginning the Creation; at its center, Christ, and, as its consummation, the judgment and transformation.

Because God had foreknowledge, he knew that man's will would be misdirected and that evil would thereby come into the world; but he also knew that through his grace good could be brought from evil.

History is divided by two cities formed by alternative loves: the earthly city by the love of self, and the heavenly city by the love of God.

It has been held that the whole of Christian thought may be seen as variations on the essential positions of two men—St. Augustine and St. Thomas Aquinas. This contention is closely related to another—that the history of philosophy is wisely seen as variations on the work of Plato and Aristotle. It is inevitable that when a religious thinker expresses the content of his faith he will use the most appropriate words, concepts, and even systems available in his culture. Consequently, St. Augustine was a Platonist, St. Thomas was an Aristotelian. Any attempt to gloss over this fundamental difference between these two leading theologians of Christendom is to pervert both.

It was St. Thomas in the thirteenth century who was most influential in establishing Aristotelian empiricism, thereby establishing a momentous division between philosophy and theology. This was quite different from the complete separation of the two to which the Protestant Reformation came in opposing the Roman Catholic synthesis. St. Thomas held that there were certain areas unique to each discipline, while other matters could be properly understood from either perspective. The Trinity and Incarnation, for example, could be known only through revelation; the nature of the empirical world was properly the jurisdiction of philosophy, almost perfectly understood by Aristotle. But God's existence, and to a certain extent his nature, could be known either through revelation or by the processes of natural reason, operating on sense perception. Thus natural theology was strongly defended as a legitimate discipline and a fitting handmaiden of the Church.

St. Augustine, however, writing eight centuries before, drew his inspiration from Plato, strongly tempered by the theology of St. Paul. For Plato, "knowledge" through the senses was inferior to intuitive knowledge, that knowledge of the essential nature of all things without which men perceive only dim shadows in a darkened cave. Coupled with this Platonic distrust of the senses was St. Augustine's preoccupation with the problem of evil and his own personal problems of morality. At first this concern had driven him to the position of Manicheanism, that philosophy holding to a metaphysical dualism of good and evil, and to the inherent evil of matter. Disillusioned by the naïveté of its spokesmen, Augustine turned to Neoplatonism, finding there a suitable explanation of evil in terms of a theistic universe, intuitively understood. "I found there," he said, "all things but one—the *Logos* made flesh."

The significance of this omission rested in Augustine's common confession with St. Paul—"I can will what is right, but I cannot do it. For I do not do the good I want, but the evil I do not want is what I do. . . . Wretched man that I am! Who will deliver me from this body of death?" Truth is not a matter simply of knowledge but of action; to anticipate the existentialists, the problem is not knowing the truth but living the truth. With this awareness came Augustine's baptism of Neoplatonism into the Christian *Weltanschauung*—the result has been called a complete break with all previous understandings of man.

Against the Greek philosophers, Augustine insisted that to know the truth is not necessarily to do the truth, for the essential nature of man is not reason but will. Man is so created that he has no option but to love, to orient his being to some object, principle, person, with an ultimate devotion. This supreme object willed by each person characterizes his total being, giving to him his presuppositions, motivations, rationale, vitality, and goal. There is no man without such a faith, "religion," "god." One does not reason *to* such an object, but reasons *from* it. No man believes in the true God, the God of moral demand, unless he wills so to do; but no amount of persuasion can change an unwilling will. Since man is essentially self-centered, he will always will something other than the true God to be god—man will create god in his own image. Only when man is touched by Divine Grace can he will God alone as true center.

Consequently, there must be no severance of theology and philosophy—there can be no reasoning to faith, to Truth. There can only be reasoning *from* faith. Only from the rightly oriented will, the mind already turned toward the redeeming God, can man discover Truth. The keystone of Augustinianism is this—"I believe in order to understand," or even better, theology is "faith seeking understanding." The same applies to morality, for every "virtue" that makes no reference to God is a vice. This insistence, essentially discounted by Aquinas and much of the medieval period, was revived as an essential proclamation of the Protestant Reformation. Through Kierkegaard it has become an adapted tenet of existentialism.

This understanding is the foundation for Augustine's magnum opus, *The City of God*. Augustine's writing career was largely consumed in apologetics, in defending orthodox (Nicene) Christianity against its antagonists both within and without the Church. Occasioned by the sack of Rome in 410, *The City of God* arose as an answer to pagan critics who insisted that Christianity was the principal cause of the weakening of the Roman Empire. The reasons documenting this charge ranged from the religious position that avowal of the Christian God had elicited the vengeance of the true pagan gods, to the secular charge that Christian otherworldliness had undermined the internal solidarity of the Empire. With a brilliant display of concerned patience, Augustine produced one of the most detailed, comprehensive, and definitive apologies ever written. Not only are major charges answered, but Augustine deals with every conceivable attack. He answered the critics in terms of the Christian position and defended his answers in detail from the writings of the honored spokesmen of the Empire throughout its history. Augustine's second purpose with this work was to help Christians themselves who had been weakened or perplexed by persecution and by the disastrous events of history.

Yet from this apology emerged what has made this not only a work of historic interest, but also a classic. *The City of God* is one of the first attempts at a theology or philosophy of history. Although Greek concepts of history differed somewhat, they were essentially in agreement that history was cyclic, characterized by an endess round of recurring events. In effect, there was no *telos*, no final goal, toward which history moved. St. Augustine's apology developed the cosmic implications of Christian revelation, defending history as a linear pattern. The Christian God is Triune; that is, God operates in the three eternal modes of Creator-Sustainer, Redeemer, Inspirer. History as the plane of divine activity has as its beginning Creation, as its center point God's redemptive act in Jesus Christ, and continues in the Spirit towards the consummation, the judgment and transformation of all into a new heaven and a new earth. From the perspective of faith the pattern of history is visible and the meaning of life perceivable. Augustine's work set the basic view of much of the Middle Ages and of Western culture as such, and he, perhaps more than any other man, provided the fundamental theology of Christendom.

The situation confronting Augustine was fraught with theological difficulties. He could easily counter petty charges, pointing to the Church as a refuge during the sacking, to Christian teachings as having tempered pagan bloodthirstiness, and to pagan respect for possessions of the Christian God. Equally easy was Augustine's proof of the moral decadence of Rome, a condition and its disastrous consequences long warned against by the Roman orators. Although Augustine may have had an apology of this scope in mind at first, the work, once begun, held vast implications. Involved here were the problems of Divine Providence, the justification of evil in a theistic world, the reconciliation of unmerited suffering, and the meaning of a history interrupted by disasters. Nothing short of a cosmology, a total world view, could do justice to the questions forcing such an apology.

The overarching problem was providence. If God does not know what evils will occur, is he God? If he does know, is God not then either impotent or evil? Augustine answers the first question in the negative—God must have foreknowledge to be God. The problem exists only if one holds that infallible foreknowledge implies necessity. For Augustine, God can know all things without undermining free will, for *the free wills themselves* are included in the order of causes which God foreknows. It is God's knowledge of a thing which gives it not only being but also its specific nature; thus, it is *the very fact* of God's knowledge of man's free will *which makes it free*—it is known as free and not as determined. Freedom does not mean uncaused but self-caused, and it is the very self which God knows even more intimately than the self does. Consequently, God's knowledge of a person is that he will sin, not that he will be forced to sin.

In this manner God's immediate responsibility for evil is met. Yet there is a larger problem, for God still permits man in his freedom to do evil. The Empire provided the framework for Augustine's answer. The Empire, at its beginning, was dedicated to truth, justice, and the good of man—it was blessed by God. But love of liberty became love of domination; desire for virtue became intoxication for pleasure; glory in well-doing became vaunted pride. Herein is por-

trayed the dilemma of man from the beginning. In the beginning God created all things, and continues to create, for all would relapse into nothingness if he were to withdraw his creative power. All that God created is good, yet mutable, for having been created from nothing, it is absolutely dependent on God. Everything was graduated according to being, and the opposition of contraries serves to heighten the beauty of the universe.

It was with the act of creation that time began, for time means movement and change—none of these apply to God. As a result, God's foreknowledge applies to *all* of time, for his eternal envisagement is unchangeable; although God knows what man in his freedom will do, he also knows what he will do to bring from every evil a greater eventual good. It is in knowing all time as present that the evil in each human present is redeemed. For Augustine, everything adds to God's cosmic whole; even sinners beautify the world.

Nothing, however, is evil by nature, for all natures are God-created. Evil can be nothing but privation, lack of good. Only the will, not one's nature, is the source of evil. Both the highest of the angels and Adam became inflated by pride in their God-given capacities, craving to become ends in themselves "ye shall be as gods." Thus evil entered the world, for men made what was good into an evil by elevating it as the *supreme* good. Sex, for example, is a good, but is made evil when claimed as the center and meaning of life. It is not the thing turned to, but the turning itself, which is evil. Since man is sustained in being by his relation to the Supreme Good, any substitution of a lesser good brings with it an ontic disruption in which man's nature is injured. Although by such action man comes to approximate a nonentity, God does not revoke his nature totally, but sustains man enough for him to be aware of his self-inflicted loss.

The result is a creature frustrated in the conflict between nature and will—"O Lord. Thou hast made us for Thyself, and we are restless until we find our rest in Thee." In first not wanting to will what he could, man now wills to do what he cannot. This is evil as privation—the impotence of an essentially good nature. Since God alone truly is, that alone which is opposed to God is nonbeing; in willing less than fullness of being, man does not create evil but gives to nonbeing the existential status of being. Expressed in another way, sin is living the lie of believing oneself to be self-created, self-sustained, self-dependent. Such confusion establishes the duality, the fall, of creation; death is the most obvious consequence. Evil then has no efficient cause but a deficient one—the will. And as man is insubordinate to God, the "flesh" becomes insubordinate to the will.

In a phrase, evil is misdirected love. At this point Augustine's theory of history emerges. Adam's sin so altered man's nature, transmitted to his posterity, that human will is incapable of redirecting itself from itself as center. For such men, history is simply cyclic. But God's foreknowledge includes not simply man's fall, but God's election of some through grace to a redirected love. For these, history is linear, marked at its center by Jesus Christ, moving toward consummation in eternal life. Thus there are two histories in God's cosmic plan, indicated by two cities. These God permitted in order to show the consequences of pride and to reveal what good can be brought from evil by Grace.

Augustine's primary definition is this: "a people is an assemblage of reasonable beings bound together by a common agreement as to the objects of their love. . . ." History, from beginning to end, is divided by the two "cities" formed by these alternative loves—"the earthly by the love of self, even to the contempt of God; the heavenly by the love of God, even to the contempt of self." Of the first parents, Cain belonged to the city of men and Abel to the city of God. But since all are condemned by God, those in the latter are there only because of God's undeserved election.

Augustine's descriptions of these cities is all the more interesting because he refuses to overstate his case. In the first place, he refuses, for the most part, to equate the human city with historic Rome or the divine city with the visible Church—the churches are "full of those who shall be separated by the winnowing as in the threshing-floor." These are invisible cities, and their members are interspersed in these institutions, to be separated only at the end of history. In the second place, he refrains from painting the human city with totally black strokes— "the things which this city desires cannot justly be said to be evil, for it is itself, in its own kind, better than all other human good. For it desires earthly peace for the sake of enjoying earthly goods, and it makes war in order to attain to this peace." This city is characterized not by its goods but by its supreme love of them.

With meticulous care Augustine traces the history of both cities, carefully exegeting scriptural history as both literal and as allegorical of the abiding presence of the city of God. Throughout, in event, figure, and word, Augustine sees Christ's coming prophesied and prepared for. Since not even the Jews held that they alone belonged to God, Augustine maintains that it cannot be denied that other men and nations prophesied concerning Christ, and thus many of these may belong to the heavenly city.

It was Christ who, after his resurrection, opened the Scriptures to the disciples so that they could understand the eternal foundation of history and God's dual plan. But most especially, it was Christ's death, resurrection, ascension, and sending of the Holy Spirit which were the instruments of God's grace to the elect. Through his Incarnation he became Mediator, partaking of humanity so that in its purification by atonement on the Cross it could be resurrected with him in glory and through faith men could participate in his divinity. Faith begins purification not only of the will, and thus of one's nature, but also of the mind. As Augustine says, impregnated with faith, reason may advance toward the truth. Theology and philosophy belong together because will and reason are inseparable, both in impotence and in restoration.

Throughout history those of the divine city will know suffering at the hands of the human city, yet, being of the elect, they will not fall again. No evil will be permitted ultimately evil results; through suffering God bears witness to himself, and through it the believer is tempered and corrected. Such members (striving for the ideal balance of contemplation and action) obey the laws of the earthly city and are concerned with the necessities which do not undermine faith. To the end, the true Church goes forward "on pilgrimage amid the persecutions of the world and the consolations of God," its life aimed at universal love, its endurance based on the hope of future happiness. The peace of the city of God is "the perfectly ordered and harmonious enjoyment of God, and of one another in God." But in this life such peace is more the "solace of misery," and righteousness consists more in forgiveness than in the perfecting of virtues. The peace of the unbeliever is earthly pleasure, but in the life to come it will be an eternal misery of the will and passions in conflict. Expressed in terms of sin, history began with man's ability to sin or not to sin; it will end for the elect with man's higher freedom, the ability not to be able to sin, for in true freedom sin no longer has delight.

With meticulous detail, often disturbing in its literalness, Augustine outlines the epochs of future history, climaxing with the "new heaven and the new earth." Such an attempt escapes the charge of speculation, Augustine believes, because it has as its point of departure scriptural revelation, interpreted from the perspective of the Christ-event. Throughout these reflections there is a tension which has its roots in Augustine's own life. On the one hand is the rejection of this world in otherworldliness, holding alone to God's unfailing omnipotence and justice, and the eternal duality of heaven and hell. On the other hand, Augustine is world-affirming, straining for a transformational vision of which God's love gives foretaste. Both have their basis expressed in one of Augustine's concluding statements, emerging not only as a statement of faith but as a yearning hope issuing from his own tempestuous life. Speaking of that which is to be, he says that "then there shall be no more of this world, no more of the surgings and restlessness of human life. . . ."

Pertinent Literature

Deane, Herbert A. *The Political and Social Ideas of St. Augustine*. New York: Columbia University Press, 1963.

Historians of political thought have disagreed sharply concerning Saint Augustine's theory of the state. In general terms, the question is whether Augustine held, with the early Church, that the sole function of the state is to preserve order by restraining and punishing evildoers, or whether, anticipating the Middle Ages, he held that the state is obliged to promote morality and religion. As Augustine said little on this subject, the actual point at issue turns out to be how far Augustine agreed with Cicero's definition of the state.

In expounding the concept *res publica*, Cicero had declared that not every assemblage of men is a commonwealth—only one which is "associated by a common acknowledgement of law and by a community of interests." Augustine replied that to make law and righteousness a criterion was, in effect, to say that Rome had never been a commonwealth, and he offered a new definition according to which the bond uniting men in states is "a common agreement as to the objects of their love. "

In discussing these passages, some writers have argued that Augustine did not mean to reject the Ciceronian definition but merely to deny that it could be applied to pagan states. According to this view, Augustine remains in the tradition, stemming from Plato, which holds that the state is part of the Cosmos, being the means nature uses to establish right order in human associations and in the souls of men. All that he meant to dispute was whether any but a Christian state could claim to be guided by this higher law. Other writers, however, have argued that Augustine found the classical theory incompatible with man's fallen condition and, setting it aside, substituted a more realistic account of what states are and what can and cannot be expected of them.

Herbert A. Deane, probably in common with most recent students of Augustine, holds to the latter view. According to Deane, Augustine retained the Platonic ideal but denied that it can be realized or even approximated except in heaven. For this reason, Augustine was free to view politics with a cold eye and to ask in the modern fashion what ends states serve and how far they are successful. According to this interpretation, Augustine has more in common with Niccolò Machiavelli and Thomas Hobbes than he does with Boniface VIII or Richard Hooker.

Deane does not restrict his study to politics nor does he draw only from *The City of God*. The first half of the book lays the foundation for Augustine's political thought in his teaching concerning man's Fall and the effect of the fall on human society. Three orders are distinguished: the natural order, prior to the Fall, in which true justice reigned; the human order, in which selfish pursuit of worldly goods eventuates in the coercive state; and the divine order, realized only in heaven, but of which the redeemed are members even now by faith. Augustine, writing at a time when the Empire was officially Christian, recognized that the number of Christians had not significantly increased and the fact that a few Christians now held important positions in the Empire did not alter the character or operation of government. Indeed, according to Augustine, the chief effect of the conversion of Constantine had been to dilute the membership of the Church.

In Chapter 4 of his book, titled "The State: The Return of Order upon Disorder," Deane takes account of the more traditional "clerical" interpretation of the City of God, citing C. H. McIlwain (*The Growth of Political Theory in the West*) as giving the most plausible version. McIlwain contends that Augustine's quarrel with Cicero amounted to no more than a dispute as to whether a pagan state ought to be called a commonwealth. He says that when Augustine redefined the commonwealth he meant the new definition to apply to pagan states only. "Great states before Christianity were *regna* (realms) but they were not true commonwealths, because there was no recognition in them of what was the one true God.

. . . No heathen state can ever quite rise to the height of a true commonwealth."

Deane raises several objections. In the first place, Augustine nowhere makes any distinction between heathen and Christian states; nor does he suggest that pagan states cannot, while Christian states can, exhibit true justice. Moreover, McIlwain does not take sufficient account of Augustine's revised definition, which Deane regards as a major contribution to political theory profoundly based on Augustine's doctrine of man. Most damaging of all, McIlwain overlooks Augustine's clear statement that "true justice has no existence save in that republic whose founder and ruler is Christ," a statement which Deane understands to mean that no earthly state meets Cicero's criterion of a true commonwealth and that only the heavenly Jerusalem does.

According to Deane, Augustine held that the state is an external order designed to achieve the social stability which all men desire in order to pursue their various goals. It depends entirely on force, being a "non-natural remedial institution." Its purpose is not to make men good, nor has it at its disposal any means to mold the thoughts and wills of its subjects. If rulers and citizens alike were truly virtuous and pious men, and were they to hear and obey God's commandments and prefer the good of others to their own, "then would the republic adorn the lands of this life with its own felicity, and mount the pinnacle of life eternal to reign most blessedly." However, as Deane notes, when Augustine speaks in this way he uses the form of a condition contrary to fact. In any case, says Deane, if this condition were to be realized the result would not be a Christian state; rather, the state would "wither away" and the anarchist ideal of a noncoercive order would take its place.

Markus, R. A. *Saeculum: History and Society in the Theology of St. Augustine.* Cambridge: Cambridge University Press, 1970.

The City of God was composed over a period of fourteen years (A. D. 413 to 426). Times were changing; and, according to R. A. Markus, it was part of the greatness of Saint Augustine that his ideas were amenable to change. Markus explains that *The City of God* grew out of two separate projects. The notion

of "two cities" appeared in his writings before the sack of Rome, and, in 411, he announced his plan to write a book dealing with that subject. But charges by pagans that Christianity was to blame for the Gothic invasions prompted him instead to begin work on a book dealing with Rome's place in history.

As this work progressed the two themes tended to coalesce.

Rome's significance in God's plan of salvation was subject to dispute in the early Church: one party identified the Empire with anti-Christ, whereas the other saw in the *pax Romana* a preparation for the spread of the gospel. The conversion of Constantine and the suppression of pagan cults by Theodosius I lend support to the latter opinion. The collapse of paganism seemed the end of an epoch; and in his early period Augustine was, says Markus, "bewitched by the Theodosian mirage." However, the chaos that followed the death of Theodosius "broke the spell" and led Augustine to develop the view that Rome's destiny was a matter of theological indifference.

According to Markus, the originality of Augustine's mature views concerning Rome lay in the distinction which he worked out between sacred and secular history. Taking it for granted that God's providence extends to all nations, he concluded that what distinguishes sacred history from world history is not any quality attached to events but has to do solely with the interpretation of events—namely with the prophetic insight which links events into a single redemptive pattern. Prophecy included Christ's life on earth and the promise of his return as King, but it was silent as to the intervening years. Therefore, the age of the Church and its relation to gentile powers belongs not to sacred but to profane history.

Augustine's theology of the "two cities" originated in a different context, having to do not with history but with society. During the reign of Theodosius, when he was inclined to see Christ's power evinced in the overthrow of paganism, Augustine had held to the Neoplatonic vision in which the social order occupies a place in nature, having for its goal the liberation of man's spiritual from his bodily elements. But gradually he abandoned this attempt to combine Christianity with the classic ideal of the *polis*. Close study of the Bible taught him to think less in terms of flesh and spirit and more in terms of sin and salvation and to see the Christian as a citizen of the heavenly Zion and as a stranger in the world. This tragic view of existence, reinforced by the troubles of the times, made it easy for Augustine to identify Rome with Babylon as the ultimate embod-

iment of the perverse and selfish loves which constitute the earthly city. Nevertheless, his attitude toward Rome remained ambiguous; and before he had completed *The City of God* he had found a way of reconciling the Christian's alienation from society with a recognition of the deep obligations which bind the Christian to the temporal order. "The heavenly city uses the earthly peace in the course of its earthly pilgrimage. It cherishes and desires, as far as it may without compromising its faith and devotion, the orderly coherence of man's wills concerning the things which pertain to the mortal nature of man; and this earthly peace it refers to the attainment of heavenly peace."

For Markus the term *saeculum*, which can be translated either as the age or the world, designates Augustine's new perspective. Heaven has receded from the earth. No longer can any people claim to enjoy God's special favor, nor can any social institution claim divine authority. History is the intermixture of two classes—those with worldly and those with otherworldly goals. The state has no particular identity, being merely a collection of individuals, some seeking one thing, some seeking another, but all agreed on the need for civil order. In its restricted area the state is autonomous; but relative autonomy also belongs to other societies, including the Church. In the language of recent theology used by Markus, church and state are irreconcilable eschatologically but not temporally: their ultimate destinations are different but their careers through history are "inextricably intertwined." It follows that the attitudes of the Christian toward the two societies must be governed not by principle but by expediency.

In a chapter entitled *Coge Intrare* ("compel them to come in"), Markus tries to resolve the conflict between Augustine's conception of a secular state and his approval of the use of coercion in behalf of the Church. That he favored Theodosius' use of force to suppress paganism and schism was compatible with his initial belief in the victorious progress of Christ's Kingdom and his Neoplatonic conception of the *polis*; but his advocacy of compulsion after he had revised these opinions raises difficulties. The concept of *saeculum*, in which the Church is seen as engaged in a "historical, perplexed, and interwoven life" with the world, provides Markus with a solution. In the first place, Augustine's new pluralistic view of society tended to dissolve the notion of the state, so that he thought less in terms of corporate action than in terms of action by individual magistrates and bishops whose duty required them to use the best means of upholding morals and religion. In the second place,

armed conflict between Catholics and Donatists being one of the facts of life in North Africa, the question for Augustine was not one of principle but of "pastoral strategy." At first he judged the results of coercion to be harmful to the Catholic cause; later he revised his opinion.

Additional Recommended Reading

Baynes, Norman H. "Political Aspects of St. Augustine's De Civitate Dei," in *Byzantine Studies and Other Essays*. London: Athlone Press, 1955, pp. 288-306. A public lecture by an outstanding historian of the period. The state, although founded on injustice, receives relative justification through its role in maintaining the peace.

Brown, P. R. L. "Saint Augustine," in *Trends in Medieval Political Thought*. Edited by Beryl Smalley. Oxford: Basil Blackwell, 1965. In Markus' judgment, a "deeply perceptive study" of political obligation.

Figgis, J. N. *The Political Aspects of St. Augustine's City of God*. London: Longmans, Green, and Company, 1921. A major contribution to the debate concerning Augustine's definition of the state. Includes a chapter on Augustine's view of history.

Löwith, Karl. *Meaning in History*. Chicago: University of Chicago Press, 1949. Chapters on leading philosophers of history from Augustine to Carl Burckhardt. "The interpretation of history is an attempt to understand the meaning of suffering by historical action."

THE PLATFORM SCRIPTURE OF THE SIXTH PATRIARCH

Author: Hui-neng (638-713)
Type of work: (Zen) Buddhist sermon, ethics, metaphysics
First transcribed: c. 677

Principal Ideas Advanced

Perfect, Buddha wisdom is in everyone.
Insight into one's original, pure nature is possible only by putting that nature into practice.
To attain insight into one's Buddha nature, one's mind must be free from attachments and error.
The practice of direct mind leads to sudden enlightenment.
Through no-thought—not being distracted by thought while thinking—one's original nature, the True Reality, is thought.
The original wisdom and such meditation are one.

The Platform Scripture of the Sixth Patriarch *(Liu-tsu t' an-ching)* is generally regarded as the basic classic of Ch'an (Zen) Buddhism. The work is reputed to be a record of the teachings of the great Ch'an Master Hui-neng, as expressed in his remarks delivered in the Ta-fan Temple in Shao-chou in or about the year 677, and as recorded by his disciple Fa-hai. The most authentic version of the work is regarded by such scholars as Wing-tsit Chan and Philip B. Yampolsky to be the *Tun-huang* manuscript, found in a cave in Tun-huang, northwest China, in 1900. (Both Chan and Yampolsky have translated the Tun-huang manuscript and have provided copious commentary. See the *Pertinent Literature* section that follows.)

Although the details of the life of Hui-neng are uncertain, and although some commentators have questioned the authorship of the *Platform Scripture*, the prevailing legends, embellished by commentators over the years, tend to agree on the following biographical items: Hui-neng was born in 638 into a humble family, the Lu family, originally in Fan-yang and later, at the time of Hui-neng's birth, in Hsin-chou in southwestern Kwangtung. Hui-neng was a firewood peddlar. In his early twenties he was inspired by a reading of the *Diamond Scripture*, and he traveled to the north to visit the Fifth Patriarch, who

was an exponent of the scripture.

Legend has it that Hui-neng was appointed Sixth Patriarch after having served a stint under the Fifth Patriarch as a pounder of rice and having subsequently impressed the Patriarch with a poem requested of all his disciples by the Fifth Patriarch. Whether or not the story is true, it appears clear that Hui-neng did "receive the robe" as Sixth Patriarch in 661, just a few months after arriving in Huang-mei to visit the Fifth Patriarch.

In 676, after several years of preaching in south China, Hui-neng moved to Canton. He had become a Buddhist priest at the age of thirty-nine. The following year (so the story goes) he was invited to lecture in the Ta-fan Temple in Shao-chou. There his remarks were recorded by his disciple Fa-hai (according to the *Platform Scripture*), and the resultant work is, or at least provided the foundation for, the *Platform Scripture of the Sixth Patriarch*.

Hui-neng is honored as the Ch'an Master who initiated the "Southern School" of Ch'an Buddhism in opposition to the Northern School led by Shen-hsiu (c. 605-706). The Northern School maintained that enlightenment would come gradually as a result of practicing formalized procedures of meditation; the Southern School argued that meditation must be free, a matter of allowing the pure Buddha-nature to reveal itself, and that enlightenment would be sudden. According to Chan, although this difference of opinion about the speed of enlightenment was present as a matter of emphasis, the two schools differed more fundamentally in their concepts of mind, the Northern School maintaining that the mind or Buddha-nature, common to all persons, cannot be differentiated and that its activities are functions of the True Reality, while the Southern School argued that the pure mind can function only in quietude or "calmness," and only after having freed itself from the false or erroneous mind with its attachments to individual thoughts. In any case, according to Chan, the Southern School became the most influential force in the development of Zen Buddhism in China from the ninth century.

As translated by Chan, the heading of the *Platform Scripture* is as follows: "The Platform Scripture Preached by the Sixth Patriarch, Hui-neng, in the Ta-fan Temple in Shao-chou, the Very Best Perfection of Great Wisdom Scripture on the Sudden Enlightenment Doctrine of the Southern School of Zen, one book, including the Giving of the Discipline that Frees One from the Attachment to Differentiated Characters for the Propagation of the Law. Gathered and recorded by disciple Fa-hai." As translated by Yampolsky, the heading is: "Southern School Sudden Doctrine, Supreme Mahäyäna Great Perfection of Wisdom: The Platform Sutra preached by the Sixth Patriarch Hui-neng at the Ta-fan Temple in Shao-chou, one roll, recorded by the spreader of the Dharma, the disciple Fa-hai, who at the same time received the Precepts of Formlessness. "

The *Platform Scripture* recounts that the Master Hui-neng lectured to more than ten thousand monks, nuns, and followers, all gathered in the lecture hall of the Ta-fan Temple. His topic was the Dharma (law) of the perfection of Wisdom (of the original, pure wisdom of the Buddha-nature). Hui-neng begins with an autobiographical account. The material is interesting, but it has little philosophical or religious import. In Section 12 Hui-neng declares that he was determined or predestined to preach to the officials and disciples gathered there in the temple, and he maintains that the teaching is not original with him: it has been handed down by the sages. Sections 13 through 19 contain the fundamental teachings of Hui-neng.

In 13 Hui-neng declares that calm meditation and wisdom are a unity, that such meditation is the substance of wisdom, and that wisdom is the function of meditation.

The Buddhist doctrine, here implicit, is that everyone shares the Buddha-nature (wisdom) and that if one can turn one's mind inward and not be distracted, one can receive enlightenment. Wisdom and meditation are one in that meditation (of the kind advocated by Hui-neng) is regarded as the function or practice of the original nature. Hence, Hui-neng declares that meditation exists in wisdom, and wisdom is within meditation. Neither gives rise to the other, he insists. If the mind and words are both good and the internal and external are one, then wisdom and meditation are one.

Hui-neng next stresses the critical importance of practicing—actively attaining—a straightforward or direct mind. A straightforward mind requires having no attachments and attending to no differentiating characters, thereby realizing that all is one; there is a unity of nature in everything. To achieve such realization in the practice of the straightforward mind is *samadhi* of oneness, a state of calmness in which one knows all dharmas to be the same. But the calm realization of oneness is not, as some people think, a matter of simply sitting without moving and not allowing erroneous thoughts to rise in the mind. To act in this way is to make oneself insentient, and that is not in accordance with the Way, the *tao*, which can work freely only if the mind is free from things. If one attempts, as some people do, to view the mind and keep it inactive, they become radically disturbed and never achieve enlightenment. (Section 14.)

Hui-neng is indirectly critical of the Northern School in his description of the meditation method which, in effect, renders people insensible and inactive; and he continues his criticism in Section 16 when he states that the deluded teachers recommend a gradual course to enlightenment, while the enlightened teachers practice the method of sudden enlightenment. In this passage Hui-neng clearly states that to know one's own mind or to know one's original nature is the same thing, and if people differ in coming to enlightenment it is because some people are stupid and deluded while others know the method of enlightenment.

Hui-neng then remarks that everyone has regarded "no-thought" as his main doctrine. His remark ties in with what he had just been saying about meditation method, for the doctrine to which he alludes is the meditation method he endorsed, a method that came to be identified with the Southern School. Put informally, the statement of method would be put injunctively, "Practice no-thought," and sense would be made of the injunction by presuming the point to be that the mind will be open to its nature, will be able to "think" (intuit) the pure nature common to all within oneself, only if it is not distracted by thoughts *about* things, including the thought about achieving enlightenment by not thinking about anything else. The truth is, one cannot achieve awareness even of the Buddha-nature by thinking *about* it.

Hui-neng speaks of no-thought as the main doctrine (of meditation), of "non-form as the substance" and of "non-abiding as the basis" (to follow Yampolsky's translation). He then adds that "Non-form is to be separated from form even when associated with form. No-thought is not to think even when involved in thought. Non-abiding is the original nature of man." Presumably, as the next passage (of Section 17) implicitly indicates, the original Buddha-nature is absolute, in no way dependent upon or related to or attached to any particular being or characteristic of being; hence, "non-abiding" (non-attachment) is the original nature of man. When involved in the thought consisting in the awareness of original nature (or while succeeding in the practice of freeing the mind), one is not thinking this or that. In that sense, the thinking of the original nature is no-thought. As Chan translates a relevant passage here, "If one single instant of thought is attached to anything, then every thought will be attached. This is bondage. But if in regard to dharmas no thought is attached to anything, that is freedom."

To be separated from forms is not to attend to the characters of things; it then happens, so Hui-neng preaches, that the substance of one's nature is pure. One must not be affected by external objects and one must not turn one's thought to them. But one must, of course, *think*—that is, one must think the pure

nature of True Reality. No-thought is thought free from the error of attending to external things and characters and from all attachment. If your pure nature is allowed to function, as it will if there is no-thought, then True Reality becomes the substance of thought.

Hui-neng then speaks of "sitting in meditation" (in Section 18). He contends that this teaching does not call for looking at the mind or at the purity of one's nature. The objects of such viewing are illusions, and to suppose that one is looking at objects or that there are such objects to look at is to be deluded. However, if delusions are avoided, then the original nature is revealed in its purity. Purity has no form, Hui-neng argues, and hence one cannot grasp the form of purity and then pass judgment on others. Deluded people are quick to find fault with others because they (the deluded) presume themselves to know the form of purity. By criticizing others, such persons violate the *tao*, the true Way.

Sitting in meditation, then, is not a matter of looking for forms or characters; sitting in meditation is, rather, to be free and not to allow thoughts to be activated. Hence (Hui-neng concludes in Section 19), true meditation is the achievement of internal calmness and purity. (To "see" the original nature and in purity and freedom to *be* the original nature—to meditate and to be wise—are one and the same. Meditation is the practice of original wisdom; wisdom is the internal subject of meditation.)

The remaining sections of the *Platform Scripture* are concerned with provoking ritualistic attention to the central features of Mahayana Buddhism or are taken up with miscellaneous material, most of it probably added by later writers to the sermon core.

Whether or not the ideas represented in the *Platform Scripture* were actually enunciated by Hui-neng and recorded by Fa-hai, they represent the central doctrines of Ch'an Buddhism of the Southern School and are of philosophical and historical interest whatever their origin. In many ways the *Platform Scripture* can be seen as an argument for intuition as the way of enlightenment, in opposition to those who argue for the way of intellect and its distinctive mode, analysis.

Pertinent Literature

Hui-neng. *The Platform Scripture*. Edited and translated by Wing-tsit Chan. New York: St. John's University Press, 1963.

Wing-tsit Chan's *Platform Scripture* is the first unabridged English translation of the *Tun-huang* manuscript (probably eighth century) discovered in 1900 in Tun-huang, northwest China. In Chan's opinion this manuscript is the most authentic and is to be preferred to the "Ming Canon" (derived from the version edited by Sung-pao in 1291), the Kosho Temple copy (of Hui-hsin's 967 version), and the Daijo Temple copy (dated 1228, with a preface dated 1116), probably also a copy of the Hui-hsin version.

The *Platform Scripture* is described by Chan as the basic Zen classic, the only Chinese work honored as a Buddhist scripture.

The chief feature of Zen Buddhism, Chan writes, is its emphasis on meditation (*dhyana* in Sanskrit, *ch'an* in Chinese, *zen* in Japanese), but it should be noted that the Zen school eventually discarded formal meditation. Zen is a way of life, Chan contends, not merely a state of mind. It is distinctive for its method, and it aims at teaching the acceptance of and insight into life. Thus, it is not accurate, he argues, to treat Zen as a specific philosophy, religion, or ethics.

As Chan summarizes the ideas of Zen, they are the following: the mind is identical with Reality; Reality is one and universal; it is the Void, beyond expression in thought or words, for Reality has no differentiated characteristics; Reality must be known directly and immediately; the mind must operate spontaneously and unconsciously if one is to attain Buddhahood. Thus, Chan writes, "the best approach to Reality is to 'have no thought,' and the best way of being is to 'have no mind.'"

Chan explains that such expressions as "no-thought" and "no-mind" are not to be taken literally because what they are intended to endorse is a method of thinking and a way of mind that is not egocentric and that is not impeded and distracted by the conscious effort to find the Way or to become a Buddha. Hence, the emphasis in Zen Buddhism is not on action but on being; it is not so much what one is to do as what one is to *be*.

Since Zen maintains that all persons have the Buddha-nature, the Buddha wisdom, and since Reality is universal, there is no particular way of seeking Buddhahood; there is only the need to be one's original, pure self. What is called for, then, is a kind of self-reliance that is nevertheless not an absorption in one's individuality but in the original Buddha-nature that one is.

Chan remarks that the influence of Zen is clear in Chinese art. In landscape painting nature is presented as a whole by way of a simple representation of the essence of Reality; there is no unnecessary color, detail, or shading.

Indian Zen techniques were introduced into China from India in the second century, Chan relates. Early Zen Masters were Tao-an (312-385) and Hui-yüan (334-416). But Zen became a distinctive Chinese school with the emergence of Bodhidharma, who arrived in Canton in the 470's and acquired devoted followers whom he advised to discard all Buddhist scriptures except the *Scripture About the Buddha Entering into Lanka*. This scripture, according to Chan, fosters the idea that the "True State or Nirvana is total Emptiness devoid of any characteristics, duality, or differentiation." Through intuition into our Buddha-nature we achieve emancipation. The method of unattached concentration is comparable to what one would achieve by facing a wall to free the mind. (Chan refers at this point to the legend of Bodhidharma's sitting in meditation for nine years while facing a wall.) By such a method the mind is free from both being and nonbeing.

Bodhidharma is usually called the First Patriarch of the Zen Buddhist school, but he was not the first Chinese Zen Master. After Bodhidharma, several generations of Lanka Masters perpetuated the doctrine, and Hui-neng, author of the *Platform Scripture* was the Sixth Patriarch, deriving the "robe" from Hung-jen (601-674), the Fifth Patriarch.

Hui-neng's family was poor, and consequently Hui-neng was illiterate, but when he heard a recitation of the *Diamond Scripture* (when he was about twenty-four) he was inspired to visit its principal exponent, the Fifth Patriarch, Hung-jen. Hui-neng so impressed the Patriarch that within a few months he was proclaimed the Sixth Patriarch, and he became a Buddhist priest in 676. In 677 (it is reported) he received an invitation from the prefect of the city of Shao-chou to lecture in the Ta-fan Temple there. Purportedly Hui-neng's disciple Fa-hai recorded the sermon, and the *Platform Scripture* is the result.

Chan offers a summary account of the lecture. Hui-neng is described as having "emphatically declared" that everyone possesses the Buddha-nature, that the "great wisdom" is nothing but this nature, and that putting the original, pure nature into practice would make one equal to the Buddha. Outside activities are useless (reading scriptures, building temples, praying, recitations, and so on); what is needed is to "take refuge in the nature within. . . ." The way to intuit one's nature is through "calmness and wisdom," attained when one frees oneself from thoughts, characters, and all attachments. True meditation is not of the conventional, ritualized sort; it consists of

the calmness that is the unattached true and original nature within. Seeing one's own nature is "sudden enlightenment." If one holds to the *Diamond Scripture* (Chan concludes his summary account), one will "attain wisdom . . . see his own nature . . . and become a Buddha in his own physical body. . . ."

Chan's Introduction to the *Platform Scripture* provides an account of the contributions to Zen Buddhism made by Hui-neng's successors, an analysis of the differences between the *Diamond Scripture* and the *Lanka* scripture (the *Diamond Scripture* emphasizing freedom of the mind from attachments, the *Lanka* emphasizing the nonduality and nondifferentiation of the True State), the differences in teachings of the Southern and Northern Schools, the later developments of Zen, and a survey of the Zen methods, including the devices of the *koan* (problem inviting an enigmatic answer), shouting, and beating.

Chan explains that the "platform" is the raised structure from which ordination is administered. The sermon part of the *Platform Scripture* is genuine; the autobiographical parts and the last sections include modifications and additions.

Hui-neng. *The Platform Sutra of the Sixth Patriarch: The Text of the Tun-huang Manuscript.* Edited and translated by Philip B. Yampolsky. New York: Columbia University Press, 1967.

Philip B. Yampolsky, at the time Lecturer in Japanese at Columbia University, provides an extensive introduction to his translation of the *Platform Sutra* (or *Scripture*). Yampolsky gives an account of the growth of Ch'an Buddhism in the eighth century, including a detailed account of the Lankavatara School and of Shen-hui, a disciple of Hui-neng and champion of what came to be called the Southern School of Ch'an Buddhism. The story of eighth century Ch'an Buddhism then focuses on Hui-neng, and Yampolsky offers a detailed and carefully documented biography of the Sixth Patriarch. In "The Making of a Book: *The Platform Sutra*," Yampolsky reviews the history of the Tun-huang manuscript (which he estimates was written between 830 and 860); he traces the developing history of versions of the work; and he offers 820 as the probable date of the *Platform Scripture*. He then discusses the *Platform Scripture* in considerable detail, concluding with a

careful analysis of content.

The contents of the Tun-huang text fall into five classes, according to Yampolsky: (1) the autobiographical material, (2) the sermons, (3) arguments against Northern Ch'an (Zen) Buddhism and in defense of the Southern School, (4) sections relating to Fa-hai (the transmitter of the book) and various miscellaneous verses and stories.

The sermons exhibit a striking similarity to passages in the works of Shen-hui, and thus Yampolsky suggests that there is the possibility that the *Platform Scripture* is derived from Shen-hui's works. Yampolsky advises that one regard the sermons of the *Platform Scripture* as representative of middle and late eighth century Ch'an thought, later organized, modified, and enlarged by subsequent Ch'an Masters.

The autobiographical section of the *Platform Scripture* tells of Hui-neng's humble beginnings, of his illiteracy, of his interviews with the Fifth Patriarch, of the Patriarch's expounding the *Diamond Scripture* to Hui-neng, of his being made Sixth Patriarch, and of his departure for the south. Throughout the remainder of the *Platform Scripture* Hui-neng is a "rather disembodied voice represented by the phrase: 'The Master said,' " Yampolsky comments.

The *Platform Scripture* contributes little to one's understanding of how the doctrine was transmitted from teacher to disciple; the teaching methods are left unclear, Yampolsky reports. However, he adds, the sermons played an important role, and by the time Hui-neng delivered his sermons at the Ta-fan Temple in Shao-chou he was "a renowned Ch'an Master, the recognized Sixth Patriarch. . . ."

Most of the central ideas in the *Platform Scripture* are taken from canonical sources, according to Yampolsky, and are presented in comparatively simple form. Other Ch'an scholars later elaborated and commented on the ideas as presented in the *Platform Scripture*.

Yampolsky summarizes the content of the sermon as follows: The identity of *prajna* (original wisdom) and *dhyana* (meditation) is said by Hui-neng to be basic in his teachings; neither comes before the other, he argues. The true wisdom is possessed from the beginning by everyone; thus, one does not attain it through meditation. Knowledge of the true nature is enlightenment. Practicing "direct mind" and having no attachments, Hui-neng taught, is the "*samadhi* of oneness," that is, concentration on the oneness of the universe. Sudden enlightenment comes to one who uses the method of direct mind (but, Yampolsky points out, Hui-neng does not suggest that the method is a quick one). Enlightenment is a state of no-thought, achieved by cutting off attachment to any instant of thought and hence attachment to thoughts and to thought itself. (Yampolsky suggests that the references to direct mind, no-thought, the original and pure nature, the Buddha-nature, and all related matters, appear to involve a conception of the Absolute as that which is beyond conception and statement in words.) Hui-neng speaks of "sitting in meditation" (*tso-ch'an*) and explains meditation as an internal seeing of the original nature by not activating thoughts. (Yampolsky points out that Hui-neng rejects the formal meditation practices of other schools of Buddhism and Ch'an, but he does not reject meditation itself.) Then the sermon turns to Mahayana Buddhism in general and to the recital of the Precepts. Throughout the sermon, Yampolsky emphasizes, the doctrine is enunciated that holds that the Buddha-nature is in all sentient beings and that to find this nature is "to see one's own original mind." The miscellaneous stories, verses, and other passages with which the *Platform Scripture* closes tend to bear out the principal ideas of the central section of the scripture and to offer points in criticism of other Buddhist schools.

Additional Recommended Reading

Conze, Edward, ed. and tr. *Buddhist Wisdom Books: The Diamond Sutra and the Heart Sutra.* London: George Allen & Unwin, 1958. A careful translation of two classic scriptures, with copious explanatory notes. Conze reports that it is said that Hui-neng achieved enlightenment by meditating on the following passage in the *Diamond Scripture*: "Therefore then, Sub-huti, the Bodhisattva, the great being, should produce an unsupported thought, i.e. a thought which is nowhere supported, a thought unsupported by sights, sounds, smells, tastes, touchables or mind-objects."

Fung Yu-lan. *The Spirit of Chinese Philosophy.* Translated by E. R. Hughes. London: Kegan Paul, Trench, Trubner & Company, 1947. The distinguished Chinese philosopher Fung Yu-lan here assumes the role of historian of thought and offers a thorough and clear account of Chinese philosophy, including a chapter on the "Inner-light School (*Ch'an Tsung*) of Buddhism."

Koller, John M. *Oriental Philosophies.* New York: Charles Scribner's Sons, 1970. Koller provides a helpful and explanatory survey of Hindu systems, Buddhist philosophies (including a chapter on Zen Buddhism), and Chinese philosophies.

Wing-tsit Chan, ed. and tr. *A Source Book in Chinese Philosophy.* Princeton, New Jersey: Princeton University Press, 1963. An excellent collection of basic writings; includes illuminating introductory sections and notes. Selections from the *Platform Scripture* are provided, together with selections from *Shen-hui yü-lu* (*Recorded Conversations of Shen-hui*).

CREST JEWEL OF WISDOM

Author: S'ankara (or Shankara, Samkara, Sankaracharya, c. 788-c. 820)
Type of work: Metaphysics
First transcribed: Unknown

Principal Ideas Advanced

*In this existence, all is illusion (*maya).

To achieve liberation the wise man will discriminate between the permanent and the transitory; he will be indifferent to the fruits of action; he will achieve tranquillity of mind, self-control, cessation of action by the mind, forbearance of suffering, faith, and deep concentration on Brahman; and he will yearn to be liberated from the bonds of ignorance and egoism.

*Liberation from this existence can be achieved only through direct perception of the oneness of the individual self (*atman) with the universal self (Brahman).

The self is none of the five sheaths of the human beings.

To achieve nirvana the disciple must overcome the feeling of "I," follow his guru's teachings, study the scriptures, and come to full awareness of the truth of the mystic formula: "This is Brahman; that thou art."

It would be incorrect to speak about "the philosophy of S'ankara" since he and other great Indian sages never claimed a philosophy of their own but were merely expounders of the great spiritual knowledge bequeathed them by a long lineage of predecessors. They differ according to the emphasis placed upon the various aspects of that knowledge, and their greatness is measured by the degree to which they mastered it. By that measure, S'ankara was perhaps the greatest of the historical Hindu sages, not including, however, Gautama the Buddha.

In the East the belief is common that there is a "soul-redeeming" *truth* which can make of its possessor a divine being, one liberated from the wheel of *samsara*, that is, from obligatory rebirth. The state of liberation, nirvana, is the supreme aim, the *summum bonum* of all six Hindu schools of philosophy, as well as of the various Buddhist sects. The Western reader must, therefore, constantly keep in mind that there are three basic doctrines of Oriental philosophy:

(1) The doctrine of *rebirth*, meaning the periodic appearance of the same human egos in new physical bodies.

(2) The doctrine of *Karma*, or moral retribution, the regulatory law under which rebirth takes place.

(3) The doctrine of *spiritual evolution* by which a relative perfection is attainable, in principle, by all beings—those of the lower kingdoms of nature included.

We can realize why no Hindu sage bothers to prove or defend these three doctrines, for they are never questioned even by an opponent. This will also explain the universal belief in India of the existence among men of advanced beings who have acquired supernormal powers (*siddhis*) and who are no longer subject to the normal laws of birth and death. Having learned the hidden secrets of nature, mainly by following the Delphic injunction "Man, know thyself!" they discovered that a thorough knowledge and understanding of their own egos enabled them to become masters not only of themselves, that is, of the actions of the outer body and the inner mind, but also of external nature to an extent that the Western reader would be inclined to call miraculous. Yet it is claimed by these sages that their supernormal powers are definitely not *supernatural*, but are exerted within the framework of nature's laws, which therefore, they are able to make use of, whenever the occasion calls for the exercise of their *siddhis*.

Such a sage was S'ankara. Because of the fact that many of his successors adopted the same name, S'ankara, there is a great confusion as to his dates as well as to his writings. Many of the writings of the later S'ankaras have been fathered upon their illustrious predecessor, not always to the benefit of the latter. Although some biographers place him as early as 510 B.C., most scholars are agreed that he was born much later, about the beginning of the ninth century.

S'ankara, by writing his commentary on the *Brahma Sūtras*, in which he stressed non-dualism (*a-dvaita*), became the founder of the Advaita system of the Vedanta school of Hindu philosophy.

S'ankara's writings consist of a number of important commentaries as well as original treatises of various lengths. Of his commentaries, the one on the *Brahma Sūtras* is of the greatest importance for his followers. Also important are the ones on some of the principal *Upanishads* as well as his commentary on the *Bhagavad Gita*.

Most of S'ankara's original treatises seem to have been written for his disciples' use only. Among these is the very short one, entitled *Ten Stanzas*, consisting of precisely ten quatrains. Somewhat longer is the *Hundred Stanzas* consisting of 101 quatrains. Of his two compendiums of Advaita philosophy, the *Thousand Teachings* consists of a part in prose of 116 numbered paragraphs and a part in verse consisting of 649 couplets arranged in nineteen chapters. The other compendium is the *Crest Jewel of Wisdom (Vivekacūdamani)*, which consists of 581 stanzas, most of which are couplets and quatrains with a few triplets interspersed.

The Vedanta viewpoint (*vedantadarsana*) was firmly established by Badarayana in his *Brahma Sutras*, also called *Vedanta Sutras*. He is claimed to be identical with Krishna Dvaipayana who is the compiler of the Vedas, to whom also the *Puranas* are attributed, not to speak of the *Mahabharata*. But the Vedas were compiled 3100 B.C., according to Brahman chronology and this is, perhaps, too early a date for the *Brahma Sūtras*.

The *Brahma Sūtras* starts with an inquiry into Brahman, the world soul, then continues with a refutation of erroneous views, after which the means of reaching union with Brahman are discussed. Finally the fourth and last part is dedicated to the nature of liberation from the rounds of rebirth, and discusses the kinds of liberated beings. The sūtras (aphorisms) are extraordinarily terse, often consisting of only one or two words, and generally without any verb. Commentators are needed to explain these riddles. But, as one would expect, commentators are wont to disagree among themselves, and so the Vedanta school split into three main systems, known as the *Advaita*, or Non-Dualistic system; the *Visistadvaita*, or Qualified non-Dualistic system; and the *Dvaita* or Dualistic system.

Of these, the first system is that of S'ankara and his commentary; the second is that of Ramanuja and his great commentary (*S'ribhasya*); the third system is that of Madhva, or Anandatirtha, and his *Sutrabhasya*.

S'ankara teaches the unity of the self of man with Brahman, and that their apparent separation is an illusion (*maya*). Ramanuja, while admitting that the self of man can unite with Brahman, claims that both are real. His system is theistic and anthropomorphic, based on religious devotion rather than on rules of logic, as is that of S'ankara. Madhva, however, teaches that the duality of man's soul and Brahman persists, that both are real and independent of each other. His dualism is unqualified and opposes S'ankara's monistic views as well as the views of Ramanuja.

There have been other commentators on the *Brahma Sutras*. Perhaps the most recent is Baladeva (eighteenth century), whose extensive commentary, known as *Govinda Bhasya*, gives the Vaisnava viewpoint, since he was a follower of S'ri Chaitanya. The *Govinda Bhasya* is therefore theistic, like the one by Ramanuja.

The *Crest Jewel of Wisdom* was written by S'ankara to assist the would-be aspirant to spiritual wisdom in his efforts to free himself from the rounds of incessant rebirths. There is a strong similarity between the teachings and methods of S'ankara and the Buddha. Both aimed to teach mankind how to conquer pain and suffering, how to reach the acme of manhood, and finally how to obtain the highest spiritual state possible while still living on earth. Both considered conditioned existence as *unreal* and stressed its illusory character (*maya*). Neither of the two had any use for personal gods (*devas*), knowing themselves superior to the latter. The Buddhists and Advaita Vedantists have been called atheists by their opponents, and Buddha as well as S'ankara discarded rituals completely. There is no real difference between the path leading to Buddhahood and the path leading to the state of a *Jivanmukta*. All this makes it more difficult to explain the nearly complete silence of the Buddha on the subject of the Self (*atman*) and the almost continuous reference to the *atman* by S'ankara. Buddha's silence led many Buddhists as well as non-Buddhists to believe that Buddha denied the existence of the *atman* and, therefore, of a soul, which, of course, would contradict Buddha's statements upon a number of other subjects.

S'ankara's writings are too metaphysical, even for the average Hindu, to be useful for any but advanced disciples in Hindu mysticism. This he frankly admits at the outset of most of his treatises, and so in the case of the *Crest Jewel of Wisdom* he directs himself to a "wise man" (*vidvan*) who strives for liberation and has renounced his desire for the enjoyment of external objects. He advises the "wise man" to apply to a true and great spiritual teacher for guidance. After some further advice of a general nature he states the qualifications necessary for success in this venture, apart from being learned and of strong intellect: (1) *Discrimination* between things permanent and transitory; (2) *indifference* to enjoyment of the fruits of one's actions in this world and in the next; (3) the six accomplishments:

S'ama (tranquillity), which is a state of mind devoted to its goal;

Dama (self-control), which is the fixing in their own proper sphere of both the organs of perception and of action, after reverting them from their objects;

The height of *uparati* (cessation), which is the spontaneous abstaining from action by the mind;

Titiksa (forbearance), which is patient endurance of all suffering, without retaliation, free from anxiety and complaint;

S'raddha (faith), which is reflection and meditation on the truth of the words of the Guru and of the sacred texts; and

Samadhana (deep concentration), which is the constant fixing of the discriminating mind (*buddhi*) upon the pure Brahman, and not the indulging of the mind (*citta*);

and (4) *yearning to be liberated* (*mumuksuta*), which is the desire to be liberated by knowing one's own real nature and the bonds made through ignorance, from egoism down to the body.

The necessary qualifications for the Guru, the teacher whom the well-equipped aspirant to liberation or nirvana must now seek, are even more severe. The Guru, through whom freedom from bondage is to be attained, must be spiritually wise, conversant with sacred knowledge, sincere, and not suffering from desires; he must know the nature of Brahman; he must be one who is at rest in the Eternal, like a fire that is tranquil when destitute of fuel, one who is a river of disinterested compassion, a friend of all living creatures.

Having found such a preceptor and having asked him for guidance, the disciple, when found worthy, is then instructed by his Master, who praises him for his desire to rid himself of the bonds of ignorance (*avidya*). He is told that liberation can only be achieved through the *direct perception* of the oneness of the individual self (*atman*) with the universal self (Brahman). Neither the Vedas, nor the scriptures (*sastras*), nor the incantation (*mantras*), nor any medicine can help him who is bitten by the snake of ignorance.

It is necessary to know how to discriminate between spirit and non-spirit, between the self and not-self.

In order to show the difference between spirit and non-spirit, the Guru outlines the visible and invisible part of nature, beginning with the grossest of man's constituent vehicles.

The *gross body* is produced from the five subtle elements, whose functions are responsible for the five senses. The Guru warns of the danger of sense enjoyments and of desires pertaining to the body, and he describes the danger in no uncertain terms.

The *internal organ* consists of *manas*, the mental

faculties of postulating and doubting; the intellect, having the characteristic of certainty about things; the ego-conforming power, producing the conception "I"; and the mind, having the property of concentration.

The *vital principle* manifests itself, according to its transformations, as one of the five "vital airs."

The *subtle or astral body* is the vehicle of the five faculties, the five sense organs, the five vital airs, the five elements, ignorance, desire, and action. It is also known as the vehicle of characteristics, and is active in dreams.

The *causal body* of the self is the unmanifested condition of the three universal qualities. Its state is that of dreamless sleep. The three universal qualities are purity, action, and darkness. When the purity is unalloyed there will be perception of the self.

The Guru now defines in many ways the Supreme Spirit (*Paramatman*) through the knowledge of which Isolation (*Kaivalya*) or Freedom is obtained.

A description follows of the five sheaths (*kosa*), another way of looking at the constituents of a human being. They are the *annamaya*-sheath, sustained by physical food—that is, the gross body; the *pranamaya*-sheath, the vehicle of the vital forces, through which the ego performs all the actions of the gross body; the *manomaya*-sheath, consisting of the organs of sensation and *manas*, the latter mental faculty being the cause of ignorance and consequently the cause of the bondage of conditioned existence, although the same *manas* when pure becomes the cause of liberation; the *vijnanamaya*-sheath, consisting of intellect and the powers of perception, the doer of actions and the cause of the rounds of rebirth, the embodied ego which has no beginning in time and which is the guide of all actions; the *anandamaya*-sheath, the reflection of absolute bliss, yet not free from the quality of darkness.

The Guru explains that these five sheaths are *not the Self*. The latter is self-illumined and remains after the subtraction of these sheaths. It is the witness of the three states, of the waking, dreaming, and deep sleep state.

The disciple is now given subtler teachings about the Self and the Supreme Spirit. In a number of stanzas is repeated, paraphrasing the *Chandogya-Upanishad*, the mystic formula: ". . . this is Brahman, that thou art (*tat tvam asi*)."

The subject of the mental impressions which are the seeds in the mind through which *karma* manifests subsequently to any act is now discussed by the Guru, and the disciple is told how to exhaust them. At the same time the disciple must overcome the feeling of "I," the power of egoism, and many stanzas are dedicated to the elaboration of this subject. Other subjects are interwoven in the discussion, such as that of *nirvikalpa samadhi*, a superior type of meditation.

The stanzas become more and more abstruse while the disciple advances in spiritual matters. The characteristics of *jivanmukta*, he who is *liberated while living on earth*, are described, and also the consequences of this achievement, especially in relation to the three kinds of *karma*.

Finally comes the moment when the disciple, through the Guru's teaching, through the evidence of the revealed scriptures, and through his own efforts, realizes the full truth and becomes absorbed in the universal self. He speaks and informs his Master about his spiritual experiences.

He tells about the Absolute (*Parabrahman*) and his spiritual bliss. He is without attachment and without limbs, sexless, and indestructible. He is neither the doer nor the enjoyer, for he is without change and without action. He is now the self-illumined *atman*. He bows down before his Guru through whose compassion and greatly esteemed favor he has achieved the goal of his existence.

The Guru, greatly pleased, explains the position of the Knower of Brahman in the remaining stanzas. At the end, the disciple salutes his Guru respectfully. Liberated from bondage, with the Guru's permission he goes away.

Pertinent Literature

Dasgupta, S. N. *Indian Idealism*. Cambridge: Cambridge University Press, 1969.

Indian Idealism contains elaborate discussion of S'ankara's monistic idealism, which finds its succinct expression in the *Crest Jewel of Wisdom*. S. N. Dasgupta traces India's idealistic thought back to the *Upanishads* and to early Buddhism and explains in what sense the Upanishadic and the Buddhist philosophies can be called "idealistic." His account of the Upanishadic idealism contains separate treatment of each of the principal *Upanishads* and prepares the ground for understanding the Vedantic idealism of S'ankara, whom he regards as the most important interpreter of the Upanishadic thought. The book also compares Buddhist idealism with S'ankara's.

In sketching the Upanishadic idealism, Dasgupta observes that the transition from the realistic and ritualistic world view of the Vedas to the mystical and idealistic philosophy of the *Upanishads* is quite explicit. In view of the Upanishadic affirmation of the transcendental reality of Being, which is claimed to be beyond thought and perception, Dasgupta wonders whether it is correct to regard such a philosophy as idealistic. Without being able to characterize the Upanishadic idealism in terms of any of the models of Western systems of idealism, Dasgupta concludes that the philosophy of the *Upanishads* may be best described as "mystical idealism." However, he notes that the *Upanishads* do not present to us a philosophy in the technical sense, as a systematic and coordinated unity of thought. Nevertheless, numerous attempts have been made to interpret the *Upanishads*. The earliest attempt at a consistent interpretation of the Upanishadic philosophy is to be found in the *Brahma Sutras* of Badarayana. The earliest available and most well-known commentary on the *Brahma Sutras* is that of S'ankara.

Dasgupta notes that in the *Mandukya Upanishad* the highest reality, Brahman, is described not even as pure consciousness but as a negation of any attempt to describe it in any way. In comparing this *via negativa* description of the ultimate reality with the nihilistic Buddhist idealism of Nagarjuna, Dasgupta finds much similarity between the two approaches.

He also points out the close similarity between the subjective idealism of the Buddhist philosopher Vasubandhu and the idealism of S'ankara. In fact, it is noted that one early interpreter of the Upanishadic idealism, Gaudapada, who was probably a teacher of S'ankara, was profoundly influenced by both Nagarjuna's and Vasubandhu's philosophies in his interpretation of the *Upanishads*. Nevertheless, Dasgupta points out some important differences between the Vedantic idealism of S'ankara and Buddhist idealism: unlike the subjective idealism and phenomenalism of the Buddhist schools, S'ankara's *Vedanta* admits of an independent objective reality, Brahman, and a quasiobjective category, *maya*, which is said to be the source of the illusory appearance of the empirical world.

Dasgupta claims that S'ankara accepts Upanishadic metaphysics, especially its monism, without proof and without question. Such monism believes in the only reality of Brahman the Absolute, which is said to be immutable, indescribable, and the true self (*atman*) of us all. We are all Brahman, and nothing other than Brahman is real. The manifold reality of the empirical world is claimed to be illusion and is explained away by S'ankara as the product of *maya*. The doctrine of *maya* helps S'ankara in affirming the only reality of Brahman. In this respect he departs from Badarayana, the author of the *Brahma Sutras*, who equally emphasizes the immanence and transcedence of Brahman.

S'ankara's philosophy espouses a twofold view of things, one referring to the ultimate reality and the other to the illusory existence of empirical entities. One's mistaken understanding of the empirical world of appearance as real is the root cause of one's desires for and attachments to things, which, in turn, is the seed for misery and loss of freedom. This is one's bondage, according to S'ankara, and the knowledge of Brahman is liberation. One's supreme task in this world is to realize one's true self as identical with Brahman.

Deutsch, Eliot. *Advaita Vedanta: A Philosophical Reconstruction.* Honolulu: East-West Center Press, 1969.

In his attempt at a philosophical reconstruction of S'ankara's *Vedata* philosophy, Eliot Deutsch selects those ideas in the *Vedanta* metaphysics, epistemology, and ethics which have central importance in the system and which are philosophically interesting on their own. He lifts such ideas from their historical and cultural settings and examines them from a critical point of view to determine their philosophical worth. The result is a book on S'ankara's *Vedanta*, which is readily understandable and appreciated by readers who are philosophically inclined but who may not have familiarity with the scholastic details of the long Vedantic tradition.

S'ankara's *Vedanta* philosophy is known as *Advaita*, meaning nondual, because it purports to show the unreality of all distinctions. Deutsch observes that the usual Upanishadic and Vedantic characterization of Brahman as existence-bliss-consciousness is inappropriate if it is meant to isolate the nature of Brahman, which is, *ex hypothesi*, limitless. However, he believes that such attribution in positive terms is not really aimed at capturing the "essence" of Brahman, but, from experiential and pragmatic points of view, is geared to direct a seeker of truth toward Brahman and to steer him away from the opposites of these positive attributes. Deutsch notes that it is the *via negativa* approach toward Brahman, first found in the *Mandūkya Upanishad* and later widely used by the Advaitins, which ensures the undifferentiated nature of the highest reality.

For *Advaita Vedanta*, even though the world of appearance is not real, it is not unreal either. From the standpoint of appearance, which is a state of ignorance, there are three fundamental modes of being: reality, which is Brahman; appearance, which accounts for the empirical reality of the world; and unreality, like a logical contradiction. The world is apparently real to those people who are yet to attain the realization that all is Brahman. However, once Brahman-realization is obtained, all distinctions between the levels of reality disappear. Any differentiation belongs to the realm of appearance; in reality, only Brahman exists.

The usual account of creation of the world in the

Advaita literature—that the world evolved out of Brahman through the latter's creative potency (*maya*)—is to be taken only as an apparent truth, like the status of the world itself. There is no real modification of Brahman; hence, all change, including creation, is only apparent. Deutsch believes that such an analysis of the relation between Brahman and the world is philosophically valid once it is affirmed that Brahman is the only reality. If one accepts the possibility of a nondual spiritual experience and believes that such experience reveals the really real, then one must accept that the world of our ordinary experience is something less than real.

Consistent with its nondualistic position, S'ankara's *Vedanta* affirms an identity between one's true self (*atman* the Self) and Brahman. The Self is One and is Brahman, whereas one's phenomenal or empirical self (*jiva*), due to misidentification of itself with things other than the Self, perceives itself to be limited and fragmented. This is one's bondage which is due to ignorance (*avidya*). Deutsch observes that S'ankara does not so much explain the nature and existence of empirical self as he describes the process whereby one comes to be aware of one's self-existence. S'ankara's analysis takes the form of phenomenology of consciousness. S'ankara attempts to show how one comes to accept something as true which is in fact an illusory appearance.

The central concern of *Advaita Vedanta* is to establish that reality is one and to guide people to a realization of it. Even though the world is claimed to be an appearance, yet within the phenomenal world the Advaitins are not subjective idealists but realists. A variety of philosophical theories are used, including those of *maya*, the levels of reality, the hierarchy of knowledge, and *karma* (Deutsch believes that *Karma* is a convenient fiction in the *Advaita* system), which help in interpreting and ordering experiences but which in themselves are no more real than those experiences themselves. The path to Brahman realization is through Self-knowledge; however, any device which helps in ordering and understanding experience and taking one closer to the path of Self-realization is helpful and is considered good.

Organ, Troy W. *The Self in Indian Philosphy.* The Hague, The Netherlands: Mouton, 1964.

Troy W. Organ introduces his study of self in Indian philosophy with a saying attributed to S'ankara: Man is on a pilgrimage to his own self. The author believes that both the Western and the Indian traditions have been concerned with the nature and existence of the self even though their emphasis and treatments have differed. Western man, in spite of his traditional interest in the self, has been more interested in the outward than in the inward, especially during the last five hundred years. The Indians, on the other hand, have been preoccupied with investigation of man's inner nature, which is the self. This is evident in their perception of philosophy as self-knowledge. Consequently, Organ thinks that it is not too unrealistic if in approaching the philosophy of India one expects to discover a better understanding of the self. However, he cautions that such an approach must be based on solid scholarship and not on superficial interests or blind faith.

Organ's study spans eight different, but often closely related, views of the self in Indian philosophy, including those of the *Upanishads* and S'ankara's *Advaita Vedanta*. He observes that the Upanishadic seers were in quest of a reality quite different from the Vedic gods, who were mostly deified symbols of external nature. The Upanishadic search took a transcendental form, from phenomenal reality to the Absolute. Its metaphysical approach affirmed Being as the basis of all becomings; but such Being, from a psychological point of view, was also understood as the inner core of the self. Hence arose the Upanishadic realization that *atman* the Self is Brahman the Absolute, the knowledge of which was viewed as leading to liberation from the bondage of the phenomenal world.

At the outset of his study of the *Advaita Vedanta* view of the self, Organ comments that he will not try to assess S'ankara's reliability as an interpreter of the *Upanishads*; rather, he examines S'ankara's ideas on their own strengths. Central to S'ankara's philosophy of the self is the idea that since the existence of the self is a presupposition of all experience and reasoning, it is self-proven. It cannot be doubted, because even the very act of doubting proves it. Hence, unlike René Descartes', S'ankara's position implies that it is more natural first to accept self's existence and then to conclude that therefore the self thinks, than the other way around. It is the self's nature which needs to be proved, not its existence.

Against the nonsubstantive "bundle" theory of the self as found in Buddhism, S'ankara argues for an unchanging substantive self which is the basis of a continuous person. He believes that the common experience of memory proves that not everything in a person is transitory. Regarding S'ankara's observation that the self is a subject, Organ comments that, as subject, the self cannot then be an object of knowledge. That is, the self cannot be known through our usual cognitive processes based on a subject-object distinction. Further, the self as a subject can reveal the objects of knowledge, but it cannot create them. This explains, according to Organ, why S'ankara's doctrine of the priority of consciousness is compatible with his realistic belief in an independent world. Organ further observes that the self as subject must have consciousness as its essence, and he notes that S'ankara is well aware of this implication because the latter attempts to prove that consciousness does not lapse even during the deepest sleep.

The difference between the individual self (*jiva*) and the Self (*atman*) is an illusory one because any difference, in the *Advaita* philosophy, belongs to the realm of appearance. However, even though *jiva* and *atman* are both spiritual in nature, the latter is mistakenly thought to be the former because people usually take their real selves to be finite and fragmented. Such misidentification is the source of bondage; accordingly, liberation from bondage is attained through self-realization. Because the Self is Brahman, and Brahman is One, the moral implication of the *Advaita* philosophy is that one ought to treat others as oneself.

Additional Recommended Reading

Deutsch, Eliot and J. A. B. van Buitenen, eds. and trs. *A Source Book of Advaita Vedanta*. Honolulu: The University Press of Hawaii, 1971. Contains essays on the philosophical and cultural background of *Advaita Vedanta*, as well as relevant selections, in English translation, from the source materials of all important *Advaita Vedanta* schools, including S'ankara's. Each selection is properly introduced.

Isherwood, Christopher and Swami Prabhavananda, eds and trs. *Shankara's Crest-Jewel of Discrimination*. New York: New American Library, 1970. A nontechnical and readable introduction to Sankara's philosophy, with a liberal translation of his *Crest Jewel of Wisdom*.

Murty, K. Satchidananda. *Revelation and Reason in Avaita Vedanta*. New York: Columbia University Press, 1959. A scholarly and faithful exposition of S'ankara's *Advaita Vedanta*.

Raju, P. T. *Idealistic Thought of India*. Cambridge, Massachusetts: Harvard University Press, 1953. A study of the historical as well as the logical development of the main schools of India's idealistic metaphysics. Contains a detailed exposition of S'ankara's philosophy.

THE BOOK OF SALVATION

Author: Avicenna (ibn-Sina, 980-1037)
Type of work: Metaphysics, philosophy of mind, epistemology
First transcribed: Early eleventh century

Principal Ideas Advanced

God is the eternal, unmoved First Mover, who exists necessarily by his own nature and who eternally generates the first created being, a pure intelligence, by a creative act of thought.

The First Intelligence creates the Second Intelligence and also the first celestial sphere as its soul; the Second Intelligence produces the Third Intelligence and the second celestial sphere; the process continues to the Tenth Intelligence, the giver of forms.

Souls are vegetable, animal, and human; the human soul is characterized by the faculties of growth, reproduction, nutrition, motion, perception, and reason.

There are five external senses and five internal senses; the internal senses are common sense, representation, imagination, estimation, and recollection.

Reason has two faculties: the practical and the theoretic; the theoretic faculty may develop to the stage of actual intellect, as activated by the Tenth Intelligence; knowledge then consists of discovering the necessary relations between universals.

In the year 529 Justinian closed the Schools of Athens, but fortunately for the West, Greek learning had been transmitted to the Near East, principally through the institutions of Alexandria and the Christian communities of Syria and Persia. Later, after the advent of Islam, this learning was fostered and developed by various Islamic philosophers and eventually carried across North Africa into Spain, where it flourished in such places as Toledo and Cordova. From the eleventh to the thirteenth centuries it trickled and then flooded into Western Europe to augment the Christians' meager and unbalanced knowledge of Greek philosophy.

Avicenna was, perhaps, the most important Islamic philosopher. Besides being a prolific writer on philosophy and religion, he was a court scholar and physician, an active politician, a civil administrator, and the writer of medical texts which were standard works in Europe through the seventeenth century. Of his approximately one hundred works the two most important are the philosophic encyclopedia, *Kitab al-Shifa (The Book of Healing),* the bulk of which

was known to late medieval thinkers, and an abridgment of it, *Kitab al-Nadjat (The Book of Salvation).* The present essay is based primarily on the section of the *Nadjat* dealing with his philosophy of mind, a section published under the title *Avicenna's Psychology* (1952).

Before we can discuss Avicenna's philosophy of mind and his epistemology it will be necessary to outline the system within which it is elaborated. Avicenna regarded himself as an Aristotelian, but his Aristotelianism, like that of both his predecessors and successors, was influenced by the pressure of religious considerations and by the fact that the Aristotle transmitted to him had become colored by Stoic and Neoplatonic elements.

The modifications in Aristotle are evident in Avicenna's notion of God, his doctrine of creation, and his cosmology. He describes God not only as an eternal, unchanging, immaterial Unmoved Mover, but also as a being whose existence is necessary because his essence is identical with his being, as the One who is indivisible, as True Perfection, as Pure

Benevolence, and as a continuously active agent intellect who, by emanation, creates the cosmos and all that is in it. Since intellect and will are identical in a pure intelligence, God can create simply by thinking. When he contemplates himself he automatically generates the first created being which is, because it stems from him, a pure intelligence.

The first created intelligence, too, can create by contemplation, but since it is a finite intelligence it can contemplate and create in different ways. In contemplating God, it creates the Second Intelligence; in contemplating its own essence and in knowing that it is a contingent being characterized by potentiality, it creates the body of the first celestial sphere; and in contemplating itself and in knowing its existence as necessary in that it flows necessarily from God, it generates the soul of the first celestial sphere.

Since the celestial sphere is attached to a body, its soul is not a pure intelligence and therefore does not create, but it does seek to emulate the perfection of its creator, the First Intelligence. It does so by contemplating the Intelligence and by perfecting its own body. Since the only change simple, celestial matter can undergo is a change of position, the soul perfects celestial matter by circular motion. Hence, the First Intelligence is the final cause of both the existence and motion of the first sphere. The Second Intelligence, by contemplating the First Intelligence and by contemplating itself in the twofold manner, produces the Third Intelligence and the body and soul of the second celestial sphere, that containing the stars. In a similar manner, further intelligences and spheres are produced as the creative process works down through the spheres of Saturn, Jupiter, Mars, the sun, Venus, Mercury, and the moon. The Tenth Intelligence does not produce a sphere but it does produce sublunar things by providing souls and forms and by uniting them with suitably disposed complexes of sublunar matter. These complexes of matter come about as the four Aristotelian elements combine and recombine under the influence of the celestial spheres. The Tenth Intelligence is the Agent Intellect or Giver of Forms which looms so large in Avicenna's psychology and which provides a linkage between Aristotle's active intellect and the active intellect of the Scholastics.

Avicenna agrees with Aristotle and disagrees with the theologians in claiming that this creative process is not a temporal process and that it is not creation *ex nihilo* (out of nothing). Creation is not a temporal event, since time is the measure of change and thus presupposes the existence of matter, and it is not a temporal process because a cause must be contemporaneous with its effect. Furthermore, creation is not *ex nihilo* since form can only be imprinted on matter that is already available. Consequently, God, matter, the cosmos, and creation itself are eternal. Things exist because God exists, because he contemplates himself necessarily, and because their existence flows directly or indirectly from this contemplation. Insofar as it explains why things exist, the theory of emanation suggests a nontemporal sequence of active, efficient causes grounded in the supreme efficient cause, but it also suggests a hierarchy of essences following from one another in sequence. When God contemplates his own essence he sees the network of implications that flow from it and thus, unlike Aristotle's God, knows the cosmos in detail.

Avicenna's views influenced much subsequent philosophy. Many, if not all, of the later Christian philosophers appreciated the proof of God's existence from the existence of contingent things, the notion of God as an agent, the step in the direction of a suitable creation theory, the doctrine of intelligences as a foundation for a study of angels, God's knowledge of the world, and the identity of essence and existence in God but their sharp separation in other things. They objected to the eternity of the world, the denial of creation *ex nihilo*, the piecemeal emanation of the created world, the determinism, and the doctrine of the Agent Intellect.

Avicenna's reliance on Aristotle, and in particular on the *De anima*, is evidenced from the beginning of his psychology when he classifies souls as vegetable, animal, and human. The vegetable soul is characterized by the faculties of growth, reproduction, and nutrition; the animal has, in addition, those of motion and perception; and the human being is completed by the faculty of reason. There are really two faculties of motion in the animal soul: a psychic one characterized by desire and anger which incite motion towards objects or away from them, and a physical one that actually moves the body by contracting and relaxing the muscles. There are five external senses, each operative when the form of the sensed object is impressed on the physical sense organ. For instance, when light falls on an object it transmits an image through the transparent medium and this image is impressed on the vitreous humor of the eye where it is apprehended by the psychic faculty of sight.

Avicenna's analysis of the internal sense goes considerably beyond that of Aristotle, who did not distinguish explicitly between internal and external senses, and it anticipates in considerable detail that of the Scholastics. There are five internal senses: fantasy or common sense, representation, imagination, the estimative sense, and the recollective or retentive sense. These are unique faculties, each being associated with a different part of the brain. The common sense receives images transmitted to it by the five external senses, enabling us both to know that they differ from one another and to collate the data received from them. The function of representation or sense memory is to preserve the data received by the common sense. An external sense, such as vision, abstracts the form of a particular object from its matter, but it can do so only in the presence of the object, seeing the form with all the determinations imposed upon it by that matter and seeing it as being present in matter. The form in the representative faculty is still particular but it is not seen as being present in or presented by matter. This further abstraction makes memory possible. Imagination is the faculty that enables us to separate and combine the images preserved by representation.

The estimative faculty detects the intentions of animate things and the effects of inanimate ones, thus enabling us to discover their significance for our welfare. On the first occurrence of such an insight, such as the sheep's recognition that the skulking wolf means it no good, the response is an instinctive one in which the estimative sense operates on the images of common sense or representation to abstract the intention. Later it also seems to work by association, for after sense memory has stored up past correlations of a certain sort of visual data, say, with subsequent pain, the occurrence of such a visual datum will trigger the associated image of pain in the imagina-

tion and the estimative sense will then note the evil of that object.

Avicenna and the Scholastics note that intentions are not the objects of any of the five external senses, yet they insist, without explaining how it is possible, that intentions can be grasped only by attending to the images of common sense or representation. These intentions are particulars, but since they are nonsensible, our apprehending them marks a yet higher degree of abstraction for here we are abstracting an immaterial thing from a material thing in which it exists only accidentally. Avicenna also points out that noncognitive judgment is involved here and that this is the supreme judging faculty in the animal. Furthermore, it is the function of this faculty to guide the two motive faculties. The function of the recollective or retentive faculty is to retain the judgments or insights of the estimative faculty, just as the representative retains the images of sensible things.

The apprehension of particulars occurs only through bodily organs, for a spatial thing can be present only to another spatial thing. This is so even in the case of the faculties of imagination, representation, and estimation, despite the fact that they operate in the physical absence of the object. This point may be shown thus: imagine two squares of exactly the same size, but separated from each other, and then ask yourself how it is possible for there to be two separate squares. Since the difference cannot be accounted for as a difference of form, it must be the consequence of the same form being manifested in two different places. That is, there must be two images impressed on different areas of the middle ventricle of the brain, which is the physical seat of the psychic faculty of imagination. The point is a general one: the determinate features of our imagery can be accounted for only if the form perceived by the faculty is at the same time a form manifested in matter. This line of reasoning, which does not appear in Aristotle, influenced the Scholastics and reappears quite explicitly in Descartes.

Reason is divided into practical and theoretic faculties. With the help of the theoretic faculty the practical faculty elaborates basic moral principles such as "Tyranny is wrong," "Lying is wrong"; it considers purposes, deliberates, initiates behavior, and produces in the faculty of appetite such responses as shame and laughter.

The theoretic faculty can occur in various degrees. It may be dormant; it may develop to the point where it possesses the primary principles of thought, such as "The whole is greater than its part" and "Things equal to a third are equal to one another"; or it may perfect its potentiality by grasping the secondary principles as well, and thus be in a position to think without the further acquisition of any other principles. These are the various degrees of the Potential Intellect. Finally, the intellect may actually think, exercising the capacities it has perfected at the prior stage. It is then called the Actual or Acquired Intellect. As we shall see later, this last stage is not attained unless the Potential Intellect is activated by the Agent Intellect, the Tenth Intelligence.

In order to achieve its end of contemplating pure forms, theoretic reason must complete the process of abstracting forms from matter, a process already initiated by the external and internal senses. That is, it must turn to the imagination, to the images of particular objects, and, through the agency of the Agent Intellect, grasp the forms appearing there free of all the materially imposed determinations they still exhibit. This process of abstraction can be by-passed only by highly gifted individuals, such as the prophets, whose intellects are illuminated directly by the Agent Intellect, the Giver of Forms. Reason recognizes that these pure forms could be manifested in many particular cases, so it regards them as universals; but it also sees that these forms need not have been manifested at all, and therefore that they are, in themselves, neither particular nor universal.

Though he departs from Aristotle in holding that a form is not restricted to its occurrence in matter, Avicenna is not quite a Platonic realist, for he does not admit that a form can exist or subsist by itself. He introduces the famous doctrine of *ante rem, in rebus,* and *post rem*, a doctrine accepted later by Aquinas and others as the solution to the problem of universals. The essences are *ante rem* insofar as they are the exemplars in the Giver of Forms, *in rebus* insofar as they are manifested in sensible objects, and *post rem* insofar as they are grasped free of material considerations by the human intellect.

Knowledge involves the discovery of necessary relations between universals, relations noted directly by intuition, which is a kind of illumination, or established indirectly by syllogistic reasoning. While his model seems to be that of a body of knowledge derived by reason alone from universals and self-evident truths, Avicenna does point out that much of our knowledge about the world, though certain, is based partly on experience. Having noted the constant conjunction between things such as man and rationality, and day and being light, and constant disjunctions such as its not being both day and night, we cannot avoid concluding that the noted constancy reveals a necessary conjunction or disjunction. Thus we are forced to acknowledge necessary truths about the world, truths such as "Man is rational," "If it is day, then it is light," and "Either it is day or it is night." But apart from this sort of assistance, and the assistance of the internal senses as providers of data, the intellect does not need the assistance of the body. It does not operate through a physical organ, for it can know itself and is not disrupted by strong stimuli, as the physical organ of sight is disrupted by a dazzling light. Furthermore, as is required by a faculty that apprehends pure forms, it is an immaterial faculty.

In defending his view that the soul is an immaterial substance, Avicenna invokes his famous "man in the void" argument. Suppose, he says, that a man is created in a void and suppose that his feet, hands, and other physical parts are separated from him in such a way that he has no sensation of them. Under these circumstances he would have no experience of an external world and no experience of his body; nevertheless, he would still be conscious of himself. Consequently, the self he is conscious of must be an immaterial thing. Furthermore, since he can think of himself without thinking that he has a body, having a body is not essential to being a self and therefore is excluded from the nature of the self. That is to say, the immaterial self exists in its own right independently of other things and is therefore a substance. If it is associated with a body, the association is accidental. The soul is an entelechy because it governs and guides the body, but it is no more the form of the body than the pilot is the form of the ship.

This soul did not exist prior to the existence of its body, for if there were a number of preexisting souls, they would have to differ from one another; to do so is impossible since they would not differ in form nor would they be individuated by matter. If there were one preexisting soul, it would have to be shared by all men—an absurd idea. Therefore, the individual soul is created when there is a body suitable for it. By binding itself closely to its body the soul is influenced permanently by the peculiar nature of the body and the particular events that befall it. Since the soul is a simple substance it survives the death of the body, carrying over into the hereafter the individuality it has acquired.

In these various respects Avicenna departed from the Aristotelian view of the soul in order to satisfy the requirements of theology. Thus the later Jewish and Christian philosophers welcomed his guidance when they encountered Aristotle. There is also a remarkable coincidence between Avicenna's position and arguments and those of Descartes. The influence of the "man in the void" argument is particularly evident.

To complete the survey of Avicenna's psychology, one must consider the relationship between the human intellect and the Active Intellect. The human intellect does not achieve its highest status, that of apprehending universals and the relations between them, unless it is activated by the Tenth Intelligence, which is the Active Intellect or Giver of Forms. Avicenna describes the Active Intellect as radiating a power which illuminates the potentially intelligible but actually sensible forms of imagination, thereby making them intelligible and thus present to a suitably prepared mind. In this way our potential intellect becomes an actual or acquired intellect. In this process, images are important for two reasons: first, we must abstract the form from an image of the object if we are to grasp the form as the form of an object, and second, we must compare and contrast images in order to raise our intellect to a level where the divine illumination is able to enlighten it. It is to be noted that the Active Intellect, not the human intellect, abstracts the intelligible form from the image in the imagination. Our dependence on the Giver of Forms is evinced further by the fact that since we have no intellectual memory we must re-establish contact with it every time we think. Later, Thomas Aquinas and others objected to Avicenna's Active Intellect and insisted on fragmenting it into individual active intellects occurring as faculties of individual human souls, thus making man himself responsible for the activating of his potential intellect. They also feared, though Avicenna himself did not, that as long as we all shared the same Active Intellect, personal immortality was jeopardized. Also, they introduced intellectual memory and insisted that when intellection occurs the knower and the known become one.

Since the human intellect is able to contact the Giver of Forms more easily on subsequent occasions, it is able to perfect itself, approaching the ideal of constant contemplation of the forms. By thus emulating the Giver of Forms, which contains all intelligible forms, the soul prepares itself to enjoy a higher and more worthy status when it leaves the body. Insofar as it is the emulated intelligence, the Giver of Forms is a final and formal cause as well as an agent, and insofar as it functions in these ways it brings the human soul into the sequence of efficient, formal and final causes that stems from and culminates in God.

Besides influencing later Jewish and Christian philosophers in the various ways already indicated, Avicenna had a great influence on the work of Averroës, the other great Islamic philosopher. Anyone interested in a critical but sympathetic evaluation of Avicenna, should turn to Averroës.

Pertinent Literature

Avicenna. *Avicenna's Psychology.* Translated by F. Rahman. London: Oxford University Press, 1952.

In this book F. Rahman presents an English translation of the section of *The Book of Salvation* which corresponds to Aristotle's *On the Soul.* He also provides an introduction and a commentary with notes.

The main themes dealt with by Avicenna in this section of *The Book of Salvation* are the definition of the soul, the classification of its faculties, sensation, intellection, prophecy, the relation between body and soul, and the immortality of the soul.

In his Introduction, Rahman provides the historical background required to understand the evolution of some of these key issues and to compare Avicenna's and Aristotle's positions. He first focuses his approach on the relation between soul and body and its analogy to the relation between a sailor or a pilot and his ship alluded to by Aristotle in *On the Soul*, II, 1, 413 a 9. The points of view of Aristotle, Alexander of Aphrodisias, Plotinus, Simplicius, and Philoponus are discussed and explained by referring to their uses of the analogy of the pilot and his ship. The link between the different conceptions of the relation between soul and body and an acceptance or rejection of the immortality of the soul is clearly indicated. Avicenna's position is compared to and contrasted with the positions of his predecessors. Rahman sees Aristotle arguing in favor of a mutual dependence of the body and the soul and thus denying the immortality of the soul. Avicenna, on the contrary, holds that the human soul is incorporeal, substantial, independent from the body, and therefore immortal.

Since the human soul is incorporeal and substantial, it is also self-conscious, as it is shown by the famous argument of "the man in the void." Rahman is thus led to discuss the conception of self-consciousness among some of Avicenna's predecessors: Aristotle, Strato, Alexander of Aphrodisias, Simplicius, and Philoponus. He claims that these philosophers did not really grasp the essential unity and persistence of self-consciousness and therefore did not have a real theory of the Ego; Avicenna somehow builds such a theory and is thus original.

Finally, Rahman offers clarifications of some aspects of Avicenna's theory of intellection: the grades of abstraction, the active and the passive intellect, and the practical intellect.

The detailed notes at the back of the volume provide for each chapter a summary of the chapter and then further clarifications and comments on difficult passages. It is in these notes that one can find some enlightenment on the main issues which are not discussed in the Introduction.

Rahman shows very clearly how Avicenna's psychological and epistemological conceptions in *The Book of Salvation* are, on the one hand, embedded in the Greek tradition of the commentaries on Aristotle's *On the Soul* and, on the other hand, constitute a truly original contribution to the solution of difficult and perennial problems.

Davidson, Herbert A. "Alfarabi and Avicenna on the Active Intellect," in *Medieval and Renaissance Studies*. III (1972), pp. 109-111, 154-178.

Herbert A. Davidson claims that Aristotle's statement on the necessity, on epistemological grounds, of the existence of an active intellect in *On the Soul*, III, 5, is very ambiguous. All subsequent philosophers try to make sense of it and to relate it to Aristotle's metaphysical positions. Focusing his study on the active intellect, Davidson is therefore led to discuss many aspects of Avicenna's epistemology and metaphysics. To do so he makes use not only of *The Book of Healing* and *The Book of Salvation* but also of all the other Arabic philosophical works of Avicenna. He really presents a synthesis of Avicenna's main tenets and an explanation of the basic arguments used to defend them. Davidson's work is therefore much broader in scope and depth than Rahman's, which limited itself to a quick introduction to one section of *The Book of Salvation*.

According to Davidson, Avicenna's active intellect is the cause, with the help of the heavenly bodies, of (1) the matter of the sublunar world and (2) the forms occurring in matter, including the souls of all animated beings and, therefore, the cause of the soul of the human being. Furthermore, but this time only by itself, the active intellect is the cause of the existence and actualization of the potential human intellect. It actualizes this intellect in providing it with the universal concepts or intelligibles. These intelligibles emanate directly from the active intellect into the human one. Therefore, there is no abstraction by the human intellect of the universal concepts from experience or images. Images are useful only to prepare the human intellect for the reception of what emanates from the active intellect. The human mind is therefore basically passive but can reach a high level of development by means of a conjunction with the active intellect, or, more exactly, by the light emanating from the active intellect and transmitting the intelligibles.

The actualization of the human intellect by the active intellect is consistent with Avicenna's contention that the human soul is independent from the body and therefore immortal. The existence of the body is only the occasion of the emanation of the human soul, and the use of images is only the requirement for the preparation of the soul for the reception of the emanation of the intelligibles from the active intellect. Once the human intellect has reached a high level of conjunction with the active intellect and so can reach

it at will, preparation by the use of images is no longer necessary. Also, at the level the human intellect is no longer subject to the limitations of discursive thought but reaches the highest stage and becomes endowed with intellectual prophecy, which is an illuminative or intuitive stage.

Davidson shows very clearly how Avicenna's conception of the immortality of the human soul and of prophecy are linked to his epistemological positions and in contrast to the positions of one of his most famous predecessors, al-Farabi, who claims that only people who grasp the right philosophical ideas or their imaginative representation will achieve immortality.

Davidson's presentation is very detailed and carefully documented. It is also critical and indicates how on some points of detail Avicenna's position does not seem to be fully consistent, although Davidson assumes that Avicenna's philosophy is basically a unified and coherent one.

Zedler, Beatrice H. "The Prince of Physicians on the Nature of Man," in *The Modern Schoolman*. LV, no. 2 (January, 1978), pp. 165-177.

Beatrice H. Zedler examines Avicenna's conception of man not only in his philosophical texts, as do F. Rahman and Herbert A. Davidson, but also in the medical ones. For the philosophical approach she bases her presentation exclusively on the Latin version of the sections *On the Soul* and *Metaphysics* of *The Book of Healing*. In what concerns the medical aspect she uses the best-known Latin versions of some of his medical books, such as the *Canon of Medicine*. Her work is therefore based only on medieval Latin translations and some references to a few modern translations.

From the philosophical texts she concludes that for Avicenna, the body, although needed for the individuation of the human soul and for the reception of most intelligibles, is not a part of the essence of man. Avicenna compares the body to an animal that one needs to ride in order to reach some place but which, once one has arrived at this place, is no longer needed and even becomes an encumbrance. In such a conception man is essentially spirit and the body a mere tool which is only temporarily needed.

From the medical texts emerges the picture of man as a being of nature whose physical well-being assures him his full realization. Nothing except a higher level of complexity distinguishes him from other beings of nature. Man seems to be a mere body, reducible to his physical elements.

Zedler claims that such a discrepancy between the medical and the philosophical approaches is not a sign of a lack of unity in Avicenna's thought. A closer reading of both kinds of texts shows that the philosophical texts include statements which imply that man is also a being of nature and that medical texts do not deny that; although man is a being of nature, there is more to be said about other aspects of him. Furthermore, in his *On the Divisions of the Rational Sciences* Avicenna considers both the study of medicine and the study of the soul as divisions of natural philosophy and therefore acknowledges that they are dealing with different aspects of a reality somehow related to matter and nature. He is therefore fully aware of holding two different positions, but, rather than considering them as completely different positions, he sees them as distinct emphases on different aspects of man. Man, on the one hand, is one of the intellectual substances; but he is the lowest one and therefore still in need at some stage of a body. On the other hand, he is a being of nature, a body which should be taken care of since it is needed by the soul—at least for a while—for its own development.

Finally Zedler claims that Avicenna's awareness of his duality of positions as emphases on different aspects of man does not lead him to reconcile that duality and to articulate clearly the relation between soul and body. She concludes that Avicenna simply juxtaposes the two aspects of man and that one has to wait for Thomas Aquinas to find a solution to the tension between a spiritualist and a naturalist approach and thereby reach a truly unified conception of man.

Additional Recommended Reading

Afnan, Soheil Muhsin. *Avicenna, His Life and Works.* London: George Allen & Unwin, 1958. The standard general presentation of Avicenna and his various works with an emphasis on the Eastern influences.

Avicenna. *Liber de Anima seu Sextus de Naturalibus.* Edited by S. Van Riet. Louvain-Leiden: E. Peeters and E. J. Brill, 1968-1972. Critical edition of the medieval Latin translation of the section *On the Soul* of *The Book of Healing*, with a very good presentation of Avicenna's psychological doctrine.

_____. *Liber de Philosophia Prima sive Scientia Divina.* Edited by S. Van Riet. Louvain-Leiden: E. Peeters and E. J. Brill, 1977. Critical edition of the medieval Latin translation of the metaphysical section *The Book of Healing*, with a very good presentation of Avicenna's conception of metaphysics.

_____. *La Métaphysique du "Shifa."* Translated by Georges C. Anawati. Paris: Vrin, 1978. French translation from the Arabic of the metaphysical section of *The Book of Healing*, with an introduction showing the influence of this text in both the East and the West.

Goichon, Amélie Marie. *The Philosophy of Avicenna and Its Influence on Medieval Europe.* Translated by M. S. Khan. Delhi: Motilal Banarsidass, 1969. Translation of three lectures given for a broad public by a specialist. Insists on Avicenna's influence on Western Europe.

Morewedge, Parviz. *The "Metaphysica" of Avicenna (ibn Sïnä).* New York: Columbia University Press, 1973. Translation of the metaphysical section of Avicenna's chief Persian work, which presents a concise outline of his philosophy.

MONOLOGION and PROSLOGION

Author: Saint Anselm of Canterbury (1033-1109)
Type of work: Theology
First transcribed: *Monologion*, 1076, *Proslogion*, c. 1077-1078

Principal Ideas Advanced

Since everything good must have a cause, and since the cause is goodness, and since God is goodness, God exists.

Since whatever exists must have a cause, and since a cause depends upon the power to cause, and since God is that power, God exists.

Since degrees of value or reality depend upon reference to absolute excellence and reality, and since God is absolute excellence and reality, God exists. [From the Monologion.]

Since God is the being than whom no greater can be conceived, and since it is better to exist in fact than merely in the imagination, God must exist in fact. [The ontological argument.]

God is not substance but Essence (the Father) and a set of essences (the Son); as Father he is the efficient cause (the creator) of all that exists; as Son he is the formal cause (the idea).

St. Anselm was an Augustinian who was unaware of Plotinus and who lived just before the great influx of Aristotle's works through the Arabian and Jewish philosophers. His fame rests to a great extent on his belief that faith is prior to reason, a belief he expresses thus in the well-known words of the *Proslogion*: "For I do not seek to understand that I may believe, but I believe in order to understand. For this I also believe—that unless I believed, I should not understand." After we have accepted on faith the revelations given through Scripture and through the Fathers, reason is able to fulfill its secondary role of clarifying meanings and providing proofs. Yet Anselm was an ambivalent figure, for despite his emphasis on the priority of faith, he felt a very strong need to support it with proofs. Indeed, he extended the scope of reason considerably farther than did the Scholastics who followed him, for they would not have thought of trying to prove doctrines like those of the Trinity and the Incarnation. His rationalism led others to characterize him as the first of the Scholastics.

This summary will concentrate on the other element that contributed to Anselm's fame, the ontolog-

ical argument as developed in the *Proslogion*. But since they are relevant, the three proofs given in his earlier work, the *Monologion*, will be considered first.

According to the first argument, the goodness of things in this world must be caused and must therefore stem from one thing that is good, or from many. But if many causes have their goodness in common, it is by virtue of this goodness that they cause good things; therefore, we must assume a common source. In either case, whether the cause be one or many, we are led to a single, unitary source of goodness. Since it is the source of all goodness, this source is not good because of something else, but is itself Goodness. (Notice that this argument depends upon a realistic doctrine of essences which will allow an essence such as *goodness* to function not only as a form but also as an active First Cause.) God is Goodness itself, not merely something that possesses goodness.

The second argument follows a similar course with respect to existence. Since whatever exists must have a cause and since an infinite regress of causes is impossible, there must either be one ultimate, nonfinite cause or several causes. If there is but one cause, we have encountered God. If there are several, then either they support each other mutually or they exist independently. The former is impossible, for that which is supported cannot be the cause of that which supports it. But if there are several independent ultimate causes, each must exist through itself, and therefore they must share this common power. Now, since it is this common power that is the source of all else, there cannot be several causes, but only one. (This proof also depends upon the above mentioned doctrine of essences.) God is not something that has this supreme power; he is this power.

The third proof depends upon the fact that things in the world can be ranked according to their degrees of "dignity," goodness, or reality. For instance, he says, all will admit that a horse represents a higher degree of reality than a piece of wood, for the horse is animate; similarly, a man outranks a horse, for he is rational. However, the sequence of degrees of reality cannot be an infinite one, for there must be some boundary, some limiting value by which all the rest are measured, a value which is real absolutely. If there should be several things that share this degree of reality, it is nevertheless the case that they are equal because of the common excellence they share. This excellence is the absolute reality which is the source of all relative degrees of reality.

Apparently Anselm thought these proofs too complex, for he tells us in the *Proslogion* that he searched a long time for a simpler proof. The result is the well-known ontological argument. When we think of something, Anselm says, and we are really thinking of it and not just uttering the associated verbal symbol, that thing is in our understanding. Of course, we need not understand that it exists, for we may be thinking of something which we believe does not exist, as in the case of the fool who says in his heart that God does not exist, or we may be thinking of something about whose existence we are uncertain. But in any of these cases, if we are thinking of something, if we understand *it*, then *it*, and not something else, is in the understanding. This point applies to our thought of anything, including God. However, in the case of God, we are thinking about a unique thing, for we are thinking about the greatest thing conceivable, the being "than which nothing greater can be conceived." Now if a being exists in the understanding alone, it cannot be the greatest conceivable thing, for a being that exists in reality as well as in the understanding would be greater. Consequently, since God is the greatest being conceivable he must exist in reality as well as in the understanding. Or, to put it another way, if the greatest conceivable being exists in the understanding alone, then it is not the greatest conceivable being—a conclusion which is absurd.

This argument met opposition from the beginning in the person of the monk Gaunilo, who criticized Anselm in his *In Behalf of the Fool*. First, Gaunilo says that because God's nature is essentially mysterious we do not have an idea of him. We may think we do, but we have only the verbal symbol, for when we hear the word "God," what are we to think or imagine? The proof fails, then, for the term "God" does not denote any *conceivable* thing. Second, he says that if the argument were sound, we could prove the existence of other things. By way of example he invites us to think of an island which is blessed with more good features and is therefore better than any actual land with which we are acquainted; then he suggests that we must admit its existence, since if it exists in the mind alone it would not be as good as lands which we know to exist. Third, he says that an idea or concept is only a part of the understanding itself, and that the existing object, if there is one, is something else. From the fact that an idea occurs it does not follow that something quite different in status also occurs. The fact that I am thinking of a being, thinking of it as the greatest conceivable being, and therefore thinking of it as existing necessarily, does not provide the slightest evidence that there actually is such a being, for the thought of a necessarily existing being is one thing and a necessarily existing being is another.

Anselm replies to the first objection by saying that the proof does not require a complete understanding of God, but only that we understand this much: that whatever else he may be, God is such that no greater being than he can be conceived. Even the fool must admit this much before he can refuse to believe. In reply to the second objection he says that God, unlike the blessed isle, is not thought of simply as the greatest thing of a certain type, or even as the greatest thing of all, but as the being than which nothing greater can be conceived. This latter concept can refer to only one thing, and that thing quite obviously is not the blessed isle. Later proponents of the argument, such as Descartes, make the same point by asserting that existence is contained in the essence of only one thing; namely, the greatest conceivable being.

The third objection, which has ever since been a standard one, is more difficult to handle. It seems to pinpoint an obvious defect, yet Anselm and many others were not daunted by it. In his reply to Gaunilo, Anselm hardly seems aware of it, for he simply repeats again, as if the objection had not been raised, that if we understand a thing, then it exists in the understanding. Since we are likely to feel more at home with Gaunilo's theory of ideas than with Anselm's, it will be necessary to reconstruct Anselm's doctrine in order to see why the objection seemed so unimportant to him. To do so we must explore a little further the nature of the divine being whose existence is supposed to be proved by the argument.

Anselm regarded God as self-caused, but the nature of this causation is quite mysterious. God could not have functioned as his own efficient, material, or instrumental cause, for all these causes must be prior to their effect, and not even God could exist prior to himself. For a similar reason God did not create himself. Yet he does exist through himself and from himself. By way of explication, Anselm presents us with a model, that of light. Light lights another thing by falling on it, but it also lights itself, for it is lucent. Its lucidity must come from itself, though, of course, it does not fall upon itself. Now, he says, in God the relation between *essence*, *to be*, and *being* (*existing*) is like the relation between *the light*, *to light*, and *lucent*. The implication is that the essence of God, the being he enjoys, and the generating of this being are one and the same thing. Like his master Augustine, Anselm conceived of God as an active essence, an activity which necessarily exists, not simply because it is active, but because its activity is the activity of existing.

In other places, too, Anselm indicates quite clearly that God is not a substance having matter and form.

First, he points out that if God were such a substance he would be composite, a state impossible in a being that is the unitary source of all and in a being that has no prior cause. Furthermore, God cannot be a substance possessing such qualities as justness, wisdom, truth, and goodness; for if he were, he would be just, wise, true, and good through another and not through himself. God does not *possess* justness and wisdom; he *is* justice and wisdom. That is, as was indicated in the earlier proofs, God is identical with these essences, and since in him they are one and the same essence, God is an Essence.

We are led to this same conclusion by another route, that of creation. As pure spirit, God creates the matter of the world *ex nihilo*, but he creates it according to a model he had in mind prior to the creation. That is, as Augustine had said earlier, all the essences that are manifested in the world existed in God's thought prior to the creation. Insofar as this network of essences is the model according to which the world is created, it is the formal first cause of the world (Augustine had called the divine ideas "the reasons"), and as first cause it is identical with God. Following Augustine, Anselm says that insofar as God *is* this expression of the world he has an intelligence; he is Wisdom, the Word, the Son. But the important point as far as the ontological argument is concerned is this: God is not thought of as a substance in the ordinary sense, but as an Essence (the Father) and also as a set of essences (the Son) that function respectively as efficient and formal cause of the world. Again, as in the proofs of the *Monologion*, God the Creator is thought of as an acting essence. It is to be noted that we have in God the Father the highest degree of reality an essence can enjoy—that of an eternally acting essence that exists in and through itself.

Anselm's doctrine of creation throws still further light on the ontological argument. It is to be noted that the essences that exist prior to creation are not created, for they are the eternal exemplars. As the Son, they are sustained by God insofar as he is the ground of all, but since they *are* the intellect of God, they are not the products of a mind and they do not depend for their existence on being in a mind. Thus, there are essences which do not enjoy the highest degree of reality, but which do enjoy a degree higher than that which they would if they were mind dependent. As Anselm says, prior to their manifestation in matter, they were not nothing. Since they are consubstantial with God, they are beings in their own right. Anselm leans as far in the direction of a Platonic realism as his theology will allow him.

Anselm was not clear about the manner in which we apprehend general ideas, but he insists that these ideas are the essences we have just discussed. This follows not only from his realistic doctrine of ideas, but also from his theory of truth. When we apprehend a thing truly, we apprehend its nature, but if it exists truly, then it manifests truly the essence God intended it to manifest. Hence, when we think truly we are apprehending one or more of the essences that constitute the intellect of God. (Thus, God is Truth.) This is not to say that we apprehend essences as they exist in God, for there they are exemplars, but what we apprehend does come directly or indirectly, clearly or obscurely, from God. Since the ideas in our understanding come into our understanding, their existence does not depend upon our understanding and is not restricted to their occurrence there. This is what Anselm means when he says that the things we understand are in our understanding.

In speaking as if we already knew that these essences constitute the mind of God, it might seem that we beg the question which is to be settled by the ontological argument, but an account of Anselm's doctrine of creation serves to illuminate the way in which he thinks of God and of essences. In both the *Proslogion* and the *Monologion*, Anselm emphasizes the proposition that essences are characters that may be shared in common by many things and that they are ontologically prior to these things. And we may assume that he would agree with Augustine, whom he follows in so many respects, that the eternity and immutability of self-evident truths and of the essences involved in them, and the fact that many minds can share the same ideas, are sufficient evidence that general ideas are not created by mutable and independent minds. At any rate, the argument presupposes that since they are not mind dependent, essences can occur elsewhere than in minds. Thus, we can conceive of an essence enjoying a higher

degree of reality, such as existing in the physical world or, perhaps, existing in such a way that it is self-sustaining. That some of the essences we apprehend also enjoy a higher degree of reality cannot be denied, for they are manifested as material objects. The only question, and the interesting one, is whether any essence we can apprehend also enjoys the supreme degree of reality. It would be worth examining the various essences we apprehend to see if there is any case where this is so. Anselm says we are led to a positive answer in the case of one and only one essence, that of the "being than which none greater can be conceived," for in this case alone the essence is such that it necessarily exists.

If we are to do justice to Anselm and understand the strong appeal this argument had for him and many others, we must be clear about the fact that throughout the argument he is talking about an essence. The premises are premises about an essence and the conclusion is a statement about this very same essence. It is not, as Gaunilo insisted, a conclusion about something else. Gaunilo's objection would be valid, as it is in the example of the blessed isle, if Anselm had concluded that an essence has been manifested in matter. But since manifestation in matter is always an accident, this is not something that could be discovered by examining an essence alone. It is crucial to the argument that existence in matter should not be thought of as the highest level of existence and that the being concerned should not be thought of as a composite of form and substance. The argument can move only from essence to Pure Essence, or *Essentia*. That is, it can only reveal to us something more about essence, and this is just what it does when it shows that one of the essences we apprehend is an active self-sustaining essence.

This discussion does not show that Anselm's argument is sound, but perhaps it does show that the whole question centers around two radically different theories about ideas, essences, and objects. Historically, philosophers who have found Anselm's argument acceptable have leaned toward a Platonic or Neoplatonic realism in which the role of essences is emphasized and that of matter minimized. The proof was not accepted by the Aristotelians who dominated the philosophic world for four or five centuries after

Anselm, nor by the nominalists and empiricists who have dominated so much of philosophic thought in the last three hundred years; but it is adopted in one form or another by Descartes, Liebniz, Spinoza, and Hegel, who, despite the fact that they diverge radically from one another, are each influenced, directly or indirectly, by Plato, Plotinus, or Augustine.

Pertinent Literature

Hopkins, Jasper. *A Companion to the Study of St. Anselm*, Minneapolis: University of Minnesota Press, 1972.

The past few years have witnessed a flurry of Anselmian studies coming from quite different quarters. Among philosophers and logicians there has been a revival of interest in Saint Anselm's ontological proof for the existence of God. Meanwhile, stimulated by the appearance of a new critical edition of Anselm's writings, historians have been busy reconstructing his life and thought. Jasper Hopkins' *A Companion to the Study of St. Anselm* is an informed and critical introduction to both spheres of activity. Of particular interest to students of philosophy are his chapters on Faith and Reason and on the Ontological Argument.

Anselm's formula, "I believe in order that I may understand," is, as Hopkins shows, more complicated than might at first appear. Belief may signify only intellectual assent, but it may also include the conversion of the will. Moreover, understanding, as used by Anselm, is broad enough to include probable as well as necessary reasoning. Hopkins, after tracing the formula through Anselm's writings, concludes that it is meant to affirm both the reasonableness of the Church's teaching and the need for faith in one who is to understand that teaching. This last consideration Hopkins explains along lines similar to those which lead modern-day apologists to define faith as interpretation. One who is committed to the teaching of the Church, says Hopkins, perceives his destiny in a new light and is able to appreciate the meaning of grace and mercy. Thus, when Anselm says that belief leads to experience and experience to understanding, he has in mind not merely understanding that something is, but understanding what it is for something to be of that kind.

This interplay between faith and reason has led some contemporary scholars to inquire more closely into the intentions underlying Anselm's philosophical writings. The first question is whether his method in the two treatises is the same. Whereas the *Proslogion* begins with the profession of believing as the condition of understanding, the *Monologion* simply announces the author's intention to proceed by reason alone without appeal to authority. Some have seen a conflict here and have argued that Anselm's conception of the relation between faith and reason changed from one work to the other. A second question is whether both works envisaged the same public, which is another way of asking whether both were intended to demonstrate the truth of the faith to unbelievers. Karl Barth has maintained that in neither work was Anselm addressing unbelievers, it being Barth's contention that argument neither brings a man to faith nor strengthens the faith that a man has but rather brings to the believer the joy of understanding. A. Stolz, on the other hand, distinguishes between what he sees as the rationalistic method of the *Monologion* and the devotional method of the *Proslogion*, the latter being in his opinion no argument but merely an attempt to understand the implications of the divine name, "He who truly is." Hopkins denies that there is any fundamental change in purpose between the two works and concludes that, although Anselm intended the arguments in the first instance to strengthen the faith of Christians, he also thought that to the degree that they were valid they must convince the honest skeptic.

In his chapter on the ontological argument Hopkins calls attention to the debate among philosophers in our time as to whether there is more than one argument in the *Proslogion*. As stated in the summary above, the proof in *Proslogion* 2 turns on the definition of God as "that than which nothing greater can be conceived." But in *Proslogion* 3, Anselm makes the further claim that this being, conceived of as existing, "cannot be thought not to exist." This latter claim is not introduced in the framework of a proof, but only as a further statement about the greatness of God. However, in his *Reply to Guanilo*, Anselm does argue that if it is conceivable for God to exist, then it is necessary that he exist; and this argument, restated in contemporary terms, has been defended independently by Norman Malcolm and by Charles Hartshorne, who refer to it as Anselm's second proof.

In evaluating the two proofs, Hopkins is mainly concerned with Anselm's use of key words. In the first proof, as Anselm recognized, there is a possibility of confusion arising from his use of the words think (*cogitare*) and understand (*intelligere*); and in *Proslogion* 4, in order to explain how the Fool could say in his heart what he could not think, Anselm distinguished between thinking, which concerns the meaning of words, and understanding, which concerns the essences of things. In the first sense, but not in the second, God can be thought not to exist. The distinction was taken up by Guanilo, who in effect accused Anselm of basing his refutation of the Fool on an equivocation. According to Hopkins, there should have been a further step in the first argument, permitting the Fool to say that he understands the use of the term but denies that there is any essence corresponding to it.

Hopkins' discussion of the second argument centers on Anselm's use of the term "necessity," and on how Anselm's argument differs from Saint Thomas Aquinas' Third Way, which also turns on the difference between possible and necessary being. Both philosophers, he contends, "become entangled in the linguistic web of their respective versions of these modal terms." Nor, in Hopkins' opinion, have Anselm's modern defenders done more than camouflage the proof's flaw behind their modal definitions. For, as in the first proof, the Fool can admit the claim construed linguistically while denying that it is valid construed according to fact.

Evans, G. R. *Anselm and Talking About God.* Oxford: Clarendon Press, 1978.

"Talking about God" covers two concerns: the speculative problem, what man can say about God, and the practical problem, how the teacher can best suit theological truths to the minds of his readers. According to G. R. Evans, Saint Anselm answered the former question to his satisfaction in the *Monologion* and the *Proslogion*, his first two works, and had no need to raise it again in subsequent studies; but the practical problem was ever with him, and in Evans' opinion, the care with which he framed his expositions to the understanding of monastic brethren who shared his interests but lacked his technical training helps to explain the perennial appeal of his writings.

The ontological proof for God's existence, although not central to the author's undertaking, does receive special notice, and her treatment of it draws together much of what she has to say concerning the question of what man can say about God.

As Anselm explains, the distinguishing feature of the *Proslogion* is that in this work, unlike the *Monologion* where a chain of arguments was used, only one argument comes into play. Most readers have understood the expression *unum argumentum* as referring to the proof in *Proslogion* 2-4. Evans, however, who approaches the work against the background of her studies in the arithmetic and geometry of the eleventh and twelfth centuries, takes it to mean "a single axiom," and argues that what was original in the *Proslogion* was Anselm's attempt to find "a single, generally accepted notion" that would enable him to deduce by rational necessity not merely God's existence but also, as he is careful to say, God's goodness, and the other divine qualities which, in the earlier work, had been deduced from a number of axioms.

Evans is not disquieted by the fact that Anselm nowhere expressly formulates his new axiom. She thinks that the well-known Augustinian principle according to which God is "that than which nothing greater can be thought" is not the axiom but its first application, and that the axiom proper, which has to bear the weight not merely of Chapters 2-4—but of the whole treatise, can be stated as, "God is 'more than' whatever we can conceive of as a good." Evans suggests the formula, "for whatever *a* we can imagine, God is $a + x$." Thus, taking for granted the absolute $a + x$-ness of God, Anselm is arguing in *Proslogion* 2 that if it is better to be in reality than in thought alone, God must exist in reality; and, in Chapter 3, that if that the nonexistence of which is unthinkable is greater than that the nonexistence of which is thinkable, then God's nonexistence must be unthinkable. In *Proslogion* 5, Anselm says explicitly that God is "whatever it is better to be than not to be," and he goes on to apply the principle to omnipotence, mercy, and other biblical attributes of God.

Evans does not suppose that in reformulating the proof she has done anything to appease its critics. If the proof merely unfolds implications already present in a single axiom, then obviously the existence of God has been taken for granted from the beginning. But this, she thinks, is entirely as it should be, given the views about language set forth in the *Monologion*, according to which God's existence, his goodness, and his faithfulness are presupposed every time we use language significantly. For Anselm, language is not merely a device for making statements about reality; created by God so that men might know and worship him, it has its own reality on a level with other things.

Human language, according to Anselm, is a repetition of divine speech. Anselm's description of the process by which God created the world parallels the activity of a human craftsman to the point of equating God's thought with a kind of internal speech. God could not have created the world out of nothing had there not existed in him from the first an expression (*locutio*) of all things that were to be. This power of thinking directly of things, in God and in rational creatures, Evans calls primary language.

The parallel between divine and human speech does not remove the gap between Creator and creature. When God speaks, he creates; his words are realities. When man speaks, using the language of *naturalia verba*, or universal ideas, he comes as close to reality as is possible for the created mind; but reality always lies beyond.

Anselm regularly equates thinking and speaking, whether he is talking about God or about man. This need causes no difficulty if we keep in mind Anselm's observations concerning the three ways in which men may be said to speak: we speak in sensible signs, or inwardly by thinking these signs, or by contemplating things directly without their signs. These three constitute a kind of "ladder of language," says Evans, with the natural words (what we would call innate ideas, although Anselm did not have the word "idea"), assumed to be present in every man's mind, being closest to the thoughts of God himself.

All of this, Evans allows, adds up to little more than taking a position on the interdependence of thoughts and things. The axioms which Anselm lays down, largely on the authority of Augustine, are assumptions so fundamental that they can be neither proved nor disproved. But Evans is interested chiefly in understanding Anselm in his historical situation. As prior, he was in the habit of discussing theological questions with his monks. Presumably the monks were in a hurry to get their questions answered, but they were listening to a philosophical genius who was willing to let the answers wait until he was satisfied as to the legitimacy of the questions. The *Monologion* provides a basis for speaking about God. At the same time it leaves room for doubt as to how far ordinary words can be used of the Creator. The most Anselm allows is that "huge abstractions" such as eternity, omnipotence, and truth can be spoken of God. Certain though he is that language is a gift provided to help man draw near God, Anselm denies that we can talk about God as he is.

Additional Recommended Reading

Barnes, Jonathan. *The Ontological Argument*. London: Macmillan and Company, 1972. Restatement of traditional and contemporary formulations and refutations of the argument.

Barth, Karl. *Fides Quaerens Intellectum*. Translated by I. W. Robertson. London: Student Christian Movement, 1960. Views Anselm as a confessing Christian rather than as a philosopher.

Hartshorne, Charles. *The Logic of Perfection*. La Salle, Illinois: Open Court, 1962. Chapter Two presents a symbolic expression of the ontological argument and a defense of the argument as valid.

Henry, Desmond Paul. *The Logic of Saint Anselm*. Oxford: Clarendon Press, 1967. An important contribution to the history of logic; includes an original interpretation of the Ontological Argument.

_____. *Medieval Logic and Metaphysics*. London: Hutchinson University Library, 1972. An experiment in applying the logic of S. Lesniewski to selected problems of medieval philosophy, including Anselm's proof.

Hick, John, and A. C. McGill, eds. *The Many-Faced Argument: Recent Studies on the Ontological Argument for the Existence of God*. New York: Macmillan Publishing Company, 1967. Includes selections from Barth, Stolz, Malcolm, Hartshorne, and others.

McGreal, Ian P. *Analyzing Philosophical Arguments*. San Francisco: Chandler Publishing Company, 1967. McGreal devotes Chapter Seven to a line-by-line semantical and logical critique of Anselm's ontological argument and argues that the argument fallaciously exploits the ambiguity of the expression "understand to exist."

Schufreider, Gregory. *An Introduction to Anselm's Argument*. Philadelphia: Temple University Press, 1978. Summarizes the present state of the Anselmian question and seeks by a renewed study of the text to reach the truth of the matter.

THE INCOHERENCE OF THE INCOHERENCE

Author: Averroës (ibn-Roshd, 1126-1198)
Type of work: Theology, metaphysics
First transcribed: Twelfth century

Principal Ideas Advanced

Since any series of causes necessary through another cause must ultimately depend upon a cause necessary in itself (a first cause), God, as the first cause, exists.

God did not create the world in time, either by willing it at the moment of creation or by willing it eternally, for to act in time is to change, and God is changeless because he is perfect.

God, as first cause and unmoved mover, does not act in time, but he produces immaterial intelligences which, because of their imperfection, can change in time.

The being of existent things is inseparable from their essence.

Averroës, the last of the great Islamic philosophers, lived roughly one hundred and fifty years after Avicenna, his philosophic rival, and about three generations after Ghazali (1058-1111) the greatest of Moslem theologians. In his controversy with these two men he concerned himself primarily with the defense and purification of Aristotle, whom he followed as closely as he could. Since he, too, accepted such spurious works as *The Theology of Aristotle*, his interpretation is still permeated by Neoplatonic elements, but to a lesser extent than that of Avicenna. The success of his endeavor is indicated by the fact that he was known to scholastic writers as *the* Commentator and that no less a person than Thomas Aquinas had him constantly at hand as he wrote his *Summa contra Gentiles* (c. 1258-1260) and his various commentaries on Aristotle.

The Incoherence of the Incoherence was written in reply to Ghazali's book, *The Incoherence of the Philosophers*, a book in which Ghazali had attacked the philosophers, and in particular Avicenna, for advocating doctrines that were incompatible with their faith. As the title of his own book suggests, Averroës came to the defense of the philosophers by attacking the incoherence of *The Incoherence*. Adopting a position similar to that of the later medieval thinkers who distinguished between revealed and natural theology, Averroës scrupulously avoided denying any tenet of his faith; nevertheless, he sided firmly with the philosophers. His interpretations of religious doctrines were so far removed from those of the theologians that even though he was studied carefully by Hebrew and Christian philosophers, he was not recognized to any great extent by his Islamic contemporaries. Averroës' book plays a very important role in the long controversy between the philosophers and the theologians, since it is concerned chiefly with the nature and existence of God, and with the relationship between God and the cosmos. Averroës does not spell out his position in detail, for he agrees on the whole with the earlier commentators on Aristotle and with the version of Aristotle he receives from them. In particular, he agrees largely with Avicenna, disagreeing on those points, and they are important points, where he thinks Avicenna departs from Aristotle. (The reader is referred to the article on Avicenna in this book.)

Averroës agrees with Aristotle that there is a First Cause, and he accepts a modified version of Avicenna's proof from contingency. Objects whose existence is contingent rather than necessary must have a cause. If the cause is itself contingent, and if its cause is contingent, and so on, there would be an infinite regress and therefore no cause at all, a conclusion which, it can readily be seen, denies the assumption that contingent objects must have a cause. Hence, any series of contingent objects must be preceded in existence by a necessary cause which is either necessary through another or necessary without a cause—necessary in itself. But if we have a series of causes each of which is necessary through another, once more we have an infinite regress and thus no cause. Hence, any series of causes necessary through another must depend upon a cause necessary in itself—a First Cause.

The nature of this First Cause and of the way in which it causes is illuminated by Averroës' discussion of creation. Averroës agrees with the philosophers against Ghazali that the world was not created in time. The philosophers had argued that if the world was created in time, it was created directly or indirectly by God, since an infinite regress of causes is impossible. If God created it in time, then he acted at a time and therefore underwent a change in time; but unquestionably, this is an impossible state of affairs since God is perfect and changeless. To Ghazali's objection that God did not act in time, but decreed from all eternity that the world should come into being at a certain time, Averroës replies that even if God had so willed from all eternity, he must also have acted at the time of creation in order to implement his decision, for every effect must have a contemporaneous cause. Consequently, the philosopher's objection cannot be avoided. It can be shown similarly that the cosmos is incorruptible; that is, that there is no time at which it will come to an end, for this too would require a change in God. Change occurs only within the world and then only when one thing is changed into another. The world itself is eternal and everlasting.

Ghazali had already attacked Avicenna on this point, asserting that the followers of Aristotle now have a problem on their hands, for they must give some account of how an eternal First Cause produces things that have a beginning in time. The problem is complicated by the fact that Averroës and Avicenna agreed with Aristotle that since the world is eternal, infinite temporal sequences do occur. For instance, there was no time when the celestial sphere began to move and no time when the first man appeared. Why

not, chides Ghazali, agree with the materialists that since there is an infinite sequence of causes, a First Cause is not only superfluous but impossible?

In reply, Averroës asks us to consider the case of the infinite sequence of past positions of a celestial sphere. Like Avicenna, he says that so far as the sphere is concerned this sequence is an accidental infinite, for the motion of the sphere at any given moment does not cause the motion it has at any other moment. First, if motion did cause motion there would be an infinite regress of causes and therefore no cause at all. Second, since motion is continuous, there are in it no discrete units that have a beginning and an end and therefore no units that could stand in a causal relationship to one another. Finally, since the cause must be contemporaneous with the effect, the causal relation cannot span an interval of time, and past motion cannot influence present motion. In the case of the celestial sphere, the motion it has at any given moment follows, not from the motion it had at some previous moment, but from its desire at that moment to emulate the perfection of the associated Intelligence. Through all eternity this Intelligence has sustained it in motion from moment to moment by continuously acting as its final cause. Since this Intelligence is itself a being whose existence is necessary through another, we are led back to the First Cause, the Unmoved Mover who stands behind the world. The Mover itself does not operate in time nor does it cause time directly, but it does produce an Intelligence which, because it is immaterial, is changeless, but which, because it is imperfect, is able to produce change of position in the sphere and thus to produce change in time.

Averroës' treatment of the infinite sequence of man begetting man is somewhat different from the preceding argument, for in this case there are discrete objects which do seem to cause one another successively. But here, too, Averroës says the sequence is, in itself, an accidental infinite. To be sure, the sequence does depend upon man, but only in several secondary senses. First, as he puts it, the third man can come from the second only if the first man has perished. That is, since the amount of matter in the universe is limited, human bodies can continue to come into existence only if others perish. Second, through the phenomena of conception and growth, man is the instrument by which God produces other men. But having functioned in both cases as a material cause by providing suitable matter, man's role is complete, for no body can produce a form in another. Directly or indirectly, the First Mover is the source of the eternal form that, when individuated by matter, animates that matter. Here again Averroës describes the Mover or one of the Intelligences as operating eternally as a final cause, again and again drawing forth from complexes of matter the form that is contained in them potentially.

Averroës then considers the question raised by Ghazali as to how it is possible for the plurality in the world to arise from the Mover, who is simple. Avicenna had argued that only one thing can emanate from God, but that this thing, the First Intelligence, is able to generate more than one thing by contemplating both itself and the Mover. Averroës replies, first, that since thought and its object are identical, the Intelligence is really identical with its thought of God and with its thought of itself and, therefore, that these thoughts are identical with each other. Hence, there is no plurality of thought and no plurality of creation. Second, he says that when Avicenna insists that only one thing can come from God, he is thinking of the Supreme Intellect as if it were a finite empirical one, but this concept is a mistake. Since our intellect is limited by matter, any particular mental act can have only one object, but since God is not so limited he can think all things even though his simplicity and changelessness preclude a plurality of acts. If it be replied that to think of all things is to have many thoughts, and that since thinker and thought are identical, God must be plural, Averroës replies that when God thinks all things he does not think them discursively as we do. In our case either we entertain images, a process which unquestionably involves spatial apprehension and thus spatial plurality, or we understand concepts by genus and species, a process which again introduces plurality. In either case, since we apprehend the object of thought by abstracting it from its material context, we apprehend it imperfectly. God, who is perfect, does not apprehend the natures of things in these ways and therefore does not apprehend them as either individual or universal. In

some manner which we do not understand, he comprehends that which is plural to us but does not comprehend it as numerically plural. (This is a particular application of the general principle that any property or capacity we attribute to God must be attributed only by analogy.) God, then, is the source of all plurality even though he is simple and changeless.

Averroës accepts the Avicennian cosmology in its general outlines. The First Mover produces a number of pure Intelligences which may produce others and which cause the motions of their respective spheres or, in the case of the Agent Intellect, preside over generation and corruption in the sublunar world. The Mover is the efficient cause of these Intelligences, producing them by means of a power that it emanates, and the final and formal cause insofar as it is the thing they seek to emulate. They in turn are the efficient, final, and formal causes of the motion of the spheres. Averroës agrees with Avicenna that though prime matter is not created, the existence of material things depends upon the Mover in that he is the source of the forms and also the agent, final, and formal cause of the manifestation of any form in matter.

But despite this agreement Averroës disagrees with Avicenna on a number of points. Some, such as the number of Intelligences (over forty), and the nonlinear order of the Intelligences (the Mover may have produced all of the Intelligences of the principle spheres directly) are unimportant, but others are crucial. As we have already indicated, Averroës insists that the Intelligences really are simple in that they do not contemplate themselves in several essentially different ways. It follows that the spheres are not composites of soul and body even though they are animate, and that God is the source of plurality. Consequently, God does not function as Avicenna says he does. Whether by intention or not, Avicenna left the impression that God's role in the creative process was completed when he produced the First Intelligence and that the further creative acts were contributed piecemeal by the various Intelligences acting from their own natures. In locating the source of plurality in God, Averroës is insisting that direct responsibility for the whole creative process rests with God. It is true, he says, that the Intelligences are creative agents, but they are the Mover's subordinates who, out of respect for him, implement his commands throughout the cosmos. Setting aside the theological analogy, we understand a theory such as this to mean that God's essence functions as the efficient, formal, and final cause of the First Intelligence, that this intelligence is an imperfect manifestation of the essence of God, that God as thus reflected functions once more as the efficient, formal, and final cause of an Intelligence or soul inferior to the first one, and so on down through the hierarchy.

Averroës also differs from Avicenna in a respect which anticipates the contrast between Spinoza and Leibniz, for he loosens the Avicenna bonds of necessity. To be sure, in some sense God does what he does necessarily, but this is not logical necessity, for the world he contemplates and thus produces is the best of all possible worlds. Similarly, the various intelligences respond to God, not because it would be contradictory not to, but because they respect him. There is a definite normative element permeating the system. On the general issue of the relation between God and the world Averroës does not differ from Avicenna as greatly as he frequently says he does; nevertheless, his modifications are important and they do result in a weakening of the Neoplatonic elements, a fact that was appreciated by later Aristotelians.

Another historically important feature of Averroës' philosophy is his rejection of Avicenna's sharp distinction between essence and existence. Avicenna had insisted that except in the case of God, existence is an accident that happens to an essence. For Avicenna, existence is a condition that must be satisfied by an essence before it can occur outside a mind, a property that must be added to it. Thus, the existence of a material object does not stem from its essence, but from what happened to its essence. On the other hand, Averroës insists that the very being of an existent thing is its essence, that its being depends upon the essence and not upon what happens to the essence. For him the terms "being" and "existence" are not verb terms, but substantives applied primarily to the object itself and secondarily to the essence that makes it the sort of thing it is. Since the object is a being or existent in virtue of its essence, it is impossible to

separate essence and existence save in thought. The essence itself may be regarded as an existent in a secondary sense of that term, but in this case it is impossible to separate essence and existence even in thought.

This difference between the two men is reflected in their views, inasmuch as Avicenna is very much concerned with how things come into existence and Averroës shows himself to be more concerned with the manner in which things change. Thus, in their proofs of the existence of God, Avicenna moves from the contingent existence of things to a necessarily existing ground, whereas Averroës proceeds from the occurrence of motion to an unmoved mover. Again, whereas Avicenna's Giver of Forms is bringing essences into existence by impressing them upon suitably prepared matter, Averroës' Agent Intellect is coaxing out forms nascent in complexes of matter. Averroës insists correctly that Avicenna is moving away from Aristotle and that he himself is truer to their common master. Later, Thomas Aquinas and his followers follow Avicenna in making a sharp distinction between essence and existence, but they acknowledge Averroës' objection by transforming existence from a property into an act of being that is prior in principle to essence. On the other hand, Ockham and the Averroists of the fourteenth, fifteenth, sixteenth, and seventeenth centuries insist that Averroës is right and that Avicenna and Thomas are wrong.

Another historically important feature of Averroës' philosophy is his disagreement with several aspects of Avicenna's psychology. First, and not so important, he believes that Avicenna added a superfluous faculty to the animal soul when he attributed an estimative sense to animals, a sense paralleling the cogitative sense in man. The ancients were correct, he says, in maintaining that imagination can detect intentions as well as sensible forms and that it can make judgments about these intentions. More importantly, Averroës gives a radically different account of the theoretic intellect. He agrees with Avicenna that the individual human intellect is activated only by the Agent Intellect which is external to us and acts on all of us alike, but he disagrees about the nature of the intellect that is activated. According to Avicenna, it is the potential intellect, an immaterial intellect, that can survive the body; but according to Averroës, it is the passive intellect, a corporeal faculty, that cannot survive the body. Averroës does admit an immaterial potential intellect in addition to the corporeal passive intellect; but it is not a personal faculty, for it is simply the Agent Intellect insofar as it individuates itself when it illuminates the passive intellect in order to prepare it for the reception of intelligible forms. Averroës thinks of the immaterial soul as being individuated when it strikes a physical object. Thus, there is no personal immortality, for individuality within

the immaterial intellect disappears when the corporeal passive intellect dies. From the point of view of the Christian philosophers of the twelfth and thirteenth centuries, Averroës is correct insofar as he gives the potential and agent intellects a common status, but incorrect insofar as he denies that they are personal faculties. They preferred to modify Avicenna by eliminating the Tenth Intelligence and endowing each human being with an individual agent intellect to accompany the individual potential intellect he already has.

Pertinent Literature

Averroës. *Tahafut al-tahafut (The Incoherence of the Incoherence)*. Translated by Simon Van den Bergh. London: Luzac, 1969.

Simon Van den Bergh presents a full translation of Averroës' reply to most of Ghazali's arguments in *The Incoherence of the Philosophers*. He also gives the translation of Ghazali's arguments, so that the book is self-contained and one does not need first to read a translation of Ghazali's *The Incoherence of the Philosophers* to be able to understand fully Averroës' answer in *The Incoherence of the Incoherence* to Ghazali's criticisms. For each issue discussed one finds Ghazali's argument or arguments and then Averroës' criticism or criticisms. The main theses and arguments of Averroës' *The Incoherence of the Incoherence* are analyzed in the Introduction, and further clarifications on more particular points and details of argumentation can be found in the notes located in the second volume.

In his Introduction, Van den Bergh first presents the historical background to the controversy in Islam between the theologians and the philosophers. According to the author, the controversy has its roots in the dispute between two main late Greek philosophical streams: (1) the Neoplatonic Aristotelianism which is somehow adopted by the Muslim philosophers and (2) the Skeptic Stoic School used by the theologians.

Van den Bergh claims that Ghazali's criticisms of the philosophers in *The Incoherence of the Philoso-*

phers are of a rather piecemeal kind and do not aim at a systematic destruction of philosophy by an attack on its foundations. Ghazali simply deals one by one with the issues on which philosophers hold positions contrary to the Islamic faith. By the philosophers Ghazali means Aristotle and his best Arabic interpreters, al-Farabi and Avicenna. So Ghazali's attack is not so much an attack on philosophy as such as it is an attack on Neoplatonic Aristotelianism. On each of the twenty disputed issues—sixteen in theology and four in natural philosophy—Ghazali tries to show the inconsistency of the position of the "philosophers." He goes from one issue to another but does not indicate connections between them; nor does he relate them to a general basic approach.

Averroës' reply to Ghazali's *The Incoherence of the Philosophers* follows the same pattern and does not present an articulate and unified defense of his philosophical positions. It is to other works that one should look for a systematic exposition of Averroës' thought.

For most of the disputed issues Van den Bergh gives an interpretation of the basic arguments of both Ghazali and Averroës and a critical evaluation thereof. He also shows the perennial character of the issues in drawing parallels between Ghazali's or Averroës' position and the position of some ancient, modern, or contemporary philosophers.

His main contention—a rather unusual one—is that, although Ghazali and Averroës seem to be in great disagreement, they basically hold the same position but let formulations divide them. Their quarrel was about words not substance. Both, in fact, present a philosophical approach; but their ways of treating philosophy differ. Ghazali, who is, according to Van den Bergh, mainly a theologian and therefore under Stoic influence, looks for a philosophy of the heart which does not so much seek abstract truth as

a God of Pity. Averroës, on the other hand, who is a philosopher in the Neoplatonic Aristotelian line, seeks a sort of disembodied truth. So Van den Bergh presents Ghazali as the champion of some sort of existential philosophy and Averroës as the champion of some sort of dry rationalism.

According to Van den Bergh, the dispute between Ghazali and Averroës is not a dispute between theologians and philosophers, or between faith and reason, but a dispute between representatives of two approaches to philosophy.

Averroës. *On the Harmony of Religion and Philosophy.* Translated by George F. Hourani. London: Luzac, 1961.

The Incoherence of the Incoherence is a reply to Ghazali's criticisms of the philosophers. It presents a discussion of some issues on which the philosophers hold positions contrary to the faith. It does not try to articulate a general theory of the relation between philosophy and religion. The texts translated in *On the Harmony of Religion and Philosophy* do so.

The first text, known as *The Decisive Treatise*, according to George F. Hourani is a juridical defense of the study of philosophy. It is a defense of philosophy written by a lawyer for other lawyers in function of the categories of Islamic law. It attempts to demonstrate that the study of philosophy, according to Islamic law, is obligatory.

The first part shows that the Law commands the study of philosophy considered as a demonstrative science. By philosophy Averroës means Aristotelian and therefore Greek philosophy. If sometimes philosophy leads to harm it is purely accidental, just as the taking of a medicine can cause harm by accident. Philosophy will cause harm only to people who are unable to follow demonstrative arguments. Therefore, although the study of philosophy is obligatory for anyone who is qualified, it should be forbidden to those who are not qualified to use demonstrative arguments.

The second part contends that, contrary to appearances, philosophy contains nothing opposed to Islam. If the apparent meaning of the Koran and the Traditions conflicts with the conclusions of philosophy, one must interpret that meaning allegorically. The

three main points of contention between Ghazali and the philosophers (God's ignorance of particulars, the assertion of the eternity of the world, and the denial of the bodily resurrection, issues that are discussed in *The Incoherence of the Incoherence*) are dealt with, and the lack of real conflict between faith or religion and philosophy in what concerns them is argued for. Averroës also elaborates some basic principles for the allegorical interpretation of the Scriptures in case of opposition with sound philosophical positions.

The third and final part insists on the fact that such allegorical interpretation should be reserved to the philosophers and hidden from the masses, whom it would confuse. For them the literal meaning is enough, and safer.

The second text translated in this book is the *Appendix* to *The Decisive Treatise*; it again deals with the problem of God's knowledge of the particulars. The third and last text deals with the allegorical interpretation of the bodily resurrection as an expression of the immortality of the soul and provides some more principles of allegorical interpretation of the Scriptures and criteria to determine when the Scriptures require such an intepretation.

In his Introduction to these texts, Hourani offers a historical background and some evaluation of Averroës' position. He first maintains that both in *The Incoherence of the Incoherence* and in *The Decisive Treatise* Averroës presents his true philosophic positions, although he exercises caution in discussing them, and, therefore, is rather involved and sometimes obscure. Hourani also contends that *The Decisive Treatise* shows that Averroës is a believing Muslim and that his text gives an impression of sincerity.

According to Hourani, *The Decisive Treatise* is the only book in Medieval Islam that attempts to give an answer to the problem of the harmony of Sunnite Islam with Greco-Arabic philosophy. Philosophy, on the one hand, is the last resort in case of conflict between the literal meaning of the Scriptures and itself, although its study should be reserved for the intellectual elite. Philosophy thus gives the true meaning of the Scriptures. Ordinary Islam, on the other hand, and therefore literal meaning, should lead the masses because they are unable to understand philosophy. Basically, for Averroës, there is only one truth; and it is philosophy which brings about, when necessary, the true meaning of religion, a meaning beyond the reach of the ordinary man. This of course excludes a "double truth" interpretation of Averroës, as some had proposed.

Tallon, Andrew. "Personal Immortality in Averroës' 'Tahafut al-Tahafut,' " in *The New Scholasticism.* XXXVIII, no. 3 (July, 1964), pp. 341-357.

One of the main contentions of Ghazali in his *The Incoherence of the Philosophers* is that philosophers not only deny the bodily resurrection but furthermore are also unable to explain individual immortality of the soul (pp. 333-363). In *On the Harmony of Religion and Philosophy* Averroës explains that the true meaning of the bodily resurrection is the immortality of the soul. But in what exactly does the immortality of the soul consist for Averroës?

In his commentary on Aristotle's *On the Soul*, Averroës states that there is only one Active Intellect for the whole of mankind, and also only one Passive Intellect. This Passive Intellect is "outside" the human being and thinks through this being by making use of the images produced by man. Only imagination, which is not a part of the intellect, is individual; but it is also mortal.

Since there is some question as to whether Averroës holds the same positions in his Aristotelian commentaries written for philosophers as he does in his defenses of philosophy written for a broader public, such as *The Incoherence of the Incoherence* and *The Decisive Treatise*, Andrew Tallon tries to determine his position on immortality in *The Incoherence of the Incoherence*.

Tallon first maintains that Averroës' text is difficult, obscure, and ambiguous. He then contends that Averroës states that intellect is separate and one for all men, although it is not an aspect of the soul since it is separate from it. The question then becomes: Is soul immortal for Averroës? Tallon indicates a few passages in which Averroës states that the soul as such is immortal, but does man have an immortal individual soul or only a collective one? Here Tallon argues that Averroës' concern is for the species and not for individuals, even though he does not say so.

To understand Averroës' position one needs to consider what his metaphysical conception of individuation implies. It is clear that for Averroës the sole principle of individuation is matter. Soul is by itself immaterial and immortal and so cannot be individuated by matter or bodies; therefore it cannot be individuated at all. Thus, Averroës believes that the soul too is separate. In other passages, however, Averroës describes the soul as *in* the body. What does Averroës mean by that? Tallon suggests that the soul is *in* a body as light is *in* a mirror. As there is one light which can be reflected in many mirrors, there is one soul which is temporarily reflected in diverse bodies. Thus, when Averroës claims that the soul is the form of the body, he is no longer holding a traditional hylomorphic position in which form and matter are interdependent, but asserting the temporary relation of the separate immaterial and immortal soul to many individual bodies.

Tallon concludes that the wording of Averroës' statement, as well as the internal coherence of his metaphysical positions, prevent him from asserting an individual immortality since *the* Soul, although immortal, is not individual.

Yet, according to Tallon, the ambiguities of Averroës' text probably indicate that Averroës the philosopher and Averroës the man are in conflict. As a philosopher Averroës does not see any way to argue in favor of an individual immortality of the soul and therefore claims only the immortality of *the* Soul. Such an immortality is an immortality of the species, not of individuals. On the other hand, as a man and a Muslim, Averroës either believes in personal immortality or wants to do so. The ambiguities are therefore not in Averroës' philosophy but in Averroës the man. Tallon is convinced that Averroës has not realized the true harmony between Averroës the believer and Averroës the philosopher, and between his intellectual integrity and his religious beliefs or desires. Such claims imply that, according to Tallon, Averroës, in what concerns his conception of the soul and of the intellect and their immortality, holds basically the same position in *The Incoherence of the Incoherence* as in his commentaries on Aristotle. In both, he defends what is traditionally known as monopsychism, or the theory that there is only one soul for all mankind and therefore no individual souls and no personal immortality.

Additional Recommended Reading

Aquinas, Saint Thomas. *On the Unity of the Intellect Against the Averroists (De Unitate Intellectus contra Averroistas)*. Translated by Beatrice H. Zedler. Milwaukee: Marquette University Press, 1968. Translation of Thomas' attack against some of his adversaries who were defending Averroës' monopsychism. Shows the influence of Averroës on the West and includes a criticism of his epistemology.

Arberry, A. J. *Revelation and Reason in Islam*. London:George Allen & Unwin, 1957. A standard presentation of diverse approaches in Islam to this question.

Averroës. *Destructio Destructionum Philosophiae Algazelis,* in *the Latin version of Calo Calonymos*. Edited by Beatrice H. Zedler. Milwaukee: Marquette University Press, 1961. Transcription of the Venice 1550 Latin edition, with a historical introduction.

Ghazali. *Tahafut al-Falasifah (The Incoherence of the Philosophers)*. Translated by Sabih Ahmad Kamali. Lahore: Pakistan Philosophical Congress, 1963. Complete English translation of *The Incoherence of the Philosophers*, including the Introduction and the arguments not included in Averroës' *The Incoherence of the Incoherence*. Allows an examination of Ghazali's work for its own sake.

Ivry, Alfred L. "Towards a Unified View of Averroës' Philosophy," in *The Philosophical Forum*. IV, no. 1 (Fall, 1972), pp. 87-113. A new and controversial interpretation of Averroës which tries to present a synthetic outlook.

SUMMA THEOLOGICA

Author: Saint Thomas Aquinas (c. 1225-1274)
Type of work: Metaphysics, theology
First transcribed: c. 1265-1274

Principal Ideas Advanced

Man requires more than philosophy in his search for truth; certain truths are beyond human reason and are available only because of divine revelation; theology, which depends on revealed knowledge, supplements natural knowledge.

The existence of God can be proved in five ways: by reference to motion (and the necessity of a first mover), by reference to possibility and necessity, by reference to the gradations of perfection in the world, and by reference to the order and harmony of nature (which suggests an ordering being who gives purpose to the created world).

God alone is the being whose nature is such that by reference to him one can account for the fact of motion, efficient cause, necessity, perfection, and order.

God's principal attributes are simplicity (for he is noncorporeal and without genus), actuality, perfection, goodness, infinitude, immutability, unity, and immanence; but the created intellect can know God only by God's grace and only through apprehension, not comprehension.

It is a difficult task to comment on Thomas's *Summa Theologica* briefly; it has meant and can mean many things to many people. Partly this is due to its length; it runs to many volumes. And partly it is due to the scope of the questions considered; they range from abstract and technical philosophy to minute points of Christian dogmatics. The situation is further complicated because of Thomas's style. Such works were common in his day, and his is only one of many which were written in this general form. The work consists entirely of questions, each in the form of an article in which the views Thomas considers important are summarized and then answered. Objections to the topic question are listed, often including specific quotations, and then an equal number of replies are given, based on a middle section ("I answer that") which usually contains Thomas's own position; but this, in turn, is sometimes based on some crucial quotation from a philosopher or theologian.

Out of this complexity and quantity many have attempted to derive Thomistic "Systems," and both the commentators and the group of modern Thomists form a complex question in themselves. Thomas was considered to be near heresy in his own day, and his views were unpopular in some quarters. From the position of being not an especially favored teacher in a very fruitful and exciting era, he has come to be regarded as perhaps the greatest figure in the Catholic philosophy and theology of the day. His stature is due as much to the dogmatization and expansion of his thought which took place (for example, by Cardinal Cajetan and John of St. Thomas) as it is to the position Thomas had in his own day. Without this further development his writing might have been important, but perhaps it would be simply one among a number of significant medieval works. The Encyclical Letter of Pope Leo XIII, "On the Restoration of Christian Philosophy," published in 1879, started the Thomistic revival. The modern developments in philosophy had gone against the Church of Rome, and Thomas Aquinas was selected as the center for a revival and a concentration upon Christian philosophy. Since that time Thomas has been widely studied, so much so that it is sometimes hard to distinguish Thomas's own work from that of those who followed him.

Part I contains 119 questions, including treatises

on creation, on the angels, on man, and on the divine government. The first part of Part II consists of 114 questions, including treatises on habits and law, and in general it covers ethical matters as against the metaphysical and epistemological concentration in Part I. The second part of Part II is made up of 189 questions, and Part III contains ninety. These cover laws, the ethical virtues, and questions of doctrine and Christology. Taken as a whole, it is hard to imagine a more comprehensive study, although it is important to remember that Thomas wrote a second *Summa*, "against the Gentiles," which was intended as a technical work of apologetics for those who could not accept the premises of Christian theology. The works overlap a great deal, but a comparative study cannot be made here. The *Summa Theologica*, then, has as its unspoken premise the acceptance of certain basic Christian propositions, whereas the *Contra Gentiles* attempts to argue without any such assumptions.

The influence of any single philosopher or theologian on Thomas's thought is difficult to establish, and probably too much has been made of Thomas's use of Aristotle. It is true that Aristotle is quoted in the *Summa Theologica* more than any other pagan author and that Thomas refers to him on occasion as "the philosopher." The availability of Aristotle's writings in fairly accurate translation in Thomas's day had a decided influence upon him and upon others of his era. Plato's works as a whole were still unrecovered, so that Aristotle is one of the few outside the Christian tradition who is quoted. Particularly in psychology and epistemology Thomas seems to have followed at least an Aristotelian tradition, if not Aristotle himself. But the authors Thomas quotes with favor cover a wide range, including frequent citations of the Neoplatonic pseudo-Dionysius and Augustine. Moreover, in a theologically oriented *summa*, the Bible and church tradition must play a major role, so that to sort out and label any strain as dominant is extremely difficult in view of the peculiar nature of a *summa*. There are positions which can clearly be recognized as Thomas's own, but the real perplexity of understanding Thomas is to grasp the variety of sources blended there and to hold them altogether for simultaneous consideration and questioning as Thomas himself did.

The first question, consisting of ten articles, is Thomas's famous definition of the nature and the extent of sacred doctrine or theology, and it opens by asking whether man requires anything more than philosophy. Thomas's contention that the Scriptures are inspired by God and are not a part of philosophy indicates the usefulness of knowledge other than philosophy. Scriptural knowledge is necessary for man's salvation, for Scripture offers the promise of salvation and pure philosophic knowledge does not. Philosophy is built up by human reason; certain truths necessary for man's salvation, but which exceed human reason, have been made known by God through divine revelation. Such knowledge is not agreed to be reason; it is by nature accepted only on faith.

Now the question arises: Can such revealed knowledge be considered as a science (a body of systematic knowledge) along with philosophy? Of course, such a sacred science treats of God primarily and does not give equal consideration to creatures. This means that it is actually a speculative undertaking and is only secondarily a practical concern. Yet it is the most noble science, because of the importance of the questions it considers, and in that sense all other forms of scientific knowledge are theology's handmaidens. Wisdom is knowledge of divine things, and in that sense theology has chief claim to the title of "wisdom." Its principles are immediately revealed by God, and within such a science all things are treated under the aspect of God.

Naturally there can be no argument on these terms with one who denies that at least some of theology's truths are obtained through divine revelation, for such a person would not admit the very premises of theology conceived of in this fashion. That is the sense in which this *summa* is a *summa* of theology intended for Christians. Since its arguments, at least in some instances, involve a claim to revealed knowledge, the *Summa* may be unconvincing to the non-Christian. Thus, the reception of grace, sufficient to become a Christian, is necessary to understand the arguments. In the Christian conception, the reception of grace enables the receiver to accept the truth of revelation. But Thomas's famous doctrine here is that such reception of grace does not destroy nature (natural knowledge) but perfects or completes it. Nothing is countermanded in philosophy's own domain; grace simply adds to it what of itself could not be known.

As compared with other classical theologians Thomas believed in a fairly straightforward approach to questions about God. However, Thomas did admit the necessity of the familiar "negative method," since where God is concerned what he is *not* is clearer to us than what he is. The proposition "God exists" is not self-evident to us, although it may be in itself. The contradictory of the proposition "God is" can be conceived.

In this case Thomas seems to oppose Anselm's ontological argument, although the opposition is not quite as straightforward as it seems. Thomas denies that we can know God's essence directly, even though such vision would reveal that God's essence and existence are identical and thus support Anselm's contention. But the ontological argument, he reasons, is built upon a kind of direct access to the divine which human reason does not have.

The existence of God, then, needs to be demonstrated from those of his effects which are known to us. Thomas readily admits that some will prefer to account for all natural phenomena by referring everything to one principle, which is nature herself. In opposition he asserts that God's existence can be proved in five ways: (1) the argument from motion, (2) the argument from the nature of efficient cause, (3) the argument from possibility and necessity, (4) the argument from the gradations of perfection to be found in things, and finally (5) the argument from the order of the world. Without attempting an analysis of these arguments individually, several things can be noted about them as a group. First, all are based on the principle that reason needs a final stopping point in any chain of explanation. Second, such a point of final rest cannot be itself within the series to be accounted for, but it must be outside it and different in kind. Third, in each case it is a principle which we arrive at, not God himself, but these principles (for example, a first efficient cause) are shown to be essential parts of the nature of God. God's existence is agreed to by showing reason's need for one of his attributes in the attempt to explain natural phenomena.

It is probably true that Thomas's five proofs have been given a disproportionate amount of attention, for following them Thomas goes into elaborate detail in a discussion of the divine nature and its primary attributes. Simplicity, goodness, infinity, and perfection are taken up, and then the other chief attributes are discussed before Thomas passes on to the analysis of the three persons of the trinitarian conception of God. Taken together, these passages form one of the most elaborate and complete discussions of God's nature by a major theologian, and it is here that much of the disagreement about Thomas's philosophy centers, rather than in the more formal and brief five proofs.

In spite of Thomas's use of Aristotelian terms, he indicates his affinity with the Neoplatonic tradition by placing the consideration of "simplicity" first. This is the divine attribute most highly prized and most stressed by Neoplatonists, and Thomas concurs in their emphasis. God's simplicity is first protected by denying absolutely that he is a body in any sense, since what is corporeal is by nature subject to division and contains potentiality, the opposite of God's required simplicity and full actuality. Nor is God within any genus, nor is he a subject as other individuals are. The first cause rules all things without commingling with them.

God's primary perfection is his actuality, since Thomas accepts the doctrine that a thing is perfect in proportion to its state of actuality. All created perfections preexist in God also, since he is the source of all things. As such a source of the multitude of things in this world, things diverse and in themselves opposed to each other preexist in God as one, without injury to his simplicity. This is no simple kind of simplicity which Thomas ascribes to his God as a perfection. God is also called good, although goodness is defined primarily in terms of full actuality, as both perfection and simplicity were. Everything is good insofar as it has being, and, since God is being in a supremely actual sense, he is supremely good. An object can be spoken of as evil only insofar as it lacks being. Since God lacks being in no way, there is in that sense absolutely no evil in his nature but only good.

When Thomas comes to infinity he is up against a particularly difficult divine attribute. By his time infinity had become a traditional perfection to be ascribed to God, but Aristotle had gone to great lengths to deny even the possibility of an actual infinite. Without discussing Aristotle's reasons here, it can be noted that Thomas makes one of his most significant alterations at this point in the Aristotelian concepts which he does use. Aristotle had considered the question of an actual infinite in the category of quantity. Thomas agrees with him: there can be no quantitative infinite and the idea is an imperfection. Form had meant primarily limitation for Aristotle, but here Thomas departs. The notion of form, he asserts, is not incompatible with infinity, although the forms of natural things are finite. In admitting the concept of the form of the infinite, Thomas departs from Aristotelian conceptions quite markedly and makes a place for a now traditional divine perfection. Nothing besides God, however, can be infinite.

Turning to the question of the immanence of God in the natural world, Thomas makes God present to all things as being the source of their being, power, and operation. But as such, God is not in the world. For one thing, God is altogether immutable, whereas every natural thing changes. He must be, since he is pure act and only what contains potentiality moves to acquire something. It follows that in God there is no succession, no time, but only simultaneous presence. God's unity further guarantees us that only one such God could exist. Of course a God of such a nature may not be knowable to a particular intellect, on account of the excess of such an intelligible object over the finite intellect; but, as fully actual, God is in himself fully knowable. The blessed see the essence of God by grace; for others it is more difficult. However, a proportion is possible between God and man, and in this way the created intellect can know God proportionally. This is not full knowledge, but it established the possibility for a knowledge relationship between God and man.

The created intellect, however, cannot fully grasp the essence of God, unless God by grace unites himself to the created intellect, as an object made intelligible to it. It is necessary in the case of God only that, for a full grasp, the natural power of understanding should be aided by divine grace. Those who possess the more charity will see God the more perfectly, and will be the more beatified. Here is Thomas's statement of the famous goal of the beatific vision. Even here God is only apprehended and never comprehended, since only an infinite being could possess the infinite mode necessary for comprehension, and none is infinite except God. God alone can comprehend himself, yet for the mind to attain an understanding of God in some degree is still asserted to be a great beatitude. God cannot be seen in his essence by a mere human being, except he be separated from this mortal life. Thomas here follows the famous Exodus XXXIII:2O passage: "Man shall not see Me, and live."

For Thomas faith is a kind of knowledge, since we gain a more perfect knowledge of God himself by grace than by natural reason. Such a concept of faith has had wide implications. That God is a trinity, for instance, cannot be known except by faith, and in general making faith a mode of knowledge has opened to Christianity the claim to a more perfect comprehension than non-Christians possess.

Names can be applied to God positively on Thomas's theory, but negative names simply signify his distance from creatures, and all names fall short of a full representation of him. Not all names are applied to God in a metaphorical sense, although some are (for example, God is a lion), but there are some names which are applied to God in a literal sense (for example, good, being). In reality God is one, and yet he is necessarily multiple in idea, because our intellect represents him in a manifold manner, conceiving of many symbols to represent him. However, univocal predication is impossible, and sometimes terms are even used equivocally. Others are predicated of God in an analogous sense, according to a proportion existing between God and nature.

In the first thirteen questions Thomas considers God as man approaches him. He then considers the world as it is viewed from the standpoint of the divine nature. Even the attributes of perfection which Thomas discussed, although they truly characterize God's nature, are not separate when viewed from the divine perspective. Now we ask how God understands both himself and the world, and the first thing which must be established is that there actually is knowledge in God. This might seem obvious, but the Neoplatonic tradition denies knowing to its highest principle as implying separation and need. Thomas admits a mode of knowing into the divine nature but he denies that God knows as creatures do. God understands everything through himself alone, without dependence on external objects; his intellect and its object are altogether the same and no potentiality is present. God's knowledge is not discursive but simultaneous and fully actual eternally. This is true because of God's role as the creator of the natural world; God's knowledge is the cause of things being as they are. God knows even some things which never were, nor are, nor will be, but it is in his knowledge not that they be but that they be merely possible.

God knows future contingent things, the works of men being subject to free will. These things are not certain to us, because of their dependence upon proximate, contingent causes, but they are certain to God alone, whose understanding is eternal and above time. There is a will as a part of God's nature, but it is moved by itself alone. The will of man is sometimes moved by things external to him. God wills his own goodness necessarily, even as we will our own happiness necessarily. Yet his willing things apart from himself is not necessary. Supposing that he wills it, however, then he is unable not to will it, since his will cannot change. Things other than God are thus "necessary by supposition." God knows necessarily whatever he knows, but does not will necessarily whatever he wills. And the will of God is always reasonable in what it wills. Yet the will of God is entirely unchangeable, Thomas asserts, since the substance of God and his knowledge are entirely unchangeable. As to evil, God neither wills evil to be done, nor wills it not to be done, but he wills to permit evil to be done; this is good because it is the basis of man's freedom. We must say, however, that all things are subject to divine providence, not only in general, but even in their own individual selves. It necessarily follows that everything which happens from the exercise of free will must be subject to divine providence. Both necessity and contingency fall under the foresight of God.

It should not be overlooked that Thomas devotes considerable time to a consideration of the nature and function of angels. Part of his reason for doing so, of course, is undoubtedly their constant presence in the biblical record. Part of his interest comes from the necessity of having intermediary beings between God and man. Having assigned to God a nature so different from man's nature, beings who stand somewhere in between are now easy to conceive. When Thomas comes to describe the nature of man, he follows much of the traditional Aristotelian psychology, which he finds more amenable to Christianity than certain Platonistic theories. Angels are not corporeal; man is composed of a spiritual and a corporeal substance. The soul has no matter, but it is necessarily joined to matter as its instrument. The intellectual principle is the form of man and in that sense determines the body's form. Since Thomas claims that the intellect in each man is uniquely individual, he argues against some Arabian views of the universality of intellect. In addition to a twofold intellect (active and passive), man has appetites and a will.

The will is not always moved by necessity, but in Thomas's views it is subject to the intellect. When he turns to the question of free will, Thomas's problem is to allow sufficient causal power to man's will without denying God's providence and foreknowledge. His solution to this problem is complicated, but essentially it involves God's moving man not directly and by force but indirectly and without doing violence to man's nature.

To obtain knowledge the soul derives intelligible species from the sensible forms which come to it, and it has neither innate knowledge nor does it know any forms existing independently from sensible things. The principle of knowledge is in the senses. Our intellect can know the singular in material things directly and primarily. After that intelligible species are derived by abstraction. Yet the intellectual soul cannot know itself directly, but only through its operations. Nor in this present life can our intellect know immaterial substances directly. That is a knowledge reserved for angels, but it means that we cannot understand immaterial substances perfectly now (through natural means). We know only material substances, and they cannot represent immaterial substances perfectly.

The soul of man is not eternal; it was created. It is produced immediately by God, not by any lesser beings (as is suggested in Plato's *Timaeus*, for instance). Soul and body are produced simultaneously, since they belong together as one organism. Man was made in God's image, but this in no way implies that there must be equality between creator and created. And some natures may be more like God than others, according to their disposition and the direction of their activities. All men are directed to some end. According as their end is worthy of blame or praise, so are their deeds worthy of blame or praise. There is, however, one last fixed end for all men; and man must, of necessity, desire all that he desires for the sake of that last end. Man's happiness ultimately does not consist either in wealth, fame, or honor, or even in power. Thomas never doubts that the end desired is to be happy, but he does deny that the end can consist of goods of the body. No created good can be man's last end. Final and perfect happiness can consist in nothing else than the vision of the Divine Essence, although momentary happiness probably does depend on some physical thing.

Now, it is possible for man to see God, and therefore it is possible for man to attain his ultimate happiness. Of course, there are diverse degrees of happiness, and it is not present equally in all men. A certain participation in such happiness can be had in this life, although true and perfect happiness cannot. Once attained, such happiness cannot be lost since its nature is eternal, but man cannot attain it by his own natural powers, although every man desires it.

Next Thomas considers the mechanics of human action, voluntary and involuntary movement, individual circumstances, the movement of the will, intention and choice. His discussion forms an addition to his psychology and a more complete discussion of the ethical situation of man. When he comes to good and evil in human action, Thomas easily acknowledges that some actions of man are evil, although they are good or evil according to circumstance. As far as man's interior act of will is concerned, good and evil are essential differences in the act of will. The goodness of the will essentially depends on its being subject to reason and to natural law. The will can be evil when it abides by an erring reason, The goodness of the will depends upon its conformity to the divine will.

In his more detailed psychology, Thomas discusses the nature and origin of the soul's passions, joy, sadness, hope, fear, and then love and hate. Pleasure, pain or sorrow, hope, despair, and fear all are analyzed in a way that anticipates Spinoza's famous discussion of the emotions. When Thomas comes to virtue, his opinion is largely based on Aristotle's. There are intellectual virtues and moral virtues, and to these he adds the theological virtues of faith, hope, and charity. Moral virtue is in a man by nature, although God infuses the theological virtues into man. For salvation, of course, there is need for a gift of the Holy Ghost.

Thomas continues with a discussion of sin, its kinds and causes. Such discussion has been extremely important both to church doctrine and in church practice. Not all sins are equal; therefore, sins must be handled in various ways. The carnal sins, for instance, are of less guilt but of more shame than spiritual sins. Mortal and venial sins are distinguished, but the will and the reason are always involved in the causes of sin. "Original sin" as a concept is of course extremely important to Christian doctrine, and Thomas discusses this in detail.

The treatise on law is one of the more famous parts of the *Summa Theologica*, for it is here that Thomas develops his theory of natural law. First, of course, there is the eternal law of which natural law is the first reflection and human (actual legal) law is a second reflection. The eternal law is one and it is unchanging; natural law is something common to all nations and cannot be entirely blotted out from men's hearts. Human law is derived from this common natural law, but human law is framed to meet the majority of instances and must take into account many things, as to persons, as to matters, and as to times.

A brief survey such as this cannot do justice even to the variety of topics considered in the *Summa Theologica*, nor can it give any detailed description of the complex material presented or of the views Thomas distills from them. The impression which the

Summa Theologica gives is that of an encyclopedia to be read and studied as a kind of source book for material on a desired issue. In fact, the only way for any reader to hope to understand Thomas and his *Summa Theologica* is to become engrossed and involved in it for himself—undoubtedly what Thomas intended.

Pertinent Literature

Gilson, Étienne. *The Christian Philosophy of St. Thomas Aquinas.* Translated by L. I. Shook from the fifth edition of *Le Thomisme.* New York: Random House, 1956.

As Professor of the History of Medieval Philosophy at the University of Paris, Étienne Gilson was largely responsible for bringing the philosophy of St. Thomas Aquinas to the attention of secular scholars. Meanwhile, by calling his fellow Catholics back from the schematized doctrines found in their handbooks to the life and teaching of the thirteenth century master, he helped raise official Thomism to a new plane. Medieval philosophy was not taught at the Sorbonne when Gilson was a student, and his acquaintance with Aquinas' writings began when he undertook to explore for his dissertation the influence of medieval thought on the philosophy of René Descartes. A series of lectures published in 1914 under the title *Le Thomisme*, the first of the five editions through which the present book has passed, is noteworthy, says its author, only as a monument to his ignorance. But ignorance of medieval philosophy was widespread: one of his reviewers denied that Aquinas had a philosophy distinct in any way from the scholastic synthesis which he shared with his contemporaries.

The words "Christian philosophy" in the English title highlight the author's conviction that one can understand Thomas' philosophy only if one approaches it through the faith of the Church. Earlier representatives of the Thomist revival, eager to prove to their secular counterparts that Catholics can philosophize like anyone else, argued that Thomas' philosophy, which they closely identified with that of Aristotle, was completely independent of his theology. As a historian, Gilson challenged this interpretation, maintaining that, not indeed in his commentaries but in his *Summas*, Thomas philosophized as a theologian, taking up into Christian doctrine such philosophical truths as could be used to amplify and explain what God had revealed through the Church.

The present work is a detailed exposition of Thomas' philosophy against the full background of Greek, Christian, and Arabian thought. But special attention is always given by Gilson to points at which Thomas went beyond his predecessors. This appears in each of the three parts into which Gilson divides his book: God, Nature, and Morality.

Gilson plunges the reader at once into what he considers Thomas' greatest contribution to philosophy: his revolutionary conception of being. Aristotle had, indeed, pointed the way when, in his analysis of substance, he affirmed that matter owes its existence to form and that form exists only in conjunction with matter. Aristotle, however, had failed to answer the question of how existence can arise from what does not exist. Had he pursued his analysis he must have arrived at existence as "the ultimate term to which the analysis of the real can attain." Thomas, in insisting that forms, by which matter is actuated, are themselves actuated by existence exposed the inadequacy of earlier essential ontologies and for the first time presented an existential ontology.

Much of Gilson's book is devoted to showing the consequences of this metaphysical innovation. One result is that God is no longer defined as Perfect Being or as Pure Act but as "the act of being that He is." "Like whatever exists, God is by His own act-of-being; but in His case alone, we have to say that *what* His being is is nothing else than that by which He exists, namely the pure act of existence." A further result is that the existence of God cannot be proved, in the strict sense, and that the five ways are not to be understood as a demonstration but rather as "a search beyond existences which are not self-sufficient, for an existence which is self-sufficient and which, because it is so, can be the first cause of all others."

A chapter entitled "Creation" serves Gilson as a transition from the doctrine of God to the doctrine of Nature. The notion that everything in the world depends on God both for its nature and its existence was foreign to the Greeks; and one of Thomas' major achievements was his doctrine of concurrent causes, by which he combined the Christian doctrine of dependence with the Greek assumption of a self-sustaining cosmos. God causes everything; but he does so in a manner that preserves the potentiality and actuality proper to each thing. In this way the creature's autonomy is secured and the groundwork is laid for a doctrine of natural law.

Thomas' moral philosophy, based on his philosophy of nature, is not to be confused with what is commonly called Christian ethics, for in the *Summa* Thomas treats the theological virtues (faith, hope, and love) separately from the moral virtues (prudence, fortitude, temperance, and justice). The law for every creature is a function of that creature's nature. Lower creatures obey it unconsciously; human beings, en-

dowed with reason, have to "find out what they are so that they may act accordingly." As a moral philosopher, Thomas gave full scope to all types of human fulfillment, showing princes, merchants, scholars, artists—persons of every type—"at grips with the problem of doing well whatever they have to do, and above all with the problem of problems, not to ruin the only life it is theirs to live." Much of his practical philosophy parallels that of Aristotle. Still, there are differences, as when, in considering justice, Thomas internalizes and personalizes what for the Greeks remained primarily a civic virtue.

In his concluding chapter, "The Spirit of Thomism," Gilson opposes Thomas' existentialism to that of Søren Kierkegaard and Martin Heidegger, but finds in it affinities to that of Blaise Pascal as preserving the ineffability of the individual against the tendency of reason to stop at the level of abstract essence. Viewed in this way, his philosophy is not limited by what the human mind knew about the world in the thirteenth century; no more, by what it knows in the twentieth. "It invites us to look beyond present day science toward that primitive energy from which both knowing subject and object known arise."

O'Connor, D. J. *Aquinas and Natural Law.* London: Macmillan and Company, 1968.

In this college paperback, D. J. O'Connor has abstracted St. Thomas Aquinas' views on ethics from the rest of his philosophy and undertaken to interpret and criticize them in the light of contemporary philosophical assumptions. The longest chapter is given over to the problem of natural law, but others provide enough background material to make the book a suitable introduction to Aquinas' thought, which, as the author points out, has proved of interest to many contemporary philosophers who do not share his religious beliefs. In a time when, as O'Connor writes, "fashionable and influential moral philosophers have abandoned objectivist theories of morals," Aquinas' views offer a special challenge to the critical philosopher.

O'Connor does not linger over the problem of faith and reason. The only way that one could support the claim that certain truths are divinely revealed would be by producing historical evidence, such as

miracles. Although Thomas says that miracles "nourish faith by way of external persuasion," he falls back at last on grace, which, he says, is the "chief and proper cause of faith," moving a person to assent inwardly. This prompts in O'Connor the usual question as to how one is to judge between the claims of rival faiths. Felt conviction, he says, is not a sufficient criterion.

We shall find that O'Connor raises the same objection to the theory of natural law that he brings against religious belief. All objectivist theories of morality, he says, rest on moral intuition, which is merely a private feeling, allowing of no independent test. There are, according to O'Connor, two kinds of moral intuitionism. The modern kind likens moral awareness to sensory awareness and implies that moral qualities are "objective and directly knowable features of experience." The analogy breaks down, however, because there is no "acceptable and public test for resolving disagreements" about moral qualities, as there is about, say, whether a thing is yellow or merely appears so. The older kind of intuition, which underlies the theory of natural law, O'Connor finds more difficult to refute since it does not imply that moral judgments are self-evidently true but that there are self-evident moral principles, and that particular judgments are derived from these by syllogistic arguments. This kind of intuitionism raises all the questions which have traditionally divided empiricists from rationalists and nominalists from realists.

O'Connor argues that if one is to maintain that moral judgments can be proved to be correct, he must present us, first, with a list, of the principles which he holds to be self-evident, and second, with a set of rules by means of which he proposes to deduce secondary moral truths from the former. As to the first, O'Connor points out the ambiguities involved in calling any proposition self-evident, and shows that the ones which Thomas offers as examples ("good is to be pursued and evil is to be avoided"; "one should do evil to no man") are tautologies, true in virtue of the meaning of their terms. As to the second, O'Connor credits Thomas with recognizing the problem, as when he distinguishes between the logical deduction of conclusions and the practical application of principles: for example, one concludes that one must not kill from the principle that one should do harm to no man; but one applies the principle that the evildoer should be punished by determining a suitable penalty. As O'Connor understands him, Thomas held that only the method of logical deduction preserves the force of natural law. On this ground we may ask how Thomas was able to leap from the principle that one should do harm to no man to the conclusion that one should not kill—this being the very claim which a defender of euthanasia or suicide would reject. "And in general, no conclusions can be obtained, by derivation, from the master principle, 'Good is to be done

and evil avoided,' without the help of other more disputable propositions."

Thus, despite its strong *prima facie* appeal to common sense, Thomism cannot stand up to modern criticism. "The rise of natural science, mathematics, and formal logic" has made clear to us both the limits of rational argument and the kind of evidence we can appropriately use as material for reasoning. Thomas, O'Connor states, "had the bad luck to be born too early." Underlying his theory of law is the claim that morality must be based on metaphysics; more precisely, that knowledge of man's duties must be derived from knowledge of man's nature. The notion that there are natures or essences to be grasped by intellectual intuition, however, is unacceptable to modern man.

The Humean objection to any reasoning which attempts to derive moral conclusions from factual premises applies to the theory of natural law. O'Connor allows that Thomas is in a better position than most philosophers to meet this criticism because he has grounded his account of moral dispositions in a description of human nature. We do, in fact, tend to apprehend as good those things to which our nature inclines us; but once more, says O'Connor, the principle is useless unless we are shown in detail which inclinations entail which duties.

The relation between natural law and positive law is not discussed by O'Connor, except in the conclusion, where he mentions a kind of minimal natural law, developed by H. L. A. Hart in *The Concept of Law* according to which certain facts about human nature (man's vulnerability, his need for society, his limited power and foresight) make necessary certain rules for living. However, says O'Connor, although Hart has made natural law uncontroversial, he has done so by extracting from it "the mainspring of morality." No reasons are contained in it why anyone should act in a particular way.

Additional Recommended Reading

Aquinas, Thomas. *Basic Writings of St. Thomas Aquinas.* Edited by Anton C. Pegis. New York: Random House, 1945. Contains an introduction and annotations by Anton C. Pegis.
Copleston, F. C. *Aquinas.* Harmondsworth, England: Penguin Books, 1955. A general introduction with a good

chapter on morality and society.

Gilson, Étienne. *Being and Some Philosophers*. Toronto: Pontifical Institute of Medieval Studies, 1949. A study of essential and existential ontologies.

Kenny, Anthony, ed. *Aquinas: A Collection of Critical Essays*. Garden City, New York: Anchor Books, 1969. Papers by contemporary analytic philosophers sympathetic with Thomism. The last two papers deal with Aquinas' moral philosophy.

WILLIAM OF OCKHAM: SELECTIONS

Author: William of Ockham (c. 1280-c. 1350)
Type of work: Logic, epistemology
First transcribed: Early fourteenth century (Selections from his writings)

Principal Ideas Advanced

All abstractive cognitions (knowledge derived from experience, made possible by reflection upon experience) depend upon prior intuitive cognitions (sense experience of things).

Our knowledge of the existing world is contingent upon God's will, for he can affect our intuitive cognitions whatever the facts may be.

Predication occurs only if the predicate term of a sentence refers to the object referred to by the subject term, and if the predicate term refers to the object not by naming it, but by referring to some feature of it.

Universals are not single properties common to many things, but signs which have application to a number of things.

An explanation involving fewer assumptions than an alternative explanation is preferable to the alternative. [Ockham's "razor."]

William of Ockham was born at Ockham, Surrey, became a Franciscan, attended Oxford, and taught there for several years until he was summoned to the papal court at Avignon to answer charges of heresy arising from his writings and teaching. He was not formally condemned, but during his stay in France he became embroiled in a controversy that split his order into bitter factions, a controversy over the ideal of poverty espoused by its founder, St. Francis. After strenuously opposing both the Pope and the majority of his order on this issue, he and several others found it expedient to flee to the court of the Emperor of Germany, who had just installed an anti-Pope and who was glad to accept their assistance in his battle with the Pope. Excommunicated by the Pope and his own order, Ockham lived in Munich until his death. In his last years he was trying to reconcile himself with his order, but apparently he died before he was successful. Ockham wrote a great deal, but very little of it is available to the reader of English. Such a reader is limited to several books of selections: *Ockham: Philosophical Writings,* by P. Boehner; *Ockham: Studies and Selections,* by S. C. Tornay; *Selections from Medieval Philosophers,* by R. Mc-

Keon; and T. B. Birch's translation of *De sacremento altaris.*

Ockham is known for his famous "razor," for his logic, and for his nominalistic and empirical viewpoint. Living in the fourteenth century, he was the dominant figure in the movement away from Albertus Magnus, Thomas Aquinas, and John Duns Scotus, the great system builders of the thirteenth century. He was the inspirer of an empirically and nominalistically inclined movement that contended with the Thomistic, Albertist, Scotist, and Averroistic schools of the next several centuries. Although he has been called the Hume of the Middle Ages, Ockham was not a skeptic. Negatively, he undermined and rejected most of the metaphysics and a good deal of the natural theology of his contemporaries, but positively, he was a theologian who accepted the traditional Christian dogmas on faith and who preferred to accept them on faith alone rather than to argue for them on dubious philosophic grounds.

His basic inclination toward empiricism is revealed in the distinction between intuitive and abstractive cognitions. When we are looking at Socrates, he says, we can see that he is white. In this case we are aware of the existence of Socrates, of the occurrence of the quality, and of the fact that this individual, Socrates, is white. That is, the senses enable us to know with certainty a contingent fact about the world. This is an instance of what Ockham calls *intuitive cognition*. But we can think of Socrates when he is not present, and of white when we are not seeing it, and we can think of Socrates as being white. In this case we are cognizing the same things, Socrates and white, and we are entertaining the same proposition, but we do not know that Socrates still exists or that the proposition is true. This is an instance of what Ockham calls *abstractive cognition*, abstractive not because the terms are abstract, but because we have abstracted from existence.

The terms of the intuitive cognition are sensed and are particular, while the terms of the abstractive cognition are not sensed and are common. In intuitive cognition the cognition is caused in us by action of the object on our sensory and intellectual faculties, a process that culminates naturally, without any initiative on our part, in the knowledge that Socrates is white. No judgment, at least no explicit one, is involved here, for we simply see that Socrates is white. On the other hand, in abstractive cognition the cognition is not caused by the object, for either the object is absent or, if present, it is not sufficiently close to produce a clear sensation. Under such circumstances we scrutinize the data given by memory or sensation and, perhaps, go on deliberately to judge or refrain from judging that something is the case.

In abstractive cognition an apparently simple idea, such as the concept "Socrates," must be understood as a complex of common terms, for neither Socrates nor any other individual is operating on us to produce the cognition of him. In such a cognition we are entertaining such common terms as "intelligent," "snubnosed," "white," and "Athenian" which, when taken together, constitute a complex abstractive term limiting our attention to the one desired individual.

By contrast, in intuitive cognition we apprehend Socrates in a different manner, for in this case the object itself is producing in us a simple noncomplex idea of itself. Indeed, we obtain the terms appearing in abstractive cognitions only by attending to and separating in thought the various features of the sensation. Thus, Ockham concludes, all abstractive cognitions depend upon prior intuitive ones, and intuitive cognition must be the source of all our knowledge about the world. Furthermore, Ockham says that we intuit or sense nothing but individual things, and these are either sensible substances such as Socrates, or sensible properties such as the sensed whiteness of Socrates. Even relations are regarded as properties of groups of individuals.

When we add to all these considerations Ockham's famous "razor"—"What can be explained by the assumption of fewer things is vainly explained by the assumption of more things"—his nominalistic and empiricistic views follow immediately, for now we have an epistemology that not only makes us start with the senses but also prevents us from going very far beyond them. The senses reveal to us a multitude of sensible individuals and provide us with a great deal of information about them and about their temporal and spatial settings, but they do not reveal any necessary connections, causal or otherwise—and the razor prevents us from assuming any. This epistemology obviously limits the scope of metaphysics but does not quite eliminate it, for the metaphysician can still tell us a little about God. Given the terms "being," "cause," and "first," all of which are derived from experience, and assuming that they are univocal terms, as Ockham does, we can form the complex idea of a being who is a first cause. Furthermore, given intellectually self-evident principles such as "Every thing has a cause," we can demonstrate the existence of a first cause that exists necessarily and which, as the most perfect existent, has intellect and will. However, we cannot prove that there is only one such God or that there might not have been a greater God, and we cannot demonstrate that he has the various features required by Christian dogma.

The sort of world suggested by Ockham's epistemology is also required by his theology. Like Scotus before him and Descartes after him, Ockham emphasizes God's will rather than his intellect. God can do nothing that is contradictory, but this fact does not limit his will, for his ideas are not of his essence and are not exemplars between which he must choose. They are his creatures and the world is whatever he has cared to make it. Consequently, the world does not exist necessarily, and within this world nothing follows necessarily from anything else and nothing requires the existence of anything else. This radical contingency stems from God's complete power over the circumstances in which things shall or shall not come into existence. God ordinarily uses instruments to produce in us the experiences we have, but he could, if he wished, dispense with them and operate on us directly. For instance, Ockham says, it would require a miracle but God could make us see a star even where there actually is no star. That is, we could have exactly the same cognition that is normally caused in us by the star even if there were no star or any other physical cause. Since the seeing of the star is one distinct event and the star itself is another, it is not impossible that either should exist independently of the other.

The possibility of cognition without a corresponding fact reveals a limitation of intuitive cognition, for even though such a cognition makes us certain that something is the case, we could nevertheless be mistaken. Ockham skirts around the threat of skepticism by remarking that although an error of this sort can occur if God interferes with the natural order, miracles are rare. Consequently, the probability of error is insignificantly low. Yet, he acknowledges, it is still the case that our knowledge of the existing world is contingent upon God's will.

There is a remarkable agreement between Descartes and Ockham concerning the contingency of our knowledge. Because Descartes held a more extreme doctrine about the power of God, he took skepticism more seriously, but, of course, he believed he could escape by using reason. On the other hand, Ockham regarded the risk of empiricism as slight and claimed that it is better to exercise a little faith than to accept the grave risks of rationalism.

In his writings, Ockham, who was probably the best of medieval logicians, commences his discussion of logic by considering the nature of terms. First, he distinguishes between written, spoken, and conceptual terms. The latter are mental contents that function as private signs of things. Since these mental signs are not deliberately produced by us, but come about naturally through the operation of the object on

us, they are called *natural signs*. Since spoken signs, on the other hand, are sounds which have been conventionally attached to particular mental signs, they are *conventional signs*. They denote the same object as the associated concept, thus enabling us to communicate what would otherwise be private. Written signs have a similar relation to spoken signs. Ordinarily, when Ockham speaks of terms he has in mind such terms as "man," "animal," "whiteness," and "white," which signify or denote things and which can function as the subject or predicate of a proposition. These terms, which he calls *categorematic* terms, are to be contrasted with *snycategorematic* terms such as "every," "insofar as," and "some," which do not denote anything when they stand by themselves. He also distinguishes between concrete terms such as "white" and abstract terms such as "whiteness," and between discrete terms such as "Socrates" and common terms such as "man."

A more important distinction is that between absolute terms and connotative terms. An *absolute term* is one that denotes directly, whereas a *connotative term* is one that denotes one thing only by connoting another. "Socrates," "man," and "whiteness" are absolute terms for they are used to point to, respectively, a specific individual, any one of a number of similar individuals, or to a property. A connotative term such as "white" is not used as a label, for there is no such thing as white. When it is used in a proposition such as "Socrates is white," it denotes the same object as does the subject term, but it does so by connoting a property of the object; namely, whiteness. The distinction can be formulated in another way. At least some absolute terms, such as "man," have real definitions in which each term, such as "rational" and "animal," can denote the same objects as the defined term. Connotative terms have only nominal definitions, for the definition will require a term in the oblique case that cannot denote the same object as does the defined term. Thus "white" may be defined as "that which has the property whiteness," but "whiteness" does not denote the white thing. In certain definitions connotative terms may occur, but these can always be defined in turn until we reach definitions that contain absolute terms only. That is, language is grounded in terms that denote only, and cognition is basically a matter of being aware of objects and features of objects by intuitive cognition.

This distinction also brings us back to Ockham's epistemology by indicating the way in which a proposition is related to the world. Since there are only particulars in the world, each term of a true proposition, such as "Socrates is white," can refer only to one or more individuals. Such a proposition does not assert that two different things are identical, nor that the subject and predicate are one and the same thing, nor that something inheres in or is part of the subject. In our example, "white" is not another name for Socrates, it is not the name of another individual, and it is not the name of the property *whiteness*; but it must denote something, It can only denote Socrates, but not, of course, as "Socrates" does. That is, it denotes him indirectly by connoting his whiteness. Predication occurs only if (1) the predicate term denotes the very same object as the subject term, and (2) the predicate term denotes the object not by naming it but by connoting some feature of it.

In the above discussion we have mentioned abstract terms such as "whiteness" that are absolute and that denote properties rather than substances. Lest it seem that Ockham was a realist after all, we must turn to his discussion of universals. He denies emphatically that there are universals of either Platonic or Aristotelian varieties, for both doctrines require that something simple be common to many things. This state of affairs, he says, is impossible unless that simple something be plural, a condition which itself is impossible. Furthermore, he says, the problem should be turned around, for since the world is composed of particulars only, the problem is not the way in which some universal thing becomes particularized, but our reason for attributing universality to anything in the first place. The only thing to which we can attribute it is a sign, and even here only by virtue of its function as a sign, for as a mere existent it is as particular as anything else. Thus a universal is a sign or concept that has application to a number of things.

The nature of this universal concept, or common term, can be understood better by considering what

it is and how it is produced. First, as a result of intuitive cognition there occurs in sensation, and then in memory, sensations or images that function as natural signs of the individual objects that cause them. Now, through the medium of these images the intellect notices the similarity of the objects so signified and notes that there could be still other entities similar to them. In noting these similarities it produces naturally another entity that resembles the particulars in such a manner that it might very well be used as an exemplar for the construction of similar things. Ockham is not clear about the nature of this new entity, but he says that it is produced by ignoring the differences between the similar particulars. The new sign, or universal, is an indeterminate image that could represent any of the determinate particulars that fall under it. But whatever it is, since it is a natural rather than a conventional sign, this resemblance has come into being as a sign that denotes indifferently any of the particulars it resembles. Ockham says this entity is a fiction only, for since it is not a particular sign produced in us by a particular object, it has no literal counterpart in the world. In Ockham's terms, if we say "Man is a universal," and insist that we are saying something is common to many things, then in this proposition the concept "man" refers to itself (it has "simple *supposition*") and not to men (it does not have "personal *supposition*"), and the concept "universal" is of the second intention (it refers to a mental sign) rather than of the first intention (it does not refer to something other than a sign). That is, the universal "man" is only a concept that can be applied to many things; in the world there are only men.

It is to be noted that Ockham is not a nominalist of the Berkeleian-Humean sort, for his general ideas are not particulars standing for other particulars. Perhaps it would be more accurate to say that he holds to a kind of conceptualism. It is to be noted also that later in his life he applied his razor to his own doctrine to eliminate the fictitious entity we have just described, for he then argued that since the act that produces the generalized picture must be able to generalize without the assistance of such a picture, such pictures must be superfluous. In the end, then, universals turn out to be acts of the intellect; the other features of his earlier doctrine are retained.

Finally, it is to be noted that though they have different grammatical functions, concrete substantives and their abstract counterparts (such as "man" and "manness") denote exactly the same things (men). Nonsubstantive qualitative terms such as "white" denote indifferently individuals such as Socrates and this piece of paper; and their abstract counterparts, such as "whiteness," denote indifferently similar features of individuals, such as a certain sensible feature of Socrates and a similar sensible feature of this piece of paper. In these ways all common terms, whether they be concrete or abstract, denote particulars and particulars only.

Ockham discusses terms in greater detail than this summary statement suggests, and he goes on to discuss propositions and arguments. He was concerned primarily with formal syllogistic reasoning, but he did make a number of observations which impinge on the areas we know in symbolic logic as the propositional calculus and modal logic. Among other things he discussed the truth conditions of conjunctive and disjunctive propositions, reduced "neither-nor" to "and" and "not," discussed valid arguments of the form "p and q, therefore p," "p therefore p or q," and "p or q, not p, therefore q," pointed out the related fallacies, and stated Augustus

De Morgan's laws explicitly. At the end of his treatment of inference he discussed some very general nonformal rules of inference. Assuming in appropriate cases that we are speaking about a valid argument, they are as follows: (1) if the antecedent is true the conclusion cannot be false; (2) the premises may be true and the conclusion false; (3) the contradictory of the conclusion implies the contradictory of the premise or conjunction of premises; (4) whatever is implied by the conclusion is implied by the premises; (5) whatever implies the premises implies the conclusion; (6) whatever is consistent with the premises is consistent with the conclusion; (7) whatever is inconsistent with the conclusion is inconsistent with the premises; (8) a contingent proposition cannot follow from a necessary one; (9) a contingent proposition cannot imply a contradiction; (10) any proposition follows from a contradiction; and (11) a necessary proposition follows from any proposition. He illustrated the last two with these examples: "You (a man) are a donkey, therefore you are God," and assuming God is necessarily triune, "You are white, therefore God is triune." Ockham concluded his discussion by saying that since these rules are not formal they should be used sparingly.

Pertinent Literature

Weinberg, Julius R. *Ockham, Descartes, and Hume: Self-knowledge, Substance, and Causality.* Madison: University of Wisconsin Press, 1977.

Representative realism posits ideas which interpose between our consciousness and its objects of awareness, insofar as these objects are physical. Julius R. Weinberg notes that many experiences were appealed to in order to show the necessity of positing ideas; in particular Peter Aureoli (d. 1322) listed several, and William of Ockham responded to the arguments based on appeal to them.

In a long summary statement, Weinberg informs us that the experiences appealed to were these: (1) When a person is riding in a boat on a river, the river and trees sometimes appear to be moved; (2) when an ignited stick is rapidly moved in a circular manner,

a circle appears to the observer; (3) a half-submerged stick appears to be broken; (4) if we press against one eye while looking at a candle, there appear to be two candles; (5) there appear to be a multitude of colors on the neck of a pigeon; (6) virtual images produced by concave and convex mirrors sometimes appear to be behind the mirror and sometimes to be between the mirror and the observer; (7) a person who stares at the sun and then looks away sees spots which soon vanish; (8) if one looks at something red or something latticed and then reads a book, one then sees the letters on the pages as red, or as latticed. That there are such experiences, Weinberg points out, may be taken as common ground by opponents in the dispute over whether there are "ideas" in the sense not of "thoughts," but of intracognitive items which are intermediaries between perceiving minds and perceiving objects. The question, he adds, concerns how one accounts for, analyzes, and explains the experiences in question. Weinberg reports that Aureoli, arguing for positing ideas, claims that: (1) the trees and bark do not move, and the eyes do not perceive themselves, although they perceive something that moves but is not the trees or bark; (2) the circle is not in the stick, the air, or the eyes; it must be something (since it is seen) but is not in physical space; (3), and also (5), are cases of "seeing" things which must be something or other (we see the bentness, and the colors) but are not properties of the physical objects (the stick, the pigeon's neck) that we see; (4) we "see" two candles where there is only one, so the second candle must be in "intentional" being—it must be an idea; (6) the mirror images are not physical objects in physical space, but we experience them, so they must be "intentional" or "apparent" beings; regarding (7) and (8), physical objects do not appear and then vanish as do the spots and lattices, and we do "see" them.

The gist of the argument, then, is clear enough from Weinberg's exposition. We "see" things which are not actual physical objects or properties or states of physical objects. These things are not in physical space. But we can refer to them, describe them, and specify conditions under which others will see things just like those that we see. So there are such things—things which exist and are nonphysical and have "intentional" or "apparent" being. (That they are intermediaries between us and physical objects is another, apparently very natural, step; but it will not be a plausible step unless the argument for positing intentional beings, as developed so far, is successful.)

According to Weinberg, Ockham denies that such experiences as these do justify one in claiming that there are intentional or apparent intermediaries between perceiving minds and perceived physical objects. His account of Ockham includes the following reasoning: everyone agrees that perceptual judg-

ments, sometimes mistaken ones, are made. Consider, then, the first experience. The trees are seen successively on the bank as one moves along in the boat. They are not seen to move, since they do not. There is nothing the motion of which is observed. Trees on a bank, observed under the described conditions, can make one mistakenly judge that the trees are moving. Perceiving stationary trees under the described conditions elicits a response in the sensory organisms much like that elicited by actually moving trees. Thus one may be caused to judge, falsely, that the trees on the bank are traveling. The circle of fire case is treated analogously, as are the straight stick looking bent and the one candle appearing as two, and so on through the others, except that Ockham held the colors actually to be on the neck of the pigeon.

It comes down to this: when there is only one candle and there appear to be two because we press one eye, pressing the eye stimulates it (or the sensory mechanism as a whole) in much the way that it would be stimulated by two candles. Under these circumstances, one may, although one need not, judge that two candles are present. And similarly for other cases of its appearing that something is there which is not, or its appearing that some fact has a property which it lacks.

The main objection, then, that Weinberg finds Ockham offering to the positing of ideas as intermediaries between perceiving minds and perceived objects is that one need not posit them in order to describe, analyze, and explain the experiences which allegedly involve them. Both parties to the dispute, Weinberg notes, admit that perceptual judgments are made, sometimes erroneously. He adds that the judgments—in the experiences cited, erroneous ones—explain (in the context of sensory organs being stimulated by external objects) what needs explanation. To posit, in addition, intentional or apparent intermediaries, Weinberg reports Ockham as contending, posits entities beyond what is necessary to explain what calls for explanation. Hence, Weinberg explains, they may be shaved from our theory by "Ockham's razor."

Moody, Ernest A. "Empiricism and Metaphysics in Medieval Philosophy," in *The Philosophical Review*. LXVII, no. 2 (April, 1958), pp. 145-163.

Ernest A. Moody recounts that the late thirteenth and early fourteenth centuries witnessed a decline of metaphysics and a rise of empiricism. He reports that historians of the period tend to speak of this period as a time of intellectual disintegration, and the assumption behind this evaluation is that the rationale of medieval philosophy is the provision of a metaphysical justification for Christianity. After all, most major thinkers were professional theologians. Thus, he suggests, when an empiricist criterion of knowledge is developed on which one cannot develop the sort of connections between knowledge and faith present in the metaphysical systems of the earlier Middle Ages, the analysis is that an intellectual breakdown has occurred. The major figure of the rise of empiricism, and so of the "breakdown," Moody reminds us, was William of Ockham.

In fact, however, the empiricists, according to Moody, were themselves participants in theological teaching and debate, and their empiricism was itself theologically motivated. Moody says that the philosophy of René Descartes and John Locke in the seventeenth century was in fact radically different from that of the Greeks; and the influence of Christianity and the work of medieval theologians in between were significant in bringing about this change. But why this influence brought about fourteenth century empiricism, he says, requires explanation. He holds that this explanation should conform to the fact that in theology, logic, mathematics, physics, and political theory, there was great activity in the fourteenth century.

Moody suggests that four terms require definition before providing the explanation: (1) *theology* is "the systematization and elaboration of the beliefs constitutive of religious faith"; (2) *philosophy* is "a type of inquiry which seeks to develop a body of general statements whose claim to acceptance is based on no other ground than the kind of evidence that is open to public corroboration by all men through their natural cognitive powers"; (3) *metaphysics* will include "any theory concerning the existent as such"; and (4) "empiricism" is "a theory of method in the

aquisition and evaluation of knowledge."

With these definitions in mind, and particularly since some of the scholastics did criticize metaphysics, Moody maintains that it is appropriate to ask whether it was uniformly the aim of scholasticism to develop a metaphysical support for theological positions. Christianity, he says, offered doctrines concerning a supersensory realm based on the authority of revelation, not as one philosophy among many philosophies all of which appealed to the same data. The dominant philosophy, he reports, was Neoplatonism, to which the Church was hostile on the whole, and which played little role in even Saint Augustine's Christian scheme of education. From the sixth through the twelfth century, Moody tells us, the Western Church had no rivals against which to defend its doctrines, and what occurred within it in terms of speculative thinking was theological in nature. Philosophy reentered in the twelfth century by way of the Arabs, with pagan philosophers translated into Latin. The Church did not welcome the reentry. The concern of theologians with philosophy, Moody indicates, was limited to viewing it as partly a threat to the faith and partly a source of ideas and arguments adaptable to theological uses. One line of defense against philosophy was to set up an impossible divide between the two, with philosophy and theology having each its own purposes, methods, evidences, and intellectual terrain. Another was a critique of the nature and scope of human knowledge intended to show that theological claims could be neither established nor refuted by philosophical arguments. (These, of course, are not incompatible tactics.)

Moody emphasizes that Ockham did not invent empiricism; what he did was to provide a technique of logical analysis which allowed him to state empiricism with a new force and clarity. Hitherto, psychological description was the empiricist method; Ockham replaces psychological description with logical analysis.

One doctrine Ockham propounded, Moody remarks, was that necessary truths are formal, and existential truths are contingent. If a statement expresses a necessary truth, then it is a statement of what can be the case, not of what is the case; its truth does not entail the existence of any actual item. If a statement is existential, entailing the existence of some actual item, then it is logically contingent; it can be denied without the denier involving himself in any contradictions.

Another of Ockham's doctrines, according to Moody, was that we cannot properly construct inferences whose premises are confirmed by experience and whose conclusions do not concern anything that can be experienced. We cannot, for example, infer from the observed order of nature the existence of an unobserved and unobservable Author of natural order. Nor can we infer from the existence of an observable item—a star or a tree—the existence of an unobserved and unobservable Uncaused Cause of that item. Moody notes that, for Ockham, one cannot even infer the existence of our own souls. Hence, Moody declares, Ockham rejects metaphysics insofar as this involves accepting a realm of unobserved and unobservable beings on the basis of inference from the observable properties of observable items (plus some principles which provide the rails of inference).

Further, Moody indicates that Ockham offered a powerful critique of the doctrine that our knowledge of external objects is mediated by internal objects, called "ideas," which the external objects cause in us. George Berkeley and David Hume, four centuries later, were to offer very similar arguments. The doctrine that such ideas are needed is called "representative realism"; it contends that the existence of objects independent of minds are represented to us by acquaintance with mind-dependent "ideas." The gist of Ockham's critique, Moody tells us, is that unless we can know some external object independent of its being represented to us by an internal object, we have no way of knowing that there are any external objects to be represented.

Further, Moody informs us, Ockham held that any knowledge we gain of causal relations—of what is caused by what—must be gained by observation. No statement expressing a causal relationship expresses a necessary truth, and from no one thing does the existence of anything else follow. A thing or event of one sort is said to be the cause of a thing or event of another sort when we have experienced the first accompanied by the second, but have never experienced the second unchaperoned by the first.

No necessary existential truths; no inference from the observed to the unobserved and unobservable; no necessary causal propositions; no necessary connections between things or events: this, Moody suggests, amounts to a rejection of natural theology.

According to Moody, Ockham's empiricist perspective was partly motivated by the sort of critique already mentioned. It was also in part motivated by more theological considerations of the following sort. If the natural order is created by God in a free act of creation—an act he need not have performed, but performed graciously—the existence of the natural order must be both logically and causally contingent. Its nonexistence would involve no contradiction; its existence will depend on God's activity; it will not be an emanation which inevitably overflows from God's nature. These ideas, Moody adds, were denied by varieties of theological necessitarianism.

Moody concludes that, for Ockham, religion was a matter of faith. He interpreted theology as a matter of developing syntax for a semantical system for which no empirical interpretation is available. So, Moody tells us, Ockham found nothing inconsistent in his being both a believing theologian and an empiricist, and he offered as the theological sanction for empiricism the consideration that it avoids theological necessitarianism and allows for the free creation of the world by God.

Additional Recommended Reading

Boehner, Philotheus. *Collected Articles on Ockham*. Bonaventure, New York: Franciscan Institute, 1970. A
    useful collection of essays by a leading Ockham scholar.
Copleston, Frederick C. *A History of Medieval Philosophy*. New York: Harper & Row Publishers, 1972. A

one-volume survey by the foremost contemporary general historian of philosophy writing in English.

Gilson, Étienne. *History of Christian Philosophy in the Middle Ages*. New York: Random House, 1955. A comprehensive discussion, with copious footnotes, by one of the greatest medievalists.

Henry, D. P. *Medieval Logic and Metaphysics*. London: Hutchinson University Library, 1972. A valuable selective discussion, with references to Ockham, especially concerning the topic of formal distinction.

Moody, Ernest A. *The Logic of William of Ockham*. London: Sheed and Ward, 1935. A careful treatment of Ockham's logic and its intellectual context by a distinguished scholar.

_____. "Ockham, Buridan, and Nicholas of Autrecourt," *Franciscan Studies*. VII (June, 1947), pp. 113-146. An astute comparison of Ockham with two other medieval thinkers, especially concerning the Parisian Statutes of 1339 and 1340.

THE PRINCE

Author: Niccolò Machiavelli (1469-1527)
Type of work: Political philosophy
First published: 1532

Principal Ideas Advanced

In order to win and retain power a man is fortunate if he is born to power, for a man who rises to power by conquest or treachery makes enemies who must be eliminated.

If a prince must be cruel—and sometimes he must to retain power—he should be cruel quickly, and he should cause great injuries, for small injuries do not keep a man from revenge.

A prince should be concerned for the people he governs only to the extent that such concern strengthens his hold on the state.

Although a prince can sometimes afford to be virtuous, flattery, deceit, and even murder are often necessary if the prince is to maintain himself in power.

Great political thinkers often write about specific historical situations and yet succeed in making recommendations which apply to times other than their own. Niccolò Machiavelli must be numbered among such thinkers. An Italian patriot deeply involved in the diverse political maneuvers of sixteenth century Italy, he addresses advice to Lorenzo de' Medici which, first written in 1513 and later published as *The Prince* five years after his death, marks him as one of the most controversial, enduring, and realistic political theorists of the modern world.

In this short book Machiavelli undertakes to treat politics scientifically, judging men by an estimate of how in fact they do behave as political animals rather than by ideal standards concerned with how they ought to act. The hardheadedly consistent refusal of the author to submit political behavior to moral tests has earned the name "Machiavellian" for amoral instances of power relations among nation states and other organized groups. The power divisions of Machiavelli's Italy are now seen to have been prophetic of the massive national rivalries which followed in the Western world. The problems encountered by Renaissance princes endured long after the princes themselves fell before more powerful enemies. Machiavelli understood how success is al-

ways a minimal condition of political greatness. In *The Prince* he presents a manual of advice on the winning and retention of power in a world containing extensive political factionalism and lust for dominion.

Critics who are clearly aware of the amoral aspects of Machiavelli's political recommendations sometimes attempt to gain him a sympathetic hearing in unfriendly quarters. They do so by placing *The Prince* in its limited historical setting and relating its contents to certain biographical facts about the author. They tell us how Machiavelli longed for one ultimate goal—the eventual political unification of Italy as an independent state under one secular ruler, strong enough to rebuff the growing might of powerful neighbors like Spain and France. The armies and policies of these neighboring countries had already seriously influenced internal affairs even in Machiavelli's beloved Florence. Critics often suggest that Machiavelli's subordination of religion to the temporal aims of princes followed from his hatred of the political machinations of the Roman Catholic Church, which, by maintaining a series of temporal states, helped to keep Italy divided. The Church situation also invited foreign intrigues and corrupted the spiritual life of the Italians. In this context, another peculiarity of *The Prince* deserves mention. It is its total unconcern for forms of government other than monarchical ones. This might suggest that Machiavelli favored the monarchical form over the republican form. But such a view would be false. In the *Discourses on the First Ten Books of Titus Livius*, Machiavelli openly expressed preference for republics whenever the special conditions for their existence could be obtained. He tells us, in *The Prince*, that he has discussed republics elsewhere.

Such historical insights help to gain for *The Prince* a more understanding reading by those who reject its sharp separation of politics from morals. Yet the fact is clear that—whatever the author's motives—*The Prince* does ignore all moral ends of organized life and rather emphasizes the need to maintain sovereignty at all costs. Coldly, calculatingly, Machiavelli tries to show princes the means they must use in seeking power as an end-in-itself. He does not discuss moral rules. Discouraging to unsympathetic critics is the extent to which actual political life often seems to fit Machiavelli's somewhat cynical model.

Machiavelli classifies possible governments as either republics or monarchies. In *The Prince* he confines his analytic attention to the latter. Any monarch with a legitimate inheritance of power and traditions is most favored. The reason is that, unlike newly risen rulers, he need offend the people less. Established rulers reap the benefits from forgotten past abuses which led to the established system. Men who rise to power by virtue of conquest or favorable circumstances must confront incipient rebellions. They must also make more promises than the established ruler, thus falling under various obligations. Machiavelli believed newly created rulers must perform their cruelties quickly and ruthlessly. They must never extend cruelties over a long period of time.

Machiavelli insists that if a prince must cause injuries, he should cause great injuries, for small injuries do not keep a man from revenge. In any case, what the prince does must fit the circumstances and the nature of his particular dominion. Not all princes should attempt to use the same methods. All princes must act, however. For example, they should never postpone war simply to avoid it. In political conflicts, time is neutral regarding the participants; it produces

"indifferently either good or evil."

Newly created monarchs often find themselves involved with members of a mixed state. Extreme difficulties confront a ruler in such situations. Mixed monarchies usually require rule over possessions whose citizens either share the monarch's language or they do not. A common language and nationality help to make ruling easier for the monarch, especially if his subjects' experience of freedom has been a limited one. There are two general ways in which to treat subjects who lack the monarch's nationality and language. One is that the monarch can take residence among the subjects. To do so permits a ready response to contingent problems and allows the subjects to identify themselves with the person of the ruler. The other is for the ruler to establish select colonies at key positions in the subjects' territory. Such colonies cost little. Their injured parties are also often scattered, thus proving easier to handle. If he maintains such colonies, the monarch should use diplomatic maneuvers aimed at weakening the stronger neighbors and protecting the less powerful ones. Machiavelli uses historical examples here, as he does elsewhere in *The Prince*. For example, he admires the manner in which the Romans anticipated contingencies in governing their colonies and acted promptly, if sometimes brutally, to meet them. On the other hand, Machiavelli asserts that Louis XII of France made basic blunders in a similar situation.

There will be times when the ruler must govern subjects accustomed to living under laws of their own. Machiavelli coldly suggests three methods of ruling these. First, the ruler can totally despoil them, as the Romans did to certain rebellious cities. Second, he can make his residence among the subjects, hoping to keep down future rebellions. If he chooses neither of these alternatives, the ruler must permit the subjects to live under laws of their own. In this event he must exact tribute from them. If possible, he should also put control of the laws in the hands of a few citizens upon whose loyalty he can count. It is dangerous to ignore the activities of men accustomed to living in freedom if they are part of one's sovereign state. The reason is that "in republics there is greater life, greater hatred, and more desire for revenge; they do not and cannot cast aside the memory of their ancient liberty, so that the surest way is either to lay them waste or reside in them."

Machiavelli shows great interest in how men acquire their rule over possessions. Methods of ruling must be made adaptable to differences in manner of acquisition. For example, a ruler may obtain his power as a result of someone else's abilities; or he may win power by his own abilities. Machiavelli judges the "do it yourself" method as the surest. There is no substitute for princely merit. Also, the prince should command his own military forces without depending too heavily on aid from allied troops. The wise prince will imitate great personal models, since life is primarily a matter of imitative behavior. The prudential prince must show careful regard to the right circumstances for seizing power. Once in power, he can use force if he possesses soldiers loyal to himself. Machiavelli warns princes to beware the flattery of their subjects. Especially should they show suspicion of the flattery of their ministers, who are supposed to advise them. Machiavelli's model of the state seems to be the Renaissance city-state—small in population and territorial extent. As an example of a ruler who arises by virtue of talent, he mentions Francesco Sforza, of Milan. Cesare Borgia is used to illustrate the nature of successful ruling by a prince whose power initially results from conditions created by others.

In all, there are four ways in which a prince can attain to political power. These ways are: by one's own abilities; by the use of fortunate circumstances (wealth or political inheritance); by wicked conduct and outright crime; and by the choice of one's fellow citizens. Machiavelli does not condemn the ruler who succeeds by using criminal techniques. Thus, Agathocles the ancient Sicilian used such methods in rising from a military rank to kill off the rich men and senators of Syracuse. Yet Agathocles used such excessive cruelty that Machiavelli warns scholars not "to include him among men of real excellence." Instances of power criminally seized and successfully held lead Machiavelli to suggest that cruelty is intrinsically neither good nor bad. Cruelty must be said to have been used well "when all cruel deeds are committed at once in order to make sure of the state and thereafter discontinued to make way for the

consideration of the welfare of the subjects."

Nonetheless Machiavelli never asserts that cruelty is the best means of attaining to power. His judgment here as elsewhere is a hypothetical one: if the situation is one requiring cruelty for the realization of power, then the prince must do what is necessary. Thus, although Machiavelli prefers methods which do not involve cruelty, he refuses to condemn the Prince who uses cruelty.

The conditional nature of Machiavelli's recommendations about seizing power becomes evident when he discusses the case of the prince who rises by the consent of his fellow citizens. This makes the most promising situation for a prince. But it rarely happens. Thus, this case cannot serve as a universal model. Chosen in such a manner, a prince need not fear that men will dare to oppose or to disobey him. "The worst a prince can fear from the people is that they will desert him." On the other hand, if his power stems from the nobility, the prince must fear both their possible desertion and their possible rebellion. In order to prepare for a rebellion the people obviously require trained leaders. Thus, a prudent ruler supported by the people must attempt to retain their favor. A prince initially supported by the nobles can win over the people by making himself their protector. If he succeeds, he may end up stronger than the prince originally chosen by the people; for the people will appreciate the benefactor who guards them against internal oppression. Machiavelli is never so cynical as to argue that a wise prince can endlessly ignore the needs of his own people. Yet he justifies a concern for the people solely in terms of its value toward guaranteeing a continuing rule. Realistically, Machiavelli insists that the prince must lead an army. This is true even of churchmen who manage ecclesiastical states. Force or the threat of force serves as the basis of the state. Times of peace should never be permitted to divert the ruler's mind "from the study of warfare." In peaceful times the prudent ruler estimates future events. By thought and preparation he gets ready to meet such events.

A morbid sense of the contingency of human events runs through the book. Any ruler must show concern for changes of fortune and circumstance. The prince should show caution in delegating any of his own powers. Machiavelli hardly ever discusses economic or ideological problems. Normally, the prince of whom he writes is a single man bent on political self-preservation and the quest for methods by which to coerce his enemies into submission or inaction. The picture is one of a ruler feverishly studying the histories and actions of great men to be ready for the possible day when relatively stable conditions may alter for the worse. The reader concludes that, in Machiavelli's view, stability in politics is extremely rare. Yet Machiavelli understands that no prince can stand completely alone. Some powers must be delegated. Some men must be favored over others. How the prince treats his friends and subjects will always influence future political events. The prince should work to create a character able to make sudden adjustments in terms of his own self-interest. The most successful ruler must "be prudent enough to escape the infamy of such views as would result in the loss of his state." He must never cultivate those private virtues which, in a public man, can prove politically suicidal. He should develop vices if these will help to perpetuate his rule.

Generosity is a value in a prince only if it produces some benefit and no harm. A wise ruler will tax his subjects without becoming miserly. Yet he should prefer the name "miser" to a reputation for generosity which may prevent him from raising monies needed to maintain security. Generosity can more easily lead to the subjects' hatred and contempt than can miserliness. The prince can even show mercy if it is not interpreted as mere permissiveness. The cursedly cruel Borgia proved more merciful than the Florentine rulers who lost the city to foreigners. As long as he keeps his subjects loyal and united the ruler may sometimes act strenuously against them. Especially is this necessary in newly created monarchies. Machiavelli's advice goes something like: try to be both loved and feared, but choose being feared if there is no other alternative. The subjects obey a prince who can punish them.

In maintaining order the prince has some rules of thumb to follow. He should keep his word unless deceit is specifically called for. He should use admired private virtues if they do not interfere with the play of political power. A conception of human nature operates here. Machiavelli thinks the plain man is capable of some loyalty to a ruler. But such a man is easily led. "Men are so simple," Machiavelli writes, "and so ready to follow the needs of the moment that the deceiver will always find someone to deceive." A prince must know how and when to mingle the fox's cunning (the ability to avoid traps) with the lion's strength (capacity to fight the wolves). He should often conceal his real motives. Internally, he must avoid conspiracies. Externally, he should keep enemies fearful of attacking. Against conspirators the prince always has an advantage. Conspirators cannot work in isolation; thus they fear the existing laws and the threat of detection. Only when the population shows some open hostility need the prince genuinely fear conspirators.

Machiavelli realizes that men seldom get to choose the circumstances most favorable to their political hopes. They must settle for what is possible rather than for the ideal. Princes must avoid the lures of utopian political constructions—"for how we live is so different from how we ought to live that he who studies what ought to be done rather than what is done will learn the way to his downfall rather than to his preservation." Machiavelli regards men as weak, fickle, and subject to changing loyalties. These psychological traits are the bedrock on which a wise prince must build his policies.

Nonetheless the author of *The Prince* understands that success in politics, however rationally pursued, is beyond the complete control of any man. The Renaissance worry about "Chance" and "Fortune" haunts the final pages of Machiavelli's book. Large-order events in the world often seem to drive men onward much like "the fury of the flood." Yet not all events happen fortuitously. Men are half free to shape their political lives within the broader forces of the universe. That prince rules best, therefore, whose character and conduct "fit the times." It will be better for the ruler to be bold rather than cautious. Fortune is like a female—"well disposed to young men, for they are less circumspect and more violent and more bold to command her." Thus Machiavelli argues for a partial freedom of will and action within a world largely made up of determined forces.

The Prince stands as a classic example of realistic

advice to rulers seeking unity and preservation of states. Its picture of human nature is somewhat cynical, viewing man as vacillating and in need of strong political direction. Yet the work is not modern in one sense; namely, it fails to discuss ideological aspects of large-scale political organization. Machiavelli's prince is one who must learn from experience. His

conclusion is that ruling is more like an art than like a science. What is somewhat modern is the realistic emphasis on tailoring political advice to the realization of national ends whose moral value is not judged. *The Prince* is therefore a fascinating if sometimes shocking justification of the view that moral rules are not binding in the activities of political rulers.

Pertinent Literature

Cassirer, Ernst. *The Myth of the State.* New Haven, Connecticut: Yale University Press, 1946.

Written against the background of modern totalitarianism, this book was an attempt to explain the recrudescence of myth in modern times. The significance of Niccolò Machiavelli, according to Ernst Cassirer, was that he helped to demythologize politics, preparing the way for the rational understanding of the state which guided Western thought until it was challenged by the romantic reaction in favor of political myth.

Cassirer has no patience with modern scholars who obscure the significance of Machiavelli's thought by representing him as writing only for his generation and saying pretty much what others had said before. Machiavelli believed that what he was saying was new and that it was true for all time to come. Moreover, readers as discerning as Cardinal Richelieu, Catherine de Medicis, and Charles Talleyrand were of the same opinion. Galileo was to say of his own *Dialogues* that they "set forth a very new science dealing with a very ancient subject." Cassirer believes that Machiavelli could have made the same boast respecting *The Prince*. As the one laid the foundations for modern physics, so the other paved the way for political science.

Clearly, Machiavelli was not simply pandering to men's penchant for evildoing: already there were books which extolled the role of tyrants. What excited Machiavelli and his readers was the conception of politics divorced from medieval notions of divine right and natural law. Political changes were then taking place which adroit rulers such as Cesare Borgia had learned to accommodate. Machiavelli was the

first thinker to understand the changes and to explain that they entailed a reversal of the relation between might and right. Appearance of right remained one of the constituents of power, but the substance was gone; a strong ruler, at least briefly, could do without even the appearance of right. *The Prince* shocked many readers simply by telling things the way they were. But according to Cassirer, besides describing facts, the book offered its readers a whole new theory and art of politics.

Medieval social theory no less than medieval cosmology took for granted a natural hierarchy of being. The boldness of Machiavelli lay in the fact that a hundred years before Galileo he destroyed the cornerstone of this tradition, denying the theocratic principle and asserting the independence and sovereignty of the temporal power. Frederick II had long before this achieved complete secularization of the state: Christians, Jews, and Saracens shared in his administration. No theory, however, had accompanied that development. Machiavelli was the first to define the state without reference to theological ideas, going so far as to treat religion simply as a tool in the hands of political architects. In Cassirer's words, the secular state henceforth existed not only *de facto* but also *de jure*.

It was one thing, of course, to declare the state independent of religious authority; but it was another thing to view the state as fully autonomous. Here, according to Cassirer, lay the danger of Machiavelli's position. A state has roots in the organic needs of human existence. Machiavelli, in his zeal to free it from religious and metaphysical ties, cut it loose from the economic, moral, and cultural life of the people as well. Politics was treated much like a game of chess. It made no difference to Machiavelli who the players were or who won. Fascinated by the game, he rallied the prospective prince, reminding him that the strategy included fraud and treachery, and urging him to play with no thought but to win. Unfortunately, says Cassirer, he forgot that politics is played not with pieces of ivory but with human beings.

There is, Cassirer recognizes, a real question as to how a man of Machiavelli's nobility of character could openly counsel princes to commit criminal acts. The conventional answer is that in the author's eyes these acts were justified because they served the common good. But this answer, in Cassirer's opinion, blurs the distinction which Machiavelli insisted upon between the viewpoint of the prince and that of the private person. When someone said that Napoleon's execution of the Duke of Enghien was a crime, Talleyrand is supposed to have remarked that it was worse than a crime: it was a mistake. This, says Cassirer, well expresses Machiavelli's view. Machiavelli insisted that if a person is unwilling to perform criminal acts when necessary he had better leave politics alone. He makes this clear in what he has to say about being beastly to beasts: his reference to Chiron, the Centaur, as the first preceptor of princes shows how radically his view of the art of government differs from that of Plato, who made Socrates the preceptors, and who equated the art of ruling with the highest wisdom. Plato and his followers saw the state as founded on law. Discarding this ideal, Machiavelli started from the fact that actual politics has always been full of crime and concluded that if such things are to be done they should be done well. This meant that the arts of practical control, even when criminal from the conventional point of view, should be included in the art of governing, and taught as such.

Cassirer doubts whether Machiavelli realized the full implications of his teachings and draws a distinction between his teachings and Machiavellism as we know it today. Politics in Italy was small in scale compared with what it came to be under the great monarchs and more recently under the great dictators, and techniques of political crime were in their infancy. Moreover, there remained in Europe strong moral and intellectual forces which worked to keep governments within the bounds of law. Then, in the nineteenth century, romantic philosophers, reacting against the Enlightenment, launched their attack against theories of natural law. In this way, the last barrier to the triumph of Machiavellism was removed.

Meinecke, Friedrich. *Machiavellism: The Doctrine of Raison d'État and Its Place in Modern History.* Translated by Douglas Scott. New Haven, Connecticut: Yale University Press, 1957.

As Friedrich Meinecke uses it, the term "reason of state" designates the particular course of action which an official must take in order to preserve the health and strength of the state on a given occasion. Because the state is an independent organism pursuing its own ends, reason of state presupposes an understanding of the state and its environment. Thus, what began as statecraft led on to a theory of the state and its place in nature. Like man, the state is amphibious, living partly in the realm of nature, partly in the realm of mind. Machiavelli, the first to grapple profoundly with this polarity of the physical and the spiritual in man, was, so far as modern history is concerned, the discoverer of reason of state.

What gave Niccolò Machiavelli's work its historical power was the fact that he fully explored both the bright and the dark aspects of political life. Machiavelli understood the uses of power, but he despised senseless greed for power and insisted that it be subordinated to the common well-being. Although he is usually thought of as a realist, that side of his work cannot, in Meinecke's opinion, be rightly estimated without recognition of his fundamental idealism.

Central to this idealism was his concept of virtue (*virtù*) drawn from pagan antiquity where there was no conflict between politics and ethics because everyone regarded participation in civic life as his main good. The originator of reason of state, says Meinecke, had to be heathen; and this was eminently possible during the Italian Renaissance, with its romantic attitude toward the past. Virtue, as Machiavelli elaborated it, was a dynamic force which raised man's native impulses to the level of a code of values for rulers and citizens. No great civic achievements, he maintained, are possible without virtuous citizens, men and women capable of great labors and sacrifices for the common good; but in addition to the virtuous citizens, there must be leaders with special virtues—men capable of founding and ruling states. Machiavelli's argument with himself concerning republics and monarchies was resolved in the light of these considerations. His judgment with respect to Italy in his day seems to have been that because citizens lacked the proper virtues, republics were doomed. He held, however, that by means of their special virtue, princes create virtue in their subjects. Indeed, the development of virtue was the one completely self-evident purpose of any state, whether republic or monarchy.

Virtue so conceived exists only in tension with necessity; and it is what Machiavelli had to say about causal determination that makes him appear to us to be a realist. Human beings are not wicked; they are sluggish and will never do anything unless they are driven to it, either by hunger and poverty **or** by the lash of a taskmaster. The only break in the causal order is the creative power of the great man who is able to change the sluggard into a citizen. Thereafter, physical necessity is absorbed by the necessity of the state; and if rulers are to follow the real truth of things, they must "learn how not to be good" when this necessity constrains.

Necessity is the intelligible feature of circumstance. But for heads of state there are unknown and unpredictable features to be reckoned with as well. These are known as fate or fortune. Hence, the great leader must be a gambler. Fortune overcomes where

men have not much virtue, and this explains the instability of most states. As we are told in the *Discourses*, however, "sooner or later there will come a man who so loves antiquity that he will regulate fortune." Fortune is malicious; so must virtue be. When it is a question of winning, unclean methods are allowed.

Meinecke is aware of the sinister aspects of reason of state. Granted that there are occasions when the common good makes immoral measures necessary, there is a temptation for rulers to employ this principle to justify immoral acts which, although expedient, are not necessary. That the sanctity of moral law is not permanently impaired when law is made to yield to supraempirical necessity was the judgment of scholastic thinkers; but when truth and justice are treated simply as elements in the empirical situation, to be weighed against material advantages, then the gates are opened to forces of active evil which traditional morality had opposed. Meinecke finds here the source of a new dualism which plagues modern civilization. By declaring their independence from any transcendent law, secular states have achieved a degree of rational organization inconceivable to the Middle Ages. At the same time, the indispensable foundation for this achievement remains the fidelity of the mass of mankind to values regarded as absolute.

Meinecke finds further fault with Machiavelli because of his failure to demand of rulers a certain moral restraint. It was vicious to tell princes that they need not possess loyalty and sincerity although they must appear to have these qualities. Meinecke would have liked to find in Machiavelli some recognition of the fact that a truly great leader does not ride roughshod over his fellows but knows how, when occasion demands, to take on himself some of the suffering, even to the point of accepting personal disgrace if that is the only means of saving the people. Apparently the ability to think in terms of inner conflicts and tragic sacrifices was beyond Machiavelli.

Additional Recommended Reading

Berlin, Isaiah. "The Question of Machiavelli," in *The New York Review of Books.* Special Supplement, XVII, no. 7 (November 4, 1971), pp. 20-32. Argues that Machiavelli shocks his readers mainly because he makes it clear that mankind has to choose its values.

Butterfield, Herbert. *The Statecraft of Machiavelli.* London: G. Bell and Sons, 1955. Stresses Machiavelli's use of history in political analysis.

Jensen, De Lamar, ed. *Machiavelli: Cynic, Patriot, or Political Scientist?* Boston: D. C. Heath and Company, 1960. A useful selection of contemporary writings about Machiavelli.

Maritain, Jacques. "The End of Machiavellianism," in *The Review of Politics.* IV, no. 1 (January, 1942), pp. 1-32, According to Maritain, politics is not an art in the technical sense as Machiavelli takes it to be, but a branch of ethics.

Pitkin, Hannah Fenichel. *Fortune Is a Woman: Gender and Politics in the Thought of Niccolo Machiavelli.* Berkeley: University of California Press, 1984. A critical exploration of important, but often neglected, themes in Machiavelli's political philosophy.

NOVUM ORGANUM

Author: Francis Bacon (1561-1626)
Type of work: Philosophy of science
First published: 1620

Principal Ideas Advanced

To acquire knowledge about the world one must interpret the particulars given in sense experience.

Various false ideas and methods have handicapped man in his attempt to study nature impartially; they are the Idols of the Tribe (conventional beliefs which satisfy the emotions), the Idols of the Cave (erroneous conceptions resulting from individual predilections), the Idols of the Market Place (confused ideas resulting from the nonsensical or loose use of language), and the Idols of the Theatre (various systems of philosophy or other dogmatic, improperly founded assertions).

The discovery, investigation, and explanation of Forms (the properties of substances) by controlled observation and experimentation, utilizing tables of instances by reference to which inductive generalizations can be made, is the philosophical foundation of all knowledge.

This important work in scientific methodology was part of a larger work, *The Great Instauration*, which was proposed in six parts (the *Novum Organum* to be the second) but never completed. Even this work itself is partial, as is indicated by the fact that the author listed in Aphorism XXI of Book II a number of topics which he proposed to discuss, but never did, either here or in his other works. The content of the book clearly indicates that he considered it to be a correction of, or a supplement to, Aristotle's logical writings, the *Organon*. A large portion of Bacon's text is devoted to a demonstration of the futility, if not the error, of trying to understand nature by the deductive method. We cannot learn about the world, he insists, by arguing, however skillfully, about abstract principles. On the contrary, we must *interpret* nature by deriving "axioms from the senses and particulars, rising by a gradual and unbroken ascent, so that the method arrives at the most general axioms last of all. This is the true way, but as yet untried." It was a new "inductive logic" whose rules Bacon proposed to disclose.

The work is divided into two Books, the first concerned mainly with setting down the principles of the inductive method and the second with the method for collecting facts. Book I is further divided into two parts, of which the first is designed to purge the mind of the wrong methods (Aphorisms I-CXV), while the second is planned to correct false conceptions of the method which Bacon is proposing (Aphorisms CXVI-CXX).

He begins by showing that the relation of man to nature is such that man can know the world only by being its servant and its interpreter. In man knowledge and power meet, for man can control nature only if he understands it; "nature to be commanded must be obeyed." Man can modify nature only by putting natural bodies together or by separating them. Moreover, his control over nature has been very much limited because man has chosen to spend his time in "specious meditations, speculations and glosses," which are well designed to systematize the knowledge which he already has but poorly designed for the discovery of new ideas. The syllogism, for example, serves only to give stability to the errors of tradition; it deals with such unsound notions as substance, quality, action, passion, and essence, rather than with those which have been abstracted from things by the proper inductive methods.

Bacon writes that there are three methods commonly employed for understanding nature. He describes these metaphorically in Aphorism XCV as those of the ant, the spider, and the bee. The ant is an experimenter, but he only collects and uses. The spider is not an experimenter, but he makes cobwebs out of his own inner substance. The bee takes the middle course; he gathers material from the flowers but transforms and digests this by powers of his own. Natural philosophy is exemplified neither by the ant nor by the spider; it does not gather material from natural history and from mechanical experiments and store it away in memory, nor does it rely solely on the powers of the mind. It alters and digests the particulars which are given in experience and then lays them up in memory.

In further clarification of his method Bacon suggests that there is an important distinction between the *Anticipation of Nature* and the *Interpretation of Nature. Anticipations* are collected from very few instances; they are sweeping generalizations which appeal to the imagination and thus produce immediate assent. Indeed, if all men went mad in the same manner they might very well agree on all anticipations. But *Interpretations* are obtained from widely dispersed data; they cannot produce consent since they usually disagree with accepted ideas. *Anticipations* are designed to be easily believed; *Interpretations* are designed to master things.

One of the contributions to scientific methodology for which Bacon has become most famous is his doctrine of the *Idols*. These are false notions and false methods which have taken possession of our minds, have become deeply rooted in them, and strongly resist our efforts to study nature impartially. Bacon believes that we can guard against these only if we are aware of what they are and how they mislead thinking. He calls them the *Idols of the Tribe*, the *Idols of the Cave*, the *Idols of the Market Place*, and the *Idols of the Theatre*. The first have their foundation in human nature itself, the second in the individual man, the third in the vagueness and ambiguity of language, and the fourth in the dogmas of philosphy and the wrong rules of demonstration.

The *Idols of the Tribe* are exemplified in the following: the beliefs that all celestial bodies move in perfect circles, because we are predisposed to find

more order and regularity in the world than we actually find; superstitions, which are accepted because we are reluctant to abandon agreeable opinions even when negative instances arise; unwillingness to conceive of limits to the world, or of uncaused causes, and the resulting eternal search for principles which are ever more and more general; the swaying of our beliefs by emotions rather than by reason; the deceptions which arise because of the dullness and incompetency of the sense organs; and our proneness to prefer abstractions to the concrete realities of experience.

The *Idols of the Cave* are due to the mental and bodily peculiarities of the individual. Men become attached to certain beliefs of which they are the authors and on which they have spent much effort. Some men see resemblances and overlook difference; others reverse these; both err by excess. Some men worship the past and abhor novelty; others reverse these; truth, however, is to be found in the mean between these extremes. Similar examples are to be found in the respective overemphasis on particles as against structure, both of which distort reality.

The *Idols of the Market Place* are the most troublesome of all. They are of two kinds: words which are names of things that do not exist (Fortune, Prime Mover, Element of Fire), and words which are names of things that exist but which are vague and confused in their meanings. The latter can be exemplified by the word *humid*, which may apply in its many meanings to flame, air, dust, and glass.

The *Idols of the Theatre* are subdivided into those of Systems of Philosophy and those of False Arguments. Among the former are the *Sophistical* (exemplified by Aristotle, who corrupted philosophy by his logic and his theory of the categories), the *Empirical* (exemplified by the alchemists and all those who leap to generalizations on the basis of a few, "dark" experiments), and the *Superstitious* (exemplified by those who employ their philosophies to prove their theologies). The False Argument idols are found when men improperly extract the forms of objects from the objects themselves, and when, in a spirit of caution, they withhold judgment even though a truth has been well demonstrated, or dogmatically assert a conclusion without sufficient grounds. The only true demonstration is experience, not by means of careless experiments, or experiments in play, or experiments performed repeatedly with only slight variations until one wearies in the process, but by planned and controlled experiments whose motive is true understanding rather than an "overhasty and unreasonable eagerness to practice."

Bacon shows that if we examine the traditional natural philosophy we can easily see why it has not met with success. In the first place, it was largely disputational—a feature which is most adverse to the acquisition of truth. It was primarily dialectical, described by Dionysius as "the talk of idle old men to ignorant youth." Much of it was argued by itinerant scholars, who put their wisdom up for sale and were primarily concerned with defending their own schools of thought. In addition, these men had the disadvantage of there being no historical knowledge, other than myths, on which they could base their conclusions, and they had very limited geographical knowledge. Furthermore, such experimental knowledge as existed was largely a kind of "natural magic" which had almost no utility, philosophy not having realized, apparently, that it, like religion, must show itself in works. Indeed, it proved sterile, not only of mechanical progress but also of theoretical development; it thrived under its founders, remained stagnant for a few years, then declined and disappeared. As a result, many of its advocates not only apologized for the limited character of their knowledge by complaining of the subtlety and obscurity of nature, and of the weakness of the human intellect, but also argued defensively that nature was completely beyond the reach of man and essentially unknowable. To claim that the soundness of Aristotle's philosophy has been demonstrated by its long survival is fallacious, Bacon argues; it has survived not because of the consensus of the judgments of free minds (the only real test of truth), but only because of the blind worship of authority. "If the multitude assent and applaud, men ought immediately to examine themselves as to what blunder or thought they have committed."

Why, then, has science not progressed more rapidly in the long period of its history? Bacon argues that several reasons may be advanced. In terms of the total history of the race, of course, the few centuries which have elapsed since the Greeks is not a long period; we should therefore not be too hasty in disparaging the meager results of man's attempt to understand the world. The poverty of results in natural philosophy can be explained by the great concentration of effort on study in the other areas of thought—religion, morals, and public affairs. Furthermore, the sciences have failed to progress because the natural philosophy on which they must be based for sound support has not been forthcoming; astronomy, optics, music, and the mechanical arts lack profundity and merely glide over the surface of things. In addition, the sciences have remained stagnant because their goal has not been clearly formulated, and the method for attaining this goal has not been stressed; men have tended to rely mainly on their wits, on an inadequate logic, and on simple experiment (which is like a broom without a band). "The true method of experience first lights the candle, and then by means of the candle shows the way; commencing as it does with experience duly ordered and digested, not bungling or erratic, and from it educing axioms, and from established axioms again new experiments; even as it was not without order and method that the divine word operated on the created mass."

Any tendency to praise the accomplishments of the mechanical arts, the liberal arts, and alchemy should be tempered by the recognition of how ignorant we still are in these areas; we know much, but there is so much that we do not know. Much of which poses as knowledge, Bacon insists, has been set forth with such ambition and parade that one easily comes to feel that it is more nearly complete and perfect than it really is; its subdivisions seem to embrace all fields, but many of these fields prove to be empty and devoid of content. Even worse, much of what is practiced in the arts is pure charlatanism, claiming without grounds to prolong life, alleviate pain, bring down celestial influences, divine the future, improve intellectual qualities, transmute substances, and much more. The main defects of such arts are to be found in their combination of littleness of spirit with arrogance and superiority; they aspire to very little, but claim to accomplish very much; they engage in trifling and puerile tasks, but claim to solve all problems.

On the positive side, Bacon believes that there are strong grounds for hope. Knowledge is so obviously good that it bears the marks of Divine Providence on its surface. All that is required is that men should realize that we need a new science, a new structure built on a new approach to experience. The old science is inadequate. "Nothing duly investigated, nothing verified, nothing counted, weighed, or measured, is to be found in natural history: and what in observation is loose and vague, is in information deceptive and treacherous." Accidental experiments must be replaced by controlled experiments "of light" rather than "of fruit," which are designed simply for the discovery of causes and axioms. Data should be arranged in *Tables of Discovery* (which Bacon discusses in Book II), and from these we should ascend to axioms educed from these particulars by a certain rule, and then descend again to new particulars. In this activity the understanding, prone to fly off into speculation, should be hung with weights rather than provided with wings. The induction which is based on simple enumeration of accidentally gathered data is a childish thing; it should be replaced by one which examines the axioms derived in this way to see whether they are applicable to new particulars not included in the original enumeration, and whether they should be extended to wider areas or modified and restricted to what the new experience discloses.

The second section of Book I is devoted to a correction of the misconceptions of the Baconian method. Bacon assures the reader that he is not trying to set up a new sect in philosophy and not trying to propose a new theory of the universe. He is not even willing to promise any new specific scientific discoveries which may occur as a result of the introduction of the new method. He grants that his method probably contains errors of detail, though he believes these to be minor in character. Among the results which he is able to show, some will be claimed by others to be trivial, some to be even mean and filthy, and some to be too subtle to be readily comprehended. In reply to these charges Bacon repeats the statement of the poor woman who, having asked for a grant from a haughty prince and been rejected on the grounds that such an act would be beneath his dignity, replied, "Then leave

off being king." If Bacon is criticized on the grounds that his method is presumptive, since he claims with one blow to have set aside all previous sciences and all earlier authors, his reply will be that with better tools one can do better things; thus, he is not comparing his capacities with those of his predecessors, but his skill at drawing a perfect circle by means of a compass with that of his predecessors who would draw a less perfect one without this instrument. And to the charge that in urging caution and suspension of judgment he is really denying the capacity of the mind to comprehend truth, he can answer that he is not *slighting* the understanding but *providing for* true understanding, not taking away authority from the senses but supplying them with aids.

Book II is concerned with the method for collecting facts. In order to explain this method Bacon first shows what he means by *Forms*. Every body may be regarded as a collection of "simple natures." Gold, for example, is yellow, malleable, heavy, nonvolatile, noncombustible. These constitute the Form of gold, for in gold these properties meet. Anyone who knows what these properties are, and is capable of transforming a body which does not possess these properties into one which does, can create gold. The Form of gold can therefore also be called the "law" of gold, for it is a description of the nature of this substance and of the various ways in which it may be created or generated. While it is true that in the world itself there exist only bodies, not empty Forms, nevertheless the discovery, investigation, and explanation of Forms is the philosophical foundation of all knowledge and all operations on objects. There is in the world a limited number of "simple natures," or Forms, and every body can be understood as a compound of such natures.

"The Form of a thing is the thing itself, and the thing differs from the Form no other wise than as the apparent differs from the real, or the external, or the thing in reference to man from the thing in reference to the universe." In view of this fact we must set up procedures which will enable us to distinguish the true Form from the apparent Form. These procedures are employed in the setting up of *Tables and Arrangements of Instances*. These are obtained by the collection of particulars discovered in nature. "We are not to imagine or suppose, but to discover, what nature does or may be made to do." But since nature is so various and diffuse it tends to distract and confuse us as it presents itself. Consequently the particulars must be arranged and organized in order that understanding may be able to deal with them. In this way it is able to use induction and to educe axioms from experience. There are three kinds of such tables. *Tables of Essence and Presence* consist of collections of all known instances of a given nature, exhibiting themselves in unlike substances. As an example, Bacon gives a long list of instances of heat—in the sun, in meteors, in flame, in boiling liquids. A second kind of collection is a *Table of Deviation, or of Absence in Proximity.* These instances are cases where heat is absent; for example, in moonlight, light from the stars, air on mountain tops, and so on. Finally, there are *Tables of Degrees* or *Tables of Comparisons.* These involve noting the increase or decrease of heat in the same substance, or its varying amount in different subjects. For example, different substances produce different intensities of heat when burned; substances once hot, such as lime, ashes, and soot, retain their former heat for some time; dead flesh, in contrast to living flesh, becomes cold. These three *Tables* are devices by which we assure ourselves that where the nature is present the Form will be present, where the nature is absent the Form will be absent, and where the nature varies quantitatively the Form will vary quantitatively. On data thus arranged we go to work by the inductive process. If we proceed simply on the basis of affirmative cases, as we are naturally inclined to do, the results will be fancies, guesses, and ill-defined notions, and the axioms must be corrected every day. God and the angels may have the capacity to extract Forms solely from affirmative cases; but man must proceed by affirmation, negation, and variation. What we obtain by this process, however, is only the *Commencement of Interpretation* or the *First Vintage.* Bacon presumably means by this what present-day scientists would call a "hypothesis"; that is, a tentative interpretation which we employ as a guide to the selection of further instances (such as *Prerogative Instances*, which he discusses in great detail). On the basis of the hypothesis we then proceed either to collect the instances by controlled observation or to produce them by experimentation.

Pertinent Literature

Anderson, Fulton H. *Francis Bacon: His Career and His Thought.* Los Angeles: University of Southern California Press, 1962.

This volume is the most complete biography and overall interpretation of Francis Bacon's achievements presently available. Fulton H. Anderson tries to show that, in spite of many detractors, Bacon was actually an original systematic thinker. He was, according to Anderson, a political thinker actively seeking to work out definite and consistent philosophical views, and he was not, as he has been accused of being, a self-seeking opportunist.

The first two-thirds of Anderson's volume deals with Bacon's political career, defending his actions from unfair interpretations. Anderson tries to show that Bacon's political actions during the reigns of Elizabeth and James I were based on his theory of royal prerogative and on his view that sovereigns are to be obeyed because they are God's agents. Anderson believes that even in the most notorious events in Bacon's political career, the Essex affair and the struggle with Coke and the Howards, Bacon behaved virtuously or, at least, was philosophically justified. Even the events that led to Bacon's political fall, his taking of bribes, are interpreted here not as indicating dishonesty, but as the outgrowth of a philosophical defense of royalism.

After dealing with Bacon as the "philosophical" politician, Anderson devotes the last third of the book to Bacon's philosophy. Starting with Bacon's early dissatisfactions with what he studied at Cambridge, Anderson follows his career up to the revolutionary proposals in the *Novum Organum.* He shows how

Bacon kept working on his scientific writings all through his political career and how he kept seeking political support for educational reforms that would give man dominion over nature. Anderson contends that Bacon's view was a rich, coherent, original system of thought involving both a pluralistic philosophy and a metaphysical naturalism. The latter was materialistic in character, influenced by Democritus, but was also based on inductive procedures that Bacon developed in much detail, and not on philosophical speculation.

Anderson contends that the bulk of Bacon's philosophical contribution is original. To make this case, Anderson carefully delineates the new advances Bacon made over the various ancient philosophers he had studied. Bacon's views are also considered in relation to many of the Renaissance naturalistic theoreticians of the time—thinkers whose theories were being taken very seriously in the late sixteenth and early seventeenth centuries, thinkers such as Paracelsus, William Gilbert, Girolamo Cardano, Giordano Bruno, Bernardino Telesio, and Tommaso Campanella. As Anderson presents the case, Bacon seems most impressive and original when compared to them. Bacon's naturalism, and the means he proposed for studying nature, have turned out to be more fruitful and more intellectually revolutionary than the views of contemporaries who presented inspired, strange, wild speculations about the nature of the universe and how to control it.

Frances Bacon, seen against this background, appears (at least in Anderson's rendition) to be a somber, careful thinker, employing inductive products to unravel the universe. Rejecting speculations and inspired interpretations, Bacon sought knowledge by a most deliberate and monumental inspection of the Kingdom of Nature, through gaining all of the facts and then making careful inductions. Only through this procedure, Bacon thought, would one discover the springs and principles of nature and be able to realize the dream of Dr. Faustus that knowledge is power.

Jardine, Lisa. *Francis Bacon: Discovery and the Art of Discourse*. Cambridge: Cambridge University Press, 1974.

Lisa Jardine accepts at face value Francis Bacon's claim that his *Novum Organum* is a logic, in which the author claimed to be making great innovations over his predecessors and contemporaries. By a very careful examination of the logic texts available in the sixteenth century, Jardine shows that Bacon was neither as completely original as Fulton H. Anderson has claimed, nor as thoroughly involved with his contemporaries as Paolo Rossi has declared him to be. By very detailed historical scholarship, Jardine attempts to establish Bacon's place in intellectual history. She maintains that she is offering a consistent rather than a revolutionary reading of Bacon's works. By reconstructing the intellectual background against which Bacon set forth the particular methodological questions in which he was interested, we are able, Jardine believes, to appreciate the originality and ingenuity of the solutions he offered. She also contends that seeing Bacon in this manner restrains us from reading back into his work concerns that in fact only later became important in the development of method in science and philosophy.

First the dialectic handbooks in use in sixteenth century schools are examined, with special attention to what is now called "methodus," a newly introduced term transliterated from the Greek. The Aristotelian and Ramist books circulated widely. Among textbook reformers the subject of dialectical methods received much attention, as in Rudolf Agricola's *De Inventione Dialectica* of 1515, which is based more on Cicero and Quintilian than on Aristotle. Agricola heavily emphasized invention. The Reformer Philipp Melanchthon followed out Agricola's approach. Jardine details the various kinds of approaches throughout the century, devoting considerable time and space to Peter Ramus and his followers, as well as to such late Italian commentators as Giacomo Zabarella. The background material is used to show that there was a dispute in Cambridge in the late sixteenth century between Everard Digby and William Temple concerning the nature and use of dialectical method. The dispute, Jardine asserts, provides some significant clues for understanding Bacon's polemical response to the discussion of dialectic. Bacon rarely cited what he was reading, and few of his books have survived. He did attack what he saw as the artificiality of some of the elements of the dialectical tradition, and he saw his own inductive method of discovery as a natural method by which people operate. Bacon proposed to establish progressive stages of certainty in the sciences by means of taking advantage of the inherent human capacities of the natural faculties. Bypassing human tendencies to err, or the Idols, Bacon sought to develop the basis for what he called "true and legitimate induction," "the very key of interpretation." Jardine carefully shows how Bacon's theory of knowledge can be seen, and perhaps be better understood, in the light of sixteenth century discussions about method.

Much of the book consists in applying the interpretation of Bacon's proposed method for understanding nature to the actual scientific procedure. In so doing, Jardine illuminates the novelty in Bacon's program. Besides clarifying Bacon's contribution to the development of natural science (and making clearer what he did not accomplish), Jardine also examines the use of Bacon's methods in ethics and civics. One must always remember that Bacon was a major political figure who wrote a great deal about moral matters. The limited possibilities of inductive moral and political sciences are discussed by Jardine, and the reasons for these limitations are examined. The role of the parable in Bacon's examination of what people can understand is dealt with in a worthwhile chapter. Other applications of Bacon's method, his kinds of examples, and his ultimate view of rhetoric are also considered. The book closes with an important chapter on Bacon's method in the *Essays* showing that what he was doing there can be seen as part of his overall method of discovery and discourse.

Rossi, Paolo. *Francis Bacon: From Magic to Science*. London: Routledge & Kegan Paul, 1968.

Paolo Rossi's study of Francis Bacon stresses that Bacon's scientific theory must be understood in its historical and social context. Even more, Rossi insists that Bacon's theory is more than the theme of one book of the *Novum Organum*: his theory is the sum of a life's work, starting when he was a rebellious college student wanting to reform all knowledge, and ending when he was a retired Lord Chancellor trying to show mankind how to deal with the inordinate varieties of nature and the basic limitations of human nature. Rossi traces many fascinating themes through the whole corpus of Bacon's writings, not merely through the few works that have become famous as classic accounts of the scientific method.

As the subtitle indicates, this study begins by placing Bacon's early works among those of the Renaissance magicians. Then it is shown why Bacon rejected the magicians for their esoteric doctrines, their elitism, and their failure to see that the progress of human knowledge requires joint undertakings. Certain elements of the magicians' beliefs remained with Bacon, however, and in his last work, *Sylva silvarum*, he borrowed from those he had so vehemently attacked.

Rossi deals extensively with Bacon's treatment of mythology. Bacon's attitude towards the significance of classical mythology changed from seeing it as primitive and useless to regarding it as meaningful parable. Bacon came to see mythology as an important way in which philosophical proposals were diffused. Bacon, however, regarded Greek philosophy, with the possible exception of Democritus' theory, as inadequate. (Some of Bacon's views about mythology were adopted by Giovanni Battista Vico.)

The reform that Bacon felt was needed in the intellectual world had to be built on more than the classical fable. It was in the logic, rhetoric, and methodology of his time that Bacon found the materials for his revolutionary proposal. It was not that Bacon discovered the inductive method, but that he saw how it could be adopted. From the rhetoricians, especially Peter Ramus, Bacon saw the value of method. In his new scientific logic, Bacon incorporated some of the typical concepts of traditional rhetoric. He substituted the collection of natural data, however, for the use of empty rhetorical devices. He used his tables, or instruments of classification, as ways of organizing reality, as ways by which memory could assist in the intellectual understanding of nature.

Bacon rejected deduction and the deductive science of mathematics and failed to appreciate what Galileo or Copernicus had accomplished. Instead, he saw his own method as a "thread" that could guide mankind through the "chaotic forest" and "complex labyrinth" of nature.

Bacon, Rossi points out, was challenging an implicit connection between deductive methods and a tendency to accept classical traditions and theories (such as Aristotle's) blindly. Bacon's real contribution, Rossi believes, lies not simply in being the spokesman for induction, "but in his courageous rejection of pre-established limitations to scientific enquiring." Bacon designed a logic as a human instrument to enable man to dominate a resisting, recalcitrant nature. He saw abstract theoretical methods as inadequate in natural research and as a result appealed to experimental data and used elaborate tables of data in his attempt to understand nature.

Rossi's book is most helpful in placing Bacon's contribution in a broader context than that provided by simply examining his proposals in the *Novum Organum*. By tracing Bacon's views through all his writings, and by seeing him in relation to the magicians, alchemists, mythologists, rhetoricians, and deductive scientists of his time, Rossi makes Bacon's contributions much clearer.

Additional Recommended Reading

Anderson, Fulton H. *The Philosophy of Francis Bacon*. Chicago: University of Chicago Press, 1948. A careful and thorough examination of Bacon's new logic of inquiry.

Broad, C. D. *The Philosophy of Francis Bacon*. Cambridge: Cambridge University Press, 1926. An interesting, although brief, critical account.

Farrington, Benjamin. *Francis Bacon: Pioneer of Planned Science*. London: Weidenfeld and Nicolson, 1963. The author of *Francis Bacon: Philosopher of Industrial Science* (New York: H. Schuman, 1949) continues his account of Bacon's contribution to the modern temper in science.

Rossi, Paolo. *Francis Bacon: From Magic to Science*. Translated from the Italian by Sacha Rabinovitch. Chicago: University of Chicago Press, 1968. Emphasizes Bacon's logic, rhetoric, and method.

MEDITATIONS ON FIRST PHILOSOPHY

Author: René Descartes (1596-1650)
Type of work: Metaphysics, epistemology
First published: 1641

Principal Ideas Advanced

Perhaps everything we believe is false.

There seems to be no way of avoiding the skeptical consequences of systematic doubt.

But if one is doubting, one exists.

This is the starting point for a philosophy based on certainty.

But if one exists, one is a thinker, a mind; and since one conceives of a God whose conception is beyond one's powers, there must be such a being.

But if God exists, then we can count on our sense experience and our reason, provided we are careful to believe only what is clearly and distinctly true.

The complete title of this work, *Meditations on the First Philosophy in Which the Existence of God and the Distinction Between Mind and Body Are Demonstrated*, prepares the reader for an essay in metaphysics. And we shall not accuse Descartes of mislabeling his product. But in order to understand Descartes' interest in these questions, and therefore the fuller import of the work, one must be prepared to find that he is actually reading an essay in epistemology, or the theory of knowledge. Is there such a thing as knowledge? If so, what distinguishes it from opinion? How is error to be explained? Such questions as these seem to have been uppermost in the author's mind. But in order to answer them, to validate knowledge, to lay hold on the necessity which to Descartes (quite in the Platonic tradition) was the mark of truth, it was necessary to raise the fundamental questions of Being.

In choosing to set down his thoughts as meditations, Descartes shows the greatest consideration for his reader. He represents himself as seated before a fire in a cozy Dutch dwelling, wrapped in his dressing gown, freed from worldly care, and devoting himself to a task which he had for some time looked forward to—a kind of mental housecleaning. On six successive days he pursues his meditation, taking us with him step by step. He pursues the task of clearing his mind of all error.

From *Discourse on Method* we learn that the work was actually composed in circumstances much like those here alleged. In 1628 Descartes was in his thirties and living in Holland, to which he had withdrawn from the more active life for the special purpose of carrying on his philosophical and scientific investigations. The *Meditations* was circulated in manuscript, and when it was published (1641) it included a lengthy appendix composed of objections by leading philosophers—including Thomas Hobbes and Pierre Gassendi—together with Descartes' replies.

The "First Meditation" is, in a way, distinct from the rest. It describes Descartes' effort, which in fact engaged him for many years, to accustom himself not to think of the world in the imagery of the senses or according to the notions of common sense and the traditions of the schools.

Can it be, Descartes wonders, that all beliefs which he had formerly held are false? Perhaps not: but if he is to achieve his goal of building up a body of incontrovertible truth, he must exercise the same rigor toward beliefs that are merely uncertain as toward those which are demonstrably untrue. That is to say, he must make *doubt* his tool. Instead of allowing it to hang over him, forever threatening, he must grasp it firmly and lay about until he has expunged from his mind every pretended certainty.

The first to go are those beliefs that depend on our senses—notably our belief in the existence of our own bodies and of everything that appears to our sight and touch. Our habitual judgment protests. What can be more certain, Descartes asks himself, than that I am seated by the fire holding this paper in my hand? But, he writes, when we reflect that our dreams are sometimes attended with equal confidence, we are forced to conclude that there is no infallible mark by which we can know true perceptions from false.

Of course, what one doubts is, in this case, only that one's ideas *represent* something beyond themselves. Descartes is one of the first philosophers to use the word "idea" in the modern sense. He means by it "whatever the mind directly perceives." But he distinguishes between the idea taken only as a mode of thought, and the idea as a representation of reality. Even in dreams we cannot deny the former of these. What we challenge is the "truth" of the ideas—Descartes calls it "objective reality"—and of judgments based on them. And his question is, whether there is anything in our sense-images that testifies unmistakably to the truth of what they represent. Obviously not, in those that we ourselves initiate in dreams and fantasies. But no more, in those that come from without, through the senses—else how could we make mistakes as to sounds and sights?

There is, he says, another class of ideas which we seem neither to originate ourselves, nor to receive from without, but to be born with—those, for example, which make up the sciences of mathematics. Two and three are five even in dreams: for this sum does not require material counters to make it true. Yet, the ideas of numbers profess to be something besides modes of thought. They do have "objective reality." Moreover, we have been mistaken about mathematical matters. No more than sense-images are they self-authenticating. Our habitual trust in them is not unlike that which we place in our senses, and has the same foundation, namely, that we are creatures of a benevolent deity who would not deceive us. Suppose that this is not the case, and that mathematics is merely a fancy of my mind. Or, worse, suppose it is an illusion deliberately imposed upon us by a malicious demon who has access to the workings of our minds. This is not unthinkable.

These are the thoughts with which the "First Meditation" leaves us. Instead of supposing that the good providence of God sustains his thinking, Descartes resolves to hold fast to the hypothesis that he is constantly being deceived by an evil spirit, so that all his ordinary beliefs are false. In this manner, while he seems to make no progress in the knowledge of truth, he at least habituates himself to suspend judgment concerning things that he does not certainly know. But this is not easy. Descartes pleads with his readers (in the replies to his objectors) not merely to give the exercise such time as is required for reading the meditation through but to take "months, or at least weeks" before going on further. How loath one is to break old habits of thinking he suggests in the figure of a slave who, when sleeping, dreads the day, and conspires to weave the sounds of gathering dawn into his dreams rather than to embrace the light and labors which it brings.

The daylight enterprise that lies before him in the "Second Meditation" is to discover, if possible, some foundation of certainty which doubt is powerless to assault. He has doubted the reality of the world presented to him through his senses. Shall he affirm that some God (or devil) must exist to put these ideas into his mind? That hardly seems necessary, for perhaps he has produced them himself. One thing, however, seems now to loom up in Descartes' mind: "I myself, am I not something?" Suppose all my ideas are hallucinations, whether self-induced or planted in me by some God or devil: in this, at least, I cannot be deceived: "I am, I exist, is necessarily true each time that I pronounce it, or that I mentally conceive it."

Here, then, for the first time, we have encountered a self-validating judgment. It is the unique instance in which man immediately encounters the existence which is represented to him by an idea: I have an idea of "myself." Like other ideas, this one claims to have objective reality. But unlike other ideas, this one's claim is open to inspection—by me. Both the idea and the existence which it represents are present each time I think them. In a simple act of "mental vision" (to use Descartes' expression) I know that I exist. As Locke will say, I know my own existence intuitively.

With this certitude to serve as a cornerstone, Descartes proceeds to raise his palace of Truth. Let man explore the structure of his own inner consciousness, and he will find the clue to universal Being. For instance, we can ask the question, "What am I?" And the answer lies at hand. "I am a thing that thinks." For was it not in the act of thinking (taken broadly to include all conscious activities) that I found the reality of the idea of myself? Contrast with this the traditional view that man is a body indwelt by a subtle essence—a very fine grade of matter—known as spirit. What confusion surrounds the whole conception! There is nothing certain, or even intelligible, about it. In fact, we have only to press ahead with our methodical doubt to discover that most of the ideas which we habitually associate with matter are illusory. Take a piece of wax fresh from the comb: we think of it in terms of color, taste, odor, texture. But none of these is essential to the wax. Place it near the fire, and all the qualities which engross the imagination are altered. All that remains unchanged, so that we can call it essential to the wax, is "something extended, flexible, movable"—properties that are knowable to the intellect and not to the senses. In any case, whether I have a body, it is not as body that I know myself when I behold myself as existing. The realm of being which I discover there has nothing about it of extension, plasticity, mobility. I am a thinking being, Descartes concludes, a mind, a soul, an understanding, a reason: and if the meaning of these terms was formerly unknown to me it is no more.

These are very important results of the second day's meditation, especially when we remember that the forward progress was all made along the path of doubt, for it was the act of doubting that gave Descartes both the certainty that he existed and that his nature was mind. But we have not yet exhausted the implications of his consciousness of doubt. Does not doubt carry with it, and actually presuppose, the idea of certainty, just as error carries with it the idea of truth? Descartes finds in his mind the idea of a perfect being by comparison with which he is aware of his

imperfections, a self-sufficient being by which he knows that he is dependent. Following this lead, he proceeds in his "Third Meditation" to demonstrate the existence of God.

His argument takes two forms. First, he asks directly concerning the *idea* of a perfect being, whence it could have come into his mind: From some other creature? From himself? Or must there exist a perfect being to originate the idea? His answer is obscured for the modern reader by the late—medieval philosophical framework in which it is expressed. The idea of God contains more "objective reality" than any other idea (including my idea of myself). But a more perfect idea cannot be generated by a less perfect being. Therefore, the idea of God in his mind must have been placed there by God himself.

The second form of the argument proceeds from the contingent quality of his own existence, made up as it is of fleeting instants, no one of which is able either to conserve itself or to engender its successor. Much in the argument reminds one of the traditional Aristotelian proof; but there is this difference, which makes it clear that the new argument is only another version of the first—it is not merely the existence of a contingent being that has to be explained, or of a thinking being, but of "a being which thinks and which has some idea of God." Thus, the principle that there must be at least as much reality in the cause as in the effect precludes the possibility that any being less perfect than God could have created Descartes —or any man.

The argument here abbreviated is of scarcely more than historical interest. And the same is true of the further argument (from the "Fifth Meditation") that, since existence is a perfection, the idea of a Perfect Being entails the existence of that Being. But we would not be just to Descartes if we did not point out that behind the framework of traditional theistic proof lies a claim which rationalistic philosophers have found valid even in our own time. "I see that in some way I have in me the notion of the infinite earlier than the finite—to wit, the notion of God before that of myself. For how would it be possible that I should know that I doubt and desire, that is to say, that something is lacking to me, and that I am not quite perfect, unless I had within me some idea of a Being more perfect than myself, in comparison with which I should recognize the deficiencies of my nature?" Here, in effect, is a new kind of reasoning. The scholastics were committed to demonstrate the existence of God by syllogisms; and, whether through expediency or inadvertency, Descartes makes a show of doing the same. But in Descartes a new, quasi-mathematical way of reasoning was pushing the syllogism to one side, as the quotation (which could be matched with several others) makes clear. His true ground for affirming the existence of God was not that it *follows from* but that it is *implicit in* his consciousness of himself.

Pascal's famous memorial which insists that the God of the philosophers is not the God of faith is a useful reminder to the general reader. There is no need, however, to suppose that Descartes needed it. The certainty of God's existence is a great triumph—but for scientific, rather than for religious, reasons. It is the *sine qua non* of all further knowledge, since "the certainty of all other things depends on it so absolutely that without this knowledge it is impossible ever to know anything perfectly." We saw earlier that such obvious mathematical truths as two plus three equals five are not self-validating, because they bear no evidence of the competency of our thought. An atheist cannot be sure; hence his knowledge cannot be called science, Descartes tells us in replying to his objectors: doubt may never rise to trouble him; but if it does, he has no way of removing it. But the doubt is removed when a person recognizes that his mind owes its constitution and working to the creativity of God, and that God is no deceiver.

For the rest, the *Meditations* is chiefly devoted to determining just how far man can trust the faculties which the beneficent Deity has implanted in him.

First, one must distinguish between impulses which incline us to belief (such as "the heat which I feel is produced by the fire") and insights into necessary truths (such as "a cause must be as great or greater than its effect.") Both are natural, and owing to the good offices of our Creator. But the former can be doubted, even after we have discovered the truth about God; the latter, which Descartes speaks of as "the light of nature," cannot be doubted at all. They are the principles of reason in our minds by which we arrive at knowledge. We have no other means of distinguishing between true and false.

Second, one must consider the causes of error. It is axiomatic that God can never deceive us and that if we make proper use of the abilities he has given us we can never go wrong. Yet obviously, he has chosen to make us fallible. How does this happen? From the fact that our intellects are finite, together with the fact that our wills (as free) are infinite. One can see why both these things must be and how, as a consequent, man does not easily stay within the narrow realm of truth. The crux of the matter is that, for Descartes, judgment involves the will (in the form of "assent" or "dissent"). It is within our power to withhold judgment when convincing evidence is wanting, and to give it only when the light of reason demands. Indeed, as Thomas Huxley and William Kingdon Clifford were to say again in the nineteenth century, Descartes held that we have a duty to bring judgment under this rule. Failure to do so involves not merely error but sin.

Third, we come to a nest of problems having to do with our knowledge of the external world. We have mentioned the famous passage in which Descartes examines a piece of wax in order to find what constitutes the essence of matter. He observed that the sensible qualities which we most readily believe to be in matter are not part of the nature of wax, as are such attributes as extension, figure, and mobility, which are not properly sensible but intelligible. Comparing the two ways of thinking about things in nature, Descartes concludes (following the lead of Galileo) that by the senses we have only the most confused notions of matter—they arise from the influence upon the mind of the body to which it is united rather than from the mind's apprehension by its own light of the necessary attributes of being. It is by the latter that we obtain true knowledge of nature, which henceforth is seen to possess only those qualities which can be described in mathematical terms. In other words, the physical world has to be envisaged as a vast, complicated machine—but not (let us remind ourselves) the way our senses view machines, rather the way they are viewed on the drawing board and in the mind of the engineer.

So far reason leads us, Descartes says. If we are

correct in supposing that there is a material world, its nature must be as classic mechanics conceives it. But it does not follow that a material world actually exists. It is conceivable that each time I receive and recognize the idea of a body, God himself impresses it upon my mind. Nothing in the idea of matter is inconsistent with its nonexistence. All that I can discover which inclines me to assent to its existence is an instinctive impulse such as attaches to all our sense perceptions: and this, of course, is no reason.

Descartes' only recourse is to appeal to the good faith of God. Thus, he writes that if God were the cause of our ideas of matter, he would undoubtedly have given us the means of knowing that this is the case, for he is no deceiver. In granting us free wills, he has, indeed, opened the door to falsity and error: but he has not permitted any error without placing within our reach the means of avoiding it, or, at least,

correcting it once it has been made. The claims of our sense-images, which reason disproves, is an example. But no analysis disproves the natural inclination which we have to believe that corporeal objects do exist. Hence, we are justified in affirming, along with the existence of finite mind (one's own) and infinite Being, the actuality of the material world. (Apparently, for Descartes, the existence of other minds is never more than an inference.)

The upshot of the *Meditations* is, then, to replace the commonsense picture of nature with one that is amenable to rational investigation. The new cosmology which was being shaped by men such as Kepler, Galileo, William Gilbert, and others rested upon fundamental assumptions which were not clear to the investigators themselves. It was the task of Descartes to give these principles their classic formulation.

Pertinent Literature

Rée, Jonathan. *Descartes*. London: Allen Lane, 1974.

Contemporary English-speaking philosophers will readily allow that modern philosophy (as distinct from ancient and medieval philosophy) began with René Descartes. Further, since the *Meditations* is clearly Descartes' central philosophical work, these same Anglo-American philosophers will regard and study that work as the source of the modern philosophical tradition.

It is certainly not wrong to see Descartes as the first modern philosopher, nor is it wrong to think of the *Meditations* as the founding work in the present philosophical tradition. But it is shortsighted to see both Descartes and the *Meditations* in only that way. All such philosophers know that Descartes did not think of himself as solely a philosopher; they know that he was also a scientist and a mathematician. His work covered what we today would regard as a wide and disparate range of disciplines. Moreover, Descartes certainly did not think of his work as scattered over unconnected fields of investigation. That is, he saw his philosophical ideas and scientific investiga-

tions as thoroughly interconnected.

Descartes' own image for this interconnectedness was that of knowledge as a tree: metaphysics or first philosophy (the full title of Descartes' work is *Meditations on First Philosophy*) is the root of the tree of knowledge; physics or second philosophy is the trunk; and the other special studies are branches of various sizes of one and the same tree.

One of the interesting and important features of Jonathan Rée's book on Descartes is that he attempts to see Descartes' philosophical work, especially the *Meditations*, in its connections with Descartes' scientific ideas and interests. In fact, there is no other work on Descartes in English which is an equally serious attempt to treat the science and the metaphysics as a unit.

In fact, Rée goes even farther. He tends to regard Descartes as primarily a scientist, as someone whose main aim and interest was to give an account of the behavior of physical phenomena. Hence he tends to describe Descartes' views on the various philosophical issues discussed in the *Meditations* as though those views were determined by the needs of his scientific program. Now that is certainly a significant thesis about how to understand and examine the philosophical parts of Descartes' writings. But there is reason for thinking that Rée has carried his ambition of uniting Descartes' philosophical and scientific works too far. In Descartes' own image of the tree, it is philosophy (that is, metaphysics) which stands at the root of knowledge, determining how the upper parts of the tree develop. Rée's version of the story tends to invert the relationship. Of course, it might be shown that in fact Descartes' physical conceptions did shape his metaphysics contrary to his own metaphor of their relationship; but that does need to be argued.

There are at least two other innovations in Rée's book when it is compared with most other philosophical writings in English on Descartes. Not only is the context of understanding broadened to include Descartes' scientific activities but also it is broadened to include some social and economic developments. Most especially, when Rée turns to write of Descartes' account of the self, he attempts to show how the Cartesian conception of the self was connected with the rise of a capitalist economic system in Europe. There clearly is some such connection, but most writings in English on Descartes tend to ignore such matters completely. Second, Rée finishes the book by saying something of the history of Descartes' reputation. He reminds us that we tend to forget what Descartes was celebrated for in the seventeenth century and what seems close to the truth: that Descartes founded a wholly new world view.

Kenny, Anthony. *Descartes: A Study of His Philosophy.* New York: Random House, 1968.

The *Meditations* has undoubtedly played a significant role in a variety of historical, cultural, and intellectual developments and consequently ought to be studied in light of those developments. For example, it is true that René Descartes was a great scientist, and so the *Meditations* must be examined in relation to his scientific activities and views. Nevertheless, the work is a piece of philosophy, a piece of metaphysics and epistemology, and was intended by Descartes as a reasoned account of the fundamental nature of reality and our knowledge of it. Consequently, at some point in one's study of the work it is necessary that it be subjected to philosophical scrutiny, its claims and arguments closely examined for their truth and adequacy.

In the English-speaking world the training of many philosophers has involved a heavy and early investigation of the *Meditations*. One of the results of that practice has been the production of a number of very good critical examinations of Descartes' main philosophical work. One of those is Anthony Kenny's book. It is a clear and patient exposition of Descartes' claims and arguments and, along with that, an intelligent critical examination of those claims and arguments.

There is nothing strikingly innovative in the organization of Kenny's book; he follows that standard procedure of taking up themes and topics in the order in which they arise in the *Meditations*. The interest comes from how Kenny handles the exposition and criticism of those topics.

As is well known, the *Meditations* opens with a process of doubt which does not, however, lead to a skeptical conclusion, since Descartes comes to the fact of his own thought (consciousness) and holds that accordingly his own existence is beyond doubt. He expressed that "first truth" in the famous phrase *cogito, ergo sum*. One of the problems that arises for anyone attempting a critical examination of Descartes' arguments is what the status of that phrase is. The word *ergo* ("therefore") signals that there is an inference from "I think" to "I am"; and there is other textual evidence for that view. On the other hand, the majority of scholars in interpreting the *Meditations* have held that the *cogito* is not an inference but is rather an intuition, something immediately apprehended as true. There is also textual evidence for this view.

One of the excellences of Kenny's book is that he very patiently works through the various ways of interpreting the phrase as an intuition and shows that none of them will stand up. He then reverses the matter and shows that the inference interpretation does, contrary to most opinion, meet the text. The result of this is that we learn that the *cogito* is not literally the *first* truth Descartes comes across but is only the first truth which asserts that something *exists*.

Descartes' first proof of the existence of God is what traditionally has been called a cosmological proof: that is, it proceeds from the existence of something, in this case the idea of God which Descartes has, to the necessity of there being a divine cause of that thing. Descartes argues that he could not have the idea of a God unless there is a God to give it to him. One of the criticisms of that argument, made by some

of Descartes' contemporaries, is that, strictly speaking, we have no idea of God; that is, we have no idea of a supremely perfect being. Descartes has an argument to show that we do have that idea. It goes from the fact of his doubting through the idea that doubt is an imperfection to the claim that he therefore has an idea of a contrasting being, one without imperfections.

That argument, when fully written out, has seemed to many to be persuasive. Kenny, however, quite clearly demolishes the Cartesian argument. He shows (see Chapter 6) by a parallel argument that we could similarly "prove" that we have a coherent idea of a being who has every conceivable shape. Consequently *that* particular way of proving that we have an idea of God will not work.

Balz, A. G. A. *Decartes and the Modern Mind*. New Haven, Connecticut: Yale University Press, 1952.

The student of the *Meditations* must know not only how its argument proceeds step by step but also the broader context in which the work was undertaken. This context includes René Descartes' other, more scientific, aims and writings. No doubt it also includes the fact of a rising new economic and social system. But there is still more to the context in which the *Meditations* must be seen. It is in that regard that A. G. A. Balz's book *Decartes and the Modern Mind* should be read.

The standard way of organizing the outlines of the history of Western civilization is in terms of the Ancient World, The Medieval World, and the Modern Period. (There is presently an argument as to whether we have moved into a Post-Modern phase.) On the whole, writers will say that the first of the modern centuries was the seventeenth century. Balz accepts that general scheme and adds to it his own theses: namely, that the broadest features of the modern mind were first exemplified by Descartes, and that our ways of thinking owe more to Descartes than to anyone else. Descartes, that is, was the first modern man and did more than any other to produce our general intellectual outlook.

It is easy for historians to get carried away by their efforts to mark out the new elements in Descartes (or anyone else, for that matter) and forget the carry-over

from the past. Balz does not make that mistake. While he does insist on the role of Descartes in ushering in a new style of life and mind, he is fully aware that, and is concerned to show how, Descartes' ways of thinking still bore strong signs of the medieval period. Balz argues that this backward-looking element is especially strong in Descartes' view of the nature of faith and in his account of the relation of faith and reason. Descartes, although on a voyage of reason, was not able, as were many philosophers who came after him and who drew upon his work, simply to throw off faith; he still had to find some way of accommodating both.

There is one other reason for reading Balz in connection with the *Meditations*. The form of the book will not be strange to one who has read through the type of books usually written in English about Descartes (for examples, Jonathan Rée and Anthony Kenny). All of the writers, Balz included, work their way through the *Meditations*, meditation-by-meditation, step-by-step; but otherwise Balz's style and outlook are greatly different from what one will find in those other works. The reason is that although Balz writes in English, he is writing from the French perspective on Descartes. (See how few English books are cited in Balz's bibliography.) And the French manner of writing and thinking about Descartes is considerably different from that in the English-speaking tradition. After all, Descartes is a culture hero to the French. Anyone who wants to understand the *Meditations* must see how it looks through the eyes of a quite different intellectual tradition from the one in which we are immersed.

Additional Recommended Reading

Buchdahl, Gerd. *Metaphysics and the Philosophy of Science*. Oxford: Basil Blackwell, 1969. See Chapter III for a discussion of the relations of Descartes' method, metaphysics, and science.

Ring, Merrill. "Descartes' Intentions," in *Canadian Journal of Philosophy*. III, no. 1 (September, 1973), pp. 27-49.

Rorty, Richard. *Philosophy and the Mirror of Nature*. Princeton, New Jersey: Princeton University Press, 1979. This seminal critique of the Enlightenment tradition includes important insights about Descartes' theory of knowledge and philosophy of mind.

Ryle, Gilbert. *The Concept of Mind*. London: Hutchinson's University Library, 1949. The classic statement of opposition to Descartes' views on mind and body.

Wilson, Margaret D. *Descartes*. London: Routledge & Kegan Paul, 1978. A recent critical scrutiny of the arguments in the *Meditations*.

LEVIATHAN

Author: Thomas Hobbes (1588-1679)
Type of work: Political philosophy
First published: 1651

Principal Ideas Advanced

A man is a group of material particles in motion.

The state—the great Leviathan—is an artificial man in which sovereignty is the soul, officers the joints, rewards and punishments the nerves, wealth its strength, safety its business, counselors its memory, equity and law its reason and will, peace its health, sedition its sickness, and civil war its death.

Reasoning is the manipulation of names; truth is the correct ordering of names.

Desire is motion toward an object, and aversion is motion away; the good and bad are understood by reference to desire and aversion.

In a state of nature there is a war of every man against every man; to secure peace men make contracts establishing a sovereign power who is not subject to civil law since by his will he creates law.

Of the three forms of sovereignty, monarchy, aristocracy, and democracy, monarchy is the most effective in securing peace.

The *Leviathan (Leviathan, or the Matter, Form, and Power of a Commonwealth, Ecclesiastical and Civil)* is primarily a treatise on the philosophy of politics. It also contains important discussions, some brief, some extended, on metaphysics, epistemology, psychology, language, ethics, and religion. Hobbes develops his views from a metaphysics of materialism and a mechanical analogy in which everything is a particle or set of particles moving in accordance with laws. Though he was at one time secretary to Francis Bacon, English philosopher and essayist, his inspiration came from Galileo Galilei, Italian mathematician and physicist. Hobbes was unusual in being an early empiricist who recognized the importance of mathematics.

In the *Leviathan* the realism of Niccolò Machiavelli, Florentine man of affairs and political writer, the emphasis on sovereignty of Jean Bodin, French legalist and politician, and the attempt of Hugo Grotius, Dutch jurist, to modernize the conception of natural law by relating it to mathematics and the new science are combined and developed with great originality, clarity, and flair for pungent statement to constitute one of the masterpieces of political philosophy.

Hobbes divides all knowledge into two classes, Natural Philosophy and Civil Philosophy. The former is the basis for the latter and consists in turn of two parts, First Philosophy, comprising laws of particles in general such as inertia, causation, and identity; and Physics, which deals with the qualities of particles. These particles, singly or in combination, may be permanent or transient, celestial or terrestrial, with or without sense, with or without speech. A man is a group of particles that is permanent, terrestrial, sensible, and loquacious. Physics contains not only optics and music, which are the sciences of vision and hearing in general, but also ethics, which is the science of the passions of men, poetry, rhetoric, logic, and equity. The four last are respectively the study of man's use of speech in elevated expression, in persuading, reasoning, and contracting. Civil Philosophy deals with the rights and duties of the sovereign or of subjects.

Hobbes makes extensive use of the mechanical model in constructing his system. Life is motion.

Therefore, machines have artificial life. The heart is a spring, the nerves are strings, the joints are wheels giving motion to the whole body. The commonwealth is an artificial man in which sovereignty is the soul, officers are the joints, rewards and punishments are the nerves, wealth is its strength, and safety is its business; counselors are its memory, equity and law are reason and will, peace is its health, sedition is its sickness, and civil war is its death. The covenants by which it comes into being are the counterpart of the fiat of creation.

It is apparent that the model is highly oversimplified. This is, in fact, the basis for much of the force it carries. Hobbes does not hesitate to ignore the model if ill-suited to his purpose, as it is in many cases where he has to deal with the details of psychology, religion, and social and political relations.

The simplest motion in human bodies is sensation, caused by the impact of some particle upon a sense organ. When sensations are slowed by the interference of others they become imagination or memory. Imagination in sleep is dreaming. Imagination raised by words is understanding and is common to man and beast.

Ideas ("phantasms" for Hobbes) proceed in accordance with laws of association or of self-interest, as in calculating the means to a desired end. Anything we imagine or think is finite. Any apparent conception of something infinite is only an awareness of an inability to imagine a bound. The name of God, for example, is used that we may honor him, not that we may conceive of him.

Hobbes considered speech the most noble of all inventions. It distinguishes man from beast. It consists in the motion of names and their connections. It is a necessary condition of society, contract, commonwealth, and peace. It is essential to acquiring art, to counseling and instructing, and to expressing purpose. It is correspondingly abused in ambiguity, metaphor, and deception.

When a man manipulates names in accordance with the laws of truth, definition, and thought he is reasoning. Truth is the correct ordering of names; for example, connecting by affirmation two names that signify the same thing. Error in general statements is self-contradiction. Definition is stating what names signify. Inconsistent names, such as "incorporeal substance," signify nothing and are mere sounds. The laws of thought are the laws of mathematics, exemplified best in geometry, generalized to apply to all names. Reasoning is carried on properly when we begin with definition and move from one consequence to the next. Reasoning is therefore a kind of calculating with names. According to Hobbes everything named is particular but a general name can be imposed on a number of things that are similar. He anticipated fundamental distinctions of Hume, Scotch philosopher and skeptic, and later empiricists in maintaining that conclusions reached by reasoning are always conditional.

Hobbes extended the mechanical model in his discussion of the passions by holding that endeavor begins in the motions of imagination. Desire, which is the same as love, is motion toward an object which is therefore called "good." Aversion, which is the same as hate, is motion away from an object which is therefore called "bad." Other passions are definable in terms of these two. Fear is aversion with the belief that the object will hurt; courage is aversion with the hope of avoiding hurt. Anger is sudden courage. Religion, a particularly important passion, is publicly allowed fear of invisible powers. When the fear is not publicly allowed, it is superstition. The whole sum of desires and aversions and their modifications carried on until the thing in question is either done or considered impossible is deliberation. In deliberation, the last appetite or aversion immediately preceding action is will. In searching for truth the last opinion is judgment.

Since desires are endless, happiness is not a static condition but a process of satisfying desires. All motivation is egoistic. Man's basic desire is for power which, like all other desires, ends only in death.

Hobbes completes the foundations for the development of his political theory with an analysis of religion. It is invented by men because of their belief in spirits, their ignorance of causes, and their devotion to what they fear. This explains why the first legislators among the gentiles always claimed that their precepts came from God or some other spirit, and how priests have been able to use religion for selfish purposes. Religion dissolves when its founders or leaders are thought to lack wisdom, sincerity, or love.

Hobbes develops his political theory proper in terms of the time-honored concepts of equality, the state of nature, natural law, natural rights, contract, sovereignty, and justice. In his hands, however, they receive treatment that is very different from his predecessors, the Greeks, St. Thomas Aquinas, Jean Bodin, and Hugo Grotius, as well as from his successors, John Locke, English philosopher, and his followers in the liberal tradition. Machiavelli's views on egoism and the need for absolute power in the sovereign anticipated Hobbes, but were not worked out in detail as a general political philosophy.

In their natural state, according to Hobbes, men are approximately equal in strength, mental capacity, and experience, and everyone has an equal right to everything. If they were without government the conflict arising from their desires, their distrust, and ambition would lead to a state of war of every man against every man. In it there would be no property, no justice or injustice, and life would be "solitary, poor, nasty, brutish and short." Fortunately, both passion—in the form of fear of death, desire for a long and reasonably pleasant life, and hope of achieving it—and reason—in the form of knowledge of the articles of peace in the form of the laws of nature—combine to provide a basis for the establishment of civil society and escape from universal strife.

The first law of nature is to seek the peace and follow it. The second, a necessary means to the first, is *"that a man be willing, when others are so too, as farre-forth as for Peace and defence of himself he shall think it necessary, to lay down this* [natural] *right to all things; and be contented with so much liberty against other men as he would allow other men against himselfe."* This is to be done by making contracts with others. A necessary condition for the operation of the second law of nature is that men perform their contracts, which is the third law of nature. For contracts to be valid it is necessary, in turn, that a sovereign power be established who will make it more painful to commit injustice, which is the breaking of a contract, than to live justly, which is the keeping of contracts. Contracts without the sword, Hobbes reminds us, are only words which

guarantee no security. The first three laws of nature, then, combined with the nature of man as a complex set of particles moving in accordance with various sets of laws—not only strictly mechanical laws, but also what might be called egoistic and hedonistic laws—are the source of society, sovereignty, and justice.

Further laws of nature, subordinate to the first three, or special cases, though not specified as such by Hobbes, require the practice of fidelity, gratitude, courtesy, forbearance, fairness, justice, equity, the recognition of natural equality, and the avoidance of contumely, pride, and arrogance. The whole doctrine of natural law, called by Hobbes a "deduction," can be summarized in the general law: do not unto another what you would not want him to do to you. Hobbes considers these laws of nature "eternal and immutable," because breaking them can never preserve the peace. The science of laws is true moral philosophy. He concludes this discussion of natural law with a remark whose significance has usually been ignored, but which must be appreciated if Parts III and IV of the *Leviathan* are to be understood. These "laws," so far, are not properly named; they are only theorems, binding to be sure, *in foro interno*, that is, to a desire they should be effective; but not *in foro externo*, that is, to putting them into practice. If, however, it can be shown that they are delivered in the word of God, who by right commands in all things, then they are properly called laws and are in fact binding.

In working out the details of the second and third laws of nature Hobbes maintains that to achieve peace, contentment, and security it is necessary that men agree with one another to confer their power upon a man or group of men of whose acts each man, even a member of a dissenting minority, will regard himself the original author. "This is the Generation of that great LEVIATHAN or rather (to speak more reverently) of that *Mortal God*, to which we owe under the *Immortal God* our peace and Defence." We may consequently define a commonwealth as *"One Person, of whose Acts a great multitude, by mutuall Covenants one with another, have made themselves every one the Author, to the end he may use the strength and means of them all, as he shall think*

expedient, for their Peace and Common Defence."
This person is sovereign. All others are subjects.

The covenant generating the sovereign is not between the sovereign and the subjects, but only between subjects that they will obey whatever ruling power the majority may establish. The covenant may be explicit, actually written, or it may be implicit, for example, by remaining in a conquered country. The covenant is an agreement to refrain from interfering with the sovereign's exercise of his right to everything. The concept of consent is not present, at least not in the sense it carried later with Locke. Making the covenant is the one political act of subjects. Their proper role is to obey as long as the sovereign is able to protect them, unless he should order them to kill, wound, or maim themselves or to answer questions about a crime they may have committed. Even these are not restrictions of the sovereignty of the ruler, but only liberties that subjects retain under the laws of nature. Politically and legally, in Hobbes's system, there is and can be no legal limitation on sovereignty. There is no right of rebellion, for example, since the sovereign is not bound by any contract, not having made one. Subjects have only the legal rights granted them by the sovereign. The sovereign is the only legislator; he is not subject to civil law and his will—not long usage—gives authority to law.

More specifically, the sovereign must have the power to censor all expression of opinion, to allocate private property, to determine what is good or evil, lawful or unlawful, to judge all cases, to make war or peace, to choose the officers of the commonwealth, to administer rewards and punishment, to decide all moral or religious questions, and to prescribe how God is to be worshiped.

There are, says Hobbes, only three forms which sovereignty may take, monarchy, aristocracy, and democracy. Other apparent forms merely reflect attitudes. For example, if someone dislikes monarchy, then he calls it tyranny. Although his arguments would support any absolutism, Hobbes shows a strong preference for monarchy in claiming that it is the best means of effecting peace. The interests of the monarch and his subjects are the same. What is good for the monarch is good for the people. He is rich, glorious, or secure if they are, and not if they are not.

He will have fewer favorites than an assembly. He can receive better advice in private than any assembly. There will be no argument and disagreement in making decisions and they will stand more firm. Divisive factionalism and the consequent danger of civil war will not arise. Hobbes admits that monarchy has some problems about succession but says they can be met by following the will of the sovereign, custom, or lineage.

Hobbes maintains that a commonwealth established by acquisition in acts of force or violence differs from one established by institution, peaceably and with something approaching explicit covenant, only in having its sovereignty based upon fear of the sovereign rather than upon mutual fear of the subjects.

No matter how established or what its form, however, there are certain causes of dissolution which Hobbes warns must be avoided: insufficient power in the sovereign to maintain peace, permitting subjects to judge what is good or evil, considering violation of individual conscience a sin, considering supernatural inspiration superior to reason, considering the sovereign subject to civil law, permitting subjects absolute property rights, dividing sovereign power, regarding tyrannicide as lawful, permitting the reading of democratic books, believing there are two kingdoms, spiritual and civil.

The all-important task of showing that there are not two different kingdoms and at the same time showing that the theorems of the first two Parts of the *Leviathan* are in fact laws and as such binding obligations, are Hobbes's main points in discussing the nature of a Christian commonwealth. The essential mark of a Christian is obedience to God's law. God's authority as lawgiver derives from his power. His laws, which are the natural laws, are promulgated by natural reason, revelation, and prophecy. In the first two Parts of the *Leviathan* knowledge of natural laws and their implications have been found out by reason. Laws are, therefore, only conditional theorems. To be shown to be unconditional laws they must be shown to be the will of God. In fact, Hobbes argues, using extensive quotation and acute, though one-sided, analysis of terms in Scripture and in common speech, all theorems of reasoning about the conduct of men seeking happiness in peace are to be found in Scripture. He concludes that there is no difference between natural law known by reason and revealed or prophetic law. What is law, therefore, depends upon what is Scripture.

Scripture, Hobbes argues, again with extensive quotation, analysis, and interpretation, is what is accepted as Scripture in a commonwealth and is nothing apart from its interpretation. If it is interpreted by conscience, we have competition and a return to the state of nature with its war made fiercer by religious conviction and self-righteousness. All the same arguments for commonwealth apply in particular, therefore, more strongly to the generation of a Christian commonwealth. This is a civil society of Christian subjects under a Christian sovereign. There is no question of opposition between church and state because there is no distinction between them. There are not two laws, ecclesiastical and civil—only civil. There is no universal church since there is no power on earth to which all commonwealths are subject. Consequently, obedience to civil law is necessary for man's admission into heaven. Even if a sovereign is not Christian, it is still an obligation and law for a Christian to obey him, since those who do not obey break the laws of God.

When these truths are obfuscated by misinterpretation of Scripture, demonology, or vain philosophy then, says Hobbes, a kingdom of darkness arises. He applies, in some detail, the test of asking, "Who benefits?" to a number of doctrines in each category and concludes that the Presbyterian and Roman clergy, particularly the Popes, are the authors of this darkness, for they gain temporal power from its existence. Hobbes adds that the errors from which the darkness arises are to be avoided, in general, by a careful reading of the *Leviathan*. Some of the darkness arising from vain philosophy, for example, can be remedied by more careful attention to Hobbes's doctrines of language. These will show that the function of the copula can be replaced by the juxtaposition and ordering of words, thus removing the darkness that arises from the reification of "esse" in its counterparts "entity" and "essence." These words, says Hobbes, are not names of anything, only signs by which we make known what we consider to be

consequences of a name. Infinitives and participles similarly are not names of anything. When men understand these and other facts about language they can no longer be deluded by mistaken interpretations of Scripture, demonology, or vain philosophy. In this instance they will no longer be deluded by the doctrine of separated essence and consequently will not be frightened into disobeying their sovereign.

There are flaws in Hobbes's philosophy. He is often crude in his vigor, achieving a logical solution of a problem by omitting recalcitrant details. His errors, however, are usually due to oversimplification, not to being muddle-headed, superstitious, or unclear. No matter how wrong, he is never unintelligible. Moreover, he could not in his own day, and cannot now, be ignored. Puritans and Cavaliers could both condemn him but both Cromwell and Charles II could draw on his doctrines. Abraham Lincoln appealed to his doctrines of covenant and unity of the sovereign power to justify the use of force in dealing with secession.

His philosophy, in its outline, development, method, and logic, very strongly affected the later developments of political and ethical thought. It is doubtful that anyone has stated so strongly the case for political authority or more strongly supported the thesis that unity, not consent, is the basis of government, and conformity to the sovereign will is its strength. His influence is clearly apparent in the doctrines of sovereignty and civil law formulated by John Austin, English writer on jurisprudence. His methods of argument about the nature of law prepared the way for Jeremy Bentham, English ethical and social philosopher, and the movement for scientific legislation based on pleasure, pain, and self-interest. In moral philosophy it is not too much to say that the subsequent history of ethics would not have been the same without Hobbes. Reactions by Richard Cumberland, British moralist and quasirationalist, and the Cambridge Platonists on the one hand, and by Lord Shaftesbury, English essayist, and Francis Hutcheson, British moralist and empiricist, on the other, developed into the eighteenth century opposition between reason and sentiment which is reflected in many of the problems occupying moral philosophers in the twentieth century.

Pertinent Literature

Oakeshott, Michael. "Introduction to *Leviathan*," in *Hobbes on Civil Association*. Berkeley: University of California Press, 1975.

Published initially in 1946 with his critical edition of the text of *Leviathan*, Michael Oakeshott's "Introduction" challenged the popular picture of Thomas Hobbes as a materialist and atheist and stimulated new interest in the subject. In Oakeshott's view, Hobbes, far from being a dogmatic materialist, was essentially a skeptic who developed his mechanistic system because causal connection seemed to him the only principle by means of which man can arrive at knowledge. Where the causal principle cannot be applied—for example, to the origin of the world—reason is silent, and man is left to faith. In this view, the second half of *Leviathan,* treating of the Christian Commonwealth and the Kingdom of Darkness, is integral to Hobbes's ethical and political thought.

That the body politic falls within the compass of reason follows from the fact that, as a human construction, it can be traced to man's nature as its cause. Oakeshott follows Hobbes's argument in some detail, but focuses particularly on "the predicament of man" which arises out of the unavoidable conflict between human nature, which is solitary, and the human condition, which is social. Language and reason, by expanding man's fears and hopes, cause the predicament; but they also reveal the nature of the conflict and suggest the means by which it can be resolved.

Having articulated Hobbes's argument, Oakeshott takes up several historical and critical questions, two of which have general interest. In a section entitled "Individualism and Absolutism," Oakeshott locates Hobbes firmly in the nominalist camp, noting that unlike nineteenth century individualists, whose libertarianism was based on a belief in the unique value of each human being, Hobbes held simply to the assumption that only individual substances are real. In society individuals may unite for one purpose or another and may agree for one person to act in place of another; but such arrangements do not alter the individual's point of view, nor is the association they form a new entity. Thus, according to Oakeshott, the authority of Hobbes's sovereign, although absolute as opposed to the individual's claims of right, is not absolute in the vicious sense of denying legitimacy to private views and aspirations.

Of particular interest to philosophers is the section entitled "The Theory of Obligation." Here Oakeshott dismisses as an oversimplification the attempt to interpret Hobbes's theory in terms of self-interest. Holding closely to Hobbes's statement that there is "no obligation on any man, which ariseth not from some act of his own," Oakeshott defines obligation as an external constraint imposed by a man on himself, directly or indirectly. Restraints imposed contrary to a man's will do not oblige him; nor do internal constraints, whether dictated by fear or by reason, oblige him in the sense given by Hobbes to the term. For this reason, Hobbes would not allow that the law of nature imposes obligations apart from sanctions, either political or divine.

Warrender, Howard. *The Political Philosophy of Hobbes: His Theory of Obligation.* Oxford: Clarendon Press, 1957.

As the subtitle indicates, this book is not concerned with Thomas Hobbes's philosophy as a whole but is an attempt to discover "the logical structure of his argument in one of its central aspects, namely, his theory of obligation." The burden of Hobbes's philosophy, says Howard Warrender, is that citizens *ought* to obey the law, adding that if the argument is worth anything, it must be consistent with itself.

There have been those who would question whether obligation is central to Hobbes's philosophy. Impressed with his mechanistic account of the origin of both man's thoughts and his passions, they have overlooked his numerous references to moral concerns or have reduced these to psychological terms as one must do when he reads Jeremy Bentham. Many scholars reject this interpretation, however, holding that alongside his psychological account of man's motivation Hobbes gives a more or less traditional account of his duties and rights. Some have even ventured that Hobbes's moral theory is close to that of Immanuel Kant. In between these two classes are those who, like Michael Oakeshott, allow obligation a limited place in Hobbes's world view, notably when a person binds himself to perform certain acts by a promise or a covenant.

In Warrender's view, Hobbes's entire moral and political system rests on natural law, understood not as something that man invents but as something that he discovers. Without denying the originality of Hobbes's interpretation of this law, he questions whether his understanding of it is as revolutionary as has often been supposed. As Hobbes interprets it, natural law is simply the sum of those conditions under which it is possible for men to form societies. Those individuals who do not have sufficient rational capacity to understand this law are not bound by it, and their social behavior must be determined by external controls. But unless there were, besides these incompetents, a sizable number of people with the capacity for understanding natural law and recognizing the obligation that it imposes, political society could never have come into being, nor could it function.

Hobbes answers the question how far natural law binds man in a prepolitical condition by pointing out that actual obligations vary according to circumstances. To make Hobbes's teaching clear, Warrender distinguishes between the grounds, the conditions, and the instruments of obligation. As he interprets Hobbes, questions of security are conditions of obligation, and the covenant functions instrumentally to determine these conditions. Neither of these is the ground of obligation, which is the law of nature itself, known to reasonable beings.

Hobbes invites confusion, Warrender admits, when he says that natural law discoverable by each individual through reason remains a mere theorem until it becomes the command of the sovereign. If this statement be taken as strictly true, says Warrender, it puts Hobbes in the position of having to say that the law of nature which dictates keeping of covenants does not have the force of law until the sovereign, whose authority rests on the covenant, commands it. The argument is circular, and Hobbes's entire theory of sovereignty and of the obligation of subjects is left without foundation in reason. But other passages in Hobbes, notably those in which he holds that natural law is recognizably instituted by God for the government of creatures who are both rational and passionate, make it possible for Warrender to represent Hobbes's whole system as resting on a prior law of nature.

In working out his interpretation, Warrender finds it helpful to keep distinct what the individual is obliged to do and what he cannot be obliged to do. This is, roughly, the distinction between duties and rights, but Warrender gives it a new turn by suggesting that what one is obliged to do is prescribed by law, whereas what one cannot be obliged to do is determined by analysis of the concept of obligation. It is often pointed out that some rights are such that one person's right follows from other person's duties. Rights of this kind follow directly from some law. But other rights are merely exemptions from obligation. These rights, which Hobbes calls liberties, are implicit in the validating conditions under which obligations are known to hold, among which is the condition that the individual must have a sufficient motive to perform the action prescribed by the obligation—a condition which precludes a person's ever being obliged to act contrary to what he regards as his best interest, whether that be understood in a temporal sense as the preservation of one's life or in an eternal sense as the salvation of one's soul.

Gauthier, David P. *The Logic of Leviathan: The Moral and Political Theory of Thomas Hobbes*. Oxford: Clarendon Press, 1969.

Acknowledging that it was Howard Warrender's book which aroused his interest in Thomas Hobbes,

David P. Gauthier carries the analysis of Hobbes's argument to a new level of precision. Warrender is correct, according to this author, in maintaining that Hobbes's moral theory follows its own necessity, which is different from the causal necessity that governs his psychology. Nevertheless, Gauthier regards as hopelessly wrong-headed the attempt to show that Hobbes kept the two separate in working out his theory of the state.

What is required, and what Gauthier undertakes in this rewarding study, is an analysis which will show how far Hobbes's moral theory can be made to stand on its own foundation, and at what points it depends on the theory of human nature which he has taken such care to elaborate. His procedure is to work out two sets of definitions for ethical terms, one which he calls *formal*, the other *material*. For example, the formal definition of good, in Hobbes, is "an object of desire," whereas the material definition is "an object enhancing vital motion." After an initial chapter on Hobbes's doctrine of Man, the book is given over to the analysis first of his moral then of his political concepts, with a final chapter given to God and Divine Law. Obligation and authorization are taken as the basic concepts respectively of Hobbes's moral and political theories.

The formal definition of obligation, constructed by Gauthier from several passages in the *Leviathan*, turns on the negation involved in laying down one's right: "A has an obligation not to do X" means "A has laid down his right to do X." What strikes Gauthier as noteworthy is that by means of this definition Hobbes is able to explain how obligations emerge immediately in a situation where no prior obligation existed. "Covenants oblige necessarily," says Gauthier. Obligation is a human creation, and there is no need to look for some prior law of nature or divine command requiring that agreements be kept.

Material definitions, in Gauthier's account, flesh out the formal definitions by making clear what, in view of his nature and condition, man ought to do. Thus, a law of nature defined formally as "a precept laying down the requirements of reason" is defined materially as "a precept laying down what is required for preservation." Similarly, the material definition of obligation includes a prudential element, intimating that not all right can be given up and dictating that covenants must be combined with security.

With these definitions of obligation in hand, Gauthier is able to illuminate the problem which has preoccupied Hobbesian studies in recent times; namely, whether morality for Hobbes reduces to prudence. No one doubts that considerations of interest are the motives which lead Hobbesian man to assume obligations, although it would be wrong to infer from this that prudence enters the definition of "ought" even for Hobbes. What needs to be cleared up, however, is whether Hobbes thinks that there are other motives besides self-interest for fulfilling obligations which one has assumed. As Hobbes does not show that there are other motives, Gauthier concludes that his moral system is one of universal prudence.

In treating Hobbes's political philosophy, Gauthier proceeds in the same manner, giving both formal and material definitions for such terms as actor, author, sovereign, and subject. What is of interest here is that the central-notion, authorization, admits only of a formal definition, "that procedure by which one man gives the use of his right to another man," and that there is nothing in this definition which prevents authorization from being limited. It is only when the means of the sovereign to uphold covenants become a consideration that authorization is understood as a kind of blank check.

Additional Recommended Reading

Brown, Keith C., ed. *Hobbes Studies*. Cambridge, Massachusetts: Harvard University Press, 1965. Papers by contemporary scholars with various points of view.

Hood, F.C. *The Divine Politics of Thomas Hobbes*. Oxford: Clarendon Press, 1964. Interprets the *Leviathan* as a specifically Christian philosophy of the state.

Peters, Richard. *Hobbes*. Baltimore: Penguin Books, 1956. A readable introduction to the man and his work.

Strauss, Leo. *The Political Philosophy of Hobbes*. Translated by Elsa M. Sinclair. Chicago: University of Chicago Press, 1952. Traces the development of Hobbes's thought.

Watkins, J.W.N. *Hobbes's System of Ideas*. London: Hutchinson University Library, 1965. A study of the political significance of Hobbes's philosophical ideas.

PENSÉES

Author: Blaise Pascal (1623-1662)
Type of work: Theology
First published: 1670

Principal Ideas Advanced

There are two essential religious truths: there is a God, and there is a corruption of nature which makes men unworthy of him.

Reason is of little use in showing either the existence or the nature of God, but it does reveal man's finiteness and his separation from God.

It is a reasonable wager to stake everything on God's existence, for God either exists or he does not; if God is, then the man who believes in him wins everything, while if God is not, the man who believes in him suffers only a finite loss.

In knowing that he is miserable, man achieves greatness.

Since man's will is subject to his passions, it is important for men to obey custom simply because it is custom, and to obey the law in order to avoid sedition and rebellion.

Pascal's reflections on religion make up a large body of notes, written between 1654 and his death in 1662, intended to form a never-finished work to bear the title, *Apologie de la Religion Catholique*. Composed at different times after a moving mystical experience, the contents of the *Pensées* appeared in print posthumously. These reflections reveal Pascal as belonging to the group of fervently Christian writers who reject the usual claims of natural theology in order the more sharply to separate faith from reason.

Pascal's thought expresses the influence of the Jansenists, a seventeenth century Catholic order indebted to the theological views of John Calvin, one of the Protestant reformers. A group in conflict with the Jesuits, the Jansenists lived at Port Royal, near Paris, where they taught several central beliefs: man's total sinfulness, salvation through God's predestination, grace as sole means to salvation, and the need of the faithful to hold to a Christian belief which can never be proved by reason.

Though never an official member of the Jansenist community, Pascal visited them frequently (his sister belonged) and wrote in their defense in a bitter controversy with the Jesuits. Pascal was a brilliant mathematician as well as a religious writer, aware of the significant mathematical developments of his day. Living an austerely self-disciplined life, he gave away his wealth in an effort to exclude all pleasure and vanity from his practices.

The *Pensées* express numerous reflections concerning a few central themes. The Christian religion as known by Pascal teaches men two essential truths: "that there is a God, to whom men may attain, and that there is a corruption of nature which renders them unworthy of him." Pascal insists that if men deny either of these truths, they must fall into atheism, end up with the philosophers' god so popular among deistic thinkers of his time, or find themselves reduced to a complete pessimism. The Christian God worshiped by Pascal does not require a philosopher's proof of existence, and he writes, "It is a wonderful thing that no canonical author has ever made use of nature in order to prove God." Pascal argues that man's miserable state does not justify total pessimism for the reason that the God worshiped by Christians, as by Abraham, Isaac, and Jacob, is one of love and consolation.

Pascal claims that God becomes available to men only through the mediation of Jesus Christ. Although Pascal makes clear that man is a "thinking reed," man's thinking capacity can nevertheless function religiously only to make clear his absolute finiteness, his total separation from God's actual infinity. In writing about faith, Pascal stresses the utter uselessness of reason for religious purposes. "Faith is a gift of God," he insists. "Believe not that we said it is a gift of reason." Yet reason is never to be disparaged, since it performs its own important functions and provides the key to whatever dignity man may achieve.

Nevertheless, Pascal sometimes does come close to a kind of reasoning about God—as in his famous wager argument for belief in God's existence (although this argument was intended primarily for skeptics who deny the importance of religious belief). In another place Pascal treats the relation of man's miserable condition to his finitude in such a way that he gives something resembling an argument for the necessity of God's existence. This latter argument rests on the awareness that the "I" of Pascal is really a thought. Had Pascal's mother died before his birth, the "I" of Pascal would never have existed. The conclusion is that Pascal is clearly not a necessary being. Pascal sees also that he is neither eternal nor infinite. He asserts that "I see plainly that there is in nature one being who is necessary, eternal, and infinite." This approximation to one of the classical demonstrations of God's existence indicates that Pascal was more concerned to argue that proofs cannot induce one to accept the Christian faith than to claim that proofs are unqualifiedly impossible of formulation. Such proofs, even if possible, turn out to be religiously useless and unimportant.

Pascal contends that men know *that* there is a God without knowing *what* God is. (In this claim he is inconsistent; he also asserts in one place that man can never *know* God's existence.) He insists that men also can know there is an infinite while remaining ignorant of its nature. Numbers cannot be brought to an end. This means simply that men can never mention a number which is the last one. So number must be infinite. Similarly, aware of the infinite's existence and unable to know its nature, men fail to know God's

nature and existence because God lacks extension and limits. Men have absolutely no correspondence with the God which Christians worship in faith. The Christians who refuse to give reasons for their faith are essentially right, according to Pascal. They present their God as a "foolishness" to a world which often complains because the Christians cannot prove this God's existence. Some critics reasonably criticize Christians for holding beliefs which are beyond proof. Pascal attempts to reply to these critics by arguing that it is reasonable to believe. This he does primarily by producing his famous wager argument.

The stakes are clear, in Pascal's view. "God is, or He is not." The agnostic can argue that, since reason is unable to decide the issue, one need make no choice either way. Pascal insists that this will not do—that men must wager. They must choose. "It is not optional; you are committed to it." Pascal claims that men own two things as stakes in such a wager: their reason and their will (blessedness). They have two things to lose: the true and the good. Man's nature involves also two things to avoid: error and misery. Now, according to Pascal, since reason is unable to make the decision, the issue must turn on man's blessedness. How is this to be decided? The answer is that if man wagers on God's existence, he stands to win everything, losing nothing. Thus, to wager for God's existence means either the possibility of finite loss (if God does not exist) or infinite gain (if God does exist). Man's wager stakes a possibility of finite loss against one of infinite gain; namely, happiness. Man can therefore make only one wager—that God does exist.

What Pascal set out to prove was not that God exists, but that men *ought to believe* in God's existence. Once made, however, the wager does not necessarily bring one to the Christian God, as Pascal was clearly aware. Yet the wager is a fruitful beginning. The doubter who makes the wager can still use the possible way of "seeing through the game" associated with the reading and study of Scripture. He can also seek to control his passions. In this present life the man who wagers will be better off for having made the wager. Such a man will be driven to associate with others who have already been cured of their malady. Like them, he must act as if he believed.

According to Pascal, no harm can come to such a man, for he will be "faithful, honest, humble, grateful, benevolent, a sincere and true friend."

To read Pascal as if he sought to debase the functions of human reason would be to read him wrongly. Because reason is incapable of knowing what God is does not alter the fact that man's greatness is tied to reason. Pascal insists that thought is not derived from body. Thought is its own kind of entity. Reason alone permits man to know the misery which marks his condition, but this very knowledge accounts for his dignity: "To be miserable is to know one's self to be so, but to know one's self to be miserable is to be great." Only man can possess this kind of knowledge which is denied to the other elements in nature. What makes Christianity the solely adequate religion, in Pascal's view, is that Christianity teaches the otherwise peculiar doctrine that man's misery and his greatness are inseparable. Men need to come to terms with their miserable condition, though they cannot fundamentally alter it. This gives both men and religion something important to accomplish. The central religious problem is to learn to control the human will rather than to pile up theological knowledge by reasoning. To cure pride, lust, and ego-centered aggressiveness remains the fundamental task of the Christian religion.

Concern about human willfulness occurs in numerous passages in the *Pensées*. Unlike the reasoning powers, the will operates according to man's perspective. Man finds himself in bondage to his passions. For this reason, custom is a most important necessity of any possible social existence. Against Montaigne, Pascal argued that men should obey custom simply because it is custom and not because it is reasonable. Men should also obey law as law in order to avoid sedition and rebellion. Pascal insists that classical philosophers such as Plato and Aristotle wrote about politics with many reservations. "If they wrote of politics, it was as if to regulate a hospital for madmen." Pascal could not believe that such men thought reasoning about politics the most serious business of life.

Though he understood the limited possibilities of reasoning, Pascal never degraded reason. Reasoning allows men to encircle the universe in certain ways,

but "instinct" and "the heart" are essential allies. "How few demonstrated things there are!" Pascal laments in one place. Men are as much automata as minds. No one should ridicule custom in view of this fact. Agreeing with a philosopher such as David Hume, Pascal says it is custom which permits men to believe that tomorrow will dawn and that men must die. Custom influences men to act, while reason directs only the mind. Habit, including religious practice, remains a routine needed in every day and age. "We have to acquire an easier credence,—that of habit,—which without violence, art, or argument, makes us believe things and inclines all our powers to this belief, so that our mind falls into it naturally." Pascal claims that life would be easier for men if reason were unnecessary; but since nature has not so arranged matters, men need to supplement intuited first principles with limited demonstrations.

Pascal makes a distinction between knowledge and judgment. For example, geometry is a matter of the mind, while subtlety is a function of intuition. Men must judge things either literally or spiritually. Honoring reason, men should accept its limits, knowing what it can and cannot accomplish. Although there is criticism of the Pyrrhonists (skeptics) for some of their beliefs, Pascal shows that he was favorably disposed to a partial skepticism concerning the powers of reason. Men can at most achieve a "learned ignorance." Different from the natural ignorance of all men at birth, a learned ignorance is gained by a few "lofty souls who, having traversed all human knowledge, find that they know nothing. . . ." This is a self-aware ignorance. Between these two kinds of ignorance dwell the great numbers of the intelligent who "disturb the world and judge wrongly of everything." Genuine philosophers are those who learn how to laugh at philosophy.

The imagination and human sickness are two important elements which shape man's constant susceptibility to deception. The wisest men can hope only to modify, never to eradicate these two sources of illusion. Man tends naturally towards wrong judgment. He finds it difficult, if not impossible, to escape the binding conditions of his own vanity. His actions are motivated by self-love. What makes the Christian view of Incarnation important is the radical cure it suggests for man's pridefulness. Men must hate religion as long as it teaches what it must—that the misery of man is objective and absolutely ineradicable except by God's grace. This side of Pascal's thought shows a relation to the long tradition in Western thought concerned with the numerous psychological and cultural obstacles in the way of genuine discovery of self-knowledge. These obstacles are, for Pascal, as much connected with the human will as with the mind. It is as if men want, in some deep and buried way, to judge things wrongly.

Pascal mentions atheism and deism as the greatest competitors of a genuine Christian faith. He understands how atheism may be a mark of a strong intellect, though only up to a point. The atheist has blind spots when he comes, say, to the notion of immortality. Pascal asks why the atheist should deny dogmatically the possibility that a man might rise from the dead. He wants to know which is the more remarkable—that a living being should appear at all, or that a once-living being should be reborn. By custom the atheist accepts the fact that there are living beings and then seems astounded by the religious notion of rebirth. Here the atheist puzzles Pascal. On the other hand, the deist seeks to know God without revelation, meaning without the mediation of Jesus Christ. The deist thus misunderstands Christianity, ending with the philosopher's God of proofs and first principles rather than with the God of redemption. Pascal clearly aligns himself with those who assert that the Christian faith cannot fully be translated into philosophical terms.

Affirmation of the original sin of all men is a necessity for Pascal. The evidence for this affirmation is that all men are born disposed to seek their own interests, a disposition which runs counter to the necessary conditions of order. Wars and revolutions arise from the individual's pursuit of self-interest even when his reason tells him that he should attend to the needs of a commonwealth. Men should usually seek the general as opposed to the particular interests of a community, but most often they do not. Facts like these Pascal takes as indicative of some basic flaw in human willing. The glory of the Christian religion stems from its insistence on man's inherent sinfulness. "No religion but ours has taught that man is born

in sin," Pascal writes; "no sect of philosophers has affirmed it, therefore none has spoken the truth." This dark doctrine, so stressed by Pascal and borrowed from contemporary Calvinism, helped to bring him into disrepute among the Jesuits, who thought he emphasized it disproportionately. Yet he was quite aware of the nonrational nature of this doctrine and made no effort to prove it.

What makes Pascal's *Pensées* an enduring work is the classical manner in which one aspect of the Christian tradition in theology receives forceful and passionate presentation. Its confessional and personal nature also makes it a work which can help individuals who, like Pascal, find themselves caught up in a struggle to make sense of Christian faith once they have abandoned belief that natural proofs of God's existence are possible. One-sided in emphasis, Pascal's work tries to show that Christian faith is reasonable on its own terms even though not susceptible of rational proofs divorced from reasons of the heart. No matter how extremely emphasized, Pascal's views about the depravity of the will help to counterbalance the more optimistic humanistic conceptions of human perfectibility.

Through the *Pensées* runs a sense of the fragility of human life—a constant reminder of something most men know when they think about it but which they often wish to forget. A sense of the contingency of life, of uncertainty about its duration, pervades Pascal's writings. A mystical sense that there is more to finite existence than meets the finite eye drives Pascal to fall back on intuition and feeling when reason proves unable to establish the kinds of certainty many religious persons hope to find.

Pascal's portrait of man's misery involves a kind of metaphysical sickness. Reasoning man is caught between the finite and an infinite whose nature he can never hope to fathom. He owns a will to self-deception, marked by an endless pursuit of means by which to divert attention from this very fact. On the other hand, a critic may well say that Pascal is too much a puritanical thinker—unwilling or unable to point out the genuinely redeeming features of natural processes. The Pascalian picture of man illustrates the more somber side of puritan thought and feeling. "Imagine a number of men in chains, and all condemned to death, of whom every day some are butchered in sight of the others, those remaining seeing their own fate in that of their fellows, regarding each other with grief and despair while awaiting their turn; this is a picture of the condition of man."

Obviously, some of Pascal's thoughts reflect events of his own biography. He shunned pleasure and picked up the radically austere notions of the Jansenists. Nevertheless, his version of Christian faith remains a recurring theme in the long, unresolved competition between those who argue for a natural theology and those others who insist that revelation is not to be explained in philosophical terms. Pascal's *Pensées* is the expression of a troubled man who seemed to need this specific version of Christian faith to find life itself a meaningful affair. Man's very misery made sense out of the Christian promise, according to Pascal. Unlike many other writers, Pascal attempted to live according to his beliefs. Many men in the twentieth century, including those who would disagree with Pascal, are finding that to live according to one's beliefs is no small achievement.

Pertinent Literature

Broome, J. H. *Pascal*. London: E. Arnold, 1965.

The two central chapters (VI and VII) of J. H. Broome's work on the life and thought of Blaise Pascal are concerned specifically with the *Pensées*. We are presented with a detailed and solid interpretation of the lasting significance of Pascal's most famous work. Broome's main concern is to capture the spirit of Pascal's religious enterprise and to communicate it to the reader in whatever way he can. Such an enterprise implies that some of the textual problems long associated with the *Pensées* must be overlooked in the conviction that even if an authoritative and complete version of the work had been passed down to us, the central issues involving the structure and spirit of Pascal's religious thought would to some extent have remained beneath the surface, necessitating the kind of interpretative approach Broome sees himself carrying out here.

Broome begins his analysis by suggesting that we think of the *Pensées* as a record of a rescue operation, a literary attempt to save not persons or groups of persons but humanity in general, threatened through original sin with the loss of the hope for redemption. Thus, the *Pensées* is to be seen primarily as the work of a devoted and ingenious thinker trying desperately to capture the attention of an audience assailed by contemporary freethinking and somehow at least to point them in the direction of possible salvation. Broome argues that the major division of the *Pensées* into the nontheological first part in which Pascal presents a series of arguments in dialectical form (including the celebrated Wager argument) and the second traditional part in which most of the arguments are based on Scripture (and in which Pascal's fundamentalism is strongest), arises naturally from an intention first to break down the defenses of the skeptic and then to strike home with the evidence and arguments from Scripture. While Broome acknowledges that this picture of Pascal's plan in the *Pensées* tends to oversimplify and even formalize it, the picture is in the long run most satisfactory, expressing as it does the *charitable* spirit of the whole enterprise, an enterprise Broome understands to be a product of the intellectual structure of the work on the one hand, and of the work as a dynamic but practical undertaking in charity (a work of the heart) on the other. Broome also considers it to be Pascal's own view that the structures are not incompatible and that the stronger the intellectual structure is the stronger and more efficient the work of charity will be.

Ultimately, however, Broome concludes that Pascal's fragments fail to convince many people who are not already convinced; although Broome asserts that what really matters with respect to the reader's reaction to the *Pensées* is that there be *some* response, since Pascal himself recognized that even a hostile reaction is better than no reaction at all. Furthermore, Broome is at pains to point out that although Pascal seems at times to hold out little hope for the majority of mankind, the contemporary impression of him as a philosopher of *angoisse* (thanks in part to his being treated as a forerunner of existentialism) must be resisted. The *Pensées* is not a philosophy of despair without any consolation whatsoever, for the wretchedness of man's natural state can be contained and transcended by a recognition of the order of the heart (love, charity), the third and supernatural order. To reach the point in our spiritual lives where it becomes possible to recognize this third order (the first two orders being mind and body) and to accept grace is, for most, a lifelong task. Man must first recognize that he is sick and must be cured. The *Pensées* is rife with this sort of tragic imagery—man is a prisoner of his own selfishness; he is balanced precariously between infinity and nothingness; man is walking a plank over a precipice—in short, man is in a predicament. Broome emphasizes Pascal's sense of man's disorientation and lack of perspective and sees it as providing the *Pensées* with the urgency to get on with the business of salvation.

Accepting that man is indeed in Pascal's predicament (and Broome never questions this premise), how *practically* is man to extricate himself and initiate the push toward salvation? At this point Broome introduces the analogy of a bridging operation to explain what in effect is Pascal's theory of the Three Orders. Broome postulates two structures of evidence used by Pascal in the *Pensées*: evidence from nature and evidence from Scripture. The two independent structures support each other by a counterpoise effect, thus producing at the center and out of instability a fragile yet provisional stability. It is not a bridge that can be walked on, for only the center is stable; the only way to proceed is upwards from the center.

To clarify the analogy: man is in a natural state of wretchedness; this is his predicament. The proper use of reason and instinct—human ingenuity—can take man only so far along the road to possible salvation, but the completion of the rescue depends in the end not on anything we can do through the use of reason and instinct. Only the operation of grace in human lives can save man from himself, from his own nature; and such grace in turn appears to be only partially the result of our own efforts (through prayer, for example), although Broome is quick to state that Pascal was himself unclear on the point. The operation of grace is the province of the third and supernatural order, the order Pascal adds to the traditional two orders of mind (reason) and body (instinct).

There are obvious problems with an analogy of this sort, and Broome does raise some of them. On what in real life is the bridge structure of the analogy based? The answer, according to Broome, is that the structure is indeed a structure in the void, and for Pascal this corresponds with the Spirit of God, his love and his grace. It is as if Pascal were suggesting that this is how man experiences the void.

Once man's ingenuity has taken him as far as he can go (as in the Wager argument where Pascal constructs an argument to show that our self-interest must impel us to wager for God's existence since we have almost everything to gain and only our wretchedness to lose), he is, so to speak, left hanging in the void, for whatever belief he can summon forth is based only on intellectual assent (rather than its coming from the heart). The rescue (and the bridge) can be completed only by turning toward God through Christ, and this is possible only by appeal to the Scriptures and by constant prayer. Indeed, Broome suggests that Pascal, in the second part of the *Pensées*, comes to treat prayer as the one way in which a certain relationship with God can be built up. We can thus approach a relationship, or possible contact with, God; but of this there can be no guarantee. For Pascal, such a possibility (which is supernatural) must ultimately depend on the intuitions of the heart for those who endure the struggle to the end.

Krailsheimer, A. J. *Pascal*. Past Masters Series. Oxford: Oxford University Press, 1980.

The central thesis of A. J. Krailsheimer's study of Blaise Pascal is that the apparently radically different phases of Pascal's life actually form a coherent whole and, most important, that the *Pensées* could only have been produced by someone who had lived just such a life. In brief, Pascal's unusual life and the *Pensées* are essentially and intimately connected. Krailsheimer argues that Pascal's early work in science, mathematics, and technology is crucially important for a full understanding and proper appreciation of the *Pensées* because it is in the early work that Pascal developed the patterns of thought and the intellectual habits which were to inform much of his later work in religion. Easily the most significant and influential of these early developments is the tripartite theory of knowledge—Pascal's continual recognition of the three ways to truth and knowledge (mind, body, and heart), so radically opposed to René Descartes' dualism of mind and matter. It is this conception of knowledge and truth which eventually links up with the famous Three Orders of the *Pensées*.

For Krailsheimer the concept of the Three Orders is central to the *Pensées* and to an understanding of the interdependence of Pascal's work on mathematics, science, morality, and religion. In rejecting the dualism of mind and body (whether it be Descartes', Michel de Montaigne's, or Plato's) Krailsheimer argues that Pascal was rejecting the supremacy of either the body (impulse) or the mind (reason) in man's nature, and was at the same time recognizing the need for a third order which would allow human beings to overcome the inadequacies of their existence imposed by a slavish submission to the first two orders. The third order, variously described by Pascal in the *Pensées* as the order of the heart or the order of charity, is the order through which we can be moved by the grace of God acting through Christ. Through grace the heart can be turned or inclined upward to charity and the life of the spirit (recognizing Christ as the savior) or downward to the life of the flesh. In this way, the heart can affect (and ultimately ground) the operations of the mind so that the mind can be put to its proper use, which it would not do of its own accord because it is by nature corrupt. Here we come up against an important aspect of Krailsheimer's view of the *Pensées*. Krailsheimer wishes to maintain that although the *Pensées* represents a rejection of the claims of rationalism with respect to man's ends, it would be a serious error to see this as a wholesale rejection of reason (as has been done). Pascal does not reject reason itself so much as its misuse; indeed, intended as they were for the freethinkers of the seventeenth century, the *Pensées* would have to make an appeal to reason and to satisfy its basic requirements if Pascal were to entertain any hope that these fragments would win over his carefully selected audience. Thus in the *Pensées*, Krailsheimer declares, Pascal employs his own form of dialectical argument to exemplify his theory of the Three Orders, which is designed not to rest on any particular conclusion (for the dialectic never stops at any stage) but to persuade gradually by a continuous appeal to the problems of real life. The *Pensées*, it must be remembered, was meant to communicate not a set of doctrines but a way of life that could possibly lead to God. Each of the orders must be used as it was meant to be used, leading to the emergence of a clear hierarchy of excellence wherein faith is experienced as the outcome of God turning our hearts rather than persuading our minds. It follows, according to Krailsheimer, that all rational arguments for the existence of God are totally irrelevant to true Christianity, founded as it is on faith and divine grace. Reason can (and indeed must) strive to explain natural phenomena; but faith and the "heart" belong to the third and most important order, the supernatural. Thus the importance of the proper use of the Three Orders.

Krailsheimer is adamant that the *Pensées* does not form a linear argument. The dialectic is the dominant form of argument: two contradictory positions are stated—usually two contradictory truths about man. Pascal then proceeds to show that the contradiction can be resolved only by a third position which contains and yet transcends the other two. Despite the dialectic, however, the *Pensées* does presuppose that one accept a fundamental premise about the nature of man: that man without God is wretched. The problem here, as Krailsheimer is quick to point out, is that one could just as easily construct a case which would show no less convincingly that happiness is the natural state of man. In any case, Pascal's argument for the wretchedness of man's natural state rests on his conception of man as a creature constituted by two opposing powers or orders, reason and instinct. Whether the one or the other is thought to be man's natural state, it is impossible for man to escape his wretchedness.

The only solution lies in the awareness of a third order, an order outside both reason and instinct. The paradox that man reveals a mixture of skepticism and dogmatism, of reason and instinct, is shown to be the dualism of grace and corruption, of greatness and wretchedness. Man, once knowing happiness, fell into (original) sin so that he is now in the hopeless and agonizing position of continuously striving to retrieve the lost state of grace. If man had never known it, he would have no need to search for it. The only possible solution, the only means of transcending this dualism, is to listen to God and accept his grace; thus the third order transcends the first two. The refusal to submit and accept grace (humility) results in natural selfishness, with each man left to himself.

Krailsheimer presents a lively and comprehensive commentary on the three central themes of the *Pensées*: the theory of orders, with the supernatural order overcoming the natural orders of mind and body; the need for individual men to see themselves as part of a historical process, the most important aspect of which is the fall from grace into original sin; and the crippling effect of the failure to overcome one's natural limitations and selfishness. Inevitably, however (and Krailsheimer does not shy away from this difficulty), the weakest element in the scheme of the *Pensées* is the historical evidence advanced for the truth of Christianity. Pascal thought it absolutely crucial that there be a first Adam. Pascal was, in effect, a fundamentalist, and this attitude does indeed show itself rather disturbingly throughout the *Pensées*. Nevertheless, Pascal's conversion to fundamentalism in no way altered his acquired scientific approach, his respect for facts, and his intellectual openness.

Pascal's third order, the order of faith, charity, and ultimately of divine love, was, according to Krailsheimer, meant to be understood as the only possible escape from wretchedness. By acknowledging his wretchedness, man becomes humble and thus acquires true pride; above all, by freeing himself of his own inadequacy, he submits to the love of God, looking upward instead of inward.

Additional Recommended Reading

Adam, Antoine. *Grandeur and Illusion* . London: Weidenfeld and Nicolson, 1972. A translation of the very good *Histoire de la littérature française au XVIIe siècle,* II, Paris: Del Duca, 1962. The English version is much abbreviated but nevertheless supplies an excellent picture of the literary, philosophical, and social background of the age.

Mesnard, Jean. *Les Pensées de Pascal.* Paris: Societe d'édition d'enseignement Supérieur, 1976. An admirable analysis of text and background.

_____. *Pascal, His Life and Works.* New York: Philosophical Library, 1952. A solid general book.

Miel, Jean. *Pascal and Theology.* Baltimore: Johns Hopkins University Press, 1969. This book is very useful on specific technical issues.

ETHICS

Author: Benedictus de Spinoza (1632-1677)
Type of work: Ethics, theology
First published: 1677

Principal Ideas Advanced

Whatever is the cause of itself exists necessarily.
Only substance is self-caused, free, and infinite; and God is the only substance.
God exists necessarily, and is possessed of infinite attributes.
But only two of God's infinite attributes are known to us: thought and extension.
Since thought and extension are features of the same substance, whatever happens to body happens also to mind as another phase of the same event.
A false idea is an idea improperly related to God; by achieving adequate ideas we become adequate causes of the body's modifications: this is human freedom, freedom from the human bondage to the passions.
The highest virtue of the mind is to know God.

Spinoza's *Ethics* is a truly amazing work. In a field which is subject to great differences of opinion, it has always been recognized as a classic by people of most diverse interests. While other philosophers come and go in popularity, Spinoza maintains a stable place, always attracting the interest of serious students. He did not write a great deal, and of his works, few receive much attention except the *Ethics*. It stands as a single work exacting a place of influence usually reserved for a more extensive collection of philosophical writings.

The figure of Spinoza has often attracted as much attention as his work, and he stands, along with Socrates, as one of the few genuine heroes in a field not much given to hero worship. A Jew, ostracized by his own people and excluded from his homeland, he insisted on following his own ideas despite their heretical tendencies. Moreover, the *Ethics* remained unpublished in Spinoza's lifetime. Upon this single posthumous work his great reputation and reservoir of influence depend. Hegel and many of the later romantics acknowledge Spinoza as the modern thinker whose thought suggests the direction for their later developments.

Widespread interest in Spinoza remains even today, despite his central theological orientation and the recent unfashionability of such an approach. Many men who find traditional religious beliefs unacceptable discover in Spinoza a rational and a naturalistic form of religion. His views on God, man, and the human emotions have widespread popular influence. Although Spinoza is sometimes called "the philosophers' philosopher" because of the abstract and technical nature of the *Ethics*, it is still true that few philosophers' general views are more widely known than are his among the nonphilosophical public. It is true that his views are often oversimplified, but it is also true that they are circulated extensively.

A great deal of argument has been generated by the style or form in which Spinoza chose to write the *Ethics*. The Continental Rationalists (Descartes, Leibniz, and Spinoza) were all much impressed by the exciting developments in mathematics, and all of them reflect something of the geometric temper in their writings. Spinoza elected to write the *Ethics* as a geometrical system— definitions, axioms, propositions, and all. Some argue that this form is essential to Spinoza's doctrines; others feel that the *Ethics* can just as easily be read in essay style. All seem agreed that the work does not really have the full deductive rigor of geometry; yet the form indicates Spinoza's desire to be clear and simple in his expression, to be straightforward in his assertions, and to connect the various parts of his thought systematically. All this he achieves with the barest minimum of explanation and with little external reference.

Fortunately we do not need to understand fully Spinoza's own attitude toward this geometrical method of philosophizing, or to appraise its success, in order to grasp the central features of Spinoza's thought. It is true that the geometrical method represents an attempted revolution in philosophical thought. In his unfinished *On the Improvement of the Understanding,* Spinoza agreed with the other modern revolutionaries of his era in stressing methodology and the need for a thorough reexamination of traditional philosophical and theological methods. His break with the scholastic method of the *Summas* is complete. Spinoza firmly believed that the human intellect can be carefully examined and improved and thereby made able to produce a more rigorous and more complete understanding of things—all this through its own strengthened power.

Properly corrected, reason is self-sufficient, its own guide and its own judge. And this is, for Spinoza, as true in ethical affairs as in speculative matters. He does not belong in the class of dogmaticians; there is no indication that he believed his own views to be either complete or final. What is evident is his trust in the human intellect to work out an acceptable and a comprehensive schema. Spinoza depended heavily on previous theological views, but his modern temperament transformed them by placing them in a new humanistic perspective.

The five parts of the *Ethics* take up in order God, the nature and origin of the mind, then the emotions, and finally the twin questions of human bondage and human freedom. In beginning with a consideration of the divine nature, and then developing all other theories in this light, Spinoza was influenced by medieval theology. Theory of knowledge and attention to human powers of knowing received a more prominent place with Spinoza, but systematically speaking a theory of the divine nature is still first. Spinoza called his first principle sometimes God,

sometimes substance. Aristotle had defined "substance" as that capable of independent existence. Spinoza interpreted this with absolute rigor and asserted that only God, a substance of infinite attributes, could fulfill this definition exactly.

The *Ethics* opens with the traditional distinction between that which requires no external cause to account for its existence (cause of itself) and that which owes its existence (causally) to another being. That which is the cause of itself exists necessarily and needs nothing other than itself to be conceived. This Spinoza calls substance. On the other hand, what is finite is what is capable of being limited by another thing of its own kind, whereas substance is absolutely infinite, in that it possesses infinite attributes.

Spinoza defines an "attribute" as that which the mind sees as constituting the essence of substance. A "mode" is some modification of substance. "Freedom" means to exist from the necessity of one's own nature alone (only substance as cause of itself fulfills this requirement) and to be set in action by oneself alone. Only substance, or God, is perfectly free, dependent on nothing else for its existence or action; it is absolutely infinite and thus one of a kind.

From here Spinoza turns to a classical definition of knowledge: we can say we know something only when we understand it through its causes. After this he begins his famous proof that there could be only one substance which would be absolutely infinite and thus be its own cause. These "proofs" are simply a modern version of the traditional arguments for God's existence, although in the *Ethics* they take a novel form. The burden of Spinoza's point is that either nothing exists or else a substance absolutely infinite exists. Something does exist, and the presence of such an absolutely infinite substance precludes the existence of more than one such, and it includes everything else as part of itself.

Since God, or substance, consists of infinite attributes, each one of which expresses eternal and infinite essence, God necessarily exists and excludes the existence of anything else not a part of it. Spinoza goes on to argue that such a substance cannot be divided, nor can the existence of a second such substance even be conceived. From this Spinoza turns to the statement of perhaps his most famous doctrine: whatever is, is in God, and nothing can either be or be conceived without God. Popularly this belief is called "pantheism," but such a doctrine (that the world taken as a whole is God) is too simple to express Spinoza's view. It is not enough to say that the natural order as a whole is God, for what really is true is that Spinoza takes all of the usual transcendental qualities of a traditional God and, combining them with the natural order, calls the sum of these God or substance absolutely infinite.

Spinoza's famous doctrine of the infinite attributes of God is easy proof against a simple label of pantheism. In addition to God's infinity in each kind (in thought and extension), Spinoza posits an infinity of attributes as belonging to God, only two of which (thought and extension) are known directly in our natural world. Thus God, as Spinoza conceives him, is infinitely larger than our natural order, since the world we are familiar with actually represents only a very small part of his vast nature. This is a speculative doctrine, as intriguing as it is baffling.

Since everything must be conceived through, and has its existence in, God, the knowledge of any natural event requires a reference to the divine nature. It is for this reason that Spinoza begins the *Ethics* with a discussion of God's nature, since the understanding of everything else, including man's ethical life, depends upon this. Nothing can be understood in isolation, and all adequate understanding involves locating the particular events and their immediate causes within the larger scheme of a substance absolutely infinite. God in traditional theology was used to explain the natural world as a whole; now every phenomenon is to be seen as a part of him and is to be explained on a part-whole analogy. What it is true to say about the divine nature, then, is also in some sense true of every part of the natural world.

Nothing remains unrealized in such a divine nature. Infinite numbers of things in infinite ways will all become real in the course of time, and time is without beginning or end. Rejecting medieval theories of creation, Spinoza returned to a more classical view of the world as eternal. The natural order is equal in duration with God. One side of his nature is timeless, but the side which includes the natural order is temporal. Time applies to God, but only to one aspect. And there are no alternatives to any natural fact, since infinite possibilities will all be realized eventually. God's existence is necessary and so is his production of the natural order as a part of his nature.

Although this production of the natural order is necessary and its pattern without alternative, nothing outside God's own nature compels him to act, and in that sense God's activity is free. Yet God is absolutely the only genuinely free agent; in nature there is nothing contingent, but everything is determined necessarily in whole or in part by factors and causes outside its own nature. "Will" had been stressed as a causal agent by Duns Scotus; again Spinoza reverts to a more classical doctrine and denies that will can be a free cause. Will, he says, is nothing other than reason's tendency to recognize and to accept a true idea. Things could have been produced, by God or by man, in no other manner and in no other order than they are and were.

In the Appendix to Book I, which contains the discussion of God's nature as it includes the world as a part, Spinoza goes on to elaborate his famous refutation of teleology. Christian doctrine necessarily depicts God as acting to achieve certain ends, or otherwise the drama of sin, atonement, and salvation would be difficult to present. God acts to accomplish his purpose, according to the orthodox conception. All of this Spinoza denied. According to the *Ethics*, thought is only one of God's infinite attributes, so that although he is a personal being in some sense, he is so only in part. Will has been denied and thought is not dominant; such a being cannot be said to act purposefully to attain an end unachievable without his conscious action. What happens in nature is simply the necessary outpouring of the divine, absolutely infinite substance, to which there is no alternative conceivable. Although Spinoza's first principle is different, he is very close to the traditional Neoplatonic theories of the necessary (although good) emanation of the world from God.

In Book II, Spinoza begins to trace the nature and the origin of the mind, one of the infinite things which necessarily follow from the nature of God. Although the mind is only one attribute among an infinite number, Spinoza readily admits that it concerns us most and is vitally important for ethical conduct. First he must distinguish between an idea (a concept of the mind) and an adequate idea (one which has all the internal signs of a true idea). Such a distinction is extremely important, since from it will come the whole of the later ethical theory.

For more traditional thought, God alone was considered perfect and all the natural order somehow less perfect (as is implied by a doctrine of original sin). Spinoza takes a radical position here and actually equates reality with perfection. This departure is perfectly understandable. Nothing in nature has an alternative or can be different from what it is, and all things are a part of God and follow necessarily from his nature. God could not be complete without the whole natural order. Thus, it is logical that each part of God (each aspect of the natural order) should be just as perfect as it is real.

Then Spinoza turns to another radical idea: God is extended, or material things are a part of his nature. Christian views had to make God responsible for the creation of the physical world, but none had made God himself material even in part. Within Spinoza's view, the material world is no longer somehow less perfect, and so it can be made a part of God without lessening his perfection.

And every material thing has an idea paralleling it, although ideas affect only other ideas and physical things affect only things physical. The attribute of extension is reflected fully in the attribute of thought, although the two are only parallel and do not intersect each other. Substance thinking and substance extended are one and the same substance, now comprehended under this attribute, now under that. Nothing can happen in the body which is not perceived by the mind, and the essence of man consists of certain modifications of the attributes of God. We perceive all things through God, although some perceptions may be confused.

How is such confusion as does arise to be corrected? All ideas, insofar as they are related to God, are true. Thus, correct understanding means to take the idea and to place it in its proper locus within the divine nature, rather than to treat it as an independent phenomenon. No idea in itself is false; it is simply improperly related to other ideas if it is confused. For instance, men are sometimes deceived in thinking

themselves to be free, but this simply reflects their ignorance of the total causal chain within the divine nature of which their actions are a part. When actions are viewed in isolation, such confusion is possible, although no idea in itself is false.

It is the nature of reason to perceive things under a certain form of eternity and to consider them as necessary. Temporal viewpoints and a belief in contingency simply reflect an unimproved reason, unable to assume its natural viewpoint. For the human mind is actually able to possess an adequate knowledge of the eternal and infinite essence of God. In many previous theological views, the human mind was thought incapable of comprehending God. For Spinoza the human mind is to be seen as a part of the divine intellect, and as such it has within its own nature the possibility for grasping the whole of the divine mind, although to do so requires a great deal of effort.

When Book III begins to discuss the emotions, we begin what ordinarily we would call the ethical part of the work proper. Even here, however, Spinoza's approach is not standard; he claims that no one before has determined both the nature and the strength of the emotions or has treated the vices and follies of men in a geometrical method. And the emotions (hatred, anger, envy) follow from the same necessity as do all other things in nature. Aristotle and others thought that conduct was not amenable to scientific knowledge, but Spinoza's natural necessity, plus the connection of every event with the divine nature, subjects the emotions to the same laws as those which govern all natural phenomena.

Spinoza says that we act when we are the adequate cause of anything; we suffer when we are the cause only partially. An emotion is a modification of the body's power to act. The emotion is an action and the body's power is increased when we are the adequate cause of the modification; the emotion is passive and the body's power of acting is decreased when we are only partially the cause. Our mind acts when it has adequate ideas; it suffers necessarily when it has inadequate ideas.

The law of existence, Spinoza tells us, is that everything should do its utmost to persevere in its own mode of being. This striving is the very essence of every living thing. We feel "joy" when we are able to pass to a higher state of being; we feel "sorrow" when through passivity and suffering we pass to a lower state. Joy, sorrow, and desire are the primary emotions. Love attaches to the things which give us joy (an active and a higher existence); hatred attaches to what gives us sorrow (a passive and a lowered existence). Naturally we endeavor to support those things which cause joy, and just as naturally we tend to destroy whatever we imagine causes us sorrow. Love can overcome hatred and thus increase our joy, and Spinoza recommends that we attempt to return love for hate for that reason. On the other hand, Spinoza feels that the traditional Christian virtue of humility produces impotence and sorrow and is to be avoided for that reason.

Spinoza is often thought of as an unrestrained optimist concerning the powers of human reason, but his treatment of human bondage in Book IV should correct any such impression. In one of the longest books in the *Ethics*, Spinoza outlines in detail the inevitable causes which bind men to the blindness of their emotions and work against any attempted liberation. Good and evil are defined here as, respectively, what is useful to us and what hinders us from possessing something good. Appetite is what causes us to do anything, and virtue and power are defined as being the same thing. Here we have a classical definition of a naturalistic ethical theory.

If our only virtue is whatever power we possess naturally, and if good means only what is useful to us, what on earth could bind men? Spinoza says that there is no individual thing in nature not surpassed in strength and power by some other thing, which means that our power is always threatened and our current well-being always subject to loss. Other things are stronger than we are and continually challenge our powers, which places us in bondage to the passive emotions (sorrow) which necessarily accompany any such threat. The force which we have at our disposal is limited and is infinitely surpassed by the power of external causes. We suffer insofar as we find ourselves to be merely a part of nature surpassed in power and thus threatened by the other parts.

An emotion can be restrained or removed only by an opposed and stronger emotion. Thus our ability to withstand the pressures around us, to prevent sorrow, depends upon our natural power to oppose the emotions surrounding us with an equal vigor. Such a task never ceases and any victory is constantly in danger of being reversed in a weak or lax moment. Yet the highest virtue of the mind is said to be to know God. Why? Simply because such knowledge renders our ideas more adequate; and, as our ideas become more adequate, our power of action is increased. Men disagree as far as their ideas are disturbed by emotions; when guided by reason they tend to understand and thus to agree.

In Book V Spinoza turns finally to an appraisal of the powers of the intellect which make it free, since freedom comes only through the possibility of increased understanding. The primary fact upon which he bases his hope for human freedom is that an emotion which is a passion, and thus destructive of our power, ceases to be a passion as soon as we form a clear idea of it. Thus, we cannot prevent the constant challenge to our power to continue our existence, but we can come to understand all the causes which play upon us. To the extent to which we understand the causes impinging on us, just to that extent we can successfully oppose any threat to our freedom or our power.

There is nothing of which we cannot, theoretically speaking, form an adequate idea, including of course God himself. The way toward increasing freedom is open and is identical with an increased understanding. Such striving toward an increase of our understanding has for its object all or part of God. This is the highest effort of the mind and its highest virtue, since it is the source of the individual's increased power of existence. Such understanding is rarely achieved and is exceedingly difficult, but its unobstructed possibility is a challenge to men and is the source of such freedom as man may have.

Pertinent Literature

Wolfson, Harry Austryn. *The Philosophy of Spinoza: Unfolding the Latent Processes of His Reasoning.* Cambridge, Massachusetts: Harvard University Press, 1934.

In this enormously erudite work, written with clarity and good humor, Harry Austryn Wolfson set out to answer three questions about Benedictus de Spinoza's chief work, the *Ethics:* what he said, how he came to say it, and why he said it that way. Spinoza's use of the geometrical method of exposition, though intended to aid clarity as well as rigor, in fact by its terseness often led to baffling obscurity. Moreover, Spinoza is unique among the great philosophers of the European tradition in having been importantly influenced by the Talmud and medieval and renaissance Jewish writers who in their turn incorporate teachings of the Islamic philosophers; and so back to the Neoplatonists and Aristotle. Thus Wolfson's historicocritical method, whereby Spinoza's doctrines are exhibited as developments in these series, demands a rare combination of scholarly abilities. His aim is no less than the reconstruction of the scholasticorabbinical treatise which, he maintains, would express the actual manner in which Spinoza did his thinking.

The first volume in its entirety is devoted to proposition-by-proposition discussion of *Ethics*, Part I, "Of God." Beginning with consideration of the definitions of *substance* as what is in itself and conceived through itself, and of *mode* as in and conceived through another, Wolfson interprets "conceived through" as referring to the relation of genus to species. He consequently holds that substance for Spinoza is related to modes as genus is to species. Substance or God, as highest genus, is not conceivable at all. The attributes of thought and extension, which the intellect perceives as if constituting God's essence, are held to be subjective: inventions of the mind, not discoveries. Although he does not mention Immanuel Kant in this connection, Wolfson's interpretation seems to make Spinoza an anticipator of the doctrine of space and time as forms of intuition.

The second volume is a commentary, briefer but still very full, on Parts II-V of the *Ethics*. In his concluding chapter, "What is New in Spinoza?," Wolfson summarizes the results of his study in the contention that Spinoza's originality consisted not in advancing new philosophical principles but in relentlessly drawing the logical conclusions of premises accepted by his predecessors. In particular he is credited with four "acts of daring": 1. Attributing extension to God. 2. Denying design and purpose in God. 3. Denying the separability of body and soul in man. 4. Denying freedom of the will. These theses eliminate all the traditional dualities from philosophy: mind/body, God/creation, teleology/mechanism, and freedom/necessity. What results is a philosophy of nature as an infinite unified organic whole. God-Nature-Substance manifests itself to our limited intellects in two types of action: thought and motion, each of which is subsumable under necessary laws. This conception is of course most acceptable to the scientific spirit. It is, however, one that theologians can hardly accept, even if logically implied by their principles. On this view God, while conscious, lacks personality—he does not, for example, reward and punish. Spinoza's theology, then, is essentially a return to Aristotle's, which Wolfson characterizes as that of God as "an eternal paralytic." Wolfson maintains that Spinoza failed to realize the extent to which his thought was a breaking away from traditional theology, believing—naïvely in Wolfson's estimation—that the dictates of reason would provide effective guides to conduct, and that the indestructibility of mind-stuff would afford the same kind of emotional reassurance in the face of death that was purveyed by the traditional doctrine of immortality.

Curley, E. M. *Spinoza's Metaphysics: An Essay in Interpretation.* Cambridge, Massachusetts: Harvard University Press, 1969.

This elegant study looks at Benedictus de Spinoza "through lenses ground by Russell, Moore, and Wittgenstein," presenting an original and provocative interpretation.

E. M. Curley begins by rejecting two conceptions of the substance/mode relation. He contends that the view of Pierre Bayle and H. H. Joachim, according to which substance is ontologically that in which attributes and modes inhere and logically the designatum of the subject in propositions whose predicates refer to attributes and modes, should not be attributed to Spinoza, who neither speaks of "subjects" nor distinguishes substance from attributes. Spinoza was in fact the first to break with the tradition, going back to Aristotle, that conflated the different distinctions substance/mode and subject/predicate. The Harry Austryn Wolfson interpretation, that substance is highest genus, of which the modes are species, is attacked with seven arguments, of which the most telling point out conflicts with the text. Wolfson's account has the consequence, drawn explicitly by its author, that substance-God is indefinable and unknowable. Spinoza specifically inveighed against this view, however, and even purported to prove that the human mind has an adequate idea of God's essence. Curley draws the moral that the historical approach can be overdone.

Turning to his positive account, Curley takes as the basis of his interpretation Spinoza's repeated assertion that substance is the cause of the modes, and his assimilation or at least analogy of cause-effect to ground-consequent. The author sets up a "model metaphysic" having these features: A set of propositions completely describing the world of extended objects is assumed to exist. Some of the propositions will describe singular facts (not things), some accidental generalizations ("All the bodies in this room weigh less than 150 pounds"), some nomological generalizations (laws of nature). Nomologicals are necessary truths and thus support counterfactual inferences. They are not reducible to truth functions of singulars. Every singular proposition follows from a nomological plus another singular. The nomologicals

can be organized into a deductive system. General nomological facts correspond to the nomological propositions.

This model, which amounts to an ideal of unified science, is applied to Spinoza's system by equating the basic (most general) nomological facts to the attribute of extension; the derivative nomological facts to the infinite modes; and the singular facts to the finite modes. Thus the finite modes (facts) can be deduced from axioms and theorems (expressing the nature of God) plus singular propositions (other finite modes, that is, God insofar as modified by finite modifications). Spinoza's determinism thus consists in affirming that everything that happens can in principle be explained by laws of nature plus a specification of antecedent conditions.

Is the model an exact fit? Curley discusses whether it captures Spinoza's conception of necessity. In the model, nomologicals are absolutely necessary, but singulars are necessary only relative to their singular causes. From this it follows that there is more than one possible world—contrary, so it seems, to Spinoza's view. Curley suggests, however, that Spinoza meant only that there could not be another world besides the existent one. He concludes, nevertheless, that Spinoza was wrong if he supposed that there is in principle an answer to the question "Why does the world containing just these facts exist, rather than some other consistent set of facts?" There must be at least one brute fact, after all.

On the question of the divine attributes, Curley considers and rejects the view that the identity of thought and extension can be translated into the current theory of mind-body identity, for the reason that watches (for example) do not have thoughts (and Spinoza, so Curley insists, was aware of the fact). Curley's view is that the attribute of extension is the set of facts; ideas (the attribute of thought) are true propositions describing the facts. He holds, furthermore, with most commentators, that consciousness is not ideas but ideas of ideas. These conscious ideas, he suggests, express propositional attitudes: for example, if p is an idea, then the idea of the idea might be of the form "A knows that *p*."

Curley tries to explain the Spinozistic doctrine of immortality, but in the end confesses to finding it "completely unintelligible." In a postscript he indulges in historical criticism to the extent of explain-

ing Spinoza's philosophy as principally a reaction against René Descartes: in particular, Spinoza insisted that the world is thoroughly intelligible, contrary to the Cartesian account which rests its nature ultimately on the inscrutable will of God.

Hampshire, Stuart. "A Kind of Materialism," in *Proceedings and Addresses of the American Philosophical Association*. XLIII (1970), pp. 5-23.

In this short paper, his Presidential Address to the American Philosophical Association, Stuart Hampshire takes up the problem of how a consistent materialist can hold both that his thoughts and sentiments are embedded in a physical, determined order, and also strive, and exhort others to strive, to alter those thoughts and sentiments for the better. He attributes his answer to Benedictus de Spinoza "rather freely interpreted."

The starting assumption of the consistent and self-conscious materialist is that human acquisition of knowledge must be studied like any other capacity of a living organism: by looking at the observable, therefore physical, mechanisms involved. These will be complex, perhaps of types not yet recognized in physics. At the same time, the materialist keeps himself in focus both as observer and observed. He thinks of people as intricate instruments reacting to environment, but also as internally determined to explore the world in light of their stored knowledge. If knowledge is determined by interests and purposes, however, and the latter also by the former, how can he get out of the circle? By considering the reflexive forms of thought: he knows that even in elementary perceptual situations he must make allowances for his own physical situation. Thus he can distinguish the real from the apparent order of things, whether in ordinary perception or at the highest level of scientific inquiry.

Let us think of all thought, not just perception, as entailing the reflective use of a physical mechanism. All thought thus becomes a kind of perception, although abstract thought is relatively independent of the immediate environment. Knowing brain physiology would enable the philosopher to make corrections analogous to those in perception. We already do this with the more obvious emotions.

The crass materialist tries to eliminate reference to thoughts and feelings in favor of physiological descriptions. The self-conscious materialist, however, replies that while physical knowledge can be put to use in correcting thought, it cannot substitute for what it corrects, any more than the listener can substitute acoustical theory for listening. True, one can make the substitution when merely observing someone else, but not in one's own case. If, for example, the philosopher knows the physiology of anger and becomes angry at someone, he will evaluate his angry thoughts in light of his belief about the physical causes, distinguishing the case where the anger is a mere physical reaction from that in which it is a standard mode of perception of the offending object.

Science has shown us how to correct our perceptions—for example, of the size of the sun. Indeed, the scientific man sees the sun differently from the way the child or savage sees it. Analogously, in the psychology of the sentiments another Copernican revolution is needed. We presently do not think of passions as psychophysical phenomena issuing from complicated causes. Interpretation in light of physiology would correct these self-centered perceptions. The self-conscious materialist would grow more detached. This does not mean that the first impression would vanish; but it would be understood and corrected if correction were needed.

The self-conscious materialist will regard other people as organisms whose sentiments are alterable by changes in their physical states, and also by arguments convincing them that their thoughts about the causes of those states are erroneous. In the materialist's own case, the two methods of correction collapse into one.

Thinking about the causes of one's psychophysical states changes those states. If I think of my fear as causally independent of the feared object, I bracket my fear of that object. Even if the fear does not vanish, it at least is altered, becoming more complicated.

The materialist, however, does not regard the relation between the sentiment and the physical state as a causal one. It is much closer. Knowing that such is the case, the self-conscious materialist knows that his limited power to change his psychophysical states depends on his power to bring more systematic knowledge of their causes to bear. Such power must itself be embodied in an internal physical structure. It is therefore not pointless or inconsistent for the materialist to urge men to recognize their powers of reflection, to be active, not passive. This is the sense and point of Spinoza's so-called double aspect theory of personality, and the thought behind *Ethics,* Book II, Proposition 22: "The human mind not only perceives the affections of the body, but also the ideas of these affections."

Additional Recommended Reading

Allison, Henry E. *Benedict De Spinoza.* Boston: Twayne, 1975. Intended for the general reader and student.
Bidney, David. *The Psychology and Ethics of Spinoza.* New Haven, Connecticut: Yale University Press, 1940. The most thorough study of *Ethics,* Parts III-V.

Bennett, Jonathan Francis. *A Study of Spinoza's Ethics.* Indianapolis: Hackett Publishing Company, 1984. A detailed critical study of Spinoza's moral philosophy and metaphysics.

Freeman, Eugene and Maurice Mandelbaum, eds. *Spinoza: Essays in Interpretation.* La Salle, Illinois: Open Court, 1974. Contains a good bibliography of works on Spinoza published 1960-1972.

Hampshire, Stuart. *Spinoza.* Harmondsworth, England: Penguin Books, 1951 . A general introduction by a leading Spinoza scholar.

Harris, Errol. *Salvation from Despair: A Reappraisal of Spinoza's Philosophy.* The Hague, The Netherlands: Martinus Nijhoff, 1973. An interpretation emphasizing the ethical and religious significance of Spinoza's philosophy.

Joachim, Harold H. *A Study of the Ethics of Spinoza.* Oxford: Clarendon Press, 1901. A meticulous study, the standard commentary before Wolfson's, and still very worth reading.

Kashap, S. Paul, ed. *Studies in Spinoza.* Berkeley: University of California Press, 1972. The first collection of essays on Spinoza, including a number of classical studies.

McKeon, Richard. *The Philosophy of Spinoza.* New York: Longmans Green, 1928. A lucid study emphasizing the close connection of science and ethics, in Spinoza and in general.

Mark, Thomas C. *Spinoza's Theory of Truth.* New York: Columbia University Press, 1972. The author proposes a view according to which Spinoza held neither a correspondence nor a coherence but an "ontological" theory of truth—"truth as being."

Pollock, Sir Frederick. *Spinoza: His Life and Philosophy.* London: C. K. Paul, 1880. A valuable general survey.

Shahan, Robert W. and J. I. Biro, eds. *Spinoza: New Perspectives.* Norman: University of Oklahoma Press, 1978. A collection of essays.

Van Der Bend, J. G., ed. *Spinoza on Knowing, Being and Freedom.* Assen, The Netherlands: Van Gorcum, 1974. A collection of papers read at a Spinoza symposium held in the Netherlands.

AN ESSAY CONCERNING HUMAN UNDERSTANDING

Author: John Locke (1632-1704)
Type of work: Epistemology
First published: 1690

Principal Ideas Advanced

At birth the mind is a blank tablet; no one is born with innate ideas.

All of our ideas come from experience, either from sensation or by reflection.

All simple, uncompounded ideas come from experience; and the mind, by combining simple ideas, forms new complex ideas.

The qualities of objects are either primary or secondary: primary qualities—solidity, extension, figure, mobility, and number—are inseparable from objects; but secondary qualities—such as colors and odors—are in the observer.

The substance of objects is a something—we know not what—which we have to assume as the support of an object's qualities.

Locke's *An Essay Concerning Human Understanding* is the first major presentation of the empirical theory of knowledge that was to play such an important role in British philosophy. The author had studied at Oxford, and later he became a medical doctor. Although he did not practice much, he was greatly interested in the developments current in medical and physical science, and there is some evidence that he first began to formulate his theory of knowledge in terms of considerations arising from medical researches of the day. Locke was a member of the Royal Society of England where he came into contact with many of the important experimental scientists, such as Robert Boyle and Sir Isaac Newton. A discussion with some of his friends seems to have been the immediate occasion of the writing of *An Essay Concerning Human Understanding,* in which Locke attempted to work out a theory of knowledge in keeping with the developing scientific findings and outlook. The completed version of the work dates from the period when Locke, along with his patron, the Earl of Shaftesbury, was a political refugee in Holland. After the Glorious Revolution of 1688, Locke returned to England, and was quickly recognized as the leading spokesman for the democratic

system of government that was emerging in his homeland. The *Essay*, first published in the same year as Locke's famous work in political philosophy, *Two Treatises of Government,* quickly established the author as the foremost spokesman for the new empirical philosophical point of view that was to dominate English philosophy from then on.

The question to which Locke addressed himself in his essay is that of inquiring into "the original, certainty, and extent of human knowledge, together with the grounds and degrees of belief, opinion, and assent." By using what he called "this historical, plain method," Locke hoped to discover where our ideas and our knowledge come from, what we are capable of knowing about, how certain our knowledge actually is, and when we may be justified in holding opinions based on our ideas. The value of such an undertaking, Locke asserted, is that one would thus know the powers and the limits of the human understanding, so that "the busy mind of man" would then restrict itself to considering only those questions with which it was actually capable of dealing and would "sit down in a quiet ignorance of those things" which were beyond the reach of its capacities.

Before commencing his investigations, Locke pointed out that human beings do, in fact, have adequate knowledge to enable them to function in the condition in which they find themselves. Therefore, even if the result of seeking the origin, nature, and extent of our knowledge leads us to the conclusion that we are unable to obtain complete certitude on various matters, this should not be grounds for despair, for skepticism, or for intellectual idleness. Too much time, Locke insisted, has been wasted by men in bemoaning their intellectual situation, or in disputing in areas in which satisfactory conclusions are impossible. Instead, he said, we should find out our abilities and our limitations, and then operate within them.

The first book of the *Essay* deals with one theory about the origin of our ideas, the thesis that our knowledge is based upon certain innate principles, which are supposed to be "stamped upon the mind of man." Locke severely criticized this theory, especially in the form in which it had been presented by thinkers such as Herbert of Cherbury (1583-1648). Adherents of this theory of innate ideas had maintained that the universal agreement of mankind regarding certain principles showed that these must be innate. Locke argued in opposition that the fact of universal agreement would be insufficient evidence as to the source of the principles in question. He also argued that, in fact, there actually are no principles that are universally agreed to, since children and idiots do not seem to know or believe the principles that are usually cited as examples of innate ideas. The way in which children acquire knowledge about the principles in question, through the learning process, further indicates that they are not born with innate ideas.

After having criticized the innate idea theory, Locke turned next to the positive side of his investigation. We do have ideas (an idea being defined as whatever is the object of the understanding when a man thinks); this is beyond any possible doubt. Then, if the ideas are not innate, where do they come from?

The second book of the *Essay* begins the development of a hypothesis about the origins of human knowledge; namely, the empirical theory. Let us suppose, Locke said, that the mind initially is just a blank tablet *(a tabula rasa)*. Where, then, does it obtain its ideas? From experience, Locke proclaimed. Experience comprises two sources of ideas, sensation and reflection. We receive many, if not most, of our ideas when our sense organs are affected by external objects. We receive other ideas by reflection when we perceive the operations of our minds on the ideas which we have already received. Sensation provides us with ideas of qualities, such as the ideas of yellow, heat, and so on. Reflection provides us with ideas such as those of thinking, willing, doubting, and so on. These two sources, Locke insisted, give us all of the ideas that we possess. If anyone has any doubts about this, let him simply inspect his own ideas and see if he has any which have not come to him either by sensation or reflection. The development of children also provides a further confirmation of this empirical theory of the origin of human knowledge. As the child receives more ideas from sensation, and reflects on them, his knowledge gradually increases.

Having thus answered the question concerning the origin of our ideas, Locke proceeded to investigate the nature of the ideas that we possess. All of our ideas are either simple or complex. A simple idea is one that is uncompounded, that contains nothing but one uniform appearance, and that cannot be distinguished into different ideas. An example of a simple idea would be the smell of a rose. A complex idea, in contrast, is one that is composed of two or more simples, such as a yellow and fragrant idea. The simples, Locke insisted, can neither be created nor destroyed by the mind. The mind has the power to repeat, compare, and unite the simples, thereby creating new complex ideas. But, the mind cannot invent simple ideas that it has not experienced. The simples, in the Lockian theory of knowledge, are the building blocks from which all of our complex and compounded ideas can be constructed and accounted for.

Many of the simple ideas are conveyed by one sense, such as the ideas of colors, sounds, tastes, smells, and touches. One crucial case that Locke argued for is the idea of solidity, which he claimed we receive by touch. This idea is that of a basic quality of bodies. It is not the same as the space that bodies occupy, nor is it the same as the subjective experience of hardness that we receive when we feel objects. Instead, for Locke, solidity is akin to the fundamental physical notion of "mass" in Newtonian physics. It is that which makes up bodies. To anyone who doubts that he is actually acquainted with such an idea, Locke suggested that he place a physical object, such as a ball, between his hands, and then try to join them. Such an experience, presumably, will give one a complete and adequate knowledge of solidity or, at least, as complete and adequate an idea as we are capable of obtaining of any simple idea. The importance of this idea in Locke's theory will be seen shortly with regard to his theory of primary and secondary qualities.

Some of our ideas are conveyed by two or more senses. Locke included in this group the ideas of space or extension, figure, rest, and motion, which, he said, we receive by means of both sight and touch. Other ideas come from reflection. And still others are the result of both reflection and sensation. Included in this later group are the ideas of pleasure and pain, and the idea of power (which we gain from reflecting on our experience of our own ability to move parts of ourselves at will).

If these are the types of ideas that we possess, classified according to their sources, can we distinguish those ideas which resemble actual features, or qualities of objects, and those which do not? The qualities of objects are divided by Locke into two categories, the primary and the secondary ones. The primary ones are those that are inseparable from bodies no matter what state the object may be in. This group includes solidity, extension, figure, mobility, and number. In contrast, the secondary qualities "are nothing in the objects themselves, but the powers to produce various sensations in us by their primary qualities," as, for example, the power of an object, through the motion of its solid, extended parts, to produce sounds, tastes, and odors in us when we are affected by it. Thus, on Locke's theory, objects possess primary qualities, the basic ingredients of Newtonian physics, and they possess secondary ones, which are actually the powers of the primary qualities to cause us to perceive features, such as colors, odors, and so on, which are not "in" the objects themselves. In terms of this distinction, we can say that our ideas

of primary qualities resemble the characteristics of existing objects outside us, whereas our ideas of secondary qualities do not. The primary qualities of things are really in them, whereas the secondary qualities, as perceived sensations, are only in the observer. If there were no observers, only the primary qualities and their powers would exist. Hence, the rich, colorful, tasteful, noisy, odorous world of our experience is only the way *we* are affected by objects, not the way objects actually are. The distinction between our ideas of primary and secondary qualities led Locke to argue that some of our ideas give us genuine information about reality, while others do not.

In the remainder of the second book of the *Essay*, Locke surveyed the various other kinds of ideas that we possess, those gained by reflection, those that are complexes, and so on. The most important, in terms of his theory, and in terms of later philosophy, is the complex idea of substance. The idea of substance originates from the fact that in our experience a great many simple ideas constantly occur together. We then presume them to belong to one thing, since we cannot imagine how these simple ideas can subsist by themselves. Therefore, we accustom ourselves to suppose that there must be some *substratum* in which the ideas subsist, and we call this substratum a substance. When we ask ourselves what idea we actually have of a substance, we find that our idea is only that of a *something* which the constantly conjoined ideas belong to. When we try to find out what this something is, we discover that we do not know, except that we suppose it must be a something which can support or contain the qualities which could produce the collection of simple ideas in us. If we attempt to find out something more definite about the nature of substance, we discover that we cannot. What do color and weight belong to? If we answer, to the extended solid parts, then to what do these belong? It is like, Locke suggested, the case of the Indian philosopher who said that the world is supported by a great elephant. When asked what supported the elephant, he replied that it rested on a great tortoise. And, when asked what the tortoise rested on, he conceded and said, "I know not what." This, Locke asserted, is all that can finally be said of the nature of substance. It is something—we know not what—which we suppose is the support of the qualities which we perceive or which we are affected by.

Each constantly conjoined group of qualities we assume belongs to some particular substance, which we name "horse," "gold," "man," and so on. We possess no clear idea of substance, either in the case of physical things or of spiritual things. But, we find that we cannot believe that either the physical qualities or the mental ones which we always experience together can exist without belonging to something. And so, although we have no definite ideas, we assume that there must be both bodies and spirits underlying and supporting the qualities that give rise to our ideas. Our inability to obtain clear ideas of substances, however, forever prevents us from gaining genuine knowledge about the real nature of things.

At the end of the second book of the *Essay,* Locke evaluated what he had discovered about the nature of our ideas. This evaluation commences the examination of the problem of the extent and certitude of our knowledge, which is developed at length in the fourth book. Our ideas are real, Locke contended, when they have a foundation in nature and when they conform with the real character of things. In this sense, all simple ideas are real, since they must be the result of genuine events and things (since the mind cannot create them, but receives them from experience). But not all real ideas are necessarily adequate representations of what does in fact exist. Ideas of primary qualities are both real and adequate. Ideas of secondary qualities are real, but only partially represent what is outside us. They represent powers that exist, but not corresponding features to the ones that we perceive. The ideas of substances that we have are very inadequate, since we are never sure that we are aware of all the qualities that are joined together in one substance, nor are we sure of why they are so joined. Hence, some of our ideas tell us what is really outside us whereas other ideas, caused by what is outside us, or by our reflection on our ideas, do not adequately represent "real" objects. Later philosophers, such as George Berkeley and David Hume, were to argue that once Locke had admitted that some of our ideas were neither representative of reality nor

adequate to portray reality, he could not then be certain that *any* of our ideas actually correspond to real features of the world. Hence, they contended that Locke, in trying to build from an empirical theory of knowledge to genuine knowledge of reality, had actually laid the groundwork for a skeptical denial of the contention that man can know anything beyond the ideas in his own mind. Locke's theory rested on maintaining that our ideas of primary qualities resemble genuine characteristics of reality. But, the opponents argued, primary qualities are really no different from secondary qualities, as we know them, and hence we have no assurance from the ideas themselves that some are real and adequate and others are not.

The third book of the *Essay* appears to deal with some unrelated topics, those concerning the nature of words and language. This book, which has begun to evoke more interest in recent years because of the present-day concern with linguistic philosophy, covers problems normally dealt with in anthropology, psychology, linguistics, and philosophy.

Two points that are raised are of central importance to Locke's main theme of the nature and extent of our knowledge, and played a role in the later history of empirical philosophy. One of these is Locke's theory concerning the meaning and referent of general terms, such as "man," "triangle," and so on. All things that exist, Locke asserted, are particular, but by abstracting from our ideas of things, by separating from them particular details or features, we finally form a general idea. In this way we arrive at the general abstract ideas that we reason about. Berkeley and Hume both challenged Locke on this point and insisted that we do not, in fact, possess any abstract general ideas. Hence, they insisted that an empirical account of our ideas of so-called general terms must be developed from the particular ideas that we have.

One of the general terms that Locke claimed gained some meaning from the abstracting process is that of "substance." But, when he analyzed what we might mean by the term, Locke distinguished between what he called "the nominal essence" and "the real essence" of a substance. The nominal essence is that abstract general idea of a substance formed by abstracting the basic group of features that constantly occur together. The real essence, in contrast, is the nature of the object which accounts for its having the properties that it does. The nominal essence describes what properties a substance has, whereas the real essence explains why it has these properties. Unfortunately, Locke pointed out, we can never know the real essence of anything, since our information, which we abstract from, deals only with the qualities that we experience, and never with the ultimate causes which account for the occurrence of these properties. Thus, our knowledge of things is sure to be sharply curtailed because of the fact that we will never discover the reasons why things have the characteristics that they do.

The fourth and last book of the *Essay* deals with knowledge in general, with the scope of knowledge, and with the question as to how certain we can be of such knowledge. Our knowledge deals only with ideas, since these are the only items that the mind is directly acquainted with. What constitutes knowledge, according to Locke, is the perception of the agreement or disagreement of two ideas. Ideas may agree or disagree in four ways. They may possibly be identical or diverse. They may be related in some respect. They may agree in coexisting in the same subject or substance. And, fourthly, they may agree or disagree in having a real existence outside the mind. All of our knowledge, Locke insisted, falls under these headings. We know either that some ideas are the same or different, or that they are related, or that they always coexist, or that they really exist independently of our minds.

If these are the kinds of items that we can know about, how can we gain such knowledge? One source of our knowledge is intuition, the direct and immediate perception of the agreement or disagreement of any two ideas. The mind "sees" that black is not white and that a circle is not a triangle. Also, "this kind of knowledge is the clearest and most certain that human frailty is capable of." Anyone who demands more certainty than that gained by intuition "demands he knows not what, and shows only that he has a mind to be a skeptic, without being able to be so." All certain knowledge depends upon intuition as its source and guarantee.

We acquire knowledge not only by directly inspecting ideas, but also through demonstrations. According to Locke, when we know by demonstration, we do not see *immediately* that two ideas agree or disagree, but we see *immediately*, by means of connecting two ideas with others until we are able to connect them with each other. This process is actually a series of intuitions, and each step in a demonstration is therefore certain. However, since the steps occur successively in the mind, error is possible if we forget the previous steps, or if we assume that one has occurred which actually has not. Intuition and demonstration are the only two sources of certain knowledge.

However, there is another source of knowledge that has a degree of certitude assuring us of truths about particular experiences. This kind of knowledge goes beyond bare probability but does not reach genuine certainty. It is called "sensitive knowledge," which is the assurance that we have on the occurrence of specific experiences, that certain external objects actually exist which cause or produce these experiences. We cannot reasonably believe, Locke insisted, that all of our experiences are imaginary or are just part of a dream. Hence, we have sensitive knowledge, a degree of assurance that something real is going on outside us.

In terms of these kinds of knowledge, types of sources, and degrees of certainty, it is now possible to outline the extent of human knowledge and to evaluate what we can actually know about the real world. We can gain knowledge only to the extent that we can discover agreements or disagreements among our ideas. Since we can neither intuit nor demonstrate all the relations that ideas can have with one another, our knowledge is not even as extensive as our ideas. In almost all cases, we can determine with certainty whether our ideas are identical or different from one another. We can tell if our ideas are related to others only when we can discover sufficient intermediary ideas. In fields such as mathematics, we keep expanding our knowledge as more connections between ideas are intuited or demonstrated. The areas in which we seem to be most limited in gaining knowledge are those dealing with the coexistence and real existence of ideas. Since we can never know the real essence of any substance, we can never know why any two ideas must necessarily coexist. We never discover why particular secondary qualities occur when a specific arrangement of primary qualities exists. We are aware of the fact that certain ideas occur over and over again in combination, but we do not know why they do this. With regard to real existence, we are, Locke maintained, intuitively certain of our own existence and demonstratively certain that God exists. We are only sensitively certain that anything else exists, which means that we have serious assurance that objects other than ourselves and God exist only when we have experiences which we feel must be caused by something outside us. Our assurance in these cases is limited to the actual moment when we are having these experiences. Once an experience is over, we have no certitude at all that the object which caused the experience still continues to exist. All that we can know about an object when we know that it exists is that at such times it actually possesses the primary qualities that we perceive, together with the power to produce the other effects that we experience.

This assessment of the extent of our knowledge indicates, according to Locke, that we can never know enough to develop a genuine, certain science of bodies or of spirits, since our information about their existence and their natures is so extremely limited. Since we can, however, obtain sufficient knowledge and probable information to satisfy our needs in this world, we should not despair or become skeptical just because investigation has revealed how limited our knowledge actually is and how uncertain it is in many areas.

Locke's *Essay* represents the first major modern presentation of the empirical theory of knowledge. In developing an account of human knowledge in terms of how it is derived from experience, what its nature is, and how limited it is, Locke provided the basic pattern of future empirical philosophy. In attempting to justify some basis for maintaining that we can have some knowledge of some aspects of reality, Locke raised many of the problems that have remained current in philosophical discussions up to the present time. Empiricists after Locke, such as Berkeley and Hume, showed that if one consistently followed out the thesis that all of our knowledge comes from experience, one could not be certain that substances exist or that anything exists beyond the ideas directly perceived. Locke's *Essay* is the source of many of the methods, ideas, and problems that have prevailed in philosophy, especially in British and American epistemology, ever since its first publication.

Pertinent Literature

Gibson, James. *Locke's Theory of Knowledge and Its Historical Relations.* Cambridge: Cambridge University Press, 1917.

James Gibson's book is one of the most important commentaries on John Locke's *An Essay Concerning Human Understanding,* and the work also includes a helpful group of discussions of Locke's relations with various seventeenth century thinkers, and an examination of Locke's influence on Immanuel Kant. The first seven chapters present a detailed commentary and interpretation of the *Essay.*

Gibson begins by attacking the view that the *Essay* simply dealt with a theory of the genesis of ideas, in which the mind was completely passive, an interpretation that makes Locke the founder of empiricism. However, this interpretation does not entirely represent either Locke's aim or the theory he developed. After all, Locke was seeking complete certainty about something real. The knowledge he sought was of certain and universal propositions. What Gibson sees as original in Locke's starting point was that he put the investigation of the nature of knowledge prior to the investigation of reality. Nevertheless, from the outset Locke insisted that the mind and the rest of reality exist. However, since these two kinds of substances can have no direct relation with each other, ideas are needed to mediate between the two.

Gibson then carefully examines Locke's polemic

against innate ideas. (Although Gibson contends that it was principally directed against the Scholastic philosophers, more recent research, especially that of John Yolton, has shown that there were several philosophers contemporary with Locke who advocated the view.) Gibson then carefully fits the various elements of Locke's theory of ideas into his interpretative framework. One of the most interesting chapters is that dealing with the ideas of substance, causality, and identity. Gibson shows how Locke moved from claiming that we suppose some substratum to our ideas, to the much stronger claim he made in his answer to Bishop Edward Stillingfleet that we cannot conceive how ideas could subsist alone. Gibson points out that the basic problem for Locke is neither that we appear to have to believe that there are substances holding our ideas together, nor that these substances are known either by sensation or reflection. The real problem is that although Locke's theory admits of ideas that are not data of immediate experience (namely, relations), it is genuinely difficult to reconcile this with what he says concerning the idea of substance. He could never justify the claim that there is complete knowledge about the supposed substance.

Difficulties such as those involved in accounting for what we can know about substances pervade Locke's account of our very limited knowledge of real existences. Gibson claimed that Locke never realized the difficulty of bringing knowledge of real existences into line with his general theory of knowledge. The former would transcend any ideas we might possess, whereas the latter would deal only with the perception of the agreement or disagreement of ideas that we have. As Gibson outlined Locke's gradual admission of how little we can actually know (based on Locke's standards), he concluded that Locke had shown us what perfect knowledge would be like. Then, unfortunately, according to Gibson, Locke pointed out not only that perfect knowledge is unattainable by human beings, but also, even worse, that we are not able even to conceive of the conditions under which it would be possible.

The second half of Gibson's book is a very interesting series of historical chapters dealing with Locke's relations with various seventeenth century intellectual movements. Gibson starts with the Scholastics, then discusses René Descartes and the Cartesians, then the English philosophers of Locke's day, such as Robert Boyle, Henry More, Sir Isaac Newton, Thomas Hobbes, and Joseph Glanvill. Then he presents two chapters on G. W. Leibniz, mostly on his lengthy critique of Locke's *Essay.* Finally, the work ends with a chapter on the ideas of Locke and Kant. Much of the historical material would have to be reconsidered in the light of more recent historical scholarship on almost all of these topics. Most important, one would have to reexamine the material in the light of the wealth of data in the Locke papers. The new edition of all of the writings of Locke, now under way, should enable one to reevaluate Locke in the context of his time.

Aaron, Richard I. *John Locke.* Oxford: Clarendon Press, 1971.

Richard I. Aaron's work on John Locke, originally published in 1937, has been substantially changed in this edition by taking into account a great deal of new information about Locke that has become available since the discovery of the Lovelace papers in 1935. Aaron's work is both a most important study of Locke's intellectual development and an excellent commentary on and interpretation of Locke's *An Essay Concerning Human Understanding,* as well as his other philosophical writings.

In Appendix I Aaron explains how he discovered the existence of the Lovelace papers. These consisted of thousands of letters Locke had received, together with a great many of Locke's manuscripts, some of which had never been published, and others which showed different versions of Locke's views. The papers were given to the Bodleian Library at Oxford and presently are being used in the publication of a new and much more complete edition of the works of Locke.

Aaron, using some of this material, is able to give a much improved picture of how Locke developed his ideas and how he went about composing the *Essay.* Three drafts exist, two written in 1671 and a third in

1685, which show that the *Essay* began after a discussion with some friends in 1671. The two drafts of that year both break down over the problem of the extent of human knowledge. The major content of Books III and IV are not in these early drafts. Locke did a great deal of work during 1675-1679 during his French visits and went back to the manuscript in the mid-1680's. The work was substantially finished in 1686, although Locke kept making changes until it was published in 1690.

Aaron stresses that Locke considered that what he was doing was preliminary to philosophy rather than setting forth a philosophical system; he also felt that the practical aspect was all-important. Aaron goes on to present a commentary on the work. Since some of the basic problems emerge, such as those connected with Locke's theory of perception, Aaron suggests that Locke held to difficult and seemingly contradictory views not because he was overfond of them, but because he felt that they were inevitable.

Locke's empiricism, Aaron contends, has often been misunderstood and portrayed as a copy theory—a theory that all mental experience can be broken down into identifiable sensory units. Rather, Aaron maintains, Locke held that thought content is based on sense experience in that sensory and reflective experience is essential if we are to have any knowledge at all. Aaron contends that since Locke tried to use this view as a means of explaining what we know about modes, substances, and relations, his treatment was far from adequate.

The ultimate outcome of Locke's analysis, Book IV of the *Essay*, is not part of the original draft of 1671. Aaron tries to trace the stages by which Locke came to his epistemological conclusion as a way of avoiding some of the skeptical pitfalls: We can intuit some information; we can know that an idea is itself; we can know some necessary relations between ideas, as in mathematics. We can, however, find no necessary relations between our ideas and an external world, and therefore no science, in Aristotle's or René Descartes' sense, is possible.

Aaron follows Locke's struggle to secure what Locke called "sensitive" knowledge and what Aaron labels "existential" knowledge, and he shows that Locke could not make his whole theory of knowledge consistent. The more practical theory that Locke closed with, regarding probabilities and the causes of errors, allows for the practical achievement of his undertaking. Much ignorance and mistaken views, according to Locke, can be eliminated; and although one may not possess knowledge of many things, one may still know enough to live happily and successfully. Aaron then goes on to deal with Locke's moral, political, and religious views.

Aaron's commentary presents significant analyses of the course of Locke's theory. In this edition Aaron has added several important notes and appendices based on both the newly examined manuscript material and some recent interpretations of specific sections of Locke (such as Appendix III on "Locke and Modern Theories of Number"). The volume is virtually indispensable for studying Locke's philosophy.

Yolton, John W. *John Locke and the Way of Ideas.* Oxford: Clarendon Press, 1956.

This very important study attempts to place John Locke's philosophy in the intellectual world of the England of his day. John W. Yolton shows that Locke's concerns, starting with the analysis of innate ideas, grew out of discussions then taking place in England. He then follows the impact of Locke's views on English thinkers (and also on several Continental ones) at the end of the seventeenth and the beginning of the eighteenth centuries. Using some of the manuscript materials of Locke in the Lovelace Collection at Oxford, Yolton is able to show Locke's reactions to some of his contemporary critics.

Yolton first surveys the nature and scope of the early reactions to Locke's *An Essay Concerning Human Understanding,* showing how they involved concerns about Locke offering views that would lead to either religious or epistemological skepticism. From the first reactions onward, those who discussed Locke's view were often highly critical. (Locke's theory was first presented in 1688 in a French summary and was criticized immediately because of Locke's denial of innate ideas.)

Yolton then examines the controversy that had been going on in England concerning whether there are innate ideas. He shows that the usual view of the history books, that Locke was criticizing René Descarte's theory, is doubtful. Yolton believes that it is more likely that Locke was dealing with the then-current version of the innate ideas theory. When Locke's view appeared in Book I of the *Essay*, Locke was widely attacked by many philosophers and theologians, mainly because of the possible criticisms of basic theological notions that could result from his denial of innate ideas. Yolton points out that few writers of the time could evaluate Locke's epistemological views without considering their effect on religion.

In tracing the reaction of Locke's contemporaries to the *Essay,* Yolton next examines those criticisms contending that Locke's epistemology leads to a skepticism about the possibility of gaining knowledge. Step by step, critics such as Henry Lee, John Seargent, John Norris, and others sought to show how Locke's positive theory of knowledge, from his theory of ideas to his classification of kinds of knowledge, all lead to skepticism. Locke did not attempt to answer his critics, except for his controversy with Bishop Edward Stillingfleet, who, like the other critics, deplored the religious skepticism that seemed sure to follow acceptance of Locke's epistemological doctrines.

Yolton then examines the opponents who raised the religious issue, dealing with everyone from Stillingfleet to the eccentric critic, William Carroll, who was convinced that Locke was a Spinozist. Those who claimed that Locke's views led to religious skepticism argued that Locke's doctrine of substance, as well as his view on the limitations of human knowledge, had serious consequences for religious beliefs. Furthermore, as vindication of the views of the orthodox opponents of Locke, some portions of his epistemology were taken over by Deist thinkers. Many Christian writers sought to show that there were Lockean elements in the latest publications of the Deists. Yolton also shows that some orthodox thinkers, including Bishop George Berkeley, adapted some of Locke's views as ways of defending Christianity.

In examining the reception of Locke's philosophy, and especially the criticism of it, Yolton follows the arguments of the subject down to the middle of the eighteenth century. By then Locke's views and the attacks on them had become part of the basic features of philosophical discussions. Also, Yolton insists, Locke's views had become part of the radical and revolutionary Deist views. The Deists, using some of the epistemological doctrines of the *Essay*, altered the presuppositions thought to be necessary for religion. Locke himself was not a Deist, though he seems to have been sympathetic with some of their beliefs. The epistemological problems raised by Locke led to an important shift in the religious, moral, and logical attitudes in the eighteenth century.

Additional Recommended Reading

Cranston, Maurice. *John Locke: A Biography.* New York: Macmillan Publishing Company, 1957. Best biography available, based on much manuscript material.

O'Connor, Daniel John. *John Locke.* New York: Dover Publications, 1967. A good overall presentation of Locke's thought.

Wood, Neal. *The Politics of Locke's Philosophy: A Social Study of "An Essay Concerning Human Understanding."* Berkeley: University of California Press, 1983. Draws out the political and moral implications of Locke's theory of knowledge.

Yolton, John W. *Locke and the Compass of Human Understanding: A Selective Commentary on the "Essay."* London: Cambridge University Press, 1970. A careful discussion of Locke's theory of knowledge by one of the most important scholars of Locke's ideas.

_____, ed. *John Locke: Problems and Perspectives: A Collection of New Essays.* Cambridge: Cambridge University Press, 1969. A fine collection of essays on various aspects of Locke's thought by leading contemporary scholars.

OF CIVIL GOVERNMENT: THE SECOND TREATISE

Author: John Locke (1632-1704)
Type of work: Political philosophy
First published: 1690

Principal Ideas Advanced

In the state of nature all men are free and equal; no man is by nature sovereign over other men.

The law of nature governs the state of nature; reason reveals the law of nature, which is derived from God.

In a state of nature no one ought to harm another in his life, health, liberty, or possessions—and if anyone does harm another, the one he harms has the right to punish him.

By his labor a man acquires as his property the products of his labor.

In order to remedy the inconveniences resulting from a state of nature in which every man is judge of his own acts, men enter into a contract, thereby creating a civil society empowered to judge men and to defend the natural rights of men.

If a government violates the social contract by endangering the security and rights of the citizens, it rebels against the people, and the people have the right to dissolve the government.

The "glorious revolution" of 1688 saw the expulsion of James II from the throne of England and the triumph of Whig principles of government. James had been accused of abandoning the throne and thus violating the original contract between himself and his people. Two years later, Locke's *Of Civil Government: The Second Treatise* came out and was looked upon by many as a tract which justified in philosophical terms those historical events. The first *Treatise* had been an argument against the view that kings derive their right to rule from divine command, a view held by the Stuarts, especially James I, and defended with no little skill by Sir Robert Filmer in his *Patriarcha* (1680). From a philosophical point of view it is of little consequence whether Locke intended his defense of the revolution to apply only to the events in the England of his day or to all men at any time; certainly we can study his principles for what they are and make up our own minds as to the generality of their scope.

After rejecting Filmer's thesis, Locke looked for a new basis of government and a new source of political power. He recognized that the state must have the power to regulate and preserve property;

that to do so it must also have the right to punish, from the death penalty to all lesser ones. In order to carry out the laws passed, the force of the community must be available to the government, and it must also be ready to serve in the community's defense from foreign injury. Political power by which the government performs these functions ought to be used only for the public good and not for private gain or advantage. Locke then set out to establish a basis for this power, a basis which he considered moral and just.

He turned to a concept used by political theorists since the time of the Stoics in ancient Greece: natural law with its concomitants, the state of nature and the state of war. The state of nature has been objected to as a concept by many because history does not indicate to us such a state existed. In this treatise Locke tries to answer this sort of objection by pointing to "primitive" societies known in his day, the nations of Indians living in the New World. But this is not a strong argument and was not really needed by Locke. The concept of the state of nature can be used as a device to set off and point up the difference between a civil state in which laws are enacted by the government and a contrasting state in which either these laws are absent in principle or another set of laws prevails. In this way the basis of civil enactments and the position of the individual within society may be better understood. This applies also to the other concepts mentioned, the state of war and natural law. At any rate, Locke holds that in the state of nature each man may order his own life as he sees fit, free from any restrictions that other men might impose; in this sense he and all others are equal. They are equal in a more profound sense from which, as it were, their right to act as independent agents comes; that is, as children of God. By use of his reason, man can discover God's commands by which he should order his life in the state of nature. These commands we call the "laws of nature." Thus, although one is free to act as he pleases in the state of nature, he is still obligated to act according to God's commands. This insures that his actions, although free, will not be licentious. The basic restriction that God's laws place upon an individual is that he treat others as he himself would like to be treated. Since men are equal and independent, they should not harm one another regarding their "life, health, liberty, or possessions. . . ."

Man's glory as well as his downfall has been free will, whereby he may choose to do or not to do what he ought to do. To preserve himself from those who choose to harm him, one has the right to punish transgressors of the law. Reparation and restraint are the two reasons that justify punishment when an individual by his acts has shown that he has agreed to live by a law other than that which common reason and equity dictate; that is, he has chosen to violate God's orders. The right to punish is thus a natural right by which men in the state of nature may preserve themselves and mankind from the transgressions of the lawless. This right is the basis for the right of governments to punish lawbreakers within the state; thus Locke provides a ground for one aspect of political power which he had noted earlier.

When an individual indicates through a series of acts which are apparently premeditated that he has designs on another's life or property, then he places himself in a state of war, a state of enmity and destruction, toward his intended victim. In the state of nature men ought to live according to reason and, hence, according to God's commands. Each man

must be the judge of his own actions for on earth he has no common superior with authority to judge between him and another when a question of aggression arises, and when relief is sought. His conscience must be his guide as to whether he and another are in a state of war.

In The Declaration of Independence, the American colonists proclaimed that men had natural rights granted them by their Creator, that governments were instituted by men with their consent to protect these rights. Locke, as pointed out, held these rights to be life, liberty, and property, whereas the Declaration proclaims them to be life, liberty, and the pursuit of happiness. It is interesting that Jefferson pondered whether to use "property" or "pursuit of happiness" and in an early draft actually had the former set down. Much of Locke's discussion in this treatise influenced the statesmen and leaders of the Colonies during the period of the American Revolution.

Locke seems to use various senses of "property" in his discussions. Speaking quite generally, one might say that whatever was properly one's own (this might mean whatever God had endowed an individual with or whatever the legislature of the commonwealth had declared as legal possession) no one else had a claim to. In spelling out this idea, Locke starts first with one's own body, which is God-given and which no one has a claim upon; a man has a right to be secure in his person. Included in this idea, of course, is the fact that life itself is a gift to which no one else has a claim, as well as the freedom to move about without restriction. There is next the more common use of "property," which is often rendered "estate" and which refers to the proper possessions which one gains in working the earth that God has given man to use for the advantage of his life and its convenience. Since working for one's own advantage and convenience involves the pursuit of happiness, it can be seen in what way the terms "property" and "pursuit of happiness" are interchangeable. This more common use of "property" is, nonetheless, related to the first use in Locke's theory. What is properly a man's own may be extended when, with regard to the common property that God has blessed men with for their use, a man mixes his labor with it and makes it his own. Divine command prescribes, however, that he take no more than he needs, for to take more than one's share may lead to the waste of God's gift and result in want for others. Locke believed that there was more than enough land in the world for men but that it should be used judiciously; he does complicate matters, however, by stating that disproportionate and unequal possessions may be acquired within a government through the consent of the governed. Locke's embryonic economic theory may be looked upon as an early statement of the classical or labor theory of value. This is especially so if we remember that aside from the "natural" or God-given articles of value that man has, he creates objects of value by means of his own labor; more succinctly, labor creates value. This view was held by such influential thinkers in economic history as Adam Smith, David Ricardo, and Karl Marx. Before we leave this aspect of Locke's theory we should note that he has again provided a ground for the use of political power to regulate, preserve, and protect property in all its aspects by establishing its place in the state of nature prior to the institution of the commonwealth.

Locke has shown that although men ought to live according to divine commands, some do not and thus they turn the state of nature into one of war. Since there is no common superior on earth to whom one can turn for restitution, men are often left helpless. It is obvious that not every injury imagined is a wrong, that two individuals in conscience may disagree, that those instances of obvious wrongs are not always rectifiable when men have only their own judgments and strength to depend upon. A disinterested judge supported by more power than a single person has alone may provide people with a remedy for the insecurity that exists in the state of nature. In the most general sense of "property," a commonwealth may provide the solution to its preservation and security by making public the laws by which men ought to live, by establishing a government by which differences may be settled through the office of known and impartial judges who are authorized to do so, and by instituting a police force to execute the law, a protection absent in the state of nature. Men give up their rights to judge for themselves and to execute the laws of nature to the commonwealth, which in turn is obligated to use the power which it has gained for the ends which led to the transference of these rights. In giving up their rights, men consent to form a body politic under one government and, in so doing, obligate themselves to every member of that society to submit to the determinations of the majority. Note that everyone who enters into the society from the state of nature must consent to do so; hence, consent is unanimous and anyone who does not consent is not a member of the body politic. On the other hand, once the body politic is formed, its members are thenceforth subject to the vote of the majority.

In discussing consent and the general question, "Who has consented and what are its significant signs?" Locke uses the traditional distinction between tacit and express consent. Although he is somewhat ambiguous at times, his position is apparently as follows. There are two great classes or categories of individuals within society, those who are members and those who are residents but not members. (A convenient and similar distinction would be those who are citizens and those who are aliens.) Both these two groups receive benefits from the government and hence are obligated to obey it. By their presence they enjoy the peace and security that goes with a government of law and order, and it is morally and politically justifiable that that government expect of them that they obey its laws. Those who are merely residents may quit the body politic when they please; their tacit consent lasts only as long as their presence in the state. Members, however, by their express consent create and perpetuate the society. They are not free to be or not be members at their whim, else the body politic would be no different from the state of nature or war from which its members emerged, and anarchy would prevail. Citizens usually have the protection of their government at home and abroad, and often, at least in the government Locke preferred, a voice in the affairs of their nation. Locke points out, however, that the people who form the commonwealth by their unanimous consent may also delegate their power to a few or to one (oligarchy or monarchy); but in any case it is their government.

There are certain aspects of government which Locke believed must be maintained to insure that it functions for the public good. (1) The legislative, which is the supreme governmental power, must not use its power arbitrarily over the lives and fortunes of the people. The law of nature still prevails in the governments of men. (2) Nor should power be exercised without deliberation. Extempore acts would place the people in as great jeopardy as they were in the state of nature. (3) The supreme power cannot take from a man his property without his consent. This applies also to taxation. (4) The legislative power cannot be transferred to any one else, but must remain in the hands of that group to which it was delegated by the people. In so acting, the legislature insures the people that political power will be used for the public good.

Locke believed that the interests of the people would be protected more fully in a government in which the three basic powers, legislative, executive, and federative, were separate and distinct in their functions. The legislature need meet only periodically, but the executive should be in session, as it were, continually, whereas the management of the security of the commonwealth from foreign injury would reside in the body politic as a whole. Strictly speaking, the federative power —treaty-making and so forth—need not be distinguished from the legislative. It is interesting that the three branches of government in the United States include the judiciary rather than the federative, which is shared by the executive and legislative branches of government. This shows that Montesquieu as well as Locke influenced the Philadelphia convention.

Government, which is made up of these three basic powers, of which the legislative is supreme, must not usurp the end for which it was established. The community, even after it has delegated its power, does not give up its right of self-preservation, and in this sense it retains forever the ultimate power of sovereignty. This power cannot be used by the community which is under obligation to obey the acts of the government unless that government is dissolved. It must be pointed out that the community is for Locke an important political concept. The exercise of its power after the dissolution of government is as a public body and does not involve a general return to the state of nature or war by its members. But in what way is a government dissolved?

When a government exercises power beyond right, when public power is used for private gain, then tyranny prevails. Such acts set the stage for the dissolution of government. It should be pointed out that in forming a community and in delegating power to a government, the people, especially in the latter case, enter into an agreement or, analogously, into a social contract with their government to provide them with security, preservation, and those conveniences that they desire, in exchange for the transference of their rights and the honor, respect, and obligation which they render to the government. The violation of their part of the contract leads government to declare them (as individuals) outlaws, to use its police force to subdue them, and its courts to set punishment for them.

In discussing dissolution in general, Locke points out that it can apply to societies and communities as well as to governments. It is seldom that a community is dissolved. If it does happen, it is usually the result of a foreign invasion which is followed by the utter destruction of the society. Governments, on the other hand, are dissolved from within. Either the executive abandons his office (as was done by James II) and the laws cannot be carried out, or the legislative power is affected in various ways which indicate a violation of trust. If, for example, the property of the subjects is invaded, or if power is used arbitrarily, then government is dissolved. Obviously, it falls upon the community to judge when this power is being abused. Generally, Locke holds, the people are slow to act; it takes not merely one or two but a long series of abuses to lead them to revolution. In fact, he points out that the term "rebellion" indicates a return to a state of war and a denial of the principles of civil society. But when this happens in the dissolution of government, it is the government that has rebelled and not the community; it is the community that stands for law and order and puts down the rebellion. Thus Locke rather cleverly concludes his treatise, not with a justification of the right of rebellion but, rather, with the right of the people to put down unlawful government, unlawful in that it violates the trust and the law of nature, leading to tyranny, rebellion, and dissolution.

Pertinent Literature

Strauss, Leo. "Modern Natural Right," in *Natural Right and History.* Chicago: University of Chicago Press, 1952.

In one of the classics of modern historical analysis of political philosophy, Leo Strauss concludes that John Locke did not recognize any law of nature in the proper sense of the term—a conclusion which he himself concedes stands in shocking contrast to what is generally thought to be Locke's doctrine, especially as that doctrine is expounded in the *Second Treatise.* According to most of Locke's critics, Locke is full of illogical flaws and inconsistencies.

These inconsistences are of such an obvious nature that Strauss believes that it is inconceivable that a man of Locke's stature and sobriety could possibly have overlooked them.

Although Locke seems to reject Thomas Hobbes's theory of natural law in favor of a more traditional view of the law of nature, there are certain flaws in his exposition of his views on that subject. Locke says, for example, that the law of nature or the moral law is capable of being developed into a science which would proceed from self-evident propositions to a body of ethics that would incorporate all the duties of life, a code that would contain, for example, the natural penal law. But Locke never seriously attempted to elaborate that code.

Locke also says that the natural law has been given by God, is known to have been given by God, and has as its sanctions divine rewards and punishments in the next life—sanctions which are of infinite weight and duration. Yet he says that immortality cannot be proven by rational demonstration. One can know of it only through revelation. Moreover, we can know of the sanctions for the law of nature only through revelation. It would follow, then, that we cannot come to know the law of nature through reason unassisted by revelation. Elsewhere, Locke attempted to demonstrate that the New Testament contains the entire law of nature and that it is revealed there in perfect clarity and plainness. One would have thought, therefore, that Locke would have written a commentary on the New Testament rather than a treatise on government.

Strauss's explanation for this is Locke's personal caution—his pragmatic refusal to do anything that would jeopardize his safety or his ability to propound his beliefs, Locke was prepared to be cautious in his writings if unqualified frankness would render his entire noble enterprise incapable of execution or if more direct and clear expression of his views would endanger the public peace or expose him to persecution. Thus, even if Locke had believed that unassisted reason was man's only "star and compass" and was all that was necessary for leading man to perfect happiness; even if he rejected revelation as superfluous or doubtful; he might nevertheless have written as he did, claiming to accept New Testament teachings as true. And even if he personally believed those teachings to be true, he was undoubtedly concerned to make his teachings as independent of Scripture as possible.

A further problem arises out of the fact that Locke enumerates certain particular laws as being laws of nature, but fails to show how they might be derived from the text of the New Testament, where, according to his teaching, they ought to be found. For example, according to Locke, one of the laws of God and nature is a requirement that the government not raise taxes on property without the consent of the people or their deputies—but nowhere does he even attempt to show where this might be found in Scripture. Similarly, in regard to marriage, Locke says that according to natural law the purpose of conjugal society is procreation and education. From this, it merely follows that men and women be tied to a longer conjunction than other creatures. But he does not tell us how firm the conjugal bonds should be. Nor does a firmer bond between men and women than between male and female animals of other species require a prohibition against incest. Indeed, Locke mentions nothing at all about incest, but agrees with Hobbes that civil society is the sole judge of which "transgressions" deserve punishment and which do not. And as for the biblical command that one honor one's ⸗arents, Locke makes it conditional: in the *Second Treatise,* he states that mere biological parenthood is not sufficient to entitle one to be honored by one's children; rather, that claim derives from the "care, cost, and kindness" which the parent has shown to the child. So, Strauss points out, the categorical imperative, "Honor thy father and thy mother," is transformed into a hypothetical imperative: "Honor thy father and thy mother if they have deserved it of you."

Needless to say, all of these and more are not identical with the teachings of Scripture. Locke calls these teachings the "partial law of nature." Since the law of nature is supposed to be set out in the New Testament *in toto,* it would seem to follow that the "partial law of nature" is not actually a part of the law of nature at all. And unlike the law of nature properly so called, it would not have to be known to have been given by God. Indeed, it would not require belief in God at all. Thus, the partial law of nature might be known even to non-Christians, such as the Chinese. According to Locke, all that is necessary for a nation to be civilized is that it know the partial law of nature. Hence, it is possible for the Chinese to be civilized, as Locke concedes them to be.

Thus Strauss arrives at the puzzling conclusion that Locke did not recognize the law of nature properly so called. Strauss explains the paradox by suggesting that in the *Second Treatise* Locke did not present his philosophical doctrines on politics, but what he calls Locke's "civil" presentation of his political doctrine. Locke writes not as a philosopher but as an Englishman, and therefore, writing for a popular audience, he appealed to popularly accepted traditions.

Nevertheless, Strauss maintains that Locke actually deviated from traditional natural law teaching in the *Second Treatise* and followed Hobbes to a greater extent than is ordinarily realized. Locke recognized the state of nature—so much so, in fact, that he said that "all men are naturally in" the state of nature. Moreover, he affirms that every man has the right to be "executioner" of the law of nature—that is, that each man has the right to impose sanctions upon those who violate the laws of nature. No law worthy of the name can exist in the absence of sanctions. Conscience is not identical with God's will, accord-

ing to Locke, and therefore conscience cannot suffice as a sanction for acts violative of the law of nature. Besides, conscience is nothing more than private opinion. Meaningful sanctions in this world, at least, must be enforced by men. If the law of nature is to be effective at all in the state of nature, then it must be enforced by private persons—private since there is not yet a civil society. The natural law is given by God, but it need not be known that God has given it, for human beings must enforce it. If human beings are to enforce it, they must know it. Indeed, no law can be a law unless it is known. Hence, the law of nature must be knowable in the state of nature.

The state of nature, however, far from being the golden age which some might imagine it to be, is perfectly dreadful, just as Hobbes said it would be. Peace exists only in civil society. The state of nature, by contrast, is "full of fears and continual dangers," and those who live in it are "needy and wretched." If men only knew the laws of nature, they would live by them; but the laws of nature are not implanted in men's minds, and most men do not have the leisure to work out the proofs for the laws of nature if they live in that awful state. Although the law of nature is at least theoretically knowable in the state of nature, then, in actual fact, the continual dangers and penury of the state of nature make it impossible for the law of nature to be discovered. Since an unpromulgated law is not law at all, the law of nature is not, in the end, a law at all in the proper sense of the term.

According to Strauss, Locke holds a rather peculiar theory of hedonism. (It is surprising that Locke should be characterized as a hedonist at all.) Good and evil he defines as pleasure and pain. But the greatest happiness consists not in enjoying the greatest or the most intense or even the highest pleasures, but in "having those which produce the greatest pleasures." These words appear in a chapter entitled "Power." Locke's thesis is that the greatest happiness consists in the greatest power, power consisting of a man's possessing the means to obtain some "future apparent good." Like Hobbes, Locke rejected the notion of a *summum bonum.* Pleasure and pain, he maintained, differ from one person to another, and even from one time to another in a given individual's life. We cling to life not because of the natural sweetness of living but because of the terrors of death. The ultimate goal of desire is not the good life, but escape from pain. The only way to stave off pain is to suffer pain—the pain of work, the work of striving to ward off even worse pain. There are no pure pleasures. Therefore, the good life is quite compatible with the coercive society of a civil state, The relief of pain through painful labor culminates not in having great pleasures but in "having those things which produce the greatest pleasures." And so, Strauss concludes, "Life is the joyless quest for joy."

Locke, John. *Two Treatises of Government*. Edited by Peter Laslett. Cambridge: Cambridge University Press, 1963.

Peter Laslett's critical edition and annotated text of the *Two Treatises of Government* is introduced by an essay which sets the work in its historical context and offers a fresh interpretation of John Locke's social and political theory. This Introduction conveys the excitement with which a historian greets a new find—in this case, Locke's own corrected copy of the *Two Treatises of Government* and the consequent recovery of his personal library. Taken with Locke's private papers, these are important because, as Laslett tries to show, they upset three conventional assumptions about Locke's political writings. First, the *The Treatises of Government* was not written in 1689 with a view to justifying the "Glorious Revolution;" second, it was not written with a view to rectifying the teachings of Thomas Hobbes; and third, it was not intended to be read as a philosophical work.

That Locke was a political refugee in Holland when James II was forced to abdicate is well known, but the extent to which he was implicated in the revolt against the Stuarts has not been fully understood. According to Laslett, it was as a confidant and aide to the Whig leader, Anthony Ashley Cooper, Lord Shaftesbury, in the late 1670's and early 1680's when the revolt was brewing, that Locke turned his mind to the problem of political obligation; and in Laslett's opinion only flight saved Locke from the fate of Algernon Sidney, who was executed for having written a book of similar import to that of the *Two Treatises of Government*.

Laslett argues that the *Second Treatise of Government* was begun in 1679 and completed the next year. In 1680, Sir Robert Filmer's *Patriarchia* appeared, and Locke began the phrase-by-phrase refutation of that work which was to become the First Treatise of the two-part work. Two copies of the manuscript were left behind when Locke took flight in 1683, but only part of one manuscript remained when he returned in 1689. Fortunately, all that was missing was the latter part of Locke's lengthy refutation of Filmer.

Hobbes and Filmer were both defenders of absolutism, but according to Laslett it is almost always Filmer's form of absolutism that Locke is concerned to refute. Hobbes at this time had no following, but Filmer was enjoying a great vogue not only among the royalists but also among others who, on religious grounds, held to the principle of passive obedience. Filmer had argued that God sets kings over men just as he sets father over children. This, of course, is what Locke denies when he argues, in the *Second Treatise*, that in the natural state no adult has authority over another. The argument in this treatise is empirical and rational: experience shows that the superiority of fathers is only temporary, and reason shows why this must be so. But because religious authority carried weight with so many people, Locke found it wise even in the *Second Treatise* to undergird his conclusions by quoting the highly respected churchman, Richard Hooker. Certainly it was the religious dimension of the controversy which led Locke to write the lengthy *First Treatise* in which he supported the conclusions of the *Second Treatise* by appealing to divine revelation.

That Locke was influenced by Hobbes need not be denied. Although he had probably read the *Leviathan* when he was young, he seems to have had no recent contact with any of Hobbes's works when he wrote the *Two Treatises of Government*. Hobbes's influence, Laslett suggests, was like the gravitational influence exercised by a large body at some distance. On the whole, the influence was positive. English defenders of liberty have usually viewed the state in terms of its constitutional history. Locke learned from Hobbes to think of it in abstract terms, with the result that his response to what was an immediate political situation reads as if it were a statement of universal truth. This, says Laslett, makes the book unique and accounts for its wide influence.

The *Two Treatises of Government* and *An Essay Concerning Human Understanding* both appeared in 1690. The former, however, did not bear Locke's name; nor was Locke willing publicly to acknowledge his authorship until shortly before his death. Part of the reason for such secrecy, Laslett suggests, could have been that James II's return remained a possibility; but more significantly, he believes, is the fact that the doctrine of the *Two Treatises of Government* was difficult to reconcile with the theory of knowledge advanced in *An Essay Concerning Human Understanding*. The doctrine, for example, that the mind is a blank table on which experience alone can write leaves little room for the doctrine that reason teaches a Law of Nature to all who will consult it.

In Laslett's opinion, Locke could have explained that the object of *An Essay Concerning Human Understanding* was to limit our claims to theoretical knowledge in order better to determine "those things which concern our conduct," and the *Two Treatises of Government* fitted into this program by showing how people ought to behave. In any case, says Laslett, Locke's philosophy was not meant to be a system, as Hobbes's was, but an attitude—the conviction that the universe, including human relations, is to be found out by experience and understood according to reason.

The thirty pages which Laslett devotes to expounding Locke's political theories are noteworthy as an attempt to avoid reading back into Locke the views of subsequent thinkers. Laslett emphasizes what he calls Locke's doctrine of natural political virtue, according to which individual persons, whether in formal or in informal groups, tend to be favorably disposed toward each other and ready to cooperate in the most effective way. Custom, trust, and implicit assent emerge as more basic than explicit assent and contractual agreements.

Additional Recommended Reading

Aaron, Richard I. *John Locke*. Oxford: Clarendon Press, 1971. Chapter 2 of Part III, devoted to a discussion of Locke's political theory, not only provides an excellent exposition of Locke's views but also puts them in the setting of contemporary religious and political thinking.

Dunn, John. *The Political Thought of John Locke: An Historical Account of the Argument of the "Two Treatises of Government"*. Cambridge: Cambridge University Press, 1969. A superb analysis of Locke's views by an author who is fully conversant with all the pertinent literature and is not at all hesitant to differ from other leading authorities.

Gough, J. W. *John Locke's Political Philosophy*. Oxford: Clarendon Press, 1973. An extended analysis of eight major themes in Locke's political philosophy, including, among others, the law of nature, individual rights, consent, property, and sovereignty.

Macpherson, C. B. *The Political Theory of Possessive Individualism: Hobbes to Locke*. Oxford: Clarendon Press, 1962. Chapter 5 is devoted to an analysis of Locke's theory of property rights, natural rights, the state of nature, and various other political questions. The essay is in the context of others dealing with Locke's predecessors.

O'Connor, D. J. *John Locke*. London: Penguin Books, 1952. Chapter 9 contains an excellent summary of Locke's political theory, a critical and well-balanced analysis in the tradition of current British analytical philosophy. The book as a whole is excellent, with biographical as well as philosophical information about Locke.

Steinberg, Jules. *Locke, Rousseau, and the Idea of Consent: An Inquiry into the Liberal-Democratic Theory of*

Political Obligation. Westport, Connecticut: Greenwood Press, 1978. In Chapter 3, "Locke and the Idea of Consent," the author attempts to demonstrate that Locke used consent theory merely as a means to convey his theory of obligation, consent being equivalent to "what individuals ought to do" or "what is morally right," regardless of whether the persons concerned had consented to anything in the ordinary sense of the word.

THEODICY

Author: Gottfried Wilhelm von Leibniz (1646-1716)
Type of work: Theology, metaphysics
First published: 1710

Principal Ideas Advanced

The truths of philosophy and theology cannot contradict each other.
If God is all-good, all-wise, and all-powerful, how did evil come into the world?
The answer is that some error is unavoidable in any creature less perfect than its creator; furthermore, all possible worlds contain some evil, and evil improves the good by contrast.
Since man has free will, he is responsible for his acts; God's foreknowledge of the course of man's inclinations did not involve predestination.
The soul is coordinated with the body by a preestablished harmony.

In some philosophical circles Leibniz's *Theodicy* has been much neglected. This fact is not strange in view of the lack of interest, until recently, in traditional theological questions. It is strange, however, in view of the centrality of the *Theodicy* in Leibniz's own thinking. A good case could be made out that in his own mind it represented his most important, as well as his most characteristic, work. Without it there is much of importance left to Leibniz, to be sure: the pure metaphysician, the logician, the epistemologist, and the mathematician. Yet a balanced view of Leibniz's thought demands that the *Theodicy* be restored to its rightful place as central in his systematic effort.

For all of the continental rationalists (Descartes, Spinoza, and Leibniz), God occupied a large and a systematic place. Much could be made of all that these men owe to medieval theology, but the point is that all these men were centrally interested in the nature of God and his relationship to the natural world. The way in which this problem is worked out by Leibniz has a great deal to do with his solution to other problems. Moreover, there is evidence that Leibniz looked upon himself (to a considerable extent) as a theologian and was most proud of his contributions there. He wished to bring peace between Catholics and Protestants, and his writing has had some effect along this line. Particularly, Leibniz wanted to give rational solutions to traditional theological issues, and more than almost any other man he made it his major goal to provide a reconciliation between traditional religious views and philosophical thought, through demonstrating their essential harmony.

The *Theodicy* has a unique place among the classical writing in philosophical theology, for it is one of the first attempts to "justify the ways of God to man" in straightforward and philosophical terms. All theological views, to be sure, had dealt with the issue of God's choice and his creation of this particular natural order; but many had bracketed the question as being beyond rational scrutiny, and few had set out to answer it directly and in detail. Theodicy, the discussion of God's orderings insofar as they concern man's purposes, became a major part of philosophical theology after Leibniz's treatise.

Leibniz was among those of his age who considered Christianity's merit to be its rational and enlightened nature, as contrasted with at least some other religions. Along with rationalism went a tendency to minimize the differences in nature between God and man. Leibniz shared in this tendency, stating that the perfections of God are those of our soul, even though he possesses them in boundless measure. Leibniz was also an optimist about the essential goodness of man and the possibility of his perfection, and it is probably this view of the nature of man which more than any other single factor led Leibniz into his "best of all possible worlds" doctrine.

The freedom of man and the justice of God form the object of this treatise, and Leibniz's aim was to support both while minimizing neither. To do this would justify God's ways to man; man would be more content to receive what God has ordained, once the logic and harmony of God's plan were grasped. God does whatever is best, but he does not act from absolute necessity. Nature's laws allow a mean between absolute necessity and arbitrary decrees. In this way both God's and man's actions were to be explained and reconciled.

God (for Leibniz) is deeply involved in the affairs of men, continually creating them, and yet he is not the author of sin. Evil has a source somewhere other than in the will of God; God permits moral evil, but he does not will it. Leibniz hoped that this view would offend neither reason nor faith. Consciously, Leibniz set out to modify the strictness of the necessity he found in Hobbes, Spinoza, and Descartes. These philosophers had not been interested in a Christian doctrine of evil, for such a doctrine requires that man be given greater freedom in order to remove evil from God's immediate responsibility.

In the *Theodicy* Leibniz assumes that the truths of philosophy and theology cannot contradict each other. God acts in creation according to general rules of good and of order. Mysteries may be explained sufficiently to justify belief in them, but one cannot comprehend them. In explaining this, Leibniz distinguishes between logical or metaphysical necessity (whose opposite implies contradiction) and physical necessity. Even miracles must conform to the former although they may violate the latter. Reason is the ultimate norm: no article of faith must imply contradiction or contravene proofs as exact as mathematics.

When we come to consider evil, we do so by asking what just reasons, stronger than those which appear contrary to them, may have compelled God to permit evil. God is subject to the multitude of reasons and is even "compelled" by them. Leibniz infers that God must have had innumerable considerations in mind, in the light of which he deemed

it inadvisable to prevent certain evils, for nothing comes from God which is not consistent with goodness, justice, and holiness. God must have been able to permit sin without detriment to his perfections; the weight of the reasons argues for it. Men are essentially in the same circumstance in which God was in finding it necessary to permit certain evils.

Since reason is a gift of God even as faith is, Leibniz argues, contention between them would cause God to contend against God. Therefore, if any reasoned objections against any article of faith cannot be dissolved, then the alleged article must be considered as false and as not revealed. Reason and faith can be reconciled. Yet reason is still faced with its central problem: How could a single first principle, all-good, all-wise, and all-powerful, have been able to allow evil and to permit the wicked to be happy and the good unhappy? Since Leibniz's time, philosophical inquiry into theological problems has often begun with this question.

Leibniz did not attempt to make the connection between God and moral evil an indirect one, which has been the traditional method. An evil will, he says, cannot exist without cooperation. An action, he asserts, is not for being evil the less dependent on God. Thus Leibniz makes the solution to the problem of evil directly a matter of accounting for God's action, since nothing can come to pass without his permission. God is the first reason of things.

The cause of this world, Leibniz writes, must be intelligent, for the first cause has to consider all possible worlds and then fix upon one to create. Such an intelligence would have to be infinite and, united to a goodness no less infinite, it cannot have chosen other than the best of all possible worlds.

It may be, for instance, that all evils are almost as nothingness in comparison with the good things which are in the universe. Whence did evil come then? We must consider that there is some original imperfection, due to the creature's limited nature, in the creature before sin. Leibniz adopts this view of "original sin," that some error is unavoidable in principle in a creature which must be less perfect than the being who creates it.

Other reasons for evil may be given: There is evil in all of the possible worlds, and so no choice could avoid it entirely. Evil often makes us savor good the more because of it—evil in that sense being necessary to any good. Man's will is responsible for its own actions; but this explanation simply leads Leibniz into a consideration of the divine foreknowledge and the question of divine predestination. Here Leibniz indulges in hairsplitting, distinguishing between what is certain and what is necessary. The will is inclined toward the course it adopts, and in that sense its action is and always has been "certain" in God's knowledge. But the action of man's will is not necessary, although this means merely that its opposite does not involve a logical contradiction. Such "contingency" Leibniz allows to remain.

God always chooses the best, but he is not constrained so to do. This is the extent of his freedom. Another natural sequence of things is equally possible, in the logical sense, although his will is determined in the choice it makes by the preponderating goodness of the natural order he chose; that is to say, the natural order that we actually have. Everything is certain and determined beforehand in man's action, although this is not the absolute necessity which would find any alternative logically contradictory. The necessity comes from the goodness of the object chosen.

The prevailing inclination always triumphs. In that sense Leibniz cannot conceive of either God or man acting irrationally, and hence the actions of both God and man are necessary. The whole future is doubtless determined. But since we do not know what it is, nor what it is that God foresees or has resolved, we must still do our duty, according to the reason God has given us and the rules he has prescribed. In the midst of an expansive metaphysical doctrine of possible worlds and the infinity of possible choices open to God, Leibniz adopted as conservative a theological view of predestination as the tradition has seen. A radical in metaphysics, he was almost a reactionary in his view of the fixed relation of God to the world.

Like many conservatives, Leibniz tried—and believed that he had succeeded—to reconcile absolute foreknowledge on God's part with human freedom. His answer is as old as Augustine's. We are free in that our actions flow from our own will, but the action

of the will in turn is dependent upon its causes, which ultimately run back to God. Notwithstanding this dependence of voluntary actions upon other causes, Leibniz still believed that the existence within us of a "wonderful spontaneity" is not precluded. This makes the soul independent of the physical influence of all other creatures, although Leibniz was careful not to say that it is also independent of God.

The doctrine of preestablished harmony is introduced to reconcile the difficulty. It was predestined from the beginning that God's design and man's volition should coincide: to Leibniz this seems to be a satisfactory solution. It is the typical solution of the rationalist. A reason has been given, and the whole scheme is seen to fit into a logical framework in which there is no contradiction or ultimate disharmony. Whereas a contemporary might begin with the premise that human freedom must at all cost be allowed for, Leibniz begins with the idea that all factors should be accounted for by a rational framework.

Preestablished harmony again accounts for the coordination of the soul and body. Like Spinoza's "parallel attributes," God ordained at the time of creation a logical ordering in which the soul's actions coincide with the body's movements. Like Descartes and Spinoza, Leibniz was thoroughly convinced that there is no interaction but there is a rationally determined plan of agreement. God has arranged beforehand for the body to execute the soul's orders. God has accommodated the soul to the body. Actually, the design of the world is simply an extension of God's perfection. Just as the rationalists of this era saw God and the human soul as being very close by nature, so also they viewed the natural order as an extension of the divine nature through creation. Although it is less than God, the created order essentially exhibits the same qualities as does divinity itself.

God is inclined toward every possible good, in proportion to the excellence of that good. God, before decreeing anything, considered among all the possible sequences of things that one which he afterwards approved. God grants his sanction to this sequence (our present natural order) only after having entered into all its detail. From such a description of God's rational selective activity comes the doctrine of the best of all possible worlds.

In most traditional accounts of ultimate origin (as, for example, in Plato's *Timaeus*), the first cause moves because he is good and outgoing, not grudging. But in all classical and in most medieval schemes such a god has no real choices to make. Leibniz presents a modern metaphysical framework in that he stresses the infinitely wide range of alternatives open to God's choice. The philosophical solution, however, is traditional. God selects according to fixed norms. It makes sense to say that classical thinkers also considered this world to be the best possible, but they believed that God had no alternatives. Leibniz simply set classical theory into a wider context of possibilities, but continued to agree to God's fixed goodness and to his necessary selection and creation.

In the *Theodicy* Leibniz also takes up traditional and primarily theological questions concerning Christ and salvation. His answers here are not startlingly novel, except that Leibniz transferred miracles, belief in the nature of Christ, and a Christian doctrine of salvation into a thoroughly rational framework. Leibniz wanted the doctrines of traditional Christianity to be amenable to his philosophical scheme of metaphysics. In the process of demonstrating this mutual harmony, like all philosophical theologians, he was pushed into giving some rather far fetched accounts of some rather difficult religious notions—for example, the assertion of the existence of all human souls in seed in their progenitors since the very beginning of things. Obviously such an idea would be helpful in establishing a religious notion of original sin in Adam; but it is hardly likely to be confirmable by the microscopic observations Leibniz's rationalism suggests.

It is not in the slightest an exaggeration to say that both Leibniz's questions and his answers are repetitious. The *Theodicy* sets out to refute certain doctrines which Leibniz opposed (particularly those of Pierre Bayle). Leibniz did this partly by reference to and elaboration of certain of his famous theories (preestablished harmony, the essential goodness of God's choice), but primarily his weapon was the repetition of his own position. As a rationalist Leibniz evinced the traditional irritation at finding that someone else did not find his reasoning as persuasive as he himself did and that his opponent continued to hold different theories. Despite this defect, the *Theodicy* illustrates how important works do not always have the technical rigor and logical tightness that one might suppose. Leibniz repeats his maxims and principles; he does little to explore them in detail. Yet Leibniz is dealing with questions of great moment and common interest, and his proposed solutions are interesting and suggestive. More precise and cogent pieces of philosophical analysis have proved to be less interesting over the years, but Leibniz's sometimes tedious and often loose reflections on the crucial issues of theology are still very much alive.

Pertinent Literature

Russell, Bertrand. *A Critical Exposition of the Philosophy of Leibniz*. London: George Allen & Unwin, 1900.

A Critical Exposition of the Philosophy of Leibniz is one of the most important secondary works on Gottfried Wilhelm von Leibniz's philosophy. The chief value of this work lies in its analyses of Leibniz's logic and metaphysics. According to Bertrand Russell, Leibniz's metaphysics—his monadology—is almost entirely derived from his logic. Russell does not think highly of Leibniz's theodicy; in his mind it represents an unsatisfactory compromise between Christian dogma and the "impieties" to which, Russell claims, Leibniz's own logic should have led him. Still, Russell presents a brief analysis of Leibniz's understanding of evil and its relation to an all-powerful, entirely good, God.

Russell maintains that in Leibniz's system, moral and physical evil (sin and suffering) are necessary results of metaphysical evil (imperfection). According to Leibniz, moral evil (that is, sin) is a consequence of judging wrongly, for if one were to judge rightly one would always act rightly. However, one is bound to judge wrongly since, because one is imperfect, one's perceptions are confused. Pain necessarily accompanies wrong actions. Thus metaphysical evil—imperfection—is the source of moral and physical evil.

Russell maintains that Leibniz's notion that moral and physical evil are necessary results of metaphysical evil is problematic. It stands in opposition to the traditional Christian account of evil and it poses the question whether imperfection is really evil. According to Russell, since imperfection is nothing more than finitude, Leibniz has no basis for asserting that imperfection is a type of evil. If existence is good, as Leibniz states, then everything is good by virtue of its existence. Internal consistency should have precluded the existence of evil in Leibniz's system altogether. Yet for Leibniz to deny that there is real evil in the world is to contradict Christian dogma. In order to stay within the bounds of Christian thought, Leibniz is forced into affirming the existence of something that his system cannot support.

A second problem arises from Leibniz's commitment to the Christian tradition. According to Leibniz, moral evil (sin) is the result of metaphysical evil. One sins because one is finite. According to traditional Christian dogma, sin is not necessary but contingent; that is, it is the result of free action. In Russell's estimation, Leibniz is not successful in his attempt to show that metaphysical necessity and freedom are compatible. Russell states: "The Ethics to which he [Leibniz] was entitled was very similar to Spinoza's; it had the same fallacies and similar consequences. But being the champion of orthodoxy against the decided atheist, Leibniz shrank from the consequences of his view, and took refuge in the perpetual iteration of edifying phrases."

A Critical Exposition of the Philosophy of Leibniz does not devote a great deal of attention to Leibniz's theodicy because Russell does not believe that it merits much attention. Nevertheless, what Russell does have to say is interesting and should be considered.

Lovejoy, Arthur O. *The Great Chain of Being.* Cambridge, Massachusetts: Harvard University Press, 1936.

The Great Chain of Being has an excellent chapter on the philosophies of Gottfried Wilhelm von Leibniz and Benedictus de Spinoza and a chapter on eighteenth century optimism which includes a brief treatment of Leibniz's theodicy. Anyone interested in Leibniz's thought will profit greatly simply from reading these two chapters. However, a complete reading of *The Great Chain of Being* is strongly recommended since the notions of plentitude, continuity, and gradation—notions which are immensely important for Leibniz—have a long history in Western thought. *The Great Chain of Being* is devoted to uncovering that history.

Arthur O. Lovejoy contends that the notion of plentitude—that everything which could possibly exist does exist—can be traced back to Plato, and that the idea of continuity—that there are no gaps in creation—can be deduced from Plato's notion of plentitude and found in some of Aristotle's teachings. The notion of gradation—that there is a hierarchy of being—is present in certain of Plato's writings and, to a larger extent, in Aristotle's works. In Neoplatonism all three of these notions are clearly present and are fully organized into a coherent philosophical doctrine.

According to Lovejoy, Western philosophy up to the nineteenth century is rationalistic in the sense that the questions "Why is there an actual world?" and "What principles determine the number of kinds of beings that make up the actual world?" are meaningful and can be answered. The answer to the second of these two questions usually involves the notions of plentitude, continuity, and gradation. The answer to the first question usually involves the notions of goodness and self-sufficiency, and, for the Christian philosopher, the idea of an omnipotent God.

Leibniz's philosophy illustrates the Christian brand of rationalism. The reason that there is a world at all is that there is a good God and that the principles that characterize the world are plentitude, continuity, and gradation. The world is full, there are no empty niches, and there is a definite hierarchy of being.

Leibniz's famous contention that "This is the best possible world" is derived from the principles of God's goodness and of plentitude. Because God is good by definition, God chooses to create the best possible world. Because the world contains as many types of actualities as possible, this is the best possible world. For Leibniz variety is one of the important aspects of the best, and no other possible world could have as many types of actualities as the present world does.

In his *Theodicy* Leibniz addresses the issue of how there can be evil in the world if it is created by an all-powerful God who is entirely good. His solution to this quandary is that (with the exception of metaphysical evil) what is meant by "evil," that is, by sin and suffering, is necessary for the sake of plentitude. Leibniz writes: "It is true that one can imagine possible worlds without sin and suffering, just as one can invent romances about Utopias or about the Sevarambes; but these worlds would be much inferior to ours." Like Plotinus, who said that "the whole earth is full of a diversity of living things, mortal and immortal, and replete with them up to the heavens," Leibniz insists on the necessity of everything that is and on its essential goodness.

The Great Chain of Being is an informative inquest into a set of ideas which have played an important role in Western thought; in the process, it sheds a great deal of light on Leibniz's theodicy.

Griffin, David Ray. *God, Power, and Evil: A Process Theodicy.* Philadelphia: Westminster Press, 1976.

In *God, Power, and Evil: A Process Theodicy*, David Ray Griffin reviews and criticizes the most famous and influential theodicies of the past, concluding with a consideration of a theodicy based on the process philosophy of Alfred North Whitehead. In addition to Gottfried Wilhelm von Leibniz's theodicy, Griffin examines the biblical and Greek sources on the nature of God and the reality of evil and the traditional theodicies of Saint Augustine, Thomas Aquinas, Benedictus de Spinoza, Martin Luther, John Calvin, Karl Barth, John Hick, James Ross, Emil Fackenheim, and Emil Brunner.

Griffin believes that most scholars have misinterpreted Leibniz's theodicy. The dominant interpretation of Leibniz's position is that although there is sin and suffering in this world it is still the best possible world since any other possible world would include even more sin and suffering. God cannot create a world that is better than this world because God is limited by the possibilities that exist, many of which are "incompossible," that is, mutually exclusive. Leibniz does not doubt God's moral perfection—God chose to create the best possible world—but he does question God's omnipotence when "omnipotence" is taken to include the ability to do the impossible. The dominant interpretation of Leibniz's theodicy, then, is that real sin and suffering exist because God is limited by the types of things that can coexist and that sin and suffering are a result of this limitation.

Griffin argues very convincingly against this interpretation. According to Griffin, Leibniz's solution to the problem of evil—the problem of how to reconcile the fact of evil with the existence of an all-good, all-powerful being—is not to deny God's omnipotence but rather to deny the reality of genuine evil. God could have created a world with no sin or suffering (moral and physical evil), but he did not do so because it would not be "'proper." A world with sin and suffering in it is better, *all things considered*, than any possible world without sin and suffering. Moral and physical evil add to the overall perfection of the world and hence are not genuinely evil. (Metaphysical evil, Griffin argues, is not genuinely evil since it is nothing more than finitude.)

Griffin is also interested in examining and explicating Leibniz's views on the relation of faith and reason and on contingent events and God's knowledge of the future. Griffin concludes that the difference between Leibniz's claim that faith should never be contrary to reason and the traditional position that faith is often unreasonable is "more verbal than real." Griffin's interest in Leibniz's contention that God knows the future in every detail, even the future of contingent events, is "less with the validity of Leibniz's arguments that this can happen without the contingency of these events being undercut than with the presupposition it requires about the nature of 'actual events.' " Griffin concludes that God could know everything that will happen only if the sufficient reasons for those things precede the occurrence of those things. If some of the sufficient reasons for any event lie within the event itself, then the event cannot be fully known before it occurs.

Griffin's work is scholarly—well-reasoned and well-documented—and accessible. The fact that it presents an alternative "process theodicy" which the author feels is entirely credible in the contemporary world is also significant. Even though Griffin takes exception to Leibniz's solution to the problem of evil, he shares Leibniz's concern that evil be explained in light of God's existence.

Additional Recommended Reading

Carr, Herbert Wildon. *Leibniz*. Boston: Little, Brown and Company, 1929. Carr discusses Leibniz's historical situation, his philosophy, and his influence. He understands Leibniz's theodicy as a corollary of Leibniz's philosophy which may be rejected without damaging Leibniz's philosophical system.

Hick, John. *Evil and the God of Love*. New York: Harper & Row Publishers, 1966. Hick's book is an account of the major Christian theodicies and a statement of his own position. Hick understands Leibniz as compromising God's power and therefore holding to a "sub-Christian" concept of God.

Hostler, John. *Leibniz's Moral Philosophy*. New York: Barnes & Noble, 1975. Hostler's well-written book explores the ethical implications of Leibniz's philosophy.

Rescher, Nicholas. *The Philosophy of Leibniz*. Englewood Cliffs, New Jersey: Prentice-Hall, 1967. This is a systematic introduction to Leibniz's thought. Rescher gives an excellent account of how the various aspects of Leibniz's philosophy, including his theodicy, are related to each other.

THREE DIALOGUES BETWEEN HYLAS AND PHILONOUS

Author: George Berkeley (1685-1753)
Type of work: Metaphysics
First published: 1713

Principal Ideas Advanced

The universe is composed not of matter but of minds and spirits. Material objects, conceived of as nonmental substances existing outside consciousness, do not exist.

The universe of sensible objects is a projection of the mind. The existence of sensible objects is comparable to that of objects in dreams or hallucinations.

The view that tables, chairs, and other sensible objects exist independently of being perceived leads to skepticism about the existence and nature of such a realm.

Perceptions are not caused by material substances.

An infinite being causes and coordinates all perceptual experiences.

In this book the view is defended that matter does not exist. The universe contains minds or spirits but no realm of atoms and molecules. George Berkeley argues that things which are normally considered material objects—stones, trees, shoes, apples—have no existence outside the minds and experiences of conscious beings. Like an object in a dream, a stone has no existence outside consciousness. If all conscious beings were to stop perceiving some sensible object—the moon, for example—that object would cease to exist. Although Berkeley's book owes its philosophical greatness to the many important arguments which are presented in support of the main thesis, the work is also notable for the simplicity and clarity with which the ideas are conveyed. The ideas are presented in the form of a dialogue between Hylas, a materialist, and Philonous, the representative of Berkeley's idealism.

The main argument in the work centers around an examination of the set of properties of which sensible objects are composed. Berkeley first examines the properties which philosophers have called "secondary qualities" (heat, taste, sound, smell, color) and argues that these properties have no existence outside sensations and perceptions in the minds of perceivers. He then argues that the same sorts of considerations will show that what have been called the "primary qualities" of sensible objects—extension (length and width), shape, hardness, weight, motion and other characteristics—also have no existence outside the perceptions of conscious beings. In arguing that *every* property which a sensible object has exists only as a sensation or a property of a sensation within a mind, Berkeley is showing that the entire sensible object has no existence outside of the mind. For Berkeley a cherry is nothing over and above the sensations experienced in connection with it. "Take away the sensations of softness, redness, tartness, and you take away the cherry," he writes.

Berkeley begins his argument by reference to heat. Intense heat like intense cold is a pain; it is intrinsically unpleasant. Pain, like pleasure, is a kind of experience; it is something which cannot exist outside of someone's consciousness. Therefore, when someone feels intense heat or intense cold, Berkeley reasons, what he feels is in his own mind, not in some inert, unfeeling object existing outside his consciousness. To be aware of intense heat is simply to be aware of a particular kind of pain sensation.

To the objection that intense heat is a *cause* of pain and not itself literally "pain," Berkeley replies that when a person is perceiving intense heat, the heat of which he is aware is not distinguishable from the pain sensation of which he is aware. In perceiving the heat the person is not aware of *two* things, heat *and* a pain sensation, but of only one thing, a painful sensation.

The temperature which an object appears to have differs under different circumstances, Berkeley proceeds. If a person's left hand is hot and his right hand cold and he then immerses both hands into a bowl of water, the water seems cool to the left hand and warm to the right hand. From this fact Berkeley concludes that the heat which the person feels cannot be a feature of some object existing outside his mind. No single object could have the incompatible properties of warmth and coolness at once. Berkeley concludes that the warmth and coolness which the person perceives are sensations within his own experience. What people think of as *the* "temperature" of the water is simply the sensation experienced in connection with the water. The sensation is in the consciousness of the person perceiving the temperature, not in an unfeeling object outside his consciousness.

These arguments concerning heat can be paralleled for the other secondary qualities of sensible objects. A sweet taste is a form of pleasure; a bitter taste is intrinsically unpleasant or painful. Since pleasure and pain are necessarily mental phenomena, a sweet or bitter taste, because it is a pleasure or pain, must itself be a mental phenomenon, Berkeley reasons. Furthermore, the taste which people perceive in an object varies under different conditions. A food which someone finds sweet at one time he may find bitter or tasteless at another time. The taste a food has to a person when he is sick is different from the taste it has to him when he is well, Berkeley writes. What differs in the two cases, he reasons, is not the alleged external object but the experience had when tasting the food. In each case one has different taste sensations, and these taste sensations, which *are* the taste of the food, exist in the mind of the person doing the tasting. The fact that some people delight in the same food which others find repulsive Berkeley considers further proof that the taste of a food is not a property inherent in the object which allegedly exists outside people's minds but a sensation undergone by the people who taste the food. Similar considerations can be appealed to in support of the claim that odor or

smell is a sensation within someone's mind.

As happens with other secondary qualities, the *color* which an object appears to have varies under different conditions. A cloud which appears some shade of white under most conditions may appear red or purple when perceived at sunset, Berkeley writes. Someone who holds that color is an inherent property of the clouds will need to say that not all the colors that may be perceived in an object are the true color of the object and that some of these colors are only apparent.

How then is the true color to be distinguished from the colors which are said to be merely *apparent?* It might be suggested that the true color is the one the object presents when it is viewed under white light. But this suggestion raises problems. An object presents a somewhat different color under candlelight from that which it presents under daylight, Berkeley notes. Indeed, there are many different intensities and shades of what we call "white light," and each of these intensities and shades is as normal and common as the others. Yet each shade and intensity leads to a somewhat different color being perceived in an object.

One might reply that the true color of an object is the color that is perceived when the object is given the most close and careful inspection possible. But this suggestion also runs into serious problems. To examine an object in the closest and most careful manner possible is to examine the object under a microscope, Berkeley writes. However, when an object is examined under a microscope, the microscope does not simply present *one* color to the eye, a color which one could label the true color; rather, the microscope (like the naked eye) presents numerous colors to the eye, and the particular color one sees in an object depends on the magnification one gives to the microscope. To pick out one color from the various colors which are perceived and call it the true color of the object would require a choice which has no justification.

A further problem for someone who maintains that color is a property inherent in objects exterior to minds is the fact that objects under the same conditions present different colors to different perceivers. Objects which appear yellow to people with jaundice appear other colors to people without jaundice, Berkeley writes. Furthermore, given the structural differences between the eyes of animals and those of people, it is probable that some animals perceive colors in objects that are different from those which people perceive. To pick out any of these perceived colors and call it the true color would involve an arbitrary, unjustifiable decision. The view that an object has a true color Berkeley considers untenable in face of the above facts. From these considerations Berkeley concludes that *all* colors perceived in sensible objects are simply visual sensations in the minds of those perceiving the color.

The accounts which scientists give of perception are often consistent with his account of secondary qualities and may even be interpreted as supporting it, Berkeley writes. Although scientists do, of course, believe in a material world existing external to consciousness which causes people to hear sounds and see colors, they often think of hearing or seeing as a matter of having certain auditory or visual *sensations*. Scientists say, for example, that when an object causes air to move in a certain manner and this air strikes the ear drum, a certain neurological activity is produced and the neurological activity causes one to experience *the sensation of sound*. Color is seen, they say, when light rays, after being reflected off some object, enter the eye and stir the optic nerve such that a message is communicated to the brain, upon which the person experiences *the sensation of color*. To say, as these scientists do, that sound and color are *sensations* is to say that they are mental phenomena.

The view that "secondary qualities" are nothing but sensations in the minds of conscious beings, although queer in relation to common sense, did not originate with Berkeley. The view had been previously defended by John Locke. Berkeley's most radical departure from previous philosophical opinion was in his claim that all properties of sensible objects, including the "primary qualities," could be shown to have no existence outside the minds of perceivers.

If the existence of perceptual variation is reason to conclude that the secondary qualities do not exist outside minds, Berkeley reasoned, then philosophers have the same reason to conclude that the primary qualities also lack existence outside minds. Like the secondary qualities, the primary qualities give rise to radical perceptual variations. The extension which an object appears to have varies as the object is perceived from different positions, Berkeley explains. The visible extension which a tree has, the extension which it has in relation to the expanse of a perceiver's field of vision, grows larger as the perceiver approaches the tree and shrinks as the perceiver moves away from the tree. When a perceiver is near, a tree may appear to be a hundred times larger than it does from a great distance. (Imagine how much larger the moon would look if you could see it from a distance of only ten miles.) It does not help to reply that the tree has the same size in *feet* and *inches* whatever one's distance from it. For the visible extension of a foot or an inch itself is not a constant and it too goes through the same variations as one approaches or recedes from it. A twelve-inch ruler looks large from very close but tiny when perceived from a distance. Furthermore, Berkeley argues, a sensible object may present differing visible extensions at one and the same time. The foot of a mouse, which seems tiny to a man, would seem to be of considerable extension to the mouse. An object which extends over a large portion of the field of vision of a mouse would extend over a small portion of the visual field of a man. Berkeley concludes that the extension of a sensible object is not a property of an object which exists outside our consciousness but a property of a sensation in the mind of a perceiver.

The types of considerations which show that the extension of a sensible object has no existence outside a mind also show that shape, hardness, and the other primary qualities are only properties of sensations within the minds of perceivers. The shape, hardness, and motion which an object appears to have also vary from one perceiver to another and vary for a single perceiver when the object is viewed under different conditions.

One might think that the fact that objects are perceived as being *at a distance* from the person perceiving them proves that the objects cannot be inside the perceiver's mind. Berkeley responds to this objection with the observation that even in dreams and hallucinations objects are experienced as being at a distance and outside of the mind, yet in spite of these appearances these imagined objects do not exist outside of the mind of the person imagining them. Thus it clearly is possible for an object to be experienced as being at a distance from oneself even when the object is really not outside one's own mind.

Another reason why the primary qualities must be in the mind with the secondary qualities, Berkeley writes, is that all sensible qualities coexist. When a person perceives a table the extension and shape which he perceives are *joined* to the color. The shape outlines the color. If the color which is perceived is in the person's mind, then so are the extension, shape, and motion which are experienced as being together with the color.

It might be supposed that when someone perceives an object he has an image in his mind which *copies* or *mirrors* a material world existing outside his mind—a world which is the cause of the image. Although it is the mental image and not the material world a perceiver is directly aware of, the image provides accurate information about the external, material world, it may be said. Berkeley finds serious problems in this view. First, if it is admitted that all the primary and secondary qualities of objects exist only within minds, then there are no properties remaining for this so-called "material substance" outside the mind to have. Talk of "material substance" in this context becomes meaningless. Furthermore, it is not possible, Berkeley argues, for an image which is continually undergoing radical changes (which our perception of sensible objects is doing) to be a copy of some set of objects which remains unchanged throughout this period (as the alleged material substance is assumed to do).

A further problem with this view, Berkeley argues, is that the model of perception which it presents leads to a severe skepticism about the alleged material world. According to this view a person perceiving a sensible object is not directly aware of the material world but only of the image in his mind. That this image which is said to be a copy of a material world outside the mind does indeed copy or resemble the object alleged to be the original could not be known. If our knowledge of the alleged original is derived entirely from our familiarity with the image which is said to be the copy, there is no independent means of checking that the "copy" is actually like the original. Indeed, since in this view people are never directly aware of the alleged material world, it follows that it is not possible even to know whether this outside, unexperienced world exists. The existence of a mental image does not itself guarantee that there is an external object causing the image, for it is logically possible for someone to have exactly the same perceptions or mental images even if no world of material objects exists.

If what we consider *real* objects are like objects in dreams and hallucinations in having no existence outside the mind, how then does Berkeley distinguish the former from the latter? Berkeley explains that the perceptions we consider real are vivid and consistent in a way that those which we do not consider real are not.

What then is the cause of people's perceptions of sensible objects if not a world of material substance corresponding to those perceptions? Berkeley reasons that because a person does not cause or coordinate his own sensations, his sensations must have a cause outside himself, and this cause, Berkeley concludes, is an omnipresent infinite spirit. From the order, beauty, and design with which our sensations appear Berkeley concludes that the designer is wise, powerful, and good "beyond comprehension."

Pertinent Literature

Hamlyn, D. W. *Sensation and Perception: A History of the Philosophy of Perception.* London: Routledge & Kegan Paul, 1961, pp. 94-116.

In this survey of the various theories which philosophers have had about perception and its relation to objects of perception, D. W. Hamlyn offers various criticisms of the arguments which George Berkeley uses in his attempt to prove that the sensible world has no existence outside the minds of those who perceive it. One of the arguments in *Three Dialogues* Berkeley bases on a claim that secondary qualities sometimes are inherently unpleasant or painful. (To perceive intense heat is to feel a kind of pain, Berkeley writes.) Since pain has no existence outside the mind, Berkeley reasons, the secondary qualities which are pains have no existence outside minds. Because intense heat **is** a kind of pain, it is nothing but a feeling in the mind of one who perceives it, he concludes. Hamlyn writes that this argument—an argument which Berkeley picks up from John Locke—is invalid. Although people may have certain feelings or sensations while perceiving heat, the warmth or heat which they feel is not just the sensation they experience. Even if it were true that a feeling of intense heat cannot be distinguished from a feeling of pain, *both* feelings, Hamlyn writes, are distinguishable from the heat in the object which causes the feelings. From the fact that a sensation of heat is a mental phenomenon, it does not follow that its cause is a mental phenomenon. To refer to "the heat" is to refer to the *cause* of the sensations and not to the sensations themselves. Hamlyn gives a similar account of the other secondary qualities which Berkeley says may be inherently painful or unpleasant. When people find a certain taste unpleasant or "painful" the taste is the property in the object which causes the unpleasant experience and not the experience itself. The unpleasantness experienced is not itself the taste but an effect of the taste.

Hamlyn explains that Berkeley is wrong to assimilate perceiving to the having of sensations. Like Locke, Berkeley thinks of the pain which someone feels when he perceives intense heat as a part or the whole of his perceiving of the heat. However, perceiving an object is not the same thing as having certain sensations, Hamlyn writes. To have a pain is not in itself to perceive anything, Hamlyn states.

Berkeley based another of his arguments on the fact that our perceptions of objects are variable. That the color, taste, shape, and other qualities that an object appears to have may vary under different conditions Berkeley presents as further proof that it could not be a single (material) object that is being perceived in all these instances. Hamlyn objects that the conclusion Berkeley draws does not follow from the premises. From the fact that an object may appear to have different properties under different conditions it does not follow that none of the properties it appears to have are truly inherent in the object. All that follows is that not all of the properties perceived are inherent in the object. How then can one determine which of the various properties that an object may appear to have are really inherent in the object? The property which is inherent in an object is the one which is perceived when the object is examined under normal conditions, Hamlyn writes.

Hamlyn commends Berkeley for observing that Locke had been inconsistent in failing to notice that the primary qualities are like the secondary qualities in being subject to perceptual variations. If perceptual variation is reason for concluding that secondary qualities have no existence outside minds, then there is the same reason for concluding that primary qualities also have no existence outside minds. However, Hamlyn writes, from the fact that the primary qualities are like the secondary in their perceptual variations it would have been wiser for Berkeley to conclude that both qualities are properties of external objects than it was to conclude that both exist together in the mind.

Moore, G. E. "Proof of an External World," in *Philosophical Papers*. London: George Allen & Unwin, 1959.

In this paper, originally published in 1939, G. E. Moore argues that chairs, stars, mountains, and all the other things which people consider material objects exist outside the minds of conscious beings. Moore does not examine or criticize the arguments which George Berkeley and other philosophers have used in support of the contrary position but simply offers a positive argument in favor of his own position—the position of common sense.

In his attempt to prove the existence of external objects, Moore distinguishes the idea of an object's being "presented in space" from the idea of an object's being such that it may be "met in space." To prove that there are objects of the latter sort is to prove that there are external objects; objects of the former sort are not external objects. After-images and toothaches are objects which are "presented in space" because they are objects having spatial locations. (An after-image appears as being outside one's head, in front of one's eyes; a toothache is experienced as being in or near one's tooth.) But after-images and toothaches are not "to be met with in space." An object that is "to be met with in space" is one which would be seen or felt by any person of normal perceptual apparatus who is in the right position. It is not possible for another person directly to perceive my after-images or pains, but if there are objects that can be perceived by more than one person then these objects are "to be met with in space." If there are objects which are "to be met with in space," then there are objects external to our minds.

External objects, objects which can "be met with in space," are objects which can exist without being perceived, Moore explains. Part of the meaning in the distinction between an object's existing only "in someone's mind" and an object's being "external to people's minds" is that in saying that an object exists only "in someone's mind" we *mean* that it does not exist at times when he is not experiencing it, whereas in describing an object as "external to our minds" we mean that it can exist at moments when it is not being perceived.

To prove that there are external objects, Moore writes, it is sufficient to prove that there are "physical objects." If one can prove that there is a human hand, a soap bubble, a shoe, a sock, or any other "material object," then one has proven that there are things which "are to be met with in space" and which exist

"outside us," Moore writes. The sentence "There is a soap bubble" entails "There is a material object" and "There is an external object." The meaning of "soap bubble" is such that an object would not be a soap bubble unless it were something which could in principle be perceived by more than one person. The meaning of the word is such that it is not a contradiction to speak of a soap bubble as existing at times when it is not perceived.

Can one prove that there are soap bubbles, hands, or other material objects? To do so is easy, Moore writes. To prove to another person that there are material objects, one need only hold up a hand and say "Here is a hand." An additional argument could be added by raising one's other hand and saying "Here is another hand." There is no better proof, Moore argues. The statement which is the premise in the argument ("Here is a hand") differs from the statement which is the conclusion ("Here is an object external to our minds"); the premise is known to be true (it would be absurd to suggest that a person does not know that he has two hands, Moore writes), and the conclusion follows from the premise.

Could a person *prove* the premise of this argument (that he is holding up one of his hands)? Moore admits that he is not confident that a person can prove that he is holding up a hand; but even if he cannot prove this, he can know it to be true. Some things one can know to be true without being able to offer a proof for them, Moore writes. It would be absurd to claim of a normal conscious person that he could not know if he is holding up a hand, Moore writes. A philosopher who is dissatisfied with this proof of the external world, merely because the premise has not itself been proven, has no grounds for dissatisfaction.

Moore, G. E. "A Defence of Common Sense," in *Philosophical Papers*. London: George Allen & Unwin, 1959.

George Berkeley's view that there are no material objects and his claim that even if there were material objects we could not know of their existence are among the views G. E. Moore attacks in this article. Other philosophical theses which sharply clash with common sense are also attacked in the paper.

Berkeley's view that there are no external, material objects *must* be wrong, Moore argues, because there are many propositions known to be true which entail that there are material objects. Among the propositions which Moore says he knows with certainty to be true are that he has a body, that his body was smaller when he was a baby than it is at the time of his writing this article, that his body has been in contact with the earth or near the surface of the earth during his whole life, and that during his life his body has been at various distances from other objects such as his bookcase and pen. Moore writes that, first, he knows with certainty that these and other propositions are true and that, second, each of these propositions entails the existence of external objects. The propositions that he has a body and that his body has been in close contact with the earth imply the existence of material things (namely, his body and the earth). Moore writes that he knows that many other people also know with certainty the same propositions about themselves—namely, that they have bodies, that these bodies have been in contact with the earth, and so forth. The reality of material objects is also entailed by these propositions which other people know to be true. A philosopher who denies that there is a material world *must* be wrong, Moore writes, simply because the above propositions and many related propositions are known with certainty to be true.

Philosophers like Berkeley who say that they do not know if there is an external world or who deny the existence of such a world regularly say things inconsistent with these claims, Moore writes. When an Idealist assumes the existence of other philosophers or of the human race he is being inconsistent with his Idealism, since being a philosopher or any other human being entails being a creature with a body. When referring to "we" or to "us," an Idealist is speaking in a way that is inconsistent with his Idealism since he is alluding to other human beings—that is, to other bodily creatures who live on the earth.

Moore is not simply accusing Idealists of being *careless* when they say things which are inconsistent with their thesis. Rather, Moore is saying that a philosopher who maintains that there are no material objects or that we do not know whether there are any such objects is defending a thesis which is inconsistent with many propositions *that he knows to be true.* An Idealist who refers to other philosophers or who speaks in terms of "we" thereby betrays the fact that he, like Moore, *knows* that there are other people (other embodied creatures). When a philosopher claims that "no human being has ever known whether material objects exist" he is making a claim that is not simply about himself. In saying this he is claiming, first, that there are in addition to himself other persons (other beings with bodies who live on the earth) and, second, that none of these other persons knows if there are material objects. Thus, the Idealist betrays the fact that he considers it certain that there are other embodied creatures, Moore contends. Since *all* people—even philosophers who deny the existence of a material world—know that they have bodies and that there are other people with bodies, it is inevitable that they will betray their knowledge of these facts, Moore writes, and thus it is inevitable that they will say things which are inconsistent with their Idealism.

The view that there are no material objects is not self-contradictory, Moore writes. It is logically possible that there might not have existed material objects. Moore explains that his reason for saying that he knows with certainty that there are material objects is the fact that he knows with certainty that his statements "I have a body," "There are other persons with bodies," and similar, related statements are true.

Additional Recommended Reading

Bennett, Jonathan. "Substance, Reality, and Primary Qualities," in *American Philosophical Quarterly.* II, no. 1 (January, 1965), pp. 1-17. An examination of the arguments which Berkeley and Locke use in defending their views on perception.

Broad, C. D. "Berkeley's Denial of Material Substance," in *The Philosophical Review.* LXIII, no. 2 (April, 1954), pp. 155-181. A critical discussion of Berkeley's theory.

Lean, Martin. *Sense Perception and Matter.* New York: Humanities Press, 1953. A detailed critique of the thinking that leads philosophers to skepticism over the existence of material objects.

McGreal, Ian P. *Analyzing Philosophical Arguments*. San Francisco: Chandler Publishing Company, 1967. Contains a detailed examination of Berkeley's argument, including a reconstruction of the argument, premise-by-premise appraisal, and logical analysis. The key to the argument is the ambiguity of the term "sense quality," according to McGreal.

Moore, G. E. "The Refutation of Idealism," in *Philosophical Studies*. London: Routledge & Kegan Paul, 1922. Moore points to certain confusions which he says have had important roles in all defenses of Idealism.

Russell, Bertrand. *The Problems of Philosophy*. London: Oxford University Press, 1912. In a style free from technical words Russell clearly explains the philosophy of Idealism.

Warnock, G.J. *Berkeley*. Harmondsworth, England: Penguin Books, 1953. An illuminating, thorough exposition of Berkeley's philosophy.

A TREATISE OF HUMAN NATURE (BOOK I)

Author: David Hume (1711-1776)
Type of work: Epistemology
First published: 1739

Principal Ideas Advanced

All of our knowledge comes from impressions and ideas; the impressions are more forceful and lively than the ideas.

By the use of memory and imagination we preserve and arrange our ideas.

We have no abstract, general ideas but only ideas of particular things which can be considered collectively by the use of general terms.

Certainty comes from the intuitive recognition of the similarity or differences in ideas, or from the demonstrative process of connecting a series of intuitions—as in arithmetic and algebra.

Our knowledge of causal relationships is simply the habit of expecting events of one kind to follow events of another kind with which they have been observed to be conjoined; there are no necessary relationships between events.

We have good reason to be skeptical about all conclusions reached by the use of reason or on the basis of sense experience.

Hume's *A Treatise of Human Nature* is his earliest philosophical work and the one that contains the most complete exposition of his views. Apparently it was planned when he was in his early twenties, when he claimed to have discovered a "new scene of thought." The work was composed during a sojourn in France from 1734 to 1737 and was revised shortly thereafter in an unsuccessful attempt to gain the approbation of Bishop Joseph Butler. The first book of the *Treatise* was published in 1739, and the other two the next year. Hume had hoped that his views would attract a great deal of attention; instead, the work "fell dead-born from the presses." His novel theories did not attract attention until after he had published a more popular version in *An Enquiry Concerning Human Understanding* in 1748. The *Treatise* was subjected to a full-scale attack by Thomas Reid in 1764. By this time, Hume was so successful as an author, especially on the basis of his essays and his *History of England* (1754-1762), that he refused to defend his first book, and called it a juvenile work. Over the years it has become more and more important as the fullest and

deepest statement of Hume's philosophical views; in fact, Book I of the *Treatise* has come to be regarded as one of the finest achievements of English philosophy.

On the title page of Book I, Hume announces that the *Treatise* is "an attempt to introduce the experimental Method of Reasoning into Moral Subiects." In the Preface, he explains that he intends to develop a "science of man" by applying Sir Isaac Newton's experimental method to human mental behavior. Following in the footsteps of various English and Scottish moral philosophers, and of the French skeptic Pierre Bayle, he hoped to discover the limits of human knowledge in such areas as mathematics, physics, and the social sciences (the moral subjects). By scrupulously observing human life, Hume thought he could discover certain general laws about human thinking and behavior. He admitted at the outset that it was probably not possible to uncover "the ultimate qualities of human nature," but he thought it should be possible to learn something about the origin and nature of what we think we know.

All of our information, Hume writes, is composed of impressions and ideas. The only difference between these is that the former strike us more forcefully and with greater vivacity than do the latter. Ideas and impressions can be simple or complex, the simple ones being those which cannot be divided into parts or aspects, while the complex ones are composed of simples. There is a great deal of resemblance between the impressions and the ideas. The simple ideas, in fact, exactly resemble simple impressions in all respects except with regard to their force and vivacity. Further, in terms of their appearance in the mind, the simple impressions always precede the simple ideas (except for one unusual case that Hume brings up). The complex ideas are composed of simple parts which are exactly like the simple ingredients of impressions that we have already experienced, though the complex idea itself may not actually be a copy of any complex impression. These discoveries about impressions and ideas indicate, Hume says, that all of our ideas are derived from experience (the world of impressions), and that we have no innate ideas in our minds; that is, ideas that are not based on what we perceive.

In the first part of the *Treatise*, Hume proceeds to explore the bases of our knowledge. We possess two faculties, memory and imagination, for dealing with the ideas that we receive. The memory preserves the ideas in the exact order in which they entered the mind. The imagination, on the other hand, is free to arrange the ideas in any manner that is desired. But, contrary to what might be expected, our imaginations do not function at random. Instead, we imagine ideas in ordered sequences, so that whenever a particular idea comes to mind, other related ideas automatically follow it, according to certain principles of the association of ideas that Hume calls "a kind of ATTRACTION, which in the mental world will be found to have as extraordinary effects as in the natural." Ideas tend naturally to be associated when they are similar, or contiguous in time or space, or when they stand in the relation of cause and effect. The importance of association is brought out when Hume comes to discuss causality in Part III.

Before applying these "discoveries" about the way we think, Hume takes up a few other questions.

He argues first for a point Bishop Berkeley had previously made, that we possess no abstract general ideas, but only ideas of particular things. General terms, such as "man" or "triangle," designate the collections of similar particular ideas that we have acquired from experience.

Hume then tries to explain mathematics as being about particular experiences. He knew relatively little about mathematics and based many of his views on comments in Pierre Bayle's *Dictionary* (1695-1697). Hume's empirical mathematical theory has generally been regarded as, perhaps, the weakest part of his book, though he was always proud of having shown that mathematics is "big with absurdity and contradiction." Hume conceived of arithmetic as being a demonstrable science dealing with relations of quantity, whereas geometry was thought of as an empirical science dealing with observable points. Because of the limitation of our ability to see and count the points, the theorems in geometry are always to some degree uncertain.

The most famous part of the *Treatise* is the third part of Book I, which treats "Of Knowledge and Probability." Genuine knowledge is gained by an intuitive inspection of two or more ideas to see if they stand in a particular relationship to each other. We can be completely certain by intuition that two ideas do or do not resemble each other, or that they differ from each other, or that one has more or less of a given quality than another, as, for instance, that one is darker than another. Such knowledge is certain in that it depends solely on what one "sees" when two or more ideas are brought together by the imagination, but it gives us relatively little information. By connecting a series of intuitions, we gain the sort of demonstrative knowledge that occurs in arithmetic and algebra. Intuition and demonstration are the sole sources of complete certainty and knowledge.

Our information about the causal relation of ideas does not arise from an intuitive examination of our ideas, and almost all of our information about what is happening beyond our immediate experience is based upon causal reasoning. How do we decide which ideas are causally related? When we examine two ideas, or two impressions that we think are so related, we find that we do not perceive any necessary or causal connection between them. We perceive only that the ideas are contiguous and successive. We do not, however, perceive that they are necessarily connected in any way, although we do feel that there must be more to the sequence than merely one idea following after another. We believe that one of the ideas must make the other occur. But, Hume asks, what evidence do we have for such a belief, and where do we acquire the belief? If we admit that we do not perceive any necessary connection between events, then Hume suggests that we ought to ask ourselves why we believe that every event must have a cause and why we believe that particular causes necessarily must have certain effects.

When the first problem is examined, we discover something that is surprising. Even though we all believe that every event must have a cause, this proposition is not intuitively obvious, nor can it be demonstrated. When we conceive of events, we neither see them as caused nor necessarily think of them in terms of their causes. Because of the freedom of our imagination, each event can be thought of separately and independently. If events can be thought of as uncaused, it is also possible that they occur uncaused. If that is a genuine possibility, then there can be no valid demonstration proving the impossibility of uncaused events. The demonstrations that had been offered by previous philosophers, Hume believed, are all unsatisfactory. They beg the question in that they assume what they are attempting to prove; namely, that every event has a cause. Apparently, the causal principle, which is not self-evident nor demonstrable, is so basic that we all accept it for reasons that seem to be unknown.

To explore the matter further, Hume turns to the other problem: What is the basis for our belief that particular causes have particular effects, and how do we infer one from the other? The actual constituents of our causal reasoning, he asserts, are a present impression of sense or memory, an imagined idea of a related event, and an unknown connection between them. When we hear a certain sound, we think of somebody ringing the doorbell. Why and how do we infer from the impression to its supposed cause? Many other ideas might have come to mind. When we hear the sound, we do not, at the same time,

experience its cause, yet we implicitly believe that said cause must also be occurring to produce the perceived effect. This reasoning process is not a logical one, Hume maintains, since there is no *reason* for us to think of one idea rather than another when a particular experience takes place.

If reason cannot be what makes us connect events causally, perhaps experience is responsible. We find that when a sequence of events is constantly repeated in our experience, and when the events are conjoined, we tend to associate ideas about them in our minds. Then, when we experience just one of the events, we also think of the other. One of them we call the cause and the other, the effect. What is there in the fact that certain events have been constantly conjoined in the past that leads us to think of them as being causally related? Hume points out that if the process involved were a rational one, we would have to presuppose that the principle of the uniformity of nature was true. This principle asserts *"that instances, of which we have had no experience, must resemble those, of which we have had experience, and that the course of nature continues always uniformly the same."*

Hume next questions whether we possess any evidence that this principle is true, or that it has to be true. Since we can readily imagine that the world might change in many respects in the future, it is not possible to demonstrate that nature must be uniform. Our experience up to the present moment does not constitute evidence as to what the future course of nature will be, or must be. Just because the sun has risen every day up to now does not prove that it has to rise tomorrow. We can only judge the future if we know that nature is uniform. But our information up to this point is only that, so far, nature has always been uniform. Experience can provide us with no clue about what has to be the case in the future. Hence, we can neither demonstrate nor prove from experience that the all-important principle of the uniformity of nature is true, even though much of our reasoning about the world depends upon it.

The acceptance of this principle, Hume contends, is a fundamental characteristic of human nature. We have a habit or custom that operates upon us for unknown and unknowable reasons. After we have experienced the same sequence of conjoined events several times, then, when we perceive one of the conjuncts, habit or custom leads us to think of the other, and to think of it in a lively and forceful way. Although we are able to think of any idea we wish, we are led psychologically to think only of a particular conjoined idea and to conceive of it with some of the force and vivacity of its conjoined impression. Such force and vivacity constitute our belief in the actual occurrence of the conjoined item. In terms of this explanation, the principle of the uniformity of nature is more a principle about how we think and feel than it is one about the order of events in the world.

Hume uses his discovery of the psychological origins of our belief in the uniformity of nature to explain the basis for our conviction that there is a necessary connection between events. The necessary connection is never perceived, no matter how often the same sequence is observed. But, after a constant conjunction of events has been perceived many times, we then feel that one of the conjuncts causes or produces the other. It is not any discoverable fact about the events that makes us believe this, but rather our psychological attitude toward the events. We possess a fundamental propensity or determination of the mind to think of a conjoined idea after experiencing the conjunct or thinking of it, once we have perceived the constant conjunction of the two in our experience. This determination, which is a strong feeling, is the necessary connection that we think exists between events. Although it is felt in us, we have a tendency to conceive of it as existing in the events themselves. This idea is actually a feature of the way we think about events, rather than a feature of them. Thus, the term "cause" can be defined as "*An object precedent and contiguous to another, and so united with it in the imagination, that the idea of the one determines the mind to form the idea of the other, and the impression of the one to form a more lively idea of the other.*"

In Hume's explanation of causality, he joins Father Nicolas Malebranche's contention that there is no necessary connection between events with his own psychological account of how we react to the uniformities in experience. Because of our habits, we expect the future to resemble the past, and we feel that when we observe certain events, their constant conjuncts must also be taking place, even if we cannot observe them. We have no actual knowledge of what is taking place, but only beliefs. Since we can never be completely sure that our beliefs correspond to the actual state of affairs, our causal information is always, at best, only probable.

Hume sees the task of the sciences as that of carefully establishing bases for "reasonable belief" by collecting data about the constant conjunctions that occur in human experience, and organizing such data in terms of scientific laws. These laws provide a form of rational expectation, in that they allow us to predict the future course of events on the basis of detailed information about what has happened up to now. The scientist, like anyone else, expects, because of his habits and propensities, that the future will resemble the past. Science, for Hume, is not the search for the "real" cause of events, but for the best available probable predictions about the course of nature, founded on correlations of constant conjunctions of events and the psychological habits of human beings.

After presenting his explanation of the source of our information, the nature of our beliefs about the world, and the character of scientific "knowledge," Hume turns in Part IV of the *Treatise* to the full statement of his skeptical views. He first presents a series of reasons to show why we should be doubtful of the conclusions that we come to because of our reasoning and those that we come to because of our sense experience and our attitudes towards it. Then Hume contends that though there are basic difficulties with regard to both our reason and our senses, we still have to believe many things because of our psychological structure. Unfortunately, what we believe is often either indefensible or contradictory.

The argument offered to engender a "skepticism with regard to reason" purports to show that even the most certain conclusions of reasoning are actually only probable and that their degree of probability diminishes the more that we examine them. Since we all make mistakes, every time we reason there is a possibility that we may err. When we check our reasoning, it is still possible that we have erred in our checking, and that we will err in checking our checking, and so on. Each judgment that we make about the merits of our reasoning is merely probable, and the combined probability, Hume says, will get smaller and smaller the more we judge our judgments of our judgments of our judgments. Hence, if this checking process were carried on indefinitely, we should begin to lose confidence even in our most certain reasonings in arithmetic or algebra.

With regard to our sense information, Hume insists that we are naturally convinced that the objects we observe exist continuously and independently of us. But as soon as we begin to examine this belief we find that it is completely unjustified and that it conflicts with what we know about our impressions. Neither sense information nor valid reasoning can supply any basis for concluding that there are independent and continuous objects. If our imaginations, through some propensities, supply us with this belief, it is still "contrary to the plainest experience." All that we ever perceive are impressions which, as far as we can tell, are definitely dependent on us. An alteration in our sense organs, or in the state of our health, changes what we perceive. In view of this, we should not think that our perceptions are things that exist independently from us, continuing to exist even when not perceived. But, Hume observes, no amount of argument on this subject makes us give up our natural belief in the existence of the external world.

The discussions of the bases for skepticism indicate that for Hume even complete skepticism is impossible because of the force of natural belief. "Nature, by an absolute and uncontrollable necessity has determined us to judge as well as to breathe and feel." Nature forces us to accept certain views, in spite of the evidence for or against them. Philosophy, Hume said elsewhere, would make us into complete skeptics, were not nature so strong. Philosophy would make us completely skeptical about the status of the objects that we perceive with our senses, but nature prevents us from taking the philosophical arguments seriously.

In his discussion of our knowledge of ourselves, Hume brings out a similar point. We all believe that we possess a personal identity that continues throughout our lives. But when we try to discover the entity we call "ourselves," we discover that all that we are acquainted with is the succession of impressions and ideas. By certain psychological habits and propensities, we have created a fiction which makes us believe that we are also aware of an identical self that perseveres through all our various experiences.

Hence, there is a type of complete skepticism that results from a careful and profound study of human nature. In theory, we realize that there is inadequate evidence to support the bulk of what we believe about the world. Our reasoning and our senses are too unreliable to support these beliefs, which are due to our psychological character and not to any legitimate conclusions of rational processes. Some of these natural beliefs conflict with one another. Hume contends that the factors which make us connect events causally in our experience should make us disbelieve in the continuous and independent existence of sense objects. The more we examine human nature, the more we should realize how dubious and unreliable human opinions are. In the conclusion to Book I of the *Treatise*, Hume points out that his skepticism even undermines his faith in his psychological findings.

But nature prevents us from carrying out this skeptical attitude to its final destructive conclusion. Regardless of the difficulties, in practice we find that we have to believe all sorts of things, even incompatible things. When we go out in the world, the skeptical doubts lose their force; we are overwhelmed by our natural feelings and beliefs, and we act and live in the same way as anyone else. Hume's final advice is that one should be skeptical when one has to be, and be a natural believer when one must, while realizing that neither of these attitudes has any final justification. In periods when doubts are not being taken seriously, one can go on and examine other aspects of the human world, as Hume does in Books II and III of the *Treatise*, and seek for laws about human passions. (One of his findings in this regard is that reason is, and ought only to be, the slave of the passions.)

The *Treatise* has been a rich source of many contemporary views. The more empirical side of it has greatly influenced the logical positivists and the language analysts. Some of the psychological analysis of human belief and behavior has influenced the pragmatists and instrumentalists. The extreme skepticism and irrationalism have had some impact on neoorthodox theologians. It is for these reasons that *A Treatise of Human Nature* is regarded by many as perhaps the best philosophical work in the English language.

Pertinent Literature

Chappel, V. C., ed. *Hume.* Garden City, New York: Anchor Books, 1966.

This collection of twenty-one essays on David Hume by scholars from different parts of the English-speaking world contains several essays which are important for studying the fundamental issues that appear in Hume's *A Treatise of Human Nature*, Book I. T. E. Jessop, the bibliographer of Hume, seeks in his essay "Some Misunderstandings of Hume" to show that although modern critics constantly attack the *Treatise* for its inconsistencies, it is nevertheless Hume's basic work, setting forth his philosophical goals. Further, Jessop argues for the value of the basic theme of the *Treatise*, Hume's naturalistic analysis of human nature.

R. H. Popkin's essay on Hume's Pyrrhonism and critique of Pyrrhonism tries to delineate exactly what kind of skepticism Hume advocated and to show how such advocacy could be reconciled with Hume's constant jibes at the Pyrrhonian skeptics in all of his works. Popkin argues that Hume developed a "consistent" Pyrrhonism, consistent in that his arguments and analyses indicated the inability of human beings to find truth and certainty in any area whatsoever. Sextus Empiricus, after pointing this out in case after case, declared that therefore we should suspend judgment. Hume saw that this consequence did not follow and that we could only actually do what nature allowed us to do. Our natural propensities could be analyzed but not justified. Popkin then tries to show that Hume's "consistent" Pyrrhonism was compatible with his naturalism.

The article by R. P. Wolff on Hume's theory of mental activity attempts to show that what Hume held to was more than associationism or the copy theory of ideas, even though he began his inquiry in the *Treatise* with these views.

Four of the essays are directly on Hume's analysis of causality. Three concern the two definitions of cause that Hume presented at the end of Book I, Part III, Section XIV of the *Treatise*, and one of the essays is on Hume's defense of causal inference. J. A. Robinson begins his discussion of Hume's two definitions of cause by pointing out that many of the peculiarities of the text in the *Treatise* are due to the fact that Hume was seeking to propound empirical laws of psychology at the same time that he was trying to give a philosophical analysis of the concept of "cause." Robinson claims that this confusion of tasks misled Norman Kemp Smith in his commentary on Hume. An answer to Robinson by T. H. Richards is presented, together with a further answer by Robinson. The discussion is very helpful in clarifying what Hume may have intended to accomplish. The essay by J. W. Lenz on Hume's defense of causal inference broadens the discussion and clarifies some of the possible interpretations of the theory. Hume's analysis of causality leads to his theory of probability and induction, at least as it is presented in Part III of Book I in the *Treatise*. D. Stove's essay on this point argues that by now Hume is credited with having proven much more on this subject than he actually did in his discussion of inductive arguments. Hume is usually portrayed as having developed a skepticism about all inductive arguments. Stove instead contends that there are probable inductive arguments that are not canceled out by Hume's analysis.

The essay by T. Penelhum treats Hume's discussion on personal identity in the *Treatise*, Book I, Part IV, Section VI. Penelhum is concerned to evaluate Hume's arguments on the subject. He very carefully examines what Hume's case rested on and finds that it was on a confusing notion of identity, which led to Hume's denying that we can discover any personal identity within us. (Hume appeared to have second thoughts about this point.) Penelhum offers a way of avoiding Hume's skeptical results.

The remaining essays by A. C. MacIntyre, R. F. Atkinson, Anthony Flew, Geoffrey Hunter, W. D. Hudson, Bernard Wand, and F. A. Hayek deal with crucial issues that appear in Books II and III of the *Treatise* and in Hume's later essays. The last three items in the volume—James Noxon, "Hume's Agnosticism"; William Capitan, "Part X of Hume's *Dialogues*"; and G. J. Nathan, "Hume's Immanent God" are important and stimulating discussions of Hume's religious or irreligious views, especially as they appear in the *Dialogues*.

Stroud, Barry. *Hume*. London: Routledge & Kegan Paul, 1977.

Barry Stroud's work presents a general interpretation of David Hume's theory of knowledge and his theory of morals and passions. The study deals with Hume's two main philosophical statements, the *Treatise of Human Nature* and the two *Enquiries*. Issues in these texts are related to current philosophical discussions of similar questions. Six of the ten chapters deal primarily with the theory Hume set forth in the bulk of the *Treatise*, Book I.

Stroud, from the outset, sets out to show that Hume was not simply an arch skeptic offering negative views about everything. He was also, and more important, a philosopher of human nature attempting to establish a Newtonian science of man which would account for all of human behavior. Hume sought to build on the work of John Locke, Lord Shaftesbury, Bernard Mandeville, Francis Hutcheson, and Joseph Butler. Stroud follows out Hume's attempt to develop his new science at the beginning of the *Treatise*, carefully examining Hume's contentions about the origin and nature of our ideas. Stroud points out that Hume never really questioned his own theory or gave much evidence for it and that there are serious problems in the theory that Hume never grappled with. Hume's theory of the association of ideas also is full of difficulties, according to Stroud, which Hume often acknowledged but did not resolve.

When Hume came to deal with the central issue of how we think about causal relationships, he was, of course, first of all very negative in the sense that he showed that such thinking is not a rational process that can be justified as deductive or inductive. Stroud turns from this to the positive side of Hume's theory of causal belief; namely, Hume's presentation of the psychological process by which we "connect" causes and effects. Many difficult or baffling parts of Hume's analysis are clarified in Stroud's account. For example, his interpretation of the kind of necessity that Hume believed existed between cause and effect makes more sense of the matter than Hume's text appears to do. One may doubt this interpretation and some of the others that Stroud offers, but usually they are illuminating and helpful in getting Hume's often confusing and sometimes seemingly contradictory explanations into a coherent pattern. Stroud traces several of these difficulties back to confused starting points of Hume. By showing how Hume could have overcome the difficulties, Stroud sets forth a more consistent analysis that Hume could have presented. In the case of causality, Stroud attempts to suggest a way for Hume to avoid psychologism while retaining his ideas about necessity.

Similarly, with the difficult discussions in Hume's *Treatise* of our knowledge of the existence and nature of external and internal objects (bodies and minds), Stroud patiently examines Hume's steps. He blames skeptical conclusions on Hume's facile acceptance of the Cartesian model of how we know about the external world. Stroud asserts that one should follow the spirit of Hume's work, examine how we do function in ordinary life, and then use what we find as a source of naturalistic explanation.

The discussion of the problem of personal identity is even murkier in Hume. Stroud ably shows how Hume was unable to find a satisfactory answer in his own terms and finally, in the Appendix to Book I of the *Treatise*, was ready to give up. Stroud contends that at this point Hume should have recognized "a fatal deficiency" in his theory of ideas.

Having presented a lucid and careful examination of the many strands of the *Treatise*, Book I, Stroud devotes the rest of his study to Hume's second and third books on man's moral and emotive behavior and to the application of Hume's naturalistic analysis of how human beings act to their actions in society. Stroud stresses the importance of Hume's naturalistic science of man for providing a program for examining the human situation rather than for offering specific answers to specific problems. Hume's own skepticism, even about this positive achievement, Stroud believes, could not really be taken seriously, even by a Humean.

Smith, Norman Kemp. *The Philosophy of David Hume: A Critical Study of Its Origins and Central Doctrines.* New York: Macmillan Publishing Company, 1941.

Norman Kemp Smith's study of the most important of David Hume's ideas, especially as they are expressed in *A Treatise of Human Nature*, Book I, deals both with interpreting Hume's overall views and with revealing their likely sources. Kemp Smith had been arguing since the beginning of this century that Hume was not really a skeptical thinker trying to destroy all positive views. Instead, Kemp Smith insisted, Hume was a naturalist who believed that reason is and ought only to be the slave of the passions. (Thus by analyzing how the passions function, we ought to be able to understand how the whole intellectual world functions.)

In developing such a reading of Hume, Kemp Smith also argued that Hume's sources, principally the writings of the Scottish moralists and of Pierre Bayle, formed the basis for a naturalistic point of view. One of the main lines by which Kemp Smith approached his subject was to argue that Hume developed his philosophy from concerns about ethical questions rather than from epistemological ones. From Francis Hutcheson, Hume learned that moral judgments were not rational but were based on feelings. Hume then went on to evaluate rational judgments as also based on feelings, and he took over the experimental method of John Locke and Sir Isaac Newton. Also, Hume used some of the most paradoxical portions of Pierre Bayle's *Dictionary,* especially the articles on Benedictus de Spinoza and Zeno of Elea, to show that even our most basic notions, such as those of space and time, are unintelligible.

From these different ingredients, Kemp Smith sought to construct a theory of the order in which Hume actually developed his ideas. It is central to Kemp Smith's interpretation to contend that Hume's theory of the role of the passions was his basic discovery. Through his theory of the actions of the passions Hume could explain all of human nature, including so-called rational behavior. Such an explanation was a positive naturalistic view and not the skeptical position with which Hume is usually credited. Hume later worked out the epistemological views of Book I of the *Treatise.* Carefully analyzing the discussions in this book, Kemp Smith brings out how they differ from what was said in Books II and III. He also stresses how these discussions led to unsatisfactory and skeptical results, or to Hume's emphasis on natural belief. The latter, his positive view, is what Kemp Smith sees as connecting the two parts of the *Treatise.* Natural belief is the result of strong feelings, and it is this kind of belief which Hume said "peoples our world." Hume's theory of belief became its author's explanatory device for the major problems of knowledge and metaphysics. It is, Kemp Smith stresses, essentially the same kind of naturalistic explanation that Hume offered in ethics. At the same time, Kemp Smith admits that there were so many conflicting tendencies in Hume from his empirical, his naturalistic, and his skeptical sides that he failed to work out one overall consistent document.

Kemp Smith's emphasis on Hume's naturalism flies in the face of the skeptical interpretation of Hume that has been popular for more than two hundred years. Kemp Smith has given a strong provocative statement of his case. Those who disagree have been forced to examine the texts most carefully to see if they can be given other interpretations. In spite of the disagreement of many scholars with Kemp Smith's interpretation, it remains perhaps the major commentary on Hume in this century.

Additional Recommended Reading

Capaldi, Nicholas. *David Hume: The Newtonian Philosopher.* Boston: Twayne Publishers, 1975. Interesting recent interpretation of Hume in terms of the science of his time.

Hall, Roland. *Fifty Years of Hume Scholarship.* Edinburgh: Edinburgh University Press, 1978. Best available bibliography of recent writings on Hume.

Hendel, Charles W. *Studies in the Philosophy of David Hume.* Indianapolis: Bobbs-Merrill, 1963. An important interpretation of Hume.

Leroy, André. *David Hume.* Paris: Presses Universitaires de France,1953. The most complete interpretation of Hume by a French scholar.

Noxon, James. *Hume's Philosophical Development.* Oxford: Clarendon Press, 1973. A controversial work on how Hume's views developed.

Passmore, John A. *Hume's Intentions.* Cambridge: Cambridge University Press, 1952. A highly critical evaluation of Hume.

Penelhum, Terrence. *Hume.* New York: St. Martin's Press, 1975. A general presentation of Hume by a major contemporary philosopher.

AN ENQUIRY CONCERNING THE PRINCIPLES OF MORALS

Author: David Hume (1711-1776)
Type of work: Ethics
First published: 1751

Principal Ideas Advanced

The purpose of ethical inquiry is to discover those universal principles on which moral praise and blame are based.

Benevolence is approved partly because of human sympathy and partly because of its social utility, but justice is approved for its utility alone.

Utility accounts for the worth of such virtues as humanity, friendship, integrity, veracity—and it is by its utility that government is justified.

Theories which attempt to explain all human conduct as springing from self-love are mistaken.

Whatever is worthwhile is so in virtue of its utility or its agreeableness.

Moral judgment is essentially a matter of sentiment, not reason.

Hume's *An Enquiry Concerning the Principles of Morals* is a philosophical classic which grows older without aging, which remains lively with a wisdom that speaks to the present. It is not the most profound of Hume's works or the most original, being to some extent a revision of Book III of Hume's masterpiece, *A Treatise of Human Nature*. But its author considered it the best of his works, and many critics have agreed with this judgment.

Dealing decisively with major ethical issues the *Enquiry* presents in clear, carefully organized form an analysis of morals. It continues the attack begun by Bishop Butler against the self-love theory (psychological egoism) of Hobbes, and in so doing achieves a measure of objectivism frequently either overlooked or denied by Hume's critics. On the other hand, after preliminary recognition of the significant but auxiliary role of reason in moral judgment, Hume sides with the eighteenth century school of sentiment against the ethical rationalists, on grounds shared today by those who regard ethical judgments as emotive utterances. But while Hume is frequently cited as a predecessor of the latter philosophers, he avoids the utter relativism and moral nihilism frequently, but erroneously for the most part, attributed

to them. Hence, although it would be worthwhile to read the *Enquiry* for its historical importance alone, it also has a unique relevance to some fundamental problems of mid-twentieth century ethical philosophy, particularly to those concerning the nature of moral judgment.

While the *Enquiry* can be clearly understood without previous reading of Hume's other works, it is an application to ethics of the theory of knowledge and methodology presented in *A Treatise of Human Nature* and *An Enquiry Concerning Human Understanding,* and its interest is enhanced by familiarity with these books. Like them, the present *Enquiry* contains a measure of skepticism which, while fundamental, has been greatly exaggerated and widely misunderstood. Indeed one of the chief merits of Hume's philosophy lies in the "mitigated" skepticism which recognizes the limits of human reason without succumbing to what he calls "Pyrrhonism" or excessive skepticism, which in practice would make belief and action impossible. But those who accuse Hume of the latter skepticism must ignore one of his chief aims: to apply the Newtonian method of "philosophizing" to a study of human nature.

The object of the study is to trace the derivation

of morals back to their ultimate source. Hume's proposed method was to analyze the virtues and vices of men in order "to reach the foundation of ethics, and find those universal principles, from which all censure or approbation is ultimately derived." Since this was a factual matter it could be investigated successfully only by the experimental method, which had proved itself so well in "natural philosophy," or physical science.

This "scientific" approach will appeal to many modern readers, but herein lies an ambiguity which, in spite of the clarity of Hume's style, has misled some critics. One must realize that Hume was at this point writing of ethics as a descriptive study *about morals*—about acts, characters, and moral judgments. In this sense ethics is a behavioral science and its statements are either true or false. This may suggest what today would be called an objectivist position, but Hume was not describing the way in which moral attitudes are affected; moral judgments, strictly speaking, are matters of sentiment, although before they can properly occur reason must furnish all the available relevant information. To avoid misinterpretation, it is hardly possible to over-emphasize this distinction between inductive conclusions *about* moral acts and judgments, on the one hand, and moral approvals and disapprovals themselves, on the other.

Hume's analysis begins with an examination of the social virtues, benevolence and justice, since their explanation will have relevance to other virtues as well. Such benevolent sentiments and characters as are described by words like "sociable" or "good-natured" are approved universally. But it is not the mere fact of approval but the principle underlying it which is the object of investigation. We approve benevolence in part because of the psychological principle of what Hume calls *sympathy*, an involuntary tendency in an observer to experience the same emotions he observes in a fellow man, but the more immediate reason for such approval is that we perceive the utility (usefulness, conduciveness to happiness) of this virtue. When we praise a benevolent man, Hume says, we always make reference to the happiness and satisfaction he affords to society. Since benevolence is regarded as one of the highest virtues, it reflects in turn the fundamental importance of utility. Even in our nonmoral judgment of value, usefulness is a paramount consideration.

In cases of uncertainty about moral questions, Hume adds, there is no more certain way of deciding them than by discovering whether the acts or attitudes involved are really conducive to the interests of society. Hume describes several reversals in the estimation of practices, such as generosity to beggars, when it was seen that their tendencies were harmful rather than helpful, as had been supposed at first.

Whereas benevolence is approved partly but not exclusively for its beneficial consequences, justice has merit for no other reason. (One must realize that Hume conceives justice as concerning only property relations, thus omitting "fair play" and equality, ordinarily considered essential to the concept; actually he accounts for impartiality by his account of truly moral judgment, as is shown below.) To prove this apparently controversial claim, Hume cites a number of cases in which the connection of justice and utility is demonstrated by their joint occurrence or non-occurrence, increase or diminution. Too many and too lengthy to admit adequate recapitulation here, Hume's arguments may be suggested briefly by a few illustrations: In situations of superfluity or of dearth of material goods, the observation of property distinctions becomes useless and is suspended; a virtuous man captured by outlaws flouting justice would be under no restraint from justice if the opportunity to seize and use their weapons arose, since regard for ownership would be harmful; societies suspend international justice in times of war because of its obvious disadvantages.

Examination of particular laws confirms this explanation of justice; they have no other end than the good of mankind, to which even the natural law theorists are forced to appeal ultimately. Particular laws would in many cases be utterly arbitrary and even ridiculous, were it not that the general interest is better served by having specified rules rather than chaos. In individual cases the fulfillment of justice may even be detrimental, as when an evil man legally inherits a fortune, and abuses it, but consistent observance of the law is ultimately more useful than is deviation.

Were individuals completely self-sufficient, again justice would not arise, but actually men mate and then rear children; and subsistence of the family requires observance within it of certain rules. When families unite into small societies, and societies engage in commerce, the domain of utilitarian rules of property enlarges accordingly. Thus the evolution of social groups shows a direct proportion between utility and the merit of justice.

In finding the essence of justice and its moral obligation in utility alone, thus making it of derivative rather than intrinsic value, is Hume degrading this virtue? Not so, he insists: "For what stronger foundation can be desired or conceived for any duty, than to observe, the human society, or even human nature, could not subsist without the establishment of it; and will still arrive at greater degrees of happiness and perfection, the more inviolable the regard is, which is paid to that duty?"

At the end of his section on justice he repeats his conclusion that utility accounts for much of the merit of such virtues as humanity, friendship, and public spirit, and for all that of justice, fidelity, integrity, veracity, and some others. A principle so widely operative in these cases can reasonably be expected to exert comparable force in similar instances, according to the Newtonian method of philosophizing. Hume then finds utility to be the basic justification for political society or government, and he notes that "the public conveniency, which regulates morals, is inviolably established in the nature of man, and of the world, in which he lives."

But is utility itself a fundamental principle? We may still ask *why* utility is approved, to what end it leads. The alternatives are two: it serves either the general interest or private interests and welfare. Hume recognizes the plausibility of the self-love or self-interest theory holding that all approvals are ultimately grounded in the needs and passions of the self, but he claims to prove decisively the impossibility of thus accounting for moral judgments.

The skeptical view that moral distinctions are inculcated through indoctrination by politicians in order to make men docile is very superficial, Hume says. While moral sentiments may be partially controlled by education, unless they were rooted in human nature the terminology of ethics would awaken no response.

But granted this response, must it still be traced to self-interest, perhaps an enlightened self-interest that perceives a necessary connection between society's welfare and its own? Hume thinks not. We often praise acts of virtue in situations distant in time and space, when there is no possibility of benefit to ourselves. We approve some virtues in our enemies, such as courage, even though we know that they may work to our harm. When acts praised conduce to both general and private welfare, our approbation is increased, but we still distinguish the feelings appropriate to each. Now if the first two considerations are rejected by arguing that we approve what is not really to our own interest by imagining our personal benefit had we been in the situation judged, Hume replies that it is absurd that a real sentiment could originate from an interest known to be imaginary and sometimes even opposed to our practical interest.

Even the lower animals appear to have affection for both other animals and us; surely this is not artifice, but rather disinterested benevolence. Why then deny this virtue to man? Sexual love produces generous feelings beyond the merely appetitive, and common instances of utterly unselfish benevolence occur in parent-child relationships. It is impossible, Hume holds, to deny the authenticity of such affections as gratitude or desire for friends' good fortune when separation prevents personal participation.

But if the evidence is so clear, why have self-love theorists been so persistent? Hume blames a love of theoretical simplicity. The self-love theory, as Butler forcibly argues, mistakenly attempts to reduce all motivation to this one principle, and so is psychologically false. Man has physical appetites each having its own object; that of hunger is food, that of thirst is drink; gratification of these needs yields pleasure, which may then become the object of a secondary, interested desire—self-love. Unless the primary appetites had occurred, there could have been no pleasures or happiness to constitute the object of self-love. But the disinterested primary passions also include benevolence or desire for others' good, satisfaction of which then similarly yields pleasure to the self. Hence self-love actually presupposes specific and independent needs and affections, which complexity is again shown by occasional indulgence of some particular passion, such as the passion for revenge, even to the detriment of self-interest.

Since self-love cannot account for our moral approval of utility, then the appeal of the latter must be direct. In any theoretical explanation some point must be taken as ultimate, else an infinite regression occurs; hence we need not ask why we experience benevolence—it is enough that we do. Actually, however, Hume further explains it by reference to sympathy, the almost inevitable emotional reaction to the feelings of others. Yet Hume is careful not to claim that "fellow-feeling" is necessarily predominant over self-love; both sentiments vary in degree. But in normal men there is close correlation between strong concern for one's fellows and sensitivity to moral distinctions. Benevolence may not be strong enough to motivate some men to *act* for the good of another, but even they will feel approval of such acts and prefer them to the injurious.

Having admitted not only interpersonal differences in sympathy, but acknowledging also intrapersonal variations of feelings for others, how can Hume account for any uniformity and objectivity in our moral judgments? Here he offers one of his most significant contributions to ethics. Even while our sentiments vary we may judge merit with practical universality, analogously to judgmental correction of variations in sensory perception. Though we do not all, or always, perceive the same physical object as having the same color, shape, or size, as when we approach an object from a distance, we do not attribute the variations to the object; instead we imagine it to have certain stable, standard qualities. Such adjustment or correction is indispensable to mutual understanding and conversation among men.

Likewise, men's interests and feelings vary. Thus, moral discourse would be impossible unless men took a general rather than a private point of view: "The intercourse of sentiments . . . in society and conversation, makes us form some general unalterable standard, by which we may approve or disapprove of characters and manners." Although our emotions will not conform entirely to such a standard, they are regulated sufficiently for all practical purposes, and

hence ethical language becomes meaningful: "General language . . . being formed for general use, must be molded on some more general views, and must affix the epithets of praise or blame, in conformity to sentiments, which arise from the general interests of the community." In order for this standard to be effective there must of course be a sentiment or emotion to implement it, and here again Hume produces a telling argument against the self-interest theory. Self-love is inadequate to the prerequisites of the concept of morals, not from lack of force, but because it is inappropriate. Such a concept as this implies (1) that there be in existence a universal sentiment producing common agreement in approving or disapproving a given object, and (2) that this sentiment comprehend as its objects actions or persons in all times and places. None but the sentiment of humanity will meet these criteria. Hume's account of a "general unalterable standard" based principally on social utility and hence on benevolence is strongly objectivistic and balances subjectivistic strains in his ethics; it also provides the impartiality apparently neglected by his definition of justice.

Having thus accounted for our approval of qualities conducive to the good of others, Hume continues his analysis of virtues and finds three other classifications. "Qualities useful to ourselves" ("ourselves" here meaning persons exhibiting the qualities) may be approved also for general utility, but primarily for benefit to the agent; examples are discretion, frugality, and temperance. Now a second major division and two other categories of virtues are added: the "agreeable" (pleasant or enjoyable) to their possessors or to others. "Qualities immediately agreeable to ourselves," approved primarily for the satisfying feelings aroused, are such as greatness of mind and noble pride, though some like courage and benevolence may also be generally useful. Good manners, mutual deference, modesty, wit, and even cleanliness illustrate "qualities immediately agreeable to others."

Only when the analysis is almost completed does Hume offer the first formal definition of "virtue" as "*a quality of the mind agreeable to or approved by every one who considers or contemplates it.*" A second definition, better summarizing the *Enquiry's* results, is that "Personal Merit consists altogether in the possession of mental qualities, *useful or agreeable* to the *person himself* or to others." A definition of value in general follows: "Whatever is valuable in any kind, so naturally classes itself under the division of *useful* or *agreeable,* the *utile* or the *dulce. . . .*"

Readers familiar with the history of ethics will thus see hedonistic and utilitarian themes which received subsequent expression in Bentham and Mill. The only goal of Virtue, Hume says, is cheerfulness and happiness; the only demand she makes of us are those of careful calculation of the best means to these ends and constancy in preferring the greater to the lesser happiness. Such an obligation is *interested,* but the pleasure it seeks, such as those of peace of mind, or awareness of integrity, do not conflict with the social good, and their supreme worth is almost self-evident.

Having discovered what he calls the true origin of morals through the experimental method, Hume is now ready to return to the Reason vs. Sentiment issue he mentions at the beginning of the *Enquiry* but defers for settlement until the end. Throughout the book statements occur which indicate his final position, but unfortunately there are also a number which appear to make moral judgment a matter of reason. This ambiguity is dispelled by Hume's final treatment showing that moral judgment proper is noncognitive and affective in nature. It is true that reason is indispensable to approval or disapproval, for it must provide the facts which pertain to their objects. Very detailed and precise reasoning is frequently required to determine what actually is useful in a given case; nothing other than reason can perform this function. In view of the importance of the question, of whether moral judgment is rational or sentimental (affective), to both the eighteenth century and ours, Hume's full recognition of the auxiliary role of reason must be kept in mind. But he cannot agree with those rationalists who hold that moral judgments can be made with the same mental faculties, methods, and precision as can judgments of truth and falsity, and who frequently make comparisons between our knowledge of moral "truths" and those of mathematics and geometry.

Besides the evidence of the origin of moral senti-

ment from benevolence, there are perhaps even more cogent arguments based on comparison of the two types of judgment. The judgments of reason provide information, but not motivation, whereas blame or approbation are "a tendency, however faint, to the objects of the one, and a proportionable aversion to those of the other." That is, moral "judgment" is essentially affective and conative, while rational judgments are neither. Although reason can discover utility, unless utility's *end* appealed to some sentiment the knowledge would be utterly ineffective.

Rational knowledge is either factual or relational (logical or mathematical) in nature; its conclusions are either inductive or deductive. But the sentiment of blame or approbation is neither such a conclusion nor an observation of fact; one can examine at length all the facts of a criminal event, but he will never find the vice itself, the viciousness, as another objective fact in addition to those of time, place, and action. Neither is the vice constituted by some kind of relation such as that of contrariety, for example, between a good deed and an ungrateful response, since an evil deed rewarded with good will would involve contrariety but the response then would be virtuous. The "crime" is rather constituted such by the sentiment of blame in the spectator's mind.

In the process of rational inference, we take certain known facts or relations and from these deduce or infer a conclusion not previously known; but in moral decisions, says Hume, ". . . after every circumstance, every relation is known, the understanding has no further room to operate, nor any object on which it could employ itself. The approbation or blame which then ensues, cannot be the work of the judgement, but of the heart; and is not a speculative proposition or affirmation, but an active feeling or sentiment." This is one of the clearest and most definitive statements of Hume's position on moral judgment.

Finally, reason could never account for ultimate ends, as can be shown very shortly by asking a series of questions about the justification of an act. For example, if one says he exercises for his health, and is asked why he desires health, he may cite as successive reasons its necessity to his work, the necessity of work to securing money, the use of money as a means to pleasure. But it would be absurd to ask *why* one wished pleasure or the avoidance of pain. Similarly we have seen that virtue appeals to sentiments which neither have nor require any further explanation. Whereas the function of reason is to discover its objects, that of moral (and aesthetic) sentiment (or taste) is to confer value.

Hence, in a radical sense, moral distinctions are subjective, but the subject from which they derive is the whole human race, and individual subjectivity is

corrected by the general unalterable standard. The *Enquiry* thus affords both a naturalistic, empirical description of the origin of moral values and a persuasive account of an ethical norm by which consistent judgments may be made, without appealing to a doubtful metaphysics. It is in this eminently sane recognition of the functions and limits of both reason and emotion that modern readers can learn much from David Hume.

Pertinent Literature

Glossop, Ronald J. "Hume, Stevenson, and Hare on Moral Language," in *Hume: A Re-evaluation.* Edited by D. W. Livingston and J. T. King. New York: Fordham University Press, 1976.

Ronald J. Glossop observes that although a focus on ideas was as philosophically popular in David Hume's time as a focus on language is in ours, Hume paid a considerable amount of attention to language, especially in his work on ethics. In this article, Glossop compares what Hume said about moral language with what more recently has been said in C. L. Stevenson's *Ethics and Language* and R. M. Hare's *The Language of Morals.* In the course of making such comparisons, Glossop attributes to Hume a form of ethical naturalism. (Ethical naturalists claim that any moral prescription is equivalent to or reducible to some kind of descriptive statement.)

Both Stevenson and Hare, Glossop says, claim that Hume not only was concerned with the issues in which they are interested but also held views about them which are in general similar to their own. Glossop denies that Hume's moral theory is importantly similar to that of either Stevenson or Hare. With regard to Hume, Glossop makes the following claims.

In the *Enquiry* (and in *A Treatise of Human Nature* as well), Hume recognizes that his concerns are what we should call metaethical rather than normative, and his sensitivity to issues of linguistic usage is evident in the most central aspects of his ethical theory. Although Hume describes in three different ways the procedure he intends to follow to discover the general principle of morals—namely,

compiling a list of virtues on the basis of (1) the evaluative meanings of terms, (2) the sentiments of a single disinterested spectator, and (3) the moral judgments of all persons—it seems clear that he would have believed the results would be the same regardless of what procedure he used, since he believed that terms used to describe virtues simply reflect approbation which everyone feels toward certain qualities because nature has made such feelings universal among human beings. Even those who reject "qualified spectators" and "unanimous approbations" would be unlikely to disagree that terms such as "generous" and "industrious" have favorable (positive) evaluative meanings, while terms such as "selfish" and "lazy" have unfavorable (negative) evaluative meanings. Hume examines the list he compiles to try to discover what the favorable evaluative meanings have in common.

Hume then offers three arguments all of which conclude that everyone, when not constrained by particular biases, in fact approves of whatever promotes the welfare of humankind. His first argument involves the claim that sympathizing with other people is an essential aspect of being human. The second is a summary of the overall argument of the *Enquiry*: What is common to all the virtues is that directly or indirectly they promote the happiness of their possessor himself or of others. The third is concerned with moral language. Hume argues that a logical requirement for both stable thought for the individual himself and communication with others is that our moral language reflect a general point of view which includes a concern for the good of the human species. (A similar argument, Glossop points out, can be found in *A Treatise of Human Nature.*) That is, Hume argues that even if we cannot "correct" our sentiments (cannot overcome the effects of our biases on our feelings), stable thought and interpersonal communication require that the linguistic formulation of our moral judgments reflect a concern for human happiness.

The third argument does not depend on the first two. Even if people in fact did not sympathize with others or approve of what promotes the general welfare, the private and interpersonal use of moral language presupposes a common viewpoint.

Glossop then considers Stevenson. Stevenson takes "X is good" to be roughly synonymous with "I approve of X; do so as well." He appears not to recognize that "approve" suggests a disinterested rather than a personal point of view; he claims that the term may be used to indicate what he calls a peculiarly moral attitude, but that such an attitude differs from others in being more intense, or an attitude about other attitudes. Hume, however, explicitly states in *A Treatise of Human Nature* that moral sentiment differs from other kinds of sentiment in that moral sentiment can arise only from a disinterested point of view. As mentioned above, he later argues in the *Enquiry* that even where one cannot "correct" his sentiments, his moral *judgments* must reflect a disinterested or general viewpoint.

According to Glossop, Stevenson's failure to recognize that moral language reflects a disinterested point of view leads him to a misinterpretation of Hume's theory. He "correctly sees that for Hume only the sentiments of *informed* spectators are trustworthy indicators of virtue and vice, but he fails to note that for Hume a distinct point of view is indicated by the notion of approbation." Not only does Stevenson's misinterpretation lead him incorrectly to identify Hume as a fellow emotivist but (Glossop claims to show) his criticisms of Hume's theory can also be seen to be inapplicable on the correct interpretation.

Turning to Hare, Glossop argues that although Hare would not agree with such an assessment, Hare and Hume differ with regard to the relation between statements of fact and moral judgments. Hare holds that all naturalistic ethical theories are mistaken, that moral language is irreducibly prescriptive, and that there is an unbridgeable gap between prescriptive and descriptive language. On the other hand, Hume, when correctly interpreted, does not claim that one can never get an "ought" statement from an "is" statement, but rather claims that such an important move has not been given sufficient attention by moral theorists. Hume claims, further, that such a move cannot be made on the basis of reason alone: we move from "is" to "ought" on a bridge of sentiment rather than reason.

Glossop describes what he takes to be Hume's ethical theory as a theory which involves an analytical part in which the term "virtue" is defined and a synthetic part in which a generalization is drawn with regard to all human qualities called virtues. Glossop says that once Hume's list of virtues has been drawn up on the basis of his definitions (the list includes such terms as benevolence or generosity, justice, discretion, industry, frugality, honesty, prudence, dignity, courage, and wit), Hume concludes that what is common to all virtues is that they are useful or agreeable to oneself or others. Then Glossop attempts to imagine how Hume would attack Hare's claim that a naturalistic approach to ethics fails because in making moral judgments descriptive, it leaves out their commending function.

Glossop argues that if one adopts Hume's definitions of "virtue," in attributing a virtue to a particular person one is making a *descriptive* statement which is itself *commendatory*. Hare is simply assuming that language cannot be both descriptive and prescriptive, and Glossop offers arguments which conclude that there is good reason for the naturalist or anyone else to reject such an assumption.

Either Stevenson or Hare, Glossop admits, might now raise the issue of resolving disagreement about moral issues. That is, they might ask Hume: "How are we to determine that any particular person has become a completely informed, completely disinterested, perfectly normal spectator?" Glossop proposes that Hume could answer as follows. Although we cannot determine *exactly* when one is completely informed, completely disinterested and perfectly normal, we can understand when one person is *better* informed, *more* disinterested, and *less* abnormal than another. So we can determine when some persons' value judgments are *more likely* to be correct than others', and we can know what we must do to *improve* our own value judgments. Furthermore, there would be something wrong with any view which said that when some person who is "completely qualified" says "P is true," he *cannot* be mistaken. So the fact that the Humean definition cannot make such a claim

is an asset rather than a liability.

One thing which Hume did not do, and should have done, according to Glossop, was to distinguish between what *are* virtues and what are *thought* to be virtues. What one *thinks* is a virtue, he says, depends on what arouses one's approbation; what arouses one's approbation depends on what one *thinks* is useful and agreeable, and that in turn depends on one's metaphysical views about the nature of reality. So modified, Glossop contends, Hume's views might receive wider acceptance because "one would no longer feel bound to accept Hume's own metaphysical views as a basis for what is useful."

Norton, David Fate. "Hume's Common Sense Morality," in *Canadian Journal of Philosophy*. V, no. 4 (December, 1975), pp. 523-543.

David Fate Norton contends that David Hume's moral theory, taking into consideration both *A Treatise of Human Nature* and the second *Enquiry*, is explicitly and fundamentally a commonsense theory. Norton claims to show how three features of that theory come together to form an outlook which is appropriately so designated. Two of those features—Hume's claim that moral distinctions rest on sentiments, and that it is by means of the principle of sympathy that the sentiments of a person come to be experienced by others—are, he says, widely accepted; whereas the third—Hume's concern to refute moral skepticism and his explicit use, for this purpose, of appeals to "common sense"—has to a great extent been overlooked.

In support of his claim, Norton argues that Hume is not, as is usually supposed, a moral "subjectivist"; that, quite to the contrary, his intention is to establish morality's "objectivity." In addition, Norton gives detailed consideration to Hume's concern with moral skepticism and his appeals to common sense. Finally, he argues for the fundamental role, at least in the original formulation of Hume's theory, of the principle of sympathy. The reader is warned against taking Norton's arguments as supporting the claim that, in Hume's philosophy as a whole, reason is thoroughly subordinated to feeling and instinct. That concept, he argues, is incorrect.

Skeptics doubt that there is something which is

known or is real. Commonsense philosophers counter by showing or insisting that something is known or is real. Therefore, if it is correct to describe Hume as a commonsense moralist, then it must be shown that he is a moral realist; that is, that he holds the distinction between virtue and vice to be not merely subjective or entirely dependent on private psychological factors.

Such a task may appear to be an impossible one, Norton writes, because of Hume's comparison of vice and virtue to perceptions of sounds, colors, heat, and other sense properties in *A Treatise of Human Nature*. An examination of his immediately following statements, however, calls for a careful consideration of which of obviously inconsistent claims better represents his position; for there Hume holds that vice, far from being a sentiment, is the (independent) *cause* of the sentiment. The choice must go against the subjectivistic claim, for Hume suggests in more than one way that virtue and vice are themselves independent of the sentiments which nature has provided for their recognition. In addition, Hume argued in *A Treatise of Human Nature* that virtue and vice are quite independent of the mind of an observer who states that the acts or character of another are virtuous or vicious; "virtuous" and "vicious" are terms, Hume claims, which refer to actions reflecting or proceeding from the enduring *qualities* or *character* of moral agents. A character, he says, is not virtuous because it pleases; rather, it pleases because it is virtuous.

Norton goes on to show that Hume's account in *A Treatise of Human Nature* of the indirect passions—pride, humility, esteem, hatred—as well as his discussion there of the unusual nature of our moral sentiments, supports the claim that epistemologically as well as metaphysically Hume is a moral realist. Hume believes, Norton contends, that when oneself and others manage to assume a disinterested stance, an interchange of sentiments enables the formation of a "general unalterable standard" of morality. Hume holds, he continues, that although we may not always feel or act as the standard suggests, its effectiveness as a standard is not thereby impaired.

Hume's theory is formulated not only in opposition to rationalist moral theory, an opposition generally recognized, but also against egoistic moral theories. His "anatomical" approach to morality in *A Treatise of Human Nature*, Hume himself believed, made that work appear to lack "Warmth in the cause of Virtue," an appearance he attempted to explain away and made sure did not infect the *Enquiry*. The latter begins by finding the viewpoint of those who deny the reality of moral distinctions so absurd that Hume recommends leaving them alone, in the belief that it is highly likely that they will in time "come over to the side of common sense and reason" on their own. However, the position of the ethical egoist, whom Hume also considers a moral skeptic, is subjected to a sustained attack in the *Enquiry*.

In *A Treatise of Human Nature*, common sense is employed as a primary weapon against moral skepticism both indirectly (Norton cites numerous passages) and directly: Hume holds that there are general principles which are "authorized by common sense, and the practice of all ages," giving as an example the right of people to resist a tyrannical ruler. Those who deny such a right, he says, "have renounced all pretensions to common sense and do not merit a serious answer." Serious arguments involving appeals to common sense, however, are given by Hume, not only in *A Treatise of Human Nature* but also in other works.

The systematic importance in Hume's moral theory of reliance on commonsense is shown by his claim that our commonsense views rest on an absolutely fundamental and natural principle: sympathy. Sympathy makes possible intercommunication of sentiments and understanding between human beings. Sympathy enables the creation of a common point of view, the pursuance of common interests, and the creation of a common moral standard by which to determine the rightness or wrongness of acts. From our observation of another's passions and our perceptions of the usual causes of such passions, we are led to the perception of the usual effects and feel the passion itself. It is through sympathy that we know and care about the good of mankind; consequently, sympathy causes us to approve of that which has a tendency toward the good of mankind. It is through sympathy that we know and care about the good of someone who may even be a stranger to us; and sympathy causes us to approve of that which has a tendency toward the good of only the stranger himself. The principle of sympathy, then, according to Hume, enables us to escape the perspective of our own narrow interests, to know and share the judgments, opinions, and feelings of others, and to establish a general and intersubjective standard of right and wrong.

Norton concludes that if we grant that Hume's principle of sympathy exists and that it functions as he claims, "then we can see that his appeals to common sense are not merely casual appeals, nor appeals to mere vulgar prejudice. They are, rather, appeals to the collective judgment and feeling of a mankind equipped to produce disinterested and intersubjective judgments of an objective moral reality."

Additional Recommended Reading

Capaldi, Nicholas. *David Hume: The Newtonian Philosopher*. Boston: Twayne, 1975. Capaldi argues that in the *Enquiry* the passions are no longer an essential feature of Hume's moral theory.

Frankena, William K. *Ethics*. Englewood Cliffs, New Jersey: Prentice-Hall,1973. Frankena's view is similar to that of Glossop in the paper summarized above, although Frankena does not consider Hume an ethical naturalist.

Glossop, Ronald J. "The Nature of Hume's Ethics," in *Philosophy and Phenomenological Research*. XXVII, no. 4 (June, 1967), pp. 527-536. Glossop doubts that Hume can be considered an ethical naturalist in the strictest sense.

Harrison, Jonathan. *Hume's Theory of Justice*. New York: Oxford University Press, 1981. A helpful discussion of Hume's moral and political philosophy.

King, James T. "The Place of the Language of Morals in Hume's Second *Enquiry*," in *Hume: A Re-evaluation*. Edited by D. W. Livingston and J. T. King. New York: Fordham University Press, 1976, pp. 343-361. King holds that although in some respects *A Treatise of Human Nature* and *Enquiry* views are similar, their logical and epistemic ordering is not. As one consequence, he argues, the problem in *A Treatise of Human Nature* of correction of the sentiments does not arise in the *Enquiry*. King denies that Hume is in the strictest sense an ethical naturalist.

Noxon, James. *Hume's Philosophical Development*. Oxford: Clarendon Press, 1973. Noxon observes that in the *Enquiry*, as opposed to *A Treatise of Human Nature*, Hume's method involves the observation of moral, not psychological, phenomena.

THE SOCIAL CONTRACT

Author: Jean Jacques Rousseau (1712-1778)
Type of work: Social philosophy
First published: 1762

Principal Ideas Advanced

Whatever rights and responsibilities the rulers and citizens have in a state are derived from some agreement; no social right is derived from nature.

In a state of nature men live to preserve themselves; to make cooperation possible and to assure common security, states are instituted by social contracts.

According to the contract, when a man places himself under the control of a sovereign, he is placing himself under the control of himself and his fellow citizens, for a sovereign exists in order to safeguard the citizens.

The sovereign is limited to the making of general laws; he cannot pass judgment upon individuals.

As a result of the joining of wills by the social contract, a general will, distinguishable from a collection of individual wills, comes into being.

The ideal government is a small, elected group; and the ideal state is small enough to allow the citizens to know one another.

Jean Jacques Rousseau is the most interesting and the most important political thinker of the eighteenth century. He is known for his famous *Confessions* (1784) and for his discussion of education in *The New Héloïse* (1760) and *Émile* (1762), but he is best known today, in philosophical circles at any rate, for *The Social Contract,* which is one of the great classics in the field of political philosophy. Rousseau was very much concerned with the relationship between the state on the one hand and the individual on the other. He recognized that the state has tremendous power over the individual, that it can command him, coerce him, and determine the sort of life he is to live, and also that the individual makes many demands on society, even if he does not have the power to back them up. But surely, he insisted, the relations between the state and the individual cannot be simply those of naked power, threats, coercion, arbitrary decrees and fearful or cunning submission, for we do speak of justified authority, the legitimate exercise of force, the rights of citizens, and the duties of rulers. The big question, then, is this: What is the source of the rights and responsibilities of both the citizen and the ruler?

In *The Social Contract,* Rousseau repudiates those who argue that the stronger have the right to rule the weaker, insisting that strength as such amounts to coercion and not justified coercion. If a highwayman brandishing a pistol leaps at me from a thicket and demands my purse, I am forced to hand it over, but his strength does not justify his act and my weakness does not make my reluctance blameworthy. Nor does this right of society over the individual flow from nature. True, the simplest social group, the family, does rest upon the natural requirement that the parents care for the child—survival is the first law of nature—but since the family usually holds together much longer than is needed to satisfy this requirement, it is evident that the rights and obligations that continue to exist within the family organization are not supported or required by nature. Rather, these obligations and rights depend upon tacit agreements between parents and children that certain relationships shall be maintained and respected within the group, agreements tacitly admitted when the son chooses to stay within the family and the father welcomes his continued presence. Agreements of this sort mark the transition from the amoral state of power and submission to power to the moral state of acknowledged rights and responsibilities. What is true of the family is also true of that larger society, the state, for whatever rights and responsibilities the rulers and citizens possess could only have evolved as the result of some agreement among men. Rousseau insists, like Thomas Hobbes, John Locke, and many others, that society is based upon some implicit contract.

This contract delivers us from a prior state of nature. Before men lived in societies they were motivated primarily by the basic urge to preserve themselves, an urge that manifested itself in physical appetites and desires and released itself instinctively through actions designed to satisfy these. Man was not governed by reason or by moral considerations, for there were no rights or moral relationships to be respected. Rousseau does not claim that pre-societal man was vicious or the natural enemy of every other man, or that he had no gregarious instincts at all, but he does claim that the life of the individual was dominated by the amoral, unreflective pursuit of his own welfare. As a result of this marked individualism and the rude circumstances of nature, life was uncertain and precarious, cooperation impossible, and aggression common. Such a state could be transcended only by instituting, by common consent, some sort of body politic within which cooperation would be possible and security guaranteed.

According to Rousseau, the society instituted by the contract brings about a marked transformation in man, for rational behavior replaces instinct, a sense of responsibility replaces physical motivation, and law replaces appetite. Latent capacities and faculties finally flower, and out of "a stupid and dull-witted animal" there emerges "an intelligent being and a man." In these respects Rousseau differs from Locke and Thomas Jefferson, who maintained that prior to the contract man is already rational and moral and already possesses rights. The contract does not change man or affect his rights; it only safeguards what he already has. But for Rousseau man's debt to society is far greater, for rights, morality, and his very status as a man are consequences of his being a member of a body politic. Rousseau also differs from

Hobbes, not about the nonexistence of morality in a state of nature, but about human nature. The Hobbesian man is so egoistic that he can only be restrained, not transformed. For Hobbes, Locke, and Jefferson, man is essentially individualistic, whereas for Rousseau he is essentially a social creature. This view leads to two different conceptions of the function of political society. In the former, social institutions have only the negative function of securing what man already has by controlling excessive individualism, whereas in the latter, social institutions have the positive function of enabling man to fulfill his nature. In the former, political institutions are a necessary evil, but for Rousseau they are a blessing.

In the contract that establishes the state, men agree with one another to place both themselves and their possessions under the complete control of the resultant body politic, and to give to it the power and responsibility of safeguarding them and of providing the framework within which they can jointly pursue their common welfare.

It may sound as if Rousseau were advocating a rather extreme despotism, but this is not so. In the first place, according to the terms of the contract, civil power and responsibility are not turned over to a king or to some small group of persons, but are kept in the hands of the contractors themselves, who thus become jointly sovereign. Consequently, when a man contracts to place himself under the control of the sovereign, his action means only that he, like every other person, places himself under the control of himself and his fellow citizens.

Secondly, while the state shall have control over the individual, the scope of its control is limited to matters pertaining to the preservation and welfare of all. If it transgresses these limits, the contract is void and the citizen is released. Thus, for instance, while the new citizen hands all his possessions over to the state, the state immediately hands them back and, by giving him title to them, institutes property rights as distinguished from mere possession. According to the contract, the state retains control only in the sense that it has the right to appropriate the individual's property if the public interest should require that it do so. Similarly, the state can command the individual only to the extent that control is needed for the public welfare. At all other times and in all other respects it guarantees his freedom from the encroachment of the government and of other individuals. In this way the contract brings human rights into being and specifies their scope.

Again, the individual is safeguarded insofar as the function of the sovereign group is restricted to the making of laws and insofar as the object of the law is always general. The sovereign power can pass laws attaching rewards or punishments to types of action and privileges to certain offices, but it cannot pass judgment upon individuals. The latter is the function of the executive or administrative branch, not that of the legislative. Rousseau maintains emphatically that the legislative and administrative functions shall not be discharged by the same group.

The transformation wrought in the individual and the nature of the sovereign act are both expressed in what is perhaps the most nearly basic of Rousseau's concepts, that of the "general will." Even though man is initially motivated by self-interest, the awareness that a contract is desirable forces him to think about others and their interests. Once the contract is made and the mechanism of democratic assemblies put into practice the individual will be forced to consider those other interests more seriously than ever before. This consideration may result from prudence alone in the first place, but the deliberate joining of lots, the debating, the compromises to accommodate others, and the conscious recognition that they have common ideals cannot fail to encourage a genuine concern for the welfare of all. Man becomes a social creature with a social conscience, and what would otherwise have been a mere collection of individuals with individual goals and individual wills becomes a collective person with a single general will and a single goal. There comes into being a *res publica*, a republic, a body politic with many members.

Rousseau stressed the point that man is not really a citizen so long as he accepts society from prudence alone, that he becomes a real citizen only when he develops a genuine concern for the welfare of all. There is an emphasis here that is not found in the English and American social contract writers. Of course, Rousseau does not write that man's interest in himself will disappear; he claims, rather, that a new

dimension has been added. Insofar as he is still self-centered, man must be a subject, but insofar as he is a socially conscious person he can assume his responsibilities as a sovereign.

Rousseau insists that the general will must be distinguished from the many individual wills. If the citizens jointly form a body politic, the general will is the will of that body, a will that comes into being when they jointly concentrate their attention on the needs of that body. This will exercises itself through democratic assemblies of all the citizens and lets its intentions be known through the decisions of such assemblies. An assembly expresses the will of the whole people and not that of a part, but it requires only the voice of the majority *if* the views of the minority have been fairly heard and fairly considered. The general will cannot be ill-intentioned; it is concerned with the good of all, and it cannot be mistaken unless it is ill-informed. Simple, unsophisticated men are quite capable of exercising sovereign power provided that they are socially conscious, and well informed, and provided further that they act after full discussion, and are not subject to pressure groups. Since sovereignty is the expression of the general will, and the general will is the expression of the will of all, sovereignty cannot be alienated by anyone or delegated to anyone—king or elected representative.

While he sometimes spoke in a rather idealistic manner, Rousseau could also be rather hardheaded. He was quite aware that the conditions just mentioned are not always fulfilled. Pressure groups do occur; citizens become so indifferent or so preoccupied with their own concerns that they fail to discharge their civic responsibilities, and administrators seek to control those they are supposed to serve. In these and other ways sovereignty can be destroyed. No human institution, he writes, will last forever. In addition, it is not likely that simple men can themselves establish the proper kind of state. Some well-intentioned and exceedingly gifted lawgiver is needed to provide a constitution, help establish traditions, and guide the fledgling state with a hidden but firm hand until the people have developed the ability, stability, and desire to carry on for themselves.

Through the expression of their general will, then, the people exercise the sovereignty which they have and must retain in their own hands, but as we have already noted, they do not administer the resultant laws. To do so they establish an executive branch that functions as their agent. The form and structure of the administration will depend upon the size of the state, and, other things being equal, the number of rulers tolerable for efficiency will vary inversely with the number of citizens. This is so since a larger state will require the tighter administrative control that can be achieved only if the executive power is restricted to a small number of administrators. On the other hand, a very small state might get along by allowing all the citizens to take part in the administration. Having in mind a moderately sized city-state, such as his native Geneva, Rousseau suggests that the ideal government would be a small elected group. He says that the function of the executive is restricted to the support and administration of the law and to the preservation of civil and political liberty, and that the sovereign assembly is restricted to legislating, but he does not specify these functions in detail nor does he discuss the relationship between them. Furthermore, he does not discuss a judiciary, but this is presumably included in the administrative complex.

He is clear, though, in his insistence that the administrator be the servant of the assembly. To ensure that this be so, the people enter into no contract with their administrator and, unlike the Hobbesian contractors, transfer no rights to him. They extend to him nothing more than a revocable commission, thereby retaining control over him without being bound by him. When the sovereign assembly meets, as it does very frequently, all commissions granted by it at previous meetings become void until they are renewed.

Rousseau favors a moderately sized state something like the communes of Switzerland wherein every citizen can come to know all the others, for in the large state relations between citizens become impersonal, and their interests, problems, and fortunes become diversified. If there are many provinces, mores will not be uniform and one body of law will not be sufficient. The number and levels of subordinate government will multiply, and as the cost increases liberty will decrease. Chains of command become attenuated to such an extent that administra-tion at the bottom levels becomes indifferent, weak, or corrupt, and supervision from the top becomes difficult. The control of the government by the people becomes impossible, as does the democratic legislative process. Indeed, a very large state cannot avoid being a dictatorship both legislatively and administratively, and that is the best form of government for it. If a state is to be a democratic state it must be small, as small as it can be without inviting encroachment by its neighbors.

It is interesting to speculate about what Rousseau would say of modern democracies which have millions of citizens and embrace hundreds of thousands of square miles. He would perhaps admit that contemporary means of communication obviate some of the difficulties he had in mind, and that security usually requires a considerably larger state than was necessary then. Quite possibly he would admire many of the ingenious ways by which we have delegated both legislative and administrative powers and controlled these powers, but he might argue sadly that we are bedeviled by many of the difficulties inherent in size. Gone forever is the small autonomous political group with its intimacies, its personal concern, its shared interests and problems, and its joint endeavors.

Rousseau's views have influenced many thinkers and political movements, partly because of the central problem with which he was concerned and partly because of the vigor and clarity with which he wrote. But his influence is due also to the fact that unresolved tensions in his thought have permitted partisan readers to place rather different interpretations upon him. On the one hand, his emphasis on equality, liberty, and the supremacy of the citizen made him a favorite author among the leaders of the French Revolution, and these emphases plus those on democracy and the control of the administrators have always made him attractive to those who have supported a republican form of government. On the other hand, his claim that man realizes his full nature only by participating in the life of a society has impressed those who believe that the state should play more than a negative regulatory role. This claim, along with his assertion that the individual is under the complete control of the sovereign power, and his sometimes near deification of the general will have seemed to others to foreshadow the engulfing national spirit of Hegel and his followers and to be congenial to the recent German and Italian cult of the Fatherland. The truth, of course, is that each of the above views requires that the interpreter select his passages and, in some cases, stretch them considerably, whereas in fact, Rousseau presents us with a rich array of ideas that are not worked out completely or consistently. These fresh ideas are what make *The Social Contract* one of the great classics of political philosophy.

Pertinent Literature

Plamenatz, John. "On le forcera d'être libre," in Maurice Cranston and Richard S. Peters' *Hobbes and Rousseau: A Collection of Critical Essays*. Garden City, New York: Anchor Books, 1972, pp. 318-332.

John Plamenatz dedicates this essay to dissipating the shocking effect of Jean Jacques Rousseau's famous contention that people may be forced to be free. Rousseau's critics have been divided about his true meaning. Some have accused him of being a traitor to liberty, allowing its suppression in its own name. Plamenatz feels that this accusation is misguided, since Rousseau insisted that genuine liberty exists only when every man (or perhaps one should say every citizen) is a member of the legislative assembly. Everyone who was not excluded from the assembly and was free to vote his conscience without unreasonable pressure or coercion was obliged to abide by the laws enacted by it.

Nevertheless, Plamenatz concedes that the expression "forced to be free" is obscure, and that if one takes it literally, it is impossible to make any sense of it. In order to understand it, he suggests that it not be taken literally, and argues that if his meaning is properly understood, it will lead to new insights into Rousseau's theories on the connections between law, duty, and freedom, and more especially to a greater appreciation of the novel contributions Rousseau made to the concept of liberty.

Rousseau distinguishes three kinds of liberty: natural, civil, and moral. Natural liberty, a state in which men are totally independent of one another, can exist only in a state of nature, where there are no laws. In such a state, where rules, rights, and obligations are unknown, man is not yet a moral being. Civil liberty consists of the right to do that which the rules permit. Moral liberty is obedience to rules imposed by the individual upon himself. The essential difference between civil liberty and moral liberty, then, is that civil liberty is conditioned by the laws or social rules imposed by the state or other citizens through some form of collective action and the threat of sanctions, while moral liberty concerns only the individual's relation to himself. According to Plamenatz, Rousseau's paradoxical slogan about forcing a man to be free has to do only with moral liberty.

In the state of nature, man enjoys natural liberty or independence because he can satisfy his relatively simple wants without the assistance of others. In such a state he is not a slave to his passions, not because he totally lacks passions, but because the passions he has are moderate to begin with, like those that brute animals have. Only in society, where men become vain and grasping, can they become true slaves to their passions. Of course, man in the state of nature has no conception either of freedom or of slavery; but men who live in civil society can look back upon the state of nature and, realizing their own acquired needs and desires and the extent to which they have become dependent upon others for their satisfaction, can reflect upon the state of nature and recognize the fact that in that state men enjoyed a kind of freedom which is denied to them.

To be free in the complete sense of that word, man must want only what he can get. He must not have insatiable appetites or desires that are incompatible with one another. Such appetites and desires are acquired only in civil society, where men develop the "unnatural" passion to be preferred over all others—a passion which is unnatural since it does not exist in the state of nature. This passion is also unnatural in that it prevents man from achieving the very goal for which he presumably organized himself into civil society—happiness.

If a society could produce two conditions, it could be said to be truly free: if it could prevent the development in its members of needs that they could not satisfy, and if it could meet those demands that its members did have, then in the sense discussed above, its members would be free, for they would not be dependent upon one another for the satisfaction of unmet needs.

In actual societies, however, there is a tendency for people to develop passions and wants which cannot be satisfied, and for inequalities to develop which result in jealousies and the consequent desire on the part of those who do not have all that their neighbors enjoy to acquire a greater share of the wealth (however that term may be defined). Inequalities give rise to prejudices, passions, and laws which serve to perpetuate the very inequalities which create the problems they are designed to treat. This leads inevitably to even greater unhappiness.

It is therefore reasonable for men in civil society to be equalitarian—to be recognized by others as equals, and to treat them equally—in short, to require of others no more than they would be willing to concede to them. No matter how rich or powerful one may be, someone always has greater power or wealth (in some sense); so, according to Rousseau, it is to everyone's interest to invoke the principle of equality.

How, then, can a man in civil society be free? He can be free in obeying the law if the law itself expresses his will. But since the laws govern all, and since equality is a reasonable goal for men to pursue (in their own self interest), it follows that it is best if *all* men are free—which means that the law must express the will of all alike. Thus, all the citizens must take part in making the law. This, of course, is the sense of Rousseau's conception of the general will.

But suppose a man has voted against a law which was enacted by the majority. Or suppose he changes his mind and no longer approves of a law which he approved of when it was first enacted. The law then—it would seem—no longer expresses his will, and his obedience to it is no longer an expression of

his freedom, but is rather an instance of coercion and enslavement. Plamenatz argues that, according to Rousseau, one who participates in the deliberations that lead to a decision (for example, a piece of legislation) binds himself to accept that decision even if he votes against it. In a sense, then, he has freely accepted the conclusions arrived at by the legislature.

As for the lawbreaker, or the one who no longer wishes to be bound by the dictates of a particular law, Plamenatz interprets Rousseau to be saying that even he respects the law. He may want to abide by the law, and at the same time want what he cannot have unless he breaks the law. Consider, for example, the citizen who is making out his tax return—wanting, on the one hand, to be honest and to fulfill the mandates of the law, and on the other hand wishing that he could keep some of the money that an honest tax return obliges him to pay to his government. If he is honest, he regrets the loss of the funds he would otherwise have and the goods and services he might have purchased with them; and if he cheats on his return, he feels guilty or tries to find some excuse for his behavior.

It is precisely this sort of situation which Plamenatz feels Rousseau draws to our attention more than any other writer before him. We feel both thwarted and liberated by our sense of duty. A person who has a sense of duty does not submit to anyone else's will, but nevertheless feels bound to abide by the rule, even when he fears no sanctions. At the same time, he wants everyone else to abide by the rule as well. Thus, men not only adopt and live by rules because of their self interest; but also they wish to keep the rules because they are moral beings—despite the fact that their appetites are such that they feel thwarted by the very rules which they want so strongly to adopt and to obey. Even when their appetites overwhelm their moral sense of duty, they wish that they were law-abiding. It is this feeling that Rousseau calls the *constant will*—a will to abide by the law even when one disobeys it.

In *The Social Contract*, Plamenatz says, Rousseau describes the social and political conditions most likely to lead men to feel this way about the laws they must obey. Those conditions, he says, are also unfavorable for the development of those passions which induce men to disobey the law. Where all men are equal, they are most likely to want only what they are capable of achieving and to do what they wish to do. To get what he wants, the citizen of such a state is not dependent upon the favors of others, and is therefore independent in Rousseau's sense of the word—although he is dependent upon laws which they and he desire be obeyed.

The phrase "to be forced to be free" cannot be taken literally, then. It can, however, be understood to express Rousseau's explanation of those conditions which are necessary for men to find a moral support in the laws established in a just society for the discipline they need to be free of the passions that would otherwise enslave them.

Cassirer, Ernst. *The Question of Jean-Jacques Rousseau.* Translated and edited by Peter Gay. New York: Columbia University Press, 1954.

The question referred to in the title is whether it is possible to reconcile discordant elements in Jean Jacques Rousseau's thought. Rousseau insisted on the unity of his work, but well-known scholars have argued that the political system sketched in *The Social Contract* is a foreign element, out of harmony with Rousseau's passion for individual freedom. Ernst Cassirer holds that Rousseau's assessment was correct, that although his thought was always in motion and cannot be reduced to a system, the movement is nevertheless continuous and gives organic unity to his writings. Rousseau wrote by impulse and, at the beginning, had no notion of his goal; but gradually he perceived the direction he must take and was able to give objective and universal expression to the problems which caused him such personal anguish.

According to Cassirer, what mainly disturbed Rousseau was the shallowness and falsity of the Enlightenment view of man, first as he met it in Parisian society and later as he listened to his friends the Encyclopedists. The success which he had enjoyed in the salons did not blind him to the fact that this highly touted existence was a kind of slavery, and when by chance he saw the notice of an essay contest on the question "Has the restoration of the sciences and the arts helped to purify morals?" he was ready with his answer. This essay, known as the *First Discourse,* was a popular success mainly because of its eloquence and passion. Cassirer says, however, that there was nothing novel in the thesis that man, naturally good, is corrupted by society; that was what many advanced thinkers were saying. The assumption of the Enlightenment was that, like other creatures, man has a fixed nature, and that in order to

discover it we need only think what he was like in his natural condition. The real shock came when, in the *Second Discourse,* "The Origins of Inequality," Rousseau denied the fixity and intelligibility of human nature and argued that what sets man apart from other creatures is that his nature is unfinished. Rousseau was the first, says Cassirer, to oppose the static eighteenth century view of the world, setting against it his own dynamic view according to which man's form and essence are plastic. In other words, he had come to consider that it is not possible to consider what man *is* apart from the question of what man *ought* to be.

For the most part, Rousseau's readers missed the main point. When he exalted the natural man over the artificial man, railed against the learned, set feeling over intellect, and called upon individual persons to free themselves from the bondage of custom and dare to live their own lives, he was understood as advocating capricious subjectivism at best and amoral self-seeking at worst. According to Cassirer, however, Rousseau was speaking a new language. The natural man which he held up in opposition to the product of civilization was not a creature of instinct and passion but one who had freed himself from his animal condition by establishing for himself a moral law; the feeling to which he appealed was not sympathy or sentiment, but conscience; and the freedom which he cherished was not arbitrary self-will, but a canopy of voluntary submission to law which the person erects over himself.

From the beginning, says Cassirer, Rousseau maintained the primacy of the ethical will over both passion and empirical knowledge. "Virtue! Sublime science of simple souls!" he cried in the *First Discourse*; "To learn your laws, is it not enough to return to ourselves and to listen to the voice of conscience in the silence of passions?" The truth must be apprehended by each person for himself, but it is denied to no one because it belongs to man's essence. All that we need in order to discover what is right is to remove hindrances that stand in our way. That was the thesis of *Émile*, his work on education; it was also the foundation of his political thought. In the *Confessions* he says that he was not long in discovering that human existence is a political achievement. Past states have grown up as battlegrounds for men's ambition and self-love, with the result that states have been oppressive; but man can control his destiny and transform a curse into a blessing. "The great question seemed to reduce itself to this: which is the form of government fitted to shape the most virtuous, the most enlightened, the wisest, and, in short, the 'best' people?" The Encyclopedists, Cassirer points out, were also interested in political reform, but where they were looking for ways to increase men's happiness, Rousseau was looking for ways to make men good. In the state that he envisaged, legislation, giving voice to the General Will, would not merely focus the wills of people but would form them,

enabling men to raise themselves above the life of appetite and desire.

According to Rousseau, law, when it is the expression of moral reason, does not diminish spiritual freedom. Rousseau hated servility as much as the next person. He could endure natural evils; indeed, he saw it as part of man's greatness that he can learn to absorb the shocks of nature. What he could not endure was having to submit to the arbitrary wills of other men. Law, as the expression of ethical will, is not arbitrary, however; one need not even think of himself as having to *obey* the law if the law is one that has been arrived at in a way that expresses the ethical will.

Cassirer mentions the high compliment which Immanuel Kant paid to Rousseau when he said that just as Sir Isaac Newton was the first to see order in the seemingly irregular motions of the heavenly bodies, so "Rousseau was the first to discover in the variety and shapes that men assume the deeply concealed nature of man and to observe the hidden law that justifies Providence." It is well known that Kant learned from Rousseau to respect the moral judgment of the common man. Cassirer brings out other parallels between the writings of the two men.

Additional Recommended Reading

Chapman, John W. *Rousseau: Totalitarian or Liberal.* New York: Columbia University Press, 1956. Contrasts Rousseau's liberalism with the classical British variety.

Cobban, Alfred. *Rousseau and the Modern State.* London: George Allen & Unwin, 1934. Considers the relevance of Rousseau's principles to the problems of modern democracies.

Gildin, Hilail. *Rousseau's Social Contract: The Design of the Argument.* Chicago: University of Chicago Press, 1983. A detailed account of central issues in Rousseau's political thought.

Grimsley, Ronald. *The Philosophy of Rousseau.* Oxford: Oxford University Press, 1973. A professor of French literature surveys Rousseau's ideas, with emphasis on his social thought.

Hendel, Charles W. *Jean-Jacques Rousseau: Moralist.* Indianapolis: Bobbs-Merrill, 1962. Detailed account of the development of Rousseau's philosophy. Useful for the advanced student.

Masters, Roger D. *The Political Philosophy of Rousseau.* Princeton, New Jersey: Princeton University Press, 1968. A commentary on pertinent writings of Rousseau by a political scientist.

DIALOGUES CONCERNING NATURAL RELIGION

Author: David Hume (1711-1776)
Type of work: Philosophy of religion
First published: 1779

Principal Ideas Advanced

The argument from design is an argument which attempts to prove God's existence on the basis of signs of adaptability in nature, but it is an unsatisfactory argument because, although plausible, it does not demonstrate with logical certainty the truth of the claim that the universe was designed.

Furthermore, if we try to deduce the nature of God from the characteristics of nature regarded as his handiwork, God must be finite, imperfect, incompetent, and dependent.

It is possible that order in nature is the result of a natural generative process.

A priori arguments designed to prove God's existence are inconclusive and establish only that something, not necessarily God, may have been a first cause.

Although the cause of order in the universe probably bears some resemblance to human intelligence, nothing can be concluded concerning the moral character of such a cause.

Hume's *Dialogues Concerning Natural Religion* is one of the most famous works criticizing some of the arguments offered by philosophers and theologians to establish the existence and nature of God. Hume, who was known as the "Great Infidel" in his own time, began writing the *Dialogues* around 1751. He showed the manuscript to several of his friends, who dissuaded him from publishing it because of its irreligious content. Over the years, he revised the manuscript many times and finally, just before his death in 1776, he made his final revisions. He was very much concerned to make sure that the work would be published shortly after his death. In his will, he first requested his friend, the economist Adam Smith, to arrange for the publication of the *Dialogues*. When Smith refused, Hume next tried to get his publisher to do so, and when he also refused, Hume altered his will, instructing his nephew to take charge of the matter if the publisher had not done so within two years of his death. Finally, in 1779, the work appeared, gaining both immediate success and notoriety. It has remained one of the classic texts in discussions about the nature of the evidence pre-sented to prove the existence of God and the character of his attributes.

The *Dialogues* are patterned after Cicero's work on the same subject, *The Nature of the Gods,* in which a Stoic, an Epicurean, and a Skeptic discuss the arguments about the nature and existence of the gods. Both Cicero and Hume found that the dialogue form enabled them to discuss these "dangerous" subjects without having to commit themselves personally to any particular view. They could allow their characters to attack various accepted arguments and positions, without themselves having to endorse or reject any specific religious view.

Hume begins the *Dialogues* with a letter from Pamphillus, a young man who was a spectator at the discussion, to his friend Hermippus. Pamphillus explains that the dialogue form is most suitable for discussing theology, because the subject, on the one hand, deals with a doctrine, the being of God, that is so obvious that it hardly admits of any dispute, while on the other hand, it leads to philosophical questions that are extremely obscure and uncertain regarding the nature, attributes, and decrees and plans of God.

The dialogue form, presumably, can both inculcate the "obvious" truth, and explore the difficulties.

After having Philo and Cleanthes debate the merits of skepticism in Part I, Hume presents Philo and the orthodox Demea as agreeing that human reason is inadequate to comprehend divine truths. They concur in the view that there is no doubt concerning the existence of a deity, but that our natural and rational information is insufficient to justify any beliefs concerning the nature of the deity. Philo sums up the case by asserting that our ideas are all based upon experience and that we have no experience at all of divine attributes and operations. Thus, the nature of the Supreme Being is incomprehensible and mysterious.

Cleanthes immediately objects and states the theory that Hume analyzes in great detail throughout the *Dialogues*. The information and evidence that we have about the natural world, Cleanthes insists, enable us to infer both the existence and nature of a deity. He then presents what is called "the argument from design," an argument that had been current in both ancient and modern theological discussions, but which had become extremely popular in the form in which it was stated by Sir Isaac Newton. Look at the world, Cleanthes declares, and you will see that it is nothing but one vast machine, subdivided into smaller machines. All of the parts are adjusted to one another, so that the whole vast complex functions harmoniously. The adaptation of means to ends through all of nature exactly resembles the adaptation which results from human design and intelligence. Since natural objects and human artifacts resemble one another, we infer by analogy that the causes of them must also resemble one another. Hence the author of nature must be similar to the mind of man, though he must have greater faculties, since his production is greater.

Philo proceeds to criticize the argument from design by pointing out first that the analogy is not a good one. The universe is unlike a man-made object, such as a machine or a house. Also, we discover causes only from our experience; for example, from seeing houses being built or machines being constructed. We have never seen a universe being produced, so we cannot judge if it is made analogously

to human productions. We have perceived many causal processes other than human design, processes like growth, attraction, and so on. For all that we can tell from our experience, any of these may be the cause of the natural world.

Cleanthes insists, in Part III, that the similarity of the works of nature to the works of human art is self-evident and undeniable. When we examine various aspects of nature in terms of the latest scientific information, the most obvious conclusion that we come to is that these aspects must be the result of design. By citing several examples, Cleanthes tries to show the immense plausibility of the argument from design. (In other works such as the *Natural History of Religion*, 1755, Hume always stressed the fact that a reasonable man could not help being impressed by the order and design in nature, and could not avoid coming to the conclusion that there must be some sort of intelligent orderer or designer of nature. However, Hume also insisted, as he did over and over again in the *Dialogues*, that no matter how convincing the argument may be, it is not logical, and can be challenged in many ways.)

To counterattack, Hume has Demea point out another failing of the argument from design. If we gained knowledge about God by analogy with the human mind, then we would have to conclude that the divine mind is as confused, as changeable, as subject to influence by the passions, as is man's. Such a picture of God is incompatible with that presented by traditional religions and by the famous theologians. In fact, as Philo and Demea point out in Parts IV and V, if the argument from design is accepted, then strange theology will ensue. Since man's mind is finite, by analogy so is God's mind. If God's mind is finite, he can err and be imperfect. If we have to judge God's attributes from the effects that we are aware of, what can we actually ascertain about God's nature? We cannot determine, from looking at the world, whether it represents a good achievement, as we have no standards of universe-construction by which we can judge. We cannot tell if the world that we perceive was made by one God or by many deities. If one takes the analogy involved in the argument from design seriously, all sorts of irrelevant conclusions are possible and any conclusion about the type of designer or designers is pure guesswork. "This world, for aught he [man] knows, is very faulty and imperfect, compared to a superior standard; and was only the first rude essay of some infant Deity, who afterwards abandoned it, ashamed of his lame performance; it is the work only of some dependent, inferior Deity; and is the object of derision to his superiors: it is the production of old age and dotage in some superannuated deity; and ever since his death, has run on at adventures, from the first impulse and active force, which it received from him. . . ." These and all sorts of other hypotheses are all possible explanations, by means of the argument from design, of the order in the universe.

Philo, in Parts VI-VIII, maintains that other explanations can be offered to account for the order in the world besides the explanation of a designer, and that these alternatives can be shown to be at least as probable. Two theories are considered, one that order results from a generative or growth process, and the other, that order is just the chance result of the way material particles come together. Over and over again we see order develop in nature as the result of biological growth. Seeds grow into organized plants. We do not see any outside designer introduce the order. Hence, if we judge solely by our experiences, one genuine possibility is that order is an unconscious result of the process of generation. The world, for all that we can tell, generates its own order just by developing. Since every day we see reason and order arise from growth development, as it does in children maturing, and never see organization proceeding from reason, it is a probable as well as a possible hypothesis to suppose that the order in the world comes from some inner biological process in the world, rather than from some designing cause outside it.

Even the ancient hypothesis of Epicurus, that the order in the world is due to "the fortuitous concourse of atoms" and that there is no external or internal designing or organizing force, suffices to account for the world as we know it. From our experience, it is just as probable that matter is the cause of its own motions as that mind or growth is. Also, nothing that we perceive proves that the present order of things did not simply come about by chance. Philo con-

cludes the discussion on this point by asserting that an empirical theology, based solely on information gained from experience, would be inadequate to justify acceptance of any particular hypothesis about the source or cause of order in the world, or any particular religious system about the nature of the force or forces that govern the universe.

Demea, the orthodox believer, who has agreed with Philo's attack up to this point, now contends, in Part IX, that there are rational *a priori* arguments, not based on any empirical information whatsoever, that show that there must be a divine being. Demea states the classical theological argument that there must be a first cause, or God, that accounts for the sequence of causes occurring in the world. Hume has Cleanthes challenge this argument by introducing some of the skeptical contentions about causality and the inconclusiveness of *a priori* arguments that Hume had presented in his *A Treatise of Human Nature* (1739) and his *An Enquiry Concerning Human Understanding* (1748). Further, Hume points out that even if the *a priori* were legitimate, and even if it actually proved that there must be a first cause, or a necessarily existent being, it still would not show that this being had to be God. Perhaps the material world is itself the first cause, the cause of itself.

With this criticism, Hume concludes his considerations of arguments purporting to establish the existence of God, and turns to what can be known about God's nature or attributes. At the beginning of Part X, Philo and Demea rhapsodize about the misery and weakness of man, which Demea presents as the reason why man must seek God's protection. Philo uses the same information about man's plight to indicate that we cannot infer moral qualities of a deity from what is going on in the human world. If we knew what the deity is like, we might be able to explain, in terms of his perfect plan, why the evils of this world occur, and why there is so much human misery. But, since we do not know God's nature, we are not able to infer that he is perfect, wise, and good, from our limited knowledge of man's dismal and painful existence. Demea offers a religious explanation of the evils; namely, that our present existence is just a moment in the course of our existence. The present evil events will be recompensed and rectified in another realm, in an afterlife. But, Cleanthes insists, if man is to judge of divine matters from his experience, he has no information to support this religious supposition. The only way in which man can accept a belief in a benevolent deity is to deny Philo and Demea's thesis that human life is absolutely miserable. To this, Philo replies that the occurrence of any evil, any misery, any pain, no matter how small a part of human life it might be raises difficulties in ascertaining if God has the moral attributes accepted by traditional religions. If God possesses infinite power, wisdom, and goodness, how does anything unpleasant happen?

Cleanthes argues, in Part XI, that if one goes back to his analogy between man and the deity, an explanation can be offered. If the author of nature is only finitely perfect, then imperfections in the universe can be accounted for as being due to his limitations. Philo, in turn, argues that present experience provides no basis whatsoever for any inference about the moral attributes of the deity, and that the more we recognize man's weaknesses, the less we are capable of asserting in support of the religious hypothesis that the world is governed by a good and benevolent deity. If we knew that a good and wise God existed, then we might be able to account for the evils in this world by either the theories of Demea or Cleanthes. But if we have to build up our knowledge and our hypotheses from what we experience, then we will have to admit that there are four possibilities concerning the first causes of the universe: that they are completely good, that they are completely bad, that they are both good and bad, and that they are neither good nor bad. The good and the evil events in human experience make it difficult to conclude from our experience alone that one of the first two possibilities is the case.

As Philo explores the four possibilities and seems to be leaning toward the last, Demea realizes with dismay that he and Philo are not really in accord. Demea stresses the incomprehensible nature of God, the weakness of man's intellectual capacities, and the misery of his life as the basis for accepting orthodox theology. Philo employs the same points to lead to an agnostic conclusion, that we cannot know, because of our nature and God's, what he is actually like, and whether there is any explanation or justification for the character of the experienced world. Demea apparently accepted revealed information as the basis for answering the questions that man, by his own faculties, could not, while Philo turned only to man's experience for the answers and found that no definite ones could be given. As soon as Demea sees how wide the gap is between them, he leaves the discussion, and Philo and Cleanthes are left on the scene to evaluate the fruits of their arguments.

In the last part, XII, Philo offers what has been taken as a summary of Hume's own views about religion. Everywhere in nature there is evidence of design. As our scientific information increases, we become more, rather than less, impressed by the order that exists in the universe. The basic difficulty is that of determining the cause or source of the design. The difference between the atheist and the theist, and between the skeptic and the dogmatist, on this matter, is really only a verbal one. The theist admits that the designer, if he is intelligent, is very different from a human being. The atheist admits that the original principle of order in the world bears some remote analogy to human intelligence, though the degree of resemblance is indeterminable. Even a skeptic like Philo has to concede that we are compelled by nature to believe many things that we cannot prove, and one of them is that there is in the universe order which seems to require an intelligent orderer. And the dogmatist has to admit that there are insoluble difficulties in establishing any truths in this area as well as in any other. The skeptic keeps pointing out the difficulties, while the dogmatist keeps stressing what has to be believed.

When these arguments are taken into account, Philo points out, we are still in no position to assess the moral character of the designer. The evidence from the observable world is that works of nature have a greater resemblance to our artifacts than to our benevolent or good acts. Hence, we have more basis for maintaining that the natural attributes of the deity are like our own than for maintaining that his moral attributes are like human virtues. As a result, Philo advocates an amoral, philosophical, and rational religion. In 1776 Hume added a final summation: "the whole of natural theology . . . resolves itself into one simple, though somewhat ambiguous, at least undefined proposition, *that the cause or causes of order in the universe probably bear some remote analogy to human intelligence*." Nothing more can be said, especially concerning the moral character of the cause or causes.

The dialogue concludes with two perplexing remarks. Philo announces as his parting observation that "To be a philosophical skeptic is, in a man of letters, the first and most essential step towards being a sound, believing Christian." This contention, which was made by all of the Christian skeptics from Michel de Montaigne to Pierre Bayle and Bishop Pierre-Daniel Huet, may have been a sincere conviction on their part. In Hume's case, there is no evidence that his skepticism led him to Christianity, but rather that it led him away from it.

At the very end, Hume has Pamphillus, the spectator, evaluate the entire discussion by saying that "PHILO'S principles are more probable than DEMEA'S; but . . . those of CLEANTHES approach still nearer the truth." Critics have variously interpreted this ending, pointing out that Pamphillus and Hume may not agree, and that this conclusion may have been intended to quiet possible critics. Others have held that Hume himself may have felt, in spite of his devastating criticisms of Cleanthes' position, that it contained more truth than Philo's almost complete skepticism.

The *Dialogues Concerning Natural Religion* has been a central work in discussions about religious knowledge ever since its publication. It is generally recognized as presenting the most severe criticisms of the argument from design, in showing its limitations as an analogy and as a basis for reaching any fruitful conclusions about the nature of the designer of the world. Since Hume in the *Dialogues* discusses only the natural evidence for religion, some later theologians, especially Søren Kierkegaard, have insisted that Hume's arguments only make more clear the need for faith and revelation as the sole basis of religious knowledge.

Pertinent Literature

Smith, Norman Kemp, ed. "Introduction," in David Hume's *Dialogues Concerning Natural Religion*. Indianapolis: Bobbs-Merrill, 1977.

This essay, first published in 1935, is probably the most important study on the *Dialogues Concerning Natural Religion*. First, Norman Kemp Smith corrects the published text of the work by comparing it with the manuscript in David Hume's own hand. (This is one of the very few works of Hume for which the manuscript has survived.) Thus Kemp Smith is able to show that some of the most skeptical portions of the *Dialogues* were added during the last years of Hume's life, when he knew he was dying.

Second, Kemp Smith makes a significant attempt to place Hume's critical views about religion in the context of the Scottish Calvinist background in which he was reared, and in the general Enlightenment background in which he flourished. Third, he compares the discussion in the *Dialogues* with the other major discussions of religion in Hume's writings, such as *The Natural History of Religion* and *An Enquiry Concerning Human Understanding*, which contain some apparently divergent views on the subject. Fourth, Kemp Smith carefully traces out some of Hume's sources for his *Dialogues*, especially Hume's use of the format in Cicero's *Nature of the Gods* and his use of fundamental arguments taken over from Pierre Bayle's *The Historical and Critical Dictionary*.

In analyzing the content of the *Dialogues*, Kemp Smith insists, in contrast to most of the interpreters of his time, that the skeptic, Philo, represents Hume's views from the beginning of the *Dialogues* to the perplexing end of the work. On the other hand, Kemp Smith claims that the Newtonian empiricist, Cleanthes, is Hume's mouthpiece only when he explicitly agrees with Philo. The drama of the *Dialogues* is the result of using both Cleanthes and Demea as foils, so that the reader will see that the arguments in favor of religion, especially the argument from design, are not adequate to support any serious religious conclusions. Nature produces some conviction about the source of the order in the universe, but this conviction cannot support any definite, unambiguous claim about *an* or *the* Author of Nature. According to Kemp Smith, Hume stated his skeptical view about religious knowledge, both in the *Dialogues* and in *The Natural History of Religion*, with the least possible emphasis. This was done presumably so that the reader would have the least difficulty in first accepting Hume's devastating critique of arguments for religion, and then following on to Hume's quite negative view of religion. The conclusions of both the *Dialogues* and *The Natural History of Religion* indicate the inability of human reason to penetrate the enigma of religious knowledge. Hume placed the problem in the context of the rest of his philosophy and showed the basic limits of human reason. In the *Dialogues* as a whole, Kemp Smith points out, Hume indicated that the traditional arguments for religion are logically defective. At this point, it is up to the reader to decide whether to go along with Hume into a thoroughgoing skepticism about religious and other matters, or whether to consider the *Dialogues* as simply instructive of the defects of certain kinds of theological arguments. This second alternative could lead, as it does in the case of Demea, to a negative way to faith. In any case, Kemp Smith insists, Hume's analysis of religious argumentation and its influence on Immanuel Kant has greatly affected discussions of Divine Existence from the late eighteenth century on.

Pike, Nelson. "Hume on the Argument from Design," in David Hume's *Dialogues Concerning Natural Religion*. Edited by Nelson Pike. Indianapolis: Bobbs-Merrill, 1970.

Nelson Pike's essay deals primarily with the argument from design, which was David Hume's primary consideration in the *Dialogues*, and with Hume's reflections on that argument. Pike very carefully examines both Hume's formulation of the argument, in contrast to other significant versions of the time, and Hume's criticisms of the version of the argument he had stated. He begins by showing that one of the key weapons that Hume employed, that of separating the way terms are used to describe the Deity from the way they were normally used, had been analyzed by theologians such as St. Thomas Aquinas and Bishop Berkeley, who had patiently explained how the terms could be used significantly without the need for a separate and distinct meaning when referring to God.

Further, Pike insists that Hume unfairly criticized the empirical and scientific character of the analogy involved in the argument from design. Working carefully through the debate between Cleanthes and Philo (Demea's contribution is rarely considered), Pike attempts to show that a version of the argument from design could and did survive all of the challenges. Pike notes several dubious steps taken by Philo, or acceded to by Cleanthes, which, if rejected, would give the argument more force.

Similarly with the discussion in Dialogues X and XI, Pike carefully considers whether Philo had eliminated all possibilities for holding that God is moral in the face of human suffering, and contends that there is still a defensible religious position. The view of Philo in Dialogue XII becomes, for Pike, Hume's own attenuated theism, which is taken over from positions Cleanthes had held earlier in the work.

Contrary to Norman Kemp Smith, Pike argues that Hume was not giving a sop to the religions in the last dialogue. He stresses that the *Dialogues* was the one work Hume knew would be published only after his death; therefore, he had no reason at all to dissimulate. Further, in *The Natural History of Religion* and in his letter to his friend Gilbert Eliot in 1751, when he began working on the *Dialogues*, Hume clearly seemed to accept the argument from design as convincing to any rational person. The letter to Eliot can be read—and Pike has done so—as saying that Cleanthes, the believer in the argument, is supposed to represent Hume. From this evidence and from his very careful examination of the way the argument proceeds in the *Dialogues*, Pike concludes that Hume and Philo rejected the "scientific" version of the argument that contended that the same kind of empirical reasoning as used in science could be used in theology to prove that an intelligent designer exists. In contrast, from the time of his letter to Eliot onward, Hume was talking of an "irregular" argument that would lead from design to designer. Philo's espousal of the argument at the end, Pike argues, was on this basis. And he also stresses, as Philo also did, that this "irregular" argument from design provides very little, if any, support for a Christian theory.

The position that Pike sees Hume working out through the central discussion of the *Dialogues* was rather close to that set forth in portions of George Berkeley's dialogue on religion, *Alciphron*. Although Hume did not refer to that work in any of his writings on religion, Pike nevertheless offers the amusing suggestion that the best answer to the query "Who speaks for Hume in the Dialogues?" is not Philo or Cleanthes but rather Bishop Berkeley.

This essay provides both a very careful analysis of the mainstream of the argument in the *Dialogues*, and a most thought-provoking interpretation.

Yandell, Keith E. "Hume on Religious Belief," in *Hume: A Re-evaluation*. Edited by D. W. Livingston and J. T. King. New York: Fordham University Press, 1976.

Writing on the occasion of the two hundredth anniversary of David Hume's death, Keith E. Yandell declares that "There is no universal consent as to what view of religion Hume embraced." He then shows that apparently conflicting claims stated in Hume's *Dialogues* and *The Natural History of Religion* have been employed to support widely differing interpretations. Yandell insists that in spite of what appears in the texts, Hume had one clear view, often stated with studied ambiguity because of the emotional factors involved. This clear view can be found in a careful examination of Hume's way of expressing himself.

One thing that has led other commentators astray, Yandell asserts, is that they have first asked which of the characters in the *Dialogues* speaks for Hume. A variety of answers have been given, pointing to all of the characters except Demea. However, Yandell insists that no single character is always Hume's spokesman. Cleanthes, who states some of Hume's views, does hold to a very un-Humean thesis—that morality is dependent on religion, no matter how corrupted religion may be. Hume had attacked this view in his major works. Philo, in the early part of the *Dialogues*, had contended that one could suspend judgment about religious belief. Later, he joined Cleanthes in denying that position.

In the light of the conflicting data, Yandell holds that each of the characters, Cleanthes, Demea, and Philo, is at various times Hume's spokesman. To understand Hume's message, one should look into the significance of the *Dialogues* in the context of Hume's other writings on religion. His *The Natural History of Religion* asserts explicitly what the *Dialogues* say only implicitly. For Hume, the basic question here is, How is religious belief related to human nature? Hume contended in *The Natural History of Religion* that there is a propensity of all mankind to believe in some kind of invisible, intelligent power—which might be said to constitute a minimal theism. Beyond that, there are contrary propensities, built upon ignorance, hope, and fear, which lead people to develop more elaborate religious beliefs and to anthropomorphize their conception of the deity.

In terms of the sources of our beliefs, what does Hume (through Philo in the last dialogue) seem to believe? Has Philo (or Hume) suddenly changed his mind on the value of the argument from design? Yandell attempts to show that Hume is thoroughly consistent in having Philo at the end be a severe critic of natural theology and at the same time be a spokesman for natural religion. The latter arises naturally; but the attempt to interpret it as a set of theistic beliefs always remains open to a devastating Humean attack. Natural religion is not based on arguments; it rests only on passions and propensities. Philo (or Hume) in defending a minimal theism in the last dialogue is not thereby defending any kind of natural theology—only a natural belief. Even this natural belief, like belief in causality, the existence of the external world, and personal identity, is in conflict with other beliefs. Hume's thrust in all of his works was to show that we can never obtain adequate reasons for believing; yet we have to believe. Natural religion, as analyzed in both *The Natural History of Religion* and the *Dialogues*, rests on natural propensities; but beyond the most minimal theism is "a riddle, an enigma, and inexplicable mystery." Yandell contends that Hume in the *Dialogues* was advocating his general theory that although basic beliefs cannot

be justified, neither can they be avoided. What can be examined is what these beliefs represent in terms of human nature. To appreciate what Hume accomplished in the area of religion, Yandell insists, the *Dialogues* should be examined not simply by reference to the views of the characters, but also by the consideration of Hume's other works on religion and philosophy.

Additional Recommended Reading

Hurlbutt, Robert H. *Hume, Newton, and the Design Argument*. Lincoln: University of Nebraska Press, 1965. A study of the discussions of the design argument among the Newtonians and Hume.

Mossner, Ernest C. *The Life of David Hume*. Oxford: Clarendon Press, 1980. The definitive biography; extensive quotations from letters and other materials.

_____. "The Religion of David Hume," in *Journal of the History of Ideas*. XXXIX, no. 4 (October-December, 1978), pp. 653-663. An attempt to characterize what Hume actually believed.

Penelhum, Terence. "Hume's Skepticism and the *Dialogues*," in *McGill Hume Studies*. Edited by David Norton, *et al*. San Diego: Austin Hill Press, 1979. An examination of whether Hume's discussion in the *Dialogues* is compatible with his skepticism.

Taylor, A. E., *et al*. "Symposium: The Present-Day Relevance of Hume's *Dialogues Concerning Natural Religion*," in *Aristotelian Society Proceedings*. XVIII (1939), pp. 179-205. A collection of discussions by some leading scholars of Hume's views about religion.

Tweyman, Stanley. *Scepticism and Belief in Hume's "Dialogues Concerning Natural Religion"*. Boston: Martinus Nijhoff, 1986. A lucid interpretation of Hume's major work on religion.

Wollheim, Richard, ed. "Introduction," in *Hume on Religion*. New York: World Publishing Company, 1963. A helpful explanatory introduction to a collection of Hume's writings on religion.

CRITIQUE OF PURE REASON

Author: Immanuel Kant (1724-1804)
Type of work: Metaphysics
First published: 1781

Principal Ideas Advanced

To establish the possibility of metaphysics as a science, it must be shown that synthetic a priori *truths are possible.*

Synthetic a priori *truths are universally and necessarily true (hence,* a priori*), but their necessity cannot be derived by analysis of the meanings of such truths (hence, they are synthetic).*

The two sources of knowledge are sensibility and understanding.

Space and time are the a priori *forms of sensibility (intuition); we are so constituted that we cannot perceive anything at all except by casting it into the forms of space and time.*

The a priori *conditions of our understanding are called the categories of our understanding; the categories of* quantity *are unity, plurality, and totality; of* quality*: reality, negation, and limitation; of* relation*: substance and accident, cause and effect, and reciprocity between agent and patient; of* modality*: possibility-impossibility, existence-nonexistence, and necessity-contingency.*

The principles of science which serve as presuppositions are synthetic a priori*; the possibility of such principles is based upon the use of* a priori *forms of intuition together with the categories of the understanding.*

Immanuel Kant's *Critique of Pure Reason* is an established classic in the history of epistemology. First published in 1781 and then revised in 1787, it is the fruit of Kant's later years and as such clearly reflects the insight and wisdom of a mature mind. It is a work in which the author attempted to conciliate two conflicting theories of knowledge current at his time—British empiricism as represented by Locke, Berkeley, and Hume; and Continental rationalism as represented by Descartes, Leibniz, and Wolff. The latter theory maintained that important truths about the natural and the supernatural world are knowable by pure reason alone, independently of perceptual experience, whereas the former held that perceptual experience is the source of all our legitimate concepts and truths of the world. Kant believed that both these doctrines were wrong, and he tried in the *Critique of Pure Reason* to correct the pretensions of each while saving what was sound in each. We can best see to what extent Kant succeeded in this undertaking by reviewing the main arguments of this great work.

Kant began his inquiry by asking why metaphysics had not kept pace with mathematics and natural science in the discovery of facts about our world. Celestial mechanics had been developed by Kepler at the beginning of the seventeenth century and terrestrial mechanics by Galileo later in the same century, and the two theories were soon united into one by Newton. These developments represented astonishing progress in natural science, but Kant could detect no parallel progress in metaphysics. Indeed, in metaphysics he saw only interminable squabbling with no apparent method for settling differences. So he asked whether it is at all possible for metaphysics to be a science.

Metaphysics can be a science, Kant reasoned, only if there exists a class of truths different in kind either from the straightforward synthetic truths of nature discoverable through sense-experience or from the straightforward analytic truths which owe their validity to the fact that the predicate term is contained in the subject term of such judgments—in other words, to the fact that they are true by virtue of the meanings of their terms, true by definition. This distinction is illustrated by the statements "Peaceful resistance is effective" (synthetic) and "Peaceful resisters shun violence" (analytic). This distinction had been recognized by Hume, who regarded it as exhausting the kinds of statements that can be true or false. But Kant believed that there are statements neither empirical nor analytic in character—synthetic *a priori* statements. These are statements which are true neither by definition nor because of facts discoverable through sense-experience. Rather, they can be seen to be true independently of sense-experience; in this sense they are *a priori* and necessarily true since no sense-experience can possibly confute them. Kant believed that all mathematical statements are of this sort—for example, "Seven plus five equals twelve." He also believed that synthetic *a priori* truths constitute the framework of Newtonian science, as we shall see shortly. But if such truths exist, Kant next asked himself, how are they possible?

They are possible, he said, if it can be shown that human knowledge is dependent upon certain concepts which are not empirical in origin but have their origin in human understanding. But even before he revealed the existence of such concepts he attempted to show in the first major division of the *Critique of Pure Reason,* entitled the "Transcendental Esthetic," that *a priori* considerations form the basis even of human perception or sensibility. This view was important to Kant, for in his proposed Copernican revolution in epistemology the two sources of knowledge are sensibility and understanding working in inseparable harness together. He had already written in the introduction to the *Critique* that all knowledge begins with experience, but it does not necessarily arise out of experience.

What are these *a priori* foundations of sensibility? According to Kant they are space and time. He reasoned that all objects of perception are necessarily located in space and time. Such objects may vary over a period of time in color, shape, size, and so on and still be perceptible objects, but they cannot be deprived of space and time and still remain perceptible. Even to establish ourselves as perceivers, and objects in our environment as objects of perception,

requires the use of spatial and temporal terms; hence, the concepts of space and time. As percipients we regard perceived objects as separate from or distant from us; and we realize that our perceptions themselves, whether of external objects or of our own thoughts and feelings, succeed one another in time. We cannot represent them otherwise and still sensibly preserve the meaning of the terms "perceiver" and "object of perception." In this sense space and time deserve recognition as presuppositions of sense-experience. All our empirical, descriptive characterizations of perceptible objects take for granted their fundamental nature as objects in space and time. This is why Kant calls space and time *forms of intuition* in order to distinguish them from the *contents* of sense-experience. To be sure, portions of space and moments of time can be perceived, but such parts must always be understood as forming parts of an underlying continuum of space and time. (British phenomenalists like Berkeley and Hume were not in agreement with this interpretation of space and time, but whether we can agree with Kant in the details of his argument, we probably can agree with him that the perception of anything presupposes the existence of space and time.)

Believing that he had already exhibited the dependency of human knowledge upon conditions prior to immediate sense-experience, Kant next proceeded to a consideration of the *a priori* conditions of human understanding. We saw above that, in Kant's view, all knowledge is the product of human understanding applied to sense-experience. Does the understanding organize the contents of sense-experience according to its own rules—rules which must originate elsewhere than in sense-experience if their function is to categorize it? Such rules exist indeed, declared Kant, and he called them the *categories of the understanding.* He argued that there are twelve such categories and that they can be discovered and classified by careful scrutiny of the logical forms of the judgments we characteristically make about the world. For example, if we look at our categorical judgments we see that they contain a referring expression which we call the grammatical *subject* and a characterizing expression which we call the *predicate.* In "Beethoven was a great composer" the referring or subject term is of course "Beethoven," and our characterizing or predicate term is "great composer." Now a tremendous number of the factual claims we normally make are of this same basic form—*substance* and predicated *property*—and for Kant, therefore, the concept of substance deserves the status of a category of knowledge. Under it are subsumed all the substance-words in our conceptual scheme of things, such as "table," "tree," "moon," "nail," and so on, which denote material objects in our environment. It is thus a family-like concept denoting all those objects which have *substantiality* in common, something which none of the individual terms in this category does.

Much the same point can be made about the concept of *causality,* to take another of Kant's categories, which he derived from the form of hypothetical or conditional judgments—our "if . . . then" judgments. "If water is heated under normal atmospheric conditions to 212°F, it will boil" and "If one suppresses his guilt-feelings he will become neurotic" are examples of hypothetical judgments which assert a causal connection between the states of affairs mentioned by the antecedent and consequent of such judgments. Such judgments also appear frequently in our factual reports on the world and suggest that the concept of causality is an important and fundamental concept in our way of recording experience. It is a concept embracing numerous words in our language, such as "create," "produce," "bring about," "make," and so forth, all of which are causal terms. By virtue of designing such a large family of terms the concept of causality must be regarded as one of the relatively few root concepts or categories at the basis of our conceptual scheme which give this scheme its flavor by influencing it throughout. The importance of causality is something which Kant clearly saw, even though it had been missed by the British phenomenalists.

Many philosophers have disagreed with Kant over his number and selection of categories as well as his method of arriving at them, but they have not taken issue with him as to the existence of categories in our conceptual framework and their importance in any account of human knowledge. But many others have rejected Kant's major contention that human knowledge is dependent upon such categories as substance

and causality and so have sided with Hume, who, not finding anything answering to such categories in immediate sense-experience, proceeded to dismiss them as fictitious. Kant, of course, agreed with Hume that substance and causality are not to be found *in* sense-experience, but he insisted nevertheless that they are necessary ingredients in a world about which we can hope to have knowledge. The Kantian point is sometimes made by saying that unless one assumes that the general features referred by one's judgments persist in time and are public entities independent of any particular percipient, there can be no confirmation judgments and consequently no knowledge at all. Kant saw this simple but essential point when he stated that the categories are necessary conditions for our having any knowledge whatsoever.

He also saw that categories such as substance and causality are by no means arbitrary impositions upon sense-experience, as is sometimes implied by Hume and his followers, but are useful concepts since sense-experience testifies to a great amount of orderliness in the world rather than to a befuddling chaos. It is the presence of order observable by all which vindicates the use of such ordering principles as substance and causality—they would have no utility whatever in a chaotic world.

It is chiefly as ordering principles that Kant viewed the categories. What they order or synthesize in his partly phenomenalistic theory of knowledge are the items of experience—colors, shapes, sizes, sounds, tactile impressions, odors, and so on. But Kant believed that there is a problem in showing how such *a priori* principles can be applied to empirical data, and he thought that the answer to this problem is to be found in the mediatory power of time which, as seen above, is an *a priori* ordering form which is a necessary condition of sense-experience. Kant proceeded to relate the categories to the concept of time, and it was this merger of the concepts of substance, causality, and time which paved the way to his discussion of the presuppositions of Newtonian science. Kant believed that there are three such presuppositions; namely, the principles of the conservation of matter, of universal causality, and of the universal interrelation of all things making up the natural world. (We recalled that in the Newtonian view of the universe all objects were considered to be made up of material particles governed in their behavior by the universal laws of motion and attraction.)

Such principles are not analytic truths, according to Kant, since their denials are not self-contradictory, nor are they empirical generalizations since we know them to be necessarily true, and no empirical generalization is ever necessarily true. They must therefore be genuine synthetic *a priori* truths, and their possibility arises from the fact that they utilize *a priori* concepts whose use is indispensable to human knowledge and yet whose only sanctioned cognitive use is in relation to the objects of sense-experience in the manner dictated by the principles in question themselves.

Kant's argument in this respect is somewhat circular, though it has been defended as illuminating by thinkers who believe that any examination of basic principles must inevitably be circular in that they must be elucidated in terms of one another. But his argument has not been convincing to many others who, although granting that Kant isolated the main presuppositions of the scientific thinking of his day, do not concede that the presuppositions are synthetic *a priori*. Such critics argue that is it one thing to show that certain concepts are not empirical in origin and another to show that the judgments in which they figure are *a priori*. Concepts such as substance and causality may indeed underlie our factual discourse about the world and so be necessary and ineradicable concepts to intelligible and informative discourse, but it is not at all evident that the principles in which they occur—such as that the quantity of substance remains invariant throughout all physical transformations—are necessarily true. Such principles may be fruitful guide-posts in scientific inquiry, yet not be true or false judgments at all, merely heuristic rules in the way that Kant himself was to regard certain metaphysical concepts as we shall see shortly.

Up to this point Kant's concern was to explore the foundations of scientific knowledge and to disclose the dependency of such knowledge upon a handful of forms, concepts, and principles. In this exploration he clashed sometimes head-on, sometimes obliquely, as we have seen, with accounts of human knowledge provided by British empiricists. But his conclusions

thus far were also brewing trouble and embarrassment for Continental rationalism as well. For what follows from showing that concepts such as causality and substance are presuppositions of empirical knowledge? It follows, Kant said, that their use independent of sense-experience is illegitimate and can only result in conceptual difficulties and empty noise. We recall that Kant's initial concern was to determine whether men can fruitfully engage in metaphysical speculation. In his time such speculation chiefly revolved around such matters as the immortality of the soul, the origin and extent of the universe, and the existence and nature of God. Was a science of such matters really possible? In the third and concluding portion of his inquiry, called the "Transcendental Dialectic" (that dealing with the categories and principles he had termed the "Transcendental Analytic"), Kant's answer to this burning question was an unequivocal "No!"

Kant identified the main concepts of the above-mentioned metaphysical issues as the psychological idea, or *soul*; the cosmological idea, or *world*; and the theological idea, or *God*; and he considered the author of such ideas to be human reason rather than human understanding or sensibility. But why is human reason unable to develop these ideas cogently and scientifically? Kant's chief explanation for this debility was that nothing in sense-experience corresponds to the ideas of pure reason and thus there can be no control over their speculative use.

Cartesians and Leibnizians, for example, argued that the soul was an immaterial, simple, therefore indestructible substance. But where is the empirical support for such claims? It does not exist, said Kant, and furthermore the reasoning leading up to such conclusions is wholly fallacious. These Cartesians and Leibnizians have treated the "I think" or *cogito,* that is presupposed by all acts of knowing, as the logical subject of our judgments analogous to the way in which "Beethoven" is the subject of the judgment "Beethoven became deaf in his later years"; further, Cartesians and Leibnizians have argued that just as "Beethoven" designates a real person, so does the knowing subject of the *cogito*. Kant's rebuttal to this argument consisted of saying that it is an analytic truth that acts of knowing presuppose a knower, but the existence of the knower is an empirical question which cannot be inferred from an analytic truth whose validity is founded upon the meaning of terms. The existence of the soul as well as its properties must remain an empirical question, and the concept of substance is properly applied only to the self that **is** the object of empirical psychology.

Kant next turned to metaphysical speculation about the universe at large. Men have always asked themselves with respect to the universe whether it had a beginning in time or has always existed, whether it is finitely or infinitely extended in space, and whether it was created. Kant showed that no definitive answers are possible to such questions. Indeed, he argued that reasoning can establish with equal cogency alternative answers to such questions. His explanation for such a disconcerting and paradoxical state of affairs in metaphysics was that one cannot regard the universe as a substance or given entity in the way a desk, for example, can be so regarded. It is of course meaningful to ask when a certain desk was made, how it was made, and what its spatial boundaries are. Such questions can be settled empirically, for we can trace the history of the desk and have it before us to measure. But this investigation of the properties of the desk and the countless ones like it which we undertake in our daily lives occur within the framework of the universe, so that the questions that can significantly be raised about things within the universe cannot significantly or profitably be asked of the universe itself. If the categories of substance and causality have as their proper epistemic function the characterization of given and possible objects of perception, it is an improper use of such categories to apply them to what is neither a given nor even a possible object of perception such as the universe. Because it is not such an object, the universe cannot serve as a check or control upon our speculations about it; and it is this basic consideration again which explains reason's incompetence in this area.

Can human reason do any better, then, in the area of theological speculation? Can it, in the absence of empirical evidence, produce convincing arguments for God's existence, his benevolence, omniscience, and so forth? Kant surveyed the standard arguments or alleged proofs for the existence of God and con-

cluded that none of them have any real force. He found that arguments which use the facts of existence, design, and causality in nature to support claims on behalf of divine existence not only make an unwarranted leap from the known to the unknown, but also fall back on the ontological argument for the existence of God as propounded successively by Saint Anselm, Descartes, and Leibniz. This famous and captivating argument begins with the premise that God is the being greater than which nothing is conceivable, and with the help of a subordinate premise to the effect that existence in the real world is better than existence merely in idea proceeds to the conclusion that God must exist, for if he did not he would not then be the greatest conceivable entity.

Kant's rebuttal of the ontological argument consists of saying that all existential statements of the form "X exists" are synthetic *a posteriori* and must be established on empirical grounds. If the major premise of the ontological argument is analytic, then existence is included in the definition of "God" and one has in effect defined God into existence. But, Kant asked, can we by definition define anything into existence, or must we not look beyond our concept of something in order to determine whether it genuinely exists? Kant added that it is in any case a mistake to view existence as a predicate like any other, since in all statements in which referring expressions such as "God" occur as subject terms the existence of the denoted object(s) is not asserted by such statements but rather taken for granted in order to see what is attributed truly or falsely to the denoted object(s). But if existence is taken for granted in this way, then as far as the ontological argument is concerned one has assumed the very point in question and the argument is question-begging.

The results of Kant's inquiry into classical metaphysics prompted him to reject the view that the leading concepts of such speculation have any constitutive place in human knowledge at all. Such concepts do not enter into the weblike structure of our knowledge of the world, as do the categories in his view. But Kant did not progress further to the Human conclusion that metaphysical works containing these concepts should therefore be consigned to the flames. On the contrary he argued that although such concepts do not have a constitutive role in human knowledge, they nevertheless have a vital regulative function in the scientific quest, for they posit a systematic unity to the world and so stimulate scientists to look for connections in nature, even between such diverse elements, say, as falling apples and orbiting planets. It is pure reason with its concept of an ordering, purposeful, and wholly rational God, for example, which proposes for investigation the idea that the world created by God must be rationally constructed throughout and so reward experimental inquiry by men similarly endowed with reason. No other faculty of the mind was for Kant capable of such a stirring vision.

In this remarkable conclusion to his inquiry into the contributing factors of human knowledge, Kant plainly conceded enormous importance to pure reason, although not that exactly which rationalists defended. He therefore no more appeased the rationalists than he did the British empiricists.

Many philosophers since Kant have appreciated his middle road between rationalism and empiricism, even if they have not been able to accept the details

of this reasoning, and they have credited Kant with the rare ability to raise problems worthy of philosophical investigation.

But other philosophers have not been impressed by Kant's strictures against rationalism and empiricism, and they have borrowed from his meticulous genius (happily wedded to broad vision) what suits their purposes while ignoring what does not. Thus Hegel, for example, was stimulated by Kant to seize upon pure reason's dialectical tendencies—so futile in Kant's view—and erect upon such tendencies a complete picture of history and the world—quite often at the expense of empirical facts. And latter-day phenomenalists such as John Stuart Mill and Bertrand Russell have persisted in the search for the foundations of human knowledge among sense-data (more lately in conjunction with formal logic), which in all their fleeting transiency are so much unlike Kant's enduring and causally ordered substances.

But most philosophical critics assent to the rich stimulation of Kant's ever surprising fertile mind and rank him among the great philosophers of all time.

Pertinent Literature

Ewing, A. C. *A Short Commentary on Kant's Critique of Pure Reason*. London: Methuen, 1938.

In his Preface, A. C. Ewing acknowledges his indebtedness to Norman Kemp Smith for his *Commentary to Kant's Critique of Pure Reason* (1918) and to H. J. Paton for his *Kant's Metaphysic of Experience* (1936), but he notes that their influence "often operates in reverse directions." Paton's commentary changed many of Ewing's ideas that were influenced by Kemp Smith's commentary, but Ewing admits that he was strongly influenced by both.

Ewing's Introduction points out that Immanuel Kant wrote the *Critique of Pure Reason* as a preliminary investigation of the human faculties of knowledge to prepare the way for the intellect's most important task—that of constructing a satisfactory metaphysics; but Kant realized, when his work was completed, that there was no room for any further metaphysics: the *Critique of Pure Reason* had done

it all.

Although originally profoundly influenced by Gottfried Wilhelm von Leibniz's views, Kant was led by accounts of David Hume's *Treatise of Human Nature* to deny the possibility of *a priori* knowledge of the real world. He designed the *Critique of Pure Reason* to answer two fundamental questions (according to Ewing): (1) How can the *a priori* categories be applied to appearances in advance of experience, and (2) Is there any justification for applying the *a priori* categories to reality?

Ewing argues that despite verbal inconsistencies in Kant's work (composed over an eleven-year period), it is possible to put together a consistent doctrine, and it is reasonable to assume that had the work been purged of its contradictions, it would have been so unified.

According to Ewing, the *Critique of Pure Reason* has two main aims: (1) to provide science with a philosophical basis in the *a priori*, and (2) to provide faith with adequate grounds even though such grounds fell short of knowledge. The latter aim, if achieved, was to prepare the way for the ethical arguments of the *Critique of Practical Reason*, and Kant hoped that in solving the problem of freedom, by showing freedom to be compatible with causality, he would make sense of ethics.

Kant realized that although it can be shown that the categories apply to objects of experience and that the *a priori* rests on that possibility, the categories could not be referred to in the attempt to prove propositions having to do with God, freedom, and immortality, for the categories did not apply to matters falling outside the realm of experience.

Ewing compares Kant's effort in "critical" philosophy to that which would be made by investigators who compared objects they saw clearly with objects they saw dimly and then made generalizations about the two kinds of objects so seen, and explained by reference to a theory of vision why the one kind was seen clearly and the other dimly.

The author warns the reader that his work is intended to be a commentary to be read in conjunction with Kant's work and not as a self-contained essay on the *Critique of Pure Reason*. It falls between the more detailed and extensive commentaries of Edward Caird, Kemp Smith, and Paton on the one hand, and the brief accounts given by Robert Adamson and A. D. Lindsay on the other. He also comments that his work is one of exegesis, not criticism, although occasionally, for the sake of clarity, some criticism is advanced.

Ewing describes Kant's claim to completeness and certainty (in the Preface to the first edition) "audacious," and he points out that even a great philosopher may commit errors (and hence can hardly lay claim to certainty) and that there is always something more to be said about any important subject.

Among the most useful comments made in Ewing's Introduction is that having to do with the term *Anschauung,* usually translated "intuition." Ewing indicates that the sense of the term in Kant is different from the sense of the term "intuition" in English

(an *a priori* insight not based on conscious reasoning). In Kant the term *Anschauung* means, Ewing suggests, "awareness of individual entities" (as by looking at something). But Ewing rejects the use of the word "perception" in translation since it is at least possible that there are beings other than human beings that are aware of individual entities without having to perceive them.

Ewing's discussion of the question as to whether there are synthetic *a priori* judgments (propositions) is also interesting and useful. Many philosophers confuse two possible meanings of the term "analytic proposition," according to Ewing: some think that an analytic proposition is that which yields no new knowledge, while others suppose it is a proposition that becomes self-contradictory when denied. Ewing claims that the proposition that a judgment which is analytic in the second sense must be analytic in the first sense is itself a synthetic judgment—hence, the effort to deny synthetic *a priori* propositions yields a synthetic *a priori* proposition.

The distinction between "transcendent" and "transcendental" is also important, Ewing points out. The term "transcendent" refers to what is not a possible object of knowledge, while the term "transcendental" refers to the necessary conditions of experience. Hence, transcendental knowledge is possible, according to Kant, in that by reference to the conditions of knowledge one understands how synthetic *a priori* propositions are possible as applying to the "appearances" or objects of experience.

Ewing's commentary is careful and thorough, and he is particularly careful to point out differences between what terms in translation ordinarily mean and what they mean in the context of Kant's thought. He is also determined to show the development of Kant's thought even in cases—and perhaps especially in cases—in which the development or transition is not clear in the *Critique of Pure Reason*.

In his commentary Ewing discusses "The Transcendental Aesthetic" (which has to do with perception, not beauty), "The Transcendental Deduction of the Categories," "The Individual Categories and Their Proofs," "Kant's Attitude to Material Idealism. The Thing-in-Itself," "The Paralogisms and the Antinomies," and "Theology and the Ideas of Reason."

Weldon, T. D. *Introduction to Kant's* Critique of Pure Reason. Oxford: Clarendon Press, 1945.

In the Preface to the first edition of his study of Immanuel Kant's *Critique of Pure Reason*, T. D. Weldon disclaims any intention of writing another commentary; he cites H. J. Paton and Herman Jean de Vleeschauwer as having provided substantial and authoritative commentaries. Weldon's intention is to discuss the *Critique of Pure Reason* as an account of Critical Philosophy, and he maintains that such an account must make clear the context in which Kant's book was written (as influenced by René Descartes, Gottfried Wilhelm von Leibniz, and Sir Isaac Newton—not Albert Einstein, Werner Heisenberg, and Erwin Schrödinger).

Weldon's book begins with a discussion of the European influences (Descartes, Leibniz, John Locke, and David Hume) and the "local" influences (Christian von Wolff, A. G. Baumgarten, and G. F. Meier) on Kant. The problem for the Europeans, Weldon suggests, was that of reconciling the new experimental methods of science (including the use of mathematics) with metaphysics and theology. Many of the problems were of the sort we now call linguistic, Weldon claims, but he warns that it is an oversimplification to presume that the linguistic approach does justice to the issues. (One notes, however, that in his conclusion to the book Weldon claims that Kant's distinction between things-in-themselves and phenomena was "not a distinction between two types of entity but a distinction between two alternative ways of talking about the world.")

Weldon then comments on Kant's early works—from the *Correct Method of Calculating the Active Force of Bodies* (1747) through *Dreams of a Spirit-Seer* (1766, an examination of issues raised by the doctrines of Emanuel Swedenborg) to the Dissertation of 1770 (*De mundi sensibilis atque intelligibilis forma et principiis*). Weldon points out that although in the *Dissertation* Kant argued that things *qua* sensuous are apprehended through sensibility, he was inclined to think that through pure reason one could know independently existing real objects *qua* intelligible. The transition to the viewpoint of the Critical Philosophy was perhaps incited by Hume's work, Weldon suggests.

In Part II Weldon summarizes and discusses in detail the argument of the *Critique of Pure Reason*, including the Prefaces, the *Aesthetic,* the *Analytic,* and the *Dialectic*.

Weldon describes Kant as a "logician rather than an epistemologist" in the formulation and answering of the fundamental question about the limits of knowledge and the consequences of limitation to beliefs in God, freedom, and immortality. Although Kant argued that only phenomena can be known—and that they are known *a priori*: "objects must conform to our knowledge"—the distinction between things as they appear and as they are "in-themselves" made it possible to argue that belief in God and immortality, and hence the belief in freedom, was compatible with the limitation of knowledge to the phenomena.

The aim of the *Aesthetic* is described by Weldon as that of demonstrating that the axioms of arithmetic and geometry are applicable to phenomena; the aim of the *Analytic* is to do the same for physics. (The solution, of course, was to refer to the forms of space and time as imposed on what is given in experience, and to the concepts of the understanding as making possible the derivation of the axioms of physics.)

The purpose of the *Dialectic*, Weldon writes, was to account for the transcendent ideas of God, freedom, and immortality, and to explain how metaphysics can yield knowledge. Just as the *Aesthetic* developed the "transcendental implications of sensibility," and the *Analytic* the transcendental implications of the understanding's use of concepts, so the *Dialectic* develops the transcendental implications of reason's capacity for inference.

In Part III, "Inner Sense and Transcendental Synthesis," Weldon examines Kant's assumption of an "inner sense" and his unanalyzed assumptions about modes of perception. Weldon contends that if Kant had concentrated on the *function* of "models," such as the Newtonian model of physical reality, instead of on the *origin* of such models (in the "transcendental imagination") he would have come closer to what modern scientific theory concentrates on and would thus have avoided many of the problems occasioned by adopting a deficient or unclear empirical psychology.

Weldon contends that Kant's achievement was that of making clear what happens in the course of scientific thinking and in emphasizing (although, Weldon says, he did not realize that he was doing so) ways of talking about the world. His work provides a foundation for the philosophical analysis of scientific method. Insofar as Kant falls short, Weldon states, he did so because he was handicapped by the limitations of Newtonian physics, Aristotelian logic, and the empirical psychology of Locke, Hume, and J. N. Tetens.

Additional Recommended Reading

Allison, Henry E. *Kant's Transcendental Idealism*. New Haven, Connecticut: Yale University Press, 1986. An important study of Kant's theory of knowledge and metaphysics.

Cassirer, H. W. *Kant's First Critique*. New York: Humanities Press, 1954. A commentary on the *Critique of Pure Reason* that emphasizes both Kant's contributions and his errors and weaknesses.

Paton, H. J. *Kant's Metaphysic of Experience*. New York: Humanities Press, 1936. A widely used commentary on the first half of the *Critique of Pure Reason*. Paton argues, in opposition to Kemp Smith, that the *Critique of Pure Reason* is a coherent work and that its critical method provides the philosophy of science with a useful tool.

Smith, Norman Kemp. *A Commentary to Kant's "Critique of Pure Reason"*. London: Macmillan and Company, 1918. One of the standard commentaries despite Kemp Smith's adoption, at least in part, of what Paton calls the "mosaic or patchwork" theory defended by Erich Adickes and Hans Vaihinger—the theory that the *Critique of Pure Reason,* especially the "Transcendental Deduction" of the first edition, was put together by combining passages written at different times and sometimes conflicting.

FOUNDATIONS OF THE METAPHYSICS OF MORALS

Author: Immanuel Kant (1724-1804)
Type of work: Ethics
First published: 1785

Principal Ideas Advanced

Nothing is unconditionally good except the good will.

The good will, which is the rational will, acts not merely in accordance *with duty but* from *duty.*

The good will wills as obedient to the moral law.

Duty consists in observing the categorical imperative: Act only according to that maxim by which you can at the same time will that it should become a universal law.

A second form of the categorical imperative is: Act so that you treat humanity, whether in your own person or that of another, always as an end and never as a means only.

A third form of the categorical imperative is: Act always as if you were legislating for a universal realm of ends.

Ethics, like physics, so Immanuel Kant holds in the *Foundations of the Metaphysics of Morals (Grundlegung zur Metaphysik der Sitten),* is partly empirical and partly *a priori*. This work deals only with the *a priori* part in that it is based entirely on the use of reason without recourse to experience. Everyone must recognize, Kant writes, that since moral laws imply absolute necessity, they cannot be merely empirical. For example, "Thou shalt not lie" applies not merely to all human beings but to all rational beings. Its ground, therefore, must be found in pure reason. Moreover, what is done morally must be not only in accordance with law but also done for the sake of law; if this were not its motivation, different circumstances of the agent would call forth different responses.

This book, issued as a preliminary to an intended metaphysic of morals, the *Critique of Practical Reason* (1788), comprises a critical examination of purely practical reason and establishes the supreme principle of morality. The order of inquiry is from common moral knowledge to the supreme principle (analysis), then back to application in practice (synthesis).

Kant begins by claiming that "Nothing in the world—indeed nothing even beyond the world—can possibly be conceived which could be called good without qualification except a *good will*." Not intelligence, wit, judgment, courage, or the gifts of fortune; possession of them is a positive evil if not combined with good will, which indeed is the indispensable condition even of worthiness to be happy. And although moderation, self-control, and calm deliberation are all conducive to good will, they can also characterize the cool villain and make him even more abominable. The goodness of the good will does not depend on its accomplishments; it "would sparkle like a jewel in its own right, as something that had its full worth in itself," even if external circumstances entirely frustrated its actions.

The good will is the rational will. Why has nature appointed reason to rule the will? Not for the sake of adaptation, which would be more efficiently accomplished by instinct. Moreover, when a cultivated reason makes enjoyment its end, true contentment rarely ensues. Reason, then, is intended for something more worthy than production of happiness. Being a practical faculty, yet not suitable for producing a will good merely as a means (instinct would do better), reason must be given us to produce a will good in itself. Everyone knows, at least implicitly, according to Kant, the concept of a will good in itself. We need only bring to light that to which we give first place in our moral estimate of action.

Kant considers the concept of duty, distinguishing between what is done *in accordance with* duty (but motivated perhaps by a natural inclination or a selfish purpose) and what is done *from* duty. Moral import is clearly seen only in those cases where on account of absence of inclination, duty is exhibited as the motive. It is our duty to be kind, and amiable people are naturally inclined to kindness. But do they act from duty or inclination? Ordinarily we cannot be sure which; however, suppose that someone in such deep sorrow as to be insensible to the feelings of others yet tears himself out of this condition to perform a kind action. We see then that his action has genuine moral worth. Or we know a man who by nature is unsympathetic yet behaves beneficently: he must be acting from duty, not inclination.

Moral worth attaches to action from duty even with respect to the pursuit of happiness, according to Kant. Everyone has an inclination to be happy, and particular inclinations toward what are regarded as the particular constituents of happiness. Still, all these subtracted, the duty to pursue one's happiness would remain, and only the dutiful pursuit would have true moral worth. (Pursuit of happiness is a duty because unhappiness could tempt to the neglect of other duties.) The commandments to love our neighbors and our enemies should be read as requiring us to exercise beneficence from duty; love cannot be commanded.

A central idea in Kant's work is that the moral worth of action performed from duty lies not in its purpose but in the maxim (rule, principle) by which it is determined. Otherwise, moral worth would depend on inclinations and incentives, which, as we have seen, cannot be the case. "Duty is the necessity of an action executed from respect for law," writes Kant, I cannot have respect for a mere consequence or inclination, but only for what can overpower all inclination: this can be no other than law itself. To be an object of respect is the same as to be valid as a source of command. The law determines the will objectively; subjectively I am determined by respect for the law; this subjective element is the maxim of my action, that I ought to follow the law whatever my inclination may be. Respect, the conception of a worth that overrides self-love, can be present only in a rational being.

The only kind of law the conception of which is capable of determining the will without reference to consequences must be the notion of conformity to law as such. That is to say: Never act in such a way that you could not also will that your maxim should be a universal law requiring everybody in these circumstances to do this action. This is what the common reason of mankind has constantly in view in moral matters, Kant claims.

For example: May I extricate myself from a difficulty by making a false promise? A prudential calculation of consequences might or might not recommend this course. But to determine whether it is consistent with duty I need only ask whether I could wish that everyone in difficulty might extricate himself similarly. I see that the maxim would destroy itself, for if it were a universal law, no one could derive any help from lying, since no promise made in a difficult situation would be believed. So there is no difficulty in deciding whether a proposed course of action would be morally good; I need only ask myself whether my maxim could become a universal law. If not, it must be rejected and the action forgone. Reason compels respect for universal legislation. Every other motive must defer to duty.

Common reason habitually employs this test: "What if everybody did that?" It is the advantage of practical over theoretical reason to be everybody's possession. Ordinary people are as likely to hit the mark as philosophers—indeed, more so, being less liable to be led astray by subtle fallacies. Nevertheless, philosophy is called upon to buttress reason against the assaults of inclination and against specious arguments on their behalf. That is why a metaphysic of morals is required.

Although only what is done from duty has moral worth, it is not possible to be certain in even one instance that an action was in fact done from duty. Some philosophers have indeed attributed all motivation to self-interest. They may be right as a matter of psychology; for how can we be sure that what we most sincerely and carefully conclude to be action from duty was not in reality prompted by some hidden impulse of inclination?

Duty, therefore, is not an empirical concept, according to Kant. Moreover, its universality and necessity also show its nonempirical nature. Nor could it be derived from examples: How would we know in the first place that the cases were fit to serve as examples, if we did not presuppose knowledge of the concept? Even if we consider the actions of God himself, we must antecedently possess the concept of duty in order to judge them as moral. Duty, therefore, is a concept *a priori*. While this fact is obvious, it nevertheless needs to be explicitly argued for on account of the popularity of empirical rules recommended as bases of morality. It is a mistake to try to popularize morality by holding out the inducement of happiness. On the contrary, the picture of disinterested duty has the strongest appeal even to children, because here reason recognizes that it can be practical.

Kant argues that if reason, which tells us what principles of action are objectively required, infallibly determined the will, we would always choose the good. But in fact the will is affected also by subjective incentives that clash with the dictates of reason. Thus the will when not completely good (as it never is in human beings) experiences the pull of reason as constraint. This command of reason, the objective principle constraining the will, is also called an imperative. A perfectly good or "holy" will, being always determined to action only by objective laws, would not experience constraint.

According to Kant, imperatives are either *hypothetical*, commanding something to be done in order to achieve a desired end: if you want X, do A; or *categorical*, commanding an action as objectively necessary: Do A (never mind what you desire). Hypothetical imperatives are further subdivided into rules of skill, which tell what to do in order to achieve some end which one may or may not wish to achieve: heal a person, or poison him; and counsels of prudence, telling what to do to achieve happiness, the one end that all rational beings in fact do have. But the counsels of prudence are still hypothetical, depending on what the agent counts as part of his happiness. Only the categorical imperative is the imperative of morality.

How are imperatives possible—how can reason constrain the will? There is no problem with respect to rules of skill, since it is an analytic proposition that whoever wills the end wills the indispensable means. Because the notion of happiness is indefinite and infallible, means for attaining it cannot be prescribed; counsels of prudence do not strictly command, but only advise. Still, there is no difficulty here as to how reason can influence the will. The puzzle arises only with respect to the categorical imperative.

We cannot show by any example that a categorical imperative does influence the will. When someone in trouble tells the truth it is always possible that not the categorical "Thou shalt not make a false promise" influenced his will but the hypothetical "If thou dost not want to risk ruining thy credit, make no false promise." Hence the question of the possibility of the categorical imperative must be investigated *a priori*. Moreover, the categorical imperative is synthetic *a priori*—*a priori* in that the action prescribed is necessary, synthetic in that the content of this action is not derived analytically from a presupposed volition.

The categorical imperative is simply the demand that the subjective principle of my action, my maxim, should conform to the objective law valid for all rational beings. Therefore, Kant contends, there is only one categorical imperative: "Act only according to that maxim by which you can at the same time will that it should become a universal law." Here are some of Kant's examples:

1. Suicide. Maxim: Out of self-love I shorten my life. But a system of nature in which this maxim was a law would be contradictory: the feeling impelling to improvement of life would destroy life. Therefore the maxim could not be a law of nature, and the action is contrary to duty.

2. False promises. A universal law of nature that people in trouble escape by making false promises is incoherent, as they would never be believed.

3. Is it all right to amuse myself at the expense of failing to develop my talents? While it could be a law of nature that all people do this, a rational being could not *will* it to be a law of nature, for rationality entails willing that faculties be developed.

4. Should we help other people, or is "Every man for himself" morally permissible? A world could exist without altruism; but again, a rational person could not will it, for his will would conflict with itself: there must often be occasions when he needs the love and sympathy of others, from which he would be cutting himself off.

Examples 1 and 2, in which the idea of the maxim as law of nature is self-contradictory, show strict duties. Examples 3 and 4, where the maxim could be law of nature but not willed to be, illustrate meritorious duties. If we were perfectly rational, then every time we thought of transgressing duty we would notice a contradiction in our will. But in fact we experience no such contradiction but only antagonism between inclination and what reason prescribes. This does show us, however, that we acknowledge the validity of the categorical imperative.

Kant contends that the form of the categorical imperative can also be deduced from the consideration that "rational nature exists as an end in itself." Rational beings (persons) do not exist as mere means to some other end but as themselves bearers of absolute worth. Everyone thinks of his own existence in this way, and the rational ground for his so doing is the same for all others. It is therefore not a merely subjective principle of action, but objective. The categorical imperative can thus be phrased as "Act so that you treat humanity, whether in your own person or in that of another, always as an end and never as a means only." This principle also condemns suicide (which is using oneself merely as a means to maintaining a tolerable life up to its conclusion) and false promising, and shows the merit of self-development and altruism.

The notion of rational beings as ends leads in Kant's ethics to a third formulation of the categorical imperative. We can form the conception of a universal realm of ends, an ideal society of completely rational beings. Such beings would act toward each other not from interest but from pure practical reason; that is, they would always do their duty. This action would be in conformity to the laws of reason, which they had imposed upon themselves. Therefore: "Act always as if you were legislating for a universal realm of ends."

The categorical imperative, in all its forms, is the principle whereby a rational being gives a law to himself: it is thus the principle of autonomy (self-legislation). All other principles, based on interest, are heteronomous (other-legislation), the "other" being the object determining the will: riches, say, or happiness, or any external object of interest. All heteronomous principles are spurious. The worst is that based on happiness, which is neither empirically nor conceptually connected with morality and virtue. It undermines morality by making the difference between virtue and vice to be a mere matter of calculation instead of a difference in kind. The appeal to a moral sense can furnish neither an objective standard of good and bad nor a basis for valid judgment; nevertheless it does have the merit of ascribing intrinsic worth and dignity to virtue. Morality based on an ideal of perfection is empty and involves circular reasoning, as it does not explain our moral ideals but pre-supposes them. Theological morality, based on the notion of the divine will, either presupposes an independent standard or tries to base morality on the notions of glory, dominion, might, and vengeance—a system directly opposed to morality. All these heteronomous moralities look not to the action itself but to the result of the action as incentive—"I ought to do something because I will something else" is a hypothetical imperative, and hence not a moral imperative.

Kant attempts to show not that the autonomous will is actual but that it is possible. To show even this much is difficult, Kant admits, inasmuch as if nature is a system of effects following by natural laws from their causes, and if human beings are part of nature, it seems that every human action is necessitated by natural causes, and thus could not be otherwise than it is. The will could not then be autonomous, "a law to itself," unless it is free.

Kant's strategy in establishing the possibility of freedom depends on the distinctions, elaborated in the *Critique of Pure Reason*, between things as they are in themselves and things as they appear to us. With regard to conceptions that come to us without our choice, such as those of the senses, we can know only how they appear, not how they are in themselves. This applies even to the individual's concept of himself: he knows himself only as he appears to himself and is ignorant of the reality underlying the appearance. However, man finds in himself the faculty of reason, which transcends the conceptions given through the senses. Man must therefore conclude that his ego as it is in itself belongs to the intelligible world (world of things in themselves). The upshot is that man has a dual citizenship: in the world of the senses his actions are explainable in terms of natural causation, thus heteronomously; but as a denizen of the intelligible world, the causality of his will is and must be thought of under the idea of freedom, as autonomous.

If we belonged only to the intelligible world, all our actions would conform to the law of freedom and would be moral. If we belonged only to the sensible world (as nonrational animals do), all our actions would be effects of natural causation—that is, determined by incentives. Belonging as we do to both worlds, we experience the dictates of practical reason as *ought*: even in following material incentives we are conscious of what reason requires. We must assume, although we cannot prove, that there is no ultimate contradiction between natural necessity and freedom in human action. And the assumption is justified, for there is no contradiction in a thing-in-itself's being independent of laws to which the thing-as-appearance must conform. In this way we can "comprehend the incomprehensibility" of the unconditional necessity of the moral imperative.

Pertinent Literature

Ebbinghaus, Julius. "Interpretation and Misinterpretation of the Categorical Imperative," in *The Philosophical Quarterly.* IV, no. 15 (April, 1954), pp. 97-108.

There is no question about what Immanuel Kant's concept of a categorical imperative is: a law unconditionally valid for the will of every rational being. Julius Ebbinghaus contends, however, that there is controversy about its contents and the inferences to be drawn from it. The opinion has been heard that Kant's philosophy is typical of—or even responsible for—the notorious German fondness for obedience to superiors, and hence for National Socialism.

But the categorical imperative, Ebbinghaus points out, is an expression of the notion of what it is to be under a moral obligation. It does not say what in particular our moral obligations are. If Kant was wrong, the consequence is not that some principles of obligation other than those which Kant acknowledged are the right ones; rather, it is that there is no such thing as being under a moral obligation of any kind.

Every moral philosophy must begin with a characterization of duty. The first misinterpretation of Kant's moral philosophy, according to Ebbinghaus, is that it is empty formalism—it does not go beyond this characterization. But the special feature of Kantianism is that it abstracts not only from the matter of will: from all purposes or ends.

In a moral theory based on a necessary end, such as Aristotle's or John Stuart Mill's, duty is whatever promotes the final end. But can other ends conflict with the final end? If they can, there must be a superfinal end to resolve the conflict, and the allegedly final end is not final after all. If they cannot, then there is no such thing as duty: the will is necessarily (in fact) in all its decisions subordinated to the highest end. This is why, according to Ebbinghaus, Kant determined the form of ethical obligation not by ends but by fitness to be universal law. This does not mean that obligation has no content: it has precisely *this* content.

Ebbinghaus reports Mill's criticism that when Kant attempts to deduce actual duties of morality, he fails to show that there would be any contradiction in the adoption by all rational beings of obviously immoral rules of conduct. Georg Wilhelm Friedrich Hegel makes a similar objection. And John Dewey, also believing that the categorical imperative is empty of content, supposes that it naturally lends itself to being filled up by whatever authority, specifically the national leader, may prescribe; these dictates then become unconditionally binding. This reasoning, however, as Ebbinghaus points out, is exactly contrary to Kant, whose doctrine forbids a man to subject his own will to the will of any other person. That would be for the will to will its own annulment, which Kant held to be self-contradictory. The obedience required by the categorical imperative is thus the exact opposite of subjection to arbitrary power.

But, then, must not the autonomous will be able to legislate for itself anything it likes? Mill supposes that it can—and that Kant admitted as much in bringing in consideration of the agent's advantage in his examples. In showing the wrongness of hard-heartedness Kant allegedly appealed to the agent's self-interest, a piece of "commonplace egoism." Ebbinghaus replies: (1) It is at any rate not "commonplace egoism," for there is no contention that the agent wills his own happiness exclusively. (2) But Kant's argument is that insofar as happiness is an end for the agent, he cannot possibly will to be abandoned in need. (3) What Kant says is that the will to hard-heartedness would be "in conflict with itself." (4) The universalized maxim of hardheartedness would be: Everyone who feels himself immune from need may be deaf to the need of others. This cannot be willed, as it would be a will to let oneself be abandoned, in a case that for all one knows might actually arise. One could indeed assent to this formulation : I will never help anyone who is immune from need—but that offers no difficulty to Kant.

Ebbinghaus claims that Kant's critics overlook the word *through* in the categorical imperative: Act only on that maxim *through* which you can at the same time will that it should become a universal law. This means that the reason for the possibility of willing the maxim as law must be found in the maxim itself, not in external circumstances of the agent. This condition is not met in hard-heartedness; anyone able

to will it must feel himself immune from need, and this is an external circumstance.

All, then, that is left of the egoism charge is that Kant holds that a man cannot will to be abandoned. To be sure, Kant does insist that we be prepared to sacrifice our happiness—but never as a possible end altogether. And that would be required were hard-heartedness universalizable.

The categorical imperative indeed abstracts from all ends, Ebbinghaus insists; but this is not to be confused with saying that the categorical imperative demands that my will have no ends at all, which would be not to be a will at all.

Utilitarians say, in effect, according to Ebbinghaus, "You must help others because it will promote your own happiness." Kant says, in effect, "You must help others whether it promotes your own happiness or not, because to will the maxim of hard-heartedness as a universal law contradicts your inevitable (and permissible) end." The difference is this: while for Kant there can be no taking into account the consequences for my happiness of willing the maxim as a law, nevertheless I must consider whether the maxim as law would make it impossible to take my own happiness as an end.

Ebbinghaus argues as follows: I will my own happiness. I *can* will the happiness of others. But in willing my own happiness I will on the principle that others should also will my happiness. Suppose now I do not will the happiness of others: I cannot then will that others should act on my maxim, for then they would not will my happiness. Thus to will my happiness and not will the happiness of others is (if the categorical imperative is valid) a contradiction. Therefore it is a definite command of duty that I must include the happiness of others in my own end of personal happiness. This shows how it is, after all, possible to deduce particular precepts from the categorical imperative.

Harrison, Jonathan. "Kant's Examples of the First Formulation of the Categorical Imperative," in *The Philosophical Quarterly*. VII, no. 26 (January, 1957), pp. 50-62.

According to Immanuel Kant, Jonathan Harrison reminds us, there are duties to oneself and to others, and perfect and imperfect duties. There are therefore

four kinds of duty: perfect duty to oneself, perfect to others, imperfect duty to oneself, imperfect to others. Kant gives one example of each. Kant holds it to be impossible that everybody adopt the maxim of an act that infringes on a *perfect* duty; but although it is possible for everybody to adopt the maxim of an act that infringes on an *imperfect* duty, it is not possible to *will* that everybody should adopt such a maxim.

The first form of the categorical imperative is supposed to be the supreme principle of morality. It is not just the demand that moral principles be general, which Kant takes for granted. This formula, moreover, is used by Kant not to test alleged moral principles, but to test maxims. He takes for granted that moral principles must be universal, and endeavors only to show what maxims are universalizable. Maxims are rules that I make for myself. They are not true or false. They are not moral principles: maxims can be made, but moral principles cannot. Maxims, however, can conform to moral principles. Maxims apply only to the person making them.

According to Harrison, Kant held that a maxim is morally unacceptable if it cannot be universalized and that it is acceptable (that is, *may*—not must or ought to be—adopted) if it can be universalized. He may also have thought that it must be adopted if its "contradictory" is not universalizable. Presumably Kant meant this by "impossible to will": Were I able to bring about a certain state of affairs, I could not bring myself to do so. There are maxims that it is logically impossible for everyone to act on: for example, Be first through every door. There are others which I would be unlikely to act on if as a result everybody else did: for example, Consume without producing.

In Kant's example of suicide, Harrison writes, we must expunge the words "From self-love I make it my principle," as this phrase has nothing to do with the maxim but only with motives for adopting it. The maxim is: " To shorten my life if its continuance threatens more evil than it promises pleasure." Now, what contradiction would result from universal adoption of this rule? None at all, Harrison claims; nor does Kant attempt to show it. All he does try to show is that it contradicts the statement that the purpose of self-love is to stimulate the furtherance of life, which amounts to saying that the purpose of self-love is to prevent people from committing suicide. But even here there is no contradiction. Things can have pur-

poses that they do not, or do not always, fulfill. Besides, the maxim is not simply to commit suicide, but to do so if I would be happier dead—and people in this situation are presumably a minority. The universal adoption of the maxim, then, would not lead to universal suicide, or even have the consequence that self-love usually or frequently caused people to commit suicide.

Harrison comments on Kant's other examples follow.

On false promises: Contradiction arises only if certain contingent statements are true; for example, people frequently find themselves in circumstances where they can obtain services in no other way than by making false promises. Furthermore, people are egotistical; they remember what promises have been made. These contingent statements are no doubt true. But that aside, there is still trouble for Kant, since the rule as he put it was "when you find yourself in certain circumstances..." which is an antecedent that could be vacuously satisfied even if nobody believed promises.

Never to help others in distress: Kant is not here appealing to self-interest; he says rather that the will would be at variance with itself, for it would also necessarily will to receive aid in distress. However, one often does things in spite of motives not to do them. All "variance with itself " means is that one could not will this maxim wholeheartedly, not that one could not will it.

Neglecting to develop my natural gifts: Kant says one cannot will the universal neglect of talents, because talents are useful. This is odd; the usefulness of talents to oneself is a better reason for not neglecting one's own than for not willing that others should neglect theirs. Further, Kant says that "as a rational being" one cannot will to neglect one's talent, evidently because it is obvious that as a partially nonrational being one can. But the "as a rational being" qualification begs the question.

According to Harrison Kant does not appeal to consequences. Although in the third example Kant points out that failure to develop one's talents would have harmful consequences for the agent, this is not a utilitarian argument: it does not say anything about harmful consequences for society.

Moreover, the harmful consequences do not provide the reason why the maxim is *wrong*—they show why one cannot will it. Nor does Kant appeal to the bad consequences of everybody's adopting a maxim, according to Harrison.

Furthermore, although Kant mentions purposes he never argues that something is wrong because it is contrary to what something was intended for. Kant seems to think that if maxims are wrong, then the question of the morality of actions falling under them is settled. But it cannot be, Harrison commends. One can do the right thing for the wrong reason. Moreover, for every wrong action, a universalizable maxim enjoining it can be found.

Additional Recommended Reading

Broad, C. D. *Five Types of Ethical Theory.* London: Routledge & Kegan Paul, 1930. Chapter 5 is a penetrating discussion of the Kantian ethics.

Duncan, A. R. C. *Practical Reason and Morality.* London: Nelson, 1957. A brief but authoritative exposition and criticism of the *Foundations*.

Levin, Michael E. "Kant's Derivation of the Formula of Universal Law as an Ontological Argument," in *Kant-Studien.* LXV, Heft 1 (1974), pp. 50-66. Argues that Kant illicitly derived the existence of a categorical imperative from the mere concept of a rational action.

Paton, H. J. *The Categorical Imperative: A Study in Kant's Moral Philosophy.* London: Hutchinson, 1946. The definitive commentary.

Sullivan, Roger J. *Immanuel Kant's Moral Theory.* New York: Cambridge University Press, 1989. A thorough examination of Kant's ethics.

AN INTRODUCTION TO THE PRINCIPLES OF MORALS AND LEGISLATION

Author: Jeremy Bentham (1748-1832)
Type of work: Ethics
First published: 1789

Principal Ideas Advanced

The first principle of moral philosophy is the principle of utility which states that every man is morally obligated to promote the greatest happiness of the greatest number of persons.

The principle of utility takes account of the fact that all men are governed by an interest in securing pleasure and in avoiding pain.

Only the consequences of acts are good or bad; intentions are good or evil only insofar as they lead to pleasure or pain.

Since suffering is always bad, all punishment is bad; but punishment must sometimes be administered in order to avoid the greater suffering that an offender against society might bring to others.

Bentham's aim in writing *An Introduction to the Principles of Morals and Legislation* was to discover the foundations for a scientific approach to penal legislation. Because he found these in human nature, rather than in statutes and precedents, his work is also a book on morals.

Two distinct elements appear in Bentham's theory. The first is a psychology of motivation according to which all the actions of men are directed toward pleasures or away from pains. The second is a principle of social ethics according to which each man's actions ought to promote the greatest happiness of the greatest number of persons. That the two principles are independent in their origin and application is not altered by the fact that happiness, according to Bentham, consists in nothing other than pleasure and the avoidance of pain.

The obligation to promote the happiness of the greatest number Bentham called *the principle of utility*. In the manner of the eighteenth century, he frankly admitted that this first principle of his philosophy cannot be proved, because a chain of proof must begin somewhere, and there can be no principle higher than a first principle. The principle, he said, is part of "the natural constitution of the human frame," and men embrace it spontaneously in judging others

if not in directing their own actions. Bentham believed that, in addition to this principle, there are in man social motives, including "goodwill" or "benevolence," which work in harmony with the principle of utility; but the inclination to kindness is one thing, and the principle of utility something else. The latter is an intelligible rule which lies at the foundation of all morals; hence, also of legislation.

What chiefly distinguished Bentham from other eighteenth century moral philosophers was, first, that he recognized only one ultimate principle of morals and, second, that the principle which he maintained was one which admitted of empirical application. The "Age of Reason" commonly appealed to a whole array of self-evident principles, intuitive convictions, and laws of nature. But Bentham complained that none of them provided an external standard which men could agree on. In many instances, the alleged truths of nature were an expression of the principle of utility: but at other times they were nothing but expressions of private feelings, prejudices, and interests. The principle of utility, on the other hand, made it possible to define good and evil, right and wrong, in terms which everyone understood and accepted. "Nature has placed mankind under the governance of two sovereign masters, *pain* and *pleasure*. . . . The *principle of utility* recognizes this subjection, and assumes it for the foundation of that system, the object of which is to rear the fabric of felicity by the hands of reason and of law."

These fundamentals having been laid down, Bentham devoted the remainder of his work to detailed analyses of the psychology of human behavior, chiefly as it bears upon problems of social control. His aim was to find the natural divisions of his subject and to arrange the matter in tables which would be of help in drawing inductions.

First, he treated of pleasures and pains. The legislator, he said, has a twofold interest in these. Inasmuch as the general happiness consists in pleasure and the avoidance of pain, the legislator must consider these as ends or final causes; but since, as legislator, he has to employ motives, he must also consider them as instruments or efficient causes. It is the latter consideration especially that makes it necessary to consider the *sources* of pain and pleasure. The legislator is advised that, in addition to such internal motives as men have toward benevolence, there are several external forces or "sanctions" which reinforce virtue and right. The physical sanction is the pain and loss which nature attaches to certain imprudent acts; the religious sanction is fear of divine displeasure or hope of divine favor; the popular sanction is the favor or disfavor of our fellow men. Political sanction is a fourth source of pain and pleasure, being the rewards and punishments which the ruling power of the state dispenses in cases where the other sanctions are not effective.

The *value* of particular pains and pleasures is obviously relevant in connection with the ends of legislation, but not less so in connection with the means, since the deterrent must be made to outweigh the temptation to crime if it is to serve its purpose. Bentham believed that it is possible to estimate the amount of a pain or pleasure, and he suggested seven calculable factors: intensity, duration, certainty, propinquity, fecundity, purity, and extent. Besides the quantitative side of pain and pleasure, Bentham recognized that there are different kinds of pains and pleasures, and he devoted a chapter to tabulating them. Perceptions, he held, are usually composite, made up of more than one pain or pleasure or both.

He undertook to analyze them into their simple parts, and to enumerate these. Besides pleasures of the senses he noted pleasures of acquisition and possession, of skill, of friendship, of a good name, of power, and even of malevolence. Besides pains of the senses, he recognized the pains of privation (desire, disappointment, regret), and the kinds of pains that are opposite to the pleasures listed above. The lawmaker, according to Bentham, must have all these in view. When he considers an offense, he must ask what pleasures it tends to destroy and what pains to produce in order, on the one hand, to estimate its mischief to the public, and, on the other, its temptation to the wrongdoer. Furthermore, when he considers the punishment, he must take into account the several pains which it is in the power of the state to inflict.

Besides these accounts of the general value of pains and pleasures, a special chapter **is** devoted to individual differences. Bentham listed thirty-two factors which influence men's sensibilities to pain and pleasure, reminding lawmakers that there is no direct proportion between the cause of pain or pleasure and its effect, since differences of health, sex, education, religion, and many other conditions must be taken into account.

Bentham then considered human *action*. The legislator is interested in acts in proportion to their tendency to disturb the general happiness; hence, his judgment has regard only to consequences, not to motives. Bentham distinguished carefully between the intention of an act and its motive. The intention of an act, he maintained, may have two things in view, the act and its consequences, but not equally: one must intend at least the beginning of the act, as, for example, when a person begins to run; but he may have none of the consequences in view, and rarely does he have more than a few. To make his point, Bentham took the story of the death of William II of a wound received from Sir Walter Tyrrel when they were stag-hunting, diversifying it with different suppositions. Had Tyrrel any thought of the king's death? If not, the killing was altogether unintentional. Did he think, when he shot the stag, that there was some danger of the king's riding in the way? If so, the act was intentional but obliquely so. Did he kill him on account of hatred and for the pleasure of destroying him? If such was true, the deed was ultimately intentional. Such examples show that intention involves, besides the motive or will to act, an understanding of the circumstances in which the action takes place. It is the latter which, according to Bentham, must chiefly be taken into account when an intention is praised or blamed, for it is the consequences which are properly good or evil; the intention is good or evil only in so far as the consequences were in view from the start.

Bentham maintained that the will or motive of an intentional act is neither good nor evil. One desire is as legitimate as another, and the pleasure which a man receives from injuring an enemy is, considered by itself, a good, however we may judge the act in terms of its consequences. Bentham was alert to the role which fictitious entities play in human discourse, and noted the difficulties which they place in the way of exact analysis. For example, "avarice" and "indolence" are supposed to act as motives, although they correspond to nothing in the heart of man. Similarly, real motives, such as the pleasure of eating or of sexual satisfaction or of possession are obscured by calling them "gluttony," "lust," and "covetousness." To help clear up the confusion, Bentham went over the whole catalog of kinds of pleasures and pains, and noted how many of them have several names. Thus, pleasures of wealth are called "pecuniary interest" (a neutral term), "avarice," "covetousness," "rapacity," "lucre" (terms of reproach), and "economy," "thrift," "frugality," "industry" (terms of approval), according to the circumstances and our estimate of their consequences. But the motive, in each case, is the same, and may neither be praised nor blamed.

Nevertheless, some motives are more harmonious with the principle of utility than others. Bentham classified the motives as *social* (good will, love of reputation, desire for friendship, and religion), *dissocial* (displeasure), and *self-regarding* (physical desire, pecuniary interest, love of power, and self-preservation). But not even the purest social motive, good will, always coincides with the principle of utility, particularly when it confines itself to the interests of a limited set of persons.

Bentham recognized that when a man is contemplating an act, he is frequently acted on by many motives which draw him in different directions. Some of them are more likely to prompt mischievous acts, others to oppose them. The sum of the motives by which a man is likely to be influenced make up his disposition. "Disposition" was, in Bentham's view, another fictitious notion which represents no more than one man's estimation of how another man is likely to behave. Nevertheless, so far as it can be estimated, the disposition of an offender is important to know. And Bentham admitted that judgments of good and bad do apply to dispositions, as they do not to single motives. He suggested that the degree of depravity of a criminal's disposition is inversely proportional to the strength of the temptation needed to prompt him to a mischievous act.

True to the principle of utility, however, Bentham maintained that, strictly speaking, only the *consequences* of an act are good or bad. Pleasures and pains are real, as dispositions are not. And acts and intentions, which are internal to the doer, are good or evil only as they attach to consequences. Bentham devoted approximately the last half of his book to distinguishing and classifying mischievous acts. The main division is between primary mischief, which is suffered by one or more individuals whose happiness is directly affected by the offense, and secondary mischief, which is the alarm or danger apprehended by the citizenry from the presence of the offender at large in their midst. Penal legislation must take account of both, since the latter diminishes the general happiness (by disturbing men's sense of security) no less than the former.

Bentham's principles for penal legislation are frankly calculative. The lawmaker must estimate the strength of temptation to do mischief, and make the punishment sufficiently severe to act as a deterrent. Bentham argues that there is no kindness in making the punishment light because if it is strong enough persons disposed to crime will not have to endure it, whereas if it is too light, they will. Severity, of course, is not the only thing to be considered. Applying his method of calculating the amount of pleasure and pain, Bentham argued that the certainty and proximity of the punishment must also be taken into account, as well as its appropriateness.

There is no detailed account in the *Introduction* of

the purposes of punishment. But in a footnote, referring to a separate work called *The Theory of Punishment,* the author explains that the principal end of punishment is to control action, whether that of the offender or of others who might be tempted to similar misdeeds. It may work through reformation of the man's disposition, through prohibiting action, or through making him an example. Bentham recognized that vindictive pleasure is also a good, but he could not tolerate making it a basis for punishment.

Like his liberal disciple John Stuart Mill (as in *Essay on Liberty*, 1859), Bentham held that all punishment is mischief and to be admitted only for the exclusion of greater evil. In many cases, to use his words, "punishment is not worth while." This is the case when the act was freely entered into by the party injured, or when the penalty cannot be efficacious (for example, when it comes too late), or when the evils of detecting and prosecuting the crime are more costly than the evils they are intended to prevent. In some cases the mischief is better countered in other ways—for example, the disseminating of pernicious principles should be overcome by educating people in wholesome ones.

The limitations of effective penal legislation were a matter of primary concern to Bentham. He emphasized private ethics and education as more important than legislation. His view of ethics is usually designated "enlightened self-interest" because he maintained that in most instances a man's motives for consulting the happiness of others are dictated by his own interest. But he conceded that there are occasions when social motives act independently of self-regarding motives. Private ethics he called the art of self-government; education, the art of governing the young. Admittedly these do not always achieve their full intention; but it is dangerous and unprofitable to try to make up for their defects by criminal procedures.

Bentham was especially critical of the jurisprudence that existed at the time, and he distinguished his approach to the subject by coining a new name. A book of jurisprudence, he said, could have one of two objects: to ascertain what the law is, or to ascertain what it ought to be. Most books are devoted to the former—he called them "expository"; his was devoted to the latter—he called it "censorial" jurisprudence, or the *art of legislation.*

Pertinent Literature

Plamenatz, John. *The English Utilitarians.* Oxford: Basil Blackwell, 1958.

Jeremy Bentham has always been considered important as a reformer and as the head of the philosophical movement known as utilitarianism; but many, including John Stuart Mill, have not regarded him as, properly speaking, a philosopher. John Plamenatz agrees with this estimate in *The English Utilitarians*, where he represents Bentham as a practical man who embraced whatever doctrines of the Enlightenment suited his purpose without subjecting them to serious criticism. The famous hedonistic calculus is an example: Bentham's rough indication as to how it would work seems to imply that putting it into practice is a mere detail, whereas, says Plamenatz, "the truth is that even an omniscient God could not make such

calculations, for the very notion of them is impossible."

Bentham's greatest confusion lay in trying to employ an egoistic psychology and an altruistic theory of morals at the same time. According to Plamenatz, Bentham did not notice that there was any difficulty here, because he was too busy showing the world how to form a society in which selfish interests can be so harmonized that as a matter of fact everyone will desire what as a matter of right he ought to desire. Plamenatz says, however, that even if it could be brought about that men's selfish interests were perfectly harmonized, it would still be impossible to reconcile egoism and utilitarianism in principle.

The English Utilitarians remains an important statement of the philosophical issues to which Bentham's *Introduction* gives rise, even though the conclusion seems to be "that it is not possible to make sense of what Bentham is saying." In *Man and Society* Plamenatz tries, as he says, to be more sympathetic and more adequate, which he does by distinguishing two lines of argument, one of which he finds relatively free of philosophical difficulties.

Insofar as Bentham believed that it is possible to deduce moral propositions from psychological observations, he was surely mistaken. His initial enterprise was to define value terms in such a way as to eliminate emotive and intuitive connotations and to give to each an objective, empirical content by way of reference to the tendency of an act or a thing to increase pleasure or diminish pain. This would have been legitimate had he been content, as David Hume was, merely to give a descriptive account of moral phenomena. Bentham, however, was primarily a reformer; and, having stipulated new meanings for the words "good" and "right," he proceeded to use them in the old way, according to which what is good ought to be desired and what is right ought to be done. In this manner he convinced himself that his utilitarian rule followed logically from his empirical definitions.

Plamenatz, however, allows that there is another strain of thought in Bentham's *Introduction*. In some passages Bentham takes his stand boldly on naturalistic assumptions about the world and man. When arguing in this vein he assumes that everyone, willy-nilly, seeks pleasure, and that ethical terms need to be redefined so that men can pursue pleasure more efficiently and without bad conscience. Taken in this second way, the utilitarian scheme is no longer an attempt to derive moral rules from psychological truths, for in this view morality in the traditional sense is an illusion which must disappear when men throw off their superstitious beliefs about God and about natural law.

Taken in a naturalistic sense, the utilitarian principle is merely a prudential rule and, as such, is compatible with psychological egoism. If "I ought to do this" means no more than that there is a social rule of which I generally approve, it is possible for me to will my own pleasure in every case while affirming that I ought to will other people's pleasure also. The possibility turns on keeping in mind the difference between what I will as a means and what I will as an end. The function of a rule is to achieve social control; and it is in my interest to support such a rule even when it deprives me of some pleasures. Stated in these terms, Bentham's system is self-consistent.

Nevertheless, in Plamenatz's opinion, utilitarianism, in both its psychological and moral claims, rests on rather simple mistakes. Against egoism, he argues that, while it is a truism that when a person gets what he wants he is satisfied, it does not follow from this that what he wants is his own satisfaction, and that therefore he is selfishly motivated. Similarly, against hedonism, he argues that although it may be the case that one always experiences a pleasant feeling when one gets what one wants, it does not follow that what a person wants is a pleasant feeling. On account of confusions such as these, together with the absurdity of the attempt to measure and sum up pleasure, Plamenatz finds himself obliged to reject the greatest happiness principle. He proposes an emendation, however, which he thinks might have received Bentham's approval. Instead of trying to calculate what would make everyone happy and acting accordingly, why not follow the rule of trying to help others "get what they want according to their own preferences"? To a modern liberal such as Plamenatz, there is something sinister about one person trying to help another get what the former thinks is good for him.

Plamenatz believes that the spirit of Benthamism is against any system which would result in sacrificing the happiness of people to an abstract scheme or program. For this reason, he regards utilitarianism as more promising than John Locke's appeal to natural law. He even suggests the possibility of reframing the doctrine of natural law in the light of his improved reading of Bentham: Act so as to help other people get what they want and not what you think is good for them.

Lyons, David. *In the Interest of the Governed: A Study in Bentham's Philosophy of Utility and Law.* Oxford: Clarendon Press, 1973.

This closely reasoned study attempts to differentiate between Jeremy Bentham's utilitarianism and that of the school which goes by his name. David Lyons' "new interpretation" finds no place in Bentham's own thought for either egoism or the greatest happiness of the greatest number. He arrives at this view by focusing attention on two main passages from the *Introduction*—the initial sections of the first and last chapters respectively. In the former passage, Bentham defined "utility" as the principle which judges actions by reference to "the happiness of the party whose interest is in question," mentioning two parties, the community in general and the particular person. In the latter, Bentham defined "ethics" in terms that, although similar, are significantly different: that is, as "the art of directing men's actions to the production of the greatest possible quantity of happiness on the part of those whose interest is in view." Then he proceeded to divide ethics into two parts, the art of directing one's own actions (private ethics), and the art of directing the actions of other human beings (the art of government). Both of these passages speak of those whose interest is concerned; but the latter, by emphasizing the notion of directing actions, defines the utility principle in a way that would otherwise remain obscure.

The traditional interpretation, according to Lyons, assumes that when Bentham spoke of the happiness of those whose interests are in view, he meant persons who are affected by a given act. Interpreted in this way, Bentham has been understood in a universalistic sense. Lyons shows, however, that, even in the first chapter, Bentham's intention was parochial—that is, limited to one's own community. When, in addition, the passages from the final chapter are taken into account, it appears that he was guided neither by universal nor by parochial interest but by what Lyons calls a dual standard. This means that Bentham envisaged the principle of utility as applying, in the first instance, to acts of government proper, and in the second to what may be called self-government. Lyons admits that, in this interpretation, Bentham was silent respecting other areas of activity where a person is responsible for directing the interests of others—for example, the family or the school—but he sees no difficulty in extending the application. What is excluded is the universalistic interpretation, according to which the rightness or wrongness of a particular act is said to be measured by the total lot of happiness it is thought of as producing.

Much of the book is given over to showing, by an examination of texts, how the dual standard of ethics can be derived from the general principle of utility. Lyons finds a useful clue in the division by Bentham of acts of government into two classes—those of the government considered as an individual, and those of individual government officials. Here, at least, is a precedent for the twofold division of ethics. The argument assumes that, in his earlier writings, which dealt with law and government, Bentham had not seriously thought of making utility the basis for private morality and that the novel feature of the *Introduction* was his attempt to generalize the principle.

Incidental to his argument for the dual standard, Lyons maintains that Bentham was not committed to egoistic hedonism. Admittedly, he was a determinist; but when he said that every act is determined by the desire for pleasure or for the avoidance of pain, he was using the term "pleasure" loosely, as equivalent in meaning to "happiness" or "welfare." Moreover, Lyons finds clear evidence in the *Introduction* that Bentham acknowledged, with David Hume and against Thomas Hobbes, that men are often motivated by sympathy with other people's pleasure and pain. Lyons also points out that in later writings Bentham admitted to finding men more self-centered than he had originally supposed, thereby showing that he regarded it as an empirical question whether and how far man is an egoist.

With the "loosened, non-egoistic hedonistic theory of goals" which he attributes to Bentham, Lyons is in a position to reject the charge that Bentham's psychology and his ethics are necessarily in conflict. A similar question, however, arises on the ethical plane: namely, whether it is possible for one person to follow two independent rules, one of which directs him to seek his own happiness, and the other which directs him to seek the happiness of the community as a whole. Here Lyons takes up the problems of modal logic involved in determining the sense in which two or more "ought" statements can be said to conflict. For the rest, he reduces the problem to a question of fact: Is the world so constituted that private interests can be harmonized with those of the community at large? According to Lyons, Bentham, when he wrote the *Introduction*, believed that it is. Another question, related to this one, has to do with the adequacy of legislation, and how far, in specific circumstances, a person is obliged to obey the law.

Lyons believes that, with the current renewal of interest in ethical theories which provide a "standard for judging what is right and wrong," as opposed to the philosophical analysis of value-terms, the time is ripe for a reexamination of Bentham's writings. Nevertheless, he argues, until there is understanding, the time has not come for a comprehensive exposition of Bentham's doctrines.

(As the subtitle indicates, Lyons' book includes a study on law, based on a separate work by Bentham, entitled *Of Laws in General*. The two parts of the book are independent, and the present review deals only with the study of utility.)

Additional Recommended Reading

Baumgardt, David. *Bentham and the Ethics of Today*. Princeton, New Jersey: Princeton University Press, 1952. Stresses the scientific pretensions of Bentham's work. See the review by Everett W. Hall, in *Ethics*. LXIII, no. 4 (July, 1953), pp. 308-311.

Long, Douglas G. *Bentham on Liberty*. Toronto: Toronto University Press, 1977. Views Bentham as a social theorist and designer of culture.

Mack, Mary P. *Jeremy Bentham: An Odyssey of Ideas*. New York: Columbia University Press, 1963. Full-scale intellectual biography.

Parekh, Bhikhu, ed. *Jeremy Bentham: Ten Critical Essays*. London: Frank Cass, 1974. Includes papers by J. S. Mill, H. L. A. Hart, and others.

PHENOMENOLOGY OF SPIRIT

Author: Georg Wilhelm Friedrich Hegel (1770-1831)
Type of work: Metaphysics, philosophy of history
First published: 1807

Principal Ideas Advanced

As the science of appearances, phenomenology is distinct from metaphysics, which is the science of being.
Phenomenology of spirit observes and describes the forms of unreal consciousness and the necessity which causes consciousness to advance from one form to another.
Knowledge of the dialectical structure of reality makes possible the scientific study of the forms in which consciousness appears.
In its evolution, mind has passed through three moments: consciousness of the sensible world; consciousness of itself and of other selves; and consciousness of the identity of the self and the sensible world.

While Napoleon was defeating the Prussians outside the walls of Jena, G. W. F. Hegel inside the walls was completing his *Phenomenology of Spirit*. Napoleon's victory signified for Hegel the triumph throughout Europe of enlightened self-rule and marked the beginning of a new social era; and in the Preface to the *Phenomenology of Spirit* he drew a parallel between Napoleon's achievement and his own. "It is not difficult to see that our epoch is a birth-time and a period of transition," he wrote. "The spirit of man has broken with the old order of things and with the old ways of thinking." Changes leading up to the present had, he said, been quantitative, like the growth of a child in the womb, but recent events had marked a qualitative change such as happens when the child draws its first breath.

When Hegel made this optimistic assessment of his own achievement, he was thinking not merely of the book in hand but of the system of knowledge for which he was later to become famous and which, even then, he was expounding in university lectures. The *Phenomenology of Spirit* was to introduce the system to the public. Originally he had planned to include it in the first volume of his *Logic*, but the project outgrew the limits of an introduction and was published as a separate work. Today it lives not as an introduction to the system but as a classic in its own

right. Indeed, many who appreciate the *Phenomenology of Spirit* find nothing to their taste in the system. Jacob Loewenberg, for example, speaks of the need "to save Hegel from the Hegelians—nay, from Hegel himself," adding that the insights that abound in the *Phenomenology of Spirit* make the task well worth attempting. This is somewhat like eating the filling of a pie and leaving the crust, for the Hegelians are undoubtedly correct in insisting that, read as it was intended to be read, the *Phenomenology of Spirit* is very much a part of the system.

Like Immanuel Hermann von Fichte and F. W. J. von Schelling before him, Hegel was a metaphysician in the tradition that stemmed from Parmenides. The problem of philosophy in the broadest sense had to do with the identity of being and knowing. Admitting that the way of mortals is mere seeming, each of the three in his own way was trying to expound the way of truth. For Fichte, the Absolute (ultimate reality, the Kantian thing-in-itself) is the self which produces the phenomenal world and then overcomes it. For Schelling, the Absolute is the common source of the self and the world. Both men held that the task of philosophy is to lead the finite mind to the level of immediacy at which the difference between knowledge and being disappears in vision. Hegel thought that both men went too far in their attempts to abolish diversity. In his opinion, an intuition which leaves all difference behind is ignorance rather than knowledge. He said, rather unkindly, that Schelling's Absolute is "the night in which all cows are black." He agreed that knowledge demands immediacy but he denied that the distinctions present in human consciousness are incompatible with the unity demanded of knowledge, it being sufficient that the logic of thought and the logic of being are the same. In short, when one thinks dialectically he thinks truly. This, as is often pointed out, was also Aristotle's solution to the Parmenidean problem. According to Aristotle, divine mind—mind fully actualized—"thinks itself, and its thinking is a thinking of thinking" (*Metaphysics* XII.9).

An obvious difference between Aristotle and Hegel is that for the latter the divine mind is immanent in the world process. Hegel expresses this by saying that Substance and Subject are one. Spirit, which is Hegel's Absolute, is said to be "the inner being of the world." It exists in itself (*an sich*) as Substance, but it also exists for itself (*für sich*) as Subject. "This means, it must be presented to itself as an object, but at the same time straightway annul and transcend this objective form; it must be its own object in which it finds itself reflected." The process Hegel describes as a circle which has its end for its beginning. What he means is that when the movement begins Spirit is one, and when it ends it is again one, while in between it is divided and tormented by the need to end the division. From Hegel's point of view, the circular movement was not in vain. In the beginning Spirit was potentially everything but actually nothing. Only by means of the processes which we know as nature and history does Spirit attain to actuality.

All of this is metaphysics. Like Parmenides, Hegel, when he speaks of Absolute Spirit, views the world not as it *appears* to mortals but as it is *known* by the gods. Metaphysics, which is the science of reality, is not phenomenology, which is the science of appearances. In the *Phenomenology of Spirit* Hegel, without abandoning the standpoint of one who knows, observes and describes the opinions of finite spirits in their multiplicity and contrariety. It is like history, says Hegel, in that it includes the sum of

human experience, both individual and communal; but, whereas history views these experiences "in the form of contingency," phenomenology views them "from the side of their intellectually comprehended organization." Most of the book is a far cry from metaphysics; and if one finds some parts indigestible, the explanation is usually that Hegel is alluding to things we have never encountered in our reading. Incidentally, it is an advantage of the German word *Geist* that, unlike our words "mind" and "spirit," which translators have to use in its place, it covers the whole range of human concerns. Psychology, history, philology, sociology, theology, ethics, and aesthetics, each of which Hegel manages to illuminate, are all referred to in German as *Geisteswissenschaften*— "sciences" of *Geist*.

The *Phenomenology of Spirit*, therefore, is the story of mankind. It is concerned directly with finite spirits and only indirectly with the Absolute, which must be thought of as hidden behind these appearances. Nevertheless, in order to understand the layout of the book, one needs to keep in mind what he is told in the Preface about the movement of the Absolute realizing itself in a threefold process: first, a process of positing itself as a living and moving being, in constant change from one state to its opposite; second, a process of negating the object and becoming subject, thereby splitting up what was single and turning the factors against each other; third, a process of negating this diversity and reinstating self-identity. This final movement, Hegel reminds us, is a new immediacy, not the immediacy with which the process began. "It is the process of its own becoming, the circle which presupposes its end as its purpose and has its end for the beginning; it becomes concrete and actual only by being carried out, and by the end it involves."

In the *Phenomenology of Spirit* the three movements are designated not from the standpoint of Absolute Spirit but from the standpoint of man. Part A, "Consciousness," is concerned with man's attempts to achieve certainty through knowledge of the sensible world. Part B, "Self-consciousness," has to do with man as doer rather than as knower, but it is mainly concerned with the self-image to which man's action leads. Part C, not titled in Hegel's outline, exhibits the stage in which man sees himself reflected in the external world. Hegel explains that these three moments are abstractions arrived at by analysis; he does not mean for us to think that the dialectic which he traces in the development of consciousness was anterior to that which he traces in the development of selfhood. On the other hand, because what is meaningful in history comes from man's efforts to attain self-knowledge, the great moments in history may be seen as illustrative of this triadic movement. Thus, the extroverted mind of pre-Socratic Greece serves to illustrate the first stage; the introverted mind of late antiquity and the Middle Ages, the second; and the boisterous, self-assertive mind of modern man, the third. The plan was simple, but the execution is complicated by Hegel's tendency to loop back into the past in order to give a fuller exhibition of the dialectic.

Part A, "Consciousness," is an essay in epistemology. Specifically it is a critical history of man's attempt to base knowledge on sensation. Although it seems probable that Hegel first envisaged the problem as it appeared to Plato in the *Theaetetus*, his exposition makes full use of the light shed on it by modern empiricism. In three chapters Hegel traces man's attempt to find certainty through knowledge, first on the level of sensation, then on the level of perception, then on the level of scientific understanding. Sensations are indeed immediate; but they cease to be such the moment we make them objects of knowledge. The object of perception, of which common sense is so sure, turns out to be a congeries of properties. And the chemical or physical force in terms of which man tries to explain these properties turns out to be unknowable and has to be abandoned in favor of descriptive laws, which, although satisfactory from a practical standpoint, are unsatisfactory to consciousness bent on knowledge. In the end, consciousness learns that the sensible world is like a curtain behind which an unknown inner world "affirms itself as a divided and distinguished inner reality," namely, self-consciousness. But, says Hegel, to understand this "requires us to fetch a wider compass."

In Part B, "Self-consciousness," Hegel makes a new start. The wider compass means taking account of man's animal condition. Life, says Hegel, is an overcoming. The animal does not contemplate the sensible world but consumes it. Self-consciousness dawns when man's appetites turn into desires. Unlike appetites, desire is universal. What man desires is the idea of overcoming. He is not content to consume what he needs: he destroys for the sake of proving that he is an overcomer; but not satisfied with proving it to himself, he needs to prove it to others. Thus, says Hegel, self-consciousness is a double movement. In order to be certain that he is a self, man needs to be recognized as such by other selves.

Hegel works through the dialectic of self-consciousness in a famous section titled "Lordship and Bondage." It is by killing a rival in life-and-death combat that primitive man attains to selfhood. If the rival lacks mettle and cries out to be spared, the double movement is still accomplished: the rival survives not as a self but as a slave who exists only to serve the lord's desires. The slave, however, although he has no independent existence at first, learns to value himself as a worker and through the skills that he acquires gradually wins the recognition of his master. In the end, the master, who wanted nothing more than to be independent, finds himself dependent upon his slave.

Much has been made, by Friedrich Wilhelm Nietzsche and others, of the two types of consciousness, that of the master and that of the slave. For Hegel, however, this section is scarcely more than an introduction to the one which follows, entitled "The Freedom of Self-consciousness." Failure of consciousness to find independence in the mutual relation between the two selves leads to the negation of the double movement. "In *thinking* I am free, because I am not in another but remain simply and solely in touch with myself." This bold attempt to recover immediacy Hegel illustrates by reference to the subjective philosophies of late antiquity, when culture was universal and life was burdensome to master and slave alike. In Stoicism, thought affirmed itself indifferent to all the conditions of individual existence, declaring its universality. In skepticism, individuality reasserted itself in the giddy whole of its disorder. In Christianity, the attempt was made to combine the universality of the former with the facticity of the latter, giving rise to the consciously divided self which Hegel calls "the unhappy consciousness." For example, the Apostle cries out (*Romans* VII), "O wretched man that I am! Who shall deliver me from the body of this death? For I delight in the law of God after the inward man; but I see another law in my members warring against the law of my mind." Devotion, ceremony, asceticism, mysticism, and obedience are viewed by Hegel as means of overcoming this rift; but the healing remains a mere "beyond." Meanwhile "there has arisen the idea of Reason, of the certainty that consciousness is, in its particularity, inherently and essentially absolute." And so man enters the last stage of his pilgrimage.

Part C, left untitled by Hegel, is the synthesis of consciousness and self-consciousness; but the synthesis, insofar as it falls within the compass of the *Phenomenology of Spirit*, is incomplete. This incompleteness must be kept in mind when we consider the titles which Hegel gave to the three subdivisions of Part C. They are: AA. Reason; BB. Spirit; CC. Religion. The titles are part of the passing show, banners around which modern men are accustomed to rally.

Reason, as understood in this major division, is the reason of newly awakened modern man. In contrast to the ascetic soul of the Middle Ages, modern man **is** blessed with sublime self-confidence, certain of his vocation to pull down the rickety structures of the past and to build new ones on the foundation of reason. Hegel discusses the rise of science, modern man's pursuit of pleasure, and the doctrine of natural law. This section is memorable mainly for the comical situations into which man's zeal and good intentions get him. Disregarding his objective nature, he plunges like Faust into life, only to find himself mastered by fates beyond his control. Retreating somewhat, he takes refuge in "the law of the heart" which the cruel world refuses to understand. Or, as the "knight of virtue," he engages in sham fights with the world. All of this appeal to immediacy, Hegel says, is "consciousness gone crazy, . . . its reality being immediately unreality." A delusory objectivity is achieved in the third section of this division when the individual undertakes to find meaning in life by devoting himself to some worthy cause. Hegel's title for this section, "The Spiritual Zoo, or Humbug!" indicates

that high-mindedness has its low side. Loewenberg catches the flavor in his heading, "Animal Behavior in the Realm of Reason."

The excessive claims made for reason provoked reactions, known historically as pietism, illuminism, and romanticism. These are all dealt with in the section "Spirit," which represents man looking for the truth within himself. The fact that Hegel loops back in time in order to draw a contrast between the conscientiousness of the Greek heroine Antigone and that of the "beautiful soul" cherished and cultivated by German romantics somewhat obscures the dialectical movement. We may take up the story with court life in France under the ancien régime, which, for Hegel, is a brilliantly orchestrated variation on the old theme of self-alienation. To be recognized as a self one had to sacrifice himself to society, either by fighting or by working or by talking. Almost everybody who was anybody chose the third way. The prerevolutionary salon, as J. N. Findlay comments, made Paris "the most agreeable city in the world" to outsiders such as David Hume; but to insiders such as Rameau's nephew in Denis Diderot's classic, it was a snake pit. Hegel points out that the revolt against the meanness and duplicity of the existing order was two-pronged—religious and philosophical. Wilhelm Bossuet exemplifies one party, François Marie Arouet de Voltaire the other. But the difference, Hegel tries to show, was superficial. Both parties were otherworldly, taking flight to the Absolute, whether it was called the Trinity or the Supreme Being. The philosophical party was to triumph as the party of Enlightenment. It lacked cohesion, however, and splintered into political sects which stoked the fires of revolution and, in their pursuit of absolute freedom, were consumed in the Terror.

Absolute freedom is undoubtedly what every self demands. But the lesson Hegel draws from the Enlightenment is that the individual cannot claim to be absolute: the truth that is in him must be in everyone else as well. And this was the new morality from Königsberg just then enjoying great success in romantic circles. Morality has the task of harmonizing thought and inclination. It recovers the wholeness known to the ancient Greeks but it does not do so by means of custom but by means of the voice of conscience, moral reason present in every man.

This section of the *Phenomenology of Spirit* is important chiefly for its criticism of deontological ethics. Universal law raised above all the contingency and duty divorced from all advantage made obvious targets for Hegel's satire. Far from harmonizing the soul, morality gives rise to dissemblance. The beautiful soul is divine in conception—the "self transparent to itself" is similar to Hegel's definition of the Absolute. Unfortunately, reality did not match the concept, as everyone must recognize when he judges his fellows, but also occasionally when he judges himself. On such occasions the conscientious person wants to confess his fault and ask forgiveness; and this can be rewarding, except when one has to do with one who is hard-hearted, and who "refuses to let his inner nature go forth." Here, as Hegel points out, morality anticipates religion.

Hitherto, consciousness has conceived of itself alternately as object and subject, as individual and social. At each level spirit has taken into itself more of the content of human experience, although it continues to mistake each new experience for the whole toward which it aspires. This wholeness Hegel finds in "Revealed Religion," by which he means Christianity. But once again he loops back in time and, in the final section, presents an entire phenomenology of religion.

Religion had been of major concern to Hegel from the time when, as a theological student, he had found difficulty reconciling biblical revelation with Greek *paideia*. His survey traces religion through three stages: the cosmological stage represented by Persia and Egypt; the anthropological stage represented by classical Greece; and the revelational stage represented by Christianity. We merely note that the first stage removed the divine too far from man and that the second brought it too close (for example in classic comedy), leaving it for the gospel of the incarnation of God's Son to find the proper distance. For Hegel, the doctrine of the Trinity—one God revealed to man simultaneously as being, as being-for-itself, and as the self knowing itself in the other—comes as close as religion can possibly come to Absolute Knowledge. However, in religion self-consciousness is not fully conceptualized. The self does not yet know itself directly but only as appearance.

"The last embodiment of spirit," Hegel explains in a brief concluding chapter, "is Absolute Knowledge. It is spirit knowing itself in the shape of spirit." Consciousness, which in religion is not perfectly one with its content, is here "at home with itself." Although the particular self is "immediately sublated" to the universal self, however, it is not absorbed into it, for the latter also is consciousness; that is to say, "It is the process of superseding itself." But here we have left phenomenology and are on the threshold of the System.

Pertinent Literature

Royce, Josiah. *Lectures on Modern Idealism*. New Haven, Connecticut: Yale University Press, 1919.

The three lectures in this series which Josiah Royce devoted to G. W. F. Hegel's *Phenomenology of Spirit* have served successive student generations as an introduction to this work, the entire series providing much-needed background in post-Kantian idealism. Like Immanuel Hermann von Fichte and F. W. J. von Schelling, Hegel started with the assumption that "the world of reality is to be defined in terms of whatever constitutes the true nature and foundation of the self." Immanuel Kant had spoken of a single consciousness the laws of which determine the conditions of all experience, and the boldest of his successors went on to formulate the conception of an impersonal Absolute as the ground and source of human personality.

Royce protests against the common impression that these idealists were arbitrarily imaginative and calls attention to the philosophically important use to which they put the dialectical or antithetical method. One finds the method, says Royce, in Plato's dialogues, which often develop and compare antithetical doctrines not merely in order to expose ignorance but also for the sake of winning a view of truth in its complexity. But while Plato restricted the dialectical process to human thinking, the idealists took it to be inherent in the nature of truth itself. According to Royce, this was partly owing to Kant's declaration, in connection with the antinomies of pure reason, that reason always expresses itself in antitheses; but it was also partly due to the storm and stress of the Napoleonic era, which brought to the light a host of contradictions deeply rooted in human nature.

Royce's chapters on Schelling are helpful to the student of the *Phenomenology of Spirit* in view of Hegel's famous description of Schelling's Absolute as "the night in which all cows are black." Royce, it should be said, does not prejudice his readers by approaching Schelling through Hegel, but takes two lectures to show how, applying the dialectic to the problem of the unity between the self and the universe, Schelling, after affirming that the world is simply the objectification of the "I" whose true nature is to know and not to be known, went on to distinguish between the "I" as conscious and the "I" as unconscious. As the artist loses himself in his work, so the intelligent activity of the self forgets itself in its product. Philosophy transcends these distinctions. The Absolute, Schelling concluded, is neither subject nor object but Indifference.

Hegel, however, held out for difference. By means of the dialectic he showed that the Absolute becomes aware of itself only by passing through a process of inner differentiation into many centers of selfhood, each of which affirms itself in a manner that when taken in isolation is false and self-contradictory but when taken as a stage in the series is true and justified.

Royce's extended tour through the *Phenomenology of Spirit* is picturesque. Taking his cue from the way in which Hegel speaks of consciousness as "passing over" from one stage to another, Royce uses the metaphor of transmigration and imagines the World-Spirit as undergoing repeated incarnations. Hegel's use of the term "world-spirit" was, according to Royce, purely allegorical, portraying consciousness as subject to historical change—a kind of Everyman, appearing successively as master and slave, as monk and pleasure seeker, as rationalist and romantic. In Hegel's Absolute all the diversity of life is

preserved—every struggle, every sacrifice, of the vanquished as well as of the victor.

In his own philosophy, Royce tries to bring knowledge and action together; hence, it is not surprising that he finds the same tendency in Hegel's dialectic. For example, the lower stages of consciousness are divided by Royce into two types according to whether the finite spirit is too practical or too theoretical in its attitude toward life. In those stages in which it is excessively practical man appears as enthusiastic, hopeful, and even heroic, but also blind, failing to understand what he is doing. On the other hand, in those stages in which spirit is excessively intellectual, man's life is empty of content and he finds himself estranged from the world. The Absolute, says Royce, is "the world of human life . . . characterized by a complete unity or harmony of what one might call a theoretical and practical consciousness."

A further point Royce liked to make and which he finds emphasized in the *Phenomenology of Spirit* is that man attains to full consciousness of self only in a social context. Even the headhunter, says Royce, referring to Hegel's early chapter on self-consciousness, depends on his neighbor to furnish him another head. But it is in the later chapters, dealing with society and the state, that this social consciousness attains full realization. All previous stages, says Royce, were "a sleep and a forgetting of the unity upon which all individual life is based. An organized social order is the self for each one of its loyal subjects. The truth of the individual is the consciousness of the people to which he loyally belongs." And what appears on the social plane appears once again on the level which we call culture, notably in religion, which in its higher forms Hegel regarded as "an interpretation of the world by the social self and by the individual only as he identifies himself with the social self."

In his own philosophy of religion, Royce maintains that the Absolute is a superhuman consciousness which, although including the consciousness of individuals, is more than the sum total of individual consciousnesses. He admits that this teaching is not explicit in the *Phenomenology of Spirit*, where Hegel seems to think that the Absolute finds its highest expression in the consciousness of individuals who have attained to awareness of the rational nature of the world. Still, he regards it as implicit in Hegel's thought and argues that it is explicit in his later writings. Royce is careful to point out that this is not traditional theism: the Absolute is not thought of as being first perfect by itself and then as creating an imperfect world; rather it becomes perfect in the process of bringing man to a realization of his place in the Divine life.

Kojève, Alexandre. *Introduction to the Reading of Hegel: Lectures on the Phenomenology of Spirit*. Edited by Allan Bloom. Translated by James H. Nichols, Jr. New York: Basic Books, 1969.

Alexandre Kojève's lectures at the *École Pratique des Hautes Études* helped to bring G. W. F. Hegel to the attention of the intelligentsia in France during the late 1930's. His lectures contrast nicely with those of Josiah Royce, because Kojève denies that Hegel was an idealist.

According to Kojève, Hegel anticipated Karl Marx's dictum that life is not determined by consciousness but consciousness by life, because he fully understood that the spirit or mind is from first to last a false consciousness, and that the motivating principle of history is not thought but action. History ends not in a higher state of consciousness but in man's return to the unconsciousness proper to his animal nature. Kojève suggests that the *Phenomenology of Spirit* might as well have been entitled "Phenomenology of Man" or "Anthropogenetics" because it is an account of the experience of the animal called man which set out to master nature and succeeded at last but had to overcome innumerable difficulties along the way. Marx erred, says Kojève, in viewing man's victory as yet future, Hegel having correctly perceived that the struggle had come to a virtual end with Napoleon.

Kojève is also at some pains to show that Hegel anticipated Martin Heidegger in his comments on being and time. In the *Phenomenology of Spirit*, although not in his later writings, Hegel identified nature with space and history with time. By discourse and by action man reveals being in thought, and time is generated by these means. Although René Descartes had already identified space with static being, it was Hegel who first opposed self (thought and time) to being (space), concluded that man is nonbeing or nothingness, and exhibited history as man's attempt to preserve his nothingness by overcoming being—namely, by transforming it into something new in a nonexistent, nonspatial past.

Kojève finds in the *Phenomenology of Spirit* four irreducible premises which, taken together, explain history: first, the revelation of being by speech, which results from man's attempt to seize the world given through the senses; second, nonbiological desire, which arises as man attempts to become a self; third, the existence of many individuals aspiring after selfhood, each seeking the destruction of every other; and fourth, the difference in quality of desire between those individuals whose aspiration after selfhood is stronger than their natural desire after life, and those in whom the opposite is the case—that is, between future masters and future slaves. History, and therefore humanity, came into existence with the first fight which resulted in one self consenting to be the slave of another. History is the dialectical relation between mastery and slavery. And history will be completed as soon as the synthesis of these two is realized in the "whole man, the citizen of the universal and homogeneous states created by Napoleon."

The specifically human, nonbiological desire which is the moving force of history is desire for recognition. The master gets recognition from the slave and by means of the slave's work his biological desires are also satisfied, but, as Hegel showed, there is more future in being a slave than in being a master. The human ideal, which arose in the master, of being recognized and also of having one's animal desires satisfied, is completely realized only by the specifically human activity of work, which is the province of the slave, who in the course of serving his master not merely rises above nature but transforms nature and mankind in the process. That the slave acts means that he obeys an idea, and in the course of his action he creates a nonnatural, technical, humanized world. His acceptance of the idea of slavery created a social order; his techniques gave birth to reason; even the glimpse of his own nothingness which led him to choose slavery rather than death anticipated the wisdom of posthistorical man.

The editor gives special prominence to Kojève's lectures on mastery and slavery and to those lectures which trace the history of the state from pagan to modern times. Here the dialectic of master and slave appears as the dialectic of universality and particularity, mastery corresponding to the former and slavery to the latter. It is noteworthy that the two concepts are dialectically present in the desire for recognition: each self wants his particular value to be recognized universally. Thus, in order for mankind to find satisfaction and bring history to an end, a society must be formed in which the individual worth of each is respected by all. Kojève notes that it was not actual slaves but self-employed bourgeoisie with highly individualistic ideologies who completed the historical evolution of mankind by realizing the ideal of a self-satisfied citizenry.

In footnotes written later, Kojève spells out for the uninitiated what he means when he speaks of the end of time and the cessation of history. To be sure, the results of the French Revolution had to be extended geographically: two world wars and numerous large and small revolutions were needed to bring its benefits to backward civilizations. But in all this time nothing new has taken place. Historical action has come to a halt and with it the conflict of ideologies, including philosophy. With light irony Kojève points to "the American way of life" as prefiguring the "eternal present" which eventually all humanity will come to enjoy, the final Marxist communism in which everyone appropriates what seems good to him without working any more than he pleases.

Additional Recommended Reading

Findlay, J. N. *Hegel: A Re-examination*. New York: Macmillan Publishing Company, 1958. Chapters V and VI on *The Phenomenology of Spirit* are the best brief guide in English. The author is a philosopher in the analytic tradition.

Hyppolite, Jean. *Genesis and Structure of Hegel's* Phenomenology of Spirit. Translated by S. Cherniak and John Heckman. Evanston, Illinois: Northwestern University Press, 1974. Full-length commentary, essential for a close study of the text.

Kaufman, Walter. *Hegel: Reinterpretation, Texts, and Commentary*. Garden City, New York: Doubleday & Company, 1965. A detailed treatment of the Preface of the *Phenomenology of Spirit*, with much information concerning the circumstances under which the book was written.

Loewenberg, Jacob. *Hegel's Phenomenology: Dialogues on the Life of the Mind*. La Salle, Illinois: Open Court, 1965. The dialogue form permits the author to raise objections which might occur to a nonphilosophical reader and to answer them in a nontechnical manner. Rewarding for the careful student.

Solomon, Robert C. *A Study of G. W. F. Hegel's Phenomenology of Spirit*. New York: Oxford University Press, 1983. Provides a thorough and lucid analysis of Hegel's most important work.

THE WORLD AS WILL AND IDEA

Author: Arthur Schopenhauer (1788-1860)
Type of work: Metaphysics
First published: 1818

Principal Ideas Advanced

The world is my idea—this is a truth for every man, since the world as it is known depends for its character and existence upon the mind that knows it.

By his understanding man forms the world of phenomena, and by his reason he achieves harmony in a world of suffering.

The entire world of phenomena, including the human body, is objectified will.

The will is a striving, yearning force which takes various forms according to its inclinations.

By losing oneself in objects, by knowing them as they are in themselves, one comes to know the will as Idea, as eternal form.

In his Preface to the first edition of *The World as Will and Idea,* Schopenhauer states that his chief sources are Kant, Plato, and the *Upanishads*. He does indeed blend these three into his own philosophical system, but he gives the whole his own philosophical interpretation.

The opening book is entitled, " The World as Idea," and in it Schopenhauer presents his modified scheme of Kant's "Copernican Revolution" in philosophy. Kant had held that the world of phenomena which we perceive is to be understood as a world which is made known to us through various features of our understanding. Events appear to us as in space and time; for Kant these were ultimately to be understood as forms of intuition or perception which, as it were, gave to events their spatial and temporal characteristics. In his famous analogy, the forms of intuition are the spectacles through which we view the world in its spatial and temporal aspects. In addition, we know the world in terms of traditional categories among which cause is a primary one; for Kant these categories are also of the understanding. Thus, the world of appearances is in the final analysis one in which undifferentiated "stuff" is formed in space and time and categorized by the understanding into the related events that science studies. But, to repeat, at bottom it is a mind-formed world. Schopenhauer accepted the Kantian view of the world, and rather brilliantly reduced the twelve categories to the *Critique of Pure Reason* to one, that of the principle of sufficient reason (causation). This principle, with its fourfold root in science, logic, morality, and metaphysics, formed the basis of Schopenhauer's analysis of the world of phenomena.

"The world is my idea" means, then, that the world of objects that I perceive depends for its existence as a perceived system of things upon the mind of consciousness that perceives it. Schopenhauer follows Kant in that he distinguishes mere sense impressions from perceptions (or ideas). Sense impressions are received by the mind from the external world; through the forms of space and time and the principle of sufficient reason, the understanding gives form to sensations, making them into ideas. Since it is the understanding which makes ideas what they are, perception is essentially intellectual. The subject or conscious mind becomes aware of object or body first through sense knowledge of its own body. Schopenhauer believed that the subject infers from sense effects immediately known to the self's body and to other bodies. It is in this way that the world of ideas is constructed. The world of ideas may be considered in two ways. The understanding itself contains the potentiality to form a world of perceptions. But it would remain dormant, as it were, did not the external world excite it. In this sense, then, there is an objective side to the possibility of knowing the world; the world must be capable of acting upon the subject to make perceptions possible. The subjective expression of the world, however, actually converts this possibility into a world of phenomena, for the law of causality springs from and is valid only for it. This means that the world of events as existing in space and time and causally related to one another is formed by the understanding. Additionally, as we noted, the sensibility of animal bodies makes possible the body as an immediate object for the subject.

Although the understanding makes meaningful the world of objects (there would be but undifferentiated sensations otherwise), there is yet another aspect of mind which has an important role to play, and that is reason. Reason distinguishes man from other animals in that by its use he is able to deal in abstract ideas or concepts, and thus to plan, choose, and build—in general, to act prudently. If he merely perceived the world of objects through his understanding he would never be able to transcend and contemplate it. In the quiet life of contemplation, he rises above the hustle and bustle of everyday activities; he can achieve stoical calm, peace, and inner harmony in a world of pain and suffering.

In the second book, " The World as Will," Schopenhauer considers the reality behind the world of appearances, what had been for Kant unknowable, the thing-in-itself. It is traditional for philosophers to speculate upon the why of things, to try to understand what makes things what they are. For Schopenhauer, this question cannot be answered by searching within the world of phenomena, but only beyond that world. The key is to be found in the subject himself who, as an individual, has knowledge of the external world rooted in the experience of his body—object to his self. Body is given to the individual in two ways. As we have seen, it is given (1) as an idea; an object among objects subject to the law of objects, that is, to the law of cause and effect. It is also given (2) as an act of will; when the subject wills, the apparent result is a movement of the body. This aspect of

Schopenhauer's philosophy can also be found in Kant. Kant had held that for morality to be possible, the will must be autonomous and not subject to the same laws as phenomena. Otherwise our actions would be causally explainable, and hence no more morally responsible than a rolling stone's action. As autonomous, the will is part of the noumenal world of things in themselves and is thus free. The result of willing, for Kant, was a physical movement subject to scientific laws, part of the world of phenomena. The cause of the movement was not itself part of the world of phenomena; hence, not a cause in the scientific sense, it was thus morally free.

We must understand that the term "cause" has a curious history in philosophical works. There is a sense of cause which we might term the creative sense, that which brings an event into being and keeps it existing. In this sense the word is often used to refer to something outside the world of events (usually a being such as God) regarded as responsible for the creation and continuity of that world. But there is another sense of "cause" which while not original with David Hume has since his time been in more popular use among many philosophers. That is cause as a constant conjunction of events within the world of phenomena; what there might be outside that world as a cause of it is held to be subject not to knowledge, but perhaps to faith. It is a religious sense of cause. When Kant refers to the autonomous action of the will, he refers to an action that is not part of the world of events, yet one which has a consequence there—a bodily movement. The sequence of bodily movements is a sequence of events (or ideas) that is subject to causal analysis in the second sense mentioned above; but since the will is not part of the world of phenomena its activities are free from scientific analysis, and thus responsible. It is this sense of the Kantian notion of will that Schopenhauer accepts.

Since an act of will is known as a movement of body which is itself an idea, Schopenhauer regards the body as objectified will. He states also that the entire world of ideas, the realm of phenomena, is but a world of objectified will. For Schopenhauer, the world of noumena is nothing but a world of will, that which is "beyond" the world of events, yet its very ground. We also have knowledge of the noumenal world; there is a unique relationship between the subject and his body in which he is aware of his "noumenal" willing and the resulting physical movements. It is possible to look upon the entire world of events, including other subjects known only as ideas, as one's own world. But Schopenhauer would not be satisfied with solipsism.

In holding that body is but objectified will, Schopenhauer argues that the various parts of the body—for example, teeth, throat, and bowels—are but expressions of will, in this case of hunger. For Schopenhauer, there is a force in all things which makes them what they are: the will. Recall, however, that phenomenally this force is not perceived; since all we know are events subject to the principle of sufficient reason, the will here is groundless. But in self-consciousness the will is not hidden but is known directly, and in this consciousness we are also aware of our freedom. We are aware of an activity that cannot itself be part of the world of events that follows from that activity.

Although it has been customary in the history of philosophy for philosophers to raise questions concerning the purpose or end of existence, of creation, Schopenhauer claims that such questions are groundless. In effect they refer to the activity of the will; but the will has no purpose. It moves without cause, has no goal; it is desire itself, striving, yearning, wanting without rhyme or reason.

The third book of Schopenhauer's work is also entitled, "The World as Idea," but "idea" is now seen as a product of reason rather than as a perceptual event. It is here that Plato's concept of the idea or form is used by Schopenhauer, and his prime purpose is to develop his theory of art by means of it. He begins by pointing out that the will is objectified not only in the many particulars that we come to know as events in space and time, subject to change and, hence, explainable under the principle of sufficient reason; but it also manifests itself in universals, which are immutable and thus not susceptible to causal analysis. Schopenhauer holds that the will as universal presents us with a direct objectification, a Platonic form, whereas as a particular it is indirect.

How is the individual to know these direct objec-

tifications? He may gain knowledge of them by transcending the world of events, of space and time and causality, and looking at things as they are in themselves. He does so by losing himself in the object, by giving up his own subjectivity and becoming one with that which he perceives. In such a state, Schopenhauer holds, the individual becomes the pure will-less, painless, timeless subject of knowledge. He becomes a knower of ideas or forms, and not of mere particulars; the object to him is now the *Idea*, the form, of the species. This seems to be something like the sort of knowledge that has been attributed to the mystic, and, no doubt, the influence of the Far East upon Schopenhauer can be seen here also; but he likens the apprehension of forms to art. The artist repeats or reproduces Ideas grasped through pure contemplation; knowledge of the Ideas is the one source of art and its aim is the communication of this knowledge. With this in mind we can see that Schopenhauer's definition of "art" fits closely with his views. It is the way of knowing things independently of the principle of sufficient reason. The man of genius is he who by intuition and imagination most completely frees himself from the world of events to grasp the eternal present within it.

Schopenhauer writes that the aesthetic mode of contemplation involves two features: (1) the object known as a Platonic idea or form and (2) the knowing person considered not as an individual in the ordinary sense, but as a pure, will-less subject of knowledge. When the knower gives up the fourfold principle of sufficient reason as a way of knowing things and assumes the aesthetic mode of contemplation, he derives a peculiar pleasure from that mode in varying degrees depending upon the aesthetic object.

Ordinarily it is difficult and, for most persons, impossible, to escape from the world of desires and wants, the world which gives rise to our willing and which can never be satisfied. Our wants are without satiation; thus, suffering, frustration, and a sense of deficiency are ever-present to us. But if by some external cause or inner disposition we are raised above the cares of the daily world, our knowledge is freed from the directives of will and the temporal aspects of events, and we can achieve that transcendent state of peace, the painless state that separates the world of forms from that of suffering. This is the state of pure contemplation that the great Greek philosophers spoke of.

The artist who has attained this state and then represents it to us in his works allows us to escape the vicissitudes of life and to contemplate the world of forms free from the machinations of the will. His work of art is a means by which we can attain his heights. Nature, too, in certain circumstances, can present us with her objects in such a way that we transcend the world about us and enter into the realm of forms. But the slightest wavering of attention on our part once more returns us to the world of phenomena; we leave contemplation for desire. Aesthetic enjoyment can also be obtained in the remembrance of things past. Schopenhauer points out that the individual in contemplating his memories finds them freed from the immediate tinges of suffering and pain that events often have. Generally speaking, aesthetic pleasure arises whenever we are able to rise above the wants of the moment and to contemplate things in themselves as no longer subject to the principle of sufficient reason; pleasure arises from the opposition to will; it is the delight that comes from perceptive knowledge. When a contemplated object takes on the Idea of its species, we hold it to be a beauty. The nineteenth century aestheticians were concerned with the sublime also; Schopenhauer sees it in the exaltation which arises when one forcibly and consciously breaks away from the world of events and enters the world of forms. The object transfigured in this contemplative act yet carries an aura of its existence as an event created by will. As such it is hostile to the perceiver, yet in being "made" into a form it is the object of pleasure and beauty. If the hostility crowds out the beauty, then the sublime leaves. When the sublime is present we recognize our own insignificance alongside that which we perceive, yet, Schopenhauer feels, we also recognize the dependence of the object upon us as one of our ideas. We are both humble and monumental in its presence.

Tragedy is the summit of poetical art; it presents the terrible side of life, the pain and evil, the want and suffering. We see in nature the all-consuming war of will with itself. When we learn of this inner struggle through tragedy, we are no longer deceived by the phenomena about us. The ego which is so involved in the world of events perishes with that world as we see it for what it is. The motives which keep the will striving are gone; they are replaced by knowledge of the world. This knowledge produces a quieting effect upon the will so that resignation takes place, not a surrender merely of the things of life, but of the very will to live. (This is not to be confused with a "desire" to commit suicide, which is a definite, if ill-advised, act of will tormented by the world of events; rather, it is a renunciation of all desire as one becomes one with the eternal.)

The last book is also entitled, like the second, "The World as Will," but in the second aspect of will Schopenhauer further examines the renunciation of the will to live. In this particular book, Schopenhauer emphasizes the Eastern religious and philosophical view of denial and renunciation. He also concentrates on the idea of life as tragic. It is interesting that Schopenhauer develops a theory of the act of generation as an assertion of the will to live. His discussion is reminiscent of Freud's account of the libido as a general drive manifesting itself throughout mankind and accounting for much, if not all, of human behavior. Freud is supposed to have been shown the passages in Schopenhauer which were similar to his. He claimed not to have read Schopenhauer, but he did acknowledge the similarity of the views.

Schopenhauer believed that in each phenomenal object the will itself is present fully, in the sense that the object is the reification of the will. But the will in its noumenal nature is most real; in inner consciousness the individual, as we noted, is directly aware of the will. The individual within the world of events, aware of pure will in himself, desires everything for himself. Schopenhauer believed that in this way selfishness arises. Recall that each has within himself, for himself, the entire world of phenomena as ideas as well as the world as will. Recall, too, that all other selves are known by the individual as his own ideas—thus he hopes to have all, to control all. His death ends all for him, although while he lives he seeks the world for himself. In this eternal war with one another men deserve the fate which the world as will has for them: a life of tragedy, of want, of pain and suffering. Ultimately, also, the will, in trying to express itself at the expense of others, punishes itself.

As we saw, only those who can rise above their principle of individuation, above the world of cause and effect, who can see the world as one of woe and suffering, can triumph over it. Once one has seen the world for what it is, there is no need to go on willing and striving. One renounces the world of ideas and of will; knowledge quiets the will. This freedom found outside the world of necessity is akin to grace, therein, believed Schopenhauer, lies one's salvation.

Pertinent Literature

Copleston, Frederick C. *Arthur Schopenhauer: Philosopher of Pessimism.* London: Burnes, Oates & Washbourne, 1946.

Frederick C. Copleston, S. J., Professor of the History of Philosophy at Heythrop College at the time of publication, presents a careful and authoritative analysis of Arthur Schopenhauer from a Roman Catholic perspective. Copleston's interest is in presenting an objective exposition of "that system of philosophy which Schopenhauer propounded in *The World as Will and Idea*" and in criticizing it; the result is as Copleston intended: the criticism does not intrude on the exposition. The book is valuable, then, both as a discerning report on Schopenhauer's ideas and as a source of penetrating criticisms well worth serious attention.

Copleston concludes that for Schopenhauer, since life is the manifestation of "the Will to live," and since such a manifestation entails suffering and evil, the ideal would be "nothingness." Accordingly, the view is in radical contrast to that of Georg Wilhelm Friedrich Hegel: "Instead of optimism, pessimism and the worst possible world; instead of Reason, irrational Will; instead of the manifestation of the Idea, the goal of nothingness."

It is impossible so to interpret Schopenhauer's philosophy as to arrive at a positive view of deep import, Copleston claims. The author himself made the effort after having composed his exposition of Schopenhauer's philosophy: he attempted to interpret Schopenhauer as meaning by "Will" force or energy, or the *élan vital,* life itself—or as propounding a psychological doctrine, or an ethic or theory of value—and in every case the doctrine developed by Schopenhauer frustrated Copleston's effort.

Some persons have attempted to see Schopen-hauer as an "esoteric" Christian, but Copleston rejects that view as absurd; Christianity, he contends, is the opposite of Schopenhauer's pessimistic denial of the value of life.

Copleston considers the effect of Schopenhauer's philosophy on the views of Eduard von Hartmann (1842-1906, author of *The Philosophy of the Unconscious*) and Friedrich Nietzsche. Neither thinker salvages anything of worth from the philosophy of Schopenhauer, Copleston concludes. In fact, he writes, Hartmann, although making Idea correlative to Will (the Will must have an end by way of Idea), posited an unconscious Absolute and then, while accepting Schopenhauer's pessimism, agreed also with Gottfried Wilhelm von Leibniz in regarding this world as the best of all possible worlds. Such a view is a "fantastic dream, that passes under the name of philosophy."

As for Nietzsche, according to Copleston, the effort to achieve an optimistic position by venerating the Superman as the ultimate expression of the will to power amounts to nothing more than a futile effort to give priority to the body's biological function of consciousness and, from an atheistic viewpoint, to endorse as the moral ideal the emancipation of moral "prejudices."

Copleston's study of Schopenhauer begins with a survey of the philosophic situation prior to Schopenhauer: Continental Rationalism, on the one hand (despite radical differences in thought among the rationalists), and British Empiricism, on the other. Copleston traces the development from Immanuel Kant (who emphasized the creativity of the individual human mind and insisted on the "thing-in-itself") through J. G. Fichte, F. W. J. Schelling, and Hegel, to Schopenhauer. Although Schopenhauer began with Kant's *Critique of Practical Reason* (in contrast to Fichte and Hegel, who developed ideas from the *Critique of Pure Reason*, thereby ending up with a rationalistic metaphysics) and developed a metaphysics of Will, Copleston warns the reader that Schopenhauer's conception of will is quite different from Kant's.

In a brief biography, Copleston recounts Schopenhauer's efforts to correct the philosophical tendencies of his contemporaries and calls attention to his misanthropy (he had no real friends). Copleston attributes the misanthropy in part to Schopenhauer's strong will and egoism, and he finds the remainder of the explanation (and, in fact, the persistence of the egoistic will) in the conflicts between Schopenhauer and his mother (which also may have stimulated Schopenhauer's relentless diatribes against women).

Copleston's account of Schopenhauer's proposition that "the world is my idea" is fair and detailed, and the author makes an effort to find what is acceptable in the idea that the world is phenomenon, including the objectified will; but Copleston argues that although the world is known by a subject and thus by way of phenomena, matter-in-itself—that is, an independent world existing apart from any subject, even the infinite Subject, God—is a "dream world."

The relation of the pessimistic attitude which pervades Schopenhauer's work to the ideas developed in his work and especially to the affirmation of will as fundamental is spelled out by Copleston under the title "The Tragedy of Life." Copleston then writes of art as providing Schopenhauer a "partial escape" through his idea that the arts express different grades of the Will's objectification (except for music, which expresses the Will itself, and hence is the highest of the arts).

The book concludes with discussions of Schopenhauer's ideas of morality and freedom, right and wrong, the state, and virtue and holiness. The summary judgment Copleston makes is that Schopenhauer's philosophy, despite its radical failure to be in accord with Christianity, is "the most striking statement of the pessimistic *Weltanschauung* in the history of human thought."

Hamlyn, David. *Schopenhauer.* London: Routledge & Kegan Paul, 1980.

David Hamlyn, of Birkbeck College, London, argues that although there is some truth in the claim that Arthur Schopenhauer was not a systematic thinker, a continuous argument runs through *The World as Will and Idea* that constitutes his central philosophical position, and Schopenhauer's other works in one way or another can be seen as filling out that central view.

Hamlyn emphasizes Schopenhauer's doctoral dissertation *The Fourfold Root of the Principle of Sufficient Reason* (written in 1813, revised and enlarged, 1847) as an introduction to Schopenhauer's main work (in line with Schopenhauer's own insistence). Although *The Fourfold Root* says little of Schopenhauer's developed metaphysical view, it provides the first stage of the argument in support of that view.

The principle of sufficient reason is expressed in the words of Christian Wolff: "Nothing is without a reason why it should be rather than not be." According to Hamlyn, Schopenhauer regarded this principle as having a single basic role, and he proceeded to specify this role by reference to its "fourfold root." He does not attempt to prove the principle, for he presumed it to be presupposed in any proof. Hamlyn argues that there is but one root of the single principle; the root, however, may take any one of four forms. Since Schopenhauer regarded the mind as having four and only four kinds of objects, he argued that there must be four and only four kinds of reason or ground.

All knowledge involves a relation between knowing subject and object of knowledge, and all objects of knowledge are "representations." (The term *Vorstellung,* translated as "Idea" in the title of Schopenhauer's masterpiece, covers, Hamlyn claims, perceptions, concepts, images: in short, any object of consciousness, not just intellectual conceptions; hence, Hamlyn prefers the term "representation," as in the translation by E. F. J. Payne, *The World as Will and Representation*).

The four forms of the principle of sufficient reason are (in the order urged by Schopenhauer, although not followed in his exposition) the principle of reason of (1) *being*, (2) *becoming*, (3) *acting*, and (4) *knowing*. The latter, Hamlyn explains, involves representations from (or of) representations; the former three are concerned with immediate representations. The principle of reason of "being" is concerned with time and space; "becoming," with causality; "acting," with the will and law of motivation; and "knowing" with reason and truth.

Hamlyn presents Schopenhauer as suggesting that since the principle of sufficient reason makes reference to a knowing consciousness and its objects and since its objects are "representations" (but not the representations of something-in-itself—and, hence, one might say "presentations"), the principle cannot apply to a world beyond representations, a world-in-itself. Schopenhauer's idealism develops logically from his starting point in the principle of sufficient reason as related to the knowing consciousness, but, Hamlyn points out, Schopenhauer does not make that idealism explicit in *The Fourfold Root*; nor does he argue for it in that work.

After a discussion of the profound influence of Immanuel Kant's work on Schopenhauer's own ideas, Hamlyn proceeds to discuss under the title "The World as Representation" the development of the defense of the central thesis that "The world is my idea (representation)" and hence "my will." The will becomes, for Schopenhauer, the only "thing-in-itself," and his transcendental idealism is a rational development of the basic position that the world *is*

will. (The chapter "The World as Will" provides a careful account of Schopenhauer's conception of the will as the underlying reality.)

Hamlyn discusses also the introduction of the Platonic Ideas into Schopenhauer's philosophy of reality and argues that for Schopenhauer the Ideas are "grades of objectification of the will." Since the Ideas are themselves representations, they do not become another fundamental reality; all that is real and thing-in-itself is will, and the representations are "objects for a knowing consciousness. . ." Through contemplation of the Ideas, made possible chiefly through the use of the intellect and the artistic faculties, the subject (knowing subject) frees itself from the will and its demands.

Art separates the Ideas from reality, Schopenhauer maintains; thus, art produces a peaceful state of mind because the Ideas free the subject from subjection to the will. Music is to be distinguished from the other arts in that music does not copy Ideas; it is an expression of the will itself.

According to Hamlyn, the notion of the freedom of the will is essential in Schopenhauer's ethics because the moral objective is the will's free denial of itself. The denial of the will entails, of course, the denial of representations and of the world as representation; hence, the resultant nothingness is a positive gain compared to the misery of existence prior to the will's denying itself.

Hamlyn's final appraisal of Schopenhauer and his philosophy is that despite the invalidity of certain lines of thought and despite the austerity and even mysteriousness of Schopenhauer's views, his mind was a "great mind indeed" and his philosophy a "magnificent intellectual construction. . . ."

Additional Recommended Reading

Gardiner, Patrick L. *Schopenhauer.* Harmondsworth, England: Penguin Books, 1967. Hamlyn endorses Gardiner's book as one of the few good books in English on Schopenhauer.

Safranski, Rudiger. *Schopenhauer and the Wild Years of Philosophy.* Cambridge, Massachusetts: Harvard University Press, 1990. This insightful study, which places its subject's life and thought in historical context, is the first biography of Schopenhauer to appear in English in the twentieth century.

Taylor, Richard. "Schopenhauer," in *A Critical History of Western Philosophy.* Edited by D. J. O'Connor.

London: Collier-Macmillan, 1964. Both Hamlyn and Gardiner cite Taylor's article as an important contribution.

Tsanoff, R. A. *Schopenhauer's Criticism of Kant's Theory of Experience*. New York: Longmans, Green, 1911. An interesting and scholarly study of Schopenhauer as critic of Kant.

THE PHILOSOPHY OF HISTORY

Author: Georg Wilhelm Friedrich Hegel (1770-1831)
Type of work: Philosophy of history, metaphysics
First published: 1832

Principal Ideas Advanced

Spirit is freedom and self-consciousness acting to realize its own potentiality.

The real is the rational, and the rational is the real; Idea or Reason is the formative principle of all reality.

The goal of history is the liberation of Spirit from its confinement in Nature in order that Spirit might be reunited with its essence as Idea.

The Spirit could not realize its reunion with Idea were it not for the force of Will, as derived from human passions.

The individual as individual is unimportant; only the historically decisive actor, the hero, makes a significant difference in history; but whether a man be a conventional citizen, a courageous person, a hero, or a victim, he is nothing but the Spirit's instrument.

The embodiment of the Spirit's freedom is the State; the State is the concrete unity of freedom and passion.

History is understood by Hegel as the movement of Spirit toward the attainment of self-consciousness. To comprehend world history as the progress of the consciousness of Spirit it is necessary to arrive at a conceptual grasp of the three constitutive elements which structure historical movement: (1) The Idea of Spirit, (2) the means of actualization, and (3) the State as the final and perfect embodiment of Spirit.

Hegel begins his discussion with a formulation of the abstract characteristics of the Idea of Spirit. The peculiar quality of Spirit is grasped when it is seen in contrast with its opposite—matter. The essence of matter is gravity, which means that it has its center outside itself and thus is dependent upon a central point toward which it tends. The essence of Spirit is freedom, which designates a self-contained existence.

Another characteristic of Spirit is self-consciousness. It is of the essence of Spirit to know itself or be conscious of itself. The self-contained existence of Spirit as freedom is thus self-consciousness. Now in the phenomenon of self-consciousness two modes must be distinguished—the fact *that I know* and *what I know*. There is the self which is conscious, and there is also the self of which the self is conscious. Insofar as in self-consciousness the self is conscious of itself, these two modes are merged into a unity. The self has itself within itself. Self-consciousness is a unity, but it is a unity which expresses a reduplication. I can know myself, I can love myself, and I can hate myself. Spirit as freedom is self-reflexive or self-reduplicative. As it is the nature of Spirit to know itself, so also it is the nature of Spirit to actualize itself. Spirit forever drives beyond that which it is *potentially* to make itself what it can become *actually*. Spirit yearns for actualization. "The very essence of Spirit is activity; it realizes its potentiality—makes itself its own deed, its own work—and thus it becomes an object to itself; contemplates itself as an objective existence."

Hegel's definition of Spirit must be understood in its context of a rational philosophy which proclaims an identification of reason and reality. In the Hegelian system the laws of logic are at the same time the laws of being. This undergirding principle of Hegel's philosophy was first formulated in his *Phenomenology of Spirit* (1807), and he expressed it thus: the real is the rational and the rational is the real. This principle also governs his interpretation of history. In *The Philosophy of History* he writes : "The only Thought which Philosophy brings with it to the contemplation of History, is the simple conception of *Reason*; that Reason is the Sovereign of the World; that the history of the world, therefore, presents us with a rational process. . . . That this 'Idea' or 'Reason' is the *True*, the *Eternal*, the absolutely *powerful* essence; that it reveals itself in the World, and that in that World nothing else is revealed but this and its honor and glory—is the thesis which, as we have said, has been proved in Philosophy, and is here regarded as demonstrated." Idea or Reason thus constitutes the primary formative principle in Hegel's philosophical system. This Idea expresses itself first in Nature but also in Spirit. The triadic unity of Idea, Nature, and Spirit thus defines the whole of Hegel's system. Expressed in terms of his dialectical logic, Idea is the thesis, Nature the antithesis, and Spirit the synthesis. Nature exhibits the emergence of the Idea in space; Spirit exhibits the actualization of the Idea in time and history. The primary category for Nature is space. The primary category for Spirit is time. Through the workings of Spirit the Idea is wrested from its localization in space and becomes temporized and historicized. Both Nature and Spirit are subject to a development under the impetus of the Idea; but the development in Nature is that of a quiet and subdued unfolding, whereas Spirit expresses a dynamic self-realization in which conflict and alienation are integral movements. "Thus Spirit is at war with itself; it has to overcome itself as its most formidable obstacle. That development which in the sphere of Nature is a peaceful growth, is in that of Spirit, a severe, a mighty conflict with itself. What Spirit really strives for is the realization of its Ideal being; but in doing so, it hides that goal from its own vision, and is proud and well satisfied in this alienation from it." Spirit is alienated from the Idea in its subjugation or bondage to Nature, but in the process of self-realization through which it attains self-consciousness Spirit becomes sovereign over Nature, subordinates Nature to its purposes, and thus drives to a reconciliation of itself with the Idea. It is in the historical consciousness of the Hebrew people, as we shall see later, that Hegel finds the first liberation of Spirit from Nature. In the Hebrew doctrine of creation Nature is understood as a creature and a servant, and Spirit appears as the creator and the master.

The aim or goal of history is the actualization of Spirit as freedom, wresting itself from its confinement in Nature, and seeking reunion with itself as Idea. This aim or goal defines at the same time God's purpose for the world. Hegel's philosophy of history thus takes on the function of a theodicy—a justification of the ways of God. God's providential activity in the world is the self-realization of Spirit. Hegel converts the truths of philosophical categories and seeks to establish a conceptual justification for the suffering and sacrifices which occur in the course of world history. "Itself is its own object of attainment, and the sole aim of Spirit. This result it is, at which the process of the World's History has been continually aiming; and to which the sacrifices that have ever and anon been laid on the vast altar of the earth, throughout the long lapse of ages, have been offered. This is the only aim that sees itself realized and fulfilled; the only pole of repose amid the ceaseless change of events and conditions, and the sole efficient principle that pervades them. This final aim is God's purpose with the world; but God is the absolutely perfect Being, and can, therefore, will nothing other than himself—his own Will. The Nature of His Will—that is, His Nature itself—is what we here call the Idea of Freedom; translating the language of Religion into that of Thought."

The second constitutive element of the world-historical process is that of the means of actualization. The Idea of Spirit, as the aim or goal of history as such, is merely general and abstract. It resides in thought as a potentiality which has not yet passed over into existence. We must thus introduce a second element—actualization. The source of power which drives Spirit from its potential being into actuality is Will. The author defines Will as "the activity of man in the widest sense." In this definition he seeks to keep the ranges of meaning sufficiently broad so as to include the needs, instincts, inclinations, and passions of men. "We may affirm absolutely," asserts the author, "that *nothing great in the World* has been accomplished without *passion*." Two elements are thus disclosed as essential for an understanding of history. The one is the Idea of Spirit; the other is the complex of human passions. Hegel speaks of the former as the warp and of the latter as the woof of the cloth of universal history. The concrete union of these two provides the third and final element of world history—freedom embodied in the State. The means or material of history is thus the passions and interests of men, used by Spirit for the attainment of its end. Individual men, activated by their inclinations and passions, constitute the power plant for the world-historical process. But these individuals are, in the final analysis, sacrificed for the end or goal of history. History is the slaughter bench at which the happiness and welfare of each individual is sacrificed. The individual constitutes but a moment in the vast general sweep of world history. He remains historically unimportant. "The particular is for the most part of too trifling value as compared with the general: individuals are sacrificed and abandoned. The Idea pays the penalty of determinate existence and of corruptibility, not from itself, but from the passions of individuals." Spirit uses the passions of men to attain its final selfconsciousness. It sets the passions to work for itself. This integration of human passions with the aim of Spirit is accomplished through the "cunning of Reason." The cunning of Reason weaves together all the expressions of passion and makes them contributory to the final goal.

The passions which are put to work by the cunning of Reason arise from the wills of particular individuals, as they play their diversified roles and carry out their variegated functions. These particular individuals are classified by Hegel into four distinct, yet interrelated, historical categories: the citizen, the person, the hero, and the victim.

The *citizen* is subject to what the author calls customary morality. The determinant of action for the citizen is the will of society, the will of a nation-state, or the will of a religious institution. The citizen has not yet apprehended his subjective existence, and consequently has no consciousness of freedom—neither personal nor universal.

The *person* is the individual who can transcend the morality of his particular society and act on the basis of a morality grounded in subjectivity. It is in the person that subjective freedom makes its appearance. The morality of the person is not subordinate. It is determined by a personal consciousness of freedom. The person exhibits an implicit awareness of the Idea as Spirit, and thus drives beyond the static customary morality of the citizen. Hegel finds in Socrates the example par excellence of the person who has been liberated from the confining morality of the citizen. "Though Socrates himself continued to perform his duties as a citizen, it was not the actual State and its religion, but the world of Thought that was his true home."

But it is only when we come to the *hero* that we find the "world-historical individual." The hero is the historically decisive actor. Like all other men, he is motivated by private gain and interest, but his actions express at the same time an attunement with the will of the World-Spirit. His own particular will involves at the same time the larger issues of world history. The heroes of history are practical and political men. They are neither philosophers nor artists. They have no theoretical understanding of the Idea which they are unfolding. But they have insight into what is timely and needed, as well as courage to act decisively on the basis of their convictions. They know what their age demands, and they commit themselves to its challenge. Caesar, Alexander the Great, and Napoleon were such men. They responded to the requirements of their times and shaped the history of the world through their decisive actions. After seeing Napoleon ride through the streets of Jena, Hegel retired to his study and wrote: "Today I saw the World-Spirit riding on horseback." Napoleon was an instrument, used by the cunning of Reason, in the actualization of the self-consciousness of freedom. To become heroes or world-historical individuals these men had to sacrifice personal happiness. "If we go on to cast a look at the fate of these World-Historical persons, whose vocation it was to be agents of the World-Spirit—we shall find it to have been no happy one. They attained no calm enjoyment; their whole life was labor and trouble; their whole nature was nought else but their master-passion. When their object is attained they fall off like empty hulls from the kernel. They die early, like Alexander; they are murdered, like Caesar; transported to St. Helena, like Napoleon."

The *victim*, who comprises the fourth category, moves solely in the realm of private desires and inclinations. He has no interest in and offers no contribution to the customary morality of the citizen, nor to the subjective morality of the person, nor to the march of universal freedom exhibited by the hero. He is abandoned to his private situation. His goal is private success and happiness. Hegel has few good words for this type of individual. Obviously, he cannot become historically decisive. In a sense history moves on without him, but in another sense he remains part of the historical pattern insofar as the cunning of Reason must use all the material which passion provides. In the final analysis Spirit makes use of the hero and victim alike. There is a real sense in which both the hero and victim are "victims." The victim is a "victim" of the hero and the age; the hero in turn is a "victim" of the World-Spirit. In all this we see the emergence of the implicatory principle of Hegel's philosophy of history that the individual as individual is unimportant.

As Kierkegaard, the chief of all critics of Hegel, has later demonstrated, the existential significance of the individual is sacrificed to the universal and the general. A frank admission of this disregard for individuality is expressed when Hegel writes: "The History of the World might, on principle, entirely ignore the circle within which morality and the so much talked of distinction between the moral and the politic lies—not only in abstaining from judgments, for the principles involved, and the necessary reference of the deeds in question to those principles, are a sufficient judgment of them—but in leaving Individuals quite out of view and unmentioned."

The third constitutive element of world history is the State. The aim or goal of history is Spirit as freedom; the means of actualization are the passions of mankind; the embodiment or fulfillment of this freedom is found in the State. The State, as understood by Hegel, is the concrete unity of universal, objective freedom and particular, subjective passion. Thus the State synthesizes at one and the same time freedom and passion, the universal and the particular, the objective and the subjective. In the State universal freedom becomes concretized and is given substance. The freedom of subjective passion is mere arbitrari-

ness and caprice. The actualized freedom of universal history, on the other hand, is *organized* liberty, or freedom structured by a State.

In the final analysis, the entities which are under consideration in Hegel's philosophy of history are "peoples" or cultural totalities. The State rather than the individual embodies universal freedom. The State does not exist for its subjects—it exists for its own sake. It is its own end. The subjects of a State are means towards its end. It is important not to confuse Hegel's definition of the State with an individual bureaucratic political organization. Such a political organization—British Monarchism, French Constitutionalism, American Democracy—may express the will of a state, but the two are not identical. The State, for Hegel, designates a cultural complex which integrates the art, religion, politics, and technology of a people into a unified selfconsciousness. The Third Reich of Hitler, for example, according to the Hegelian philosophy, must be understood as a ghastly distortion of the true meaning of a State. Nazism constituted a pseudostate—a State without cultural content. The State, for Hegel, becomes the foundation for any organization—political or otherwise. The State is responsible for all cultural activities. The implication of this is the subordination of personal morality, personal religion, and political self-determination to a corporate or group substance. This group substance or State, insofar as it provides the foundation for all of man's temporal activities, is understood as an expression of God's purpose for the world. The State is thus defined to be the divine Idea as it exists on earth. There is no room for personal religion and personal morality in Hegel's system. The individual as individual stands outside morality, and outside history itself. Only as a moment in the march of universal freedom, embodied in the State, does the individual become significant. The State or the culture, rather than the individual, is, for Hegel, the bearer of history.

In formulating his philosophy of history Hegel traces the development of the consciousness of freedom as it moves from Eastern to Western civilization. History travels from East to West. Oriental civilization is the childhood of history. Greek civilization marks the period of adolescence. In Roman civilization history develops to manhood. Germanic civilization appears as the fourth phase of world history—old age. The Orientals had acknowledged only *one* man as being free—the despot. And insofar as the freedom of the despot expressed itself in the recklessness of passion, it must be accounted as mere caprice; hence, in Oriental civilization we do not yet find freedom, properly understood. In Greece and Rome, the consciousness of freedom manifested itself in the acknowledgement that *some* men are free. Slavery, with its restriction of freedom, was an accepted institution in both Greece and Rome. It is not until we come to the Germanic nations that we find the acknowledgement that *all* men are free. Germanic civilization, under the influence of Christianity, attained the consciousness of universal freedom.

Among the peoples of China and India, who comprise Oriental civilization, we find only the first glimmerings of a historical consciousness; history as such does not begin until the rise of the Persians. In China and India, the Idea remains bound to Nature. The peculiar determinants of Spirit are lacking. In China, morality is equated with legislative enactments, individuals are stripped of personality, and the will and the passions of the emperor constitute the highest authority. The emperor as the supreme head of political affairs is also at the same time the chief priest of religion. Religion is thus subordinated to the despotism of a particular bureaucratic organization. Such an organization, according to Hegel, is the very negation of a historical State as a cultural unit. The civilization of India exhihits a similar bondage to Nature. This is expressed particularly in the institution of the caste system. The individual does not choose his particular position for himself. He receives it from Nature. Nature is the governing power. Thus, in Oriental civilization the universal idea emerges in Nature, but it does not drive beyond itself to the self-consciousness of Spirit.

The Persians are the first historical peoples. This historical consciousness is expressed in their use of Light as a symbol for the Good *(Ormuzd).* Light provides the condition for the exercise of choice, and it is precisely choice, action, and deeds which constitute the stuff of history. Historical states are what their deeds are. The Persians understood history as a struggle between Good and Evil, in which the actors were confronted with the inescapability of choice. There is a deficiency, however, in the historical consciousness of the Persians. They failed to grasp the higher unity in which the antithesis of Good and Evil is synthesized. Judaism, which took its rise in the same geographical and cultural milieu, provides a further advance in the progressive development of the consciousness of freedom. In Judaism, Spirit is liberated from Nature and is purified. Both the individual man and Israel as a nation come to a consciousness of themselves as distinct from Nature. Jehovah, as the quintessence of Spirit, is understood as the Lord of Nature. Nature is subordinated to the role of creature. Spirit is acknowledged as the Creator. "The idea of Light has at this stage advanced to that of 'Jehovah'—the *purely One.* This forms the point of separation between the East and the West; Spirit descends into the depths of its own being, and recognizes the abstract fundamental principle as the Spiritual. Nature—which in the East is the primary and fundamental existence—is now depressed to the condition of a mere creature; and Spirit now occupies the first place. God is known as the creator of all men, as He is of all nature, and as absolute causality generally."

Judaism thus marks the transition from East to West. Spirit is acknowledged in its separation from Nature, but neither Spirit nor Nature are yet fully comprehended. In Greek civilization another advance becomes apparent. Greece, as the adolescent period of the historical process, introduces the principle of subjective freedom or individuality. This principle is expressed both in the personal or subjective morality of Socrates (as contrasted with the customary morality of society), and in the rise of Athenian Democracy. As despotism was the peculiar characteristic of the political life of the Orient, so democracy is the peculiar characteristic of the political life of Greece. Spirit becomes introspective and posits itself as particular existence, but it posits itself precisely as the ideal and thus suggests the possible triumph over particularity through a comprehension of universality itself. But the universals of Greek thought are fixed and static essences; hence they are still fettered by the limitations of Nature. They still

remain dependent upon external conditions. Therefore, the new direction projected by the consciousness of the Greek Spirit still retains natural elements.
A concrete expression of this principle is the continued practice of slavery, which grants freedom to
some but not to all. In Rome, in which history attains
its manhood, an advance is made from democracy to
aristocracy. The institutions of the people are united
in the person of the emperor. In the will of the
emperor the principle of subjectivity, enunciated in
Greek thought, gains unlimited realization. The will
of the emperor becomes supreme. But insofar as
subjectivity is universalized and objectivized at the
expense of the claims of art, religion, and morality,
the State which emerges in Roman civilization is still
an inferior State, lacking in cultural content.

The State, understood as the concrete embodiment of subjective and objective freedom, comes to
its full realization in the German Spirit. The German
Spirit, like the Greek, apprehended the principle of
subjectivity, but unlike the Greek it became the
bearer of the Christian ideal and thus universalized
the principle to mean that *all* men are free. The
Greek and Roman Spirit still kept some men (the

slaves) in chains. The individual interests and passions of men thus find their fulfillment only in the
German Spirit. This fulfillment is the unification of
the objective Idea of freedom, as the aim of history,
with the particular and subjective passions of mankind, in the concrete embodiment of a cultural
whole. Subjective freedom, without objective order,
is mere caprice—expressed either in the will of a
despot or emperor, or in the chaos of anarchy. Thus,
subjective freedom cannot be realized until it finds
its place within a structured whole—the State.
"This is the point which consciousness has attained,
and these are the principal phases of that form in
which the principle of Freedom has realized itself;
—for the History of the World is nothing but the
development of the Idea of Freedom. But Objective
Freedom—the laws of *real* Freedom—demand the
subjugation of the mere contingent Will—for this is
in its nature formal. If the Objective is in itself
Rational, human insight and conviction must correspond with the Reason which it embodies, and then
we have the other essential element—Subjective
Freedom—also realized."

Pertinent Literature

Marcuse, Herbert. *Reason and Revolution: Hegel and the Rise of Social Theory.* London: Oxford University
Press, 1941.

No full-length study of Georg Wilhelm Friedrich
Hegel's *The Philosophy of History* exists in English.
This is due not merely to the fact that the book in
question consists of a series of lectures Hegel delivered and, as such, were never authorized for publication by him. The deeper reason is that Hegel's *The
Philosophy of History* can scarcely be understood
apart from Hegel's system as a whole, and in particular apart from the teleology of his political theory.

Herbert Marcuse's book is a seminal work of
political theory as well as a sympathetic treatment of
the aims and motives of Hegel's philosophy of history and of the state. Marcuse writes from *within* the
Hegelian-Marxist tradition and from the perspective
of a political philosopher rather than a metaphysician

or an epistemologist.

Reason and Revolution was written because the
rise of Fascism in Europe called for a reinterpretation
of Hegel which would demonstrate that his basic
concepts were hostile to Fascist theory and practice.
Marcuse's book is in this respect a sort of informed
refutation not only of attempts to picture Hegel as a
protofascist ideologist but also of later equally misguided attempts to portray him as an enemy of the
open society, as was done by Karl Popper, for example. Finally, the book was written not merely to revive
an interest in Hegel—which it succeeded in doing—
but in the hope of reviving what Marcuse called the
power of negative thinking, the essence of the dialectic. In this view, thinking is essentially negation.

Marcuse argues that Hegel's most abstract concepts are saturated with experience of a world in which the unreasonable becomes reasonable, in which unfreedom is the condition of freedom and war is the condition of peace. Philosophical-dialectical thinking begins with the refusal to accept this prescribed universe of discourse.

Reason and Revolution consists of two parts. Part I consists of eight chapters which are devoted entirely to Hegel, under the title "The Foundations of Hegel's Philosophy." The first introductory chapter covers the sociopolitical and philosophical setting in which Hegel lived and worked; Chapter II examines Hegel's early theological writings; Chapter III and Chapter IV examine the early attempts at a philosophy of mind, morality, and nature; Chapters V-VII then cover, in turn, Hegel's phenomenology of spirit, his logic, his political philosophy, and his philosophy of history. Part II then consists of two long chapters: "The Foundations of the Dialectical Theory of Society" and a concluding chapter called "The End of Hegelianism." The chapter on the dialectical theory of society covers the negation of philosophy, Søren

Kierkegaard, Ludwig Feuerbach, and a brilliant discussion of Karl Marx. The concluding chapter discusses British neoidealism, the revision of the dialectic, and Fascist "Hegelianism," and concludes, appropriately enough, by contrasting National Socialism with Hegelianism.

Marcuse's discussion of Hegel's philosophy of history occupies the book's central chapter (VII) spatially. The emerging *Weltgeist* concretizes the interest of reason and freedom, it is argued, and national history must therefore be understood in terms of universal history. For while Hegel's logical writings had shown the identity of idea and being, the idea unfolds itself "in space" as nature and "in time" as mind. But to exist in time is to exist in the temporal process of history. History, thus, is an exposition of mind in time. The *Logic* demonstrates the structure of reason; *The Philosophy of History* expounds the historical content of reason.

Marcuse's reading of Hegel's philosophy of history as the story of liberty repays close study not only for the power of its exposition but also for its penetrating critical appreciation of Hegel.

Findlay, John N. *Hegel: A Re-examination.* New York: Macmillan Publishing Company, 1958.

John N. Findlay's twelve-chapter study of Georg Wilhelm Friedrich Hegel's philosophy is one of the two most important books on Hegel written in the English language in the past thirty years or so; and it almost certainly joins the ranks of earlier works on Hegel by John M. E. McTaggart, G. R. G. Mure, W. T. Stace, and Jean Hyppolite as classics in the study of Hegel.

The first, introductory chapter not only covers Hegel's life and writings but also attempts to liberate Hegel from the chief misconceptions which have come to dominate an understanding of his philosophy. The misconceptions include treating Hegel as a transcendent metaphysician, or as some sort of subjectivist who thought that our mind or God's made up the universe. Hegel is equally misunderstood if he is treated as a rationalist who deduces the structure and details of experience, or as a political reactionary whose system masks his reactionary intention. What Findlay proposes instead is to relate Hegel's ideas

and language to our own time in order to show that he has as much to say to us as to previous generations.

Chapter II treats Hegel's notion of Spirit (*Geist*); Findlay discusses what Hegel says about it, what he means by it, and the historical circumstances which require the notion of Spirit; and, finally, he disposes of standard objections to Hegel's conception. Chapter III treats the dialectical method in detail; Chapters IV and V are devoted to penetrating expositions of Hegel's *Phenomenology of Spirit*; Chapters VI, VII, and VIII are expositions of Hegel's logical writings, *The Science of Logic* and the pertinent sections of the *Encyclopedia of the Philosophical Sciences in Outline*; Chapter IX adumbrates Hegel's philosophy of nature; Chapter X treats Hegel's psychology, under the title "The Philosophy of Subjective Spirit"; Chapter XI compresses Hegel's philosophy of law, state, and history, under the title "The Philosophy of Objective Spirit"; Chapter XII treats his aesthetics, philosophy of religion, and history of philosophy.

The Philosophy of History is discussed in the fifth section of Chapter XI. The point is insisted upon by Findlay that the philosophy of history is a part of the teleological movement of Hegel's system as a whole, of the particular teleology of his political theory. For Hegel here passes from the supreme self-objectification of Spirit—the developed State—to a study of the less developed States that lead up to it. Thus, the philosopher of history is a theodicist, for Hegel, in that he can fathom the deep-set drift which leads to more developed political arrangements and also believes he can articulate the new states of consciousness that events are producing. The philosopher of history follows the Cunning of Reason, in short, but does so with the full consciousness often denied those world-historical figures who labor in its service.

Findlay stresses in his discussion that there is but one single historical line of States, in Hegel's philosophy of history, which represents the unfolding of the State-Idea. Only a single State embodies the State-Idea for its time, the rest serving as satellites or as observers. While Findlay rightly observes that Hegel's philosophy of history is a philosophical re-seeing of data, it is not an attempt to write a factual history. Nevertheless, it seems a pity, Findlay thinks, that Hegel was unable to recognize the temporal coexistence of independently significant historical cultures—the Incas and Mayas, for example, in relation to Western European culture. It is also regrettable that Hegel was unable to see that several ordering principles might account for historical data in alternative ways, and that he did not appreciate sufficiently the disruptive and dysteleological features of history.

Taylor, Charles. *Hegel.* Cambridge: Cambridge University Press, 1975.

Charles Taylor's *Hegel* is probably the most comprehensive and thorough study in English. It amounts to almost six hundred large printed pages which are divided into twenty chapters; these, in turn, are organized into six parts.

Part I—" The Claims of Speculative Reason"—consists of three chapters. Chapter I describes the aspirations of the young Romantics of the 1790's, from whom Georg Wilhelm Friedrich Hegel emerged and against whom he defined himself. Chapter II—"Hegel's Itinerary"—sketches Hegel's development; and Chapter III—"Self-positing Spirit"—attempts an outline of his main ideas. Here Hegel is related to earlier figures in the history of philosophy and to the intellectual issues of his time, which are characterized in terms of a pervasive tension between the ideals of individuality and national autonomy on the one hand, and a profoundly felt need to recover unity with nature and within society on the other hand. This pervasive tension between autonomy and unity is taken by Taylor as basic to understanding the Odyssey of self-positing Spirit. Moreover, this tension and longing are not only fundamental to understanding Hegel and his times, but also help to illuminate our own, it is argued.

Part II treats Hegel's *Phenomenology of Spirit* in six chapters; Part III examines his logical writings in five chapters; Part IV treats Hegel's philosophy of history and politics, and the insight he had into modern societies, in three chapters; the three chapters of Part V—"Absolute Spirit"—discusses Hegel's philosophies of art, religion, and the history of philosophy. Part VI, the book's conclusion—"Hegel Today"—argues that Hegel's philosophy is an essential part of the recapitulative conflict of interpretations through which we try to understand ourselves as a civilization.

Chapter XV, "Reason and History," contains a substantial discussion of *The Philosophy of History.* The drama of the sweep of history builds toward Hegel's philosophy of politics, in Taylor's view. The problem is how to reconcile the freedom of the individual who recognizes himself as rationality with a restored *Sittlichkeit. (Sittlichkeit,* ethics, is carefully defined by Taylor as the morality which holds all of us in virtue of our being members of a self-subsistent community, to which we owe allegiance as an embodiment of the universal.) History's main drama is then opened by the breakdown of Greek *Sittlichkeit,* the emergence of the individual with universal consciousness. This, in turn, develops in succeeding centuries in individuals and institutions which embody *Sittlichkeit*; and the two—the individual and the institutional—are eventually reconciled in the rational State.

On the wider scale, history can be seen as the succession of communities in which the earlier are imperfect expressions of what is embodied by later ones. Such communities are *Volksgeister*, the spirit of a people. Thus the Idea *qua* history is realized only through the dialectical unfolding of historical civilizations. Despite the looseness of fit between history and logic, Taylor argues that the dialectic of history is to be understood as reflecting the conceptually necessary stages in the self-unfolding of the Idea. And on the widest possible scale, that of the *Weltgeist*, the cunning of Reason is expressed by and expresses itself in the greatness of world-historical individuals, persons whose unconscious motivation—sometimes perceived through a glass darkly—articulates the next stage in the self-unfolding of the Idea.

Additional Recommended Reading

Avineri, Shlomo. *Hegel's Theory of the Modern State*. Cambridge: Cambridge University Press, 1972. One of the most lucid expositions and appraisals of Hegel's theory of the State available in any language.

Bosanquet, Bernard. *The Philosophical Theory of the State*. New York: Macmillan Publishing Company, 1899. A reading of Hegel's philosophy of history by a British idealist which situates the philosophy of history within Hegel's philosophy of right (*Recht*).

Croce, Benedetto. *History as the Story of Liberty*. Translated by Sylvia Sprigge. London: George Allen & Unwin, 1941. An important work by Italy's leading Hegelian.

Kaufmann, Walter. *Hegel: Reinterpretation, Texts, and Commentary*. Garden City, New York: Doubleday, 1965. A general treatment which stresses the *Phenomenology of Spirit* and pays less attention to Hegel's idealism or to the dialectic.

Lukács, Georg. *History and Class Consciousness*. Translated by Rodney Livingstone. Cambridge, Massachusetts: MIT Press, 1971. This classic of Marxist thought was repudiated by its author because it treats Marxism as an application of Hegel to history. This is the fountainhead of Western Marxist humanism, against the reigning Soviet orthodoxies.

Marx, Karl. *The German Ideology*. New York: International Publishers, 1933. A standard introduction to Marx's understanding of Hegel and the Hegelians.

PHILOSOPHICAL FRAGMENTS

Author: Søren Kierkegaard (1813-1855)
Type of work: Existential theology
First published: 1844

Principal Ideas Advanced

Men can be separated into three groups, depending on the values they hold: the aesthetes want entertainment, pleasure, and freedom from boredom; ethical men live for the sake of duty, taking on obligations in order to be bound to discharge them; and religious men live in order to obey God.

The Socratic idea of religious truth is that truth in religious matters is not unique, that one learns religious truths by recollection of what one has learned in the realm of Ideas.

The alternative position (the Christian view) is that God in time (Jesus Christ) is the teacher of men, that faith is an organ of knowing, that knowledge comes through the consciousness of sin, and that in a moment of decision a man's life can be changed.

Søren Kierkegaard's *Philosophical Fragments* is the central work in a series of books which are marked by a consistent theme, a most unusual manner of presentation, pervasive irony, and a single-minded effort to present Christianity in a fashion which requires the reader to reach some sort of decision about it. The irony of Kierkegaard is evident even in the title of the book: *Philosophical Fragments*. Very few philosophers would entitle their main work a "fragment," or try to present in less than one hundred pages the core of their position.

In order to read Kierkegaard with some degree of understanding, it is necessary (for most readers, at any rate) to have some knowledge of the general plan of his literary work. One of the essential features of his philosophical position is the doctrine of the "Stages." Kierkegaard believed that men can be separated into three groups, depending on what values they hold as fundamental. He calls these three groups "aesthetes," "ethicists," and "religionists."

The *aesthete* is a person who lives for the interesting; he wants entertainment and variety in his life, and he seeks to avoid boredom as the worst evil that can overtake him. He lives to find immediate satisfactions and he avoids making any long-term commitments. All men have the aesthetic as the basic material of their lives; many remain in the aesthetic stage throughout life. But some men move into another sphere, the ethical.

The *ethicist* lives for the sake of doing his duty; he replaces the interesting versus the boring with the good versus the bad. The kind of man Immanuel Kant had in mind when he urged us to do our duties rather than follow our inclinations is the kind of man Kierkegaard called the ethical man. The ethicist's life is successful if he takes on as many obligations to other men as possible and does his best to discharge these obligations.

Kierkegaard contrasted the ethical man with the aesthete in his first book, *Either/Or* (1843), by posing the question of love and marriage. The aesthete falls in love, lives for a multitude of engagements (but no marriages), wants romance in the Hollywood sense. The ethical man does not fall in love, but rather chooses to love, wants a short engagement so that he may enter the state of being married (and thereby become duty bound to another person for the remainder of his days), and finds his romance in the daily routine rather than in secret, passionate moments.

A great many persons with this kind of ethical concern base the ethical rules which govern their lives in God's will. For such persons, there is no difference between being ethical and being religious. However, Kierkegaard felt that the Christian religion demanded a different orientation from that which characterizes the ethical man. Kierkegaard did not believe that the Christian concept of sin could be explained by saying that to sin is to break an ethical rule. Sin is not violation of rule, but violation of the person of God. Kierkegaard contrasted the ethical man's orientation with the religious man's orientation in his book *Fear and Trembling* (1843), where he considered the problems arising out of Abraham's intended sacrifice of his son, Isaac. As Kierkegaard saw it, Abraham had to choose between the ethical demand to avoid murder and the religious command from God that he sacrifice his son. Kierkegaard raised the question whether it might not be the case that religious commitment sometimes requires a man to suspend his ethical concern. The religious man may at times face the temptation to be good rather than holy.

Such is the doctrine of the stages in Kierkegaard's philosophy. There is one other feature of Kierkegaard's writing that should be pointed out before considering *Philosophical Fragments* in more detail. It is the technique Kierkegaard called "indirect communication." Considerable time might be spent elaborating it, but for the present purpose it will be sufficient to point out that the technique implied that the doctrine of the stages should not be stated directly. The representatives of the various stages should not be described from the point of view of an external observer, but presented "from within," so to speak. To this end, Kierkegaard often adopted pseudonyms in his books. He felt he could best present the aesthetic stage by imagining an aesthete, then writing out what such an aesthetic man would say. *Either/Or*, for example, is an extended correspondence between "a young man" and his older friend, "Judge Wilhelm." Kierkegaard does not directly enter the picture at all, and he offers no judgment between the two views of life presented by the young man and the judge; the reader is left to decide. Kierkegaard was quite successful in this matter, even presenting the imaginary characters with different writing styles. The young man writes beautifully, is poetic, sensitive, and lyrical; the judge writes in a pedestrian style, lecturing as

he goes, paying little attention to literary graces.

The pseudonymous author of the *Fragments* is Johannes Climacus—one who is writing about something which is at the climax of the total problem that concerned Kierkegaard throughout his entire literary and philosophical production. Climacus is detached, ironic, and supposedly uncommitted on the immediate problem he is considering; namely, the possibility of giving a different view of religious truth from that presented by Socrates. Socrates is used in the book as a foil, as a man holding a position against which an alternative view can be seen more sharply. Christianity, as Kierkegaard understood it, is the alternative, of course, but, although the reader understands this quite early in the book, the position is not called Christianity until the last paragraph of the book.

The "Socratic" position which Climacus assumes in the book is a rather common interpretation of the Socrates of Plato's dialogues. It may be put briefly as follows: Truth in religious matters does not differ from other kinds of truth. The point of religion is to hold true beliefs about God and to act in accordance with them. Coming to hold true beliefs, in religion as in other areas of human concern, is essentially a matter of recollection, of remembering what a man knew in the realm of the Ideas before birth but forgot when the soul was imprisoned in the body. The teacher, in this case, does not introduce anything new to the learner, but merely serves as midwife, helping the learner to recall what he once knew. After the recollection occurs, the learner adjusts to the true propositions, and the teacher drops out of the knowing relation. The teacher is an occasion, but not a condition, for knowing.

The essential elements in the (Christian) alternative position regarding religious truth are set forth quite openly by Kierkegaard's pseudonym in the "Moral" which he appends to the *Fragments*. The Christian "hypothesis" (as Climacus calls it) differs from the Socratic position, as sketched above, in assuming *faith* as an organ of knowing, in presupposing that there can be in men a *consciousness of sin*, in supposing that there can be a *moment of decision* which changes the course of a man's life, and in assuming a different kind of *teacher* from Socrates— namely, God in time (that is, Jesus Christ). The detachment of Climacus can be seen in the fact that he states these new assumptions so clearly in this "Moral," thus enabling the reader to reject Christianity simply and yet with understanding, if he so desires. Furthermore, Climacus merely states that the hypothesis he has been elaborating differs from Socrates' position in these respects. The question of which hypothesis is true is an entirely different question, he says, and he makes no effort to settle this latter question.

Now if Socrates is right, Climacus argues, the truth is within a man. The teacher merely helps the pupil to realize what he had known all along. In such a case, a man is in the truth rather than in error. In addition, the teacher is not important, since he does not remove the learner from error nor does he introduce him to new truth. Further, the time at which a learner recalls the truth is not important. All in all, the situation is similar to what happened with most, if not all, of us when we learned the basic elements of arithmetic; we can no longer remember who taught them to us or when we were taught. The important thing is that two and two make four, and they always have and always will.

The alternative to this view obviously involves assuming that man is not naturally in the truth but is naturally in error. If this is the case, then the teacher must first give the learner the condition for leaving error and apprehending truth. Then the teacher must provide the truth for the learner to apprehend. The moment at which the learner leaves error and apprehends truth is now quite important and decisive for the learner. And the teacher must be more than an ordinary man, since he is essential to the learner's apprehension of the truth. Indeed, the teacher is so crucial that he is even necessary in order that the learner may recognize that he is in error. Such a teacher, Climacus says, we could appropriately call "Savior."

These elements in Climacus' alternative hypothesis are obviously elements in the traditional Christian account. The fact that one is naturally in error rather than in the truth and also that one does not even recognize such a condition clearly refer to the Christian doctrine of sin, and Climacus does call being in error "sin." The truth that one gains from the teacher is just as obviously the faith that Christians possess. The very unusual teacher who is essential to coming into the truth is, as Climacus calls him, "God in time"; that is, Jesus of Nazareth. And the crucial moment in which a man leaves error for truth is the conversion experience that is the object of so much preaching in the Christian churches. Climacus leaves no doubt that these identifications are appropriate, since he often speaks to the reader about what he has written, citing the original sources of the "hypothesis" he is developing.

In outline, then, the account in the *Fragments* is a very familiar one, differing from the usual Christian account only in the words used to express it and in the reference to the Socratic alternative. There are, however, some implications of Climacus' simple account which are deserving of further treatment. Two matters should be looked into further here: Climacus' account of "the Absolute Paradox," and the question of the "disciple at second hand."

The Absolute Paradox is a discussion of the philosophical significance of the Christian claim that God was incarnate in Jesus of Nazareth. One of the implications of the Socratic view that the truth is somehow within man and needs only to be drawn out by a skillful teacher such as Socrates is that the human mind is adequate for knowing the truth, even religious truth. If, on the contrary, man does not have the truth within himself in some sense, then what a man ought to know or needs to know is beyond man himself—it is the unknown. Or, as Climacus calls it, it is "the other," the absolutely other. But if it is the absolutely other than man, then man's reason is not competent to know it. Yet man, if he is to achieve the truth, must come to know this absolutely other. To this end, so Christians hold, God—the absolutely other—became incarnate in man; that is to say, the absolutely other became not absolutely other. This requires us to say, then, that the Unknown (God) is both absolutely other and not absolutely other than man. And this statement, clearly, has the form of a self-contradiction.

One of the senses of the word "paradox" is such that a paradox is an apparent contradiction which is seen, on examination, not to be a contradiction. Thus, it is paradoxical to say of a certain member of a group, who is very talkative, that he says less than anyone else in the group. Here, at first glance, it looks as if we are saying that the person both talks a great deal and does not talk a great deal. But the puzzle is resolved quickly when attention is called to the way the words "talk" and "say" are used; namely, although he *talks* a great deal, he *says* very little. Most of his talk is insignificant, it is idle chatter. Such a paradox, then, can be resolved by making some kind of distinction between the apparently incompatible predicates.

In saying that his paradox is "Absolute," however, Climacus seems to be saying that it cannot be resolved. The reason the paradox cannot be resolved lies in the uniqueness of the particular paradox in question. It is essential to Climacus' paradox that the word "absolutely" be included. God both is and is not *absolutely* other than man. If we said of Jones that he is other and not other than Smith, we could go on to specify the similarities and differences between the two men: both are philosophers, but one is interested only in logic, while the other is interested only in ethics. They are alike, yet they differ. But if Jones were said to be *absolutely* other than Smith, then no comparisons could be made at all. When we use the expression "totally different" in ordinary speech, we usually mean to emphasize strongly a difference which is really only partial. We mean that two things differ fundamentally in *some* (but not all) respects. But Climacus is using "absolutely other" in a rather strict way, and this means that even to express the total difference is to go beyond the strict limits of language and understanding. Strictly speaking, we cannot even mention a total difference between two things; the very mention of them indicates at least one respect in which they are not totally different; namely, they are alike in that they can be talked about.

If this is the case, however—that God or the unknown is both totally like and totally unlike man, and yet that we should not even be able to state this—then the paradox Climacus is expressing cannot be resolved. It cannot be resolved because the very language of this paradox, in one sense at least, does not have meaning. The paradox is absolute. Yet we must express ourselves. Or at least Christian men feel that they must express themselves. There is an urge

in men, Climacus feels, which drives them to try to express the inexpressible. (Reason, Climacus says, seeks its own downfall.) To come at this point in a somewhat different way, most men can remember trying to express the uniqueness of their beloved in a language which has its power in virtue of expressing the common features, the repeatable elements, the universally instanced qualities of experience. We try to express the unique in terms of the common, and the result is often the paradoxical or the trite. This is why the modern suburbanite's calling his wife "Honey" is at once so full of significance for him, and yet so trite to his neighbors.

If Christianity is true, then its central claim—that God was incarnate in Jesus of Nazareth—leads to a paradox, a paradox which cannot be resolved as paradoxes usually are. But there is also another sense of the word "paradox" which is involved in the discussion in the *Fragments*. Another meaning of the word (its etymological meaning) is "contrary to the received opinion." The Absolute Paradox is paradoxical also in this sense, and this leads to another point Climacus makes in connection with the paradox. Climacus' discussion of the Absolute Paradox is followed by a section in which he claims that man's response to the paradox is to be offended. The religious man, when he has passed through the "moment" and has changed from being in error to being in the truth (to having faith), has his ordinary value commitments upset. Some of Jesus' remarks, at least as they are reported to us in the Christian Scriptures, surely run counter to the prevailing values of everyday life. Common sense—perhaps we have a sample of it in Polonius' advice to his son Laertes in Shakespeare's *Hamlet*: "This above all, to thine own self be true . . ."—surely does not suggest that we turn the other cheek when a man strikes us, nor does it agree that the meek shall inherit the earth. What men usually adopt as a pattern for life is in conflict with the pattern set forth in the Christian Gospels. Men usually want "success" rather than "peace" (in the Christian sense). And so the Christian recommendation, based on its being a revelation from a transcendent God, offends man. Why should one love his neighbor rather than sell to him at a profit? Because God says so. But this recommendation is unreasonable. True enough, but who is to say that God is reasonable? Did not God reveal himself in a most unexpected way? Namely, as the apparently illegitimate son of a poor Nazarene woman, born outside wedlock and in the ancient equivalent of a garage? The Christian account is so contrary to the received opinion of what is of real value that it offends the hearer. Such is Climacus' observation.

Another consequence of the Christian account is that if God revealed himself in Jesus of Nazareth, then it seems he gave special advantages to those men who were contemporary with Jesus and knew Jesus personally, advantages which are denied to the rest of us who are not contemporaries of Jesus. Climacus argues that the immediate followers of Jesus, the "contemporary disciples," enjoyed no advantage over the noncontemporary, the "disciple at second hand." The paradox is the key to Climacus' position here. What the contemporary *saw* was not God, but the man Jesus. It was not apparent or obvious to a normal observer that Jesus is or was more than simply a good man. The divinity which Christians attribute to Jesus was not evident to the senses, but represented an additional characteristic about Jesus which men recognized only in the light of what traditionally has been called the gift of grace from God. Men did not naturally look at Jesus and see his divinity; they beheld only his manhood. Only if God granted grace to the observer, did the observer "see" the divinity of Jesus. Again using the traditional Christian terminology, we can say that even the Apostles could not recognize the divinity of Jesus without having been enlightened by the Holy Spirit. Thus, the contemporary disciple enjoyed no advantage over the disciple at second hand insofar as Jesus' divinity is concerned. The only advantage the contemporary enjoyed concerns Jesus' manhood, his historical existence. Indeed, if there is any advantage, it is the advantage

which the disciple at second hand enjoys in having the testimony of several generations that the man Jesus is also God. The reiteration of this claim brings it home as a possibility in a way that the contemporary disciple did not experience.

Such, then, is the position set forth by Kierkegaard, through the pseudonym "Johannes Climacus" in the *Philosophical Fragments*. It is what is at the heart of the (religious) "existentialist" position Kierkegaard gave the name to. The position is elaborated, by the same pseudonym, in a much longer and more involved book, *The Concluding Unscientific Postscript to the Philosophical Fragments* (1846)—which runs to 550 pages as compared with the ninety-three pages of the *Fragments*—but it is the same position nevertheless. It is stated clearly and succinctly in the *Fragments* as a hypothesis; in the *Postscript* an attempt is made to discuss what would happen to a sophisticated person were he to attempt to put into operation in his own life what is discussed merely as a possibility in the *Fragments*. In *The Concluding Unscientific Postscript to the Philosophical Fragments* Climacus concerns himself with the personal question: How do I become a Christian? But the *Postscript* depends upon the *Fragments*, and the *Fragments* is really the central statement of Kierkegaard's position. Rarely does one find such an important question as the philosophical account of Christianity stated with the precision, clarity, and wit which Kierkegaard exhibits in the *Fragments*. Kierkegaard was possessed of a keen intellect, a logical passion, and an ability to give expression to one of the most significant alternatives in Western Civilization in a manner that retains the kernel of Christianity yet makes possible its discussion in the modern milieu. To have done this is a philosophical and literary achievement of the first order.

Pertinent Literature

Thomas, John Heywood. *Subjectivity and Paradox*. Oxford: Basil Blackwell, 1957.

John Heywood Thomas' *Subjectivity and Paradox* affords a lucid, elegant profile of Søren Kierkegaard's contribution to the philosophy of religion, and is a convincing reply to those scholars who would sharply distinguish between the religious character and the intellectual expression of his thought. The book is also a polemic against those who would contend that religious assertions lack cognitive significance and are reducible merely to statements of inner feeling. Thomas uniquely demonstrates how Kierkegaard by his efforts to communicate to his age about Christian faith and discipleship shows in a concrete way the possibility for meaningful religious discourse. Through a careful examination of two themes—subjectivity and paradox—central to the *Fragments* and to Kierkegaard's work as a whole, Thomas advances a coherent and insightful interpretation of Kierkegaard's view of religious faith and what it means to become a Christian. Documentation is solid and opposing accounts are duly considered.

In an early chapter Thomas supports the view that Kierkegaard's work developed as a powerful criticism of Georg Wilhelm Friedrich Hegel's philosophy of religion. Whereas Hegel's God is totally impersonal, being equated with Absolute Reality or Absolute Spirit, Kierkegaard's God of Christianity is infinitely personal and capable of being appropriated only through an act of intense personal commitment. Hegel acknowledged the Christian doctrine of Incarnation, but for him this meant that God is incarnate in all men and indeed in everything finite, since the world of finitude is nothing other than one moment in the dialectical development of God's nature. For Hegel, Jesus Christ is God incarnate for the simple reason that all men are so; but other than as bearing witness to a metaphysical truth—the unity of God and man—Hegel gave little religious value to the history of Jesus. In dramatic contrast, one of the crucial theses in Kierkegaard's *Fragments* is that for Christianity the Incarnation stands as a unique, momentous, decisive event in history: a necessary condition through which alone it is possible for a person to achieve an intimate relationship with God. Finally, according to Hegel, faith is a form of knowledge; it is spirit knowing spirit, a symbolic type of knowledge which constitutes the first stage on man's road to Ultimate Reality, where the final stage is the appropriation of Absolute Spirit by Reason. It is against precisely this view that Kierkegaard posits his definition of faith as "an objective uncertainty held fast

in an appropriation-process of the most passionate inwardness."

The fundamental concern in the *Fragments* is the meaning of Christian faith, although the overt discussion deals with the nature of truth and how far the truth admits of being learned. Thomas acutely perceives that for Kierkegaard the crucial question is not what is truth, but rather what is the individual's proper relation to the truth *qua* Christianity. Kierkegaard brilliantly illustrates that for Christianity truth is not something which can be acquired in the manner of learning information. A truth relationship can never be objective, detached, abstract, or impersonal; rather, from the viewpoint of Christianity truth requires of the person a subjective appropriation, and intense concern—which is nothing other than faith itself. Thomas is therefore able to justify his contention that the principle of subjectivity is rudimentary to unlocking Kierkegaard's concept of faith.

Because for Kierkegaard the very notion of subjectivity implies passion, commitment, and risk, it readily follows that in his view the object of faith by definition must be something uncertain. In an interesting manner Thomas delineates two types of assertions that Kierkegaard makes when describing the object of Christian faith as an objective uncertainty. One type of assertion is that the object of faith is necessarily incapable of being logically demonstrated or objectively known by any sure means. This seems to be what he implies when he speaks of the person's "faith in God," since presumably the existence of God is an objective uncertainty. But in his discussion of the Absolute Paradox he gives every indication of implying that the object of faith is indeed a logical impossibility. Thus in the *Fragments* he proclaims that faith's object is an "offense" to reason; the object of faith is posited not merely as an inherent uncertainty but as an outright absurdity, at least from any objective point of view. Thomas sensibly suggests that Kierkegaard is using this latter description to characterize uniquely the Christian's "faith in Christ," given the fact that to a nonbeliever the Incarnation and the possibility of an eternal being existing in time pose an enigma, a rational incoherence. Interpreting Kierkegaard in this way helps clarify what otherwise might foster perplexities in trying to decipher his discussion of faith, particularly within the context of the *Fragments* and the *Concluding Unscientific Postscript*.

Christian faith means subjectivity for Kierkegaard; but more than that it signifies paradox. Critics have disagreed widely as to what Kierkegaard intended by designating Christianity as a religion of paradox. Thomas gives an account which is at once revealing and provocative by interconnecting paradox, faith, and subjectivity to create a vision of what for Kierkegaard it means to become a Christian. Two uses of the term "paradox" are distinguished. The first points to a paradox proper or, in other words, an apparent contradiction which actually can be resolved upon closer scrutiny. Broadly speaking, the paradoxical nature of faith is manifest by the person's complete and decisive affirmation of faith's object in spite of the fact that the object exists as an objective uncertainty. Uncertainty, then, is an essential condition of faith. Yet in the *Fragments* Kierkegaard makes it quite clear that the subjective appropriation of the truth bears an inner certainty derived from passion although such certainty is very different from that of logic or mathematics, or even science. Viewed in this way, faith appears to involve a paradox by being simultaneously an instance of certainty (inner certitude) and of uncertainty (lack of knowledge). This "paradox" is resolved, obviously, by characterizing faith first by its subjective quality, then by its objective quality.

Kierkegaard employs the notion of paradox more narrowly in a second sense to describe uniquely the faith of Christianity. It is in this sense that he often speaks of Christian faith as faith in the "Absolute Paradox." Here, Thomas argues, Kierkegaard intends a type of paradox which rationally cannot be removed, dissolved, or surmounted. In Christianity Jesus Christ is the Absolute Paradox: he is an existing being who at one and the same time is entirely God and entirely man, who is wholly eternal yet wholly temporal. From the point of view of reason the Incarnation is an absurdity, a logical impossibility—yet through faith it acquires the highest degree of certitude for the believer. Kierkegaard is able to conclude that while all faith involves paradox in the broadest sense, Christian faith alone has as its object the Absolute Paradox.

In concluding his discussion of paradox Thomas points out that even though the Absolute Paradox objectively is a blatant contradiction, it is not without meaning for the believer. By virtue of subjectivity, in the "leap" of faith, what before appeared as an absurdity now is grasped with the fullest understanding; what before appeared as an impossibility now is an utmost necessity; and what before appeared as the grossest error ever thought now is appropriated as the highest truth to which a person can attain. In Kierkegaard's thinking, all of this is part of what it means to become a Christian.

Stack, George J. *On Kierkegaard: Philosophical Fragments*. Atlantic Highlands, New Jersey: Humanities Press, 1976.

Contrary to what the title might imply, George J. Stack's book is not a commentary on Søren Kierkegaard's *Fragments*. In a series of six exploratory essays the author sympathetically and imaginatively discusses certain fundamental recurring philosophical themes which he finds interwoven throughout Kierkegaard's works. Emphasis is explicitly given to the philosophical as opposed to the theological dimensions of Kierkegaard's thought. Stack succeeds in his attempt to illuminate the central core of what might be regarded as Kierkegaard's philosophical anthropology. This fresh, revealing study

offers a discerning analysis of basic "existential categories" (possibility, necessity, actuality, irony, concern, repetition, and others) which Kierkegaard incorporates in his description of what is man. The book justifies its assumption that Kierkegaard in his pseudonymous works was trying to create a philosophical foundation for prescribing how it is possible for a person to achieve authentic self-realization.

Deserving of serious critical consideration is Stack's suggestive thesis that Kierkegaard's philosophy be interpreted as a response to nihilism. The basic claim is that Kierkegaard's phenomenology of the "stages on life's way" is the product of his constant struggle—both intellectual and personal—with the problem of nihilism. It was Kierkegaard (and not Friedrich Nietzsche) who first recognized the threat of nihilism and existential meaninglessness as an underlying malaise in the world of his time. And it was in Christianity that Kierkegaard saw a genuine possibility for overcoming nihilism, for the passionate resolve and type of ethical-religious commitment necessary to generate and intensify meaningfulness in human existence. Stack advances the same line of thought in a more recent publication, *Kierkegaard's Existential Ethics,* University of Alabama Press, 1977.

Stack's point of departure is *The Concept of Irony*, which he perceives as an initial expression of Kierkegaard's confrontation with nihilism. It is common knowledge that Socrates—dialectician and ironist supreme—represents for Kierkegaard the existential thinker *par excellence*. The key notion in Kierkegaard's interpretation of Socrates is that of irony. In Socrates irony is more than a rhetorical device to show up the ignorance of other people. Rather, it is a mode of being, a perspective which has to be lived through to be fully understood. The ironic standpoint becomes ultimately one of negation, in that it seeks to annul all unexamined assumptions, undermine all certainties, and corrode the secure belief that human reason is the way to Truth. It is in this respect that Kierkegaard views Socratic irony as being essentially nihilistic. The person who has taken up irony into his own existence encounters nihilism head on: a dissolution of all absolutes, a loss of universally accepted values, a psychological sense of the meaninglessness of existence, and a pervasive skepticism about all things. This is not the end of the matter for Kierkegaard, but the beginning.

Kierkegaard realizes that the positive function of irony is to turn the individual back upon himself, to transform the abstract into the personal, and to engender self-consciousness, self-discovery, and the permanent possibility for self-realization. The dominant modality of ironic thought and existence is *possibility*. On the one hand, irony is profoundly nihilistic, seeming to preclude a personal commitment to anything: in the absence of objective certitude and in the midst of infinite negativity and nothingness, what is left for man to embrace? On the other hand, by transposing human existence into the realm of the infinitely possible, irony paves the way for transcending nihilism through a radical affirmation of an objective uncertainty which harbors, nevertheless, meaningfulness in the highest degree. By "nihilating" the actuality of objective truth, the dialectic of irony paradoxically reveals the possibility for subjective truth. The goal of Socrates was not to uncover absolute or metaphysical truths, but to arouse in the person the need for resolution, self-discovery, and a personal truth which can be taken up into one's life to give meaning to one's existence. Irony for Socrates is part of that dialectical process of self-realization. Stack is quick to point out that this is echoed in Kierkegaard's ethics of subjectivity. Thus one sees in Kierkegaard an intimate relationship among irony, possibility, and authentic existence.

As a mode of being, nihilism is not something which can be overcome by thought or reason. What is required is a transformation of the self, a resolute choice of one's own existence or, as Kierkegaard would be most apt to say, a subjective inwardness that holds fast to a truth for which one can live and die. The significance of the negativistic standpoint is that it brings the individual to the brink of despair, hopelessness, and indifference; but in so doing it points the way to meaningfulness and value—that is, subjectivity, commitment, and a passionate striving to become the self one has the potentiality to be.

In the remaining sections of his book Stack discusses Kierkegaard's concept of the aesthetic; then he traces the influence of Aristotle upon Kierkegaard's conception of the ethical; and finally he explicates the concept of existential possibility as the basis for both authentic ethical existence and the "dialectical movements" of religious faith. Still, his most noteworthy contribution is his thesis that Kierkegaard's existential "philosophy of subjectivity" is the result of his confrontation with nihilism and his ensuing quest for meaning.

Additional Recommended Reading

Collins, James. *The Mind of Kierkegaard*. Chicago: Henry Regnery Company, 1953. Widely recognized as a superb and reliable commentary on the central themes in Kierkegaard's work, Collins' study remains one of the best available general introductions to Kierkegaard's philosophy. The author establishes a basis for critical evaluation by positioning Kierkegaard's views against the historical, intellectual, and moral background of the Western tradition.

Evans, C. Stephen. *Kierkegaard's "Fragments" and "Postscript": The Religious Philosophy of Johannes Climacus*. Atlantic Highlands, New Jersey: Humanities Press, 1983. A clear account of two of Kierkegaard's most important works.

Lowrie, Walter. *Kierkegaard*. New York: Oxford University Press, 1938. A monumental biographical and interpretative work by the translator who has done more than anyone else to make Kierkegaard known to the English reader. This exceedingly thorough, highly detailed study is indispensable as a guide to Kierkegaard's life and thought.

_____. *A Short Life of Kierkegaard*. Princeton, New Jersey: Princeton University Press, 1942. A compact and lucid portrait of Kierkegaard's psychological and spiritual development which provides penetrating insights into the nature of his writings. In Lowrie's words, this short biography is "not merely an abstract or condensation" of the earlier *Kierkegaard*, but a fresh approach to the events which influenced Kierkegaard's thinking.

Swenson, David F. *Something About Kierkegaard*. Edited by Lillian Marvin Swenson. Minneapolis: Augsburg Publishing House, 1945. As a pioneer Kierkegaard translator and scholar, David Swenson's contribution to the understanding and appreciation of Kierkegaard's significance is immeasurable. The present collection of essays is especially valuable for its explanation of Kierkegaard's existential dialectic and the thought-provoking exposition of Kierkegaard's doctrine of the three stages on the way of life.

Taylor, Mark C. *Kierkegaard's Pseudonymous Authorship: A Study of Time and the Self*. Princeton, New Jersey: Princeton University Press, 1975. A scholarly, carefully wrought treatise which persuasively argues that Kierkegaard's pseudonymous works form a coherent whole. The unifying theme as perceived by Taylor is the temporality of the self as it is revealed in the different stages of existence. Taylor's aim is to show that by entering into the dialogue created by Kierkegaard's pseudonyms it is possible to achieve a meaningful clarification of time and the self, with the ultimate result that the reader will be led to a deeper understanding of himself as an existing individual.

Thompson, Josiah, ed. *Kierkegaard: A Collection of Critical Essays*. Garden City, New York: Doubleday & Company, 1972. This is a well-rounded collection of interpretative papers on Kierkegaard's philosophy of religion, including discussions of such topics as indirect communication, the meaning of subjectivity, the concept of irony, and Kierkegaard's existential ethics.

CONCLUDING UNSCIENTIFIC POSTSCRIPT

Author: Søren Kierkegaard (1813-1855)
Type of work: Existential theology
First published: 1846

Principal Ideas Advanced

The subjective thinker is an engaged thinker, one who by his activity commits himself to an understanding of the truth which, by the manner of his existence, he is; he seeks to comprehend himself, not as an abstraction, but as an ethically engaged, existing subject.

Only individuals matter; existence is individual in character.

An existent individual is one in the process of becoming; he moves into an uncertain future.

Since death is imminent every choice has infinite worth, and every moment is a unique occasion for decisive action; each individual achieves his being through decision.

In his development the thinker may pass through the aesthetical stage (in which he experiments but does not commit himself), the ethical stage (in which he acts decisively and commits himself), to the religious stage (in which his sin is acknowledged and he commits himself to God).

Kierkegaard has been called the "Danish Socrates." The *Concluding Unscientific Postscript to the Philosophical Fragments,* which is the central point of his whole authorship, bears out Kierkegaard's legitimate claim to this title. In the *Postscript* Socrates is acknowledged as the illustrious Greek who never lost sight of the fact that a thinker remains an existing individual. The Socratic maieutic method, with its use of ignorance, irony, and dialectics, pervades the whole work. The Athenian gadfly reappears in these pages in a modern counterpart.

The Socratic method is used by Johannes Climacus (Kierkegaard's pseudonym) to elicit from the reader an awareness that truth is subjectivity. The doctrine of "the subjective thinker" stands at the center of this classic, and it provides the pivot point around which all the themes revolve. The subjective thinker is the *engaged* or *involved* thinker whose thought, directed toward a penetration of his inner consciousness, moves in passion and earnestness. He finds in the theoretical detachment of objective reflection a comic neglect of the existing individual who does the reflecting. Objective reflection tends to make the subject accidental and transforms his exis-

tence into something indifferent and abstract. The accent for the subjective thinker falls on the *how;* the accent for objective reflection falls on the *what.* Objective truth designates a "what" or an objective content that can be observed in theoretical detachment. Subjective truth is a "how" that must be inwardly appropriated. Truth as subjectivity thus becomes inward appropriation. Truth, subjectively appropriated, is a truth which is *true for me.* It is a truth which I *live,* not merely observe. It is a truth which I *am,* not merely possess. Truth is a mode of action or a manner of existence. The subjective thinker lives the truth; he *exists it.*

One need not proceed far into the pages of the *Postscript* to become aware that Kierkegaard's arch enemy, against whom his Socratic, ironical barbs are directed, is Hegel. Johannes Climacus finds in the systematized, objective and theoretical reflection of Hegel's philosophy a fantastic distortion of truth and an ingenious system of irrelevancy. Climacus never tires of harpooning the System. The Hegelian, in neglecting the crucial distinction between thought and reality, erects a system of thought which comically excludes his own existence. He seeks to comprehend himself as an expression of abstract, universal, and timeless categories; thus he loses himself as a concrete, particular, and temporal existent. "One must therefore be very careful in dealing with a philosopher of the Hegelian school, and, above all, to make certain of the identity of the being with whom one has the honor to discourse. Is he a human being, an existing human being? Is he himself *sub specie aeterni*, even when he sleeps, eats, blows his nose, or whatever else a human being does? Is he himself the pure 'I am I?' . . . Does he in fact exist?" The Hegelian affords an instance of philosophical comedy in which we have thought without a thinker. He erects a marvelous intellectual palace in which he himself does not live. The subject, in Hegel's objective reflection, becomes accidental, and truth as subjectivity is lost.

Descartes shares Hegel's fate of falling under the Kierkegaardian irony and devastating intellectual harpooning. It was Descartes who provided modern philosophy with the *cogito, ergo sum* for its foundation. Now either the "I" which is the subject of the *cogito* refers to a particular existing human being, in which case nothing is proved (If I *am* thinking, what wonder that I *am!*) or else the "I" refers to a universal pure ego. But such an entity has only a conceptual existence, and the *ergo* loses its meaning, the proposition being reduced to a tautology. The attempt by Descartes to prove his existence by the fact that he thinks leads to no real conclusion, for insofar as he thinks he has already abstracted from his own existence. Descartes had already prepared the stage for the later Hegel's identification of abstract thought and reality. Contra Descartes, Climacus is ready to defend the claim that the real subject is not the cognitive subject, but rather the ethically engaged, existing subject. In both Descartes and Hegel he finds that cognition and reason have been viciously abstracted from the concrete particularity of existence.

The subjective thinker emphatically rejects the rationalists' reification of reason, but he in no way denies the validity of thought so long as it is existentially rooted. The subjective thinker is indeed a thinker who makes use of thought in seeking to penetrate the structures of his subjectivity and so to understand himself in his existence. The nobility of the Greek thinker (particularly Socrates) is that he was able to do this. He existed in advance of speculation and the System. The subjective thinker is at the same time a thinker and an existing human being. This is a truth, says Climacus, a statement which, deserving emphasis, cannot too often be repeated, and the neglect of which has brought about much confusion. Kierkegaard was by no means an opponent of thought. He insisted only that thought be placed back into existence, following its vicious abstraction by Hegel. "If thought speaks deprecatingly of the imagination, imagination in its turn speaks deprecatingly of thought; and likewise with feeling. The task is not to exalt the one at the expense of the other, but to give them an equal status, to unify them in simultaneity; the medium in which they are unified is *existence.*"

When the subjective thinker thus makes the movement of understanding himself in his existence, he discovers that in the order of reality (as distinct from the order of abstract thought) individuals—and individuals alone—exist. Existence is indelibly individual in character. Kierkegaard's philosophy is a crusade for the reality of the concrete individual. "The individual" (*Enkelte*) was Kierkegaard's central category. It is in this category that he saw bound up any importance that he as a subjective thinker might have. This category was so decisive for his whole literary effort that he asked that it be inscribed on his tombstone (and it was). The human self is not humanity in general. Humanity does not exist; only individual human beings exist. Existential reality resides not in the genus or in the species but in the concrete individual. Universals, like crowds, are abstractions which have neither hands nor feet.

To exist means to be an individual, but to exist also means to be in the process of becoming. "An existing individual is constantly in process of becoming; the actual existing subjective thinker constantly reproduces this existential situation in his thoughts, and translates all his thinking into terms of process." Although Hegel in his *Logic* had much to say about processes in which opposites are combined into higher unities, his doctrine of becoming is ultimately illusory because it does not understand process from the point of view of concrete existence. Logic and pure thought can never capture the existential reality of becoming, for logical entities are *states of being* which are timeless and fixed. In the moment that Hegel wrote his *Logic*, with the intention of encompassing the whole of reality, he forfeited the concrete becoming in which the subjective thinker finds himself disclosed. But this intractable reality of concrete becoming remains as a source of profound embarrassment for the Hegelian—particularly when he is ready to write the last paragraph of his system and finds that existence is not yet finished! Kierkegaardian irony reaches its height when Climacus undertakes to satirize the System. "I shall be as willing as the next man to fall down in worship before the System, if only I can manage to set eyes on it. Hitherto I have had no success; and though I have young legs, I am almost weary from running back and forth between Herod and Pilate. Once or twice I have been on the verge of bending the knee. But at the last moment, when I already had my handkerchief spread on the ground, to avoid soiling my trousers, and I made a trusting appeal to one of the initiated who stood by: 'Tell me now sincerely, is it entirely finished; for if so I will kneel down before it, even at the risk of ruining a pair of trousers (for on account of the heavy traffic to and fro, the road has become quite muddy),'—I always received the same answer: 'No, it is not yet quite finished.' And so there was another postponement— of the System, and of my homage." System and finality are correlative concepts. But existence, which is constantly in the process of becoming, is never finished. Thus, an existential system is impossible. Reality itself is a system—but a system only for God. There can be no system for an existing individual who always stands in the throes of becoming.

As existence involves individuality and becoming, so assuredly does it involve the future. One exists in a process of becoming by facing a future. The subjective thinker is passionately and earnestly interested in the time of immediate experience as it qualifies his existence. Time for the existing subject is not a time in general—an abstract, cosmic time which is spatialized through objectivizing categories. His interest has to do with the time of his inner experience —time as it is concretely lived rather than abstractly known. In the subjective thinker's immediate experience of time, the future has priority. His life is lived primarily out of the future, for in his subjectivity he understands himself as moving into a future. This future generates uncertainty and anxiety. Tomorrow may rob me of all my earthly goods and leave me desolate. The subjective thinker, when he penetrates to the core of his subjectivity, thus finds the uncertainty of life itself. Wherever there is subjectivity, there is uncertainty.

Death is one of the most ethically significant uncertainties of life. Subjective thought discloses death as an imminent possibility. But for the most part man devises means of concealing this imminent possibility. He approaches the fact of death through the eyes of objective reflection and thus conveniently transforms it into something in general. Viewed *objectively*, death is a general and universal occurrence which befalls all forms of life. Viewed subjectively, death is an imminent uncertainty which pertains to my particular existence and which makes a difference for my individual decisions. Death is thus apprehended not as a generalized empirical factuality, but as a task or a deed. "If the task of life is to become subjective, then the thought of death is not, for the individual subject, something in general, but is verily a deed." Death, subjectively understood, becomes a task in that it is defined in terms of its ethical expression. It is experienced and appropriated in an anticipatory conception in such a way that it transforms the whole of man's life. When death is existentially appropriated, then every decision receives a singular importance. If death is imminent every choice has infinite worth, and every moment is a unique occasion for decisive action. Death makes a difference for life.

In the subjective movements of his engaged existence the subjective thinker discloses his existence as qualified by individuality, becoming, time, and death. Already in these movements the pathway is opened for decisive action. The category of decision becomes a centralizing concept for the subjective thinker. In facing a future the existing subject is called to decision. Thus the subjective thinker is at the same time an ethical thinker. He understands his personal existence as a task and a responsibility. He must choose in order to attain his authentic selfhood. His essential humanity is not given. It is achieved through decision. The greatness of man is that he has an *either/or*. This either/or becomes a matter of indifference for the Hegelian. In Hegel's timeless categories there is no place for decisive action or ethical commitment. "Ethics has been crowded out of the System, and as a substitute for it there has been included a something which confuses the historical with the individual, the bewildering and noisy demands of the age with the eternal demand that conscience makes upon the individual. Ethics concentrates upon the individual, and ethically it is the task of every individual to become an entire man; just as it is the ethical presupposition that every man is born in such a condition that he can become one." The objective reflection which is so peculiar to the System transforms everyone into an observer. But existing individuals are actors as well as observers. They make choices which affect the whole of their lives. They are engaged in action which is decisive for themselves as well as for others. The ethically existing subject is thus of utmost importance; but for the Hegelian, who is concerned with the general developments of world history and the meditation of opposites in this world history, the ethical subject remains unacknowledged.

Kierkegaard regarded the existentially decisive act for the ethically engaged subject as not an external action but rather as an internal decision. It is inward passion rather than external consequences which constitutes the criterion of ethical action. The person who does not own a penny can be as charitable as the person who gives away a kingdom. Let us suppose, says Climacus, that the Levite, who found the man that had fallen among thieves between Jericho and Jerusalem, was inwardly concerned to help sufferers in distress. Let us suppose further that when he met the victim he was frightened at the possibility of robbers nearby and hastened on lest he also become a victim. He failed to act, giving no help to the sufferer. But after having left the victim he was overcome by remorse, and hurried back to the scene, but arrived too late. The Samaritan had already helped the victim in his distress. If this were the sequence of events would one not have to say that the Levite acted? Indeed he acted, says Climacus, and in an inwardly decisive sense, even though his action had no external expression.

Much time is devoted in the *Postscript* to a delineation of the "stages" or "existence spheres"—a delineation which Kierkegaard had already undertaken in two of his earlier works, *Either/Or* (1843) and *Stages on Life's Way* (1845). However, for the first time in his writings we have an analysis and description of irony and humor as transitional stages between the aesthetical and the ethical, and the ethical and the religious, respectively. The aesthetical stage is the stage of experimentation. The aestheticist is one who experiments with various possibilities but never commits himself in passionate choice. He experiments with love but never commits himself in marriage. He experiments with thought but never commits himself in action. A constant flight from the responsibility of decision characterizes the aestheticist. Thus he lacks the decisive content of subjectivity—inwardness, earnestness, and passion. It is only in the ethical stage that these decisive determinants appear. The transition to the ethical stage is by way of irony. Climacus speaks of irony as the "boundary zone" between the aesthetical and the ethical. The purpose of irony is to rouse man from his unauthentic aesthetical floundering to an ethical consciousness. Irony elicits the discrepancy between the inward and outward, as this discrepancy is expressed in the life of man. Irony makes man aware of the discrepancy between his inward lack of wisdom and his outward claim of its possession. It makes man aware that his outward profession of virtue betrays an inward lack of it. Irony constitutes the first awareness of the ethical, seeks to bring these suppressed discrepancies to light, and thus drives beyond itself to the next stage.

The ethical stage is the sphere of decisive action and self-commitment. The ethical man has resolutely chosen himself and exists in passion and in inwardness. The personality of the aestheticist is dispersed because of his floundering in possibilities. The personality of the ethical man is unified or centralized because he has been able to commit himself in definite modes of action. But the ground of this unification and the ultimate source of this commitment is not disclosed until the self apprehends itself in the movements of the religious sphere. Although in tension, the ethical and the religious are so close, says Climacus, that they are in constant communication with one another. It is for this reason that the two stages are often hyphenated and designated as the ethico religious sphere. The "boundary zone" between the ethical and the religious is humor. The ethical thinker drives beyond the ethical to the religious through the expression of humor, in which there is a protest against the externalization of ethical norms and standards. The humorist is aware of this externalization, which tends to become identified with the religious, contests it as the proper measure, but still is unable to establish a God relationship in terms of religious passion *stricte sic dictus*. (Kierkegaard's provocative book, *Fear and Trembling*, 1843, incomparably expresses this suspension of an externalized ethics through the movement of faith, exemplified by Abraham in the intended sacrifice of his son Isaac.) Only when the existing subject has apprehended his relationship to God as a relationship qualified by inwardness and passion does he proceed to the religious stage.

The new determinant which is introduced in the religious stage is the determinant of suffering. Suffering is the highest intensification of subjectivity. In it we see the fullest expression of inwardness. The suffering which is acknowledged in this stage, however, must not be confused with the poetic representations of suffering peculiar to the aesthetical stage, nor with the reflection *about* suffering which is always qualitatively different from the fact of suffering, nor with suffering as a simple outward ethical manifestation. Religious suffering is an expression of an inward God-relationship, like that of Job, which remains opaque to the aesthetical and ethical consciousness.

The religious stage is internally differentiated by two levels of existence—religiousness A and religiousness B. Religiousness A is the religion of immanence. Religiousness B is the "paradoxical religiousness," that in which the qualitative distinction between God and man is disclosed, and God's presence in time is revealed in the paradox of Christ. The distinction between A and B also expresses the corresponding distinction between guilt-consciousness and sin-consciousness. Guilt, prop-

erly understood, is a determinant of religiousness A; sin is a determinant of religiousness B. Guilt is a disrelationship of the subject with himself. It points to an internal fissure within consciousness which results because of an alienation from his absolute *telos*. It is still a movement within immanence. In religiousness B guilt becomes sin. The disrelationship of the subject with himself is now apprehended as a disrelationship with God. The existing subject can acquire a guilt-consciousness through the purely human movement of dialectics in which he understands himself as alienated from himself in the process of becoming. But sin-consciousness requires a disclosure by God so as to reveal to man that his guilt is at one and the same time an implication of sin. The pagan can have no consciousness of sin. Sin-consciousness emerges only in the subject's awareness of himself as existing in a disrelationship with God. This God is a God who has entered time and history. It is thus that religiousness B finds its supreme expression in Christianity, with its teachings of the "Absolute Paradox" or "Deity in time." As the "paradoxical religiousness," religiousness B affirms a qualitative distinction between God and man. God is wholly and utterly transcendent to the temporal order. Thus, religiousness B breaks with religiousness A. There is no natural kinship between the eternal and the temporal. And so the advent of eternity in time is disclosed as a paradox. Christ is the absolute paradox who reveals God in time, makes man aware of his sin, and calls him to faith and decisive commitment through which sin is overcome.

In his analysis and description of the religious stage as the crown and culmination of the three stages (which must be understood not in terms of temporal sequences of successive development, but rather in terms of copresent qualifications of subjectivity), the author makes his central intention quite apparent. The leading question which concerns Climacus is already put to the reader in the introduction. "The subjective problem concerns the relationship of the individual to Christianity. To put it quite simply: How may I, Johannes Climacus, participate in the happiness promised by Christianity?" It is significant that in the appendix, "For an understanding with the reader," the question is reiterated : "Now I ask how I am to become a Christian." This is indeed Kierkegaard's central question, posed not only in the *Postscript*, but in all of his other writings. Explaining his own perspective as an author, Kierkegaard informs

his readers in his book *The Point of View* (1849) that underlying the whole of his literary work is the central concern of how to become a Christian—a task which is extremely difficult in Christendom.

Pertinent Literature

Johnson, Ralph Henry. *The Concept of Existence in the Concluding Unscientific Postscript*. The Hague, The Netherlands: Martinus Nijhoff, 1972.

Ralph Henry Johnson's interpretation of the *Concluding Unscientific Postscript,* while at times going against the grain of traditional Kierkegaardian scholarship, is intelligible, illuminating, and well-defended. In the main he accomplishes his stated goal, which is to clarify the concept of existence as presented in the *Postscript.*

The title page of the *Postscript* lists the author as "Johannes Climacus," one of Søren Kierkegaard's pseudonyms. Much has been written concerning his use of pseudonyms. Kierkegaard himself discusses the subject in *The Point of View for My Work as an Author*, wherein he cautions readers not to equate the views of his pseudonyms with his own. On this point Johnson takes Kierkegaard quite literally. Whereas most modern critics suppose that in the *Postscript* Kierkegaard actually is speaking for himself, Johnson argues that the separation between Climacus and Kierkegaard should be kept strict and rigid. This becomes the starting point for Johnson's examination of the concept of existence in the *Postscript*—Climacus' concept, he admonishes, but not necessarily Kierkegaard's.

The central, yet often overlooked, theme of the *Postscript,* according to Johnson, is that men have forgotten what it means to *exist*. In this context the term "exist" is not intended in the loose sense of mere presence or being in the world, but rather in a higher, more strict sense that requires elucidation. The significance of the *Postscript*, on Johnson's interpretation, is Climacus' illustration of the "forgetting-claim" through examples from science, philosophy, and religion, with the result being an indirect communication of what individual human existence means in the

strictest sense of the term.

Climacus' analysis of human existence is seen by Johnson as a polemic against the type of abstract, systematic, objective thinking exhibited in speculative philosophy and modern science where the individual becomes lost and forgotten. Men need to be reminded, notes Climacus, that to exist as a human being is to exist as an individual. In a chapter which deviates from the content of the *Postscript* but which is interesting nevertheless, Johnson imaginatively considers the differences between science (or the scientific community as an entity) and the individual. His purpose is to show that the more a person gets caught up in scientific thinking, the greater tendency there is to forget that one is a finite and temporal being who must face up to the prospect of death, who is limited in knowledge and understanding (particularly self-understanding), and who exists as more than a cognitive organism. What must not be forgotten is that beyond thinking and knowing, man is fundamentally an emotive and ethical being.

At the heart of Climacus' position is the claim that men have forgotten how to think subjectively. Indeed, in the strictest sense, to exist as a human being is to think subjectively, as opposed to objectively. This is what is meant by the proclamation that truth is subjectivity. Whereas objective thought is externalized, directed away from the thinker's own existence toward something else, subjective thought is characterized by reflective inwardness. In objective thought the relationship between subject and object is one of indifference; but in subjective thought there is an intense, active concern in which the very being of the subject is at stake. The objective thinker is essentially defined by his status as a knowing subject, while the subjective thinker is an ethically existing subject.

In philosophy there is a long history which has it that the kind of thinking that is essential for a truly human existence is abstract thinking; but because not all men are endowed by nature with the ability to think abstractly (or can develop it), it would follow in that view that not all men are capable of achieving a truly human existence. As for Climacus, the kind of thinking that is essential for a truly human existence is subjective thinking, and because all men have the ability to think subjectively, the implication is that every person is, in principle, capable of fully existing as a human being in the strictest sense of the term.

Shmuëli, Adi. *Kierkegaard and Consciousness*. Translated by Naomi Handelman. Princeton, New Jersey: Princeton University Press, 1971.

This intriguing study develops an unconventional but extremely suggestive interpretation of Søren Kierkegaard's thought. Adi Shmuëli views Kierkegaard's philosophy primarily as a theory of human consciousness. The book begins with an examination of the aesthetic, ethical, and religious modes of consciousness, then turns to the problem of alienation, and culminates with a characterization of Christian consciousness as it is actualized through faith, love, and intersubjectivity.

Aesthetic consciousness, which is the lowest level, is defined in terms of immediacy, the here and now. It arises with the momentary awareness of given phenomena, sensations, emotions, volitions, or thoughts. At this stage there is no reflection or self-awareness; the individual is "invisibly present" but "not yet discovered." Thus Kierkegaard depicts the aesthetic life as an unconnected succession of ephemeral experiences, each passing away as quickly as it comes. For the aesthete, the only time is the present, the only truth is the moment, and the only reality is today.

The mark of ethical consciousness is reflection, whence comes self-awareness. Whereas aesthetic consciousness is more a passive apprehension or contemplation, reflective consciousness realizes itself through action. In ethical consciousness there is a positing of ideals and a choosing of a way of life. The future rather than the present takes on the greatest significance for the individual; the ultimate concern shifts from what *is* to what *will be*.

Religious consciousness designates the highest level. In the *Postscript,* Kierkegaard distinguishes between two sorts of "religiousness," what he calls religiousness A and religiousness B. One of the most valuable parts of Shmuëli's study is his penetrating account of this distinction. Religiousness A is basically a deepening and intensification of reflective consciousness, with an additional factor being an awareness of God, the Absolute. Such awareness, however, is neither direct nor transparent. Reflection upon one's own finitude leads the individual to the Infinite; awareness of his temporality brings him to the Eternal; and recognition of his imperfection impels him toward the Perfect. In religiousness A, man's "ethical" choice comes in the form of resignation and surrender to the Absolute.

Religiousness B, on the other hand, which has expression only in genuine Christianity, is constituted by a faith relationship with God. By the miracle of the Incarnation, God—the Absolutely "other"—becomes known to man through Jesus Christ. It is this "absolute relationship with the Absolute" that signifies the consummate form of consciousness for an existing individual.

Shmuëli goes on to explain how for Kierkegaard the actualization of consciousness in the highest form requires a religious "leap" of faith whereby the gap is bridged between the finite and the infinite, the immanent and the transcendent. Until man makes this leap he shall remain forever far from God, hence alienated from the ground of his very being. Disillusionment, melancholy, guilt, and ultimately despair is the tragic finale of alienated consciousness. Only by becoming a Christian is it possible to overcome alienation and achieve total self-realization. Following this line, in the latter sections of his book Shmuëli expands upon Kierkegaard's meaning of Christian consciousness. All in all, the book demonstrates in its own way how Kierkegaard's entire philosophy is directed toward answering the question of what it means to become a Christian.

Solomon, Robert C. "Kierkegaard and 'Subjective Truth,' " in *Philosophy Today*. XXI, no. 3 (Fall, 1977), pp. 202-215.

What does Søren Kierkegaard mean by his claim that "truth is subjectivity?" When he contrasts "objective truth," which is suprapersonal, necessary, and universal, with "subjective truth," which is intrinsically personal, not necessary, and not universally acceptable, what does he mean by subjective truth? What does he mean when he contends that objective truth is truth for anyone and that subjective truth is truth for an individual? These are the guiding questions in Robert C. Solomon's compact disquisition on Kierkegaard's concept of subjective truth. By combining elements from Hegelian and Kantian philosophy with ideas drawn from contemporary philosophy of language, he offers a fresh approach to what is probably the most fundamental feature of Kierkegaard's thought.

Solomon exposes the fact that even in G. W. F. Hegel the notion of "truth" is understood in more than just an epistemological sense. In science, mathematics, and the like, truth is conceived as a reality or set of facts sought to be known. However, such "cognitive truth" is but one kind of truth. Equally intelligible are the kinds of truth found in morality, religion, art, and music. In morality, truth is right action; in religion, truth is a special relationship with God; in art and music, truth is beauty. Similarly, Kierkegaard's subjective truth must be understood in an extended sense of the term. Kierkegaard is not seeking to reject objective (cognitive) truth totally as it applies in its proper domain, which is science and mathematics. What he does wish to deny is that objective truth is the only kind.

The most provocative section of Solomon's essay is one in which he uses J. L. Austin's celebrated doctrine of "speech acts" as a vehicle for interpreting Kierkegaard. Austin distinguishes between "descriptive" statements (which enable a person to *describe* something) and "performative" statements (which enable a person to *do* something). The statement "Water freezes at thirty-two degrees Fahrenheit" is descriptive. However, a groom uttering the words "I do" during the course of a marriage ceremony is not describing or reporting on a marriage; he is actually engaging in it. In saying those words he is doing something: namely, making a promise, a commitment. Descriptive statements correspond to Kierkegaard's concept of objectivity, while performative statements correspond to subjectivity.

Following through on Solomon's interpretation, it can be said that objective truth is characterized by a "correctness" of description, the final proof being the facts as they exist. Subjective truth, on the other hand, is defined by the sincerity and success of a performative act. A person who says "I promise to repay the loan on Friday" but has no intention of doing so is not "truly" making a promise. Objective truth, quite clearly, is impersonal by nature. The truth that the earth is ninety-three million miles from the sun is not dependent on any particular astronomer, and the truth of Euclidean geometry is not dependent on Euclid's existence. Yet subjective truth is intensely personal by its very definition. In making a promise, it is *my* promise in a way in which no objective truth can ever be mine: it is my commitment, my life, and my decision. Subjective truth depends totally on the particular individual. This approach to Kierkegaard gives new perspective to his doctrine of subjectivity.

Additional Recommended Reading

Elrod, John W. *Being and Existence in Kierkegaard's Pseudonymous Works*. Princeton, New Jersey: Princeton University Press, 1975. A thoughtful study which argues that at the heart of Kierkegaard's pseudonymous works is an ontology which serves as a unifying principle for understanding the aesthetic, ethical, and religious modes of existence; focus is upon Kierkegaard's concept of the self and its dialectical development as reflected by the different "stages" of human existence.

Lowrie, Walter. *Kierkegaard*. New York: Oxford University Press, 1938. A monumental biographical and interpretative work by the translator who has done more than anyone else to make Kierkegaard known to the English reader. This exceedingly thorough, highly detailed study is indispensable as a guide to Kierkegaard's life and thought.

McCarthy, Vincent A. *The Phenomenology of Moods in Kierkegaard*. The Hague, The Netherlands: Martinus Nijhoff, 1978. An insightful examination of the meaning, function, and interrelationship of four cardinal moods (or states of mind) perceived by Kierkegaard as integral to the emergence of religious subjectivity. The first major study of its kind, this readable, clearly conceived treatise delineates Kierkegaard's idea that spiritual growth is occasioned by personality crises reflected by a sequence of moods—irony, anxiety, melancholy, and despair. A unique contribution toward an understanding of Kierkegaard's philosophical anthropology and religious psychology.

Malantschuk, Gregor. *Kierkegaard's Thought*. Edited and translated by Howard V. Hong and Edna H. Hong. Princeton, New Jersey: Princeton University Press, 1971. A magnificently detailed presentation which examines the dialectical nature of Kierkegaard's writing and the manner in which his individual works coherently fit together as parts of a unified whole. Malantschuk masterfully lays out the basic presuppositions of Kierkegaard's methodology, with a focus upon his progressive shift of emphasis from the objective to the subjective elements which bear on man's existential development. Fully to understand and appreciate this fine piece of scholarship, prior acquaintance with Kierkegaard is essential.

Stack, George J. "The Meaning of 'Subjectivity is Truth,' " in *Midwestern Journal of Philosophy*. (Spring, 1975) pp. 26-40. A scholarly essay which develops the notion of subjectivity in Kierkegaard's thought. The author distinguishes between the subjectivity of authentic ethical existence and the subjectivity of faith, showing how the first is preparatory to the second.

ESSAY ON LIBERTY

Author: John Stuart Mill (1806-1873)
Type of work: Political philosophy
First published: 1859

Principal Ideas Advanced

An individual's liberty can rightfully be constrained only in order to prevent his doing harm to others.

Certain areas of human freedom cannot rightfully be denied: the freedom to believe, the freedom of taste, and the freedom to unite (for any purpose not involving harm to others).

Open expressions of opinions should not be repressed, for if the repressed opinion is true, one loses the opportunity of discovering the truth; while if the repressed opinion is false, discussion of its falsity strengthens the opposing truth and makes the grounds of truth evident; furthermore, the truth may be divided between the prevailing opinion and the repressed one, and by allowing expression of both, one makes recognition of the whole truth possible.

Important political thinkers often write like men who are convinced that a bedrock of significant issues underlies the otherwise multitudinous details of human political life. How such men estimate the nature of that bedrock accounts for the important differences of viewpoint among the great political philosophers from Plato to contemporary minds. John Stuart Mill thought long and hard about the theoretical and the practical problems connected with liberal democratic government. Actual service in the British Parliament brought him into intimate contact with applied politics. Beneath the surface of nineteenth century British political experience Mill came upon the one problem he considered central to all men's long-range interests. The clarity with which he stated this problem in the *Essay on Liberty* has earned for him a justified reputation as defender of the basic principles of Liberalism. "The struggle between Liberty and Authority," he wrote in that work, "is the most conspicuous feature in the portions of history with which we are earliest familiar, particularly in that of Greece, Rome, and England." The individual's relation to the organized power of state and popular culture requires that men draw the line between what in principle rightly belongs to each. The liberal task concerns how men are to meet the necessary demands of organized life without destroying the rights of the individual.

Mill mentions two ways in which men gradually subdued sovereign power after long and difficult struggles. First, select groups within a given political domain worked to compel the rulers to grant them special immunities. Second (and historically a later phenomenon), men managed to win constitutionally guaranteed rights through some political body which represented them. These historical tendencies limited the tyrannical aspects of sovereign power without raising questions about the inherited right of the sovereign to rule.

A later European development involved the replacement of inherited rulers by men elected for periodic terms of governing. This was the aim of popular parties in modern European affairs, according to Mill. Men who once wanted to limit governmental powers when such government rested on unrepresentative principles now put less stress on the need of limitation once government received its justification by popular support—say, through elections. "Their power was but the nation's own power, concentrated, and in a form convenient for exercise." Yet Mill criticizes European liberalism for failing to understand that popularly supported governments may also introduce forms of tyranny. There can be what Mill's essay refers to as "the tyranny of the majority." The earlier question went: Who can protect men from the tyranny of an inherited rule? Modern Europeans can ask the question: Who will protect men from the tyranny of custom? The individual citizen's independence is threatened in either instance. He needs protection from arbitrary rulers and also from "the tyranny of the prevailing opinion and feeling." Even a democratic society can coerce its dissenters to conform to ideals and rules of conduct in areas which should belong solely to the individual's decisions.

The chief concern of modern politics, then, is to protect the individual's rights from governmental and social coercion. Mill argues that the practical issue is even narrower—"where to place the limit" which liberal minds agree is needed. Mill understands that organized life would be impossible without some firm rules. Men can never choose to live in a ruleless situation. "All that makes existence valuable to anyone, depends on the enforcement of restraints upon the actions of other people." But *what* rules are to prevail? To this important question the satisfactory answers remain to be realized. Existing rules, which will vary from one culture and historical epoch to another, tend to become coated in the clothing of apparent respect through force of custom; they come to seem self-evident to their communities. Men forget that custom is the deposit of learned ways of acting. Few realize that existing rules require support by the giving of reasons, and that such reasons may be good or bad. Powerful interest groups tend to shape the prevailing morality in class terms. Men also often act servilely toward the rules created by their masters.

Mill credits minority and religious groups, especially Protestant ones, with having altered customs by their once heretical resistance to custom. But creative groups out of step with prevailing modes of action and thought often sought specific changes without challenging in principle the existing rules of conduct. Even heretics sometimes adopted a bigoted posture toward other theological beliefs. As a result many religious minorities could simply plead for "permission to differ." Mill concludes that religious tolerance usually triumphed only where religious

indifference also existed side by side with diversified bodies of religious opinion.

A criterion by which rightful interference in a man's personal life can be determined is offered by Mill. Individuals and social groups may so interfere only for reasons of their own self-protection. Society has a coercive right to prevent an individual from *harming* others, but it may not interfere simply for the individual's own physical or moral good. In this latter domain, one may attempt to persuade but not to compel an individual to change his views or his actions. Mill adds a further qualification; namely, the individual must possess mature faculties. Children, insane persons, and members of backward societies are excluded from the use of the criterion. Moreover, the test whether interference is proper can never involve abstract right but only utility—"utility in the largest sense, grounded on the permanent interests of man as a progressive being." Failures to act, as well as overt acts causing harm to others, may be punished by society.

The question is then raised as to how men are to interpret the notion that unharmful acts belong solely to the agent. What are the rights belonging to a man which can never lead to harm to others? There are three broad types of such rights, according to Mill. The types are: one, "the inward domain of consciousness"; two, "liberty of tastes and pursuits"; three, "freedom to unite, for any purpose not involving harm to others." Mill insists that no society or government may rightfully deny these areas of fundamental human freedom. Men must be permitted and even encouraged to seek their good "in their own way." This means that the repressive tendencies of institutions, including churches and sects, must continually be curbed. Mill points out how even Auguste Comte, the famous French sociologist, encouraged a form of despotism over individuals in society in the name of positivistic rationality. Mill insists that any successful resistance to the individual's coercion by opinion or legislation requires defense of the right to think and to express one's views in the public marketplace.

Mill's famous book addresses several aspects of the problem concerning the relation of authority to the individual: first, the nature of man's freedom of thought and public discussion of controversial ideas; second, the ways in which human individuality is a necessary element in man's well-being; third, the limits of society over the individual. There is then a concluding chapter which shows some practical applications of the liberal principles which Mill has defended.

The first argument against repression of open expression of opinion is that the repressed opinion may be true. Those who silence opinion must act on the dogmatic assumption that their own viewpoint is infallible. But if a given opinion happens to be true, men can never exchange error for its truth so long as discussion is curtailed. On the other hand, if the controversial opinion is false, by silencing discussion of it men prevent more lively truths in existence from gaining by the healthy collision with error. No government or social group should be permitted to claim infallibility for the limited perspective which any given group must inevitably hold toward events. "The power itself is illegitimate," Mill argues, insisting that "the best government has no more title to it than the worst."

Mill lists a number of possible objections to his first argument in defense of free discussion: One should not permit false doctrines to be proclaimed; men should never allow discussion to be pushed to an extreme; persecution of opinion is good in that truth will ultimately win out; and only bad individuals would seek to weaken existing beliefs which are useful. None of these objections proves persuasive to Mill. He answers by asserting: There exists a difference between establishing a truth in the face of repeated challenges which fail to refute it and assuming a truth to prevent its possible refutation; open discussion holds significance only if it applies to extreme cases; many historical instances show that coercive error can interfere with the spread of true opinions; and, finally, the truth of an opinion is a necessary aspect of its utility. Mill reminds men how very learned persons joined with those who persecuted Socrates and Jesus for holding opinions which, later, won many adherents. Such persecution often involves the bigoted use of economic reprisals in many cases, about which Mill says: "Men might as well be imprisoned, as excluded from the means of earning their bread."

Mill's second argument for open discussion concerns the value it holds for keeping established truths and doctrines alive. Such discussion challenges men to know the reasons for their beliefs—a practice which forms the primary basis of genuine education. Without challenge, even accepted religious doctrines become lifeless, as do ethical codes. Discussion of false opinions forces those holding existing truths to know *why* they hold the opinions they do. Mill points out that even in the natural sciences there are instances when alternative hypotheses are possible. Experience indicates that in religious and moral matters one should expect a great range of viewpoints. Organized intolerance of opinions which conflict with the official views kills "the moral courage of the human mind." Mill agrees with the critics who assert that not all men can hope to understand the reasons for their received opinions, but he reminds the critics that their own point involves the assumption that someone is an authority regarding those reasons. Consolidation of opinion requires open discussion. Mill's judgment is that with no enemy at hand, "both teachers and learners go to sleep at their post."

The third argument for free discussion rests on the possibility that competing views may share the truth between them. Even heretical opinions may form a portion of the truth. To the objection that some opinions are more than half-truths, like those associated with Christian morality, Mill replies by stating that this morality never posed originally as a complete system. Christian morality constituted more a reaction against an existing pagan culture than a positive ethical doctrine. Men's notions of obligation to the public stem from Greek and Roman influences rather than from the teachings of the New Testament, which stress obedience, passivity, innocence, and abstinence from evil. Mill's conclusion is that the clash of opinions, some of which turn out to be errors, proves helpful to the discovery of truth.

The question about how freely men may act is more difficult. Mill agrees with those who insist that actions can never be as free as opinions. Actions always involve consequences whose possible harm to others must receive serious consideration. Men need long training in disciplined living in order to achieve the maturity required for a responsible exercise of their judgmental capacities. Yet individuality constitutes an inescapable element in the end of all human action, which is happiness. For this reason men must not permit others to decide all issues for them. The reasons are that others' experience may prove too narrow or perhaps it may involve wrongful interpretations; prove correct and yet unsuited to a given individual's temperament; or become so customary that men's passive acceptance of the experience retards their development of numerous unique human qualities. The man who always acquiesces in others' ways of doing things "has no need of any other faculty than the ape-like one of imitation."

What concerns Mill—a concern prophetic of contemporary difficulties in organized social life—is that society shows a threatening tendency to curb individuality. The pressures of social opinion lead to a deficiency of individual impulses, a narrowing of the range of human preferences, and a decline in spontaneity. At this point Mill, who usually speaks favorably of Protestant resistance to earlier orthodox doctrines, singles out Calvinism for harsh criticism. Modern society evinces dangerous secular expressions of the earlier Calvinist insistence that men perform God's will. The emphasis was on strict obedience. So narrow a theory of human performance inevitably pinches human character. As an ethical teleologist and a Utilitarian, Mill holds that the value of human action must be determined by its tendency to produce human self-realization. Obedience can never be an adequate end of human character.

Mill insists that democratic views tend to produce some conditions which encourage the loss of individuality. There is a tendency "to render mediocrity the ascendent power among mankind." Political democracy often results in mass thinking. To protect human individuality, men must show a great suspicion of averages; for the conditions of spiritual development vary from person to person. In fact, Mill argues that democracy needs an aristocracy of learned and dedicated men who can guide its development along progressive paths. What Mill calls "the progressive principle" is always antagonistic to the coercive stance of customary modes of thinking and acting. Such a principle operates only in contexts which

permit diversity of human types and a variety of situations. Mill laments that the latter condition seems on the wane in nineteenth century England. He suggests, also, that the slow disappearance of classes has a causal relation to the growing uniformity in English society. His general conclusion, expressed as a warning, is that the individual increasingly feels the compulsions of social rather than governmental coercion.

To what extent may society influence the individual? Mill asserts that society can restrain men from doing damage to others' interests as well as require men to share the burdens of common defense and of protection of their fellows' rights. Society may rightfully establish rules which create obligations for its members insofar as they form a community of interests. Education aims at developing self-regarding virtues in individuals. Individuals who are persistently rash, obstinate, immoderate in behavior, and filled with self-conceit may even be subject to society's disapprobation. But society must not punish a man by legal means if the individual acts in disapproved ways regarding what he thinks to be his own good. "It makes a vast difference both in our feelings and in our conduct towards him," Mill warns, "whether he displeases us in things in which we think we have a right to control him, or in things in which we know that we have not." Mill rejects the argument that no feature of a man's conduct may fall outside the area of society's jurisdiction. A man has the right to make personal mistakes. Finally, Mill argues that society will tend to interfere in a person's private actions in a wrong manner and for the wrong reasons. Religious, socialistic, and other forms of social censorship prove unable to develop adequate self-restraints. A full-blown social censorship leads, in time, to the very decline of a civilization.

Mill concludes his work by pointing out the circumstances under which a society can with justification interfere in areas of common concern. Trade involves social aspects and can be restrained when it is harmful. Crime must be prevented whenever possible. There are offenses against decency which should be curbed, and solicitation of others to do acts harmful to themselves bears watching. Mill writes: "Fornication, for example, must be tolerated, and so must gambling; but should a person be free to be a pimp, or to keep a gambling-house?" The state may establish restrictions of such activities, according to Mill. Finally, Mill argues that the state should

accept the duty of requiring a sound education for each individual.

Pertinent Literature

Wolff, Robert Paul. "Liberty," in *The Poverty of Liberalism*. Boston: Beacon Press, 1968.

The argument with which John Stuart Mill attempts to demonstrate his libertarian principle fails to do what Mill intended it to do, according to Robert Paul Wolff. Mill's argument hinges upon the distinction he draws between the internal sphere of private consciousness and those actions which affect the individual alone, on the one hand, and the individual's interactions with other persons, on the other. In the first, according to Mill, society has no right whatever to interfere, while in the latter, society's guiding rule must be the principle of utility. Indeed, the entire argument of the *Essay on Liberty* is based, according to Wolff, upon the utilitarian principle.

Wolff contends that Mill's defense of the liberty of thought and discussion is based upon a premise that Mill never makes explicit, but which is essential to his argument: that knowledge makes men happy. If, contrary to this assumption, an increase in knowledge would contribute to unhappiness, then, on utilitarian grounds, men ought to refrain from pursuing it. Since Mill does not articulate any evidence in support of this premise, Wolff concludes that the entire argument rests upon an article of faith, one which is at least subject to some doubt in view of the debates among nuclear physicists and geneticists as to the likelihood of further explorations in their fields producing greater misery than happiness among their fellow human beings.

Moreover, a religious believer who is also a utilitarian ought to be opposed to religious liberty, since he would be committed to a belief that adherence to the dogmas of his religion would be more conducive to human happiness than the erroneous beliefs of atheists, agnostics, and members of other cults. Furthermore, it is not clear that even scientific advances depend as much as Mill thought upon absolute freedom of speech and debate. Our schools do not follow

Mill's principle, which Wolff suggests would require the establishment of departments of astrology (and, one might add, of creationism and Lamarckian biology) and permission for medical quacks and faddists to practice their arts without official hindrance.

Even in politics, where Wolff concludes that Mill is right, Mill is right for the wrong reasons: It is not truth, but justice, which is served by free and open debate among opposing interest groups.

Wolff concludes by arguing that the weight of empirical evidence is against a strictly utilitarian defense of extreme libertarianism; that welfare-state liberalism is a natural outgrowth of Mill's libertarianism; and that modern American "conservatives" are "merely nineteenth-century Milleans who have refused to admit the facts, and have elevated to the status of absolute and inviolable principles the doctrines which Mill sought to maintain on empirical grounds."

Wolff begins the attack by accusing Mill of failing to distinguish carefully between different types of interests. Mill fails, that is, to observe that the true distinction between the inner and the outer spheres is really a matter of rights or norms, and not of facts. And this causes Mill to blur other important distinctions and to arrive at conclusions which are not supported by the evidence. More importantly, perhaps, Wolff challenges Mill's fundamental assumptions at the root, suggesting, for example, that Mill's personal attachment to the value of individuality misled him into supposing that the absence of all constraint is conducive to its development, whereas it may well be that judicious restraints may be more effective in this regard. In other areas, too, a little meddling may result in considerable reduction of the pain that imprudent persons inflict upon themselves. Even Mill recognized this, as illustrated by his remarks on paternalism vis-à-vis children and savages. Modern welfare-state liberals have rejected Mill's claim that government interference results in greater unhappiness, as evidenced by their adoption of such programs as social security and other forms of regulation; while the conservatives have accepted Mill's factual assessment of the dangers of governmental intrusion into economic and other affairs.

Oddly enough, Mill adopts a paternalistic attitude toward education and culture, which he feels must be imposed upon every child, but tends to be much more liberal (adopting a thoroughly *laissez-faire* position)

with regard to material things. Modern liberals, on the other hand, have been loath to impose their aesthetic or doctrinal positions upon the masses, but have not hesitated to regulate drugs, dishwashers, and airfares. Even more paradoxical is Wolff's finding that modern liberals who defend the publication of pornographic materials on the ground that they have "redeeming artistic merits" or "social value" have thereby forsworn the doctrine of absolute freedom of expression, replacing it with appeals to their superior standards of taste—an approach which Mill would have found appalling.

Himmelfarb, Gertrude. *On Liberty and Liberalism: The Case of John Stuart Mill.* New York: Alfred A. Knopf, 1974.

Gertrude Himmelfarb's major thesis is that there is a conflict between the John Stuart Mill of the *Essay on Liberty* and the "other" John Stuart Mill, the bulk of whose work represents a very different trend of liberal thought. Mill's liberalism is suffused with an ambivalence which Himmelfarb maintains has continued to plague liberals to the present day. Her book is divided into three parts: a detailed exposition of the *Essay on Liberty* and an analysis of its contents in the light of Mill's views on the same subjects as expressed in his other writings; an attempt to account for the "extraordinary disparity" between Mill's doctrines in the *Essay on Liberty* and those he expressed in his other writings; and finally, a discussion of the impact Mill's doctrines have had on modern philosophical, social, and legal thinking and the institutions of the Western world.

Much of Himmelfarb's analysis in Part One of her book invokes biographical information and historical settings as well as Mill's own words in order to illuminate the theories he was proposing and the conflicts between his various pronouncements. For example, focusing upon Mill's frequent references to society, Himmelfarb notes that this is a radical departure from the views of Mill's father, James Mill, and of James Mill's mentor, Jeremy Bentham, who had regarded "society" as a fiction, insisting that only individuals exist, and that the rulers should be accountable to the people and reflect the interests and the will of the people. It was precisely this notion that

Mill inveighed against most fiercely, for in his view, the tyranny of the majority was the greatest evil of all. Society, then, is the chief antagonist in the *Essay on Liberty,* the greatest threat to the individual.

In some of his earlier writings, Mill had contended that there was too much literature and that the public read too much to digest what it read and to exercise its critical faculties over the material upon which it "gorged" itself. He therefore condemned the public for its failure to listen to those who spoke most wisely, preferring instead to listen to those who spoke most frequently. This seems to be quite at variance with Mill's thesis, in the *Essay on Liberty,* that the truth will ultimately prevail if all views are given a free and unimpeded opportunity to be expressed. He even went so far as to recommend the establishment of a "clerisy" supported by the state with the purpose of cultivating and transmitting the national culture, preserving and enlarging the stock of knowledge, and instructing their lesser colleagues, who would serve as residents, guides, guardians, and instructors in their communities. Moreover, Mill had refused to join a writers' society—whose aim was to bring together writers of conflicting opinion—on the ground that he was not interested in assisting anyone in diffusing opinions contrary to his own, but only in promoting those which were "true and just."

At the very time that the *Essay on Liberty* was being published, Mill endorsed the principle that reforms should always be adapted to the framework of the existing constitution. It is "an almost indispensable condition of the stability of free government," he said, to have an "attachment resting on authority and habit to the existing constitution." This appears to be radically at variance with Mill's defense of individualism in Chapter 3 of the *Essay on Liberty*. He argues elsewhere that a "restraining discipline" ought to be the main ingredient of a proper education—and also that when the system of discipline failed on the national level, the disintegration of the state was the inevitable result, with the "natural tendency of mankind to anarchy" reasserting itself. It was therefore necessary, he said, for the state to maintain internal discipline if it was to avoid decline and eventual submission to a despot or to a foreign invader.

Turning to the "applications" Mill makes of his doctrine, Himmelfarb observes that most of these applications seem to be curiously out of touch with the Victorian society in which Mill lived. Indeed, the entire book sounds as though it was aimed at some other society, for, according to Himmelfarb, the Victorians (contrary to prevailing stereotypes) were remarkably liberal in virtually every sense: they engaged openly and sometimes notoriously in extramarital affairs; prostitution was commonplace; they were very free to adopt radical political, religious, and social ideas and to publish them; there were no fetters on scientific inquiry; and people were very free to engage in all kinds of social experimentation. The only norms that were rigidly enforced appear to have been relatively trivial ones which Mill never mentions. Mill himself, in response to some of his critics who made the same points, once claimed that the book was directed at some possible future society which might be more repressive than the one in which he himself was living.

Curiously enough, the one area in which Victorian society was genuinely subject to criticism for its illiberality was almost entirely overlooked by Mill in the book—namely, the equality of women. In other essays, Mill had argued for greater equality of opportunity for women, but in the *Essay on Liberty*, except for a few casual remarks (such as those in connection with polygamy among the Mormons), he has nothing to say about it.

Himmelfarb concludes her book with a look back at the intellectual ancestors of Mill's theory, including John Milton, John Locke, Benedictus de Spinoza, Thomas Jefferson, and Thomas Paine, among others, and at the impact the theory has had upon other thinkers, from Mill's contemporaries to our own time. She distinguishes the kinds of liberty with which he did not choose to deal—political liberty, civil liberties (in the sense of judicial protection of the rights of defendants), and others. Finally, she offers some "paradoxes and anomalies," including a discussion of the controversy over the legalization (or decriminalization) of homosexuality, in which Mill's doctrines played such an important role.

Additional Recommended Reading

Berlin, Isaiah. *Four Essays on Liberty.* London: Oxford University Press, 1969. Original essays on some of the issues raised by Mill in the *Essay on Liberty*.

Devlin, Patrick. *The Enforcement of Morals.* London: Oxford University Press, 1968. A recent attack on some of Mill's principal doctrines, in the context of the controversy over the legalization of homosexual relations in Great Britain.

Hart, H. L. A. *Law, Liberty, and Morality.* Stanford, California: Stanford University Press, 1969. A response to Devlin and others, and a defense of Mill's theory, by one of the most distinguished legal philosophers of our time.

Ryan, Alan. *J. S. Mill.* London: Routledge & Kegan Paul, 1974. An excellent summary of Mill's life and works, including a historical and literary analysis of the *Essay on Liberty*.

Schneewind, Jerome B., ed. *Mill: A Collection of Critical Essays.* Garden City, New York: Anchor Books, 1958. A very good collection of recent articles by various authorities on many aspects of Mill's philosophy.

UTILITARIANISM

Author: John Stuart Mill (1806-1873)
Type of work: Ethics
First published: 1863

Principal Ideas Advanced

Those acts are right and good which produce the greatest happiness for the greatest number of persons.
An act derives its moral worth not from its form but from its utility.
Although it is the intrinsic worth of pleasure which gives value to acts conducive to pleasure, some pleasures are better than others in quality.
The proof of the value of pleasure is that it is desired, and the proof of the claim that some pleasures are better than others is that experienced, rational men prefer some pleasures to others.
Justice is the appropriate name for certain social utilities by which the general good is realized.

The central aim of John Stuart Mill's *Utilitarianism* is to defend the view that those acts are right and good which produce the greatest happiness of the greatest number. This ethical position did not originate with Mill. An influential predecessor, Jeremy Bentham, earlier championed pleasure and pain as the sole criteria for judging what is good and bad. The utility yardstick measures good by asking: Does an act increase pleasure, and does it decrease pain? Bentham's crude "Push-pin is as good as poetry" interpretation of the yardstick led to numerous criticisms. Therefore, Mill states the principle of utility in its most defensible form both to counter some specific criticisms of it and to make clear what are the sanctions of the principle. He also offers a proof of the principle. The work concludes with a discussion of the relation of utility to justice.

The ethics of Utilitarianism influenced a large number of public men and helped to shape important reform legislation in nineteenth century British political life.

Utilitarianism opens with the author's lament that little progress has occurred through centuries of ethical analysis. Ethical philosophers seeking to define the nature of "good" have left a number of incompatible views to their intellectual posterity. Mill admits that history of scientific thought also contains confu-

sion about the first principles of the special sciences. Yet this is more to be expected in the sciences than in moral philosophy. Legislation and morals involve practical rather than theoretical arts. Since such arts always aim at ends of action rather than thought, they require agreement about a standard by which the worth of those ends can be evaluated. There is greater need of fixing the foundation of morals than of stating the theoretical principles underlying bodies of scientific knowledge. The sciences result from accumulation of many particular truths, but in moral philosophy "A test of right and wrong must be the means, one would think, of ascertaining what is right or wrong, and not a consequence of having already ascertained it."

Ethical intuitionists insist that men possess a natural faculty which discerns moral principles. Against them, Mill argues that appeal to a "moral sense" cannot solve the problem of an ultimate ethical standard for judging acts. No intuitionist claim about knowledge of moral principles can provide a basis for decisions regarding cases. Intuitionist and inductive moral theorists usually disagree about the "evidence and source" grounding moral principles. Clearly, then, the main problem facing moral philosophers is that of justifying our judgments in the light of a defensible principle.

Mill asserts that even those philosophers must invoke the greatest happiness principle who wish to reject it. For example, the German philosopher Immanuel Kant claimed that the basis of moral obligation involves a categorical imperative: "So act that the rule on which thou actest would admit of being adopted as a law of all rational beings." Mill insists that numerous, even contradictory, notions of duties can follow from this imperative. Kant's noble effort thus leads to decisions which can be shown to be immoral only because the consequences of some universally adopted acts would be unwanted by most men.

The fact that men tacitly employ the utility yardstick is not the same as a proof of its validity. Mill offers to present such a proof. He makes clear that no absolutely binding proof, "in the ordinary and popular meaning of the term," is possible. To give a philosophical proof means to advance reasons directed at man's rational capacities. Philosophical proofs are their own kinds of proofs. It is in this sense of proof that Mill promises to make good after he has first more fully characterized the Utilitarian doctrine.

Mill must first perform an important polemical function in replying to critics who find problems with the Utilitarian doctrine. The polemic is to serve the persuasive goal of winning over critics to a proper understanding of Utilitarianism, whose basic view of life is "that pleasure and freedom from pain are the only things desirable as ends." A corollary to this claim is that all things desirable are so either for the pleasure they can directly produce or for ways in which they serve as means to other pleasures or preventions of pain. Aware that some thinkers view his idea as a base moral conception, Mill states a number of outstanding objections to it. He argues that the objections represent either misunderstandings of the Utilitarian doctrine or, if they contain some truth, views which are not incompatible with it.

Mill rejects the argument that Utilitarianism chooses to picture human nature at the lowest animal level. Clearly, animals are incapable of experiencing many pleasures available and important to men. Every "Epicurean theory of life" also admits that intellectual pleasures are more valuable than those of simple sensation. "It is quite compatible with the principle of utility to recognize the fact that some kinds of pleasure are more desirable and more valuable than others." Pleasures must be judged in terms of quality as well as quantity. Mill suggests a way in which the value of two possible pleasures may be determined. Only that man can decide who, out of wide experience, knows both pleasures and can thus state a comparative judgment. Apparently Mill believed this test is adequate. He assumed that the man of experience actually knows the worth of competing pleasures in a manner which is not simply psychological but objective. Rational beings should choose pleasures of higher quality. Not all men are equally competent to render decisive judgments. In a striking sentence Mill writes: "It is better to be a human being dissatisfied than a pig satisfied."

A summary statement of important criticisms of the Utilitarian doctrine, along with brief descriptions of Mill's replies, is here in order. First, the Utilitarian "greatest happiness" principle is said to be too exalted in expecting human beings to adopt a disinterested moral posture. Mill's reply is that in serving the interests of one's fellow creatures the motive may be either self-interest or duty. The resulting act rather than the motive must be judged, though the motive of duty can influence us to honor also the character of the doer. Men can promote the general interests of society without always fixing "their minds upon so wide a generality as the world, or society at large." Second, to the charge that Utilitarianism will make men cold and unsympathizing, Mill answers that men should show interest in things other than those concerned with standards of right and wrong. Yet it is necessary to emphasize the need of making judgments of right and wrong and to supply moral standards for human behavior. Third, Mill calls simply false the view that Utilitarianism is a godless doctrine. Religiously inclined men can use the Utilitarian standard to determine what in detail the will of God means for human action. Fourth, some critics complain that Utilitarianism will end in expediency. Mill's rebuttal is that the utility principle does not justify acts which result only in the pleasure of the lone individual. The social standard must always operate. Fifth, Mill argues that Utilitarianism can account even for the actions of martyrs and heroes. Heroism and martyrdom involve individual sacrifices whose ultimate aim is the increase in the happiness of others or of society as a whole. Other criticisms—that Utilitarianism overlooks lack of time for men to decide the results of given actions and that Utilitarians may use the doctrine to exempt themselves from moral rules—are shown to apply equally to other ethical doctrines.

Mill goes on to admit that other questions about a moral standard can be raised. For what reasons should any person adopt the standard? What motivates one to apply it? Such questions about the sanctions of a moral standard Mill treats as if they are meaningful. There are two possible kinds of sanction for Utilitarianism—an external and an internal one. Desire of favor and also fear of displeasure from one's fellows, or from a sovereign God, constitute the Utilitarian principle's external sanctions. Given feelings of affection for other men or awe for a God, men may act also out of unselfish motives which can "attach themselves to the Utilitarian morality, as completely and powerfully as to any other."

Conscience makes up the internal sanction of the principle. Mill defines conscience as "a pain, more or less intense, attendant on violation of duty." This sanction is really a feeling in the mind such that any violation of it results in discomfort. Even the man who thinks moral obligation has roots in a transcendental sphere acts only conscientiously insofar as he harbors religious feelings about duty. There must be a subjective feeling of obligation. But is this feeling of duty acquired or innate? If innate, the problem concerns the objects of the feeling. Intuitionists admit that principles rather than the details of morality get intuited. Mill argues that the Utilitarian emphasis on regard for the pleasures and pains of others might well be an intuitively known principle. Some regard for interests of others is seen as obligatory even by intuitionists who insist on yet other obligatory principles. Mill thought that any sanction provided by a transcendental view of the origin of obligation is available to the Utilitarian doctrine.

Nevertheless, Mill's view was that men's notions of obligation are actually acquired. Though not a part of man's nature, the moral faculty is an outgrowth of it. This faculty can arise spontaneously in some circumstances as well as benefit from proper environmental cultivation. The social feelings of mankind provide a basis of natural sentiment which supports the Utilitarian doctrine. "Society between equals can only exist on the understanding that the interests of all are to be regarded equally." Proper education and social arrangements can encourage the moral feelings toward virtuous activity. By education men can learn to value objects disinterestedly which, in the beginning, they sought only for the sake of pleasure. Mill claims that virtue is one good of this kind.

In *Utilitarianism* Mill raises the peculiar question as to whether the utility principle can be proved. It is difficult to understand what kind of question Mill thought he was asking here. The setting for this question appears to involve something like the following: When someone asks if the principle has any sanctions, it is as if he were to ask: "Why should I seek the good even if the utility principle is sound?" But when someone asks for a proof of the principle, it is as if he were to inquire: "How can I know *that* the utility principle is true?" Strangely, this question comes up only after Mill has already refuted a whole range of criticisms of the Utilitarian doctrine as well as shown the sanctions which support it.

Mill argues that "the sole evidence it is possible to produce that anything is desirable, is that people do actually desire it." One difficulty with this assertion concerns the word "sole." Even if it is true that nothing can be desirable which is not desired by someone, would it follow necessarily that one's desire of an object is sufficient evidence of its desirability? If not, what besides desire would account for an object's desirability? Contextually, it would appear that Mill might have to agree that though everything desirable must be desired, not everything desired need be desirable. This would follow from his earlier claim that some pleasures are qualitatively better than others. A human being who desired to live like a pig would seek to evade realizing the highest kind of happiness available to him. To this argument Mill might have wanted to reply that, in fact, no man really does want to live like a pig. Yet the most controversial aspect of Mill's proof occurs when he insists that "each man's happiness is a good to that person, and the general happiness, therefore, a good to the aggregate of all persons." Some philosophers call this statement an example of an elementary logical fallacy—attribution of a property applicable to the parts of a collection to the collection itself. The Utilitarian stress on men's obligation to seek the happiness of the greatest number raises a question about the relation of individual pleasures to social ones. A man may desire to drive at high speeds as an individual, yet not have grounds for making desirable the changing of the speed rules. What Mill wants to underline is that in conflicts between social and individual interests, the individual interests must often give way.

Ultimately a conception of human nature must serve as justification of Mill's use of the utility principle. The proof runs to the effect that men are, after all, naturally like that. If they do not seek happiness directly, they seek other ends as a means to it. To a skeptic convinced that the principle cannot be proved by an appeal to human nature, Mill might have said: "Obviously, you misunderstand what you really desire." In this case the utility principle is proved in that it conforms to what men are like. On this basis, however, it seems peculiar to want to argue that men *ought* to use the principle in making moral judgments. To say that men ought to act in a given way is to imply that they may not.

The concluding chapter of *Utilitarianism* discusses the relation of justice to utility. The idea of justice tends to impede the victory of the Utilitarian doctrine, according to Mill. Men's sentiment of justice seems to suggest existence of a natural, objective norm which is totally divorced from expediency and hedonistic consequences. Mill's task was to indicate how the Utilitarian doctrine could accommodate this sentiment and nevertheless remain the sole acceptable standard for judging right and wrong.

One must examine objects in the concrete if he wants to discover whatever common features they may contain. This is true of the idea of justice. Several fundamental beliefs are associated in popular opinion with notions like "just" and "unjust." Justice involves respect for the legal and moral rights of other people. It implies the wrongfulness of taking away another's moral rights by illegal or even legal means. There can be bad laws. The notion of desert is also important. This notion entails belief that wrongdoing deserves

punishment and the doing of right, reciprocation in good acts. Justice cannot mean doing good in return for evil, according to Mill. Nevertheless men may waive justice when they are wronged. Furthermore, men ought not to break promises which are willingly and knowingly made. This is so even in the case of implied promises. Justice precludes breach of faith. Finally, justice implies impartiality and equality in the treatment of men and claims. This means that men ought to be "influenced by the considerations which it is supposed ought to influence the particular case in hand." Mill concludes that several general features rather than one are common to these opinions about justice. Turning to the etymology of the word, he asserts that the primitive meaning of justice is "conformity to law." The Greeks and Romans, recognizing the possibility of bad laws, came to view injustice as the breaking of those laws which ought to be obeyed. The idea of justice in personal conduct also involves the belief that a man ought to be forced to do just acts.

To say that justice accepts the idea of the desirability of compelling someone to do his duty tells men what justice is about. Yet it does not mark off the peculiar nature of justice from other branches of morality. According to Mill, justice involves the notion of perfect obligation. Duties of perfect obligation imply the existence of a correlative right in a person or persons. "Justice implies something which it is not only right to do, and wrong not to do, but which some individual person can claim from me as his moral right." This view of justice admits a distinction between moral obligation and the domains of beneficence and generosity. In men the sentiment of justice becomes "moralized," spread over a social group or community. Justice then involves the feeling that one ought to punish those who harm members of that community. Men's need of security plays a role here. The idea of right does also. Justice involves a belief that there are rights which morally society must defend. Thus justice is compatible with the utility principle, for "when moralized by the social feeling, it only acts in directions conformable to the general good."

The idea of justice requires belief in a rule of conduct applicable to all men, plus a sentiment which sanctions the rule. This sentiment, which insists that transgressors be punished, is compatible with the utility principle if the idea of justice is taken to refer to special classes of moral rules. These are the rules without which the realization of the general good would be impossible. An important example of such rules would be those forbidding one person to harm another. Such rules presuppose the Utilitarian doctrine that one person's happiness must be considered as important as another's. Mill's conclusion is that "Justice remains the appropriate name for certain social utilities which are vastly more important, and therefore more absolute and imperative, than any others are as a class."

Utilitarianism is a book of significance for thinkers concerned about the problem of moral fairness in a social setting. Mill attempted to show that men's notions of obligation can be made compatible with the utility principle. What animates the work is Mill's clear conviction that even the more exalted moral claims of intuitionists and Kantian moralists make sense only if the Utilitarian doctrine is the true one. Only with justice and binding rules of obligation can man achieve the greatest happiness of the greatest number.

Pertinent Literature

Albee, Ernest. *A History of English Utilitarianism.* London: Sonnenschein, 1902.

Just as Ernest Albee's book *A History of English Utilitarianism* offers a survey of its general subject matter, so Chapters X-XII present a survey of the more specific topic of John Stuart Mill's version of Utilitarianism. In doing so they give their reader considerable information concerning the relationships between Mill's theories and those of other writers within the Utilitarian tradition, as well as a view of the development of Mill's own thinking on ethical issues. Finally, in these chapters Albee offers a systematic explanation and a detailed critical analysis of Mill's central tenets in moral philosophy.

Chapter X is devoted to Mill's early essays on ethical topics, which consist mainly of commentaries on the views of contemporary writers such as Jeremy Bentham, Samuel Taylor Coleridge, and William Whewell. Albee makes a point of emphasizing that in these essays Mill is not only beginning to formulate the positions that he will develop fully later but that, in the process, he is also commencing the task of transforming Utilitarianism from a relatively narrow and rigid conception of morality into one that is broader and more humane. Of particular interest is the discussion of Mill's essay *Bentham* (1838), for Albee makes it clear that even at such an early date Mill, far from being a slavish disciple of his mentor, was acutely aware of major weaknesses in the Ben-

thamite position.

In Chapter XI Albee turns to more mature expressions of Mill's ethics that appear in several writings, beginning with an examination of his views on the controversy between determinism and free will, and the conclusions he draws from them regarding the possibility of developing a science of human nature. It was Mill's conviction that such a science is possible, Albee emphasizes, that was to determine the direction that his subsequent reasoning in ethics would take. It also, Albee adds, explains the ultimate failure of Mill's enterprise; for since ethics cannot be reduced to the natural sciences, it cannot be dealt with through a methodology patterned on theirs.

According to Albee, Mill had come to recognize the impossibility of basing his ethics simply on an analysis of human nature by the time he completed his essay *Utilitarianism*. As far as the details of the theory presented in that essay are concerned, Albee attaches considerable importance to Mill's departure from Bentham, embodied in his claim that pleasures differ from one another qualitatively as well as quantitatively. In Albee's opinion, such a view, besides being inconsistent with Mill's stated hedonism, is historically significant because it represents a break from the narrower Utilitarianism of the past to a wider form of the theory yet to be successfully articulated. Albee continues his account with detailed remarks on the various issues raised in *Utilitarianism,* taking special note of Mill's emphasis on sympathy as a motivating force for moral action, a view that also set him apart from earlier Utilitarians, with their conception of universal psychological egoism. Albee does not devote much space to Mill's argument in support of hedonism that appears in Chapter IV of *Utilitarianism*, offering little criticism of it—a lacuna in his account that was filled shortly afterwards by G. E. Moore. His substantive discussion of Mill's ethics ends with some remarks on Mill's attempt to incorporate the duty of justice within the framework of his hedonistic ethics, as this appears in the final chapter of *Utilitarianism*. Albee sums up Mill's special contribution to our philosophical tradition with the comment: "Seldom, indeed, has a personality accounted for more in the whole history of Ethics."

Moore, G. E. *Principia Ethica*. New York: Cambridge University Press, 1903.

The classic critique of John Stuart Mill's ethics appears in Chapter III of G. E. Moore's *Principia Ethica*. Until recently the criticisms Moore levels there against Mill's case for hedonism in *Utilitarianism* have been considered by most moral philosophers to be so decisive as neither to require further supplementation nor to countenance successful defense of the views they attack.

Moore's main objection to hedonism, which he states at the beginning of the chapter, is that the arguments by which it is generally supported commit the naturalistic fallacy; they mistakenly identify the concept of "good" with that of "pleasure" and by doing so consequently fail "to distinguish clearly that unique and indefinable quality which we mean by good." Pursuing his case in detail, Moore concentrates his attention on Chapter IV of *Utilitarianism*, which contains Mill's celebrated "proof" of the principle of utility. After having noted that Mill assumes, for the purpose of his argument, that the term "desirable" is equivalent to "good," he points out that Mill then reduces the notion of what is desirable to that of what is in fact desired. In doing so he commits the naturalistic fallacy, being led into this error through drawing a false analogy between the meaning of "desirable" on the one hand and that of "audible" and "visible" on the other. The falsity of the analogy, of course, lies in the fact that the first concept is normative and the second two are descriptive; it is this confusion on Mill's part that motivates Moore's description of his error as an example of the naturalistic fallacy.

Turning to the second step in Mill's argument, the attempt to establish that pleasure is the only thing that we desire, hence (by his first argument) the only thing good, Moore begins by pointing out that Mill actually denies his own thesis through his admission that we do in fact desire things other than pleasure. To repair this flaw in his argument he goes on to contend that, ultimately, we do desire nothing but pleasure because, in desiring these other things, we are desiring them as a part of our pleasure. Moore examines Mill's reasoning on this issue at length, laying bare a number of confusions in it, including particularly Mill's mistaken view that pleasure is the object of our desires, rather than the view, for which support can be given, that it is a cause of our desires, and the even more egregious error that leads him to affirm that money (that is, physical coins), when desired for its own sake, must be identical with feelings in our consciousness. Against such fallacious argumentation, Moore considers the best antidote to lie in an epigram taken from Joseph Butler, which he reproduces on the title page of *Principia Ethica*: "Everything is what it is, and not another thing. "

On the positive side, Moore argues that the question of whether hedonism is true or false, even though it cannot be resolved by the type of argument that Mill employed in *Utilitarianism*, is susceptible to rational adjudication. Ultimately, he contends, the issue must be settled by an appeal to intuition or direct insight into values. We are capable of such insight, and our capacities can be heightened by deliberate effort and buttressed by argument. At their best, Moore concludes, they reject Mill's hedonistic thesis that pleasure is the only good thing good as an end.

Ryan, Alan. *J. S. Mill*. London: Routledge & Kegan Paul, 1974.

Alan Ryan's approach to the ethics of John Stuart Mill is representative of a relatively recent trend toward viewing Mill's contribution to Utilitarianism with greater sympathy than had critics under the influence of G. E. Moore. Ryan does not refrain from criticism, but he also tries to evaluate individual arguments in terms of the total context of Mill's thought, with the result that their deficiencies do not appear so glaring as they had to Moore. His general perspective is that, despite the numerous logical errors he committed in defending his position, Mill made a major contribution to one of the most important theories in the history of ethics.

Ryan begins his discussion of *Utilitarianism* by pointing out that it is necessary to an understanding of Mill's line of argument to appreciate the general intellectual setting in which it was written and the kind of audience to whom it was addressed. To gain acceptance for his Utilitarian view Mill believed it necessary to resolve three problems, all of them associated with a perceived antagonism between a secular ethics such as Utilitarianism and the traditional Christian creed, which had become embodied in the intuitionistic moral pronouncements of eighteenth century English divines. (1) The appeal to consequences as a guide to moral action lacks the clarity and immediate authority of an appeal to rules of conduct already laid down. (2) Such an appeal also runs the danger of undermining the individual's sense of duty, and hence of encouraging immorality. (3) The Utilitarian goal of the maximization of pleasure was considered by many to be morally obnoxious, as witness Thomas Carlyle's description of Utilitarianism as a "pig philosophy." If, in reading *Utilitarianism*, one imaginatively puts himself into the historical situation in which it was written, Ryan contends, he will recognize that Mill's case was largely shaped by his attempts to find answers to these objections to his theory.

Ryan views Mill's ethics as forming a central component of a wider interest, which he calls "the Art of Life." Mill is not clear about what is included within this broader domain, but indicates that, in addition to morality, it comprises prudence and aesthetics. In all of these realms the standard by which our actions should be guided, according to Mill, is that of the maximization of good (pleasurable) consequences.

On the vexed question of Mill's "proof" of the principle of utility, Ryan accepts the verdict of critics that the argument in Chapter IV of *Utilitarianism* is rent with errors, but suggests that some plausibility can be given to Mill's effort if we turn to other passages in which he states his case in a different form. Specifically, if we remember that in his *Logic* Mill had offered an inductive argument in support of induction, we can view him in *Utilitarianism* as doing the same for the principle of utility, defending the appeal to consequences as the ultimate justification of moral action on the grounds that people tacitly do accept such an appeal already. The difficulty with this form of inductive argument, however, lies in its inability to draw a vital distinction—between the grounds on which we actually make moral judgments and the grounds on which we ought to make them.

Ryan concludes his chapter with a review of Mill's Utilitarian explanation of justice. Of it he writes: "Mill's account of justice is one of the most interesting parts of his moral theory; it is also better argued than most. . . ." He nevertheless does not agree with Mill's interpretation but rather finds it deficient in two related respects. First, he agrees with most critics in finding unacceptable Mill's attempt to explain the concept of "desert" (for example, in justifying rewards and punishments) in terms of the good consequences that a just procedure will produce and an unjust procedure prevent. Second, he argues that Mill's Utilitarianism cannot explain either the rules we have for what we discern to be cases of just ways of acting or our obligation to follow these rules in practice.

Additional Recommended Reading

Anschutz, R. P. *The Philosophy of J.S. Mill*. Oxford: Clarendon Press, 1953. A survey of Mill's philosophy, beginning with a chapter on his ethics.

Berger, Fred R. *Happiness, Justice, and Freedom: The Moral and Political Philosophy of John Stuart Mill*. Berkeley: University of California Press, 1984. Provides helpful insights on Mill's theories of utilitarianism and liberty.

Britton, Karl. *John Stuart Mill*. London: Penguin Books, 1953. A short account of Mill's philosophy with a chapter devoted to his ethics.

McCloskey, H. J. *John Stuart Mill: A Critical Study*. London: Macmillan and Company, 1971. A critical account of Mill's thought, including his ethics.

Plamenatz, J. P. *The English Utilitarians*. Oxford: Basil Blackwell, 1949. A brief history of the main Utilitarian writers with a chapter devoted to Mill.

Schneewind, J. B., ed. *Mill: A Collection of Critical Essays*. Garden City, New York: Anchor Books, 1968. Nineteen essays on Mill by contemporary scholars, concentrating primarily on his ethics.

Stephen, Leslie. *The English Utilitarians*. London: Duckworth and Company, 1900. A classic survey of the English Utilitarians in their social and historical settings; most of Volume III is devoted to Mill.

THE METHODS OF ETHICS

Author: Henry Sidgwick (1838-1900)
Type of work: Ethics
First published: 1874

Principal Ideas Advanced

Modern man uses three different methods of ethics, three ways of resolving moral problems: egoism, intuitionism, and utilitarianism.

Egoistic hedonism, the theory that one ought to seek his own pleasure, is one of the natural methods of ethics; its primary disadvantage is the difficulty of measuring and evaluating pleasures.

The ethics of right and duty employs an a priori *method, utilizing intuition, or direct cognition, as a way of discovering duties; but it is difficult to find moral principles that do not need qualification and that do not admit exceptions.*

Certain moral principles are manifestly true: the principle of impartiality, the principle of prudence, and the principle of benevolence.

Utilitarianism is true to the principles of impartiality and benevolence; but it is difficult to reconcile egoism and utilitarianism.

Henry Sidgwick held that ethics has to do with the reasons which men use in deciding between two courses of action and that the study of ethics is the attempt to bring these reasons together in a coherent system. Modern Western man uses three different "methods" of ethics; that is, three different ways of answering the question, "Why should I do such and such?" He may reason with a view to self-interest; he may ask what his duty is; he may try to estimate the effect of the action in question on the general well-being. Sidgwick held that the ordinary man does not find it necessary to choose between these methods: on some occasions he uses one, and on other occasions another.

Professed moralists, however, have condemned this slackness and have insisted that all ethical reasoning should proceed from one principle and employ one method. Some have maintained that ethics is the reasoned pursuit of happiness, whether one's own or that of all mankind. Others have denied this and maintained that man's reason knows immediately what acts are right and what are wrong. In Sidgwick's view, neither of these approaches could be carried through consistently without unduly constraining the moral intention of ordinary men. He accepted the ideal of unity and consistency which governs all theoretical inquiry; but he was wary of Procrustean solutions, and thought it better to leave certain questions unresolved than to do violence to important aspects of moral experience. Thus, instead of championing only one method, he sought to find a higher unity in which the distinctive contribution of each of "the methods of ethics" is preserved.

A work with such a thesis might have turned out to be a tiresome piece of eclecticism. Actually, it is a masterpiece in philosophical analysis, a pioneer work which set the style for philosophy at Cambridge University for at least two generations afterwards. Sidgwick aimed at synthesis, but his conclusions were modest and imperfect. The strength of his work lies in the sympathetic treatment which he accorded each method, the care he expended in defining and testing claims, and the hopeful and tentative manner in which he developed rival positions.

Sidgwick broke with the practice, which had prevailed in English philosophy before his time, of treating moral philosophy as an adjunct of metaphysics, or of divinity, or of psychology. Whether moral law has its foundation in the will of God or in the evolution of society, whether the will of man is an efficient cause, whether man is naturally selfish or social are questions which do not enter into ethical inquiry. Ethics is a search for "valid ultimate reasons for acting or abstaining." Problems concerning God, Nature, and Self belong not to ethics but to general philosophy. "The introduction of these notions into Ethics is liable to bring with it a fundamental confusion between 'what is' and 'what ought to be,' destructive of all clearness in ethical reasoning."

Limiting his field, therefore, to what would today be called "the phenomenology of morals," (see Husserl, *Ideas*), Sidgwick brought under review three methods of ethical reasoning and their corresponding principles. He called them, for brevity, egoism, intuitionism, and utilitarianism. British ethical opinion, when his book first appeared, could fairly well be summed up in these three positions. The neo-Hegelian position, represented by T. H. Green and F. H. Bradley, had not yet challenged the "national philosophy." When it did, beginning with the publication in 1875 of Green's *Introduction to Hume's Treatise*, the picture was no longer so simple. In subsequent editions (the sixth appeared posthumously in 1901), Sidgwick undertook to refute the new philosophy. But historians question whether he could have conceived and written the kind of book he did if idealism had taken root in England a decade earlier.

The first method discussed by Sidgwick is egoistical hedonism. We have mentioned Sidgwick's concern to separate ethical questions from psychological ones. But historically, ethical hedonism has always been closely connected with psychological hedonism and has been thought to draw support from it. For example, Jeremy Bentham maintained that "the constantly proper end of action on the part of any individual" is his own happiness. This is an ethical proposition. But Bentham also said that "on the occasion of every act he exercises, every human being is inevitably led to pursue that line of conduct which, according to his view of the case, taken by him at the moment, will be in the highest degree contributory to his own greatest happiness." This is a psychological proposition. Sidgwick said that, if the psychological statement be construed strictly, the ethical statement is meaningless: there is no point in maintaining that one "ought" to pursue the line of conduct which will bring him the greatest happiness if he is incapable of following any other line. But even if the psychological law is taken in a weak and approximative sense, "there is no necessary connection between the psychological proposition that pleasure or absence of pain to myself is always the actual ultimate end of my action, and the ethical proposition that my own greatest happiness or pleasure is for me the *right* ultimate end."

Ethical hedonism does, however, deserve consideration as a method of ethics apart from the alleged psychological law. When a man makes "cool self-love" the ordering principle of his life, he is, according to Sidgwick, using one of the "natural methods" by which men judge between right conduct and wrong. And the philosophical egoist who defines the good in terms of pleasure is doing no more than stating this view in clear and meaningful terms.

One problem, for example, that is implicit in the popular conception of estimating satisfactions—say, the relative value of poker and poetry—is to find a common coin by which they can be measured. Pleasure, conceived of as "the kind of feeling that we seek to retain in consciousness," serves as that coin. To give the theory further applicability, pain may be regarded as commensurable with pleasure, along a scale on either side of a "hedonistic zero."

Sidgwick submitted these notions to searching criticism, the most damaging of which, in his estimation, was that methodical and trustworthy evaluation of the pleasures involved in two different courses of action is impractical. He did confess, however, that "in spite of all the difficulties that I have urged, I continue to make comparisons between pleasures and pains with practical reliance on their results." But he concluded that for the systematic direction of conduct other principles were highly desirable. He thought that this would be recognized by the man who is concerned only with his own happiness.

Common morality, however, although it allows a place for reasonable self-love, does not admit that a man has the right to live for himself alone. This brings us to the second "method" of ethics, which Sidgwick called intuitionism. From this point of view, right conduct has very little to do with desires and selfish enjoyment. What matters to it is duty and virtue.

Sidgwick held that the notions of "right" and "ought," which are fundamental to the intuitionist point of view are "too elementary to admit of any formal definition." They cannot be derived from the idea of the good, if this is understood to consist in happiness. If, on the other hand, it is understood to consist in excellence, this is merely another way of referring to what ought to be. The judgment that a certain course of action is right presents itself as a direct cognition. It may be accompanied by feelings, such as sympathy or benevolence, but it is itself a dictate of reason. Unlike egoistic hedonism, which reasons *a posteriori* in its effort to estimate future good, the ethics of right and duty employs an *a priori* method, reasoning from self-evident truth. Sidgwick called it, therefore, the method of intuition.

Sidgwick maintained, however, that it is one thing to recognize the *prima facie* claims of moral insight —that they are simple and categorical—and something else to grant that their claims are veridical. The point he wished to make is that man would not have the notions of morally right and wrong (as distinct from instrumentally right and wrong and logically right and wrong) except for some kind of direct moral insight.

The systematic moralist soon discovers that not all moral intuitions are trustworthy. There are, said Sidgwick, three levels on which the claims of obligation present themselves to man's conscience. First, there is the kind of judgment ordinarily referred to as the voice of conscience, which functions after the analogy of sense perception and testifies to the rightness or wrongness of single acts or motives. But the slightest experience with men is enough to convince us that conscience, in the sense of an intuitive perception, is not infallible. Virtuous men differ in their judgment of a course of action. In their effort to persuade one another, they appeal from the particular instance to general rules which seem to be self-evident. This is the second level of intuitive moral reasoning. It comprises rules such as these: that we govern our passions, obey laws, honor parents, keep promises, and the like.

To the unreflective mind, these rules seem unexceptionable. But a serious attempt to give them precise meaning and application discloses at once their ambiguity. For example, it is said to be intuitively certain that "the promiser is bound to perform what both he and the promisee understood to be undertaken." But on examination, all sorts of qualifications come into view, which are just as obviously reasonable as the original principle. The promisee may annul the promise if he is alive; and there are circumstances in which it seems that promises should be annulled if the promisee is dead or otherwise inaccessible. Again, a promise may conflict with another obligation. Or, a promise may have been made in consequence of fraud or concealment. Sidgwick explored these and other possibilities in detail, and concluded "that a clear consensus can only be claimed for the principle that a promise, express or tacit, is binding, if a number of conditions are fulfilled," and that "if any of these conditions fails, the consensus seems to become evanescent, and the common moral perceptions of thoughtful persons fall into obscurity and disagreement."

Recognizing the weakness of common moral axioms, philosophers, ancient and modern, have sought to raise the principle of intuition to the level of an axiomatic science by formulating abstract principles of morality so clearly that they cannot conceivably be doubted or denied. For example, "we ought to give every man his own," and "it is right that the lower parts of our nature should be governed by the higher." These alleged axioms are self-evident, but only because they are tautologies. Sidgwick called them "sham axioms." They are worth even less than popular moral rules.

It might seem, from this analysis, that the entire attempt to base ethical reasoning upon intuition was a mistake and should be abandoned. Such, however, was not Sidgwick's contention. "It would be disheartening," he said, "to have to regard as altogether illusory the strong instinct of common sense that points to the existence of such principles, and the deliberate convictions of the long line of moralists who have enunciated them." And if the "variety of human natures and circumstances" is so vast that rules are not helpful in determining particular duties, there are, nevertheless, "certain absolute practical principles, the truth of which, when they are explicitly stated, is manifest."

The first such principle is that of justice or impartiality. It states that "if a kind of conduct that is right for me is not right for someone else, it must be on the ground of some difference between the two cases other than the fact that I and he are different persons." Sidgwick saw this as an application of the principle of the similarity of individuals that go to make up a logical whole or genus.

The second principle is that of prudence. It states "that Hereafter *as such* is to be regarded neither less nor more than Now." In other words, a man ought to have a care for the good of his life as a whole, and not sacrifice a distant good for a nearer one. Sidgwick said that this was an application of the principle of the similarity of the parts of a mathematical or quantitative whole.

The third principle is that of benevolence, and follows from the other two. If we combine the principle of justice (equal respect for the right of every man) with the principle of the good on the whole, we arrive at "the notion of Universal Good by comparison and integration of the goods of all individual human—or sentient—existences." "I obtain the self-evident principle that the good of any one individual is of no more importance, from the point of view of the universe, than the good of any other. . . . And it is evident to me that as a rational being I am bound to aim at good generally."

In Sidgwick's opinion, these formal principles of intuition are an indispensable part of systematic ethics, providing the rational necessity on which the whole structure is based. Egoistic hedonism would have no kind of rational foundation apart from the axiom of prudence here expressed. Nor would universal hedonism, or utilitarianism, without the other two axioms, those of justice and benevolence.

But the axioms of intuition do not offer practical guidance by themselves. They must be given content and direction in terms of the good—not merely in terms of the formal concept of the good as "excellence," but in terms of the material concept of the good as "happiness," that is, "desirable con-

sciousness." We have seen the validity of this concept in connection with egoism. All that remains is to accept it as the ultimate criterion or standard which ought to govern our actions toward our fellowmen.

Sidgwick's discussion of utilitarianism, the third of his three "methods," is brief. It need not be extensive because its main principles have already been stated—that the good is pleasure was shown under egoism and that the right action has regard to the happiness of the whole was shown under intuitionism. As we have seen, Sidgwick does not try to base our duty to mankind at large on "feelings of benevolence," or "natural sympathy." It rests on a moral cognition, as Jeremy Bentham, because of his affinities with the Age of Reason, saw better than John Stuart Mill. Sidgwick declared that utilitarianism requires a man to sacrifice not only his private happiness but also that of persons whose interests natural sympathy makes far dearer to him than his own well-being. Its demands are sterner and more rigid than traditional notions of duty and virtue. And the Utilitarian who follows his principles will find the whole of organized society rising up against him "to deter him from what he conceives to be his duty."

The fact that he found the rationale of utilitarianism implicit in the axioms of intuitionism was, for Sidgwick, a great step toward bringing the diverse methods of ethics into a higher synthesis. That egoism finds its rule of prudence among them was also encouraging. But one fundamental breach remained to be healed. How to reconcile egoism with utilitarian duty?

Theologians have resolved the problem by the doctrine of immortality and eternal rewards. But Sidgwick refused that solution in the interests of preserving the autonomy of ethics. He did not deny the desirability of such an arrangement but he saw no rational evidence for it. "It only expresses the vital need that our Practical Reason feels of proving or postulating this connection of virtue and self-interest, if it is to be made consistent with itself. For," he says, "the negation of this connexion must force us to admit an ultimate and fundamental contradiction in our apparent intuitions of what is Reasonable in conduct."

That would be tantamount to admitting that rational ethics is an illusion. It would not mean abandoning morality, "but it would seem to be necessary to abandon the idea of rationalizing it completely." And this, in turn, would have the practical consequence that in a conflict between duty and self-interest, the conflict would be decided by "the preponderance of one or other of two groups of non-rational impulses."

Sidgwick's conclusion has about it the inconclusiveness of many a Socratic dialogue. He suggested that we may be faced with the alternative of accepting moral propositions "on no other grounds than that we have a strong disposition to accept them," or of "opening the door to universal scepticism."

Pertinent Literature

Broad, C. D. "Sidgwick," in *Five Types of Ethical Theory*. Paterson, New Jersey: Littlefield, Adams & Company, 1959.

C. D. Broad's pioneering critical study of Henry Sidgwick's *The Methods of Ethics* originally appeared in 1930, and it is still the most detailed and thoroughgoing critical work on *The Methods of Ethics,* and among the fairest and most lucid. Broad's overall opinion of the work is extremely high; he ranks it as the best treatise on ethics ever written. Nevertheless, he disagrees with Sidgwick on a number of important points of substance and method and assesses his arguments as inconclusive or even fallacious in some cases.

Broad arranges his critique into seven major topics, three of which will be touched upon here: Sidgwick's classification of the methods of ethics, discussion of the three methods, and examination of the relations among the methods.

Broad says that Sidgwick's method of classification of the various methods of ethics uses both epistemic and ontological distinctions and results in crossdivisions. Broad prefers a distinction of methods into deontological and teleological, and he classifies Sidgwick as primarily a teleologist who accepts certain highly abstract deontological principles about the proper distribution of happiness.

Broad agrees in the main with Sidgwick's critique of the morality of common sense. Sidgwick lays down several requirements for genuine moral axioms: they must be clear and determinate, the principles must continue to seem self-evident no matter how closely they are examined and in the face of whatever difficulties confront them, and they must be mutually consistent. Sidgwick finds that the dog-

matic intuitionistic principles of commonsense morality do not fulfill the requirements. It is for that reason that Sidgwick turns to the alternative of a teleological view supplemented with a very few deontological principles about distribution. Broad suggests a different alternative. He argues that the dogmatic intuitionist makes two fundamental mistakes: he simply identifies rightness with fittingness of an action to the situation in which it occurs and fails to notice that utility is also a relevant consideration; he also takes it for granted that the fittingness of an action to its situation is a simple function of its relation to only a very short train of events, what Broad calls the initial situation or the phase that immediately succeeds the action. But remote consequences are also relevant to its fittingness as well as to its utility. These mistakes can be rectified by a view which holds that the rightness or wrongness of an action is a function of both its fittingness and its utility. Deontological principles will cease to be absolute and instead concern the tendencies of certain kinds of acts to be right or wrong. Estimates of rightness and wrongness in particular cases will become very complex and uncertain. No doubt this alternative is not so simple as Sidgwick's utilitarianism, but it may be closer to the truth.

Broad devotes a great deal of thoughtful discussion to Sidgwick's universal hedonistic view of intrinsic goodness. Sidgwick holds that the one and only intrinsically good thing is the experience of pleasure, and that nothing is relevant to the intrinsic value of an experience but its hedonic quality—its pleasantness or painfulness. With Jeremy Bentham he also holds that nothing is relevant to the goodness or badness of an experience as a means except its fecundity, by which he means its tendency to produce pain or pleasure in the future. Broad thinks that this cannot be true and that Sidgwick and others who try to show that it is true commit a fallacy. His telling counterexample is the case of malice. Suppose someone takes pleasure in thinking of the undeserved suffering of another. Is malice not an intrinsically bad state of mind precisely because it is pleasant and the more pleasant the more intrinsically bad? On the other hand, the sorrowful contemplation of the undeserved suffering of another is not intrinsically bad. Therefore, Broad concludes, we must be prepared to accept the possibility that there is no single simple feature of an experience necessary and sufficient to make it intrinsically good or bad; the goodness or badness will depend on the constituents of the experience and how they are related. Attempts to prove that pleasantness is sufficient for intrinsic goodness seem to follow this line of reasoning: For any particular nonhedonic quality, an experience can be intrinsically good if it is pleasant but lacks that quality. Therefore it could be intrinsically good if it lacked all such nonhedonic qualities. That is fallacious, Broad thinks, in the same way that it would be fallacious to argue that since something can be round without having any particular area, it could be round without having any area at all. Broad thinks that Sidgwick is guilty of this fallacy and that the doctrine of hedonism is almost certainly false.

Broad distinguishes three forms of hedonism: egoistic, altruistic, and universalistic. He notes that common sense regards egoism as "grossly immoral" and altruism as Quixotic. It is not sure about the universal form. While Sidgwick thinks the principles of egoistic hedonism and universalistic hedonism are both self-evident, he confesses that they are clearly contradictory, and he can find no way of refuting egoism. Broad thinks that egoism, far from being self-evident, is plainly false, and that universalistic hedonism is not obviously true. For example, he thinks that although the total net happiness in a group could be increased by increasing the size of the group but diminishing the average happiness of its members, to do so would be plainly immoral. Broad also thinks that fecundity is not the only relevant consideration in deciding how to distribute happiness. For example, he thinks that a very unequal distribution is *ipso facto* somewhat objectionable even though it might finally be justified on utilitarian grounds. Thus Broad believes that Sidgwick's theory cannot be the whole truth about ethics.

Darwall, Stephen L. "Pleasure as Ultimate Good in Sidgwick's Ethics," in *The Monist*. LVIII, no. 3 (July, 1974), pp. 475-489.

Henry Sidgwick regards himself as an intuitionist, or at least a utilitarian on an intuitionist basis, thus dissociating himself from empiricism. Despite that, argues Stephen L. Darwall, Sidgwick's utilitarian view is largely analogous to an empiricist epistemology and arises from his account of pleasure and its role as the ultimate good. Darwall believes that Sidgwick's view is mistaken and that to understand it as the analogue of epistemological empiricism enables one to see why it is mistaken.

Briefly, Sidgwick defines pleasure as a feeling a sentient being, at the time of feeling it, apprehends to be desirable, when considered merely *as* a feeling, irrespective of its objective conditions or consequences. It is not a particular kind of feeling; what makes various experiences or feelings pleasures is their relation to desire. Darwall says that this account of pleasure has the merit of being able to explain how pleasure can be a reason for action as well as solving some of the difficulties inherent in psychological hedonism. The account seems true in many instances, but seems implausible in many others, among them some of the most important for moral philosophy.

For example, one takes pleasure in the thought that the war is over or that one has helped a friend or done a good job. Darwall says that on Sidgwick's account, in all these cases if I am to get pleasure from these thoughts, I apprehend my having these thoughts as desirable *however they might happen to have come about*. This he thinks is clearly untrue; if I am to get pleasure I must believe the thoughts to be correct or justified. What I take pleasure in, what I apprehend as desirable, is not a feeling or thought at all, but rather some objective condition, some state of affairs.

Sidgwick holds that pleasure is the ultimate good and that (roughly) rightness consists in promoting it, so that his view about rightness is essentially teleological. One line of support he gives for that view is that the mere existence of human organisms is not in itself desirable, but is desirable only because it is accompanied by consciousness. He concludes that therefore this consciousness is what must be regarded as the ultimate good. Darwall sees this argument as a *non sequitur*, as had James Seth before him. It does not follow from the fact that I cannot take pleasure in some state of the world unless I am aware of it, that what I apprehend as ultimately desirable is my awareness of it. Darwall suggests that Sidgwick's acceptance of this fallacious argument, together with his claim that pleasure is the ultimate good, constitutes an empiricism comparable to epistemological empiricism—this not-withstanding the fact that Sidgwick himself remarks that experience cannot tell us that anyone ought to seek pleasure. Pleasure plays the role of the "given" and the foundation of morality just as sense data play the role of the "given" and the foundation of knowledge. Naturally then, according to Darwall, Sidgwick's view falls prey to some of the same problems which beset empiricism. Egoistic hedonism becomes the same vexing problem for

Sidgwick that solipsism became for the empiricists. It is one's own pleasure which is presented in experience as desirable. How, then, can one come to know, or can one know at all, that the aggregate pleasure of all persons is good? Sidgwick concedes that the egoist may decline to agree that there is any such thing as the universal good, and he admits that if the egoist does so decline, he knows of no way to prove him mistaken. Sidgwick ultimately acknowledges the possibility of a fundamental and irredeemable contradiction in our intuitions about what is reasonable in conduct.

The lessons to be learned from Sidgwick's errors are similar to those Immanuel Kant taught about early empiricism. Moral philosophy ought to begin not with the question of what presents itself to us as in itself desirable, but with the question of what constitutes *practical* experience which we can reason about. Darwall says that if there are principles which govern practical experience, these principles are surely relevant to a theory of the right, and they cannot be found in the direction in which Sidgwick is looking for them. That is because their ground is that they are constitutive principles of practical experience of rational agents and not that they are apprehended as desirable. Sidgwick's teleological approach, then, must actually reverse the proper order of inquiry. As Darwall puts it, "A theory of the right is prior to a theory of value."

Raphael, D. D. "Sidgwick on Intuitionism," in *The Monist*. LVIII, no. 3 (July, 1974), pp. 405-419.

D. D. Raphael discusses Henry Sidgwick's account of intuitionism and its role in relation to the particular sort of utilitarianism that Sidgwick himself embraces. Sidgwick attempts a kind of reconciliation between intuitionism and utilitarianism, calling himself a utilitarian on an intuitionist basis. He distinguishes three kinds of intuitionism: perceptual, dogmatic, and philosophical. Perceptual intuitionism is the view that in each particular case we apprehend what is right without employing general rules to reason to conclusions. Dogmatic intuitionism holds that there are several general, independent, and self-evident moral principles and that we refer to these

principles in making judgments about particular cases. Sidgwick thinks that this is the method used by enlightened common sense, but that it is defective in several important respects. The principles do not form a coherent system; indeed, they often conflict with one another, and the method gives no guidance about how the conflicts should be settled. The principles are often indeterminate in their application to particular cases; and upon close scrutiny, the principles raise skeptical doubts about their supposed self-evidence.

Philosophical intuitionism finally attempts to refine dogmatic intuitionism by providing a set of principles which are undoubtedly self-evident, co-herent, clear, and determinate, that will enable us to resolve conflicts and show us the relationships of the rules of morality to one another. Sidgwick's own version of philosophical intuitionism attempts to remedy the defects of dogmatic intuitionism by combining principles of justice, prudence, and rational benevolence. Justice as a principle separate from utility is purely formal; it amounts to impartiality—treating like cases alike. Substantive justice, Sidgwick believes, is grounded entirely on utility. Departures from equality of treatment can be justified, according to Sidgwick, only on some reasonable ground. Raphael points out that such a ground can only be utilitarian, for any other ground would require additional self-evident principles beyond those Sidgwick is willing to admit. Further, says Raphael, as a utilitarian Sidgwick must hold that when such reasonable grounds exist, discrimination is not only permissible but also morally required, and consequently equity as an independent moral principle becomes trivial. Sidgwick's principle of impartiality seems on the surface to require impartiality in cases in which common sense also requires it, but if utility is the one and only reasonable ground for discrimination, there can be cases in which the agent's own personal satisfaction in acting partially toward one of several parties, say, because he likes him, can tip an otherwise equal balance of utility and justify or, indeed, require discrimination.

Even if we ignore such cases, Raphael believes Sidgwick's principles to be still relatively trivial, for they require equal treatment only when the consequences of alternatives appear to be equal with regard to happiness. That is because a difference in utility, in Sidgwick's view, is always a sufficient reason for preferring one course of action to another. Raphael thinks that, on the contrary, equity and utility can give rise to opposed claims, requiring a striking of a balance between them.

This consideration leads Raphael to his last and most significant comment on Sidgwick's argument for utilitarianism as a way of rationalizing the morality of common sense. Sidgwick, when describing the principles of commonsense morality, does not include the principle of utility among them, and can therefore introduce the principle as a higher order, one which is able to act as moral arbiter when commonsense principles conflict. Sidgwick does not take into account the real possibility of conflict between the principle of utility itself and other moral principles. Sidgwick seems to make the assumption that the principle of utility plays no role at the lower level of commonsense morality, an assumption Raphael regards as absurd. It is true that practical moral conflicts are sometimes settled by appeal to the principle of utility, but this is an appeal to one principle already belonging to the morality of common sense, not a new, higher level principle. Sidgwick likewise overlooks the fact that sometimes conflicts are also settled by appeal to other principles, such as justice or conscientiousness. Thus, according to Raphael, Sidgwick's attempt to rationalize dogmatic intuitionism by appeal to utility as a higher order principle at once self-evident, providing the main foundation for morality, and capable of resolving conflicts, falls to the ground.

Additional Recommended Reading

Havard, William C. *Henry Sidgwick and Later Utilitarian Political Philosophy*. Gainesville: University of Florida Press, 1959. Mainly historical rather than critical. Defines Sidgwick's place in the British utilitarian and Liberal tradition. On Sidgwick's differences with Bentham and Mill and his reconciliation of utilitarianism with intuitionism, see especially Chapter 4, "Reconstruction of the Utilitarian Ethic."

The Monist. LVIII, no. 3 (July,1974). Entire issue devoted to Sidgwick. Contains several excellent historical and critical articles by J. B. Schneewind, W. K. Frankena, M. Singer, and P. Singer, among others, in addition to those reviewed above.

Schneewind, J. B. "First Principles and Common Sense Morality in Sidgwick's Ethics," in *Archiv fur Geschichte der Philosophie.* XLV, Heft 2 (1963), pp. 137-156. Gives an account of the methodology Sidgwick uses to support utilitarianism.

_____. *Sidgwick's Ethics and Victorian Moral Philosophy.* Oxford: Clarendon Press, 1977. Gives the historical context for the problems Sidgwick was addressing. Contains the longest and possibly the best expository interpretation of *The Methods of Ethics* itself, as well as a brief account of Sidgwick's later disagreements with T. H. Green, F. H. Bradley, and Herbert Spencer.

THUS SPAKE ZARATHUSTRA

Author: Friedrich Wilhelm Nietzsche (1884-1900)
Type of work: Ethics
First published: Parts I and II, 1833; III, 1884; IV, 1885

Principal Ideas Advanced

Life is the will to power, and he who would truly live must overcome the beliefs and conventions of common men; he must become an overman (or "superman").

Those who teach the Christian virtues of pity and meekness seek to corrupt man, to destroy his will to power, and to make him submit to those who prosper from the conventional way.

Men who do not have the courage to live seek to escape by sleeping, by prizing the soul more than the body, and by seeking peace instead of war.

The overman is virtuous when he frees himself from the belief in God and from the hope of an afterlife; he is nauseated by the rabble, and his joy comes from surpassing those who live by false hopes and beliefs.

Worship of any sort is a return to childhood; if men must worship, let them worship donkeys if that suits them.

It is difficult to decide whether Nietzsche is greater as a literary figure or as a philospher. He was a literary master of the German language. He influenced such writers as Bernard Shaw, H. L. Mencken, Theodore Dreiser, Robinson Jeffers, Frank Norris, and Jack London. He is neither a systematic philosopher in the sense of Hegel, nor a meticulous critical philosopher in the sense of Ernst Mach, the philosopher of science. Nietzsche belongs rather to the traditon of philosophers who wished to tell men how to live. His injunction is for one to become an individual, and to follow one's own desires—if necessary, through the destruction of others.

Nietzsche is often inconsistent, sometimes contradictory; but he is almost always provocative. His criticisms of nineteenth century institutions remind the reader of those of his contemporaries, Søren Kierkegaard and Fyodor Dostoevski, and like theirs often seem to apply to our own century. His positive doctrine is rejected by most people and is accepted not, as Nietzsche had hoped, by potential leaders but by those hopelessly defeated by modern civilization.

There are three principal themes in *Thus Spake Zarathustra*: the will to power, the consequent revaluation of values, and the doctrine of eternal recurrence. Life is essentially a will to power, the feeling that one is in command of oneself and of the future. In controlling the future, one finds that the values which most people accept are inadequate and that one must adopt a new, in many cases opposite, set of values. But neither power nor the new set of values is desirable for its consequences. If one were to use power to accomplish some final end, one would no longer need it; if one were to realize the new values, one would no longer need them. For Nietzsche there are no final ends. Power and the revaluation of values are good in themselves; and, consequently, there is no millennium, nothing but an eternal recurrence of people, things, and problems.

These three themes are developed carefully in *Thus Spake Zarathustra*. This exposition will follow Nietzsche's manner of development which is both self-conscious and purposive.

The main theme in Part I is that the individual stands alone with his fate in his own hands. He can expect no help from others either in this life or in some imagined future life. He must "make himself" to use the phrase of the modern existentialists. As Part I opens we find that Zarathustra has spent ten years on a mountain in meditation. His companions have been his eagle, a symbol of pride, and his serpent, a symbol of wisdom. He has just decided to go into the world of men to teach some of the wisdom that he has acquired during his period of meditation.

On the way down the mountain, he meets a saint who tells him that the way to help men is to stay away from them and to save them through prayer. Here Nietzsche announces one of his important ideas, that the individual can expect no supernatural help because God is dead.

Zarathustra reaches a town where, finding a crowd engaged in watching a tightrope walker perform his act, he says to them, "I teach you the overman. Man is something that shall be overcome." He explains that man has evolved from apes but that he is still apelike. Man is poisoned by those who teach that salvation is found not in this world but in the next, and by those who teach the Christian ethics of virtue, justice, and pity. But the people in the crowd are not ready for Zarathustra's message. They think that he is announcing the tightrope walker's act. He reflects that they cannot be taught since they are not ready to take the first step toward learning by recognizing that their present beliefs are false. What Zarathustra must find is those "who do not know how to live except by going under, for they are those who cross over."

The tightrope walker falls and is killed. Zarathustra and the corpse are left alone in the marketplace. Zarathustra then realizes that one of his great problems will be to communicate his message to people too indifferent or too stupid to understand him. But his purpose remains firm, "I will teach men the meaning of their existence—the overman, the lightning out of the dark cloud of man." Since he cannot teach the multitude, he decides that he will have to select a few disciples who will follow him "because they want to follow themselves. . . ."

Throughout the rest of Part I, Nietzsche expresses a series of more or less disconnected criticisms of the men of his time. Most people are sleepers because sleep robs them of thought, makes them like inanimate objects, and imitates death. Man uses sleep as a means of escape, just as God created the world as a diversion, as an escape from himself.

Another sort of escape is found by accepting the injunction to renounce the body and love the soul.

But the soul is only a part of the body; and one must love the whole more than one loves any part. Love of the soul to the exclusion of the body is a kind of renunciation of life. Another is the belief that life is full of suffering. So it is, but the overman will see to it that his is not one of the sufferers. War brings out many of the best qualities in men, Nietzsche argues. "You should love peace as a means to new wars— and the short peace more than the long. . . . You say it is the good cause that hallows even war? I say unto you : it is the good war that hallows any cause."

The state, another escape from reality, is one of the greatest enemies of individualism. It tells the citizen what to do, how to live; it replaces his personality with its own.

Another renunciation of life is dedication to the ideal of chastity. To deny the lust of the flesh is often to affirm the lust of the spirit. Why deny lust? Nietzsche asks. Women are only half human at best, more like cats or cows. What is great is the passion of love between men and women, for all creation is the result of passion. The solution to all of women's problems is childbearing; and this is the only interest women ever have in men. A man needs two things, danger and play. His interest in woman is that she is "the most dangerous plaything." She is "the recreation of the warrior. . . ." Her hope should be that she will bear the overman. Men are merely evil, but women are bad. That is why they are dangerous. Men can overcome them only by subjugating them completely. An old crone agrees with Zarathustra and adds her advice, "You are going to women? Do not forget the whip!"

How should one die? Only when one has perfected his life; but if one cannot live a perfect life, then it is best to die in battle. Death must come because one wants it.

Part I ends with the injunction that through Zarathustra's teaching one should not become merely a disciple and imitator of the prophet, but should learn through him to understand oneself. The section ends on a note that has become familiar: "'*Dead are all gods: now we want the overman to live*'—on that great noon, let this be our last will."

In Part II Nietzsche develops the notion of the will to power. The first part is largely negative, but the second part provides the positive doctrine. It begins with the idea that the conjecture of God is meaningless because it defies the imagination. However, the conjecture of the overman is within the scope of the human mind if one first eliminates error. One cause of error is pity; but the overman is willing to sacrifice himself, and so he is willing to sacrifice others. Priests cause error. They have taken death as their God's triumph; they need to be redeemed from their Redeemer. They are virtuous because they expect a reward in the afterlife, but there is no reward. For the overman, to be virtuous is to be true to oneself and to follow where the self leads. The mass of people want power and pleasure too, but they want the wrong kinds. The overman must seek the higher powers and pleasures. He must be nauseated by the rabble that is around him.

This category of nausea is also found in works by Dostoevski and Jean-Paul Sartre. In *Notes from the Underground*, the sickness is caused by the loathsomeness of life; in Sartre's *Nausea*, it is caused by the meaninglessness of existence. For Nietzsche, the malaise comes from seeing the rabble as one would see a field of dead, decaying animals, from seeing their "stinking fires and soiled dreams. . . ."

Nietzsche's statement of his positive doctrine is often interrupted by fell criticisms. The contrast between the desires of the masses and those of the overman reminds him of the belief that all men are equal. But if men were born equal, there could be no overman. Those who have preached equality have told the people what they wanted to hear rather than the truth. The truth can be discovered only by the free spirit that wills, desires, and loves. Such a free spirit finds that not all things can be understood, and that some must be felt. The will to truth is just one aspect of the will to power. Such a will carries the free spirit beyond truth and falsity and beyond good and evil as well. The slave thinks that he can conquer his master by his servility; he has the will to power, but in its lowest form. The forerunner of the overman has the will to be master, the will to command, the will to conquer. Since he is incapable of positive action, the slave can do neither good nor evil. The master with his capacity for evil has a capability for good. If the good requires positive action, so does the beautiful.

Zarathustra asks, "Where is beauty?" and answers, "Where I must will with all my will; where I want to love and perish that an image may not remain a mere image."

If one cannot find truth among those who tell the people what they want to hear, still less can one find it among the scholars, who have removed themselves from the possibility of action and who "knit the socks of the spirit." Neither can one turn to the poets. They know so little they have to lie to fill the pages they write. They are the great mythmakers; they created God. Zarathustra's mission is to lead men away from myths toward an assertion of the will. Men who accept the myths are like actors who play the parts assigned to them but who can never be themselves. The man who exercises the will to power can do so only by being himself.

The Third Part of *Thus Spake Zarathustra* introduces the theme of eternal recurrence, but it is almost obscured by other themes. The main question is: What does one experience when one travels? Zarathustra decides that no matter where one travels one can experience only oneself. But if this is the case, then the individual is beyond good and evil, both of which require some absolute standard or criterion of judgment. There is none. Man lives in a world, not of purpose, knowledge, law, and design, but of accident, innocence, chance, and prankishness. "In everything, one thing is impossible; rationality." Of course one may use a little wisdom, but only as a joke.

But what of people who cannot accept this doctrine because they are weak in body and in mind? They cannot be expected to accept the truth; they talk but cannot think. They ask only for contentment and refuse to face life. They expect teachers of contentment, flatterers who will tell them they are right. They want those who will condemn as sins the acts that they never commit, and who will praise their small sins as virtues. But Nietzsche continues. " 'Yes, I *am* Zarathustra the godless!' These teachers of resignation! Whatever is small and sick and scabby, they crawl to like lice, and only my nausea prevents me from squashing them."

Although much that Nietzsche says is negative and critical, he constantly warns the reader that criticism should be given only out of love and in preparation for a positive doctrine to follow. Condemnation for its own sake is evidence only of an interest in filth and dirt.

If God is dead, how did he die? Here Nietzsche cannot resist a criticism of the musician Wagner, with whom he had been closely associated and with whom he had finally quarreled. Wagner had written an opera, *Götterdämmerung (The Twilight of the Gods)*. It is a highly dramatic story of the destruction of the Norse gods. Nietzsche says that the gods did not die in the way that Wagner describes. On the contrary, they laughed themselves to death when one of their number announced that there was only one god. This jealous god had lost his godhead by saying the most godless word; and the other gods died laughing.

What are often considered evils turn out on close examination by Nietzsche to be goods. Sex, which is cursed by "all hair-shirted despisers of the body," is a virtue for the free and innocent. Lust to rule, which destroys civilizations, is a fit activity for the overman. Selfishness, a vice only of masters as seen by their slaves, is a necessary virtue of great bodies and great souls. The first commandment is to love yourself; the great law is "*do not spare your neighbor!* Man is something that must be overcome."

Nietzsche turns at last to the doctrine of eternal recurrence. The theory that history repeats itself in identical cycles is familiar to us through Plato, who derived it from the writings of Egyptian and Babylonian astronomers. It requires a concept of time that has not been congenial to Western thought ever since it was attacked by Saint Augustine. For us, time seems to move in a straight line that has no turnings. Nietzsche, knowing that his doctrine would not be well received, stated it first of all as coming from Zarathustra's animals: "Everything goes, everything comes back; eternally rolls the wheel of being." Whatever is happening now will happen again and has happened before. The great things of the world recur, but so do the small. The recurrence of the small things, of the men farthest removed from the overman, seems at first impossible for Zarathustra to accept. That the return is exactly the same—not that the best returns, not that the part returns, not that all except the worst returns, but that *all*, best and worst, returns—is difficult for him to acknowledge. But at

last he is willing to abandon the doctrine of progress for the truth of eternal recurrence.

The Fourth Part of *Thus Spake Zarathustra*, not intended by Nietzsche to be the last, is concerned with the consequences of accepting some portion of Zarathustra's teachings without accepting the whole. One must take all or none. Much of this part consists of parodies of Christian views—for example, that one must become like a little bovine to enter the kingdom of heaven.

Zarathustra, who is still concerned with the overman, wonders what he will be like. As he goes from place to place in the world, he sees that man is fit only to be despised unless he is the prelude to the overman. Man is not to be preserved; he is to be overcome. Man must be brave even though there is no God; man must be strong because he is evil; and he must hate his neighbor as a consequence of the will to power.

But once more, this doctrine is too strong for the people who listen to Zarathustra. Although God is dead, it is necessary for them to make a god of their own; and this time they choose a donkey. The animal fulfills all of the requirements for a god. He is a servant of men. He does not speak and therefore is never wrong. The world, created as stupidly as possible, is in his own image. Everyone is able to believe in the donkey's long ears. Zarathustra, after upbraiding the people for worshiping a donkey, is told by them that it is better to worship some god, even a donkey, than no god at all. At least here is something that the worshiper can see, touch, hear, and even smell and taste if he wants to. God seems more credible in this form. The first atheist was the man who said that God is spirit.

Zarathustra replies to this plea for the donkey by pointing out that worship of any sort is a return to childhood. The overman has no wish to enter the kingdom of heaven; he wants the earth. However, if the people need to worship, let them worship donkeys if such a belief helps them.

No man except Zarathustra has seen the earth as it is. But the overman will come, and he will see it. He will command the earth and it will obey. With this vision in mind, Zarathustra turns again to the world to search for and bring into perfection the overman.

Pertinent Literature

Kaufmann, Walter. *Nietzsche: Philosopher, Psychologist, Antichrist.* Princeton, New Jersey: Princeton University Press, 1950, 1974.

Any discussion of Friedrich Wilhelm Nietzsche's reception in English-speaking countries must acknowledge Walter Kaufmann's pioneering book. It remains the most widely read work on Nietzsche by English-speaking persons to this day. When Kaufmann's book first appeared in 1950 Nietzsche was in eclipse in Europe and censured in the United States as a protofascist ideologist. He was seldom taken seriously philosophically, at any rate. This book changed all that; and, coupled with eleven elegant translations that he produced, Kaufmann's contributions remain a bench mark for Nietzsche scholarship.

Kaufmann's work situates Nietzsche in the mainstream of Western thought, argues that he was a great philosopher, and relates his thought to Socrates and Plato, Martin Luther and Jean Jacques Rousseau, Immanuel Kant and Georg Wilhelm Friedrich Hegel, Johann Wolfgang von Goethe, and Heinrich Heine. In doing this Kaufmann emancipates Nietzsche from Charles Darwin, Arthur Schopenhauer, and Adolf Hitler alike, by reference to whom he had previously and typically been understood.

The book is divided into four parts, preceded by a "prologue" and succeeded by an "epilogue." The Prologue, "The Nietzsche Legend," undermines the various distortions of Nietzsche which had then gained widespread currency. Part I, "Background," treats three preliminary matters: Nietzsche's life as the background of his thought, Nietzsche's method, and the death of God and the Revaluation. Part II, "The Development of Nietzsche's Thought," examines his views on art and history, *Existenz* versus the State, Darwin, and Rousseau, and introduces Nietzsche's initial discovery of the will to power. Part III, "Nietzsche's Philosophy of Power," then examines the will to power in several contexts: in relation to morality and sublimation; sublimation, *Geist*, and Eros; power versus pleasure: the master race; overman and eternal recurrence. Part IV, "Synopsis," treats Nietzsche's repudiation of Christ and his atti-

tude toward Socrates. The "Epilogue" treats Nietzsche's heritage.

Thus Spake Zarathustra is discussed throughout, but crucially in the last chapter of Part II and all of Part III. These chapters constitute the philosophical core of the book; for Kaufmann argues that the will to power is *the* core of Nietzsche's philosophy, and Zarathustra is its teacher. Hence *Thus Spake Zarathustra* is a central (perhaps *the* central) Nietzschean *opus*.

Zarathustra was chosen as the great protagonist, Kaufmann suggests, because of Nietzsche's own dualistic tendencies, which he sought to overcome through the doctrines of will to power and eternal recurrence. For the will to power is developed by Nietzsche not only as a psychological concept of sublimation but as nothing less than a generic definition of morality, all morality. Common to all moral codes—that of the Greeks, the Persians, the Jews, and the Germans—is the generic element, will to power *as* self-overcoming. Nietzsche proposed to explain all human behavior in terms of will to power, according to Kaufmann.

The process of self-overcoming which the will to power expresses is *sublimation*, and Kaufmann spends considerable time elucidating the manifold ways in which the concept of sublimation is forged by Nietzsche, anticipating, for example, Sigmund Freud's later development of sublimated sexuality. Nietzsche suggests over and over in *Thus Spake Zarathustra* and elsewhere that the sexual impulse could be channeled into creative spiritual activity, instead of being fulfilled directly. Olympic contests, the rivalry of tragedians, and the Socratic-Platonic dialectic could be construed as sublimated strivings to overwhelm one's adversaries, for example.

Nietzsche is a dialectical monist, according to Kaufmann, and the philosophy of power which Nietzsche has Zarathustra articulate culminates in the dual vision of the overman (*Übermensch*) and the eternal recurrence.

According to Kaufmann, Nietzsche's overman is not some new species or higher type; rather, it is the person who, like Goethe, has overcome his animal nature, has sublimated his impulses, has organized the chaos of his passions, and has given "style to his life." In its quintessential expression, being an overman is to be an artistic Socrates or, to vary the metaphor, Christ's soul in Caesar's body.

The doctrine of eternal recurrence is referred to by Kaufmann as "the Dionysian faith." The overman, the person who has transmuted his life into a beautiful totality, would also want to affirm all that is, has been, or will be, in affirming his own being. Those who achieve self-perfection want an eternal recurrence out of the fullness of their own being, out of their delight in the moment. Thus, Kaufmann argues, eternal recurrence was for Nietzsche less an idea than an experience: the experience of a life supremely rich in suffering, pain, agony, and their overcoming.

But it was not only an experience. Kaufmann argues that the doctrine of eternal recurrence was a "meeting place" of science and philosophy. He maintains that Nietzsche thought that the doctrine of eternal recurrence was implied by modern science. If science assumes a finite amount of energy in a finite space and an infinite time, it might follow that only a finite number of configurations of the power quanta is possible. Thus, argues Kaufmann, Nietzsche regarded the doctrine of eternal recurrence—despite the experiential thrust stressed in *Thus Spake Zarathustra*—as "the most scientific of all possible hypotheses." And, of course, Zarathustra was its prophet and its teacher.

Alderman, Harold. *Nietzsche's Gift*. Athens: Ohio University Press, 1977.

Harold Alderman's *Nietzsche's Gift* is an extremely difficult book to describe, primarily because it is a work which insists that philosophy is a kind of theater of self-enactment rather than a statable series of issues about questions which are decidable in principle. The chief reason for including it here, then, is that it is the *only* book-length treatment of Friedrich Wilhelm Nietzsche's *Thus Spake Zarathustra* available in the English language. It moves within the orbit of the phenomenological tradition and is most indebted to Martin Heidegger. Its principal "adversaries" are commentators like Arthur C. Danto on the one hand—persons who try to see the argument beneath the surface prose and try to relate this to perennial questions in the history of philosophy—and Walter Kaufmann on the other hand. Kaufmann's book would be characterized by Alderman as a "historical-comparative" study, one which he wishes to contrast with his "philosophical" study. Books about Nietzsche, Alderman asserts, are not books of philosophy, a deficiency he seeks to remedy in treating Nietzsche as the foremost "philosopher of philosophy."

Alderman's investigation of *Thus Spake Zarathustra* emerges against the background of three questions: What do we do in trying to deal theoretically with the diffuse problems and perplexities we encounter in one another and the world? What are the conditions and limitations of our theoretical explications of our *praxis*? What does it mean to be serious about thinking?

In seeking to answer such questions, Alderman argues that *Thus Spake Zarathustra* is itself an exhibition of the structures of philosophical experience. As a result, the narrative content of *Thus Spake Zarathustra* becomes an essential feature of its meaning, and the voiced character of an idea is central to understanding the sense in which a thinker becomes both free and responsible in acknowledging the playful character of his philosophizing.

The book consists of eight chapters. The first chapter, "Nietzsche's Masks," is concerned primarily to differentiate Alderman's reading from other readings. It is suggested that *Thus Spake Zarathustra* is Nietzsche's *magnum opus*, that it is the touchstone for any interpretation of Nietzsche's work. It also argues suggestively how Nietzsche's dictum—whatever is profound loves masks—applies self-referentially in that Nietzsche's aphoristic style, along with the use of allegories and metaphors, constitutes his masking device.

The second chapter, "The Camel, the Lion, and

the Child," takes Zarathustra's opening speech—
"On the Three Metamorphoses"—as its hermeneutic
guide in order to illustrate the cyclical structure of
experience, which must necessarily be reenacted in
the process of self-encounter. According to Alderman, the three metamorphoses state the structure of
"the theatre of philosophy." The section of *Thus
Spake Zarathustra* to which this speech belongs,
Part I, culminates with the speech "On Voluntary
Death." Here, Alderman argues, we are confronted
on the literal level with human finitude and on the
metaphorical level with the temporary character
of all self-conceptions and ideas. Alderman suggests that Nietzsche's injunction—"Die at the right
time!"—indicates that a genuine human life is not to
be measured by the length of its duration; but it also
suggests for him that within the boundaries of a finite
existence no permanent meaning may be assumed.
This latter point may be generalized to identify Alderman's approach. He argues throughout that it is
Nietzsche's view that all meanings are finite which
are invoked to cope with human finitude. There are
no final, univocal interpretations of life and world
available, as long as the need to interpret life remains.

Chapter III, "Silence and Laughter," advances
Alderman's historicist theme further. It is argued that
to understand Nietzsche's doctrines we must understand why they are spoken, understand that in *Thus
Spake Zarathustra* a philosophical revolution occurs
through the rediscovery and exploration of the range
and limits of human speech.

Chapter IV, " The Thinker at Play: Value and
Will," explores the relationship between value and
will to power within the existential-phenomenologi-
cal matrix. Alderman offers an interesting list of the
identifying characteristics of the "slave" and "master" moralities—a list which is of course meant to be
neither exhaustive nor logically necessary:

Slave/Master

1. resentful/expresses anger directly
2. reactionary (negative)/creative (positive)
3. other-directed/self-directive
4. other-worldly/this-worldly
5. self-deceptive/self-aware
6. humble (meek)/proud (*not* vain)
7. altruistic/egoistic
8. prudent/experimental
9. democratic (self-indulgent)/aristocratic (value
   hierarchy)
10. confessional/discrete (masked)
11. morality of principles/morality of persons
12. weak-willed/strong-willed
13. Good (weakness) vs. Evil (strength)/Good
    (strength) vs. Bad (weakness)

The remaining four chapters cover "The Drama of
Eternal Recurrence," "The Comedy of Affirmation,"
"Philosophy as Drama: Nietzsche as Philosopher,"
and an epilogue, "Who is Nietzsche's Zarathustra?"
The doctrine of eternal recurrence is discussed in
detail and it is argued not only that the cosmological
version is untenable but also that Nietzsche never
intended to teach a cosmological doctrine.

Chapter VI is a detailed discussion of Part IV of
Thus Spake Zarathustra. It is argued that Nietzsche's
serious and comedic recapitulation of his major
themes indicates the personal conditions under
which affirmation of any doctrine may be appropriately made. Chapter VII briefly relates Alderman's
construction of *Thus Spake Zarathustra* to four other
works Nietzsche published: *The Birth of Tragedy,
Beyond Good and Evil, The Gay Science,* and *Toward
a Genealogy of Morals*. The epilogue, Chapter VIII,
is Alderman's attempt to differentiate his interpretation from that of Martin Heidegger.

Additional Recommended Reading

Danto, Arthur C. *Nietzsche as Philosopher*. New York: Macmillan Publishing Company, 1965. An attempt to
    relate Nietzsche's thought to the analytic tradition and to isolate the specifically philosophical features of his
    work.
Heidegger, Martin. *Nietzsche*. 2 vols. Pfullingen: Neske, 1961. One of the world's most influential interpretations

of Nietzsche by one of its major twentieth century philosophers. Now being translated into English, in four volumes, for Harper & Row.

Jaspers, Karl. *Nietzsche: An Introduction to the Understanding of His Philosophical Activity.* Tucson: University of Arizona Press, 1965. This translation of Jasper's seminal work on Nietzsche provides the other influential interpretation of Nietzsche by a famous existential philosopher.

Magnus, Bernd. *Nietzsche's Existential Imperative.* Bloomington: Indiana University Press, 1978. An interpretation of Nietzsche which focuses on his doctrine of eternal recurrence and takes *Thus Spake Zarathustra* as its principal source.

Morgan, George A. *What Nietzsche Means.* Cambridge, Massachusetts: Harvard University Press, 1941. Less philosophical than the others mentioned so far, but a clear and sympathetic attempt to understand Nietzsche.

BEYOND GOOD AND EVIL

Author: Friedrich Wilhelm Nietzsche (1844-1900)
Type of work: Ethics
First published: 1886

Principal Ideas Advanced

Ideas which preserve life and add to a man's power are more important than ideas sanctioned by logicians and seekers after the absolute.

The metaphysical interest in the freedom of the will should give way to an interest in the strength of the will.

Men must turn conventional values upside down in order to live creatively; the established values of society were invented by the weak to enable them to triumph over the strong.

Scientific minds are weak when they fail to pass judgment; whoever denies the will denies the power of life.

Progress in life is possible only if there are men of action who have the courage to trust will and instinct; new values arise which go beyond conventional good and evil when the will to power asserts itself.

Friedrich Nietzsche holds a commanding historical significance in modern thought in spite of a continuing controversy about his stature as a philosophical mind. Many scholars refuse to judge Nietzsche's brilliant writings as serious philosophical contributions. They prefer to view him as a poet, or as a critic of culture and religion, or even as a superb master of the German language. Yet some contemporary scholars insist on Nietzsche's importance as a genuine philosophical figure—a lonely, disturbed thinker who anticipated contemporary criticism of the classical ideal of a rigorously deductive model of philosophical knowledge and of the accompanying belief in the possibility of a completed metaphysics. Nietzsche felt keenly the impact of Darwinian evolutionary views which so stirred many nineteenth century thinkers in a number of intellectual fields. As a philosopher, he must be included in that group of thinkers for whom the philosopher's primary function is to lay bare the unexamined assumptions and buried cultural influences lurking behind supposedly disinterested moral and metaphysical constructions. Symptomatically, *Beyond Good and Evil* begins with a chapter entitled "About Philosophers' Prejudices." Written during Nietzsche's intellectual maturity, hard on the heels of a lengthy literary

development yet prior to the tragic illness which ended his career and made him a mental case, this book reflects the many important central tendencies of his thought. Its contents illustrate the surprisingly wide range of Nietzsche's intellectual interests—the origin and nature of moral valuations, the history and psychology of religion, the psychology of human motivation, and the relation of man and historical processes. Nietzsche often uses aphorisms (as he does in the fourth section of *Beyond Good and Evil*) which, though unsystematic from a logical point of view, manage to express a tolerably consistent philosophical viewpoint.

Nietzsche's writings contain numerous passages which suggest similar positions worked out in greater psychotherapeutic detail by Sigmund Freud. Frequently he shows greater interest in the question, "What are the motives of philosophizing?" than in "What do philosophers say?" When he turns to an analysis of moral judgments, Nietzsche worries about what may hide submerged in such valuations—much as a student of icebergs wants to discover what exists beneath the surface. Perhaps the valuations produced by moralists always represent a perspective on things in the sense that there may exist no final metaphysical standpoint from which to render such valuations. In a similar manner, the philosophical quest after truth may peculiarly express what Nietzsche terms the "will to power" rather than a disinterested description of things. Even assuming that genuine truth can be obtained in principle, Nietzsche points out that the value of an idea has greater significance than the truth of the idea. The value perspectives by which individuals live may be necessary and yet not objective. "Un-truth" may carry greater value than "truth" in many situations. Such perspectives must be judged in terms of the degree to which they are life-furthering. "Even behind logic and its apparent sovereignty of development stand value judgments," Nietzsche suggests early in *Beyond Good and Evil*; "or, to speak more plainly, physiological demands for preserving a certain type of life." On this supposition, a psychologist would ask of any belief whether it is conducive to sound health (a therapeutic matter) rather than whether it is true. " True" and "health-producing" become synonymous in Nietzsche's treatment of ideas.

Nietzsche criticizes a philosopher like Immanuel Kant for having assumed existence of an unknowable "thing-in-itself " behind the phenomenal universe available to science. Similarly, he shows scorn for Hegel, who sought to find in the antithetical aspects of existence (passions, ideas, moral valuations) the expressions of a more fundamental rational reality. The tendency toward dualism, by which the "I" as subject stands independent of that which is perceived (as well as logically distinct as "subject" over against "object"), receives criticism as a possible grammatical prejudice erected into a false and misleading metaphysical argument. Rather than philosophizing in "the grand manner," Nietzsche encourages piecemeal treatment of a host of specific, clearly stated problems. Physiology may hold the key to solution of a number of old and baffling questions, including moral ones.

A philosophical investigator must forgo easy solutions happening to fit his prejudices—just as physiologists must cease thinking that the basic drive behind organic life is that toward self-preservation. The will to power may prove more fundamental than desire of self-preservation. The will to power expresses an expansive, assimilating, positive, value-creating tendency in existence, nonhuman as well

as human. There may also be no immediate certainties like the philosopher's "I think" or "Schopenhauer's superstition, 'I will.' " The older superstition that thinking activity results from a human will requires sophisticated and subtle analysis, for "A thought comes when 'it' and not when 'I' will." Indeed, even to say, "*It* is thought," instead of "I think," may cause another set of misleading metaphysical puzzles to arise. Nietzsche also argues that the metaphysical question about freedom of the will results from misuses of terms like "cause" and "effect," which are simply concepts. These concepts are fictions useful for the facilitation of common understanding but not as explanations. Men must stop creating myths about an objective reality based on pure concepts useful for other ends. There is neither "free" nor "non-free" will, according to Nietzsche, but simply "strong will and weak will."

Psychological investigations done previous to Nietzsche's day are found suspect because of the subtle ways in which their conclusions reflect human prejudices and fears. This theme sounds constantly throughout Nietzsche's writings. Nietzsche wanted a new kind of psychologist able to resist the unconscious forces in himself influencing him to accept conclusions dictated by his "heart." The evidence is what must count in such investigations. He asks his readers to imagine an investigator in physiology-psychology who possesses the courage to believe that greed, hatred, envy, and such passions are "the passions upon which life is conditioned, as things which must be present in the total household of life." So, too, the new philosophical breed will approach the study of the origins of morals with a ruthless honesty.

In a later book, *Toward a Geneology of Morals* (1887), Nietzsche in practice attempted the kind of historical-genetic investigation his *Beyond Good and Evil* recommends in principle. In the former book it is suggested that the concepts "good" and "bad," as well as "good" and "evil," arose out of a spiteful transvaluation of classical values by the meek and the lowly. "Bad" is the valuation placed on acts previously termed "good" in an aristocratic, healthy culture. Jewish and Christian priests, expressing their hatred of life, described as "evil" those biological functions fundamental to creation and healthful strength.

The central suggestion in *Beyond Good and Evil* is that another transvaluation of human values must now follow from the evolutionary notion of the will to power—that the cultural standpoint of Western Europe so influenced by Christian valuations must undergo a deep change certain to usher in gigantic, even sometimes cataclysmic, alterations in the table of values. Man is seen as a being who must "get beyond" existing valuations in order to live creatively and even dangerously. A culture whose established values are foundering, in which the faith in metaphysical absolutes wobbles unsteadily on aging legs, throws up the question whether the belief in the possibility of an objectively justifiable morality is not an illusion. Never does Nietzsche say that men can live without making valuations. Nor does he argue that moral valuations are unqualifiedly relative— one as good as another. His point is psychological and critical. Nietzsche believed that man's nature, a product of evolution, demands the constant creation of new valuations even in the face of the absence of absolute standards. This aspect of his thought brings to mind contemporary existentialist thought which, however differently expressed by numerous existentialist writers, responds to the anguish of the human situation by making value judgments possible even though absolutes are lacking.

Nietzsche warns that the new philosopher must guard against some of the characteristics of the "intellectuals." This is a theme expressed early in his literary life (in *The Use and Abuse of History*, 1874, for example), when Nietzsche cautioned against bringing up a German generation so preoccupied with history that the *value* of those things whose history is studied could receive neither affirmation nor denial. Intellectualistic pursuit of objective knowledge tends to weaken the critical and evaluative capacities needed by men as a basis for living. Nietzsche never ridicules the scientific quest after objective knowledge as such. What he warns against is the production of scientific minds unable to make judgments about better and worse. Objective knowledge functions valuably only as a means to some other end or ends, like those which actualize human potentiality in all its possible varieties. Scientific knowledge fails to show men what things they should

say "Yes" and "No" to from a valuational standpoint. Judgment is a function of the will—something which the scientific man can never determine.

For long centuries men decided on the value of actions by reference to their consequences. Nietzsche calls this the *pre-moral* period. Since he elsewhere caricatures English utilitarian thought, one must assume that Nietzsche thinks little of a value standard based on the tendency of acts to produce pleasure rather than pain. A second period, lasting for the past ten thousand years (according to Nietzsche who made no anthropological survey of such an enormous space of historical time), is marked by a predominant tendency to judge the value or worthlessness of an act by its origins. "The origin of an action was interpreted to rest, in a very definite sense, on an *intent*." Such an intentional yardstick for judging actions reflected an aristocratic stance. In his own time, Nietzsche believed neither the intent nor the consequences of an act would play the crucial role. This would be the *amoral* period. In a famous passage, Nietzsche characterizes the nature of the philosophers who would conduct new amoral analyses of human valuations: "A new species of philosopher is coming up over the horizon. I risk baptizing them with a name that is not devoid of peril. As I read them (as they allow themselves to be read—for it is characteristic of their type that they wish to remain riddles in some sense), these philosophers of the future have a right (perhaps also a wrong!) to be called: *Experimenters*. This name itself is only an experiment, and, if you will, a temptation." These thinkers will view pain and suffering as the necessary preconditions of any new valuations. They will also issue commands rather than simply describe or explain.

Nietzsche's treatment of what he calls "the peculiar nature of religion" bears a crucial relation to his prophesied transvaluation of existing values. According to Nietzsche, a student of religious phenomena should develop that kind of malicious subtlety which the moral investigator needs in all times and places if he is to succeed in his work. Although he despised the moral values taught by traditional Christianity, Nietzsche nonetheless admired the psychological self-discipline of the Christian saints. Religious phenomena fascinated him. The faith demanded of early Christians, a rarely attained reality, provides an example possessing peculiarly tough and lasting appeal. Nietzsche writes that contemporary men lack the corresponding toughness to appreciate the paradoxical statement of faith: God dies on a cross. Early Christian faith demanded qualities found in a modern Pascal, according to Nietzsche. In Pascal this faith "looks in a horrible way like a continuous suicide of the reason, a tough, long-lived, worm-like reason which cannot be killed at one time and with one blow." Nietzsche believed that such a faith would require careful study if the new experimenters were to learn how to succeed in their own transvaluation of Christian values. Especially intriguing are the three restrictions associated with what Nietzsche calls "the religious neurosis"—solitude, fasting, and sexual abstinence. For a student to understand the earlier historical transvaluation which occurred he must answer the question: "How is the saint possible?" Genuinely to understand how from the "bad" man one gets, suddenly, a saint requires one to compare Christianity's valuations to the lavish gratitude characteristic of earlier Greek religion before fear made Christianity a possibility.

Nietzsche argues that the study of moral and religious phenomena can never be the work of a day or a brief season. Modern thinkers can hope only to assemble the necessary evidence, slowly and painstakingly. Their first concern is the statement of a morphology of morality rather than the former ambitious attempt to give a philosophical justification of the derivation of a morality. Only "the collection of the material, the conceptual formalization and arrangement of an enormous field of delicate value-feelings and value-differences which are living, growing, generating others, and perishing" is possible at the present time along with some observations about recurrent features of these value growths. Investigators must know where to look for the proper evidence. For this task, the scientific man lacks the capacities needed for directing the investigations. The scientific man functions best as an instrument—an enormously valuable one. Yet the instrument "belongs in the hands of one who has greater power"—one who commands what uses the instrument shall be put to. Most philosophers also fail to qualify for this

kind of moral analysis. The reason is that they have reduced philosophizing to theory of knowledge, which produces a value skepticism when what is required is action—value-commanding and value-judging.

The whole problem of understanding moral valuations is reminiscent of the older Faith versus Reason controversy in theology. Does "instinct" (the tendency to act creatively without always knowing how to give reasons for one's actions) hold a more important place in the subject matter of moral analysis than reasoning (the capacity to give reasons for one's valuations)? This problem emerges early in the character of Soctrates—a philosopher whom Nietzsche admires for his magnificent irony and dialectical skills even though Nietzsche denounces "Socratism," the dogma that beliefs are valuable only insofar as they are capable of logical justification. Nietzsche considers Socrates a much greater figure than Plato. Socrates knew how to laugh at himself, realizing that his superior powers failed to discover the means by which to justify many beliefs he held important. Plato was more naïve than Socrates. Plato left a moral prejudice which Nietzsche simply rejects: the view that instinct and reason ultimately seek the same end—"God" or "*the* Good." Plato, in thus dissolving all that Nietzsche finds fascinating in the Faith-Reason controversy, made possible a later Christian institutionalization of herd-morality.

Fundamentally, Nietzsche distrusted individuals who venerate reason and deny the value of instinct. He insists that men of action illustrate the gap that exists between those who merely know (intellectually) and those who act. Any existing morality needs a horizon provided by men of action who say: "It shall be thus!" This command source of any morality must itself go unjustified and unquestioned. Any existing morality is in this sense always "problematic." By this Nietzsche probably meant that after reasons for the existing valuations have been given, there must remain, at last, a self-justifying command for which no further reasons are possible. Indeed, all morality containing progressive aspects stems from an aristocratic type of commanding. Every command requires a commander, some individual who supplies the necessary value horizon which others must simply accept. There can be no objectively grounded perspective of all perspectives. Life as an expanding process requires the cutting off of deliberative procedures at some point.

Nietzsche was willing to accept some of the painful consequences of this view of the command origin of all moral valuations. One consequence is that any existing morality requires sacrifice of numerous individuals and of many nuances of feeling and human tendency. Morality requires the application of command in such a way that not all legitimately natural instincts can find total expression at any one time. It also rests on exploitation as a necessary element in the creation of values. Some instincts must give way to others—and the commanding ones ought to be domineering and aristocratic. There must occur "the forcing of one's own forms upon something else."

Nietzsche's analysis of morality led him to dislike equalitarian democracy and herd-utilitarianism ("the greatest happiness of the greatest number"). An order of rank must exist. Between commander and commanded must arise a social distance based upon the former's greater value. The new philosopher seeking to transform valuations must stand "against his own time"—finding a value standpoint "beyond" the accepted valuations of his own era. To do so requires hardness and patient waiting. Philosophical success is thus partly a result of circumstances beyond any individual philosopher's control. *What* his creative response shall be is a function of what the situation is in which he finds himself. In this sense the philosopher must always be a lonely man, "beyond" the good and evil of conventional morality. This loneliness will produce anguish.

In *Thus Spake Zarathustra* (1883-1885), Nietzsche describes the anguish which results from the discovery that no God is found beyond good and evil. Nor is there a higher, more ultimate Platonic har-

mony. The new philosopher must learn to embrace existence for its own sake. Nietzsche attempts to express the nature of this love of existence through a doctrine of "eternal recurrence," which seems sometimes to function even mystically in his thought. The philosopher of existence must say "Yea" to reality while knowing that "God is dead." Any new values which arise in the evolutionary process do so as expressions of man's self-commanding capacity. Error and pain inevitably and necessarily are aspects of existence. "That everything recurs, is the very nearest approach of a world of Becoming to a world of Being: the height of contemplation," he wrote in the second volume of *The Will to Power* (a work published by Nietzsche's sister, 1901-1904, from remaining notes). The new philosopher of "beyondness" needs this doctrine of eternal recurrence, since he must command new values in an existence which expresses the will to power rather than a rational scheme of things.

In Nietzsche's style one finds a brilliance to match his intellectual daring—a wealth of suggestion, irony, maliciousness, a fine balancing of value antitheses, and playful criticism coupled with the most serious intention. The understanding of Nietzsche's works requires that one attempt to read them sympathetically, returning to them again and again. If he is to be judged severely for his unsystematic methods and for the disordered expression of his complex anxieties, his age and culture must also be so judged. Nietzsche was (as he says all men are) a philosopher who worked from an inner necessity to achieve self-understanding. Of philosophers he wrote: "But fundamentally, 'way down below' in us, there is something unteachable, a bedrock of intellectual destiny, of predestined decision, of answers to predestined selected questions."

Pertinent Literature

Kaufmann, Walter. *Nietzsche: Philosopher, Psychologist, Antichrist*. Princeton, New Jersey: Princeton University Press, 1950.

Walter Kaufmann's *Nietzsche: Philosopher, Psychologist, Antichrist* is the most thorough study in

English of Friedrich Wilhelm Nietzsche's work. It brings Nietzsche's philosophy into focus while also tracing his development and actively criticizing other major interpretations of his thought.

In Part III, "The Philosophy of the Will to Power," Kaufmann makes his most extensive use of *Beyond Good and Evil*. There he is concerned, perhaps over-zealously, to show that Nietzsche was not an irrationalist. Although Nietzsche repudiates the traditional dualism of reason and impulse and explains all human behavior in terms of the will to power, it nevertheless remains true that he regarded reason as the highest manifestation of the will to power, for reason gives man power not only over nature but also over himself. Those who stand at the top of the power scale, according to Nietzsche, neither act on impulse nor extirpate their passions, but, in a manner reminiscent of Aristotelian man, act rationally by instinct, through an "attained unconsciousness" or "second nature." Nietzsche, who never prescribes moral norms but finds human conduct reflected universally in nature, often equates the will to power that nature displays with the "instinct of freedom" or with Eros. For him all life is a striving to transcend and perfect itself. Accordingly, "Nothing that is alive is sufficient unto itself," but everything strives to overcome itself as it denies itself gratification for more life and more power. Human life is a dialectic of commanding and obeying. Although most men, contenting themselves with the strength of the herd in their bid for power, obey other men's laws, genuine creativity generates its own standards. Thus, Kaufmann maintains, "One of the most significant connotations of the phrase 'beyond good and evil' is that all established codes must forever be transcended by men who are creative."

Kaufmann gives scant attention to Nietzsche's master and slave moralities. He emphasizes that Nietzsche in no way identifies with the master despite his polemic against weakness. Every man would in fact be a mere animal were it not for the ambiguous marvel of bad conscience which imposes itself on an intransigent, suffering material, burning a "No" into the soul. For Nietzsche what is called "higher culture" rests on the channeling and spiritualizing of cruelty. Here Kaufmann finds grounds for saying that Nietzsche's very evaluation of suffering and cruelty springs out of his respect for rationality.

The offspring of man's self-inflicted travail is the "overman" or superman, humanity in its highest form. This overman may possibly be willed and bred in the future, but until now it has appeared only as a fortunate accident of history in the human being who has inherited the supra-abundant power of passion and reason stored up from the experience of generations. Such a one, glimpsed in Caesar and perhaps Goethe, in performing "his unique deed of self-integration, self-creation, and self-mastery," overcomes the highest resistance from his epoch and from the ordinary humanity in himself. Just as he redeems his every impulse in the wholeness and sublimity of his own nature, so he believes that likewise every particular may have meaning in the vast macrocosm of nature as a whole. He therefore joyously affirms the fatality allotted him in embracing what is at once the most nihilistic and *"most scientific of all possible hypotheses,"* the eternal return of the same. Simultaneously the overman realizes his full power as the "single one." And this is the only goal that history can have. Kaufmann sees both the overman and the eternal recurrence as denying, equally, indefinite progress and the eternal beyond. Both express the repudiation of any depreciation of the moment, the finite, and the individual. Hence Kaufmann sees Nietzsche's dual vision, whose foci might seem antithetical in character, as one of complete rational consistency.

Danto, Arthur C. *Nietzsche as Philosopher.* New York: Macmillan Publishing Company, 1967.

Arthur C. Danto's *Nietzsche as Philosopher* is the first book to attempt an analytical assessment of Friedrich Wilhelm Nietzsche's philosophy. Much of it is an indictment of Nietzsche for his inconsistency, vagueness, erroneous assumptions, and rhetorical excesses. Throughout Nietzsche's books, Danto writes, there is the sense of "an irresponsible shifting of ground and an infuriating skeptical juggling in which the juggler is part of what he manages to keep aloft through some miraculous feat of light-handedness."

Although Nietzsche claims that morality belongs to a stage of ignorance in which the concept of reality is lacking, his own *perspectivism*, "the doctrine that there are no facts but only interpretations," makes it impossible, Danto says, for Nietzsche himself to distinguish the real from the imaginary. In his teaching about the *Üebermensch* (overman) Nietzsche leaves singularly unspecific the goal for life that he proclaims. His contrasting of this ideal with the contemporary herd crassly revives the ancient idea that some men (now the bulk of mankind) are natural slaves. However, Danto insists, the notion that simply because the common man is not exceptional, he is sick, weak, or impotent is "as nakedly a fallacious inference as could be drawn." Again, Nietzsche's assertion that the strong simply are their acts of strength, when coupled with his denial that the subject is the agent of action, appears to offer a mere triviality of logic as the foundation of a metaphysics of morals. Danto finds Nietzsche's anti-Darwinism to be based on little more than a pun, and his counterdoctrine, that the weak prevail over the strong, to be manifestly illogical. Furthermore, he considers that Nietzsche, in exhorting the strong to passionate action, is guilty of assuming that the gratuitous causing of suffering is justified by the mere fact of metabolism and that any antisocial impulses can suffice to provide new moral horizons.

For all this, Danto maintains that most of Nietzsche's irrationality lies not in his thought but in his misuses of language. Although Nietzsche wrote "what seem to be bald apologies for and exhortations to lust, cruelty, violence, hatred, and brutality of every sort," in his approach to morality, through the juxtaposing of reason to passion, he scarcely deviated from a tradition that goes back at least as far as Socrates. Repeatedly he resorted to excessive language in order to drive home his points. Danto

believes that out of self-indulgence and self-dramatization he often overestimated the difficulties of his own thinking. On the other hand, his utterances do sometimes verge on the mystical, offering us enigmatic paradoxes, for he was actually groping toward a breakthrough in thought.

Danto states that *Beyond Good and Evil* represents Nietzsche's most mature philosophy. He takes as his task the reconstructing of a Nietzschean system that he finds embedded in its aphorisms. That system's central concept is total nihilism, the recognition that "every taking-for-true (*Fuer-wahr-halten*) is necessarily false; because there is no true world at all." Accepting this insight need not lead to a will to nothingness. Rather it should lead to an embracing of fate, to a Dionysian affirmation of the world just as it is. Precisely this yes-saying to the world as sheer chaos and meaninglessness opens the way to creativity, for it includes the view that the world is an infinity of "power quanta" whose essential characteristic is "the will to overpower and to resist being overpowered." Danto takes no real cognizance of Nietzsche's notion of self-overcoming as intrinsic to the will to power or of Nietzsche's portrayal of the will to power as a single force coursing through all phenomena. He speaks only of isolated centers of will, each seeking to organize the world solely from its own perspective and each locked in perpetual combat with the rest. The key to creativity is knowing that the only source of form, meaning, and value lies in this contest. In ably propounding this interpretation, Danto continually introduces a metaphysical framework largely alien to Nietzsche's thinking. Paradoxically enough, this structuring allows a host of Nietzschean pronouncements that fit readily into Danto's schema simultaneously to qualify Nietzsche as a progenitor of some branch or other of contemporary analytical philosophy.

Camus, Albert. "Nietzsche and Nihilism," in *The Rebel*. Translated by Anthony Bower. New York: Vintage Books, 1956.

Albert Camus, in the section of *The Rebel* entitled "Nietzsche and Nihilism," portrays the Friedrich Wilhelm Nietzsche of the period of *Beyond Good*

and Evil as the philosopher in whom "nihilism becomes conscious." Nietzsche was the first complete nihilist of Europe because he refused to evade the outlook common to all men of his time, which was not the simple belief in nothing but, rather, the inability to believe in what exists. Determined to live as a rebel and to destroy everything that kept nihilism from view, Nietzsche made it his mission to bring men to awareness of their lack of faith in God, while simultaneously he attacked the ideals of traditional morality for undermining faith in the world.

But the active nihilist who casts out God and the enslavement to moral idols finds, in anguish, that to be without law also is to lack freedom. Rather than live under the servitude of moral anarchy in a world of pure chance, he chooses complete subordination to fate. An eager embracing of total necessity becomes his definition of freedom. His rebellion thus culminates in the asceticism that transforms Karamazov's "If nothing is true, everything is permitted" into "If nothing is true, nothing is permitted."

To be sure, under this deification of fate, the individual is annihilated, submerged in the destiny of a species, lost in the vast ordering of the cosmos as a whole. Yet through this same acquiescence the individual becomes divine, since he participates in the divinity of the world. In saying yes to the world, he re-creates the world and himself. He becomes the great artist-creator.

In this "magnificent consent" Camus sees something analogous to the Pascalian wager. It involves a heroic game of mental subterfuge. The lucidity that began by rebelling against illusions ends by finding evasions of its own. Writing during the aftermath of the Nazi atrocities, Camus notes that this man who claimed to be the last antipolitical German, in accepting evil as a possible aspect of the good "dreamed of tyrants who were artists." He remained blind to the fact that "tyranny comes more naturally than art to mediocre men." The same Nietzsche who, with his mind only, said yes even to murder, had also to admit that, in fact, he could not bear even to break his word. But the moment Nietzsche said yes to the world as it is, he opened the way to others who could bear to lie and kill and who would actually gain strength from such acts. Originally Nietzsche's rebellion had been a protest against a lie. His affirmative, "forgetful of the original negative, disavows rebellion at the same time that it disavows the ethic that refuses to accept the world as it is."

Nietzsche's responsibility extends still further. As the solitary man of lucidity, he seemed to assent to the world quite uncomplicatedly just as it was. But accepting the world included accepting history, and accepting history included accepting the will to power as the sole legitimate motivation for human action. "Nietzscheanism," Camus contends, "would be nothing without world domination." Nietzsche, as the prophet of nihilism, knowing its internal logic, foresaw its ascendency and sought to transform the sordid apocalypse that threatened into a renaissance by redirecting it toward a superior type of humanity. Ironically, he could not prevent the "free-thinkers" whom he detested from taking hold of the will to power for themselves and, through the very logic of nihilism and the doctrines of social emancipation, ushering in their own superhumanity. Thus there are those today, Camus writes, who have corrected Nietzsche with Karl Marx and who choose to give assent solely to history instead of to the whole of creation. Camus believes that such an alliance could happen only because Nietzsche, like Marx, had replaced the Beyond with the Later-On. Once this great rebel had emancipated himself from God's prison, his immediate concern was to construct yet another, the prison of history and reason. Sanctioning tyranny, he ended by camouflaging and consecrating the very nihilism that he claimed to have overcome.

Additional Recommended Reading

Heidegger, Martin. *Nietzsche*. Translated by David Farrell Krell. Vol. I. New York: Harper & Row Publishers, 1979. In this monumental work, Heidegger is often doing what he calls "thinking the unthought in a thinker's thought." He nevertheless provides numerous insights into Nietzsche.

_____. "Nietzsche's Word: 'God is Dead,' " in *The Question Concerning Technology and Other*

Essays. Translated by William Lovitt, New York: Harper & Row Publishers, 1977. Heidegger explicates Nietzsche's philosophy in the light of Nietzsche's avowed intention to overturn traditional metaphysics through his revaluing of all values. In so doing he goes on to show from his own point of view that Nietzsche actually still stands squarely in that tradition and indeed embodies its culmination.

Hollingdale, R. J. *Nietzsche*. London: Routledge & Kegan Paul, 1973. Quoting extensively from *Beyond Good and Evil*, Hollingdale considers it and *Toward a Genealogy of Morals* to be probably Nietzsche's best books.

Jaspers, Karl. *Nietzsche: An Introduction to the Understanding of His Philosophical Activity.* Translated by Charles F. Wallraff and Frederick J. Schmitz. Chicago: Henry Regnery Company, 1969. In Jaspers' book we are to realize in dialogue with Nietzsche that genuine freedom and authenticity are found only in creativity; Jaspers makes extensive use of *Beyond Good and Evil*.

Löwith, Karl. *From Hegel to Nietzsche: The Revolution in Nineteenth Century Thought.* Translated by David E. Green. New York: Holt, Rinehart and Winston, 1964. A brief but penetrating analysis dealing with nihilism, the herd, work, education, and the Superman in Nietzsche.

Magnus, Bernd. *Nietzsche's Existential Imperative*. Bloomington: Indiana University Press, 1978. Magnus sees the doctrine of the Eternal Return as the central theme in Nietzsche's thought.

Morgan, George A. *What Nietzsche Means*. Cambridge, Massachusetts: Harvard University Press, 1941. Morgan provides one of the most cogent and richly documented analyses of Nietzsche's thought available anywhere.

Nehamas, Alexander. *Nietzsche: Life as Literature.* Cambridge, Massachusetts: Harvard University Press, 1985. An influential work in contemporary studies of Nietzsche.

Solomon, Robert C., ed. *Nietzsche: A Collection of Critical Essays*. Garden City, New York: Anchor Books, 1973. A superb collection of essays on Nietzsche written from a wide range of perspectives.

Stern, J. P. *A Study of Nietzsche*. New York: Cambridge University Press, 1979. Stern singles out *Beyond Good and Evil* for special attention, providing in Chapter V an invaluable sketch of all nine parts.

MARX: SELECTED WORKS

Author: Karl Marx (1818-1883)
Type of work: Philosophical anthropology, philosophy of social science, social and political philosophy,
     philosophy of history
First published: Various times

Principal Ideas Advanced

The postulation of transcendent divine beings is a function of incomplete and distorted self-identification among men.

Incomplete human self-identification is a function of nonegalitarian and incompletely developed modes of production.

The state is the ideologically legitimated power of ruling classes over laboring classes; its disappearance under genuine egalitarian and advanced productive and social conditions is thus necessary by definition.

Socially mediated production on the basis of foresight and skill distinguishes human from animal production; blockages in the development and expression of these basic capacities, reaching a peak in capitalism, are entitled "alienation."

Human history can be represented and explained as a sequence of changes in the modes of human production, upon which are raised corresponding sociopolitical structures and modes of thought.

The capitalist mode of production and its corresponding social and ideological forms will predictably give way to a socialist order which expresses human capabilities and thus overcomes alienation.

A number of circumstances have until recently led to an underestimation of the philosophical dimensions and interest of Karl Marx's work. First, the general disrepute of "speculative" as opposed to "empirical" thought in the later nineteenth century led Friedrich Engels and his collaborators to stress the hardheaded empiricism, scientism, and even positivism of Marx's work when they undertook to turn it into the ideology of a mass movement during the 1880's. Marx himself was probably involved in this effort. In any case, its success was ensured by consolidation of power in Russia by a group of Marxists schooled exclusively in this view. Second, the manuscripts of Marx which could shed a different light on the origins and foundations of Marx's thinking were not published until this century. This fact is obviously not unconnected with the first. Here Marx's complicity derives from his habit of keeping his philosophical way of thinking out of view in the works he prepared or authorized for publication, largely in order to preclude any intimation of idealism, which he felt would undermine the urgency of his message to the working class. The publication in the last fifty years of four groups of Marx's manuscripts, however, has thrown much new light on his deeper philosophical roots, commitments, and habits, and has given rise to a scholarly enterprise in which the expertise of philosophers has been particularly prominent and effective. These "manuscript clusters" are (1) Marx's *Critique of Hegel's Philosophy of Right* (written 1843, published 1927), together with the "Introduction" to it which Marx did publish shortly after completing the larger manuscript; (2) the famous *Economic and Philosophic Manuscripts of 1844* (published in 1932) together with some related papers, especially the essay "On the Jewish Question," which appeared in 1844, and the "Notes on James Mill," which did not; (3) the complete text of *The German Ideology* (written 1846, published in full 1932), which Marx wrote with Engels, along with the short but important "Theses on Feuerbach," which Engels found and published in 1886; and (4) the *Grundrisse* or "Rough Draft of Capital," a rich but unwieldly group of notebooks (written in 1857, published ineffectively in 1939 and effectively in 1953, and translated in full by 1973). It is on these works that the following sketch is based.

Like his Young Hegelian companions, Marx as a graduate student began to suspect that Georg Wilhelm Friedrich Hegel's philosophy leads to the unwarranted positing of transcendent entities—notably, Absolute Spirit. The point is not that Hegel takes this line; it is that he is unable, whatever his intentions, to escape it. By 1843 Marx had become especially intrigued by Ludwig Feuerbach's *causal* explanation of the positing of transcendent objects. For Feuerbach they are projections, roughly, of an "ideal self" displaced into another world because of factual restrictions placed on self-recognition and self-validation in this world. These restrictions come about generally from the domination of nature over man, but more particularly they arise whenever some men systematically dominate others. Given such an artificial division within the species "man" (as if differences between classes or races or other social groupings were like, or took the place of, differences between whole species) individual human beings are prevented from seeing in themselves what is characteristic of all men and seeing in all men what is characteristic of themselves. Full recognition and expression of one's "species being," then, is blocked. (An assumption of this argument is that rational persons basically experience themselves and other beings in terms of categories like natural kinds.) This blockage is expressed by the ascription of ideal human characteristics to divine beings. For Feuerbach, the degree of progress in history, then, is marked by stages in which men take back into self-characterizations predicates that had been projected onto fantastic beings. This process culminates in the refusal to countenance, however bloodlessly and undescriptively, any divinity at all. In such ideal circumstances, there will, by definition, be no religion. Further, the only entities which will be ontologically certified are those which have their roots exclusively in sensory experience and which can be referred back to sensory particulars as their subjects. Hegel's philosophy, since it fails to pass this ontological test, is not nearly as far beyond religious thinking as its author hopes. Meanwhile, however, Feuerbach's own theory remains deeply ambiguous about the relation it posits between empiricism and the demand that our experience is categorized in essentialistic terms such as "species being." The basic problem is that one may talk about kinds in ontological terms (roughly essentialism) without thoroughgoing empiricism, and vice versa. Feuerbach seems never to have faced this tension squarely, or even to have recognized it fully. The ambiguity is passed on to Marx. Feuerbach's theory does, however, propose a test for its own verification. It will be verified if there comes to exist a social reality which is jointly characterized by (a) a throughgoing empiricism, (b) the disappearance of religion, and (c) sufficiently democratic political institutions to express social equality—that is, by hypothesis, seen as underlying the joint existence of the first (a) and (b), and so providing an arena for complete mutual recognition among human beings.

What is crucial is that Marx deeply accepted this complex hypothesis. Some of his first works are an attempt to *further* Feuerbach's analysis by showing why *merely formal democracy* is not sufficient to bring about (a) and (b). Marx became convinced, on the basis of contemporary sociological information, especially about America and France, that formal democracy not only can coexist with religion, but can bring about an intensification and interiorization of religious belief. These apparent countercases to Feuerbach's theory never led Marx to suspect the general thesis itself, but did propel him to find some additional factor (d) which is alleged to be preventing the joint coexistence of (a), (b), and the "real or true democracy" needed for (c). Under the increasing influence of socialist literature, Marx came to find this additional factor in *pure private property*.

Thus, already in his crucial interpretation (in 1843) of Hegel's political philosophy, Marx shows that Hegel's countenancing of transcendent objects and his contempt for empiricism—indeed his whole "upside down" ontology and epistemology, which makes particular space-time substances dependent on abstract universals rather than the opposite—is of a piece with his justification of antidemocratic politics and private property. The one supports the other. Within the political theory itself, moreover, where Hegel promises a solidarity between rulers and ruled, Marx finds marked "alienation" and "division." Deceptive idealist rhetoric to the contrary, there is no common mind in the state portrayed by Hegel—only the domination of some by others, and naked self-interest by all. This estrangement at the political level, Marx concludes, is integrally connected to the justification of private property that Hegel built into his state-construct. It is at this point that Marx commits himself to the thesis that political community (in a Rousseauean sense) is possible if and only if private property is dismantled. Although he speaks of this as a *fulfillment* of democracy (as had the extreme left wing of the popular party during the great French Revolution, to whose views Marx's here hark back), it is unclear whether Marx at this time is speaking of a fulfillment of democracy in a democratic *state*; or had already come to believe what he later clearly proclaimed—that such a "democracy" requires the disappearance and delegitimation of the state itself. The state, in this latter view, comes *by definition* to refer to an institution functioning to restrict property to a particular class or set of classes. Its disappearance, therefore, in genuinely equal social conditions is analytically guaranteed.

However one analyzes Marx's views on "true democracy," it is certainly the case that by the time of his essay "On the Jewish Question" Marx held, in opposition to his former mentor Bruno Bauer, that formal democracy as a political institution exists *merely* to preserve bourgeois property rights. As these lead to human separation, competition, and the privatization of experience, they result in the religious-displacement illusions postulated by Feuerbach and in a political life which is something apart from, and dominating, the activities of the individual.

In the *Economic and Philosophic Manuscripts of 1844* Marx deepened this analysis by showing *why* private property in its developed bourgeois form (where entitlement to property rests on no qualification beyond formal personhood) leads to this sociopolitical and religious alienation. He first situates this

kind of private property in its larger context: that production and distribution system we call *laissez-faire* capitalism. He does this by way of an analysis of the writings of the political economists. He then more generally lays down what he thinks has since the beginning distinguished the human species from other animal species: a productive capability which is characterized by (1) the intervention of intelligence and foresight into the productive process; and (2) a thoroughgoing social organization of production. (Marx couples these two characteristics in such a way that without the one, the other will not continually change and develop.) These conjoint capacities express themselves in the creation of a "humanized nature" in which men *cooperate* to transform the found materials of their environment into objects which are media for self-expression and which thus permit mutual human recognition in a public sphere. In creativity conceived along artistic lines, then, Marx locates the *sine qua non* of the full mutual recognition that, in different ways, Hegel and Feuerbach were concerned to make possible. Marx's insistence on "social *praxis*" centers on this view of "transformative activity" as the locus of human expression, development, and recognition. This is man's "species being." Indeed, in a productive system that appears *most* distinctively human, self-expression and mutual recognition provide the motive for production, and the securing of more basic needs appears as a concomitant and by-product of the achievement of these recognition-needs. Conversely, where human production is centered on the preservation of "mere existence," human life appears less distinguishable from that of other species, and human production approximates the narrowness of animal production.

Marx goes on to show that this latter pole is most closely approached in capitalism. Because of the complete dominance of pure private property under capitalism, the worker is alienated (1) from the product of his work, since he does not own it, and it cannot therefore express him, (2) from the process of his work, since he sells his own labor capacity which is his most basic human ("inalienable") attribute, and (3) from other men, since although capitalist production is *de facto* enormously cooperative and thus socialized, (1) and (2) prevent it from being experienced as the work of consciously cooperating human beings and as a product of their joint activity. Indeed, on the contrary, the economic system appears as something to which men subject themselves as to a fact of nature. It therefore becomes a fetish to them. Socialism, Marx concludes, *by removing private property*, allows the basic defining dispositions of human beings to operate freely. This is a program whose time has come, because the skills, tools, and productive capacity of capitalism itself provide the necessary conditions for this fulfillment of human aspiration. Marx found such a call in contemporary communist propaganda literature, which, although frequently written by intellectuals, he took to be a genuine and spontaneous expression of the experience and intelligence of the working class itself. He was also delighted to find in this literature a concomitant rejection of religion and of formal democracy, and thus a confirmation not only of Feuerbach's thesis, but also of his own interpretation of it. Marx's enormous and lasting confidence in the working class—which has presented great problems for twentieth century Marxists—derives, one is tempted to conclude, from his astonishment that the working class had independently arrived at Feuerbach's and his own insights.

Marx's strategy of situating types of property relations within larger and more comprehensive types of productive relations, first used in 1844, when combined with the judgment that man's productive activity is the most central aspect of his experience, suggests a larger project still: redoing Hegel's and Feuerbach's accounts of the historical development of humankind toward full self and mutual recognition on the basis of these presuppositions. Against Hegel, it will be stressed by Marx that successive types of consciousness do not unfold out of their own conceptual resources, but rather on the basis of changes in man's socially mediated interchange with the environment. Marx believed that Hegel had at one point grasped this, in a left-handed way, in the *Phenomenology of Spirit*, when he spoke of the slave's sense of self-identification as superior to the master's, because the former's transformative interaction with nature gives him a solidly achieved sense of self, while the latter is subject to the shifting tides of honor

and opinion in an elitist world cut off from its productive roots. But these ideas were soon buried, and Hegel constructs his history as the history of consciousness moving on its own steam toward "theoretical" self-appropriation. (See *1844 Manuscripts,* "On Hegel's Dialectic.") Against Feuerbach, it will be stressed that the progressive taking back of alienated human properties from postulated divinities cannot be displayed as moving toward a passive, sensationalistic empiricism of the English sort, with its concomitant pleasure ethic, political indifference, and historical blindness. For Marx, men recognize their own essence ("*Wesen*") in and by their productive activity, and therefore progressively in proportion as they make nature a home that expresses themselves ("humanized nature"). This Marx calls "active or practical materialism," as opposed to Feuerbach's "speculative" materialism. (See Marx's "Theses on Feuerbach," 1886.)

The first attempt to carry out this historical project occurs in *The German Ideology* (1846), on which Marx collaborated with Engels. What stands out in this account is a conscious attempt both to suppress the essentialistic language which had hitherto characterized Marx's thinking and to insist upon the empiricist credentials of the authors. What is to be traced is a *factual* history of the human race, in which changing forms of production determine corresponding sociopolitical patterns and legitimating ideologies. Essentialistic language would automatically imply, it is asserted, that the determination works the other way around, as in Hegel, and (it is now insisted) in the Young Hegelians as well. Nevertheless, looked at more closely, what we actually find here is a history with a high degree of quasilogical and dialectical patterning, and a suspicion arises that the forecast of the coming socialist order with which the work culminates is derived as much from his dialectical machinery as from the empiricistic data base on which we are merely *told* that it rests. It is plausible to think, then, that some essentialism, and indeed some Hegelian dialectic of consciousness, lurks inside these empiricist trappings. The resolution of this tension between contingent empirical fact and necessary quasilogical unfolding in accounting for human history constitutes the most difficult and vital problem in the analysis of Marx's mature philosophical commitments. Two other problems are associated with it. (1) How is either empiricism or quasilogicism consistent with Marx's claim that human agents freely make their own history? and (2) How is Marx capable of exempting his own analyses from the sociopolitical and economic determinism on which, in his view, it would appear *all* intellectual products rest?

Orthodox Marxism had long committed itself and Marx to a rather deterministic theory of the kind worked out by Engels in *Anti-Düring* and *The Dialectics of Nature*, and had thus allowed Marx's insistence on free human activity to escape from view. The problem of self-referencing was also bypassed by simply asserting that Marxism is a "science" which grounds its judgments in the way that natural science does. The publication of the early manuscripts may well have scandalized proponents of these views, but it was always possible to take the tack of calling these manuscripts juvenilia. For several decades the central issue in Marx scholarship,

then, centered on where precisely to draw the line between the young Marx and his mature scientific-deterministic successor, who presented in *Das Kapital* the laws by which capitalism inevitably gives way to socialism. The publication of the *Grundrisse,* however, demonstrated that the habits of mind frequently associated with the younger Marx were still operating in Marx's thinking while he was writing *Das Kapital*, if somewhat behind the scenes. Those who still wished to speak of two Marxes were then driven to think of them as two alternating sides of a single Marx which vied with each other until the end. More challenging approaches, however, have tried to demonstrate that the new understanding of *Das Kapital* that the study of the *Grundrisse* makes possible shows a coherence of the later view with the earlier one at the expense of Marx's alleged scientism. The main point is to challenge the quasideterministic interpretation of *Das Kapital* itself. The correct disposition of these issues, however, is still far from accomplished.

Pertinent Literature

Avineri, Shlomo. *The Social and Political Thought of Karl Marx*. Cambridge: Cambridge University Press, 1968.

Shlomo Avineri's study is based largely on a detailed reading of Karl Marx's *Critique of Hegel's Philosophy of Right* (1843). It is the first major study to investigate the bearing of this early manuscript on Marx's subsequent thought. It is an important part of Avineri's thesis to show that Marx later remained faithful to what he had already worked out in this *Critique*.

Avineri's interpretation of the *Critique* is built on the premise that Marx means what he says in terming his an internal critique of Georg Wilhelm Friedrich Hegel's political philosophy. It accepts Hegel's own premise—that reality *qua* reality is penetrated with reason—and demonstrates that the sociopolitical vision of the modern state that Hegel articulates and recommends in the *Philosophy of Right* is still irrational when judged by standards that Hegel himself

should accept. The demonstration of this irrationality is accomplished by Marx's use of Ludwig Feuerbach's "transformative method." In this interpretive device, Hegel's habit of ascribing existential import to concepts apart from their instantiations, and of treating the latter as deductions from, or at best exemplifications of, the concepts, is replaced by treating what Hegel regards as "predicates" as "subjects." Thus, the concept of the monarch is nothing other than an abstraction from real, earthly monarchs, and less attractive on that account. This technique is taken over by Marx and used to strip Hegel's *Philosophy of Right* of an appearance of rationality that it does not yet deserve, since rational social life is not yet realized.

The chief dimension of irrationality is the gap between the real "material" life of civil society and the separation from it of political "form." This dialectic between state and civil society, which is central to Marx's argument, yields a theory of historical development that, according to Avineri, throws much light on Marx's later materialist theory of history. In classical Greco-Roman society, no civil society emerges in contradistinction to the political life of the citizen. That is where his real identity is. In the Middle Ages, there is also no split between civil and political life: political life expresses itself entirely in terms of the work roles of civil society, rather than the reverse (guilds, corporations, and the like). Modern society, however, is basically characterizable as a mutual separation of state and civil society, the state becoming alien to the concrete life of the social individual, while the economic life of civil society becomes itself more and more abstract, one-sided, and non-self-expressive as pure private property and capitalism emerge. Marx goes on to speak of their reunion both as "true democracy" and as "communism" ("*Gemeinwesen*").

Thus Avineri believes that the issue of whether Marx at this time was a left-wing democrat or a communist is empty. Common productive life, on the basis of the anthropology soon to be worked out in detail in the *1844 Manuscripts, fulfills* political life while trancending it as a separate kind of life, while the communizing of productive and economical life makes it humanly expressive in a way that classical political theory, including Hegel's, must either promise without delivering, or ignore with peril to its own claim to rationality.

In turning to how a rational society is to be realized, Avineri interestingly points out how Marx assigns to the proletariat the role of "universal class" that Hegel had reserved in the *Philosophy of Right* for the bureaucracy. The connection is in the role assigned to both to bring about rationalization of the sociopolitical structure, and in the claim that Hegel makes for the bureaucrats and Marx for the proletarians that they have in mind the interest of the whole society (hence "universal"). What is different, of course, is that in Hegel's case the method for rationalizing is administrative domination, while in Marx's case it is revolutionary liberation. According to Marx, Hegel's bureaucrats are really corrupted by and embedded in the egoism of a society based on private property. Marx's proletarians do not fall back into this because they have nothing to protect; they also can acquire positive cooperative and fulfilling values in the transformative activity of work itself.

Avineri believes that Marx remains faithful in his later works to the theory worked out in 1843-1844, although terminology, accent, and matters of details do shift. One interesting argument that Avineri proposes about the later Marx is designed to undercut the idea that Marx moved, in *Das Kapital*, to a kind of deterministic scientism. Avineri argues that *Das Kapital* is a model of a free-market society already approximated by the England of the 1850's. The *projection* toward socialism proceeds by noting ways in which the free-market model tries, by many devices, to rectify its own instability and inherent mutability. These interventions, however, bring about by their very nature an integration of collective political decision-making and the economic infrastructure. Thus socialism grows up within the world of capitalism itself.

It would be small exaggeration to conclude that, for Avineri, Marx came not to reject Hegel but to fulfill him—to mark out what a truly rationalized society would be like, where rationality is conceived of as an organic unity between social matter and political form.

Ollman, Bertell. *Alienation: Marx's Conception of Man in Capitalist Society.* Cambridge: Cambridge University Press, 1971, 1976.

In combating the common interpretation of Karl Marx's historical materialism, which holds that the sociopolitical and ideological superstructure are causally determined and explained by the economic base, Bertell Ollman takes a daring tack: this *cannot* be the case for Marx because this model of causal explanation assumes an ontology in which one (sort of) thing has effects on another that is fully discriminable from it. Marx, Ollman argues, consistently subscribed to an ontology of "internal relations" in which any one "thing" is simply the totality of its relations. No entity, that is, has defining properties which are statable in nonrelational terms. Casual analysis of the type referred to, then, is to be replaced by accounts of inherently changeable and constantly changing configurations of "elements" that are themselves relations. Ontologies of this sort were most fully articulated by British Hegelians at the turn of the century. Ollman holds that, like them, Marx read such a doctrine out of Georg Wilhelm Friedrich Hegel, as when, for example, he refers to the sun and plants in the *1844 Manuscripts* as mutually "objects" to each other. An object (*Gegenstand*) is for Marx that to which an entity is related in order to be what it is, and without reference to which it would have no identity conditions sufficient to posit it as existing at all.

Such a view has advantages in enabling us to separate Marx's "essentialism" from the usual sense of a preestablished entelechy which limits the development and operation of any kind of being in precise directions. It thus preserves, within a broader sense of "essentialism," Marx's insistence that man's "nature" is constantly changing as the range of the "objects" with which man deals, and to which he relates himself, is increased. It also helps make sense of Marx's reiterated insistence that the individual person is not something constituted prior to or apart from his social relations, but comes to be an individual precisely in and through those relations. What speaks against the thesis are, first, the possibility that a doctrine of internal relations is not formulatable in a way that does not depend on an idealism which Marx trenchantly rejects, at least in his maturity. Second, any such doctrine takes upon itself the perhaps unfulfillable task of preserving a sense for "individuation" which squares with our experience.

To the first of these objections, Ollman replies by taking seriously Friedrich Engels' attempt to work out a "materialist dialectic," and Marx's approval of that chore. (Thus Ollman makes a more positive assessment of Engels' work than is customary among nonorthodox Marxists.) As to the second problem, Ollman believes that although "individuation" is indeed always relative to a point of view on the ontologically constituted whole, such points of view can do justice to the way we break up our experience for purposes of understanding it and dealing with it. Putting these two points together, Ollman arrives at an account in which a "materialist" doctrine of internal relations is seen as truly reflecting and reporting how the whole of experience coheres with and can be best explained from *the perspective of human productive activity*. On the basis of this general theory, Ollman offers an interpretation of the key Marxian concept of "alienation," as it is worked out in the *1844 Manuscripts* and as it is presumed to underlie Marx's thinking thereafter. Alienation, roughly, is a condition in which human productive activity in interaction with "objects" is narrowed, contracted, and reduced below what human needs, wants, and capacities are, *at any given time*, capable of. In such a condition, and especially under capitalism, experience becomes "abstract" or "one-sided." Thus, in Ollman's reading, Marx's frequent attacks on "abstraction" refer to a separating off of aspects from a concrete whole, as notably the separation of the "commodity" in capitalism from the reference of social production to social life. Such separated elements cannot adequately explain matters presumed to be separated from them, or in turn be explained by other "abstractions." Thus the conventional model of historical materialism frequently assumed to be Marx's is for Ollman contrary to his view.

Rader, Melvin. *Marx's Interpretation of History*. New York: Oxford University Press, 1979.

In addressing himself to the conflict between traditional interpretations of Karl Marx and more recent readings which stress Marx's roots in Georg Wilhelm Friedrich Hegel, Melvin Rader suggests that we might distinguish between several "models" of historical process which Marx uses heuristically

and alternately. Thus Rader separates the traditional "base-superstructure" model from a more Hegelian "organic totality" model. The former may take either a fundamentalist or a more sophisticated form. In its fundamentalist version, the base-superstructure model severely separates out the various strata of social reality and ascribes to the lowest stratum, the stratum of "forces of production," all causal and explanatory roles. The more sophisticated version, preferred by Friedrich Engels, may be called "dialectical" at least in the rather weak sense that it permits of causal interaction among the strata, while nevertheless insisting on the ultimate weight of the base "in the long run." The strength of the base-superstructure model generally is that it maintains the characteristically Marxian stress on the role of modes and forces of production in historical process. Its weakness is its tendency to reductionism, and, in the case of the fundamentalist version, to epiphenomenalism. Moreover, the rules for separating out and then relating the various strata have proved to be very difficult to formulate and to use with sufficient precision.

The "organic totality" model does away with these problems at a stroke; but it does so only by getting into the turgid area of "internal relations." Nevertheless, this model is, for Rader, more faithful on the whole to Marx's work both early and late. Rader takes pains, then, to clarify Marx's views about internal relations.

First, he argues that neither in the early nor the mature writings does Marx's theory of internal relations—relations such as constitutively obtain among parts of organisms and in social relations—extend as far as a universal ontology committed to the view that anything and everything is logically incomplete except by its relation to everything else. Rader casts doubt on Bertell Ollman's ascription of such a view to Marx. (See above review of Ollman's *Alienation*.) Marx's invocation of internal relatedness focuses on the world of human activity and its situation within the wider sphere of organic activity; and even in these restricted contexts Marx is quite open about the degree of interpenetration that needs to be postulated for explanation in particular cases. Degrees of internal relatedness are a matter for empirical investigation rather than *a priori* legislation.

Second, Rader is concerned to point out that there is less inherent tension between Marx's two models than one might assume. In Marx's early period, the dominant use of the organic totality model is nevertheless accompanied by insistencies that employ, or at the very least foreshadow, the base-superstructure model. For example, in his very early critique of Hegel's political theory Marx traces defects in Hegel's state-construct to underlying economic and property relations. Conversely, in *Das Kapital* Rader finds much use of organic conceptualization. Indeed, it is only that model which can provide the normative foundations for Marx's attack on capitalist societies and his approbation of socialist ones. Without being buffered by the expressive humanism available in that model, the exclusive use of base-superstructure talk to explain historical process might be taken as involving an "economic determinism" in which the stages of history unfold by alleged immutable laws of social development into a socialist order whose desirability is, in this account, both beside the point and ungrounded in relevant sorts of arguments. Rader holds that Marx never envisioned the matter in this deterministic light.

Indeed, Rader is concerned to point out that there are areas of real compatibility between the organic totality and the base-superstructure models. There can be hierarchical dependence between the parts of organisms without undermining their internal relatedness. Some organs and functions are more basic to the preservation and functioning of a living whole than others, and thus play greater causal-explanatory roles. So too in societies, the "forces of production" are basic to social functioning. Where this works eufunctionally we see a harmony among the various aspects of social life, and between individual and society, that can best be represented in terms of the descriptions available in the organic totality model. Where it is dysfunctional we see the social organism separate into "abstract" relations which can best be described and explained in terms of the base-superstructure model. The separability of the elements featured in this model describes and explains dysfunctional relations within a presumed, but defective, organic totality. It thus plays a significant role in explanations of periods of social revolution.

Additional Recommended Reading

Cohen, G. A. *Karl Marx's Theory of History: A Defense*. Princeton, New Jersey: Princeton University Press, 1978. Well-argued functionalist interpretation of the traditional base-superstructure model.

Elster, Jon. *An Introduction to Karl Marx*. Cambridge: Cambridge University Press, 1986. A solid overview of Marx's economic and political philosophy.

Gould, Carol. *Marx's Social Ontology: Individuality and Community in Marx's Theory of Social Reality*. Cambridge, Massachusetts: MIT Press, 1978. Seeks insight into Marx's use of internal relations in his connection with Aristotle.

Lichtheim, George. *Marxism: An Historical and Critical Study*. New York: Frederick A. Praeger, 1961. A view of subsequent streams of Marxist thought built up on a sound reading of Marx himself.

McLellan, David. *Karl Marx: His Life and Thought*. New York: Harper & Row Publishers, 1974. Reliable and nontendentious biography.

_____. *The Young Hegelians and Karl Marx*. New York: Frederick A. Praeger, 1969. Traces influence on the early Marx of such figures as Bruno Bauer, Moses Hess, Arnold Ruge and Feuerbach, as well as Hegel.

Schmidt, Alfred. *The Concept of Nature in Marx*. London: New Left Books, 1973. Refutation of dialectical materialist interpretation of Marx's ontology and epistemology.

THE WILL TO BELIEVE

Author: William James (1842-1910)
Type of work: Ethics, philosophy of religion
First published: 1897

Principal Ideas Advanced

Decisions between hypotheses proposed to our belief are genuine options when they are living (of vital concern to us), forced (no third alternative is possible), and momentous (presenting a unique opportunity of considerable importance).

Whenever a genuine option cannot be settled on intellectual grounds, it is right and necessary to settle it according to our passional inclinations.

The religious option concerning the belief in God is a genuine option which promises most to the person who has the passional need to take the world religiously.

Men possess free wills which are not determined; determinism—the theory that decisions are causally determined—fails to account for the sense of human freedom.

Now a classic, this work takes its title from the first ten separate essays written at different times. Originally presented as lectures to academic clubs, these essays express "a tolerably definite philosophic attitude" which James named *radical empiricism*—an ordinary man's empiricism which takes experience as it comes, "seeing" even matters-of-fact as subject to possible future reinterpretation; yet radical for its rejection of dogmatic monism in the face of the obvious plurality of the things making up the universe. James also wanted to make a case for the right of men to believe some moral and religious postulates for whose certainty the evidence can never fully be on hand. Sympathetic to a wide range of philosophical viewpoints, James sought to give intellectual significance to the role of the emotions in specified contexts. He also criticized the prevailing academic opinion that only scientific methods can produce an adequate understanding of the human condition.

The first four essays ("The Will to Believe," "Is Life Worth Living?," "The Sentiment of Rationality," and "Reflex Action and Theism") are concerned directly with religious problems. Two others ("The Dilemma of Determinism" and "The Moral Philosopher and the Moral Life") also give some attention to religious aspects of ethical problems. A final essay ("What Psychical Research Has Accomplished") defends scholars who inquire into the possibility that mental life may involve phenomena which escape our ordinary scientific criteria. The remaining essays ("Great Men and Their Environment," "The Importance of Individuals," and "On Some Hegelisms") show James's concern to find commonsense facts philosophically interesting; to criticize some unexamined assumptions of rationalism; and to resist the spread of absolutist and totalist theories which swallow up the individual in an "environment," overlook human differences by stressing only similarities, and ignore diversity in emphasizing unity.

Three broad types of subject matter receive treatment in James's book. These are the nature and motives of philosophizing, the justification of religious and moral beliefs, and the nature of the moral enterprise. A common theme also runs through what would otherwise be a collection of unrelated essays. This theme is the problem of the relation of evidence to specific human beliefs. If the book has a positive thesis, it is that men may rightfully hold certain religious, moral, and metaphysical beliefs even when conclusive evidence for their adequacy is absent.

James resists the positivistic tendency of his age to assume that scientific methods will prove able to decide all important questions about existence. Similarly, he expresses criticism of any extreme rationalistic reliance on logic as the sole criterion of philosophical adequacy. There are some beliefs which are truths-in-the-making. "And often enough our faith beforehand in an uncertified result *is the only thing that makes the result come true*," he writes. One comes to understand that James is moved to philosophical activity by a desire to justify the rightness of certain beliefs—that God exists, that men possess free will, that moral effort represents a genuinely objective worthiness, that pain and evil cannot justify suicide, and that practical as well as theoretical needs ought to influence one's philosophical outlook.

The book's historical influence partly stems from the nature of the problems addressed by the author. Most of these problems are close to ordinary human experience. James also reassures those thinkers who, unconvinced that a completed metaphysical system is really possible, want to resist making a forced choice between philosophical certainty and philosophical skepticism. Philosophical argument can take place fruitfully somewhere on this side of certainty, according to James. Yet such argument need not lapse into arbitrariness. Logic is a subservient instrument. It is subject to the felt needs of religious, moral, and practical demands. James argues that a qualified moral idealism need not lead to sentimentalism in escaping the twin threats of pessimism and nihilism. Some philosophical viewpoints are relatively more adequate than others even though no one viewpoint can hope to exhaust the whole domain of reality. Such a generous spirit animates James's essays that even critics who are unpersuaded by some of the arguments nevertheless recognize in them the evidences of a rare and gifted philosophical mind.

The book's opening essay is crucial for the broad way it sketches the nature, purposes, and possibilities of philosophizing. Written in 1879, "The Sentiment of Rationality" states convictions which are presupposed in James's more restricted discussions of topics in religious and moral philosophy. A number of basic questions caused James to write this essay.

What is the philosophic quest really about? What are the conditions which any philosophy must meet if it is to be accepted? How can one know that the philosophic demand for a peculiar kind of rationality has been satisfactorily met?

Philosophic pursuit of a rational conception of existence marked by universality and extensiveness succeeds whenever a feeling of intellectual "ease, peace, rest" is the result. Any adequate philosophy must satisfy two kinds of human distress. One is theoretical—the intellectual concern to form a general conception of the universe. The other is practical—the moral and religious desire to include men's passional natures in any philosophical consideration of how men are to act and what they should believe.

Two cravings gnaw at the philosopher. Intellectual simplification is always one philosophic need. Simplification requires reduction of the world's numerous details to fewer significant abstractions which stress similarities. Theoretical life would be an impossibility without such abstractions. The other need is the clear demand for recognition of the perceived differences among things. Philosophic rationality results only when each of these competing impulses receives serious consideration. James insists that philosophizing involves a continuous, yet never fully successful, synthesizing of these two cravings—a mark of whose successful handling is the feeling that some original puzzlement no longer proves irritating to the mind. As an activity, philosophizing must involve the whole man. Philosophizing must therefore often give way to hosts of other intellectual quests since its own unique function is to discover a general picture of "the hang of things."

An important conviction operates at this point in James's development. It is that any metaphysical conception must remain open to future possible theoretical anxiety. Man's need of a philosophic view of the nature of things results only in partial and temporary satisfaction. Any instance of the feeling of rationality can itself founder on the shoals of the question about its justifiability. Even if the world *is* a certain way, it *might* yet be otherwise. Thus the worry about "nonentity" arises, named by James "the parent of the philosophic craving in its subtilist and profoundest sense." Through awareness of a possible other state of affairs, men can lose the feeling of rationality once gained. No single logically consistent system can still man's theoretical demands when he is faced by the query: Why just this sort of world and no other? "Every generation will produce its Job, its Hamlet, its Faust, or its Sartor Resartus." Mystical ecstasy can realize the psychological equivalent of the feeling of rationality when logic proves inadequate. Yet "empiricism will be the ultimate philosophy," for even the mysteriousness of existence depends on an irreducible fact about a universe which is dissatisfying to our theoretical demands.

Exclusive concern with the theoretical impulse leads men to skepticism or to a sense of wonder about the universe. One or the other arises when a completed metaphysical system begins to wane. Does the matter end here? Denying that it does, James argues that now the practical life acquires a heightened rational significance. Practical demands play a role in one's choice of a philosophy when systems exist whose logical methods are equally sound. Men's belief that their wills can influence the future must receive justification in any important philosophical system. Men can adopt that philosophy which most fully satisfies certain moral and aesthetic requirements of human nature.

The better philosophy is always relevant to men's expectations about the future. Yet there is no one, final, "better" philosophy. For example, a philosophy which retains the notion of substance will remain a perennial contender for human acceptance. Similarly, idealism will remain a challenging possibility for thinkers requiring an identification of the universe with our personal selves, materialism for thinkers wanting an escape from selves. James concludes that temperamental differences are important in the quest after the sentiment of rationality. To be humanly acceptable, a philosophy must limit moral skepticism and satisfy men's belief that they "count" in the creation of a future world. According to James, no philosophy can succeed which ignores the practical craving after a world which is partly responsive to men's future expectations, their human faiths, and their commonsense conviction that moral striving genuinely counts for something.

Take the question: Does God exist? James rejects the agnostic argument that one ought never to hold beliefs for which conclusive evidence is lacking. Reasonable persons seek both to avoid error and to attain the maximum amount of truth. Yet there may be questions such that neither "yes" nor "no" replies are justified by existing evidence but to which men may rightfully give an affirmative belief-response. James insists that the matter of God's existence is such a question, as are questions about the importance of the individual, the value of life versus suicide, and the possible existence of human free will. *How* men treat such questions is important. James argues that men may believe certain statements for reasons of the heart when conclusive evidence is lacking and the beliefs help to initiate future discoveries of a practical kind. This thesis forces James to consider the problem of the relation of evidence to belief.

Belief involves a willingness to act on some hypothesis. James insists that any proposition may serve as a hypothesis—though he is not always clear about the form of such a hypothesis. Ordinarily, a proposition like "This litmus paper is blue" is not considered a hypothesis because it lacks a proper hypothetical form. A proposition of the form: "If this litmus paper is put into a given solution, it will turn red," is a hypothesis capable of some testing provided the proper details are supplied. But James had in mind statements of moral and religious belief whose adoption by men might result in bringing about a desired truth. One may help to make another person's attitude friendly towards himself by adopting a believing attitude toward the statement: "X is friendly towards me." Belief in some propositions is a requirement of their future possible verification. According to James, religious beliefs may often be of this kind. Religious beliefs involve one in assenting to statements for which conclusive evidence is absent. James wants to defend the right of men to hold such beliefs if they meet specified conditions. A man has an option to believe certain hypotheses in religion and morals if the hypotheses are living rather than dead, forced rather than avoidable, and momentous rather than trivial.

What makes a hypothesis "living," "forced," and "momentous" is its relation to a thinker's interests.

The test here seems to be predominantly psychological and cultural, for an individual's interests are what they are, however caused. James admits that not all men will find the same hypothesis living, forced, and momentous—giving the example of a Christian confronted with the command: "Be a Theosophist or be a Mohammedan." Yet James insists that the God-hypothesis confronts men with a genuine "option," meaning that such an option is living, momentous, and forced. He argues that the agnostic who neither affirms nor denies God's existence has already decided against such an existence. The agnostic decides to give up all hope of winning a possible truth in order to avoid a possible error in a situation for which evidence must in principle be inconclusive. The agnostic's right to disbelieve in this case is no greater than the religious man's right to believe.

A critic may say at this point that James's way of arguing may encourage men to choose their beliefs by an individualistic criterion of psychological comfort—something on the order of the command: "Believe what you need to believe." James warns his readers that he is countering academic people's disregard of the passional aspects in human decision-making and that the right to believe occurs only in a matter which "cannot by its nature be decided on intellectual grounds." James apparently thinks the genuine religious option concerns the *thatness* of God's existence rather than the choice of an existing institutional means for expressing one's decision to believe in God's existence. Yet he does seem to argue, on the other hand, that those who are agnostics choose to treat the God-hypothesis as a dead one. Moral and religious options are such that, if the believer takes an affirmative stance regarding a belief, they promise that the better aspects will win out in the universe and a man will be better off for believing. One might put even the God-hypothesis in a psychological form: "If you believe that God exists, even now you will be benefited." Yet it is not clear that James would wish to regard the force of the central religious hypothesis as purely psychological.

In discussing features of the moral landscape, James once again shows his distrust of intellectual abstractions and generalizations. He is convinced philosophers can never produce an airtight, finished moral system. Nor can moral philosophers dogmatically solve all issues in advance of actual situations. Yet James openly defends two general moral notions. One is that human demands and obligations are coextensive. The second is that men have a right to believe they are free. Any genuinely moral philosopher places his own cherished ideals and norms in the scales of rational judgment even as he realizes that no one standard measure is attainable which will apply to all occasions. The moral philosopher holds no privileged status for deciding concrete instances of conflict in human demands. James insists that the moral philosopher "only knows that if he makes a bad mistake the cries of the wounded will soon inform him of the fact."

James advances the thesis about coextensiveness of demands and obligations in the essay "The Moral Philosopher and the Moral Life." There are no intrinsically "bad" demands, since demands are simply what they are. Without them, there could be no basis of moral life. Here James seeks to give due recognition to biological and psychological facts. He wants an "ethical republic." Terms like "good" and "bad"——whose meanings constitute the metaphysical function of moral philosophizing—refer to objects of feeling and desire. Only "a mind which feels them" can realize moral relations and moral law. James insists that the moral philosopher must "vote for the richer universe"——that which can accommodate the widest possible range of human wants. Yet James fails to make clear how the philosopher may determine what should pass as the richer universe if all demands have equal status in principle. On this issue James seems to appeal to intuition, for he argues that "the nobler thing *tastes* better"—indicating that he recognized that some demands are more appealing than others.

The most suggestive essay concerned with a moral issue is "The Dilemma of Determinism," in which James argues that, though no proof is possible, man does possess free will. This is a unique defense of indeterminism which presupposes a metaphysical position; namely, that the universe is in reality a pluriverse containing objective possibilities of novelty. The problem which concerns him is that of the relation of freedom to chance rather than of freedom to cause. "Chance" is a relative word which tells one nothing about that of which it is predicated. "Its origin is in a certain fashion negative: it escapes, and says, Hands off! coming, when it comes, as a free gift, or not at all." James disliked the contemporary distinction between "hard" and "soft" forms of determinism. The "soft" form of determinism argues that causality is quite compatible with responsible action and ethical judicability. What James wanted to discover is the metaphysical view necessary to determinism. He concluded it is a view which takes possibilities never actualized as mere illusions. James insists that determinism is unable to give adequate account of human feelings about possibility—the feeling that the universe contains genuine choices or alternatives, objectively real risks. Indeterminism insists that future volitions can be ambiguous, and "indeterminate future volitions *do* mean chance."

According to James, determinism results in an unavoidable dilemma. It must lead either to pessimism or to subjectivism. Men share a universe which daily calls for judgments of regret about some things happening in it. But if events are strictly necessitated, they can never be otherwise than what they are. Taken seriously, human regrets suggest that though some feature of the universe could not have been different, yet it would have been better if it were different. This reasoning leads to pessimism. James argues that men can give up pessimism only if they jettison their judgments of regret. Men can perhaps regard regrettable incidents—including the most atrocious murders—as teleological links in a chain leading to some higher good. Murder and treachery then cease to be evils. But a definite price must be paid for such a teleological optimism. The original judgments of regret were themselves necessitated, on the determinist's position. Some other judgments should have existed in their place. "But as they are necessitated, nothing else *can* be in their place." This means that whether men are pessimists or optimists, their judgments are necessitated.

One escape from this pessimism-optimism impasse is to adopt subjectivism. The practical impulse to realize some objective moral good can be subordinated to a theoretical development of an understanding of what is involved in goodness and evil. The facts of the universe can be valued only insofar as they produce consciousness in men. Subjectivism emphasizes the knowledge of good and evil in order to underscore the nature of human involvement. Experience rather than the objective goodness or badness of experience becomes the crucial factor for any moral subjectivism. But the indeterminist must reject subjectivism because it fails to do justice to men's empirical notions of the genuinely *moral* significance of human experiences. In addition, subjectivism leads to mere sentimentality and romanticism.

James concludes that common sense informs men that objective right and wrong involve real limits. Practical reason insists that "conduct, and not sensibility, is the ultimate fact for our recognition." Only indeterminism can make sense out of this practical insistence on objective right and wrong. Yet indeterminism does not argue that Providence is necessarily incompatible with free will. In an example involving chess, James shows how Providence can be like a master chess player who, though knowing the ultimate outcome of the game, must face unpredictable moves by an amateur player. On the other hand, James concludes that indeterminism gives men a special view—"It gives us a pluralistic, restless universe, in which no single point of view can ever take in the whole scene." James concludes that men have a right to be indeterminists and to believe in free will even in the absence of a persuasively final proof.

Pertinent Literature

Madden, Edward H. "Introduction," in William James's *The Will to Believe and Other Essays in Popular Philosophy*. Edited by Frederick H. Burkhardt. Cambridge, Massachusetts: Harvard University Press, 1979.

This volume, the sixth in a series entitled "The Works of William James," uses modern critical techniques to provide a definitive edition of the collected essays published by William James in 1897. Edward H. Madden's Introduction discusses all ten of them, showing how they advanced James's philosophy and how his critics responded.

Although these articles were prepared for diverse occasions between 1879 and 1896, Madden finds their unifying theme in James's conviction that all intellectual activity is affected by volition and emotion. Thought serves desire and need: willing directs thinking and at times even feeling. Madden notes that James explores these motifs in a free and often breezy style, but not without the care that makes serious philosophy. Thus, the articles are "popular" in the sense that James intended them to deal with fundamental topics that concern us all: for example, good and evil, freedom, and religious faith.

Madden thinks James's essays must be understood in terms of the author's ambivalence toward science. It is true that James himself was a scientist, but he was also skeptical about claims made by some of his scientific colleagues, particularly those who would condemn as illegitimate any beliefs for which sufficient evidence is lacking. According to Madden, James does not deny that one can obtain objective conclusions from critical inquiry, but he does defend a person's right to believe what needs require, if after consulting available evidence the outcome remains inconclusive.

Such a position drew criticism because some philosophers suspected that James's view would close off inquiry, thus legitimating belief without a continuing unbiased search for evidence. Granting that James may not have done full justice to such criticism, Madden does not ascribe this possible oversight to some presumed tendency of James's to believe too much too soon. In fact, Madden asserts, James had the greatest difficulty making up his mind on any issue.

In addition to discussing "The Will to Believe" (1896), Madden calls special attention to "The Dilemma of Determinism" (1884) and "The Moral Philosopher and the Moral Life" (1891), two articles he takes to be among James's most significant. The central concern of the former is whether the future is open or closed, whether possibilities are concretely real or illusory. Putting the issue in this way, Madden believes, was a sound move for James to make in defending human freedom against determinism. Unfortunately, James did not carry the analysis far enough. As Madden sees it, he failed to develop an adequate theory of human agency to go with his open-ended universe. James goes on to defend the reality of a finite God, and Madden finds that possibility intriguing. However, Madden also believes that some of James's early critics were correct: things come out too neatly when James makes divine power both limited enough to excuse God from responsibility for evil and yet sufficient to guarantee the ultimate significance of moral values.

As for "The Moral Philosopher and the Moral Life," Madden states that James's ethical theory aims at the maximum fulfillment of human desire. James rejects, however, the classical utilitarian emphasis on pleasure and advocates instead a strenuous mood that battles evil sacrificially and heroically. Madden notes John Dewey's attraction to James's conviction that moral theory cannot be fully developed in advance of paying attention to actual desires and circumstances. Nevertheless, Madden also sees problems in James's position. In particular, although James argues that our sense of the good must be constructed and revised in light of actual needs and circumstances, it seems to Madden that James's fundamental and apparently unchangeable commitment to maximize everyone's satisfaction may not be consistent with his empirical orientation.

Smith, John E. *The Spirit of American Philosophy.* New York: Oxford University Press, 1963.

This classic study interprets the philosophies of Charles S. Peirce, Josiah Royce, John Dewey, and Alfred North Whitehead, as well as the thought of William James. Attempting to locate a common American spirit among these varied thinkers, John E. Smith finds it in the belief that thought not only interprets life theoretically but also directs it practically. His chapter on James, subtitled "Purpose, Effort, and the Will to Believe," relates this thesis to James's analysis of human experience.

Smith acknowledges James's thought to be far less simple than a first glance may suggest, but he also indicates that James should have formulated his central tenets with greater rigor. Nevertheless, James's philosophy is distinctively American because it underscores the vitality and variety of experience and accepts the challenge of adventure in an open-ended existence. According to James, everyone has a right, even a duty, to be guided by personal experience. For James, Smith adds, human plans and purposes are dominant forces. We use them to discover and to create a rational world where we can feel at home as much as possible.

A consistent voluntarism, Smith believes, characterizes James's philosophy, but an emphasis on the active elements in thought and feeling is not without difficulty as it is illustrated in James's "will to believe." Although no idea of James's, or of American philosophy generally, is as well known, neither has any concept been so frequently misinterpreted. If the fault does not lie entirely with James, at least some of it does, and Smith sifts the wheat from the chaff.

James's accent on the will left him vulnerable to criticism that it was acceptable for belief to be arbitrary. Thus, Smith agrees that James's second thought—namely, to speak instead of "the right to believe"—would have served him better. A right involves not only what one may do; it usually entails boundaries and responsibilities as well. In fact, Smith

asserts, James did limit the right to believe, not perfectly, perhaps, but better than some criticisms imply. Smith notes James's provisions that the will or right to believe should come into play only if one faces an option that is live, forced, and momentous, and only if reason alone cannot give a final verdict. Then he draws out some significant characteristics of the actual situations in which James would think a choice is essential to determine belief.

Some of James's examples do not ring true, Smith argues; but James is on the right track in holding that there are times when belief is a necessary condition for having experience that can provide convincing evidence. Knowing whether God is real or whether it is valid to say that "love never fails," Smith suggests, are two examples where James's account is reliable. Unless we are willing to consider the possiblility that God exists or that love never fails, it is unlikely that we will ever be able to have the experience that could support such beliefs.

James also argues that belief is sometimes crucial for creating facts as well as for discovering them. Belief in oneself or in what another person is going to do is often critical in directing action. James's position does not deny that some situations may involve limits that we cannot control. Still, the will can be decisive in determining what possibilities will become actualized in a particular set of circumstances.

More carefully than James did himself, one must distinguish between cases where belief is necessary to discover facts and where belief is necessary to create them. In addition, one must recognize that such circumstances are not the only ones, although undeniably they are correctly described by James as momentous. Appreciation of these limits, Smith argues, goes far toward making James's analysis intelligible and trustworthy.

Davis, Stephen T. *Faith, Skepticism, and Evidence: An Essay in Religious Epistemology.* Lewisburg, Pennsylvania: Bucknell University Press, 1978.

Stephen T. Davis does not provide an overview of William James's essays as Edward H. Madden's article (see above) has done; nor does he share John E. Smith's concern to detect what is distinctively American in James's thought. Instead, utilizing the logical techniques of analytic philosophy, Davis probes James's essays, particularly "The Will to Believe," to show how those writings clarify the nature of religious faith and the possible justifications for religious belief. He shares Smith's appraisal: If correctly interpreted, James's argument in "The Will to Believe" is sound. Davis goes into the greater detail, however, in applying James's thought to issues concerning evidence and religious belief.

James wonders whether it is ever rational to believe a proposition on other than intellectual grounds. As Davis sees it, in asking whether one is ever intellectually justified in believing a nonevident proposition, James's aim is to defend the rationality of religious belief, at least in certain circumstances, although his argument is not restricted to religion.

Later philosophers have seen an important distinction in "The Will to Believe." James, they argue, did not notice sufficiently that there are two main arguments in the essay. Following Gail Kennedy, Davis refers to them as "the will to believe argument" and "the right to believe argument. "

The first holds that faith is sometimes self-verifying. In certain cases one's belief can be a causal factor in that belief's becoming true. For example, if you believe that a particular person likes you, your belief may help to bring about that person's liking you. Or, your belief that you can leap across a chasm can help to bring about your success in doing so.

A second argument, Davis says, focuses on what James calls a genuine option. This part of James's analysis asserts that it is sometimes rational to believe on the basis of passional need rather than on the basis of objective evidence alone. Before defining a genuine option, it is important to note that James limits such cases to those that cannot be decided solely on intellectual grounds. He is interested in propositions whose truth value is unknown and where the available evidence bearing on their truth value is ambiguous.

Davis proceeds to interpret James's understanding that a genuine option must be live, forced, and momentous. In addition to possessing some sense of truth, a live option makes a real and serious appeal. Moreover, if such an option is also forced, it will permit no third alternative. For example, if you say, "Either call my theory true or call it false," the option is avoidable because I can decide not to call your theory anything at all. But if you say, "Either accept this truth or go without it," there is no middle way. If I decide *not* to decide whether to accept that truth or to go without it, I will go without it. Finally, if the option is also momentous, it is unique and cannot be duplicated exactly.

Taking note of James's argument that in the case of a genuine option one has the full intellectual right to believe something on the basis of passional need, Davis next explores James's opinion that "the religious hypothesis" is a genuine option. For James, such a hypothesis entails belief that perfection is eternal, that the best things in the universe are the more eternal things, and that we are better off even now if we believe that perfection is eternal. Understood in this way, Davis asserts with James, religious beliefs are rationally justifiable.

The key to Davis' argument is that the "'liveness' and 'momentousness' criteria" are superfluous for James. If an option is forced and the evidence bearing on it is ambiguous, those conditions are sufficient for James's appraisal to be valid. James's skeptical opponents want suspended judgments in all cases where evidence is ambiguous. But surely, Davis argues, in the case of an option that is both forced and ambiguous, James is correct. If the evidence is ambiguous, one cannot decide what to believe on the basis of evidence. And if the option is forced, one cannot decide to suspend judgment. The only alternative is belief on some basis other than evidence, which is exactly what James is trying to justify.

Additional Recommended Reading

Beard, Robert W. " 'The Will To Believe' Revisited," in *Ratio*. VIII, no. 2 (December, 1966), pp. 169-179. This article is an insightful appraisal of James's criteria for "genuine" options.

Clive, Geoffrey. *The Romantic Enlightenment: Ambiguity and Paradox in the Western Mind (1750-1920)*. New York: Meridian Books, 1960. Clive's chapter, "The Breakdown of Empirical Certainty: William James and the Leap," links James's analysis of "the will to believe" to Søren Kierkegaard's existentialism.

Conkin, Paul K. *Puritans and Pragmatists: Eight Eminent American Thinkers*. Bloomington: Indiana University Press, 1976. More than any other major American philosopher, Conkin argues, James exalted the human will, but his voluntarism often left him on shaky philosophical ground.

Kennedy, Gail. "Pragmatism, Pragmaticism, and the Will to Believe—A Reconsideration," in *The Journal of Philosophy*. LV, no. 14 (July, 1958), pp 578-588. Kennedy's essay carefully analyzes a distinction between situations in which beliefs are self-verifying (the *will* to believe) and circumstances in which one is justified in believing more than evidence strictly warrants (the *right* to believe).

O'Connell, Robert J. *William James on the Courage to Believe*. New York: Fordham University Press, 1984. An insightful analysis of James's controversial concept of "the will to believe."

Roth, John K. *Freedom and the Moral Life: The Ethics of William James*. Philadelphia: The Westminster Press, 1969. Roth provides an extensive discussion of "The Moral Philosopher and the Moral Life" and accentuates James's emphasis on our freedom to develop meaningful lifestyles of our own choosing.

Roth, Robert J. *American Religious Philosophy*. New York: Harcourt, Brace & World, 1967. In a chapter on "William James and the God of Pragmatism," Roth gives special attention to "The Sentiment of Rationality," "Is Life Worth Living?" and "Reflex Action and Theism," as well as to "The Will to Believe."

Russell, Bertrand. *A History of Western Philosophy*. New York: Simon and Schuster, 1945. Russell says that James's analysis in "The Will to Believe" is a specious defense of religion.

Stroh, Guy W. *American Philosophy from Edwards to Dewey: An Introduction*. Princeton, New Jersey: D. Van Nostrand Company, 1968. *The Will to Believe and Other Essays in Popular Philosophy*, argues Stroh, clearly manifests the humanism in James's philosophy.

Wild, John. *The Radical Empiricism of William James*. Garden City, New York: Doubleday & Company, 1969. Interpreting James's psychology and its similarities to European phenomenology and existentialism, Wild sees James's essays as fundamental expressions of his convictions about the freedom of the mind and the strenuous life.

THE WORLD AND THE INDIVIDUAL

Author: Josiah Royce (1855-1916)
Type of work: Metaphysics
First published: Vol. I, 1900; Vol. II, 1901

Principal Ideas Advanced

Being can be understood as an absolute system of ideas which embody the fulfillment of purposes.
All knowledge is of matters of experience.
The individual self must be defined in ethical terms by reference to a life plan.
As a free individual each person by his will contributes to the world and to God's will.
Although no perfection is to be found in the temporal world, the Eternal Order is perfect.
Because we are finite, union with the infinite God is realized.

Professor Josiah Royce of Harvard University has proved to be the most durable American proponent of what is, for the most part, an outworn metaphysical creed: Absolute Idealism. *The World and the Individual* is composed of two series of Gifford Lectures delivered before the University of Aberdeen in 1899 and 1900, the first entitled " The Four Historical Conceptions of Being," and the second, "Nature, Man, and the Moral Order." In these lectures Royce developed, with some significant changes, earlier ideas which he had presented in such works as *The Religious Aspects of Philosophy* (1885) and *Studies of Good and Evil* (1898).

A statement of the core of Royce's philosophical position appears in the last lecture of the second volume: "The one lesson of our entire course has thus been the lesson of the unity of finite and of infinite, of temporal dependence and of eternal significance, of the World and all its Individuals, of the One and the Many, of God and Man. Not only in spite, then, of our finite bondage, but because of what it means and implies, we are full of the presence and the freedom of God."

This is a truly revealing statement considered not only as a condensation of Royce's central claim, but also as indicating the characteristic mode of argument which gives Royce's philosophy its individual content and flavor, distinguishing it from other Hegelian idealisms. For what does Royce maintain?—That from man's finitude, God's infinite presence and freedom follow. Royce supposed that the finite, the limited, is conceivable only by comparison with an actual infinitude. It is as if he had argued that man, in virtue of his limitations, suggests the actual unlimited, the Absolute—otherwise, there would be no sense in saying that man is "limited," that he does not come up to the mark. We are reminded of Descartes' argument that knowledge of man's imperfection leads to knowledge of the actuality of God's perfection and, hence, of God's existence.

If we consider the general character of Royce's argument, we can see that it takes the form of the claim that from imperfection, knowledge of perfection follows. Hence, from knowledge of purpose, knowledge of fulfillment follows; from knowledge of error, or of its possibility, knowledge of the actuality of truth follows; from knowledge of the partial, knowledge of the Absolute; from knowledge of the individual, knowledge of the community—and from knowledge of the unfulfilled and finite individual and community, knowledge of the fulfilled, infinite, "Individual of Individuals," God himself, follows.

To appreciate the character of this argument, used by Royce in these several ways, we have only to turn to an earlier essay, "The Possibility of Error." In this essay, a chapter from *The Religious Aspect of Philos-*

ophy, Royce argued that the possibility of error implies the actuality of "an infinite unity of conscious thought to which is present all possible thought." Royce suggested that an error is a thought which aims at being a complete thought in regard to its chosen object, and it is only by comparing the incomplete or inadequate thought with a complete or adequate thought that the incomplete thought can be known to be erroneous. Furthermore, not only could the error not be *known* to be erroneous were there not a complete thought present to a thinker who could compare the complete thought with the erroneous thought, but the error could not even be an error were there not such an actual complete thought and actual, knowing thinker. For how could the idea be incomplete by reference or comparison to *nothing*, or by reference to something other than a thought; no, for an error to be an error, an actual, adequate thought (and thinker) must exist. Since "there must be possible an infinite mass of error," there must be *actual* an infinite, all-knowing thought.

A pragmatist such as William James or Charles Sanders Peirce would say that a belief can be understood to be erroneous *if* what one *would* receive in the way of experience, *were* one to act appropriately, *would* run counter to one's expectations. But the mere *possibility* of a more satisfactory and adequate experience was not enough for Royce. Unless there were *actually* a complete idea, no belief could possibly be erroneous, for no belief could fail to measure up to a complete idea unless there actually were such a complete idea.

In the Preface to *The World and the Individual* Royce writes: "As to the most essential argument regarding the true relations between our finite ideas and the ultimate nature of things, I have never varied, in spirit, from the view maintained in . . . *The Possibility of Error*. . . ." He goes on to refer to a number of books in which the argument was used, and then states that "In the present lectures this argument assumes a decidedly new form. . . ." The argument in its new form is presented in Chapter VII of the first volume of *The World and the Individual*, the chapter entitled "The Internal and the External Meaning of Ideas." Here the argument concludes with the fourth (and final) conception of Being considered by Royce:

"What is, or what is real, is as such the complete embodiment, in individual form and in final fulfillment, of the internal meaning of finite ideas." The three conceptions of Being which Royce examined and rejected prior to settling upon this final idea were those of realism, mysticism, and critical rationalism. The fourth conception of Being, for all of the novelty of its presentation, is fundamentally that with which readers of Royce's earlier works are familiar; and the argument in its support is, strictly speaking, not a new argument distinguishable from the one to be found in "The Possibility of Error" and *The Conception of God* (1897), but—as Royce himself wrote—the argument in "a decidedly new form."

To understand the argument in its new form a distinction must be drawn, in Royce's terms, between the "internal and external meaning" of ideas. According to Royce, an idea "is as much an instance of will as it is a knowing process"; that is, an idea is a partial fulfillment of the purposive act of desiring to have an adequate conception of something. By the "internal meaning" of an idea Royce meant the "conscious embodiment" of the purpose in the idea. If I try to get a clear idea about someone, then to the extent that my thoughts are directed by that interest and come to have something of the content they would have were I entirely clear in my conception, then to that extent my idea has internal meaning. Unless to some extent I fulfill the purpose of my thought by thinking accurately, I cannot be said to have an object of thought: in thinking about someone, I have to think accurately enough, at least, to identify him as the object of my conception. Internal meaning, then, is a function of, and consequence of, human will and purpose.

But ideas refer beyond themselves to something external, not part of their content. And Royce asks, "How is it possible that an idea, which is an idea essentially and primarily because of the inner purpose that it consciously fulfills by its presence, also possesses a meaning that in any sense appears to go beyond this internal purpose?" The answer is that the external meaning of an idea is the "completely embodied internal meaning of the idea." Or, in other words, a finite thought fulfills itself to some extent by managing to be *about* something; but what the thinker aims at is a more complete and adequate idea, a fuller conception, one that fulfills his purpose in thinking. Yet unless there is such an adequate idea, such an external meaning, then the incomplete thought, the unfulfilled idea, the partial conception, aims at nothing; and if it has no objective, it cannot fail; and if it cannot fail, it cannot be incomplete or partial. Hence, the possibility of unfulfilled internal meanings implies the actuality of external meanings; and the totality of external meanings is God. God is the "Other," the fulfillment of purpose, which alone can be the object of thought. An idea is true to the extent that it "corresponds, even in its vagueness, to its own final and completely individual expression."

Royce built his conception of God in such a manner that God, or that Being which is the absolute fulfillment of all individual wills, "sees the one plan fulfilled through all the manifold lives, the single consciousness winning its purpose by virtue of all the ideas, of all the individual selves, and of all the lives."

Another insight which serves to illuminate Royce's philosophy and his method is the realization that for Royce, "the world is real only as the object of true ideas." This proposition is not peculiar to us because we tend to interpret the word "object" as we choose in order to adjust the claim to our own philosophies. But realize that, for Royce, to be the "object" of an idea is to be that at which the idea aims, its objective; and the objective of the idea (of the thinker) is a completely adequate thought, one that fulfills his original purpose in thinking. Hence, if "the world is real only as the object of true ideas," the world is real only as an absolutely adequate thought, itself an expression of will. The consequence is that God alone is real—but, then, insofar as any individual or any thought fulfills the purpose which has being because of the finite individuals and wills, then just to that extent the finite individual or thought has Being, is part of Being. Thus, unity is achieved despite the variety and finitude of things. The individual contributes to the Being who fulfills the purposes of the individuals.

With the final conception of Being, the first volume of *The World and the Individual* comes to a close. In *Nature, Man, and the Moral Order,* the second volume of these Gifford Lectures, Royce worked out the implications of his conception in order to present an idealistic theory of knowledge, a philosophy of nature, a doctrine about self, a discussion of the human individual, a portrait of the world as "a Moral Order," a study of the problem of evil, and some conclusions concerning the bearing of these matters on natural religion.

Royce's idealistic theory of knowledge is a reaffirmation of his central predisposition to accept as real only that which fulfills the purpose of an individual will. Realists talk about "hard" facts, he writes, but analysis shows that "hard" facts are understandable as facts which enable us "even now to accomplish our will better than we could if we did not acknowledge these facts." A fact is *"that which I ought to recognize* as determining or limiting what I am here consciously to do or to attempt." A distinction is drawn between the ethical Ought, definable by reference to a more rational purpose than our own, and a theoretical Ought, definable by reference to a world of recognized facts which embodies and fulfills purposes. To know, then to apprehend a fact, is to come to have the thought which the present thought would be were its purpose (its internal meaning) fulfilled by further considerations (the external meaning); to know is to think what you *ought* to think relative to the purpose of your thought. Facts are *objective* in that they are *"other than"* the present, incomplete thoughts; our grounds for acknowledging facts are *subjective* in that they are related to our purposes, the intentions of our wills; but the objective and subjective are synthesized by "the essential *Teleological* constitution of the realm of facts..."—a teleological constitution which is understood once reality or Being is recognized as absolutely ordered and fulfilling will.

Royce argues that to us who see the reality in a fragmentary fashion, facts appear to be disconnected; but there is, he claims, a linkage of facts which illuminates the particular character of each fact. Analogously, through temporal failures and efforts the reality of eternal fulfillment is won.

To Royce it appears that our wills are such that they cannot be satisfied by the mere addition of content, additional facts; for the full expression of will, other wills are necessary. Finally, fulfillment comes only from a system of wills which is such that Being is a unity, a one out of many, a will (the

Individual of Individuals) which is the infinite, eternal embodiment of individual wills which, by their temporal efforts, have contributed to the reality of the whole.

According to Royce, the idea that nature is hopelessly divided between matter and mind is itself the product of a scientific enterprise motivated by social concerns. The fulfillment of that social concern is best served by recognizing the unsatisfactory character of a conception which maintains a diversity in nature, an irreconcilable tension between matter and mind. The conception of the natural world "as directly bound up with the experiences of actually conscious beings" is more in accord with the Fourth Conception of Being which the first series of lectures was designed to advance. The idea of a nonconscious, nonliving, nonwilling reality is unacceptable, for to *be*, to be *real*, is to be the conscious fulfillment of purpose. Thus, if nature is real, nature is the conscious fulfillment of purpose.

The idea of the human self is constructed not by reference to any "Soul Substance" but, as we might expect, by reference to an "Intent always to remain another than my fellows despite my divinely planned unity with them. . . ." There is no conflict between individual selves and the Divine Will, "for the Divine Will gets expressed in the existence of me the individual only in so far as this Divine Will . . . includes within itself my own will, as one of its own purposes."

In order to justify the claim that reality exhibits a moral order, Royce insists that every evil deed must sometime be "atoned for" or "overruled" by some individual self; in this manner, perfection of the whole is realized. The evil of this world is in its incompleteness, its partial fulfillment of purposes—but since the incomplete, the unfulfilled, make sense only by reference to an actual Absolute, by being incomplete they make Being possible as an ordered whole.

Royce regarded God, or Absolute Being, as a person, that is, as "a conscious being, whose life, temporally viewed, seeks its completion through deeds. . . ." God is the totality of all conscious efforts, but viewed eternally, God is an infinite whole which includes temporal process. Man is also a person, but not absolute; his reality finally consists in God's reality—God and man are one.

Since the self possesses individuality, a uniqueness of purpose, it can be satisfied only by what is Other, by what fulfills that purpose, namely, God. But God is eternal. Consequently, the immortality of self is assured.

One can come to understand, provided he views Royce's arguments with sympathetic tolerance, how if the self is realized only in God, there is a sense in which the self (the individual) and God are one—although viewed from the varying perspectives of time and purpose, they are distinct. But if the self and God are one, then, in the respect in which they are one, they are alike: God's eternity, then, is man's; and this is man's immortality. Although the individual self, in being distinguished from other selves by his peculiar purposive striving, is only partial; yet, in contributing to the reality of the Absolute and in becoming unified with the Absolute, it is itself absolute. The part is equal to the whole, even though, considered otherwise than by reference to the final unity, the part is distinguishable from the whole.

One cannot fail to be persuaded of Royce's moral sincerity and intellectual acumen for *The World and the Individual* is eloquent witness to both. Fantastic as the idealistic image is to the realist who presupposes an unconcerned and unconscious material world as the barren scene of his pointless adventures, it has a certain intellectual charm and moral persuasiveness to one who is willing to sympathize with the interest that leads a man such as Royce to fail to understand how anything could be *real*, could be worthy of the honorific name "being," which did not show itself to be a conscious effort to go beyond the limits of fragmentary knowledge and experience to a recognition of and identity with the whole of such effort. If such a proposition as, "All Being is the fulfillment of purpose," is taken not as a description of the facts of the matter in regard to the kind of world the physicist studies, but as a suggestion that all human effort be directed to the ideal cooperation of all seekers after truth and goodness, *The World and The Individual* comes to be recognizable as a revolutionary manifesto directed to the human spirit— something quite different from the naïve speculative expression of an idealistic philosopher remote from the world of hard facts and hard men.

Pertinent Literature

Marcel, Gabriel. *Royce's Metaphysics*. Translated by Virginia Ringer and Gordon Ringer. Chicago: Henry Regnery Company, 1956.

In 1956 the existential thinker Gabriel Marcel added a foreword to this study of Josiah Royce, which he had published in French nearly forty years earlier. The great value of Royce's philosophy, he asserted, was that it marked "a kind of transition between absolute idealism and existentialist thought." Most scholars agree that "transitional" is a good term to describe *The World and the Individual*, the massive two-volume work based on Royce's Gifford Lectures of 1899-1900. This book, it is often claimed, belongs to a middle period in the development of his thought. In it one can see Royce advancing ideas originally set forth in *The Religious Aspect of Philosophy* (1885), but the positions that he offers on knowledge, God, and community have not yet achieved the richness and novelty that they would come to possess in *The Problem of Christianity* (1913). Nevertheless, Marcel's appraisal of Royce's thought also fits *The World and the Individual*: ". . . his philosophy is an important landmark in the development of contemporary thought."

Marcel's overview of Royce's metaphysics leads him to concentrate on three aspects of *The World and the Individual*. The first is Royce's theory concerning the relation between an idea and its object. Royce sees, correctly in Marcel's view, that an idea has not only a representational aspect but also volitional and intentional qualities. Marcel concurs that the relation between these "external" and "internal" meanings points toward an inescapable issue—namely, the question of what is the true connection between them.

The author underscores the point that Royce's book attempts to undercut all ultimate forms of dualism. In so doing Royce argues that external meanings are actually a reflection of internal meanings. Indeed, in the final analysis the universe is the manifestation

of the purpose and will of an Absolute Knower or God. In this context, Marcel is particularly attracted to Royce's treatment of the ancient problem of "the one and the many" in the Supplementary Essay appended to Volume I of *The World and the Individual*. Although Marcel does not find Royce's treatment completely persuasive, which helps to explain why he sees Royce's philosophy as involved in a transition from absolute idealism to existentialism, he is intrigued by Royce's attempt to fathom what the life of an Absolute Knower might be.

Royce's account of a "self-representative system" tries to show that infinite multiplicity can be grasped without contradiction. The core of his argument, Marcel suggests, is that there really are purposes whose meaning is both logically sound and dependent upon comprehension of an infinite multitude of particulars. Marcel is willing to agree that an actual, graspable infinite is not unthinkable, but he does not believe that such reality squares with "the contingency of finite individuals." He acknowledges that Royce's analysis of time and eternity seeks to clarify how the full meaning of becoming could only be possessed by a form of knowing that can comprehend change as a succession and as a totality. But as Royce attempts to cope with the meaning of individual contingency in this setting, it still seems to Marcel that the all-encompassing Absolute Individual does more to compromise the individuality of other beings than to guarantee it, as Royce promises.

More to Marcel's liking is Royce's differentiation between "description" and "appreciation," a distinction established earlier but elaborated in *The World and the Individual*. He applauds Royce's emphasizing that these two perspectives, far from being separable or ultimately in conflict, are complementary in a way that Royce perceived in especially insightful ways. What Royce calls "the world of description" is dependent upon and even an expression of "the world of appreciation"; the latter level of social understanding and value is a precondition for the objectivity of abstract reflection and scientific research which characterize a descriptive awareness and give us powerful tools to carry out our purposes. Marcel suggests that as Royce emphasizes these diverse aspects of consciousness and reality, he is feeling his way toward a less rigid notion of the Absolute and is at the same time articulating views akin to existential theories that emerged later in the twentieth century.

Smith, John E. *Royce's Social Infinite*. New York: The Liberal Arts Press, 1950.

John E. Smith's book is a good companion for Gabriel Marcel's commentary on *The World and the Individual* because it gives special attention to the problem of community in Josiah Royce's thought. Although Royce's later works—*The Philosophy of Loyalty* (1908), *The Sources of Religious Insight* (1912), and *The Problem of Christianity* (1913)—predominate in Smith's study, the author stresses that *The World and the Individual* is pivotal in the development of Royce's thought about God. This development, Smith argues, moves away from a conviction that the Absolute is an encompassing awareness that grasps all truth simultaneously and reconciles at once every conflict of finite wills.

As Royce revises his earlier position, he emphasizes the point that existence is an actual infinite in the sense of being a well-ordered system or community which has its roots in a form of interpretation that is triadic. Smith agrees with Marcel in believing that the place where Royce breaks much of his new ground is in the Supplementary Essay to the first volume of *The World and the Individual*. More than Marcel, however, Smith stresses that Royce seems to realize now that the Absolute cannot grasp everything immediately—by "appreciation," if you will—but must have a form of awareness that places greater emphasis on mediation, interpretation, and even description.

In Royce's early writings, Smith asserts, the Absolute Self is portrayed as fully actualized truth and goodness, so that the finite progress made by human beings toward knowledge and excellence constitutes no real progress for God. Royce's accent is on the completeness of thought that characterizes the Absolute. Such awareness grasps immediately and intuitively what a finite form of consciousness could comprehend only in a mediated and discursive way.

This view carries forward into *The Spirit of Modern Philosophy* (1892). Drawing on the distinction between description and appreciation, it implies that the mode of God's awareness is an eternal appreciation of all existence.

The World and the Individual, Smith believes, does not relinquish Royce's conviction that God is primarily to be understood in terms of wholeness, unity, and inclusiveness of insight. The latter quality, moreover, still entails immediacy and appreciation. But novel elements now begin to appear in Royce's conception of God. System and order become more pronounced as characteristics of God's awareness, thus suggesting that a more mediated and discursive quality may be present in the Absolute's life. These new factors, Smith believes, put Royce on the course that eventually results in a theory that comes to see reality as both an infinite system and a community of interpretation.

These changes enter Royce's view of God, Smith notes, partly in response to Royce's desire to buttress his conviction that the Absolute is not simply a knowing consciousness but also a willing self. As a willing God, Royce's Absolute expresses itself in multiple purposes and activities. The dynamism implied by such an emphasis on will in *The World and the Individual* evidently led Royce to move even further away from a focus on the immediate awareness of all-encompassing thought and toward a theory that would make God's awareness no less thorough but better able to do justice to the moving texture of experience.

Although *The World and the Individual* takes its bearings primarily from epistemological and metaphysical issues, as Royce intensifies his stress on the Absolute-as-Will and on the notion that a dynamic communal conception of existence must be accentuated, elements of his ethic of loyalty can be discerned. While only latent in *The World and the Individual*, Smith implies, this substantive work of Royce's mid-dle period is also an essential step on the way to his mature moral philosophy.

Kuklick, Bruce. *Josiah Royce: An Intellectual Biography*. Indianapolis: Bobbs-Merrill, 1972.

This book, supplemented by the author's *Rise of American Philosophy* (1977), is the most detailed recent study of Josiah Royce. It revolves around three main themes: (1) the centrality of logical problems in Royce's work; (2) the significance of Immanuel Kant in setting many of the issues that concerned him; and (3) the relationship between pragmatism and idealism as these trends developed at Harvard around the turn of the century. Bruce Kuklick's discussion of *The World and the Individual* reflects them all. As it does so, Kuklick also accents Royce's understanding of specifically human existence.

Kuklick underscores Royce's belief that ideas are volitional. Human thought expresses purpose: thus both knowing and willing are not separable affairs and human beings actually participate in the construction of their own world. Kuklick points out that in Royce's view knowing is activity; but this fact leaves us always short of full comprehension even as we may move toward increased understanding. Ultimately the completeness that we seek is found in the Absolute, and Royce's argument in *The World and the Individual* intends to ensure the notion that our finite experience can only have the sense that it actually possesses if the Absolute is real. Kuklick is not convinced by Royce's metaphysical arguments; he is somewhat more impressed by Royce's suggestions about the nature of human consciousness.

According to Kuklick, Royce provides a view of human consciousness not significantly different from the theory of William James. At least in its human form, consciousness is in process, and it is characterized by selective attention. Ideas emerge as possible plans of action. That is, to have an idea means that there is a self prepared to take action so as to fulfill an aim related to the object of the idea. In so doing, the world takes shape through human agency, although not, of course, in accord with just any interpretation that we can muster. We encounter factors of resistance in our experience, and thus a distinction between volition and cognition emerges which Royce prefers to analyze in terms of the internal and external meanings of ideas.

What we seek, Kuklick interprets Royce to say, is a correspondence between internal and external meanings; but the correspondence that we seek is still intelligible only in terms of purpose. An idea can be true only if it corresponds to its referent in the fashion that the idea intends. Herein lies the basis for Royce's claim that he was not less a pragmatist than James. However, Royce added the qualification that his was an "absolute" pragmatism. He did so because he believed that the correspondence we finite selves actually do experience in time can have the validity it clearly does possess only if there is a full correspondence between knowledge and volition. That full correspondence, Royce argues, can exist only if the Absolute is real.

Royce's Absolute involves a union of finite and fragmentary selves. The human individual, Kuklick understands Royce to argue, is aware of the world and itself, but the constraints of time keep the awareness partial and incomplete. Royce turns this existential predicament to the best, however, by interpreting our sense of finitude so that it implies a place for us within something much larger and much more inclusive. Neither James's pragmatism nor the thought of Gabriel Marcel's existential colleagues would be likely to find so near at hand Royce's optimistic assurance that human finitude is transcended by a meaningful Absolute in whose life we participate. Nevertheless, Kuklick's account of *The World and the Individual* helps to show that Royce's reading of human existence is related to other philosophical trends from the recent past, even if its metaphysical resolutions are far removed from them.

Additional Recommended Reading

Buranelli,Vincent. *Josiah Royce*. New York: Twayne, 1964. Buranelli accentuates Royce's conviction in *The World and the Individual* that "ideas are like tools. They are there for an end." He sees Royce's "pragmatism" as akin to that of Charles Sanders Peirce.

Clendenning, John. *The Life and Thought of Josiah Royce*. Madison: University of Wisconsin Press, 1985. A leading account of Royce's life and work.

Cotton, James Harry. *Royce on the Human Self*. Cambridge, Massachusetts: Harvard University Press, 1954. As Cotton spells out Royce's theories of selfhood, he also argues that there is not a sharp break between *The World and the Individual* and *The Problem of Christianity* but "only a seeming one."

Flower, Elizabeth and Murray G. Murphy. "Josiah Royce," in *A History of Philosophy in America*. Vol. II. New York: G. P. Putnam's Sons, 1977, pp. 695-769. The authors cite the second volume of *The World and the Individual* as a "major advance" in Royce's account of "appreciation" and "description" but conclude that he leaves unsettled as many problems as he solves.

Fuss, Peter. *The Moral Philosophy of Josiah Royce*. Cambridge, Massachusetts: Harvard University Press, 1965. *The World and the Individual*, says Fuss, contributes foundational elements that committed Royce to the basically "self-realizationist" moral philosophy elaborated more completely in his later works.

Jarvis, Edward A. *The Conception of God in the Later Royce*. The Hague, The Netherlands: Martinus Nijhoff, 1975. Jarvis provides a detailed analysis of the theological developments in *The World and the Individual*, sharing the view of other commentators that it points a way toward the more adequate perspective of *The Problem of Christianity*.

Roth, John K., ed. *The Philosophy of Josiah Royce*. New York: Thomas Y. Crowell, 1971. The editor suggests that the lasting contributions of Royce's *The World and the Individual* are to be found more in his analysis of finite human experience than in his metaphysical conclusions about the Absolute.

Royce, Josiah. *The Basic Writings of Josiah Royce*. Edited by John J. McDermott. Chicago: University of Chicago Press, 1969. McDermott comments on the "herculean task" Royce set for himself in *The World and the Individual*: nothing less than to provide a complete account of the nature of experience.

Schneider, Herbert W. "Josiah Royce," in *A History of American Philosophy*. New York: Columbia University Press, 1963, pp. 415-424. Schneider sees the Supplementary Essay of *The World and the Individual* as a reworking of Royce's entire philosophy in the light of suggestions about logic that he absorbed from Charles Sanders Peirce.

PRINCIPIA ETHICA

Author: George Edward Moore (1873-1958)
Type of work: Ethics
First published: 1903

Principal Ideas Advanced

The adjective "good" names an indefinable, unanalyzable, simple, unique property.

The term "naturalistic fallacy" is applied to any theory which attempts a definition of good, for if good is simple, it has no parts to be distinguished by definition.

Sometimes the value of a whole is not simply the sum of the values of its parts. [The Principle of Organic Unities.]

One's duty, in any particular situation, is to do that action which will cause more good than any possible alternative.

The ideal good is a state of consciousness in which are combined the pleasures of aesthetic contemplation and the pleasures of admiring generous qualities in other persons.

That G. E. Moore's *Principia Ethica* has attained the status of a modern classic is amply attested by the number of references made to its central concepts and arguments. Moore's central contention is that the adjective "good" refers to a simple, unique, and unanalyzable property. He claims that propositions containing value terms and ethical predicates are meaningful and can be found to be either true or false, even though the word "good" names an indefinable property knowable only by intuition or immediate insight. Moore also argues that the truth of propositions predicating intrinsic goodness—that is, that something is good on its own account, quite without reference to its value as a means—must likewise be seen immediately and without proof. The term "naturalistic fallacy" is proposed to name the error of mistaking some property other than goodness for goodness itself. Any definition of "good" would involve reference to something having distinguishable aspects or parts—hence, not simple; but since goodness is simple, any such definition would be false, an instance of the naturalistic fallacy.

The failure of previous systems of ethics, Moore alleges, is attributable to their imprecise formulations of the questions peculiar to ethics. His objective is to discover and lay down those basic principles according to which any scientific ethical investigation must proceed. Ethics should be concerned with two basic questions: "What kinds of things ought to exist for their own sakes?"—which presupposes knowledge of good—and "What kinds of actions ought we to perform?"

The first task of ethics, then, is to determine what "good" means. The only relevant type of definition is not a verbal definition but one which describes the real nature of what is denoted by stating the parts constituting the whole referent. But in this sense of "definition," "good" cannot be defined. It is a simple notion, not complex. The word "good," like "yellow," refers to an object of thought which is indefinable because it is one of many similarly ultimate terms presupposed by those complex ones which can be defined. True, one can give verbal equivalents of these notions; for example, yellow can be described in terms of light vibrations of certain frequencies—as the physicist might describe it—but light waves are obviously not identical with yellow *as experienced*.. One either knows yellow in his experience or he does not, for there is no substitute for the visual experience. Likewise, while there are other adjectives, such as "valuable," which can be substituted for "good," the property itself must be recognized in an act of direct insight.

With respect to the notion of good (as a *property* indicated by the adjective—not as a substantive, "a good" or "the good"), and to propositions predicating intrinsic goodness, Moore is an intuitionist. Such propositions are simply self-evident; proof is neither possible nor relevant. But in other respects Moore rejects intuitionism; he denies that such propositions are true *because* they are known by intuition. Holding that this, like any other way of cognizing, may be mistaken, he also denies that propositions in answer to the second basic question—concerning what *ought* to be done—can be known intuitively, since it is a question of means involving intricate causal relations and variable conditions and circumstances. Judgments about intrinsic goodness are true universally if true at all, but in order to know what we ought to do, that is, to know that any given action is the best, we would have to know that the anticipated effects are always produced and that the totality of these reflect a balance of good superior to that of any alternatives. Such judgments can be only probable, never certain. Thus, both types of ethical judgment presuppose the notion of good, but in ways not always clearly distinguished. The situation is complicated because various combinations of intrinsic and instrumental value and disvalue or indifference may occur. Obligatory acts may have no intrinsic value at all, and acts which are impossible and thus not obligatory may have great intrinsic goodness.

But things having this simple, unique quality of goodness also have other properties, and this fact has misled philosophers into what Moore terms "the naturalistic fallacy." To take any other property, such as "pleasant" or "desired," no matter how uniformly associated with good, as *definitive* of "good," is to make this error. These other properties exist in space and time, and hence are in nature; on the other hand, good is nonnatural; it belongs to that class of objects and properties which are not included in the subject matter of the natural sciences. Thus, when someone insists that "good" *means* "pleasant," or in the substantive sense, "pleasure," he is defining good in terms of a natural object or property; that this is

fallacious may be seen by substituting for the meaningful question, "Is pleasure good?" the question implied by such a definition: "Is pleasure pleasant?" Clearly we do not mean the latter, Moore insists, or anything like it, and can by direct inspection see what we do mean—we are asking whether pleasure is qualified by an unanalyzable and unique property.

That we can have this notion of good before our minds shows that "good" is not meaningless. The idea that it names a complex which might be analyzed variously must be rejected because we can always ask about any proposed definition of good as complex, "Is X good?" and see that the subject and predicate were not identical. For example, suppose "good" were defined as "that which we desire to desire." While we might plausibly think that "Is A good?" means "Is A that which we desire to desire?" we can again ask the intelligible question, "Is it good to desire to desire A?" But substituting the proposed definition yields the absurdly complicated question, "Is the desire to desire A one of the things which we desire to desire?" Again, obviously this is not what we mean, and direct inspection reveals the difference between the notions of good and desiring to desire. The only remaining alternative is that "good" is indefinable; it must be clear, however, that this condition applies only to what is meant by the adjective "good," not to "*the* good"; were the latter incapable of definition and description, ethics would be pointless.

Moore calls attention to another source of great confusion, the neglect of what he calls the "principle of organic unities." This is the paradoxical but most important truth that things good, bad, and indifferent in various degrees and relationships may constitute a whole in which value of whole and parts are not regularly proportionate. Thus, it is possible for a whole made up of indifferent or even bad parts to be good, or for one containing only good parts to be indifferent or bad, and in less extreme cases, for parts of only moderate worth to constitute wholes of great value. Crime with punishment may make a whole better than one of these two evils without the other; awareness of something beautiful has great intrinsic goodness, but the beautiful object by itself has relatively little value, and consciousness may sometimes be indifferent or bad. The relationship of part to whole is not that of means to end, since the latter consists of separable terms, and upon removal of a means the same intrinsic value may remain in the end, which situation does not obtain for part and whole. Failure to understand the principle of organic unities causes erroneous estimation of the value of a whole as equal to that of the parts.

The foregoing principles and distinctions form the core of Moore's ethics and underlie both his criticism of other views and the final elaboration of his own. He argues that naturalistic theories which identify good with natural properties must either restrict the sense of "nature" if they define "good" in terms of the natural, since in other respects the evil is just as "natural" as the good, or else must select some special feature of nature for this purpose, as does Herbert Spencer in describing the better as the more evolved. In any case the naturalistic fallacy occurs. Hedonism, the view that "pleasure *alone* is good as an end...," is by far the most common form of ethical naturalism, and it receives more detailed treatment. Hedonism is initially plausible, Moore concedes; it is difficult to distinguish being pleased by something from approving it, but we do sometimes disapprove the enjoyable, which shows that the predicate of a judgment of approbation is not synonymous with "pleasant." But most hedonists have fallen into the naturalistic fallacy. John Stuart Mill furnishes a classic example when he asserts that nothing but pleasure or happiness and the avoidance of pain are desirable as ends, and then equates "desirable" with "desired." Actually Mill later describes other things as desired, such as virtue, money, or health; thus, he either contradicts his earlier statements or makes false ones in attempting to show that such things as virtue or money are parts of happiness. He thus obliterates his own distinction—and one upon which Moore insists—between means and ends.

Moore writes that of the hedonists only Henry Sidgwick recognized that "good" is unanalyzable and that the hedonistic doctrine that pleasure is the sole good as an end must rest on intuition or be self-evident. Moore here freely admits what others might regard as a serious limitation in the intuitionist method—that Sidgwick's and his own intuitions conflict and that neither is able to prove hedonism

true or false. But this is disturbing primarily because of the disagreement rather than the lack of proof, Moore adds, since ultimate principles are necessarily incapable of demonstration. The best we can do is to be as clear as possible concerning what such intuited principles mean and how they relate to other beliefs we already hold; only thus can we convince an opponent of error. Mill had rejected Jeremy Bentham's view that the only measures of value in pleasure are quantitative, and he had suggested that there are differences in kind; we learn these by consulting competent judges and discovering their preferences. But if pleasure is really the only desirable end, differences in quality are irrelevant; thus, Sidgwick reverted to the simpler form of hedonism, but specified that the ultimate end is related essentially to human existence. Moore submits reasons for rejecting Sidgwick's intuitions. The first objection is that it is obvious that the most beautiful world imaginable would be preferable to the most ugly even if no human beings at all were there to contemplate either. It follows that things separable from human existence can be intrinsically good. But pleasure cannot be good apart from human experience; it is clear that pleasure of which no one was conscious would not be an end for its own sake. Consciousness must be a *part* of the end, and the hedonistic principle is thus seen to be false: it is not pleasure alone but pleasure together with consciousness that is intrinsically good.

The importance of this conclusion lies in the method used to achieve it—that of completely isolating the proposed good and estimating its value apart from all related objects—for the same method shows that consciousness of pleasure is not the only good. Surely no one would think that a world consisting of nothing but consciousness of pleasure would be as good as one including other existents, and even if these were not intrinsically valuable, the latter world could be better as an organic unity. Similar methods of analysis refute other forms of hedonism—egoistic and utilitarian; Moore concludes that, at best, pleasure would be a criterion of good were pleasure and the good always concomitant, but he regards this as very doubtful and supposes that there is no criterion of good at all.

The chief remaining type of ethics Moore criticizes is what he calls "metaphysical ethics" positing some proposition about a supersensible reality as the basis for ethical principles. He admits that the metaphysicians are right in thinking that some things that *are* are not natural objects, but wrong in concluding that therefore whatever does not exist in nature must exist elsewhere. As noted above, things like truth, universals, numbers, and goodness do not exist at all. But metaphysical ethicists such as the Stoics, Spinoza, and Kant have tried to infer what is good from what is ultimately real and thus have committed a variant of the naturalistic fallacy, for whether the reality involved is natural or supernatural is irrelevant. To the second basic ethical question, "What kind of actions ought we to perform?" a supersensible reality might be relevant, but typical metaphysical systems have no bearing on practice. For example, if the sole good pertains to an eternal, perfect, Absolute Being, there is no way by which human action can enhance the goodness of this situation.

Perhaps the metaphysical ethicists have thus erred through failing to notice the ambiguity of the question, "What is good?" which may refer either to good things or to goodness itself; this ambiguity accounts for the inconsistency between such propositions as that the only true reality is eternal and that its future realization is good, when what is meant is that something like—but not identical with—such a reality would be good. But in this case it becomes clear that it is fallacious to define good as constituted by this reality. While "X is good" is verbally similar to other propositions in which both subject and predicate stand for existents, it is actually radically different; of any two existents so related we may still ask, "Is this whole good?" which again shows the uniqueness of the value predicate.

Because of Moore's precise analytical method, the details of his criticism of other positions cannot be treated adequately here, but they are in principle germane to the lines suggested above, as is also his account of practical ethics. It is essential to remember that in answering the question as to what we ought to do once we know intuitively what things are good as ends, a different method must come into use. Since practical ethical judgments assert causal relations between actions and good or bad effects, the empirical method affording probability, never certainty, is indicated. Thus, Moore differs from traditional intuitionists both in his definition of "right" and in his account of how it is known. Right is not to be distinguished from the genuinely useful, and duty is "that action, which will cause more good to exist in the Universe than any possible alternative." In practice our knowledge of right and duty is most limited, so we must consider as duties those acts which will *usually* yield better results than any others. Such limitations do not excuse individuals from following the general rules, but when the latter are lacking or irrelevant, attention should be redirected to the much neglected intrinsic values of the foreseeable effects. It follows, of course, that virtue, like duty, is a means rather than an end, contrary to the views of some Christian writers and even of Kant, who hold inconsistently that either virtue or good will is the sole good, but that it can be rewarded by something better.

It remains to state Moore's conception of "*the* good" or the ideal. He notes that he will try to describe the ideal merely as that which is intrinsically good in a high degree, not the best conceivable or the best possible. Its general description follows: " The best ideal we can construct will be that state of things which contains the greatest number of things having positive value, and which contains nothing evil or indifferent—*provided* that the presence of none of these goods, or the absence of things evil or indifferent, seems to diminish the value of the whole." The method of discovering both the intrinsically valuable and its degrees of value is that previously mentioned: the method of isolation. It will show that "By far the most valuable things, which we know or can imagine, are certain states of consciousness, which may be roughly described as the pleasures of human intercourse and the enjoyment of beautiful objects." Moore stresses the point that it is these wholes, rather than any constituents, which are the ideal ends.

In aesthetic appreciation there are cognition of the object's beautiful qualities and also an appropriate emotion, but neither of these elements has great value in itself compared to that of the whole, and to have a positive emotion toward a really ugly object constitutes a whole which is evil. Beauty is thus not a matter of feeling: "the beautiful should be *defined* as that of which the admiring contemplation is good in itself," and whether an object has true beauty "depends upon the *objective* question whether the whole in question is or is not truly good, and does not depend upon the question whether it would or would not excite particular feelings in particular persons." Subjectivistic definitions of beauty commit the naturalistic fallacy, but it should be noted that beauty can be defined as it is above, thus leaving only one unanalyzable value term, "good." Consideration of the cognitive element in aesthetic appreciation shows that knowledge adds intrinsic value; aside from the value of true belief as a means or that of the actual existence of the object, it is simply and clearly better to know it truly rather than merely to imagine it. Thus appreciation of a real but inferior object is better than that of a superior but imaginary one.

The second and greater good consists of the pleasures of personal affection. All the elements of the best aesthetic enjoyments plus the great intrinsic good of the object are present here. Part of the object consists of the mental qualities of the person for whom affection is felt, though these must be appropriately expressed in the bodily features and behavior. Since "Admirable mental qualities . . . consist very largely in an emotional contemplation of beautiful objects . . . the appreciation of them will consist essentially in the contemplation of such contemplation. It is true that the most valuable appreciation of persons appears to be that which consists in the appreciation of their appreciation of other persons . . . therefore, we may admit that the appreciation of a person's attitude toward other persons . . . is far the most valuable good we know. . . ." From these assertions it follows that the ideal, contrary to tradition, must include material properties, since both appreciation of beauty and of persons requires corporeal expression of the valuable qualities.

Since the emotions appropriate to both beautiful objects and to persons are so widely varied, the totality of intrinsic goods is most complex, but Moore is confident that "a reflective judgment will in the main decide correctly . . ." both what things are positive goods and the major differences in relative values. But this is possible only by exact distinction of the objects of value judgment, followed by direct intuition of the presence, absence, or degree of the unique property, good.

Twentieth century students of ethics have benefited immeasurably from Moore's attempt to be clear and precise in the analysis of ethical principles and from his redirection of attention to the really basic questions. Some critics cannot accept certain major conclusions concerning the indefinability of "good," its presence to intuition, its objective status, and the consequent treatment of the "naturalistic fallacy," but even the nature and the extent of the disagreement he has aroused testify to Moore's stature as a philosopher of ethics.

Pertinent Literature

Schilpp, Paul A., ed. *The Philosophy of G.E. Moore* (The Library of Living Philosophers). Vol. IV. London: Cambridge University Press, 1968.

Each volume of The Library of Living Philosophers contains not only articles written for that volume critically examining the works of a philosopher but also the philosopher's replies to those critics. The points George Edward Moore selects for rejoinder are those he regards as most important; nearly a third of his "Reply to My Critics" is on ethics, and most of that is on his *Principia Ethica*. Contributors to the Paul A. Schilpp volume who deal with *Principia* *Ethica* include C. D. Broad, Charles L. Stevenson, William K. Frankena, H. J. Paton, and Abraham Edel. Here we can only sample the exchanges of views rather than give comprehensive coverage to this admirable volume.

Broad focuses on two questions: What is the distinction between a "natural" and a "non-natural" characteristic? and, what, if any, is the connection between the doctrines that "good" is simple and unanalyzable and that it is nonnatural? Failing to find clear and detailed answers, Broad sets out to supply the basis for an explanation. He posits nonethical "good-making" characteristics, whose presence may make the object possessing them intrinsically good. But if "good" is a simple quality present in the intrinsically good thing, not definable at all, it will hence not be definable in natural terms; thus there is indeed a connection between the claim that "good" names a simple quality and the claim that it names a nonnatural quality.

On Moore's hypotheses, some important features follow. *If* good is a characteristic, it is nonnatural; one accepting this is committed to believing that there are *a priori* notions, of which goodness is one; and because of the necessary connection between the natural good-making characteristics of an object and its nonnatural goodness, judgments of its goodness are *synthetic a priori* judgments (necessarily true, although not true by definition). The alternatives for those unwilling to accept these implications are that either goodness is a natural characteristic or that the connections between goodmaking characteristics and the goodness that these determine is only contingent, not necessary.

Stevenson exhibits some of Moore's arguments in such a way as to show that Moore's affirmations are compatible with that sort of naturalistic view that regards emotive meaning as the meaning of "typically ethical" expressions. Thus Moore cannot hold up his intuition of goodness as a nonnatural quality as the only alternative to existing, defective naturalisms. Alleging that Moore has confined himself systematically to cognitive meanings as the substance of typically ethical utterances, Stevenson suggests, Moore has shut himself off from an alternative preferable to declaring "good" indefinable.

Frankena investigates the relation of "good" (or "value") to obligation. This principle of Moore, on the strength of which he is often called a utilitarian but not a hedonistic utilitarian, is that the act which an agent ought to do is always the one that promotes the most possible intrinsic good in the universe. Frankena analyzes Moore's conception of "good" at some length, concluding that if good is simple, as Moore insists, then it does not have external relations

to moral agents; it does not suffice as a basis of judgments of what is right and therefore of what ought to be done; hence its presence cannot compel an act by a moral agent. Thus, goodness has no obligatoriness and is not normative. And if not, then there is no reason to call it indefinable or nonnatural.

Paton asks whether the goodness of a thing might not vary with varying circumstances. Moore's later description of good as "worth having for its own sake" seems to assume a relation to a mind or self. Paton does not see that it is proven in *Principia Ethica*, or follows from the view that goodness is simple and unanalyzable, that good does not vary. He himself finds that the only thing good in all circumstances, not varying according to those circumstances, is, as Immanuel Kant suggested, a good will. Otherwise there are cases of good objects whose goodness depends on relations to other, variable things.

Paton also explores the relation of good to will. Is it the case that to be good is to be willed in a certain way (say, rationally), or is it the case that to be willed in a certain way is to be good? While Moore regards such a relation to be only empirical, he has not ruled out by argument the possibility that there might be a necessary reciprocal connection. Paton would call for exploration of the possibility that a thing to be good must satisfy some desire, will, or need. Acknowledging this possibility, he says, still need not commit the naturalistic fallacy.

Edel makes a thorough examination of Moore's entire ethic, treating it as a logical system and extracting and arranging its terms, definitions, postulates, and rules for the formation of ethical statements and procedures for interpretation and for determining the truth and falsity of ethical statements within the logical structure. Edel essays to discover whether any values are expressed in the structure itself or by its adoption. Screening out considerations of instrumental values while preservng intrinsic value, Moore's postulates (Edel finds) require the absolute constancy of value. From this foundation flow several consequences that make the logical structure a vehicle for (in Edel's terms, not Moore's) several broad values. These consequences are that the doctrine encourages contemplative vision rather than practical problem-solving in ethical matters; the only possible type of interpretation of value relations is intuitive; the ultimate function of ethics becomes an aesthetic experience of contemplating conceived worlds and intuiting their intrinsic good; duties are little explained, but the difficulty of knowing them becomes impressive; existing conventional moralities, even when practiced in the face of rational criticism of their provisions, are greatly supported, while innovation in action is strongly discouraged; yet bold speculation and openness to newly conceived values may elevate the human spirit despite its bonds to mundane morality.

Now it is Moore's turn. In reply to both Broad and Frankena on the relation of "good" and "ought," Moore essays to give more information about the meaning of "good." He introduces the comparative form "better," and offers a sense of "better" of which "good" is the positive degree. Examples: "This world is better than any other possible world would have been," and (in paraphrase) "If there were two worlds, neither containing any pleasure but one containing more pain than the other, the other would be better." Thus it would be true of a "good" world that it is a world whose existence is better than if no world exists at all. Yet Moore refuses to *define* "good" in terms of this sense of "better"; he wishes only to *exhibit* this sense to us.

Moore finds Stevenson persuasive, but decides he has reasons to remain with his early view that "good"

is indeed a characteristic. He plies Frankena with a great number of queries as to Frankena's meanings, and challenges Frankena's step from the view that statements of the presence of value do not include and are not identical with statements about obligation, to the view that such statements are not normative. Moore in fact disputes virtually all of Frankena's points, with the exception of the point that since "good" is simple it cannot be defined in terms of obligation.

As for Paton, Moore now concedes that the proposition that there exists a state of affairs which is good entails the proposition that some experience does exist—in other words, that good must be related to mind. In elaborating one of Paton's examples, Moore gives an instance of the good which underscores his insistence that an object be seen on the whole before being judged as to goodness. In the case given, he places the good in the motive rather than in the carrying out of the act. He asserts that the whole combination would have been equally good, intrinsically, no matter what the circumstances under which it occurred.

Moore disclaims understanding Edel's essay sufficiently to reply. Edel has undertaken the impossible task of searching for structure where no structure existed or was intended, and in doing so has produced a fantastic misrepresentation of Moore's doctrines.

White, Alan R. "Ethics," in *G. E. Moore: A Critical Exposition*. Oxford, Basil Blackwell, 1958.

Alan R. White treats George Edward Moore principally as a founding spirit of the British analytical movement in contemporary philosophy. Setting forth Moore's conceptions of analysis as processes of inspection, division, and distinction, White finds that as early as 1903, in *Principia Ethica,* Moore was already applying these methods to ethical investigations.

Defining the field of ethics by the question "What is good?" Moore is interested in "good" only in one sense—ethical, simple, and indefinable—known only by intuition. Yet Moore does not claim that an ethical truth is true *because* it is known by intuition; thus he is not a traditional intuitionist. Moore mentions many other senses of "good." White objects that these are not the many meanings of one ambiguous term, but rather that "good" has one meaning only, its valuative meaning, and that these variations are differences in the applicability of that meaning under differing circumstances.

White protests again that Moore does not actually stick to the view that good (goodness) is unanalyzable, but actually analyzes good by the method of distinguishing it from other notions. White finds the naturalistic fallacy to be the equating of any two notions or terms that are actually distinct. He shows clearly the close relation of this conception to the "open question" method, upon which Moore depends to reveal the fallacy—that is, to show that any naturalistic notion is not the same as "good."

White claims that Moore confused meaning with naming, taking the meaning of any word to be that thing—either physical or mental—that it names, and, upon being unable to find a physical meaning for "good," arrogated it to the status of a property that had a mental, although objective, meaning. He did not consider any third possible thing that could comprise its meaning. This explains many of the criticisms of "good" as a character, simple, indefinable, and independent. It also helps to explain why Moore is almost persuaded by Stevenson that he should heed emotive meaning, where he might find the sort of meaning he could not more clearly exhibit in the sphere of cognitive meaning. Moore need not insist that propositions about good are true or false, in the sense of a correspondence theory of truth, for ordinary language—which ought to be Moore's standard—has many other well-established usages.

In examining Moore's conception of the "intrinsically good," White commends the substitute expression "if quite alone" for "intrinsically." It best expresses Moore's intended meaning, and makes evident the relation of intrinsic goodness to the test by isolation for anything alleged to be intrinsically good. Actually, White suggests, the phrase "intrinsically good" does not convey one particular sense of "good," but rather signals a particular type of reason for applying the word. It expresses the claim that for *this* good object, the claimant discerns ultimate good, beyond which there is no further ground, hence no further explanation. Basically, White concludes, Moore is trying to show us that all the various reasons to apply "good" correctly rest upon these ultimate judgments, expressed in the application of "good" without a reason.

Additional Recommended Reading

Broad, C. D. "Is 'Goodness' a Name of a Simple Non-Natural Quality?," in *Proceedings of the Aristotelian Society*. N.S. XXXIV (1934), pp. 249-268. A careful discussion of the issue raised by Moore's contention that goodness is simple and unanalyzable.

Frankena, W. K. " The Naturalistic Fallacy," in *Mind*. XLVIII, no. 192 (October, 1939), pp. 464-477. A penetrating and influential statement.

Hudson, W. D., ed. *New Studies in Ethics*. Vol. II. New York: St. Martin's Press, 1974. Chapter by J. N. Findlay on "Moore, Rashdall and Ross," and chapter by G. J. Warnock on "Intuitionism." Two careful critiques of Moore's ethics.

Jones, E. E. C. "Mr. Moore on Hedonism," in *The International Journal of Ethics*. XVI (July, 1906), pp. 429-464. Concentrates on the degree to which Moore's view approaches a hedonistic utilitarianism.

Lewy, Casimir. *G. E. Moore on the Naturalistic Fallacy*. Oxford: Oxford University Press, 1965. Another thoughtful analytic examination of the "fallacy" named by Moore.

THE LIFE OF REASON

Author: George Santayana (1863-1952)
Type of Work: Metaphysics, philosophy of history
First published: 1905-1906

Principal Ideas Advanced

The philosophy of history is an interpretation of man's past in the light of his ideal development.

The life of reason, which gives meaning to history, is the unity given to existence by a mind in love with the good.

By the use of reason man distinguishes between spirit and nature, and comes to understand his own wants and how to satisfy them.

Instinct which originally showed itself only in animal impulses takes on ideal dimensions and leads man into service for society and God.

Finally, in art, which is the imposing of form on matter, but most of all in science, which puts the claims of reason to the test of fact, the life of reason reaches its ideal consummation.

In his autobiography, Santayana says that *The Life of Reason* had its origin in a course which he gave at Harvard University entitled "Philosophy of History." It drew heavily from Plato and Aristotle, but also from Bacon, Locke, Montesquieu, and Taine. We may add Schopenhauer (who was the subject of Santayana's PhD dissertation), and his professor William James, whose biologically oriented psychology left a strong impression on Santayana.

For Santayana, the philosophy of history implies no providential plan of creation or redemption but is simply "retrospective politics"; that is to say, an interpretation of man's past in the light of his ideal development. It is the science of history which deals with events inferred from evidence and explained in terms of causal law. But not content with a mere knowledge of what has happened, man has a strong propensity toward trying to find meaning in events as if history were shaped to some human purpose. Admittedly, it is not; still, the exercise is profitable, for it is one of the ways in which we discover what goals we wish to pursue in the future. The failures and successes of our forebears, as their acts will appear when measured by our ideals, can help us to appraise our standards, as well as to enlighten us with

respect to how far they can be attained. But it can serve its function only if we remember that it is ideal history—an abstract from reality made to illustrate a chosen theme—rather than a description of actual tendencies observable in the world.

The theme which Santayana selects as giving meaning to history is the rise and development of reason. Unlike his idealistic counterparts, who think of nature as the product and embodiment of reason, he conceives reason as a latecomer on the evolutionary scene and very much dependent upon what has gone before. This is not to say that there is no order in nature prior to the dawn of consciousness in man. Santayana's contention, on the contrary, is that reason, which is too often thought of in the abstract, schoolmasterly fashion, is in reality an extension of the order already achieved in organized matter. In its earliest phase, it is nothing more than instinct which has grown conscious of its purposes and representative of its conditions. For in the dark laboratories of nature, life has already solved the hardest problems, leaving to its strange child, reason, nothing to do at first but amuse itself with the images which drift through the mind while the body goes about its accustomed business. We can scarcely call it reason until, distinguishing these mental states from objects, reason gradually sees what the parent organism is about, what it runs from, what it pursues, and how it manages each new eventuality. Then it begins to play its role. Where instinct is dependent on present cues, reason can summon thoughts from afar, suggest short cuts, and balance likelihoods. Often its well-meant suggestions lead to destruction; but, on the other hand, its occasionally fruitful counsels tend to perpetuate themselves in habits and customs, as a shelter of branches which, devised for one night's protection, remains standing and becomes a rudimentary home. It is in this way that reason, an adjunct of life, comes to have a "life" of its own.

Reason, by this accounting, is the servant of will or interest. It is these that determine what is good. Santayana calls the Life of Reason the unity inherent in all existence.

Santayana traces reason's career through five phases. He devotes one book to each.

Reason in Common Sense may be regarded as introducing the other books. It outlines the origins of the two realms, nature and spirit, whose fortunes are followed through the rest of the work. Out of an originally chaotic experience, man learns to distinguish first the stable, predictable realm of nature. Regularity and order are present there; and things occurring repeatedly can be identified and their habits noted. But in a great part of experience, images come and go in no discernible pattern, and combine in innumerable ways. This remainder we come to designate as spirit: it is the seat of poetry and dreams, and later of philosophy and mathematics.

Human progress may be viewed as the gradual untangling of these two realms. The rich garment of sight and sound under which nature appears to our senses conceals its structure and beguiles man into supposing that trees and rivers have spirits and pursue purposes not unlike his own. It is practical experience—fishing and agriculture—that gradually teaches him otherwise, enabling him to strip off irrelevant qualities, and discern the mechanical process underneath. Not surprisingly, he is sometimes reluctant to leave behind the more congenial picture of poetry and myth. But insofar as he becomes aware of his advantage, he learns to prefer things to ideas,

and to subordinate thinking to the arts of living.

Almost as difficult as discerning nature is the task of deciding what is good. Before consciousness awakened, instinct guided the body toward the satisfaction of genuine, if partial, needs. But when ideas appeared, impulse was diverted, and moral perplexity began. False gods arose, which exist only in imagination, and these must be set aside in favor of ideas which live up to their promises. And there is the further problem of subordinating the claims of competing goods under a common ideal. Reason has not to go beyond human nature to discover the truth and order of values. By understanding man's wants and the limits of his existence, it points him toward his highest fulfillment, that is, his happiness—than which he has no other end.

Viewed in these larger aspects, the rational life is sanity, maturity, common sense. It justifies itself against romanticism, mysticism, and all otherworldliness which betoken a failure to distinguish between ideal and real, or a misguided flight from nature to the world of dreams.

Reason in Society follows the course of man's ideal attachments from the passionate love of a man for a maid to the fancies of a man of taste and finally to the devotions of a saint. The instincts which unite the sexes, bind parents and offspring, and draw the lonely from their isolation into tribes and cities, when illuminated with the flame of consciousness, take on ideal dimensions and give rise to love, loyalty, and faith. It is the mark of love to combine impulse and representation; and no one who has truly loved can be entirely deaf to the voice of reason or indifferent to the liberal life toward which it calls.

Santayana groups societies into three classes. The first, which he calls *natural* societies, includes not merely the family, but economic and political groups. In these, association is more instinctive than voluntary: but they serve reason well when the regimen that they prescribe becomes the means of fashioning strong, reliant individuals who, without disloyalty to their origins, form *free* societies based on mutual attachments and common interests. Such persons, in possession of their own wills, may go further and create *ideal* societies, which is what we do when, forsaking the company of men, we make beauty or truth our companion.

In its social expressions, perhaps more than anywhere else, reason has to draw the fine line between crude fact and irresponsible fancy. Somewhere between the shrewd materialism of Sancho and the lofty madness of Don Quixote, there is a way of living which incorporates the ideal in the actual, whether in love or in politics. Therein lies the liberal or free life for man.

Reason in Religion develops the view, which is perhaps as characteristic of Comte as it is of Hegel, that religion is a half-way station on the road from irresponsible fancy to verifiable truth. It is neither to be rejected out of hand as imbecile and superstitious, nor rationalized and allegorized until it agrees with science. In the story of human progress it fulfills a civilizing function, but under serious disabilities: for although it pursues the same goal as reason, it relies upon imagination instead of logic and experiment. On the positive side, its occasional profound insights into moral reality have spurred mankind to needed reforms; but this gain is offset by its stubborn adherence to an anthropomorphic view of nature which closes the way to systematic advance.

A lifelong student of the religions of the West, Santayana illuminates his theme with detailed criticisms of the major traditions. The Hebrew religion gets high marks for its wholesome emphasis upon morals, but is censured for its dogmatic and intolerant spirit. The Christian gospel, which dramatizes man's efforts to transcend his nature, is an important step toward the goal of freedom; but it needs to be blended with pagan ritual if man is not to lose sight of his moral dimensions. Along the Mediterranean shores, such a paganized Christianity developed. But it remained strange to its converts in the northern forests. Gothic art, philosophy, and chivalry are, by contrast, a barbarized Christianity, and have as their proper motif the native religion of the Teutons. This it was that, coming of age, threw off the world-denying gospel and emerged in its proper sublimation, first as Protestantism, then as romanticism and Absolute Egotism. Less mature, and further divorced from reality than Catholicism, Gothic Christianity lingers on in various idealisms—moral, political, philosophical—obscuring the path of reason.

Reason in Art is broadly conceived to include every activity which "humanizes and rationalizes objects." For Santayana, with his classical bias, artistic activity consists in imposing form upon matter. Like religion, art is preoccupied with imagination; but its concern is more wholesome because, instead of mistaking fancies for facts, it fashions facts according to its ideal preferences. Thus, each genuinely artistic achievement is a step forward toward the goal of rational living.

Man's earliest constructions must have been clumsy and unprepossessing, not even rivaling the spontaneous products of nature. Compared, for example, with the prancing of a stallion, the movements of a savage in his dance are crude and ridiculous. But when art frees the dance from the excitement of war or courtship, and makes the intention its study, a new form of discipline and social control appears which purges the soul. So man tames his own spirit and gladdens it with sights and sounds.

The advance of civilization is not always friendly to free creation. Customs, acquiring almost the force of instincts, stifle invention; and products have a way of enslaving their producers. A society which looks upon art as truancy from business condemns the artist to vagrancy and robs his genius of its normal incentive. It has entered a post-rational phase because it has lost touch with man's genuine needs. Art is no mere pleasurable accessory to life. Man is engaged in liberal and humane enterprise in the measure that, transcending his animal needs and vulgar ambition, he becomes the master of the conditions of his existence, visits on them his kind of perfection, and renders their tragic aspects endurable by clothing them in intelligible and regular forms.

Reason in Science brings the Life of Reason to its *logical* conclusion; for, as Santayana defines science, it is the consummation of the rational ideal in the light of which the other phases of human life have been interpreted and alongside which they have been judged. Insofar as the standard has been presupposed all along, this final volume is somewhat anticlimactic. What saves it from this lot is the feeling of contemporaneousness that goes with the word "science," together with the belief (characteristic of the period in which the work appeared) that mankind has *actually* entered the scientific era for which all previous history was but the prelude. Science, says Santayana, is practically a new thing: only twice in history has it appeared—for three hundred years in Greece and for a comparable time in the modern West. Art and religion have had their day—nothing more is to be expected from them. They bow before the new techniques of measurement and verification. The fruits of science, however, have scarcely begun to appear; and the morrow is sure to bring many surprises.

Santayana's purpose, however, was not primarily to trumpet the dawn of a new day. Optimism with respect to the future was never one of his characteristics. But he was concerned to defend tough-minded naturalism against tender-minded idealism and against all kinds of compromise. Perhaps we might say that his trumpet blast is an effort to frighten off the enemies of science who, he thought, would yet have their way.

To this end, he stresses the sharp distinction between the realm of nature and the realm of spirit. There is a science corresponding to each of these which, using classic terms, he designates respectively as *physics* and *dialectic*.

The ideal expression of physics is mechanics, because the laws governing the behavior of matter are there made perfectly intelligible. But mechanics is exceptional, true only in the gross. The forms and repetitions of nature are never simple and never perfect. Nevertheless, all knowledge which has to do with facts must adopt a mechanical principle of explanation. This is true, Santayana insists, even in the sciences that treat of man—notably history and psychology. There are no special "historical forces," such as idealists are wont to suppose: historical causation breaks up into miscellaneous natural processes and minute particular causes. Similarly, there are no "moral causes," such as biographers and literary psychologists presume: the part of psychology which is a science is physiological and belongs to the biology of man.

As physics comprehends all sciences of fact, dialectic includes all sciences of idea. Its perfect expression is mathematics, which makes possible the deductive elaboration of hypotheses in physics. But another branch of dialectics elaborates the relationship between conflicting human purposes or ideals. Socrates, who pioneered in its development, first established rational ethics. Purely a normative science, it sheds great light on human undertakings, and is presupposed in any study (such as the present one) which attempts to deal intelligently with problems of good and evil. But it is limited to ideas, and cannot take the place of observation and experiment in questions that have to do with existence.

As between questions of fact and questions of purpose, the latter are by far the more fateful, since it is within their domain to decide whether the Life of Reason is to be pursued. Here Santayana considers at length the subject of post-rational ethics and religion. The age of the Greeks passed. In mathematics, physics, and medicine, knowledge continued to progress; but meanwhile a sense of world-weariness descended upon men's minds, causing them to turn their backs on worldly enterprise and seek consolation in pleasure or compensation in ecstasy, or to deaden disappointment by asceticism and obedience. The humanism of Socrates gave place to Stoicism, Epicureanism, Skepticism, and to a revival of pagan cults, all founded on personal or metaphysical despair. In Christianity a similar experience of disillusion forced the imagination to take wings and seek its hope beyond the clouds.

In Santayana's judgment these post-rational systems are not to be condemned. They witness to the fact that life is older and more persistent than reason and knows how to fall back on more primitive solutions to its problems when its bolder experiments fail. And, even in retreat, they hold on to certain conquests of reason, which they fortify and furnish in rare fashion. So, true sages can flourish and true civilizations can develop in retrogressive times, and supernaturalism can nourish a rational and humane wisdom.

This, however, is not to admit that the post-rational systems are an advance over the rational even in the solution of man's spiritual enigmas. And when the same despair breeds arbitrary substitutes for physical science, it is time to cry alarm. Santayana's final chapter, "The Validity of Science," is devoted to criticisms of science, particularly from theologians and transcendental philosophers. The former wish to combine scientific explanation with relics of myth, and so preserve a sanction over moral and political behavior. What the latter seek is less clear. Their attack consists in showing (what was never in doubt) that the findings of science are relative; such philosophers, apparently, aim at freeing their minds of intelligible notions so that they can swim in the void of the vegetative and digestive stage of consciousness.

Science is not beyond criticism. A healthy skepticism respecting the claims of reason is ever in order.

It is an integral part of science to review its findings, and purge itself of arbitrariness and bad faith. For its whole aim is to free the mind from caprice by bringing it under the control of objective principles. Santayana quotes Heraclitus' saying, "Men asleep live each in his own world, but when awake they live in the same world together." Religion and art are too much like dreaming; when man brings his dreams under the control of the real world, on the one hand, and the principle of contradiction, on the other, he passes from mere faith and aspiration to knowledge and expectation.

Pertinent Literature

Kirkwood, M. M. *Santayana: Saint of the Imagination.* Toronto: University of Toronto Press, 1961.

M. M. Kirkwood has designed her book in order to realize two purposes: (1) to portray the man George Santayana by complementing his own autobiographical account with materials drawn from his letters, and (2) to explicate the significant strands in his philosophical thought. Her major thesis is summed up in the subtitle of her book—that Santayana was a "saint of the imagination." On the philosophical level, she holds that for Santayana the naturalist it is imagination which, with its creative power, lifts man above the other animals and unleashes his creative capacity to create culture as it unfolds in the institutions of art, religion, and science, and which also enables him to live the spiritual life absorbed in the contemplation of essences. On the biographical level, she sketches the imaginative life of Santayana the man and attempts to show the continuity of his career. She depicts Santayana as more a poet than a philosopher, but always as a person who was constant in his naturalist convictions, courageous and sincere about his religious feelings, and unremittingly creative until the end.

Chapters 9 and 10 are devoted to the exegesis of *The Life of Reason*, as it appeared in the first edition in 1905 and 1906, published in five volumes. The general title of both chapters reveals the author's line of interpretation: "The Imagination Producing a Philosophy."

Chapter 9 treats *Reason in Common Sense* and *Reason in Society.* Kirkwood canvasses Santayana's definitions of reason as she expounds the epistemology and theory of values contained in *Reason in Common Sense*; she seeks to trace and elucidate his descriptions of the office of reason in the creation of human culture—an office conspicuous in the quest for harmony of human impulses among themselves and also with the natural environment. In her exposition of *Reason in Society* she pauses to remark that, since the book is replete with remarkable judgments of humane wisdom together with direct, practical applications, it is more interesting than its more profoundly philosophical antecedent.

Chapter 10 takes up *Reason in Religion, Reason in Art,* and *Reason in Science.* Kirkwood observes that Santayana may have been influenced by his parents to regard religions as artificial and fictitious, but that he nevertheless experienced deep religious feelings which he would not gainsay. Although Santayana's naturalistic convictions repudiated the supernatural, he persisted in the appreciation of the value of religion as fundamental to human civilization, locating its validity not in the facts it alleges but in the ideal values it posits, values manifest in the religious virtues of piety, spirituality, and charity.

Kirkwood finds *Reason in Art* a less striking volume than *Reason in Religion;* but in her brief exposition she associates its themes with the argument of Santayana's earlier work, *The Sense of Beauty*. She rounds out her treatment of *The Life of Reason* with a discussion of the final volume, *Reason in Science*. Here she focuses on Santayana's moral philosophy, attending to his tripartite division of prerational morality, rational ethics, and postrational morality, and delineating his preference for rational ethics.

Methodologically, Kirkwood stays close to the text, summarizing each volume of *The Life of Reason,* and interspersing her summary with numerous quotations from Santayana. These are selected to underscore the role of the imagination, which is twofold: (1) imagination as Santayana's own faculty enabling him to create, and (2) imagination as a special agency in human culture. Religion may serve to illustrate her theme. Santayana as a naturalist did not believe in religion as a doctrinal creed stating truths about existence. Disbelief in Santayana's case, however, did not seduce him to discount the imagi-

native power of religion as a vessel of beauty and a vehicle of moral significance.

In Chapter 14, Kirkwood considers the abridged, one-volume edition of *The Life of Reason*, which appeared in 1954. Following the account of its publication reported by Daniel Cory, she relates that the aged philosopher worked over the Triton edition with a red crayon while his literary secretary, Cory, assisted him. She esteems the one-volume edition as the occasion for the philosopher to complete his task by remaking an early, basic work in order to round out his thought. While Chapter 14 does not mention every revision, it outlines the major differences between the earlier and later editions and calls attention to the most significant changes and deletions. Particularly noteworthy is that in the 1954 edition Santayana dropped the term "mechanism" and its derivatives in numerous passages and substituted the terms "materialism" and "naturalism" and their derivatives.

Munitz, Milton K. *The Moral Philosophy of Santayana.* New York: Humanities Press, 1958.

Milton K. Munitz regards George Santayana as primarily a moral philosopher who sought to understand the conditions of life and to estimate its possible goods. He finds two strands running through Santayana's thought which contribute to both its strengths and weaknesses: naturalism and eclecticism. The naturalism draws upon traditional views of man, knowledge, and nature associated with the Greeks, particularly with Aristotle; it portrays man as a being in nature whose impulses and desires point to ideals or goals as their satisfactory fulfillment; it is realistic in the theory of knowledge; and it proposes the ideal of a good life which, grounded in nature, embraces both the theoretical and practical functions of man. The eclecticism, on the other hand, introduces doctrines which are incompatible with the naturalism— a Platonic doctrine of essence, an epistemological dualism characteristic of British empiricism with its implication of skepticism, and a theory of spirituality which is otherworldly. The eclecticism is alleged to split Santayana's thought into an untenable metaphysical, epistemological, and moral dualism. Munitz clearly favors the naturalistic strand in Santa-

yana's thought, and criticizes or reinterprets the eclectic factors along consistently formulated naturalistic lines.

This compact book is divided into three parts: (1) naturalism and dualism, (2) the life of reason, and (3) the spiritual life. It is the second part which concentrates on *The Life of Reason*, although comments which illuminate this work appear in other chapters. In Chapter 1, for example, Munitz distinguishes three stages in the development of Santayana's thought. The first is otherworldly and pessimistic; the second is naturalistic and humanistic; and the third reverts to the outlook of the first. It evinces, to use Santayana's term, a "post-rational" mind—one disappointed in the ability to attain natural happiness and seeking solace in mystical self-absorption.

According to Munitz, *The Life of Reason* belongs to the second stage; it is the best expression of Santayana's humanism and naturalism. In Chapter 2 Munitz concentrates on this masterpiece. He opens with an attempt to ascertain the meanings of "the life of reason." He locates its roots in Santayana's famous statement that "everything ideal has a natural basis and everything natural an ideal development." This principle is traced in its various ramifications through the historical progress of mankind; it is also delineated in the possible ideal not yet attained, in personal ethics and in social morality, in concrete particular values and in general principles. The life of reason, based on nature, involves, on the one hand, the acceptance of the specific natural conditions of life, values stemming from fundamental natural impulses, and, on the other, the operation of intelligence which finds the means to satisfy fundamental impulses and desires and, further, criticizes them in order to transform them into a harmony—among themselves and with external reality. Since, therefore, the ideal emerges within a natural process as the desired or desirable terminus or goal, it is no transcendent entity but a practical function.

Unfortunately, according to Munitz's interpretation, Santayana strayed from his naturalism and humanism. Taking off from themes to be found in his earliest works but also present in *The Life of Reason*, he propounded a doctrine of spirit and of spirituality which proposes escape from natural life to purely mystical and aesthetic contemplation of essences. Hence Munitz charges that Santayana's later works undermined the naturalism and humanism of his middle period. Untenable dualisms result: essence is separated from existence and mind from its objects; and the natural ideal of the good as happiness consisting in the harmonious satisfaction of desires is replaced with the mystical ideal of absorbing the individual in the passive contemplation of pure essences.

Singer, Beth J. *The Rational Society: A Critical Study of Santayana's Social Thought.* Cleveland: The Press of Case Western Reserve University, 1970.

This critical study of George Santayana's social and political philosophy covers *The Life of Reason*, in particular *Reason in Society*, and *Dominations and Powers*. Beth J. Singer, unlike Milton K. Munitz, finds Santayana's later thought continuous with the earlier and stresses its persistent naturalism. By naturalism she means a materialist interpretation of reality, extended to morality, society, and politics. Whereas Singer acknowledges that there are ambiguities in Santayana's materialism, she discounts them and emphasizes instead the constancy of his advocacy of epiphenomenalism as the key to his steadfast naturalism. For epiphenomenalism restricts causation to the physical order, so that mind, reason, and its ideals, although they are natural effects of physical causes, have no causal efficacy. Of course she does not deny the difference between Santayana's social and political philosophy in *The Life of Reason* and that in the later *Dominations and Powers*. The difference, however, consists in his abandonment of the moral ideal of inclusive harmony, best represented in Greek rational ethics, which he upheld in *The Life of Reason*, for a kind of moral relativism. When Santayana wrote *The Life of Reason*, he used the ideal of Greek rational ethics to judge

other moral ideals, but subsequently he became disillusioned about the practicality of any ideal service as a standard to evaluate other ideals.

While comments on *The Life of Reason* are strewn throughout this compact volume, Chapters 4 through 6 are particularly germane to an understanding of this masterpiece. It is in Chapter 6, "Moral Idealism and Moral Rationality," that Singer presents her thesis that the change in Santayana's moral philosophy assumes a form different from that alleged by Munitz. Santayana is not embroiled in a contradiction between naturalism and eclecticism, but he did revise his concept of moral rationality. He ceased to identify spirituality, attended by moral idealism, with the life of reason. Still he retained them together not as successive and mutually exclusive stages of life, but rather as two complementary dimensions. Nevertheless, Singer's interpretation concedes that, because of the epiphenomenalism (which is indeed the essential element of Santayana's naturalism), it is difficult to explain how reason could be practical.

Chapter 4, "Natural Society," is an exposition and critical interpretation of Santayana's classification of the three stages of society presented in *Reason in Society*: the natural, the free, and the ideal. Natural society is the outgrowth of natural needs: individuals associate for the sake of nutrition, reproduction, and governance. In the discussion of natural society Santayana's antipathy for liberalism and democracy surfaces, as does his preference for a hierarchical social order dominated by a natural aristocracy. Free society in Santayana's sense is an association of persons by affinity rather than necessity—by devotion to common goals or interests; it occurs despite separation in space and time. Ideal society is composed of those vast institutionalized systems of symbols which make up civilization—art, religion, and science.

In Chapter 5, "Biology and Civilization," Singer scrutinizes Santayana's conception of race and his view of its role in the history of civilization. Santay-

ana held that biology undergirds morality, society, and civilization. He even went so far as to claim that races, defined as kinds of individuals molded by breeding and selection, shape the characters of the individuals they embrace and actually determine their destinies. Espousing this doctrine of race in *Reason in Society*, Santayana divided the white race (or people) from the black, and he praised Jews, Greeks, Romans, and the English for their superiority. The doctrine of race survives and is reinforced in the later work, where Santayana grounded morality on race. Critical of Santayana's racism, Singer remarks that Santayana confused the transmission of social custom with biological heredity and erroneously equated national character with pedigree.

Additional Recommended Reading

Howgate, George W. *George Santayana.* New York: A.S. Barnes & Company, 1961. First published in 1938, this is an early exposition and interpretation of Santayana's moral philosophy in *The Life of Reason* with stress on the Spanish and individualistic features.

Lachs, John, "Santayana's Moral Philosophy," in *The Journal of Philosophy.* LXI, no. 1 (January 2, 1964), pp. 44-61. A systematic but sympathetic treatment of Santayana's ethics which draws upon other works in addition to *The Life of Reason.*

McCormick, John. *George Santayana: A Biography.* New York: Paragon House, 1988. Shows the links between Santayana's life and thought.

Moore, A. W. Reviews of *The Life of Reason,* Vols. I-IV, in *The Journal of Philosophy.* III, no. 7 (March 29, 1906), pp. 211-221; and Vol. V, in *The Journal of Philosophy.* III, no. 17 (August 16, 1906), pp. 469-471. Book reviews by a distinguished member of the "Chicago School" of pragmatists who criticized Santayana sharply for making reason impotent rather than efficacious in human life and culture.

Reck, Andrew J. "Realism in Santayana's *Life of Reason,*" in *The Monist.* LI, no. 2 (April, 1967), pp. 238-266. An examination of the realisms, epistemological and metaphysical.

Sprigge, Timothy L. S. *Santayana: An Examination of His Philosophy.* London: Routledge & Kegan Paul, 1974. A critical formulation and appraisal of Santayana's materialism and ethical theory in *The Life of Reason.*

Vivas, Eliseo. "From *The Life of Reason* to *The Last Puritan,*" in *The Philosophy of George Santayana* (The Library of Living Philosophers). Edited by Paul A. Schilpp. La Salle, Illinois: Open Court, 1940, pp. 315-350.

Woodward, Anthony. *Living in the Eternal: A Study of George Santayana.* Nashville, Tennessee: Vanderbilt University Press, 1988. A helpful interpretation of Santayana's theory of knowledge and worldview.

CREATIVE EVOLUTION

Author: Henri Bergson (1859-1941)
Type of work: Metaphysics
First published: 1906

Principal Ideas Advanced

The attempt to understand the self by analyzing it in terms of static concepts must fail to reveal the dynamic, changing character of the self.

There is an interesting force that shows itself in living things, an élan vital *that has endured through the ages, accounting for the creative evolution of life and of instinct and intelligence in living things.*

Instinct is limited in that although it grasps the fluid nature of living things, it is limited to the individual; but intellect is limited in that although it constructs general truths, it imposes upon life the static character of concepts.

But by the capacity of intuition, a disinterested and self-conscious instinct, a kind of knowledge is made possible which is superior to that provided by either instinct or intellect working separately.

At the time of his death in 1941, in the France dominated by the Nazis, Bergson was a relatively forgotten man, forgotten by the cultivated public and given little attention by the professional philosopher. Yet in the first two decades of this century he was lionized by the former and respected and often received enthusiastically by the latter. His fame was made by his immensely popular *Creative Evolution*. In this book he engages in metaphysical speculation on the grand scale, projecting his views back into the remote past and forward into the future. He speculates about matters that are difficult to speak about and impossible to verify in any of the traditionally accepted ways. Indeed, he mounts a concerted attack on traditional philosophic assumptions and techniques, insisting in particular that the dominant mechanistic and materialistic approach can lead only to a gross misrepresentation of reality. The chief villain here is intellect itself, for it can operate only through the use of concepts, and concepts are fixed, static categories that cannot contain fluid reality. There was a strong strain of anti-intellectualism in Bergson.

These basic views are expressed first in his discussion of the self. Perhaps the most noteworthy feature of our own inner life is the unceasing change that occurs there, the unceasing flow of thoughts, feelings, perceptions, and volitions. It is quite natural to think of this change as a succession of states in which each state holds the stage for a while before it is followed by its successor. Pursuing this analysis, we are led to think of the states themselves as internally static and changeless, for change is just the replacement of one state by another. Similarly, we are led to think of time as a succession of moments within which temporal change does not occur. Having cut the self into a collection of independent and static atoms of experience, we then wonder how this collection can constitute a unified, dynamic self, but we solve this difficulty by postulating the existence of an unexperienced mental substance that supports them, holds them together, and accounts for the manner of their succession.

We have gone astray, Bergson says, because we have tried to describe the dynamic, pulsating self by using concepts that inevitably impose their foreign rigidity upon it. Change in the self is not a process in which unchanging blocks are successively cast into and out of existence. Rather, it is a continuous process occurring in a self in which "states" (if we must use this term) are not units demarcated by sharp lines, but are at most centers of intensity trailing off indefinitely within the unbroken fabric of experience. Because it is growing, the self is changing in a direction that cannot be reversed, the past accumulating around the present as snow accumulates around a rolling snowball. To be such a changing thing is to be a self, and to experience such irreversible change is to have a history. This dynamic snowballing time, this time that counts, is real time or "duration," as Bergson calls it to distinguish it from the conceptualized, static, essentially reversible time of the mathematician. Memory is not the recalling of experiences that have long departed, but is the past living on in the present, affecting our present behavior. Consequently, in the self there is no exact repetition of past patterns, and novelty is the rule. Man is free, for in using the past he creates the future. We can discover all this for ourselves if we attend to our own inner life and are not misled by the concepts intellect would like to impose. Duration is not to be thought about; it is to be experienced, for only experience can reveal it to us.

Compared with the self, physical objects do not grow and change, they do not have memories, they do nothing new, they do not have histories, and they do not endure, for time makes no difference to them. The planets revolve as they always have, and they will continue to do so, except insofar as they are subject to changing external forces. The static concepts of mathematics and physics apply quite appropriately to them because they lend themselves to description in just such terms. These differences between physical objects and the living self indicate the presence of something in the latter that is not in the former, some dynamic element that makes the difference between the accumulative, purposeful, creative behavior of the one and the passive, repetitious, monotonous existence of the other. If we turn to biological phenomena and especially to the evolution of living things, we will discover overwhelming evidence in support of this thesis. One of the main examples is that of the evolution of the eye. Both the complex arrangement of otherwise useless components and the long history of increasingly complex sensory organs cannot be explained plausibly unless we assume some sort of integrating force that is moving in a definite direction.

Bergson cites the biological evidence that supports the fact of evolution, but we are not concerned with the fact itself as much as we are with what it presupposes. Darwin's theory of the survival of the fittest is all right as far as it goes, but it does not explain why mutations should occur in the first place or why many of them survive when they have no immediate survival value.

Bergson rejects three theories before he offers his own. First, he says that no mechanistic or materialistic account will do, for such an account forces the dynamic processes of life into the straitjacket of physical concepts and, in insisting that the future is determined completely by the past, repudiates the duration, freedom, and creation that are evident in the realm of living things. Second, Bergson rejects any finalistic view that describes the world as being attracted or directed toward some future goal, some end it cannot avoid, for such a view replaces one form of determinism by another. Finally, he repudiates the vitalism that was current in the biology of his day, for the postulation of a vital principle whose function is restricted to explaining the organization of parts and drives within the individual does not explain the fact of evolution.

Bergson's own view is a sort of cosmic vitalism in which the vital principle or *élan vital*, as he calls it, is life itself as it has endured through the ages, and evolution is the history of the effort of life to free itself from the domination of matter and to achieve self-consciousness. Beginning as the dimmest spark distinguishing the living from the dead, thrusting itself out in various directions, the *élan vital* has tried one by one the experiments represented by the divergent branches of the evolutionary tree. Many of the resultant forms have long ago been rejected as unsuitable, and others have been allowed to stagnate as the *élan* has continuously diverted its energies into the more promising ones. It pushed out into the vegetable and animal kingdoms and found that the latter allowed it greater scope. It discovered that the storage and explosive release of energy lead to freedom, that motion and consciousness are better than a sedentary torpor, that defense through high mobility and dexterity is better than that of armor, and so on through a host of minor and major alternatives. The most significant dichotomy of all has been that between the arthropods which have developed through the various insect forms to culminate in the hymenoptera, and the vertebrates which have diversified but culminated in man. This dichotomy is significant because the culminating species embody the best solutions the *élan* has yet found in its long struggle to emancipate itself from the matter that drags it down, the solutions represented by instinct and intelligence.

Both instinct and intelligence emerged as instruments for manipulating matter. Intellect fulfills this function through its ability to apprehend problems and to produce the mechanical devices needed to solve them. In fact, according to Bergson, intelligence is the faculty of making objects—such as tools to make tools—and of varying the manufacture at will. Arising from the animal's hesitation in a dilemma, intelligence expresses itself in thought rather than in action; developing the technique of language, it can operate when the original stimulus is no longer present; becoming aware of this subjective process it develops self-consciousness; concentrating on relations and forms, it frees itself from matter and develops the ability to generalize; and finally, using these resources and indulging its aroused curiosity, it turns from practical to theoretical matters. Instinct, too, operates through the use of tools, but the tools in this case are integral parts of the body, tools designed for a specific use and limited to that use. The instinctive reactions of the insect are sure and precise, but their scope is both limited and invariant. Instincts are released directly in action and function unconsciously. Yet they do involve an important kind of knowledge—not knowledge *about*, but an unconscious empathy with their object.

Both intellect and instinct have their advantages as well as their disadvantages. Among the great advantages of intellect are its consciousness and its ability to discover general truths, but it has disadvantages stemming from its inability to grasp things except through forms that are suggested to it by the object but crystallized into sharply defined concepts by itself. Thus, it is limited in two respects; it can grasp only the external form of a thing, and it cannot avoid seeing in the thing the static nature of the concept through which it is seen. Instinct has the advantage of grasping the fluid nature of living things, but it is limited to the individual and has not attained consciousness.

The production of instinct and intelligence is an experiment in which the *élan* has been articulating divergent but complementary tendencies that have lain dormant in it from the beginning. Through the resultant clarification it is readying itself to combine the desirable features of each in a new capacity that will transcend both. This new capacity already appears fleetingly in man. It is the capacity of intuition, a capacity that may be described briefly as instinct that has become disinterested and self-conscious. Artists to a greater extent, and most men to a lesser, are able to place themselves in a sort of divining sympathy with things and with other people. Intuition manifests itself in situations in which men are not dominated by disinterested thought—in the crises of life where problems press in and drastic action is required, and in moments of intense joy, sadness, or commiseration. In such cases and for a brief time we know our own inner being and that of others in a much more intimate fashion than we do when we sit in our studies and describe ourselves. Life then becomes aware of itself, of duration, and of the world, not through the distorting mediation of concepts, but directly and immediately. Man in his present state cannot maintain such insight for long, but if the *élan* is successful it will develop beings who can. What the nature of that intuition will be, and whether the *élan* will attain its goal of complete self-consciousness and complete dominance over matter, we cannot tell. We cannot tell for we are manifestations of the *élan*, and it does not know. It is striving less blindly than it did in past ages, but still, it does not know.

In the first half of his book, when he pits the *élan* against matter, it appears as if Bergson were maintaining that the world is composed of two radically different and independent principles. But in the latter half he makes it clear that he does not maintain such a metaphysical dualism. The distinction he has made between the *élan* and matter shares the defect of all distinctions made by the intellect—it is overdrawn. On the one hand the physical world around us is not quite as static and inert as it appears in the enclosed systems of the physicist, for if we regard it over long periods and great expanses we will find that it does not repeat itself quite as monotonously as we sometimes think it does. On the other hand, the self is not a continuously creative, pure-burning center of energy, for it can lapse into periods of lethargy during which it approaches the status of a physical thing. This is not to deny that there is a big difference between *élan* and matter, but it is to deny that the difference is an absolute one. It has the signs of being a difference in degree rather than one in kind.

If we retrace our steps in time we will find that the difference was even less long ago. Did the first organic things differ radically from the inorganic compounds from which they arose? Did not their emergence presuppose some prior creative activity? Indeed, Bergson speculates, life and matter stem from a common inarticulated source that contained neither as we know them, even though it did contain the tendencies from which they have evolved. Feeling dimly a need for creation, the primal substance began to stir, and gathering strength erratically but gradually, it generated life and matter by processes that are the inverse of each other.

Sometimes Bergson writes as if the quickening in the original indeterminate source has led to its articulation into parts that vary in their vitality, the less vital lapsing into relatively passive matter that resists the efforts of the more vital to move it or to move through it. At other times he writes as if the resistance to life stems from life itself. It is pictured as a frail element that overextends itself, that depletes itself, and that lapses into lethargy before it can gather itself together for another spurt. Matter is tired life. If the *élan* is a flowing current, then matter is a congealing of it. If the *élan* is a cosmic tension, then extension is the interruption or disappearance of that tension.

Bergson expresses himself in two particularly vivid metaphors. The first is that of a vessel of steam from which live jets escape, travel through space, lose their energy, condense into water and fall, only to provide a cooling medium that saps the energy of the jets that in penetrating it try to carry it with them in their upward thrust. Thus, through the ages, both life and matter have come from an inexhaustible reservoir, generated by processes that are the inverse of each other, and having inverse effects upon each other. The other, and perhaps better, metaphor is that in which the emerging *élan* is likened to a series of skyrockets. Imagine an original skyrocket that rises, slows down, and bursts, scattering its exhausted fragments through the sky. Imagine also that as it bursts it releases a number of rockets that gather speed and mount upwards in various directions through the debris. Some of these, retarded by their own weight and slowed by the resisting ashes of their predecessors, will simply fizzle out, doomed to do no more than scatter debris yet higher in the sky. But, in a final burst, some will release still others that will probe the upper reaches before they too die, barrenly or fruitfully. In this fashion the original urge to life has climbed through the ages, fighting its own lethargy, thrusting through or by the static remnants of its past endeavors, gathering strength to go off in new directions, sometimes succeeding and sometimes failing in its attempt to attain higher levels of consciousness.

Bergson's reliance on vivid metaphors of this sort accounts in part for the immediate impact the book had, but it also gives rise to some of the more severe criticism leveled at him. Metaphors are suggestive, but they are not accurate. Time and the self may both be like a rolling snowball rather than like a series of beads on a string; matter may be like congealing jelly or life like a river seeking the easiest path through the constraining land, and the *élan* may be like steam or skyrockets, but such suggestions should be followed by hard-headed, nonmetaphorical analyses. Although Bergson was often a good critic of others' speculations, the exposition of his own doctrine remains both ambiguous and vague. The concepts of duration, matter, *élan vital*, and intuition are never entirely clarified, and different images of them are not really reconciled. Furthermore, the distinction between epistemological and metaphysical considerations is not maintained, particularly in the discussion of matter where it is often unclear whether the villain is our concept of matter or matter itself. His criticism of the mathematician's account of space and time is based on an inadequate knowledge of the mathematics of the continuum, for apparently he believed all series must be discrete series. Finally, his attacks on the extent and accuracy of intellectual knowledge, and in particular his assumptions that the intellect must distort and that it is the blind captive of its own distortion, seem too extreme.

Perhaps Bergson would reply that although the intellect is capable of giving us knowledge of a sort, better knowledge may be achieved by intuition. Perhaps he would defend his use of metaphors in this way also, arguing that in using them he deliberately intends to lead us away from conceptual analysis, which must fail, toward intuition which alone can succeed. Intuition, duration, the self, or the *élan* cannot accurately be described simply because they are indescribable; he can only point to the sort of experience in which they are immediately known, and urge us to discover them for ourselves.

Pertinent Literature

Chevalier, Jacques. *Henri Bergson.* Translated by Lilian A. Clare. New York: Macmillan Publishing Company, 1928.

In his book *Henri Bergson*, Jacques Chevalier seeks to defend Henri Bergson's philosophy from those who would understand it as a type of anti-intellectualism, pure intuitionism, radical indeterminism, or idealism. Chevalier admits that all of these elements are, to some extent, involved in Bergson's philosophy, but he contends that the thrust of Bergson's thought is much more balanced and realistic. In Chevalier's opinion, Bergson's philosophy is the most adequate philosophy of its time.

Chevalier begins his book with a study of the intellectual milieu of France toward the end of the eighteenth century and then proceeds to give an account of Bergson's life and the development of his thought. According to Chevalier, there were a number of factors in Bergson's environment which led him to champion intuition, freedom, and duration, as opposed to intellectualism (the doctrine that all knowledge is conceptual), determinism (the doctrine that everything that happens could not have happened otherwise), and mechanism (the doctrine that "life" is simply a complex machine). Bergson did not wholly reject intellectualism, determinism, and mechanism. Rather, he maintained that, in addition to conceptual knowledge, there is direct knowledge; in addition to some things being determined, other things are free; and in addition to there being mechanistic aspects of life, there are spiritual aspects.

Chevalier maintains that Bergson's philosophy is realistic in both its method and its doctrines. Bergson's method is realistic in that it begins with what is given in experience and also in that it builds upon information obtained through scientific experiments. According to Chevalier, Bergson's realistic method is his greatest contribution to philosophy.

Moreover, Chevalier is convinced that the substance of Bergson's philosophy—the content of his doctrines—is realistic. At the heart of Bergson's philosophy stands his doctrine of knowledge, his epistemology. Unlike Immanuel Kant and those who followed him, Bergson maintains that it is possible to know things as they are in fact. Kant taught that what is known is shaped by universal categories of understanding, and therefore it is not possible to know things as they are in themselves, but only as they appear. Bergson, on the other hand, holds that through intuition it is possible to know things in themselves.

In Chevalier's final section, "The Trend of Bergsonian Thought: God and Man's Destiny. The Metaphysical Revival," the religious dimensions of Bergson's philosophy are considered. In Chevalier's estimation, one can discern an implicit doctrine of God in Bergson's works *Time and Free Will, Matter and Memory,* and *Creative Evolution.* In these works, Bergson implies the existence of a God who is characterized by personality—or, rather, superpersonality—freedom, and creativity. Bergson is neither a monist nor a pantheist; he believes that God created the world and is active in the world, but is not identical with the world.

In the first part of this century Bergson's philosophy was very controversial. A few persons, most notably George Santayana and Bertrand Russell, were highly critical of it; but a great many others were extremely impressed by it and considered themselves "Bergsonians." Jacques Chevalier's book *Henri Bergson*, stands as a classic work in the tradition of the Bergsonians.

Gunter, Pete A. "The Heuristic Force of *Creative Evolution*," in *The Southwestern Journal of Philosophy*. I, no. 3 (Fall, 1970), pp. 111-118.

Scientists and philosophers have generally agreed that Bergson's understanding of biological matters is unscientific. In his article "The Heuristic Force of *Creative Evolution*," Pete A. Gunter argues that this is not the case. A careful study of Bergson's most famous work, *Creative Evolution*, Gunter contends, reveals that Bergson's vitalism is not unscientific and that, in fact, it is capable of explaining certain scientifically accepted facts and of leading the way to the discovery of new facts. Gunter develops his argument around four aspects of Bergson's thought: his concept of matter and life, his treatment of physics and biology, his concept of intuition and its relevance to the natural sciences, and his concept of biological time.

Gunter's first point is that Bergson's understanding of matter and life is not dualistic. The apparent dualism between Newtonian atoms and vital impulses disappears when one recognizes that, according to Bergson, matter and life are both characterized by dynamic movement. Gunter maintains that Bergson judges there to be a "natural contrast" between living organisms and nonliving matter, but that this natural contrast falls short of a metaphysical dualism.

Gunter's second concern is to show that, for Bergson, physics and biology are similar disciplines. Although there are passages in *Creative Evolution* which suggest that physics is precise and scientific while biology is not and never can be, this is not Bergson's position. Precision is more difficult to achieve in biology than in physics because living things are more dynamic than are nonliving things; nevertheless, both sciences approximate real objects and both sciences are subject to certain limitations.

The third issue with which Gunter deals is Bergson's concept of intuition and its relevance to the natural sciences. Bergson maintains that intuition plays a role in all scientific explanations. Apart from intuition there simply are no explanations. This is not to say that all branches of science are equally dependent upon intuition or that intuition alone is sufficient. According to Gunter, Bergson maintains that the amount of intuition that is required for explaining a fact depends upon the amount of life in the fact to be explained; that intuition may be checked against information obtained according to scientific methodology. When properly understood, then, Bergson's appeal to intuition in the life sciences is not unscientific.

Gunter's fourth concern is to discuss Bergson's concept of biological time as the internal pace of an organism. Unlike physical or clock time, biological time is not comprised of equal units; instead, it accelerates in the developmental stages of an organism and decelerates in the decaying stages. Gunter cites various studies dealing with "biological clocks" which appear to support Bergson's theory of biological time.

In Gunter's estimation, Bergson's understanding of biological events is still relevant and deserves careful consideration by members of the scientific community. Gunter's thesis is well argued.

Santayana, George. *Winds of Doctrine: Studies in Contemporary Opinion*. New York: Charles Scribner's Sons, 1913.

Included in his work *Winds of Doctrine* is George Santayana's celebrated and unsympathetic critique of Henri Bergson's evolutionary philosophy. Santayana recognizes Bergson as the most representative and remarkable philosopher of the period just preceding World War I, yet he takes issue with virtually every aspect of Bergson's philosophy. He strongly opposes Bergson's evolutionary understanding of reality, introspective method, anthropomorphic tendencies, mysticism, and assessment of science and reason.

Santayana raises two important objections to Bergson's evolutionary understanding of reality: he objects to Bergson's phychophysical dualism and his conclusion that human beings are the final stage of evolution. Santayana believes that Bergson undercuts his own evolutionary theory on both accounts. A truly evolutionary position would not be dualistic: it would explain life in terms of matter. By contending that life is not a natural expression of material being but rather is the natural expression of a "life force" which is nonmaterial, Bergson's philosophy is less evolutionary than it could be. Bergson's evolutionary position is further undermined by his assumption that human beings are the final product of evolution. A truly evolutionary philosophy would hold that the process which has led up to human beings will continue beyond human beings. An evolutionary process cannot have final ends. In Santayana's estimation, Bergson's evolutionary position is internally inconsistent.

According to Santayana, Bergson's notion that evolution culminates in human beings is tied to his introspective method and his anthropomorphic tendencies. Bergson "turns inward"—becomes introspective—because he is afraid to look outward. He is afraid of space, mechanism, necessity, death, reason, and the discoveries of science. In Santayana's words, Bergson suffers from "cosmic agoraphobia." Bergson escapes these fears by turning inward and by concluding that this inner world is finally the most real world, that everything actual must resemble it in some fashion. Bergson's "metaphysics," then, is simply a projection of his personal psychology onto the world at large. According to Santayana, Bergson spoils his psychology by pretending that it is a metaphysics.

Santayana recognizes the attractiveness of Bergson's philosophy. It would be nice if evolution were simply a process to create human beings and if everything actual resembled our inner selves. It also would be nice if scientific discipline were unnecessary and if the truth concerning anything could be obtained through careful introspection, as Bergson contends. But is this actually the case? Is there any reason to think that Bergson is correct? Santayana firmly believes that there is not, that Bergson's philosophy is almost entirely specious.

Santayana's essay raises many important objections to Bergson's philosophy. One need not accept his judgment of Bergson's thought, but one must deal with the issues he has raised.

Additional Recommended Reading

Carr, Herbert Weldon. *The Philosophy of Change: A Study of the Fundamental Principle of the Philosophy of Bergson*. London: Macmillan and Company, 1914. A sympathetic and careful study of Bergson's major philosophical doctrines.

Gunter, Pete A. *Henri Bergson: A Bibliography*. Bowling Green, Ohio: Philosophy Documentation Center, 1974. This work contains an introduction which includes a biographical sketch; a list of works by Bergson; and a complete list of works published about Bergson.

Hanna, Thomas, ed. *The Bergsonian Heritage*. New York: Columbia University Press, 1962. *The Bergsonian Heritage* is a collection of three essays and seven short papers dealing with the importance of Bergson's thought. The essays are: "What Bergson Means to Us Today," by Edouard Morot-Sir; "Bergson Among Theologians," by Jaroslav Pelikan; and "Bergson and Literature," by Enid Starkie.

Lindsay, Alexander D. *The Philosophy of Bergson*. London: J. M. Dent & Sons, 1911. Lindsay's thesis is that Bergson's thought is best understood by comparison with Kant's. Like Kant, Bergson was interested in resolving the antinomies found in uncritical thought by reassessing the limits of philosophy and by establishing a new method.

Maritain, Jacques. *Bergsonian Philosophy and Thomism*. Translated by Mabelle L. Andison in collaboration with J. Gordon Andison. New York: Philosophical Library, 1955. This is a translation of *La Philosophie Bergsonienne*, which was first published in 1914. The book presents an explication of Bergson's thought and a critical examination of his major doctrines. As the English title indicates, Maritain draws upon Thomistic Philosophy in his critique of Bergsonian doctrines.

Vandel, Albert. "L'Importance de *L'Evolution créatrice* dans la genèse de la pensée moderne," in *Revue de Théologie et de Philsophie*. IX, no. 2 (1960), pp. 85-108. Vandel traces the history of evolutionary theory since Jean Baptiste Lamarck. He also discusses Bergson's contribution to evolutionary theory and the influence of Bergson's thought on F. Leenhardt, G. Mercier, and Pierre Teilhard de Chardin. Unfortunately, this article has not been translated into English.

PEIRCE: COLLECTED PAPERS

Author: Charles Sanders Peirce (1839-1914)
Type of work: Logic, epistemology, metaphysics
First published: (1931-1958, eight volumes)

Principal Ideas Advanced

A belief is a habit of action; different beliefs give rise to different modes of action.

Our idea of anything is our idea of its sensible effects; objects are distinguished according to the difference they make practically.

True ideas are those to which responsible investigators, were they to push their inquiries far enough, would finally give assent; reality is what true ideas represent.

Of the four methods of fixing belief—the method of tenacity, of authority, of a priori judgments, and the method of science—the scientific is preferable as providing critical tests of procedures.

By the conceptions of Firstness, Secondness, and Thirdness, a metaphysics of cosmic evolution can be developed; Firstness is the individual quality of a thing, Secondness is the relatedness of a thing to something other than itself, and Thirdness is the tendency to mediate, to contribute to law.

There is a chance in the universe (tychism); the universe begins in a chaos of unpersonalized feeling and develops habits or patterns of action (synechism); finally, as laws develop, the universe moves toward a condition of perfect rationality and symmetry (agapasm).

Although it is almost a century since Charles Sanders Peirce—in conversation with William James, Chauncey Wright, Nicholas St. John Green, and Oliver Wendell Holmes at informal meetings of the "metaphysical club" in Cambridge, Massachusetts—developed and brought to clear expression the central ideas which became the core of pragmatism, the pragmatic philosophy continues to prevail as the predominant American philosophy. Of course, if one were to make a survey, it might very well turn out that the majority of American philosophers would deny being pragmatists, although few would deny having been influenced by the ideas of Peirce, James, and John Dewey. But idealism in America is practically dead, despite some isolated champions in its behalf; and the new linguistic empiricism—which represents the emphasis of the Vienna positivists on grounding philosophical claims in experience (and manipulating statements according to an impartial logic), together with the emphasis of the British philosophers on the study of ordinary language in the multiplicity of its uses—comes very close to being a sophisticated, latter-day version of the American pragmatism which Peirce invented and defended.

But Peirce was more than the creator of pragmatism; he was a scientist, mathematician, logician, and teacher—although his career as a professor was limited. He lectured at Harvard and The Johns Hopkins University. Peirce's failure to find, or to be offered, a university position suitable for one of his talents, was a consequence of his independent and undisciplined nature. The result of his being free from academic restrictions was perhaps both fortunate and unfortunate: as an outsider, his creative powers had no formal limits, but his intellect was brilliant, and he knew where to stop in his inventions and speculations; but because he was an ousider, he had neither the security nor the incentive to fashion his essays into any coherent whole. Although he attempted, in later life, to write a great, single work in which his views on logic, nature, science, man, and philosophy would be developed in some mutually illuminating and supporting fashion, his poverty and isolation—together with his iconoclastic stubbornness—combined to frustrate his great ambition.

The most comprehensive collection of Peirce's papers is the *Collected Papers of Charles Sanders Peirce* (eight volumes, 1931-1958), edited by Charles Hartshorne and Paul Weiss, but other selections from his essays are available, including *Chance, Love, and Logic: Philosophical Essays by the Late Charles S. Peirce* (1923), edited by Morris R. Cohen, and *The Philosophy of Peirce* (1940), edited by Justus Buchler.

Although the critical interest in Peirce's writings is as lively now as it has ever been, and the attention given to the papers has intensified since the publication of the *Collected Papers*, so that new discoveries are constantly being made and new enthusiasms are frequently aroused, most editors of Peirce's essays and most commentators on his work are agreed on the importance of certain essays as being particularly characteristic of Peirce at his best. Among the early essays are "The Fixation of Belief," and "How to Make Our Ideas Clear," and among the later, "The Architecture of Theories" and "The Doctrine of Necessity Examined." Since these essays contain some of the most famous and revealing statements of Peirce's basic opinions, an examination of them will serve as an introduction to other significant essays.

Peirce's thought, varied and original as it was, falls naturally into four categories: the pragmatic, the epistemological, the logical, and the metaphysical. The poles are the pragmatic ideas of meaning and truth (ideas which condition the epistemological conceptions), and, at the other extreme of his thinking, the metaphysical ideas. The effort to relate these poles to each other rewards the student of Peirce with a synoptic idea of Peirce's philosophy which illuminates the otherwise confusing variety of essays to be found in the *Collected Papers*.

In the essay "How to Make Our Ideas Clear," which first appeared in the *Popular Science Monthly* for January, 1878, Peirce set out to clarify the unclear conception of clarity to be found in Descartes' writings on method. The first step was to clear up the conception of belief. Peirce began by speaking of doubt as a kind of irritation arising from indecisiveness in regard to action; when a man does not know

what to do, he is uneasy, and his uneasiness will not leave him until he settles upon some mode of action. Belief is "a rule for action," and as it is acted upon repeatedly, each time appeasing the irritation of doubt, it becomes a habit of action. Thus, Peirce concluded, "The essence of belief is the establishment of a habit, and different beliefs are distinguished by the different modes of action to which they give rise."

In a previous essay, "The Fixation of Belief," which appeared in the *Popular Science Monthly* for November, 1877, Peirce had written of doubt as a state of dissatisfaction from which we try to free ourselves, and of belief as a satisfactory state. The struggle to remove the irritation of doubt and to attain belief, a rule of action, was described as "inquiry," and the settlement of opinion was set forth as the sole object of inquiry.

It was Peirce's conviction that logic, as the art of reasoning, was needed to make progress in philosophy possible; he anticipated logical positivism in urging that only "a severe course of logic" could clear up "that bad logical quality to which the epithet *metaphysical* is commonly applied. . . ."

Thus, the first step in learning how to make our ideas clear is to come to the realization that belief is a habit of action, the consequence of a process of inquiry undertaken to appease the irritation of indecisiveness. Since the entire purpose of thought, as Peirce conceived it, is to produce habits of action, it follows that the meaning of a thought is the collection of habits involved; or, if the question has to do with the meaning of a "thing," its meaning is clear once we know what difference the thing would make if one were to become actively, or practically, involved with it. Peirce's conclusion was that "there is no distinction of meaning so fine as to consist in anything but a possible difference of practice."

As an example, he referred to the doctrine of transubstantiation and to the Catholic belief that the elements of the Communion, though possessing all of the sense properties of wine and wafers, are literally blood and flesh. To Peirce such an idea could not possibly be clear, for no distinction in practice could be made between wine and wafers, on the one hand, and what *appeared* to be wine and wafers, on the other. He argued that no conception of wine was possible except as the object of the reference, "this, that, or the other, is wine," or as the object of a description by means of which certain properties are attributed to wine. But the properties are conceivable only in terms of the sensible effects of wine; "Our idea of anything is our idea of its sensible effects. . . ." Consequently, "to talk of something as having all the sensible characters of wine, yet being in reality blood, is senseless jargon." The rule for attaining clearness of thought, Peirce's famous pragmatic maxim, appears in "How to Make Our Ideas Clear" as follows: "Consider what effects, which might conceivably have practical bearings, we conceive the object of our conception to have. Then, our conception of these effects is the whole of our conception of the object."

Peirce's discussion of his maxim, centering about examples, makes it clear that the rule for the clarification of thought was not designed to support a simple phenomenalism. Although Peirce used sentences such as "Our idea of anything *is* our idea of its sensible effects. . .," he did not use the expression "sensible effects" to mean sensations merely. By conceiving, through the use of the senses, the effects of the action of a thing, we come to understand the thing; our habit of reaction, forced upon us by the action of the thing, is a conception of it, our belief regarding it. The object is not *identifiable* with its effects—that is not even proper grammar, and Peirce was aware of the relation of linguistic practice to philosophical perplexity—but the object can be conceived as "that which" we conceive only in terms of its effects.

Peirce's pragmatic rule should be distinguished from William James's version of the same principle. James stressed an idea's becoming true; he used the misleading expression "practical cash-value" to refer to the pragmatic meaning of a word, and he sometimes emphasized the *satisfactoriness* of an idea, as constituting its truth, in such a way that no clear line was drawn between sentimental satisfaction and the satisfaction of a scientific investigator.

Peirce, on the other hand, in developing the ideas of truth and reality made careful use of the contrary-to-fact conditional in order to avoid any loose or emotional interpretation of the pragmatic method.

He wrote, in "How to Make Our Ideas Clear," that scientific processes of investigation "if only pushed far enough, will give one certain solution to every question to which they can be applied. . . ." Again, in clarifying the idea of reality, Peirce came to the conclusion that " The opinion which is fated to be ultimately agreed to by all who investigate, is what we mean by the truth, and the object represented in this opinion is the real." In other words, those opinions to which systematic, responsible investigators *would* finally give assent, *were* the matter thoroughly investigated, are true opinions. It was Peirce's dissatisfaction with the tender-minded versions of the pragmatic method that led him finally to give up the name "pragmatism," which he invented, and to use in its place the term "pragmaticism."

Peirce's preference for the scientific method of inquiry is nowhere more clearly expressed and affirmed than in his early essay, " The Fixation of Belief." Regarding the object of reasoning to be the discovery of new facts by a consideration of facts already known, and having argued that a belief is a habit of action which appeases the irritation of doubt or indecisiveness, he went on to examine four methods of fixing belief: the method of tenacity, which is the method of stubbornly holding to a belief while resisting all criticism; the method of authority, which consists of punishing all dissenters; the *a priori* method, which depends on the inclination to believe, whatever the facts of the matter; and, finally, the method of science, which rests on the following assumption: "There are real things, whose characters are entirely independent of our opinions about them; those realities affect our senses according to regular laws, and, though our sensations be as different as our relations to the objects, yet, by taking advantage of the laws of perception, we can ascertain by reasoning how things really are, and any man, if he have sufficient experience and reason enough about it, will be led to the one true conclusion."

Peirce strongly endorsed the scientific method of inquiry. He argued that no other method provided a way of determining the rightness or wrongness of the method of inquiry itself; the test of a procedure undertaken as scientific is an application of the method itself.

In support of the realistic hypothesis on which the

method of science is based, Peirce argued that the practice of the method in no way cast doubt on the truth of the hypothesis; furthermore, everyone who approves of one method of fixing belief in preference to others tacitly admits that there are realities the method can uncover; the scientific method is widely used, and it is only ignorance that limits its use; and, finally, the method of science has been so successful that belief in the hypothesis on which it rests has been strengthened proportionately.

These passages should be of particular interest to those who suppose that Peirce, as the founder of pragmatism, was absolutely neutral in regard to commitments ordinarily regarded as metaphysical. He did not claim to know the truth of the realistic hypothesis, but it did seem to him eminently sensible, accounting for the manner in which nature forces experience upon us, and making uniformity of opinion possible. (However, his theory of cosmic evolution, as shall be seen, is a peculiar kind of realism.)

In the essay "The Architecture of Theories," published in *The Monist* in January, 1891, Peirce introduced the critical conceptions of First, Second, and Third, which he described as "principles of Logic," and by reference to which he developed his metaphysics of cosmic evolution. He defined the terms as follows: "First is the conception of being or existing independent of anything else. Second is the conception of being relative to, the conception of reaction with, something else. Third is the conception of mediation, whereby a first and second are brought into relation."

Arguing that philosophical theories should be built architectonically, Peirce offered the conceptions of First, Second, and Third as providing the logical principles of construction. Any adequate theory, he maintained, would order the findings of the various sciences by the use of the principles of First, Second, and Third. Thus, in psychology, "Feeling is First, Sense of reaction Second, General conception Third, or mediation." Significantly, as a general feature of reality, "Chance is First, Law is Second, the tendency to take habits is Third," and, Peirce maintained, "Mind is First, Matter is Second, Evolution is Third."

Peirce went on to sketch out the metaphysics which would be built by the use of these general conceptions. He wrote that his would be a "Cosmogonic Philosophy," and that it would describe a universe which, beginning with irregular and unpersonalized feeling would, by chance ("sporting here and there in pure arbitrariness"), give rise to generalizing tendencies which, continuing, would become "habits" and laws; the universe, such a philosophy would claim, is evolving toward a condition of perfect rationality and symmetry.

Four more papers, all published in Cohen's selection, *Chance, Love, and Logic*, develop the ideas introduced in "The Architecture of Theories." They are "The Doctrine of Necessity Examined," "The Law of Mind," "Man's Glassy Essence," and "Evolutionary Love."

In "The Doctrine of Necessity Examined," Peirce argued for the presence of chance in the universe. But Peirce's conception of chance was not the usual conception of the entirely uncaused and irregular, acting without cause or reason. He wrote of chance as "the form of a spontaneity which is to some degree regular," and he was careful to point out that he was not using the conception of chance as a principle of explanation but as an element in the description of a universe in which there is the tendency to form habits and to produce regularities. The doctrine of absolute chance was named "tychism," and the doctrine of continuity was named "synechism." The essay "The Law of Mind" develops the latter doctrine.

In "The Law of Mind," Peirce argued that there is but one law of mind, that ideas spread, affect other ideas, lose intensity, but gain generality and "become welded with other ideas." In the course of the article Peirce developed the notion of an "idea" as an event in an individual consciousness; he argued that consciousness must take time and be in time, and that, consequently, "we are immediately conscious through an infinitesimal interval of time." Ideas are continuous, Peirce claimed, and there must be a "continuity of intrinsic qualities of feeling" so that particular feelings are present out of a continuum of other possibilities. Ideas affect one another: but to understand this, one must distinguish three elements within an idea (Firstness, Secondness, and Thirdness make their appearance again); the three elements are, First, the intrinsic quality of the idea as a feeling, its *quale*; Second, the energy with the idea affects other ideas (its capacity to relate); and, Third, the tendency of an idea to become generalized (its tendency to be productive of law). Habits are established by induction; general ideas are followed by the kind of reaction which followed the particular sensations that gave rise to the general idea. Mental phenomena come to be governed by law in the sense that some living idea, "a conscious continuum of feeling," pervades the phenomena and affects other ideas.

Peirce concluded "The Law of Mind" with the striking claim that matter is not dead, but it is mind "hidebound with habits."

In the essay "Man's Glassy Essence" Peirce argued that mind and matter are different aspects of a single feeling process; if something is considered in terms of its relations and reactions, it is regarded as matter, but if it is understood as feeling, it appears as consciousness. (This is a more sophisticated philosophy than James's radical empiricism, which resembles Peirce's hypothesis in some respects.) A person is a particular kind of general idea.

If it seems intolerable to suppose that matter is, in some sense, feeling or idea, one must at least consider that for Peirce an idea must be considered not only in its Firstness, but in its Secondness and Thirdness as well. In other words, an idea or feeling, for Peirce, is not *simply* a feeling as such; that is, a feeling is more than its quality, its Firstness. A feeling is also that which has the tendency to relate to other feelings with which it comes in spatial and temporal contact, and it works with other feelings toward a regularity of development which can be known as law. It does not seem likely that Peirce can be properly interpreted so as to delight a physical realist who maintains that matter is in no way feeling or mind; but his philosophy is much more acceptable, to one concerned with the multiplicity of physical phenomena, than an idealism which regards ideas as static individuals existing only in their Firstness (merely as feelings).

In "Evolutionary Love," Peirce maintained that his synechism calls for a principle of evolution that will account for creative growth. How is it that out of chaos so irregular that it seems inappropriate to say that anything exists, a universe of habit and law can emerge? Chance relations develop, the relations become habits, the habits become laws; *tychism* emphasizes the presence of chance, *synechism* emphasizes the development of relations through the continuity of ideas, and *agapasm* (Peirce's term) emphasizes the evolutionary tendency in the universe. Thus, we discover how the logical (ordering) principles of Firstness, Secondness, and Thirdness make intelligible not only the idea (with its *quale*, its relatedness, and its tendency to contribute to the development of law), but also the person (who is a general idea), matter (which is mind hidebound with habits), and the character of the universe. The logical principles become metaphysical.

Peirce is important in contemporary thought primarily because of his pragmatic, logical, and epistemological views. There is a great deal of material in the *Collected Papers* that remains to be explored, and those who would picture Peirce as the forerunner of linguistic and empirical philosophy can find much to support their claims in his essays. His metaphysics is regarded as interesting, though as pragmatically insignificant; but this is partly a matter of current taste. When interest in metaphysics revives, and there is no methodological reason why it cannot revive and be respectable, the metaphysics of Charles Sanders Peirce, his theory of cosmic evolution or agapasm, will certainly be reconsidered.

Pertinent Literature

Barnes, Winston H. F. "Peirce on 'How to Make Our Ideas Clear,' " in *Studies in the Philosophy of Charles Sanders Peirce*. Edited by Philip P. Wiener and Frederic H. Young. Cambridge, Massachusetts: Harvard University Press, 1952, pp. 53-60.

At the heart of Charles Sanders Peirce's philosophy is his principle of clarification, or, as it is sometimes referred to, his pragmatic principle, which was first enunciated in an early essay from his *Collected*

Papers entitled "How to Make Our Ideas Clear" as follows: "Consider what effects, that might conceivably have practical bearings, we conceive the object of our conception to have. Then, our conception of these effects is the whole of our conception of the object." Winston H. F. Barnes seeks to clarify this principle of clarification.

Peirce recognizes three grades of clearness of apprehension. The first grade of clarity is familiarity with a concept, the second grade comes from the definition of a concept, and the third grade implies the possible concrete utilization of a concept of actual affairs. Peirce's principle is a rule for attaining clarity of the third (and highest) degree.

Barnes quickly dismisses two common misinterpretations of Peirce's principle. The first suggests that the meaning of a concept is to be equated with the volitions or actions to which it gives rise. Barnes explains that although the spirit of the maxim is that clarity of apprehension manifests itself in purposeful action, Peirce does not mean that acts constitute the meaning or purport of any given word (as a linguistic symbol). A second misinterpretation proposes that the meaning of a concept consists solely in its effects upon the senses. Peirce himself repudiates this interpretation by his emphatic statement that concepts cannot be explained by anything but concepts. In other words, ideas are not clarified by percepts, images, or any effects on the senses.

Shifting only slightly from the paths laid by the above two misinterpretations, Barnes demarcates two much more plausible translations, what he terms the *Conceptual Pragmatic* view and the *Conceptual Experiential* view. In the former view, the meaning of a concept becomes clarified in terms of *conceiving* the volitions or actions to which it gives rise, whereas in the latter, clarification is in terms of *conceiving* possible effects on the senses. Both of these accounts have certain strengths. Although Barnes does not totally commit himself to one or the other, he confesses that the experiential account has somewhat greater plausibility.

Peirce tells that to clarify our conception of an object we must substitute our conception of those sensible effects that under certain conditions of practical importance an object would have. Stated in this way, there seems to be a close parallel to the logical positivist principle that the meaning of a proposition is its method of verification. The meaning of "chlorine," then, would consist of our conception of the sensible effects chlorine would produce in us—namely, its color, odor, and the like, along with the sensible effects resulting from contact with other materials (turning clothes white, creating hydrochloric acid when mixed with hydrogen, and so forth). While this is on the right track, Barnes claims that Peirce intends something more.

On the Conceptual Pragmatic Interpretation the meaning of a concept is linked with a conceived conditional disposition. To have a concept is to have a particular belief regarding what sensible effects would arise should a certain type of action be performed. To clarify the concept is to clarify the belief and to bring that belief into consciousness as a *conceived* conditional disposition. Hence the concept of chlorine becomes understood as a conceived belief that "if I should wish to bleach clothes, then I should use a certain yellowish-green liquid, irritating to the nose, and capable of turning clothes white." The occasion for using the chlorine may never arise, and we may never use chlorine, but the concept is essentially tied to possible action.

The Conceptual Experiental Interpretation casts the rule for clarifying concepts in terms of a conceived conditional *expectation*, instead of a *disposition*. Again using the example of chlorine, the concept is to be understood by conceiving *what I would expect* to happen "if I should take this yellowish-green liquid, which is irritating to the nose, and capable of turning clothes white, and add it to the water when washing my clothes." Instead of being tied to a conceived disposition to act in a certain way, as on the Conceptual Pragmatic Interpretation, the meaning of chlorine is exhibited by a conceived expectation.

Using Barnes's example, the difference between the two plausible views can be illustrated in the following ways. Given a singular belief such as "These are coals," and assuming that combustibility is a part of the meaning of the concept of coal, then (1) according to the experiential theory "These are coals" is clarified by a conceived conditional expectation: for example, "If these were in contact with flame, they would burn." (2) According to the pragmatic theory, the same meaning is clarified by a conceived conditional disposition: for example "If I wished to obtain heat, I would bring these into contact with flame." Whichever interpretation may be correct, Barnes concludes, the principle of clarification stands as one of the most provocative and foundational aspects of Peirce's philosophy.

Davis, William H. *Peirce's Epistemology.* The Hague, The Netherlands: Martinus Nijhoff, 1972.

The question of skepticism stands as one of the major issues in the history of Western philosophy. Is knowledge of reality possible and if so, how? Throughout his career, Charles Sanders Peirce was forced again and again to wrestle with the intractable problem of knowledge. In a penetrating analysis of Peirce's epistemology, William H. Davis brings into focus a set of ideas which he believes can serve as a key to uncovering the nature of human knowledge. Davis' work is more than simply an exposition of Peirce's philosophy; it is itself a commendable essay in epistemology.

In his *Collected Papers*, Peirce attacks the traditional "intuitionist" theory of knowledge that has its paradigm in René Descartes. Descartes sought to base all knowledge on primitive intuitions, what he called "clear and distinct ideas." Peirce's alternative is that knowledge is a process of flowing inferences. By "inference" he does not mean merely conscious abstract, logical thought; he means any cognitive activity whatever, including perceptual cognition and even subconscious thought processes. The inferential process whence derives all knowledge he terms "synthetic thinking," which implies a continuous activity of comparing, connecting, and putting together thoughts and perceptions. Knowing simply cannot be immediate and intuitive, he argues, for if nothing else it is a temporal process occurring over a period of time. No experience whatever is an instantaneous affair. Supposing that Peirce is correct, the question then becomes: What can be said about synthetic thinking?

Peirce recognizes three kinds of reasoning processes: deduction, induction, and abduction, the latter being original with him. He holds a generally orthodox view of deduction and induction. He agrees that deduction is analytic in essence and therefore yields no new knowledge. New knowledge comes from synthetic thinking, which he divides into two categories, inductive and abductive. Abduction is understood basically as a creative hypothesis-building process. The main difference between induction and abduction is that in the former "we generalize from a number of cases of which something is true and infer that the same thing is true of a whole class," whereas in the latter "we find some curious circumstance which would be explained by the supposition that it was a case of a certain general rule, and thereupon adopt that supposition." Davis pursues this distinction by showing that actually every induction involves an abduction, that in a sense induction is best viewed as a form of abduction. Such being the case, it follows that all new knowledge arises by way of abduction. Because of the importance Peirce attaches to abduction, Davis spends a great deal of time examining that notion and relating it to Peirce's pragmatism.

Davis' study probably more than any other has demonstrated the truly revolutionary significance of Peirce's doctrine of abduction and the implications and consequences it has for philosophy in general and epistemology in particular. The book is divided into five chapters: I. Inference: The Essence of All Thought; II. Hypothesis or Abduction: The Originative Phase of Reasoning; III. Fallibilism: The Self-corrective Feature of Thought; IV. Concrete Reasonableness: Cooperation Between Reason and Instinct; and V. The Cartesian Circle: A Final Look at Scepticism.

Murphee, Idus. "The Theme of Positivism in Peirce's Pragmatism," in *Studies in the Philosophy of Charles Sanders Peirce, Second Series.* Edited by Edward C. Moore and Richard S. Robin. Amherst: University of Massachusetts Press, 1964, pp. 226-241.

What is the connection between Charles Sanders Peirce's pragmatism and his professed positivism? Depending on how Peirce's *Collected Papers* are interpreted, there will be different answers to this important question. It might be thought, for example, that pragmatism and positivism are at odds with each other. Whereas the language of pragmatism emphasizes belief, action, and practical effects, the language of positivism stresses the accumulation of positive evidence, experimentation, and scientific verification. Idus Murphee takes the position that the basic concepts underlying Peirce's pragmatism do not blunt in any way his strong commitment to experimentalism, but in fact serve to emphasize and reinforce that commitment.

Peirce's idea of belief is that of conviction which is fixed by perceptual evidence. All belief is "expectative" in the sense that the meaning of a belief comes down ultimately to the practical effects which can be expected or anticipated in such case that the belief is acted upon. Hence meaningfulness, on the pragmatic formula, is a function of practical considerations. At the same time, Murphee points out, what any concept or proposition claims must be translated in terms of positive evidence. By this Peirce implies that beliefs are in essence forms of scientific hypotheses, whereupon their meaning embodies laboratory methods of verification; to believe such and such is to assert that if a given experiment were carried out, an experience of a given description would result. Furthermore, since belief implies conviction, or assent, the belief itself hinges upon the evidence which has proven

sufficient to insure the requisite commitment to action. In this way Peirce's pragmatism fundamentally intertwines with his positivism.

Murphee goes into much detail to show that when Peirce speaks of the evidence for belief he means phenomena or observations which in theory are open to the public. Commitment to action is not enough to qualify a conviction as a belief. While Peirce acknowledges that beliefs may be mistaken, and that erroneous beliefs may really be believed, he observes that every belief is at least thought to be true by the person holding it. Given Peirce's definition of truth—namely, that to which a community of investigators would give assent, based upon the results of their cooperative inquiry—it clearly follows that, in Murphee's words, "a claim to truth is a public claim which only a public can verify." The evidence for any such claim, therefore, and the basis for the correlative conviction to action, must of necessity lie in the public domain, open to scrutiny by a community of inquirers. Private nuance, introspection, and the like are insufficient for "fixing" belief and creating meaning.

In sum, there is no contradiction for Peirce, in phrasing pragmatism in the language of positivism. Pragmatic meaning is preliminary to verification, and the conditions under which truth and falsity may be asserted (in specific terms, the conditions for scientific inquiry, experimentation, and verification) are precisely those which Peirce intends the pragmatic formula to specify.

Additional Recommended Reading

Bernstein, Richard J. *Beyond Objectivism and Relativism: Science, Hermeneutics and Praxis.* Philadelphia: University of Pennsylvania Press, 1985. Sees American pragmatism, and Peirce's philosophy in particular, as providing a view of knowledge and knowing that is neither objectivistic nor relativistic.

Buchler, Justus. *Charles Peirce's Empiricism.* London: Kegan Paul, Trench, Trubner & Company, 1939. Justus Buchler is recognized as a leading authority on the philosophy of Peirce. The present study organizes and clarifies those ideas in Peirce which serve as a foundation for the empiricism he espoused. Exposition is limited to the methodological side of Peirce's thought, focusing on his commonsensism, his pragmatism, and his theory of the formal sciences.

Feibleman, James K. *An Introduction to the Philosophy of Charles S. Peirce.* Cambridge, Massachusetts: M. I. T. Press, 1970. The most comprehensive introduction to Peirce's philosophy available. Part of the aim of this book is to exhibit the system which the author finds inherent in the seemingly disordered collection of Peirce's philosophical writings. This is a revision of an earlier work on Peirce published in 1946.

Moore, Edward C. and Richard S. Robin, eds. *Studies in the Philosophy of Charles Sanders Peirce, Second Series.* Amherst: University of Massachusetts Press, 1964. This second volume of Peirce studies updates the previous series (Wiener and Young, 1952) by bringing into focus the heightened interest in Peirce's scientific contributions. Themes discussed include logic, probability and induction, perception and belief, Peirce's evolutionism, and his scientific metaphysics.

Scheffler, Israel. *Four Pragmatists: A Critical Introduction to Peirce, James, Mead, and Dewey.* New York: Humanities Press, 1974. A competent discussion of those ideas in Peirce most crucial to his pragmatism, including his cosmology, his theory of inquiry, and his so-called "pragmatic maxim."

Thompson, Manley. *The Pragmatic Philosophy of C. S. Peirce.* Chicago: University of Chicago Press, 1953. An impressive commentary aimed toward a systematic construction of Peirce's philosophy. Peirce's disparate writings are organized and interpreted in relation to the chronological development of his pragmatism.

Wiener, Philip P. and Frederic H. Young, eds. *Studies in the Philosophy of Charles Sanders Peirce.* Cambridge, Massachusetts: Harvard University Press, 1952. One of the early major achievements of the Charles S. Peirce Society, this book is a collection of twenty-four fine essays which expound, elaborate, and critically assess important aspects of Peirce's philosophy.

PRAGMATISM

Author: William James (1842-1910)
Type of work: Epistemology, philosophy of philosophy
First published: 1907

Principal Ideas Advanced

Pragmatism is both a philosophical method and a theory of truth.

As a method, it resolves metaphysical disputes by asking for the practical consequences of alternative resolutions.

Once a distinction of practice is made, theoretical difficulties disappear.

As a theory of truth, Pragmatism claims that ideas are true insofar as they are satisfactory; to be satisfactory, ideas must be consistent with other ideas, conformable to facts, and subject to the practical tests of experience.

Occasionally a book succeeds in giving influential expression to an attitude and a set of principles which eventually make up a historically important philosophical movement. This is the case with William James's *Pragmatism*. Borrowing the term from his philosophical contemporary, Charles S. Peirce (1839-1914), James attempts in a series of published lectures to popularize and defend "a number of tendencies that hitherto have lacked a collective name." Pragmatism came to dominate the American intellectual scene for more than two decades as well as to gain recognition as a uniquely American philosophical position. To this historical phenomenon of the pragmatic movement James's book still serves as a sympathetic if sometimes polemical introduction. Its eight related essays discuss the origin and meaning of Pragmatism as well as suggest how the pragmatic method can be applied to troublingly perennial problems in metaphysics and religion. The contents give evidence of James's belief that philosophizing, as a technical concern, must always involve consequences for the life of common sense and common men.

Given the question: Can a philosopher settle all philosophical disputes disinterestedly?—James replies in the negative. The point here is not that philosophers ought to ignore claims of logic and evidence. Rather, the point is that philosophical

"clashes" involve more than logic and evidence. James insists that no philosopher can wholly "sink the fact of his temperament," however responsibly he seeks to give "impersonal reasons only for his conclusions." A philosophical attitude necessarily becomes colored by a man's temperament. In "The Dilemma in Philosophy," which opens *Pragmatism*, James argues that a fundamental opposition in temperament has marked the history of thought—that between rationalism and empiricism. The rationalist values "abstract and eternal principles"; the empiricist, "facts in all their crude variety." Aware that so hard and fast a distinction can serve only a rough-and-ready use, James suggests that clusters of traits tend to distinguish the rationalist from the empiricist. Rationalists are "tender-minded," "intellectualistic," "idealistic," "optimistic," "religious," "free-willist," "monistic," "dogmatical." Empiricists are "tough-minded," "sensationalistic," "materialistic," "pessimistic," "irreligious," "fatalistic," "pluralistic," "skeptical."

This rule of thumb distinction between two attitudes James applies to his view of the existing philosophical situation. This situation is one in which even children "are almost born scientific." Positivism and scientific materialism tend to dominate the scene, favoring the empirically minded outlook. Yet men also seek to preserve an element of religiousness. James insists that a philosophical dilemma arises which is unacceptable to his contemporaries: adopt a positivistic respect for empirical facts which ignores religion or keep a religiousness which is insufficiently empirical. James will settle for neither alternative. He asserts that "in this blessed year of our Lord 1906" the common man as philosopher demands facts, science, and religion. The ordinary man cannot find what he needs in the philosophical country store. Materialists explain phenomena by a "nothing but" account of higher forms in terms of lower, while religious thinkers provide a choice between an empty transcendentalist idealism (whose Absolute has no necessary relation to any concretely existing thing) and traditional theism (whose compromising nature lacks prestige and vital fighting powers). Rationalist elements in idealism and theism emphasize refinement and escape from the concrete realities of ordinary, everyday life. The result is that for the common man's plight "Empiricist writers give him a materialism, rationalists give him something religious, but to that religion 'actual things are blank.' "

For this dramatically staged intellectual predicament James has a philosophical hero ready in the wings. It is "the oddly-named thing pragmatism." Pragmatism is offered as a philosophy which can salvage the religious values of rationalism without perverting man's many-sided awareness of facts. It can also take account of the way temperamental demands inevitably affect foundations of philosophical systems. What James promises for his generation is a kind of philosophical synthesis which locates personal ways of seeing things squarely in the heart of philosophical subject-matter. What this involves he describes in two essays: "What Pragmatism Means" and "Pragmatism's Conception of Truth."

Pragmatism is both a method and a theory of truth. The method can be used by men holding widely different philosophical persuasions. Its function is chiefly that of settling metaphysical disputes which seriously disturb men. Metaphysical arguments involve "notions" about which one can always ask whether the notions lead to any practical consequences. Such notions must be shown to make a difference in human conduct if they are to prove meaningful. Two Jamesian examples can illustrate

what is meant here. One example concerns an argument about whether, if a man circles a tree around whose trunk a squirrel is also moving, one can say the man "goes round" the squirrel. James shows how the answer depends on what is meant by "round." Mean by "going round" that the man is in successive places to north, east, south, and west of the squirrel, then he does go round the animal. Mean, on the other hand, that the man is behind, then to the right of, then in front of, and then to the left of the squirrel, then the man may not actually go round the squirrel—since the animal may move simultaneously with the man's movements. James concludes that an argument of this kind, if analyzed, turns out to be a verbal one.

Another example illustrates how the pragmatic method is compatible with many possible results. James asks his readers to view the method as being like a corridor in a hotel, whose doors open into many rooms which contain thinkers involved in a variety of intellectual pursuits. These pursuits may be metaphysical, religious, or scientific. Metaphysically, one room may harbor a man working out an idealistic system, while another may shelter a thinker attempting to show that metaphysics is an impossibility. James insists that the pragmatic method is neutral regarding the kinds of thought going on in the rooms. Nevertheless, he insists that as a theory of truth Pragmatism favors the nominalist's preference for particulars, the Utilitarian's stress on what is useful, and the positivist's dislike of metaphysical speculations and merely verbal solutions of problems. James believes men wanting to employ words like "God," "Matter," "the Absolute," "Reason," and "Energy" should use the pragmatic method in seeking to show how such notions can have practical effects.

As an instrumentalist theory of truth, Pragmatism views sharp distinctions between logic and psychology with great suspicion. Ideas are instruments which help to dispel doubt when inherited bodies of opinion no longer produce intellectual ease. Belief means the cessation of doubting. But what makes a belief true? James asserts that an idea is true if it permits the believer to attain "satisfactory relations with other parts of our experience." This genetic conception of truth—influenced by Darwinian biology—sees ideas as true for specified situations, always in principle subject to change and reevaluation. Some critics interpret James's emphasis on the contextual truth of an idea as meaning a man may believe whatever happens to make him comfortable. James rejects any wish-fulfilling conception of pragmatic truth. He states conditions which any idea must satisfy to qualify as workable. These conditions are quite conservative: Ideas must prove consistent with other ideas (including old ones) conformable to existing facts, and subject to experiential corroboration and validation.

James is mostly critical of rationalistic metaphysical ideas leading to no observable differences in domains of human conduct. He rejects claims about *the* Truth. Nevertheless he will consider even theological ideas as possibly true as long as their proponents can show them to affect some actual person's behavior. "Truth lives, in fact, for the most part on a credit system." Truth concerns matters of fact, abstract things and their relations, and the relations of an idea to the entire body of one's other beliefs. Ideas unable to conform to men's factual knowledge simply cannot have what James calls "cash-value. "

James's relevant essays about truth sometimes raise questions which they do not satisfactorily answer. Some critics accuse him of advocating a subjectivist theory of truth. Elsewhere, James defends his views by suggesting two kinds of criteria for testing the meaning of any sentence. First, a sentence has meaning if it leads to observable consequences in experience. Second, a sentence is meaningful if someone's belief in it leads to behavioral consequences. James seems to employ the first view when he writes about scientific and factual knowledge. He uses the second view when discussing certain moral and religious beliefs. It is the second view which worries some critics, who think that—if taken literally—it can justify as true any psychologically helpful belief.

The bulk of the remaining essays in *Pragmatism* seek to illustrate how the pragmatic method and theory of truth may be applied to specific problems. These are predominantly philosophical rather than scientific problems. In "Some Metaphysical Problems" and "The One and the Many" he applies the generous theory of meaning to such problems as the meaning of substance, the relative values of materialism and spiritualism, the problem of evil, the debate about freedom of the will, and the merits of monism and pluralism as cosmological notions. "Pragmatism and Common Sense" discusses three kinds of knowledge whose truth-claims are perennial. "Pragmatism and Humanism" and "Pragmatism and Religion" indicate how Pragmatism can mediate in disputes among hard-headed empiricists and abstract rationalists.

Taking the traditional puzzles about substance, design in nature, and free will, James argues that such metaphysical issues often lead to no genuine consequences for action if treated in solely intellectual terms. "In every *genuine* metaphysical dispute some practical issue, however conjectural and remote, is involved." Metaphysical arguments thus concern something other than what seems the case. Influenced by the thing-attribute aspect of grammar, men worry about substance because they suppose a *something* must support the external and psychological objects of our perceivable world beyond what these objects are experienced as. James asks us to imagine that a material or spiritual substance undergoes change without altering our perceptions of its supposed attributes. In such a case our perception of the properties would be the same as before. It follows that the notion of substance as standing for something beyond perceived qualities of objects can add nothing to our actual knowledge of the things in the world. Only in the Catholic claims about the Eucharist can the notion of substance have any practical use—a religious one. Similarly, arguments whether God or matter best explains the origin and development of the universe are unimportant so far as the observable facts go. Only one's expectations about the future can make the theist-materialist issue important. The pragmatic method leads to a slight "edge" for theism, according to James, since the belief in God "guarantees an ideal order that shall be permanently preserved." *What* the world is like, even if God created it, remains a matter for patient scientific labors to discover. The theistic conception of the world's origin permits men a kind of enjoyment which materialism excludes. Morally, theism is preferable since it refuses to take human disasters as the absolutely final word, while materialism denies the eternity of the moral order.

The question whether there is design in the world is also pointless if raised with scientific intent. The design issue is really a religious one. It is not open to purely rational solution. The significant aspects of the issue concern *what* that design may be, as well as *what* the nature of any possible designer. James applies a similar treatment to the determinism versus free will controversy. For him, this is an out-and-out metaphysical issue rather than interesting solely in relation to the discussion of moral judicability. To decide in favor of free will means to accept a faith that the universe can be improved through human effort. James calls this faith in improvability "meliorism." In turn, such a belief requires rejection of any absolute monistic conception of the cosmos. It requires belief in the notion that reality is a multiverse. The universe is neither simply one nor an absolute randomness. It is a pluriverse which contains specific kinds of unity as well as directly experienced "gaps." It is not *now* an absolute unity in light of our experience, but men may hope for such a completed unity as a possible future cosmic event.

James insists on the misleading nature of traditional metaphysical disputes. Metaphysical arguments seem to concern problems which human intellect can solve if only that intellect "gets them right." Yet, they are really practical problems. They are significant only when found to express hidden religious and moral issues. The pragmatist favors a decision for free will, belief in God's existence, faith in an increasing unity in a pluralistic universe, and hope that elements of design exist as grounds for one's belief in meliorism. Faith may rightfully decide when human reason proves insufficient. The reason is that such faith expresses confidence in the promise of the future and results in beneficial consequences for our present living.

James rejects metaphysical monism for moral and religious reasons. Monism implies a certain completedness about the universe even now. This completedness requires the denial of free will and, if God exists, of a worthwhile God. Nevertheless, James's pluralism includes the view that many kinds of unity

compose the universe. Intellect aims neither at variety nor unity, but at totality. The world contains important unities but is not a total unity. Some parts of the world are continuous with others, as in space-time; practical continuities appear (as in the notion of physical gravity); and there are systems of influence and noninfluence which indicate existence of causal unities. Furthermore, there are generic unities (kinds), unities of social purpose, and aesthetic unities. These are experienced. Yet, James says, we never experience "a universe pure and simple." Pragmatism therefore insists on a world as containing just as many continuities *and* disjunctions as experience shows to exist.

The only ultimate unity may be an absolute knower of the system. Even the system may not always be considered to be a necessary unity, since the world may exist as eternally incomplete—actually subject to addition and loss. Our knowledge of such a world grows slowly, through scientific criticism, common sense, and philosophic criticism. No one can demonstrate conclusively which, if any, of these ways of knowing is the truest. Common sense builds up customary ways of organizing the materials of experience. It uses such concepts as thing, same or different, kinds, minds, bodies, one time, one space, subjects and attributes, causal influences, the fancied, the real. Scientific criticism adds more sophisticated notions, like "atoms" and "ether," say, casting some doubt on the adequacy of commonsense concepts. The philosophical stage gives no knowledge quite comparable to the other two. Philosophical criticism does not make possible description of details of nature. Our decisions about which philosophical views to adopt must turn on practical rather than theoretical criteria. On the other hand, choice between common sense and scientific notions will rest on existence of kinds of corroboration which, in principle, will always be lacking in the cases of competing philosophical claims.

The essays in *Pragmatism* express a loosely stated yet consistent philosophical viewpoint. Through them runs the excitement of discovery that, if only the pragmatic method be adopted, many old and perplexing issues can be translated into practical ones. James seems eager to help men discover the metaphysical views which will conform to their experienced needs. On the other hand, he wants to insist on binding tests when the pragmatist handles common sense and science. He is less insistent on such tests in religious and moral domains. His major thesis is that "all true processes must lead to the fact of directly verifying sensible experience *somewhere*, which somebody's ideas have copied." His generosity remains attractive even to some critics who reject his philosophical conclusions.—*W.T.D*.

Pertinent Literature

Thayer, H. S., ed. "Introduction," in William James's *Pragmatism*. Cambridge, Massachusetts: Harvard University Press, 1975.

In his Introduction to this volume, which is the first in a recent series of critical editions of the writings of William James, H. S. Thayer notes that the publication of *Pragmatism: A New Name for Some Old Ways of Thinking* (1907) unleashed a storm of controversy. Disputes about the merits of the work still swirl. Thayer sorts out the issues by setting James's book within the context of his full philosophical career.

For nearly thirty years prior to the appearance of *Pragmatism*, writes Thayer, James had explored the problems and themes that would culminate in his pragmatic theories of meaning and truth. Early on, James became convinced that knowing is an activity in which human emotions and practical concerns play a governing part. We cannot make reality conform completely to the heart's desire, but human aims are significant. Inquiry functions in their service. By 1885, Thayer believes, James was already advancing a view that would locate the truth of propositions in their ability to lead us successfully toward obtaining fulfillment of the practical expectations they entail.

Humanistic concerns are salient in James's book, and Thayer claims that one of its major goals was to explore how pragmatism might clarify religious problems. In themselves these aims would not have been sufficient to provoke the debate that *Pragmatism* has caused, but those objectives were linked to James's unique theory of truth, which said more than enough to set philosophical nerves on edge. Thayer contends, however, that much of the ensuing conflict has been due to misunderstandings that can be largely corrected by keeping three points in mind.

The first is that James's own statements about truth do not all fit together easily because, by his own admission, the theory was never formulated completely. Indeed, Thayer's second point is that James probably chose unwisely in calling his suggestions about truth a *theory* at all. For James intended to give no exhaustive account or definition of truth, asserts Thayer, but rather to elucidate what other theories had neglected or failed to explain. Third, James sought in particular to make more intelligible the traditional position that true propositions "agree" with reality.

Elaborating on his third point, Thayer explains that such agreement is found when ideas guide human activity into satisfactory adjustments to reality. What James wanted to provide, Thayer emphasizes, is a critical and intersystematic interpretation of what those relationships entail. Consistency, coherence, and simplicity, along with the pressure of stubborn fact and the weight of everyday experience, all exert their influence in James's account.

Thayer does not deny that James also believed that our judgments about truth and reality rightly include some relativity. Not only do people carve existence up in different ways, depending on their needs and interests, but also basic beliefs, religious ones for example, may be true for some persons and false for others. Contrary to the usual criticisms, Thayer argues, James's handling of these aspects of experience was neither a logical muddle nor a defense of capricious subjectivism. James took with utmost seriousness the fact that truth depends on objective relations, but such relations are often formed in a decisive way by the drives, projects, and expectations of individuals. Consequently those relations may differ, and as they do so, the resulting truth also varies.

No doubt, says Thayer, problems remain in James's account of truth. Two instances are James's tendencies to identify the true with the useful and to equate truth and verification. Even in these cases, however, Thayer's interpretation remains sympathetic, for he implies that patient and detailed reconstruction may save James's ideas from error without giving up their intended meanings. Thayer does not provide that reconstruction here, but he concludes that *Pragmatism* is an extraordinary philosophical statement because of James's unflagging concern to address "the real perplexities, the uncertainties and resurgent hopes that permeate ordinary human experience."

White, Morton. *Science and Sentiment in America: Philosophical Thought from Jonathan Edwards to John Dewey.* New York: Oxford University Press, 1972.

The most intriguing dimensions in the history of American philosophy, Morton White suggests, are the responses American thinkers have made to challenging developments in modern science. William James provides a case in point, for he came to philosophy by way of physiology and psychology and was well equipped to appreciate the power and value of scientific method. Nevertheless, that recognition did not lead James to champion science over every other form of human experience. In fact, James's background in the sciences moved him to warn against reductive tendencies in scientific theory. Thus, White notes, James's *Principles of Psychology* (1890) and his essays in *The Will to Believe* (1896) defend the rightful authority of sentiment or feeling to determine moral, religious, and metaphysical beliefs.

According to White, James's early writings advocated not a dualism but a "trialism" where the fixation of belief is concerned. James held that, in addition to cases where beliefs are properly determined by individual feeling that goes beyond public empirical evidence or the insight of pure reason, there are areas where belief is and should be formed only by the two latter elements. White finds places in *Pragmatism* where this "trialism" persists, but he is most fascinated by a more radical thesis that James was exploring in 1907, namely, that *all* beliefs are colored by personal sentiment. The provocative claim that intellect, will, taste, and passion mix and mingle in all human knowledge prompts White to subtitle his chapter on William James: "Pragmatism and the Whole Man."

A "holistic" theory of knowledge is what White sees James developing in *Pragmatism*. He argues, moreover, that James's position culminated a struggle that had gone on in American philosophy for more than 150 years, initiated when Jonathan Edwards tried to locate a distinctive base for religious knowledge by appealing to a "Sense of the Heart." The core of James's holistic epistemology, White contends, exists where James argues that the process of arriving at a belief, or of finding a belief to be true, involves an appraisal that involves our whole stock of opinions. Human beliefs and challenges to them are continually being weighed in relation to one another. Equilibrium depends on the ability of the total stock of beliefs to accommodate emotional desires, needs for consistency, aims to anticipate experience, and aesthetic yearnings for elegant explanation. Thus, White interprets James to say, the truth of scientific theories, far from being imposed upon us, now takes on qualities similar to that of religious or moral convictions. Human opinion is uncoerced by experience not only in the latter realms but in the former as well. In meeting or failing to meet James's holistic conditions, scientific theories, too, fall under James's pragmatic theory of truth.

The crux of the matter, White asserts, is James's emphasis that beliefs are never tested in isolation but always as parts of a stock of opinions. The stock of opinions is not absolutely fixed, but neither is it totally malleable. Experience entrenches some beliefs much more firmly than others. To gain status as a personal or a public belief, either a new claim will have to be one that can be accommodated to existing beliefs or it will require older beliefs to be revised or scrapped. What distinguishes James's pragmatic theory of truth, White contends, is that he developed his notion of coherence so that our existing stock of beliefs may be challenged, and rightly so, not only by logical inconsistency or stubborn fact but also by unsatisfied desire. Nor did James think that any elements in the stock of beliefs could be deemed immune from these diverse challenges. If new beliefs had to battle their way to acceptance against previously established views, James also held that metaphysical beliefs and even convictions about physical realities or logical principles might be subject to alteration or abandonment if they came into conflict with facts or feelings of sufficient authority.

The major contribution of James's *Pragmatism*, White infers, is the insight that the whole person appraises opinion by appeal to many different factors. Sentiment can always be one of them. As never before, White observes, James gave feeling and immediate experience a central role in American philosophy, so much so that he "represented the triumph of Romanticism in American thought."

Wild, John. *The Radical Empiricism of William James*. Garden City, New York: Doubleday & Company, 1969.

John Wild's book has done more than any other to relate the philosophy of William James to the insights of European phenomenology and existentialism. Differing from many interpreters of James's thought, Wild gives primary attention to *The Principles of Psychology*; but far from ignoring James's *Pragmatism* and its sequel *The Meaning of Truth* (1909), he finds that their major theses are defensible provided one corrects the excesses that left James open to legitimate criticism.

When Wild refers to James's "radical empiricism," he has in mind his lifelong concern to describe and clarify human experiences as they are actually lived through. Distrusting systems of thought constructed by reason alone, James placed a premium on open empirical investigation. Wild sees James's pragmatic theories of meaning and truth as part and parcel of that priority. For example, Wild points out, James understood that neither sense perception nor rational conceptualization grasps reality completely. Existence always shows itself to have further depths and relations that are presently unknown, and thus investigation must continue if our knowledge is to advance. That investigation requires perception and conceptual analysis to work in tandem. The former is clarified only when the light of conceptual analysis is shed upon it but the adequacy of concepts and theories is validated only when they lead to fulfilled expectations in concrete experience.

James, says Wild, shared the existential insight that there is no necessary connection between meaning and being. What that insight meant for James,

Wild explains, is that truth is not a property that every proposition possesses or lacks automatically. James saw that truth exists only if a match between a meaning and an actually existing reality turns up somewhere in experience. Admittedly we do at times speak of truth as eternal and complete. No human person, however, encounters any verification that is absolutely final. Complete knowledge and absolute truth, James held, are best regarded as regulative ideals. The strength of such proposals, Wild finds, is that James's remarks about truth were firmly based in descriptions of what actually occurs as we seek knowledge and inquire after truth.

Nevertheless, Wild does not believe that James kept everything in focus as well as could be desired. Preoccupied with moral and religious issues, James was correct to think that there is no corroboration within human experience apart from activities that men and women perform; but Wild thinks that James should have placed greater stress on the role that facts play in validating most empirical judgments.

Wild anticipates White's proposition that James's earlier writings made sharper distinctions among the different kinds of belief that confront us. He agrees, too, that *Pragmatism* tends to blur those distinctions in favor of an increased authoritative role for feeling and sentiment; but on the whole Wild has less sympathy for James at this juncture than does Morton White. On the other hand, Wild joins both White and H. S. Thayer in holding that indictments of "subjectivism" commonly brought against James usually rest on misinterpretations. James did not believe,

Wild argues, that a belief is ever sufficiently justified merely if one feels satisfied by it. Critical testing that brings a belief into coherent relationships with life's many dimensions is always required. That convic-tion, Wild maintains, is further evidence of James's desire to develop a philosophy that is constantly in touch with the lived experience of individuals and groups.

Additional Recommended Reading

Allen, Gay Wilson. *William James: A Biography.* New York: The Viking Press, 1967. This study of James's life cites four major elements in his philosophy—pluralism, radical empiricism, tychism, and theism—and underscores how James's *Pragmatism* interprets the universe as one of flux and change.

Ayer, A. J. *The Origins of Pragmatism: Studies in the Philosophy of Charles Sanders Peirce and William James.* San Francisco: Freeman, Cooper & Company, 1968. This noted British philosopher argues that James's concern to find a place for religious belief, without compromising empirical evidence or sound intellectual standards, is a chief motivation behind *Pragmatism*, which contains a consistent and even tenable view of truth if James's theory is properly interpreted.

Dooley, Patrick K. *Pragmatism as Humanism.* Chicago: Nelson-Hall, 1974. The pivotal ingredient in James's thought, and the key for understanding *Pragmatism*, the author suggests, is his distinctively humanistic outlook.

Earle, William James. "William James," in *The Encyclopedia of Philosophy.* New York: Macmillan Publishing Company, 1967. Earle sees James's *Pragmatism* as an exploration of what it means to believe and in particular what it means in actual experience to find ideas true or false.

Flower, Elizabeth and Murray G. Murphy. *A History of Philosophy in America.* 2 vols. New York: G. P. Putnam's Sons, 1977. Flower and Murphy suggest that James's *Pragmatism* can still alert us to the subtlety and richness of experience, the purposeful quality of thought, and the active character of knowing.

James, William. *The Writings of William James: A Comprehensive Edition.* Edited by John J. McDermott. New York: Random House, 1967. McDermott sees James's *Pragmatism* as an epistemological elaboration of themes and principles set forth earlier in *The Principles of Psychology.*

Morris, Charles. *The Pragmatic Movement in American Philosophy.* New York: George Braziller, 1970. While James extended pragmatism beyond the parameters of C. S. Peirce's outlook, Morris argues that the two thinkers ended up with highly similar theories of meaning.

Myers, Gerald E. *William James: His Life and Thought.* New Haven, Connecticut: Yale University Press, 1986. An extensive study of James's thought and the milieu in which it appeared.

Rorty, Amelie, ed. *Pragmatic Philosophy.* Garden City, New York: Doubleday/Anchor Books, 1966. In her comments in this anthology, the editor judges James's writings, including *Pragmatism*, to be engaging but not always precise and rigorous.

Roth, John K. *American Dreams: Meditations on Life in the United States.* San Francisco: Chandler and Sharp, 1976. The author discusses James's pragmatic outlook in the context of James's meliorism, a middle position between an optimism that sees progress as inevitable and a pessimism that finds gloom and doom ahead.

IDEAS: GENERAL INTRODUCTION TO PURE PHENOMENOLOGY

Author: Edmund Husserl (1859-1938)
Type of work: Metaphysics, epistemology
First published: 1913

Principal Ideas Advanced

Natural sciences are, by nature, dogmatic; the phenomenologist must undertake a critical study of the conditions under which knowledge is possible.

To distinguish within experience that which experiences from that which is experienced, one must suspend natural beliefs; this suspension of belief is made possible by a method of bracketing by which we talk not about trees and selves as items external to experience but of the "trees" and the "perceptions" of experience.

Noema, *that which is perceived, is dependent upon* noesis, *the perceiving; but* noema *has the kind of being peculiar to essences.*

The absolute forms of essences which owe their actuality in consciousness to acts of perceiving are Eideia, *eternal possibilities of quality, related to other* Eideia *by external relations.*

The term "phenomenology," as it is used by Husserl and his disciples, designates first of all a principle of philosophical and scientific method. The usual method of natural science proceeds from a body of accepted truth and seeks to extend its conquest of the unknown by putting questions to nature and compelling it to answer. The phenomenological method adopts a softer approach. Setting aside all presuppositions and suppressing hypotheses, it seeks to devise techniques of observation, description, and classification which will permit it to disclose structures and connections in nature which do not yield to experimental techniques. It has been widely fruitful in psychology and the social sciences, as well as in epistemology and value-theory.

Husserl, in his *Logical Studies* (1900-1901), did much to advance general phenomenological studies. But he had in view a specifically philosophical application of the technique which many of his associates did not completely grasp, or failed to share. *Ideas* was written with a view to clearing up the distinction between phenomenological psychology, which he regarded as a legitimate, but secondary, science, and phenomenological philosophy, which, he was prepared to maintain, is the foundation of all science.

When a sociologist or psychologist conducts a phenomenological investigation, he puts aside all the usual theories and assumptions which have governed research in that field: but he cannot rid himself of all presuppositions (such as, for example, the belief in the existence of the external world, the constancy of nature). As Plato saw, every science must proceed upon some assumptions—except philosophy. To fulfill its promise, the phenomenological approach must bring us at last to an absolutely presuppositionless science. Pure phenomenology, or phenomenological philosophy, is, in Husserl's opinion, precisely that. (It has long been the aspiration of philosophers to make their science an absolute one, one that rids itself of all presuppositions and stands with open countenance before pure Being. Husserl stands in this tradition.)

Phenomenology is not to be confused with "phenomenalism," a name sometimes given to extreme forms of empiricism, such as that of Ernst Mach, which maintains that nothing is real except sense-data. In fact, this is one of the misconceptions which phenomenology is designed to overcome. If the empiricists are right, the unity and order which we are accustomed to find in the world are not given in experience but put there by the activity of the mind. Genetic psychology, which seeks to explain the origin of our various mental habits and responses, would therefore hold the key to understanding our whole view of the world. A good example is J. S. Mill, who in his *A System of Logic* (1843) undertook to explain the force of syllogistic reasoning in terms of associationist psychology. Other positivists and pragmatists have attempted to give a psychological theory of knowledge and of valuation. Husserl argued, however, that the empiricists were wrong, that they did not come to their conviction about the absence of order and intelligibility in the pure data of experience by examining what is given there, but had it as an Idol of the Theater (to use Francis Bacon's term). It follows that they have misconceived the task of psychology in supposing that it can discover in the mind laws which give rise to the meaning of the world, and that it is incumbent upon us to set about developing new accounts of logic, knowledge-theory, aesthetics, and ethics which stand on their own evidence. In place of *psychologism* (a misconceived psychology or science of the soul) what is needed, if justice is to be done to experience, is *phenomenology* (science of phenomena, or appearances).

Husserl takes his place, then, in the forefront of those twentieth century philosophers who have sought to reaffirm the autonomy of various philosophical disciplines over against psychology. He was equally concerned to turn back the tide of the popular-scientific view of the world which he called naturalism. The particular sciences, by nature, are dogmatic. That is to say, they proceed without examining the conditions under which knowledge is possible. This is not to be held against them. But when anyone attempts to build a natural philosophy on the findings of the sciences, his uncritical procedure opens the way to skepticism, because the categories in terms of which we grasp natural events are unsuited to take account of conscious events, including the pursuit of scientific truth. It seems innocent enough to explain consciousness in terms of natural causes until we recollect that matter and the laws which govern its behavior are themselves part of our experience. This, according to Husserl, is the point at which the philosopher must step in. His primary task, in fact, will be to distinguish within experience the part that experiences from the part that is experienced.

There are many overtones of Descartes in Husserl's writings. The former philosopher, in order to escape from the ambiguities and uncertainties of our ordinary, natural experience, developed a method of doubting. By bringing under question the whole phenomenal world, he laid bare a world of logical forms which he could not doubt. Husserl adopts a similar method. He talks of "suspending" our natural beliefs, including the fundamental conviction of every healthy mind that there is a world "out there," that there are other selves, and so on. We are asked to "alter" this natural standpoint, to "disconnect" our beliefs about causation and motion, to "put them out of action." This is, of course, only a methodological procedure, in order to help us overcome our animal bias and make it possible for us to take a coolly intellectual view of things. Greek philosophy used the term *epoche* to indicate the suspense of judgment. Husserl presses this term into his service.

To make his meaning clear, he uses the example of looking with pleasure into a garden where an apple tree is blossoming. From the natural standpoint, the tree is something that has transcendent reality in space and time, and the joy of perceiving it has reality in the psyche of a human being. But Descartes has reminded us that perceptions are sometimes hallucinations. We pass, therefore, from the natural to the phenomenological standpoint, bracketing the claims of both the knower and the known to natural being. This leaves us with "a nexus of exotic experiences of perception and pleasure valuation." We can now speak of the content and structure of the situation without any reference to external existence. Nothing is really taken away from the experience, but it is all there in a new manner. In order to indicate this, the use of quotation marks is helpful. We can now speak of "tree," "plant," "material thing," "blossoming," "white," "sweet," and so forth, and be sure that we are talking only about things that belong to the essence of our experience. Similarly, at the opposite pole, we can distinguish "perceiving," "attending," "enjoying," and other ego-acts. These each have their special characters, and repay analysis.

Husserl was at one time a student of Franz Brentano (1838-1917), who had said that what distinguishes mental acts from nonmental acts is that the former invariably refer to something other than themselves. Drawing from the scholastics, he said that they are "intentional." Husserl makes constant use of this discovery. To designate the ego-acts, which are not limited to cognition but include as well various attitudes such as doubting and supposing, as well as volitions and feelings, he uses the Greek word *noesis* (literally, a perceiving). To designate the corresponding objects, for instance, "tree," "fruitful," "charming," he uses the corresponding word *noema* (literally, that which is perceived). An important part of the analysis of consciousness consists in tracing the relation between these. In each case, the *noesis* is real and fundamental, but *noema* is dependent and, strictly speaking, unreal. In our example, "the perceiving of the tree" is actual and constitutive of "the tree perceived." But conversely, though it does not have reality, *noema* has being, which is lacking to *noesis*: that is to say, it is composed entirely of essences, which are eternally what they are and stand in necessary or *a priori* relations with each other. The same thing is true of volition and other modes. "The valuing of the tree" is a *noesis*. It has the same reality as "the perceiving of the tree." Correspondingly, "the value of the tree" is a *noema*. It does not have reality, but it has the same kind of essential being as the structure and properties have which make up the object of cognition. The value-characters likewise take their place in an *a priori* system together with other values.

As long as our interest, as philosophers, is directed primarily toward the life of the mind, we shall be chiefly interested in exploring the various *noeses*. Husserl's delineation of these is subtle and perceptive, and goes a long way toward persuading the reader of the necessity of this descriptive groundwork, although as is sometimes true of the drawings of a microscopist we may have difficulty in recognizing in it the familiar features of the mind. His account of "meaning," for example, should be studied by those who are interested in semantics, and his analysis of "sentiment" and "volition" provides an instructive approach to the question of the relation between emotions and values. One thing is common to all *noeses*, according to Husserl: all are at bottom *thetic*, or postulational; Husserl speaks of them as *doxa* (Plato's word for "opinion"). This does not imply that some of our *noeses* are not characterized by "certainty," just as others are characterized by a "sense of likelihood" or "doubt. " But in any case, it is what we commonly call a "moral certainty. " The conviction is a mode of the "perceiving" rather than a function of anything lying in the "perceived."

But in the present work Husserl does not consider mental acts *per se*. He studies them because they provide the key to the various grades and types of objects which make up the *noemata*; for, corresponding to "perception" there is the realm of "colors," "shapes," and "sizes"; and corresponding to "perceptual enjoyment" there are "dainty" pink and "gloriously" scented. These qualities owe their actuality in consciousness to the *noeses*; but they are part of an order of being which is absolute and independent. Husserl calls all such absolute forms or essences *Eideia*, to avoid the ambiguities of such words as Ideas and Essences. They are eternal possibilities, each perfectly definite and distinct from every other, but also linked with every other in a system of eternal relations. Thus, "pink," "white," "green" are species under the genus "color"; and "color" itself stands in a hierarchy of perceptual "qualities. " A similar hierarchical structure embraces the *noema* of value.

Husserl, who began his philosophical studies as a logician, was preeminently interested in the grammar of meaning. He claims that, on a very abstract level, all *noema* exemplify universal relations which can be formulated in a *Mathesis Universalis* such as Leibniz conceived. But the theorizing logician does not do justice to the wealth of formal relations which lie before the phenomenologist. "Its field is the analysis of the *a priori* shown forth in *immediate* intuition, the fixing of immediately transparent essence and essential connexions and their descriptive cognition in the systematic union of all strata in pure transcendental consciousness. " It begins by distinguishing various regional ontologies—of which the "formal region" exploited by the logician is only one. "Material regions" are numerous. The region of the physical *Thing* will serve as an example. The question presents itself as follows: "How are we to describe systematically the *noeses* and *noemata* which belong to the unity of the intuitively presenting Thing-consciousness?" Leaving aside the *noetic* factor, the problem is to analyze the essential connections by which "appearances" present themselves as "one and the same thing." The analysis discloses that a mere *res extensa* is conceivable apart from the idea of a *res materialis* and a *res temporalis*. Yet as a matter of fact, a thing as presented to "us humans" involves all three of these. So, there are "strata" and "formations" constituting the thing. And it is necessary to analyze each of these unities in turn. The problem of "presentation in space" has here to be faced. Although, according to Husserl, its meaning has never yet been completely grasped, it now appears in clear light—namely by "the phenomenological analysis of the *essential* nature of all the noematic (and noetic) phenomena, wherein space exhibits itself intuitionally and as the unity of appearances. "

In the present volume, as is proper in an introduction, Husserl is able only to indicate the direction which the investigation must take. And one must look to his other works, and those of his disciples, to see the analyses carried out in detail. While Husserl

worked chiefly in the field of epistemology, his disciples carried the method into axiology and philosophical anthropology (Max Scheler), aesthetics (Theodor Lipps), sociology (Karl Mannheim), comparative religion (Rudolph Otto), and ethics (Nicolai Hartmann), not to mention the "existentialism" of Martin Heidegger and Jean-Paul Sartre. For the ordinary reader, these developments are more interesting and fruitful than pure phenomenology. But that is because it is difficult for most people to exercise themselves about the sheer possibility of knowledge. Husserl's significance, as a philosopher, is that, like Descartes and Kant, he appeared at a time when the foundations of science were themselves threatened, and irrationalism, skepticism, and nihilism threatened the very nerve of Western civilization. He sought to revive knowledge, to make possible once again a rational view of the world and of the human enterprise. He was conscious of being the continuer of a long tradition, and with some reluctance admitted to falling under the classification of idealist. He most resembles Kant, and his work can be summed up as the search for the transcendental conditions which make "meaning" (scientific, ethical, aesthetic, religious) possible.

Pertinent Literature

Kohák, Erazim V. *Idea and Experience: Edmund Husserl's Project of Phenomenology* in *IDEAS I*. Chicago: University of Chicago Press, 1978.

Phenomenology is at once a concrete philosophy of experience and a formal method of inquiry founded upon radical reflexivity. During the past fifty years phenomenology has become the dominant philosophical force in Western Europe, while in England and America it has had a profound impact through its applications in psychology, sociology, and the other human sciences. The name most commonly associated with phenomenology as it is known today is Edmund Husserl. Yet it is not easy to penetrate his philosophy, or even to describe what he means by phenomenology. Because of the magnitude and complexity of his work, together with a technical terminology which is often obscure and bewildering,

understanding Husserl can be at times nearly impossible. For this reason Erazim Kohák's commentary is most welcome. He cuts through Husserlian verbiage and carefully presents Husserl's ideas using ordinary language, thus opening the doors to Husserlian phenomenology for those who are not scholars in the field.

Kohák guides the reader through the first nine chapters of Husserl's influential *Ideas: General Introduction to Pure Phenomenology*. The aim is to retrieve and elaborate the simple, basic insight crucial to all of Husserl's work—namely, that *to know means to see*. For Husserl, the primordial starting point of all knowledge, the ultimate source of the validity of all rational assertions, is not speculation, not pure reason, but a kind of direct "seeing," an experiential awareness which people sometimes acknowledge with the startling exclamation, "Oh, *now I see!*" In a sense, Husserl's phenomenology evolves as an anatomy of *direct seeing.*

Kohák's presentation is unique in that he actually utilizes the method of phenomenology in his study of phenomenology. Much has been written concerning the so-called "phenomenological method." Husserl, in fact, many times refers to his own work as a study of method. Kohák, however, rightly points out the mistake in thinking of phenomenology's "method" as a special set of techniques or procedures. More accurately, what is intended by the term "method" is a certain stance or perspective, a manner of orientation. As a descriptive science of human experience, phenomenology proposes a fundamental cognitive reorientation; and the goal, as in any science, is to promote *seeing and grasping clearly*. In a similar manner, by approaching Husserl from a phenomenological perspective, Kohák's goal is to enable the reader to "grasp" more clearly the main features of Husserl's philosophy, or way of philosophizing.

The subject matter of phenomenology is lived experience; the task is a scrupulous examination and clarification of what and how we actually experience in our most ordinary daily living. Husserl's slogan "Back to the things themselves" means "Back to experience. " Any answers to our questions are to be found in experience itself: if not there, then nowhere. The trouble is that as we live it, experience is highly elusive, and as it is represented by poets, scientists, and philosophers it seems to change from account to account. Too often our descriptions do not faithfully record our experience as actually lived. Kohák gives the example of marriage. As lived, marriage is a *way of being*; it is a mode of existence for two people. Yet when the "facts" of the marriage are being described—the living arrangements, the rights and obligations, who cooks and who washes dishes, who earns the money—the lived reality of *being married* seems to evaporate. We need a special focus, a special perspective on experience to see it as it is lived. Husserl would say we need a rigorous, radically reflexive, phenomenological perspective.

Phenomenological seeing requires effort, just as does ordinary seeing. We frequently see indistinctly and unclearly, and accordingly we need to look again, carefully, painstakingly, directing our focus until the object emerges clearly. This is also the case in phenomenological reflection, where the "object" we are looking for is our own experience as actually lived. Pure experience, however, cannot be grasped by any ordinary means of attentiveness. What is required, according to Husserl, is a radical shift in viewpoint and a suspension of what he calls the "natural standpoint."

The natural standpoint is the conventional, habitual, commonsense point of view evident in ordinary, everyday experience. The most pervasive feature of the natural standpoint is the attitude that there exists a real world "out there," constantly there to be seen, touched, and heard, a world not subjectively invented but objectively given. From the natural standpoint, the objects of our world are encountered as spatially and temporally ordered, all things exhibiting an identity, a history, and a causal origin. From the natural, customary point of view, the world is experienced as a shared world, an inter-subjective world, a world which is there for all of us and to which all of us belong.

The problem with the natural standpoint, according to Husserl, is that in a subtle way it turns the subject away from lived experience. As lived, reality is the *experiencing of* an object. From the natural standpoint, reality is *the object*; the experiencing is purely incidental to it. But if we are to achieve knowledge of reality, we must "see" reality as it is given, as actually lived—or, as Husserl puts it, we must look at it "in brackets."

Phenomenological bracketing, or *epoche,* is a methodological suspension of the natural standpoint, a shift away from the habitual stance we assume toward the world, and a shift toward pure, unadulterated experience in its brute givenness. Using Kohák's illustration, bracketing is a "switching off," as when we switch off an electric lamp. The lamp is still there, but now as one of the objects in the room, not as that which illuminates everything else. In suspending the natural standpoint, the phenomenologist in a sense is "switching off the world." *Epoche* does not imply denying or canceling out the world. The world, like the lamp, is still there, but no longer as that which illuminates or explains experience. On the contrary, it becomes a datum to be explained. Phenomenological bracketing allows us to "grasp" the reality of the world *as experience* or, in Husserl's terminology, *as phenomenon.*

Once the need and justification for bracketing is clearly seen, it will require no further explanation. Yet, as Kohák acutely recognizes, seeing is rarely accomplished at a glance. So to further help the reader to understand the idea of *epoche*, he goes on to consider possible applications of bracketing in areas such as theology, sociology, and physics. the main point which comes out of his discussion is that knowing is seeing, and that sometimes seeing can be achieved only through a radical shift in focus.

In other chapters of the book Kohák explicates Husserl's ideas on experience and intersubjectivity, reflection, intentionality, transcendental subjectivity, and the relation of phenomenology to empiricism and idealism. At each step of the way his commentary is lucid, straightforward, and insightful. As a whole, this book deserves to be ranked as one of the finest introductions to Husserl's phenomenology.

Natanson, Maurice A. *Edmund Husserl: Philosopher of Infinite Tasks.* Evanston, Illinois: Northwestern University Press, 1973.

The basic principle of phenomenology is the intentionality of consciousness, the idea that all consciousness is consciousness of *something*. In itself this is not too astounding. But the emphasis which Edmund Husserl brings to bear upon this principle is that the objects of consciousness—that is, the *intentional objects*—must be understood as part of the unified structure of consciousness itself. This is due to the fact that the intentional object is endowed with *meaning*. In his book on Husserl, Maurice Natanson provides a fine exposition of the meaning and implications of the principle of intentionality.

When it is said that consciousness is intentional, one of the important things meant is that consciousness by its very nature *directs* itself toward its object. The principle signifies that between consciousness and its object there is an essential relationship which can be described metaphorically as "aiming toward." " Any given experience, for example, seeing a tree, involves even at the most elementary level a sense of direction such that I see *this* rather than *that*. Insofar as I am seeing something (some object), it is correct to say that I am *directed toward* the object I am conscious of—in this case, the tree.

Husserl distinguishes between the intentional object, in his words, the "noema," or object as *meant*, and the real, or "transcendent," object. After agreeing that consciousness is necessarily *of something*, the question arises as to what can be said about this "of something. "

Husserl asks us to suppose that we are looking at a blossoming apple tree in the garden. From the natural standpoint—that is, from the ordinary, everyday way of looking at things—the apple tree is something that exists in the reality of space. Real relations are thought of as subsisting between us and the real tree. Husserl refers to our "real" tree as a transcendent object, insofar as its existence is conceived as being completely independent of our perceptual experience. Now the ordinary person firmly believes, and rightly so, that when we speak about objects of consciousness we are referring at least sometimes to actual entities like the apple tree. But if we go on to identify our "intentional object" as being the real apple tree, a difficult problem arises with regard to the possibility of hallucination.

Under conditions like those described above, it is not contradictory to suppose that the so-called perception may be in fact a mere hallucination, in which case the "perceived" object—the apple tree which is believed to stand before us—does not actually exist. But how can one be said to "perceive" an apple tree if no apple tree actually exists? Husserl resolves the apparent perplexity by carefully distinguishing between the real object (which may or may not actually exist) and the objective *meaning* of the perceptual act, the latter being the intentional correlate of consciousness. Real tree or not, the intentional structure of the perceptual experience remains intact, such that there is a consciousness of "this apple tree in bloom." To speak of the intentional object, in other words, is to speak of the *sense* or *meaning* of the perceptual experience.

Natanson illustrates how at the base of all perception is perceptual *meaning*. By its very nature the act of consciousness harbors within itself a meaning of some sort, and this meaning is the intentional (noematic) element present in all determinate modes of concrete consciousness. Thus the internal structure of consciousness is fundamentally the relationship between consciousness and its objective meaning: a relationship which sees consciousness always directed toward, reaching toward, or groping for a meaningful content.

In one of the most illuminating sections of his book, Natanson demonstrates how intentionality makes it possible for us to experience sameness, and thus to enjoy a world of familiar, repeatable, and expectable events. An intentional object is not something which appears and disappears with a given act of consciousness, but something which remains identical through different modes of consciousness and moments in time. Although conditions under which I perceive something may vary considerably, the identity of the intentional object is unaffected. In the apple tree *as meant*, we have something which can be thought of as the same throughout an indefinite number of presentative acts. Natanson gives the following illustration. Suppose I am on a bus and casually glance at the face of the woman sitting across from me. I see her face, now from the front, now in profile. As the bus goes through a tunnel, the light changes, her face looks different—yet it is the same face. Changes in light, vantage point, or time do not affect the identity of the object *as meant*. I may close my eyes and reopen them, I may turn my head and then look back again, and still the intentional object remains invariant. The prize of intentionality, stresses Natanson, is identity.

The principle of intentionality is only one aspect of Husserl's phenomenology. Other important topics which Natanson addresses include Husserl's phenomenological method, bracketing and the suspension of the natural standpoint, the concept of *Lebenswelt* (life-world), and the manner in which phenomenology provides a critique of traditional philosophy and a foundation for the human sciences.

Additional Recommended Reading

Edie, James M. *Edmund Husserl's Phenomenology: A Critical Commentary.* Bloomington: Indiana University Press, 1987. An important interpretation by a leading Husserl scholar.

Elliston, Frederick and Peter McCormick, eds. *Husserl: Expositions and Appraisals.* Notre Dame, Indiana: University of Notre Dame Press, 1977. Both in title and content, this work joins exegesis and criticism. The essays are grouped into three parts, dealing respectively with general philosophical themes in Husserl, specific phenomenological concepts and methodological considerations, and comparisons and contrasts with other major figures and traditions in contemporary philosophy. Of the twenty-three articles included, eleven are published for the first time.

Kockelmans, Joseph J. *A First Introduction to Husserl's Phenomenology.* Pittsburgh: Duquesne University Press, 1967. This book succeeds in giving a relatively clear and concise overall picture of the main themes and topics in Husserl's philosophy,

Kolakowski, Leszek. *Husserl and the Search for Certitude.* New Haven, Connecticut: Yale University Press, 1975. The book, which is a set of three lectures delivered at Yale University, takes as its point of departure Husserl's quest for the absolutely unquestionable foundation of knowledge. Kolakowski argues that Husserl's attempt to attain epistemological certitude not only failed but was bound to fail.

Ricoeur, Paul. *Husserl: An Analysis of His Phenomenology.* Translated by Edward G. Ballard and Lester E. Embree. Evanston, Illinois: Northwestern University Press, 1967. Ricoeur ranks as one of the giants in the phenomenological movement. This collection of nine individual essays provides a unified interpretation of the most influential elements of Husserl's phenomenology, along with creating a link in the development of Ricoeur's own existential phenomenology.

Sokolowski, Robert. *Husserlian Meditations: How Words Present Things*. Evanston, Illinois: Northwestern University Press, 1974. A philosophical commentary on the work of Edmund Husserl. Sokolowski conjoins interpretation with criticism as he investigates Husserl's doctrines for the purpose of advancing truthfulness. The chapters on internal time-consciousness and the phenomenological reduction (viewed as a move from mundane experience to genuine philosophical reflection) are especially fruitful.

TRACTATUS LOGICO-PHILOSOPHICUS

Author: Ludwig Wittgenstein (1889-1951)
Type of work: Logic, philosophy of philosophy
First published: 1921

Principal Ideas Advanced

The world is made up of atomic facts; atomic facts are facts which are incapable of analysis into more elemental facts.

Propositions are logical pictures of (possible) facts; what is common to a proposition and the fact it pictures is logical structure.

A proposition does not express the form of a possible fact; it shows it.

To give the general form of proposition is to give the essence of all description and of the world; any proposition whatsoever can be formed by drawing from the class of elementary propositions and using various logical operations.

Philosophy is a process of clarification; the propositions of natural science are meaningful, but the attempt to say something meaningful in ethics, aesthetics, or metaphysics is bound to fail, for any such attempt involves the impossible task of talking about the world from the outside.

This is an unusual book, both in content and in style. In content it is about logic, though the author finds the chance in discussing this subject to say much about the theory of signs, epistemology, metaphysics, and philosophy in general. Furthermore, in talking about logic Wittgenstein indicates that there are many things which we cannot say about logic, not because we do not know them, or even because we do know them but cannot find words by which to express them, but because they are literally *inexpressible* by means of *any* language. Consequently we must remain silent about them.

In style the book is also strange. The sentences (or sometimes groups of sentences) are all numbered in accordance with a plan. For example, a certain sentence has the number 3; this follows sentences 1 and 2 in the order of the natural numbers. But between 2 and 3 are sentences numbered, for example, 2.0122 and 2. 151 . Sentence 2.0122 is a statement referring to statement 2. Statement 2.151 follows statement 2.1 and is a comment on it; but 2.1, in turn, is another comment on 2, and follows it. All statements are in this way arranged in a unique, linear order based on the decimal notation, and the reader is able to determine by the number attached to each sentence what *general* topic is being considered, what *special* aspect of this general subject is involved, and so on, sometimes to the fourth level of specialization.

Furthermore, because of the unusual meanings associated with many of the terms employed by the author, the editor has chosen to publish on facing pages the original German text and its parallel English translation. This permits the reader who is familiar with German to improve his understanding of the text by checking with the original German and in many cases to detect fine shades of meaning which might otherwise have escaped him. In a book where such common words as "fact," "object," "meaning," and "truth" occur in great abundance and are employed with somewhat unusual connotations, the parallel translation is of great help. The book also contains a valuable introduction, written by Bertrand Russell, which both summarizes the text and criticizes it on some important points.

For convenience of discussion it will be well to combine Wittgenstein's discussion of Proposition 1 and the remarks on it, with Proposition 2 and all of the remarks contained in Propositions numbered 2.0. Proposition 1 states that the world is everything that is the case; Proposition 2 asserts that what is the case, the fact, is the existence of atomic facts. The world, then, is made up of atomic facts and is constituted by them. Atomic facts are facts which are incapable of analysis into more elemental facts. This does not mean that atomic facts cannot be analyzed, but only that they cannot be analyzed into other atomic facts. An atomic fact is itself a combination of objects (entities, things), each of whose essence lies in its being a constituent of an atomic fact. But the objects which are elements of atomic facts cannot themselves be analyzed, since they form the substance of the world. If we take advantage of the illustration of an atomic fact which Russell gives in his introduction (Wittgenstein does not give illustrations of atomic facts), we may say that it is what is asserted by the proposition "Socrates is wise." This contains two objects, *Socrates* and *wise*, each of which, in its own unique way, unites with the other to form the atomic fact. Traditional philosophy would call these objects "substances" and "qualities." Wittgenstein states that however different from the real world an imaginary world might be, it must have something, its form, in common with the real world. Since the form is given by the objects, we may presume Wittgenstein to be saying that any imaginable world would have to contain substances and qualities, however these might differ from those in our real world. The world is the totality of atomic facts; it also determines the nonexistence of atomic facts, for the nonexistence of an atomic fact is a kind of fact. Reality, therefore, is the totality of atomic facts plus the fact that these are *all* the atomic facts.

Beginning with Proposition 2. 1, continuing more or less explicitly through Proposition 4, and extending implicitly through the rest of the book, Wittgenstein examines what is meant by saying that a proposition is a picture of a fact. He describes this picturing relation variously as "modeling," "standing for," "representing," "corresponding with," "depicting," and "projecting." We should note, first, that a proposition is itself a fact. By this is not meant the propositional sign which expresses the fact, though

Wittgenstein admits that propositions can be expressed perceptibly through the senses, but rather the *sense* of the proposition. The point is, of course, that the proposition is a *logical* picture of the fact, not a *visual* one or an *audible* one. He says that it represents the fact in "logical space"—a metaphor which he uses repeatedly throughout the book. Its representative character lies in its form or structure, which means a coordination of the elements in the picture with the objects in the fact, and an identity of logical form exhibited by both the picture and the fact. Thus the proposition "Socrates is wise" pictures the fact of Socrates' wisdom because "Socrates" represents Socrates, and "wise" represents wisdom, and the form exhibited by "Socrates" and "wise" in the propositional relation is the same as that exhibited by Socrates and wisdom in the fact. That this is a logical form rather than a spatial form is to be seen in the fact that while the sentence "Socrates is wise" has a spatial order of its elements, neither the *meaning* of the sentence nor the *fact* asserted by the sentence is spatial; what is common to the meaning and the fact is a logical structure.

More precisely, the proposition does not strictly represent the fact, but rather the *possibility* of the fact, the possibility of the existence and nonexistence of atomic facts. A proposition whose expression mentions a complex is not nonsense if this complex fails to exist, but simply false. A proposition represents what it represents independently of its truth or falsity, through its form of representation, through its *sense*. Furthermore, by virtue of the identity of form which runs through various facts, the picture represents every reality whose form it has; thus "Socrates is wise" also pictures the fact that Plato is human.

"The logical picture of the facts is the thought" (Proposition 3). To say that an atomic fact is thinkable means that we can imagine it. And if it is thinkable it must also be logical, for anything which is "unlogical" could not be expressed at all. Language cannot express anything which "contradicts logic" any more than a spatial figure can represent anything which contradicts the laws of space, or can represent the spatial coordinates of a point which does not exist.

The sign through which thoughts are expressed is the propositional sign. Both the proposition and the propositional sign are facts. In the propositional sign the elements (the words) are combined in a definite way so that the objects of the thoughts correspond to the elements of the propositional sign. The simple signs used in propositional signs are called "names." Objects can only be named and spoken about; they cannot be asserted. Names cannot be further analyzed; they are primitive signs. They have meanings only in the context of propositions.

A propositional expression presupposes the forms of all propositions that it expresses, and thus it may be said to characterize a form and a content; the form is constant, and everything else is variable. If every constituent part of a proposition is changed into a variable, the logical form (the logical prototype) remains. Thus, to use an example which Russell gives elsewhere, if we change the proposition "Socrates drank hemlock" into the proposition "Coleridge ate opium," the form of the proposition, "ARB," remains. This may be called a "propositional variable."

In the language of everyday life the same word often signifies in two different ways, and different words signify in the same way. For example, the verb "to be" appears sometimes as the sign of equality, sometimes as the expression of existence, sometimes as an intransitive verb, and sometimes as a sign of identity. Words of this kind are the cause of some of the most fundamental confusions in thought, especially in philosophical thought. The only way to avoid these difficulties is to invent a special symbolism—a symbolism which obeys the rules of *logical* grammar (logical syntax). Such rules follow of themselves if we know only how every sign signifies. Bertrand Russell and the mathematician, Gottlob Frege, have invented such logical symbolisms, but even these do not exclude the possibility of error.

The great advantage of a logical language is that it calls our attention to formal properties of objects and facts. This is not because propositions express the form of facts, but because they "show it" and do not state it. No proposition is capable of representing its form of representation, for this would require something which is impossible—the picture would have to place itself outside its form of representation. "The proposition *shows* how things stand, *if* it is true." The existence of a structure in a possible state of affairs is not *expressed by* the proposition which presents the state of affairs; it is *shown* in the proposition by means of its structure. The identity of form which is exhibited by the proposition and by the fact accounts for the representation of the fact by the proposition, but this does not give the proposition a *formal property* of representing the fact. It would be as meaningless to ascribe a formal property to a proposition as to deny it of the proposition. And it would be equally meaningless to assert that one form has a certain property and another form has a different property, for this assumes that there is sense in asserting that either form has either property. We do not ascribe properties to forms nor do we ascribe forms to propositions or states of affairs. In this respect formal concepts differ from proper concepts. The proper concept "man" can be expressed by a propositional function, for example, "x is a man"; but the formal concept "object" cannot be expressed by "x is an object.": In this expression "x" is a sign of the pseudo-concept *object*, and to say that a rose is an object (thing, entity) is to utter nonsense. The same holds true of such words as "complex," "fact," "function," and "number," which should be represented in symbolism by variables, not by proper concepts. Recognizing these as variables shows the absurdity of making such statements as "There are objects" (supposedly patterned after "There are books") or "There is only one 1" (which according to Wittgenstein is as absurd as it would be to say "2 plus 2 is at 3 o'clock equal to 4"). To summarize, then, the great advantage of a precise logical symbolism is that it prevents us from talking nonsense. The correct use of the symbols, as was said above, follows immediately if we know how every sign signifies.

A further consequence of the notion that "object" is a pseudoconcept is the impossibility of finding some "property" which all "objects" possess. We have already seen that atomic facts are complex and contain objects as elements of a certain structure. These objects are unanalyzable. Consequently, to name a certain atomic fact is to presuppose the truth of a certain atomic proposition, namely, the proposition asserting the relatedness of the constituents of the complex; and this, in turn, presupposes the naming of the constituents (object) themselves. But now, according to Wittgenstein, since the concept "object" is a pseudoconcept, there is no way by which we can describe the totality of things that can be named. This means that we cannot say anything about the totality of what there is in the world. There is no property, such as self-identity, which all objects possess. To say that if all objects were exactly alike they would be identical, and there could be only one object in the world, is to assert not a logical truth, but an accidental characteristic of the world. Consequently, we cannot use self-identity as a property by which we can "locate" an object. Instead, we signify objects by means of letters, and different objects by different letters.

The simplest proposition, the elementary proposition, asserts the existence of an atomic fact. Such a proposition is a concatenation of names and is incapable of analysis into further propositions. Now it is an important thesis of Wittgenstein that all propositions are truth-functions of elementary propositions and can be built up from them. (An elementary proposition is a truth-function of itself.) Truth-functions are obtained in the following way: Suppose all elementary propositions were given. Each of these could be either true or false. Therefore a proposition containing three elementary propositions *p, q, r* could have a truth-function T,T,F, or T,F,T, and there would be eight such possible truth-functions; in case there were four elementary propositions there would be sixteen truth-functions. Starting with any group of elementary propositions the truth-functions formed from them may be arranged in a series.

Of the propositions, two kinds are particularly important. One of them, called a "tautology," is a type of proposition which is true for all the truth-possibilities of the elementary propositions. The other, called a "contradiction," is a proposition which is false for all the truth-possibilities of the elementary propositions. The truth of a tautology is *certain*; the truth of a contradiction is *impossible*; the truth of all other propositions is *possible*. Here we have the serial arrangement of propositions which forms the basis for a theory of probability. An example of a tautology is "It is either raining or it is not raining"; this is always true regardless of whether the *p* and the *not-p* which it contains are true or false. A tau-

tology, therefore, "says nothing" about the world, for it is true of all possible states of affairs. An example of a contradiction is "It is both raining and it is not raining"; this is false regardless of whether the *p* and the *not-p* which it contains are true or false. A contradiction therefore also "says nothing" about the world, for it is false for all possible states of affairs. Tautologies and contradictions are without sense. "Contradiction is the external limit of the propositions, tautology their substanceless center."

Logical operations are those which produce propositions from other propositions. For example, "denial" (not), "logical addition" (either-or), "logical multiplication" (and) are all logical operations. Thus, operations do not assert anything; the *result* of an operation, a proposition, does assert something; and what it asserts depends upon the elementary propositions on which it is based. We can thus express the general form of all propositions; this is a propositional variable whose values would be all possible propositions. Wittgenstein states this form in abstract symbols; it means, according to Russell's statement in the *Introduction*, "whatever can be obtained by taking any selection of atomic propositions, negating them all, then taking any selection of the set of propositions now obtained, together with any of the originals—and so on indefinitely."

We saw above that language cannot express anything that contradicts logic. Wittgenstein now resumes the discussion of this topic and points out that we cannot say what we cannot think. We cannot say that there is *this* in the world but there is not *that*, for such a statement would imply that logic can exclude certain possibilities from the world; but in such a case logic would have to "get outside the limits of the world"; that is, it would have to consider these limits from both within and without the world. However, logic cannot go beyond itself; "logic fills the world: the limits of the world are also its limits." This principle also has applications for solipsism. Solipsism is correct, but cannot be asserted; it can only be "shown." The subject who knows is the limit of the world; he does not belong to it. The best example of this theory is the field of vision: there is nothing *in the field of sight* that permits us to conclude that it is seen by an eye.

Reality, for Wittgenstein, proves to be very loose-knit. No atomic fact contradicts any atomic fact, and no atomic fact can be inferred from an atomic fact. There is no causal nexus in nature, and belief that there is such a thing is superstition. Induction is a process of assuming the simplest law that can be made to describe the regularities of nature. But there is no necessity in this process. The only necessity is a *logical* necessity, and the only impossibility is a *logical* impossibility; and these presumably do not exist in the world.

The *sense* of the world lies outside the world. If there were *value* it would have to "lie outside all happenings and being-so. For all happenings and being-so is accidental." As a consequence, ethics and aesthetics cannot be expressed, and are transcendental.

What, then, is philosophy? It seems to have two tasks. One is to show that every proposition is a picture of a fact. This cannot be *said*, for no proposition can say anything about itself. That a proposition has, for example, the subject-predicate form cannot be said in a proposition, and that a proposition has the form "*p* or *q*" cannot be said in a proposition. Nor can it be said how a proposition pictures reality. A sentence has no *apparent* pictorial character. But neither does a musical score, or a phonograph record; and neither does a pattern of sound waves obviously picture the sound themselves. Yet all of these stand to that which they represent in a relation which can be seen in the similarity of structure holding between them and the facts. There is a "law of projection" which enables us to translate the picture into the fact, though this *law* cannot be stated. And since the law cannot be stated, we should not try to do so. Wittgenstein therefore concludes with proposition 7, "Whereof one cannot speak, thereof one must be silent."

But there *is* another task for philosophy. Philosophy is not a theory, like one of the natural sciences, ending in a series of conclusions which can be called "philosophical propositions." It is an activity, a process of clarification, in which we try to delimit thoughts which are obscure and confused. If philosophy finds that the *answers* to its questions cannot be expressed, it should realize that its *questions* have not been properly expressed, for "if a question can be put at all, then it *can* also be answered." To doubt where there are no questions is absurd. To insist that the problems of life have not been touched by the sciences, and yet to be unable to formulate these problems which remain in a language which is clear enough to permit an answer is really to say that there is no problem left. This is precisely what Wittgenstein says. "The solution of the problem of life is seen in the vanishing of this problem." The right method of philosophy is to turn all of the things which can be said over to the scientists, who will *say* them, and then when anyone asks a metaphysical question, to point out to him that his question is meaningless. Philosophy will then "see the world rightly."

Pertinent Literature

Ramsey, Frank P. "Critical Notice of Ludwig Wittgenstein's *Tractatus Logico-Philosophicus*," in *Mind*. XXXII, no. 128 (October, 1923), pp. 465-478.

Frank P. Ramsey's "Critical Notice" remains the best short introduction **to** Ludwig Wittgenstein's *Tractatus*. He begins by noting that the "attractive epigrammatic flavor" of the book may detract from Wittgenstein's explanations of his technical terms and theories, but that the Introduction to the book written by Bertrand Russell and printed with it may partly make up for the deficiency of its discursive style. However, Ramsey was also among the first—Wittgenstein himself evidently *was* the first—to call attention to the fact that there are serious errors in Russell's Introduction. The most important of these is that Russell evidently thought that Wittgenstein's investigation of symbolism was directed at discovering "the conditions that would have to be fulfilled by a logically perfect language." This is certainly false; Ramsey attributes the error to a too quick generalization from the few passages in which Wittgenstein *is* concerned with a logically perfect and not just any language, "e.g., the discussion of 'logical syntax' in 3.325ff." (All decimal references herein refer to the numbered passages of the *Tractatus*.) He goes on to argue that many other passages, notably 4.002ff, indicate that the *Tractatus'* doctrines are intended to apply to ordinary, natural languages and indeed to language as such. Ramsey does appear to agree with Russell in supposing that the book's fundamental thesis is that "in order that a certain sentence should assert a certain fact there must, however the language may be constructed, be something in common between the structure of the sentence and the structure of the fact." Since this thesis depends on Wittgenstein's notions of a "picture" and its "form of representation," Ramsey addresses most of the balance of his review to a critical examination of them.

According to the *Tractatus*, all meaningful sentences are used to represent facts pictorially. However, a picture itself is a fact, "the fact that its elements are combined in a definite way." The elements of the picture are coordinated with the constituents of the fact which it pictures, and "These co-ordinations constitute the representing relation which makes the picture a picture." In Ramsey's interpretation, "a picture represents that certain objects are combined in a certain way" means "the elements of the picture are combined in that way, and are co-ordinated with the objects by representing relation which belongs to the picture." Ramsey argues that Wittgenstein's use of "form of representation" is ambiguous between: (1) "the (possibility of the) way in which the elements of the picture are combined"; and (2) "the possibility that the things [that is, the constituents of the fact pictured] are so combined with one another as are the elements of the picture." He then points out that, according to the first interpretation, Wittgenstein would be saying only that the picture is itself a fact; and his claim "that we cannot represent or speak about the logical form of representation" would amount to "no more than that we cannot talk about what makes a fact a fact, nor ultimately about facts at all, because every statement apparently about facts is really about their constituents." Ramsey is certainly correct both in suggesting that Wittgenstein believed these doctrines when he wrote the *Tractatus* and also in his

further claim that Wittgenstein intended a good deal more than this by his claim that "the picture has the form of representation in common with the pictured." This is brought out by Wittgenstein's second use of "form of representation" noted above, for, as Ramsey points out, it implies "that the things with which its [the picture's] elements are co-ordinated by the representing relation are of such types that they *can* be combined in the same way as the elements of the picture." Ramsey sees this as Wittgenstein's principal reason for the important claim that "the picture contains the possibility of the state of affairs which it represents" [2.203]. (This doctrine is central to the *Tractatus* for it is the book's explanation of the fact that we are able to produce and to understand novel sentences, ones—such as the present sentence—with which we have never before been acquainted.)

Next, Ramsey introduces C. S. Peirce's distinction between type and token in order to clarify Wittgenstein's use of the word "proposition." This sentence begins with a token of the word "this"; all the tokens of that word may be grouped together—on the basis of physical similarity and conventions associating certain noises with certain shapes—into a single type, the word "this." According to Ramsey, Wittgenstein uses the term "propositional sign" for reference to what we would ordinarily call a "sentence" in order to make clear that he is talking about sentences—not in the sense in which they have "the same nature as the words of which they are composed," but rather as tokens of propositions whose "instances consist of all propositional sign tokens which have in common, not a certain physical appearance, but a certain *sense*."

This brings Ramsey to one of the most important theses of the *Tractatus*: namely, that "a thought is a type whose tokens have in common a certain sense, and include the tokens of the corresponding propositions." (As Max Black and others have noted, "here if anywhere we can see the beginning of the 'linguistic turn' in modern [analytic] philosophy," for the *Tractatus* was the first work to systematically argue that all discussion of thought can be replaced with discussion of propositions expressed by propositional sign tokens which picture facts in exactly the same way, share precisely the same pictorial relationship to facts, as thoughts.) As Ramsey points out, Wittgenstein thus reduces the analysis of judgment to the question "What is it for a proposition token to have a certain sense"? Ramsey paraphrases Wittgenstein's answer to this question as "a proposition token is a logical picture; and so its sense should be given by the definition of the sense of a picture; accordingly the sense of a proposition is that the things meant by [that is, referred to by] its elements are combined with one another in the same way as are the elements themselves, that is, logically." (This corresponds to the second use of "form of representation" attributed to Wittgenstein by Ramsey and noted above.)

Ramsey notes that Wittgenstein's definition is not a complete definition in two respects. First, it applies only to elementary proposition tokens, for only such proposition tokens can have *all* their elements correlated with objects, there being no "objects" to correlate with logical constants such as "any," "all," "if," "and," "or," and "not," according to the *Tractatus*. Moreover, because of the redundancy and enormous complexity of ordinary (natural) languages, there are even words in some apparently noncomplex proposition tokens which seem to fail to have "objects" correlated with them. For example, in "a connects b with c," the names "a," "b," and "c" may be correlated with the objects a, b, and c respectively, but it is not clear that there is any "object" to be correlated with "...connects ... with. . . ." Setting aside this latter problem on the Tractarian grounds that a completely analyzed non-complex proposition token of any language—whether ideally constructed or colloquial—must reduce to simple signs (names) each of which refers to an object, Ramsey notes that one aim of the *Tractatus* theory of truth-functions is to show that there are no "objects" to be correlated with logical constants in truth-functionally complex proposition tokens. This the *Tractatus* attempts to accomplish as follows: an elementary thought or proposition token "p" says that p is the case; such a thought or proposition token is true if p is the case (in other words if its sense agrees with reality; that is, the possible state of affairs it represents is the actual one), and it is false if p is not the case. When a truth-functionally complex proposition is built up using elementary propositions, its truth value is determined by the truth values of its elementary propositions. In a given truth-functionally complex proposition, there will be 2^n combinations of the truth values of its elementary components, and correspondingly 2^n possibilities of existence and nonexistence of the atomic facts whose possibility they picture. The logical constants used in its construction do not themselves refer to "objects" (as do the names out of which the elementary proposition tokens themselves are constituted). Instead, the logical constants determine a unique truth value for each of the truth value combinations of the complex's elementary components, and correspondingly picture the possibility of a (complex) fact. Unlike Gottlob Frege, Wittgenstein does not suppose that propositions refer to abstract entities—"The True" and "The False." Instead, in Wittgenstein's view, the proposition (complex or elementary) is true if the fact it represents exists, and false otherwise. From a Tractarian point of view, the "problem of defining truth" is dissolved once we understand the way in which propositions picture facts. (Chapter 2 of G. E. M. Anscombe's *Introduction to Wittgenstein's* Tractatus uses a game analogy to clarify Wittgenstein's elimination of the abstract, Fregean truth values; see additional readings.)

Next, Ramsey turns to the two extreme cases to which this analysis leads. If the proposition disagrees with all truth possibilities, it is contradictory; and, if it agrees with them all, it is tautologous. In either case, the proposition does *not* say anything—about how the world is, about what is the case. Ramsey acknowledges that Wittgenstein's discovery of the tautologous nature of (many of) the propositions of logic was a remarkable achievement, but he argues that it is doubtful that Wittgenstein's analysis is adequate. First, outside the context of an ideally constructed language, the Tractarian theory does not yield a unique analysis even for propositions which are only truth-functionally complex. Second, in the case of proposition tokens which express propositional attitudes—that is, attitudes towards propositions—Wittgenstein's reduction of, for example, "A asserts 'p' " to "'p' says that p" can at most amount to an analysis of "A asserts 'p' using a certain logical notation." (Wittgenstein presumably would not have seen this as a problem at the time that he wrote the

Tractatus, for—whatever logical notation or language someone might use in asserting, thinking, or believing "p"—the proposition expressed would have the same logical form and sense because it would picture the same fact.) Third, and more importantly, the *Tractatus* fails to take account of the relation between the person who has a propositional attitude and the proposition toward which he or she has that attitude: for example, A's believing "p and q" may just amount to A's believing "p" and also believing "q"; but A's believing "p or q" is not the same as A's believing "p" or A's believing "q," for A may believe "p" while believing "not-q." Moreover, A believes "not-p" is clearly not the same as its not being the case that A believes "p," for in the former case A believes "p" is false while in the latter case A may have no belief whatever as to the truth value of "p." (Considerations such as these may have been instrumental in Wittgenstein's eventual rejection of the *Tractatus*' view of propositions.)

The balance of Ramsey's "Critical Notice" is devoted to the following: a criticism of Wittgenstein's remarks on the mystical, a criticism in which Ramsey traces the pseudopropositions which Wittgenstein calls attempts to express the mystical to mundane consequences of our linguistic practice; a remarkably incisive discussion of Wittgenstein's treatment of identity; a discussion of his treatment of necessity and possibility; an examination of the *Tractatus*' account of philosophy, in which Ramsey argues that philosophical activity may result in philosophical propositions even if the Tractarian view is correct; and a very brief account of Wittgenstein's general view of the world. One of the most startling conclusions of the *Tractatus*, of course, was that there are no philosophical propositions as such: according to 6.54, although the "propositions" in the *Tractatus* "serve as elucidations . . . anyone who understands me eventually recognizes them as nonsensical, when he has used them—as steps—to climb up beyond them. (He must, so to speak, throw away the ladder after he has climbed up it.)" Ramsey seems to have misunderstood the *Tractatus* on this point for he evidently thought that a substantial analysis of " 'p' is significant" is consistent with the Tractarian view, whereas one of its major theses is that it is not possible to *say* what the significance of a proposition is. This thesis presumably follows from other more basic theses of the *Tractatus*—for example, that the sense of any (significant) proposition is (nothing but) the fact whose possibility it pictures.

Ramsey acknowledges that the *Tractatus* includes "remarks, always interesting, sometimes extremely penetrating, on many other subjects, such as the Theory of Types, Ancestral Relations, Probability, the Philosophy of Physics, and Ethics," but he does not include a review or criticism of Wittgenstein's remarks on these topics.

Black, Max. *A Companion to Wittgenstein's* Tractatus. Ithaca, New York: Cornell University Press, 1964.

After a brief general introduction, very helpful comments on Bertrand Russell's Introduction, and a comparison of Ludwig Wittgenstein's problems with Russell's philosophy, Max Black provides a passage-by-passage commentary. Each "installment" of *Tractatus Logico-Philosophicus* is introduced by a brief statement which is followed by line-by-line comments on its sentences. These include explications of difficult terms and explanations of how remarks in that "installment" are related to earlier drafts of the *Tractatus* as well as to many of Wittgenstein's other works. Black also cross-references related parts of the *Tractatus* and provides pithy paraphrases of troublesome passages. These are often complemented by exegetical and critical essays in which Black excavates the *Tractatus*' foundations.

Black argues that the central motif of the *Tractatus* is its treatment of "the essence of logic," and that Wittgenstein's examination of logic and mathematics is not "merely peripheral," as Erik Stenius had maintained in his *Wittgenstein's* Tractatus: *A Critical Exposition of Its Main Lines of Thought.* Also, Black shows that G. E. M. Anscombe is far off the mark in the first edition of her *Introduction*, which takes the "principal theme" of the *Tractatus* to be the relation of thought to reality; for he shows that its main thrust is to turn this theme into the more promising problem of the relation of language to reality. He notes that

Wittgenstein's investigations began with those which occur later in the *Tractatus*—on logic, language, mathematics and probability, science, ethics, and the self. In the final conception, logic, language, and the world are "virtually inseparable," for "the ontology of the 'Tractatus' is a striking combination of an atomistic conception of the universe as an aggregate of mutually independent atomic facts, and an organic conception of logical form—or, what comes to the same, 'logical space.'" As a metaphysical text, it has few peers. Wittgenstein's conception of the world as an aggregate of facts, not of things "sets him off sharply from Aristotle, Spinoza, Descartes—indeed from any of the 'classical philosophers' who come readily to mind, the earlier Russell not excluded," Black writes; for Wittgenstein's conception of *the possibility of language*, led him to reject "the traditional conception of the universe as something that can be referred to by a name. "

Wittgenstein's investigation of the possibility of language, *any* language *as such*, resulted in the Tractarian "picture theory" of propositional meaning. He thought that this in turn revealed ("showed" but did not "say" what *is*) the necessary ontological structure of reality. This metaphysics dovetailed neatly with his Viennese *fin de siècle* speculations about God, the self, will, and life and death, as well as with the accounts of science, ethics, and the mystical which then seemed most plausible to him, while "simultaneously" explaining why nothing comparable to scientific knowledge about these matters had been produced by aeons of philosophical thought and writing. Black helpfully comments on much of this; but his treatment in LXXX-LXXXIII of Wittgenstein's remarks on science, causation, induction, and the laws of nature is essential for understanding his commitment to science over metaphysics, given the difficulty of analyzing the principles and laws of science into truth-functional compounds of elementary propositions which picture states of affairs—a task required by the "picture theory" of propositional meaning.

Equally important is Black's explication in II-IV of Wittgenstein's argument for the necessary existence of "objects as the substance of the world." In brief, Black reads the *Tractatus* as limited to an ontology of atomic facts into which the world divides

and simple objects which are their substance. Objects *(Gegenständen)* contrast with atomic facts *(Sachverhalten)*. Objects are simple; they necessarily exist; they are symbolized by names which "show" something; and they are mutually dependent. Atomic facts are complex; their existence is merely contingent; they are depicted by full sentences which "say" something; and they are mutually independent. Black notes that the *Tractatus* takes internal (logical) properties and relations to be "essentially different from" external (material) properties and relations. This is one of its major contributions to contemporary philosophy. The former are grammatical features required in order for propositions to express their sense. The latter are (nothing but) combinations of objects. An object is "spatial," "temporal," or "colored" if its form is such that it can be combined with other objects in spatial, temporal, or colored configurations. Thus, material properties and relations are not ontologically ultimate elements which inhere in objects. This is crucially important as shown by Black in LXXXV, "The Incompatibility of Colors." While writing the *Tractatus* and in the years immediately following, Wittgenstein was puzzled by the fact that "This [point in my visual field] is red" and " This [the same point] is blue" appear to exclude one another, or even to be inconsistent; whereas elementary propositions are mutually independent, as are the atomic facts which they depict. Wittgenstein at first believed that such propositions—appearances notwithstanding—were complex rather than elementary, and that analysis of them would show that their incompatibility does not involve any mutual dependence between either elementary propositions or the atomic facts which they depict. Failure to analyze away their evident incompatibility started Wittgenstein on the investigations which eventuated in his later repudiation of the *Tractatus*.

On Black's reading, Wittgenstein's consignment of philosophy to silence in the concluding remarks of the *Tractatus* is hyperbolic. In LXL Black suggests (in effect) that Wittgenstein may have been confused by the two Tractarian ways in which a proposition can fail to make sense—failing to picture facts at all *(sinnlos)* versus, as it were, "picturing" illusory "metaphysical facts" *(unsinnig)*. It seems unlikely that Wittgenstein himself could have been so confused about so fundamental a feature of the *Tractatus*. So, his remarks in 6.53-7 can probably be given a better reading. (In this regard see Russell's Introduction to the *Tractatus*.)

Additional Recommended Reading

Anscombe, G. E. M. *An Introduction to Wittgenstein's* Tractatus. New York: Harper & Row Publishers, 1959. This is an excellent short book-length introduction which was written primarily for students. It especially emphasizes the ways in which the *Tractatus* grew out of the prior works of Frege and Russell. It includes a somewhat useful glossary of Tractarian terms and symbols.

Copi, Irving M. and Robert W. Beard, eds. *Essays on Wittgenstein's* Tractatus. New York: Hafner Press, 1973. There are a number of anthologies of articles on the *Tractatus*. The Copi/Beard collection is notable not only for including perhaps the best selection of Tractarian expositions and critiques but also for an excellent bibliography and for a very useful index of references to the *Tractatus* in the anthology's contents.

Janik, Allan and Stephen Toulmin. *Wittgenstein's Vienna*. New York: Simon and Schuster, 1973. This is an excellent piece of cultural history which excavates the intellectual roots of the *Tractatus*.

Kripke, Saul A. "Naming and Necessity," in *Semantics of Natural Language*. Edited by D. Davidson and G. Harman. Dordrecht/Boston: D. Reidel, 1972, pp. 253-355. The referential theory of the relation between language and reality presented by Kripke is in certain ways like that of the *Tractatus*. However, Kripke's relata are different from Wittgenstein's for he takes ordinary things and the theoretical entities of science to be what are named by designators. His view of necessity and possibility is very different from that of the *Tractatus*. "Naming and Necessity" is especially interesting as a Russellian treatment of the problems posed by seeing language as a representation of reality.

McDonough, Richard M. *The Argument of the "Tractatus" : Its Relevance to Contemporary Theories of Logic, Language, Mind and Philosophical Truth*. Albany: State University of New York Press, 1986. Shows how Wittgenstein's early theories continue to be reflected in more recent philosophical views.

Musil, Robert. *The Man Without Qualities*. Translated by E. Wilkins and E. Kaiser. London: Secker & Warburg, 1960. The first volume of this novel was published in German in 1930. Musil was not able to complete it before his death; however, he published the second volume in 1932, and material which Musil had prepared toward a third volume was published posthumously. The first three volumes of the English translation include the parts which Musil himself completed; a fourth volume includes the unfinished conclusion of the work and some unfinished chapters. Unlike the other works cited in this review of literature pertinent to the *Tractatus*, Musil's book is neither a treatise of technical philosophy nor of cultural history, but rather a fictional work informed by the Tractarian view of the world. The story setting is the preparations in 1913 for a national celebration of the Austrian Emperor's jubilee aimed at imbuing the entire world with the lofty spirit of "our grand old Austrian culture." It encompasses only one year in time, and was to end with the beginning of World War I, but Musil's two thousand completed pages plus about twenty unfinished chapters—some of which exist in as many as twenty versions—are like an ever-expanding total picture of one year's events. The reader is left with a mystical sense that everything that did happen in 1914 and since might somehow be undone by the force of the alternate reality pictured by Musil. This perhaps differs from Wittgenstein's sense of the mystical, as in 6.44: "It is not *how* things are in the world that is mystical, but *that* it exists." Nevertheless, Musil was taken with the *Tractatus*, and *The Man Without Qualities* is an expression of the mystical in the sense of 6.45: "To view the world *sub specie aeterni* is to view it as a whole—a limited whole. Feeling the world as a limited whole—it is this that is the mystical." Musil's work is in the sense of 6.522 a struggle against the limits of our language. That is, it is an attempt to say what can only be felt—that the world is not everything, that there is something outside it, its "sense" or "meaning."

Rorty, Richard. *Philosophy and the Mirror of Nature*. Princeton, New Jersey: Princeton University Press, 1979. This is not a commentary on the *Tractatus*; it is a criticism, largely based on Wittgenstein's *Philosophical Investigations* (see below), of any view according to which nature or reality is mirrored by thought, mind, language, or logic. For the student of the *Tractatus*, the principal interest of Rorty's book is that it makes explicit some of the assumptions and presuppositions of the philosophical tradition out of which the *Tractatus* emerged.

Stenius, Erik. *Wittgenstein's* Tractatus: *A Critical Exposition of Its Main Lines of Thought*. Ithaca, New York: Cornell University Press, 1960. Although this is an interesting and provocative book, it is hardly an exposition of the *Tractatus*. Its primary contribution is that of placing Wittgenstein in the Kantian rather than the British Empiricist wing of Western philosophy.

Wittgenstein, Ludwig. *Notebooks, 1914-1916*. Edited by G. H. von Wright and G. E. M. Anscombe. Oxford: Blackwell, 1961. The *Tractatus* is to a great extent a distillation of material in the *Notebooks*. In many cases, however, the *Notebooks* represent a more tentative stage in Wittgenstein's thinking than do the fully developed views of the *Tractatus*.

_____. *Philosophical Investigations*. Translated by G. E. M. Anscombe. New York: Macmillan Publishing Company, 1953. Wittgenstein is unique among philosophers for having produced two great classics of which the second is the definitive critique of the first. The German edition of this book is printed together with the German text of the *Tractatus*. Wittgenstein suggests in the Preface to the *Investigations* that it should be read together with the *Tractatus* in order to be properly understood. Whereas the *Tractatus* focused on our use of language to refer to things and thereby picture facts, the *Investigations* focuses on other uses of language and sees the *Tractatus* as a typical result of the philosopher's craving for generality.

HUMAN NATURE AND CONDUCT

Author: John Dewey (1859-1952)
Type of work: Ethics
First published: 1922

Principal Ideas Advanced

Moralities of the past were deficient in that they were based on arbitrary rules rather than on a scientific understanding of human nature as formed within a social environment.

Human nature is continuous with the rest of nature; ethics is thus allied with physics and biology, and with sociology, law, and economics.

Vices and virtues are habits developed during the interaction of the human organism and the social environment.

Morals are ways of action invented to meet specific situations; reactions to them become habits and acquire prescriptive character.

Education must enable the organism to modify its behavior in the face of novelty.

Reflection upon conduct has as its objective the satisfying resolution of a problem arising from the incompatibility of various impulses.

In the Preface to *Human Nature and Conduct: An Introduction to Social Psychology* Dewey says that his book "sets forth a belief that an understanding of habit and of different types of habit is the key to social psychology while the operation of impulse and intelligence gives the key to individualized mental activity. But they are secondary to habit so that the mind can be understood in the concrete only as a system of beliefs, desires and purposes which are formed in the interaction of biological aptitudes with a social environment. "

Thus, to understand ourselves and others in terms of Dewey's theory, we must study human nature and the social institutions in which it functions. Both forces work to shape the individual. Morality is the interaction between the two.

Dewey criticizes the morality of the past as being based largely on arbitrary rules rather than on a scientific understanding of human beings. The few have given and administered rules which the many have obeyed with reluctance, if at all.

Such morality is largely restrictive, concerned with what should not be done. Many people conform, but others circumvent the morality in their practice, while giving lip service to it or by having a theory which avoids it. The romantic device of the glorification of impulse as opposed to knowledge is such a theory. Those who attempt to live by a morality divorced from an adequate theory of human nature inhabit a world in which the ideal and the real are sharply separated. They must renounce one world or live uneasily in a world split in two.

It is Dewey's contention that only knowledge can solve moral problems and that only scientific method holds promise of providing knowledge. The moral life operates in an environmental setting that is both natural and social. Human nature is continuous with the rest of nature, and as a result ethics is allied with physics and biology. Since the activities of one person are continuous with those of others, ethics is allied with such social sciences as sociology, law, and economics. Even the past is not irrelevant. We can study history to understand the present as derived from the past and to help us determine the structure of the future.

The moral acts of a person are closely related to

his habits. Habits are compared by Dewey to psychological functions. Both require the cooperation of the organism and its environment. Vices and virtues are not private possessions of a person; they are the result of the interaction of human nature and environment. "All virtues and vices are habits which incorporate objective forces." They can be studied and understood and, as such, can serve as the basis of moral discussion.

Everyone is familiar with bad habits. They are tendencies to action which somehow command us but which we usually have acquired without conscious intent. Since they command, they are will in a clear sense of this word. Since they are demanding, and determine what we regard as significant and what as trivial, they are the self if we are to understand that concept.

Dewey uses this view to replace the belief that will is a separate faculty which, if exercised, can achieve whatever the individual wishes to achieve. A person with a bad habit is not simply failing to do the right thing; he has formed a habit of doing the wrong thing. Habits cannot be dismissed by a simple effort of will any more than rain can be brought on by a simple act of dancing. As one must understand the conditions that cause drought and bring rain, so one must understand the objective conditions which cause and continue habit.

Neither reason nor will can be separated from habit. What one reasons about, what one decides upon, how one acts on decisions is determined by the relation of the human organism to an environment.

Many people have thought that social institutions are the result of individual habits. The contrary is true for Dewey. They are the source of information about habits, in the sense that the individual must acquire habits that conform with those of his social group. This explains the meaning of such terms as group mind, collective mind, and crowd mind. They can mean nothing more than "a custom brought at some point to explicit, emphatic consciousness, emotional or intellectual." Dewey adds, "In short, the primary facts of social psychology center about collective habit, custom."

One might expect that democracy would encourage individuality, but democracy as we live it seems, on the contrary, to encourage conformity. Conformity is due to the unfavorable influence of past custom as it affects beliefs, emotions, and purposes. An education tied to the past "becomes the art of taking advantage of the helplessness of the young; the forming of habits becomes a guarantee of the hedges of custom." But habit is not necessarily conservative. It is any ability formed through past experience. One can acquire the habit to seek new solutions to new problems as easily as the habit to attempt to solve all problems in old ways. Dewey does not describe habit as simply a way of acting; it is also a way of thinking, because thinking requires energy and energy is organized by habit.

Dewey's view of habit places him in opposition to a central contention of the great majority of moralists. They have held that ethical decisions can or must be made by the intellect, unencumbered by nonrational dispositions such as habits or customs. Morality involves relating a set of ideal laws to particular situations and deciding on a course of action which resolves the situation and is in accord with these laws. What classical moralists do not account for, Dewey contends, is the source of ideal laws. Such laws do not suddenly appear, fully formulated, carrying with them their own demand for obedience. On the contrary, they grow like language from incoherent mutterings to complex systems of communication, requiring adherence to rules which are a product of after-the-fact reflection and which acquire a prescriptive character. Morals are ways of acting invented to meet specific situations. When these situations are repeated, the reaction to them becomes a habit and acquires a prescriptive character. Morality refers to social institutions to which we must defer if we are to live. But deference is not implicit obedience. Indeed, implicit obedience to any rule of action is impossible. The rule is derived from the environment, and conditions change. In a completely static world, rules might forever remain the same; but our world is not static, and new rules arise from inevitable change.

We must distinguish between impulses and habits. All human beings love, hate, desire, and avoid; and these impulses have been embodied in social institutions. But what variety there is in these institutions!

Different societies utilize the same impulses in many ways: the communism of the South Sea islanders, the pacifism of the Chinese (these are Dewey's examples), the militarism of the ancient Persians, the variety of class morality in almost every society.

The infant is largely potentiality. It is born in an adult environment which provides channels for its impulses; indeed, without these channels the impulses have no meaning, because while an activity stems from the impulse, the nature of the activity comes from the social environment. This environment may be intensely tight, narrow, and restrictive or it may be loose, wide, and tolerant. Dewey advocates the latter sort. He says: "With the dawn of the idea of progressive betterment and an interest in new uses of impulses, there has grown up some consciousness of the extent to which a future new society of changed purposes and desires may be created by a deliberate human treatment of the impulses of youth. This is the meaning of education; for a truly humane education consists in an intelligent direction of native activities in the light of the possibilities and necessities of the social situation."

Dewey describes insistence on conformity as training, not education. Education, properly speaking, must enable the organism to modify its behavior in the face of novelty, rather than to withdraw timidly. Dewey says again and again and in article after article that no old set of habits will ever be adequate to meet new situations. One fact about the future we can be sure of is that it will contain novelty. Old rules sometimes meet new situations but only because the old rules are vague.

By defining human nature as this combination of impulses and social conditioning, Dewey is able to claim that human nature can be changed. As social conditions change, new ways must be devised to meet the change; old impulses are directed into new channels and a new human nature is formed. Indeed, the very words we use to describe human nature— selfishness, greed, altruism, generosity—are social terms and have no meaning apart from our interaction with the environment. A person acts with regard to the consequences of his acts, and a part of these consequences is what others will think of the act.

Instincts provide the motive for action but do not determine the character of the action. To attribute all business activity to the acquisitive instinct is an oversimplification, tending to obscure the study of business enterprise. Another case in point is pleasure. The moral literature of the world is full of tirades branding pleasure as evil. Certainly some excesses of pleasure do harm; but pleasure is as necessary to the human organism as work, which is often taken as its opposite. It is through art and play that new and fresh meanings are added to the usual activities of life. Both have a moral function. Both bring into use the imagination which often finds no part to play in our mundane activities. Both heighten and broaden the meaning of our ordinary concerns. Art and play release energy in a constructive way.

The constructive release of energy is in the direction of meeting new situations by modifying old ways of action. The alternatives are frozen custom or unbridled revolution. What Dewey wants is conscious, reflective reconstruction of society. We must act, but we must act constructively, guided by intelligence.

What, then, is the place of intelligence in conduct? Dewey has already discussed habits. They are related to intelligence in two ways. The first is restrictive. Habits confine intelligence to the problem at hand; but if this were its only function, the goal of intelligence would be mindless action. Intelligence offers the solution; habit takes over and repeats the solution again and again. But habit is not only restrictive. In its second function it presents alternatives. The more numerous our habits, the greater are the possibilities of action. In explaining this second function of habit, Dewey says that we "know how by means of our habits." This means that through habits of inquiry we recognize the novelty in a situation and marshal our previous experience by means of the channels of habit to meet it. This focus of habits on a problem and the solution which results is an essential function of intelligence. Unless we have habits of inquiry, there is no approach to the problem. We must learn until it becomes habit that problems can be recognized and that to solve them we must recollect, observe, and plan.

Some psychologists believe that intelligence and moral conscience are separate faculties which are unconditioned by experience but which operate on the subject matter of experience when it falls within their realm. Dewey does not share this view. For him, both develop in the human organism as the organism develops. The organism grows in height, learns to swim, evinces a desire for knowledge, accepts, and rejects. Every habit is an impulse. The child learns something, likes what he learns, and then wants to learn more. That he may want to learn more is no more mysterious than that he may want to swim better or that he may want to act morally.

To act morally is to act in the best or wisest way. Such a course of action requires deliberation. To deliberate is to examine with the mind the possible courses of action and their consequences. The possible courses of action which are considered are the result of habit. The choice of one course rather than others simply means that "some habit or some combination of elements of habits and impulse finds a way fully open. Then energy is released. The mind is made up, composed, unified." Deliberation is always the search for a way to act, not an end in itself.

Dewey disagrees with the Utilitarians. Their theory, he believes, is that the intellect calculates the consequences of various courses of action and then chooses the one that will result in the most pleasure. His first objection to this theory is that it depends on the misapprehension that reason leads directly to action. On the contrary, habit furnishes the force of action, not reason nor yet the anticipation of feelings. Secondly, there is the difficulty of predicting future pleasures. Future pleasures depend on our bodily state at some future moment and on the environment of that state. Both of these are independent of present action. "Things sweet in anticipation are bitter in actual taste, things we now turn from in aversion are welcome at another moment in our career." What makes utilitarianism seem plausible to its advocates is their assumption that the organism and its surroundings will remain constant through time. They project the present into the future.

"There is seen to be but one issue involved in all reflection upon conduct: The rectifying of present troubles, the harmonizing of present incompatibilities by projecting a course of action which gathers into itself the meaning of them all." In this sentence

Dewey summarizes his ethical theory as he formulated it in *Human Nature and Conduct*. Good means the unity that the organism experiences in an action which harmonizes incompatibilities. A moral act is the solution to a problem. Moral aims are not expressed in precepts that exist outside action but they are consequences or natural effects of action. Men like some consequences and attempt to achieve them again. In this attempt at realization, consequences function as ends. An end is a dream in which present conflict is ended; the environment is corrected; and the future is seen in terms of a concrete course of action. The dream of fixed ends at which all action should aim is another expression of men's hope for certainty in action. That this hope is vain is the subject of another of Dewey's books, *The Quest for Certainty* (1929).

The function of intelligence is to foresee the future insofar as this can be done by means of principles and criteria of judgment. These principles are like habits. When they become fixed and are regarded as changeless, they can restrict action. However, it must be remembered, Dewey warns, that these principles were derived originally from concrete situations and that they deserve the deference due to any generalization that results from experience. They are hypotheses with which to experiment and whose use is to forecast the consequences of action.

What part does desire play in moral judgment? Most theories evaluate desire in terms of its object. But reflection shows that a desire can have a variety of objects. Psychologically, desire drives the organism forward. It gives activity to life. The projected object of the desire and the attained object never agree, however close they may approach one another. Desire acting without will misses its object because action is not controlled. Desire acting with intelligence, Dewey concludes, is led toward its object.

No person who acts can control the future; his control is limited to the present. He may die before his goal is reached or he may no longer desire it as a goal. Neither can he provide all contingencies. If he attempts to do so, he will never act at all. He must act in the present. A new house may be a future goal, but it has to be built in some present if it is to be lived in. Future goals are attained by learning through action in the present. Dewey applies these ideas to education. "If education were conducted as a process of the fullest utilization of present resources, liberating and guiding capacities that are now urgent, it goes without saying that the lives of the young would be much richer in meaning than they are now." This principle can also be applied to modern industrial production. The worker confronted with article after article that he will never use soon loses the interest that might motivate him to make his work efficient. His work seems senseless.

For Dewey, the scope of morals extends to all cases in which there are alternative possibilities of action. The word "conduct" covers every act that is judged better or worse. Morality is not to be severed from other life activities. Every type of conduct incorporates value and gives for good or bad a meaning of life.

Any doctrine of moral conduct which replaces adherence to precepts with a naturalistic theory must explain the fact of freedom. Whatever happens in accord with a law of nature is not free; and if morality is not somehow separated as different in kind from natural facts, moral actions will not be free and men will have become automatons. Dewey must meet this problem. To do so, he defines the person acting freely as having three characteristics: (1) the ability to plan and act in accord with the plan; (2) the capacity to vary plans to meet new conditions; and (3) the conviction that desire and choice are a significant factor in action. The capacity to plan presupposes intelligence, and so intelligence is a precondition to freedom. There are two sorts of freedom, freedom-to and freedom-from. Freedom-from is necessary but restrictive. It must leave room for freedom to act, which requires desire, deliberation, and choice.

For Dewey, we live in a social world. We are conditioned by education, tradition, and environment. The materials on which our intelligence operates come from the community life of which we are a part. Morals are social, and the school as well as other social institutions have a responsibility towards them. The knowledge of how to fulfill moral responsibility must come from the social sciences. Just as a castaway on an uninhabited island has no moral problems, so morality is a natural outgrowth of social living. The question, "Why be moral?" has no meaning in a social context. The moral situation is a part of the social environment in which everyone lives, changing and dynamic, but always present, always presenting its obligations. Morals are actualities. In moral acts we express our awareness of the ties that bind every man to every other.

Pertinent Literature

Geiger, George R. *John Dewey in Perspective*. New York: Oxford University Press, 1958.

Although George R. Geiger (of Antioch College) in his Preface to *John Dewey in Perspective* writes that "to correct the sometimes narrow and occasionally vulgar interpretation of his philosophy there will be deliberate emphasis on the consummatory and esthetic aspects of Dewey's philosophy of experience," he is not suggesting that the work is a study of Dewey's aesthetics; the point is that critics have tended to stress the instrumental aspect of John Dewey's philosophy, while Geiger wants to show the sense of Dewey's concern with the instrumental by calling attention to his emphasis on the quality of experience, the consummatory aspect of experience as an undergoing.

This emphasis is pertinent in the consideration of Dewey's ethics. If one is lulled into presuming that Dewey emphasized morality as a matter of habits, and habits as fixed practices that may or may not survive critical examination, then one can hardly be expected to find Dewey's ethics helpful in the understanding and appraisal of morality and moralities. If, however, a study of human nature reveals no common interest and hence no universal end of conduct, only a variety of interests and objectives, changing with circumstances, and if, further, inquiry yields information by which plans of effective action can be put together, the satisfaction of which in turn yields consummatory experiences of a quality such that the term "enjoyment" applies, then morality can be seen to be most desirable when it incorporates, in the form of habits, practices which inquiry and judgment have encouraged.

Geiger begins his examination of Dewey by making clear Dewey's account of experience. Experience is not to be thought of as a purely subjective matter; as Dewey has often insisted, experience is a doing and an undergoing, an interaction of organism and environment. Since experience is *of* nature, *of* things, and is the interaction of highly developed creatures and the environment, then, as Dewey writes in *Experience and Nature* (1925), "esthetic and moral experience reveals traits of real things as truly as does intellectual experience. . . ." Again, in a pertinent passage from Dewey (quoted by Geiger), Dewey writes that "reverie and desire are pertinent for a philosophic theory of the true nature of things. . . ."

Dewey's point appears to be that our understanding of things and events is most useful, most relevant to our lives, when it is an understanding that involves acting upon and being affected by the world around us; a vital aspect of a complex experience that cannot be grasped by simply attempting to add together discrete phases of the experience is missed if one fails to recognize the suffering and enjoyment of persons. At the same time, the picture is incomplete and false if one supposes that experience is simply subjective, simply pain and pleasure, and ignores the dynamic situation that obtains when creature and environment interact, or, as Geiger suggests, "transact." (Geiger mentions that Dewey in his ninetieth year admitted that the word "experience" was bound to be misinterpreted. One wonders, though, whether a technical terminology would have provoked more discerning attention from Dewey's readers.)

An experience is unified, transactional, and closes with a consummatory phase, according to Dewey. The "esthetic" is a vital part of the complete experience; it has to do with the immediately enjoyed possession of meaning; it is an undergoing of the organism in a transaction that finally makes sense because of that undergoing. Both art and morality would be not only pointless but also impossible

without this feature of consummatory experience, what in a broad sense Dewey terms the "esthetic, "

In his account of values (as Geiger points out in Chapter 3), Dewey persisted in breaking down the walls between "the immediate and the reflective in human experience. " The point is not that there is no difference between what one likes and what, after inquiry and reflection, one would choose; the point is that "values," as distinguished from objects of passing appetite, are discovered in the course of experience; reflection enables us, on the basis of experience, to learn the relationships that obtain between persons and what they act upon and are affected by: such knowledge is the knowledge of values. Dewey has no sympathy for talk about absolute ends, ends-in-themselves, goods out of context, universal goods, and so forth. The knowledge of values is knowledge of what specific processes yield and how the outcome of activity relates to interests that develop in the course of experience.

Geiger makes it clear that Dewey endorses intelligent choice—choice based on what is discovered in experience—in preference to arbitrary choice. But Dewey was not thereby inclined to argue that reflection is an absolute, universal, necessary good. Reflection is useful; it is a process by which meaningful and satisfying experience becomes possible. Goods are specific, and they relate to individual persons in concrete situations; accordingly, it is misleading to talk of reflection (or of pleasure) as an "ultimate value" unless by doing so one succeeds in emphasizing that which is finally useful or satisfying to someone.

In Chapter 6, "Values and Inquiry," Geiger challenges the fashionable dogma that there is an unbridgeable gap between facts and values. Just as Dewey went to great lengths to challenge dichotomies (such as subjective-objective, means-ends, action-contemplation, reality-appearance) that cannot survive critical inquiry, so he labored to make clear the continuity involved in facts and values. There is, of course, no question that scientific inquiry may be *about* values; as Geiger points out, anthropology, sociology, and psychology, among other sciences, take as at least part of their subject matter the values that have been professed and the reasons that have been given and the judgments that have been made.

Dewey's point, Geiger emphasizes, is that there may be inquiry *into* values; one can come to value-conclusions in the course of inquiry; some values withstand the challenge of experiential inquiry, while others do not; values have to do with the resolution of problems, the adaptation of means to ends, the securing of enjoyments that emerge in the course of experience reflectively controlled.

Geiger's entire discussion is clear, insightful, and positive. His book closes with an endorsement of Dewey's philosophy as one that unites human beings and nature, makes humane judgment possible and sensible, and shows the meaning (the consummatory point) of applying intelligent inquiry to the resolution of problems.

Hook, Sidney, ed. *John Dewey: Philosopher of Science and Freedom.* New York: The Dial Press, 1950.

John Dewey: Philosopher of Science and Freedom is what its editor, Sidney Hook, calls a "symposium," a collection of articles written in commemoration of John Dewey's entering the tenth decade of his life. Hook states in his Preface that two themes dealt with in Dewey's work account for the vitality and relevancy of his philosophy: his emphasis on scientific method and its implications for the human generation of meaning, and his concern for human freedom and free societies and for making clear the conditions of freedom. Both of these themes are discernible within Dewey's ethics, and, as it happens, Hook's contribution to the symposium is an examination of some features of Dewey's ethics: "The Desirable and Emotive in Dewey's Ethics. "

Hook begins his essay by pointing to two causes of what he describes as the "sterility" of most discussions of value: namely, the study of human values has not been sufficiently empirical, and too many philosophers have begun their inquiry with definitions and problems of analysis.

Concentrating at the outset on problems of definition leads to sterility, Hook contends, because the appeal in such inquiry is to the common usage of terms, and in particular to the common usage of terms in English. Usage, however, can change overnight, Hook insists, and, even worse, there is no dependable connection between ethical behavior and rules of good linguistic usage. Accordingly, Hook argues, any credible ethics will be empirical; it will involve paying attention to value facts and to relevant human behavior.

Hook contends that an empirical fact of great importance for ethics is the fact that questions about values arise in problematic situations. This fact should control subsequent discussion. When habitual responses do not permit the free flow of experience, or when such responses are challenged by others and one gropes for justificatory reasons, the procedures undertaken to resolve these problematic situations serve, in effect, as the data of inquiry. Moral situations are problematic when satisfaction is to be achieved only through inquiry and resultant decision. In the course of inquiry objectives are set and a specific course of action is determined upon from a set of alternative courses of action.

Moral deliberation begins, Hook maintains, with the funded memory of goods and ends to which one is already committed; such goods and ends include values (such as friendship and art) and general rules (such as honesty and truthfulness). The moral problem is one that requires for its resolution a choice between incompatible alternatives—not, he insists, the application of a universal rule to a concrete case. Further, the moral problem requires the resolution of the conflict of ends by a choice that determines (or redetermines) the character of the agent. (Presumably, in deciding upon ends, one considers the consequences of doing so in the various alternatives, and one chooses: the kind of person you are is made out by discovering what you chose and why you chose it.)

Hook continues his analysis of moral problematic situations by calling attention to the fact (what he presumes to be a fact) that any moral decision is final and valid at the place and time it is made (that is, the moral decision does not presume to be eternally prescriptive, nor does it leave itself open for the kind of challenge that consists in calling for further reasons; that the end is decided upon and that the means are judged to be satisfactory is the end of the matter on that occasion).

Finally, every moral decision, according to Dewey (as Hook reports it), expresses an attitude, a special concern or urgency, and hence has a kind of "quasi-imperative" force. Hook quotes Dewey (in *Ethics*, Second Edition, 1932) as writing, "A moral judgment, however intellectual it may be, must at least be colored with feeling if it is to influence behavior."

It becomes clear that in Dewey's ethics, attitudes, emotive states, and feelings—although necessary to value and to the resolution of moral problems—are not sufficient; it is what one chooses while reflectively considering the results of relevant inquiry that determines values and ends for the one who decides.

Hook offers a careful criticism of views presented by Charles Stevenson and Morton G. White, views that call into question certain aspects of Dewey's ethics. In his rejoinder, Hook emphasizes Dewey's view of moral judgments as problem-solving decisions based on inquiry into causes and consequences of action, the whole making sense as related to the attitudes, interests, and decisions of the person conducting the inquiry. Hence, Dewey does not deny the importance of calling attention to emotive factors, as Stevenson does; but Dewey also succeeds in showing how problematic situations of the kind that relate to human conduct can be resolved through inquiry and intelligence by reference to what is in fact desired or in fact decided upon.

Additional Recommended Reading

Boydston, Jo Ann and Kathleen Poulos. *Checklist of Writings About John Dewey, 1887-1977.* Carbondale: Southern Illinois University Press, 1974 and 1978. Covers both published and unpublished studies *about* Dewey's work.

Dewey, John and James Hayden Tufts. *Ethics.* New York: Henry Holt and Company, 1908 and 1932. Dewey wrote Part II and Chapters XX and XXI of Part III.

Morgenbesser, Sidney, ed. *Dewey and His Critics.* New York: The Journal of Philosophy, 1977. A collection of noteworthy articles about Dewey's views, originally published in *The Journal of Philosophy*, and selected for republication by Morgenbesser. Many eminent philosophers are represented.

Schilpp, Paul A., ed. *The Philosophy of John Dewey.* New York: Tudor Publishing Company, 1939 and 1951. Another in the extremely valuable series *The Library of Living Philosophers,* this volume contains the usual features: a biography (by his daughter, Jane M. Dewey, based on material furnished by John Dewey), descriptive and critical essays (by, among others, Bertrand Russell, George Santayana, Hans Reichenbach, John Herman Randall, Jr., Stephen C. Pepper, Alfred North Whitehead, and Henry W. Stuart—who wrote on Dewey's ethical theory), "The Philosopher Replies" (almost one hundred pages of closely reasoned responses to the critical essays), and a bibliography (1882-1950).

Thomas, Milton Halsey. *John Dewey: A Centennial Bibliography.* Chicago: University of Chicago Press, 1962. A careful and thorough index to Dewey's writings.

West, Cornel. *The American Evasion of Philosophy: A Genealogy of Pragmatism.* Madison: University of Wisconsin Press, 1989. A historical and critical overview of pragmatism, which includes worthwhile perspectives on Dewey.

I AND THOU

Author: Martin Buber (1878-1965)
Type of work: Theology, epistemology
First published: 1923

Principal Ideas Advanced

There is no independent "I" but only the I existing and known in objective relation to something other than itself, an "It," or as encountered by and encompassed by the other, the "Thou."

Just as music can be studied analytically by reference to its notes, verses, and bars, or encountered and experienced in such a manner that it is known not by its parts but as a unity, so the I can relate itself analytically to something other, "It," or it can encounter the other, "Thou," so as to form a living unity.

The "Thou" stands as judge over the "It," but as a judge with the form and creative power for the transformation of "It."

Each encountered "Thou" reveals the nature of all reality, but finally the living center of every "Thou" is seen to be the eternal "Thou."

The eternal "Thou" is never known objectively, but certitude comes through the domain of action.

Since its first appearance in German in 1923, this slender volume has become one of the epoch-making works of our time. Not only does it place within one cover the best thinking of one of the greatest Jewish minds in centuries, but also, more than any other single volume, it has helped to mold contemporary theology. For example, ironically the neoorthodox tradition in recent Protestantism has appropriated in rather wholesale manner Buber's "I-Thou encounter," the "Eternal Subject," and other features. Although such men reinterpret these points from a radical Protestant context, others, such as Tillich, have developed systems that are in fundamental agreement with Buber's fuller understanding. Perhaps at no other point do liberal and orthodox Christian thinkers find so rich a place of meeting.

For Judaism, on the other hand, Buber's writings have been a new leaven. It is not true, as some have maintained, that Buber is a rebel from basic Judaism, that he is simply a Jew by birth and an existentialist by conviction. Rather, Buber is a mortar for the rich heritage of Judaism, some of it long neglected, and certain insights of contemporary thinking. No other writer has so shaken Judaism from its parochialism

and applied it so relevantly to the problems and concerns of contemporary man.

Buber's writing is often rhapsodic in quality, frustrating the searcher for clear and distinct ideas; his key work has been aptly called a "philosophical-religious poem." Yet this is as it should be, for Buber is no system builder, but the imparter of a way of life. At its center is a unique type of relation, one universally available and yet almost universally neglected. His task is not so much one of detailed and logical exposition, but one of evoking, eliciting, educing this relation which is its own proof.

Quite early, Buber's youthful mastery of Jewish thought, life, and devotion came into tension with European intellectualism, especially the thought of Kant and Nietzsche. Buber's tentative resolution was that of mysticism, particularly as developed by the post-medieval Christian mystics. But a sense of rootlessness drew him back toward Judaism, first in the form of emerging Zionism, not so much as a political movement as a cultural renaissance. Here, in the venerable roots of Jewish religioculture, Buber found an alternative to man's modern plight of over-commercialism and superintellectualism. But it was in *Hasidim* that his answer became crystalized. This pietist conservative Jewish movement, emerging in eighteenth century Poland, moved him to withdraw from active life for five years of intensive study. The teachings stressed not monastic withdrawal, but joyous life in communities of this world, worshiping in every practical activity.

At this same time Buber encountered translations of Søren Kierkegaard's work. Kierkegaard's insistence on total involvement and absolute commitment, on the priority of subjective thinking, on truth as existential or lived truth, and his stress on the centrality of the individual—all of these elements made immediate contact with Buber's newfound religious devotion. The resulting tension of existentialism and *Hasidim* was creative for Buber. The emphasis of *Hasidim* on the warmth of community tempered the cold stress of Kierkegaard on the lonely and anxious individual; the latter's pessimism concerning man was largely dissolved by the general Jewish confidence in man's God-given potential. On the other hand, the existentialist stress on authentic existence grounded in the totally free and responsible decision of the self transformed Buber's earlier concern with mystic absorption and the illusory nature of the commonplace world. In personal experiences resulting from man's seeking him out for help, Buber learned the utter necessity of religion as a this-worldly faith, as a total devotion transforming every aspect of common life together. The unique "I-Thou" was no longer understood as a state of the absorbed individual in unity with an Absolute, but as a permeating relationship with all life—a lived experience, not of loss, but of transformation and fulfillment in reciprocity. With this key awareness, Buber's religious philosophy was fully formed, and it emerged in his greatest writing, *I and Thou*.

Quite clearly, this work is an essay in epistemology; it is epistemology, however, not simply in the traditional sense of understanding the nature and ascertainable truth of commonsense perception, but in the sense of exploring in sweeping fashion the possible "modes" or types of "knowing." It is Buber's thesis that strict empiricism is only one of several kinds of relation with reality, and that a life founded upon this mode alone is anemic to the core. Although

he refuses to argue the point, Buber assumes that the plurality of modes corresponds with dimensions within reality itself. Such a contention stands within a time-honored tradition, whether it be Plato's distinction between sense impression and *noesis* or more recently Teilhard de Chardin's distinction between the "inner" and "outer" aspects of all things. Such a distinction, Buber holds, cannot be logically argued, for logic is simply the instrument of one of these modes and does not apply to others. Verification is thus intrinsic to the mode itself; it is self-verifying and requires no further "proof."

Buber's key affirmation is this—"To man the world is twofold, in accordance with his twofold attitude." This overarching attitude is expressed in every language by the words indicating "I," "It," and "Thou." "It" and "Thou" do not signify different things, Buber insists, but two different relations possible between the same self and the same "object." This is an interesting contention, first developed in detail by Kiekegaard, for in general parlance the ground for such distinction is usually held to be within the object itself. Underlying Buber's position here is a radical rejection of Descartes' famed "*Cogito, ergo sum.*" There is no such thing as an independent "I" which, internally certain of its own existence, then moves externally to God and the world. Rather, there is no I in itself but only the I existing and known in these two basic ways.

The "I-It" relation is the realm of objectivity, the realm of "experience," which is generally understood as perceiving, imagining, willing, feeling, and thinking. It includes all activities of the "I" in which there is an object, a "thing," whose existence depends on being bounded by other "things." Here one experiences and extracts knowledge concerning the "surface of things." Above all, the "I-It" experience is unilateral; in it the "I" alone is active, and the object perceived has no concern in the matter, nor is it affected by the experience.

This experience, as well as the "I-Thou," occurs in regard to three spheres—our life with nature, with men, and with intelligible forms. For example, to use Buber's most difficult illustration, in an "I-It" experience with a tree, I may look at it, examine its structure and functions, classify it, formalize the laws of its operation, see it in terms of its numerical components or control and shape it by activity. But not only may I experience the tree but I may enter into relationship with it—this is the mode of "I-Thou." Here I am "encountered" by the tree; I become bound to it, for it seizes me with "the power of exclusiveness." Although this relation is totally different in kind from the "I-It" experience, it is not strictly different in "content." In it one does not have to reject or forget the content of objective knowledge; rather, all of the above enumerated components become indivisibly united in the event which is this relation—"Everything belonging to the tree is in this: its form and structure, its colours and chemical composition, its intercourse with the elements and with the stars, are all present in a single whole."

While objective knowledge is always of the past, the relation of the "I-Thou" is always present, a "filled present." Above all, characteristic of this relation is its mutuality. Yet we cannot say that in this relation the tree exhibits a soul, or a consciousness, for of this we can have no experience. The relation is undifferentiated, and to inquire of its constitutive parts is to disintegrate what is known only as an indivisible whole. Such a wholeness is all-consuming and absolute—a "He" encountered as a "Thou" is a "whole in himself" and "fills the heavens." What Buber means is not that the "He" alone is existent but rather that this relation is such that "all else lives in *his* light."

To one not naturally inclined to Buber's way of thinking, the best available illustrations, as Buber's own examples clearly indicate, are from the arts. In fact, Buber maintains that the "I-Thou" relation is the true source of art. Music can be analyzed in terms of notes, verses, and bars; this is the realm of the "I-It." This same music, however, may be encountered in a living relation in which each component is included, yet experienced not as parts but as an inseparable unity. In artistic creativity, a form which is not an offspring of the artist encounters him and demands effective power. This calls for sacrifice and risk—risk, for endless possibility must be ended by form; sacrifice, because the work consumes the artist with a claim which permits no rest. Buber's interpretation of this artistic form is helpful in understanding the "content" of the "I-Thou" encounter. Says Buber, "I can neither experience nor describe the form which meets me, but only body it forth."

Here we begin to see Buber's transition from the exclusive relation of the "I-Thou" to the inclusive, concerned life which Buber espouses, in contrast to the mystic. The "I-Thou" is consummated in activity, activity which inevitably partakes of the "I-It" experience, but activity which is redeemed, for in being the creative and transforming ground of activity, the "I-Thou" relation is exhibited in its fullness. This creative tension of "It" and "Thou" in the practical life is exemplified in such contrasts as those between organization and community, control and mutuality, and individuals and persons. The "Thou" stands as judge over the "It," but a judge with the form and creative power for its transformation. In existential living the fathomless dimension of the "Thou" is creatively incarnated, as it were, into the common-place world of the "It." As an "It," the created object will be scrutinized with all the instruments of "objectivity," but as a living embodiment of a "Thou" it has the capacity to lift its perceiver from the common-place to the all-pervasive dimension of the Thou in which all things fundamentally participate. As Buber continually insists, such relation is not simply subjective, for then it could have no mutuality: "To produce is to draw forth, to invent is to find, to shape is to discover." This relation of "I-Thou" is subjectivity and objectivity in a totality which transcends the "I-It" quality of either in isolation.

We begin to see here that Buber is passing inevitably from the field of epistemology to that of metaphysics. If it be true that the relationship of "I-Thou" is a valid mode of apprehending reality, a relationship grounded in the very nature of reality, a further question is unavoidable—what is the relation of "Thou" to "Thou," each of which is apprehended as *the* totality and as *the* illuminator of the whole? It is Buber's answer to this question which distinguishes him from aesthetic philosophers such as Santayana, Jordan, and Bosanquet, and marks him as a religious philosopher. He begins by perceiving love as the unique quality of the "I-Thou" relation, love as a "metaphysical and metapsychical fact." This is the nature of the relationship between "Thou" and

"Thou," and the "I" as it participates in that which is the constituting relation of all. At this central point Buber comes intriguingly close to Christianity. "Love is responsibility of an I for a *Thou*. In this lies the likeness . . . of all who love, from the smallest to the greatest and from the blessedly protected man . . . to him who is all his life nailed to the cross of the world, and who ventures to bring himself to the dreadful point—to love *all men*." Or again, the "I-Thou" relation is one in which man "calls his *Thou* Father in such a way that he himself is simply Son. . . . " There can never be hatred of a "Thou"; hatred can be only against a part of a being. The "Thou," the whole, can only be loved, for this is the very nature of the mutual relation.

Since each encountered "Thou" reveals the inmost nature of all reality, we see that everything can appear as a "Thou. " This is so because in the "I" is an "inborn Thou," an *a priori* of relation. We see this, Buber affirms, as the child's fundamental guide to action from the instinct to make contact by touch and name, to its blossoming in tenderness and love, and its perfection in creativity. All of these emerge from the "I's" inherent longing for the "Thou. " Throughout life "I-Thou" encounters continue, but they are not ordered, for they are only "a sign of the world-order." Increasingly one sees this to be so, for every "Thou" inevitably becomes an "It"; but man cannot rest content with only a momentary "I-Thou" relation. The inborn "Thou" can be consummated only in a direct relation with the "Thou" which cannot become "It. " All lesser "Thou's" whet the soul for the relation which is abiding, for which all others are mere foreshadows. Through them the "I" sees that the "Thou's" are such only because they possess a "living Centre," that "the extended lines of relations meet in the eternal Thou. "

Witness to this is exhibited for Buber even in the practical realm. Men can live in mutual relation only when they first take their stand in mutual relation with a living Center. A great culture rests on an original, relational event from which a special conception of the cosmos emerges. Loss of this center reduces a culture to the impotence of a mere "It." Likewise, marriage is consummated by a couple's mutual revealing of the "Thou" to each other; only

thereby do they participate in the "Thou" which is the unifying ground in which mutual relations in all realms are possible, Whatever name one gives to this "Thou," if he really has "Thou" in mind, despite his illusions, he addresses the true "Thou" which cannot be limited by another. Even though he regards himself as an atheist, he stands in a relation which gathers up and includes all others.

This meeting of the "Thou" is a matter both of choosing and being chosen. One can prepare, yet since all preparations remain in the realm of "It," the step from that realm is not man's doing. Thus the word "encounter" is the only one appropriate. Epistemologically, the particular encounters are prior; metaphysically, the Central Thou is eternally prior. Through the former we are addressed by the latter: ours is the response. It is here that we reach the apex of Buber's position—"In the relation with God unconditional exclusiveness and unconditional inclusiveness are one." This relation means neither the loss of world nor "I," but a giving up of self-asserting instinct by regarding all in the love relation of the "Thou." The world of "It" cannot be dispensed with, nor is it evil; it becomes demonic only when the motivating drive is not the will to be related but, for example, in economics is the will to profit, or, in politics, the will to power. Buber's ethic can be clearly stated—man participating in awareness of the Thou "serves the truth which, though higher than reason, yet does not repudiate it. . . . He does in communal life precisely what is done in personal life by the man who knows himself incapable of realising the *Thou* in its purity, yet daily confirms its truth in the *It*, in accordance with what is right and filling for the day, drawing—disclosing—the boundary line anew each day." Such a life is characterized by action filled with meaning and joy, and possessions radiating with "awe and sacrificial power." These are the truths of primitive man, encountering with wonder the immediacy of life, but now purified of superstition and fitted for civilized community. To hallow life is to encounter the living God; to encounter this "Thou" is to hallow life—this is the paradox which best summarizes Buber's thought.

It is in this relation that Buber sees true theology resting. Its basis is not dogma, a content once and for all delivered. It is a compulsion received as something to be done; its confirmation is its product in the world and the singleness of life lived in obedience to it. This is the meaning of revelation, revelation which is eternal and ever available. It must be completed in theology, in objectification, but the abiding sin of religion is to substitute the objectification for the relation, to make the Church of God into a god of the church, to make the Scripture of God into a god of the scripture. The mystery at the foundation of theology cannot be dispelled, yet language can point in the right direction. For Buber the affirmations "God *and* the world" or "God *in* the world" are still in the "I-It" realm; but the declaration "the world in the Thou" points to the true relation. With hesitation, Buber attempts to say more, drawing heavily upon the artistic analogy. The God-man relation is characterized by the polarity of creatureliness and creativity, of being totally dependent upon God and yet totally free. For Buber this tension can only mean that while we need God in order to exist, God needs us for the very meaning of life. That is, "there is a becoming of the God that is"—herein is the eternal purpose of our existence. Mutual fulfillment, which is the "I-Thou" relation, must mean, in the final account, that we are co-creators with God in cosmic fulfillment.

Such declarations will raise immediate questions for the logical philosopher. Is this absolute idealism, pantheism, panpsychism, or process philosophy? In what sense is this the theistic world view of traditional Judaism, centered in the God of providence and history? Buber's refusal to be of any help here shows the degree to which he is not a philosophic system-builder but an existentialist and, above all, a religious thinker. The problem for him is not so much to know as it is to act in lived awareness of the omnipresent "Thou."

But at least this much can be said. In Buber we have the general Kantian position taken to a religious conclusion. The realm of the "Thou" is the realm of the noumenon; here is to be found no causality but the assurance of freedom. The realm of "It" is the phenomenal realm, the realm of necessity, causality, and the objectification of all according to finite categories. But for Buber the noumenal is more than a postulate or an inference. Similar to Kant's impact of the moral imperative and the encounter of beauty and sublimity in the *Critique of Judgment*, the noumenon is encountered through the total self. And finally, as in Kant, the eternal "Thou" is never known objectively, but certitude of it comes centrally through the domain of action.

Pertinent Literature

Friedman, Maurice S. *Martin Buber: The Life of Dialogue* Chicago: The University of Chicago Press, 1976.

Maurice S. Friedman is unquestionably the most influential interpreter of Martin Buber's thought. His numerous articles on Buber have not only helped to give prominence to Buber's ideas but have also, to a large extent, given rise to a dominant interpretation of his philosophy. The core of this interpretation can be found in *Martin Buber: The Life of Dialogue*, which Buber himself has called the definitive interpretation of his work.

Friedman's major concern is to disclose a concealed unity in Buber's writings, a philosophic unity which transcends even Buber's own explicit self-understanding. The mystical, existential, and dialogical phases of Buber's philosophizing are seen by

Friedman to be thematically unified by the problem of evil. Not only does this interpretation enable Friedman to give coherence to the philosophic dimension of Buber's thought, but it also allows him to integrate the religious dimension which was so influential for all of Buber's insights. This can already be seen in the first, or mystical, phase of Buber's reflections on the nature of the transcendent. The mystic, of course, aims at complete and undifferentiated unity with the ground of life. Correspondingly, evil is then the state of being in which the subject is separated from the transcendent. Even during this phase, however, Buber developed a fundamentally affirmative aspect of his thinking: namely, the belief that redemption is always possible. The basic theme in this spiritual tension between unity and separation is that evil can never gain complete dominance—an insight which was to guide Buber throughout his life. Still in keeping with his Judaic background, in the existential phase of his life Buber saw good as commitment by the whole person and evil as a directionless, purposeless wandering based on a lack of decision. In this phase the object of one's self-realization does not matter; what is considered important is the nature of one's involvement.

The real correspondence between the philosophic and Judaic elements in Buber's thinking came to the fore only in his dialogical writings. There the emphasis was on the meeting between man and God in the I-Thou relationship. One might therefore assume that the I-Thou relationship is the good and the I-It the evil. Friedman shows, however, that it is not solely the one relationship which is good, but rather the proper balance of the two. Buber recognized that no one could live permanently in the I-Thou, for reversion to the mode of I-It is a necessary moment of the dialogue. Thus it is only when the I-It predominates to the exclusion of the I-Thou that it is evil. This dialogical view also shows that God or spirit is not that which is good in itself; it is so only in relation to the world. The emphasis pointed to by Friedman is thus one of balance between a variety of tensions.

The meaning of life is revealed only by the pulsating between the Thou and the It. Thus it is the impulse to evil, the domination of the It, which contains in it the very possibility of the good. A fundamental reversal seems always to be promised by the unwavering Thou, which puts an outside limit on the movement away from good.

Through his interpretation of evil Friedman brings to light the deeper meaning of dialogue, which cannot be restricted to an understanding of the I-Thou relationship itself. He sees this confirmed in Buber's later writings, where there is an increasing emphasis on understanding evil as significant in itself, rather than simply as a negative reflection of something else. In his view, Buber's work thus began to flesh out a true philosophical anthropology, one which considered the wholeness of man, rather than only a special moment in his life. Both extremes of existence are rejected. To talk about leading a life of dialogue ultimately means not simply relation, but a dynamic relation which swings between the Thou and the It. It is this fuller understanding which, according to Friedman, is Buber's ultimate solution to the problem of evil and which designates the fundamental reality of man's existence. The very notion of evil is essential to good. What redeems man's existence is thus the fact that even the negative elements of it are essential for a complete, positive life.

Schaeder, Grete. *The Hebrew Humanism of Martin Buber*. Translated by Noah J. Jacobs. Detroit: Wayne State University Press, 1973.

Noah J. Jacobs' translation of a work originally published in German in 1966 is the most comprehensive study of the totality of Martin Buber's life and thought in print. It provides not simply an understanding of Buber's philosophy, but also comprehensively covers the cultural context and the intellectual influences which had major significance for his thought. Rather than being simply an intellectual biography or philosophic analysis, this work should be considered to be an important contribution to intellectual history. A wide-ranging discussion of Immanuel Kant, Friedrich Wilhelm Nietzsche, Wilhelm Dilthey, Georg Simmel, and Martin Heidegger, among many others, gives the interpretation of

Buber's thought a significant contextual validity.

Grete Schaeder finds a twofold emphasis in Buber's work, an emphasis which results both in incompleteness from a purely philosophical or theological perspective and in Buber's major insight —the recognition of the fundamental significance which must be given to the sphere of the Between. Although, according to Schaeder, the religious dimension always formed a backdrop to Buber's reflections, in the writings before *I and Thou* the major concern was always the impact of the religious or secular experiences on man's life. It is the effects on the future conduct of man which give a personal revelation by God their significance. The experience of the mystery has a profound renewing effect, which, however, is not explicable in terms of conceptual understanding. In the first part of *I and Thou* Buber traced the experience back to a submerged primal form of being which is present in all men. In describing the effects on man he attempted to formulate a philosophical anthropology, but given the fundamental mystery at the source of the experience, he in fact lacked a secure ontological foundation for the analysis. The emphasis on the personal aspect of the revelation brought with it an irreducible subjective element. Schaeder grants, however, that given Buber's explicit concern with the concrete life of man this lack of foundation is what must be expected.

Seen from the other, the theological, perspective the undemonstrability of that which is experienced in revelation is a hindrance as well. The revelation of the eternal Thou is seen at the same time as uniquely personal and yet transcultural. Buber was convinced that the eternal Thou functioned as the backdrop in every relationship, but that the transcendent as such could not be experienced. He was thus again driven to the subjective dimension.

Given the incompleteness or lack of objectivity of the preceding two perspectives, Schaeder argues that the focus for Buber naturally moved to the *Between*, to the "meeting" of the two dimensions. Neither man nor God can ultimately be understood as a singularity; both must be seen in the context of their communion in history. This meeting surpasses or precedes rational philosophizing and moves back to an existence within an attitudinal framework. Buber in this regard was more concerned with life as it is lived than with philosophizing about it. Ultimately, then, understanding of the I-Thou dialogue must occur on a symbolic or mystical plane. The meeting of God and man is a mystery and must remain so; but it is also a certainty that provides its own confirmation through the effects which it has on man. The notion of the I-Thou in itself indicates that in the last phase of his thought Buber recognized that it is man as he lives, as opposed to God, who provides that more fundamental understanding of himself that must surpass any philosophical anthropology.

Wood, Robert E. *Martin Buber's Ontology: An Analysis of I and Thou.* Evanston, Illinois: Northwestern University Press, 1969.

Along with other commentators on Martin Buber's thought, Robert E. Wood recognizes that Buber's primary concern was to provide a description of the I-Thou experience, to bear witness to a fundamental truth which he had experienced in his own life. Such an approach of necessity left unexplored many of the philosophic presuppositions which underpin the experience itself. In *Martin Burber's Ontology* Wood aims to explore the ontological foundations of Buber's thought through an explication of the notion of Presence as it binds together the subject and object in the sphere of the Between. While Wood's analysis is a good beginning in this direction, he makes it plain that the totality of such a task requires more than can be found in his book.

Within the context of Buber's entire corpus, his central concern was one of emphasizing the notion of unity. In varying combinations the theme of the unity of God, the world, and man is explored through the mystical, existential, and dialogical phases of his thinking. The mystical phase emphasizes primarily the question derived from Meister Eckhart of how the unity of God could be reconciled with the multiplicity of creation. Buber was here striving for unity beyond distinction. Because of his concurrent immersion in *Hasidism*, however, he also recognized that the unification had to end and a return to life be undertaken. This in turn led to the existential phase in which a genuine "I" existing in the world was Buber's goal. Man returns to a higher unity within himself where the totality of self is sufficient. In this phase the eternal Thou is not recognized as a necessity; experience of the other only draws one back into subjectivity.

In 1914, however, a key event occurred in the life of Buber which halted his drive toward subjectivism. A friend sought him out for advice which Buber felt he could not give. Shortly afterward the friend was killed in the war. Buber then recognized that his earlier way of thinking had to be transcended as a means for understanding man's condition in the world; the beginnings of his dialogical thinking were generated.

After following Buber's philosophic progress through its development, Wood undertakes a section-by-section analysis of *I and Thou* with the aim of bringing out the ontological import of the main themes discussed by Buber. According to Wood, through his experiental emphasis Buber overcame the limitations of either straightforward subjectivisim or objectivisim. In the "Between" the subject and object are united, but in an ontological sense it is this very Between which first of all lets the subject and object arise. Ontologically, then, the Between has priority and contains a surplus of meaning which would remain even should those elements be removed. However, given Buber's religious orientation, the Between is not pure Between; it is formulated only against the background of the transcendent, which provides the essential unity and which for Buber cannot be explicated but only experienced in the mode of the I-Thou. Inevitably this experiental immediacy degenerates and becomes conceptual, meaning that I-It relationships take the place of the I-Thou relationship.

It is Wood's basic thesis that the experiental unity can be grounded on a metaphysical foundation. The important point to notice in this regard is that such a metaphysics must be a historical, temporal one— that is, one which contains a dialectical recognition of the interplay between the two different modes of I-Thou and I-It. In this metaphysics the transcendent forms the absolute horizon which can be interpreted ontologically even though not as the absolute mystery which it is. Wood is searching for a philosophic completion of Buber's most important insight. The ground itself, he believes, can ultimately be explicated in terms of the relationships which arise from it. Even though Wood does not complete the required metaphysical investigation to achieve that end, he thus outlines an important direction of inquiry for the study of Buber's thought.

Additional Recommended Reading

Cohen, Arthur A. *Martin Buber.* London: Bowes and Bowes, 1957. A short introduction which concentrates on the basic themes in Buber's thought, especially the pursuit of the holy.

Diamond, Malcolm L. *Martin Buber: Jewish Existentialist.* New York: Oxford University Press, 1960. Diamond's work links the Jewish and the philosophical elements in Buber's thought.

Hodes, Aubrey. *Martin Buber: An Intimate Portrait.* New York: Viking Press, 1971. This work provides a biographic insight into Buber's life and thought by a close associate.

Kohanski, Alexander. *An Analytical Interpretation of Martin Buber's "I and Thou".* New York: Barron's Educational Series, 1975. A section-by-section discussion of *I and Thou* intended for the nonspecialist.

Moore, Donald J. *Martin Buber: Prophet of Religious Secularism.* Philadelphia: The Jewish Publication Society of America, 1974. Excellent discussion of the Jewish-Christian dialogue opened up by Buber's works.

Schilpp, Paul A. and Maurice Friedman, eds. *The Philosophy of Martin Buber* (The Library of Living Philosophers). La Salle, Illinois: Open Court, 1967. This volume contains thirty essays on Buber's thought and Buber's "Replies to My Critics." Noteworthy articles include those by Charles Hartshorne, Helmut Kuhn, Emmanuel Levinas, Gabriel Marcel, and Jean Wahl.

BEING AND TIME

Author: Martin Heidegger (1889-1976)
Type of work: Existential metaphysics
First published: 1927

Principal Ideas Advanced

The world, existentially and phenomenologically understood, is a region of human concern; man is a being-in-the-world, in that by participation and involvement the world becomes constitutive of man's being.

Man has being in an environment; and his world is a world he shares with others.

Man is a creature of concerns; in relation to environment, his concerns are practical; in relation to the communal world, his concerns are personal.

The three fundamental features of man are factuality (he is already involved in the world), existentiality (he is a project and a possibility that which has been, but also that which can become), and fallenness (he has the tendency to become a mere presence in the world, failing to make the most of his possibilities because of gossip, curiosity, and ambiguity).

Through anxiety man encounters nothingness and becomes aware of his finitude and the necessity of death; but through resolution man, who moves in time from past to future through the present, appraises himself, chooses with the whole of his being, and thereby achieves authentic existence.

The primary philosophical problem for Heidegger is the problem of being. His major philosophical treatise, *Being and Time* constitutes an attempt at a formulation of the basic questions and forms of analysis which are to lead to a clarification of the meaning and structures of Being. The form of analysis which peculiarly characterizes *Being and Time* is what Heidegger calls *Daseinsanalytik* (analysis of human being). This form of analysis is adopted because it is believed that man is the portal to the deeper levels of reality, and that only through a disciplined analysis and description of human being can the path be opened for an apprehension of Being itself.

Heidegger, in his analysis and description of human being or presence (*Dasein*), makes use of the phenomenological method. Philosophy thus becomes "phenomenological antology." The ontological content of philosophy is Being, and the method which is used to clarify and explicate the meaning of Being is phenomenology. Heidegger was a student of Husserl, and at least in part took over Husserl's transcendental phenomenology and its program of a return "To the data themselves." Adherence to this formula, argues Heidegger, will preclude abstract constructions and formulations, sterile concepts, and the adoption of pseudoquestions which tend to conceal the phenomena or the data rather than reveal them. In the use of the phenomenological method Heidegger seeks to get back to the data of immediate experience, and describe these data as they "show themselves" in their primitive disclosure. The word "phenomenon" has a Greek etymological root φαινόηενου (*phainomenon*), derived from the Greek verb φαινεόδαι (*phainesthai*), which means: that which shows itself or that which reveals itself. The original Greek meaning of λογος (*logos*), the second constitutive etymological element in the word "phenomenology," is discourse, which "opens to sight" or "lets something be seen." Thus, phenomenology, properly understood as the *logos of the phenomenon*, is the disciplined attempt to open to sight that which shows itself, and to let it be seen as it is. In using the phenomenological method, one must therefore discard all preconceived logical and epistemological constructions and seek to examine and describe the phenomena as they show themselves.

The application of the phenomenological method in the analysis of human being or *Dasein* discloses first of all the foundational experience of "being-in-the-world." Man emerges in a world of going concerns and initially discovers himself in his engagement and involvement in practical and personal projects. Heidegger's phenomenological and existentialist concept of the world should not be confused with any objective conceptualization of the world as a substance or an abstract continuum of points. It is Heidegger's persistent argument that Descartes' conceptualization of the world as a *res extensa* entailed a phenomenological falsification of the world as a datum of immediate experience. The world is not an extended substance or an objective spatial container into which man is placed. The world, existentially understood, is a field or region of human concern which is never disclosed independent of this concern. There is no world without man. Thus, to say that man's being is a "being-in-the-world" is to describe human reality in terms of a self-world correlation which underlies all concrete participation and engagement. Man is *in* the world in the sense of being *in* a profession, being *in* the army, being *in* politics, being *in* love, and the like. The relationship between man and the world is not that of a coinherence of substances or objects, but rather the relationship of existential participation and involvement. *Dasein* is in the world in the sense of "being preoccupied, producing, ordering, fostering, applying, sacrificing, undertaking, following through, inquiring, questioning, observing, talking over, or agreeing." The phenomenon of "being-in" denotes the intimacy and familiarity of "being-with" as distinct from the objective spatial proximity of "being-besides."

As the phenomenon of world is falsified when understood as a substance or objectivized entity, so also human being or *Dasein* is distorted when interpreted as a substantial self or a self-identical subject. Again, the error of Descartes' isolation of the thinking substance (*res cogitans*) is disclosed, and the spurious character of the epistemological quandaries which such a view entails is made apparent.

Man is not an isolated epistemological subject who first apprehends his own existence and then seeks proof for an objective external world. In his primordial experience man already has his world given in his immediate concerns and preoccupations. The world is constitutive of his being. It is in this way that Heidegger's phenomenology undercuts the subject-object dichotomy, bequeathed by the Cartesian tradition to contemporary epistemological theory, and liberates the self from its lonely, worldless isolation.

A phenomenological description of man's being-in-the-world shows that the world is structurally differentiated into various regions or existential modalities. There is the region of the *Umwelt* (environment), initially disclosed through the utensils which *Dasein* uses in his practical concerns. My world is disclosed in one of its modifications as an instrumental world in which utensils are accessible for the realization of my various undertakings. The German word *Zuhandensein,* which can be translated as "at-handness," designates this accessibility of utensils which constitutes an integral part of my world. Utensils are "at-hand" for one's use and application. But my *Umwelt* is also disclosed in the mode of *Vorhandensein* ("on-handness"). This modality lacks the existential proximity of "at-handness," and is epistemologically secondary and derivative. Heidegger's favorite illustration of these two modifications of the *Umwelt* or environment is his example of the hammer and the act of hammering. In man's primitive experience of his world the hammer is an instrument with which he hammers. The hammer is revealed as a utensil or instrument through the act of hammering. On this level of experience, knowledge and action, or understanding and doing, are in an inseparable unity. Action is already a form of knowledge, and knowledge involves action. One can, however, objectivize one's environmental world and view one's hammer as a physical object in abstraction from its instrumental value. When a hammer becomes a mere object or thing we can speak of it only as being "on-hand" as contrasted with being "at-hand." The hammer in the mode of "on-handness" becomes the object of a theoretical, scientific construction, and is defined in terms of the qualities of weight, composition, size, and shape which constitute it as a material substance. When we say that the hammer *as utensil* is heavy, we mean that it will render more difficult the act of hammering. When we say the hammer *as object* is heavy, we mean that it has such and such a scientifically determined weight. The mode of "at-handness" is thus man's existentially primitive mode—the mode through which *Dasein* first encounters his world in his practical concerns. The world as "on-hand" is a later construction.

Man's "being-in-the-world" thus includes a relatedness to an environmental region—either in the mode of "at-handness" or "on-handness." But man's environment does not exhaust his world. Coupled with his relatedness to an environmental region is his relatedness to a communal region. The *Dasein*-world correlation encompasses a *Mitwelt* as well as an *Umwelt*. Man's world is a world which he shares with others. Human being is essentially communal ("*Dasein ist wesenhaft Mitsein*"). The communality of human being is a pervasive phenomenon which shows itself in man's experience of aloneness as assuredly as in his experience of being-with-others. Aloneness is itself a deficient mode of being-with. Man experiences aloneness only as a privation of an original communal relatedness. Thus *Dasein* possesses an indelible communal character. In society and in solitude man is structurally a communal creature. Now for the most part man exists in the unauthentic communal mode of the "anonymous one." To exist in the mode of the "anonymous one" is to exist in one's communal world in such a way that man's unique selfness is depersonalized and reduced to the status of an "on-hand" being. In short, man transforms himself and another self into an object or a thing, thus depriving both of their unique existential freedom which alone makes authentic communication possible.

The movements of the *Mitwelt* are conceptualized in terms of the categories and relations which obtain in the *Umwelt*, and man becomes a tool or utensil which can be used by another, or a mere object or thing. The "anonymous one," thus depersonalized, moves in the realm of the customs, habits, and conventions of everyday life. He succumbs to what Heidegger calls the everydayness of existence. He simply takes on the mechanical habits, the estab-

lished customs, and the accepted conventions of everyday life. The "anonymous one" is further characterized by an "averageness" in which the average becomes the measure of his potentialities and the final standard for his creativity. He lives by a spurious "golden mean" in which social behavior is calculated on the basis of socially binding "laws of averages." This leads to a leveling process in which all superiority is flattened and all originality trivialized. Publicity is another existential quality of the "anonymous one." He "opens" himself to the public, conforms to its demands and opinions, accepts its standards, and thus retreats from personal commitment and responsible decision. *Das Man* designates that leveled and reduced self which thinks what the public thinks, feels what the public feels, and does what the public does.

In the various projects of his "being-in-the-world" *Dasein* is disclosed to himself as a creature of care or concern. His existential relation to his environmental world is a relation of practical concern, and his relation to his communal world is one of personal concern. Man's engagement or involvement in his practical and personal projects discloses *Dasein* as that being whose movements are peculiarly characterized by the existential quality of concern. Concern is the ground determinant of the being of *Dasein*. Concern permeates every modality of his "being-in-the-world. " Heidegger finds it to be significant that this existential self-understanding of human being as concern was already expressed in an old Latin myth attributed to Hyginus, the compiler of Greek mythology:

> As Concern was going across a river she saw some clay. Thoughtfully she took a piece of it and began to form it. As she was contemplating that which she had made, Jupiter appeared. Concern begged Jupiter to bestow spirit upon that which she had formed. This wish Jupiter happily granted her. But when Concern wished to give her name to that which she had made, Jupiter protested and demanded that his name be used. While Concern and Jupiter were disputing over the name, Earth arose and demanded that her name be used as it was she who had offered a piece of her body. The disputing parties sought out Saturn as judge, and he submitted the following decision: "You, Jupiter, as you have given the spirit,

shall take the spirit at death. You, Earth, as you have given the body, you shall then again receive the body. But Concern, since she has first formed this creature, may possess it as long as it lives. And as there is a dispute concerning the name, so let it be called 'homo' as it has been made out of earth (humus)."

The fable clearly expresses the point that man has his source in concern, and concern will permeate his being as long as he lives. Man's being-in-the-world has the indelible stamp of concern. Also, the fable is explicit in showing that it is Saturn (time) who submits the final decision relative to the nature of man, making it clear that temporality provides the ontological ground and inner meaning of this creature that has been formed by concern.

The peculiar task of Heidegger's phenomenological ontology is that of a delineation of the constitutive features of *Dasein*, who has been defined as Concern. The three foundational features of *Dasein*, all of which have attached to them a temporal significance, are factuality, existentiality, and fallenness.

The factuality of *Dasein* characterizes man's naked "thereness"—his abandonment or "throwness." As he discloses himself in the various concerns of his being-in-the-world, man finds that he has been thrown into a world without consultation and abandoned to the chance factors which have already constituted him. He discovers himself as already brought into being, a fact among facts, part of a going concern, involved in situations which he has not created and in which he must remain as long as he is. In Heidegger's analysis of factuality we can anticipate the significance of temporality as the final ontological meaning of concern. Factuality expresses primarily the directionality of pastness. *Dasein* reveals himself as *already* being-in-the-world. He is already begun and has a past through which he has been defined and shaped. His factuality is his destiny.

The second constitutive structure of *Dasein* is existentiality. This structure points to man's disclosure of himself as a project and a possibility. Man is that which he has been, but he also is that which he can become. Man finds himself thrown into the world, but he also experiences freedom and responsibility to transform his world and redefine himself in his concerns with it. This involves an apprehension of human being in terms of possibilities. *Dasein* as possibility is projected into the future. Thus, existentiality is temporally rooted in futurity as factuality is rooted in the past. In a sense existentiality and factuality are polar elements of human being. By virtue of his factuality man is always already thrown into a situation; by virtue of his existentiality he exists as possibility and understands himself as moving into a future.

The third structural element in the ontological constitution of *Dasein* is *fallenness*. Fallenness points to the universal tendency of man to lose himself in his present preoccupations and concerns, alienating himself from his unique and personal future possibilities. Fallen man exists as mere presence, retreating from his genuine self which always involves his past and his future. He thus becomes a reduced self. The fallenness of human being receives its most trenchant expression in the movements of gossip, curiosity, and ambiguity. Gossip is an unauthentic modification of speech which simply repeats the accepted, everyday, conventional, and shallow interpretations of the public. No decisive content is communicated, because gossip is concerned only with a reiteration of the clichés which reflect the present and restricted world horizons of the "anonymous one." Curiosity, which is always allied with gossip, indicates man's insatiable desire to explore everything in his present environment simply for the sake of discovering novelty—not for the purpose of authentic understanding, but simply to engage in pursuits which will provide momentary distraction. Ambiguity is the lack of comprehension and singleness of purpose which results when the self has forfeited its unique possibilities in its preoccupation with the present. Thus, factuality, existentiality, and fallenness constitute the three basic ontological structures of human being. These structures are correspondingly rooted in the three modes of temporality—past, future, and present. Factuality qualifies *Dasein* as already-in-the-world, having arrived from a past; existentiality qualifies him as purposive or as existing in-advance-of-himself; and fallenness qualifies him as present with the world in his everyday concerns.

A phenomenological description which seeks to penetrate to the immediate experience of being-in-the-world will need to give disciplined attention to the phenomenon of anxiety. Anxiety is described by Heidegger as a ground-determinant of the human situation. Anxiety is the basic mood which discloses the threatening character of the world by confronting man with his irremovable finitude. Anxiety, first of all, should not be confused with fear. Fear has a definite object which can be specified either within the region of the environmental world or the communal world. A utensil, an object, or a person constitutes the source of fear. But the source of anxiety remains indeterminate. That which threatens cannot be localized or specified. It remains indefinable. The source of anxiety is nothingness. Through anxiety man encounters the nothingness which is constitutive of his finitude. Anxiety, properly understood, is an intentional disclosure. It is an instance of pretheoretical intentionality, pointing to and revealing a most vital aspect of one's being-in-the-world. The theoretical intentionality of pure thought can never disclose nothingness because thought is always directed to an object, but nothingness can never be objectivized or conceptualized. It can be experienced only on a pretheoretical and preobjective level. The interior of human being remains opaque to purely theoretical analysis. It can be penetrated only through preobjective elucidation and description. This accounts for Heidegger's emphasis on the phenomenological importance of man's "preconceptual understanding of Being." The nothingness, preobjectively disclosed through anxiety, brings *Dasein* face to face with his radical finitude. The accentuation of the principle of finitude is a theme which runs throughout the whole of Heidegger's philosophy. His *Daseinsanalytik* is in its central intention a philosophy of human finitude. In this disclosure of nothingness and finitude anxiety also reveals the contingency of human existence and the threat of meaninglessness. Anxiety breaks down the superficial, surface realities which conceal man's true predicament and reveals the world as something strange and uncanny. The trusted world of everyday and mediocre concerns collapses. What was previously a refuge of security and contentment now becomes strange and puzzling. The world has noth-

ing more to offer. Its former significance is reduced to insignificance. All protections and supports vanish. Nothing remains.

As anxiety discloses man's finitude, so also it discloses his indelible transitoriness—his "being-unto-death." The death which is examined in Heidegger's phenomenological analysis is not the death of the "death-bed," or death understood as the biological termination of empirical reality. Such a view of death is an objectivized view which can be understood only by the one observing, never by the one who has to die. The "being-unto-death" of which Heidegger speaks is an experience of death which interpenetrates one's subjectivity. It is a death which one understands and appropriates in one's existential concerns. It is a mode of existence which *Dasein* takes over as soon as he is. Death is a phenomenon which embraces the whole of life and entails a responsibility for life. In anticipating his final and irrevocable limit of being-in-the-world, *Dasein* appraises himself in light of the finite possibilities which precede his end, shoulders his responsibility for these possibilities, and authentically chooses himself as a whole. As had already been taught by Kierkegaard, death makes a difference for life. The anticipation of death infuses every choice with existential urgency. Man's possibilities are limited by his final end—which is always imminent. As soon as man is born he is old enough to die. Thus, he must seek to take over his death by affirming himself with the whole of his being in every decisive moment. But for the most part man engages in a retreat or flight from his having to die. He loses himself in an unauthentic being-unto-death, whereby death is objectivized and externalized as an "on-hand" factuality which befalls man in general but no one in particular. This is the death of the "anonymous one." An authentic being-unto-death, on the other hand, is an awareness of death as a unique possibility which I, and I alone, will have to face. Numerous responsibilities are transferable and can be carried out by proxy. But no such transferability is possible for the task of dying. There is no dying by proxy. Every *Dasein* must die his own death.

Conscience and guilt play a dominant role in Heidegger's *Daseinsanalytik*. Conscience is defined as the "call of concern" which summons man to an awareness of his existential guilt. Man as such is guilty. Guilt is an inevitable and irreducible determinant of human being. The guilt which is under discussion in *Being and Time* is quite clearly not a moral quality which man may or may not possess. It is a determinant of his finite existence as such. The concept of guilt in Heidegger's analysis is a transmoral concept. The moral view of guilt is rooted in an ontology of "on-handness," wherein guilt is externalized and defined as a "thing" or an "on-hand" reality. The common expression of such an unauthentic, external view of guilt is the court scene representation in which man is pronounced guilty by an external judge. The transmoral concept of guilt understands guilt as a structural implication of finitude and nothingness. *Dasein* as a field of concern is basically a structure of finite possibilities, which he is free to actualize in his concrete choices. These possibilities are primarily rooted in the future. However, the past also holds possibilities which can be repeated. Thus, in his temporal existence *Dasein* is ever projected into one or another of his possibilities, choosing one and excluding another. Choice involves an inevitable sacrifice or exclusion of possibilities. In every choice *Dasein* is "cutting off" possible alternatives which might have been but are not. These nonchosen possibilities remain structurally a part of his being and constitute one expression of the nothingness of his existence. "The nothingness which we have in mind belongs to *Dasein*'s being-free for his existential possibilities. This freedom is only in the choice of one, which means not-having-chosen and not-being-able-to-choose the other." Conscience calls me to my possibilities, but I must always sacrifice some of these possibilities in choosing others. In actualizing one I am not actualizing another, and thereby becoming guilty. Every action implies guilt, but it is impossible to exist without acting. Thus, guilt is an irremovable quality of human being.

One would not be too far amiss in saying that the crowning phenomenological concept in Heidegger's *Daseinsanalytik* is resolution. Anxiety has disclosed nothingness and finitude, and has revealed a world without supports. The existential reality of death has made man aware of his ephemeral or transitory being. Conscience has summoned *Dasein* to an ac-

knowledgment of his inevitable guilt. But man must drive beyond these discontinuities of existence and affirm his being. He does this through resolution. Resolution thus becomes a *sine qua non* for authentic existence. This resolution is given its final meaning in Heidegger's seminal interpretation of the character of human time. Heidegger's analysis of time is in a real sense the focal point of the whole discussion in *Being and Time*. Central to Heidegger's analysis is his distinction between the quantitative, objective, and scientifically measured clock time, and the qualitative, subjective time of human concern. Quantitative time is understood as an endless, passing, irreversible succession of discrete, objectivized nows. Nows are conceptualized as "on-hand" entities, thus betraying the restriction of this view of time to the region of "*Vorhandensein.*" In "clock time" present moments are viewed as discrete entities. Some moments have gone by and we call them the past. They are no longer real. Some moments are yet to come and we call them the future. They are not yet real. Only the present is real. Qualitative or existential time, as contrasted with "clock time," understands time as an ecstatic unity. The past, future, and present are inseparable phases of the care-structure of human existence. "Temporality temporalizes itself fully in each ecstasy, *i.e.*, in the ecstatic unity of the complete temporalizing of temporality there is grounded the wholeness of the structural complex of existentiality, factuality, and fallenness, which comprises the unity of the care-structure." In existential time the past is *still* real and the future is *already* real. Whereas quantitative time gives priority to the present, existential time gives priority to the future. Man's concerns are primarily oriented to the future. However, the past retains its significance in an existential view of time. The past is never existentially finished. It holds possibilities which can be repeated. Thus, we find Heidegger insisting on the importance of the notion of repetition—a notion which was introduced into modern philosophy by Kierkegaard.

Existential time provides the ontological horizon for man's self-understanding of his historicity. *Dasein* exists historically, which means that he is always arriving from a past, moving into a future, and deciding in the present what he is to become. The authentic self faces the future in resolution. Man achieves integrity when he apprehends himself in his temporal and historical movements, acknowledges his past and future possibilities, appraises himself in light of his final possibility (death), and chooses in the moment with the *whole* of his being. Such a self is unified or authentic. Authenticity and unauthenticity thus receive their final clarification in Heidegger's discussion of time and history. The unauthentic self of the "anonymous one" is a reduced self—a self which has lost itself by virtue of its fall into the mode of "on-handness" and its consequent sacrifice to the present. The "anonymous one" exists in a depersonalized and objectivized mode, in which he has dispersed himself in present concerns to the neglect of both future and past. The time which becomes normative for the "anonymous one" is the quantitative time of the clock and the calendar. But this time applies only to the mode of "on-handness." The final meaning of unauthenticity is thus found in the tendency of man to reduce himself and other selves to "on-hand" reality—to a thing or an object—which has no temporal significance beyond its simple presence as a discrete now. The authentic time of human existence is a unique, qualitative time in which past and future are always copresent. *Dasein* exists authentically when he acknowledges the unique qualitative time of his personal being, and seeks to unify the three ecstasies which are structurally a part of his being as long as he is. These ecstasies are unified in resolute choice. The resolute *Dasein* thus achieves or wins his authenticity when he takes over his unique past, anticipates his unique future, and chooses in such a manner that his past and future are integrated. The past is held in memory, the future is courageously faced, and the moment is creatively affirmed as the "opportune time" for decisive action.

Pertinent Literature

Macquarrie, John. *Martin Heidegger.* Richmond, Virginia: John Knox Press, 1968.

This brief survey of Martin Heidegger's thought through approximately 1960 by one of the co-translators of *Sein und Zeit* provides one of the most lucid clarifications of key concepts in *Being and Time* that is available. John Macquarrie asserts, to begin with, that the quest for Being provides the unity that holds all of Heidegger's work together and that those who insist that there is little relationship between the earlier and the later work have become so bogged down in details that they do not perceive Heidegger's philosophy as pervaded by the grand strategy of the dialectic between existence and Being. The structure of this dialectic was traced out in the opening pages of *Being and Time* itself in the discussion of the "hermeneutical circle." Not to be confused with the kind of circular reasoning that consists in begging the question, the hermeneutical circular way of thinking involves a continual interpretation and reinterpretation in which understanding of Being that is already given with human existence itself is rounded out and corrected while, correspondingly, human existence itself becomes progressively understood in the light of Being.

Macquarrie's exposition of Heidegger's existential analytic proceeds along a way that nicely delineates phases of this progression. First he shows how the threefold structure of care constitutes the Being of everyday *Dasein*. *Dasein* is disclosed as ahead-of-itself in its possibility, in its projecting, and in its understanding. It is pictured as already-in-a world in its facticity, its thrownness, and its affective states. Finally it is seen as close-to-its-world, or absorbed in its world, in its falling, in its immersion in the "they," and in its scattering of its possibilities. Macquarrie stresses that up to this point Heidegger sees the analytic as confirmed by the way men generally— particularly poets—have perennially seen care to be that which is distinctively human. Yet any such delineation considers man only on the level of his routine, everyday existing, in his fragmentariness and inauthenticity. The analytic is extended beyond itself and these limits are broken through, Macquarrie points out, when Heidegger turns his attention to the phenomena of death and conscience. For it is death which allows the *Dasein* to be grasped as a whole, and it is conscience which discloses to *Dasein* the possibility of authenticity in the sense of being its own, something that it has itself expressly chosen.

Macquarrie considers Heidegger's subtle discussion of death and dying to be among the most interesting in *Being and Time*. He maintains that Heidegger does not encourage meditative brooding on death. Rather, his concern is to show that if no thought is given to death and the future stretches out indefinitely, any sense of urgency or responsibility in life is gone. *Dasein* is being-toward-death, and in recognizing this fact rather than fleeing from it *Dasein* turns toward an authentic existence, an "eschatological" existence, as Macquarrie terms it. Macquarrie considers that for Heidegger death is to be thought of as a kind of "perspective. " As the organization of a picture is found in the convergence of perspectives toward a vanishing point, so for *Dasein*, death is that unifying point that organizes all life's possibilities.

Conscience as the authentic self's calling itself back from lostness in the "they" is the opposite of the voice of society or Sigmund Freud's superego, which only dominates and stifles the individual. It is the awareness of how it is with oneself.

Neither death nor conscience, although it isolates *Dasein* from the mass in allowing the self to confront the true self, isolates *Dasein* from community. Macquarrie repeatedly emphasizes that since Being-with is one of the fundamental existentalia of *Dasein*, community for Heidegger must be an indispensable dimension of authentic existence. And, more importantly, he shows that for Heidegger the resoluteness of a whole and authentic life opens out on the history of peoples as the focus of the relationship between man and Being.

Under the heading "Temporality and History," Macquarrie shows Heidegger in *Being and Time* penetrating still further into the structure of existence as he replaces the substantial soul with temporality, thereby providing a more appropriate model for understanding the complex and dynamic character of human life. Man is not, as is the thing, simply *in* time. Only as deteriorated or fallen does man appear as scattered among his immediate concerns, hopping along from one now point to the next. Authentic *Dasein* exhibits "the unity of a future which makes present in the process of having been." Macquarrie goes so far as to say that although Heidegger's is certainly a secular philosophy, nevertheless, inasmuch as *Dasein* transcends the "now" and thus can attain to genuine selfhood, Heideggerian man realizes a kind of "eternal life" within time—yet not in isolation. It is man's temporality that unites him with the historical community. Here the hermeneutical circle again comes into view. It is only because we are historical—oriented to the future, grounded in possibility rather than in fact—that we can take up the study and interpretation of history. History as the life of peoples is what reveals to us "the authentic repeatable possibilities of *Dasein*."

Thus in all of Heidegger's later writings that deal with the past—particularly in his studies of the philosophers that compose the destruction of ontology, originally intended for the last volume of *Being and Time*—Macquarrie sees Heidegger fetching back the possibility that the past contains to make it present in our existence now. This going back through the history of philosophy permits Heidegger to find those places where the forgetting of Being has taken place so that the genuine insights of the beginning may be recovered and made creative for our time.

Biemel, Walter. *Martin Heidegger: An Illustrated Study.* Translated by J. L. Mehta. New York: Harcourt Brace Jovanovich, 1976.

Walter Biemel's book is probably the best brief study in English of Martin Heidegger's work as a whole. Its translator, J. L. Mehta, has himself written an excellent book on Heidegger. Biemel begins his chapter on *Being and Time* by stating that this is not a difficult book to read. It becomes difficult, however, when we attempt to understand it in the light of its fundamental intention, which is to inquire about the meaning of Being. Although *Dasein* is at the center of Heidegger's attention in *Being and Time*, he treats human existence not as subject or consciousness merely, but as the being that has a peculiar relationship to Being. This relationship is secured, oddly, through Being's having a relationship to itself. For unlike other entities man not only is; he *has* to be, in that his being is imposed upon him as a task. *Dasein* cannot be defined in its essence by citing "what" it is. Its essence lies in the fact that it always "has its being to be." Its being is always at issue for it.

Since the analysis of *Dasein* is intended by Heidegger as a preparation for the development of the question about the meaning of Being, it is not surprising that after pursuing a provocative account of the basic structures of human existence delineated in *Being and Time*, Biemel brings that account to culmination in a discussion of Heidegger's inquiry into the connection between Being and truth. *Being and Time*, quite properly, is shown to contain only the earliest stages of an inquiry which is elaborated and made more profound in Heidegger's later writings.

Biemel is at pains to show how, in his characteristic way, Heidegger starts with the ordinary understanding of truth which has hardened and come to appear definite, and then moves back to the primordial phenomenon as it was prior to the hardening that has covered it up. The definition of truth that was first propounded in the Middle Ages on the basis of a misinterpretation of Aristotle and that remained current well beyond Immanuel Kant is *adequatio intellectus et rei*, the correspondence of the intellect to the thing. But, Heidegger asserts, intellect and thing are in no way similar. How, then, can they correspond? Or even more baffling, since this definition of truth implies on the one side of the correspondence the act of real judging and on the other side the ideal content referred to in the act of judging, when we consider that this ideal content itself often refers in turn to something real or concrete, is it not obvious that knowing and judging often are severed into two disparate ways or "levels" of being which never can be seen capable of being united? As an interpretation of our actual experience of knowing, is this not a ridiculous distortion?

Heidegger's search for a more adequate interpretation begins with a simple phenomenological analysis of the act of coming to know that something is true. When we attempt to verify a statement such as "the picture on the wall is hanging askew," we are not concerned with a psychical event or a process of representation: We are concerned with the thing itself. The proof of such a statement lies in perceiving. Through the latter the entity in question is "discovered." It becomes accessible in its being. It is this disclosure that our statement sets forth. Thus Heidegger can say that "to be true is to-be-discovering." The stress is on the *laying open* of a thing and not on the conformity of mental processes with an ideal content which is then believed to inhere in something real.

Building on what he claims to be the genuinely Greek view of truth, Heidegger regards being-true (*aletheuein*) as a mode of being of *Dasein*. It is *Dasein* that acts in a "discovering" manner. The true in the most primal sense is the action of letting something become accessible and without cover, and only secondarily the thing that becomes uncovered. Thus Heidegger's well-known words "*Dasein* is in the truth" do not mean that *Dasein* possesses all truth. That would be absurd. Rather it means that *Dasein* is in a position to "disclose." It is able to-be-discovering only because it stands in a peculiar relation to itself as the being that is alert and open, directing itself toward possibility and, as being-in-the-world, actively encountering and showing to itself whatever comes into its ken. This is not to revert to subjectivism and to say simply that consciousness is self-consciousness, Biemel insists. It is crucial to remember that for Heidegger the fundamental structure of *Dasein* is being-in-the-world. Being-in-the-world includes the existentalia which are caught up in care and grounded in the temporalization of *Dasein*. *Dasein* projects itself forward onto its possibilities, opening up a world, and finds itself ever in a particular world which presupposes the temporalization of its "has-been." In projecting, *Dasein* may understand itself either authentically in terms of its ownmost possibilities or inauthentically in terms of the world to which it has forfeited itself. The latter mode of self-comprehension is no less definitive than is the former. The openness of *Dasein* is its primordial truth, but *Dasein* is "equioriginally in both truth and untruth. "

Heidegger names the prefix in *aletheia* (truth) the "alpha-privitive." For entities are forever being snatched out of concealment, so that discoveredness or unconcealedness is a kind of robbery. Discoveredness must constantly be wrested from illusion and guarded, lest it fall back into dissimulation.

In closing his chapter, Biemel rejoins the theme with which he began. That *Dasein* exists in the mode of being open is not only what distinguishes it from all other beings, but it is also what makes possible *Dasein's* understanding of Being. For *Dasein* finds its closest relation to Being in finding itself in or in returning to its inmost selfhood in resoluteness, which is being-toward-death—the foremost mode of being true.

Macomber, W. B. *The Anatomy of Disillusion: Martin Heidegger's Notion of Truth.* Evanston, Illinois: Northwestern University Press, 1967.

This very provocative and informative book throws light on the entire range of Martin Heidegger's philosophy through elevating a simple illustration that Heidegger uses in *Being and Time* to an absolutely key position. The analogy of the broken hammer confronts us in some way on nearly every one of its pages. W. B. Macomber is indeed right in maintaining that a unitive vision informs the development of Heidegger's thought from beginning to end, but it is somewhat doubtful that the hammer analogy is adequate to bear the weight of his demonstration of his view.

Macomber stresses that for Heidegger all things, whether natural or manmade, first appear to us as instruments. Always we are engaged in *using* the beings in our world prior to *knowing* them. For invariably they "mani-fest" themselves to the careful hand before they come into view for the speculative eye. In fact, readers of the later Heidegger are admonished not to lose sight of the fact that, as shown in *Being and Time, Dasein* first lets a being be by using it within the context of its specified project. For Heidegger, "manipulating" is originally a necessary complement to "letting-be" (*Sein lassen*).

And yet, when a thing serves a useful function it is essentially inconspicuous. For *Dasein's* ordinary encounter with the instrumental complex or "all-embracing workshop" that comprises its world is not a conscious encounter in which beings manifest their real presence. Although open to its world through a kind of practical vision which Heidegger calls "Um-sicht" (a word Macomber translates as "prudence" or "pro-vision"), *Dasein* is primordially so preoccupied with the work to be done that it takes no notice of the

instrument that it is using. The true being of a particular thing remains hidden behind its function.

Only when *Dasein* confronts an impasse and can no longer proceed with its work—when the hammer breaks or the typewriter ribbon wears out—is it called back out of preoccupation with the future-oriented project to specific awareness of the present. *Dasein* recognizes now what the individual instrument is, what end its function serves, and what its relationship is to the other instruments within the work complex. And for the first time *Dasein* becomes specifically aware of its workshop as opening out upon the environment and the world. What was previously implicit becomes explicit. Even *Dasein's* own selfhood is revealed to it in the question that it is forced to ask itself: What do I do now?

Macomber emphasizes the fleetingness of this Heideggerian moment of revelation. For the deficient tool is immediately taken up into a new human project as *Dasein* sets out to repair, process, or discard it. The instrument withdraws again from human awareness. Yet *Dasein*, in experiencing a gap in the referential structure of its world and so stumbling upon the void, encounters the primordial Nothingness from out of which all truth (*aletheia*) arises. It is in their very vanishing as usable objects that things become transciently and mysteriously present to us in their truth.

Macomber points out that only in one other realm, namely, in the revelatory sphere of the work of art, does Heidegger find truth emerging so forcefully and inescapably. But he doubts whether art, although accorded this special-role, is, after all, decisively different from the practical world where instruments hold a central place. It is not surprising, Macomber thinks, that many modern artists from the Dada movement onward have regarded their art as a broken instrument. In every other realm of human endeavor, he believes, Heidegger himself clearly finds the model of the broken instrument to be applicable. The sequence of activity, breakdown, and awareness is omnipresent in experience. To illustrate the fact, Macomber expands upon Heidegger's claim that the status of a science must be judged according to its capacity to experience crisis in its fundamental concepts, crisis originating not in cognitive difficulties or in a breakdown in thinking, as both Plato and Aristotle supposed, but grounded in a breakdown in *Dasein*'s very being-in-the-world, from out of which all thinking emerges.

Even Heidegger's own philosophy, Macomber is quick to point out, is founded on an understanding of man's relation to Being that lay beyond the grasp of previous thinkers so long as the traditional definition of man was functioning adequately. With the breakdown of the conception of man in the second quarter of the twentieth century, Heidegger has been able to glimpse man in his more fundamental dimensions. One can only say "glimpse"—and what an effervescent glimpsing it would be!—for according to Macomber's view the implication is clear that just as the instrument withdraws again when it is given a function within a new project, so the true being of man must constantly be lost sight of in Heidegger's ongoing project of elaborating a new philosophy.

Additional Recommended Reading

Farias, Victor. *Heidegger and Nazism.* Philadelphia: Temple University Press, 1989. Explores the connections between Heidegger's life and thought and National Socialism.

Fell, Joseph P. *Heidegger and Sartre: An Essay on Being and Place.* New York: Columbia University Press, 1979. The first five chapters of this impressive book throw much light on the ontology of *Being and Time* by contrasting it with that of Jean-Paul Sartre's *Being and Nothingness.*

King, Magda. *Heidegger's Philosophy: A Guide to His Basic Thought.* New York: Macmillan Publishing Company, 1964. This book provides easy access to *Being and Time* for the beginner. It is clear and accurate while still doing justice to the profundity and complexity of Heidegger's thinking.

Kockelmans, Joseph. *Martin Heidegger: A First Introduction to His Philosophy.* Pittsburgh: Duquesne University Press, 1965. This is a systematic and very readable treatment of *Being and Time* with some attempt, in the last chapters, to relate its themes to Heidegger's later works.

Langan, Thomas. *The Meaning of Heidegger: A Critical Study of an Existentialist Phenomenology.* New York: Columbia University Press, 1959. Langan restricts himself in his highly articulate analysis of *Being and Time* to an existentialist view of its principal themes. Since he regards Heidegger's later writings as substitutes for the unpublished sections of *Being and Time*, he imposes an existentialist interpretation on them also.

Marx, Werner. *Heidegger and the Tradition.* Translated by Theodore Kisiel and Murray Greene. Evanston, Illinois: Northwestern University Press, 1971. One of the best works on Heidegger in any language, Marx's book contains in Chapter II an excellent account of the way *Dasein* in *Being and Time* replaces the traditional notions of substance and subject.

Richardson, William J., S. J. *Heidegger: Through Phenomenology to Thought.* The Hague, The Netherlands: Martinus Nijhoff, 1963. The single aim of this monumental work is to reach an understanding of what Heidegger means by thought. Its eighty-page analysis of *Being and Time* is remarkably well rounded in view of its appearance as one stage along the way to that goal.

Schmitt, Richard. *Martin Heidegger on Being Human: An Introduction to* Sein und Zeit. New York: Random House, 1969. Despite its very un-Heideggerian argumentative style and its serious neglect of the theme of time, this is a good introduction to a number of concepts in *Being and Time* for the American-trained philosophy student; it contains a wealth of illustrations.

THE QUEST FOR CERTAINTY

Author: John Dewey (1859-1952)
Type of work: Philosophy of philosophy; pragmatism
First published: 1929

Principal Ideas Advanced

In the past the quest for certainty, to be achieved by the discovery of eternal truths and ultimate reality, led to the misleading distinction between theory and practice.

Science and philosophy, by becoming experimental and operational, have shown that idea and practice work together as instruments: ideas relate experiences and make predictions possible, and by experience ideas are tested.

Statements about present enjoyments are factual, while value judgments indicate attitudes to be assumed; such judgments are instrumental and corrigible.

The Quest for Certainty, considered against the background of traditional philosophies, is a revolutionary work. In his book Dewey does not claim originality for all of its ideas, but he justifiably asserts that were its program enacted, a revolution comparable to the Copernican would be effected not only in philosophy but also in the moral, social, and economic dimensions of daily life. That this claim is a valid one is partially verified by the pervasive influence of Dewey's teachings on many phases of American culture, especially on education. That Dewey's works should have such an influence is especially appropriate in view of his constantly recurring emphasis upon the importance of an intimate, reciprocal relationship between theory and practice. Whether the reader finds all of Dewey's methods and conclusions acceptable or not, it is undeniable that the author's searching criticism of older theories combined with constructive suggestions of remedial and progressive measures have profound practical import.

The quest about which Dewey writes is an ancient one, originating as a need for security from the perils of primitive life, security sought first, perhaps, by prayers and rites performed in an attitude proper to the holy, or on the other hand, by magical manipulations of fortunate or lucky tangible objects. Mystery

and glamour attended the former, while the latter were regarded as more amenable to practical control. Gradually this distinction was generalized and abstracted into that between the spiritual and intellectual on the one hand and the material and practical on the other; the distinction was also between superior and inferior respectively, and resulted in an isolation of theory and knowledge from practice which has hampered human progress ever since. Action is notoriously subject to failure or at least unforeseen results; material objects are only partially amenable to man's control. Consequently, man was led to seek certainty in an eternal, immaterial realm of thought not subject to the risks of action. This was conceived as the realm of true Being or ultimate reality, unchanging, thoroughly rational, and governed by the laws of logic, and hence alone the object of genuine science. The mundane world, on the contrary, was regarded as infected with non-being, unreality, and change; it was irrational and the object only of belief or opinion, not genuine knowledge. Moreover, the Good was identified with the real so that value was attainable only by knowledge, and both were dissociated from action.

The developments of these distinctions have had ramifications into almost every traditional philosophical theory, Dewey argues; the ideals of certainty in knowledge, various metaphysical views, theories about mind and how it knows—all of these, even when formulated by strongly opposing schools, have stemmed from the jealously guarded barrier between theory and practice erected in the quest for certainty. Since modern philosophy has accepted the conclusions of natural science while retaining doctrines about mind, knowledge and values formulated in prescientific ages, it has found itself increasingly isolated from the actual problems and values of contemporary life. Consequently, the basic problem for philosophy today is the integration of our beliefs about existence and those about values, especially since this gap has been widened by misinterpretations of certain developments of modern science.

Greek science, says Dewey, was basically aesthetic in character; its explanatory and descriptive categories, such as harmony, symmetry, and proportion, were used to organize logically the qualitative characteristics of experienced objects into kinds of species. Thus nature, considered only an inferior kind of reality patterned after the eternal forms, was known—insofar as it was an object of knowledge at all rather than of opinion or belief—by reason rather than by experience. Greek natural philosophy was also teleological, holding that things and events tended toward their own proper ends or goods and thus toward the highest and best. This outlook, lasting through the Middle Ages, fostered an attitude of acceptance rather than an art of control such as that made possible by modern science.

Galileo and other founders of the new science effected a revolution by eliminating the qualitative and purposive and by substituting the quantitative interpretation of scientific objects. Rather than classifying things into species defined by and tending toward eternal forms, the new science saw them as reducible, for its purposes, to a few basic categories of space, time, mass, and motion. Phenomena such as heat, light, mechanical motion, and electricity could be converted or translated into one another; homogeneity replaced the heterogeneity basic to the Greek view, and "All that counted for science became mechanical properties formulated in mathematical terms. . . . " The revolution was not completed at once, however. Though Newton osten-

sibly subscribed to the empirical approach, remnants of the old metaphysics were obvious in his belief that change occurred only in the external relations between particles of permanently fixed natures. This postulate of permanence was really evidence of the longstanding quest for certainty rather than a hypothesis experimentally verified. Even the most avowedly empiricist school showed this same bias; for them, knowledge was founded on sensory impressions given by an antecedent reality unaffected by knowing. Later, objective idealists held that reflective thought merely reproduces the rational structure of a universe constituted by an Absolute Reason. Even now realism holds that valid inquiry apprehends prior existence—it does not modify it. All these views presuppose that inference and judgment are not originative.

As the new science became truly experimental, however, this premise was abandoned; science now "*substitutes data for objects.*" This means that science, instead of taking qualitative objects such as stars and trees as finalities waiting only for logical classification, takes them as problematic, inviting further interpretation and investigation. The latter is undertaken in response to problems and unresolved difficulties which are never wholly theoretical but are always ultimately rooted in need for practical security; these problematic situations determine the lines of inquiry and the criteria of successful solution. Experimental knowledge, inference, or judgment then becomes originative in a very real sense; its "procedure is one that installs doing as the heart of knowing. . . . " Change, once regarded as evidence of the inferiority of the experienced world to the ideal and eternal, now becomes useful: "*The* method of physical inquiry is to introduce some change in order to see what other change ensues; the correlation between these changes, when measured by a series of operations, constitutes the definite and desired object of knowledge. " The objects of scientific knowledge are not qualitative entities, but *events*, mathematically formulated relations between changes undergone by experienced objects, and most important for our present purposes, *consequences.*

Dewey takes physical science as a model for experimental philosophy because on the whole the former yields the best authenticated and reliable knowledge we enjoy at present, while at the same time its conclusions are corrigible and its hypotheses subject to revision in the light of future evidence and problems. Besides, in its technological applications it is as a matter of fact already the dominant feature of modern life. Philosophy can learn from it, Dewey believes, how to approach the basic modern problem of reintegrating beliefs about existence with those about values, as well as how to avoid some of the more technical philosophical problems to which traditional theories inevitably led.

Dewey cites with approval Bridgman's statement in *The Logic of Modern Physics* (1927): "...we mean by any concept nothing more than a set of operations; *the concept is synonymous with the corresponding set of operations.*" The philosophical implications of such an experimental empiricism (as distinguished from traditional sensational empiricism), understood at the time by only a few thinkers such as William James and Charles Sanders Peirce, are so far-reaching as to make it "one of three or four outstanding feats of intellectual history." It shows that neither sensational empiricism nor *a priori* rationalism was wholly right or wholly wrong: ideas are empirical in origin, but sensory qualities, to be significant, must be related by ideas; the new method's concepts of scientific objects are neither *a priori* nor reducible to sensation. The object of knowledge is "eventual; that is, it is an outcome of directed experimental operations, instead of something in sufficient existence before the act of knowing." Thus the sensory and rational elements of knowledge do not compete but cooperate; the latter are used to organize and direct, the former to test and verify or correct. Conclusions, not the previously given, are *truly known*; but conclusions of former investigations become in turn instrumental to the achievement of new solutions.

The operational method makes mind a participant rather than a mere spectator in the knowing situation. As is illustrated by the Heisenberg principle of indeterminacy, the act of observation is itself an essential ingredient in what is known. From this point of view, then, nature is neither rational nor irrational as it has been described traditionally, but is, rather, intelligible; it is *to be* known through intelligence. This ap-

proach also yields new definitions of intelligence, thought, and mind. Merely mechanical and animal responses to uncertain and perilous situations are reactions or direct actions, but "response to the doubtful as such" is definitive of mind and thinking, and when responses "have a directed tendency to change the precarious and problematic into the secure and resolved, they are *intellectual* as well as mental." Misinterpretations of Newtonian science, by emphasizing the difference between ordinary perceptual experience and the scientific formulation of nature, had reinforced the metaphysical distinction between mind and body, but in Dewey's view, "There is no separate 'mind' gifted in and of itself with a faculty of thought; such a conception of thought ends in postulating the mystery of a power outside of nature and yet able to intervene within it." As defined above, thinking is observable behavior, whereas traditional theories on the contrary tried to explain the more by the less obvious. Now with our greater understanding of the relation between sensory organs and perception we are able to conceive the same relation as holding between the brain and thought.

One stronghold of the rationalistic and mentalistic schools, however, and one not adequately accounted for by traditional empiricism, was the structure of mathematics. Because mathematics seemed to rest on self-evident axioms known intuitively, and because of the universality, immutability, ideality, and logical necessity of mathematics, it was thought to demonstrate the subsistence of a realm of eternal essences and a nonphysical reality; the applicability of mathematics to the physical world, moreover, seemed to show a rational element even therein. Does the operational theory of ideas, together with its implications concerning the nature of mind and thought, break down here? Dewey thinks not. We must distinguish between overt and symbolical operations, operations to be enacted and those merely possible but without actual consequences. Just as the concepts of space, time, and motion were finally seen to be ways of correlating observations rather than as reflecting properties of Being, and their worth was found in the former function, so logical and mathematical principles and relationships may be interpreted. They may have arisen from practical needs for manipulation and organization of physical things, later to be developed more fully and independently of immediately instrumental purposes. Men then become interested in such operations as operations which, when symbolized, can be performed without any direct reference to existence. That this is the case seems most clearly illustrated by the history of geometry, which originated in the need for measurement of utilitarian objects. The formal order and internal relations such systems show are analogous to the self-consistent structure of a machine designed for a certain purpose. The means-consequence relation as exemplified in the operation of a machine may be *thought* abstractly as an operation to which the imperfections of actual machines are irrelevant; so conceived, the function has the ideality, immutability, internal necessity, and universality which characterizes the realm of essence supposedly encountered in logic and mathematics.

The worth of a machine is judged by the efficacy with which it performs the function for which it was designed, and the more abstractly this function is conceived—the more it is idealized—the more clearly it can be understood. But in the conception of function ideas for improvement are germinated. Thus, the operational or experimental method is capable of projecting new goals and values and of instituting its own standards. It is imperative that this lesson learned from science be applied in the moral, social, and political life, where it is not yet fully operative. The apparent value-sterility of quantitative and operational science can now be regarded as illusory, the illusion being rooted in the notion that science discloses reality as it is in itself. The experimental method is an effective way of thinking of things, but since it is not the only way to think of them, it is not actually inimical to qualitative experience, and it can make positive contributions to the qualitative aspects of human life by affording means of making values more available and secure. We recall that, according to Dewey, the main problem for modern philosophy is to reintegrate beliefs about existence and those about values. It is obvious now that his purpose in tracing the development of operationalism and instrumentalism is to show their significance for what he calls, typically, the "*construction*" of good, suggesting thereby that values,

like objects of knowledge, are not so much given as achieved.

By "value" Dewey means "whatever is taken to have rightful authority in the direction of conduct." But there are still rival theories about the status of values comparable to the traditional epistemological opposites, empiricism and rationalism. Some writers would equate goods with actual enjoyments, while others see them as eternal, universal, absolute. Dewey favors the empirical and subjective theories to the extent that they relate "the theory of values with concrete experiences of desire and satisfaction," but the operational approach again makes a significant emendation: values are not antecedently given, but are enjoyments attained as *consequences*. Previous goods and present enjoyments are problematic, as are immediately experienced qualitative objects in relation to knowledge. The crucial differences here are indicated in the very suffixes of terms such as "the enjoyed and the enjoyable, the desired and the desirable, the satis*fying* and the satis*factory*." This is in no sense to derogate immediate enjoyments and likings, but mere feelings have no claim over us as ideals and future goods, any more than objects as immediately experienced are adequate as scientific objects. Whereas propositions about present enjoyments are factual and may be of instrumental worth, value judgments and appraisals indicate attitudes *to be* assumed and hence do make claims on us. Dewey summarizes this view in what he describes as his main proposition: "*Judgments about values are judgments about the conditions and the results of experienced objects; judgments about that which should regulate the formation of our desires, affections and enjoyments.*"

Value judgments, then, like their counterparts in science, are relational in nature. They, too, are instrumental and never final, and are thus corrigible. There are criteria of goods—for example, genuine goods are not later regretted; in achieving goods concern is centered on the valuable object rather than on the mere feeling of satisfaction—but such criteria are never absolute and fixed. It is thus impossible to set up a detailed catalog of values in hierarchical order. Dewey's approach "would place *method and means* upon the level of importance that has, in the past, been imputed exclusively to ends," for as long as ends alone are considered ideal and of true worth, while means are scorned as merely practical, ends fail to be realized. While failure to achieve the good has been attributed to perversity of will, the real obstacle has been lack of adequate knowledge of means. Hence the traditional elevation of spirit over matter is similarly mistaken, for the material serves as means.

The traditional separation of ends and means, another reflection of that of theory and practice, has left action without the guidance afforded only by knowledge. Consequently, some means, such as material wealth, have been overvalued as ends in the absence of any adequate philosophy of values appropriate to contemporary problems. The technological applications of science have been used selfishly and irresponsibly. Nowhere is the failure properly to relate ends and means more evident than in industrial life, and the resulting tragedy is that enjoyment of the highest social and cultural values, the truly human goods, is dependent on economic conditions ignored by many ethical philosophers. Our economy tends therefore to evade moral guidance as irrelevant and to be frankly materialistic, but the remedy is not to treat economics as beneath the notice of ethics; it is rather to apply here the instrumentalist approach.

Whereas mechanistic philosophy rejected the concept of purpose as explanatory of natural events, the developments of modern science have made clear the role of the observer in knowledge; and Dewey holds that in a significant sense purpose has been restored to nature, since "distinctively human conduct can be interpreted and understood only in terms of purpose." By removing the artificial barriers between knowledge and practice, science and values, and the consequent false problems such as those of the relationships between mind and body, spirit and matter, nature can be regarded as the ultimate source of all ideals and goods. To remove such obstacles, to free men's minds and hearts from slavery to the past, to turn them from the quest for an illusory certainty to discoverable paths to enjoyable goods, is the task of contemporary philosophy. No longer in competition with science through claims to sole superior knowledge of reality, philosophy takes up the task of exploring the richly various ways of putting science to truly human use.

Pertinent Literature

Ratner, Joseph, ed. *Intelligence in the Modern World: John Dewey's Philosophy.* New York: Random House, 1939.

Joseph Ratner's "Introduction" to *Intelligence in the Modern World* is more than an introduction to the philosophy of John Dewey. It is also an example of philosophy done under the influence of Dewey's thought. Ratner is critical of Dewey's work; he recognizes that Dewey is not always consistent and that on many occasions he is not clear in his thinking. On these matters Ratner tries to improve Dewey's philosophy; but there is no doubt in Ratner's mind that Dewey's basic position—that philosophy must be scientific, that it must be experimental and self-correcting—is absolutely correct.

Intelligence in the Modern World is a selected anthology of Dewey's writings. Organized under headings such as "The Meaning of Philosophy,"

"Philosophy and Science," "Intelligence in Social Action," "Science and the Philosophy of Education," "Perception, Language and Mind," and "The Artistic-Esthetic in Experience," Ratner includes selections from Dewey's *Philosophy and Civilization* (1931), *The Quest for Certainty, Ethics, Experience and Education* (1938), *Experience and Nature* (1925), *and Art as Experience* (1934). In his Introduction Ratner seeks to introduce all of Dewey's major works by developing what he considers to be Dewey's central position. According to Ratner, all of Dewey's thought has its roots in his criticism of idealized philosophies—philosophies which concern themselves with some eternal and immutable reality. Dewey maintains that such philosophies are, at best, vacuous, and at worst, harmful. The proper domain of philosophy is the temporal, mutable reality that is the world in which people live.

Ratner gives a brief summary of Dewey's analysis of the history of Western Philosophy from the time of the ancient Greeks through modern times. In Dewey's mind it was the Greek philosophers who initiated the "quest for certainty," the attempt to find security from the hazards of the temporal world, by going beyond this world. Ratner applies this critique of Western Philosophy to the philosophies of two of Dewey's contemporaries: Bertrand Russell and Alfred North Whitehead. In Ratner's estimation both Russell and Whitehead have continued the Western tradition of going beyond the temporal, mutable world. By contrasting Dewey with two contemporary examples of "idealized" philosophy, Ratner intends to demonstrate the uniqueness of Dewey's thought.

While Ratner's interpretation of Russell's philos-ophy, and more specifically of Russell's philosophy in *The Analysis of Matter*, is sound, his interpretation of Whitehead's philosophy is highly questionable. Ratner's contention that Whitehead's "quest for certainty" takes him outside the world of experience would be disputed by virtually all of Whitehead's interpreters. The fact that one cannot rely on Ratner's understanding of Whitehead is regrettable, but it does not seriously damage his introduction to Dewey's thought. Dewey believed that the data with which philosophers ought to begin should come from ordinary life experience and that the test of a philosophy is whether or not its conclusions render these experiences more significant and our dealings with them more fruitful. Philosophies which begin with some idealized or refined experience and which never check their conclusions against ordinary experience are useless. Ratner may not understand Whitehead's philosophy, but he understands Dewey's thought very well.

Feldman, W. T. *The Philosophy of John Dewey: A Critical Analysis.* Westport, Connecticut: Greenwood Press, 1968.

W. T. Feldman's book *The Philosophy of John Dewey: A Critical Analysis,* first published in 1934, deals with John Dewey's thought from his first publication through *Experience and Nature* and *The Quest for Certainty.* Although cognizant of the tremendous influence of Dewey's work and genuinely respectful of Dewey's intellectual prowess, Feldman is convinced that there are serious problems with Dewey's philosophy which make it impossible to accept his thought as a whole. In his excellent book, Feldman aims to illuminate the ambiguities, the equivocations, and the contradictions which he detects in Dewey's work.

According to Feldman, there are three distinct meanings of "experience" in Dewey's philosophy, a fact which obfuscates Dewey's commitment to empiricism. The first meaning of "experience" presupposes an idealism similar to that of George Berkeley. Experience is the ground of being; to exist is to exist in conscious experience. The second meaning of "experience" is the "interaction of an organism with its environment." Unlike the first meaning, which presupposes a philosophical idealism, the second meaning presupposes a type of naturalism; experience is a coping with one's surroundings. The third meaning of experience, and the meaning most often employed in *The Quest for Certainty*, is immediate, self-enclosed awareness. This third meaning does not deny that experience is somehow dependent upon external events, but it does deny that these events are revealed in experience. In Feldman's estimation, Dewey's empiricism is confounded by his equivocation between experience as the interaction of an organism with its surroundings and experience as immediate, self-enclosed awareness.

Feldman also finds fault with Dewey's implicit concept of continuity and his inconsistent statements regarding value and objectivity. According to Feldman, Dewey employs a concept of continuity as a basis for criticizing most of Western philosophy without ever explicitly defining what he means by "continuity." Moreover, Dewey opposes the separation of minds and bodies, ideas and objects, and values and experiences, and yet fails to develop a concept of continuity which is capable of holding these things together. (The matter is further complicated by Dewey's doctrine of emergent intelligence. In his essay in *Creative Intelligence*, 1917, and in *Experience and Nature,* Dewey adopts the position that intelligence characterizes a level of existence separate from the organic realm out of which it evolved. This doctrine appears to introduce a dualism into Dewey's thought and thereby to undermine his commitment to continuity.)

Another aspect of Dewey's thought that Feldman finds problematic is his position concerning value and objectivity. In *The Quest for Certainty* and elsewhere, Dewey maintains that the dichotomy between objective knowledge and moral concerns is a false dichotomy. All thought is marked by a moral bias and concern. According to Dewey, it is both impossible and undesirable to construct a world view that is something other than a projection of how one believes reality ought to be. Yet Dewey also contends just the opposite: that objective knowledge is possible and that it ought to be sought. One can and should, he contends, keep one's self out of the data.

Despite Feldman's critical evaluation of many aspects of Dewey's thought, his book is a good introduction to Dewey's philosophy. His focus on the major concepts underlying Dewey's philosophy and the complexities involved in each of them is most illuminating.

Flower, Elizabeth and Murray G. Murphey. *A History of Philosophy in America.* Vol. II. New York: Capricorn Books, 1977.

Elizabeth Flower's and Murray G. Murphey's *A History of Philosophy in America* is the most complete study of philosophy in America to date. It combines a very adequate account of the careers of America's best philosophers from the Puritans to C. I. Lewis with a lucid exposition and careful analysis of their philosophies.

Critical of scholars who have tried to "encapsulate" John Dewey's philosophy, Flower and Murphey seek to illuminate the organic structure of Dewey's thought by emphasizing the centrality of his psychology to the rest of his work. The uniqueness of Dewey's thought, in their estimation, lies in his belief that a naturalistic psychology dissolves the distinction between fact and value. Since knowing and action are inseparable, and since action is always purposive and valuing, fact and value do not exist in separate spheres. To view fact and value as inhabiting distinct realms is, in Dewey's estimation, to misunderstand both.

Flower and Murphey divide their discussion of Dewey's thought into five sections: (1) Absolutism and Experimentalism; (2) A Naturalistic Psychology, Individual and Social; (3) Theory of Inquiry; (4) Ethics and Valuation; and (5) Social Philosophy.

In the first section Flower and Murphey discuss Dewey's life, particularly its intellectual and professional aspects, and they present a broad analysis of his shift from Hegelianism to a biologically oriented functionalism.

In the second section they discuss what they understand to be the core of Dewey's philosophy—his naturalistic psychology. In his early articles, which were devoted to psychology, and in his *Syllabus,* in which he applies psychology to moral judgments, Dewey lays the foundation for all of his later work. According to Flower and Murphey, Dewey's central concern in the articles on psychology is to show that the experiencing individual imports unrecognized biases into his or her experience. A related concern is to eradicate biases of philosophers and psychologists which have created artificial problems that follow from the compartmentalizing of experience. Experience for Dewey is unified; it is not divisable into acting and thinking, sensation and reflection, private and public.

The third section is devoted to a discussion of Dewey's logic. Dewey's logic deals with understanding in general; it is an inquiry into inquiries. Scientific inquiries, commonsense inquiries, and value inquiries are all of a piece for Dewey; they are all ways of adjusting to or interacting with one's environment. Dewey's investigations into the origins and boundaries of logic are, according to Flower and Murphey, a study of the dynamic interrelationship which exists between the individual and the world.

Valuation, a specific aspect of the interaction between an individual and the world, is the focus of section four, in which Flower and Murphey discuss *The Quest for Certainty*. The great significance of Dewey's ethical thought, of which *The Quest for Certainty* is one element, is its emphasis upon the developmental nature of valuation. Dewey is opposed to the notion that values are somehow permanent and unchanging. His position is that, just as scientific knowledge is "being made," values are "being made"; and just as absolutes are out of place in science, so are they out of place in ethics.

The final section is concerned with Dewey's social philosophy. By "social philosophy" Flower and cial philosophy. By "social philosophy" Flower and Murphey mean his political philosophy, his philosophy of culture, his philosophy of law, and his philosophy of education. In addition to commenting briefly on Dewey's social philosophy, Flower and Murphey note the relation between his social philosophy and his social psychology. What is important to note, they maintain, is that Dewey's thought leads inevitably to social philosophy. Dewey did not engage in social philosophy as an afterthought; rather, his philosophy is inherently social by virtue of his naturalistic psychology.

Flower's and Murphey's thesis that Dewey's naturalistic psychology is the foundation for the rest of his work deserves careful consideration. Their book serves to unify and to illuminate Dewey's life and thought.

Additional Recommended Reading

Bernstein, Richard J. *John Dewey.* New York: Washington Square Press, 1966. A sympathetic and comprehensive statement of Dewey's thought; a very good statement and analysis of Dewey's philosophy and its development.

Boydston, Jo Ann and Kathleen Poulos. *Checklist of Writings About John Dewey.* Carbondale: Southern Illinois University Press, 1978. This book should be very useful to the student interested in Dewey's philosophy. It contains a complete listing of all published and unpublished works about Dewey and lists of reviews of Dewey's books, as well as reviews of works about Dewey.

Geiger, George R. *John Dewey in Perspective.* New York: Oxford University Press, 1958. Geiger emphasizes Dewey's understanding of aesthetic experience as the key to understanding Dewey's thought as a whole.

Gouinlock, James. *John Dewey's Philosophy of Value.* New York: Humanities Press, 1972. Dewey's moral philosophy, according to Gouinlock, is integral to Dewey's understanding of nature. By developing this thesis Gouinlock seeks to clarify Dewey's moral philosophy.

Hook, Sidney. *John Dewey: An Intellectual Portrait.* Westport, Connecticut: Greenwood Press, 1971. This republication of the 1939 edition shows how Dewey the philosopher and Dewey the man and social reformer fit together. Generally regarded as the definitive delineation of Dewey.

Schilpp, Paul A., ed. *The Philosophy of John Dewey.* New York: Tudor Publishing Company, 1951 . Contains a biography of Dewey written by his daughters, a collection of seventeen essays on Dewey's philosophy, Dewey's responses to these essays, and a bibliography of Dewey's writings from 1885 to 1950. The essays are of very high quality.

PROCESS AND REALITY

Author: Alfred North Whitehead (1861-1947)
Type of work: Metaphysics
First published: 1929

Principal Ideas Advanced

Only a philosophy of organism can describe a universe in which process, creativity, and interdependence are disclosed in immediate experience.

Philosophy involves generalization from the concrete particulars we know to universals; it aims at a description of the dynamic process which is reality.

A philosophical system should be logically consistent and coherent, and it should be grounded in immediate experience.

The categories of this philosophy of organism are the category of the ultimate (creativity), the categories of existence (actual entities, prehensions, nexus, subjective forms, eternal objects, propositions, multiplicities, and contrasts), the categories of explanation (twenty-seven in number), and the categories of obligation (nine in number).

Everything but God is an actual entity occasioned by something; but God, although an actual entity, is not an actual occasion.

Every event in the creative, interdependent process is qualified by past, present, and future.

Process in reality is a creative advance in which feelings are integrated, actual occasions grow together toward a final phase of satisfaction, and God is conditioned by, and reciprocally affects, events in the temporal world.

The central aim in Whitehead's chief work, *Process and Reality,* is to replace the traditional philosophy of substance with a philosophy of organism. The thesis of the author is that only a philosophy of organism can provide clarification of a universe in which process, dynamic actualization, interdependence, and creativity are disclosed as the primary data of immediate experience.

Although Whitehead expresses some far-reaching reservations regarding traditional modes of thought, he formulates his philosophy of organism through a dialogue with the great logicians, scientists, metaphysicians, and theologians of the past. He finds the thought of Plato more decisive than that of Kant; he considers Bergson more suggestive than Hegel; he contends that Locke was closer to a philosophy of organism than Descartes; and he is ready to choose Leibniz over Aristotle. Western philosophy is defined by the author as a series of footnotes to Plato. Some of these footnotes he wishes to salvage and reformulate; others he is quite happy to see deleted. Of all the philosophical giants in the Western tradition, Kant is the least cordially received. The author makes it clear that his philosophy of organism constitutes a recurrence to pre-Kantian modes of thought. According to Whitehead, the Copernican revolution of Kant was not as revolutionary as many of his followers maintained it to be. Whitehead's philosophy is a speculative philosophy formulated into a coherent and logical system of general concepts which are intended to provide the categorial interpretation for any and all elements of human experience.

In examining the methodological foundations of Whitehead's system, we find first a procedure of descriptive generalization, and second an epistemology which expresses both a rational and an empirical side. Philosophical method involves generalization, in which there is a movement from the concrete particular to the universal. This generalization is based on description rather than deduction. Whitehead considers it to be a mistake that deduction, the primary method of mathematics, has intermittently become the touchstone for philosophical inquiry. Deduction is for the author an auxiliary mode of verification that should never be given primacy in philosophical methodology. Applied in Whitehead's philosophy of organism, this method of descriptive generalization takes the form of a description of *dynamic process* rather than of static structure. Morphological description is replaced by description of dynamic life processes.

Whitehead's epistemology contains both rational and empirical elements. The rational criterion is coherence and logical consistency; the empirical criterion is applicability and adequacy. A philosophical system must be coherent and logical. No entity can be conceived in abstraction from all other entities, nor can an entity be understood as long as its relation to other entities is not specified according to logical rules. But knowledge demands also an empirical justification. Categories must be applicable and adequate. They are applicable when they describe all related experience as exhibiting the same texture. They are adequate when they include all possible experience in their conceptual vision. Whitehead was deeply concerned to maintain an experiential basis for his philosophy: "The elucidation of immediate experience is the sole justification for any thought." Philosophy should aim at generalization, but it should not overreach its mark and lose itself in abstractions that are not grounded in experience. One of the chief errors in philosophy, contends the author, is the "fallacy of misplaced concreteness." This fallacy results when an abstraction becomes an exemplification of the system and replaces the concrete entity of which it is an abstraction. The success of philosophy, continues the author, is commensurate with the degree to which it avoids this fallacy.

Through the implementation of his method of descriptive generalization Whitehead derives a categorial scheme which sets forth the governing concepts of his philosophy of organism. His catego-

ries are classified according to a fourfold schematic division: (1) the category of the ultimate; (2) categories of existence; (3) categories of explanation; and (4) categorial obligations.

The *category of the ultimate* is creativity. Creativity is the universal of universals, the ultimate metaphysical principle which underlies all things without exception. Every fact of the universe is in some way or another an exemplification of creativity. Even God is subordinate to the category of the ultimate. As the ultimate metaphysical principle, creativity is also the principle of *novelty*. It provides the reason for the emergence of the new. In its application to the novel situation, of which it is the origination, creativity expresses itself as the "creative advance."

The *categories of existence* are eight in number: (1) actual entities; (2) prehensions; (3) nexus (plural of nexus); (4) subjective forms; (5) eternal objects; (6) propositions; (7) multiplicities; and (8) contrasts. *Actual entities,* which replace the traditional concept of particular substances, are the final facts of the universe; they are the real things of which the world is made up. *Prehensions* are the concrete facts of relatedness, exhibiting a "vector character," involving emotion, purpose, valuation, and causation. A *nexus* is a particular fact of togetherness of actual entities. *Subjective form* is the determining or defining quality of private matters of fact. *Eternal objects* are the pure potentials by reason of which facts are defined in their subjective forms. *Propositions* render meaningful the distinction between truth and falsehood; as abstract potentialities they are suggestions about the concrete particularity of actual entities. *Multiplicities* indicate the disjunctions of diverse entities. *Contrasts* indicate the mode of synthesis which occurs in a prehension or a concrete fact of relatedness. Along with these eight categories of existence Whitehead delineates twenty-seven categories of explanation and nine categorial obligations. We shall discuss the explanations and obligations as they become relevant in the development of the author's system.

Actual entities, which constitute Whitehead's first category of existence, are the building blocks of his organismic universe. Here the philosophy of organism inverts Spinoza. For Spinoza actual entities, as particulars, are inferior modes; only the Infinite Substance is ultimately real. In the philosophy of organism actual entities are the ultimate facts. These actual entities are in a process of "perpetual perishing," but as they perish they are somehow taken up in the creative advance, pass into other actual entities through the operation of prehension, and achieve objective immortality. This interpretation of a universe of flux in which actual entities come to be and pass away must be understood, according to the author, as simply an expansion of a sentence in Plato's *Timaeus*: "But that which is conceived by opinion with the help of sensation and without reason is always in the process of becoming and perishing and never really is." The universe, as it is immediately disclosed, is a universe of becoming, flux, and perishing. The category of actual entities has universal applicability. It applies to nonliving matter as well as to all instances of life. It applies to the being of man as well as to the being of God.

A significant implication of this doctrine is that God, for Whitehead, is not outside the system. He is within the reach and range of the categories. However, God is differentiated from all other actual entities in that he is not occasioned by anything. Thus, all actual entities other than God are also occasions. God is an actual entity but not an actual occasion. Every actual occasion exhibits a dipolar structure consisting of a physical pole and a mental pole. By reason of its physical pole the actual occasion prehends other actual occasions; by reason of its mental pole a prehension of eternal objects is made possible. In this description of the bipolar structure of actual occasions the author formulates an alternative to the Cartesian dualism of mind and body. God also exhibits a dipolar structure. He possesses two natures—a primordial nature and a consequent nature. His primordial nature, which consists of an envisagement of all the eternal objects and an appetition for their actualization, corresponds to the mental pole of actual occasions. His consequent nature, which is the consequence of the reaction of the world upon God, corresponds to the physical pole of actual occasions.

Actual occasions are grouped into societies or nexus through the operation of prehension. A prehension, according to the eleventh category of explanation, consists of three factors: (1) the subject which is prehending; (2) the datum which is prehended; and (3) the subjective form which designates the manner in which the subject prehends its datum. A nexus, according to the fourteenth category of explanation, "is a set of actual entities in the unity of the relatedness constituted by their prehensions of each other." By reason of their physical poles actual occasions can prehend each other and form societies or nexus. There results an organismic coinherence in which every event in the universe is a factor in every other event. All things ultimately inhere in each other. There are no isolated events. For Whitehead the universe is an interdependent universe in which all parts are interrelated. The analogy of the organism replaces the analogy of the machine. Not only, however, do actual occasions prehend each other by reason of their physical poles; they also prehend eternal objects by reason of their mental poles. Eternal objects are permanent and immutable principles of determination, clearly reminiscent of the eternal forms or ideas in the philosophy of Plato. An eternal object is a pure potential which, in itself, remains neutral to any particular fact of ingression in the temporal order. There are no new eternal objects. They are fixed in the timeless primordial vision of God. However, each eternal object is a potentiality in the history of actual occasions. An actual occasion prehends an eternal object and thus the object becomes realized in time and space. Ingression refers to the particular mode in which the potentiality of an eternal object is realized in a particular entity, contributing to the structure and definition of that actual entity. Eternal objects contribute the necessary structure which keeps the organismic process from dissolving into an indeterminate and discontinuous succession. Process does not contradict structure in Whitehead's analysis. Process and structure are interdependent concepts.

Actual occasions, and the societies which they form, are in a process of growing together until they reach a final phase which is called "satisfaction." This process of growing together, in which new prehensions constantly take place, is designated by the author as "concrescence." "In a process of concrescence, there is a succession of phases in which new prehensions arise by integration of prehensions in antecedent phases. . . . The process continues until all prehensions are components in the one determinate integral satisfaction." Each actual occasion as it is objectified in the process of concrescence exhibits a claim upon the future. The future is in some sense constitutive of the being of every actual occasion. Whitehead expresses this when he describes an actual occasion as a "subject-superject." Every occasion is at once the subject experiencing and the superject of this experience; it is the present experiential datum, but it is also the future result or the aim of its present experience. This aim or future project is called the "subjective aim," which controls the becoming of the actual occasion and lures it to its final satisfaction. All becoming thus occurs within a spatiotemporal continuum, in which all entities experience the bite of time. Each event in the universe is qualified by the past, present, and future. Although actual occasions perish, they enter into the internal constitution of other actual occasions, in which they become objectified. Every present fact of the universe is thus constituted by all antecedent phases. So also is every present fact constituted by its potentialities for future realization by its subjective aim. An actual entity is that which it can become. "That *how* an actual entity *becomes* constitutes *what* that actual entity is; so that the two descriptions of an actual entity are not independent. Its 'being' is constituted by its 'becoming.' This is the 'principle of process.' "

That all things flow is the one ultimate generalization around which Whitehead develops his whole system. This doctrine of a fluent, becoming universe, remarks the author, was already suggested in the unsystematized insights of Hebrew literature (particularly the Psalms), as well as in the early beginnings of Greek philosophy (particularly Heraclitus). Coupled with this doctrine of flux, however, is a competing notion—the permanence of all things. These two notions, contends the author, constitute the complete problem of metaphysics. Whitehead does not intend to reject the doctrine of permanence, but rather seeks to adapt it to his ultimate generalization that all things flow. This adaptation is expressed in two implicatory principles of his system—his doctrine of self-constituting identity and his doctrine of cosmic order. In his nine categorical obligations the author formulates the

category of objective identity, which asserts the essential self-identity of every actual entity as an individual constituent in the universe. Each actual entity is a cell with an atomic unity. In the process of concrescence actual entities grow together but they do not sacrifice their atomic unity. They retain their self-identity and thus give expression to a life of their own. Viewing the organismic process from the side of the cellular and atomic units which comprise it, we need to acknowledge a self-constituting individuality which indicates a permanence within the flow of all things. As there is objective self-identity in Whitehead's philosophy of organism, so also is there preestablished harmony or universal cosmic order. The latter aspect of the universe is indicated in the author's seventh category of obligation, the category of subjective harmony. The process of concrescence exhibits a preestablished harmony in which all prehensions are viewed as being contributive to a stable cosmic order, informed by the eternal objects and directed by the subjective aim. Thus does the doctrine of permanence receive another expression in Whitehead's system. His elaboration of the notion of preestablished harmony has some interesting implications for the author's position on the nature of evil. Although he does not formulate an explicit theodicy, he veers in the direction of a Leibnizian resolution to the problem. Novelty is not to be identified with creativity. The emergence of novelty in the organismic process may inhibit and delay the creative advance and thus provide the condition for the rise of evil. Evil constitutes a real fact in Whitehead's universe. Spinoza's attempt to explain away evil as an illusion arising from our finite, modal point of view is thus rejected. Evil is for Whitehead an *ens reale*, and not simply an *ens rationis*. However, when the creative advance attains its final phase or its satisfaction, the universe is the better off for the fact of evil. The satisfaction or the final phase is richer in content by reason of the particular cosmic disharmonies. All inhibiting novelties are somehow contributive to a greater good. In the creative advance of the world, particular evil facts are finally transcended.

Whitehead's philosophy of organism occupies a unique position in the history of philosophy in that it makes the sentient quality of experience decisive. His theory of prehension and his doctrine of the creative advance are governed by a notion of the pervasiveness of feeling. In the final analysis, prehension involves an objectification of feelings, and the creative advance is a process in which these feelings are integrated in an exemplification of harmony. "In the place of the Hegelian hierarchy of categories of thought, the philosophy of organism finds a hierarchy of categories of feeling." This accent on the sentient quality of experience by Whitehead has both epistemological and metaphysical implications. It entails, first of all, a rejection of the subject-object dichotomy as the foundation for knowledge. Most traditional varieties of philosophy, claims the author, give priority to the intellect and the understanding. In such a view the knowing subject is the primary datum and the philosophical task becomes a demonstration of the validity of propositions about the objects encountered by the subject. It was particularly in the Cartesian tradition that this subject-object form of statement became normative.

In Whitehead's philosophy of organism the subject is an emergent datum, rather than the foundational datum. The complex of feelings constitutes the primitive datum. The primitive element is sympathy, or feeling in another and feeling conformally with another. Intellect and consciousness arise only in the higher phases of concrescence. The universe is initially disclosed as a system of "vector feelings." This primacy of feeling is made explicit in Whitehead's doctrine of "presentational immediacy." In its immediate presentment the world is *received* as a complex of feelings. Primitive experience must thus properly be understood in terms of *sense-reception* rather than *sense-perception*. In sense-reception the interconnections of feelings are simultaneously disclosed. There is thus an internal bond between presentational immediacy and causal efficacy. Both Hume and Kant, in giving priority to the conscious subject, were unable to grasp this point. The sense-perception of the subject was for them the primary fact, and any apprehension of causation was somehow to be elicited from this primary fact. In the philosophy of organism, which gives primacy to sentient experience, causal relations are disclosed on the level of feelings. They

are directly felt on a pretheoretical or precognitive level of experience. The types of feeling are indefinite, and depend upon the complexity of the data which the feeling integrates. There are, however, three primary types of feeling which are constitutive of all more complex patterns: (1) physical feelings, (2) conceptual feelings, and (3) transmuted feelings. *Physical feelings* arise from the physical pole of the actual entity and have for their initial datum another actual entity. *Conceptual feelings* arise from the mental pole and have for their datum an eternal object. *Transmuted feelings* are akin to physical feelings in that they proceed from the physical pole, but their objective datum is a nexus of actual entities rather than a single entity. The creative advance integrates these various types of feeling in its progression toward satisfaction. This integration proceeds in such a manner that the earlier phases of feelings become components of later and more complex feelings. Thus, in each phase there is an emergence of novelty. This goes on until the final phase is reached, which is the complex satisfaction in which all earlier phases of feelings are taken up as formative constituents of a final and coordinated whole.

The categories of Whitehead's philosophy of organism receive their final exemplification in his metaphysics of theism. The doctrine of God completes Whitehead's system. In formulating his metaphysics of theism he has no intention of submitting rationally demonstrative proofs for the existence of God; rather, he intends to provide a theoretic system which gives clarification to the immediate facts of religious experience. The touchstone of religious experience is love. The author finds the most decisive expression of this religious attitude in the Galilean origin of Christianity. The theism suggested in this Galilean origin must be contrasted, on the one hand, with the theism of Aristotle, in which God is the unmoved mover who exhibits no concern for his creation and, on the other hand, with the theism of medieval theology, which, according to the author, gave to God the attributes which belonged exclusively to Caesar. The author's intention is thus to formulate a theistic view which arises from a religious experience in which love is the governing datum.

In Whitehead's philosophy this God of love is not to be treated as an exception to the categories and the metaphysical principles which they enunciate. God is the chief exemplification of the metaphysical system. In this role of chief exemplar his nature can be viewed from two perspectives—as *primordial* and as *consequent*. As *primordial*, God is unlimited or infinite potentiality. He is a unity and plenum of conceptual feelings, in abstraction from any physical feelings, and hence lacks the fullness of actuality. God as primordial is deficient in actuality. As a unity of conceptual feelings and operations he is a free creative act. He is in no way deflected by the particular occasions which constitute the actual world. The actual world presupposes the primordial nature, but the primordial nature does not presuppose the actual world. All that the primordial nature presupposes is the general and abstract character of creativity, of which it is the chief exemplification. As unlimited potentiality the primordial nature includes the eternal objects and accounts for the order in their relevance to the process of creation. So also God in his primordial nature is the *lure* for feeling or the "object of desire." He provides the condition for each subjective aim and draws the process to its final satisfaction.

Coupled with God's primordial nature is his *consequent* nature. His consequent nature is derivative. It expresses the reaction of the world upon God. The consequent nature is thus, in part, subject to the process of actualization in the actual world. By reason of his consequent nature God can share in the fullness of physical feelings of the actual world as these physical feelings become objectified in God. God shares with every actual occasion and every nexus its actual world. As consequent, God is conditioned by the world. His nature is consequent upon the creative advance of actual occasions in the process of concrescence. The primordial nature is free, complete, eternal, actually deficient, and unconscious. The consequent nature is determined, incomplete, everlasting, fully actual, and conscious. By reason of his consequent nature God establishes a providential relation to the world. His providential love is expressed through a tender care that nothing be lost. He saves everything in the world and preserves it in his own life. God's providence also manifests itself in the workings of divine wisdom. Through his infinite wisdom he puts to use even that which in the temporal world would be considered mere wreckage. The consequent nature thus makes possible a continuing point of contact and a reciprocal relation between God and the world. The events in the temporal world are transformed through God's love and wisdom, and his love and wisdom then pass back into the world. God thus receives his final definition as the great companion—the fellow sufferer who understands.

Pertinent Literature

Leclerc, Ivor. *Whitehead's Metaphysics: An Introductory Exposition.* Bloomington: Indiana University Press, 1958.

Widely acclaimed as one of the best introductions to Alfred North Whitehead's thought, Ivor Leclerc's book is a tremendous aid to those who seek to understand Whitehead's philosophy. Leclerc's book is carefully structured and well written. It presupposes some familiarity with philosophy, but it does not assume that one has any knowledge of Whitehead's metaphysics.

There are three reasons why Leclerc is so successful in his effort to explicate Whitehead's thought: (1) he presents Whitehead's various concepts in a linear fashion, (2) he relates Whitehead's ideas to the classical issues in Western philosophy, and (3) he provides quotations from Whitehead's books as a means of illustration and as a way of bringing together the introductory exposition and the original texts.

Leclerc abandons Whitehead's holistic approach in favor of the more traditional linear style of exposition. Whitehead viewed his metaphysics as a unified system in which each aspect of the system is dependent on every other aspect for its full meaning. Consequently, in his most extended statement of his metaphysics—*Process and Reality*—he introduces the whole of his system in Chapter II and then spends the remainder of this rather lengthy book trying to make his account in Chapter II intelligible. Although one can readily accept Whitehead's reason for writing *Process and Reality* in the manner in which he chose to write it, the fact remains that it is virtually impossible for anyone to read this book with any understanding of its contents. Leclerc, in his effort to make Whitehead's thought accessible to the inquiring student, limits himself to introducing only one Whiteheadian concept at a time. The benefits of this approach are immediately manifest, especially when one considers Whitehead's neologisms. Unfortunately, Whitehead's system is such that every aspect really does depend upon every other aspect for its full meaning. This limitation is important, but not fatal. Every method of exposition has its limitations as well as its benefits. The advantages associated with Leclerc's linear style of expression complement the advantages associated with Whitehead's holistic style. As long as one does not read Leclerc's book instead of, but rather in addition to, reading Whitehead's own works, one can only profit from Leclerc's account of Whitehead's metaphysics.

Leclerc's book is useful in another respect: it shows the relationships between Whitehead's thought and the classical issues in Western philosophy. Leclerc's primary thesis in this book is that Whitehead's later thought is a response to specific problems in Western philosophy. At various times Whitehead himself indicates which philosophical issues bear on his thought, but all too often he does not. By systematically noting the philosophical issues underlying Whitehead's metaphysical notions, Leclerc illuminates many facets of Whitehead's thought.

Leclerc's book is also helpful because of his use of quotations. In order to facilitate the transition from secondary material to the texts themselves, Leclerc includes in his book many passages from Whitehead's work. His use of quotations serves an additional function: not only does it help one make the transition from secondary to primary sources, but it also makes one want to read the original works.

Cobb, John B., Jr. *A Christian Natural Theology, Based on the Thought of Alfred North Whitehead.* Philadelphia: Westminster Press, 1965.

The primary purpose of John B. Cobb Jr.'s book *A Christian Natural Theology* is to construct a Christian natural theology on the basis of Alfred North Whitehead's philosophy of organism. The term "natural" is used here in contrast to "supernatural." A natural theology is one in which God exemplifies the same metaphysical principles as every other instance of actuality. Cobb favors a natural theology over a supernatural theology because he opposes a separation of religious beliefs from nonreligious beliefs. Such a split, he contends, is unnecessary and may have disastrous consequences. When persons are unable to integrate their religious beliefs with their other convictions, religious beliefs become isolated and problematic. According to Cobb, religious beliefs—for example, the concept of God and God's activity in the world—ought to be explainable in terms of the same categories which are employed in the understanding of other actualities and their relations. In that Whitehead also held this view, it is hardly surprising that Cobb chooses Whitehead's philosophy of organism as the basis of his Christian natural theology.

Cobb opens his book with an excellent introduction to Whitehead's metaphysics. Beginning with the rationale which underlies Whitehead's thought, Cobb discusses the problems associated with psychophysical dualism and the equally serious problems associated with materialism and idealism. If there are two fundamentally different types of actualities, how are they related, how do they interact? If everything actual is material, how can mentality be explained? Conversely, if everything is finally mental, how can physical things be accounted for? In light of these traditional philosophical issues, and the conceptual problems which confronted physicists at the turn of the twentieth century, Cobb presents Whitehead's understanding of "actual occasions of experience. "

What Cobb terms his "introduction" to Whitehead's philosophy is relatively brief. He devotes less than twenty pages to an explanation of "actual occasions," "physical prehensions," "propositional feelings," "corpuscular societies," and other Whiteheadian concepts. These pages are well written and they provide a general guide to Whitehead's thought, but they do not constitute a full introduction to Whitehead's metaphysics. Were this the extent of Cobb's explication of Whitehead's thought, one would be well advised to consider a more extended introduction. However, Cobb continues to explicate Whitehead's philosophy throughout his book. When, for example, Cobb discusses the human psyche, personal identity, and freedom and self-determinism, he does so in terms of Whitehead's metaphysics. Indeed, one of the major strengths of Cobb's account is his

interest in bringing Whitehead's metaphysics to bear on such topics as anthropology, ethics, and religion. By focusing on matters such as these, Cobb emphasizes the existential relevance of Whitehead's thought.

One need not fear that Cobb's Christian beliefs and his interest in constructing a Christian natural theology color his understanding of Whitehead's thought. In those parts of the book where Cobb is using Whitehead's thought as the basis for a Christian natural theology, he states very clearly that these are his thoughts and not Whitehead's. In addition to being a major Christian theologian, Cobb is one of the most respected interpreters of Whitehead's philosophy; even if one has no interest in Christian theology (natural or supernatural), one will find Cobb's book extremely useful for illuminating Whitehead's metaphysics.

Kraus, Elizabeth. *The Metaphysics of Experience: A Companion to Whitehead's* Process and Reality. New York: Fordham University Press, 1979.

Elizabeth Kraus's book is neither a popularization of *Process and Reality* nor a commentary on it. It is just what it purports to be: a companion volume intended to illuminate Alfred North Whitehead's great and extremely abstruse text. Aimed at the advanced student, *The Metaphysics of Experience: A Companion to Whitehead's* Process and Reality is too difficult to be useful to most people. Whitehead's philosophy is both complex and uncommon, and his terminology is absolutely unique. A guide to *Process and Reality*, Kraus maintains, cannot change these facts. But the difficulties that confront the reader of *Process and Reality* go beyond those posed by the originality of Whitehead's metaphysics and his new language—the structure of the book presents problems of its own. Kraus seeks to obviate those problems, which are a result of the structure of *Process and Reality.*

Except for two sections preceding the main body of Kraus's book, *The Metaphysics of Experience* has the same five-part organization as *Process and Reality*. In the Introduction Kraus presents a compact explanation of Whitehead's thought in general and of

its early development. In Chapter 1 she examines at some length Whitehead's 1925 work, *Science and the Modern World*. According to Kraus, the philosophical scheme that Whitehead develops in detail in *Process and Reality* is sketched in broad strokes in *Science and the Modern World*. Her comments on this earlier work are perceptive and helpful for understanding the technical expression of Whitehead's position in *Process and Reality*.

In Chapters 2, 3, 4, and 5, Kraus presents the most important aspects of Parts I, II, III, and IV of *Process and Reality*. Chapter 2 deals with Whitehead's understanding of speculative philosophy and his "Categoreal Scheme." Chapter 3 deals principally with his concept of societies and his modal theory of perception—perception in the mode of causal efficacy, perception in the mode of presentational immediacy, and perception in the mode of symbolic reference. In Chapter 4 Kraus presents Whitehead's genetic analysis of concrescence, and in Chapter 5 she explains his theory of extension. Whitehead's account of his theory of extension is virtually impenetrable. Most readers dismiss this section of *Process and Reality* as irrelevant. Kraus not only demonstrates the relevance of Whitehead's theory of extension; she also succeeds in shedding a great deal of light on its meaning. Chapter 5 is without question the single most helpful chapter.

Chapter 6 is devoted to Whitehead's concluding remarks concerning the relationship between God and the world. In this chapter Kraus decides to enter into an interpretive debate. The first part of this chapter is given to countering Charles Hartshorne's concept that God is a temporally ordered society of divine occasions and to speculating on the possibility of subjective immortality. Kraus argues that Whitehead's concept of God is similar to the mystical understanding of God and that subjective immortality is a real possibility. One ought to recognize that on these matters Kraus's book is not acting simply as a guide to understanding *Process and Reality*; it is venturing out on its own.

Process and Reality is definitely in need of a guide; without a guide one will almost certainly become lost. Kraus's *The Metaphysics of Experience* is a very able guide, and the advanced student will find it very useful.

Additional Recommended Reading

Christian, William. *An Interpretation of Whitehead's Metaphysics*. New Haven, Connecticut: Yale University Press, 1959. This presentation of Whitehead's philosophy is remarkable for its clarity and for its accuracy. Christian's book is an excellent introduction to Whitehead's advanced thought, especially his concepts of actual occasions, eternal objects, and God.

Hartshorne, Charles. *Whitehead's Philosophy*. Lincoln: University of Nebraska Press, 1972. Charles Hartshorne has been the major Whiteheadian scholar and commentator since 1925. This book is a collection of thirteen essays he has written on Whitehead's philosophy, including "Whitehead's Metaphysics," "The Compound Individual," "Whitehead's Idea of God," and "Whitehead's Theory of Prehension."

Lowe, Victor. *Understanding Whitehead*. Baltimore: The Johns Hopkin University Press, 1962. This book is a very good introduction to Whitehead's philosophy. Part II, "The Development of Whitehead's Philosophy," traces Whitehead's thought from his early work in mathematics up through *Process and Reality* and *Adventures of Ideas*. Lowe is not, by his own account, a Whiteheadian, but he appreciates Whitehead's genius.

Schilpp, Paul A., ed. *The Philosophy of Alfred North Whitehead* (The Library of Living Philosophers). New York: Tudor Publishing Company, 1951. This book contains a short autobiographical sketch by Whitehead, nineteen essays on Whitehead's thought, a very brief summary of Whitehead's thought, and a bibliography of Whitehead's work. Victor Lowe's essay "The Development of Whitehead's Philosophy" and Charles Hartshorne's "Whitehead's Idea of God" are particularly good.

Sherburne, Donald. *A Whiteheadian Aesthetic*. Foreword by F. S. C. Northrop. New Haven, Connecticut: Yale University Press, 1961. In this volume, Sherburne seeks to construct a theory of aesthetics on the basis of Whitehead's understanding of reality. The first four chapters are devoted to explaining Whitehead's philosophy. His sections on "Creativity," "Eternal Objects," and "God," are especially fine.

THE RIGHT AND THE GOOD

Author: William David Ross (1877-1971)
Type of work: Ethics
First published: 1930

Principal Ideas Advanced

Rightness and goodness are simple and unanalyzable properties; they cannot be explained in terms of feelings, nor are they scientifically discoverable.

We cannot discover value or rightness by the use of the senses; such properties are discoverable only by intellectual intuition.

Basic moral truths are invariant; they are not products of various cultures.

The claim that "right" means "productive of the greatest possible good" is mistaken, for some acts—such as keeping a promise—are right regardless of whether they are productive of the greatest possible good.

Moral principles, discoverable by anyone who is intellectually mature, fall into a moral order; but the moral order cannot specifically be stated, for the resolution of conflicts between moral principles must be made in the light of particular circumstances.

Sir William David Ross, one of the most influential of recent philosophers, has played a leading role in the development of contemporary ethics. He is the best-known exponent of a nonnaturalistic deontological ethical theory, a type of theory that has been at the center of philosophic controversy during most of the first half of this century.

Like H. A. Prichard and E. F. Carritt, or in an earlier period, Kant and Richard Price, Ross is a deontologist or formalist insofar as he insists that the concepts of "right," "duty," and "obligation" are fundamental concepts that cannot be explained in terms of, or derived from, other value concepts such as "good." In this respect he differs from utilitarians such as J. S. Mill and, recently, G. E. Moore, who have argued that concepts of moral obligation can be derived from "good," the primary notion. However, like Moore, Ross is a nonnaturalist insofar as he insists that properties such as right and good are not to be explained in terms of the feelings or inner states of the judge, nor are they properties that can be detected by the senses or discovered by any scientific procedure. They are, rather, "nonnatural" properties apprehended by intellectual insight. This doctrine

places him in opposition to naturalists such as George Santayana, John Dewey, Ralph Barton Perry, C. I. Lewis (to a certain extent), and to a number of sociologically inclined thinkers such as David Émile Durkheim. It also opposes him to emotivists such as A. J. Ayer and C. L. Stevenson, who deny that the ethical significance of terms is cognitive at all. Ross's views are expressed most elegantly in *The Right and the Good*, a book that has become a modern classic in the literature of ethics. They are expanded somewhat in a later book, *The Foundations of Ethics* (1939), which an interested reader will want to consult.

In this review we shall adopt Ross's order of discussion, starting with right and turning later to good. When he speaks of "right," he has in mind the closely related concepts of "right," "obligation," and "duty" which, he says, with minor qualifications refer to the same thing. He is using the term "right" not in the weaker sense of "not wrong" but in the stronger sense of "wrong not to." The property of rightness, he says, is simple and nonanalyzable, and the concept of "right" is consequently indefinable. Here he is following the pattern laid down by Moore in his *Principia Ethica* (1903), although Moore applied it there to the concept of "good" only. Furthermore, he argues, as Moore did in the case of "good," that in addition to being indefinable, "a word like 'right' . . . does not stand for anything we can point out to one another or apprehend by one of the senses." Rather, it is a property we recognize in certain types of action by an intellectual insight or intuition.

Ross believes that even though "right" is indefinable, most of us will know what it means, for most of us are moral people who constantly make moral judgments quite satisfactorily. If we are not sure, we can always consider particular cases and see that we do distinguish between moral behavior on the one hand and other kinds of behavior on the other. And if we are confused about the relationship between the notion of "right" and value concepts such as "good," once again we can clarify the issue only by attending to, analyzing, and comparing cases. Ultimately each of us must examine his own moral consciousness if he wishes to attain clarity, for, as Ross has already argued, " 'right' . . . does not stand for anything we can point out to one another." The moral insight is private in the sense that we cannot look to make sure the other person is apprehending what we apprehend. This does not mean that communication is impossible, for observation and discussion will reveal that on the whole we agree that there is moral behavior and we agree, also, on the kinds of behavior that are moral.

Ross himself discusses and criticizes several prominent philosophical views that deny one or another of the major points of his own position. Thus he argues against thinkers like Durkheim by claiming that moral insight is not to be equated with or explained away in terms of the mores a culture happens to have at some particular time. The insights men have may vary from time to time, as may the codes men lay down, but basic moral truths themselves are invariant. Against Moore's doctrine in *Principia Ethica*, that "right" means "productive of the greatest possible good," he has two arguments. First, he uses Moore's own open question technique against him, for, he says, it surely is an important question whether actions that produce the greatest good are right. This is not the trivial question it would be if the corresponding statement were analytic, and it would be analytic if the alleged definition were correct. Second, he argues that the rightness of certain actions, such as that of promise keeping, does not depend entirely or essentially upon the good produced by such actions. It is to be noted that later on, in *Ethics* (1911), Moore himself changed his mind and agreed with Ross that "right" is indefinable.

Ross also argues against the view that to say an act is right is to say that it is morally good; that is, that it stems from a morally praiseworthy motive. Here, too, he uses two arguments. First, he says that since motives are feelings or desires that cannot be summoned up at a moment's notice, it would be impossible in many cases to do what is surely our duty. Since *ought* implies *can*, it cannot be our duty to act from a good motive. (This is not to deny that it is our duty to develop our character or that we can act from good motives.) Second, it is not our duty to act from a sense of duty but rather our duty simply to do certain things, such as to return the book we have borrowed. The goodness of the act is important if we are concerned with the virtue of the agent, but this goodness must not be confused with another property the act may have, that of being right or obligatory.

Ross then turns from the question of the meaning of ethical terms to another major question: What is the criterion of right and wrong? Here too he is reacting against Moore and other utilitarians, for regardless of whether they think they are giving a definition of right, they all maintain that the goodness produced by an act is the sole criterion of its rightness. Ross replies that this is not the case with respect to a wide variety of actions. We have already mentioned promise keeping. Ross acknowledges that the consequences of keeping a promise must be taken into account when we consider whether or how we should keep it, and he acknowledges that in some cases these consequences are such that we should not keep it, but he points out that in many cases we are obliged to keep a promise even if it should result in less beneficial consequences than some other action, and that in all cases involving a promise there is a moral consideration present which has nothing to do with consequences. In the case of promises, an obligation arises because of a special sort of action in the past rather than because of future consequences, and it arises because in promising, and by promising, we "create a moral claim on us in someone else." The utilitarian ignores the fact that the act of promising is the source of an obligation. Other things being equal, then, we are obliged to keep our promises, and this obligation is not the obligation to produce beneficial consequences. Ross does assert that we are also obliged to act so as to benefit others, but this is another, quite different, obligation.

Ross maintains that there are still other sorts of obligation. First, there are obligations similar to that of keeping promises in that they stem from the particular actions of men. He writes not only of promises and contracts, but also of cases of fidelity such as the "implicit promise" underlying the understanding that we will tell the truth. Also included in the category of "special obligations" are our obligations to compensate others for the wrongs we have done them (the duty of reparation) and to return the services of those who have helped us (the duty of gratitude). In contrast to these "special obligations" which occur only if one party to the obligation has acted in a particular way with respect to the other, there are the "general obligations" we have with respect to all men simply because and insofar as they are men. In addition to the duty to benefit others, Ross mentions our obligations to distribute happiness according to merit (justice), to improve ourselves, and to refrain from injuring others. Ross believes he has given a complete catalogue of duties, but he is less concerned with defending this contention than he is with emphasizing that there are many types of obligation quite distinct from the obligation to maximize the amount of good in the world. The important point is that not one of these obligations can be explained away in terms of any of the others. The utilitarian is mistaken when he asserts that there is only one criterion of what is right, for there are many, each as fundamental and irreducible as the others.

Each of these is a moral principle, each is a moral truth. Together they express the "moral order" which is "just as much part of the fundamental nature of the universe . . . as is the spatial or numerical structure expressed in the axioms of geometry or arithmetic." Men have not always apprehended these principles,

but any who "have reached sufficient mental maturity and have given sufficient attention" to them should recognize their self-evident truth.

Since there will be many particular cases where these principles will clash, it cannot *always* be obligatory to keep a promise, or to rectify wrongs done to others, or to benefit others, and so on. For this reason, Ross says that promise keeping and other kinds of acts which are usually obligatory are *prima facie* right, meaning by this that if no stronger and contrary moral consideration is relevant to the case in point, promise keeping, or whatever it is, is morally obligatory. He draws an analogy with the parallelogram of forces in physics: the fact that one makes a promise "tends" to make a certain action right, but the fact that this same act will harm another person "tends" to make it wrong. If only the first tendency were present, it would determine the outcome and keeping the promise would be right or obligatory and not merely *prima facie* right. But since there are two opposing "tendencies" actual duty will be determined by the stronger of the two. The weaker tendency is still present, though overcome. It may be wrong to keep the promise in this situation but even so, keeping it is still *prima facie* right. This is Ross's way of maintaining the absoluteness of moral principles in the face of the obvious fact that they clash in particular cases.

Ross does not think these principles can be arranged hierarchically in such a fashion that when any two clash we know beforehand which must take precedence over the other, and he does not believe there is any principle that enables us to resolve such conflicts. He maintains that our moral life is far more complex than the systematizers of ethics imply it is. We must consider cases as they come, weigh the relative strengths of the moral considerations as they occur in the individual cases, and reach our decisions accordingly. As a result, we cannot be nearly as certain about the rightness of particular acts as we can be about the truth of the general principles, for while the latter is self-evident, the former can never be known with certainty.

In his discussion of the good, Ross is concerned primarily with "intrinsic" goodness which he, like many others, distinguishes from "instrumental" goodness. Something is intrinsically good if it is good for its own sake, quite apart from any value it might have as a means of attaining some other good. Ross believes that only states of mind or relations between them can have intrinsic value and, therefore, that anything else has value only insofar as it produces such states or relations. Thus, for instance, the physical painting has instrumental value but only the experience it produces in us has intrinsic value. It follows that a world that contained no conscious beings would be a valueless world.

When we examine our states of mind, Ross says, we will find that only four things are intrinsically valuable. The first three, in increasing order of importance, are (1) pleasure, (2) knowledge and right opinion, and (3) morally good states such as virtuous dispositions and morally good motives. Of the third, sense of duty ranks highest followed by feelings such as sympathy and benevolence. He presents "the apportionment of pleasure and pain to the virtuous and the vicious respectively" as the fourth intrinsic good. To support his view he asks us in each case to consider two universes which are equal in all respects except that the state under consideration is present in one and absent in the other, believing that in each case we will agree that the universe containing the state in question is the better one. If anything other than these four things is intrinsically good, it can only be something exhibiting several of them. Thus, for example, the intrinsic goodness of aesthetic enjoyment involves both pleasure and knowledge.

Ross's analysis of the nature of intrinsic goodness is like that of G. E. Moore, to whom he acknowledges his debt. Good is a simple, unanalyzable property of a state of mind, a property it has in virtue of the fact that it has some other property, that of being pleasant, knowing, or virtuous. Good is not to be confused with these other properties. Good is a "consequential" or "dependent" property insofar as the state of mind has goodness only because it also has some other properties, but good is not a "constitutive" property of the state of mind, as the other properties are, for it does not belong to the essential nature of the state of mind. That is, while a statement such as, "A state of knowing is a cognitive state" is an analytic statement, the statement, "A state of knowing is intrinsically

valuable" is synthetic.

Good is a simple property and the corresponding concept, "good," is indefinable. Ross defends this claim by arguing that no offered definitions have been able to survive examinations. Some fail because either they exclude actions that are right or include actions that are wrong. And all, even those in which the denotations of the *definiens* and the *definiendum* may coincide, fail because they do not express what we mean by "good." This latter argument is much like Moore's use of the open question technique which we have already mentioned in our discussion of right. Ross does not insist that we can prove that "good" is indefinable, but he does hold that the fact that all proffered definitions have failed is extremely strong evidence, especially when we consider that there is no reason in the first place why we should think that good is a complex property. In brief, Ross ends up as Moore did, by considering good to be a simple, unanalyzable, "nonnatural" property that is present in something because of the presence in it of certain other quite natural properties.

This conception of a nonnatural property and the related notions of intuition and synthetic *a priori* truths lie at the center of Ross's position, and as such have been the targets of most of the criticism directed against him. Nonnatural properties have been especially bothersome. Ross and Moore both maintain that value and moral terms refer to properties of things and actions, and yet both insist that these properties are not sensed and cannot be discovered by scientific means. Consequently, they have the difficult task, which has bothered Moore particularly, of trying to explain what such nonnatural properties are. As Moore's long puzzlement indicates, they have not succeeded even to their own satisfaction. On the other hand, they have refused to abandon the notion because they believe that the consequence would be the destruction of the cognitive significance of moral and value statements, a consequence made all too clear by the work of the later emotivists. The dominating model of significance and truth is that made familiar by empirical propositions: if a statement is cognitively significant, then it must be capable of being true; and if it is capable of being true, then it must refer, correctly or incorrectly, to things and properties. Furthermore, we must be able to observe things and their properties. Applying this model to value statements, we are forced to make a similar series of moves. If the statement "A is good" is true, then there must be such a property as good, A must possess it, and we must be able to examine A and notice that A possesses it. We may be puzzled as to exactly what sort of thing the examination reveals, but if we say that A is good, it seems that we are forced to admit that we have inspected A and have noticed that it has the property we call good.

Very recently writers such as S. Toulmin, P. H. Nowell-Smith, K. Baier, and A. I. Melden have attacked the underlying model of significance, arguing that the concepts of "reasonable," "valid," and "true" have quite legitimate and distinctive uses in moral discourse, uses which vary from the uses of these terms in scientific discourse. Thus, they contend, we can escape the postulation of puzzling non-natural properties without giving up the contention that moral discourse does differ significantly from

scientific discourse, and we can do so without denying that moral statements have cognitive significance. That is, very recent thought has broken out of the bonds indicated by our recent classification of ethical theories as being either naturalistic, non-naturalistic, or emotivist, a scheme of classification which presupposed the acceptance of the dominant model that has been mentioned.

As for Ross, no matter how severely some of his ideas are being criticized, there is no doubt that he has played a very important role in the development of contemporary ethical theory and that his influence still lives strongly. His insistence that moral and value terms differ from descriptive terms, his insistence on a deontological ethics, and his insistence that morality is far too complex to be contained by any theory which would reduce it to a single principle have been and continue to be very influential. These basic ideas persist even in the views of many who are somewhat unhappy about the epistemological framework within which Ross has expressed them.

Pertinent Literature

Pickard-Cambridge, W. A. "Two Problems About Duty," in *Mind*. XLI, nos. 161, 162, 163 (January, April, July, 1932), pp. 72-96, 145-172, 311-340.

W. A. Pickard-Cambridge believes that W. David Ross's view of duty and his criticism of ideal utilitarianism are oversimplified. Since Ross finds duty to consist in the *actual production* of a sought state of affairs, attempting is not enough—one's duty is to *succeed*. The realities of situations, however, reveal fatal flaws in this view. Ross uses "ought" to apply to that which is directly done or ought to be done. However, as simple an action as returning a borrowed book (a Ross example) requires the doing of many acts by persons other than the one responsible—a mail collector, mail handlers, a carrier—yet Ross calls all of it the primary agent's duty; and this is not how we truly understand duty. More properly, Pickard-Cambridge concludes, Ross should say that a person's duty is to *aim at* producing the sought situation by actions that may reasonably be thought *likely* to produce it. In his later work, *The Foundation*

of Ethics, Ross indeed comes around to the view that our duty is to "set ourselves" to accomplish a situation or action.

The intuitionist such as Ross argues with two advantages. First, he uses logical standards against his opponent; yet the opponent cannot use them against him, for the intuitionist claims that inspection, not argument, produces his knowledge. Second, if the intuitionist agrees with his opponent on a judgment of what a duty is, he can claim that not the opponent's argument but his own intuition is his basis. The only promising way that Pickard-Cambridge finds to argue with the intuitionist, therefore, is to compare instances of one and the same act, which must always be intuited in the same way, in which the resulting goodness or badness varies. If moral judgments of appropriate observers in these instances vary concomitantly with differences of resulting good or evil, this should be a rebuttal to the intuitionist.

Using this method, Pickard-Cambridge takes up Ross's two kinds of duty, *prima facie* and actual or absolute duty, to show that what actually determines either kind is not intuition, but the amount of good done by the action when carried out. Without defining ideal utilitarianism, he takes its principle to be that our duty is to do the act that leads to the most good, the best subsequent situation. Exhibiting in one imaginary instance after another, with significant variations, what in practice we do judge the duties of the agents to be, he shows that when we take a full range of factors of the actions into account, a utilitarian calculation of the resulting good or evil coincides with the judgments of duty. Thus, ideal utilitarianism suffices to explain satisfactorily the determinations of duty, whereas Ross himself admits that intuition has shortcomings.

Ross's examples are oversimplified. The assumption of "other things being equal" is never justified; every case involves many persons, not two only. Results accruing to other persons and to society as a whole must be heeded. So must subjective forms of good as well as objective (sometimes measurable) ones. Pickard-Cambridge's examples examine the effects of considering the abilities of beneficiaries to use the benefits well, the extent to which their desires affect our obligation, the relative moral character of alternative beneficiaries of our actions, and the like. The very fulfillment of an expectation is a good, and must be considered in the calculation.

Pickard-Cambridge finds that the intuitionist theory provides no way for differing judges to find common ground and to come to agreement. The ideal utilitarian method, however, provides a clear and intelligible principle, considerably narrows the margins of inexactness or judgmental differences, encourages us to analyze out different elements of duty, provides for expressing them appropriately for rational deliberation, and promises that we can actually come to know our duty. On the other hand, the method of intuition simply adopts an unchecked personal impression, admitting fallibility. Any moral theory which rules out the possibility of certainly knowing our duty stands condemned.

McCloskey, H. J. "Ross and the Concept of a *Prima Facie* Duty," in *Australasian Journal of Philosophy*. XLI, no. 3 (December, 1963), pp. 336-345.

Nearly all the critical response to W. David Ross has centered on his analysis of right, obligation, or duty, not on his analysis of the good. Many critics have complained that he has not made it clear what *prima facie* duty is and what is its relation to absolute or actual duty. H. J. McCloskey asserts that Ross has made a mistake in attempting to derive *prima facie* duties from actual or absolute duties; instead, he should base the latter on *prima facie* duties.

Ross makes two claims, equally unclear. (1) *Prima facie* duties are not really duties, although it is convenient even if misleading so to term them. (2) They are rather *tendencies* to be duties. Ross, however, does not mean "tendencies" in the usual causal sense, and does not explain in what sense he does intend it. Ross at times accepts the causal model, but at other times comes near to a view that McCloskey outlines and defends.

Contending that *prima facie* duties are actually not duties is the source of Ross's trouble, although he nowhere deliberately rejects the possibility that they may be duties. Most likely Ross intends merely to stress that certain acts that at first appear to be obligatory turn out not to be obligatory. McCloskey asserts that to be subject to a *prima facie* duty is to be in a moral situation and under some obligation to act in a certain way, although not being *absolutely* obligated to act in that way. This is quite different from being subject conditionally to a duty, or to being obligated sometimes or usually (*tending* to be obligated).

The qualities that determine absolute duties to be duties are present in and spring from the *prima facie* duties. There are differences, however. First, since "'ought' implies 'can,'" we are always able to carry out our absolute duties, but are not always able to carry out our *prima facie* duties. Next, although not obligated to do something other than fulfill a duty, we are always under obligation to fulfill the most important *prima facie* duty or duties in the situation. And the obligatoriness that thus binds us is the same obligatoriness that duty has as a *prima facie* duty; it does not come from somewhere else. A given *prima facie* duty does not change its nature when it is identified as the one that is most important and that therefore is to be fulfilled, to the exclusion of others. Thus Ross errs in using language suggesting that *prima facie* duties are something other than duties, but become duties under certain conditions. It is by virtue of the presence of other things, other *prima facie* duties, that one *prima facie* duty emerges as an absolute or ultimate duty.

The expression "absolute duty," then, is a short way of designating the largest sum of fulfillable *prima facie* duties, including the most important or most morally insistent. It is as the absolute or operative duty that a duty has special qualifications, not as *prima facie*. Thus an analysis of duty should base the absolute, operative duty upon the *prima facie* duties rather than the other way around.

Stocker, Michael. "Intentions and Act Evaluations," in *The Journal of Philosophy*. LXVII, no. 17 (September 3, 1970), pp. 589-602.

In making the larger point that motives play no role in the rightness or wrongness of actions, W. David Ross asserts that no morally good act is ever morally obligatory. To establish this, he appeals to Immanuel Kant's principle that " 'ought' implies 'can,' " together with the factual premise that one cannot by choice and at a moment's notice produce in himself a morally good motive.

Examining this "curious" argument, Michael Stocker tries to find what Ross consistently could have meant by it.

That X is my duty implies that I can perform X, for if X were asserted to be my duty but I could not perform it, that would be unjust, and no actual duty is ever unjust. However, " 'ought' implies 'can' " cannot imply "action from a morally good motive is never obligatory" unless we can never act from such a motive. In fact we do act at times from morally good motives. So " 'ought' implies 'can' " does not make it inconsistent to believe both that we have obligations and (what Ross denies) that our obligations may include acting from a morally good motive. Even if we do not have a *duty* to act from a good motive, we can at least sometimes perform a morally good act from a sense of duty.

All that Ross may conclude from " 'ought' implies 'can' " is that we have an obligation to perform a morally good act only when we *can* perform it—which is true of all duties. Ross believes that we have a *prima facie* duty to do whatever morally good actions we can; and such a position should admit doing some of the acts that are done from morally good motives since they are morally good acts. Examining two possible reformulations of Ross's argument, Stocker shows that one proves too much: namely, that we have no obligations at all. The second allows either for performing the obligated act simply, or else for performing it with a good motive. Ross should concede that regarding it obligatory to act with morally good intentions is consistent with "'ought' implies 'can.' "

Ross's argument that motives (good or not) never are commanded by duty cannot be correct. For example, to keep a promise one must do something with the intention of keeping the promise. To do nothing while other events merely happen to bring about the object of the promise, or to keep it by accident or by mistake, does not constitute *keeping* the promise—doing what fulfills the obligation—for the motive of intending to perform is part of what is promised. Other *prima facie* duties also may include a component of motive or intention in the content of the duty. The motive affects our evaluation of these acts.

There are other kinds of cases. Although a person fulfills an obligation from a nonconscientious motive, he might still fulfill it from a moral motive if he had not had his other motive; and if he fulfills it with a conscientious motive, we cannot argue that he does better than if he fulfills it with a lesser motive, for the quality of the motive here is irrelevant so long as the fulfillment is adequate. To perform an obligatory action with a morally good intention is to create a moral good over and above discharging one's obligation. Acting from a bad motive alone may suffice to constitute an action morally bad.

In sum, to act on good or bad intentions affects some, but not all, act evaluations. Good intention appears necessary, and sometimes sufficient, for doing a morally good act. Acting on a bad intention appears sufficient for acting wrongly; but except in the special cases where to have the intention is part of the obligation, the act that fulfills is sufficient to discharge an obligation. It need not have a morally good motive.

Additional Recommended Reading

Atwell, John. "Ross and *Prima Facie* Duties," in *Ethics*. LXXXVIII, no. 3 (April, 1978), pp. 240-249. Although various formulations of *prima facie* duty all fail (usually because they are circular), the author attempts formulations of *prima facie* wrongness, finally finding one he maintains is not circular, is sufficiently general, and is consistent with Ross.

Broad, C. D. "Some Reflections on Moral-Sense Theories in Ethics," in *Broad's Critical Essays in Moral Philosophy*. Edited by David R. Cheney. New York: Humanities Press, 1971, pp. 188-222. Starting with ought-sentences, Broad elicits and tests forms of intuitionist theories from a moral-emotivist point of view.

Ewing, A. C. *The Definition of Good*. London, Routledge & Kegan Paul, 1948. Ewing converts to his own use Ross's notion of *prima facie* duty.

_____. "The Pursuit of the Good," in *Ethics*. New York: Macmillan Publishing Company, 1953. Ewing shows that the position of Ross on *prima facie* duty and the position of the ideal utilitarian on the intrinsic goodness of an act can be brought very close together.

Johnson, Oliver A. *Rightness and Goodness: A Study in Contemporary Ethical Theory*. The Hague, The Netherlands: Martinus Nijhoff, 1959. A study of recent ethical theory to extract the valuable contributions of the intuitionistic deontologists while not embracing their doctrine.

Muirhead, John H. *Rule and End in Morals*. Freeport, New York: Books for Libraries Press, 1969. Historical and critical comment on the revolt against idealistic ethics culminating in Ross; elicits seven principles for a synthesis of the opposing positions.

Rosen, Bernard. "In Defense of W. D. Ross," in *Ethics*. LXXVIII, no. 3 (April, 1968), pp. 237-241. Alleges that Strawson's attack upon Ross (see below) is totally ineffective because Strawson misreads Ross.

Stocker, Michael. "Rightness and Goodness: Is There a Difference?," in *American Philosophical Quarterly*. X, no. 2 (April, 1973), pp. 87-98. Rather than joining the controversy over whether "good" is derived from "right," or the reverse, the author asserts that there is no moral difference, centering his argument against the antiaxiological argument on Ross's statement of it.

Strawson, P. F. "Ethical Intuitionism," in *Readings in Ethical Theory*. Edited by Wilfrid Sellars and John Hospers. Appleton-Century-Crofts, 1952. Succinct criticism of ethical intuitionism cast in the form of dialogue.

THE LOGIC OF SCIENTIFIC DISCOVERY

Author: Sir Karl R. Popper (1902-   )
Type of work: Philosophy of science and epistemology
First published: 1935 (German); 1959 (English)

Principal Ideas Advanced

The method of testing in the empirical sciences is characterized, not by inductive inference, but by deducing empirically testable claims from proposed theories.

Falsification, not verification, is crucial in science.

Scientific propositions are to be distinguished from nonscientific in that only the former are empirically falsifiable.

The asymmetry between verification and falsification makes it possible for a falsification criterion to succeed where the verification principle failed.

A scientist proposing a theory must state the conditions under which it will be appropriate to reject it.

Karl R. Popper's *The Logic of Scientific Discovery*, described by N. R. Hansen as without doubt one of the most important books ever written on the philosophy of science and by P. B. Medawar as "one of the most important documents of the twentieth century," begins with a consideration of the problem of induction. An inference is inductive, Popper explains, if it moves from a singular statement (roughly, a statement whose subject term refers to some particular concrete thing) to one or more universal statements (roughly, statements whose subject terms refer to all the members of a class of things). In science, such inferences occur when one passes from descriptions of particular experimental results to hypotheses or theories alleged to be justified by these results. *All observed swans have been white* sums up a set of particular statements which report observations of concrete particular items. *All swans are white* expresses a universal statement one might inductively infer from that summary.

Notoriously, Popper notes, such inferences are not deductively valid, and *the problem of induction* is the question of whether such inferences are ever rationally legitimate, and if so under what conditions. One widely held view, Popper notes, is that the universal statements which express natural laws, or laws of science, or well-confirmed scientific theories, or the like, are known by experience; that is, singular statements are statements known by experience from which the natural-law-expressing universal statements may somehow legitimately be derived. Hence, in this view, the problem of induction has some proper solution.

This alleged solution, Popper continues, is often expressed in terms of a *principle* of induction—a proposition known to be true which can be placed in inferences from singular to universal scientific statements and whose presence in such inference renders the inference rationally compelling. Some philosophers, Hans Reichenbach among them, have held that without some principle of induction, science would be without decision procedure and could no longer distinguish solid theory from superstition.

This alleged principle of induction, Popper notes, cannot be a logical truth or a statement true by virtue of its very form or structure (because no such proposition would legitimately lead one from *All observed A's are B* to *All A's are B*, or from singular to universal statement in any other case). It must rather be synthetic, or not contradictory to deny. How, though, Popper asks—consciously restating an argument offered by David Hume—shall we rationally justify our acceptance of this principle? It must be not a singular but a universal statement. We cannot certify its truth by logic alone. If, then, we try to justify it from experience we shall again face the very sort of derivation of universal from singular statements the principle itself was meant to sanction, and so on *ad infinitum* if we appeal to a higher-order inductive principle. Perhaps, as Reichenbach contends, an inductive principle is accepted by "the whole of science"; but, Popper asks, cannot "the whole of science" err? Nor, Popper continues, will it do to say that singular statements, while they do not *entail* universal conclusions, nevertheless render such conclusions probable, for then we should need some principle of probability, and while perhaps this would differ in content from a principle of induction, its justification would present exactly similar difficulties. Thus it is clear that Popper completely rejects the familiar inductivist view that, while not rendering universal statements certain or providing conclusive justification for them, true singular statements can provide good reason for universal statements or render them (at least to some degree) probable. Popper argues that, if some degree N of probability is to be assigned to statements based on inductive inference of some sort, then some sort of principle of induction must be somehow justified. How this is to be done remains utterly problematic, even if one weakens the alleged relationship between singular premise and universal conclusion ("providing some degree of reliability" replacing "inductively justifies") or the alleged status of the conclusion ("probable" replacing "true"). Other attempts to shore up induction, Popper feels, are equally unsuccessful.

Obviously, Popper also rejects the views that induction *needs* no justification and that universal statements are merely, albeit perhaps infinite, conjuncts of singular statements. In this respect, Popper's view agrees with an acid (but not for that reason incorrect) remark by Bertrand Russell to the effect that there are two kinds of reasoning: deductive and bad.

Rejection of inductive reasoning, Popper holds, involves much gain and no loss. Obviously, however, if he rejects inductive inferences and hence inductive confirmation of theories, Popper must replace this account of scientific method by some other. It is this positive, constructive task that is the central topic of *The Logic of Scientific Discovery.*

The basic task of the scientist, Popper contends, is to put forward, and then test, theories. Part of this task, of course, is the invention of theories, a matter Popper holds "neither to call for logical analysis nor to be susceptible of it." Study of the conditions, activities, and stages included in the invention of theories, he holds, is a matter for psychology, not philosophy. Philosophy, or the "logic of knowledge" as opposed to its psychology, is concerned with the *testing* part of the scientist's task.

This testing procedure, Popper tells us, begins by deducing consequences from the theory being tested; the theory, in effect, becomes a premise from which conclusions are deductively derived. This done, Popper continues, four lines of testing may be distinguished, First, the conclusions may be compared among themselves; this provides something of a test as to the internal consistency of the theory. Second, the conclusions may be examined to see if the theory has any empirical consequences, and so is scientific as opposed to tautological. Third, the conclusions may be compared to those of other theories to see whether the theory, if it survived empirical tests, is such that its acceptance would mean scientific advance. Fourth, the empirical conclusions or predictions, if any, are applied to experimental results to see if what the theory tells us will occur really does occur.

It is this fourth line of testing which is central for Popper. It is the *new* empirical consequences of a theory—empirical conclusions which follow from it but not from hitherto-accepted theories—that gain the assessor's attention. These predictions are compared with the results of relevant experiments, old or new; if the predictions of what would happen under certain circumstances are not correct descriptions of what did happen under those conditions, the theory, Popper notes, is falsified. (The form of deductive inference involved here is the simple and standard *modus tollens*: if p entails q, and q is false, then p is false.) If the predictions are correct, then the theory is (so far) verified. A theory which, often tested, is not falsified is *corroborated*, although this is fundamentally a matter of *not having been falsified*. This doctrine of testing procedure raises various questions, some of which we will discuss shortly. What Popper emphasizes most, however, is that the procedure outlined above contains no inductive procedures whatever, and yet—*contra* Reichenbach—does not leave the scientist, or the philosopher of science, without rational decision procedure when faced with a choice between incompatible theories.

Popper's "criterion of demarcation" requires that a genuinely scientific hypothesis must be (in principle) empirically falsifiable. Popper regards distinguishing the nonscientific (including what is logical, or mathematical, or metaphysical) from the scientific—a task he designates "the problem of demarcation"—as an epistemological problem, perhaps the most basic one. He holds that appeal to inductive reasoning provides no solution to this problem, and that his own testing-through-attempting-to-falsify account of scientific decision procedure solves it.

In contrast to traditional (for example, Humean) empiricism, which recognized as scientific only concepts analyzable in terms of sensory phenomena, Popper holds that statements, not concepts, are the basic elements of scientific theories. In contrast to contemporary empiricism, which at least to some degree replaced analysis of concepts by analysis of statements, but recognized as scientific only statements derivable from (or reducible to) elementary perceptual claims, Popper holds that any statement which entails a proposition which describes a possible experimental or observational result is scientific, whether it is itself entailed by some set of elementary perceptual claims. ("Scientific" here does not mean "part of science," and certainly not "true," but something like "within the scope of scientific interest." One might say that mathematical claims are those which, whether true or false, fall within the domain of mathematics in that they are decidable by its procedures; then one is using the word "mathematical" in a sense analogous to that in which "scientific" is used above.)

Popper is quite candid about a feature of his view which has given others pause. His criterion of demarcation, he admits, rests, if not securely, then at least squarely, on a *convention*. He distinguishes science from nonscience, he tells us, not on the basis of some discernible intrinsic difference between scientific and nonscientific propositions, but on the basis, in effect, of a decision that the science/nonscience distinction be made along the line of demarcation. This decision, he admits, is not beyond rational dispute; but he adds that any such dispute can be only among those who share his purposes, and whether one does that or not, he holds, *is* beyond rational dispute. Thus if Popper succeeds in marking off what is of scientific interest from what is not, he feels he will have been triumphant. The logical positivists, he contends, shared his purpose but, by appealing to the verification principle (which, roughly, asserts that a sentence has truth value only if it is either a tautology or is empirically confirmable or disconfirmable) as their principle of demarcation, failed to provide a basis for distinguishing science from metaphysics. The core of their failure, Popper suggests, is found in their acceptance of induction as a confirmation method. By contrast, and without claiming anything about whether metaphysical propositions have truth value, Popper holds that his own criterion does mark out the desired distinction. If one has some other end in mind, there is neither reason nor need to suppose his criterion will serve that end.

Popper, then, views science as an empirical theoretical system—a system of synthetic or nontautological statements which represents not only a possible but also our actual world of experience. That a system does represent our world is guaranteed only by its having been exposed to unsuccessful falsification attempts. This, Popper notes, falls short of the ideal of such philosophers as Moritz Schlick and Friedrich Waismann who require that meaningful statements be conclusively verifiable or in principle determined as true; it replaces this ideal by another —that a scientific statement be capable of being refuted by experience. Lest this seem to trivialize natural laws, Popper points out that the more ways there are of refuting a proposition, or the more ways there are of its going wrong, then the more information the proposition contains. Information content waxes proportionate to falsifiability potential.

The falsification strategy, Popper notes, is made possible by an asymmetry between verification and falsification; that a proposition cannot be verified or established does not entail that it cannot be falsified or refuted, and that a proposition can be falsified does not entail that it can be verified. Further, while even if we limit ourselves to propositions with empirical content, while no set of singular statements will entail a universal statement, a universal statement will entail singular statements. The failure of the verification principle, Popper asserts, is no reason to expect the falsification criterion to suffer a similar fate.

A complication, if not a problem, arises, however, when we note that, as Pierre Duhem and W. V. O. Quine have emphasized, rarely if ever does a theory all by itself entail any predictions; it does so only together with auxiliary hypotheses. Schematically, one has not that H (theory) entails P (prediction), but that T and H (auxiliary hypothesis) entails P. If, then, one deduces P from T and H, and discovers that under the relevant controlled experimental conditions, P turns out to be false, various alternatives remain open. One could reject the rule of inference by which P was derived, or claim that the experiment was not properly conducted, or deny that one's perception of the result was correct, although these alternatives may often seem (and be) radical. Or one could reject T, or else H. If one rejects H, one can retain T without recourse to any of the other alternatives noted. If one always rejects the auxiliary hypotheses, no theories will ever be falsified. To put it mildly, this would be inconvenient for Popper's perspective.

Popper, of course, is fully aware of the problem. To meet it, he specifies that, when a member of a scientific community proffers a theory, he or she also is to specify the conditions under which the theory itself (and not some other proposition, be it auxiliary hypothesis or whatever) is to be abandoned. In such fashion, those who play the game of science must be prepared to say when they will admit defeat.

Popper maintains that his view provides for the objectivity of scientific theories which, he contends, lies in their being intersubjectively testable. If science is to have an empirical basis, he continues, the propositions comprising this basis must themselves be objective, and hence intersubjectively testable. Thus they must entail predictions, and so on *ad infinitum* so that science can contain no ultimate statements. The infinite regress thus produced, he argues, is not vicious; true, every claim can be tested and testing must stop somewhere so that some claim is accepted which is not tested—some claims will be accepted as correct observational reports without their having run a falsification gauntlet. But this, Popper reminds us, violates no tenet of his philosophy of science, and (in principle) one can test any proposition one wishes. The net effect of this is that scientific knowledge is possible without its being required to rest on allegedly indubitable propositions. Popper explicitly rejects the view that science is comprised of propositions about which we are rightly epistemically certain—about which it is logically impossible that we are wrong—and his methodology in philosophy of science rules out science's having, or needing, indubitable foundations. In this important respect, as in others, he differs from classical empiricism.

It has been claimed that what Popper says often seems simple, even obvious. Perhaps it often is; but then it was not "obvious" until he said it. The above summary of Popper's views probably does not give much hint of their breadth and depth. A sense of that comes on the one hand from knowing something of the intellectual landscape he occupied—the issues and problems he dealt with and the light he threw on them—and on the other hand from reading the rich detail of *The Logic of Scientific Discovery* and the later *Conjectures and Refutations*.

Pertinent Literature

Toulmin, Stephen. "Conclusion: The Cunning of Reason," *Human Understanding*. Vol. I. Princeton, New Jersey: Princeton University Press, 1972.

Stephen Toulmin in *Human Understanding* (as we shall see) deals with some of the same fundamental issues as Karl R. Popper does in *The Logic of Scientific Discovery*, so it is natural that Toulmin should discuss Popper's views. Toulmin argues that in science as well as in ethics the actual cultural diversity of human concepts, cross-culturally and historically, poses an intractable problem for those who view *rationality* as a property of particular propositional or conceptual systems. In this view, scientific rationality is a matter of inference within scientific theories, and the history of science becomes a story of one system of propositions being succeeded by another.

Recently, Toulmin reports, philosophers have sought to extend the notion of rationality beyond the meaning provided to it by formal logic, and to develop this notion in such a way that it has application to contexts involving conceptual change. Among such philosophers are Popper, as well as Thomas Kuhn and Imre Lakatos. His own view, Toulmin notes, might be seen as fitting within this general perspective, but Toulmin finds that his own argument, in one fundamental way at least, opposes the tendency these other philosophers share. Popper and the others, Toulmin reports, begin by taking a formal logician's perspective on science, and thus they find conceptual change somewhat anomalous. Toulmin rejects this choice of a beginning, as well as the consequences he takes to follow from it.

This view, Toulmin suggests, involves a confusion or makes a mistaken identification; it misconstrues the nature of rationality. Toulmin contends that instead of being identified with a property of conceptual systems, rationality should be seen in terms of the procedures by means of which persons change from one set of beliefs or concepts to another. Failure to do this—or continuing to view (scientific) rationality as a matter of inference within scientific systems—Toulmin argues, has led to viewing the basis for choosing between scientific systems to be not rational judgment but pragmatic preference.

Popper's treatment of the logic of scientific research, Toulmin notes, focuses on problems of formal proof or disproof. He held, Toulmin continues, that the universal and timeless criterion which any genuine scientific hypothesis must meet is that of being falsifiable by experience. Rational progress in science is for Popper a matter of elimination of hypotheses. Toulmin adds that although Popper later modified his position to the extent that hypotheses may achieve a degree of positive corroboration, having some higher status than merely failing to be rejected, it is still *whether propositions are acceptable*, rather than *whether concepts are applicable*, that is Popper's concern. Ultimately, Toulmin contends, Popper imposes on science a procedure not drawn from within its own procedures and proposes a definition of the scientific which is ultimately arbitrary.

One consequence of this approach, Toulmin contends, is that lines of theoretical advance, although justified in themselves, are closed off because they do not conform to the (arbitrary) criterion for being scientific. Paul Feyerabend, Toulmin reminds us, has strongly protested against this aspect, as he sees it, of Popper's thought.

If one is committed to making rationality a characteristic not of procedures of conceptual change but of systems of substantive scientific propositions, the only alternative to Popper's own account, Toulmin suggests, is to pay closer attention than does Popper to the actual history of science—to what scientists as scientists have actually done—and hope to discern in this history some illumination concerning scientific rationality. This, Toulmin says, Lakatos and Kuhn, each in his own way, has done. Toulmin is not satisfied, however, that either has succeeded in providing a satisfactory account of scientific rationality.

Lakatos, Toulmin finds, simply continues Popper's argument, discussing the history of science in terms taken over from formal logic. Even though Lakatos stresses the importance of the actual history of science (Toulmin thinks that Popper's interest in historical episodes does not prevent his philosophy of science from being fundamentally ahistorical), his shared beginnings with Popper lead him to expect, Toulmin contends, "knock-down dialectical victories" in scientific, and particularly in philosophy-of-science, disputes. Further, Toulmin continues, while Lakatos goes so far as to say that if a demarcation criterion is inconsistent with what practicing scientists will accept as the distinction between what is and what is not scientific, then the demarcation criterion should be rejected, he does not make clear how his own criterion (based on the notion of a research program) is concretely to be applied to actual instances so as to tell what is and what is not scientifically rational. In particular, Toulmin contends, we are not told how to recognize when even majority scientific opinion, or the judgment of the "scientific elite," is mistaken; nor are we given the grounds on which such judgment should be overturned.

Toulmin finds Kuhn's position, which he claims shares Popper's sort of starting point although it differs from Popper's view in important ways, is also a failure in its endeavor to offer a satisfactory account of scientific rationality. The core of Kuhn's position, according to Toulmin, involves appeal to *what scientists normally do*, and he finds this ambiguous between *what scientists habitually do* and *what scientists properly do*. The former meaning, Toulmin contends, leads to relativism and provides no appeal beyond sheer scientific practice. The latter meaning, he adds, has Kuhn depending on criteria such as maximum predictive accuracy, and thus imposing on scientific procedures standards not discovered from a study of actual scientific endeavors.

Toulmin, then, finds Popper's own approach to scientific rationality, as well as that of Lakatos and Kuhn, whom he sees as sharing Popper's starting point, to be inadequate. His basic purpose in *Human Understanding* is to provide his own alternative account.

Lakatos, Imre. "Popper on Demarcation and Induction," in *The Methodology of Scientific Research Programmes*. Edited by John Worrall and Gregory Currie. Cambridge: Cambridge University Press, 1978, pp. 139-167.

Imre Lakatos claims that Karl R. Popper's ideas represent "the most important development in the philosophy of the twentieth century," and compares his accomplishment to David Hume's, Immanuel Kant's, and William Whewell's. Popper, he reports, discussed two basic problems in *The Logic of Scientific Discovery*—the problem of demarcation and the problem of induction; the second problem, Popper contended, was an "instance or facet" of the former, although Lakatos disagrees with this. Lakatos reports that, according to Popper, the logic of scientific discovery is comprised of a set of rules for appraisal of already-stated theories; the rules are tentative and cannot be mechanically applied.

Given Popper's work, Lakatos notes, the term "normative" in the expression "normative philosophy of science" has come to refer not to rules for coming up with solutions, but to rules for appraising solutions. Popper, he continues, proposed that a theory should be taken seriously only when a crucial experiment has been devised for it, and rejected when it fails such an experiment. Thus theories are not established or made probable, but rather are eliminated, by appeal to experience; clash with, not confirmation by, experience becomes central. Lakatos thus describes the history of science, viewed in Popperian terms, as a duel between theories and experiences in which experiences can win but theories can only survive.

What is actually tested, as Lakatos tells us Popper was aware, is not isolated statements, or even isolated theories, but clusters of theories. (The relevance of this is that if theories Tl, T2, T3 and T4 together lead to the conclusion that x will happen under condition C, and x does not happen under C, then, barring some error of inference or experiment, we must reject TI, or T2, or T3, or T4. But we do not yet know *which*.)

Lakatos reports Popper's view to be that we must decide, in advance of running a crucial experiment, which claim or theory will be abandoned if the experiment fails (that is, does not come out as the current theories require)—even should this involve a guess agreed upon by scientists. Such guesses are crucial to Popper's theory; moreover, they must be guesses as to what components of theories, not what statements of initial conditions, shall be rejected. This is required, Lakatos explains, because if whenever a theory entails that, under certain initial conditions, something x will happen, and x in fact does not occur under those conditions, we allow ourselves always to say that the descriptions of initial conditions were at fault (the actual initial conditions only *seemed* to fit the description of those under which, according to the theory, x would occur), then we shall never refute or eliminate any theory. Thus, Lakatos continues, Popper requires that a scientist who wishes his theories to be taken seriously to specify in advance of running them what crucial experiments there are whose failure to go as their theories requires will bring them to abandon those theories—and to abandon the basic assumptions they involve. This rule, he suggests, is basic among the conventions which, for Popper, define the "game of science."

Pursuing the metaphor, Lakatos notes that the opening move in the game involved the presentation of a logically consistent hypothesis or theory which, under agreed-upon conditions, would be falsified. The proposition, Lakatos continues, which expresses the experimental results which would falsify the hypothesis or theory is a *basic* proposition, and there must be unanimous agreement within the scientific community that some experimental results will yield knowledge as to the truth value of the basic statement. Then the crucial experiment is repeatedly run. If, Lakatos tells us, the experiment goes as the theory requires, the theory is corroborated, which only means that it lives to duel again; if it goes otherwise, it is falsified. Should there not be unanimity as to whether the results went as the theory requires, then either the hypothesis is withdrawn, or a new basic proposition is formulated; or perhaps unanimity is purchased at the price of expulsion from the scientific community of the members as one side in the dispute.

Lakatos adds that if a theory is falsified, its replacement must explain whatever success its predecessor had—account for what its predecessor succeeded in accounting for. Further, Lakatos explains,

it must contain new empirical content over its predecessor. Once a new hypothesis of the indicated sort has been preferred, it is tested. Science, Lakatos indicates, progresses, in Popper's view, in the sense that the replacing hypotheses have more empirical content and pose deeper questions about the world than those they replace.

Lakatos' presentation makes it clear that Popper rests the demarcation of science from nonscience on conventions or (nominalistic) definitions. Popper suggests that only those who agree on what constitutes the purpose of science will be able to develop a rational procedure for assessing his conventions or definitions; and Popper, in turn, Lakatos explains, views the adoption of such purposes as nonrational, or beyond the scope of argument. Lakatos adds that Popper never specifies a purpose for the game of science that transcends the rules of that game, nor does he provide a procedure for assessing one logically consistent set of rules over another. Popper proposed, for the first time in 1957, Lakatos indicates, that the goal of science is truth, but in *The Logic of Scientific Discovery* this was classified as a (psychological) motive of scientists, "not a rational *purpose* of science." Thus, Lakatos contends, Popper has no theory of how noncontradictory conventions are to be assessed. Putting the matter in Popperian terms, Lakatos remarks that Popper has not told us under what conditions he would abandon his own criterion of demarcation. Lakatos concludes his essay by endeavoring to supply what he has argued that Popper failed to provide.

Additional Recommended Reading

Kuhn, Thomas. *The Structure of Scientific Revolutions.* Chicago: University of Chicago Press, 1970. Presents a major alternate approach to Popper's.

Lakatos, Imre. *Philosophical Papers.* Edited by John Worrall and Gregory Currie. Cambridge: Cambridge University Press, 1978. Collection of essays developing a Popperian type of approach.

Lakatos, Imre and Alan Musgrave, eds. *Criticism and the Growth of Knowledge.* London: Cambridge University Press, 1970. Discussion of Kuhn's views, including a contribution by Popper.

Magee, Bryan. *Karl Popper.* New York: The Viking Press, 1973. An introduction to Popper's thought; in the *Modern Masters* series.

_____. *Modern British Philosophy.* New York: St. Martin's Press, 1971. Contains contributions by Popper.

Popper, Karl R. *Conjectures and Refutations: The Growth of Scientific Knowledge.* London: Routledge and
    Kegan Paul, 1963. An account of Popper's views; variations on the theme that we can learn from our mistakes.
Schlipp, Paul A., ed. *The Philosophy of Karl Popper* (The Library of Living Philosophers). La Salle, Illinois:
    Open Court, 1974. Thirty-three essays on Popper, plus Autobiography and Reply.

PHILOSOPHY AND LOGICAL SYNTAX

Author: Rudolf Carnap (1891-1970)
Type of work: Philosophy of philosophy
First published: 1935

Principal Ideas Advanced

Philosophy is the logical analysis of meaningful language.

Meaningful language is either the language of logic and mathematics (involving analytic sentences) or the language of science (involving empirically verifiable synthetic sentences).

Metaphysics and ethics are not legitimate parts of philosophy for their language is meaningless.

Logical analysis is logical syntax, and logical syntax is the study of the manipulation of signs in accordance with the rules of a language.

Rudolf Carnap's *Philosophy and Logical Syntax* is the substance of three lectures which he gave at the University of London in 1934. As a result, the book is short, presenting the essentials of the logical positivism of the Vienna Circle in outline form. It is perhaps as good an outline summary of the Vienna Circle views as is available, coming, as it does, from the pen of the best known—and perhaps the most influential—member of the group.

Logical positivism is certainly not an unknown movement to American and British philosophers. During the 1930's and early 1940's it seemed destined to sweep all other philosophical movements into the forgotten and insignificant areas of the past. Recent days, of course, have seen the movement called into question, but the ghost of the verifiability criterion of meaning and the emotive theory of ethics still stalks the philosophical world.

Logical positivism had its origin in a seminar conducted in the 1920's in Vienna by Moritz Schlick. A number of the members of this group, the original "Vienna Circle," were scientists reacting against those idealist philosophers who pontificated, sometimes in almost complete ignorance, about the aim and function of science. Part of positivism's program was the explicit rejection of this kind of irresponsible philosophizing. Another characteristic concern of the group was a strong interest in logic, an interest which

grew out of their admiration for the work which had been done on the foundations of mathematics toward the close of the nineteenth century and in the early twentieth century, particularly the work of Whitehead and Russell in their *Principia Mathematica* (1910-1913). These interests quite naturally led the Vienna group to deliberate regarding philosophy's proper business. They decided that philosophy is properly the analysis and clarification of meaningful language. By meaningful language they meant the language of empirical science together with the language of mathematics; all other language, they held, lacked cognitive meaning. The Vienna Circle philosophers gave expression to this conviction in their criterion of empirical meaning, a widely known and vigorously debated tenet of logical positivism.

Carnap spends the first of the three chapters of *Philosophy and Logical Syntax* discussing the implications of the verifiability criterion. At one point he states that only the propositions of mathematics and empirical science "have sense," and that all other propositions are without theoretical sense. However, he does not do much in the book with mathematical propositions—with "analytic" propositions, as positivists sometimes labeled the propositions of logic and mathematics. He spends most of his time with "synthetic" propositions; that is, with propositions whose truth value cannot be determined simply by referring to their logical form. As examples of this analytic-synthetic distinction we might consider here the two propositions: (1) "The ball is red," and (2) "Either the ball is red or the ball is not red." We cannot know whether the first one is true or false without in fact examining the ball, but we can know that the second proposition is true without looking at the ball. It is true in virtue of its logical form. A sentence which is true or false in virtue of its form alone is analytic; a sentence whose truth value is determined by the (nonlinguistic) facts is synthetic.

Carnap holds the view that the only synthetic propositions which make sense are those propositions whose truth value can be determined by consulting the evidence of sense. And these propositions, he further believes, are all to be found within the domain of empirical science. He uses the word "verification" in the usual logical positivist sense; that is to say, a proposition is verifiable if its truth value can be determined by reference to sense experience. The only synthetic propositions which make sense, then, are verifiable propositions, and these are all scientific propositions. This is the verifiability criterion of empirical meaning.

It is Carnap's view, then, that philosophy is the logical analysis of meaningful language, and meaningful language is restricted either to analytic propositions (logic and mathematics) or to empirically verifiable propositions (natural science). This theory implies that certain traditional areas of philosophy are no longer to be regarded as legitimate. Carnap rejects what he calls traditional metaphysics since it is made up of propositions which he feels are neither analytic nor empirically verifiable. As examples of such illegitimate metaphysical sentences he mentions sentences about "the real Essence of things," about "Things in themselves," about "the Absolute," and "such like." In addition, Carnap rejects traditional philosophical ethics. He believes the usual utterances of ethical philosophers—such as "Killing is wrong"—mislead people in virtue of their grammatical form. They look like propositions, and so philosophers have given arguments to show that they are either true or false. Carnap, however, believes that what is grammatically an assertion, "Killing is wrong," is logically not an assertion at all, but rather a disguised command, "Do not kill." However, commands are neither true nor false and hence cannot be propositions. Ethics, then, is necessarily ruled out of the domain of philosophy.

Ethics and metaphysics are thus ruled out of philosophy proper. But there must be something to them; otherwise why have people been so concerned about them? Here Carnap also has a simple answer. Metaphysical and ethical utterances express deep feelings and emotions. That is why people are so concerned about them. They express our emotions. But this, Carnap points out, is to say that they resemble the utterances of the lyric poet; that is, they express emotion, and they evoke a profound response in the reader, but they nevertheless do not make theoretical or cognitive sense—they are meaningless from a philosophical and scientific point of view.

But not only metaphysics and ethics suffer from Carnap's determination to rid philosophy of the senseless burden it has borne. Epistemology and psychology also suffer as a result of his reforming zeal. Insofar as there is a legitimate area of psychology, it is an empirical science which, as such, is not the philosopher's concern. And epistemology is, Carnap suspects, a hybrid of psychology and logic. Philosophers must continue to do the logic, but they should give over the psychology to the behaviorists. And now, finally, we reach the proper domain of the philosopher, after rejecting metaphysics, ethics, psychology, and epistemology. The philosopher is to do logical analysis on the language of the scientist. There can be no misunderstanding of Carnap's intention here, for he writes: "The only proper task of *Philosophy* is *Logical Analysis.*"

We should now try to determine what Carnap means by "logical analysis." As Carnap understands it, logical analysis is a concern with the logical syntax of a language. This claim needs elucidation.

In other of his writings, Carnap has taken some pains to identify what he means by logical syntax. In the *Foundations of Logic and Mathematics* (1939) he has perhaps made the distinctions most clearly. There he distinguishes pragmatics, semantics, and syntax as parts of the general philosophical concern with language which he calls "semiotic." The first distinction which needs to be made here is between language which is about language, and language which is not about language. One might, for example, assert the proposition: "The ball is red." In this case one would be using language to talk about the nonlinguistic world, to talk about a ball. But one might then go on to talk about the proposition which refers to the red ball; one might say: "The proposition 'The ball is red' has four words in it." In this case the proposition is not about objects such as red balls, but about language itself. Such language about language is called "meta-language"; language about objects is called "object language." The general theory of an object language, stated in a meta-language, is what Carnap means by "semiotic." But semiotic has three branches: pragmatics, semantics, and syntax. Pragmatics is an empirical study of three elements which can be distinguished in the use of a language—linguistic signs, the meanings (Carnap calls them "designata") of the signs, and the users of the signs. Pragmatics studies all three elements. Oversimplifying, pragmatics may be likened to the activity of an anthropologist constructing a dictionary for a tribe he is studying. The anthropologist studies and records how the tribesmen use words, how the words are spelled and combined, and what the words indicate.

Semantics is an abstraction from pragmatics. The semanticist (in the Carnapian sense—not to be confused with the so-called "General Semanticist") restricts his concern to the words or signs and their designata, their meanings. He abstracts from users to focus solely on the signs and their designata. There can be two kinds of semantics: descriptive semantics is an empirical study of signs and their matter-of-fact meanings in popular usage; pure semantics, on the other hand, is not an empirical study but a normative one which lays down rules regarding the signs and what their proper designata are. A pure semantical system is an artificial language consisting of rules specifying designata for a collection of linguistic signs. An example of a pure semantical sentence might be: "The predicate word 'large' designates the property of being large in a physical sense." This specifies how the word "large" is to be used in a given artificial language, and it implies that such common language expressions as "That's a large order" are incorrect in the semantical system in which the rule

occurs.

Syntax represents yet another level of abstraction. Pragmatics includes signs, designata, and users. Semantics ignores the users and focuses its attention solely on signs and their designata. Syntax ignores the designata of the signs as well as ignoring the users. It is concerned only with the signs and the rules in accordance with which they can be combined and manipulated. Again we may oversimplify and say that the subject matter of syntax is the traditional rules of logical deduction, provided we add that the rules are formulated in a more abstract and formal way than is customary. Very roughly speaking, then, we may say that pragmatics may be likened to making a dictionary of usage, that semantics may be likened to specifying the exact and unambiguous definitions of words in, say, a technical treatise, and that syntax may be likened to constructing a formal set of rules of logic.

In his second chapter Carnap attempts to characterize and illustrate logical syntax somewhat more fully. In the first place, he says, syntax is a "formal" theory. He means by this that syntax abstracts from all concern with the sense or meaning of the signs and confines itself strictly to the forms of the signs or words. It consists entirely of rules specifying how signs—regarded simply as shapes or designs or sounds—may be combined and manipulated. Within this formal theory there are two kinds of rules: formation rules and transformation rules. The formation rules, in effect, define what is to be regarded as a proper sentence. The ordinary man's rejection of Russell's well-known example of an ill-formed sentence—"Quadruplicity drinks procrastination"—is made in virtue of an appeal to the implicit formation rules of the English language. Ordinarily, of course, we all abide by the implicit formation rules of English. Carnap's formation rules are intended to make explicit these implicit rules that we follow. The other group of rules, the transformation rules, specify what manipulations can be performed on the well-formed sentences identified by the formation rules. The transformation rules are the rules of logical deduction expressed in syntactical terms. Carnap states that the two primitive terms in a logical syntax are "sentence" and "direct consequence." That is to say, syntax is concerned to identify what are proper sentences and also to specify how we are to draw their logical consequences.

There are other important syntactical terms in addition to "sentence" and "direct consequence," however. Carnap spends a fair amount of time in the second chapter defining and illustrating these additional syntactical terms. He defines "valid" as the property a sentence has if it is a direct consequence of the null class of premises. Putting this into a different logical terminology, we could say that a proposition which is validly inferred from tautologies is itself a tautology; Carnap means by "valid" what is often called "tautologous." Carnap then defines "contravalid" so that it corresponds to the usual notion of self-contradiction. These two classes of sentences, the valid and the contravalid, make up the class of "determinate" sentences; all other sentences (sometimes called "contingent sentences" by other logicians) are called "indeterminate. "

The syntactical transformation rules serve to isolate the valid and contravalid sentences. These rules are called "L-rules" by Carnap. But there are other inferences that may be made which depend, not on these logical rules, but on certain laws of natural science; for example, Newton's laws or the laws of thermodynamics. Scientific laws, such as these, which also serve to justify drawing the consequences of sentences, Carnap calls "P-rules" to distinguish them from the L-rules. Carnap is then able to distinguish additional kinds of sentences; namely, P-valid and P-contravalid sentences.

Other additional terms are defined in this second chapter. Enough have been mentioned here, however, to enable us to see what it is that Carnap is up to. He is making many of the usual distinctions and defining many of the usual terms of traditional logic. But he is doing it in a slightly different way from that characteristic of traditional logic. He has avoided the usual basic logical terms "true" and "false," since they depend on the question of the meaning of the propositions which are said to be either true or false. He has also avoided the usual logical term "implication," and has replaced it with "direct consequence." All of this is intentional and novel. Carnap sees it as being implied by his defi-

nition of syntax as a *formal* theory. He can describe a language and lay down rules for manipulating it without ever dealing with the question of the meaning of the words and sentences, and, consequently,without ever worrying about what the subject matter is that the language deals with. He is not doing physics or chemistry or biology; rather, he is manipulating symbols, symbols which might be assigned meanings later on so that they become words and sentences in a theory of chemistry or physics or biology. But, as Carnap sees it, he has sharply separated the work of the philosopher-logician from the work of the scientist. Furthermore, abstracting from the meanings of the words and sentences enables the philosopher-logician to concentrate on the properly logical matters and avoid the tangles that often impede progress in the sciences. Best of all, he has, as a philosopher-logician, a legitimate activity in which to engage, one which benefits the scientist and which also circumvents the morasses of much traditional philosophy.

Just how Carnap feels he has avoided the morasses of traditional philosophy is best seen by looking at his discussion of what he calls "pseudo-object sentences." (In his *The Logical Syntax of Language*, 1934, he calls these "quasi-syntactical sentences.") Carnap feels that many times philosophers have combined syntactical predicates with nonsyntactical subjects. The result is neither one thing nor another; they are not statements in the object language, nor are they statements in the metalanguage. They are, however, responsible for many of the disputes of traditional metaphysics about the reality or nonreality of entities such as universals. One example will perhaps illustrate Carnap's distinction fairly clearly. He distinguishes three sentences:

(1) The rose is red.	A real object-sentence in the material mode of speech
(2) The rose is a thing.	A pseudo-object sentence
(3) The word "rose" is a thing-word.	A syntactical sentence in the formal mode of speech

No disputes arise over the first sentence. It is a sensible sentence which everyone understands and knows how to handle. Nor do disputes arise over the third sentence. Most people do not speak this way, but when they do (that is, when they are philosophical syntacticians), they make sense and avoid confusion. Unfortunately, philosophers have too often spoken in the manner of the second sentence. They then believe they are speaking about roses, and they begin debating and defining, getting further and further mired in the morass of bogus entities. One should speak either with the vulgar about red roses or with the sophisticated about thing-words. But one should beware of speaking with the metaphysicians about rose-things.

Pseudo-object sentences are likely to give rise to pseudo-questions. This is the burden of the final chapter of Carnap's book. Logical positivism offers hope, he feels, for genuine progress in philosophy because it identifies the errors of earlier philosophies, and it provides a technique for avoiding them. The problem of universals, for example, is not a real problem; it is a pseudo-problem which results from confusing the "formal mode" of speech and the "material mode" of speech, from being deceived by pseudo-object sentences such as 'The rose is a thing." We should speak in the formal mode about "predicate words"; we should not speak in the material mode about universals as things.

The position Carnap states in *Philosophy and Logical Syntax* has been stated much more fully in other of his works, especially in his earlier *The Logical Syntax of Language*. In some of his later works he has also modified some of his earlier views——most notably, perhaps, by admitting semantics to philosophical legitimacy along with syntax. But in its essentials the position is as stated in *Philosophy and Logical Syntax*. It is a view which has influenced contemporary philosophy greatly, and it is a view which is genuinely novel—a notable achievement in as ancient a discipline as philosophy. It probably has not had the influence outside philosophy which the intrinsic merit of the position deserves. This lack of widespread influence is quite probably the result of Carnap's tendency, in his more extended writing, to use a formidable and forbidding battery of technical apparatus including strange terms and Gothic script. He unfortunately has not completely rid himself of a Germanic fascination with architectonics and a tendency to identify the profound with the unfamiliar. He has also suffered from a tendency to oversimplify and trivialize the views he opposes. One can understand his rejection of the excesses of some idealist philosophers, but one finds it hard to move from that to the simple "resolution" of the problems the idealists wrestled with which defines them out of existence as "pseudo-problems." But when all is said about Carnap's lack of understanding and sympathy for any philosophical problems other than his own, one must still acknowledge the great skill he has brought to bear on the problems that did interest him. Carnap is a great innovator and an original thinker of enormous stature; one can forgive him if he is not the best twentieth century historian of philosophy. And when the history of twentieth century philosophy is written, surely Carnap's attempt to develop a logic which does not rest on any prior theory of meaning will be given a most prominent place, and deservedly so.

Pertinent Literature

Quine, Willard Van Orman. "Two Dogmas of Empiricism," in *From a Logical Point of View*. New York: Harper & Row Publishers, 1963.

Modern empiricism, Willard Van Orman Quine suggests, has to a significant degree been founded on two assumptions. One, he says, is that there is a basic bifurcation between analytic truths (grounded in meanings) and synthetic truths (grounded in fact). The other (not our concern here) is reductionism—the view that each meaningful claim is constructed out of terms which refer to immediate experience. Quine rejects both; our concern will be with his critique of the former dogma.

Quine reminds us that David Hume distinguished between relations of ideas and matters of fact, Immanuel Kant between analytic and synthetic propositions, and Gottfried Wilhelm Leibniz between truths of reason and truths of fact. Leibniz held that truths of reason are true in all possible worlds, Quine notes, adding that this is tantamount to saying that they cannot be false. Analytic statements, Quine adds, are said to be those which have self-contradictory denials, although insofar as the concept of *being self-contradictory* is wide enough to serve the purpose of marking off analyticity, it is itself in equal need of clarification. Quine's view is that these various ways of marking off the analytic from the synthetic fail to do so with sufficient clarity to justify the dogma concerning them.

Kant's distinction, Quine argues, treats an analytic statement as one whose predicate conceptually contains nothing not already contained in its subject, and is thereby twice defective in that it applies only to subject-predicate statements, leaving the metaphor of containment unanalyzed.

With regard to singular terms, *meaning*, Quine contends, is one thing; *naming* another (as "nine" and "the number of planets" share referent but not meaning). An analogous distinction, he adds, arises with respect to predicates or general terms; general terms do not name, but are true of, items—the items a term is true of being its extension. But the extension of a general term is to be distinguished from its meaning, or intension, Quine insists, illustrating his point with the extensional identity and intensional distinctness of "creature with kidneys" and "creature with a heart."

Quine finds it a short step from distinguishing between meaning and reference, and theory of meaning and theory of reference, to viewing the theory of meaning as primarily focusing on analyticity of statements and synonymy of linguistic forms, and rejecting meanings as "obscure entities." So, Quine suggests, consideration of the (thus purified) theory of meaning leads us back to problems concerning analyticity.

Propositions viewed as analytic, Quine suggests, fall into two classes. One class is comprised of logical truths, such as *No unmarried man is married;* such truths remain true no matter what interpretation we give to their nonlogical components. The other class is composed of statements such as *No bachelor is married*—which can be turned into logical truths by trading synonym for synonym. But the content of

"synonymous" is not more lucid than that of "analytic."

Rudolf Carnap, Quine notes, has explained analyticity in terms of "state-descriptions." A state-description is a complete assignment of truth-values (truth or falsity) to each atomic or noncompound statement of a language. Carnap assumes, Quine explains, that the truth values of compound statements in a language will be functions of the truth values of their components, and a statement is analytic if it remains true under every state description.

Quine points out that this rendition of analyticity succeeds only insofar as the atomic sentences of the language are logically independent, unlike, say, *Suzy is a spinster* and *Suzy is not married*. Without this qualification, one could assign *true* to *Suzy is a spinster* and *false* to *Suzy is not married*, so that *No spinster is married* becomes, not analytic, but synthetic. Thus, Quine continues, the state-description account of analyticity will do only for languages "devoid of extralogical synonym pairs" of the sort exemplified by *Suzy is a spinster* and *Suzy is not married*. Quine suggests that the net result is that the state-description criterion provides an account of logical truth, not of analyticity generally. Carnap, Quine reports, is not unaware of this, and uses his state-description account as a tool for approaching topics in probability and induction. Quine's point is that the state-description account could not be proffered as a successful general account of analyticity.

Appeal to definition—"an *analytic* statement is one true by definition"—Quine argues, will not help, since definitions other than stipulative depend on already recognized but quite unanalyzed synonomy. Passing over Quine's discussion, and rejection, of the "interchangeable in all contexts without change of truth value" criterion for synonomy, we now consider Quine's treatment of Carnapian strategies regarding analyticity.

It is sometimes suggested, Quine remarks, that problems in separating analytic from synthetic statements arise from vagueness in natural language which could be removed by the precision of artificial language. A statement S will then be *analytic for* a language L, and, Quine notes, the problem then becomes giving sense to *S is analytic for L*.

Carnap's work on artificial languages and semantical rules, Quine suggests, is the natural place to look for help in this regard. Quine argues as follows. Suppose we have an artificial language L^* such that L^*'s semantical rules explicitly specify all of L^*'s analytic statements; they tell us that only such-and-such statements are the analytic statements of L^*. Then the rules will contain the as-yet-not-understood term "analytic." To grasp "A statement is analytic for L^* if and only if. . .," (where some specific analysis fills in the dots) we must first (where S and L, in contrast to L^* are, not constants, but variables) understand "S is analytic for L." Hence, Quine concludes, appeal to a Carnapian artificial language whose semantical rules specify the language's analytic statements does not provide a proper analysis of analyticity.

Alternatively, Carnap continues, one could view the semantical rule, not as specifying analytic sentences of L^*, but as a conventional definition of the simple symbol *analytic-for-L*. But this, Quine contends, will define neither *analytic,* nor *analytic for,* nor will it explicate "S is analytic for L," where S and L are variables—not even if we restrict the range of L to artificial languages.

Again, Quine suggests, we might appeal to the fact that analytic statements at least must be true, and consider a semantical rule R which simply states that such-and-such statements (along with others unspecified) are true. A statement may then be said to be analytic provided that it is not only true but also true according to R. But then, Quine claims, we must contend not with "analytic" but with "semantical rule," which is as yet unexplained. Were every rule that says that some statements are true to count as a semantical rule, Quine reports, one could easily turn all truths into analytic ones in the sense just characterized, thus ruining the strategy for marking off analytic from synthetic statements. Semantic rules, Quine suggests, at least so far as the present alternative goes, are but those which appear on a page beneath the meaningless heading "Semantical Rules."

In these (and other) ways Quine argues that appeals to semantical rules and artificial languages fail to provide a clear content to, or basis for, a clear division of all statements into the analytic, or else the synthetic, type. Indeed, he contends, that any such distinction to be made is a piece of unestablished empiricist dogma.

Bohnert, Herbert. "Carnap's Theory of Definition and Analyticity," in *The Philosophy of Rudolf Carnap* (The Library of Living Philosophers). Edited by Paul A. Schilpp. La Salle, Illinois: Open Court, 1963, pp. 407-430.

That there is a sharp division between analytic sentences and synthetic sentences, Herbert Bohnert notes, has been dubbed (by Willard Van Orman Quine) one of the "two dogmas of empiricism." Rudolf Carnap accepted the dogma, and his way of developing the distinction has had great influence among empiricists.

Bohnert holds that the analytic-synthetic distinction, while historically important and progressively more clearly articulated, was not made with precision until the late nineteenth century. One reason for this was that, at times, the motive for precision was weak, in that analytic propositions basically were discussed only to contrast them unfavorably with empirical propositions, as in John Locke and John Stuart Mill, or to distinguish them from alleged other sorts of necessary although nonanalytic claims, as in Immanuel Kant. The growth of a mathematical edifice housed with paradoxical and imaginary entities but lacking rigorous analysis was unfavorable to the offering of a lucid criterion for analyticity, as was the inclusion of geometry within mathematics, given a natural dependence on visualization in geometrical thinking. Another factor contributing to lack of precision, Bohnert notes, was the rise of psychologism, which involves taking propositions to be mental acts of judgment and supposes that such terms as "true," "valid," and "analytic" apply to states of mind, thus, in effect, putting off attempts to give precision to the notion of analyticity until the mind was better understood and, more importantly, sanctioning the mistaken view that analyticity was more a matter of psychology than of logic.

Then, Bohnert continues, mathematical analysis

was scrutinized and purified, logic took great steps forward in the work of Gottlob Frege and Bertrand Russell, among others, and the view, proffered by David Hume, that mathematics did not include matters of empirical fact was reinforced by the effort to reduce mathematics to logic. Further, the creation of logically consistent non-Euclidean geometrics produced a sharp distinction between a postulate system and its interpretation, and the relativistic revolution in physics, which seemed to show that what had appeared to be self-evident geometrical truths were actually false empirical claims, distinguished geometry from the rest of mathematics. Geometrical claims, Bohnert reports, were viewed as synthetic by some, and analytic by others, of the interpretations of the systems in which they resided. The development of the concept of a (formal) language, and of the distinction between a (first order) language and a metalanguage (or second order language), matters which received their fullest treatment at Carnap's hands, provided a full escape from psychologism by replacing judgments with sentences. Carnap, then, Bohnert notes, endeavored to develop a rigorous and consistent empiricism which accounted for necessity in mathematics and limited the role of convention in the sciences. This program, Bohnert reports, required a sharp and rigid analytic-versus-synthetic bifurcation. Bohnert adds that Carnap's development of this distinction came in two stages—one syntactical, one semantical.

The first stage, Bohnert explains, was comprised by the attempt to analyze analyticity by means of reference to an uninterpreted language or formal calculus. Bohnert indicates that it had become possible to represent inferences in a way that made it clear that they depended on logical structure rather than meaning, and that this, plus the increase in rigor a formal approach made possible, motivated Carnap to develop his syntactic strategy, as did the goal of avoiding all empirical content and reference. Also important, Bohnert adds, was the refutation of Ludwig Wittgenstein's allegation that discourse about language involved one in an effort to say what could not be said; in sharp contrast to the Wittgenstein view in the *Tractatus Logico-Philosophicus,* Carnap desired to show that any philosophically significant metalinguistic claim could be so cast as to be at least as precise as sentences in the corresponding object language.

The core of the syntactic notion of analyticity, Bohnert tells us, is provability; while the feature of *being self-evident* is rejected as requisite for analyticity, *being provable by means available to human minds* is retained. Unfortunately, Bohnert continues, this approach faced problems of a purely syntactical sort, as Kurt Gödel proved that formal systems possessed of sufficient resources to contain number theory also contained sentences which, while purely formal, were neither provable nor refutable within the system by any finite process of proof. Some such sentences would be true but unprovable so long as the law of the excluded middle (the principle that every constructible or well-formed sentence is true, or else false) is not abandoned. Some even suggested, Bohnert notes, that this law be regarded as synthetic *a priori*—that is, as both nonanalytic and yet knowable without appeal to empirical evidence. (This is not an alternative Carnap could cheerfully embrace, since empiricism apparently requires that analytic sentences be *a priori* and nonanalytic statements be *non-a priori (a posteriori)*. Carnap, Bohnert continues, endeavored to expand the notion of provability so that deductions based on infinite classes of premises could count as proofs, but he did so at the price of there being some describable, finite, general method of proof by which "provability" could be characterized. Bohnert adds that, even with this expanded concept of provability, not every sentence one would wish to label "analytic" is provable in some system thus far constructed, and some at least have doubted that this approach actually remains within the limits proscribed by linking *being analytic* and *being provable by means available to human minds*. Whatever its final status, Bohnert contends, Carnap's efforts at developing a syntactical version of analyticity was instrumental in uncovering metalogic's potential.

In any case, Bohnert reports, Alfred Tarski's work persuaded Carnap that analyticity had a semantic aspect not covered by his own purely syntactical approach; he thus came to hold that an analytic sentence is such by virtue of being true, not merely in terms of its logical structure, but by the meanings of its terms. Thus, Bohnert indicates, Carnap became interested, not in languages conceived as mere formal structures, but conceived as syntactically constructed calculi which contain terms which designate nonlinguistic objects and sentences which, if true, correspond to nonlinguistic facts.

The core of the semantic conception of analyticity, Bohnert informs us, is *having null content,* or *having zero strength,* or *conveying no information.* Making use of concepts not unlike the class-of-all-possible-worlds notion of Leibnizian fame to define such quantitative notions as the strength of a sentence, Bohnert explains, Carnap correlates the degree of strength a sentence possesses to the amount of information it contains. The result is that one can show that analytic sentences have no strength, and so convey no information. And, Bohnert adds, Carnap has proposed languages in which modal concepts necessity, possibility, contingency) become expressible in such a way that every state of affairs expressed by an analytic sentence is a necessary one.

Given this characterization of Carnap's effort to develop a semantic conception of analyticity, Bohnert devotes a substantial and technical discussion to articulating it further and defending it against Quine's influential criticisms of the analytic-synthetic distinction.

Additional Recommended Reading

Ayer, A. J., ed. *Logical Positivism.* New York: Free Press, 1959. A collection of essays by various logical positivists, including three by Carnap.

Carnap, Rudolf. *The Logical Structure of the World* [and] *Pseudo-problems in Philosophy.* Berkeley: University of California Press, 1967. A republication of two of Carnap's works, with a preface by their author.

Copi, Irving M. and James A. Gould, eds. *Contemporary Readings in Logical Theory.* New York: Macmillan Publishing Company, 1967. An excellent collection of essays on contemporary logic, including a paper by, and many references to, Carnap.

Kneale, William and Martha Kneale. *The Development of Logic.* Oxford: Clarendon Press, 1962. A comprehensive history of logic, with several references to Carnap.

Rorty, Richard, ed. *The Linguistic Turn: Recent Essays in Philosophical Method.* Chicago: University of Chicago Press, 1967. Contains two papers by Carnap and a good bibliography.

Weinberg, J. R. *An Examination of Logical Positivism.* London: Kegan Paul, Trench, Trubner & Company, 1936. A splendid discussion of logical positivism.

LANGUAGE, TRUTH AND LOGIC

Author: Alfred Jules Ayer (1910-   )
Type of work: Philosophy of philosophy, epistemology
First published: 1936

Principal Ideas Advanced

Metaphysics is impossible because metaphysical statements are meaningless.

A sentence is factually significant if and only if there is a method of verification an observer could adopt to determine the truth or falsity of the sentence; when experience cannot settle an issue, the issue has no factual meaning.

The propositions of philosophy are not factual, but linguistic; they are not factual reports, but either definitions of words in use or expressions of the logical implications of such definitions.

Value statements and statements declaring duties are neither true nor false; they express the feelings of the speaker.

Alfred Jules Ayer presents here a modified version of logical positivism that he prefers to call "logical empiricism." However, the doctrines, particularly their implications for philosophy, are largely those of logical positivism, and the work serves to bring these together succinctly and vigorously. Therefore, the book has had great importance in the twentieth century, both as a positivistic document and as a center of controversy about positivistic tenets. In it, Ayer offers to solve the problems of reality, perception, induction, knowledge, meaning, truth, value, and other minds. He presents no great new idea; rather, his are solutions others have proposed, but which Ayer has modified and brought into logical consistency. A second edition (1946) enabled Ayer, in a new introduction, to reply to his critics. He provided a further explication and changed a few beliefs, but essentially his position remained unchanged. The reader of *Language, Truth and Logic* who is unfamiliar with the field probably would prefer to reserve reading the new introduction until after examining the text itself.

Ayer attacks the possibility of metaphysics, saying that he will deduce the fruitlessness of attempting knowledge that transcends the limits of experience from the "rule which determines the literal signifi-

cance of language." The sentences of metaphysics, failing to meet this rule, are meaningless.

The criterion of meaning Ayer finds in the *verification principle*. "We say that a sentence is factually significant to any given person, if, and only if, he knows how to verify the proposition which it purports to express—that is, if he knows what observations would lead him, under certain conditions, to accept the proposition as being true, or reject it as being false." Another possible kind of meaningful sentence is the tautology. But any sentence which is neither a tautology nor a verifiable proposition (by this criterion) is a mere pseudo-proposition, a meaningless sentence.

Certain provisions qualify this tenet. Ayer distinguished practical verifiability and verifiability in principle. Some sentences are not practically verifiable, because of inconvenience or the present state of science and culture. If one could know what observations would decide such a matter if he were in a position to make them, the proposition is verifiable in principle. A further distinction is that between "strong" verifiability and "weak" verifiability. According to the "strong" theory, advanced by the Vienna Circle of logical positivists, a sentence is meaningful only if it is conclusively verifiable empirically; according to the "weak" theory, it is meaningful if experience may render it probable. Ayer chooses the "weak" theory, on the basis that since no empirical demonstration is ever one hundred percent conclusive, the "strong" theory leaves no empirical statement meaningful. By using the "weak" theory, Ayer believes he allows meaning to general propositions of science and to propositions about the past, two types which had given difficulty to previous positivistic writers. The proposed principle rules out such assertions as the statement that the world of sense is unreal, and such questions as whether reality is one substance or many. No experience could decide these issues, so they have no literal significance. The metaphysician has usually been misled by the grammar of his language, so that he posits an entity ("substance," "Being") where grammar requires a noun as the subject of a sentence, even though thought may exert no such requirement.

By the abandonment of metaphysics, the philosopher is freed from the function of constructing a deductive system of the universe from first principles. For first principles cannot come from experience, whose propositions are hypotheses only and never certain. But if they are taken *a priori*, they are only tautologies, which cannot apply to the universe as factual knowledge.

The problem of induction can be set aside as unreal. It is the attempt to prove that certain empirical generalizations derived from past experience will hold good also in the future. It must have either an *a priori* or an empirical solution. But in the first case it is improper to apply tautologies to experience, for they cannot apply to matters of fact; and in the second, we simply assume what we set out to prove. Since Ayer can conceive no test that would solve the "problem" through experience, he concludes that it is not a genuine problem. In actuality, we place our faith in such scientific generalizations as enable us to predict future experience and thus control our environment; there is no general logical problem about this practice.

A common mistake is to assert that without a satisfactory analysis of perception, we are not entitled to believe in the existence of material things. Rather, the right to believe in their existence comes simply from the fact that one has certain sensations, for to say the thing exists is equivalent to saying the sensations are obtainable. It is the philosopher's business to give a correct definition of material things in terms of sensations. He is not concerned with properties of things in the world, but only with our way of speaking of them. The propositions of philosophy are not factual, but linguistic in character—"that is, they do not describe the behavior of physical, or even mental, objects; they express definitions, or the formal consequences of definitions." Philosophy is a department of logic. It is independent of any empirical, not to say metaphysical, assumptions. Often propositions which are really linguistic are so expressed as to appear to be factual. "A material thing cannot be in two places at once" is actually linguistic, recording "the fact that, as the result of certain verbal conventions, the proposition that two sense-contents occur in the same visual or tactual sense-field is incompatible with the proposition that they belong to the same material thing." The question, "What is the nature of x?" asks for a definition, which is always a linguistic statement.

Philosophical analysis essentially provides definitions. But they are not the most frequently occurring kind; that is, *explicit* or synonymous definitions giving an alternate symbol or symbolic expression for the term to be defined. Rather, they are a special sort, *definitions in use*, which are made by showing how a sentence in which the definiendum occurs can be translated into equivalent sentences which do not contain the definiendum or any of its synonyms. An example taken from Bertrand Russell defines "author" in the sentence, "The author of *Waverley* was Scott," by providing the equivalent, "One person, and one person only, wrote *Waverley*, and that person was Scott." Such definitions clarify sentences both where no synonym for the definiendum exists, and also where available synonyms are unclear in the same fashion as the symbol needing clarification. A complete philosophical clarification of a language would first enumerate the types of sentence significant in that language, then display the relations of equivalence that hold between sentences of various types. Such a set of definitions would reveal the structure of the language examined; and any truly philosophical theory would hence apply to a given language.

Some of our symbols denote simple sense-contents, and others logical constructions, the latter enabling us to state complicated propositions about the elements of the logical constructions in a relatively simple form. But logical constructions are not inherently fictions. Rather, material things are among such logical constructions. The definition-in-use will restate the definiendum naming a material thing by translating it into symbols that refer to sense-contents that are elements of the material thing. In other words, roughly, to say something about a table is always to say something about sense-contents. The problem of the "reduction" of material things into sense-contents, long a chief part of the problem of perception, is a linguistic problem readily solved by providing definitions-in-use. To accomplish this reduction, Ayer stipulates that two sense-contents *resemble* each other *directly* when either there is no difference, or only an infinitesimal difference, between them; and *indirectly*, when they are linked by a series of direct resemblances amounting to an appreciable difference. He stipulates further that two sense-contents are *directly continuous* when within successive sense-fields there is no difference, or only an infinitesimal difference, between them, with respect to the position of each in its own sense-field; and *indirectly continuous* when related by an actual, or possible, series of direct continuities. Any two of one's sense-contents, then, are elements of the same material thing when they are related to each other by direct or indirect resemblance and by direct or indirect continuity.

Ayer assumes that the object of a theory of truth is to show how propositions are validated. Like all questions of similar pattern, the question "What is truth?" calls for a definition. Consequently, no factual theory is needed to answer it. The real question discussed most of the time in "theories of truth" is "What makes a proposition true or false?"

Ayer adopts the distinction between analytic and synthetic propositions. Each has its own validation. "A proposition is analytic when its validity depends solely on the definitions of the symbols it contains, and synthetic when its validity is determined by the facts of experience." While "Either some ants are parasitic or none are," an analytic proposition, is undubitably and necessarily true, it provides no actual information about ants. As a tautology, it has no factual content and serves only to help us understand matters of language. The valid propositions of logic are true by tautology and are useful and surprising in revealing hidden implications in our sentences. They can help us gain empirical knowledge, but it is not the tautologies which render empirical knowledge valid. Whether a geometry actually can be applied to physical space is an empirical question which falls outside the scope of the geometry itself. There is thus no paradox about the applicability of the analytic propositions of logic and mathematics to the world.

Synthetic propositions, Ayer affirms, are validated by experience. Experience is given in the form of sensations. Sensations are neither true nor false; they simply occur. Propositions about them are not logically determined by them in one way or another; hence, while these are perhaps largely dependable, they may be doubted. Similarly, they may be confirmed by additional experience. In other words, "Empirical propositions are one and all hypotheses." And, in fact, whenever a verification is carried out, it is applied to an entire system of hypotheses—a principal one, together with supplementary hypotheses which often are adjusted by the verification rather than by the principal hypothesis. Therefore, the "facts of experience" can never *per se* oblige us to abandon a particular hypothesis, since we may ever continue without contradiction to explain invalidating instances in various ways while retaining the principal hypothesis. We must of course retain a willingness to abandon it under certain circumstances because of experience, or else we make of it not a hypothesis but a definition. It must be granted that we are not always rational in arriving at belief—that is, we do not always employ a self-consistent accredited procedure in the formation of our beliefs. That a hypothesis increases in probability is equivalent to saying that observation increases the degree of confidence with which it is rational to entertain the hypothesis.

The exposition of synthetic propositions, every one of which is a rule for the anticipation of our future experience, constitutes Ayer's validation of the verification principle, for it comes to just what the veri- fication principle states, that the literal significance of an empirical proposition is the anticipated sense- contents entailed in it.

To account consistently for statements of value with empirical principles, Ayer holds that descriptive ethical sentences are empirical statements and that normative ethical sentences are "absolute" or "intrin- sic," not empirically calculable, and indefinable in factual terms. The normative symbols in a sentence name no concepts, add nothing to the factual content. Thus, normative sentences are not capable of being true or false. They simply express certain feelings of the speaker. They are not even *assertions* that the speaker has a certain feeling, for such assertions would be empirical and subject to doubt. Thus we remove the question of their having any validity at all.

But how, then, can we dispute about value? Ayer maintains that actually we never dispute about ques- tions of value, but only about questions of fact. The pattern usual in such a dispute is to exhibit to our opponent what we believe to be the facts, assuming a common framework of value statements, and at- tempt thus to bring him to our way of seeing the facts.

As to religious knowledge, we cannot appeal to tautologies for factual truth about God, for these are mere stipulations of our own. Nor can we have empirical propositions about God, for we can con- ceive of no experience which would bring us differ- ent sense-contents if God exists than if he does not. Hence, the notion is metaphysical and meaningless.

Ayer applies a complete phenomenalism to the traditional problems of the self and knowledge of the world. He denies that the given needs a logical rather than sensory justification. Further, he rejects the pattern of subject-act-object as an account of percep- tion. He defines a sense-content not as the object, but as a part of sense-experience, so that the existence of a sense-content always entails the existence of a sense-experience. Hence, the question of whether sense-contents are mental or physical is inapplicable. Such a distinction can apply only to the logical constructions which are derived from them. The difference between mental and physical objects lies in differences between the sense-contents, or in the different relations of sense-contents that constitute objects.

The self may be explained in similar terms. "It is, in fact, a logical construction out of the sense- experiences which constitute the actual and possible sense-history of a self." To ask its nature is to ask what relationship obtains between sense-experiences for them to belong to the sense-history of the same self. Rather than retain the metaphysical notion of a sub- stantive ego, we can identify personal identity simply in terms of bodily identity, and that in turn is to be defined in terms of the resemblance and continuity of sense-contents. To say anything about the self is always to say something about sense-contents. I know other selves empirically, just as I know physi- cal things and my own self empirically.

Ayer urges the unity of philosophy with the sci- ences. Rather than actually validating scientific the- ory, the philosopher's function is to elucidate the symbols occurring in it. It is essential to the task that he should understand science. Philosophy must de- velop into the logic of science.

As well as providing further exposition, Ayer's introduction to the second edition contains some modifications of doctrine which deserve notice. In the interim between editions, he came to accept a belief of the logical positivists, which he opposed in the first edition, that some empirical statements may be considered conclusively verified. These are "basic statements," referring to the sense-content of a single experience, and their conclusive verification is the immediate occurrence of the experience to which they refer. As long as these merely record what is experienced and say nothing else, they cannot be factually mistaken, for they make no claim that any further fact could confute. But this change makes little difference to the chief doctrine, Ayer maintains, for the vast majority of propositions are not of this sort.

Ayer introduces the term "observation-statement," to designate any statement "which records an actual or possible observation." To remove the objection that, as originally stated, the principle allows any indicative statement whatever to have significance, Ayer amends its expression to say that the principle of verification requires of a literally meaningful, nonanalytic statement that it should be either directly or indirectly verifiable. For it to be directly verifiable it must be an observation-statement or, in conjunction with one or more observation-statements, must entail at least one other observation-statement not entailed by the other observation statements alone. To be indirectly verifiable, first, in conjunction with certain other premises, a statement must entail one or more directly verifiable statements not deducible from the other premises alone and, second, the other premises must include no statement that is not either analytic, or directly verifiable, or indirectly verifiable independently.

Ayer gives up the position that *a priori* propositions are linguistic rules, for they can properly be said to be both true and necessary, while linguistic rules cannot be called true and are arbitrary. Descriptive linguistic statements of contingent empirical fact of language usage are, however, the basis for statements of logical relationships—which are necessary truths.

Ayer admits doubts as to whether his account of the experiences of others is correct, yet says, "I am not convinced that it is not." He confesses error in assuming that philosophical analysis consists mainly in providing "definitions in use." Such a result is the exception rather than the rule; and in fact, for statements about material things such definition becomes impossible, since "no finite set of observation-statements is ever equivalent to a statement about a material thing."

Finally, rather than classify philosophical statements alongside scientific statements, Ayer states that "it is incorrect to say that there are no philosophical propositions. For, whether they are true or false, the propositions that are expressed in such a book as this do fall into a special category . . . asserted or denied by philosophers. . . ." The lexicographer is concerned with the use of particular expressions, but the philosopher, with classes of expressions; and his statements, if true, are usually analytic.

Pertinent Literature

Evans, J. L. "On Meaning and Verification," in *Mind*. LXII, no. 245 (January, 1953), pp. 1-19.

Logical positivism was developed in the 1920's and 1930's by the philosophers (and scientists) who formed the Vienna Circle. The positivists' aim was to find a way to draw a distinction between science and metaphysics such that science would remain as *the* legitimate field of human knowledge while metaphysics (that is, most of traditional philosophy) would be ruled out as a pseudo-discipline. The weapon they devised to achieve that aim was the verification principle.

The verification principle was intended to be a test (criterion) to determine whether any given sentence is meaningful. Excluding sentences which express analytic (trivial) propositions (for example, "A red house is red"), the verification principle says that a sentence is meaningful if and only if the proposition it expresses is verifiable. That is, a sentence which expresses a nonverifiable proposition is literally meaningless, literally nonsense. (The positivists often went further and gave not only a criterion of mean-

ingfulness but also a specification of what the meaning of a sentence is. Thus it was often said that "The meaning of a sentence is its method of verification.")

This principle, at least when "verification" was interpreted as "verifiable in sense experience" (and that was the interpretation implicitly accepted by friends and foes alike), was intended to be a tool which would reveal metaphysics to be nothing but nonsense. What is the view of philosophers today about the verification principle? To put it bluntly, no one accepts it. What were the reasons that produced this unanimity in opposition to verifiability? Surprisingly, there is no one work which systematically presents the case against the verification principle. A good account of the criticisms behind the current rejection of the principle can be found in the essay by J. L. Evans.

It is helpful to make a distinction between criticisms which the positivists could respond to by altering the principle and those which could not be accommodated by a new version of the principle. (There is, of course, no sharp distinction between those types of criticism; moreover, too much patching, even if each single patch seems successful, tends to undermine any thesis.) For example, if a proposition must be verifiable to be meaningful, there are even questions about whether scientific propositions are really meaningful. We cannot check, verify, every individual crow to determine whether it is black, so how can we verify "All crows are black" ? Consequently, the positivists had to reformulate the principle to say that it did not require "complete verification." To see similar modifications in response to criticisms, see the reference to Carl G. Hempel in the bibliography following these essays.

There are other criticisms which are much harder to take into account by modifying the principle; for example, is the verification principle verifiable? If not, it is either analytic (trivial, uninformative), which no positivist would accept, or meaningless, which would be disastrous. So it must be verifiable. But then, by the positivists' own account, it cannot be more than a hypothesis; that is, it cannot be fully verifiable. Any ways around this criticism (and there are ways to remove its sting) inevitably seem *ad hoc*, invented to save the principle, and so are unsatisfying.

Probably the most decisive criticism has been the realization that there are many kinds of meaningful sentences which are quite unrelated to any issue of verification. "Pass the salt" and "How are you?" are sentences and meaningful, but talk of verifying them is completely beside the point. It becomes clear from this that verification is not a general criterion of meaning. In fact, at its best the verification principle tells us (something about) what is to count as an empirical proposition. And that means that metaphysical propositions, which do not purport to be empirical, escape from the positivists' way of condemning them.

Achinstein, Peter and Stephen F. Barker, eds. *The Legacy of Logical Positivism.* Baltimore: The Johns Hopkins University Press, 1969.

It was the aim of the logical positivists to reject metaphysics and to retain science. One of the most obvious features of the positivists' work was their extensive knowledge of and extreme regard for natural science. (A. J. Ayer is something of a rebel in this respect—there is far less of a "scientific" atmosphere in *Language, Truth and Logic* than in any of the other major positivist writings.) It is worth asking, in view of their intellectual allegiances, how their view of the nature of science has stood the tests of time and criticism.

The book under review addresses itself to this question. The papers by various philosophers which are collected in this volume are, with two exceptions, attempts to appraise the positivists' thought about the role of theories in science, about their views on the behavioral sciences, and about their contribution to the philosophy of mathematics. One of the exceptions should be noticed first. The introductory essay by Herbert Feigl, a member of the Vienna Circle, is a clear discussion of the beginnings and "spirit" of logical positivism and is well worth reading.

Before considering some of the papers specifically, there are a few general points to be noticed. All the authors agree that it is legitimate to talk about the *legacy* of positivism; that is, they agree that there are no more logical positivists. Even the former adherents, Feigl, Carl G. Hempel, and Ayer, are no longer philosophically committed to the positivists' program (no matter how much their present views are deeply shaped by those earlier ideas.) Again, all the authors represented here agree that positivism had a beneficial effect on philosophy. There is disagreement, however, on the further question of what that beneficial effect consists of. This lack of agreement appears most clearly in the papers by Hempel and Michael Scriven. Hempel, a former positivist, holds (in the conclusion to his paper) that the value to current philosophy of positivist thought resides in the detailed work done by the positivists and not in the sweeping general theories (for example, the verification principle) they offered. Scriven, on the other hand, is more representative of the other authors in that he claims that it was precisely in those broad slogans, which have turned out to be misguided, that positivism has had a good effect on philosophy. For it was these striking general views which made other philosophers rethink their fundamental views.

Of the papers on the nature of theory in science, the one most accessible to the beginner is Norbert Hanson's. The main theme of it and the others on this topic is the same: the positivists made a sharp distinction between theory and observation in science; the present authors agree that no such radical distinction between a formal structure of theory and the factual content of a science can be made. (They disagree, however, on how much of a distinction there is between theory and observation or interpretation.)

On the topic of the positivists' contribution to philosophical questions about the social sciences, the paper to start with is Scriven's. He considers several topics very critically, yet sympathetically: the positivists' doctrine of operationalism, their defense of value-free social science (Scriven's analysis and criticism of this is particularly good), and the positivist opposition to *Verstehen* theory (the idea that there is a special technique of "understanding" available to social scientists which is not available to physical scientists) .

Stephen F. Barker's paper on the positivists and their philosophy is clear and helpful, even to those not well versed in such issues. And last, the piece by Stephen Toulmin, while idiosyncratic (it is really about Ludwig Wittgenstein and Toulmin), is nevertheless very instructive about the development of twentieth century philosophy, including the role of the logical positivists.

Urmson, J. O. *The Emotive Theory of Ethics*. New York: Oxford University Press, 1969.

One of the consequences of using the weapon of verifiability was that fields of human thought other than the intended target—namely, metaphysics— were also in the line of fire. Religious propositions, for example, were regarded as not empirically verifiable and so were relegated to nonsense. Although that particular outcome probably did not distress the positivists deeply, it turned out that, according to their view, moral propositions also were not empirically verifiable and so should be regarded as literally nonsensical. But that was a shocking conclusion; and so that morality should be meaningless seemed an important objection to the verification principle. Hence it was important to the positivists' program to find an account of moral propositions which would show them not to be nonsense, without surrendering the verification principle. The result was the emotive theory of ethics.

But are ethical claims unverifiable by observation? It is clear, as J. O. Urmson shows in this excellent book, that, given the intellectual situation in the 1930's, the positivists had to conclude that moral claims are not capable of verification. G. E. Moore presumably had shown that "good" did not name any *natural* property; that is, any property discoverable by the senses. That meant that moral propositions were not verifiable since "good" is essential in moral discourse. On the other hand, positivistic empiricists could not accept Moore's alternative view: namely, that "good" names a *nonnatural* property. Such a view requires a doctrine of intuition, a notion repugnant to empiricists.

Although A. J. Ayer was not the first to formulate the emotive theory (Urmson gives the history of the notion), his account in *Language, Truth and Logic* is still the best short account, as well as having been influential at the time. According to Ayer, the problem is solved by holding that "good" and other terms *do not name* any property at all; hence, propositions containing the word "good" are not really propositions and so, of course, are not verifiable. But sentences containing "good" *do* have a function in discourse—they *express* feelings and stimulate actions. What look like propositions are really forms of command along with expressions of emotions.

Urmson is especially good at showing how the emotivist theory had roots other than those demanded by the positivists' program. One striking thing about Ayer's development of the theory was that it derived solely from considerations about sensible discourse and not from any thought about moral language itself. On the other hand, Charles Stevenson came to formulate an emotivist theory shortly after Ayer and came to do so by way of a consideration of the workings of moral language. (See Ayer's approval of Stevenson's more detailed work in a footnote to the Preface of the second edition of Urmson's book.) In fact, Stevenson turns out to be the hero of Urmson's study.

How stands the emotive theory today? Much of Urmson's criticism deals with details of formulation. But he also clearly argues that the emotivist's belief that moral sayings are neither true nor false and so are not subject to rational discourse is not acceptable. Moreover, the easy assumption that all evaluational language, including moral, aesthetic, political, and other, is to be given the same kind of account is cogently objected to by Urmson. Lastly, while the emotivists thought they were giving an analysis of the meaning of "good," Urmson argues that contemporary speech-act theory shows that they confused questions of meaning and act/use. Still, Urmson is very careful to point out that it was precisely the emotivists' realization that moral language does something other than state facts which led to the modern theory which is now being used to criticize its ancestor.

Additional Recommended Reading

Ayer, A. J. *Part of My Life: The Memoirs of a Philosopher.* New York: Harcourt Brace Jovanovich, 1977. A fairly rare type of work; very informative.

_____., ed. *Logical Positivism.* New York: Free Press, 1959. The best anthology of positivist writings with a good introduction by Ayer and an especially large bibliography.

Hempel, Carl G. *Aspects of Scientific Explanation.* New York: Free Press, 1965. Includes the important paper "Empiricist Criteria of Cognitive Significance: Problems and Changes."

Kraft, Viktor. *The Vienna Circle: The Origin of Neo-Positivism.* Westport, Connecticut: Greenwood Press, 1969. An excellent account.

MacDonald, Graham, and Crispin Wright, eds. *Essays of A.J. Ayer's "Language, Truth and Logic."* Oxford: Basil Blackwell, 1987. A series of critical and sympathetic responses to Ayer's seminal work.

AN INQUIRY INTO MEANING AND TRUTH

Author: Bertrand Russell (1872-1970)
Type of work: Epistemology
First published: 1940

Principal Ideas Advanced

Empirical knowledge has its basis in percepts (sense experiences); from basic propositions about percepts empirical knowledge is constructed.

Although basic propositions are not indubitably true, as propositions of the utmost particularity, referring to percepts, they are the most dependable propositions of empirical inquiry.

Empirical knowledge requires provision for general statements, for stating logical relationships, and for modes of inference.

Propositions are both objective and subjective; they are objective in that they indicate factually, and they are subjective in that they express the state of mind of the speaker (belief, denial, or doubt).

Sentences are true if what they indicate is the case; to know a sentence to be true one must perceive its verifier (the event the sentence indicates).

The phrase "theory of knowledge," Russell says, has two meanings. One kind of theory, the lesser, accepts whatever knowledge science presents, and seeks to account for it. Russell's concern is with the wider kind, which embraces all problems of establishing the nature and validity of all knowledge. Confining his attention in this work to empirical knowledge, he undertakes to discover two things, principally: (1) What is meant by "empirical evidence for the truth of a proposition"? (2) What can be inferred from the fact that there sometimes is such evidence?

Russell brings to the problem of a theory of empirical knowledge the full force of its counterpart, logical knowledge, to whose modern development he is a foremost contributor. He attacks the problems of his general task by translating their elements into formal logical symbols, so as to achieve a precision lacking in the language in which the problems are usually couched. Yet the book does not consider problems of logic as such, except when they are relevant to epistemology.

To talk about epistemological matters, Russell sets up a modern linguistic apparatus. He conceives a hierarchy of languages, at whose base is the object-language or primary language. Terms in the object-language include subjects and predicates. While ordinary language may provide a beginning, we should transform every subject of the object-language into a unique proper *name*, making use of coordinates in the visual field and of measures of time for discriminating the object named. The name will apply to a complex; and sometimes we must give names to complex wholes without knowing what their constituents are. We learn the names of things ostensively, and only of those things we actually perceive while hearing or coining their names. The names are employed as subjects in propositions of the simplest sort, called *atomic* propositions. We may designate their predicates *relations*. Letting R stand for the relation "above," the proposition "A R B" consists of the relation R and the names A and B, and asserts that A is above B. This is a dyadic relation. Predicates may take any number of terms. The predicate of a single name is a monadic relation: "$f(A)$" states that a characteristic f is an attribute of A.

The secondary language consists of statements about the primary language (thus it must include the primary language within it). Therefore all words for logical conceptions, such as "is true," "is false," "or," "if," belong to the secondary language. All logical truths, since they depend for their truth on rules of syntax, are at least on this level, if not higher. An important group of propositions of the secondary language are those stating *propositional attitudes*, such as "A believes proposition p."

The distinctive feature of empirical rather than logical truth is, of course, its basis in percepts, the sense images by which perception is possible. Russell adapts A. J. Ayer's phrase "basic propositions" to designate those propositions arising as immediately as possible from percepts. A basic proposition "is a proposition which arises on occasion of a perception, which is the evidence for its truth, and it has a form such that no two propositions having this form can be mutually inconsistent if derived from different percepts." Examples in ordinary language are "I am hot," "That is red." Many basic propositions may arise describing a single percept, for we perceive a sensory whole combining the entire fields of vision, touch, and so on; and within this field we identify smaller wholes of sensory complexes—the individual objects of the world. Basic propositions need not be atomic propositions. An important group includes some propositions stating propositional attitude—"I believe proposition *p*"—and thus basic propositions may occur in the secondary language as well as in the primary.

Unlike most prior writers, Russell does not affirm that basic propositions are indubitably true. He is quite willing to doubt them, particularly those involving the memory of percepts. But what distinguishes basic propositions from others is their immediacy, whereas other propositions rest to some degree on inference. The evidence for a basic proposition is the momentary percept which causes it, and nothing can ever make a percept more or less certain than it is at the moment of its occurrence. It is from basic propositions that Russell proceeds to erect the structure of empirical knowledge. Since basic propositions are based on the least questionable objects of experience, they are the most dependable propositions in empirical inquiry. Thus, empirical knowledge is founded on propositions of the utmost particularity. Russell crit-

icizes other writers for failing to screen out all traces of inference in the propositions they have regarded as basic.

A pure empiricism, depending only upon percepts for validation, would be self-refuting. It must contain some general proposition, which cannot be a basic proposition, about the dependence of knowledge upon experience; and the consequence is that such a proposition could not itself be known. Empirical knowledge requires certain additional elements besides basic propositions. These include provisions for making general statements and for stating logical relationships. Empirical knowledge, in other words, needs some epistemological premises as well as factual premises. Modes of inference are also required. These modes include the usual logical operations of deduction. More important in empirical knowledge, however, are nonlogical patterns of inference; namely, reasoning by analogy and by induction. As an example: Russell throughout assumes that things perceived *cause* perceptions, and that perceptions *cause* propositions. His notion of cause is that it is a convenient device for collecting together propositions of certain percepts; it is something that we can arrive at inductively from appropriate combinations of percepts. Without some such organizing scheme for relating percepts, we would have nothing resembling empirical science. Yet neither causality nor induction is perceived, nor are they validated by logical syntax.

An innovation, no doubt startling to logicians, which Russell finds necessary to epistemology is to supply substantial meaning rather than merely formal meaning to logical terms. He finds these in psychological fact. "Or" rises from a hesitation, a conflict between two motor impulses when the organism is suspended between two courses of action. "Not" expresses a state of mind in which an impulse to action exists but is inhibited. "True" has its psychological ground in an expectation that is fulfilled; "false" in the surprise when an expectation is defeated. Such interpretations as these become possible when we accept into epistemology not only logic but psychology and physical science, as we must in order to account for empirical rather than purely logical knowledge.

Russell is now able to develop a theory of significance. Regarded epistemologically, a proposition has two sides, objective and subjective. The objective side is what it *indicates* factually. The subjective side is what it *expresses* about the state of mind of its originator; and this is called its *significance*. What it expresses may be belief, denial, or doubt. These distinctions, not needed in logic, solve many puzzles of epistemology. The points concerning significance are independent of truth or falsity of the proposition; truth and falsity come into the relation of the proposition to what it indicates. A proposition does not necessarily consist of words; it is psychological, of the stuff of belief, not language. But words may always be found to state the belief which, as a proposition, may underlie the many possible ways of saying it, in one or in various languages. Russell provides a sample language to show that the psychological conditions of significance can be translated into precise syntactical rules.

Logical sentence-patterns can start from particular propositions recording percepts and extend our thought over material that we have not experienced, and in this way we can expand our body of statement. If we know "Socrates is mortal" we can think "Something is mortal," or "Everything is mortal," and so on. Then further inquiry so as to have new percepts may test whether the new statements should be added to belief. Simple statements of immediate percepts may be expressed with constants—particular names—and predicates. But any statement covering a percept one has not actually had must contain a variable term in place of a constant, for one can neither give nor learn a name (in Russell's sense) for an object one has not perceived. An epistemological language will need names, whereas a logical language does not deal with particulars and has no use for names. By the use of variables rather than names, it is possible to have propositions transcending one's experience. This is in fact what happens whenever one receives information from another person.

Thus far Russell has investigated meaning. In effect, he has constructed an epistemological language, so that one can know what kinds of sentences are possible as statements of percepts and their relationships. It remains to examine the relationship between meaning and truth, between language and the world.

Among the many possible theories of truth, Russell adheres firmly to a correspondence theory. Truth is defined by events, not percepts, although it becomes known by percepts. Truth is thus a broader concept than knowledge. The truth of a proposition is established by perception of its *verifier*. The sort of sentence which provides the model for truth is a spontaneous sentence that expresses what it indicates—that is, in which the subjective and the objective content coincide. Such a sentence is "I am hot!" Provided the sentence is stimulated by the immediate circumstances of the moment, there is no reason to doubt it. The verifier of a true sentence is what the sentence *indicates*; in other words, what makes that sentence true is that I was hot when I said it. Similarly, the verifier of a sentence about the future is the occurrence of what it indicates, and when that occurrence is perceived, the sentence is verified. A false sentence has no verifier, and it indicates nothing. Obviously, some verifiers may never be perceived, and there are some sentences whose truth or falsity we never know. Sentences are true if their verifiers occur, but when verifiers are not perceived the sentences cannot be said to be known. The presence of an observer, Russell affirms, is no requisite of verifiers occurring.

The verifier of a basic proposition is a single occurrence at a moment of time. As to sentences containing variables, there is (usually) not just one but a collection of verifiers for them. The actual verification of such sentences depends on what is said. "All men are mortal" says "For any x, if x is a man then x is mortal." This can never be verified by empirical knowledge because it would be impossible to examine all values of the variable—all men. "Some men live in Los Angeles" says "There is an x such that x is a man and x lives in Los Angeles." This can be verified by one of a very large number of verifiers, since any individual man living in Los Angeles can be the assigned value of the variable. In this fashion, propositions which are not basic, but which, rather, by the use of variables indicate occurrences beyond the speaker's experience, may be verified. We can give in advance a description of the occurrence which would make the proposition true, but we cannot name the occurrence. The relation between a sentence and its verifier is often much more remote than the explanation of simple cases would suggest.

Russell denies that either the verification or the verifier of a sentence constitutes its meaning. The verifier, as what the sentence indicates, relates to its truth; but we must know what the proposition means before we can know either its significance or its verifier; that is, before we can know either what it expresses or what it indicates. This knowledge is based ultimately on our ostensive learning of object-words.

Known error arises in the experience of surprise upon a disappointed expectation. Its simplest case requires a combination of expectation, perception, and memory, in which either the expectation or perception must be negative, the others being positive. This combination accounts for our perceptions which seem to be negative perceptions, such as in "There is no cheese in this cupboard." We examine every object in the cupboard having a size which might result in a percept of cheese, but in every such case the expectation is disappointed.

The relation of empirical knowledge to experience is explained by Russell as follows: I must depend completely upon my own experience for all beliefs whose verbal expression has no variables; these include only basic propositions of immediate experience and memory. Though not indubitable, they are highly trustworthy. All my knowledge of what transcends *my* experience, including everything I learn from others, includes variables. When someone tells me, "A is red," using a proper name for something I have not experienced, if I believe him, what I believe is not "A is red" since I am not immediately acquainted with A, but "There is an x such that x is red." (Future experience giving me a percept of A together with a percept of the name "A" may later entitle me to believe "A is red.") Such a view of the nature of empirical knowledge would commit us either to depleting the body of knowledge to an intolerably small set of beliefs, or else to relaxing our insistence that only the belief in true statements may be called knowledge. In order to admit the statements one believes on testimony, statements of things ever ex-

perienced anywhere by other human beings, and statements assumed in physical science, we should have to do the latter. In fact, upon examining the limitations of pure empiricism, Russell concludes there are no true empiricists.

Certain principles of logic make difficulties in our epistemological language when we attempt to apply nonsyntactic criteria of truth. They are the principles of extensionality and atomicity. Loosely, the principle of extensionality allows us to insert any atomic proposition in the place of a given atomic proposition in a sentence in the secondary language. But this will obviously not do for sentences stating propositional attitudes. "A believes p" should not entitle us to say, by substitution, that A believes any or all propositions whatever. The principle of atomicity in effect requires us to reduce the complex parts of any proposition on a higher language level to their components on the atomic level, then be governed in assessing the truth of the whole by the relationships thus exhibited. Difficulties which these two principles raise in logic have been attacked by Wittgenstein and others by distinguishing between the assertion of a proposition and the mere consideration of a proposition. Russell affirms, however, that the appropriate distinction to be made is between indication and significance. The principle of extensionality will be found to apply to all occurrences of a proposition within a larger proposition when its indication is what is relevant, but not when only its significance is relevant, as is the case with sentences of propositional attitudes. Russell is less sure whether atomicity must be accepted or denied; upon considering the immediacy of perception and, in contrast, the elaborateness of inference involved in applying the principle of atomicity, he is inclined to believe that its application is irrelevant to the theotetical construction of empirical knowledge.

Another matter arising in logic is the challenge to the law of the excluded middle (which says that a proposition must be either true or false, not a third thing). It has been suggested that sentences as yet unverified should not be called either true or false. But Russell clings to a realism, and a correspondence theory of truth, declaring that a sentence is true if its verifier occurs, even though its perception may not be part of anyone's experience. This outlook is extremely helpful in framing hypotheses, he says, and we should not attempt to do without it.

A continually recurring question in any investigation involving logical and nonlogical knowledge is whether anything about the structure of the world can be inferred from the structure of language. Since words are sensible objects, Russell believes that such inference is possible. While we confine the investigation to names and their objects, we have no reason to attempt such inference. But on examining sentences, we find that those like "A is to the left of B" cannot be explained without raising the question of universals. There is no escape from admitting relations as part of the nonlinguistic constitution. A universal is the meaning of a relation-word. "Above" and "before," just as truly as proper names, mean something in perception. Thus, in a logical language there will be some distinctions of parts of speech which correspond to objective distinctions. Again, when we ask whether the word "similar" in recurring instances means the same thing or only similar things, there is no logical escape from granting that it means the same thing, thus establishing the universal "similar." Russell concludes, although with admitted hesitation, that there are universals, and not merely general words. Knowledge must then be not of words alone but of the nonlinguistic world also. One who denies this fact must deny that he even knows when he is using a word; a complete agnosticism is not compatible with the maintenance of linguistic propositions. Hence, Russell believes that the study of syntax can assist us to considerable knowledge of the structure of the world.

With this work, given as the William James Lectures at Harvard University in 1940, Russell has performed at least three worthy services for modern epistemology. By asserting that more than one thing can be known from one experience, that there is more than a single kind of knowledge, and that the mind can attain negative knowledge through perception, he has assigned to the mind a fuller role in shaping its life than that accorded it by positivists and reductionistic philosophers. He has pointed out the necessity for a metaphysic, if only a very simple one, and in doing so has given strength to the counterclaim against logical positivism that logical positivism is itself a metaphysic. Most important, his penetrating criticism has shown the importance of the limitations upon empirical knowledge that its advocates, in their consciousness of the limitations of other kinds of knowledge, are prone to overlook.

Pertinent Literature

Einstein, Albert. "Remarks on Bertrand Russell's Theory of Knowledge," in *The Philosophy of Bertrand Russell* (The Library of Living Philosophers). Vol. V. Edited by Paul A. Schilpp. Evanston, Illinois: The Library of Living Philosophers, 1946, pp. 277-291.

Albert Einstein used the opportunity afforded by his being asked to contribute to The Library of Living Philosophers' volume on the work of Bertrand Russell to say something about Russell's attempt to resolve the problem concerning the relation of what Einstein calls "sense-impressions" to knowledge. Although Einstein is critical of Russell's reply to that question, it is evident that the great physicist was most of all concerned to generate inquiry concerning the question as to whether "pure thought," as he puts it, can contribute to knowledge—presumably to knowledge of the physical world. (One supposes Einstein must sometimes have wondered how much of what he suggested about the physical world was based on sense experience and how much was the product of his creative intelligence operating independently of any reference to sense-impressions.)

It would be a mistake to think that since Einstein was a physicist he was not therefore a philosopher. As he himself indicates in his essay, "The present difficulties of his science force the physicist to come to grips with philosophical problems to a greater degree than was the case with earlier generations." Not only was Einstein stimulated to be philosophical, but he also shows a remarkable ability to say significant and provocative things in short order.

Einstein begins his critique of Russell with a quotation from *An Inquiry into Meaning and Truth* in which Russell makes the point that we are all naïve realists in childhood but that modern science forces us to realize that the relationship between physical things and the subjective responses to them are very complex and puzzling. If what an observer observes are the effects of things on himself, then knowledge appears to stem from the subjective. Russell concludes: "Naïve realism leads to physics, and physics, if true, shows that naïve realism is false. Therefore, naïve realism, if true, is false; therefore, it is false." (By "naïve realism" Russell means the uncritical belief that "things are what they seem"; he does not explain, however, what it is to believe that things are what they seem. It is nevertheless clear that they do not, at least to a child, seem to be what later on the child learns physics says they are.)

The empirical procedure, the method of acquiring knowledge about physical things through "a working-over of the raw-material furnished by the senses" (as Einstein puts it), has worked and is generally accepted, he writes. But this success in no way implies the impossibility of acquiring knowledge of "reality" by pure speculation.

Einstein describes David Hume as having made the point that essential concepts—such as that of causality—cannot be derived from sense-impressions. That revolutionary point, Einstein claims, has influenced the *best* of the philosophers ever since—Russell included. If whatever we know empirically is not certain, one would be crushed were it not for Immanuel Kant, who maintained (although for the wrong reasons) that if any knowledge is certain, it is grounded in reason itself.

Einstein then comments that although most persons now agree that the concepts Kant thought certain are not certain, there is something correct in what Kant said—namely, that "in thinking we use, with a certain 'right,' concepts to which there is no access from the materials of sensory experience, if the situation is viewed from the logical point of view."

Einstein then goes further. He calls the concepts that make knowledge possible, concepts not derived from sense experience, "free creations of thought which cannot inductively be gained from sense-experiences." He gives as an example the series of integers, and he argues that it would be a mistake to abandon useful concepts and propositions not inductively demonstrable on the ground that they are "metaphysical." All that is required is that the concepts and propositions be such as to make the conceptual system a unified and parsimonious one.

Hence, Einstein concludes, despite Hume's skepticism the only thing to fear is the "fear of metaphysics" itself. Such fear, leading to the rejection of useful concepts that cannot inductively be established, is, he writes, a "malady" just as bad as the early philosophical practice of "philosophizing in the clouds."

The bearing of all this on Russell is that Einstein attributes Russell's conception of things as bundles of sense-qualities to be a consequence of his giving way to the fear of metaphysics. Einstein sees no reason why the "thing," as conceived by physics, cannot function as an independent concept "together with the proper spatio-temporal structure. "

(In his reply, also given in the Paul A. Schilpp volume, Russell argues that we are stimulated by experience to count—our having ten fingers led to the decimal system. He contends that it is doubtful that concepts arise independently of sense experience. And he defends his reducing things to bundles of qualities by appealing to Ockham's razor.)

Jager, Ronald. *The Development of Bertrand Russell's Philosophy.* New York: Humanities Press, 1972.

Ronald Jager's study of Bertrand Russell's philosophical development was published in the centenary year of Russell's birth in the Muirhead Library of Philosophy Series. Jager's book is ambitious and rewarding. It attempts to provide a comprehensive account of Russell's intellectual development, and although it could hardly be expected that this work would remark on everything significant accomplished by Russell, it ably surveys the basic stages of Russell's intellectual pilgrimage.

Beginning with an overview of Russell and his work, Jager proceeds to discuss Russell's early metaphysics, his theory of logic, his philosophy of mathematics, logical atomism (including theories of language and theories of knowledge), neutral monism (mind and matter, and the private and public world), politics and education, and ethics and religion. The study concludes with an account of Russell's views concerning the relations of religion and philosophy.

The study of any work by Russell profits from some acquaintance with ideas developed in other works. Hence, although Jager has little to say about *An Inquiry into Meaning and Truth*, he has enough to say about the views presented there but expressed and defended in other works to make the reading of this study all the more rewarding. The sections on truth of propositions, sense-data and constructions, the neutrality of sensations, perception and the external world, perspectival privacy and egocentricity, and structure and knowledge are especially helpful. Of the chapters "Atomism: Theory of Language," "Atomism: Theories of Knowledge," "Neutral Mo-

nism: Mind and Matter," and (especially—for here a criticism of the work figures prominently) "Neutral Monism: The Private and the Public World" are the most helpful for one studying *An Inquiry into Meaning and Truth*.

In his Introduction to Russell's philosophy Jager identifies three phases of his thought: the realist phase, the atomist phase, and the neutral monist phase. The realist phase, according to Jager, was concerned with the metaphysical doctrine of external relations; the atomist phase with logical considerations; and the neutral monist phase with the ideals of science. Jager then identifies two dominant themes in Russell's work—the idea that philosophy must begin with logical analysis and then proceed to synthesis, and the idea that technical devices (of logic and mathematics) have their counterparts in general philosophy, and *vice versa*. Jager's study is a critical examination of Russell; the attempt is made not only to explicate Russell's work but also to point out its weaknesses and strengths. The result is a very helpful and substantial work of philosophical review.

Chisholm, Roderick M. "Russell on the Foundations of Empirical Knowledge," in *The Philosophy of Bertrand Russell* (The Library of Living Philosophers). Vol. V. Edited by Paul A. Schilpp. Evanston, Illinois: The Library of Living Philosophers, 1946, pp. 419-444.

Roderick M. Chisholm, of Brown University, presents a searching and detailed examination of Bertrand Russell's account of epistemological order. It is an account which distinguishes between primitive knowledge, consisting in the knowledge of the truth of certain basic "psychological premises," and derivative knowledge based on the former. The focus is on the idea of basic propositions since a psychological premise is defined as a proposition "expressing a belief not derived from any other belief."

Chisholm not only considers what Russell said—an effort that requires speculation on Chisholm's part—but also what Russell might have said; that is, other possibilities that bear on the problem of epistemological order. The analysis throughout is careful and rewarding, and Russell wrote an extended reply (also included in the Paul A. Schilpp volume) .

The problem Chisholm considers is that of giving

an account of basic propositions such that they can be seen to be indeed basic—not dependent for their understanding or their truth on anything beyond what is given; the evidence for such a proposition was presumed by Russell to be a "perceptive occurrence" which is its cause. Such a proposition must be synthetic, known to be true independently of other propositions, and determinable by analysis as given ("postanalytically" given, as Chisholm puts it). The difficulty in giving such an account is that of formulating immediate knowledge so as to generate epistemological premises that are synthetic, do not refer beyond given sense-data, and can be logically related to the propositions of science.

Chisholm finds difficulties in Russell's suggestion in *An Inquiry into Meaning and Truth* that a basic proposition (reporting a red "patch" as given) of the form "This is red" is better expressed in the form "Redness is here"; the term "red" is a name, not a predicate, and what it names is the quality "red" itself. Such a proposition, Russell argued in his work, does not describe a substance as being red; it refers to a quality as "here-now": "There is something that is redness here-now."

Chisholm reports Russell's view as that of maintaining that in the perceptual situation we are confronted by the universal ("redness") and not by a particular or instance of the universal. Moreover, in this formulation "a more perplexing problem" arises, Chisholm argues—that of avoiding "ego-centric words" in the formulation of basic propositions. ("Ego-centric words" are such words as "this," "that," "here," "now," "I," "me," and so forth, according to Russell in *An Inquiry into Meaning and Truth*.)

As Chisholm reads Russell, Russell attempts to solve the problem of eliminating egocentric particulars by regarding the quality referred to in a basic proposition as part of a "bundle" of qualities; the bundle of qualities is the subject of the proposition, specified by a "name" (such as "this" as in "This is hot," the term "hot" naming the quality); and the judgment of perception, although a "judgment of analysis" (report of analysis) is "not an analytic judgment" (judgment by definition) because we can refer to the bundle by a name without knowing what qualities constitute the bundle.

Chisholm dismisses Russell's theory as having no plausibility. He argues that Russell appears to reintroduce the notion of substance in talking about the unexperienced parts of a whole. Chisholm also argues that not all judgments of perception are judgments of analysis and, finally, that if the "bundles" are bundles of qualities, it would be possible for such a bundle to recur (and hence the presumed basic proposition would not be concerned with a unique fact of the kind that could serve as the foundation of empirical knowledge).

Chisholm suggests, as an alternative solution to the problem of egocentric particulars, the introduction of "time-qualia," on the assumption that *times*, like colors, sounds, and so on, can be experienced immediately; the reference to a time of a quality would thus be specific without the use of an egocentric word.

In his reply to Chisholm, Russell spends more than half of the space defending the claim that there is an epistemological order. He states his agreement with most of what Chisholm writes. He denies, however, that he asserted or believes that a quality is a universal; it is a particular. He reaffirms his belief and hope that every judgment of perception is a partial analysis of a whole that is a bundle of qualities. He argues that although we can always experience the parts of such a bundle if we attend to them, it is also possible that we can identify a whole without attending to each and every one of its parts. The possibility of recurrence Russell regards as "a merit." Finally, he rejects the "time-qualia" proposal as "not . . . plausible" for two reasons: he can find no sense qualia in his experience, and the theory makes time absolute instead of relational.

Additional Recommended Reading

Pears, D. F., ed. *Bertrand Russell: A Collection of Critical Essays*. Garden City, New York: Anchor Books, 1972. An excellent anthology of critical articles by eminent philosophers: W. V. O. Quine, A. J. Ayer, D. F. Pears, Jaakko Hintikka, Anthony Quinton, Grover Maxwell, Charles A. Fritz, Jr., G. Kreisel, Rudolf Carnap, Kurt Gödel, David Kaplan, Charles S. Chihara, Jules Vuillemin, and D. H. Munro. Harru Ruja provides an excellent bibliography of works by and about Russell.

Schilpp, Paul A., ed. *The Philosophy of Bertrand Russell* (The Library of Living Philosophers). Vol. V. Evanston, Illinois: The Library of Living Philosophers, 1946. An invaluable collection of critical articles, plus Russell's autobiographical account, replies to his critics, and a bibliography of his writings to 1944. Includes material by Hans Reichenbach, Morris Weitz, Kurt Gödel, James Feibleman, G. E. Moore, Max Black, Philip P.

Wiener, Albert Einstein, John Laird, Ernest Nagel, W. T. Stace, Andrew Paul Ushenko, Roderick M. Chisholm, Harold Chapman Brown, John Elof Boodin, Justus Buchler, Edgar Sheffield Brightman, Eduard C. Lindeman, Boyd H. Bode, and Sidney Hook.

BEING AND NOTHINGNESS

Author: Jean-Paul Sartre (1905-1980)
Type of work: Existential metaphysics
First published: 1943

Principal Ideas Advanced

Being is never exhausted by any of its phenomenal aspects; no particular perspective reveals the entire character of being.

Being-in-itself (en-soi) *is fixed, complete, wholly given, absolutely contingent, with no reason for its being; it is roughly equivalent to the inert world of objects and things.*

Being-for-itself (pour-soi) *is incomplete, fluid, indeterminate; it corresponds to the being of human consciousness.*

Being-in-itself is prior to being-for-itself; the latter is dependent upon the former for its origin; being-for-itself is derived from being-in-itself by an act of nihilation, for being-for-itself is a nothingness in the heart of being.

Freedom is the nature of man; in anxiety man becomes aware of his freedom, knows himself responsible for his own being by commitment, seeks the impossible reunion with being-in-itself, and in despair knows himself forever at odds with the "others" who by their glances can threaten a man, turning him into a mere object.

The subtitle of *Being and Nothingness, An Essay on Phenomenological Ontology,* states clearly the central intention of the author. Jean-Paul Sartre is at one with Parmenides and Plato in his contention that the chief problem of philosophy is the problem of being. Significant differences, however, emerge in a comparison of the ontological investigations of the ancient Greeks with those of the contemporary Frenchman. The adjective, "phenomenological," in the subtitle of Sartre's classic, indicates one of these significant differences.

Sartre's ontology is an ontology that follows in the wake of Immanuel Kant's critical philosophy, Edmund Husserl's phenomenological reduction, and Martin Heidegger's ontology of *Dasein. Being and Nothingness* has all of the Kantian reservations about any philosophy which seeks to proceed beyond the limits of possible experience, draws heavily from the phenomenological investigations of Husserl, and exhibits basically the same form of analysis and description as was used in Heidegger's *Being and Time* (1927). Nevertheless, Kant, Husserl, and Heidegger intermittently throughout the work fall under some rather trenchant Sartrian criticism. Kant's chief mistake was his appeal to a "thing-in-itself" which somehow stands behind the phenomena. In Sartre's phenomenological ontology there is nothing concealed behind the phenomena or the appearances. The appearances embody full reality. They are indicative of themselves and refer to nothing but themselves. The Kantian dualism of phenomena and noumena, appearance and reality, is abolished, and being is made coextensive with phenomena. Husserl comes in for a similar criticism. His hypothesis of a transcendental ego is pronounced useless and disastrous. The fate of such a view, according to Sartre, is shipwreck on the "reef of solipsism." The faults of Heidegger are not as grievous as those of Kant and Husserl. As becomes apparent on every page of *Being and Nothingness*, Sartre's analysis is markedly informed by Heideggerian concepts. Yet Heidegger, argues the author, neglects the phenomenon of the lived body, has no explanation for the concrete relatedness of selves, and misinterprets the existential significance of death.

Being, in Sartre's analysis, evinces a *transphe-*

nomenal character. Although there is no *noumena* and no *thing-in-itself* which lies concealed behind the phenomenal appearances of being, being is never exhausted in any of its particular phenomenal aspects. Being, in the totality of its aspects and manifestations, never becomes wholly translucent to consciousness. Everything which has being "overflows" whatever particular categories, designations, and descriptions human knowledge may attach to it. Being evinces relationships and qualities which escape any specific determination. Although being is reduced to the whole of its phenomenal manifestations, it is in no way exhausted by any *particular* perspective that man has of the phenomena. All phenomena overflow themselves, suggesting other phenomena yet to be disclosed. This primordial being, transphenomenal in character, expresses a fundamental rupture into "being-in-itself" (*en-soi*) and "being-for-itself" (*pour-soi*).

Being-in-itself designates being in the mode of fullness or plenitude. It is massive, fixed, complete in itself, totally and wholly given. It is devoid of potency and becoming, roughly equivalent to the inert world of objects and things. It has no inside and no outside. It expresses neither a relationship with itself nor a relationship to anything outside itself. It is further characterized by an absolute contingency. There is no reason for its being. It is superfluous (*de trop*). "Uncreated, without reason for being, without connection with any other being, being-in-itself is superfluous for all eternity."

Being-for-itself is fluid and vacuous rather than fixed and full. It is characterized by incompleteness, potency, and lack of determinate structure. As being-in-itself is roughly equivalent to the inert and solidified world of objectivized reality, so being-for-itself generally corresponds to the being of human consciousness. These two modes of being, however, are not granted an equal ontological status. Being-in-itself is both logically and ontologically prior to being-for-itself. The latter is dependent upon the former for its origin. Being-for-itself is inconceivable without being-in-itself and is derived from it through an original nihilation (*néantisation*). Being-for-itself thus constitutes a nihilation of being-in-itself. Being-for-itself makes its appearance as a nothingness

which "lies coiled in the heart of being—like a worm." The being of the for-itself is a "borrowed" being which emerges from the in-itself by virtue of its power of negation. The source of the power of nothingness remains inexplicable and mysterious. The for-itself simply finds itself *there*, separated and at a distance from the absolute fullness of the in-itself. The for-itself emerges as an irreducible and ultimate datum.

One of the fateful consequences of the primordial rupture of the for-itself from the in-itself is the introduction of nothingness. Sartre makes it clear that it is through man or human consciousness that nothingness comes into the world. In his discussion on nothingness Sartre is intent upon rejecting the Hegelian dialectical approach and substituting for it a phenomenological account. For Hegel, being and nothingness are dialectical concepts which take their rise from the same ontological level of mediated reality. Sartre maintains in his phenomenological approach that nothingness is dependent upon being in a way that being is not dependent upon nothingness. Nothingness is not an abstract idea complementary to being, nor can it be conceived outside of being; it must be given at the heart of being. Nothingness demands a host, possessing the plenitude and full positivity of being, from which it borrows its power of nihilation. Thus, nothingness has only a borrowed or marginal being. Although Sartre never acknowledges his debt to Augustine on this point, his analysis seems to draw heavily from Augustinian sources. Augustine had already described evil as a tendency toward nothingness, the movement presupposing perfect being as a host in which evil exists as a privation of the good. It would indeed seem that in its basic outlines Sartre's analysis of nothingness is little more than a secularized Augustinianism. The introduction of nothingness raises the question of its relation to negative judgments.

As Heidegger had done before him, Sartre insists that nothingness is the origin and foundation of negative judgments, rather than vice versa. This foundation finds its clarification in the context of human expectations and projects. Sartre, as an example, tells of expecting to find a person (Pierre) in a cafe when in fact he is not present: my expectation of finding

Pierre has caused the absence of Pierre to happen as a real event pertaining to the cafe. I discover his absence as an objective fact. I look for him and find that he is not there, thus disclosing a synthetic relation between Pierre and the setting in which I have expected him to be. There obtains a *real* relation between Pierre and the cafe, as distinct from the relation of *not-being* which characterizes the order of thought in simple negative judgments. To make the negative judgment that Pierre is not in the cafe has purely abstract meaning. It is without real or efficacious foundation.

We have observed that it is through man that nothingness comes into the world. The question then arises: what is it about the being of man that occasions nothingness? The answer is: freedom. The freedom which is here revealed should in no way be identified with a property or a quality which somehow attaches to man's original nature. Freedom is the "nature" of man. There is no difference between the being of man and his being-free. As becomes apparent later in *Being and Nothingness*, Sartre's ontology of man is a philosophy of radical and total freedom. This consciousness of freedom is disclosed in anxiety. "It is in anxiety that man gets the consciousness of his freedom; or if you prefer, anxiety is the mode of being of freedom as consciousness of being; it is in anxiety that freedom is, in its being, in question of itself." There is thus an internal connection among nothingness, freedom, and anxiety. These are interrelated structural determinants of the being of man.

Nothingness, freedom, and anxiety provide the conditions which make possible the movement of "bad faith" (*mauvaise foi*). Bad faith is a form of self-deception which in making use of freedom denies it. Bad faith is akin to lying, yet not identical with it. In lying one hides the truth from others. In bad faith one hides the truth from oneself. In the former there is a duality of deceiver and deceived; in the latter there is a unity of a single consciousness. Bad faith does not come from the outside. Consciousness affects itself with it" In describing the pattern of bad faith Sartre develops the example of a woman who consents to go out with an amorous suitor. She is fully aware of his intentions and knows that sooner or later she will have to make a decision. An immediate

decision is demanded when he caresses her hand. If she leaves her hand there she encourages his advances; if she withdraws it she may well preclude any further relationship with the suitor. She must decide, but she seeks means for postponing the decision. It is at this point that bad faith comes into play. She leaves her hand in his, but does not notice that she is doing so. She becomes all intellect, divorces her soul from her body, and transforms her body into an object or thing—into the mode of "being-in-itself." Her hand becomes "a thing," neither consenting nor resisting. She objectivizes her body, and ultimately herself, as in-itself, and thus stages a flight or an escape from herself as for-itself. She loses her subjectivity, her freedom, and her responsibility for decision. She exists in bad faith.

The pursuit of being leads to an awareness of nothingness, nothingness to an awareness of freedom, freedom to bad faith, and bad faith to the being of consciousness which provides the condition for its possibility. We are thus led to an interrogation of the immediate structures of the for-itself as consciousness. The immediate consciousness in which the self experiences presence is what Sartre calls the nonpositional consciousness. This consciousness characterizes the level of primitive awareness, and is prior to the positional consciousness which is the reflective consciousness of the intentional action. Nonpositional consciousness is prereflective; therefore, Sartre describes it as a prereflective cogito (*cogito pre-reflexif*). This prereflective cogito quite clearly precedes the Cartesian cogito, which is a movement of reflection, and becomes the foundation for it. Positional consciousness, on the other hand, is reflective in character, directed toward some intentional object. Sartre has taken over Husserl's doctrine of intentionality and has made it central to his description of the positional consciousness. Positional consciousness is always consciousness *of* something. It is directed outward into a *world*. But the positional consciousness can also be directed reflexively upon itself. Consciousness can become conscious of itself as being conscious. It is in this way that the ego or the self is posited or derived. Both the world and the ego or self are posited by the projecting activity of the for-itself in its nonpositional freedom, and they become correlative phenomena inextricably bound up at their very source. Without the world there is no ego, and without the ego there is no world. Both the world and the ego are hypostatized through reflection as unifying, ideal limits.

One of the central structural elements of the for-itself is facticity. The for-itself apprehends itself as a lack or decompression of being. It is not its own foundation. It is a "hole" in the heart of being, infected with nothingness, abandoned to a world without justification. It discovers itself thrown into a situation, buffeted by brute contingencies, for the most part superfluous and "in the way." Facticity indicates the utter contingency and irrevocable situationality of the being of the for-itself. Without facticity consciousness could choose its attachments to the world—it would be absolute and unfettered freedom. But the freedom which the for-itself experiences is always restricted by the situation in which it is abandoned. Nevertheless, the freedom of the for-itself is a *real* freedom and even in its facticity the for-itself perpetually relates itself to itself in freedom. I do not become a bourgeois or a Frenchman until I *choose* to become such. Freedom is always present, translating facticity into possibility. In the final analysis the for-itself is totally responsible for its being.

Value and possibility provide two additional structures of the for-itself. Value is an expression of an impossible striving toward a coincidence of being. The for-itself perpetually strives to surpass itself toward reunion with the in-itself, thus achieving totality by healing the fundamental rupture in being. But this totality is an impossible synthesis. As soon as the for-itself would become coincident with the in-itself it would lose itself as for-itself. A final totality remains forever unattainable because it would combine the incompatible characteristics of the in-itself (positivity and plenitude) and the for-itself (negativity and lack). The impossible striving for reunion gives rise to the unhappy or alienated consciousness. The for-itself is "sick in its being" because it is haunted by a totality which it seeks to attain but never can without losing itself as for-itself. "The being of human reality is suffering because it emerges in being as perpetually haunted by a totality which it is without being able to be it, since it would not be able to attain

the in-itself without losing itself as for-itself. Human reality therefore is by nature an unhappy consciousness, without the possibility of surpassing its unhappy state." Now possibility, as an immediate structure of the for-itself, provides further clarification of the meaning of the for-itself as lack. The possible is what the for-itself lacks in its drive for completeness and totality. It indicates the *not yet* of human reality, the openness of its constant striving.

The structures of the for-itself are ontologically rooted in temporality, which provides their unifying ground. This temporality is understood in Sartre's phenomenological analysis as a synthesis of structured moments. The "elements" or directions of time (past, present, and future) do not constitute an infinite series of nows, or collected "givens," in which some are no longer and others are not yet. If time is understood as an infinite series of discrete nows, then the whole series is annihilated. The past nows are no longer real, the future nows are not yet real, and the present now is always slipping away, functioning only as a limit of an infinite division. In such a view time evaporates and is dissolved into an infinite "dust of instants" which are ontologically anemic. A phenomenological analysis of the time of the immediate consciousness avoids this dissolution of temporality by describing the elements of time as "structured moments of an original synthesis."

Following Heidegger, Sartre speaks of time as an *ecstatic* unity in which the past is *still* existentially real, the future *already* existentially real, and in which past and future coalesce in the present. However, Sartre differs from Heidegger in refusing to ascribe ontological priority to the future. No ecstasis of time has any priority over any of the others; none can exist without the other two. If, indeed, one is to accent any ecstasis, Sartre maintains that it would be phenomenologically closer to the facts to accent the present rather than the future. The past remains an integral part of my being. It is not something which I had or possessed at one time; it is something of which I am aware here and now. The past is always bound to my present. Man is always related to his past, but he is at the same time separated from it insofar as he engages in a constant movement from himself as past to himself as future. The past tends to become solidified and thus takes on the quality of an in-itself. It is defined as a for-itself which has become an in-itself. It takes on a character of completeness and fixity, but it still remains mine, and as long as it remains a part of my consciousness it can be recovered in an act of choice. The past provides the ontological foundation for facticity. In a very real sense the past and facticity indicate one and the same thing. The past makes possible my experience of abandonment and situationality. In contrast to the past which has become an in-itself, the present remains a full-embodied for-itself. The author defines the present as a "perpetual flight in the face of being." It exhibits a flight from the being that it was and a flight towards the being that it will be. Strictly speaking, the for-itself as present has its being outside of itself—behind it and before it. It was its past and will be its future. The for-itself as present is not what it is (past) and is what it is not (future). The future is a mode of being which the for-itself must strive to be. As a mode of being it designates an existential quality which one *is*, rather than an abstract property which one *has*. The future is a lack which is constitutive of my subjectivity. As the past provides the foundation for facticity, so the future provides the foundation for possibility. The future constitutes the meaning of my present for-itself as a project of possibilities. The future is not a series of chronologically ordered nows which are yet to come. Rather, it is a region of my being, which circumscribes my expanding possibilities, and defines me as a for-itself who is always on the way.

The temporalized world of the for-itself is not an insulated world experienced in isolation. In the world of the for-itself the "others" (*autrui*) have already made their appearance. Hence, the being of the for-itself is always a being-for-others as well. The discussion of the problem of the interrelation of personal selves occupies a lengthy and important part of *Being and Nothingness*. The author begins with an examination and criticism of the views of Hegel, Husserl, and Heidegger, and then proceeds to a positive formulation of his own. The "other" is already disclosed in the movements of the pre-reflective, nonpositional consciousness. Shame affords an example of a pre-

reflective, disclosure of the "other," as well as a disclosure of myself as standing before the other. Through shame I discover simultaneously the "other" and an aspect of my being. *I am ashamed of *myself* before the "*other*." The "other" reveals myself to me. I need the "other" in order to realize fully all the structures of my being. It is thus that the structures of being-for-itself and being-for-others are inseparable.

In the phenomenon of "the look" (*le regard*) we find another example of the prereflective disclosure of the self and the other. It is through the look that the "other" irrupts into my world, decentralizes and dissolves it, and then by reference to his own projects reconstitutes it and the freedom which I experience. When I am "looked at" the stability of my world and the freedom which I experience as for-itself are threatened. The "other" is apprehended as one who is about to steal my world, suck me into the orbit of his concerns, and reduce me to the mode of being-in-itself—to an object or a thing. "Being-seen-by-the-other" involves becoming an object for the "other." When the movement of the look is completed I am no longer a free subject; I have fallen into the slavery of the "other." "Thus being-seen constitutes me as a being without defenses for a freedom which is not my freedom. It is in this sense that we can consider ourselves as slaves in so far as we appear to the other. But this slavery is not the result of a life in the abstract form of consciousness. I am a slave to the degree that my being is dependent at the center of a freedom which is not mine and which is the very condition of my being." It is in this way that the existence of the "other" determines my original fall—a fall which can be most generally described as a fall from myself as being-for-itself into the mode of being-in-itself. My only defense is the objectivization of the "other." Through *my* look I can seek to shatter the world of the "other" and divest him of his subjective freedom. Indeed I seek to remove the other from my world and put him out of play, but this can never succeed, because the existence of the other is a contingent and irreducible fact. I *encounter* the "other"; I do not *constitute* him. The "other" remains, threatening to counterattack my defenses with *his* look. Thus there results a constant cycle of mutual objectivization. I affirm my freedom by rendering the "other" into an object. Then the "other" affirms his freedom by rendering me into an object. Then I stage an existential counterattack, and the cycle repeats itself. According to the author there seems to be no end to this sort of thing. The upshot of all this is an irreconcilable conflict between the self and the "other," with a consequent breakdown of all communication. Alienation has the last word in Sartre's doctrine of intersubjectivity. The reader who searches for a positive doctrine of community, searches in vain. All forms of "being-*with*" find their common denominator in an alienating "being-*for*."

In the relation of the for-itself with the "other" the body appears as a central phenomenon. The body is discussed in the context of three ontological dimensions: (1) the body as I exist it, (2) the body as utilized and known by the "other," and (3) the body as I exist it in reference to its being known by the "other." The body as I exist it is not the objectivized body constituted by nerves, glands, muscles, and organs. Such an objectivized body is present for the physician when he gives me a medical examination, but I do not apprehend my body in this way. I apprehend my body in its lived concreteness as that phenomenon which indicates my possibilities in the world. The body as *concretely lived* signifies a level of being which is fundamentally different from the body as *objectively known*. The body as concretely lived reveals an original relation to the world of immediate and practical concerns. I carry out my practical concerns through instruments or utensils,

Sartre, in the development of his concept of the world, draws heavily from Heidegger and defines the world of immediate experience as an instrumental world. Instruments refer to my body, insofar as the body apprehends and modifies the world through the use of instruments. My body and the world are thus coextensive. My body is spread out across the utensils which I use. My body is everywhere in the world. To have a body and to experience that there is a world are one and the same thing. However, not only do I exist my body, but my body is also utilized and known by the "other." This second ontological dimension indicates my body as a body-for-the-other. My body as known by the "other," and so also his body as known by me, is always a body-in-a-situa-

tion. The body of the "other" is apprehended within the movements of a situation as a synthetic totality of life and action. The isolated appendages and gestures of another's body have no significance outside the context of a situation. A clenched fist in itself means nothing. Only when the clenched fist is apprehended as an integral part of a synthetic totality of life movements is the lived body of the "other" disclosed. A corpse is no longer in a situation, and hence can be known only in its modality of death as an anatomical-physiological entity. The third ontological dimension indicates the reappraisal of my body as a body which is known by and exists for the "other." Thus alienation enters my world. My body becomes a tool or an object for the "other." My body flows to the "other," who sucks it into the orbit of his projects and brings about the dissolution of my world. This alienation is made manifest through affective structures such as shyness. Blushing, for example, expresses the consciousness of my body not as I live it for myself, but as I live it for the "other." I cannot be embarrassed by my own body as I exist it. Only a body which exists for the "other" can become an occasion for embarrassment.

In the concrete relation of the for-itself with the "other," two sets of contradictory attitudes make their appearance. On the one hand, there are the attitudes of love and masochism, and on the other hand, the attitudes of hatred and sadism. In the love relationship the beloved is for the lover not simply a thing which he desires to possess. The analogy of ownership breaks down in an explanation of love. Love expresses a special kind of appropriation. The lover wants to assimilate the love of the beloved without destroying his or her freedom. But this relationship of love ultimately founders because it is impossible to maintain an absolute subjectivity or freedom without objectivizing another as the material for one's freedom. This accounts for the insecurity of love. The lover is perpetually in danger of being made to appear as an object. In masochism the annihilation of subjectivity is deliberately directed inward. The masochist puts himself forward as an in-itself for the "other." He sets up conditions so that he can be assimilated by the "other"; thus, he deliberately transforms himself into an object. Hatred and sadism constitute the reverse attitude. Here there is an attempt to objectivize the "other" rather than oneself. The sadist seeks to "incarnate" the "other" by using his body as a tool. The "other" becomes an instrument in his hands and thus appropriates the freedom of the "other." But simplest form is an attempt to appropriate the freedom of the "other." But this attempt results in failure because the "other" can always turn back upon the sadist and make an object out of him. Thus, again, the reader is made aware of the futility of all attempts to establish harmonious relations with the "other." This inability to achieve genuine communication leads to a despair in which nothing remains for the for-itself but to become involved in the circularity of objectivization in which it passes from one to the other of the two fundamental attitudes.

The author concludes his phenomenological essay with a restatement and further elucidation of the nature and quality of human freedom, and a delineation of his program of existential psychoanalysis. Freedom is discussed in relation to the will, in relation to facticity, and finally in relation to responsibility. The will can never be the condition of freedom; it is simply a psychological manifestation of it. The will presupposes the foundation of an original freedom in order to be able to constitute itself as will. The will is derived or posited by reflective decision. It is a psychological manifestation which emerges within the complex of motives and ends already posited by the for-itself. Properly speaking, it is not the will that is free. Man is free. The will is simply a manifestation of man's primordial freedom. Freedom in relation to facticity gives rise to the situation. The situation is that ambiguous phenomenon in which it is impossible clearly to distinguish the contribution of freedom and the determinants of brute circumstance. This accounts for the paradox of freedom. There is freedom only in a situation, and there is a situation only through freedom. Sartre delineates five structures of the situation in which freedom and facticity interpenetrate each other: (1) my place, (2) my past, (3) my environment, (4) my fellow man, and (5) my death. Insofar as freedom always interpenetrates facticity, man becomes wholly responsible for himself. I am responsible for everything except for the fact of my

responsibility. I am free, but I am not free to obliterate fully my freedom. I am condemned to be free. This abandonment to freedom is an expression of my facticity. Yet I must assume responsibility for the fact that my facticity is incomprehensible and contingent. The result is that my facticity or my final abandonment consists simply in the fact that I am condemned to be wholly responsible for myself. Although freedom and facticity interpenetrate, it remains incontestable that freedom is given a privileged status in the Sartrian view of man.

The touchstone of existential psychoanalysis is a concentration on man's fundamental project (*projet fondamental*). This fundamental project is neither Heidegger's *Sein-zum-Tode*, nor is it Freud's libidinal cathexis. The method of existential psychoanalysis resembles that of the Freudians in that an effort is made to work back through secondary and superficial manifestations of personality to an ultimate and primary project, but the existentialist differs with Freud concerning the nature of this project. The Freudian localizes the project in a libidinal attachment which is determined by the past history of the self. The existential psychoanalyst broadens the framework of explanation to include the future projects of the self as well. The fundamental project is thus understood in the context of man's temporalized being, which includes the ecstatic unity of past, present, and future. The irreducible minimum of this fundamental project is the *desire to be*. Quite clearly, it is impossible to advance farther than being, but in having advanced thus far one has undercut the simple empirical determinants of behavior. The goal of this desire to be is to attain the impermeability, solidity, and infinite density of the in-itself. The ideal toward which consciousness strives is to be the foundation of its own being. It strives to become an "in-itself-for-itself," an ideal which can properly be defined as God. One can thus most simply express the fundamental project of man as the desire to be God. But the idea of God is contradictory, for in striving after this ideal the self can only lose itself as for-itself. Man's fundamental desire to give birth to God results in failure. He must thus reconcile himself to the fact that his is a useless passion.

Pertinent Literature

Grene, Marjorie. *Sartre*. New York: New Viewpoints, 1973.

Being and Nothingness is "one of the treasure-houses" of Western philosophy, according to Marjorie Grene. Even despite its distortion of realities through its obsession with nothingness, she contends, it reveals much about man through its occasionally brilliant phenomenological descriptions and particularly through the unusual subtlety of its arguments.

Grene's book is itself in many ways a masterful piece of argumentation. Actually, it is a critique of Jean-Paul Sartre's entire philosophy, from the early works on imagination and the emotions on through to *L'idiot de la famille,* Sartre's existential psychoanalysis of Gustave Flaubert which he never finished. The principal thrust of Grene's book is an attack on Sartre's Cartesianism. Yet she sees Sartre as a tragic figure to whom we can feel considerable indebtedness, since he, more than any other twentieth century thinker, has honestly faced the consequences of the crisis that Cartesianism has wrought in all of us. He thus may aid us in finally and completely evading those consequences ourselves.

Unfortunately, Chapter IV of Grene's book, which attempts to give a critical sketch of the whole of *Being and Nothingness* in barely thirty pages, can be followed only if the reader has the text of *Being and Nothingness* close at hand or fresh in mind; but it is here that she demonstrates most astutely that Sartre's "prereflective *cogito*," only a variant of the isolated Cartesian *cogito*, must, even as Sartre successfully overcomes all the traditional dualisms, lead him inevitably to espouse the dualism of all dualisms: the sheer surging forth of consciousness against a meaningless plenum.

In Chapter V, Grene's style is more expansive, as befits her subject matter. Here she retraces her steps to Parts III and IV of *Being and Nothingness* for a more thorough treatment of interpersonal relations, the body, and the emotions. She first points to the way in which Sartre's move out of solipsism, by way of shame, from the prereflective *cogito* to the *cogito* that reveals the Other, exactly parallels René Descartes'

move, by way of reverence, from himself to the divine Other. Of course, the contrast between the God who founds all being and Sartre's "Other" who will not let him be "because *he* would be instead" is enormous, but Grene nevertheless finds Cartesian biases sustaining the adversary relationship that pervades all Sartrean community. First, Sartre's confining of the prereflective *cogito* to the nonthetic consciousness (of) *self* completely blinds him both to that "from-to" awareness that Edmund Husserl sees as an integral part of the self-world relationship and to the already-being-out-there-with-other-people that both Michael Polanyi and Martin Heidegger portray as fundamental to the structures of human existence and prior to methodological doubt. Second, Sartre's adherence to Descartes atomistic ideals of the instant and of freedom prevent him from seeing that both the for-itself and the for-others, although never derivable from each other, both depend for their being on what Grene refers to as the "among others." Third, and this is even more basic, Sartre's acceptance of the Cartesian division of consciousness from the body brings him to the impasse expressed in his statement, "The body is the instrument which I am." As a consequence of this, Sartrean man can never live in his own body as the vehicle of knowledge and of rational activity. In his perennial conflict with the Other, therefore, he strives to reduce the Other to body in order to put him out of action and so to defeat him. He never experiences the "among-others" as the bodily-being-together of persons.

In his discussion of the emotions Sartre reaches an even more serious impasse, Grene argues. She shows that passion for Sartre can have no authentic standing; it can only be deceptively emancipated from its role as the nonthetic other-side of reason. Reason, on the other hand, is empty. Only in nihilating choice can reason assert itself as free. In the final analysis, Sartre reduces Cartesian reason to will, depriving it of all content for the sake of its autonomy. But reason must have content as well as goal. And this, despite Sartre's pressing need to force the nonthetic mode of consciousness constantly in upon itself, he can discover only as a product of the passion to become God. Grene leads her reader to see that the irony and perhaps the tragedy of Sartre is to aspire, like his mentor Descartes, to a state "free of all cares and limited by no passions" only to discover and confess in the midst of that striving that he is nothing but a useless passion. For passion not to be useless, Grene contends, it must aim to be something less than the *causa sui*. It must have an end that is both lived and known, that is grounded both in history and in community, and that assents to the embodied being out of which it grows.

Anderson, Thomas C. *The Foundation and Structure of Sartrean Ethics*. Lawrence: The Regents Press of Kansas, 1979.

Thomas C. Anderson's book offers a counter to those many critics of Jean-Paul Sartre who contend that the ontology of *Being and Nothingness* will not support an ethics. Anderson, who believes that Sartre is one of the most misunderstood of modern philosophers, makes a careful textual analysis of sections of *Being and Nothingness* which he claims can ground a moral philosophy and calls on the later Sartrean writings as well as on the writings of Simone de Beauvoir and Francis Jeanson for aid in constructing a plausible moral theory which, to his mind, is truly representative of Sartre's views. His work contains many insights and cogent arguments, but he writes with a quite Pelagian bias that can blind him to the ineradicability of grounding ambiguities in Sartre's thinking and can therefore repeatedly lead him to an overly simplistic and vitiating interpretation of it.

A principal emphasis of Anderson is that the central goal for authentic Sartrean man is not to be God but to be free. It is true that for Sartre all men desire to be in-itself-for-itself or God; but that desire is on the prereflective or "lived" level. Reflection sees that being God is an impossible ideal. But more importantly, reflection is capable of acknowledging that this ideal has value only with respect to man as a contingent being. To Anderson it follows that this ideal need not be chosen as a goal. Only those, he says, who are prey to the debilitating spirit of seriousness expressly *choose* to be God. Good faith, in contrast, asserts human freedom as the highest value because freedom is itself the source of all values, including even the aim to be God. From all this Anderson concludes that life need not, after all, be a "useless passion." Sartre's readers too often forget, he claims, that the description in *Being and Nothing-*

ness of man pursuing an unattainable end is intended only to portray man in bad faith. But here he himself fails to take seriously enough Sartre's repeated insistence that man must out of structural necessity always posit as his original choice some mode of the in-itself-for-itself.

Anderson believes that the reason why it is not sufficiently recognized that Sartre's ultimate value is freedom is that Sartrean authenticity has been too much stressed. The authentic person is simply one who accepts himself and his situation without fleeing from them. "Authentic," Anderson maintains, is an overly abstract and rather empty term used to designate the person who knows that his own freedom is the source of all values, who accepts responsibility for this, and thus makes freedom his ultimate value. The authentic person is simply one who accepts himself and his situation without fleeing from them.

Why does Sartre single out freedom as ultimate? Simply, Anderson says, because for him freedom is the source from which all meaningful values spring; and the choosing of any value logically entails the valuing of freedom as a more fundamental choice. But is not freedom, then, through this very logic, somehow elevated to the rank of an intrinsic value? On the contrary, Anderson insists. What has value has value because we choose it. It is precisely because nothing, including freedom, has intrinsic value, because all values, including the value of freedom, are created out of freedom, that freedom should be chosen first of all. Thus Anderson shows that, rather surprisingly, Sartre's very subjectivism regarding values grounds his ethics rather than rendering it impossible.

But what sense does it make to choose freedom,

according it value, when, as Sartre everywhere insists, man is already fundamentally free? Critics who ask this question of Sartre, Anderson argues, forget that if something is a fact, that does not automatically make it valuable. Sartre is not guilty of the naturalistic fallacy. Quite to the contrary, he makes a distinction between freedom as an aspect of man's ontological structure and freedom as choice related to action. Men are quite free, for example, to reject or hide from their structural freedom as they do when they choose to believe in determinism. Furthermore, Anderson shows, Sartre insists repeatedly that although man is ontologically free, he should choose to realize his freedom ever more fully through striving to remove restrictions to choice and to the attaining of his goals. But, then, is freedom seen only negatively as "freedom-from"? No, Anderson answers, freedom once liberated has a goal. It aims at exercising and developing the multifaceted features of human life. Fundamentally, this goal is not external to man. Sartre can even speak of his ideal for man as "play," the pursuing of the free expansion of human existence. It is this, Anderson points out, that Sartre calls "true and positive humanism."

Anderson has a whole array of criticisms to make of the way Sartre grounds his ethics in *Being and Nothingness*. A most telling one involves pointing out that Sartre does not use the term "value" consistently. One result of this, Anderson believes, is that

although Sartre successfully demonstrates that it is morally right for man to choose to value the capacity for choice, he has not established, as he believes, that a similar obligation exists for man to make free choice more real by changing his situation so as to increase his options for choice. Another criticism which is as important as any Anderson makes is that Sartre never explains convincingly why one must believe that logic and consistency are necessarily included in the choice of a meaningful life.

In the area of interpersonal relations, on the other hand, Anderson strongly defends Sartre, maintaining that Sartrean man is not nearly so estranged from the Other as Sartre's opponents claim. He contends that "conflict," taken in the strict sense, does not mean open hostility but means instead ontological distinctness and psychological objectification. These can, he acknowledges, be the basis for hostility; but they need not be. There is not even any necessity that men relate as being isolated against one another and striving to objectify one another. It is only those who attempt to be God who will end either by trying to dominate others or by being dominated by them. Thus, it is Anderson's firm if questionable opinion that *Being and Nothingness* leaves open the possibility for human relationships founded not on a precarious balancing of oppositions but on the uncontentious reciprocity that would allow positive harmony to prevail.

Manser, Anthony. *Sartre: A Philosophic Study*. London: The Athlone Press, 1966.

Anthony Manser's book has a way of making the analytically trained reader feel at home. The book makes a very special attempt to express Jean-Paul Sartre's thought in language as close to that of contemporary British philosophical thinking; and it tries to demonstrate that there is a closer kinship between Sartre's thinking and the empirical tradition than is generally believed. With very little distortion, Manser brings Sartre onto Anglo-Saxon ground and clarifies his thought often by contrasting him with Bertrand Russell, Ludwig Wittgenstein, A. J. Ayer, or John Austin, sometimes by pointing to similarities between Sartre and thinkers such as Gilbert Ryle, Stuart Hampshire, Norman Malcolm, and Peter Winch.

One of the most important sections of Manser's book is his excellent discussion, based on a wealth of diverse passages culled mostly from *Being and Nothingness*, of Sartre's view of language. The following is a summary of a few of its dominant themes.

Manser shows that language is no less important for Sartre than for British philosophers. Indeed, it is precisely because Sartre considers language to be so central to human life that he is not attracted by abstract linguistic arguments that stay isolated within the boundaries of language alone. I am language as I am my body, is the Sartrean contention. The same problems and ambiguities that hold for the body hold also for language. Language differs in character depending on whether we look at it from the standpoint of the speaker or writer or from that of the reader or mere listener. Speaking resembles the body in action. One who speaks or who replies directly to speaking is situated within language. To him, words are a prolongation of sense like claws or antennae. A speaker feels them from inside and operates them as he does his body. It is as though he were possessed of a verbal body of which he is only indirectly aware, just as, when walking or running, he might be peripherally aware of his hands or feet. Sometimes, of course, he is uncertain about a part of his language and must reflect on what he is going to say, or he must call to mind some rule of grammar. In these cases he is like a person performing an unfamiliar action who has to concentrate on the way he moves his arms and legs. This is particularly true of speaking a foreign language. But in any sort of ordinary communication, language never seems to be something outside us as though it were an instrument that we are using.

On the other hand, words do have established meanings, and language does have rules. These latter have been *discovered*, however, *after* the spoken word, and basically they are in the forefront only for those standing outside living conversation, and then they cannot give entry to what is being said. Whenever we are mere listeners to the conversation of others, we may know all the rules and all the dictionary meanings of the words we are hearing, and yet, because we stand outside the interchange that is taking place, we will find that our attention to rules

or meanings only blocks our understanding of it. Living language in which we participate, in contrast, is transparent; it never gets in the way. We can even find that after genuine participation in a conversation we know something that we learned through words, yet are unable to recall any of the specific words that conveyed it to us.

Too often we think of language as comprised of words that are mere units of discourse with rules that enable us to assemble them into sentences. Discourse, however, is made up of statements, questions, pleas, and commands. It is in sentences that these must be expressed; words are merely traces of the passage of sentences, in much the same way that highways were originally traces of the passage of caravans and pilgrims. Only in the sentence can the word function to designate. Outside it, it is a mere propositional function.

That language does exist independently of us is a fact. Yet being in a world full of linguistic rules and established meanings is part of what Sartre calls being in situation. Within my situation as the one speaking, I am free. *What* I say is never determined by the rules of language. When I am genuinely *saying* something, it is true that I take the orderings of grammar and meanings up into my speech, but I transcend them in my free act of speaking. In the same way, what I do physically is never dictated by my body, even though the ways in which I move are both restricted and helped along by the arrangement of my bones and muscles.

Additional Recommended Reading

Caws, Peter. *Sartre*. London: Routledge & Kegan Paul, 1979. Caws takes as his first task the reconstruction of central arguments in Sartre's philosophy in order to bring criticism to bear on them. He gives particular attention to the development in *Being and Nothingness* of themes first found in the earlier works on the imagination and the emotions.

Champigny, Robert. *Stages on Sartre's Way: 1938-52*. Bloomington: Indiana University Press, 1959. In the belief that *Being and Nothingness* is a systematization of Roquentin's grounding experience in Sartre's novel *Nausea*, Champigny attempts to show that Sartre's entire philosophy is rooted in his sensibility.

Danto, Arthur C. *Jean-Paul Sartre*. New York: The Viking Press, 1975. Commending Sartre for the strength and vision of his philosophical system, Danto explains his thought in relation to other major philosophies as he examines the way Sartre relates reality to representation, language to consciousness, the world to the human structuring of it, and so forth.

Hartmann, Klaus. *Sartre's Ontology*. Evanston, Illinois: Northwestern University Press, 1966. Concerning himself with the basic premises of Sartre's ontology, Hartmann first traces its development from Husserlian phenomenology and then interprets *Being and Nothingness* within the framework of Hegel's dialectic.

Morris, Phyllis Sutton. *Sartre's Concept of a Person: An Analytic Approach*. Amherst: University of Massachusetts Press, 1976. Morris compares Sartre with Strawson, Ryle, Shoemaker, Russell, Austin, and others with respect to his treatment of the usual problems considered by Anglo-Saxon philosophers under the heading "philosophy of mind."

Stern, Alfred. *Sartre: His Philosophy and Psychoanalysis*. New York: The Liberal Arts Press, 1953. Giving a critical analysis in the first part of his book of the formative influences on Sartre's thought, Stern then moves on to an examination of the existential psychoanalysis found in *Being and Nothingness* and compares it with the doctrines of Freud, Adler, and others.

PHENOMENOLOGY OF PERCEPTION

Author: Maurice Merleau-Ponty (1908-1961)
Type of work: Existential phenomenology
First published: 1945

Principal Ideas Advanced

The world is not (as realism contends) the cause of our consciousness of it; but neither (as idealism contends) does our consciousness "constitute" the world by providing order and meaning to intrinsically meaningless "sensations."

The human body is no mere "physical body" which can be understood in terms of purely causal relations between its parts and between itself and objects; as "lived" it is, rather, the bearer of our most fundamental grasp of and orientation to the world, which provides the basis for our more conscious, personal activities.

The human mind is not sheer mind, possessing a pure rational comprehension of the world or of itself. Human rationality is rooted in human perception, and self-knowledge is mediated through bodily expression and action in the world and through time.

Man is not determined by his past, his temperament, his situation; but neither is he radically free in relation to these motivations. His freedom is found in accepting them and taking them up in free choices, in which one proferred motivation is refused only by accepting another, and which can only gradually modify the basic direction of personality.

Phenomenology of Perception is Maurice Merleau-Ponty's second book, following *The Structure of Behavior*, a critique of psychological behaviorism published in 1942. *Phenomenology of Perception* incorporates various insights from the earlier work, but also deals in depth with many matters which it did not treat, or treated only cursorily. This work defines the main lines of the philosophical position to which Merleau-Ponty held for most of the rest of his life, with significant changes in the direction of his thinking only clearly emerging in the various fragments which were published posthumously as *The Visible and the Invisible*.

Phenomenology of Perception is in some respects less, but in many respects more, than its title suggests. It is not a systematic orderly analysis, along Husserlian lines, of perception regarded in isolation from other modes of human consciousness. Rather, it is a kind of *ontology of human existence,* in which perception is shown to play a most fundamental role. In the range of its topics—which include embodiment,

sexuality, the relation between self and other, self-knowledge, temporality, and freedom—the work is comparable to Jean-Paul Sartre's *Being and Nothingness*. Indeed, the influence of Sartre, who was Merleau-Ponty's friend and associate for many years, is often apparent, although Merleau-Ponty avoids the abstract oppositions and paradoxes of Sartre's thought and presents a subtler, more concrete conception of these matters.

In the working out of his position, Merleau-Ponty also comes to terms with such giants of modern philosophy as René Descartes, Immanuel Kant, and G. W. F. Hegel. His work reflects as well his familiarity with twentieth century French thinkers such as Henri Bergson, Léon Brunschvicg, and Gabriel Marcel, and with psychological literature, particularly that of the Gestalt school. But the most significant influence on his thinking is clearly phenomenology, as represented by Edmund Husserl, Martin Heidegger, and Max Scheler.

Merleau-Ponty's understanding of phenomenology is presented in the "Preface" to his work. Phenomenology, he says, involves an attempt to recall the prescientific experience of the world on which our scientific knowledge is based, but which is often passed over by an attitude that (mistakenly) takes scientific knowledge to be absolute. He credits Husserl with developing the method by which the absolutist pretensions of science could be criticized, but declines to follow Husserl in the idealistic direction that characterized much of his work. Phenomenological reflection does not lead, Merleau-Ponty says, to recognition of oneself as a "transcendental consciousness" somehow apart from the world, but to the revelation of our "being-in-the-world" ("being in" to be understood as meaning not simple spatial location, but "inhabiting," "being involved in"). Moreover, our reflection on "essences" does not disclose them as a separate sphere of being, but rather should serve as a means for clarifying concrete *existence*, our living experience of the world and ourselves.

The "Introduction" to *Phenomenology of Perception* is a section subtitled "Traditional Prejudices and the Return to Phenomena." Here Merleau-Ponty critically examines certain concepts and assumptions which have had the effect of obscuring, rather than illuminating, the true nature of our perceptual experience. Chief among such concepts is that of *sensation*. Sensations are usually conceived of as isolated, inner states which the perceiver undergoes as a result of external stimuli. The "constancy hypothesis" in psychology postulates that uniform stimuli produce uniform effects of this sort. But this attempt to construct a causal account of perception is inadequate, Merleau-Ponty argues; nothing in our actual experience corresponds to this concept of sensation. Our perceptual life is not composed of isolated states; in it, every element has some *meaning* in relation to the whole. Perceptual consciousness is not the sheer feeling of an inner state, but is (in the phenomenological sense) *intentional*, is directed *toward*, is consciousness *of* something other than itself. The empiricists' conceptions of "association" and "projection of memories" or the rationalists' conception of (for example) "judgment" as processes which remedy the deficiencies of sensations, only reflect the inadequacy of the concept of sensation. Associa-

tion and memory must somehow be suggested, "motivated" by present experience, which thus *cannot* be a blind sensation. Judgment is *based on* a perceptual field having some *inherent* structure, which it seeks to make explicit.

The fundamental error of both empiricist and rationalist accounts of consciousness, Merleau-Ponty argues, lies in what he calls "the prejudice in favour of the world." They *presuppose* a conception of a fully determinate "objective" world and attempt to understand consciousness on this basis—either as a mere *effect* of this world or as objective *knowledge of* it—rather than beginning with an unprejudiced examination of that perceptual experience through which there *comes to be* a world *for me*. Such reflection will disclose perception as neither the passive undergoing of sensations, nor the active, rational "constitution" of the "objective" world, but as a living relation to an ambiguous, prescientific, perceptual world.

Having thus set the essential task of his work, Merleau-Ponty turns to the crucial topic of *the body*. His discussion—which occupies the first main division of *Phenomenology of Perception*—proceeds largely through reflection on scientific findings about the body, findings which he contends have been seriously misinterpreted by scientists themselves. He attempts to establish that the human body is not an object in the world (a mere "physical object"); *that* concept of the body is an abstraction from the concrete, "*lived*" body, which is one's point of view on, one's openness to, and the base of one's orientation toward the world. Because the theory of the body and the theory of perception are of necessity closely related, Merleau-Ponty's account of the body provides an avenue to disclosure of the concrete perceived world which underlies the "objective" world depicted by science.

Merleau-Ponty's reflections on the body are extraordinarily rich, and only some of their most basic themes can be indicated here. He points to a number of considerations which preclude the body's being adequately conceived as an "object"—as something which is related to other "objects," or whose parts are related to one another, only externally and mechanically. The study of the nervous system has shown, he says, that no *simple* localization can be assigned to the ability to perceive a specific quality. Sensible qualities are not mere effects of stimuli, but require that the body be somehow "attuned" for their perception, as the hand, in moving around an object, *anticipates* the stimuli which will reveal the object to it. Merleau-Ponty provides a particularly illuminating discussion of "phantom limb" experiences, in which a person seems to feel (for example) pain in an amputated limb. He argues that this phenomenon can be explained neither in terms of mere physical factors (such as stimuli affecting the nerves which had been linked to the limb) nor purely psychological factors (such as memory of the lost limb or refusal to face its loss). Rather, a phantom limb is experienced when objects are implicitly taken to be manipulatable as they were before loss of the limb. It is a matter of our projecting ourselves into a practical environment, of our embodied "being-in-the-world," of our ambiguous concrete existence at a level prior to the abstract distinction of the "physical" and the "psychological." The body is no mere "thing"; it is a "body-subject," the seat of our habits, of our innate and acquired capacities and orientation toward the world. As such it provides the general background from which our most conscious, personal, and rational acts emerge.

Merleau-Ponty subsequently deals with the nature of bodily movement and its relation to perception. Consciousness does not move the body as one moves an "object" through space, he argues; rather, the body moves insofar as it "inhabits" space, insofar as it is oriented in relation to objects. Our perceptual powers are themselves intimately interrelated. The unity of the living body is the unity of a "style," comparable to the unity of a work of art; our powers work together in disclosure of the world.

Merleau-Ponty's account of the body concludes with discussions of sexuality and of "the body as expression and speech." His discussion of sexuality —which involves some very subtle reflections on Sigmund Freud—depicts it as a general atmosphere which suffuses life in such a way that it can neither serve as a total explanation of our existence nor be isolated from the other modes of our being-in-the-world. Neither a matter of mere "physiology" nor of sheer consciousness, sexuality is a mode of our being-in-the-world, a basic manner in which one embodied being can exist in relation to another.

In his discussion of speech, Merleau-Ponty criticizes equally empiricist psychologies which construe our use of words as the mere result of physiological processes, and rationalist conceptions which take words to be merely external accompaniments of thought, linked to it by mere association. Both of these views deprive *the word itself* of meaning. But, he argues, thought and speech—either external or internal—are essentially bound up with each other. Contrary to most of the philosophical tradition since Plato, Merleau-Ponty denies that meaningful speech must be preceded or accompanied by a *separate* process of thinking. Rather, we think in speech; and although thinking sometimes seems to run "a step ahead" of speech, it nevertheless requires linguistic expression to establish itself. The phenomenon of speech must ultimately, he adds, be understood as of a kind with other modes of bodily "gesture"—their meaning is immanent in them. The whole expressive dimension of our embodied existence stands as one more proof that the rigid Cartesian dualism of thinking substance and extended substance is inadequate.

In the second main division of *Phenomenology of Perception*, Merleau- Ponty turns to an explication of the concrete structures of the *perceived world*. Again he attempts to delineate an alternative to both empiricism and rationalism. Both views, he argues, simply presuppose a fully determinate objective world. Empiricism locates the subject as a thing in that world, construes the relation of world to subject as causal, and constructs its account of experience on that basis. Rationalism takes the world to be *for* a knowing subject and analyzes experience accordingly. Neither takes its stand *within* that ambiguous living experience in which objects come to be for us. Accepting this task, Merleau-Ponty provides accounts of our concrete experience of sensible qualities, of spatial location, depth, and movement, of shape, size, the "natural thing" as a unity of sensible qualities, and finally of the *world* as that open unity which forms the ultimate horizon of all our experiences. Preeminent in all these experiences is the role of the body— its capacity to "merge into" a given perceptual situation (as when, without any thought, it manages to grasp the true colors of things despite abnormal lighting conditions which change the "objective" stimuli which are present), to respond to the solicitation of ambiguous data, to grasp through the unity of its perceptual powers the unity of qualities in a thing, to be present through the perceptual field to a world which is ever incomplete.

The last and perhaps most interesting chapter of Merleau-Ponty's account of the perceived world deals with "the other self and the human world" and draws on many of the basic insights developed in earlier sections. We are not only conscious of natural objects, he notes, but also perceive about us the artifacts and inhabitants of a cultural and social world—a *human* world. And the first, the most basic "cultural object," he argues, must be the *body* of the *other person*; only on the foundation of our perception of others is a cultural world accessible to us. But "objective thought" would make perception of the other impossible by construing all bodies as mere objects, and the subject as a pure "for itself," a sheer self-conscious, rational surveyor of the objective world. This would make it unintelligible that a body could ever be truly *expressive* of a subjectivity, and that there could ever be another for-itself *for me*. But, as Merleau-Ponty has shown, *I* am not a sheer for-itself—I am rather an embodied, perceiving, behaving subject—and thus the *other's* body is not for me a thing, a mere in-itself. *My* experience of embodied subjectivity allows me, prior to any sort of explicit analogy or judgment, to grasp another consciousness in *its* embodiment. The perceived world, as that unity which forever outruns my determinate grasp of it, is also crucial here; as my different perspectives "slip into" one another and are united in relation to the perceptible thing, so my perspective and that of the other "slip into" one another and are united in the world, in which our communication is possible.

Language and the experience of dialogue of course play an important role. Our thoughts are woven together in living, reciprocal speech. But, Merleau-Ponty adds, the plurality of consciousnesses, their difference from one another, is an inescapable fact. The anger or grief which I grasp in another's behavior, for example, do not have the same significance for both of us; he *lives* what I merely *perceive*. We have common projects, but each participates in it from his *own* perspective. Solitude and communication, Merleau-Ponty warns, must not be taken as exclusive alternatives; rather, they are two aspects of our ambiguous human condition. Thus I can recognize that the other is *imperfectly* known by me, only if I *do* have experience *of* the other. Merleau-Ponty proceeds to criticize Sartre's claim that I must either make an object of the other, or allow his "gaze" to make an object of me; another person's gaze is felt as unbearable, he says, only if it replaces possible communication, and the latter retains its truth. He concludes by asserting that I am neither in society as one object among others, nor is society in me as an object of thought; rather, the social is a "dimension of existence" in which I live.

The third and final main division of *Phenomenology of Perception* deals with "being-for-itself and being-in-the-world." Here Merleau-Ponty discusses self-knowledge (the "*cogito*"), temporality, and freedom. Developing the position of Descartes, idealism has argued that objects must be *for* a subject which is *for itself*, which knows itself, which somehow contains within itself the key to every object that it could possibly encounter. But the mind is not a sheer for-itself, Merleau-Ponty maintains; the *cogito* does not involve an absolute and total self-knowledge. Thus he undertakes a critique of traditional doctrines of the *cogito*. He argues first that, contrary to Descartes, I can be no more certain *that* I see than the *thing* I see exists. Nor do I possess absolute self-knowledge in respect to my will or feeling; I can, for example, think that I am in love without truly being so. I do *not* know myself so much *in myself*, in some inner and immediate self-presence, as *in act*. It is by action and expression in the world and through the body that I achieve determinacy and clarity for myself, so that the *cogito* is inherently conditioned by temporality. Thus the "I think" is dependent on the "I am." Even in the sphere of so-called "pure thought"—geometrical thinking, for example—my grasp of truth is dependent on my bodily orientation to the world, through which I can fundamentally grasp what a "triangle" or a "direction" is. Moreover, thought is inherently dependent on speech, and the clarity achieved in a given thought is dependent on an always somewhat obscure context which has been formed by past acts of expression. The centrality of this phenomenon of "acquisition" in our mental life points again to the inherent temporality of all our grasp on truth.

These critical reflections on doctrines which would grant to the mind an absolute grasp of itself or of the world do not, however, lead Merleau-Ponty to reject the *cogito* altogether. There is, he says, a presence to self which precedes and conditions our explicit grasp of ourselves or of the world, a "tacit *cogito*" which precedes the "spoken *cogito*." But this tacit *cogito* is inchoate and must be expressed in a verbal *cogito* in order to attain clarity. The ultimate subject, Merleau-Ponty concludes, is not a sheer self-present nonworldly ego which "constitutes" the world, but a being which *belongs to* the world.

The fundamental role of time in relation to all sorts of phenomena is indicated throughout the *Phenomenology of Perception*, but it becomes the explicit theme of Merleau-Ponty's reflections only in the penultimate chapter of the work. He begins by arguing that time is inseparable from subjectivity; without a subject, there is no *present* in the world, and without a present there can be no past or future. But what is the fundamental relation of time and subjectivity? The subject cannot, he says, be simply located in the "now," and its consciousness of past and future explained in terms of physiological or psychological "traces" of the past. Such "traces," being purely *present*, could not ground our opening onto past or future. But neither could time be a constituted *object* for a *nontemporal* subject before whom past, present, and future were equally arrayed; for if they were all alike *present*, there would be no time. Time, then, is inseparable from a subject, but this subject is *itself* inherently *temporal*, is *situated* in time, and grasps future and past on the horizon of a flowing present which accomplishes the transition between them. There is an essential interdependence between temporality and the "thrust" of concrete subjectivity toward a world and toward a future in which it can (in both senses of the term) "realize" itself.

The final chapter of *Phenomenology of Perception* is a subtly reasoned and eloquently expressed reflection on human freedom. Initially, Merleau-

Ponty notes, the only alternative to a causal and deterministic conception of the relation between the subject and the world (a conception which would, in effect, make a thing of consciousness) is a view of human consciousness as *wholly* free, independent of all motives, of nature, of one's past temperament and history. In this view—which is essentially that expressed by Sartre in *Being and Nothingness*—even obstacles to our freedom are in reality deployed by it; it is my choice to reach a certain destination which *makes* certain objects into obstacles for me.

However, Merleau-Ponty responds, this abstract conception of freedom would in effect rule it out completely. A wholly indeterminate freedom would lack even the possibility of committing itself, since the next instant would find it again indeterminate and uncommitted. Rather, he argues, a choice once made must provide some impetus to personality, must establish a direction which tends to conserve itself. Because I am not a sheer self-conscious subject but an *embodied* being like other human beings, my free choices take place against a background of possibilities that have a kind of preliminary significance for me. Thus mountains appear high to me whether or not I choose to climb them. And because I am a *temporal* being like my established character and habits, although they do not cause, do *incline* me to certain choices.

Freedom is always, then, a taking-up of some meaning or some motivation which is offered by my situation in the world. I can reject one proferred meaning or motivation, Merleau-Ponty says, only by accepting another. And even if a man being tortured refuses to provide the information his torturers demand, this free action does not reflect a wholly solitary and unmotivated choice; it is supported by his awareness of unity with his comrades, his preparation for such an ordeal, or his long-established belief in freedom.

Man is neither a mere thing nor a sheer consciousness. Human life involves a continual synthesis of the for-itself and the in-itself, a taking-up and shaping of our finite situation, a reciprocity of self and world. We are truly free not by denying our natural and social situation, but by assuming it and living it. Thus philosophy recalls us to our concrete existence in the world, where—Merleau-Ponty suggests—our pro-per task is to commit our freedom to the realization of freedom for all.

Pertinent Literature

Kwant, Remy C. *The Phenomenological Philosophy of Merleau-Ponty.* Pittsburgh: Duquesne University Press, 1963.

Remy C. Kwant's work is a good general study of Maurice Merleau-Ponty's philosophy. Nine of its thirteen chapters deal primarily with *Phenomenology of Perception*, although they also contain supplementary references to other works published during the philosopher's lifetime. The book is in large part expository and reflects sympathy for Merleau-Ponty's insights, although Kwant also criticizes seriously some basic aspects of his philosophical position.

The first three chapters concentrate on Merleau-Ponty's account of the "body-subject." Kwant discusses the sense in which the body can be described as "subject"—namely, in that it is "a meaning-giving existence," a source of meaning for various sorts of objects. But he is careful to add that Merleau-Ponty conceives the relation of the "body-subject" to objects as dialectical; the former does not stand apart from, but *is* in its relation to the latter. Kwant develops Merleau-Ponty's use of the question-answer relation as a metaphor for the relation of body and world. The body, he says, is permeated with "questioning orientations" which the world "answers" in various ways.

In reflecting on Merleau-Ponty's approach to the "body-subject," Kwant first notes the difficulty of describing his method precisely. One aspect of this method which he stresses is Merleau-Ponty's examination of instances of abnormality (for example, the case of a brain-damaged patient which is discussed at some length in the *Phenomenology of Perception*) in order to illuminate normal existence by contrast. Kwant comments, in a way with which most readers of Merleau-Ponty can sympathize, on the somewhat "obscure nature" of his philosophy. While granting important insights to Merleau-Ponty, Kwant suggests that his ideas cannot be systematized or very clearly formulated. But this is, he suggests, due to the nature of the subject matter—the "obscure basis," the "dark soil in which are the hidden roots of our existence."

Kwant regards Merleau-Ponty's attempt to show the dependence of thought on language, and of language on the body-subject, as an important aspect of a general attempt to establish the fundamental bodily nature of man. As Kwant understands Merleau-Ponty, the latter's position ultimately implies that "man is nothing but a body-subject"—although this claim is qualified in light of the fact that Merleau-Ponty uses the term "body" in different ways, sometimes as a term for our "fixed existence," but sometimes also as inclusive of the "self-transcending" capacities of human existence.

The sixth and seventh chapters of Kwant's book are closely related; they deal with Merleau-Ponty's "rejection of the absolute" and his account of "metaphysical consciousness." In the sixth chapter, Kwant indicates that Merleau-Ponty rejects any eternal, absolute truth, any truth transcending our "acquired" truths—those which have been established through human acts of expression. In the seventh, Kwant stresses a "revolutionary" aspect of Merleau-Ponty's thought—namely, that he does not take the "intelligibility of reality" to be true *in principle*, but regards it as a contingent *fact*, inseparable from our contingent, situated, bodily being-in-the-world.

Chapters nine and ten provide useful accounts of Merleau-Ponty's relation to the phenomenological tradition and the relation of his thinking to science. The twelfth chapter compares his philosophy to Jean-Paul Sartre's. While finding Merleau-Ponty's critique of the Sartrean conception of freedom to be sound, Kwant regrets that Merleau-Ponty's own account of freedom is framed so much in terms of criticism of Sartre, and he suggests that Merleau-Ponty lacks "a description of the inner essence of the thinking and free subject."

This latter point is related to criticisms suggested by Kwant throughout this work and brought together in the concluding chapter. In general, he suggests that Merleau-Ponty has given a good account of the *roots* of our existence but has not adequately treated its *heights*. He has not, for example, described the "inner character" of rational thinking *per se*, of the universality of rational truth, or of "conscious, free subjectivity." Kwant grants "great credit" to Merleau-Ponty for showing that the human body is no simple "thing," but suggests that traditional soul-body dualism *did* have a basis in certain aspects of our existence—such as our "universal openness" to truth and our capacity for unselfish love—to which Merleau-Ponty does not give sufficient attention. Finally, Kwant is critical of Merleau-Ponty's refusal to seek any ground outside contingent human existence in the world for the intelligibility of reality. Merleau-Ponty's thought "contains a very valuable vision," he says, but this vision is incomplete.

In general, Kwant's criticisms of Merleau-Ponty seem to be weighty, but not conclusive. *Phenomenology of Perception* did not give extended consideration to the structures of thinking *per se* or to the question of rational truth. But it is not wholly silent on these topics, and the fact that Merleau-Ponty did not treat them in more detail is partially to be explained by the fact that his primary concern was *perception*. It may not be so clear, as Kwant thinks, that Merleau-Ponty identified man with the body— even the body in a very broad sense of the term; but it must be admitted that, having shown how the traditional sharp distinction between mind and body distorts our concrete (and ambiguous) existence, Merleau-Ponty does not (perhaps in principle cannot) offer any precise account of their relation.

As for questions of the absolute, of rationality and truth, and of the spiritual dimensions of existence, it should be noted that Merleau-Ponty's later works (including some of his posthumously published writings) have much to say on these matters. On the whole, the horizons of the later works are somewhat broader than those of *Phenomenology of Perception*. It is true, however, that he never achieved a systematic or clear resolution of these most important and difficult issues.

Langan, Thomas. *Merleau-Ponty's Critique of Reason.* New Haven, Connecticut: Yale University Press, 1966.

Thomas Langan's book is a somewhat brief but intensive study of Maurice Merleau-Ponty's thought. Most of the chapters deal primarily with *Phenomenology of Perception* but attempt to integrate with it some of Merleau-Ponty's other writings. Langan interprets Merleau-Ponty as standing in, and making original contributions to, the tradition of "critical" or "transcendental" philosophy, which does not deal so much directly with objects as it reflects on the experience in which objects are given to us. More specifically, Langan sees Merleau-Ponty's thinking as a response to "internal tensions" in this tradition, which derives from René Descartes and has been developed by Immanuel Kant, G. W. F. Hegel, and Edmund Husserl, but which has also given rise to Søren Kierkegaard, Friedrich Wilhelm Nietzsche, Karl Marx, Martin Heidegger, and Jean-Paul Sartre.

Remy C. Kwant's first chapter, "The Transcendental Standpoint," reflects briefly on the tradition of transcendental philosophy, pointing to the difficulty of its attempts to put aside all commonsense presuppositions. With his interpretation, Merleau-Ponty attempted to go farther in this direction than either Hegel or Husserl, who presupposed (although in rather different ways) that reality is rationally knowable. Merleau-Ponty's distinctive contribution to transcendental philosophy, Langan suggests, lies in his elaboration of a "new notion of synthesis," a new account of the relation of experience and Being. According to this account, we "synthesize" or "make sense of" Being from a position *within* Being.

With this as his guiding theme, Langan sets out to explore various aspects of Merleau-Ponty's philosophy. His second chapter, entitled "Incarnated Intentionality: The New Transcendental Aesthetic," deals with Merleau-Ponty's account of embodied consciousness and perception. He first focuses on the problem of truth, noting that the way in which

Merleau-Ponty originally poses the problem—asking how there can be an *"in-itself for us"*—indicates a basic attempt to surpass the traditional opposition of idealism and empiricism. Langan provides a helpful analysis of the way in which, according to Merleau-Ponty, our perception of a *figure* takes place (as the Gestalt psychologists had stressed) in the context of a background or *field*, with the *world* forming the ultimate background. This reference of perception to a background transcending it is important in Merleau-Ponty's account of experience as both *mine* and as pertaining to what lies *beyond* me. Langan proceeds to discuss the body as our opening onto this world, noting the impossibility of describing our embodied, living experience with clear and distinct concepts. Nevertheless, he provides an artfully constructed re-presentation of Merleau-Ponty's reflections on this topic, culminating in a discussion of intersubjectivity.

Langan's third chapter, "Analytica-Dialectica," begins with an account of Merleau-Ponty's treatment of the *cogito*, giving special attention to his conception of conceptual truth as dependent on human embodiment, perception, and expression. The fourth chapter, "Practica," discusses Merleau-Ponty's conception of finite freedom in the *Phenomenology of Perception* and then turns to his reflections on political action in later works. The fifth chapter— "Poetica: A New Montaigne"—centers around the opposition between "fascination" ("passive absorption in one's world") and "activism" (the attempt to achieve total domination of one's situation). That neither of these extremes is an adequate response to the human condition is clearly implied in *Phenomenology of Perception* but Langan finds in Merleau-Ponty's later works, particularly in his reflections on the varieties of human expression, a more developed depiction of the possibilities of existence in the tension between these polar opposites.

In his concluding chapter, "Toward the Rehabilitation of Reason," Langan resumes explicitly his discussion of the transcendental tradition and of Merleau-Ponty's place within it. In effect, he argues that, however significant Merleau-Ponty's advance over earlier philosophers in this tradition, he has failed in the task he set himself—that of explaining how there can be an in-itself for us, how we can grasp *as it is* a reality independent of ourselves. Can there be true objectivity of any sort, Langan asks, if—as Merleau-Ponty suggests—all our encounters with things are conditioned by the body and its acquisitions, culture and its "sedimentation" of past human expression? This is a complex question to which no simple answer ought to be made. It does not, however, seem that Langan has given quite enough consideration to those aspects of Merleau-Ponty's thought which point in a realistic direction—not to that scientistic "realism" which construes man and objects as causally related, but to a richer realism which attributes to human experience the power to transcend itself and grasp what is.

Additional Recommended Reading

Bannan, John F. *The Philosophy of Merleau-Ponty.* New York: Harcourt, Brace & World, 1967. A useful general exposition of Merleau-Ponty's ideas.

Langer, Monika. *Merleau-Ponty's "Phenomenology of Perception" : A Guide and Commentary.* Gainesville: University Presses of Florida, 1989. A useful introduction to Merleau-Ponty's phenomenology.

Mallin, Samuel B. *Merleau-Ponty's Philosophy.* New Haven, Connecticut: Yale University Press, 1979. An ambitious, scholarly attempt at a synthesis and reconstruction of Merleau-Ponty's philosophical position.

Merleau-Ponty, Maurice. *The Primacy of Perception.* Evanston, Illinois: Northwestern University Press, 1964. The title essay in this collection is a brief statement—read by Merleau-Ponty in 1945 to a gathering of French philosophers—of his major philosophical ideas, with the text of the (at times very interesting) discussion which followed. Other essays include a "prospectus" of work which he planned to do in the 1950's, and "Eye and Mind," a fascinating work written during the last months of his life.

Rabil, Albert. *Merleau-Ponty: Existentialist of the Social World.* New York: Columbia University Press, 1967. A solid account of Merleau-Ponty's thought which gives some attention to its development and to the political context of his work.

Sartre, Jean-Paul. "Merleau-Ponty," in *Situations..* New York: George Braziller, 1965. Sartre's eloquent and fascinating memorial essay on Merleau-Ponty.

ZEN BUDDHISM

Author: Daisetz T. Suzuki (1870-1966)
Type of work: Metaphysics, ethics
First published: 1956 (Selections by editor William Barrett from works published during the years 1949-1955)

Principal Ideas Advanced

Zen is a way of life, of seeing and knowing by looking into one's own nature.

The truth comes through active meditation, and enlightenment is sudden and intuitive.

Zen does not rely on the intellect, the scripture, or the written word, but on a direct pointing at the soul of man, a seeing into one's own nature as making Buddhahood possible.

Zen masters make the moment of enlightenment (satori) *possible by referring directly to some natural and commonplace matter; the immediate recognition of the unity of being follows.*

The chief characteristics of satori *are irrationality, intuitive insight, authoritativeness, affirmation, a sense of the Beyond, an impersonal tone, a feeling of exaltation, and momentariness.*

The methods of Zen are paradox, going beyond the opposites, contradiction, affirmation, repetition, exclamation, silence, or direct action (such as a blow, or pointing.)

Zen Buddhism shares with other philosophies and faiths which stress intuition and awareness the ironic condition of desiring to communicate what cannot be communicated. Like the theologies of the Middle Ages, it urges an understanding of true being by a kind of direct insight into one's own being, but it disdains any intellectual or formalistic methods of achieving that insight. The profession of conviction, then, is largely negative; the emphasis, insofar as discourse is concerned, is not on what can be said but on that concerning which we must be silent. A Zen master is not a lecturer; he is a director, or pointer, one who turns the attention of the disciple to some natural fact which, properly apprehended, reveals everything. Of those who have made the effort to explain Zen Buddhism, no one has been more successful than the Japanese philosopher and professor, Daisetz T. Suzuki, whose *Essays in Zen Buddhism* (1949, 1950, 1953), *The Zen Doctrine of No-Mind* (1949), and *Studies in Zen* (1955) provide the selections collected and edited by William Barrett under the title, *Zen Buddhism*. As an introduction to Suzuki's work and

to Zen Buddhism, this volume is admirably suited; it deals with the meaning of Zen Buddhism, its historical background, its techniques, its philosophy, and its relation to Japanese culture.

According to the legendary account of Zen, given by Suzuki, Zen originated in India, and the first to practice the Zen method was Sakyamuni himself, the Buddha. He is reputed to have held a bouquet of flowers before his disciples without saying a word. Only the venerable Mahakasyapa understood the "silent but eloquent teaching on the part of the Enlightened One." Consequently, Mahakasyapa inherited the spiritual treasure of Buddhism.

According to historical accounts, however, Zen Buddhism originated in China in A.D. 520 with the arrival of Bodhi-Dharma from India (the twenty-eighth in the line of patriarchs of Zen, according to the orthodox followers). The message brought by Bodhi-Dharma became the four-phrase summation of the Zen principles:

"A special transmission outside the scriptures;

"No dependence upon words and letters;

"Direct pointing at the soul of man;

"Seeing into one's nature and the attainment of Buddhahood."

These are not the words of Bodhi-Dharma, but of later disciples who formulated his teachings. The method of "direct pointing," of referring to some natural thing or event as the focal point of meditation, preparatory to an instantaneous enlightenment, continues to be the most characteristic method of Zen Buddhism.

Dharma came to be known as the *pi-kuan* Brahman, the Wall-contemplating Brahman, because of his practice of contemplating a monastery wall—reputedly for nine years. One of the most familiar stories of his teaching has to do with the persistent seeker after truth, the monk Shen-kuang, described in legend as having stood in the snow until he was buried to his knees and as having cut off his arm in order to show the sincerity of his desire to learn. Finally, gaining audience with Dharma, he said, "My soul is not yet pacified. Pray, master, pacify it." Dharma replied, "Bring your soul here, and I will have it pacified." Suzuki finishes the story: "Kuang hesitated for a moment but finally said, 'I have sought it these many years and am still unable to get hold of it!'

"'There! It is pacified once for all.' This was Dharma's sentence."

The Chinese founder of Zen, Suzuki reports, was Hui-neng (638-713), who was so deeply touched by a recitation of the *Diamond Sutra (Vajracchedika-sutra)* that he made a month-long journey to beg the patriarch Hung-jen to allow him to study under him. Hung-jen recognized Hui-neng's spiritual quality and transferred the partriarchal robes to him. (The account may not be accurate, having been composed by the followers of Hui-neng.)

It was Hui-neng who taught that Zen is the "seeing into one's own Nature." According to Suzuki, "This is the most significant phrase ever coined in the development of Zen Buddhism." Allied with this idea was the "abrupt doctrine" of the Southern school of Hui-neng. According to the *Platform Sutra,* "When the abrupt doctrine is understood there is no need of disciplining oneself in things external. Only let a man always have a right view within his own mind, no

desires, no external objects will ever defile him. . . . The ignorant will grow wise if they abruptly get an understanding and open their hearts to the truth." In opposition to the view that enlightenment can be achieved by passive or quiet meditation, Hui-neng emphasized apprehending the nature of the self while the self is in the midst of action. Hui-neng began the Zen tradition of getting at the truth directly, intuitively, not intellectually. " When the monk Ming came to him and asked for instruction," Suzuki recounts, "[Hui-neng] said, 'Show me your original face before you were born.' " Suzuki comments: "Is not the statement quite to the point? No philosophic discourse, no elaborate reasoning, no mystic imagery, but a direct unequivocal dictum."

Suzuki's essay " The Sense of Zen," which is Chapter I of Barrett's collection, states at the outset that Zen is "the art of seeing into the nature of one's own being." He argues that Zen Buddhism contains the essence of Buddhism, although it differs from other forms of Buddhism in not stressing rules, scriptures, authorities, and the intellectual approach to the truth. Zen Buddhism assents to the Buddha's "Fourfold Noble Truth" which is built on the basic claim that life is suffering and that to escape suffering one must overcome desire and find truth. There is a struggle in the individual between the finite and the infinite, so that the nature of one's being, which provides a clue to the resolution of the conflict within the self, must be directly grasped. But books are of no help, nor is the intellect; the only way to Buddhahood is through a "direct pointing to the soul of man," as one of the four statements claims. "For this reason," Suzuki writes, "Zen never explains but indicates. . . . It always deals with facts, concrete and tangible." Suffering is the result of ignorance, and ignorance "is wrought of nothing else but the intellect and sensuous infatuation. . . ."

Direct teaching or pointing is sometimes a silent reference, as with the Buddha's flower. But it may appear in the use of an apparently irrelevant, even ridiculous or apparently senseless remark. To appreciate the method of direct pointing, Suzuki cautions, one must regard the attempt to learn as no mere pastime; for Zen Buddhists, Zen is an ethical discipline, an attempt to elevate one's spiritual powers to their ideal limits. The brief answers of the masters to their students' questions were never intended to be intellectual riddles or symbolic utterances. To talk by the use of metaphorical imagery would not be to point directly. Perhaps one can say that although some of the statements attributed to the masters appear to be symbolic in import, there may very well be more direct meanings which are the significant meanings of the statements. Suzuki gives some illustrations of the Zen practice of uttering a few words and demonstrating with action: "What is Zen?" The master: "Boiling oil over a blazing fire." "What kind of man is he who does not keep company with any thing?" The master (Baso): "I will tell you when you have swallowed up in one draught all the waters in the West River."

There is perhaps no more difficult point to make than that such answers from the Zen masters are important not as charming and archaic riddles or irrelevancies, but as "direct pointings" to the truth. The tendency of the Western mind is to go at these remarks intellectually, to "make" sense out of them. But Suzuki argues with convincing sincerity that for the Zen Buddhist such remarks are instruments of enlightenment that can be comprehended simply and naturally with the "opening of a third eye," the sudden enlightenment by which one sees into the nature of his own being. The name for the moment of enlightenment or awakening is "*satori*," and the means to it is meditation of the proper sort. (As Mr. Barrett indicates, the term "Zen" comes from the Japanese term *zazen*, meaning "to sit or meditate," and is equivalent to the Chinese *ch'an* and the Indian *Dhyana*. The distinctive feature of Zen is that meditation and action are one. Suzuki says, "Zen has its own way of practicing meditation. Zen has nothing to do with mere quietism or losing oneself in a trance.")

To achieve *satori*, or enlightenment, involves "meditating on those utterances or actions that are directly poured out from the inner region undimmed by the intellect or the imagination. . . ." Again, examples from the masters are offered to suggest the direct method of Zen. Referring to his staff, Yeryo said, "When one knows what that staff is, one's life study of Zen comes to an end." Ye-sei said, "When you

have a staff, I will give you one; when you have none, I will take it away from you."

Some suggestive remarks by Suzuki put the Zen method into a perspective accessible to Western minds. If we consider that the direct method is possible for the Zen masters because *any* point of meditation, properly caught in the fullness of its being, is infinitely illuminating, we can come to appreciate the pertinence of apparently irrelevant and abrupt remarks. If one's study of Zen ends with knowledge of the master's staff, it may be that it also ends, as Suzuki suggests, with knowledge of the flower in the crannied wall. Tennyson's image may have much the same significance as the Zen master's image. Referring to the Buddhist scriptures, Suzuki argues that "enlightenment and darkness are substantially one," that "the finite is the infinite, and *vice versa*," and that "The mistake consists in our splitting into two what is really and absolutely one." All of this is reminiscent of the philosophy of the metaphysical mystics; there is a close resemblance to the views of such men as Nicholas of Cusa and Giordano Bruno. Suddenly to appreciate the unity of all being and to recognize that unity in an illuminating moment of knowing one's own nature to be the nature of all being, and therefore the nature of whatever it is to which the master's abrupt remark calls attention, is surely not an act of intellect. For intellect to "work it out" would be to spoil the whole effect, as if one were to try to embrace the quality of a rug as a whole by tracing out its separate threads and their relationships to other threads. *Satori*, if it occurs, has to be a moment of "grasping," of knowing "all at once," and it is not at all surprising that the masters of Zen have come to rely on the abrupt remark as a sudden direct pointing.

In the essay, "Satori, or Enlightenment," Suzuki defines *satori* as "an intuitive looking into the nature of things in contradistinction to the analytical or logical understanding of it." It involves a new view, a new way of looking at the universe. The emphasis of the Zen masters, as with the patriarch Hui-neng, is not on direction or on instruction, but on seeing into one's own nature in order to see the nature of all, to achieve Buddhahood and to escape the cycle of birth and death.

Here again Suzuki emphasizes the masters' methods of bringing the seekers of enlightenment abruptly to *satori*. "A monk asked Joshu . . . to be instructed in Zen. Said the master, 'Have you had your breakfast or not?' 'Yes, master, I have,' answered the monk. 'If so, have your dishes washed,' was an immediate response, which, it is said, at once opened the monk's mind to the truth of Zen." Such remarks are like the strokes and blows, or the twisting of noses, which the masters sometimes resorted to, as if suddenly to make the disciple aware of himself and of the obscuring tendencies of his old perspectives. By referring to commonplace matters in the context of a desire to know all, the masters somehow refer to all. By being apparently irrelevant, they show the relevance of everything.

The chief characteristics of *satori*, Suzuki writes, are *irrationality*, the nonlogical leap of the will; *intuitive insight*, or mystic knowledge; *authoritativeness*, the finality of personal perception; *affirmation*, the acceptance of all things; *a sense of the Beyond*, the loss of the sense of self together with the sense of all; *an impersonal tone*, the absence of any feeling of love or "supersensuality"; *a feeling of exaltation*, the contentment of being unrestricted and independent; and *momentariness*, an abruptness of experience, a sudden realization of "a new angle of observation."

In "Practical Methods of Zen Instruction," Suzuki discusses methods for arriving at the realization of the absolute oneness of things. A proper appreciation of these methods, even in outline, depends upon unabridged explanations and examples, but the methods can be mentioned. Zen sometimes utilizes *paradox*, but by concrete images, not by abstract conceptions. Another method is to attempt to think the truth without using the ordinary logic of affirmation and denial; it is the method of *"going beyond the opposites."* The third method is the method of *contradiction*, the method of denying what has already been asserted or taken for granted. The method of *affirmation* is the method frequently referred to: stating almost blithely some commonplace matter of fact in answer to an abstruse and apparently unrelated question. *Repetition* serves to return the self to what it has already seen and not recognized. *Exclamation*, particularly when used as the only answer and when the sound is meaningless, is sometimes used; and even the method

of *silence* has provoked *satori*. But of all the methods, the *direct method* of illuminating action—even though the action be commonplace or almost violent, such as a blow on the cheek of a questioner—is most characteristic of Zen, perhaps because it is the action of everything to which Zen directs attention.

The *koan* exercise is the Zen method of teaching the uninitiated by referring them to answers made by Zen masters. The student is either enlightened or encouraged to "search and contrive" in order to understand the state of mind of the master whose *koan* he is considering. Suzuki devotes an interesting chapter to a discussion of the *koan* exercise, and he offers several examples.

The basic principles of Zen, particularly as related to the teachings of Hui-neng, are examined anew in the essay, "The Zen Doctrine of No-Mind," in which the emphasis on the No-Mind, the Unconscious, brings out the essential concern with active, nondiscursive, intuitive insight. By avoiding the conscious effort to understand intellectually and by participating in ordinary action, one prepares oneself for the moment of enlightenment.

Zen differs from pragmatism, Suzuki maintains, in that pragmatism emphasizes the practical usefulness of concepts, while Zen emphasizes purposelessness or "being detached from teleological consciousness. . . ." Suzuki describes Zen as life; it is entirely consistent with the nonintellectualism of Zen that Zen has implications for action in every sphere of human life. But Zen is concerned not so much with the quality or direction of action as with the perspective of the actor. The emphasis is on "knowing and seeing." Like existentialism, Zen recognizes the antinomy of the finite and the infinite and the possibilities which that relation of apparent opposition opens up; but unlike existentialism, Zen does not involve any conception of an absolute opposition and, consequently, does not entail any "unbearable responsibility," or nausea in the face of the necessity for action. Once the division of finite and infinite, individual and other, is seen to be the consequence of intellectual analysis, so that the idea of individuality is succeeded by the idea of oneness, there is no fear of plunging into the abyss.

In his discussion of Zen and Japanese culture Suzuki shows how Sumiye painting (ink sketching on fragile paper, with no corrections possible), swordsmanship, and the tea ceremony are expressions of Zen principles.

Suzuki's essays on Zen Buddhism are exotic material for the Western reader, but taken seriously— that is, as having some bearing on practice and perspective—they can contribute immeasurably to an appreciation of Oriental religion and philosophy.

There is also the challenging possibility that these essays may lead to an understanding of the unifying intuitive mysticism which persistently runs through Western metaphysics despite its prevailing realistic and pragmatic directions. And the most hopeful possibility of all is that by a sincere effort to *learn by seeing* the Zen attitude, the Western mind may finally reach the enlightened freedom of finding that the opposition between realism and mysticism vanishes.

Pertinent Literature

Watts, Alan W. *The Way of Zen.* New York: Pantheon Books, 1957.

Although acknowledging the value of Daisetz T. Suzuki's works on Zen Buddhism, Alan W. Watts maintains that not even Suzuki has written a work providing Zen's historical background in Chinese and Indian thought. Watts's book attempts to provide such an account; in the discussion of the background and history of Zen Buddhism he considers Taoism, Buddhism, Mahayana Buddhism, and the rise and development of Zen. The second part of his book is concerned with the principles and practice of Zen. According to Watts, Zen Buddhism is "a way and a view of life"; it does not fit into the categories of Western philosophy or religion. Zen defies classification, Watts writes, because it is *not* philosophy, religion, psychology, or science; the only way to explain what Zen is, he insists, is to make clear what it is not.

Watts begins the study of the historical background of Zen by turning to its Chinese origins; it is more Chinese than Indian, and although it has been a distinctive feature of Japanese culture since the twelfth century, its Taoist origins and its Chinese flavor must be understood if Zen is to be grasped at all. Hence, Watts's first concern is with "The Philosophy of Tao." Such a philosophy is difficult for the Western mind to comprehend, he suggests, because Western thinking is of the type a Taoist would call "conventional"—dependant upon conventional signs and modes of communication. Western think-

ing requires for its expression the use of an alphabetic language, and the words used call attention to abstractions; hence, Western thinking is "linear" and "one-at-a-time," Watts contends, and is hardly suitable for grasping a universe in which everything is happening at once, revealing a complexity that escapes analysis by the use of abstract terms. Watts contrasts Taoism to Western thinking: Taoism, he contends, is unconventional knowledge, a way of life that involves understanding life directly instead of by abstract, linear, representative thinking.

The author also contrasts Taoism to Confucianism: Confucianism attempts to order life according to conventional rules and standards; Taoism attempts to counter this restrictive tradition by developing "original spontaneity, which is termed *tzu-jan* or 'self-so-ness.' "

The common origin of Taoism and Confucianism, according to the Chinese, was not the *Tao Te Ching*, attributed to Lao-tzu, but the I Ching, or *Book of Changes*. Watts writes sympathetically about the use of the *I Ching* as a book of divination, a book by reference to which decisions can be made. He emphasizes the value of intuition, of what he calls the "peripheral vision" of the mind, and he suggests that perhaps the scientific way of discovery has serious limitations, at least when what one is deciding upon is a way of life.

In Taoism the mind is used but not forced. If the

tao, the Way, the "world process," is to be grasped at all, it is by letting the mind go, by a kind of unconsciousness, a "no-mind" or un-self-consciousness.

The first principle of Taoism is the *tao* itself—the Way of life. The second is spontaneity: the *tao* operates in a spontaneous way, not according to plan. Accordingly, the intelligence that confronts the *tao* is itself spontaneous and intuitive. Watts explains *te* as a kind of "virtue" or "power" which one has who is of no-mind, whose mind is not conventional but spontaneous. The combining of Taoism, which Watts describes as "a liberation *from* convention and *of* the creative power of *te*," with Mahayana Buddhism resulted in Zen Buddhism.

In his chapter "The Origins of Buddhism," Watts explains the Four Noble Truths, the Eight-Fold Path, and the basic ideas of *karma* and *nirvana*. From the fundamental perspective that leads to the judgment "Life is suffering," or, Watts suggests, "frustration" (although, as always, no single Western term or even set of terms is sufficient), a way of life is derived that the Eight-Fold path prescribes. Everything depends on clear awareness, as in Taoism—an opening of the mind to what *is*; from such contemplation comes the right view, understanding, speech, action—and, in short, liberation, a condition of being that is *nirvana* or release from the limited ways and "desire" that inevitably involve suffering. Mahayana Buddhism concentrated on bringing about a cessation of the mind's tendency to think in a discriminative way; the effort was to find *upaya*, "skillful means" for eliminating discriminatory thought, thereby making *nirvana* accessible.

Watts declares that Zen Buddhism has a "special flavor" that resists descriptive identification, but he suggests that "directness" is the key to making the distinction between Zen and other forms of Buddhism. Zen relies on *chih-chih*, a direct pointing, a nonsymbolic action. He traces the historical development of Zen and gives numerous examples of the Zen way. His explanatory account to some degree relies on Suzuki, but his fresh and lively approach to the subject also illuminates Suzuki's writings and fills out the picture of Zen Buddhism.

Barrett, William, ed. "Introduction," in D. T. Suzuki's *Zen Buddhism: Selected Writings of D. T. Suzuki.* Garden City, New York: Doubleday & Company, 1956.

William Barrett's collection of selections from Daisetz T. Suzuki's works on Zen Buddhism is a convenient and dependable source of the most helpful of Suzuki's explanatory essays, and it is further distinguished by the quality of its introduction, in which Barrett makes the effort to connect the philosophical approach fostered by Zen Buddhism to the interests that in the West have led to a practical and cognitive effort to grasp the sense of the world of common experience and concern. The selections in *Zen Buddhism* are drawn from the following works published by Rider and Company, London: *Essays in Zen Buddhism, First Series* (1949), *The Zen Doctrine of No-Mind* (1949), *Essays in Zen Buddhism, Second Series* (1950), *Essays in Zen Buddhism, Third Series* (1953), and *Studies in Zen* (1955). (The latter work is also published in the United States by Philosophical Library.)

Barrett presents the selections under topics that provide a system of orientation for students unfamiliar with Zen Buddhism: I: The Meaning of Zen Buddhism; II: The Historical Background of Zen Buddhism; III: The Heart of Zen; IV: Techniques of Zen; V: Zen and the Unconscious; VI: Zen and Philosophy; and VII: Zen and Japanese Culture. For those familiar with Western philosophy, Chapter 9 (in Part VI, "Zen and Philosophy"), "Existentialism, Pragmatism and Zen" is especially helpful as providing a contrast that illuminates the difference between the Western philosophical method of analysis and experimentation and the Zen method of subjectivity.

Barrett regards Suzuki as unique in that Suzuki assumes that Buddhism is as pertinent and living a life spirit as it was over 2500 years ago when Gotama Siddhartha experienced enlightenment. Barrett testifies to the positive effect in his own life of his becoming acquainted with Zen through the writings of Suzuki, and he attributes much of the "freshness and vitality" of Suzuki's accounts of Zen to his having become thoroughly familiar with

Chinese Buddhism.

The "practical and concrete Chinese spirit," Barrett writes, brings Buddhism more within the grasp of the Western mind than does the "soaring metaphysical imagination of the Indians." The paradoxes and anecdotes of the Zen masters exhibit the Chinese faculty of expression through concrete imagery that provokes the kind of intuitive response that makes understanding possible.

According to Barrett, the Western tradition, with its dominant Hebraic and Greek influences, has worked against the recognition of certain basic realities of life. Both influences have been divisive, Barrett believes: the Hebrew view distinguishes God from the world (and, accordingly, God from his creatures), the Law from fallible persons, and the spirit from the flesh; the Greek, by contrast, divides matters on intellectual, not moral and religious grounds, insisting upon a radical distinction between reason and the senses. The Orientals, on the other hand, by making intuition central, have avoided the divisions that plague the Western mind and spirit.

Medieval Christianity, as influenced by Aristotle, fosters a rational, logical, and hence humanized view of reality, Barrett maintains. But modern astronomy, physics, and even mathematics are more akin to the spirit and thrust of Indian thought, which emphasizes the vastness and ultimate irrationality of the universe.

Reason generates paradoxes; intuition grasps unity. If Being is to be known, it cannot be known by intellect. The Zen approach to understanding is by a form of subjective action that the term "no-mind" can only suggest. Barrett calls attention to Martin Heidegger's philosophy and its rejection of the dichotomizing intellect, and to D. H. Lawrence's call for "mindlessness" to correct the inhibiting and distorting influence of Western rationalism, which divides subject and object. These Western thinkers—the one, a philosopher, the other, an artist—approach but do not reach the revelatory attitude that Zen Buddhism encourages and exhibits.

The language of Zen involves concreteness of expression, the use of images and examples that incite intuition, Barrett writes; but this language is not simply a means: "On the contrary, the language of Zen is of the essence, the manner of expression is one with the matter." Zen is "Radical Intuitionism," Barrett suggests—not a philosophy of intuition but intuition "in the act itself." The task for the Zen master is to "awaken the third eye," the eye of intuition; language is used to get beyond language and concepts, even to get beyond distinguishable "facts" in order to know the unity of Being.

Zen itself is not a philosophy, Barrett warns—at least, it is not a philosophy in the Western sense; it is "a philosophy to undo philosophy," an attempt to avoid the divisive tendency of the emphasis on ideas as the objects of disciplined thought by achieving an "unmediated relation to reality. . . ."

Nor is Zen a kind of mysticism, Barrett insists. Although it works toward enlightenment, *satori*, it does not involve the conception of a reality beyond the world of sense experience and the consequent necessity of a radical experience by which one leaves the world of appearance and enters into the world beyond. Zen is matter-of-fact, Barrett contends; it is not philosophy, or mysticism, or pantheism, or theism; it is a way of achieving the actuality of unity, the living of Being. Zen is "the living fact in all religions East or West," Barrett declares. "Zen touches what is the living fact in all religions." He invites the reader to discover Zen through the writings of Suzuki.

Additional Recommended Reading

Abe, Masao, ed. *A Zen Life: D. T. Suzuki Remembered*. New York: Weatherhill, 1986. Provides useful biographical background of Suzuki and his philosophy.

Beck, Lily Adams. *The Story of Oriental Philosophy*. New York: Farrar and Rinehart, 1928. Beck covers Indian thought, Buddhism, Chinese thought, and finally, in Chapter XXIX, "Buddhist Thought and Art in China and Japan: The Teachings of Zen." Beck ties Zen to the teachings of Bodhidharma and the Yoga of the early Upanishads.

Hackett, Stuart C. *Oriental Philosophy: A Westerner's Guide to Eastern Thought* Madison: University of Wisconsin Press, 1979. Hackett's account is intelligible and scholarly, and his remarks about Zen Buddhism, although brief, provide an excellent summary of the distinctive features of Zen.

Humphreys, Christmas. *Buddhism*. Harmondsworth, England: Penguin Books, 1951. A readable introduction to Buddhism with an account of the doctrines of the Southern and Mahayana schools, including a chapter on Zen Buddhism.

—————————. *Zen Buddhism*. London: Heinemann, 1949. As the title suggests, the author focuses on Zen Buddhism.

Koller, John M. *Oriental Philosophies*. New York: Charles Scribner's Sons, 1970. Chapter 13, "Zen Buddhism," explains Zen within the context of the history of Buddhism. Like Barrett, the author describes Zen Buddhism as neither a religion, a philosophy, nor a set of beliefs; it is an active way of achieving integrity and completeness in a moment of experience.

THE REBEL

Author: Albert Camus (1913-1960)
Type of work: Ethics
First published: 1951

Principal Ideas Advanced

When a person who is slave to the absurd conditions about him declares that there is a limit to what he will endure or approve, he becomes a man, he exists.

In creating value through rebellion, the rebel creates values for all men and makes himself part of the community of men.

Those who attempt to rebel by becoming nihilists or utopians fail to achieve authentic rebellion.

The genuine rebel combines the negative attitude of one who recognizes the relativity of values with the positive attitude of one who makes an absolute commitment which gives rise to spiritual values.

From Robespierre to Stalin, lovers of justice and equality have fallen time and again into contradiction and ended by outraging the humanity they were committed to save. *The Rebel* seeks to understand the failure of a century and a half of revolution and, by returning to its source in the spirit of revolt, to recover the ideal which has eluded the ideologues.

Camus' book is, in one respect, a history of the whole anti-God, anti-authoritarian movement in literature, philosophy, and government. This is clearly indicated in the subtitle, *An Essay on Man in Revolt.* The historical study is divided into three parts. The first, entitled "Metaphysical Rebellion," examines a gallery of "immoralist" authors beginning with the Marquis de Sade and ending with André Breton. A longer section, called "Historical Rebellion," traces the fortunes of political nihilism both in its individualist and its collectivist forms. A third part, "Rebellion and Art," briefly indicates the manner in which the same analysis may be carried over into the fine arts, particularly the history of the novel. Thus, the body of this considerable work is a series of essays in literary and historical criticism.

But the introductory and concluding essays are of a different sort. In them Camus conducts a phenomenological investigation into the data of Revolt, analogous to Max Scheler's study of Resentment and his own earlier analysis of the Absurd. These essays, which are the most original part of the book, provide the norm by which the failures of nihilism are judged, and point the direction of a more humane and creative endeavor.

The essay *The Myth of Sisyphus* (1942) was addressed to the problem of nihilism which engrossed the minds of intellectuals at the close of World War I. In it we are offered Camus' variant of existentialism, according to which the person who has been confronted with the meaninglessness of existence gives his own life a modicum of dignity and significance by holding the posture of revolt. An honest man, says Camus, acts according to his belief. If he affirms that the world is meaningless, he is bound to commit suicide, for to go on living is to cheat. According to Camus in this youthful work, the only honest reason for a man's putting up with the irrationality of things is to be able to feel superior to the forces that crush him—like Pascal's Thinking Reed. To the man of the Absurd, the world becomes as indifferent as he is to the world. He bears his burden without joy and without hope, like Sisyphus, who was condemned to roll his rock up the hill anew each day; but he preserves a titanic fury, refusing any of the palliatives offered by religion or philosophy or by the distractions of pleasure or ambition.

When *The Rebel* was written, ten years later, the fashionable nihilism of the period between the wars was no longer relevant. The fall of France led to the taking of sides by many intellectuals, including Camus. The problem of suicide gave way to that of collaboration. People who had cultivated indifference suddenly found that they could not overlook the difference between Pierre Laval and Charles de Gaulle.

The new concern is plainly evident in Camus' novel *The Plague* (1947), where it is abundantly clear that those who are strong ought to bear the burdens of the weak. In this pest-hole of a world, no man can stir without the risk of bringing death to someone. But although we are all contaminated, we have the choice of joining forces with the plague or of putting up a fight against it. The immediate objective is to save as many as possible from death. But beyond this, and, in Camus' eyes even more important, is the task of saving men from loneliness. It is better to be in the plague with others than to be isolated on the outside.

In *The Rebel*, Camus tries to show that solidarity is logically implied even in the absurdist position; for to perceive that life is absurd there must be consciousness, and for there to be consciousness there must be life. But the moment human life becomes a value, it becomes a value for all men. In this way, absurdism may be extended to prohibit murder as well as suicide. But it offers no creative solution to an age of wholesale exportation, enslavement, and execution. We must turn, instead, to a different kind of revolt—that which on occasion is born in the heart of a slave who suddenly says, "No; there is a limit. So much will I consent to, but no more." At this moment a line is drawn between what it is to be a thing and what it is to be a man. Human nature is delineated, and a new value comes into being. To be sure, the universe ignores it, and the forces of history deny it. But it rises, none the less, to challenge these; and in so doing so creates a new force, brotherhood. Out of rebellion Camus wrenches a positive principle of politics as Descartes had found certitude in the midst of doubt. "I rebel," says Camus, "therefore *we* exist."

Although the first stirrings of rebellion are full of promise, the path they mark out is straight and narrow, and few there be that follow it to the end. Like the moral virtues in Aristotle's *Ethics*, it is a mean between two extremes. The rebel, if he thinks out the implications of the impulse which moves within him, knows that he must never kill or oppress or deceive his fellow man. But in the actual world such a policy makes him accessory to the crimes of others. Therefore, he must on occasion perform acts of violence in the interest of suffering humanity. The difficulties of taking arms against oppression without becoming an oppressor are so great that it is small wonder most would-be rebels slip into one false position or another.

In *The Myth of Sisyphus*, Camus went to great lengths showing the inauthentic responses to the Absurd made by the existentialists Søren Kierkegaard, Franz Kafka, and Jean-Paul Sartre, who, according to Camus, rejected literal suicide, but substituted a kind of "philosophical suicide" by making believe that it is possible to escape Absurdity. Just so, in *The Rebel*, Camus' chief line of argument is to show that the great heroes in the literature of revolt and in the history of revolution, almost without exception, fall away from authentic rebellion. For some, the dominant impulse is to negate the forces that frustrate man's development: with them rebellion passes into hatred, and they can think of nothing but destruction. For others, the impulse is to enforce order and realize a standard good: love of their fellow man gives place to an abstract goal which they must achieve at any cost. The former are nihilists, the latter utopians.

Camus' discussion in "Rebellion in Art" provides a clear instance of the two kinds of false rebellion. All art, in his opinion, is essentially a revolt against reality. Art both needs the world and denies it. But contemporary art has allowed itself to be sidetracked. Formalism gravitates too exclusively toward negation, banishing reality and ending in delirium. Realism, however (he specifies the "tough" American variety), by reducing man to elemental and external reactions, is too eager to impose its own order on the world. Both arise, in a sense, out of the spirit of revolt, protesting the hypocrisy of bourgeois conventionality; both fail, as art, inasmuch as they lose touch with the springs of revolt. Proust is Camus' example of a genuine artist: rejecting those aspects of reality which are of no interest to man while lovingly affirming the happier parts, he re-creates the universe by redistributing its elements after the heart's desire. This suggests that the creative way is not that of "all or nothing" but that of moderation and limit. The order and unity which make for genuine art do minimal violence to the matter they undertake to re-form. And the artist remains, above all, a friend of man.

Camus' classification of rebels into world-deniers and world-affirmers provides only a rough basis for division when he comes to consider the great figures in the history of revolt. The difficulty is that the contradictions into which their extremism leads renders them at last almost indistinguishable. Nevertheless there is merit in retaining the groupings. Under "Metaphysical Rebellion," Sade's advocacy of universal crime and Alfred de Vigny's Satanism exemplify rebellion which took the way of negation. With them we may place Rimbaud, who made a virtue of renouncing his genius, and the surrealist Breton, who talked of the beauty of shooting at random into a street crowd. On the other side are the partisans of affirmation—Max Stirner with his absolute egotism, and Nietzsche with his deification of fate. When we turn to "Historical Rebellion," there are the anarchists and nihilists such as Michael Bakunin and Dmitri Pisarev, for whom destruction was an end in itself. But they are more than balanced by the revolutionaries, whose ambition in overthrowing the present order was but a means toward fulfilling the destiny of a race or of mankind—Robespierre and St. Just, Mussolini and Hitler, Marx and Lenin.

The section on Metaphysical Revolt deals with those whose revolt was centered in the realm of imagination. Camus finds their archetype not in Prometheus but in Cain; because rebellion presupposes a doctrine of creation and a personal deity who is held to be responsible for the human condition. Their temper is rather that of blasphemy than of unbelief; and when they go so far as to deny that there is a God, their protest, lacking an object, turns into madness. Here Ivan Karamazov is more instructive than real-life rebels. Indignation causes him to reject God on the grounds that a world that entails suffering ought never to have been permitted. But he discovers that, having rejected God, there is no longer any limit—

"everything is permitted." And Ivan acquiesces in the murder of his father—before going mad. Ivan rejects *grace* and has nothing to put in its place. This is the tragedy of nihilism.

Historical Revolt was directed less immediately against God than against the absolutism of divine right kings and the prerogatives of feudal lords and bishops. But it has its metaphysical dimension. In rejecting the old order, the revolutionaries too were rejecting grace, without, however, falling into nihilism; for instead of concluding that all things are permitted, they immediately divinized *justice*. They repudiated Christ, but retained the apparatus of an infallible institution within which alone salvation is possible. And in place of the madness of Ivan Karamazov, they find themselves swallowed up in Chigalov's despair. Their conclusion is a direct contradiction of their original premises: starting from unlimited freedom they arrive at unlimited despotism.

In Camus' opinion, just as the nineteenth century revolted against *grace*, the twentieth must revolt against *justice*. The kingdom of men which the revolutionaries sought to substitute for the kingdom of God has retreated into the distance and the goal has been brought not a step nearer. The fault is in the nature of revolution itself, which, as the word indicates, describes a full cycle. In rebellion, the slave rises against his master; in revolution, he aspires to take his master's place. Thus, the champions of justice have merely substituted a new domination for the old. And in many ways the new is less tolerable than that which it replaced. For the rule of God at least allowed man to preserve the human image; but when the sacred disappeared, man's dignity disappeared with it. Ivan Karamazov said that "everything is permitted"; Chigalov, the human-engineer, calculated that nine-tenths of the human race must be reduced to herd animals. This is what takes place when God is overthrown. It is a principle of all revolutions, says Camus, that human nature is infinitely malleable; in other words, that there is no special human nature. Under the kingdom of grace there was; and the rebel insists that there still is. This is the limit that he opposes to Caesarism. Rebellion rediscovers man, affirms that he is not a mere thing, insists that a distinctive nature sets him off from all other beings and, at the same time, unites him with every other man. From this point of view, the only alternative to grace is *rebellion.*

No doubt enough has been said about the defections into which rebels are prone to fall. Like many a preacher, Camus finds it easier to criticize the failures of others than to present a clear-cut statement of what authentic rebellion entails. We have, of course, his stories and dramas to fill out the picture. But so far as the present essay is concerned, the only vivid illustration of genuine revolt is found in his account of a group of Russian terrorists (the most exemplary were brought to trial in 1905) who combined nihilism with definite religious principles. Camus calls them "fastidious nihilists." "In the universe of total negation, these young disciples try with bombs and revolvers and also with the courage with which they walk to the gallows, to escape from contradiction and to create the values they lack." They did not hesitate to destroy; but by their death they believed they were re-creating a community founded on love and justice, thus resuming the mission the church had betrayed. They combined respect for human life in general with the resolution to sacrifice their own lives. Death was sought as payment for the crimes that the nihilists knew they must commit.

Transposed into a more moderate key, what Camus seems to be advocating is a life of tension in which contradictions may live and thrive. There must be a way between that of the Yogi and that of the Commissar, between absolute freedom and absolute justice. In this world, man has to be content with relative goods; but he does not have to give them anything less than his absolute commitment. This is humanism, though hardly of the Anglo-Saxon utilitarian variety. The values born of the spirit of rebellion are essentially spiritual. The rebel wills to serve justice without committing injustice in the process, to use plain language and avoid falsehood, to advance toward unity without denying the origins of community in the free spirit.

Politically, Albert Camus takes his stand with syndicalist and libertarian thought: as opposed to the revolutionists who would order society from the top down, he favors a society built out of local autonomous cells. Far from being romantic, he holds that a communal system is more realistic than the totalitarian, based as it is on concrete relations such as occupation and the village. Nor is it new. From the time of the Greeks, the struggle has been going on (especially around the Mediterranean) between city and empire, deliberate freedom and rational tyranny, altruistic individualism and the manipulation of the masses. It is the endless opposition of moderation to excess in man's attempt to know and apply the measure of his stature, his refusal to be either beast or god.

Pertinent Literature

Brée, Germaine. *Camus.* New Brunswick, New Jersey: Rutgers University Press, 1959.

At the age of forty-four, Albert Camus received the 1957 Nobel Prize for literature. Germaine Brée believes that Camus' international reputation rests primarily on novels such as *The Stranger* (1942), *The Plague* (1947), and *The Fall* (1956), but she also includes *The Rebel (L'Homme révolté)* in her distinguished list. Like Camus' fictional works, however, this essay in moral and political thought has attracted far less attention from professional philosophers than the work of his famous French contemporary and rival, Jean-Paul Sartre.

Although Camus will continue to be counted among the existentialists, he actually disclaimed connection with them. Brée finds that Camus' study of Edmund Husserl, Martin Heidegger, and Karl Jaspers did not run very deep. The thought of Friedrich Nietzsche and Søren Kierkegaard was better known to him, but Brée surmises that neither attracted him strongly. In fact, she suggests, Camus had relatively little interest in philosophical scholarship.

Brée notes that the appearance of *The Rebel* provoked a major controversy in France. Concerned with what she calls "the monomaniacs of revolt," Camus' book was in part a critique of the French political left, arguing that Marxist ideology could destroy freedom and result in Stalinist terror. At this time, Sartre and some of his followers were striving to combine existentialism and Marxism. Stung by Camus, they attacked him as a sentimental idealist. The ensuing debate, rancorous at times, left the friendship of Sartre and Camus in ruins. Brée stresses that the issues at stake in *The Rebel* transcended the personal disputes that split French intellectuals in the 1950's, but she does defend Camus and underscores how characteristic it was for him to root his literary concerns in the soil of his particular time and place.

The Rebel is a reflection provoked by politically inspired mass murder in the twentieth century. According to Brée, Camus argues convincingly for the book's central thesis: When revolution in the name of human freedom becomes an unlimited demand for liberty, the result is tyranny; likewise, when revolution against social injustice turns into an unbounded claim for justice, the outcome is terrorism against individual existence.

Grasping for absolutes, Camus thought, leads to madness. To avoid that tragic waste, there must be moderation. In making these claims, Brée points out, Camus was neither preaching accommodation nor rejecting his own inheritance from the left. He did,

however, question some of the latter's Marxist axioms. Camus, for example, doubted that history is predetermined to move toward one particular form of human liberation, and thus he denied that all actions are justifiable so long as they lead to the emergence of a socialist state. Camus' criticism of Marxist ideology, Brée asserts, unmasked the fallacy of sacrificing the present happiness of individuals, for whom justice was supposedly being sought, in order to pursue ends that were nebulous and problematic.

Such criticism, Brée admits, was not original with Camus. She asserts, however, that the "eminently sane" conclusion to *The Rebel* takes a more distinctive position. Dealing with broad moral considerations more than with specific political policies, it delineates Camus' democratic idea of rebellion as moderation. Freedom and justice ought to be preserved and extended, but modern men and women must recognize how life imposes limits that cannot be violated with impunity. Quite rightly, Brée implies, Camus affirms the need for law to define basic human rights and for governments to honor them as inalienable. Only by doing so will there begin to be assurance that people can enjoy "the daily measure of happiness which, in Camus's eyes, is man's greatest treasure."

Wilhoite, Fred H., Jr. *Beyond Nihilism: Albert Camus's Contribution to Political Thought*. Baton Rouge: Louisiana State University Press, 1968.

If Albert Camus has never taken center stage in academic philosophy, Fred H. Wilhoite, Jr. acknowledges that he is not often mentioned by political theorists either. Yet Wilhoite agrees with Germaine Brée in holding that political concerns were never far from Camus' attention. This book, therefore, explores whether Camus had an explicit political philosophy. The answer, Wilhoite states, must be negative if one is looking for a systematic view that discusses all the major questions that normally occupy political theory. On the other hand, he thinks Camus' sensitive reflections do contribute significantly to recent social thought.

Wilhoite says that two themes are especially important in his study of Camus. First, there is Camus'

"existential method." Here the author is not pointing primarily to a set of substantive conclusions, but rather to the fact that Camus tried hard to avoid vague abstractions. Wilhoite finds Camus "existential" because he worked from his own experience, not from *a priori* truths, and because the characters in his stories, novels, and plays give his ethical inquiry a realistic texture. The second theme, more directly applicable to *The Rebel*, is Camus' struggle to develop a normative response to contemporary nihilism, which Wilhoite describes as an outlook that finds existence bereft of intrinsic meaning and, in particular, devoid of intellectually authoritative moral standards.

The Rebel, Wilhoite claims, contains the core of Camus' existential ethic. Moving from Camus' observation that rebellion says "No!" to exploitation and thereby says "Yes!" to limits that must not be overstepped, Wilhoite holds that Camus' rebel uncovers a shared common good that transcends one's individual fate. True, rebellion may be motivated by egoistic concerns; but the rebel's willingness to die in resisting oppression implies a commitment to rights for all. Thus, the form of rebellion advocated by Camus does not seek to conquer or to destroy its opposition. Mutual respect for life is its goal instead.

Camus was impressed by the fact that men and women, at least sometimes, simply recognize wrongdoing and act to stop it. This insight, Wilhoite insists, is especially important because Camus also recognized that apparently timeless moral truths have repeatedly been negated by twentieth century history, which seems to permit anything. According to Wilhoite, Camus discovered that even in a wasteland of moral skepticism and metaphysical absurdity, rebellion assumes and reveals that human existence itself still contains a firm foundation for establishing differences between right and wrong and thus for building human solidarity.

Although Camus never wrote a systematic treatise on the subject, Wilhoite holds that his entire literary output consists of observation and comment on human nature. *The Rebel* in particular affirms universal human qualities, thus helping to explain Camus' rejection of "existentialism," which he tended to equate with the Sartrean formula that where human life is concerned existence precedes essence. On the other hand, Wilhoite also thinks that Camus' own existential leanings account for his reluctance to describe human nature as though it could be encompassed by the abstract categories of traditional philosophy. Camus chose instead to illuminate humanity's shared predicament in striving after meaning and justice. The most vital result of that effort, Wilhoite concludes, shows that even without the "certainty of divine guidance or of consensus on a metaphysical system, we need not float adrift on a sea of nihilism."

Masters, Brian. *Camus: A Study*. Totowa, New Jersey: Rowman and Littlefield, 1974.

On January 5, 1960, while traveling to Paris in a fast car driven by Michel Gallimard, Albert Camus died instantly when the vehicle crashed into a tree. He was only forty-six, and thus Brian Masters reminds us that *The Rebel* was the work of a relatively young man. Praising Camus' writing as a "hymn to life," Masters notes that Camus was joyful and not one to be downcast. He reports, too, how Camus once stated that if he were to write a book on ethics it would consist of a hundred pages. Ninety-nine would be blank, but the last one would say, "I know of only one duty, and that is to love."

The Rebel, it seems to Masters, may not stand up to rigorous philosophical scrutiny because it is less a careful study of moral and political theory than it is an autobiography. Masters views the work as Camus' attempt to solve an intolerable paradox posed by history: that people are more good than bad and yet they do more evil acts than good ones. Camus believed that this tragedy emerged from the human propensity to go to the extremes of absolutism or nihilism. He thought that his description of authentic rebellion might be the needed corrective, but as far as the political climate of Camus' own day was concerned, Masters observed that Camus was overly optimistic. The book provoked stormy attacks not only from the left but also from the political right.

Masters calls Camus a "stern moralist" who struggled to renew humane values that are under threat. Especially significant in this battle is Camus' argument that even when one starts with the Absurd, with the conviction that all transcendental values have fled from a world that is ridiculous and senseless, and unshakable conviction remains. This conviction holds that existence lacks justice, an undeniable realization that is precious to Camus because it implies that men and women do possess a common basis for understanding what justice is. The Absurd, suggests Masters, is thus seen by Camus as an affront to an inherent moral sensitivity that points toward what Camus cautiously designates as a shared human nature.

Recognition of human solidarity, however, does not solve the practical problems that remain. For example, Masters argues, Camus' rebel cannot condone injustice; but in combatting wrong, further injustices may be committed. Masters finds that Camus "is not a successful theoretician" when it comes to handling satisfactorily all the difficulties that an authentic rebel must confront in pursuing a path of moderation, a middle way between the extremes of all or nothing that absolutism or nihilism involve. He does find, however, that Camus himself was consistently guided by the rebel's aim of seeking greater *degrees* of justice, freedom, and happiness—not everything or nothing at all. Thus, Masters concludes,

he also chose means for action that were faithful to his beliefs, exhibiting a determined honesty that "opposed force from whatever quarter it came and exposed intolerance under whatever name it was cloaked."

In common with other interpreters, Masters affirms that Camus did not regard himself as the leader of a school of thought or even as a philosopher. The author thinks Camus was motivated to write *The Rebel* and all of his other books mainly because he wanted no one to live deceived or oppressed. This "transparent sincerity," Masters maintains, gives Camus' writings their special distinction.

Additional Recommended Reading

Barnes, Hazel E. *The Literature of Possibility: A Study in Humanistic Existentialism.* Lincoln: University of Nebraska Press, 1959. Although she finds that Camus' allusions to human nature present many problems, Barnes acknowledges that *The Rebel* stakes out a dynamic middle ground where one must live with the recognition that violence may at times be morally necessary even though it can never be fully legitimate.

Copleston, Frederick. *A History of Philosophy.* Vol. IX. Garden City, New York: Image Books, 1977. *The Rebel*, says Copleston, is not intended to be a political blueprint but rather a moral reflection that explores the tensions between the spirit of moderation and the passion of revolt.

Cruickshank, John. *Albert Camus and the Literature of Revolt.* New York: Oxford University Press, 1960. Although *The Rebel* reveals Camus' ethical sensitivity and nobility of mind, Cruickshank finds the book unsatisfactory because of its "lyrical flights" at the end.

Doubrovsky, Serge. "The Ethics of Albert Camus," in *Camus: A Collection of Critical Essays.* Edited by Germaine Brée. Englewood Cliffs, New Jersey: Prentice-Hall, 1962, pp. 71-84. Doubrovsky holds that Camus' writings, including *The Rebel*, speak most clearly about what persons ought *not* to do. Thus, they form an ethical prolegomenon rather than a fully developed moral theory.

Hanna, Thomas. *The Lyrical Existentialists.* New York: Atheneum, 1962. Asserting that Camus' thought is best summed up as a "philosophy of revolt," Hanna sees *The Rebel* as an extraordinary reflection on the tragic aspects and redemptive possibilities within modern European history.

Meagher, Robert E., ed. *Albert Camus: The Essential Writings.* New York: Harper Colophon Books, 1979. Meagher's commentary in this anthology interprets *The Rebel* as itself an act of rebellion, one that reveals Camus' own protests and the affirmations implicit in them.

Murchland, Bernard C. "Albert Camus: The Dark Night Before the Coming of Grace?," in *Camus: A Collection of Critical Essays.* Edited by Germaine Brée. Englewood Cliffs, New Jersey: Prentice-Hall, 1962, pp. 59-64. Citing *The Plague* and *The Rebel* as perhaps Camus' best works, Murchland underscores Camus' use of rebellion to protest against absurdity.

Olafson, Frederick A. "Albert Camus," in *The Encyclopedia of Philosophy.* New York: Macmillan Publishing Company, 1967. Olafson stresses that the taking of human life is inconsistent with Camus' true rebellion, but he thinks that Camus failed to sufficiently clarify how his rejection of violence is to be interpreted.

Thorson, Thomas Landon. "Albert Camus and the Rights of Man," in *Ethics.* LXXIV, no. 4 (July, 1964), pp.

281-291. This article finds Camus' insights about political philosophy especially pertinent for the second half of the twentieth century.

Woelfel, James W. *Camus: A Theological Perspective*. Nashville: Abingdon Press, 1975. Calling *The Rebel* Camus' "definitive philosophical essay," Woelfel sees Camus setting himself in opposition to Sartre by postulating a universal human nature.

THE COURAGE TO BE

Author: Paul Tillich (1886-1965)
Type of work: Ontology, ethics
First published: 1952

Principal Ideas Advanced

Considered from the ethical point of view, courage in a man is a sign of his caring for something enough to decide and to act despite opposition; considered in terms of its effect on his being (ontologically), courage is the self-affirmation of one's being.

These points of view are united in the conception of courage as the self-affirmation of one's being in the presence of the threat of nonbeing; anxiety is the felt awareness of the threat of nonbeing, and courage is the resolute opposition to the threat in such a manner that being is affirmed.

Three types of anxiety—ontic, moral, and spiritual (the anxiety of fate and death, of guilt and condemnation, of emptiness and meaninglessness)—are present in all cultural ages, but spiritual anxiety is predominant in the modern period.

Existential anxiety cannot be removed; it can be faced only by those who have the courage to be.

The courage to be involves the courage to participate, to be oneself, and to unite the two by absolute faith in the God above God, "being-itself."

The material in Tillich's book, *The Courage to Be,* was first presented in the form of a series of lectures given at Yale University in 1950-51, under the sponsorship of the Terry Foundation. The central task which the author has assumed in these lectures is that of a dialectical analysis and phenomenological description of courage as a structural category of the human condition.

Courage, as understood by the author, is both an ethical reality and an ontological concept. As an ethical reality courage indicates concrete action and decision which expresses a valuational content. As an ontological concept—that is, as illuminating a feature of being—courage indicates the universal and essential self-affirmation of one's being. Tillich argues that these two meanings of courage must be united if a proper interpretation of the phenomenon is to be achieved. In the final analysis the ethical can be understood only through the ontological. Courage as an ethical reality is ultimately rooted in the structure of being itself.

These two meanings of courage have been given philosophic consideration throughout the whole history of Western thought. The author provides a brief historical sketch of the attempt to deal with the phenomenon of courage by tracing its development from Plato through Nietzsche. There is first the tradition which begins with Plato and leads to Thomas Aquinas. In the thought of Plato and Aristotle the heroic-aristocratic element in courage was given priority. Plato aligned courage with the spirited part of the soul, which lies between reason and desire, and then aligned both courage and spirit with the guardian class (*phylakes*), which lies between the rulers and the produc ers. The class of guardians, as the armed aristocracy, thus gave the Platonic definition of courage an indelible heroic-aristocratic stamp. Aristotle preserved the aristocratic element by defining the courageous man as one who acts for the sake of what is noble. However, there was another current of thought developing during this period. This was the understanding of courage as rational-democratic rather than heroic-aristocratic. The life and death of Socrates, and later the Christian tradition, gave expression to this view. The position of Thomas Aquinas is unique in that it marks the synthesis of a heroic-aristocratic ethic and society with a rational-democratic mode of thought. With Stoicism a new emphasis emerges. Taking as the ideal sage the Athenian Socrates, Stoics became the spokesmen for an emphatic rational-democratic definition of courage. Wisdom replaces heroic fortitude and the democratic-universal replaces the aristocratic ideal. The "courage to be" for the Stoics was a rational courage, indicating an affirmation of one's reasonable nature, or Logos, which countered the negativities of the nonessential or accidental. But this courage to be, formulated independently of the Christian doctrine of forgiveness and salvation, was ultimately cast in terms of a cosmic resignation. The historical significance of the ethical thought of Spinoza, according to the author, is that it rendered explicit an ontology of courage. This ontology of courage was one which made the Stoic doctrine of self-affirmation central, but which replaced the Stoic idea of resignation with a positive ethical humanism. Nietzsche stands at the end of the era, and in a sense is its culmination. Nietzsche transforms Spinoza's "substance" into "life." Spinoza's doctrine of self-affirmation is restated in dynamic terms. Will becomes the central category. Life is understood as "will-to-power." Courage is thus defined as the power of life to affirm itself in spite of its negativities and ambiguities—in spite of the abyss of nonbeing. Nietzsche expressed it thus: "he who with eagle's talons *graspeth* the abyss: he hath courage."

Tillich, in formulating his ontology of courage, keeps the tradition from Plato to Nietzsche in mind. His definition of courage, as the universal self-affirmation of one's being in the presence of the threat of nonbeing, receives its final clarification only in the light of the historical background which he has sketched. In the author's definition of courage the phenomenon of anxiety is disclosed as an unavoidable consideration. Courage and anxiety are interdependent concepts. Anxiety is the existential awareness of the threat of nonbeing. Courage is the resolute facing of this anxiety in such a way that nonbeing is ultimately embraced or taken up into being. Thus, the author is driven to formulate an ontology of anxiety. There is first a recognition of the interdependence of fear and anxiety. Fear and anxiety are distinct, but not separate. Fear has a determinable object—a pain, a rejection by someone who is loved, a misfortune, the anticipation of death. Anxiety, on the other hand, has no object, or paradoxically stated, its object is the negation of every object. Anxiety is the awareness that nonbeing is irremovably a part of one's being, which constitutes the definition of human finitude. Anxiety and fear are thus distinct. Yet they are mutually immanent within each other. Fear, when it is deepened, reveals anxiety; and anxiety strives toward fear. The fear of dying ultimately ceases to be a fear of an object—a sickness or an accident—and becomes anxiety over the nonbeing envisioned "after death." And conversely, anxiety strives to become fear, because the finite self cannot endure the threatening disclosure of nonbeing for more than a moment. The mind seeks to transform anxiety into fear, so that it can have a particular object to deal with and overcome. But the basic anxiety of nonbeing cannot, as such, be eliminated. It is a determinant of human existence itself.

The author distinguishes three types of anxiety: (1) *ontic anxiety* or the anxiety of fate and death; (2) *moral anxiety* or the anxiety of guilt and condemnation; and (3) *spiritual anxiety* or the anxiety of emptiness and meaninglessness.

Fate threatens man's ontic self-affirmation relatively; death threatens it absolutely. The anxiety of fate arises from an awareness of an ineradicable contingency which penetrates to the very depth of one's being. Existence exhibits no ultimate necessity. It manifests an irreducible element of irrationality. Behind fate stands death as the absolute threat to ontic self-affirmation. Death discloses the total ontic annihilation which is imminent in every moment of our existence. For the most part man attempts to transform this anxiety into fear, which has a definite object. He partly succeeds but then realizes that the threat can never be embodied in a particular object. It arises from the human situation as such. The question then is posed: "Is there a courage to be, a courage to affirm oneself in spite of the threat against man's ontic self-affirmation?"

Nonbeing threatens on another level. It threatens

by producing moral anxiety—the anxiety of guilt, which threatens relatively, and the anxiety of condemnation, which threatens absolutely. The self seeks to affirm itself morally by actualizing its potentialities. But in every moral action nonbeing expresses itself in the inability of man to actualize fully all of his potential. He remains estranged from his essential being. All of his actions are pervaded with a moral ambiguity. The awareness of this ambiguity is guilt. This guilt can drive man toward a feeling of complete self-rejection, in which he experiences the absolute threat of condemnation. The question then arises whether man can find a courage to affirm himself in spite of the threat against his moral self-affirmation.

Lastly, there is the anxiety of emptiness and meaninglessness, which reveals the threat to man's spiritual self-affirmation. Emptiness threatens this self-affirmation relatively, meaninglessness threatens it absolutely. Emptiness arises out of a situation in which the self fails to find satisfaction through a participation in the contents of its cultural life. The beliefs, attitudes, and activities of man's tradition lose their meaning and are transformed into matters of indifference. Everything is tried but nothing satisfies. Creativity vanishes and the self is threatened with boredom and tedium. The anxiety of emptiness culminates in the anxiety of meaninglessness. Man finds that he can no longer hold fast to the affirmations of his tradition nor to those of his personal convictions. Truth itself is called into question. Spiritual life is threatened with total doubt. Again, the question arises: Is there a courage to be which affirms itself in spite of nonbeing—in this case, nonbeing expressed in the threat of doubt which undermines one's spiritual affirmation through the anxiety of emptiness and meaninglessness?

These three types of anxiety find a periodic exemplification in the history of Western civilization. Although the three types are interdependently present in all cultural ages, we find that ontic anxiety was predominant at the end of ancient civilization, moral anxiety at the end of the Middle Ages, and spiritual anxiety at the end of the modern period. The anxiety of fate and death was the central threat in the Stoic doctrine of courage; it received expression in the transition from Hellenic to Hellinistic civilization, which saw the crumbling of the independent city states and the rise of universal empires, introducing a political power beyond control and calculation; and it is present on every page of Greek tragical literature. In the Middle Ages the anxiety of guilt and condemnation was dominant, expressed in the theological symbol of the "wrath of God" and in the imagery of hell and purgatory. Ascetic practices, pilgrimages, devotion to relics, institution of indulgences, heightened interest in the mass and penance—all witness to the moral threat of nonbeing as it manifests itself in guilt and condemnation. Modern civilization, born of the victory of humanism and the Enlightenment, found its chief threat in the threat to man's spiritual self-affirmation. Here the anxiety of emptiness and meaninglessness becomes dominant. Democratic liberalism calls into question the security and supports of an absolute state; the rise of technology tends to transform selves into tools and thus displace man's spiritual center; skepticism replaces philosophical certitude. All cultural contents which previously gave man security no longer afford satisfaction and meaning. Modern man is threatened with the attack of emptiness and meaninglessness.

The author concludes his ontology of anxiety by distinguishing existential anxiety, in the three types discussed, from pathological or neurotic anxiety. Existential anxiety has an ontological character and is thus understood as a universal determinant of the human condition. Existential anxiety cannot be removed; it can only be courageously faced. Pathological anxiety, on the other hand, as the result of unresolved conflicts in the socio-psychological structure of personality, is the expression of universal anxiety under special conditions. It is the consequence of man's inability to face courageously his existential anxiety and thus take the nonbeing which threatens into himself. The neurotic self still affirms itself, but it does so on a limited scale. Such affirmation is the affirmation of a reduced self which seeks to avoid the nonbeing that is constitutive of his universal finite condition. But in thus seeking to avoid nonbeing the neurotic self retreats from the full affirmation of his being. Hence, the author's definition of neurosis as "*the way of avoiding nonbeing by avoiding being.*" The neurotic personality always affirms something less than what he essentially is. His potentialities are sacrificed in order to make possible a narrow and intensified affirmation of what remains of his reduced self. The neurotic is unable to take creatively into himself the universal existential anxieties. In relation to the anxiety of fate and death this produces an unrealistic security, comparable to the security of a prison. Since the neurotic cannot distinguish what is to be realistically feared from those situations in which he is realistically safe, he withdraws into a castle of false security so as to insulate himself from all threats of existence. In relation to the anxiety of guilt and condemnation, pathological anxiety expresses an unrealistic perfection. The neurotic sets up moralistic self-defenses against all actions which would widen the horizons of his reduced and limited actualized state, which he considers to be absolutely perfect. In relation to the anxiety of emptiness and meaninglessness, which expresses itself in a radical existential doubt, pathological anxiety drives the self to an unrealistic certitude. Unable to face the doubt regarding the contents of his cultural tradition and his personal beliefs, the neurotic constructs a citadel of certainty, from which he fends off all threat of doubt on the basis of an absolutized authority. This absolutized authority may be either a personal revelation, a social or religious institution, or a fanatical leader of a movement. In any case, he refuses to accept doubt and rejects all questions from the outside. He is unable courageously to accept the reality of meaninglessness as a universal phenomenon in existential reality.

The courage to be is the movement of self-affirmation in spite of the threat of anxiety as the existential awareness of nonbeing. This courage is conceptually clarified by the author through the use of the polar ontological principles of participation and individualization. The basic polar structure of being is the polarity of self and world. The first polar elements which emerge out of this foundational polar structure are the elements of participation and individualization. The relevance of these elements to Tillich's doctrine of courage is evident. Courage expresses itself as "the courage to be as a part," exemplifying the polar element of participation, and as "the courage to be as oneself," exemplifying the polar element of individualization. Finally, these two polar exemplifications of courage are transcended and united in "absolute faith." Absolute faith, grounded in transcendence, provides the final definition of the courage to be.

First the author examines the manifestation of courage as the courage to be *as a part*. This is one side of man's self-affirmation. He affirms himself as a participant in the power of a group, a historical movement, or being as such. This side of courage counters the threat of losing participation in his world. The social forms which embody this manifestation of courage are varied. The author briefly discusses four of these forms: *collectivism, semi-collectivism, neocollectivism,* and *democratic conformism.*

All of these forms attempt to deal with the three types of anxiety—ontic, moral, and spiritual—by channeling their individual expressions into an anxiety about the group. Thus, it becomes possible to cope with these existential anxieties with a courage that affirms itself through collective or conformal participation. The individual anxiety concerning fate and death is transcended through a collective identification. There is a part of oneself, belonging to the group, which cannot be hurt or destroyed. It is as eternal as the group is eternal—an essential manifestation of the universal collective. So, also, a self-affirmation is made possible in spite of the threat of guilt and condemnation. Individual guilt is translated into a deviation or transgression of the norms of the collective, and the courage to be as a part accepts guilt and its consequences as public guilt. The anxiety of emptiness and meaninglessness is dealt with in the same way. The group becomes the bearer of universal meaning, and the individual derives his personal meaning through a participation in the group. The ever present danger in the radical affirmation of the courage to be as a part is the absorption of the self into the collective, with the consequent loss of the unique, unrepeatable, and irreplaceable individual.

The courage to be *as oneself* expresses the other side of man's self-affirmation. This movement is made possible through the ontological polar element of individualization. The courage to be as oneself has found a concrete embodiment in *romanticism, naturalism,* and *existentialism.*

Romanticism elevated the individual beyond all cultural content, and conferred upon him a radical autonomy. In some of its extreme expressions, as in Friedrich von Schlegel, the courage to be as oneself led to a complete rejection of participation.

Naturalism, whether of the "philosophy of life" variety or of the American pragmatic variety, follows basically the same path. Nietzsche, in his definition of nature as the will-to-power, granted priority to the individual will and made it the decisive element in the drive toward creativity. In Nietzsche individual self-affirmation reaches a climactic point. American pragmatism, in spite of its roots in democratic conformism, shares much of the individualistic attitude characteristic of European naturalism. It finds its highest ethical principle in growth, sees the educational process as one which maximizes the individual talents of the child, and seeks its governing philosophical principle in personal creative self-affirmation.

It is in *existentialism* that the courage to be as oneself is most powerfully presented. Tillich distinguishes two basic expressions of existentialism—as an attitude and as a philosophical and artistic content. Existentialism as an attitude designates an attitude of concrete involvement as contrasted with an attitude of theoretical detachment. Existentialism as a content is at the same time a point of view, a protest, and an expression. But in all of its varieties existentialism is the chief protagonist for the reality of the individual and the importance of personal decision. It is concerned to salvage the individual from the objectivization of abstract thought, society, and technology alike. The existentialist struggles for the preservation of the self-affirmative person. He fights against dehumanization in all of its forms. The task of every individual, according to the existentialist, is to be himself. Heidegger has profoundly expressed this existentialist courage to be as oneself in his concept of resolution (*Entschlossenheit*). The resolute individual derives his directives for action from no external source. Nobody can provide for one's security against the threat of ontic annihilation, moral disintegration, or spiritual loss of meaning. He himself must decide how to face his imminent death, how to face his moral ambiguity, and how to face the threat of meaninglessness which strikes at the root of his existence.

We have seen that the danger in the courage to be as a part is a loss of the self in the collective. The opposite danger becomes apparent in the various forms of the courage to be as oneself—namely, a loss of the world as a polar structure of selfhood. The question then arises whether there can be a courage which unites both sides of man's self-affirmation by transcending them.

Courage understood as absolute faith exemplifies this union through transcendence. A courage which can take the three types of anxiety creatively into itself must be grounded in a power of being that transcends both the power of oneself and the power of one's world. The self-world correlation is still on this side of the threat of nonbeing; hence, neither self-affirmation as oneself nor self-affirmation as a part can cope successfully with nonbeing. The courage to be, in its final movement, must be rooted in the power of being-itself, which transcends the self-world correlation. Insofar as religion is the state of being grasped by the power of being-itself, it can be said that courage always has either an explicit or implicit religious character. The courage to be finds its ultimate source in the power of being-itself, and becomes manifest as absolute faith. As long as participation remains dominant the relation to being-itself is mystical in character; as long as individualization remains dominant the relationship is one of personal encounter; when both sides are accepted and transcended the relation becomes one of absolute faith. The two sides are apprehended as contrasts, but not as contradictions which exclude each other.

This absolute faith is able to take the threefold structure of anxiety into itself. It conquers the anxiety of fate and death in its encounter with providence. Providence gives man the courage of confidence to say "in spite of" to fate and death. Providence must not be construed in terms of God's activity, but as a religious symbol for the courage of confidence which conquers fate and death. Guilt and condemnation are conquered through the experience of divine forgiveness which expresses itself in the courage to accept acceptance. The courage to be in relation to guilt is "the courage to accept oneself as accepted in spite of being unacceptable." In relation to the anxiety of emptiness and meaninglessness the courage to be, based on absolute faith, is able to say "yes" to the undermining doubt and to affirm itself in spite of the threat. Any decisive answer to the question of meaninglessness must first accept the state of meaninglessness; this acceptance constitutes a movement of faith. "The act of accepting meaninglessness is in itself a meaningful act. It is an act of faith." Through his participation in the power of being-itself man is able to conquer emptiness and meaninglessness by taking them into himself and affirming himself "in spite of."

The content of absolute faith is the "God above God." Tillich rejects the God of theological theism, who remains bound to the subject-object structure of reality. A God who is understood as an object becomes an invincible tyrant who divests man of his subjectivity and freedom. This is the God whom Nietzsche pronounced dead, and against whom the existentialists have justifiably revolted. Theism must be transcended if absolute faith is to become a reality. The "God above God" is the power of being-itself, which, as the source of absolute faith, is not bound to the subject-object structure of reality. Being-itself transcends both self and world and unites the polarities of individualization and participation. The courage to be, which is ultimately grounded in the encounter with the "God above God," thus unites and transcends the courage to be as oneself and the courage to be as a part. This courage avoids both the loss of oneself by participation and the loss of one's world by individualization.

Pertinent Literature

Randall, John Herman, Jr. "The Philosophical Legacy of Paul Tillich," in *The Intellectual Legacy of Paul Tillich*. Edited by James R. Lyons. Detroit: Wayne State University Press, 1969.

John Herman Randall, Jr.'s lecture was the first of three given at Wayne State University under the Slaughter Foundation commemorating the first anniversary of Paul Tillich's death. Randall, who was closely associated with Tillich from the time of his arrival in this country—for many years they conducted a joint seminar on Myth and Symbol—mentions his own delight at being able to observe a true-blue German Romantic at first hand. As a historian, Randall notes that in his student years Tillich was introduced to philosophy by an expert on Johann Gottlieb Fichte, and that, having bought a set of F. W. J. Schelling at a bargain, he made Schelling the subject of both his Th.D. and Ph.D. dissertations. Martin Heidegger, his colleague at Marburg, contributed to his philosophical vocabulary.

Randall views Tillich as primarily a philosophical theologian, engaged in the perennial task of interpreting the symbols of religion in terms of contemporary philosophical thought. Tillich said that philosophy formulates an analysis of the human situation and asks the questions to which it gives rise, leaving to theology the task of finding the answers in the revelatory message. Randall, however, doubts whether the matter is that simple. In fact, the philosophy to which Tillich was attuned was that which he found in Schelling, Søren Kierkegaard, and the early Karl Marx, who were in revolt against Hegelian essentialism and the optimistic assumption that man is realizing his essence in the world process. Convinced that existential man, caught in his situation, is estranged from his essential nature, these thinkers were already giving expression to the Christian interpretation of man's fallen condition. Hence, in Randall's opinion, it is only those philosophers who are hidden theologians who will ask questions which theologians find significant.

Tillich's existentialism is, however, only one aspect of his thought. More fundamentally, he must be understood as a modern representative of the Augustinian tradition of Christian Platonism, as against the Thomistic tradition of Christian Aristotelianism. Like St. Augustine, he could admit no clear distinction between philosophy and theology. Faith is not a weaker form of knowledge, but an ontological commitment; truth is not a quality of propositions, but the power of being; knowing is not abstraction, but participation. For Tillich, no cosmological argument for the existence of God is possible because any being whose existence demands proof is finite. On the other hand, the ontological argument, although not a proof, reveals God as the Ultimate presupposed in all our encounters with reality.

Philosophically, Tillich stands in the tradition of Platonic realism. As he sees it, reality possesses a structure (*Logos*), and it is this structure which makes reality a whole. This logical realism, which affirms that subjective reason grasps the objective structure of things, says Randall, is "designedly not in the fashion of much recent nominalist philosophizing," although Randall looks favorably upon it. A more

serious problem for the modern mind is that the reason (*nous*) which grasps these higher structures by a kind of direct participation does not admit of verification in the way that technical reason (*dianoia*) does. And Tillich, aware of the problem, carefully described what he called an "experiential" (as distinct from experimental) method. What he intended, says Randall, seems close to what American pragmatism calls the method of intelligence.

On the whole, says Randall, Tillich's philosophy is so difficult for English-speaking philosophers to take seriously that his legacy is likely to consist in his wealth of specific insights rather than in his system as a whole.

Boas, George. "Being and Existence," in *The Journal of Philosophy*. LIII, no. 23 (November 8, 1956), pp. 748-759.

John Herman Randall, Jr. relates that when G. E. Moore's time came to comment on a paper read by Paul Tillich, he said, "I don't think I have been able to understand a single sentence of your paper. Won't you please try to state one sentence, or even one word, that I can understand?" George Boas is more attuned than most English-speaking philosophers to Tillich's language. His book *Dominant Themes of Modern Philosophy* (1957) concludes with a chapter entitled "The Rise of Existentialism." Boas remains, however, an unreconstructed American; and in this paper, part of a symposium of existentialist thought in which Tillich was the first participant, he holds out for the language of John Dewey and George Santayana.

Boas develops his subject, "Being and Existence," in quite traditional terms, equating being with the realm of essence and existence with the realm of fact. The realms are opposed to each other as universal is opposed to particular; but they are further opposed in that the former, which is set up by human reason in order to make sense of the latter, often fails, as when scientific theories prove false and our best-laid plans "gang agley." Such headaches, however, are no reason for despair. Boas himself is convinced that the universe is not completely intelligible, but he agrees with Dewey that what people like to call mysteries can be dissipated if we revise our assump-

tions—that is, adjust essence to existence.

Against the background of this kind of reasoning, Boas asks what Tillich can mean when, in *The Courage to Be*, he says that nonbeing is contained in being. First, nonbeing can refer only to what the ancients called becoming. It is not, of course, the logical negation, of being; hence, it must stand for coming-into-being and ceasing-to-be. That it is eternally present in "the process of the divine life" can mean only that cessation of being is always a possibility, but not an actuality; hence, it is not, strictly speaking, nothing. To say, however, that man is threatened by nonbeing when he thinks of death or guilt or meaningless is mistaken. "To be" is either a copula or a synonym for existence: taken either way, the negation of being is not what threatens us; it is the positive associations that go with our ideas of death or guilt or fate. That a person may be depressed when he thinks of any of these is understandable, but to talk as if such feelings are rationally connected with the recognition of man's finitude is wrong-headed. On the contrary, it is possible, with the Buddhists, for example, to accept nonbeing as the highest good.

Having disposed of nonbeing, Boas turns to being, in which nonbeing is said to be contained. We tend, says Boas, to hypostatize essences, and we then fall into the trap of supposing that anything that can be named, such as universe or being, can be subsumed under a more comprehensive genus. This tendency explains not merely how Tillich comes to speak of nonbeing as a correlative of being but also how he arrives at the more general concept of being-itself. But how, asks Boas, can anything be predicated of that which is supposed to transcend being and nonbeing since that which is beyond this distinction is beyond meaningful discourse? In Boas' opinion, it cannot; hence, all talk about being-itself, or the ground of being, or unconditional transcendence is literally nonsense.

Hook, Sidney. "The Atheism of Paul Tillich," in *Religious Experience and Truth.* Edited by Sidney Hook. New York: New York University Press, 1961, pp. 59-64.

There is no reason to think that Paul Tillich's denial of the God of theism, specifically the personal God of liberal Protestantism, would have scandalized either Martin Luther or St. John of the Cross. Sidney Hook is right, however, in believing that when the ordinary person reared in the Western tradition professes to believe in God, he thinks of God as a being who exists alongside the world that he has created; therefore he would call Tillich an atheist if he heard him deny that such a being exists and say that to worship such a being as God is superstitious idolatry. Hook mentions that Benedictus de Spinoza and G. W. F. Hegel, who took a somewhat similar stand, were denounced as atheists; but neither of these was a professor in a church seminary.

Hook makes no bones about his own opposition to religion, explaining that he does not belong to the Jamesian school of pragmatism which holds that "the warmth and light radiated by the beaming countenance of a cosmic confidence man is to be preferred to the stern and cheerless visage of the truth about man's tragic estate." Yet he can almost approve Tillich's kind of religion; for worshipers who hold that God is not *a* being but *being* itself would surely not persecute one another; nor would they oppose science. Moreover, on the positive side, they might well devise symbols that would provide aesthetic and emotional support for various ethical and cultural societies, whose outlook is often funereal. Nevertheless, reminding himself that there is an irreconcilable difference between even the highest religion and the secular, rational way of approaching human problems, Hook sees the danger that religious professionals will take advantage of the obscurities of Tillich's language and use it to support the very superstitions which Tillich opposed.

Hook owns that he is tired of arguing and hearing others argue with Tillich about ontology, explaining that to do so is like punching an eiderdown. When he had polemized against Tillich, with his customary mildness to be sure, always Tillich had replied, "I agree with everything you have said," and embraced him as a fellow seeker of the Grail. To an outsider, however, it seems possible that Tillich may have grown tired. Anyway, it is hard to believe that he could have given assent when Hook argued, as he does here, that being is nothing but an abstraction. Tillich, he says, sees plainly enough that, just as what all men have in common is not another man, so what all beings have in common is not another being. (This is the metaphysics lying behind his theological talk about God not being *a* being but *being*-itself.) Still, says Hook, Tillich fails to see that any answer we may give to the question "What do different beings have in common?" can never be anything but a universal or essence or definition. Furthermore, this fact is fatal to his concept of being itself as some sort of unconditioned ground of all beings: first, because an essence, no matter how purely conceived, has no ontological standing; and, second, because an essence must be differentiated from other essences, whereas Tillich's being itself is supposed to include all differences.

Unable to accept Tillich's ontology as philosophy, Hook casts a glance at German Romanticism and concludes that the unconditioned transcendent is simply the all-in-all of pantheistic spiritualism. It was typical of the Romantics, he says, to think of our individual egos as part of the Cosmic Ego, from which it is painful to be separated and in which we find peace and security when our egos are reintegrated into the whole.

Additional Recommended Reading

Kelsey, David H. *The Fabric of Paul Tillich's Theology*. New Haven, Connecticut: Yale University Press, 1967. Kelsey explores Tillich's ontological analysis in Chapter 3 as providing the framework within which Christian symbols are meaningful.

McLean, George F., O. M. I. "Paul Tillich's Existential Philosophy of Protestantism," in *Paul Tillich in Catholic Thought*. Edited by Thomas A. O'Meara and Celestin D. Weisser. Dubuque, Iowa: The Priory Press, 1964, pp. 42-84. Critical although not unsympathetic exposition of Tillich's religious philosophy, particularly the polarity between individuality and participation. Part of the Catholic-Protestant dialogue.

Margolis, Joseph. "Existentialism Reclaimed," in *The Personalist*. XLII, no. 1 (Winter, 1961), pp. 14-20. Suggests qualifications which must be made in Tillich's existentialism if it is to qualify as a philosophy.

May, Rollo. *Paulus: Reminiscences of a Friendship*. New York: Harper & Row Publishers, 1973. Tillich was one of May's advisers while he was writing his graduate thesis, later published as *The Meaning of Anxiety*. Tillich told May that *The Courage to Be* was his reply to that book.

Randall, John Herman, Jr., "The Ontology of Paul Tillich," in *The Theology of Paul Tillich*. Edited by Charles W. Kegley and Robert Bretell. New York: Macmillan Publishing Company, 1952, pp. 131-161. An earlier and more technical version of the discussion of topics treated in his Slaughter Lecture.

PHILOSOPHICAL INVESTIGATIONS

Author: Ludwig Wittgenstein (1889-1951)
Type of work: Philosophy of philosophy, philosophy of language
First published: 1953

Principal Ideas Advanced

Language is best conceived as an activity involving the uses of words as tools.

Words are used in a multiplicity of ways and are to be understood by engaging in the language "games" in which they are employed; words are not labels for things.

For a large number of cases in which the word "meaning" is used, the meaning of a word is its use in the language.

Discourse about sensations is understandable because there is a grammar of the word "sensations," and of such words as "pain" and "remember," which can be grasped by anyone acquainted with the relevant language games; no reference to what one has in mind or feels privately makes sense unless it makes sense in this way.

Expecting, intending, remembering—these are ways of life made possible by the use of language; and language is itself a way of life.

Philosophical Investigations, published posthumously, contains in Part I a body of work completed by Wittgenstein by 1945. This material includes a preface in which he comments on the book, characterizing it as an "album" of "sketches of landscapes," in virtue of its being a collection of philosophical remarks by the use of which Wittgenstein attacked the problems with which he concerned himself. Parts II and III, written between 1947 and 1949, were added by the editors, G. E. M. Anscombe (who translated the work from the German), and R. Rhees. The German and English versions appear side by side.

Although the work has been in translation only a few years, discussion of its contents preceded the publication of the work because of the appearance of the "Blue Book" and the "Brown Book," collections of typescripts and notes based on Wittgenstein's lectures at Cambridge. In part, the author's interest in the publication of the work during his lifetime came from a reluctance to rest his reputation on second-hand reports of his philosophical remarks.

An aura of mystery, then, surrounded *Philosophical Investigations* when it finally appeared—and something of the aura yet remains as arguments having to do with the interpretation of the sense and direction of Wittgenstein's remarks tend to condition the understanding of the book. Nevertheless, there is little argument about the central theme; in spite of Wittgenstein's erratic and peripatetic method, the purpose of his remarks manages to become clear. The point of the book appears to be that language is best conceived as an activity involving the uses of words as tools. There is a multiplicity of uses to which words can be put. To understand the meaning of an utterance is to understand the use to which it is put. Consequently, it is misleading and confusing to think of language as being made up of words which stand for objects. Understanding the uses of words is like understanding the rules of games, and just as confusion results when a player in a game makes up new rules as he goes along, or misapplies the rules, or conceives of the game in some static fashion—so it causes confusion and perplexity when a user of language creates new rules, violates old ones, or misconceives language. To be clear about language, one must look to its uses.

But if all that Wittgenstein meant to do with his remarks were to say this, he could have done the job with a great deal less effort and at considerably less length. The *Investigations* is not so much a report of the results of Wittgenstein's philosophical investigations, as it is itself an investigation *in progress*—and what it deals with and exhibits are philosophical investigations. In other words, Wittgenstein's remarks are used to show that certain philosophical problems arise because language is misconceived; and because of the author's adroit uses of language we are lead to conceive of language as instrumental. In a sense, then, the book *is* what it is *about*; its process, as a proof, is its evidence.

What is it to investigate *philosophically*? Wittgenstein's answer is: It is *not* to seek theses or theories, and it is *not* to find static meanings (objects) for which words are permanent labels; it is, rather, to understand by attending to the uses of language relevant to the problem at hand in order to discover how philosophical problems arise "when language *goes on holiday*"—that is, when a user of languages takes off in new, unpredictable directions as a result of failing to abide by the rules of a particular "language game." One might support Wittgenstein at this point by saying that what poets do intentionally, in order to be poets, philosophers do in ignorance—and hence are philosophers.

In the Preface to the book, Wittgenstein declares that he had hoped to bring the remarks of the book into some coherent whole, but such an attempt—he came to realize—could never succeed. He suggests that philosophical investigation involves coming at a problem from a number of different directions.

On the point concerning coherence one may justly dissent. Though it is true that escape from a static conception of language is made possible by a series of relevant demonstrations of the uses of language, there is no reason why the points of the book could not have been clearly made seriatim—even if, to do so, eccentric uses of language would have been necessary. A number of problems could then have been dealt with in the Wittgenstein fashion, a fashion which would have illuminated the eccentric uses of language. In fact, that is what *almost* happens in the *Investigations:* now and then we catch the author presenting a thesis, and it is clear that the problems he considers—suggested by his own odd uses of lan-

guage in the expression of his theses—are intended to illustrate and support his points. Yet Wittgenstein had a streak of philosophical coyness—sometimes disguising itself as a kind of insight—which led him, presumably for theoretical reasons, but more likely for effect, sometimes to withhold the moral of the tale, the destination of his philosophical wanderings.

There are two principal metaphors by the use of which Wittgenstein has sought to make his meaning clear: the metaphor of language as a game and the metaphor of language as a tool. Or, to be more accurate, the metaphors of languages as games or as tools. After describing a primitive language which could be described as involving a process of calling for objects by the use of words, Wittgenstein writes: "We can . . . think of the whole process of using words . . . as one of those games by means of which children learn their native language. I will call these games 'language-games' and will sometimes speak of a primitive language as a language-game. . . . I shall also call the whole, consisting of language and the actions into which it is woven, the 'language-game.' " (7) (In Part I, which comprises the largest section of the work, the remarks are numbered. For convenience in referring to the work—since there are no chapters, section headings, or other devices for locating oneself—these numbers are mentioned here.)

Then, in 11, Wittgenstein writes: "Think of the tools in a toolbox: there is a hammer, pliers, a saw, a screwdriver, a rule, a glue-pot, glue, nails and screws.—The functions of words are as diverse as the function of these objects."

But what is the point of using the expression, "language-game"? Wittgenstein answers: "Here the term 'language-*game*' is meant to bring into prominence the fact that the *speaking* of language is part of an activity, or of a form of life." (23) He then presents a list of some of the functions of language—for example, giving orders, describing, reporting events, making up stories, translating—and comments: "It is interesting to compare the multiplicity of the tools in language and of the ways they are used, the multiplicity of kinds of word and sentence, with what logicians have said about the structure of language. (Including the author of the *Tractatus Logico-Philosophicus*.)"

(23) Here the reference is to his own earlier work (1921) in which he defended a logical atomism—a philosophy which would elucidate problems by devising an ideal language in which for each simple object or property there would be a fixed, unambiguous symbol—ironically, the very conception of language which the *Investigations* examines and rejects.

The simile that using an utterance is like making a move in a game suggests the problem, "What is a game?" If language involves simply the use of names as labels, then there is a definite answer to that question. But if the word "game" is used in various ways, it may very well be that there is no "object," no essential nature, to which the word "game" calls attention. Indeed, this conclusion is what Wittgenstein argues. In response to the supposition that there must be something common to the proceedings called "games," he urges everyone to "*look and see* whether there is anything common to all," and he ends a survey of games by remarking: "And the result of this examination is: we see a complicated network of similarities overlapping and criss-crossing: sometimes overall similarities, sometimes similarities of detail." (66) He introduces the expression "family resemblances" to characterize the similarities.

The point is that just as games form a "family," so do the various uses of an expression. To look for common meanings, then, is as fruitless as to look for the essential nature of games. The only way of making sense out of a problem having to do with the essence of language (or the meaning of a word) is by examining language as it is actually used in a multiplicity of ways.

The theme of the *Investigations* is introduced shortly before the philosophical investigation into the essence of games: "For a *large* class of cases—though not for all—in which we employ the word 'meaning' it can be defined thus: the meaning of a word is its use in the language." (43)

To understand this critical sentence is to understand the *Investigations*. At first the claim that, as the word "meaning" is often used, the meaning of a word is its use in the language might appear to be a variant of the familiar pragmatic claim that verbal disputes are resolved by decisions as to the practical use of language. William James considered the question "Does the man go round the squirrel?" in an imagined situation in which, as the man walks round a tree, the squirrel moves about the tree trunk, keeping the tree between himself and the man. Some persons would be inclined to say that the man *does* go round the squirrel, since the man's path enclosed the squirrel's path; but others would say that the man *does not* go round the squirrel since the squirrel keeps the same part of its body turned toward the man. James would settle the issue by deciding how to use the word "round." He did not *answer* the question, but he settled the problem; he settled it by resolving the issue as a problem. In an analogous fashion, it might seem, Wittgenstein proposed resolving problems, not by answering them, but by showing that they involve confusions concerning the use of language.

But to interpret "the meaning is the use" in this manner is to fail to understand the function of the sentence in Wittgenstein's remarks. For Wittgenstein is not suggesting that meanings be determined by reference to use, or that meanings be explicated by reference to human attitudes in the use of language. What he suggests is what he says (but he says it oddly): the meaning of a word is its use in the language. For anyone who takes the word "meaning" as if the meaning of a term were an object, or a class of objects, or a property of a class of objects—in other words, something to which a word, as a label, refers—it is nonsense to say "the meaning of a word is its use." If the word "man" means rational animal, for example, what would be the sense of saying, "The meaning of the word 'man,' namely, rational animal, is its use in the language"? That is indeed philosophic garble. But if, now, we take the word "meaning" as it is used in discourse about the *meaning* of conduct, the *meaning* of an act, the *meaning* of a form of life—then it makes sense (even though it is *new* sense, since we do not usually talk about the meaning of a word in this sense of the word "meaning") to talk about the meaning of a word as being the use of the word in the language: it makes sense if by the "use" of something we mean what we would mean—more or less—in talking about the "purpose" of something. To understand a word, then, is much like understanding an act which makes no sense until one notices what the act does and, consequently, realizes what the act is *for*, what the purpose of it is, what *meaning* it has.

There is no more difficult demand upon philosopher accustomed to the sign-referent way of analyzing language than this demand that philosophers stop thinking of words as names for objects (a conception that has some use only in reference to a primitive language quite different from ours) and start thinking of words as tools that can be used in various ways and can be understood as bringing about certain changes in behavior or in ways of looking at things. Figurative description of language as a game is meant to stress "the fact that the *speaking* of language is part of an activity, or of a form of life": one does something with the use of a word that is much like what one does in making a move in a game; and just as it would be senseless to ask what the move *stands for* or *represents* (as if somehow it were a symbol for the victory toward which the player moves), so it is senseless to ask what the word, as used, *stands for* or *represents*. To be sure, conventional answers can be given to questions of the latter sort, but conventional answers are not illuminating; one comes to understand what language is and what language means in noticing (seeing) what is done with it (just as one can come to understand a machine by watching its operation).

This interpretation of Wittgenstein's remark that "the meaning of a word is its use in the language" gains strength with the realization that a considerable number of the remarks are directed against the idea that the meaning of a word is whatever the speaker has in mind or feels privately. Here again the problem "What is the essential nature of games?" is illuminating. By a survey of the various activities to which attention is called by various uses of the word "game," one comes to understand the word "game" and games; and the problem dissolves because one is satisfied with the survey of the family of games, and there is nothing more to wonder about. Similarly, to understand the meaning of the word "pain" is to have acquired the technique of using the word; there is nothing hidden or private to wonder about.

But this conclusion—that discourse about sensations is meaningful because the word "sensation" has a use in our language, and that the word "sensation"

cannot be part of a private language significant only to the speaker—is intolerable to philosophers who like to say that "Sensations are private," "Another person can't have my pains," or "I can only *believe* that someone else is in pain, but I *know* it if I am." (These are Wittgenstein's examples—which he discusses in a series of related remarks.) Wittgenstein realized that much of what he had to say is intolerable to some philosophers, but he writes that philosophers have the habit of throwing language out of gear; and sometimes the philosophical use of language is so extreme, so abnormal, that what is called for is *treatment* by one who understands that philosophical problems arise and philosophical theories are advanced when philosophers develop the disease of taking expressions that fit into the language in one way and then using the expressions in some other, problem-provoking, paradox-generating way. Hence, "The [enlightened] philosopher's treatment of a question is like the treatment of an illness." (255)

Thus, if someone comes forth with the philosophical "discovery" that "Sensations are private," what he needs is treatment: a philosopher who talks about private sensations has made the error of confusing a discovery about the "grammar" (the systematic use) of the *word* "sensation" with a nonlinguistic fact. "The truth is: it makes sense to say about other people that they doubt whether I am in pain; but not to say it about myself." (246) But it does not follow from the grammatical point—that it would be senseless to *say* that I doubt whether I am in pain—that therefore I *know* that I am in pain: the expression "I know I am in pain" has no use in our language—except, perhaps, to emphasize (do somewhat better) the job that is done with the expression "I am in pain." To confuse the use of the word "know" in such an expression as "I know he is in pain" (for he is writhing, clenching his teeth, and the like) with its use in the expression "I know I am in pain" is to breed perplexity which only an investigation into the multiplicity of uses of the word "know" can resolve.

In his discussions of understanding, memory, and sensations, Wittgenstein characteristically sketches the range of uses of the terms "sensations," "understand," and "remember." He resists the tendency to settle upon one use, one way of looking at things, one definition as somehow settling anything. For even if one considers what one takes to be a "single" use of a term, it soon develops that there are borderline cases, areas in which one use imperceptibly merges into another, so that any decision as to the use of language by way of definition settles nothing (the complex network remains) and may lead to further paradox. Philosophical difficulties in this area (as well as in others) arise when one kind of grammar is mistaken for another, when an expression appropriate in one context is used in another: "Perhaps the word 'describe' tricks us here. I say 'I describe my state of mind' and 'I describe my room.' You need to call to mind the differences between the language-games." (290)

Expecting, intending, remembering—these are ways of life made possible by the use of language; and language is itself a way of life. What we find when we try to find the criteria of these states are the uses of various expressions—or by noticing the uses of various expressions we come to learn what kind of behavior prompts our use of these terms. No reference to *inner* thoughts, sensations, intentions, or memories is necessary.

For Wittgenstein "*Essence* is expressed by grammar." (371) To understand the nature of something is to acquire the technique of using the language which prompted the question and the investigation concerning it. There are, however, no simple answers; in a sense, there are no answers at all. One gets acquainted with the multiplicity of uses and one surveys the scene accordingly: there is nothing left to wonder about.

Wittgenstein does not deny the existence of feelings, of pains, memories, and expectations. In response to the charge that "you again and again reach the conclusion that the sensation itself is a *nothing*," he responds, "Not at all. It is not a *something*, but not a *nothing* either! The conclusion was only that a nothing would serve just as well as a something about which nothing can be said. We have only rejected the grammar which tries to force itself on us here." (304) Again, in response to the query "Are you not really a behaviorist in disguise? Aren't you at bottom really saying that everything except human behavior is a fiction?" he replies, "If I do speak of a fiction, then it

is of a *grammatical* fiction." (307) The effort throughout is to argue against the tendency philosophers sometimes have of studying "inner processes" in order to acquire knowledge about sensations, memory, and so forth; the proper procedure, according to Wittgenstein, is to attend to the use of the relevant terms. If we do observe the uses of such terms as "sensation," "pain," "think," "remember," and so forth, we come to see that the technique of using these terms in no way depends upon introspecting private processes. An analagous mistake is made when it is assumed that to mean something is to think something. We can say that we meant a person to do one thing, and he did another—and we can say this even though we did not think of the possibility in question: "'When I teach someone the formation of the series . . . I surely mean him to write . . . at the hundreth place.'—Quite right; you mean it. And evidently without necessarily even thinking of it. This shows you how different the grammar of the verb 'to mean' is from that of 'to think.' And nothing is more wrong-headed than calling meaning a mental activity!" (693)

In Part II of the *Investigations* the theme of the latter section of Part I is made perfectly clear: meaning, intending, understanding, feeling, and seeing (whether it is visual apprehension or the understanding of something; and these are related) are techniques, forms of life, modes of action about which we could be clear were we not confused by misleading parallelisms of grammar. To understand, to see clearly, is to master techniques to which our attention is called when language is used; and the use of language is itself a technique.

Philosophical Investigations is Wittgenstein's mature discourse on method. It corrects the basic error of the *Tractatus Logico-Philosophicus*—the error of supposing that there are atomic facts involving unanalyzable simples, an error which arose from the mistaken conception of language as a naming of objects. This book not only makes the correction by conceiving of language as a tool and of the use of language as a form of life involving techniques, but it also exhibits the multifarious character of philosophical investigations by showing them as crisscrossing sight-seeing excursions made possible by tracing out families of similarities to which the multiplicity of language uses calls attention.

If there is a weakness in this revolutionary work, it is the weakness of glossing over the multiplicity of *limited* philosophical concerns. Not all philosophers can be satisfied with the restless philosophical excursions which so delighted Wittgenstein and at which he was so adept; many philosophers are more content to stay at home with their limiting and precising definitions, their fanciful speculations, their penchants for single uses of single terms. Nevertheless,

Wittgenstein's work can serve as a foundation for argument against philosophic dogmatism; it makes possible an *enlightened* staying-at-home. From it a philosopher can learn that there is more between heaven and earth than can be seen by the use of his vocabulary; and there is then some hope that, though he spends his days looking at the world from his single window, he will not confuse the complexity of the world with the simplicity of some grammatical fiction.

Pertinent Literature

Pitcher, George. *The Philosophy of Wittgenstein*. Englewood Cliffs, New Jersey: Prentice-Hall, 1964.

Anyone who turns to look at the *Philosophical Investigations* must have, if he is to make sense of that work at all, a few key background facts in mind. First, Ludwig Wittgenstein was, as George Pitcher says, one of the greatest of twentieth century philosophers, if not the greatest. Second, this work, the *Investigations*, is one, but only one, of two books upon which that judgment is based; his earlier book, the *Tractatus Logico-Philosophicus,* is as important in making that claim about his historical importance. Third, the *Philosophical Investigations* rejected most of the views Wittgenstein held in the *Tractatus*. This last fact is crucial. The *Tractatus* established Wittgenstein as one of the central philosophers of the century; but later he came to form philosophical views quite at odds with those which had elevated him to international recognition. And that fact, that he rejected the views of his youth to work out a wholly different set of ideas which became equally important, creates one of the strongest reasons for a claim to greatness. The reader of the *Investigations* must realize that in that work one of Wittgenstein's aims is to show how misdirected his earlier ideas had been.

It is thus very helpful for a beginning student of the *Investigations* to know something of Wittgenstein's ideas in the *Tractatus* in order to know what forms the background of the detailed work in the later book. That is where a book like Pitcher's is very helpful. By including a discussion of both books

under the same cover, Pitcher is able to make the relevant connections that assist the beginning reader of the *Philosophical Investigations* to understand the course of Wittgenstein's thinking.

Since the concern of this review is with the *Investigations*, only a few brief words about the earlier part of Pitcher's book are in order. He begins with a short sketch of Wittgenstein's life and character (and there is no doubt that Wittgenstein was a fascinating and exasperating character), and he then moves off into a discussion of the *Tractatus*. His aim in that discussion is to give the reader the broad picture of what Wittgenstein was up to, and so he omits all mention of the technical material on logic. Most briefly, the *Tractatus* is shown as a book which presents a metaphysical system based upon reflections on language and logic. Pitcher's aim is to show, in an introductory way, what Wittgenstein's views of language and logic were at that time and how those views acted to produce an account of what the world must be like in its broadest and deepest features.

It seems clear that upon finishing the *Tractatus*, Wittgenstein thought that he had solved all the central philosophical problems, and so he gave up philosophy. Other philosophers, however, deeply impressed by the book, sought him out to discuss it with him. Some of those conversations led him to start thinking about the problems once more. The upshot was that he returned to philosophy in 1929 in order to think and teach. Within the next decade he came to see that he had been radically wrong in his earlier thinking. The *Philosophical Investigations* is his attempt to work out a new set of ideas.

Pitcher organizes his discussion of the *Investigations* around several of Wittgenstein's themes, including that of the rejection of the doctrines of the *Tractatus*. The topic that Pitcher treats at greatest length is that of the nature of philosophy, allocating two different chapters to it; and there is no doubt that Wittgenstein had original things to say about what philosophy is.

Whereas metaphysicians, including Wittgenstein in the *Tractatus*, had thought of philosophy as rather like logic or as either a super-science or a study subservient to science, Wittgenstein came to the point of not accepting any of those models. For him, philosophical problems came to be best seen as puzzles (although as he says they are very *deep* puzzles.) The traditional ways of describing philosophy, including that which held philosophy necessarily to involve failure, took philosophers to be trying to answer problems *about the world*. Wittgenstein, looking back upon his own superb piece of metaphysics, came to talk of philosophical puzzlement as something not needing an *answer* but as something requiring help in finding one's way about. For Wittgenstein, in philosophy we are not faced with the problem of dealing with the unknown and our

ignorance of it; rather, the pieces of the puzzle are all there if we can but see that they are there and how to put them together.

How does it come about that we get ourselves into such a baffled condition? Wittgenstein spends a good deal of time on that question. Pitcher notes that Wittgenstein found several different sources for such a condition, but thinks that there is one which Wittgenstein emphasizes throughout the *Investigations*. Wittgenstein found there to be a very fundamental tendency in human thought toward uniformity. This craving for similarity is an attempt to smooth out or ignore differences among related objects, to make people, things, and ideas as much alike as possible. For Wittgenstein in his later work, the metaphysician is one who allows that common human tendency free rein. Philosophy is the desire to *assimilate,* and philosophical puzzlement arises simply because the phenomena which philosophers try to assimilate exhibit great and basic differences, differences which in the long run really cannot be overlooked.

With that analysis of the nature of philosophy, one can see why so much of Wittgenstein's method is that of getting people to break down the blinders with which they view the world. The *Investigations* is a work on differences in the uses of language and in the world, on how to see variety where before one saw similarity.

Cavell, Stanley. "The Availability of Wittgenstein's Later Philosophy," in *The Philosophical Review.* LXXI, no. 1 (January, 1962), pp. 67-78.

The *Philosophical Investigations* is so close to us in time and, because of the very forcefulness of its ideas, has engendered so much passion and partisanship, that there are a great number of seriously conflicting interpretations of the aim, meaning, and truth of Ludwig Wittgenstein's work. In the absence of anything approaching consensus about how to understand the book, the general reader can become lost in a sea of perspectives from which to regard it. These circumstances make Cavell's essay "The Availability of Wittgenstein's Later Philosophy" very helpful. Not only does Cavell develop a definite and important interpretative line, he also sets his view in

direct contrast to another way of reading the *Investigations*. Cavell's essay is a critical review of a book by David Pole entitled *The Later Philosophy of Wittgenstein* (London: The Athlone Press, 1950.) Since the type of interpretation offered by Pole is not unusual, a reader of Cavell's essay can see two very opposed views standing face to face. Finally, one can see in this discussion a vigorous defender of Wittgenstein replying to a strong critic of the views expressed in the *Investigations*.

Cavell's essay has two sections covering two notions crucial to an interpretation of Wittgenstein; then two sections in which he examines questions concerning "ordinary language philosophy"; and, finally, a consideration of Wittgenstein's style of writing.

Cavell takes it that Pole's aim is to show that Wittgenstein's ideas about language are wrong. Cavell argues that Pole (like other commentators) reads Wittgenstein as having held that language is essentially a system of rules which govern our linguistic behavior. On the contrary, Cavell writes, it was Wittgenstein's aim to reject just that picture of language, to show that language is not a calculus comprised of a set of rules. The consequence of such a rejection is that Wittgenstein had to spend a great deal of time trying to show how language could function without being bound everywhere by rules.

If, according to Cavell's line of interpretation, Wittgenstein did not hold rules to be the ultimate components of human understanding, what *did* he suggest is at the bottom of our language? This is where Wittgenstein's idea of a *form of life* is introduced. Following a rule is itself one kind of human activity, one form of life, or one aspect of the human form of life; the activity of following a rule cannot itself be understood as governed by rules.

An interpretation such as Pole's, which places rules at the center of the story, must also emphasize the notion of *decision*. Since a given system of rules cannot cover every relevant possible happening, it seems that occasions must arise in which the system plugs a hole in the set of rules and does so by way of a decision as to how the rules should apply to a given and anomalous case. However, Cavell argues that the concept of decision plays quite a different and less crucial role in Wittgenstein's thought. In fact, he holds that the central theoretical concepts in the *Investigations* are not rules and decisions but rather the related notions of "grammar" and (less centrally) "criteria."

A second major topic on which such critics as Pole have attacked Wittgenstein is on his views about ordinary language. The one group of interpreters will regard remarks to the effect that philosophy can only describe ordinary language and not change it as being deeply conservative and wholly opposed to the entire spirit of rationalism built into the philosophical tradition. Cavell, in this brief essay, is deliberately tentative in replying to that line of interpretation and criticism. In part, he says that interpretation of the meaning of the appeal to ordinary language on Wittgenstein's part is simply mistaken: Wittgenstein meant only that mere philosophizing cannot change language, not that the results of philosophizing cannot help in linguistic reform.

That is not a full answer to Pole's view, however, for it is plain that the philosophical tradition importantly seems to come into conflict with "commonsense" beliefs at various crucial places. And there is a clear sense generated by Wittgenstein's remarks on ordinary language that he is somehow arguing in defense of common beliefs and in opposition to the philosophical views which conflict with them. Cavell tries to work out what is going on in this dispute. Basically, he argues that Wittgenstein denies that philosophy has the upper hand in seeming conflicts with commonsense beliefs; what Wittgenstein does not do, however, is assert, like George Edward Moore, that common sense has the upper hand. Instead, he denies that there is really any conflict between philosophy and common sense; and that is because philosophical propositions are not strictly propositions at all—they are a kind of remark which has no grounding in our form of life.

Cavell wants Wittgenstein's aim in this matter to be seen as *Kantian*. Immanuel Kant maintained that the persistence of certain philosophical troubles arises because philosophers attempt to know what is beyond the limits of any conceivable experience. Many philosophical propositions for Kant are produced by misunderstanding the limits of human understanding. It is Cavell's contention that Wittgenstein's attack on the philosophical tradition is very much like Kant's (although clearly there are also differences). The appeal to ordinary language, then, is not a conservative claim, or one holding philosophy to be impotent—it is rather a claim that there are conditions of human understanding, that these are embodied in a complex way in language, and that metaphysical propositions violate them.

Cavell finds it necessary to conclude with a few remarks on the style of the *Investigations,* a style that has perplexed many readers because it seems so unphilosophical. Cavell's aim is to show that the style is not wholly new to philosophy: it is a form of the confessional style incorporating aspects of the dialogue. Moreover, Cavell holds that it was *forced* upon Wittgenstein by the nature of the argument rather than adopted out of perversity or idiosyncrasy.

Additional Recommended Reading

Baker, G. P. and P. M. S. Hacker. *Wittgenstein: Understanding and Meaning.* Chicago: University of Chicago Press, 1980. A detailed commentary of the first 184 sections of the *Investigations* (to be Volume One of a sequence.)

Cavell, Stanley. *The Claim of Reason: Wittgenstein, Skepticism, Morality, and Tragedy.* London: Oxford University Press, 1979. A brilliant but idiosyncratic application of Wittgenstein's ideas.

Fann, K. T., ed. *Ludwig Wittgenstein: The Man and His Philosophy.* New York: Dell Publishing Company, 1967. More essays from various perspectives, some stressing the biographical.

Fogelin, Robert J. *Wittgenstein.* New York: Routledge, Chapman & Hall, 1986. Offers an insightful look at Wittgenstein's life and thought.

Pitcher, George, ed. *Wittgenstein: The Philosophical Investigations.* Garden City, New York: Anchor Books, 1966. A good collection of essays.

WORD AND OBJECT

Author: W. V. O. Quine (1908-)
Type of work: Philosophy of language
First published: 1960

Principal Ideas Advanced

Translation from one language into another is indeterminate. Two schemes of translation, incompatible with each other, might be equally adequate and acceptable.

Two kinds of entities exist: physical objects and sets of objects.

Entities are posited to exist if they are empirically attested to or have theoretical utility.

First-order predicate logic with identity is a canonical notation.

A canonical notation—that is, a logically perspicuous language—makes clear the ontological commitments of a theory.

Word and Object is W. V. O. Quine's *magnum opus*. Although it is neither his first word about the topics that have dominated his philosophical life nor his last word, it is the most complete expression of his views in a single place and was written when he was at the height of his philosophical powers, roughly between 1955 and 1959.

The book continues the themes of his earlier articles in *From a Logical Point of View*; (1953), of which the two most famous are "On What There Is," which discusses criteria for ontological commitment, and "Two Dogmas of Empiricism," the first dogma being that there is a clear distinction between analytic sentences, which are true by virtue of their meanings, and synthectic truths, which are made true by facts; the second dogma being that each meaningful sentence is reducible to an equivalent sentence, all the terms of which refer to immediate experience. As these two articles make clear, Quine is equally interested in the problems of ontology and language, problems that he thinks are intertwined. Quine further elaborated and refined the views of *Word and Object in Ontological Relativity and Other Essays* (1969). In the title essay, which constitutes the first of the John Dewey Lectures, given at Columbia University in 1968, Quine admits his debt to Dewey; in *Word and Object* and other essays he expresses his debt to C. S. Peirce and his commitment to a kind of pragmatism. By his own admission Quine is in the mainstream of traditional American philosophy.

Word and Object can be seen to consist of three projects: one concerns words; one concerns objects; and one concerns the conjunction of words and objects. The first project is an attempt to give empirical foundations to language, to explain the human use of language in terms of human behavior and the perceptual environment. Quine restricts the theoretical terms of the explanation to these two because, he claims, they are the only available resources for the evidence upon which human beings learn language; thus Quine is very much concerned with reconstructing how a person—typically, but not invariably, a child—might come to learn a language. The second project concerns the classic problem of metaphysics: What kinds of objects are there? What really exists? Quine's short answer to these questions is that there are two kinds of objects that really exist: physical objects and sets or classes of objects. These first two projects come together in his discussion of the kind of language that is appropriate for expressing what there is. According to Quine, it is science that says what there is, and the language for science, what he calls "a canonical notation," is first-order predicate calculus with identity.

Quine's most famous or infamous thesis about language is what he calls "the indeterminacy of translation." The thesis is this: two systems of translating one language into another can be devised such that each system is compatible with all the speech dispositions of those who know the language; yet the two systems are not equivalent. Quine develops his thesis in the course of describing the situation with which a linguist would be confronted when first coming upon a culture wholly alien to his own. How can the linguist correlate sentences of his language with sentences of the native speaker? That is, how can the linguist come to translate between his own language and that of the native? This is the problem of radical translation.

Suppose a rabbit hops by and the native says, "Gavagai." The linguist might plausibly guess that the utterance means, "There's a rabbit," or "Look at that rabbit." Of course the linguist might be wrong; in order to determine that, the linguist has to test his guess or hypothesis by interrogating the native in some way. But how can he do this? One way is for him to say "Gavagai" the next time a rabbit appears and observe the reaction of the native. The linguist wants to see whether the native will assent to or dissent from the utterance. Assuming that a linguist can ask a native whether a given sentence is appropriate, Quine defines "affirmative stimulus meaning" as the class of stimulations that would prompt assent, "negative stimulus meaning" as the class that would prompt dissent, and "stimulus meaning" as the ordered pair of the two. Further, two utterances are stimulus synonymous just in case they have the same stimulus meaning; that is, when they would produce assent or dissent in the same situations. Although the notion of stimulus meaning is well-defined, the linguist is still faced with a cluster of problems, to which Quine is attentive. Which utterances of the native are to count as assent and which dissent? Given that "evok" and "yok" are the utterances expressing each, which is which? Another problem is that a native will not always be willing or able to respond to the query. His glimpse of the object may not have been long enough to allow him to respond at all. So, in addition to the assents and dissents there will be some lack of response. The native will sometimes make mistakes;

perhaps he was looking in the wrong direction or attending to the wrong object. Or he might lie. Because of all of these possibilities for skewed results, stimulus synonymy is not what is ordinarily meant by "synonymy."

This partial catalogue of the linguist's problem is not meant to imply that the linguist's task is impossible. The point is rather to indicate what difficulties one faces in learning a wholly alien language, what resources are available to learn it, and the strategy the linguist will employ in matching utterances with behavior. Given enough data, time, and imagination, the linguist will surely succeed in writing a manual of translation.

Quine helps us understand how the linguist will proceed with his job of translation beyond those utterances whose use is most closely tied to observation by explaining how the linguist might move from translating observation sentences like "Gavagai" to truth-functional sentences. The linguist comes to translate a linguistic element as expressing negation when and only when adding it to a short sentence causes a native speaker to dissent from a sentence previously assented to; the linguist comes to translate a linguistic element as conjunction when and only when it produces compounds from short component sentences that the native is disposed to assent to when and only when he is also disposed to assent to the components separately. The qualification "short" is added to guard against the native's becoming confused by a sentence of extreme length. And it applies only to the language-learning situation; once the terms are learned, there is no restriction on the length of the sentences to which the terms are applied.

After the observation sentences, the truth-functional ones, and some other related sorts are translated, how does the linguist proceed? Roughly, he divides the sentences he hears into those segments that he hears often repeated; these he counts as the words of the language. His task is then to correlate these words with words of his own language in such a way that the correlation conforms to his translation of the earlier sentences. Quine calls these correlations "analytical hypotheses." A further constraint on analytical hypotheses is that stimulus-analytic ones, those sentences that receive unanimous assent among the natives, should, if possible, be correlated with sentences that are stimulus-analytic for members of the linguist's own speech community; *mutatis mutandis* for stimulus-contradictory sentences. The parenthetical "if possible" is an escape clause. It is not always possible, without sacrificing the simplicity of the analytical hypothesis, to match a stimulus-analytic sentence of the natives with one of the linguist's community. It may be necessary, in the interests of simplicity, to translate a stimulus-analytic sentence of the natives as, "All rabbits are men reincarnate." Such translations, however, are a last resort. By the principle of charity, one should always avoid attributing absurd or bizarre beliefs to foreigners.

There is another problem, or rather another result, of the thought experiment involving radical translation. The most fundamental relation between language and the world, the relation of reference, is infected by a kind of indeterminacy, which Quine calls "the inscrutability of reference." Suppose that one linguist has determined that "Gavagai," whatever its other uses, translates "rabbit" when it is used as a term. It remains a possibility that a second linguist, acting on the very same evidence as the first, will determine that "Gavagai" translates "rabbit stage" and a third that it translates "undetached rabbit part." Each of these preferred translations is consonant with all of the empirical evidence, yet the references of "rabbit," "rabbit stage," and "undetached rabbit part" are different. In other words, there is no one correct answer to the question, "What does 'Gavagai' refer to?" Reference is inscrutable.

The situation of radical translation implies that the translator has a language and attempts to correlate the sentences of his own language with the sentences of a language foreign to him. In this regard the problem of radical translation is different from the situation that the infant is in when he begins to acquire his language. However, there is an important respect in which the infant is in the very same situation: he has the very same resources available to him as the linguist does. Like the linguist, the infant must learn his language on the basis of perceptual stimulation and human behavior and must construct and test

hypotheses about what an utterance means just as the linguist, but self-consciousness is not essential to the learning process.

The babbling of human beings during the end of their first year of life becomes transmuted into an incipient language by selective, positive reinforcement. Among the randomly produced verbal sounds of the infant will be "mama" and "papa," which for the infant have no significance. They acquire significance when its mother and father reward the infant for producing those vocal sounds. Like a chicken learning to pull a lever for a pellet of food, a child first acquires language. The comparison of a child with a chicken is neither facetious nor unfair. Quine's model for the first steps of language acquisition is a stimulus-response model, and he approvingly refers to the work of his Harvard colleague B. F. Skinner in this regard. In an oblique response to the criticisms of Noam Chomsky, who trenchantly criticized Skinner's work, Quine concedes that, in addition to the stimulus-response mechanism, such innate forces as the natural tendency for an infant to smack its lips in anticipation of nursing and thereby to utter "mama" and a "basic predilection for conformity" play some role in a total causal account of infant language acquisition. Chomsky, however, is not satisfied by such meager concessions; he demands a more full-blown innatism and he discusses Quine's views in his contribution to *Words and Objections,* edited by Donald Davidson and Jaakko Hintikka.

Among the most important things that the infant needs to learn are the distinctions among various types of terms. Quine distinguishes between singular terms, such as "Cicero" and "the orator who denounced Catiline," and general terms, such as "orator" and "apple." General terms, unlike singular terms, divide their reference among a number of objects. Definite and indefinite articles, "the" and "a(n)" respectively, and the plural ending, are devices for the use of general terms in English. A person does not know how to use a general term in English if he does not know how to use such expressions as "an apple," "the apple," and "apples." Mass terms, such as "gold" and "water," are a kind of middle case, a kind of grammatical hermaphrodite. Syntactically, they are like singular terms in resisting indefinite articles and plural endings; semantically, they are like singular terms in not dividing their reference. But they are like general terms in not naming one thing. The double role of mass terms extends to predication. In the subject position they are like singular terms ("Water is wet"); in the predicate position, they are like general terms ("That puddle is water").

Quine's second project is to answer the question, "What is there?" His answer that there are physical objects, that is four-dimensional spatiotemporal entities, and abstract objects, sets or classes of objects, is perhaps less interesting than his answer to several related questions, such as "What isn't there?" or, to put the question more perspicuously, "Why does Quine refuse to countenance various sorts of purported entities?" On the ground of economy, Quine does not accept sense-data; they are not needed for science. Physical objects cannot be eliminated from science, and they do all the work that sense-data do. Sense-data are not needed even to account for reports of illusions and uncertainty. Quine accounts for them with the phrase "seems that" prefixed to a sentential clause about physical objects, and he then paraphrases them away in the same way he paraphrases away propositional attitudes towards sentences. Sense-data are excess baggage.

Quine's rejection of sense-data brings his standards for adjudicating conflicting claims for thinghood into high relief. Something has a claim to being an entity if it is empirically attested to or is theoretically useful. Competing claims to thinghood have to be weighed against both considerations. Sense-data have empirical support but no theoretical use. Physical objects have at least some empirical support and a great deal of theoretical utility. Even if physical objects are not completely observable, or not "all there," positing the unobservable parts involves more conceptual continuity than inventing an abstract entity. Theoretical utility also recommends classes or objects for thinghood. Classes account for numbers and numbers for mathematics. Hence, there are classes.

There are no properties or attributes because, in contrast with classes, they do not have clear identity. Classes are identical just in case they have the same members. There is nothing similar to be said for prop-

erties. The same set of objects might have two different properties; all and only creatures with hearts are creatures with kidneys; but the property of having a heart is different from the property of having a kidney.

Also, there are no facts. Like properties, facts do not have well-defined identity conditions. There is no answer to the question, "Is the pulling of the trigger the same entity as the killing of the man?" Facts are objectionable on other grounds. "Fact" is a stylistic crutch; it helps support the word "that" in some grammatical constructions, such as "The fact that he left is no excuse," and the phrase "that fact" is a kind of standard abbreviation for a previously expressed assertion. As such, however, facts can be eliminated or altogether avoided by simple paraphrase; it also helps invigorate a prose style, as William Strunk, Jr., and E. B. White show in *The Elements of Style.*

Another question is, "Are objects given?" Quine says, "No." They are posits. To call something a "posit" is not, for Quine, to be derogatory. Although some posits are bad—theoretically unjustified— some posits are really real; we posit entities of certain sorts in order to explain phenomena. For Quine, our beliefs are replete with posits. If a posit fails to explain a phenomenon or if another posit explains it better, then its justification fails. But the best explanatory posits are justified and have the status of being real. In short, for Quine, two sorts of objects have this status: physical objects for natural sciences, and sets or classes for mathematics.

Quine's third project is to explain how a person's ontological commitments can be clearly expressed in language. His explanation is that what is required is a canonical notation which is clear, precise, and unambiguous. Such a notation is the first-order predicate calculus with identity. A canonical notation has two purposes. The first is that it allows for simplification of theory. It allows a person to iterate a few constructions a large number of times to the same effect as the use of a larger number of constructions a small number of times. The use of a larger number of constructions may allow for psychologically simpler constructions, but not a theoretically simpler one; and that is what is demanded. The second purpose of a canonical notation is clarity. There are no ambiguities and no hedged entities in a canonical notation. Everything that is meant is up front.

Quine's notion of philosophical explication is an important one in itself and important historically in contrast with some traditional notions of analysis. A philosophical explication does not purport to uncover or bring to light the hidden or implicit ideas of the people who use the problematic notion; and it does not purport to be synonymous with the problematic notion. In one stroke, Quine cuts the Gordian knot of G. E. Moore's paradox of analysis. Philosophical explication is informative because it replaces the problematic notion with unproblematic notions that serve the same purpose. The notions of the explication may well be unfamiliar to and difficult for the ordinary user, but that is irrelevant. Familiarity should not be confused with intelligibility. Philosophical explication requires philosophically acceptable notions, not familiar ones.

This view of philosophical explication introduces a certain latitude into the standard of correctness. A correct explication may not be a unique one; several nonequivalent explications may be equally acceptable, no one of which is more or less correct than the others, so long as each explication meets scientific standards and serves the original purpose. For example, it is indifferent whether one accepts Gottlob Frege's, John von Neumann's, Ernst Zermelo's, Richard Dedekind's, or someone else's definition of number—so long as the chosen one does the job. In short, explication is elimination: out goes the bad air of familiar but unacceptable notions; in comes the good air of intelligibility. Quine thinks that his view of philosophical explication is in line with Ludwig Wittgenstein's doctrine that the goal of philosophy is to dissolve a problem by showing that, contrary to appearances, there really was no problem.

Pertinent Literature

Harman, Gilbert. "Quine on Meaning and Existence," in *The Review of Metaphysics*. XXI, nos. 1 and 2 (September and December, 1967), pp. 124-151, 343-367.

Gilbert Harman's article has two parts. The first part is an exposition of W. V. O. Quine's views about meanings and propositions. The second part explains how Quine goes about answering the question, "What is there?"

Harman explains that Quine's objections to the existence of meanings and propositions is not ontologically based. Quine does not reject them because they are abstract entities; sets are abstract entities, and Quine believes that they exist. The difference between meanings and propositions on the one hand and sets on the other is that sets have explanatory value and the others have none; this is the reason why Quine rejects them. He rejects them because they do not in fact explain what they purport to explain. Believing that there are such entities as meanings or propositions is similar to believing in phlogiston or witches; such beliefs are part of an inadequate scientific theory. Worse, appeals to meanings and propositions are not simply incorrect explanations; they explain noth-

ing, although they may give the false appearance of explaining something. Instead of saying that "Copper is a metal" is true by virtue of the meanings of its words, there is nothing to prevent one from saying with equal justice that it is true by virtue of the fact that copper is a metal. Similarly, instead of saying "Copper is copper" is true by virtue of the meanings of its words, there is nothing to prevent one from saying with equal justice that it is true by virtue of the fact that everything is self-identical. The phrase "by virtue of the meanings of its words" does no explanatory work.

One argument for the existence of propositions is this: The same belief can be expressed by different sentences; thus beliefs cannot be sentences; they are what is expressed by sentences—namely, propositions. Quine claims that the postulation of propositions plays no explanatory role. What is believed are sentences, and ordinary talk allows the same belief to be identified with several sentences. The phenomenon of belief can be accounted for solely in terms of attitudes toward sentences, and hence no postulation of propositions is necessary and no postulation is justified.

In the second part of his article, Harman explains how Quine answers the question, "What exists?" Philosophy, for Quine, is continuous with science. Philosophy differs from science only in being methodologically more self-conscious and in being applied to problems more general than those which any particular science investigates. In order to answer the question "What exists?" we need to know something about science; to do this is to do philosophy of science, and, for the purposes of ontology, that is all philosophy needs to be.

These views put Quine at odds with logical positivists, for whom there is a sharp division between philosophy, which in large part consists of practical decisions about the language of science, and science. Should one choose the physical object language of science or the language of sense-data? For Quine, to choose a language is to choose a theory. A person makes decisions about what kind of language to speak on grounds of practicality, convenience, and simplicity; but these are the very same sorts of considerations that go into decisions about what scientific theory a person should accept. One can, if one likes, formulate talk about things as talk about language. And this is sometimes a useful device. The sentence "Grass is green" can be reformulated as "'Green' is true of what 'grass' is true of." Quine calls such reformulations "semantic assent." These reformulations are legitimate; they are especially helpful for parties who are arguing about ontological commitments. But at some stage a person must go down the mountain and talk about nonlinguistic things.

Scientific theory needs a regimented language, and regimentation of language serves the same purpose as scientific theory: systematization. Two marks of systematization are definiteness and regularity. Regimented language has a definiteness and regularity that ordinary language lacks; and, because the better a scientific theory the more definite and regular it is, regimented language can express sophisticated scientific theories with an ease and accuracy that is ill-suited to ordinary language. This view of regimented and ordinary language does not entail a conflict between the two. Each is well-suited to its own purposes, but it is important not to mistake those purposes nor to deny the legitimacy of either.

Strawson, P. F. "Singular Terms and Predication," in *Words and Objections: Essays on the Work of W.V.O. Quine.* Edited by Donald Davidson and Jaakko Hintikka. Boston: D. Reidel, 1969, pp. 97-117.

A central part of W. V. O. Quine's theory of a canonical notation is his distinction between singular terms (for example, "Leo" and "that lion") and general terms in the predicate position (for example, "tawny" in "Leo is tawny"). P. F. Strawson thinks this distinction rests upon concepts that Quine has not made explicit. These concepts are: first, a hierarchy of types of entities, where spatiotemporal particulars are of type 0 and their properties type 1; second, the function of singular terms to identify particulars, where identifying is to be understood as bringing it about that the audience knows what object is to receive the predication. A singular subject/predicate statement is true, then, just in case the predicate applies to the object identified by the subject term; it is false if the predicate does not apply. When the subject term fails to identify any object at all, then there is nothing for the predicate to be judged either true of or false of, and the result is what Quine calls a truth-value gap.

The existence of truth-value gaps is not the important point; it is just a consequence of what is important—namely, that singular terms and general terms in the predicate position play different roles, and that consequently their failure to function properly leads to different results. General terms, according to Quine, have the role of being true of the object that the singular term refers to; and reference is the role of the singular term. But, Strawson objects, the terms "is true of " and "refers to" are as obscure as the distinction they are intended to explain; and, worse, Quine sometimes uses them interchangeably.

The need for an adequate account of the distinction is acute because of Quine's views about canonical notation; he holds that all singular terms get eliminated in favor of variables, quantification, and general terms in the predicate position. Such elimination, however, masks the fact that we understand the role of variables only because we understand the role that singular terms have. It is important, then, to see that the elimination of singular terms, if in fact it can be carried out, does not dispense with the notion of identification, which is inextricably tied to them.

There is a further point to be made about predication. In correct predication, the predicate expresses a property that is of a type that groups or collects the object identified by the subject; and there are levels of properties that form a kind of hierarchy. First-order properties, such as being human, group spatiotemporal particulars; properties of properties, such as being a color, group properties of the first type. This fact explains Quine's choice of quantification as a test of ontological commitment. Because he is ontologically committed to spatiotemporal entities as the basic entities, he looks for a criterion that picks them out to the exclusion of other things. Quantification in first-order predicate logic offers him such a criterion, because of the type-hierarchy implicit in predication; spatiotemporal entities are of type 0; that is, they and only they can be the values of bound variables and are not things that might be expressed by a general term in the predicate position. All other kinds of entities, properties, properties of properties, and so on, can introduce entities expressed by general terms in the predicative position. Strawson wants to remind Quine, however, that such entities can also be identified by singular terms in the subject position; and this means that they too count as entities, although they are not, of course, the same type of entity as spatiotemporal particulars.

Strawson, P. F. "Entity and Identity," in *Contemporary British Philosophy*. Edited by H. D. Lewis. London: George Allen & Unwin, 1976, pp. 193-220.

P. F. Strawson claims that W. V. O. Quine's slogan, "No entity without identity," does not express a philosophically valuable principle. The slogan is susceptible to various interpretations: (1) everything is identical with itself; (2) everything belongs to some sort or kind of thing such that instances of each sort or kind are identifiable by a common or general criterion; (3) some things belong to sorts or kinds of things such that instances of each sort or kind are identifiable by a common or general criterion; and some things do not belong to such sorts or kinds. The former things are entities; the latter are not.

Strawson holds that (1) says too little to be of value; (2) says too much to be of value; and (3) is stipulative at best. (1) merits no further discussion. (2) is shown to be false by considering universal or general things. Neither character traits (wit, cheerfulness, amorousness), nor smells, nor musical *timbres*, nor ways of walking, talking, and gesturing, nor literary and architectural styles, have statable identity conditions, although competent speakers have no problem correctly applying the terms for them and saying whether, with respect to them, something is the same as or different from another thing.

Concerning (3), it is the case that there is a distinction between instances of those kinds of things for which there are specifiable criteria or identity—call them "substances"—and instances of those kinds of things for which there are not—call them "nonsubstances." This fact, however, cannot be used to establish that the former instances are entities and the latter are not. For, while it is true that identification of some nonsubstances depends upon the identification of substances, it is also true that substances themselves depend upon forms that do not themselves have specifiable criteria of identity. So, to honor substances alone with the title of "entity" is simply to stipulate what an entity is.

Why then should Quine, or anyone else, find (3) appealing? Strawson thinks it is due to conflating two very different considerations. The first consideration is that substances, material individuals, are the original entities of our acquaintance and undeniably entities; this is an ontological consideration. The second consideration is that material individuals are the subject of first-order predication; this is a logical consideration. It is not surprising, however, that the two considerations should have been conflated; each reinforces the other. Material entities are eminently predicate-worthy in the sense that they are the indispensable objects of first-order predication; and we understand first-order predication by our practice of predicating things of material entities. Material individuals, however, are not the only subjects of predication and not the only things that have specifiable criteria of identity. Earlier, Strawson had made clear that any concept expressed in a predicate can be shifted into the subject position of a sentence and thereby made a suitable candidate for predication. "Green" in "Grass is green" can be promoted to the subject position, as in "Green is my favorite color." Usually, the shift from predicate to subject position requires some grammatical readjustment—concrete common terms in the predicate position become abstract singular terms in the subject position—but that is logically unimportant. What is important is the fact that these abstract objects can be subjects for predication, and yet they do not have specifiable criteria of identity. Thus (3) fails to capture fully our notion of an entity.

There is at least one additional way in which Quine's slogan can be interpreted; namely, as saying that everything that can be sensibly talked about can be, at least in principle, identified. This, however, is not an interpretation that Quine ever intended to be put on it. It is, rather, Strawson's own view, and it is with rare immodesty that he refers to this interpretation as an admirable maxim. The immodesty is tempered, however, when he goes on to explain that the maxim has a different application for each different class of ontological kinds, and should either be dropped from the philosophical vocabulary or severely restricted in sense.

Additional Recommended Reading

Davidson, Donald and Jaakko Hintikka, eds. *Words and Objections*. Boston: D. Reidel, 1969. A collection of essays, inspired by *Word and Object*, by first generation Quinians and many of Quine's most important contemporaries.

Harding, Sandra G., ed. *Can Theories Be Refuted? Essays on the Duhem-Quine Thesis*. Boston: D. Reidel, 1976. A collection of essays discussing Quine's view that individual sentences of a scientific theory are not refuted piecemeal.

Orenstein, Alex. *Willard Van Orman Quine*. Boston: Twayne, 1977. A comprehensive introduction to Quine's philosophy.

Strawson, P. F. "Positions for Quantifiers," in *Semantics and Philosophy*. Edited by Milton K. Munitz and Peter K. Unger. New York: New York University Press, 1974, pp. 63-79. A further attack by Strawson on Quine's ontological use of quantification theory.

Shahan, Robert W. and Chris Swoyer, eds. *Essays on the Philosophy of W. V. O. Quine*. Norman: University of Oklahoma Press, 1979. A *Festschrift*, the contributors of which are second-generation Quinians and critics.

HOW TO DO THINGS WITH WORDS

Author: J. L. Austin (1911-1960)
Type of work: Philosophy of language
First published: 1962

Principal Ideas Advanced

There appears to be a contrast between merely saying something and doing something; this is the contrast between "constative utterances," such as stating, and "performative utterances," such as promising.

Detailed examination of this contrast shows that it is not fruitful: to say something is to do something; in fact it is to do many things.

Locutionary acts consist, among other things, of uttering words with a sense and reference.

Illocutionary acts are governed by conventions and include such things as promising, swearing, and stating.

Perlocutionary acts are natural acts, such as persuading or angering, consequent upon illocutionary acts.

How to Do Things with Words is a reconstruction of J. L. Austin's William James Lectures at Harvard for 1955; it was first published posthumously under the editorship of J. O. Urmson. Austin's views on the matters discussed in the lectures were first formed in 1939, and he made some use of them in his address, "Other Minds," to the Aristotelian Society (1946). Between 1952 and 1959, he lectured on the same topic, sometimes under the title "Words and Deeds." Much of Austin's philosophical reputation rests upon his incisive and acerbic criticism of the views of other philosophers, for example his withering attacks on the views of A. J. Ayer and G. J. Warnock in *Sense and Sensibilia. How to Do Things with Words,* however, is a first-class piece of constructive philosophy. Austin invented speech act theory; before him there was no such theory; and his theory has been used, revised, and extended not only by philosophers, but also by linguists, linguistic anthropologists and sociologists, cognitive psychologists, and speech communication theorists.

Austin begins his lectures in a remarkably modest way: "What I shall have to say here is neither difficult nor contentious; the only merit I should like to claim for it is that of being true, at least in parts." Coming from most philosophers, such modesty would hardly be disarming; coming from Austin, it is simply the

first of those many parts that are true. He then recounts with approval the attempts to recognize that some purported statements are strictly nonsense and to account for why they are nonsense. He also lauds the discovery that some apparent statements do not purport to state facts but to evince emotion or to prescribe or otherwise influence conduct. These efforts and discoveries have developed piecemeal, he thinks, but also amount to a revolution in philosophy, about which he says, "If anyone wishes to call it the greatest and most salutary in its history, this is not, if you come to think of it, a large claim." What he proposes to offer the revolution is a manifesto, or, to drop the metaphor, a theory that describes the utterances that masquerade as statements. He calls such utterances "performatives."

Performatives have two characteristics: (a) they do not describe or "constate" anything at all and are not true or false; (b) to utter the performative sentence is not merely to say something. Austin's first examples of performatives are "I do," uttered by a bride or groom; "I name this ship the *Queen Elizabeth*," uttered by someone smashing a bottle of champagne against the bow; "I give and bequeath my watch to my brother," as occurring in a will; and "I bet you sixpence it will rain tomorrow." Based upon these examples, it might be tempting to think that to say the right words is the same as to do the action at issue. But that is not correct. In general, the words have the proper effect only if uttered in appropriate circumstances, and only if the participants are doing certain other physical or mental things; for example, breaking the bottle of champagne. Further, for some acts, words are not necessary at all. Marrying might be accomplished by cohabiting, betting accomplished by inserting a coin into a slot machine.

Austin's examples of performatives are sufficient to prove that there is some distinction to be drawn between them and constatives: "But now how, as philosophers, are we to proceed? One thing we might go on to do, of course, is to take it all back: another would be to bog, by logical stages, down. But all this must take time."

Constatives are true or false; performatives are not; rather, because they are types of actions, they can be done well or badly. Austin, in his doctrine of infelicities, concentrates on how they can be performed badly; for one way to learn how a machine works is to see in what ways it can break. As a kind of action, performatives are subject to all the defects that any action is; as linguistic acts, they have some special problems. Without pretending that the list is exhaustive or that its items are mutually exclusive, he mentions three conditions on performatives, conditions which, if contravened, give rise to infelicities:

(A) A conventional procedure having a conventional effect must exist, and it must require that certain words be uttered by certain persons in certain circumstances; and the persons and circumstances must he the right ones for invoking the conventional procedure.

(B) The procedure must be performed correctly and completely.

(C) When the procedure requires certain thoughts, feelings, or intentions to act subsequently in a certain way, the participant must have them and in fact perform the intended action.

If an action is infelicitous for contravening either (A) or (B), the action is a misfire; the attempted performative is a failed attempt; the act is null and void. If an action is infelicitous for contravening (C), then the performative is successful but defective for "abusing" the procedure. This classification is help-

ful and instructive even though the borders between (A), (B), and (C) are not always clear, and it is not always possible to decide whether an infelicity belongs to one kind or another. It is important to be attentive to these deficiencies in the classification. "And we must at all cost avoid oversimplification, which one might be tempted to call the occupational disease of philosophers if it were not their occupation."

Although performative utterances are not true or false if they are felicitously, that is, nondefectively, performed, they are related to statements that are true. For example, if a person felicitously utters, "I apologize," it is true that he apologizes, true that the person had offended or otherwise injured the addressee, true that he commits himself to not repeating the injury, and so on. The way in which a performative is related to some true statements is analogous to the way in which constatives are related to some true statements. The sentence "All men blush" *entails* "Some men blush." Saying "The cat is on the mat" *implies* that the speaker believes that the cat is on the mat. And "All Jack's children are bald" presupposes that Jack has children (see P. F. Strawson's *Introduction to Logical Theory*). So constatives are more like performatives than first appeared to be the case; they are being assimilated.

There are other reasons for assimilating constatives. The truth of "I am stating that John is running" depends upon the felicity of the speaker's saying or having said, "John is running." So at least some constative utterances have felicity conditions. On the other side of the distinction, some performatives are false: The warning "I warn you that the bull is about to charge" is a false warning if the bull is not about to charge.

These matters raise doubts about the performative/constative distinction. Is there a way to make the distinction in grammatical terms, by grammatical criteria? Many, but not all, performatives have their main verb in the first person singular, present tense, active, indicative mood, but "You are hereby authorized. . .," "Passengers are warned. . .," "Notice is hereby given" and "Turn right" are exceptions. Thus, neither person, number, tense, voice, nor mood can be used as a simple criterion. The first-person, active, present tense remains, however, an attractive base upon which to build a criterion. For notice that there is an asymmetry between a performative verb in this form and the same verb in other persons, tenses, and moods. If I utter "I had bet," "He bets," or "They (might) have bet," I describe a certain action; but no action is described if I utter the words "I bet." Rather, to say, "I bet" (in the right circumstances, frame of mind, and so on) is, roughly, to bet. Austin's strategy for devising a criterion is, then, to make a list of verbs having this asymmetry and to "reduce" other performative utterances to this form, which Austin calls "explicit performative" form.

Explicit performatives should be considered a development of language that evolves out of "primary performatives," which are vague and less explicit because they serve more than one purpose. "I will," in contrast with "I promise that I will," can be used either for a prediction, expression of intention, or promise. Explicit performatives do the work that mood, tone of voice, cadence, adjectives, adverbs, particles, and sundry other things do in primary performatives. The imperative mood is indeterminate between giving an order, advice, permission, or consent, where the corresponding performative verb is determinate. Depending upon how the sentence "It's going to charge" is uttered (depending upon its phonological contour), the act is either a warning, a question, a charge, or a statement. The particles "therefore," "although," and "moreover" become, respectively, "I conclude that," "I concede that," and "I add that" in explicit performative form.

Although all this is instructive, it fails to serve the purpose of yielding a criterion of explicit performatives. For it is not always easy to determine whether an utterance is performative. "I assume that . . ." can be performative but may not be, and one can assume things without saying anything at all; and "I agree that . . ." may be performative or merely descriptive of the speaker's attitude. Another problem is that "I state that . . ." seems to be performative and yet is paradigmatically constative. The performative/constative distinction, then, cannot be sustained as a fruitful one, and it has, as promised, bogged down.

Up to this point Austin has been contrasting saying and doing. A new approach is required, one that focuses on the senses in which saying can be doing. Austin notices that every case of saying something, in the full sense, what he calls "the locutionary act," is a case of doing something. Every locutionary act consists of a *phonetic* act, a *phatic* act, and a *rhetic* act. The phonetic act is the act of merely uttering noises; a parrot is capable of performing a phonetic act. The phatic act is the act of uttering certain words in a grammatical sequence, that is, noises that belong to a language, and of uttering those words as belonging to a language. The *as* requirement is important; a parrot utters words but because it is not aware of them *as* words or *as* having a meaning, it does not perform a phatic act. The rhetic act is the act of uttering the words with a more or less definite sense and reference. The terms "sense" and "reference" are those of Gottlob Frege, but the doctrine is Austin's. For Frege, all meaningful words have both a sense and reference; for Austin, reference belongs to words that are correlated to objects by "demonstrative conventions"; sense belongs to those words that are correlated to general things by "descriptive conventions." For more about this see his articles "Truth" and "How To Talk: Some Simple Ways."

The difference between the phatic act and the rhetic act is brought out by the different ways of reporting them. A phatic act is reported by direct quotation: He said, "The cat is on the mat." A rhetic act is reported by indirect quotation: He said that the cat is on the mat. The difference is critical. A person who reports a phatic act is claiming, in effect, to be offering a verbatim report of the speaker's words; he is not committed to the proposition that its speaker had achieved any reference; there might have been no cat at all to refer to. A person who reports a rhetic act is not claiming that its speaker used the very words in which the report is cast; the speaker might have said, "The feline pet is lying upon the fabric used for protecting the floor." The person is committed to the proposition that the speaker's words had a definite sense and reference.

To report a rhetic act is not to report a speech act fully; for such a report leaves out the force of the utterance. Was his saying that I was to go to the store an order or merely advice or a suggestion? The force of a speech act is its "illocutionary force"; the act is an *illocutionary* act. The illocutionary act is governed by and conforms to conventions, and it should not be confused with something else that is done in a speech act, a *perlocutionary* act, which is not. A perlocutionary act is an act that produces certain effects on the feelings, thoughts, or actions of the audience, or even the speaker, as a consequence of the illocutionary act. These effects are natural consequences and not conventional ones, such as follow illocutionary acts. Although it is only a rough linguistic guide, we commonly report illocutionary acts as things done *in* saying something and perlocutionary acts as things done *by* saying something. In saying it, I *warned* him (illocutionary act); by saying it, I *persuaded* him (perlocutionary act). These linguistic formulas do not, however, yield a criterion. *By* saying something, a person might have been joking or insinuating, but joking and insinuating are not perlocutionary acts. And *in* saying something, a person might have made a mistake; but making a mistake is not an illocutionary act.

The original contrast between performatives and constatives was a false dichotomy. Illocutionary acts are performative, in Austin's original sense of that term, and some of them have truth-values. "I state that . . ." is on a par with "I argue that . . ." and "I promise that . . ." Like performatives, statements also have felicity conditions. A statement often presupposes the existence of a referent; so if no referent exists, the attempted statement fails. Further like performatives, statements require that the speaker be in a certain position; without evidence, the speaker cannot state when the world will end, although he may guess or prophesy it. Stating, it appears, is not *sui generis;* it is just one of many kinds of evaluation, and statements are not simply to be evaluated in terms of truth and falsity. Statements can be correct or incorrect, fair or unfair, exaggerated, precise, apt, misleading, or rough.

Statements belong to one category of illocutionary acts. Austin tentatively distinguishes five such categories: *verdictives, exercitives, commissives, behabitives,* and *expositives.* Verdictives, as the name implies, are typified by the kind of judgment issued by a jury, judge, umpire, or arbiter; they include estimates and appraisals. Exercitives are exercises of power; they include appointing, voting, ordering, and warning. Commissives commit the speaker to a course of action; they include promising, swearing, and declaring. Behabitives concern attitudes and social behavior; they include apologizing, congratulating, and condoling. Expositives indicate how an utterance fits into a conversation; they include arguing, replying, objecting, and stating.

Austin ends his lectures by commenting on his failure to relate his theory to traditional philosophical problems. The failure was deliberate; "I have purposely not embroiled the general theory with philosophical problems"; this should not be taken to mean that I am unaware of them. . . . I leave to my readers the real fun of applying it in philosophy."

Pertinent Literature

Searle, John R. "Austin on Locutionary and Illocutionary Acts," in *The Philosophical Review*. LXXVII, no. 4 (October, 1968), pp. 405-424.

John R. Searle thinks that J. L. Austin's distinction between illocutionary acts and locutionary acts is unhelpful and proposes to replace it with another: namely, the distinction between an illocutionary act and a propositional act. Searle's alternative distinction has, he thinks, important consequences for a number of the issues Austin discussed, including the relationship between truth (and falsehood) and statements, and the relationship between what a speaker means when he says something and what the sentence means.

Searle's first objection to Austin's distinction is that the terms are not mutually exclusive. There are some sentences in which the meaning exhausts its potential illocutionary force; for example, "I hearby promise that I am going to do it," which has the meaning of a promise. This entails that the locutionary act would be the same as the illocutionary act. And a description of the locutionary force, the meaning of the sentence uttered, would be a description of the illocutionary force of that utterance. Searle does not deny that the concepts of locutionary act and illocutionary act are different; rather, he is pointing out that the classes they denote overlap; some of their members are the same.

Searle's second objection concerns the *way* Austin tries to distinguish between locutionary and illocutionary acts. Austin holds that locutionary acts should be reported by direct quotation, while illocutionary acts should be reported by indirect quotation. Contrast this report of a locutionary act: He said, "Shoot her," with this report of the illocutionary act: He urged (advised) me to shoot her. This means that direct quotation should be wedded to locutionary acts; indirect quotation should be wedded to illocutionary acts. Austin, however, violates this; for he again deploys the difference between direct and indirect quotation to make out the distinction between the phatic and rhetic acts. Phatic acts, he holds, should be reported by direct quotation, rhetic acts by indirect quotation. Report of phatic act: He said "Get out!" Report of rhetic act: He told me to get out.

There is a further problem here. Notice that the report of the rhetic act above contains a verb expressing an illocutionary act, "told." In general, all reports of rhetic acts will contain some verb expressing some illocutionary act, even if the verb is a generic one; for example, "told" is a generic term; "order," "request," and "command" are more specific terms of that class. What this means is that the notion of an illocutionary act leaks into the notion of a locutionary act. Why does that happen? Searle's answer is that it is because every sentence has, as part of its meaning, some illocutionary force potential. The grammatical moods of indicative, interrogative, and imperative express this force. The upshot is that while phonetic acts and phatic acts can be separated from illocutionary acts, there is no rhetic act separate from an illocutionary act. There is a distinction between the literal meaning of a sentence and the intended force of its utterance, but this is only a special case of the distinction between literal meaning and intended meaning, and

it has no special relevance for speech act theory. As a consequence of Searle's criticism of Austin's distinctions, he proposes to eliminate the notions of locutionary act and rhetic act. What remains are three equally primary concepts of a phonetic, a phatic, and an illocutionary act.

Behind Searle's objections to Austin's distinction are three linguistic principles: The first, which he elaborated in his book *Speech Acts*, is the principle of expressibility, according to which whatever can be meant can be said. Often we mean more than what we say because we do not know the words or constructions to say all that we mean, sometimes because the language itself lacks the resources. Nevertheless, in theory all that we mean could be said; we could improve our knowledge of the language, or, if the language itself is deficient, improve its resources. Austin has overstressed the distinction between a sentence and the speech acts performed, to the neglect of the Principle of Expressibility. Since it is possible for a speaker completely to express what he means by uttering a sentence, what he says can include the force he means; so Austin's attempt to distinguish the force of an utterance from its meaning was wide of the mark. More importantly, the study of the meaning of sentences and the study of the illocutionary acts which are performed in uttering those sentences are not two different studies, but one and the same study from two different perspectives.

The second principle, which might be called "The Fundamental Principle of Language," is that the meaning of a sentence is a function of the meanings of its parts. The parts of a sentence include, in addition to its constituent words, syntactic and phonetic structure, roughly, the order in which the words occur and their intonation patterns. If Austin had considered this he would have been less likely to separate the illocutionary force of a sentence from its meaning. He might have seen that sentence structure, intonation, and the mood of the main verb express force and hence would have seen that the force is an inseparable part of meaning.

The third principle is that the illocutionary force of an utterance can be more or less determinate, and illocutionary acts are distinguishable by virtue of several dimensions. An illocutionary act might have the generic force of soliciting action without having the more specific force of being either a request, entreaty, or plea. Neglect of this third principle may have misled Austin into thinking that such generic illocutionary force expressions as "say that," "tell someone to do something," and "ask whether" are expressions for another kind of act: namely, locutionary acts.

The defects of Austin's distinction between locutionary and illocutionary acts notwithstanding, an important insight underlies it, Searle argues. It is the insight that most illocutionary acts can be divided into a propositional content, which consists of a sense and reference, and the force with which that content is put forward. This distinction between propositional content and force can be parlayed into accounting for why the concept of the act of making a statement has been confused with the concept of a statement, the object or product of the act of stating. A statement is a propositional content, put forward with stated force. Statements are the results or products of a particular kind of act, an illocutionary act of stating. The act of stating occurs in time and takes time to perform. The resulting statement is neither in time nor takes time. The act of stating is neither true nor false. The statement *is*.

Strawson, P. F. "Intention and Convention in Speech Acts," in *Logico-Linguistic Papers*. London: Methuen, 1971, pp. 149-169.

J. L. Austin explicity and repeatedly says that an illocutionary act is a conventional act: that is, an act done in accordance with a convention. This claim is true about a great many illocutionary acts: declarations of guilt and innocence, umpire calls, surrendering. But it is not true of all. Stating, questioning, and warning are illocutionary acts, but they are not, or at least not always, conventional acts in the sense Austin means. The only conventions associated with these acts are the conventions governing the use of the words uttered in performing the act. But these conventions determine what locutionary act has been performed; they do not make the illocutionary act conventional.

Working on the supposition that Austin did not simply overgeneralize, P. F. Strawson wants to understand what insight lay behind Austin's mistake; he finds a clue in Austin's qualified remark that an illocutionary act is conventional in the sense that it could be made explicit by the performative formula. The clue is the notion of explicitness. All illocutionary acts are communicative acts; this means that for a successful illocutionary act, it is not enough that the speaker mean something when he performs his act; it is also necessary that the audience understand what the speaker means. Further, and this is the crucial point, the mechanism by which the speaker transmits his message and the audience understands it must have a certain overtness; it must, in other words, be

avowable. This point is best explained in terms of H. P. Grice's account of "nonnatural meaning," according to which, in a speech situation, a speaker nonnaturally means something just in case he intends to produce a certain response in an audience by an utterance, intends his audience to recognize his intention, and, further, intends that the audience's recognition will be part of its reason for having the response. Strawson then complements Grice's analysis with a tentative analysis of audience uptake. For human communication is successful only when the audience recognizes the speaker's intentions. An audience understands something by an utterance only when it recognizes that the speaker intends that the audience is to recognize that the speaker intends to produce a certain response.

Strawson then uses this analysis of audience uptake to explain two features of Austin's theory: (1) Austin's view that all illocutionary acts are conventional in the sense that they can be made explicit by the performative formula, and (2) Austin's attempt to characterize illocutionary acts as something we *do*, in saying something. Concerning (1), Strawson begins by pointing out that because nonnatural meaning concerns a speaker's own intentions, he can speak of those intentions with a special kind of authority: they are his ownmost. Further, the speaker has a motive for doing so; it is one of his intentions that the audience recognize them; so, if there is a way to facilitate that recognition, the speaker will want to avail himself of it. One of these ways would be to add to the content of the message a conventional device that would signal the type of force that the message has. To the message that the audience should move, the speaker might add what looks like another comment: That's a warning (I'm warning you) or That's an order (I am ordering you). But this appearance of two comments, message and comment on message, disappears when the latter assumes its performative form: I hereby warn you; I hereby order you. When the explicit performative formula precedes the message (the that-clause), it no longer appears to be a comment on a message but a convention-governed device for *making explicit* the type of communicative force that the speaker intends. Concerning (2), Strawson contrasts illocutionary acts with showing off and insinuating, which, although not illocutionary acts, are things that are done in saying something. Showing off and insinuating are not illocutionary acts because they lack the requisite openness. It is not part of the speaker's intention to have his audience recognize his desire to impress the audience, in the one case, or to instill a belief, in the other. And such recognition may in fact frustrate the speaker's intention.

While the openness required of communicative meaning is instructive, it does not explain everything. How, for example, can "Don't go" have, on one occasion, the force of a request, and, on another, the force of an entreaty? Strawson's answer is that such cases call merely for enriching the intentional scheme already devised. In an entreaty the audience is to understand that the speaker intends it to recognize that he passionately or desperately desires something to be done and to understand that the speaker intends it to have this understanding; the same applies to requests *mutatis mutandis* except that the desire is less passionate or desperate. Orders or commands call for a further, although still quite manageable, complication. The audience is supposed to recognize, *via* the communicative intentions, the right sort of social requirements.

There is, however, a limit to how much can and should be packed into the intentions of the speaker. At a certain stage of conventionalized behavior, the requirement that the speaker have certain intentions drops out, and its work is performed, in a certain context, by mere physical gesturing. Umpires, juries, judges, bridge players, priests, and civil servants perform their assigned illocutionary acts unfettered by the requirement that they have the complex kind of intention to secure a certain response in their audience. The convention governing the gesturing behavior in a certain context is sufficient to guarantee the act.

The upshot is that there is a spectrum of cases. At one end, the illocutionary act depends heavily on the intentions of the speaker and their recognition by the audience; and the illocutionary act is in no way conventional except in the sense that the words of the utterance are bound by conventions. At the other end of the spectrum are the fully convention-governed illocutionary acts that dominated Austin's thinking. This is not to say that intentions play no role in the illocutionary act; in the standard case, they are present. But they are not necessarily present in each case, and, when they are not, the convention supplies what is lacking. The conventionalized and nonconventionalized illocutionary acts are, then, alike in possessing wholly overt and avowable intentions. They are also unalike. In a conventionalized illocutionary act, whenever the audience understands what the speaker intends, the illocutionary effect is achieved. If a runner understands that the umpire intends him to be called out, he is out. This is not the case for *non*conventional illocutionary acts. The audience might understand what response the speaker intends and yet not respond in that way. The audience might recognize that the speaker intends it to believe something and yet not believe it; or the audience might recognize that the speaker intends it to do something and yet not do it.

Strawson ends his article with a caveat. Conventionalized and nonconventionalized illocutionary acts are merely the extremes of a spectrum. There are many intermediate cases, and it is important not to lose sight of them; yet a general account of linguistic communication cannot supply every qualification that the facts might require without risking the audience's failure to understand the main point.

Additional Recommended Reading

Fann, K. T., ed. *Symposium on J.L. Austin*. London: Routledge & Kegan Paul, 1969. A volume containing contributions by many of Austin's colleagues, students, and friends, on a wide range of subjects, including several biographical accounts.

Furberg, Mats. *Saying and Meaning: A Main Theme in J. L. Austin's Philosophy*. Totowa, New Jersey: Rowman and Littlefield. 1971. The first book-length discussion of Austin's theory.

Holdcroft, David. *Words and Deeds*. Clarendon Press, 1978. A recent attempt at a comprehensive theory of speech acts that takes into account the work of Austin, Grice, Searle and others.

Searle, John R. *Speech Acts: An Essay in the Philosophy of Language*. London: Cambridge University Press, 1969. The best and most adequate extension and revision of aspects of Austin's theory of speech acts.

Vendler, Zeno. *Res Cogitans*. Ithaca, New York: Cornell University Press, 1972. In Chapter 2 Vendler uses transformational grammar to provide theoretical support for Austin's classification of illocutionary acts.

A THEORY OF JUSTICE

Author: John Rawls (1921-   )
Type work: Moral and social philosophy
First published: 1971

Principal Ideas Advanced

The principles of justice are whatever would be agreed to by rational, self-interested, and unenvious persons who knew they were to enter a society structured according to their agreement but did not know what positions they would have nor what their natural endowments and particular interests would be.

Justice is fairness.

The principles of justice are: First, equal and maximum feasible liberty for all. Second, power and wealth to be distributed equally except where inequalities would work for the advantage of all and where all would have equal opportunity to attain the higher positions.

The most ambitious and influential work in social philosophy of the later twentieth century, this book attempts to show what the principles of social justice are and why they can be satisfied only in a liberal society which partially redistributes income and wealth for the benefit of its least advantaged members. John Rawls revives the social contract tradition of John Locke, Jean Jacques Rousseau, and Immanuel Kant, in opposition to utilitarianism.

Justice, the author declares, is the first and indispensable virtue of social institutions, as truth is of theories. Even the welfare of society as a whole cannot morally override the inviolability that each person has, founded on justice. This is the reason why utilitarianism, which looks only to the sum of welfare and permits the sacrifice of the few for the good of the many, is not a tenable moral theory.

In this book Rawls is concerned with social justice only, not with the justice that individuals may display in private dealings. Society is a cooperative venture for mutual advantage: that is, if people cooperate in the production of goods, there will be more goods than if every person produces things only for his own consumption. But people do not only cooperate in the production of social goods, they also compete for them. Everyone prefers more rather than less. These facts give rise to the problem of distributive justice:

On what principles should these benefits be distributed?

There is scope for the operation of justice whenever many individuals coexist in a territory and are similar enough so that no one is able to dominate the rest. The social goods must be moderately scarce so that there will be conflicting claims that cannot all be satisfied.

Rawls makes a distinction between the *concept* of justice, on which all agree, and different concep*tions* of justice. The concept, he says, is that "institutions are just when no arbitrary distinctions are made between persons in the assigning of basic rights and duties and when the rules determine a proper balance between competing claims to the advantages of social life." Different conceptions are generated when people differ in their interpretations of what distinctions are arbitrary and what balances are proper.

The social justice of which Rawls writes has to do with the basic structure of society: the way in which major social institutions, chiefly governmental, distribute fundamental rights and duties and divide up the product of social cooperation. This is the distributive aspect of the basic structure of society, not a complete social idea. Rawls claims that his conception of distributive social justice tallies with the traditional Aristotelian notion that justice consists in giving everyone his due; for notions of what people are entitled to are ordinarily derived from social institutions.

Rawls's basic idea is that the correct principles of justice are what free and rational people, concerned to further their own interests, would agree to accept as defining the fundamental terms of their association, if their agreement were made under conditions that were fair to all parties. This is "justice as fairness." The conditions of fairness obtain when no party to the agreement is in a position where he can have any advantage over other participants in furthering his own interests. Such a fair position, which Rawls calls "the original position," demands that all participants be equal: this corresponds to the "state of nature" in traditional contract theory. But Rawls requires in addition that no contracting party shall know what his place will be in the society he is to enter, nor what class he will belong to, nor what his social status will be, nor even his fortune in the distribution of natural assets and abilities: his intelligence, strength, and particular psychological traits. This is the "veil of ignorance," drawn to prevent the parties from pressing their particular selfish interests. It would not be "fair" if the parties could be influenced in their deliberations by the morally irrelevant contingencies of natural chance (to which natural endowments are due) or social circumstances. Rawls assumes, however, that all parties know the "laws" of psychology and sociology and the general facts about social life. They are also to be mutually disinterested—that is, they take no interest in the interests of other people; and rational in the sense that they take the most effective means to whatever they put before themselves as their ends. Rawls assumes, finally, that they are not motivated by envy; that is to say, they will not forgo goods for themselves merely to prevent others from enjoying them. Although the parties are not allowed knowledge of what their particular conceptions of the good will be, they are assured motivation by a "thin theory of the good": they all want to pursue rational plans of life, in which rights, liberty and opportunity, income and wealth, and the bases of self-respect are primary goods; for it is rational to desire these things, and good is the object of rational desire. Principles of justice, then, are to regulate the distribution of these primary goods.

No actual person, of course, is ever ignorant in the ways specified, nor are actual persons equally rational, disinterested, and envy-free. But the restrictions of the original position are not arbitrary or fantastic but serve to rule out of discussion factors that we are convinced are irrelevant to justice. The conception of justice that results must be one that validates our strongest intuitions—for example, that religious and racial discrimination are unjust. We must aim for "reflective equilibrium" in which our intuitions about justice are harmonized with our principles. This may require adjustment in either or both. The conditions of the original position are those we do in fact accept, Rawls avers—or that we could be "persuaded" to accept.

There are certain formal constraints embodied in the concept of right: principles should be general, universal in application, public, capable of ordering conflicting claims, and final. These conditions are satisfied by the notion of deliberation in the original position: since the individuals cannot identify themselves, they cannot tailor principles to their own advantage; nor would there be any point in their trying to strike bargains with one another. Rawls assumes, furthermore, that as everyone is equally rational and similarly situated, each is convinced by the same arguments. Anyone—any actual person— can enter the original position at any time by arguing in accordance with its restrictions.

The parties in the original position would agree, Rawls claims, in choosing two principles of justice. The first is that everyone is to have equal right to the most extensive basic liberty (political, intellectual, and religious) consistent with equal liberty for others. The second is that social and economic inequalities are to be arranged so that they are (1) to everyone's advantage (this is called "the difference principle") and (2) attached to positions open to all. The first principle is prior to the second—that is, it must be fully satisfied before the second comes into play; no tradeoffs of liberty for economic or social advantage are to be permitted.

The general conception of justice behind this is that all social values should be equally distributed unless an unequal distribution turns out to be to everyone's advantage—for example, by providing incentive for greater production to be shared by all. Rawls defines injustice as "inequalities that are not to the benefit of all."

It is supposed to follow deductively from the specifications of the original position that the parties will vote unanimously for the two principles. The argument is this: The voters not only do not know what their position in the society they are forming will be; but they also do not even have any basis on which to calculate the likelihoods of alternatives. Moreover, Rawls claims, a person in the original position will care little for what he might gain above the minimum he can be sure of. And the situation is one of grave risk: that is, if the principles of justice allow unacceptable positions to exist in the society, every voter runs some risk—the magnitude of which he cannot even guess—of ending up in it. Under these conditions the theory of rational choice is said to dictate a "maximin solution": choose principles such that their worst outcome for the chooser will he better than the worst possible under alternative principles—in other words, choose as if your enemy is to assign you your social place.

The maximin strategy would lead to choice of equal distribution of all social goods, were it not for the fact that some inequalities may be such as to bring about the production of more social goods to be distributed, so that by permitting these inequalities it will be possible for everyone, including the worst off, to have a larger share of goods than if the distribution were equal. Since the choosers want more rather than less, and are not envious, there is no reason why they should not adopt this, the difference principle: inequalities to be permitted when everyone, including the worst off, benefits from them. This principle, being chosen under fair conditions of equality, is just.

The social good of liberty is to be distributed equally. People in the original position must adopt a principle of equal religious liberty if they are to adopt any principle at all. As for toleration, the principle is that limitations on liberty must be for the sake of preventing even greater violations of it and must be supported by arguments capable of convincing any rational person. Applying this principle to the question of tolerating the intolerant, Rawls holds that it cannot be unjust for the tolerant to suppress the intolerant in self-defense; but when the intolerant do not constitute a real threat they must be tolerated. Paternalism—governmental protection of ourselves against our own weakness and irrationality—is acceptable, as the rational persons in the original position would foresee that they might become irrational and need such help.

Only in the distribution of wealth, income, and authority are inequalities to be allowed. Here too equality is the "benchmark"—equal distribution would not be unjust, only inefficient. Rawls recognizes that people are born with unequal natural endowments, physical and mental, and that social and familiar conditions may accentuate them. But these inequalities are "arbitrary from the moral point of view"—no one deserves his natural endowments, and even a sober and industrious disposition is dependent on the accidents of nature and nurture. The "system of natural liberty," which rewards people in proportion to what they have the talent and industry to produce, thus permits distribution to be improperly influenced by the "natural lottery." The difference principle represents an agreement to consider the total pool of natural talents as a common asset in which everyone shares. While the natural lottery is neither just nor unjust, societies that base distribution of goods on it are unjust. There must be redress for the undeserved inequalities of birth and natural endowment. It is unjust that people should get more because they are born with more.

Under the difference principle, those who are less favored by nature have no ground for complaint of inequalities, for they benefit from their existence. The more favored should realize that their well-being depends on cooperation, which must be obtained on reasonable terms which the difference principle specifies. Thus the difference principle promotes fraternity, making society more like a family.

The only sense in which people can be said to deserve anything is this: if in accordance with the difference principle it has been announced that those who produce more will get more, then the higher producers deserve their differential and it would be unjust to withhold it from them.

The background institutions for distributive justice may be either democratic capitalist or socialist, but they must include a public school system, equality of economic opportunity, a social minimum, and social security. Rawls recommends a governmental organization including four branches: Allocation, to keep prices competitive and to prevent too much economic concentration, by adjusting taxes and subsidies. The Stabilization branch will guarantee full employment. The Transfer branch will correct competitive pricing (which by itself ignores need) to see that total income is allocated according to need. The Distribution branch, by taxes and adjustments in the rights of property, corrects the distribution of wealth. A proportional expenditure tax (the more you spend the higher your tax rate) is preferable to a graduated income tax.

Rawls claims that his theory is in the spirit of Immanuel Kant, who held that moral principles are the objects of rational choice by free and equal rational beings. The original position is devised in accordance with this conception. One acts autonomously when action is the expression of freedom and rationality. In the original position it is impossible to choose heteronomous principles. Moreover, the Rawlsian principles of justice are categorical imperatives: they do not assume that anyone has any particular aims. But justice as fairness improves on Kant by showing how in choosing principles of justice we

are fully expressing our natures as rational and free individuals—our noumenal selves. In justice as fairness, moreover, the basis of equality is being a moral person, which means having the capacity to have a conception of one's own good and a sense of justice. Moral persons are all persons who would be capable (contingencies aside) of taking part in the initial agreement.

To give people really fair opportunities, the family ought to be abolished; but this reform, Rawls allows, is not urgent.

The most important social good, Rawls avers, is self-respect, which he defines as "a person's sense of his own value, his secure conviction that his conception of his good, his plan of life, is worth carrying out," together with confidence in his ability to carry it out. Justice as fairness furthers the equal distribution of the bases of self-respect.

Although the assumption that persons in the original position are not motivated by envy is contrary to present facts about real persons, Rawls holds that in the just society there will be little occasion for or incitement to envy. It is not right to claim, as conservative writers do, that the modern tendency to equality is based on envy. In any case, the two Rawlsian principles of justice cannot be so based, for by hypothesis they are chosen by envy-free people.

Pertinent Literature

Nozick, Robert. *Anarchy, State, and Utopia.* New York: Basic Books, 1974.

This book shares honors with *A Theory of Justice* as a seminal work in social and political philosophy. The view advanced is the antithesis of John Rawls's: only a minimal state, one which limits its functions to common defense and protection against crime, is morally justifiable; and distributive justice is satisfied whenever a person is entitled to his holdings, which is when he produced them or acquired them through voluntary exchanges from people who were entitled to them.

At page 183 Robert Nozick pays a handsome tribute to the importance and elegance of the work of

Rawls, his colleague in the Harvard philosophy department; he then offers forty-nine pages of criticism. What, Nozick first asks, is Rawls's problem? Is it how the total product of a cooperative society ought to be distributed? Or is it only how to distribute the surplus produced over what would have been produced if there had been no cooperation? Apparently the former; but this might give some persons less than they would receive if they worked only for themselves. How can this be fair?

Why, indeed, does social cooperation create a problem for distributive justice? People who did not cooperate—who lived, for example, each on his own island—might still make Rawlsian claims to get more than they produced because they did not "deserve" their natural endowments of poorer soil, greater need, and the like. Then justice would have to counteract this "natural lottery." But such claims would obviously be without merit, since in these situations it would be clear who was entitled to what. How does social cooperation change things so that entitlement is no longer an applicable or appropriate criterion? Because everything then becomes a joint product in which individual contributions are indistinguishable? But Rawls admits that individual contributions to the social product can be identified, for he allows unequal incomes to be paid to specified persons as incentives.

Rawls says that it is not just for some to have less in order that others may prosper. But could this not be said when, in order to satisfy the difference principle, funds are transferred from a previously prosperous group to a previously depressed one? In any case, from the mere fact that A has more than B it does not follow that B is badly off *because* A is well off.

The difference principle indeed offers terms on which the less well endowed would be willing to cooperate: what better terms could there be for them? But it does not offer terms on which the better endowed would be willing to cooperate. Although everybody gains from cooperation, the difference principle does not assign the results symmetrically to the better and worse endowed. In Rawls's scenario it is proposed on behalf of the worse endowed that they should get so much that any attempt to give them more would result in their actually getting less. Why is this any fairer than if the better endowed made the reverse proposal? Rawls's explanation of why the less well favored should not complain of inequalities is that they get more than they would under equality. But he says about the more favored only that they should not complain because only thus could they expect willing cooperation from the less favored. This is not enough.

If social products fell like manna from heaven, the difference principle might be a suitable rule for their distribution. But this is not the appropriate model for deciding how to divide up the pie when the contributors to the pie are known. How do people in the original position get the *right* to make this kind of decision? Rawls assumes without argument that no entitlement theory of justice can be correct—that is, the right theory of justice must be one in which the pattern of distribution is settled in advance. This assumption, furthermore, clashes with Rawls's contract theory, for such a theory is one according to which *anything* emerging from a certain process is just.

Noting that much of Rawls's theory depends on the belief that it is the business of a just society to neutralize the baleful workings of "the natural lottery," Nozick finds an ambiguity in the claim that natural endowments are "arbitrary from a moral point of view." Is this supposed to be part of a positive argument to show that the distributive effects of natural endowments ought to be nullified, or of a negative argument to rebut any claim that they ought *not* to be nullified? A positive argument, Nozick claims, could not involve the notion that goods should be distributed according to desert, since Rawls explicitly rejects desert as a distributive basis. Hence the supposition underlying Rawls's position must be that people ought to be treated equally unless there is a moral reason why they need not be. Equality is the "benchmark"; deviation from it needs to be explained by moral forces. But why? Differential treatment of citizens by their government does indeed need moral justification; but elsewhere, it is not so clear. No moral reason need be produced to justify my patronizing one theater owner and not another. The assumption of the argument consequently fails.

Finally, Nozick questions Rawls's proposal to deal with natural assets as a pool for the benefit of all. To do so is to treat persons as mere means. contrary to Kant's prohibition. Envy of the better-endowed does after all underlie the Rawlsian conception of justice.

Matson, Wallace I. "What Rawls Calls Justice," in *The Occasional Review.* Autumn, 1978, pp. 45-57.

Wallace I. Matson contends that despite the title, John Rawls's book is not about justice. Rawls said that the concept of justice, on which there is agreement, is that of not making arbitrary distinctions between persons in the assigning of basic rights and duties and the determination of a proper balance between competing claims to the advantages of social life. Matson disagrees. Balancing claims and assigning rights and duties are primarily the business of politicians and arbitrators, not of the paradigmatic institutions of justice—namely, courts. Judges are concerned with awarding persons what is *due* them. The concept of justice is that of giving every man his due. Conceptions of justice differ as to what in particular is a person's due.

Rawls's two principles do not constitute a conception of justice, either a right one or a wrong one. The first principle, equal liberty, cannot be part of a conception of justice, since liberty and justice are independent notions—either can exist without the other: in a monastery there might be justice without liberty, and in an anarchical society, liberty without justice. Nor is the difference principle a principle of justice: it does not award people their due, nor does Rawls claim that it does. Rawls holds, rather, that except for what follows from governmental promises, no one deserves anything.

Matson concedes that a Rawlsian might admit these points but dismiss them as irrelevant on the ground that Rawls was writing explicitly about social justice, not the justice one individual shows in his private dealings with other persons. The author replies that institutions and societies can be just only in the derivative sense that they further just dealings of individuals with other individuals. The notion of "social justice" as different from, and even in opposition to, individual justice is mere cant.

Why did Rawls overlook so obvious a point? Because, Matson conjectures, he accepted a genetico-social deterministic account of human behavior, as a consequence of which the notion of desert becomes vacuous. Rawls has attempted to construct an ethics without desert. The first principle of such an ethics must be that there can be no moral reason to treat one man any differently from another: the equalitarian "benchmark." And equality would remain the principle if Rawls did not recognize the dismal fact that the intelligent and industrious cannot in practice be motivated to produce without hope of selfish gain. Hence the difference principle, the Rawlsian analogue of the Apostle Paul's grudging allowance for sex, "It is better to marry than to burn."

In the desertless ethics, fairness, which dictates distribution when desert is not in question, becomes the substitute for the vacuous notion of justice. Rawls's astonishing assertion that "Injustice is simply inequalities that are not to the benefit of all" begins to make sense once "unfairness" replaces "injustice." But it is important for Rawls to retain the *word* "justice." Such emotively appealing pronouncements as "Justice is the first virtue of social institutions" and "Each person possesses an inviolability founded on justice that even the welfare of society as a whole cannot override" lose their plausibility and attractiveness if in each case rewritten as, for example, "The *difference principle* is the first virtue of social institutions."

Johnson, Oliver A. "The Kantian Interpretation," in *Ethics.* LXXXV, no. 1 (October, 1974), pp. 58-66.

Oliver A. Johnson takes issue with Rawls on his claim to have produced a theory of justice in the spirit of Immanuel Kant's ethics. Three concepts that play a central role in Kantian ethics are autonomy, the categorical imperative, and rationality. Johnson argues that the Rawlsian theory clashes with Kant with respect to all three.

Kantian autonomy of the will refers to action done from the motive of respect for the moral law. In autonomous action the agent's wants and inclinations play no part. Rawls interprets this as meaning that the autonomous agent acts according to principles chosen by him as expressing his nature as a free and equal rational being, not because of his peculiar endowments, wants, or social position. The veil of ignorance is supposed to guarantee autonomous action. However, Johnson notes, the veil of ignorance does nothing to alter the motivation of Rawls's parties, which Rawls explicitly states to be the desire to promote their own interests. Their actions therefore remain heteronomous, since for Kant only the motive counts, not the circumstances.

Rawls's misconstruction of the autonomous/heteronomous distinction leads him to misinterpret the categorical imperative, which he supposes to be obeyed by the parties in the original position because they do not act in order to obtain particular ends but only because they desire "primary goods." But (says Johnson) that only makes their principles into what Kant calls "counsels of prudence," which are hypothetical, not categorical imperatives.

Both these Rawlsian misinterpretations stem from the misconception of Kant's notion of the role of reason in ethics. Rawls's notion of rational choice is that of taking the most effective means to given ends.

It is exemplified in the choice of a rational plan of life that will further the primary good of self-respect, thus producing happiness for the agent. But Kant explicitly rejected the notion that the role of reason in morality is to produce happiness, and he denied that in fact it could efficiently do so. He conceived the role of reason as quite different and higher: to produce a will good in itself. This is not merely different from but opposed to the role assigned by Rawls. A "Kantian interpretation" of Rawls's theory is therefore impossible. Rawls is not Kantian but anti-Kantian.

Replies to Johnson's paper were published by Bernard H. Baumrin (in *Midwest Studies in Philosophy,* I) and Stephen Darwall (*Ethics,* LXXXV). Rejoinders by Johnson appeared in Vols. II and LXXXVII of the same journals, respectively. Conclusions similar to Johnson's will be found in "Rawls' Kantianism" by Andrew Levine, *Social Theory and Practice,* III.

Additional Recommended Reading

Barry, Brian. *The Liberal Theory of Justice: A Critical Examination of the Principal Doctrines in 'A Theory of Justice' by John Rawls.* Oxford: Clarendon Press, 1973. First book-length critique of Rawls.

Daniels, Norman, ed. *Reading Rawls.* New York: Basic Books, 1975. Fourteen essays selected from the enormous Rawls literature. Contains a Rawls bibliography, 1971-1974.

Gauthier, David. "Justice and Natural Endowment: Toward a Critique of Rawls' Ideological Framework," in *Social Theory and Practice.* III, no. 1 (Spring, 1974), pp. 3-26. Argues that parties in the original position, who according to Rawls would know the general facts about natural endowments, would adopt not Rawls's principles but principles approximating those of a free market economy.

Pogge, Thomas Winfried Menko. *Realizing Rawls.* Ithaca, N.Y.: Cornell University Press, 1989. Explores ways in which the moral philosophy of Rawls can and cannot be implemented.

Urmson, J. O. "A Defence of Intuitionism," in *Proceedings of the Aristotelian Society* N. S. LXXV (1974-1975), pp. 111-119. A metatheoretical argument to show the implausibility of *any* ethics such as Rawls's based on a single principle or a few principles with a decision procedure.

Masterpieces of World Philosophy

TITLE INDEX

AUTHOR INDEX